WORLDMARK ENCYCLOPEDIA *of* National Economies

WORLDMARK ENCYCLOPEDIA *of* National Economies

Volume 3 – Asia & the Pacific

Sara Pendergast and Tom Pendergast, Editors

GALE GROUP

THOMSON LEARNING

Detroit • New York • San Diego • San Francisco
Boston • New Haven, Conn. • Waterville, Maine
London • Munich

Jeffrey Lehman and Rebecca Parks, *Editors*
William Harmer, *Contributing Editor*
Brian J. Koski, Jeffrey Wilson, *Associate Editors*
Shelly Dickey, *Managing Editor*

Mary Beth Trimper, *Manager, Composition and Electronic Prepress*
Evi Seoud, *Assistant Manager, Composition Purchasing and Electronic Prepress*

Barbara J. Yarrow, *Manager, Imaging and Multimedia Content*
Randy Bassett, *Imaging Supervisor*
Pamela A. Reed, *Imaging Coordinator*
Leitha Etheridge-Sims, Mary K. Grimes, David G. Oblender, *Image Catalogers*
Robyn V. Young, *Project Manager, Imaging and Multimedia Content*
Robert Duncan, *Senior Imaging Specialist*
Christine O'Bryan, *Graphic Specialist*
Michelle DiMercurio, *Senior Art Director*
Susan Kelsch, *Indexing Manager*
Lynne Maday, *Indexing Specialist*

Library of Congress Control Number: 2001099714

27500 Drake Rd.
Farmington Hills, MI 48331-3535
http://www.galegroup.com
800-877-4253
248-699-4253

ISBN 0-7876-4955-4 (set)
Vol. 1 ISBN 0-7876-4956-2
Vol. 2 ISBN 0-7876-4957-0
Vol. 3 ISBN 0-7876-5629-1
Vol. 4 ISBN 0-7876-5630-5
Printed in the United States of America

TABLE OF CONTENTS

Countries are listed by most common name. Official country names are listed in the entries.

PREFACE

The *Worldmark Encyclopedia of National Economies* joins the Worldmark family of encyclopedias and attempts to provide comprehensive overviews of the economic structure and current climate of 198 countries and territories. Each signed entry provides key data and analysis on a country's economic conditions, their relationship to social and political trends, and their impact on the lives of the country's inhabitants. The goal of this set is to use plain language to offer intelligent, consistent analysis of every important economy in the world.

It is our sincere hope that this set will open the reader's mind to the fascinating world of international economics. Contained within this collection are a number of fascinating stories: of Eastern European nations struggling to adapt to capitalist economic systems in the wake of the collapse of communism; of Pacific Island nations threatened with annihilation by the slow and steady rise of ocean levels; of Asian nations channeling the vast productivity of their people into diversified economies; of the emerging power of the European Union, which dominates economic life across Europe; of Middle Eastern nations planning for the disappearance of their primary engine of economic growth, oil; and many others. To make all this information both accessible and comparable, each entry presents information in the same format, allowing readers to easily compare, for example, the balance of trade between Singapore and Hong Kong, or the political systems of North and South Korea. Economics has a language of its own, and we have **highlighted** those economic terms that may not be familiar to a general reader and provided definitions in a glossary. Other terms that are specific to a particular country but are not economic in nature are defined within parentheses in the text.

This set contains entries on every sovereign nation in the world, as well as separate entries on large territories of countries, including: French Guiana, Martinique, and Guadeloupe; Macau; Puerto Rico; and Taiwan. The larger dependencies of other countries are highlighted within the mother country's entry. For example, the entry on Denmark includes a discussion of Greenland, the United Kingdom includes information on many of its Crown territories, and the United States entry highlights the economic conditions in some of its larger territories.

ENTRY OBJECTIVES

Each entry has two objectives: one, to offer a clear picture of the economic conditions in a particular country, and two, to provide statistical information that allows for comparison between countries. To offer comparable information, we have used some common sources for the tables and graphs as well as for individual sections. Even the most exhaustive sources do not provide information for every country, however, and thus some entries either have no data available in certain areas or contain data that was obtained from an alternate source. In all entries, we tried to provide the most current data available at the time. Because collection and evaluation methods differ among international data gathering agencies such as the World Bank, United Nations, and International Monetary Fund, as well as between these agencies and the many government data collection agencies located in each country, entries sometimes provide two or more sources of information. Consequently, the text of an entry may contain more recent information from a different source than is provided in a table or graph, though the table or graph provides information that allows the easiest comparison to other entries.

No one source could provide all the information desired for this set, so some sources were substituted when the main source lacked information for specific countries. The main sources used included: the *World Factbook 2000* and *2001,* which provided the common information on the countries' gross domestic product (GDP) at purchasing power parity, the division of labor, balance of trade, chief imports, chief exports, and population, unless otherwise noted in the text; the World Bank's *World Development Indicators,* which was a valued source for information about the infrastructure and consumption patterns of many countries; the *Human Development Report,* from the United Nations, which provided GDP per capita information on many countries; and the International Monetary Fund's *International Financial Statistics Yearbook,* which provided historical records of trade balances for most countries. Each entry also contains a bibliography that lists additional sources that are specific to that entry.

ENTRY ORGANIZATION

All entries are organized under 16 specific headings to make it easy to find needed information quickly and to compare the conditions in several different countries easily. (The sole exception is the entry on the Vatican, whose unique features necessitated the removal of several sections.) The sections are as follows:

COUNTRY OVERVIEW. This section includes information about the size of all land surfaces, describing coastlines and international boundaries. It also highlights significant geographical features in the country and the location of the capital. The size of the country is compared to a U.S. state or, for smaller countries, to Washington, D.C. Also included is information on the total population, as well as other important demographic data concerning ethnicity, religion, age, and urbanization. Where relevant, this section also includes information about internal conflicts, major health problems, or significant population policies.

OVERVIEW OF ECONOMY. This overview is meant to provide an analysis of the country's overall economic conditions, mentioning those elements that are deemed most important to an understanding of the country. It provides context for the reader to understand the more specific information available in the other sections.

POLITICS, GOVERNMENT, AND TAXATION. This section identifies the structure of the government and discusses the role the government, political parties, and taxes play in the economy.

INFRASTRUCTURE, POWER, AND COMMUNICATIONS. This section offers a description of the roads, railways, harbors, and telecommunications available in the country, assesses the modernity of the systems, and provides information about the country's plans for improvements.

ECONOMIC SECTORS. This section serves as an overview for the three more specific sections that follow, providing a general description of the balance between the country's different economic sectors.

AGRICULTURE. This section discusses the agriculture, fishing, and forestry sectors of the country.

INDUSTRY. This section discusses the industrial sector of the country, including specific information on mining, manufacturing, and other major industries, where appropriate.

SERVICES. This section concentrates on major components of the diverse services sector, usually focusing on the tourism and banking or financial sectors and sometimes including descriptions of the retail sector.

INTERNATIONAL TRADE. This section focuses on the country's patterns of trade, including the commodities traded and the historical trading partners.

MONEY. This section offers a brief description of the changes in inflation and the exchange rates in the country, and the impact those may have had on the economy. It also mentions any recent changes in the currency and the nature and impact of the central banking function.

POVERTY AND WEALTH. This section paints a picture of the distribution of wealth within the country, often comparing life in the country with that in other countries in the region. It includes governmental efforts to redistribute wealth or to deal with pressing issues of poverty.

WORKING CONDITIONS. This section describes the workforce, its ability to unionize, and the effectiveness of unions within the country. It also often includes information on wages, significant changes in the workforce over time, and the existence of protections for workers.

COUNTRY HISTORY AND ECONOMIC DEVELOPMENT. This section provides a timeline of events that shaped the country and its economy. The selected events create a more cohesive picture of the nation than could be described in the entries because of their bias toward more current information.

FUTURE TRENDS. To provide readers with a view to the future, the entry ends with an analysis of how the economic conditions in the country are expected to change in the near future. It also highlights any significant challenges the country may face.

DEPENDENCIES. This section discusses any major territories or colonies and their economies.

BIBLIOGRAPHY. The bibliography at the end of the entry lists the sources used to compile the information in the entry and also includes other materials that may be of interest to readers wanting more information about the particular country. Although specific online sources are cited, many such sources are updated annually and should be expected to change.

In addition, a data box at the beginning of each entry offers helpful economic "quick facts" such as the country's capital, monetary unit, chief exports and imports, gross domestic product (GDP), and the balance of trade. The U.S. Central Intelligence Agency's *World Factbook* (2000 and 2001) was the main source of this information unless otherwise noted. Each entry also includes a map that illustrates the location of the country. Since economic conditions are often affected by geography, the map allows readers to see the location of major cities and landmarks. The map also names bordering countries to offer readers a visual aid to understand regional conflicts and trading routes.

ACKNOWLEDGMENTS

We wish to thank all those involved in this project for their efforts. This set could not have been produced without the unfailing support of the publisher and our imaginative advisory board. At the Gale Group, managing editor Shelly Dickey and Peggy Glahn in New Product Development were especially helpful. We would also like to thank Gale editor William Harmer for his work in the early stages of the project, but special thanks must go to editors Rebecca Parks and Jeffrey Lehman who brought the set to publication. Copyeditors Edward Moran, Robyn Karney, Karl Rahder, Jennifer Wallace, and Mary Sugar must also be commended for their work to polish the entries into the form you see here.

COMMENTS

We encourage you to contact us with any comments or suggestions you may have that will benefit future editions of this set. We want this set to be a meaningful addition to your search for information about the world. Please send your comments and suggestions to: The Editors, *Worldmark Encyclopedia of National Economies,* The Gale Group, 27500 Drake Road, Farmington Hills, MI 48331. Or, call toll free at 1-800-877-4253.

—*Sara Pendergast and Tom Pendergast*

NOTES ON CONTRIBUTORS

Abazov, Rafis. Professor, Department of Politics, LaTrobe University, Victoria, Australia. Author, *Formation of the Post-Soviet Foreign Policies in Central Asian Republics* (1999), and annual security and economic reports, *Brassey's Security Yearbook*, and Transitions Online.

Abazova, Alfia. LaTrobe University, Victoria, Australia. Reviewed for *Pacifica Review* and *Europe-Asia Studies.*

Amineh, Parvizi Mehdi, Ph.D. Department of Political Science, University of Amsterdam, the Netherlands. Author, *Towards the Control of Oil Resources in the Caspian Region* (New York: St. Martin's Press, 1999); *Die Globale Kapitalistische Expansion und Iran: Eine Studie der Iranischen Politischen Ökonomie (1500–1980)* (Hamburg-London: Lit Verlag).

Arnade, Charles W. Adviser. Distinguished Professor of International Studies, University of South Florida. Author, *The Emergence of the Republic of Bolivia.*

Audain, Linz, M.D., J.D., Ph.D. Staff physician, Greater Southeast, INOVA Fairfax and Southern Maryland hospitals; former professor of law, economics, and statistics at various universities; editor, *Foreign Trade of the United States* (2nd ed.), *Business Statistics of the United States* (6th ed.).

Benoit, Kenneth, Ph.D. Lecturer, Department of Political Science, Trinity College, University of Dublin, Ireland.

Bouillon, Markus R. Doctoral student in international relations with a regional focus on the Middle East, St. Antony's College, University of Oxford.

Burron, Neil. Graduate student in International Development, The Norman Paterson School of International Affairs, Carleton University, Ottawa.

Campling, Liam. Lecturer in International Politics and History, Seychelles Polytechnic (University of Manchester Twinning Programme). Editor, *Historical Materialism—Special Issue: Focus on Sub-Saharan Africa* (2002). Contributor to *West Africa* and *African Business* magazines.

Carper, Mark Daniel Lynn. Instructor of Geography, Central Missouri State University.

Cavatorta, Francesco. Doctoral candidate in the Department of Political Science, Trinity College, Dublin, Ireland. Author, "The Italian Political System and the Northern League," in *Contemporary Politics,* March 2001.

Chari, Raj. Lecturer, Department of Political Science, Trinity College, Dublin, Ireland. Author, "Spanish Socialists, Privatising the Right Way?" in *West European Politics,* Vol. 21, No. 4, October 1998, and "The March 2000 Spanish Election: A 'Critical Election'?" in *West European Politics,* Vol. 23, No. 3, July 2000.

Chauvin, Lucien O. Freelance journalist, Lima, Peru. President of the Foreign Press Association of Peru.

Childree, David L. Graduate student in Latin American Studies at Tulane University, specializing in politics and development.

Conteh-Morgan, Earl. Professor, Department of Government and International Affairs, University of South Florida, Tampa, Florida. Co-author, *Sierra Leone at the End of the 20th Century* (1999).

Costa, Ecio F., Ph.D. Post-doctoral associate, Center for Agribusiness and Economic Development, Department of Agricultural and Applied Economics, University of Georgia, Athens, Georgia. Author, "Brazil's New Floating Exchange Rate Regime and Competitiveness in the World Poultry Market," in *Journal of Agricultural and Applied Economics.*

Cunha, Stephen, Ph.D. Professor of Geography, Humboldt State University, Arcata, California. Consultant, USAID, World Bank, National Geographic Society.

Davoudi, Salamander. Graduate student in Middle Eastern economics, Georgetown University, Washington, D.C. Former aid at the Royal Jordanian Hashemite Court.

Deletis, Katarina. M.I.A. (Master of International Affairs), Columbia University, New York. International communications officer, Deloitte Touche Tohmatsu, New York.

Divisekera, Sarath. Ph.D., School of Applied Economics, Victoria University, Melbourne, Australia. Author, *Income Distribution, Inequality and Poverty in Sri Lanka* (1988).

Eames, Rory. Honors student, School of Resources, Environment, and Society, The Australian National University, Canberra, Australia.

Easton, Matthew. Independent consultant, Cambridge, Massachusetts. Author, *In the Name of Development: Human Rights and the World Bank in Indonesia* (1995).

Feoli, Ludovico. Graduate student in Latin American Studies, Tulane University, New Orleans, Louisiana. Publications director and academic coordinator, CIAPA, San José, Costa Rica.

Ferguson, James. Writer and researcher specializing in the Caribbean. Author, *A Traveller's History of the Caribbean* (1999).

Florkowski, Wojciech J. Associate professor, Department of Agricultural and Applied Economics, University of Georgia.

Foley, Sean. Ph.D. candidate, History, Georgetown University, Washington, D.C. Author of various articles and a chapter in *Crises and Quandaries in the Contemporary Persian Gulf* (2001).

Foroughi, Payam. Ph.D. student in International Relations, University of Utah. International development consultant, NGOs, USAID, and the United Nations, Central Asia; freelance writer.

Friesen, Wardlow. Senior lecturer, Department of Geography, The University of Auckland, New Zealand. Author, "Tangata Pasifika Aotearoa: Pacific Populations and Identity in New Zealand," in *New Zealand Population Review,* Vol. 26, No. 2, 2000; "Circulation, Urbanisation, and the Youth Boom in Melanesia," in *Espace, Populations, Sociétés,* Vol. 2, 1994; "Melanesian Economy on the Periphery: Migration and Village Economy in Choiseul," in *Pacific Viewpoint*, Vol. 34, No. 2, 1993.

Fry, Gerald W. Adviser. Professor of International/Intercultural Education, and director of Graduate Studies, Department of Educational Policy and Administration, University of Minnesota—Twin Cities; former team leader on major Asian Development Bank funded projects in Southeast Asia.

Gazis, Alexander. Commercial specialist, U.S. Embassy, N'Djamena, Chad. Author, *Country Commercial Guides* for Chad (Fiscal Year 2001 and 2002).

Genc, Emine, M.A. Budget expert, Ministry of Finance, Ankara, Turkey.

Genc, Ismail H., Ph.D. Assistant professor of Economics, University of Idaho, Moscow, Idaho.

Gleason, Gregory. Professor, University of New Mexico. Former director, USAID Rule of Law Program in Central Asia.

Guillen, April J., J.D./M.A. International Relations candidate, University of Southern California, Los Angeles, with an emphasis on International Human Rights Law.

Hadjiyski, Valentin, Ph.D. New York-based freelance author, former United Nations expert.

Hodd, Jack. Queen's College, Cambridge, researching graphical presentations of general equilibrium models.

Hodd, Michael R. V. Adviser. Professor of Economics, University of Westminster, London, and has worked as a consultant for the ILO and UNIDO. Author, *African Economic Handbook,* London, Euromonitor, 1986; *The Economies of Africa,* Aldershot, Dartmouth, 1991; with others, *Fisheries and Development in Tanzania,* London, Macmillan, 1994.

Iltanen, Suvi. Graduate of the European Studies Programme, Trinity College, Dublin, Ireland.

Jensen, Nathan. Ph.D. candidate in political science, Yale University, and visiting scholar at UCLA's International Studies and Overseas Programs. He is currently completing his dissertation titled "The Political Economy of Foreign Direct Investment."

Jugenitz, Heidi. Graduate student in Latin American Studies, Tulane University, New Orleans, Louisiana. Research assistant, Payson Center for International Development and Technology Transfer.

Kiyak, Tunga. Ph.D. candidate in marketing and international business, Michigan State University. Research assistant, Center for International Business Education and Research (MSU-CIBER). Curator, International Business Resources on the WWW.

Kuznetsova, Olga. Senior research fellow, The Manchester Metropolitan University Business School, Manchester, UK. Author, *The CIS Handbook. Regional Handbooks of Economic Development: Prospects onto the 21st Century,* edited by P. Heenan and M. Lamontagne (1999).

Lang-Tigchelaar, Amy. Graduate student in joint MBA/MA in Latin American Studies Program, Tulane University, New Orleans, Louisiana.

Lansford, Tom. Assistant professor, University of Southern Mississippi, Gulf Coast. Author, *Evolution and Devolution: The Dynamics of Sovereignty and Security in Post-Cold War Europe* (2000).

Lynch, Catherine. Doctoral candidate in political science, Dublin City University, Ireland. Areas of interest include the political economy of implementing peace agreements, the politics of peace building, the implementation of policy, and other aspects of comparative political science.

Mahoney, Lynn. M.A., University of Michigan. Associate director of development, director of communications, American University of Beirut New York Office; freelance writer.

Mann, Larisa. Graduate student of economic history, cultural studies, and legal studies, London School of Economics. Presented "Shaky Ground, Thin Air: Intellectual Property Law and the Jamaican Music Industry" at the "Rethinking Caribbean Culture" conference at the University of West Indies, Cave Hill, Barbados.

Mazor, John. Writer and journalist specializing in economic and political issues in Latin America and the Levant. Graduated from Boston University with a degree in literature and studied intelligence and national security policy at the Institute of World Politics in Washington, D.C.

Mobekk, Eirin. MacArthur postdoctoral research associate, Department of War Studies, King's College, London, United Kingdom.

Mowatt, Rosalind. Graduate student in Economics, Wits University, Johannesburg, South Africa. Former economist for National Treasury, working with Southern African Development Community (SADC) countries.

Muhutdinova-Foroughi, Raissa. M.P.A., University of Colorado at Denver. Journalist, Radio Tajikistan; consultant, United Nations, World Bank, and Eurasia Foundation, Commonwealth of Independent Nations; freelance writer.

Mukungu, Allan C. K. Graduate student, University of Westminster, London, and has done consultancy work for the World Bank.

Musakhanova, Oygul. Graduate, University of Westminster; economist, Arthur Anderson, Tashkent, Uzbekistan.

Naidu, Sujatha. LL.M. in Environment Law, University of Utah. Ph.D. student in International Relations, Department of Political Science, University of Utah; freelance writer.

Nicholls, Ana. Journalist. Assistant editor, *Business Central Europe,* The Economist Group. Author of three surveys of Romania.

Nicoleau, Michael. J.D. Cornell Law School, Ithaca, New York. Co-author, "Constitutional Governance in the Democratic Republic of the Congo: An Analysis of the Constitution Proposed by the Government of Laurent Kabila," in *Texas International Law Journal,* Spring 2000.

Nuseibeh, Reem. Graduate student in Comparative Politics/Human Rights, University of Maryland, Maryland. Middle East risk analyst, Kroll Information Services, Vienna, Virginia.

Ó Beacháin, Donnacha. Ph.D. Political Science from National University of Ireland, Dublin. Civic Education Project visiting lecturer at the Departments of International Relations and Conflict Resolution at Tbilisi State University and the Georgian Technical University, respectively, 2000–2002.

Ohaegbulam, F. Ugboaja. Professor, Government and International Affairs, University of South Florida. Author, *A Concise Introduction to American Foreign Policy* (1999), and *Nigeria and the UN Mission to the Democratic Republic of the Congo* (1982).

O'Malley, Eoin. Doctoral candidate in Political Science at Trinity College, Dublin, and visiting researcher at UNED, Madrid, Spain. Author, "Ireland" in Annual Review section of the *European Journal of Political Research* (1999, 2000, 2001).

Ozsoz, Emre. Graduate student in International Political Economy and Development, Fordham University, New York. Editorial assistant for the Middle East, The Economist Intelligence Unit, New York.

Peimani, Hooman, Ph.D. Independent consultant with international organizations in Geneva, Switzerland. Author, *The Caspian Pipeline Dilemma: Political Games and Economic Losses* (2001).

Pretes, Michael. Research scholar, Department of Human Geography, Research School of Pacific and Asian Studies, The Australian National University, Canberra, Australia.

Sabol, Steven. Ph.D., the University of North Carolina at Charlotte. Author, *Awake Kazak! Russian Colonization of Central Asia and the Genesis of Kazak National Consciousness, 1868–1920.*

Samonis, Val, Ph.D., C.P.C. Managed and/or participated in international research and advisory projects/teams sponsored by the Hudson Institute, World Bank, CASE Warsaw, Soros Foundations, the Center for European Integration Studies (ZEI Bonn), the Swedish government, and a number of other clients. Also worked with top reformers such as the Polish Deputy Prime Minister Leszek Balcerowicz, U.S. Treasury Secretary Larry Summers, the World Bank, and OECD Private Sector Advisory Group on Corporate Governance, and with the Stanford Economic Transition Group; advisor to the Czech government (Deputy Prime Minister Pavel Mertlik), the Lithuanian parliament, and several Lithuanian governments, international organizations, and multinational corporations; founding editor, *Journal of East-West Business* (The Haworth Press Inc).

Sezgin, Yuksel. Ph.D. candidate in Political Science, University of Washington. Former assistant Middle East coordinator at the Foreign Economic Relations Board of Turkey.

Schubert, Alexander. Ph.D., Cornell University.

Scott, Cleve Mc D. Ph.D. candidate and graduate assistant, Department of History, University of the West Indies, Cave Hill Campus, Barbados.

Stobwasser, Ralph. Graduate student in Middle Eastern Studies, FU Berlin, Germany. Worked in the Office of the Chief Economist Middle East and North Africa, World Bank, Washington, D.C.

Strnad, Tomas. Ph.D. student, Department of the Middle East and Africa, Charles University, Czech Republic. Chief editor of the *Arab Markets Magazine*; author of "The Kuwaiti Dilemma," "OPEC—Main Sinner or Sheer Scapegoat?," and "Globalization in the Arab and Muslim World" in *International Policy* and other magazines.

Stroschein, Sherrill. Assistant professor of Political Science, Ohio University. Frequent contributor to scholarly journals on East European topics and a former contributor to *Nations in Transit* (1995 and 1997 editions).

Thadathil, George. Associate professor of History, Paul Quinn College, Dallas, Texas. Author, "Myanmar, Agony of a People" in *History Behind Headlines*, 2000. His research interests include South and Southeast Asia, and Asian collective security.

Thapa, Rabi. Editor and environmentalist, France. Environment/development assignments in Nepal, 1998.

Tian, Robert Guang, Ph.D. Associate professor of Business Administration, Erskine College. Author, *Canadian Chinese, Chinese Canadians: Coping and Adapting in North America* (1999).

Ubarra, Maria Cecilia T. Graduate student in Public Policy and Program Administration, University of the Philippines, Quezon City, Philippines. Research fellow, Institute for Strategic and Development Studies; case writer, Asian Institute of Management, Philippines.

Vivas, Leonardo. M.Phil., Development Studies, Sussex University (UK); Ph.D., International Economics and Finance, Nanterre University (France); fellow, Weatherhead Center for International Affairs, Harvard University.

Viviers, Wilma. Program director, International Trade in School of Economics, Potchefstroom University, South Africa.

Zhang, Xingli. Ph.D. student, University of Southern California, Los Angeles. Author, "Brunei" in *East Asian Encyclopedia* (in Chinese).

INTRODUCTION

THE POWER OF ECONOMIC UNDERSTANDING

The economies of the world are becoming increasingly interconnected and interdependent, a fact dramatically illustrated on 2 July 1997 when the Thai government decided to allow its currency to "float" according to market conditions. The result was a significant drop in the value of the currency and the start of the Asian economic crisis, a contagion that spread quickly to other Asian countries such as the Republic of Korea, Indonesia, Malaysia, and the Philippines. Before long the epidemic reached Brazil and Russia.

In this way, a small economic change in one less-developed country sent economic shock waves around the world. Surprisingly, no one predicted this crisis, though economist Paul Krugman in a prominent 1994 *Foreign Affairs* article argued that there was no Asian economic miracle and the kind of growth rates attained in recent years were not sustainable over the long term. In such an interconnected global economy, it is imperative to have an understanding of other economies and economic conditions around the world. Yet that understanding is sorely lacking in the American public.

Various studies have shown that both young people and the public at large have a low level of literacy about other nations. A survey of 655 high school students in southeast Ohio indicated that students were least informed in the area of international economic concerns, and the number of economics majors at the college level is declining. The economic and geographic illiteracy has become such a national concern that the U.S. Senate recently passed a resolution calling for a national education policy that addresses Americans' lack of knowledge of other parts of the world.

The information provided by the media also frequently reflects a distorted understanding of world economies. During the Asian economic crisis, we often heard about the collapse of various Asian countries such as Korea and Thailand. They were indeed suffering a severe crisis, but usually companies, not countries, collapse. The use of the "collapse" language was therefore misleading. In another example, a distinguished journalist writing in a prominent East coast newspaper claimed that Vietnamese women paid more in transportation and food costs than they were earning while working in a factory manufacturing Nike shoes. Such a statement, while well intended in terms of genuine concern for these women workers, makes no economic sense whatsoever, and is actually not accurate. The wages of these women are indeed extremely low by U.S. standards, but such wages must be viewed in the context of another society, where the cost of living may be dramatically lower and where low salaries may be pooled. At other times, a fact—such as the fact that a minority of the Japanese workforce enjoys employment for life—is exaggerated to suggest that the Japanese economy boomed as it did in the 1980s *because* of the Japanese policy of life-long employment. Such generalizing keeps people from understanding the complexities of the Japanese economy.

"THINGS ARE NOT WHAT THEY SEEM." In defense of this lack of economic understanding, it must be said that understanding economics is not easy. Paul A. Samuelson, author of the classic textbook *Economics* (1995), once stated about economics "that things are often not what at first they seem." In Japan, for example, many young women work as office ladies in private companies as an initial job after completing school. These young ladies often stay at home with their parents and have few basic expenses. Over several years they can accumulate considerable savings, which may be used for travel, overseas study, or investing. Thus, as Samuelson noted in his textbook, actual individual economic welfare is not based on wages as such, but on the *difference* between earnings and expenditures. Wages are not the only measure of the value of labor: one must also consider purchasing power and how costs of living vary dramatically from place to place. Without taking into account purchasing power, we overestimate economic well-being in high-cost countries such as Japan and Switzerland and underestimate it in low-cost countries such as India and Cambodia.

Consider the following examples: The cost of taking an air-conditioned luxury bus from the Cambodian capital of Phnom Penh to its major port, Sihanoukville, is less than $2. The same bus trip of equal distance in Japan or the United States would cost $50 or more. Similarly, a (subsidized) lunch at a factory producing Nike shoes in Vietnam may cost the equivalent of 5 U.S. cents in 1998, while lunch at a student union on a U.S. college campus may cost $5. Thus a teaching assistant on a U.S. campus pays 100 times more for lunch than the Vietnamese factory worker. Who is more "poorly paid" in these situations? Add to this the reality that in many developing countries where extended families are common, members of the family often pool their earnings, which individually may be quite low. To look only at individual earnings can thus be rather misleading. Such cultural nuances are important to keep in mind in assessing economic conditions and welfare in other nations.

Various economic puzzles can also create confusion and misunderstanding. For example, currently the United States has the highest trade deficit in world history: it imports far more that it exports. Most countries with huge trade deficits have a weak currency, but the U.S. dollar has remained strong. Why is this the case? Actually, it is quite understandable when one knows that the balance of trade is just one of many factors that determine the value of a nation's currency. In truth, demand for the U.S. dollar has remained high. The United States is an attractive site for foreign investment because of its large and growing economic market and extremely stable politics. Second, the United States has a large tourism sector, drawing people to the country where they exchange their currency for U.S. dollars. Several years ago, for the first time ever, there were more Thais coming to the United States as tourists than those in the United States going to Thailand. Third, the United States is extremely popular among international students seeking overseas education. Economically, a German student who spends three years studying in the United States benefits the economy in the same way as a long-term tourist or conventional exports: that student invests in the U.S. economy. In the academic year 1999-2000, there were 514,723 international students in the United States spending approximately $12.3 billion. Thus, the services provided by U.S. higher education represent an important "invisible export." Fourth, 11 economies are now dollarized, which means that they use the U.S. currency as their national currency. Panama is the most well known of these economies and El Salvador became a dollarized economy on 1 January 2001. Other countries are semi-officially or partially dollarized (Cambodia and Vietnam, for example). As the result of dollarization, it is estimated by the Federal Reserve that 55 to 70 percent of all U.S. dollars are held by foreigners primarily in Latin America and former parts of the U.S.S.R. Future candidates for dollarization are Argentina, Brazil, Ecuador, Indonesia, Mexico, and even Canada. With so many countries using U.S. dollars, demand for the U.S. dollar is increased, adding to its strength. For all these reasons, the U.S. currency and economy remained strong despite the persisting large trade deficits, which in themselves, according to standard economic logic, suggest weakness.

SYSTEMS OF CLASSIFICATION. As in other fields, such as biology and botany, it is important to have a sound system of classification to understand various national economies. Unfortunately, the systems commonly used to describe various national economies are often flawed by cultural and Eurocentric biases and distortion. After the end of World War II and the start of the Cold War, it became common to speak of "developed" and "underdeveloped" countries. There were two problems with this overly simplistic distinction. First, it viewed countries only in terms of material development. Second, it implied that a nation was developed or underdeveloped across all categories. As an example, "underdeveloped" Thailand has consistently been one of the world's leading food exporters and among those countries that import the least amount of food. Similarly, in "developed" Japan there are both homeless people and institutions to house the elderly, while in "underdeveloped" Vietnam there are no homeless and the elderly are cared for by their families. Which country is more "developed"?

Later the term "Third World" became popular. This term was invented by the French demographer Alfred Sauvy and popularized by the scholar Irving Horowitz in his volume, *Three Worlds of Development.* "First World" referred to rich democracies such as the United States and the United Kingdom; "Second World" referred to communist countries such as the former U.S.S.R. and former East Germany. The term "Third World" was used to refer to the poorer nations of Africa, Latin America, and Asia (with the exception of Japan). But this distinction is also problematic, for it implies that the "First World" is superior to the "Third World." Another common term introduced was modern versus less modern nations. The Princeton sociologist Marion J. Levy made this distinction based on a technological definition: more modern nations were those that made greater use of tools and inanimate sources of power. Thus, non-Western Japan is quite modern because of its use of robots and bullet trains. Over time, however, many people criticized the modern/non-modern distinction as being culturally biased and implying that all nations had to follow the same path of progress.

More recently, economists from around the world have recognized the importance of using a variety of factors to understand the development of national economies. Each of these factors should be viewed in terms of a continuum. For example, no country is either completely industrial or completely agricultural. The entries in this volume provide the basic data to assess each national economy on several of these key criteria. One can determine, for example, the extent to which an economy is industrial by simply dividing the percentage of the economy made up by industry by the percentage made up by agriculture. Or one can determine how much energy national economies use to achieve their level of economic output and welfare. This provides an important ecological definition of efficiency, which goes beyond limited material definitions. This measure allows an estimate of how "green" versus "gray" an economy is; greener economies are those using less energy to achieve a given level of economic development. One might like to understand how international an economy is, which can be done by adding a country's exports to its imports and then dividing by GDP. This indicator reveals that economies such as the Netherlands, Malaysia, Singapore, and Hong Kong are highly international while the isolationist Democratic People's Republic of Korea (North Korea) is far less international.

Another interesting measure of an economy, particularly relevant in this age of more information-oriented economies and "the death of distance" (Cairncross 1997), is the extent to which an economy is digitalized. One measure of this factor would be the extent to which the population of a given economy has access to the Internet. Costa Rica, for example, established a national policy that all its citizens should have free access to the Internet. In other economies, such as Bhutan, Laos, and North Korea, access to the Internet is extremely limited. These differences, of course, relate to what has been termed "the digital divide." Another important factor is whether an economy is people-oriented, that is, whether it aims to provide the greatest happiness to the greatest number; economist E.F. Schumacher called this "economics as if people mattered." The King of Bhutan, for example, has candidly stated that his goal for his Buddhist nation is not Gross National Product but instead Gross National Happiness. Such goals indicate that the level of a country's economic development does not necessarily reflect its level of social welfare and quality of life.

Another important category that helps us understand economies is the degree to which they can be considered "transitional." Transitional economies are those that were once communist, state-planned economies but that are becoming or have become free-market economies. This transitional process started in China in the late 1970s when its leader Deng Xiaoping introduced his "four modernizations." Later, Soviet leader Mikhael Gorbachev introduced such reforms, called *perestroika,* in the former Soviet Union. With the dissolving of the U.S.S.R. in 1991, many new transitional economies emerged, including Belarus, Uzbekistan, Kyrgyzstan, and the Ukraine. Other countries undergoing transition were Vietnam, Laos, Cambodia, and Mongolia. These economies can be grouped into two types: full transitional and partial transitional. The full transitional economies are shifting both to free markets and to liberal democracies with free expression, multiple parties, and open elections. The partial transitional economies are changing in the economic realm, but retaining their original one-party systems. Included in the latter category are the economies of China, Vietnam, Laos, and Cuba. This volume provides valuable current information on the many new transitional economies emerging from the former Soviet world.

KEY THEMES IN THE WORLD ECONOMY. In looking at the economies of countries around the globe, a number of major common themes can be identified. There is increasing economic interdependence and interconnectivity, as stressed by Thomas Friedman in his recent controversial book about globalization titled *The Lexus and the Olive Tree: Understanding Globalization.* For example, the People's Republic of China is now highly dependent on exports to the United States. In turn, U.S. companies are dependent on the Chinese market: Boeing is dependent on China for marketing its jet airliners; the second largest market for Mastercard is now in China; and Nike is highly dependent on China and other Asian economies for manufacturing its sports products. Such deep interdependence augurs well for a peaceful century, for countries are less likely to attack the countries with whom they do a vigorous business, even if their political and social systems are radically different. In fact, new threats to peace as reflected in the tragic terrorist attack of 11 September 2001, primarily relate to long-standing *historical* conflicts and grievances.

Conventional political boundaries and borders often do not well reflect new economic realities and cultural patterns. Economic regions and region states are becoming more important. The still-emerging power of the European Union can be gauged by reading the essays of any of the countries that are currently part of the Union or hoping to become a part of it in the coming years. This volume may help readers better understand which nations are becoming more interconnected and have similar economic conditions.

The tension between equity (fairness) and efficiency is common in nearly all national economies. In some economies there is more stress on efficiency, while in others there is more stress on equity and equality. Thus, as should be expected, countries differ in the nature of the equality of their income and wealth distributions. For each entry in this volume, important data are provided on this important factor. The geographer David M. Smith has documented well both national and international inequalities in his data-rich *Where the Grass is Greener* (1979).

Invisible and informal economies—the interactions of which are outside regulated economic channels—represent a growing segment of economic interactions in some countries. In his controversial but important volume, *The Other Path* (1989), the Peruvian economist Hernando de Soto alerted us to the growing significance of the informal economy. In countries such as Peru, research has shown that in some cases individuals prefer work in the informal to the formal sector because it provides them with more control over their personal lives. The Thai economist Pasuk Phongpaichit and her colleagues have written a fascinating book on Thailand's substantial invisible economy titled *Guns, Girls, Gambling, and Ganja* (1998). Thus, official government and international statistical data reported in this volume often are unable to take into account such data from the hidden part of economies.

In an increasingly internationalized economy in which transnational corporations are highly mobile and able to move manufacturing overseas quite rapidly, it is important to distinguish between real foreign direct investment and portfolio investment. At one point during Thailand's impressive economic boom of the late 1980s and early 1990s, a new Japanese factory was coming on line every three days. This is foreign direct investment, involving actual bricks and mortar, and it creates jobs that extend beyond the actual facility being constructed. In contrast foreign portfolio investment consists of a foreign entity buying stocks, bonds, or other financial instruments in another nation. In our current wired global economy, such funds can be moved in and out of nations almost instantaneously and have little lasting effect on the economic growth of a country. Economies such as Chile and Malaysia have developed policies to try to combat uncertainty and related economic instability caused by the potential of quick withdrawal of portfolio investments.

Some argue that transnational corporations (owned by individuals all over the world), which have no national loyalties, represent the most powerful political force in the world today. Many key transnational corporations have larger revenues than the entire gross national products of many of the nations included in this volume. This means that many national economies, especially smaller ones, lack effective bargaining power in dealing with large international corporations.

Currently, it is estimated by the International Labor Office of the United Nations that one-third of the world's workforce is currently unemployed or underemployed. This means that 500 million new jobs need to be created over the next 10 years. Data on the employment situation in each economy are presented in this volume. The creation of these new jobs represents a major challenge to the world's economies.

The final and most important theme relates to the ultimate potential clash between economy and ecology. To the extent that various national economies and their peoples show a commitment to become greener and more environmentally friendly, ultimate ecological crises and catastrophes can be avoided or minimized. Paul Ray and Sherry Anderson's *The Cultural Creatives: How 50 Million People Are Changing the World* (2000) lends credence to the view that millions are changing to more environmentally conscious lifestyles.

In trying to understand the global economy, it is critically important to have good trend data. In each of the entries of this volume, there is an emphasis on providing important economic data over several decades to enable the reader to assess such patterns. Some trends will have tremendous importance for the global economy. One phenomenon with extremely important implications for population is the policy of limiting families to only one child in China's urban areas. This deliberate social engineering by the world's most populous country will have a powerful impact on the global economy of the 21st century. The global environmental implications are, of course, extremely positive. Though there is much debate about the economic, political, and socio-cultural implications of this one-child policy, overall it will probably give China a tremendous strategic advantage in terms of the key factors of human resource development and creativity.

THE POWER OF UNDERSTANDING. By enhancing our knowledge and understanding of other economies, we gain the potential for mutual learning and inspiration for continuous improvement. There is so much that we can learn from each other. Denmark, for example, is now getting seven percent of its electrical energy from wind energy. This has obvious relevance to the state of California as it faces a major energy crisis. The Netherlands and China for a long period have utilized bicycles for basic transportation. Some argue that the bicycle is the most efficient "tool" in the world in terms of output and energy inputs. Many new major highways in Vietnam are built with exclusive bike paths separated by concrete walls from the main highway. The Vietnamese have also developed electric bicycles. The efficient bullet trains of Japan and France have relevance to other areas such as coastal China and the coastal United States. Kathmandu in Nepal has experimented with non-polluting electric buses. In the tremendous biodiversity of the tropical forests of Southeast Africa, Latin America, and Africa, there may be cures for many modern diseases.

We hope to dispel the view that economics is the boring "dismal science" often written in complex, difficult language. This four-volume set presents concise, current information on all the economies of the world, including not only large well-known economies such as the United States, Germany, and Japan, but also new nations that have emerged only in recent years, and many micro-states of which we tend to be extremely uninformed. With the publication of this volume, we hope to be responsive to the following call by Professor Mark C. Schug: "The goal of economic education is to foster in students the thinking skills and substantial economic knowledge necessary to become effective and participating citizens." It is our hope that this set will enhance both economic and geographic literacy critically needed in an increasingly interconnected world.

—Gerald W. Fry, University of Minnesota

BIBLIOGRAPHY

Brown, Lester R., et al. *State of the World 2000.* New York: W. W. Norton, 2000.

Buchholz, Todd G. *From Here to Economy: A Shortcut to Economic Literacy.* New York: A Dutton Book, 1995.

Cairncross, Frances. *The Death of Distance: How the Communications Revolution Will Change Our Lives.* Boston: Harvard Business School Press, 2001.

Friedman, Thomas F. *The Lexus and the Olive Tree: Understanding Globalization.* New York: Anchor Books, 2000.

Fry, Gerald W., and Galen Martin. *The International Development Dictionary.* Oxford: ABC-Clio Press, 1991.

Hansen, Fay. "Power to the Dollar, Part One of a Series," *Business Finance* (October 1999): 17-20.

Heintz, James, Nancy Folbre, and the Center for Popular Economics. *The Ultimate Field Guide to the U.S. Economy.* New York: The New Press, 2000.

Horowitz, Irving J. *Three Worlds of Development: The Theory and Practice of International Stratification.* New York: Oxford University Press, 1966.

Jacobs, Jane. *The Nature of Economies.* New York: The Modern Library, 2000.

Korten, David C. *When Corporations Rule the World.* West Hartford, CT: Kumarian Press, 1995.

Levy, Marion J. *Modernization and the Structure of Societies.* 2 vols. New Brunswick, NJ: Transaction Publications, 1996.

Lewis, Martin W., and Kären E. Wigen. *A Critique of Metageography.* Berkeley: University of California Press, 1997.

Lohrenz, Edward. *The Essence of Chaos.* Seattle: University of Washington Press, 1993.

Ohmae, Kenichi. *The End of the Nation State: The Rise of Regional Economies.* London: HarperCollins, 1996.

Pasuk Phongpaichit, Sungsidh Priryarangsan, and Nualnoi Treerat. *Guns, Girls, Gambling, and Ganja: Thailand's Illegal Economy and Public Policy.* Chiang Mai: Silkworm Books, 1998.

Pennar, Karen. "Economics Made Too Simple." *Business Week* (20 January 1997): 32.

Ray, Paul H., and Sherry Ruth Anderson. *The Cultural Creatives: How 50 Million People Are Changing the World.* New York: Harmony Books, 2000.

Salk, Jonas, and Jonathan Salk. *World Population and Human Values: A New Reality.* New York: Harper & Row, 1981.

Samuelson, Paul A., William D. Nordhaus, with the assistance of Michael J. Mandal. *Economics.* 15th ed. New York: McGraw-Hill, 1995.

Schug, Mark C. "Introducing Children to Economic Reasoning: Some Beginning Lessons." *Social Studies* (Vol. 87, No. 3, May-June 1996): 114-118.

Schumacher, E.F. *Small is Beautiful: Economics as if People Mattered.* New York: Perennial Library, 1975.

Siegfried, John J., and Bonnie T. Meszaros. "National Voluntary Content Standards for Pre-College Economics Education." *AEA Papers and Proceedings* (Vol. 87, No. 2, May 1997): 247-253.

Smith, David. *Where the Grass Is Greener: Geographical Perspectives on Inequality.* London: Croom Helm, 1979.

Soto, Hernando de; translated by June Abbott. *The Other Path: The Invisible Revolution in the Third World.* New York: Harper & Row, 1989.

Stock, Paul A., and William D. Rader. "Level of Economic Understanding for Senior High School Students in Ohio." *The Journal of Educational Research* (Vol. 91, No. 1, September/October 1997): 60-63.

Sulloway, Frank J. *Born to Rebel: Birth Order, Family Dynamics, and Creative Lives.* New York: Pantheon Books, 1996.

Todaro, Michael P. *Economic Development.* Reading, MA: Addison Wesley, 2000.

Wentland, Daniel. "A Framework for Organizing Economic Education Teaching Methodologies." Mississippi: 2000-00-00, ERIC Document, ED 442702.

Wood, Barbara. *E.F. Schumacher: His Life and Thought.* New York: Harper & Row, 1984.

Wren, Christopher S. "World Needs to Add 500 Million Jobs in 10 Years, Report Says." *The New York Times* (25 January 2001): A13.

AFGHANISTAN

Islamic State of Afghanistan
Dowlat-e Eslami-ye Afghanestan

CAPITAL: Kabul.

MONETARY UNIT: Afghani (Af). One afghani equals 100 puls. There are coins of 1, 2, and 5 afghanis and notes of 10, 20, 50, 100, 500, 1,000, 5,000, and 10,000 afghanis.

CHIEF EXPORTS: Opium, fruits and nuts, hand woven carpets, wool, cotton, hides and pelts, precious and semi-precious gems.

CHIEF IMPORTS: Capital goods, food and petroleum products, and most consumer goods.

GROSS DOMESTIC PRODUCT: US$21 billion (purchasing power parity, 1999).

BALANCE OF TRADE: **Exports:** US$80 million (1996 est.; does not include opium). **Imports:** US$150 million (1996 est.).

COUNTRY OVERVIEW

LOCATION AND SIZE. Afghanistan is located in southern Asia and shares a border with 6 countries: China, Iran, Pakistan, Tajikistan, Turkmenistan, and Uzbekistan. Landlocked, with an area of 652,000 square kilometers (251,737 square miles), Afghanistan is a mountainous country dominated by the Hindu Kush and the Himalayan mountain ranges to the north and arid desert to the south. Afghanistan endures the most extreme temperatures on earth. Comparatively, the area occupied by Afghanistan is slightly smaller than the state of Texas. The capital city, Kabul, is located in the northeastern part of the country.

POPULATION. The 1976 census estimated the Afghan population at 16.6 million, but 4 years later, similar research put the population at 15.5 million. In 1999, a United Nations (UN) sponsored census, carried out by the Taliban (originally, a group of Afghans trained in religious schools in Pakistan) put the population at 23 million, indicating an annual population growth of 2.8 percent. Finally, the CIA *World Factbook* estimates the population in July 2000 at 25,838,797. Doubts about the true figures stem from the war that began as a result of the invasion of the country by the Soviet Union in 1979. Not only did this war result in the loss of approximately 1 million lives but an estimated 5 million Afghans went into exile abroad, to countries such as Pakistan and Iran, thus creating the world's largest refugee population. Mass migration from the rural areas to the urban centers occurred and the population of the capital city of Kabul more than doubled after 1979. Over one-third of Afghan families have migrated to Kabul since 1995 and the share of the urban population increased from 10 percent in the 1970s to over 30 percent in 1995. The return of the Afghan refugees began in April 1992, following the victory of the mujahideen (anti-Soviet freedom fighters; from the Persian word for "warrior"), and by the middle of 1996 over half of the refugees had been **repatriated**. However, when the United States began military strikes against Afghanistan for harboring terrorist Osama bin Laden in 2001, another wave of refugees fled the country.

The principal linguistic and ethnic group in Afghanistan are the Pashtun. These people represent just over half of the population and live mostly in the south or in the east. Persian-speaking Tajiks, who live in the eastern valleys, make up 20 percent of the population; another 10 percent of the population is of Turkmen and Uzbek origin, and they live on the northern plains. There are an additional 20 other different ethnic groups of which the Baluch, the Hazaras, and the Nuristanis are the most well known, and these groups speak over 30 different languages. The vast majority—84 percent—of Aghanis follow the Sunni Muslim faith, while a significant minority—15 percent—are Shi'a Muslims.

Following the collapse of the **communist** regime in 1992, a civil war has been fought largely along ethnic lines between the Pashtuns, the Tajiks, the Uzbeks, and the Hazaras.

OVERVIEW OF ECONOMY

Following the end of 40 years of peaceful monarchical rule in July 1973, Afghanistan was plunged into a war that continued into the 21st century. The end of the monarchy was followed by the setting up of a communist-style regime that collapsed when 100,000 Soviet troops invaded the country in December 1979. For 10 years Soviet forces occupied the country and dictated its governance, but local rebel forces, known as the mujahideen, drove the Soviets out in 1989. The victory by the mujahideen brought no peace to the troubled country, however. For the next several years fighting continued between rival mujahideen factions. By 1996 the sitting government had collapsed, and effective control of the country was seized by the radical Islamic Taliban faction. The Taliban remained in power until 2001 when U.S. attacks toppled the faction from power.

In economic terms, Afghanistan is among the world's poorest countries due to the incessant fighting that has placed the economy on the verge of collapse and taken hundreds of thousands of lives. Two decades of war and political strife left the country's **infrastructure** in ruins and its people almost entirely dependent on foreign aid. The majority of administrative, economical, and social institutions were wiped out due to the Soviet invasion, mass migration, and continued fighting.

The principal source of revenue in Afghanistan traditionally came from the agricultural sector, and under normal circumstances the country is capable of producing not only enough food to feed its entire population but surplus food to export abroad. But as of 2001 the country was able to produce enough food no longer. Given that the country is heavily dependent on subsistence agriculture, the decline in income levels and the increased lack of food security (a country's ability to feed its own people) increased poverty and caused other economic difficulties. Much of the land that was previously devoted to wheat farming began to be used to cultivate opium poppies, which are used in the production of heroin. The country's transport system was almost entirely broken down, as well as most industry and the agricultural infrastructure. These sectors were so seriously damaged that only sustained massive investment could salvage them.

Before the Soviet invasion in 1979, the economy was almost entirely controlled by the government of Afghanistan, with most investments taking place within the **public sector**. The **private sector** extended only to agriculture and trade. The past 2 decades have seen the dismantling of centralized governance and an increase in private sector participation. In 2000 the private sector played a major role in the country's traditional economic activities, and there was still much room for private sector investment in small-scale industries, provided that political stability was achieved. The Taliban emerged in the mid-1990s and swept through the country, taking control in a remarkably short period of time. Political stability was then entirely dependent on the future course the Taliban chose to follow and the economic policies they chose to pursue. The Taliban movement established nominal government in most parts of the country, but it was only recognized by Saudi Arabia, Pakistan, and the United Arab Emirates.

The Afghan economy is famously dependent upon the decisions made by its neighbors' governments. In the past, the country was heavily dependent on economic relations with the former Soviet Union, and in 2001 it was sensitive to economic decisions made by the Pakistani government. An example of this dependency can be seen within the markets. An increase in the prices of essential commodities (basic foodstuffs such as bread and rice) in Pakistan led to an increase in prices of the same commodities in Afghanistan. In addition, when Pakistan devalued its currency in 1998, the value of the Afghan currency was also reduced. Because of the lack of a governmental infrastructure, there were no reliable economic indicators available for such data as GDP, foreign trade, or national income.

POLITICS, GOVERNMENT, AND TAXATION

Due to its strategic geographical position, Afghanistan has been invaded throughout history and conquered by the Persians, the Macedonians, the Parthians, the Kushan Empire, the Huns, and the Arabs. The only peaceful period in the country's recent past was between 1933 and 1973 when it was ruled by King Zahir Shah. However, following the dissolution of the monarchy in 1973, a communist-style regime was established. The watershed event in the modern era was the 1979 invasion by the Soviet Union, which was launched in order to keep Afghanistan from becoming too independent. After a long, entrenched war which many have called "the Soviets' Vietnam," the USSR finally withdrew from the country in 1989. After that, the Taliban took control of most of the country, but a protracted war still continued with opponents of the Taliban, who practiced the same kind of guerilla warfare against the Taliban that they carried out against the Soviet Union.

Afghanistan has not had an effective central government capable of exerting its authority across the entire country because the population is structured by tribes. When the communist administration in Kabul crumbled in 1992, the religious, linguistic, and ethnic differences within the country deepened, leading to the fragmentation of Afghanistan into a series of fiefdoms controlled by warlords. The Taliban originated in the refugee camps on the Pakistani border towns and was initially comprised of religious students who blamed the failure of the previous government on its unwillingness to impose the tenets of fundamentalist Islam (the religion of the world's Muslims and the chief religion in the Middle East; Islam literally means "submission to the will of God"). The Taliban played cleverly on the deep divisions within the country, and in 2000 only 10 percent of the entire country was controlled by non-Taliban groups. This student militia ran the country in accordance with the strict Islamic principles laid out in Sharia Law (Sharia is the law of Islam, based upon the Qur-an, the Sunna, and the work of Muslim scholars in the first two centuries of Islam). Their rigid and often brutal interpretation of Islam caused the Afghan people tremendous suffering, especially among women who were entirely deprived of their rights. The Taliban's successful rise to power was attributed to the substantial help that it received from the Pakistani government combined with the inability of the opposing parties to organize themselves and join together to form an effective opposition. The main political figures within Afghanistan prior to the downfall of the Taliban were Mohammad Omar, the spiritual leader of the Taliban, and Colonel Ahmad Shah Massoud, the leader of the remaining opposition forces.

Afghanistan under the Taliban regime essentially had no central government—no executive branch, no legislature, and no independent and impartial judicial system. Many critics of the regime charged that there was no rule of law, no constitution, no civil society, and no system in place to monitor human rights abuses or address grievances. The Taliban's distaste for the standards of international human rights was made clear to the international community. The UN Security Council imposed **sanctions** on the Taliban in November 1999 under

Security Council Resolution 1267. (Sanctions are imposed unilaterally or multilaterally by states onto countries that violate international norms of behavior and can take many forms, from denying government aid or other benefits to banning any form of trade.) The UN demanded that the Taliban hand over the terrorist Osama bin Laden, who is suspected of being involved in the 1998 bombing of U.S. embassies in Tanzania and Kenya and the September 2001 attacks on the Pentagon in Washington, D.C., and the World Trade Center in New York City. When the Taliban refused to comply, the UN declared that UN member states may not operate commercial aircraft in Afghanistan, and all known funds and other financial resources controlled by the Taliban outside of the country were frozen. With the downfall of the Taliban regime in 2001, an interim government composed of tribal and Northern Alliance leaders was formed to restore stability to the country. However, fighting amongst the different leaders threatened the effectiveness of this new government. It is possible that lasting peace and stability will only come to Afghanistan under the watchful eye of an international peacekeeping force stationed in the country.

There has never really been a formal tax system in this essentially tribal country. Local tribal leaders often used to **levy** arbitrary taxes on commercial goods passing through their territory, but this revenue never reached Kabul. The Taliban tried to gain popularity by removing checkpoints erected for the collection of taxes, and local traders rewarded them with large donations.

INFRASTRUCTURE, POWER, AND COMMUNICATIONS

Before the Soviet invasion in 1979, considerable investment from the United States and development agencies had been channeled into the reconstruction of the Afghan road networks. Over 2,000 kilometers (1,243 miles) of roads were built linking the principal cities, giving the country a distinctly modern feel. The long war has undone much of the work carried out by development agencies in the 1970s. In 1993, the **United Nations Development Program** (UNDP) estimated that 60 percent of the 2,500 kilometers (1,553 miles) of paved roads needed to be totally rebuilt and that minor roads linking rural areas were in very poor condition. The country has just 21,000 kilometers (12,050 miles) of total roadways. Since 1993 the condition of the roads in Afghanistan has further deteriorated and hundreds of bridges have been destroyed, cutting off many remote mountain areas.

The telecommunications infrastructure has improved since 1999, and in 2001 it was possible to phone between 2 of Afghanistan's major urban centers, Kabul and Kandahar. Telephone calls were also possible to 13 foreign countries, including the United States, the United Kingdom, Canada, and Saudi Arabia. All calls made to Afghanistan have to go through an operator, and calls out of Afghanistan must be made on satellite telephones. In 2000, the Taliban signed a contact with a company based in the United Arab Emirates to increase the number of telephone lines in the country to 1 million by September 2001. This project also aims to put the country in touch with over 99 other countries instead of just 13 within the same time frame.

The aviation infrastructure was almost completely destroyed by the war. Most of the national fleet of aircraft is now unusable or too dangerous to fly commercially. When the first round of sanctions were imposed by the United Nations in 1999, Afghanistan's national airline, Ariana, was hit badly because its airplanes were no longer allowed to fly abroad. The country has only 14 airports with paved runways and another 32 dirt landing strips.

Communications

Country	Telephones[a]	Telephones, Mobile/Cellular[a]	Radio Stations[b]	Radios[a]	TV Stations[a]	Televisions[a]	Internet Service Providers[c]	Internet Users[c]
Afghanistan	29,000 (1996)	N/A	AM 7; FM 1; shortwave 1 (1999)	167,000 (1999)	10	100,000 (1999)	1	N/A
United States	194 M	69.209 M (1998)	AM 4,762; FM 5,542; shortwave 18	575 M	1,500	219 M	7,800	148 M
India	27.7 M (2000)	2.93 M (2000)	AM 153; FM 91; shortwave 68	116 M	562	63 M	43	4.5 M
Pakistan	2.861 M (1999)	158,000 (1998)	AM 27; FM 1; shortwave 21	13.5 M	22	3.1 M	30	1.2 M

[a]Data is for 1997 unless otherwise noted.
[b]Data is for 1998 unless otherwise noted.
[c]Data is for 2000 unless otherwise noted.

SOURCE: CIA *World Factbook 2001* [Online].

Before the Soviet invasion in 1979, energy consumption per capita was among the world's lowest. However, as a result of war and the Soviets' development of the country's gas reserves, consumption levels increased. In 1992 the authorities stated that Kabul's winter requirement was 300 megawatts even though the installed capacity was only 150 megawatts. Between 1992 and 1996, much of the capital had no power. In 1993 the UNDP estimated that over 60 percent of the gas transmission lines were not functioning. In July 2000, the Taliban initiated a project to build an electrical grid from Afghanistan to Turkmenistan; however, the project has not progressed due to a lack of funds. Reports coming out of the country in 2001 indicated that the severe winter had claimed hundreds of Afghan lives.

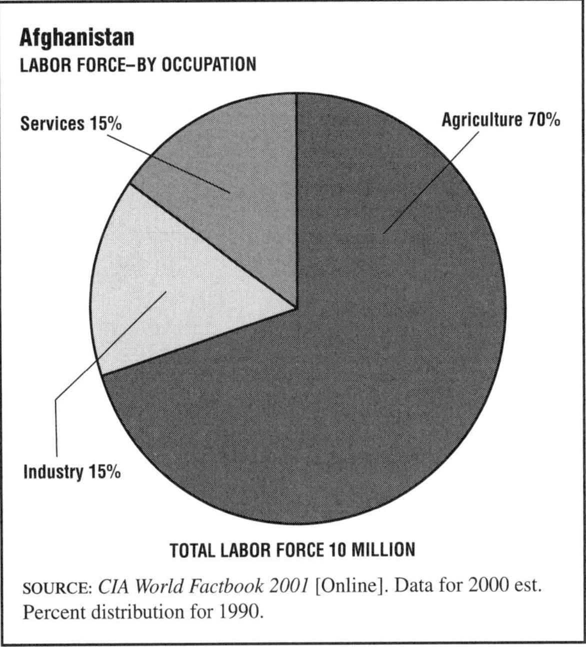

SOURCE: *CIA World Factbook 2001* [Online]. Data for 2000 est. Percent distribution for 1990.

ECONOMIC SECTORS

The economy of Afghanistan, one of the world's least developed, has never been properly documented. Prior to the Soviet invasion in 1979 the very few economic data were often wholly unreliable. Official statistics almost entirely ground to a halt in 1979 and have not been produced since the communist government fell in 1992. Nevertheless, the CIA World Factbook estimated that in 1990 the agricultural sector produced 53 percent of GDP while industry contributed 28.5 percent and services 18.5 percent. In 1980 it was estimated the 68 percent of the workforce worked in agriculture, 16 percent in industry, and 16 percent in services.

Over 2 decades of war have either destroyed or seriously damaged the infrastructures of the agricultural, industrial, and service sectors. Nevertheless, the agricultural sector is still the largest employer. Its output is largely dependant on changing political conditions and, to a lesser extent, the weather.

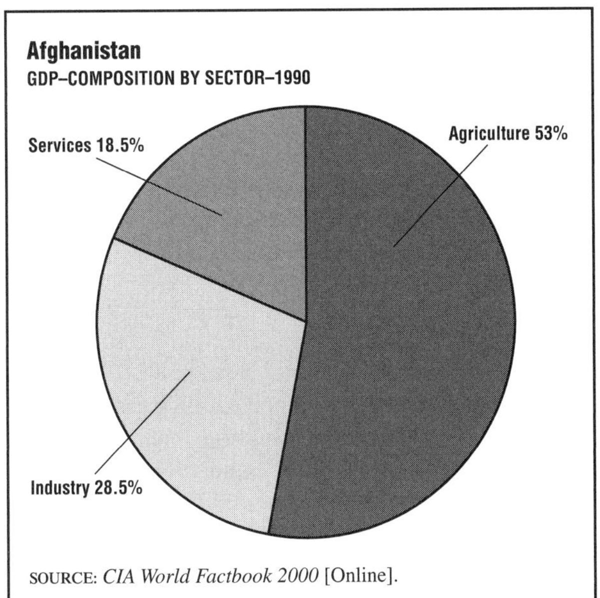

SOURCE: *CIA World Factbook 2000* [Online].

AGRICULTURE

Agriculture has traditionally driven the Afghan economy, accounting for approximately 50 percent of GDP before the Soviet invasion in 1979. Nevertheless, the agricultural sector has never produced at full capacity. Before the invasion, only 30 percent of the total arable land of 15 million hectares was cultivated. At that time the main exports were sugarcane, sugar beets, fruit, nuts, vegetables, and wool. However, the continuing war reduced production significantly. Soviet troops planted land mines all over the country, rendering large areas of land useless and forcing large sections of the population to become refugees. The resulting cut in production caused massive food shortages. Kabul University produced a report in 1988 which found that agricultural output was 45 percent less than the 1978 level. The UNDP estimated that in 1992 only 3.2 million hectares of land were cultivated of which only 1.5 million hectares were irrigated. In 2001, the principal food crops were corn, rice, barley, wheat, vegetables, fruits, and nuts. In Afghanistan, industry is also based on agriculture, along with raw materials. The major industrial crops are cotton, tobacco, castor beans, and sugar beets. Sheep farming is also extremely valuable. The major sheep product exports are wool and sheep skins.

In 2000, Afghanistan experienced its worst food crisis ever recorded because of a very severe drought. Such low levels of recorded rainfall had not been seen in the country since the 1950s. The water used to irrigate the lands comes from melting snow, and in 2000 the country experienced very little snowfall. The southern parts of the country were badly affected, and farmlands produced 40 percent of their expected yields. Half of the wells in the country dried up during the drought, and the lake feeding the Arghandab dam dried up for the first time since 1952. The barley crops were destroyed and the wheat crops were almost wiped out. In the middle of 2000, the drought's consequences were felt in Kabul, when more and more displaced people were migrating to the capital.

The prices of staple foods have also increased in different parts of the country because demand is much higher than supply. For instance, in Kabul, a family of 7 can earn US$1.14 a day if the head of the family is lucky enough to find employment, whereas a loaf of bread costs US$0.63, roughly half an individual's income per day. A large segment of the Afghan population depends on food imported from abroad or distributed by aid organizations. The civil strife and drought increased the country's food import requirements to a record 2.3 million metric tons in 2000/2001, according to the UN World Food Programme. Much of the needed imports come from the international community and the rest from Pakistan. The disruption to the flow of this international aid caused by the 2001 war between U.S.-led forces on the Taliban has threatened widespread famine and starvation to much of the Afghan population.

The number of livestock was greatly reduced during the years of war. In 1970, the total livestock population was estimated at 22 million sheep, 3.7 million cattle, 3.2 million goats, and 500,000 horses. According to a survey carried out in 1988, the number of cattle had declined by 55 percent, sheep and goats by 65 percent, and the number of oxen used to plow the fields was down by 30 percent. Much of the livestock is malnourished and diseased.

Afghanistan in 2000 was the world's largest producer of opium, used to produce the drug heroin. The total opium production for 1998 was estimated at 2,102 metric tons against a total of 2,804 metric tons in 1997. This reduction in the level of poppy production was due to heavy and continuous rains and hailstorms in some of the major poppy producing provinces. However, in 1999, the country produced a staggering 4,600 metric tons. The rotting economy forced farmers to grow the opium poppies as a **cash crop**, and this practice was supported by the Taliban until 2001, because it provided farmers with money that they would otherwise not be able to earn. However, in 2001, the Taliban ordered the country's farmers to stop growing poppies following an edict by Mullah Omar, the supreme religious leader, that opium cultivation is not permitted under Islam. While analysts contend that the reason had more to do with convincing the United Nations and the international community to lift sanctions, officials from various countries argued that this was done in order to boost the market price for heroin. Heroin still flowed from Afghanistan, only at a much higher price—after the Taliban's ban on opium growing, the price shot from $44 to $700 per kilo. This caused speculation that the Taliban had stockpiled a large supply of the drug, and the higher proceeds allowed them further funding for military and government operations. With the September 2001 attacks on the United States, opium production was believed to be resumed.

INDUSTRY

Afghanistan's significance from an energy standpoint stems from its geographical position as a potential transit route for oil and natural gas exports from Central Asia to the Arabian Sea. This potential includes the proposed multi-billion dollar oil and gas export pipelines to be built in Afghanistan by UNOCAL, an American oil company, and Bridas, an Argentinean firm. However, political instability has thrown these plans into serious question, and it is unlikely that construction will be approved until the fighting in the country stops.

GAS. Afghanistan's proven and probable natural gas reserves are estimated to be around 150 billion cubic feet. Afghan gas production reached 275 million cubic feet per day (mcf/d) in the mid-1970s. However, due to declining reserves from producing fields, output gradually fell to about 220 mcf/d by 1980. At that time, the largest field, Djarquduq, was tapped and was expected to boost Afghan gas output to 385 mcf/d by the early 1980s. However, sabotage of infrastructure by the anti-Soviet mujahideen fighters limited the country's total production to 290 mcf/d. During the 1980s, the sale of gas accounted for up to 50 percent of export revenues. After the Soviet pullout and subsequent Afghan civil war, roughly 31 producing wells were closed, pending the restart of gas sales to the former Soviet Union. In 1998, Afghan gas production was only around 22 mcf/d, all of which was used domestically. In February 1998, the Taliban announced plans to revive the Afghan National Oil Company, which was abolished by the Soviet Union after it invaded Afghanistan in 1979. The company is expected to play an important role in the resumption of both gas and oil exploration in Afghanistan.

OIL. Soviet estimates from the late 1970s placed Afghanistan's proven and probable oil reserves at 100 million barrels. Despite plans to start commercial oil production in Afghanistan, all oil exploration and development work, as well as plans to build a 10,000 barrel per day (bbl/d) refinery, were halted after the 1979 Soviet invasion. In September 1999, Afghanistan signed a deal with Consolidated Construction Company of Greece to explore for oil and gas in the area of Herat in southwestern Afghanistan near the Iranian border. This area is believed to be potentially rich in hydrocarbons (any of a variety of organic compounds—including oil and coal—that can be harnessed to produce energy). In the meantime, Afghanistan reportedly receives some of its oil imports from Saudi Arabia as foreign aid. There have also been reports that Pakistan has offered to assist Afghanistan in constructing an oil refinery, as well as in repairing damaged roads in order to facilitate transport of oil products from Turkmenistan to Afghanistan and Pakistan.

COAL. Besides gas and oil, Afghanistan is also estimated to have significant coal reserves (probable reserves of 400 million tons), most of which are located in the northern part of the country. Although Afghanistan produced over 100,000 tons of coal annually as late as the early 1990s, the country was producing only around 4,000 tons as of 1998.

MANUFACTURING. Almost all manufacturing businesses have shut down or are producing at well below capacity because of the damage caused during the war and the lack of raw materials available in the country. Before this sector collapsed, it was mainly processing local agricultural raw materials. However, the country's cotton mills, woolen textiles, and cement plants were still not producing at full capacity. In 2000, the Taliban announced the startup of 26 production and servicing projects that would create 1,500 jobs, including the production of alcohol-free beverages, printing, syringe-making, and chemical products.

SERVICES

Like the other sectors of the economy, the services sector has been devastated by years of war. There are no reliable figures for **retail** trade in Afghanistan, and the current economy cannot support anything approaching a vigorous retail trade sector. There is no tourism sector in Afghanistan because the country remains unstable, extremely volatile, and dangerous for foreigners.

FINANCIAL SERVICES. In 1932, Afghanistan's banking system was founded by Abdul Majid Zabuli, who developed the economy and imported the necessary goods to start up plants and factories. His bank eventually developed into the Afghan National Bank, which has served roles as both the country's central and commercial bank. Until the beginning of the 1990s, the Afghan National bank had 7 branches in Kabul and 10 other branches in other major cities. It also had offices in Hamburg, Paris, London, and New York. However, like all institutions in 2001, the banking system has been severely affected by the war, and it virtually collapsed when the mujahideen seized power in 1992. The other important banks in Afghanistan are the Construction Bank, the Industrial Credit Fund, the Industrial Development Bank, the Agriculture Bank, and the Export Promotion Bank. The sanctions imposed on Afghanistan in 1999 forced the smaller banks to close, and by 2001, the resources of the remaining banks were very limited, allowing them to engage only in trade-related work.

Those who provide financial services to the average Afghan are not the banks, but money changers who operate in the streets. This situation has meant that opium has become vitally important for Afghanistan's poor, who otherwise would not be able to afford basic foodstuffs. These moneylenders give out informal loans in exchange for a fixed amount of crop. Clearly, opium production or its being banned affects income levels for the poor. These effects remain difficult to determine.

INTERNATIONAL TRADE

The Soviet invasion in 1979 damaged Afghanistan's industrial and agricultural sectors significantly, and as a result the country's exports, of which gas was very important, diminished. This shift naturally meant that the import bill had to rise to provide the Afghan people with basic commodities such as food and petroleum products and most **consumer goods**. Rising imports during the 1980s resulted in a serious **trade deficit**, although accurate figures are impossible to estimate, since official statistics exclude most illegal trade. From 1985 to 1986 and from 1989 to 1990 the value of exports fell almost 50 percent from US$566.8 million to US$235.9 million, with declining natural gas exports accounting for much of the difference. Other crucial earners of foreign exchange included the sale of nuts and vegetables to Pakistan and India and sheepskins to Europe. Imports declined somewhat during the 1980s as Afghanistan and the Soviet Union became more and more integrated. Between 1989 and 1991, the USSR was consuming 72 percent of Afghanistan's exports and supplying it with 57 percent of its imports. Despite the difficulties in determining trade figures, the CIA *World Factbook* estimated imports of

Trade (expressed in billions of US$): Afghanistan

	Exports	Imports
1975	.217	.350
1980	.670	.841
1985	.567	1.194
1990	.235	.936
1995	.026	.050
1998	N/A	N/A

SOURCE: International Monetary Fund. *International Financial Statistics Yearbook 1999.*

US$150 million in 1996 and exports of US$80 million, not including opium.

When the Soviet Union collapsed in 1991 and the communist government simultaneously fell in Kabul, most imports started to flood in from Pakistan. Under the Afghan Transit Trade (ATT) agreement, signed in 1965, Pakistan allows Afghanistan to have access to the sea and to engage in commerce with the international community to the extent required by Afghanistan's economy. Most of the goods imported under the ATT are reportedly electronics and other consumer items, which cross Pakistan's territory free of **duty**.

Since the Taliban's rise to power, trade has increased significantly with Pakistan, but most of it is not officially recorded. Trade between these 2 countries involves the importation of fuel, wheat, and cement and had included the export of opium. There has been an increase in the volume of trade between Afghanistan and Turkmenistan since 1998. In September 1998, the Taliban authorities signed an agreement with the government of Turkmenistan to begin importing gasoline, diesel, and jet fuel. This action has, to some extent, reduced Afghanistan's dependency on fuel imports from Iran. According to a World Bank report, the total trade between Afghanistan and Pakistan was estimated to be US$2.5 billion in 1996–97, of which US$1.96 billion was estimated to be the value of **re-exported** goods from Afghanistan into Pakistan.

MONEY

In 1993, the official **inflation rate** was more than 150 percent. While there has been no official figure since then, one estimate put the figure at a whopping 240 percent for Kabul in 1996. This kind of skyrocketing price increase in a society is often called "hyperinflation." Thus, a loaf of bread in the capital city may have cost US$1 in 1995 and risen to US$2.50 in 1996. The value of the afghani has also plummeted against the U.S. dollar, going from 36,000 afghanis to the dollar in October, 1998, to 45,000 afghanis to the dollar 6 months later. Weaker currency values can lead to higher prices and **inflation**. Until Afghanistan establishes normal relations with the rest of the world, there is little hope that its currency will have any stability or value.

POVERTY AND WEALTH

At meeting of the World Health Organization in Copenhagen in March 1995, its director, Dr. Hiroshi Nakajima, stated that "There can be no social development or sustained economic growth without health. . . . Poverty remains the main obstacle to health development." These remarks clearly describe the situation concerning poverty in Afghanistan in 2001.

In 1996, a report published by the United Nations ranked Afghanistan as the third poorest country in the world. Very few Afghans have access to drinkable water, health care, or education. In Kabul, safe drinking water is enjoyed by only 1 out of every 8 families because the reservoirs have been polluted by the waste accumulated through war. Of all infant deaths, 42 percent are related to diarrhea and dehydration, which are caused by unsafe drinking water and unclean conditions. Unlike in the United States, children are not immunized against infant diseases such as polio or tuberculosis. There are very few polio-endemic countries left in the world today; Afghanistan is one of them.

Afghanistan has the third highest infant mortality rate in the world (185 per 1,000 live births), following Niger and Angola. It has a maternal mortality rate (number of mothers dying in child birth) of 1,700 per 100,000 live births, according to the UN. Life expectancy in 2001 was just 45 years for men and 46 years for women.

In 1997, UNICEF carried out a study in Kabul which concluded that the children of Afghanistan suffer from severe psychological trauma. Seventy-two percent of children interviewed had experienced the death of one or more family members between 1992 and 1996, and 40 percent of them had lost one parent. Almost all the chil-

Exchange rates: Afghanistan

afghanis (Af) per US$1	
Jan 2000	4,700
Feb 1999	4,750
Dec 1996	17,000
Jan 1995	7,000
Jan 1994	1,900
Mar 1993	1,019

Note: These rates reflect the free market exchange rates rather than the official exchange rate, which was fixed at 50.600 afghanis to the dollar until 1996, when it rose to 2,262.65 per dollar, and finally became fixed again at 3,000.00 per dollar in April 1996.

SOURCE: CIA *World Factbook 2001* [ONLINE].

GDP per Capita (US$)

Country	1996	1997	1998	1999	2000
Afghanistan	800	800	800	800	800
United States	28,600	30,200	31,500	33,900	36,200
India	1,600	1,600	1,720	1,800	2,200
Pakistan	2,300	2,600	2,000	2,000	2,000

Note: Data are estimates.

SOURCE: *Handbook of the Nations*, 17th, 18th, 19th and 20th editions for 1996, 1997, 1998 and 1999 data; CIA *World Factbook 2001* [Online] for 2000 data.

dren had witnessed acts of extreme violence, and all the children had seen dead bodies in the streets. Ninety percent of the children interviewed believed that they would die in the conflict. Unsurprisingly, all the children interviewed suffered from nightmares and anxiety attacks.

The Taliban forbade women to work or enter any workplace, decreeing that they should stay confined to their homes. But due to the country's critical shortage of doctors, the Taliban decided to allow some female doctors to work in public hospitals in 1997. These women doctors were allowed to treat only female patients. The U.S. Senate Foreign Relations Committee heard a report in 1998 about the mistreatment of female doctors. The report indicated that these doctors were often beaten by hospital guards in an attempt to uphold the policy of the Department of Commanding Good and Forbidding Evil. Male doctors were not allowed to treat female patients except members of their own family and female patients who actively sought medical advice were often attacked and beaten and ordered not to appear again in the street. According to Amnesty International, in 1994 a pregnant woman delivered her baby in a street in Kabul, while her husband was being beaten by the guards for trying to take her to the hospital.

WORKING CONDITIONS

Most of the Afghan **labor force** in 2001 was employed in agriculture, domestic trade, and, increasingly, cross-border trade. There are no exact figures, but it is estimated that many Afghans work as casual laborers in neighboring Pakistan and Iran. While income derived from **remittances** is not known, it is estimated to be increasing by the year. Unemployment has risen significantly in services, industries, and other formal institutions since the civil war began. Afghanistan's total workforce was estimated in 1997 as 8 million. The unemployment rate in 1995 was estimated at 8 percent, according to the CIA.

The Taliban's harshly discriminatory policies against women have affected the Afghan economy in a devastating way by cutting the labor force by almost three-quarters. The UN estimates that 60 to 75 percent of the Afghan population is composed of women, and there are hundreds of thousands of widows in Afghanistan, of whom 50,000 live in Kabul alone. Over 150,000 women in Kabul were not allowed to work under the Taliban.

COUNTRY HISTORY AND ECONOMIC DEVELOPMENT

1893. The Durand Line, created by the British and Russia, creates the border between India and the kingdom of Afghanistan.

1894. Tarzi Amanollah seizes power, becomes king, and launches a successful war against British domination.

1923. Amanollah initiates constitutional reforms, bringing Afghanistan closer to the USSR.

1933. Zahir Shah is crowned king and remains in power for 40 years.

1973. President Mohammed Daoud assumes the presidency of Afghanistan after a military coup and abolishes the monarchy. King Zahir Shah is sent into exile.

1977. A new constitution is drawn up establishing a one-party parliamentary system with additional powers given to the president.

1978. The president and his family are murdered in a military coup, and Nur Mohammed Taraki becomes president of a new communist-style regime.

1979. Soviet troops invade Afghanistan and install a government.

1980. Armed tribal groups begin a *jihad* (holy war) against the Soviet-installed government; the Afghan refugee population in Pakistan reaches 1.5 million.

1980s. Armed mujahideen groups fight Soviet and government forces; hundreds of thousands of Afghans die in the struggle, and millions more become refugees.

1986. President Mohammed Najibullah takes office.

1989. Soviet troops withdraw from Afghanistan.

1989–1992. Conflicts increase between government and opposition forces.

1992. In April, President Najibullah is replaced by a 4-member council under a United Nations plan; later, an interim government led by Professor Sebghatollah Mojadedi, takes over. Refugees begin to return to Afghanistan.

1992–1995. Intertribal fighting spreads to all major cities.

1994. The Taliban emerge as a major force in the ongoing internal conflict.

1996. The Taliban gain control of Kabul.

1998. Taliban forces capture key Northern Alliance stronghold of Mazar-e Sharif.

1998. U.S. cruise missiles strike alleged terrorist bases in Afghanistan in response to attacks on U.S. diplomatic facilities by groups led by Osama bin Laden.

1999. The Taliban rule out Osama bin Laden's extradition, leading the UN Security Council to impose sanctions restricting flights and the sales of arms.

2000. UN Security Council imposes further sanctions on the Taliban. The destruction of Buddha statues in the Bamian province by the Taliban sparks worldwide condemnation, further isolating Afghanistan.

2001. Following a devastating terrorist attack on the U.S. World Trade Center and the Pentagon by al-Qaeda terrorists in September, U.S.-led military action against the Taliban and the al-Qaeda terrorist group begins. The Taliban is forced to surrender all of its territory after attacks by U.S. and British forces, in conjunction with the Northern Alliance, a rebel group of tribal chieftains.

FUTURE TRENDS

After the September 2001 terrorist attacks on the United States, the U.S. military action initiated on Afghanistan resulted in the Taliban being stripped of their territory and power, but Afghanistan's future remains in serious disarray. Negotiations to set up an interim government began in Germany in November 2001, and while the participants claimed a desire for peace and a new beginning, Afghanistan's legacy of war and destruction certainly leaves the success of such platitudes open to doubt. Once the U.S.-led military action ends, an international peacekeeping presence will certainly be required to prevent further bloodshed. Given the volatile nature of the country and region, the international community will be called upon to help rebuild Afghanistan and protect the fledgling government that comes out of this latest conflict. Any sort of normalized economic relations are likely several years away.

The United Nations has recognized the need for massive humanitarian intervention in Afghanistan in order to prevent famine in the drought-stricken parts of the country in which 8 to 12 million people live. Of these people, 1.6 million faced starvation in January 2001. The UN made arrangements for weekly humanitarian flights to Kandahar with supplies and there was a project underway to fly extremely sick children to Germany for treatment. Many non-governmental organizations are calling for increased awareness and urgent action on the part of the international community.

DEPENDENCIES

Afghanistan has no territories or colonies.

BIBLIOGRAPHY

"Afghan Children Experience Severe Trauma." *UNICEF Information Newsline.* <http://www.unicef.org/newsline/97pr43.htm>. Accessed December 2000.

Afghan Info Center. *Structure of Economy in Afghanistan.* <http://www.afghan-info.com/Economy.html>. Accessed December 2000.

Asian Development Bank. *Key Indicators of Developing Asian and Pacific Countries.* Manila: Asian Development Bank, 2000.

Dupree, L. *Afghanistan.* Princeton, NJ: Princeton University Press, 1973.

Economist Intelligence Unit. *Country Profile: Afghanistan.* London: Economist Intelligence Unit, 2000.

Economist Intelligence Unit. *Update Afghanistan, 2001.* London: Economist Intelligence Unit, 2001.

"Human Rights and Gender in Afghanistan." *Amnesty International.* <http://www.amnesty.org/ai.nsf/index/ASA110021998>. Accessed December 2000.

International Monetary Fund. *International Financial Statistics Yearbook 1999.* Washington, D.C.: International Monetary Fund, 1999.

Newby, Eric. *A Short Walk in the Hindu Kush.* London: Lonely Planet Publications, 1981.

Office of the UN Coordinator for Afghanistan. "The State of the Afghan Economy." *Afghanistan Online.* <http://www.afghan-web.com/economy/econstate.html>. Accessed December 2000.

UNICEF. "UNICEF Humanitarian Action Update: Afghanistan, 7 December 2000." *UNICEF in Action.* <http://www.unicef.org/emerg/Afghan7Dec.pdf>. Accessed December 2000.

United Nations. "World Food Programme: Field Operations." *World Food Programme.* <http://www.wfp.org/afghanistan/default.htm>. Accessed May 2001.

U.S. Central Intelligence Agency. *World Factbook 2000.* <http://www.odci.gov/cia/publications/factbook/index.html>. Accessed April 2001.

U.S. Department of State. *Human Rights Practices for 1998 Report: Afghanistan Country Report.* <http://www.usis.usemb.se/human/human1998/afghanis.html>. Accessed December 2000.

Urban, Mark. *War in Afghanistan.* London: Macmillan, 1988.

"Women in Afghanistan: A Human Rights Catastrophe." *Amnesty International.* <http://www.amnesty.org/ailib/intcam/afgan/afg6.htm>. Accessed December 2000.

"Women's Health and Human Rights in Afghanistan." *Women's Health Information Center.* <http://www.ama-assn.org/special/womh/library/readroom/vol_280/jsc80298.htm>. Accessed December 2000.

World Bank. *World Development Indicators 2000.* Washington, D.C.: World Bank, 2000.

—Salamander Davoudi

AUSTRALIA

Commonwealth of Australia

CAPITAL: Canberra.

MONETARY UNIT: Australian Dollar (A$). One dollar equals 100 cents. There are coins of 5, 10, 20, and 50 cents, and 1 and 2 dollars. There are notes of 5, 10, 20, 50, and 100 dollars. An interesting feature of Australia's banknotes is that they are made out of thin plastic rather than paper.

CHIEF EXPORTS: Coal, wheat, gold, meat, wool, aluminum, iron ore, machinery, and transport equipment.

CHIEF IMPORTS: Machinery and transport equipment, computers and office machines, telecommunication equipment and parts, crude oil, and petroleum products.

GROSS DOMESTIC PRODUCT: US$445.8 billion (purchasing power parity, 2000 est.).

BALANCE OF TRADE: **Exports:** US$69 billion (f.o.b., 2000 est.). **Imports:** US$77 billion (f.o.b., 2000 est.).

COUNTRY OVERVIEW

LOCATION AND SIZE. Australia is a continent and a country in the Southern Hemisphere, lying to the south of Southeast Asia, and dividing the Indian and South Pacific Oceans. The total area of Australia is 7,686,850 square kilometers (2,967,892 square miles), with land constituting 7,617,930 square kilometers (2,942,282 square miles) and water 68,920 square kilometers (26,610 square miles). Australia is about the same size as the United States, not including Alaska. The only country that occupies an entire continent, the Commonwealth of Australia does not share any land boundaries with other nations. The length of the country's coastline is 25,760 kilometers (16,007 miles). The capital, Canberra, is located in the southeast corner of the nation and lies approximately halfway between the 2 largest cities, Sydney and Melbourne.

POPULATION. The population of Australia was 19,169,083 as of July 2000, with a population density of about 2.4 people per square kilometer (6.19 people per square mile). Most of the population is concentrated along the southeast coast of the country, in an arc running from the city of Brisbane to the city of Adelaide. This arc is sometimes called the "boomerang coast" because of its shape. All of Australia's large cities (those with more than 1 million people)—Sydney, Melbourne, Brisbane, Perth, and Adelaide—are on the coast. The population living inland (more than 200 kilometers, or 124 miles, from the coast) is rather small, and a large part of this region, called the Outback, is extremely sparsely populated. Australia's population is mostly urbanized, with about 88 percent of its people living in an urban area. Sydney alone has over 20 percent of the country's people.

Australia's population has become increasingly multicultural. In 2000, 21.8 percent of Australia's people were born overseas. Australia is still a land of immigrants and each year attracts new residents from all over the world. Fewer than 3 percent of the population is identified as Aboriginal or Torres Strait Islander (the latter being a Melanesian group native to northern Queensland). The country's population has doubled since World War II. With the exception of rapid growth shortly after the war, Australia's population growth has been steady at around 1 to 1.5 percent annually. The population in 1985 was 15.75 million, and in 1990 it was 17.06 million. The country's population is expected to reach 21 million by 2010. The Australian government has not found the need to create explicit population controls, given this slow rate of increase. Australia has a slowly aging population, with 21 percent between the ages of 0–14, 67 percent between 15–64, and 12 percent over the age of 65.

OVERVIEW OF ECONOMY

The Australian economy developed rapidly in the twentieth century to become relatively stable and

prosperous in world terms. Australia is characterized by an abundance of resources and a diverse yet predominantly primary sector-oriented economy. Grains, livestock, minerals, processed metals, and coal have been the mainstays of economic growth since European settlement in 1788 and continue to play the dominant role in export revenue. The **gross domestic product (GDP) per capita** continues to be high, with Australia ranked 17th out of 191 countries, with a GDP per capita of about US$17,575 in 1998. Australia's standard of living and lifestyle are similar to those of the United States and Europe.

Australia's economy depends on trade. Traditionally, Australia exported raw materials to its former colonial power, Great Britain, and to other European countries. When Great Britain joined what is now called the European Union (EU), trade between Great Britain and Australia declined. Australia has compensated by seeking new markets for its exports in Asia, especially in Japan and Southeast Asia. Japan, especially, has been a major purchaser of Australia's mineral and agricultural products. With the Asian financial crisis of the late 1990s, Australia sought to increase its exports to Europe and the United States while still maintaining a high level of trade with Asia.

Australia's geographic position and its topography have had an impact on its economy. The country is located relatively far from most world population centers and markets. Australia's immediate neighbors, with the exception of New Zealand, are developing countries. The Australian continent is generally dry and contains poor soils, limiting agricultural potential and requiring imports of water and fertilizers. Most of the continent's interior, the Outback, is unsuitable for agriculture except for limited cattle grazing. Australia is a generally flat continent with its few small mountain ranges being low in elevation; they primarily run north-south at the eastern edge of the country. Obstacles to road and railroad building are generally the great distances between population centers and between resources and population centers.

Australia's dependence on mineral and agricultural exports and the small size of the country's economy mean that it is exposed to fluctuations in world commodity prices. Fortunately, the diversity of minerals and agricultural products in Australia means that when some commodity prices are low, others are likely to be high, protecting the Australian economy from devastating shocks. Australia is self-sufficient in most resources including food and minerals; the major exception is oil, of which 20 percent of Australia's needs must be imported.

In the 1990s, the Australian government encouraged the **privatization** of government-owned companies. Large blocks of government-owned shares in the national telephone company, Telstra, and the national airline, Qantas, among other companies, were sold to the public. The Australian government has increasingly pursued a more free market approach to its economy, with fewer regulations and controls on business.

Australia's **external debt** is estimated at US$222 billion, and in 2000 the debt was estimated at approximately 3.3 percent of the GDP. The hosting of the Summer Olympic Games in 2000 contributed significantly to the rise in debt. However, Australia's debt has been declining as a percentage of both value of exports and GDP. **Debt servicing** continues but has little effect upon the performance of the economy as a whole, as it is large and strong enough to make interest payments without problems.

Australia is a contributor to global aid programs, but most aid is concentrated in the Asia-Pacific region. Australia contributes US$1.43 billion in overseas aid per year, and a significant proportion of this goes to Papua New Guinea, which is Australia's nearest neighbor and a former Australian colony. Australia is seen as a safe investment target for both domestic and overseas corporations. The mix of small, medium, and large companies is similar to that of the United States or Great Britain.

POLITICS, GOVERNMENT, AND TAXATION

The Commonwealth of Australia is a federal system with 6 states, 2 domestic territories, and a number of overseas territories, the latter consisting of small islands and a part of Antarctica. (However, the United States and many other countries do not recognize Australia's or any other country's territorial claims in Antarctica.) The 6 states are New South Wales, Victoria, Queensland, Tasmania, South Australia, and Western Australia. The 2 domestic territories are the Northern Territory and the Australian Capital Territory, the last of which, a small district containing the national capital, Canberra, is similar politically to the District of Columbia in the United States.

Australia is a constitutional monarchy with Queen Elizabeth II of England as the formal head of state. She is represented in Australia by a governor general. In practice, the political system is headed by the prime minister and the Australian parliament, which resembles that of Great Britain or Canada. Australia's parliament has 2 houses: the lower is the House of Representatives and the upper is the Senate. Australia is a member of the British Commonwealth. This organization of former British territories should not be confused with the formal name of the country, the Commonwealth of Australia. Australia's national government is usually called the Commonwealth government.

The major political parties in Australia are the Australian Labor Party, Australian Democratic Party, Liberal Party, National Party, and Green Party. The current Commonwealth government is a coalition of the conservative Liberal and National parties. The economic goals of these 2 parties are the promotion of free enterprise through reducing government regulation, privatization of government enterprises, and decentralization of government services, policies similar to those of the Republican Party in the United States. The leading opposition party, Labor, advocates policies similar to those of the Democratic Party in the United States.

Australia has a federal system, like that of the United States, which means that government income and expenditure is divided between the Commonwealth and state governments. Approximately half of the national government's revenues derive from a national **income tax**. Other leading sources of the national government's income include company taxes, sales taxes, excise **duties**, interest and dividends on investments, and various other taxes. The principal expenditures of the national government include social security programs, which account for about 37 percent of expenditures, followed by health care at about 15 percent, assistance to state governments at about 12 percent, defense at about 7.5 percent, general public services at about 7 percent, and education at about 7 percent, with other expenditures making up the remainder.

For state governments, most revenue (about 52 percent) is derived from various state taxes, followed by transfers and payments from the national government (40 percent), and income from public utilities (8 percent). The major state government expenditures are on health, education, general services, transportation, law and order, community services, and other matters including cultural and environmental issues.

The Commonwealth government has played a very active role in the development of the economy towards reduced regulation, lowering of taxation rates, and the privatization of government corporations such as Telstra, the largest telephone company. Foreign investment is generally unrestricted and the United States is the largest source of **foreign direct investment**. The government does not usually interfere with the takeovers of domestic enterprises by foreign investors, nor does it offer any tax incentives for foreign investment. The Federal Treasury, however, regulates foreign investment through the Foreign Investment Review Board (FIRB). This regulation is a screening process to ensure conformity with Australian law and policy. As with many government controls, the greater part of regulating, promoting, and developing investment has been handed down to the control of the Australian states. Recent tax reform has introduced a 10 percent Goods and Services Tax (GST) nationwide, which replaced former taxes such as payroll and wholesale taxes. Most goods and services are now taxed through the GST at the flat rate of 10 percent. Corporate income, capital gains, and branch tax rates are all 36 percent. Personal income taxes are progressive, meaning that the rates increase with the taxpayer's income.

The Australian Defense Force, comprising army, navy, and air force branches, has 54,000 personnel currently serving, and in 1997 recorded an expenditure of US$8.4 billion. The Australian Defense Force is apolitical and does not play any role in economic development. The government has recently sought to increase funding for the Defense Force because of political instability in neighboring countries such as Fiji and Indonesia.

INFRASTRUCTURE, POWER, AND COMMUNICATIONS

Australia's transport and communications **infrastructure** has developed rapidly in close conjunction with the expansion of the country's main industries. The development of transport infrastructure in Australia has been almost entirely related to moving commodities for sale in cities or to gaining access to seaports.

ROADS. In 1996, Australia had 913,000 kilometers (567,338 miles) of roads, of which 353,331 kilometers (219,559 miles) were paved. Freeways constitute 13,630 kilometers (8,469 miles) of total roads in Australia. Road infrastructure in Australia is generally very good. Both urban and inter-city roads are well developed across the country. However, congestion, especially that caused by competition between freight and passenger road users, is becoming a problem in the large cities. The main cities affected are Adelaide, Melbourne, Sydney, and Brisbane; Sydney has the worst congestion problems, followed by Melbourne, then Brisbane. Intra-urban movement constitutes about half the total tonnage of road freight in Australia.

RAIL. In 1999 there was a total of 33,819 kilometers (21,015 miles) of rail lines in Australia. Rail infrastructure exists in both urban networks (mostly commuter rail) and regional networks (mostly freight rail). Rail infrastructure in Australia has never received much government support, despite the country's relatively flat topography and large distances. The consequence has been the development of a few high demand corridors being serviced by relatively poor infrastructure. While current rail infrastructure has sufficient capacity to deal with demand, major investments, totaling at least US$2 billion, have been identified as necessary to deal with the expected in-

Communications

Country	Newspapers	Radios	TV Sets[a]	Cable subscribers[a]	Mobile Phones[a]	Fax Machines[a]	Personal Computers[a]	Internet Hosts[b]	Internet Users[b]
	1996	1997	1998	1998	1998	1998	1998	1999	1999
Australia	293	1,376	639	43.6	286	48.6	411.6	477.85	6,000
United States	215	2,146	847	244.3	256	78.4	458.6	1,508.77	74,100
India	N/A	121	69	18.8	1	0.2	2.7	0.18	2,800
Indonesia	24	156	136	N/A	5	0.9	8.2	0.76	900

[a]Data are from International Telecommunication Union, *World Telecommunication Development Report 1999* and are per 1,000 people.

[b]Data are from the Internet Software Consortium (http://www.isc.org) and are per 10,000 people.

SOURCE: World Bank. *World Development Indicators 2000.*

crease in transport demand over the next 20 years. Additionally, conflicts between commuter and freight rail operators are becoming typical of the rail transport centers of Sydney, Melbourne, and Brisbane.

AIR. Australia currently has 408 airports, 15 of which serve as major intersections and destinations. The national air carrier is Qantas Airways. The country's second largest air carrier, Ansett Airlines, also has an extensive domestic network. The primary commercial airports are Sydney, Melbourne, Brisbane, Adelaide, and Perth. There are an additional 254 regional airports with paved runways across the country. Almost all of Australia's air movements constitute passenger travel. While Australia's air infrastructure is well developed, it has become increasingly overused and overworked and faces increasing maintenance and development costs. Between 2000 and 2020, an estimated US$1.4 billion in new investment will be required to adequately service air travel demand. Of this amount, roughly 67 percent will be directed at terminal expansion for the primary international airports. Currently, Australia's largest and most congested airport, the Kingsford Smith Airport in Sydney, remains efficient by world standards. Australia's main regional airports (Canberra, Coolangatta, Cairns, Darwin, and Hobart) are operating within capacity.

SEA. Australia has 14 major seaports, including Fremantle (Perth), Darwin, Brisbane, Newcastle, Sydney, Port Kembla, Adelaide, Melbourne, Davenport, and Hobart. In addition, export-dedicated seaports are located at Gladstone, Weipa, Hay Point, Dampier, and Port Hedland. Australian seaports are currently under-utilized, and most ports have the infrastructure to meet demand for the next 2 decades. The Bureau of Transport and Communication Economics found in 1996 that spending on infrastructure development will not likely exceed US$500 million over the next 20 years.

POWER. Australia does not import or export electricity. The country produces its own electricity supply, which is generated from coal (89.85 percent), hydro-electricity (8.35 percent), and other sources, mainly renewable energy (1.8 percent). Australia does not generate or consume electricity from atomic power. Total electricity production in Australia was 186.39 billion kilowatt hours (kWh) in 1998, with total consumption being 173.34 billion kWh for the same year.

COMMUNICATIONS. In 1997, there were 9.5 million phone lines in use in Australia, representing a 15 percent increase since 1993. For the same period (1993–97), subscriptions to cellular phone networks increased 667.3 percent, with a total of 3.8 million users in 1997. Thus, Australia has one of the world's highest rates of cellular phone use. Recent upgrades to the digital phone system have achieved almost total coverage across the country. In 1999 Australia had 709 Internet service providers.

ECONOMIC SECTORS

The export of agricultural and mineral resources has been the mainstay of Australia's economy for many years and continues to be a significant contributor to the GDP. Commodities produced in these sectors generate 57 percent of the value of total exports. The services sector (driven partly by the continuing development of the tourism industry) makes up an increasingly dominant proportion of GDP. The dependence on the export value of commodities puts Australia somewhat at the mercy of fluctuations in world commodity prices. Australia's attempts to increase manufactures have met with competition from the global market. Therefore, Australia has focused on developing its service sector.

During the 1990s, many Australian government-owned or partially government-owned companies were privatized or partially privatized. Notable examples of this process include the partial privatization of the Commonwealth Bank, the national airline Qantas, and the telephone company Telstra. Currently, public enterprises account for about 10 percent of total economic output in the country.

Australian companies are regulated by a number of government agencies. Chief among these is the Trade Practices Commission, which has the responsibility of encouraging competition and preventing **monopolization** in any industry. The Trade Practices Commission is concerned with price discrimination, resale price maintenance, misuse of market power, types of exclusive dealing, and anti-competitive agreements. Another government body, the Prices Surveillance Authority, identifies prices that are deemed excessive and establishes inquiries to determine if high prices result from anti-competitive or collusive com-

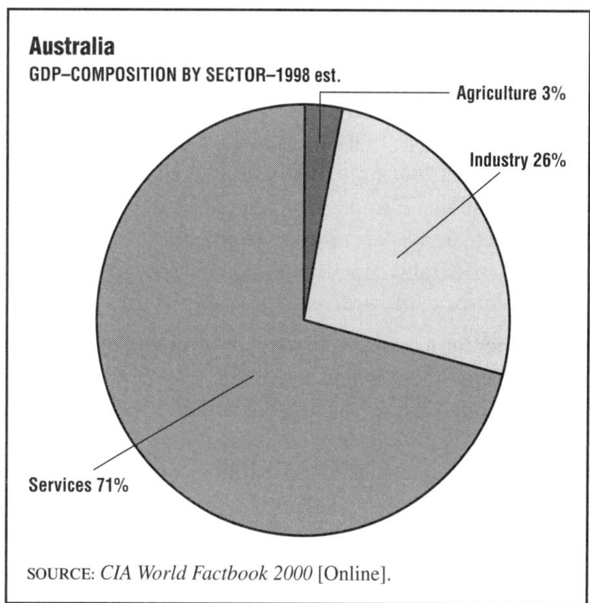

SOURCE: *CIA World Factbook 2000* [Online].

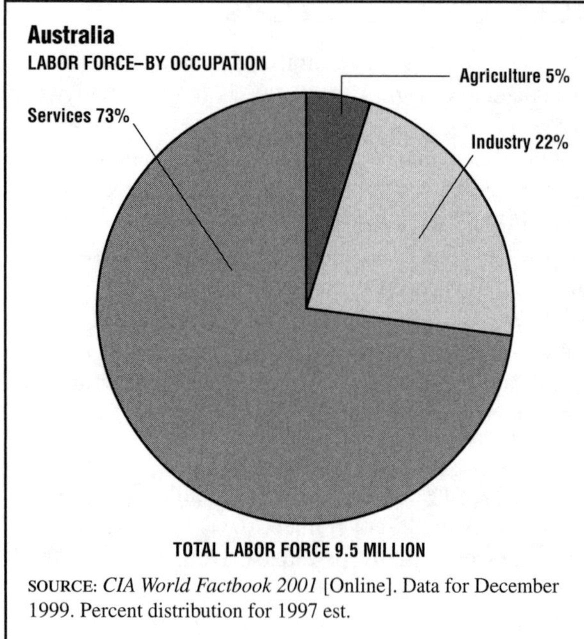

SOURCE: *CIA World Factbook 2001* [Online]. Data for December 1999. Percent distribution for 1997 est.

pany behavior. A third government body, the Industry Commission, is concerned with the allocation of resources in the economy as a whole. The Industry Commission advises the government on the setting of **tariffs** and other protective barriers needed to support Australian industry or to make it more competitive globally.

AGRICULTURE

Historically, agriculture has been as important in the development of Australia, as it was in the United States. Australia's traditional dominance in wheat and sheep continues into the 21st century. Recently Australian agriculture has become increasingly diversified. The considerable expanses of arable land have helped Australia to become a leading world exporter of grains, meats, and wool. Both grains (predominantly wheat and barley) and wool markets around the world are dominated by Australian exports. The market for cattle is more regional but is becoming increasingly important globally, given health concerns about European-produced beef. While only about 6 percent of Australia is suitable for crops and pasture, a considerable amount (60 percent) of the land area is suitable for cattle grazing.

Agriculture contributes roughly 3 percent of the GDP and employs about 4 percent of the total workforce directly. While the sector's contribution to the GDP is small, raw and unprocessed agricultural commodities contribute about a quarter of Australia's total export earnings each year. Australia exports a great deal more agricultural produce than it imports. In 1998 agricultural exports from Australia were estimated at US$15.14 billion, in comparison to the US$3.11 billion worth of agricultural imports for the same year. The main agricultural crops grown in Australia are wheat, coarse grains (barley, oats, sorghum, maize, and triticale), rice, oilseeds (canola, sunflowers, soybeans, and peanuts), grain legumes (lupins and chick peas), sugarcane, cotton, fruits, grapes, tobacco, and vegetables. The main livestock production is in sheep (wool and lamb), beef, pork, poultry, and dairy products. Exports account for over 90 percent of wool and cotton production, nearly 80 percent of wheat, over 50 percent of barley and rice, over 40 percent of beef and grain legumes, over 30 percent of dairy products, and nearly 20 percent of fruit production.

The distribution of agricultural production in Australia is largely determined by the physical environment and climate. The traditional large farm system of wheat and sheep production is spread fairly uniformly between parts of New South Wales, Victoria, South Australia, and Western Australia. Queensland, New South Wales, and Victoria produce the majority of beef, and New South Wales has the largest and most numerous poultry farms. Sugarcane and large-scale vegetable production occurs almost entirely in the tropical state of Queensland, while cotton is produced in both New South Wales and Queensland. Tropical fruits, such as mangoes and bananas, are grown in parts of New South Wales, Queensland, Western Australia, and the Northern Territory.

A notable characteristic of Australian farming and agricultural production is the extent to which net farm income varies from year to year. Australia's weather is subject to extreme fluctuations, which has an impact on annual production and ultimately on farm income.

Farm sizes range from relatively small part-time farms to operations of more than 5000 hectares. In general, Australian farming is characterized by large scale, highly mechanized and efficient operations, one of the key reasons why only a small percentage of the workforce is employed in this sector. Environmental factors have long been ignored in the production of agricultural commodities due to their importance to the economy. At the beginning of the 21st century, however, Australia is forced to pay more attention to the growing evidence of environmental stress and degradation caused by farming. In the past, the agricultural sector carried considerable political weight, being represented by the Labor and National political parties. Currently, there is increasing political pressure from urban residents to remove most **subsidies** and other forms of protection given to farmers. Australian farmers already do not receive many of the subsidies given to farmers in the United States and Europe.

INDUSTRY

MINING. Australia's mining sector is important to both Australia and the world. The mineral sector is the largest primary sector in the economy, accounting for 6.5 percent of the GDP but for more than 60 percent of export earnings. World-wide, Australia is the third largest producer of minerals and metals (not including coal and petroleum). About 80 percent of total mineral production is exported.

Australia is the world's leading producer of alumina and bauxite (both used in the production of aluminum), diamonds (mainly industrial, not gems), opals, and sapphires. The country is the world's second largest producer of lead and zinc; the third largest producer of gold and iron ore; the fourth largest producer of cobalt and uranium; the fifth largest producer of aluminum, coal, copper, nickel, and silver; and the sixth largest producer of salt. Australia is virtually self-sufficient in most minerals and metals. The main exception is oil, but Australia does produce 80 percent of its own needs, mainly from offshore wells. However, Australia does have large deposits of coal, natural gas, liquified petroleum gas, and uranium, all of which are exported.

Many minerals are widespread throughout the country, but others are concentrated in particular areas. Most mining takes place in remote or rural Australia. Bauxite, diamond, and iron ore production is concentrated in the tropical north. Coal, lead, and zinc are mined primarily in New South Wales and Queensland. Uranium production is limited to a few mines in the Northern Territory and South Australia. Every Australian state and the Northern Territory have substantial mining activity. Most of Australia's oil is found offshore. The northwestern coast of the continent and Bass Strait, between Tasmania and the mainland, are the principal locations for petroleum extraction.

Of Australia's total mineral and energy production, 40 percent consists of metals, 30 percent of petroleum group products, 25 percent of coal, and 5 percent of industrial minerals (such as construction materials, clay, and salt).

Minerals of particular interest include coal, which is the largest foreign exchange earner in the sector, accounting for 25 percent of the minerals sector and 15 percent of the country's total export earnings. Australia is the sixth largest producer of coal in the world, but the world's largest exporter, most of which is sold to Japan and other Asian countries.

Australia's uranium mining has been controversial, as much of it has been conducted in environmentally sensitive World Heritage areas (sites recognized by the United Nations Educational, Scientific and Cultural Organization [UNESCO] as having global cultural significance). Some groups have protested against Australia's mining of uranium because of its role in energy production. Australia itself does not use atomic power and operates only one experimental reactor. Australia does not sell uranium for use in weapons and maintains strict controls on exports. Foreign investment in Australia's uranium industry was allowed in 1996. Australia has the world's largest reserves of uranium, about 25 percent of world total.

With respect to the ownership of minerals and mineral rights, each Australian state owns resources in its own area, while the Commonwealth government owns resources in the territories and offshore. However, the Commonwealth government has given control over non-uranium minerals within the boundaries of the Northern Territory to the territorial government.

Mining in Australia has frequently led to conflict with Aboriginal groups over ownership of land and resources. Much of Australia's mining takes place in remote areas, including the Outback, where Aboriginal people form a high percentage of the population. Aboriginal people have protested against mining activity which disturbs or destroys sacred sites, causes environmental damage, and negatively affects the customs of Aboriginal communities. The proposed expansion of the Ranger uranium mine, at Jabiru in the Northern Territory, has been criticized by Aboriginal people living in the area. Australian legislation in the 1990s belatedly recognized Aboriginal concerns. In 1996, the *Wik* ruling of the High Court of Australia determined that mineral leases in Australia are subject to Aboriginal claims. The effect that this ruling will have on mining is still uncertain, but it will probably have little financial impact on the mining sector as a whole.

Foreign companies control a majority of mining, smelting, and refining in Australia. Many mineral companies are vertically integrated, in that they mine, refine, and distribute their products globally. Australia's largest mining company, Broken Hill Proprietary (BHP), is one of the world's largest mining companies. It operates in Australia as well as overseas. BHP's recent merger with the South African mining company, Billiton, made it one of the three largest mining companies in the world. The new company is known as BHPBilliton. Two other large mining companies, Anglo American (South Africa) and Rio Tinto (Great Britain), also have substantial investments in Australia.

MANUFACTURING. The manufacturing sector has grown substantially since the 1950s, and while it remains a key sector in terms of its contribution to the GDP and employment, it also faces fierce competition from competing regional economies, especially those in Asia.

The relatively small population of Australia, and hence its small domestic market, has traditionally limited the development of certain types of manufacturing, such as sophisticated industrial equipment and electrical goods. Otherwise Australia is well equipped locally to produce most manufactured goods competitively. Key manufacturing industries in Australia are industrial machinery, chemical production, transport equipment, food processing, and steel production. Australia has the ability to manufacture most of its needs and can obtain most raw materials domestically. About one-fifth of Australia's workforce is employed in manufacturing industries, and the growth of the sector since World War II has been fairly uniform. Australia has its own automobile industry, although foreign companies have overall control and ownership. Large investors include General Motors, Ford, Toyota, and Mitsubishi. General Motors owns the Australian automobile company, Holden, that produces its own line of Australian cars.

The manufacturing sector in Australia has been stable and sound, with a broad spectrum of industries that have had little need for tariff protection or government subsidies. However, the rapid development of similar industrial manufacturing industries in Asia has created many cheaper **import substitutes**. High levels of industry regulation (such as union-driven working conditions) and smaller margins of trade have also put the manufacturing sector under stress. Many **value-added** goods, refined fossil fuels, and metal products are now produced more cheaply in Asia, reducing the competitiveness of Australia.

The manufacturing sector in Australia is located almost completely in the urbanized regions of eastern Australia, with the exception of considerable steel and primary industry production in the state of Western Australia. Working conditions are generally very good, with "award wages" (nationally legislated working conditions and minimum wages) and Occupational Health and Safety measures addressing workers' interests. In 1998, 54 percent of employees did not take any time off work because of a work-related injury or illness. The manufacturing industry is one of the most unionized employment sectors in Australia and has taken a leading role in promoting an improvement in working conditions.

SERVICES

The service sector contributes approximately 69.2 percent of the GDP and employs an estimated 73 percent of the **labor force**. The recent growth in tourism, **retail**, and financial services contributes to a steady increase in these numbers.

TOURISM. By the end of the 20th century, tourism had become Australia's largest "resource," surpassing coal in value. In 2000 approximately 4.6 million international tourists arrived in Australia, bringing an estimated US$9.02 billion into the country, a 73 percent increase from tourist revenues in 1993. International tourist arrivals for 2001 are estimated to increase substantially to 5.2 million. International tourists come mostly from New Zealand, accounting for 17 percent, and Japan, accounting for 15 percent. Tourists come from other regions as well: the Americas, 12 percent; Asia (except Japan), 26 percent; Europe, 24 percent; and others, 6 percent. Some 99 percent of international tourists in Australia arrive by air.

The Australian Tourist Commission (ATC) is responsible for promoting Australian tourism internationally. According to their recent policy statements, the ATC "positions" Australia differently in tourism markets, meaning that they present different aspects of Australia in different countries. For example, in Japan, Australia is promoted as "close, affordable, safe," and with "inspirational experiences of nature and culture." In other overseas markets, Australia is typically positioned as "the most naturally free-spirited and liberating country in the world" and as a destination for a regular vacation rather than as the "trip of a lifetime."

Australia's scenery, variety of landscapes, distinctive animals, beach culture, modern cities, and relaxed lifestyle are all promoted as reasons to visit the country. The relatively weak Australian dollar, which has steadily declined in value against the U.S. dollar, makes Australia an affordable destination, as foreign travelers increasingly receive more Australian dollars per unit of their own currency. The 2000 Summer Olympics held in Sydney was a major factor driving an increase in international tourism to Australia. Televised events revealed many aspects of the country to potential visitors. The success of Australian films, particularly the *Crocodile Dundee* series, and television programs such as *Survivor II* and *The Crocodile Hunter* have also sparked an interest in visiting Australia. International tourists are forecast to increase by an average of 7.8 percent per year until 2010.

RETAIL. Australia has a diverse range of retail enterprises, similar in complexity to that of the United States or Great Britain. Australian-owned national retailers are numerous but are considerably outnumbered by smaller retailers. Small businesses (those employing fewer than 20 people) accounted for 95 percent of total retail businesses but only 38 percent of total retail income in the period 1998–99. For the same period, large businesses (those employing more than 200 people) made up less than 1 percent of total retail businesses but generated 41 percent of total retail income. The remaining 4 percent of retail businesses and 21 percent of income was attributable to medium-size businesses (21–200 employees).

The larger retail businesses in Australia are mainly comprised of department stores and supermarkets, which contribute 99.6 percent of total income. At the end of June 1999, there were 98,289 retail businesses in the country, generating about US$90 billion in revenue. Since 1991–92, the number of retail businesses has increased by 18 percent, and employment in this sector has increased by 33 percent, with an annual sector-wide revenue growth rate of 5 percent. In the same period (since 1991–92) the operating profits of Australian retailers doubled.

Small businesses are most numerous and tend to dominate the total income for domestic repair and service industries, such as household equipment repair and motor vehicle services and maintenance. Small businesses also comprise the greater part of the total income for recreational goods, specialty foods, furniture, housewares, and appliances. Small enterprises and the large national retailers alike are subject to "award conditions" which specify minimum wages and employment conditions. The retail industry, while having a very high union membership rate, is not controlled by unions, and the Commonwealth government and business alike support moves towards direct employer-employee workplace agreements.

FINANCIAL SERVICES. Financial services is a growing sector in the Australian economy. With respect to commercial banking, the sector is dominated by 4 large private banks: the National Australia Bank, Commonwealth Bank (partially government owned), Westpac, and ANZ Bank. Together these 4 account for about 70 percent of market share and provide both retail and wholesale banking services (services to individuals and to companies). In an increasingly globalized economy, Australia's banks face international competition but have generally thrived. Australia's banking system has been consistently modernized by technological developments. For example, checks and checking accounts are no longer widely used, and Automated Teller Machines (ATMs) and electronic banking have replaced both the use of checks and in-person banking transactions.

Australia's financial services sector also includes many non-bank financial institutions. These include financial intermediaries such as building societies, credit unions, money market dealers, and finance companies. Building societies, similar to Savings and Loan companies in the United States, have generally been declining as they are no longer competitive and have been bought out by banks. Funds managers and trusts are other non-bank financial institutions. These institutions manage insurance funds, superannuation (retirement) funds, and real estate assets, among other matters.

Australia's central bank is the Reserve Bank of Australia, similar in concept to the Federal Reserve system in the United States. The Reserve Bank's functions include managing and issuing the currency, controlling the money supply, supervising the private banks, assisting the government in formulating economic policy, providing banking services to the government, managing the foreign **exchange rate**, and managing the Australian government's overseas financial holdings. The overall objectives of the Reserve Bank are to maintain the stability of Australia's currency, maintain **full employment** in the country, and ensure the economic prosperity of Australia.

INTERNATIONAL TRADE

Historically, Australia's largest trading partners were Great Britain and the rest of Europe. This historical trading relationship reflected Australia's colonization by Great Britain and the British need for new markets for manufactured goods as well as sources of raw materials. The cultural affiliation between Australia and its "mother country" also contributed to this historic trading pattern. Since the 1970s, however, Australia's international trade has shifted towards Asia and Pacific countries. When Great Britain joined what is now known as the European Union in the 1970s, Australia lost many trading advantages with that country and sought new markets closer to home. Japan, Singapore, other Southeast Asian countries, and the United States have all become important Australian trading partners. The composition of Australia's exports has largely remained the same, but new markets (including more recently South America and the Middle East) have been sought. The marked failure of some key Southeast Asian economies, particularly Indonesia, Thailand, and Hong Kong in the late 1990s, has had only a limited effect on the Australian economy. As of 2001, political events outside Australia, such as disturbances in the neighboring countries of Indonesia and Fiji, have had almost no impact on Australia's trade.

Australia's principal exports are meat, wheat, cotton, machinery and transport equipment, coal, iron ore, aluminum, gold, and other minerals. The largest destination for exports is Japan, which purchased almost US$9 billion worth of Australian products in 1999. The United States was the second-largest purchaser, at about US$4 billion, followed by South Korea, New Zealand, Taiwan, Hong Kong, China, Singapore, Great Britain, Indonesia, Malaysia, and Italy. Eight of the top twelve importers of Australian products are in Asia.

Trade (expressed in billions of US$): Australia

	Exports	Imports
1975	11.948	10.697
1980	21.944	22.399
1985	22.604	25.889
1990	39.752	41.985
1995	52.692	61.283
1998	55.895	64.668

SOURCE: International Monetary Fund. *International Financial Statistics Yearbook 1999.*

Australia's main imports are machinery and transportation equipment (mostly motor vehicles), computers and office machines, telecommunications equipment, oil and petroleum products, medical and pharmaceutical products, aircraft and related equipment, and clothing. Australia's largest source of imports is the United States. Australia imported nearly US$10 billion worth of goods from the United States in 1999. Other leading sources of imports to Australia are Japan, Great Britain, China, Germany, South Korea, New Zealand, Indonesia, Taiwan, Singapore, Italy, and Malaysia. With the exceptions of Hong Kong and Germany, Australia's top twelve trading partners are the same for both exports and imports.

The recent (2000) sharp drop in the value of the Australian dollar, especially against the U.S. dollar, could have an impact on Australia's current **trade deficit**. A devalued currency means that Australia's exports become relatively cheaper, while imports become more expensive. Thus, a weak Australian dollar may give the country a competitive edge over Canada, the United States, and other countries in selling raw materials to Japan, to take one example. However, the flip side is that imported products become more expensive, as Australians require more dollars to purchase the same product. For example, a product selling for US$100 would be the equivalent of A$153 in 1999, assuming all other factors to be equal. But with the drop in the value of the Australian dollar, the same US$100 product would be the equivalent of A$192 in 2001. Therefore, many Australian consumers might find imported products too expensive and stop buying them. If this situation continues, Australia's exports could increase and its imports decrease, leading to a decline in the amount of the trade deficit.

MONEY

Australia's economic performance depends on the world prices of mineral and agricultural commodities. The value of Australia's currency can considerably affect the value of export earnings. Australia has also managed to steer clear of **recession** and sharp fluctuations in the rate of **inflation** during the past 2 decades. Government policies of the 1990s, including allowing the value of the currency to fall, **deregulating** industry, and encouraging foreign investment, allowed Australia to weather the Asian economic crisis of that decade. In this period, inflation was low, averaging between 1 to 3 percent per year. Inflation is a controversial topic among economists and is still not clearly understood. However, within the past 2 years price increases in Australia have been attributed to the introduction of the Goods and Services Tax (GST) of 10 percent on most products and services; the fall in the value of the Australian dollar, which makes imports more expensive; and the increase in world oil prices, which are passed on to Australian consumers. Nevertheless, steady economic growth of around 4 percent per year has characterized the greater part of economic performance.

Australia has an established stock exchange. The Australian Stock Exchange (ASX) opened in 1987 through the merger of smaller, very well established (100 years or so of trading) exchanges. In 1998, there were 1,162 companies listed on the exchange.

POVERTY AND WEALTH

Australia has sometimes been called a "classless society," though this is not strictly true. Class in Australia is generally defined on the basis of income or self identification. The terms "working class," "middle class," and "upper class" are all in use, but are difficult to define statistically. Social mobility in Australia is high and there are no formal or cultural obstacles to movement between social or economic classes. Australia's high level of multiculturalism, with many recent immigrants, also contributes to class mobility. Immigrants are often concerned to get the best possible education for their children so that they will move upwards economically. There are some differences in standards of living between rural and urban residents, as the cost of providing basic services to rural areas is generally higher. Rural regions often have more limited services and higher prices for **consumer goods**.

In Australia the general living standards are very high, but differences remain between the country's richest and poorest. Moreover, the gap between rich and poor

Exchange rates: Australia

Australian dollars (A$) per US$1	
Jan 2001	1.7995
2000	1.7173
1999	1.5497
1998	1.5888
1997	1.3439
1996	1.2773

SOURCE: CIA *World Factbook 2001* [ONLINE].

GDP per Capita (US$)

Country	1975	1980	1985	1990	1998
Australia	14,317	15,721	17,078	18,023	21,881
United States	19,364	21,529	23,200	25,363	29,683
India	222	231	270	331	444
Indonesia	385	504	603	778	972

SOURCE: United Nations. *Human Development Report 2000; Trends in human development and per capita income.*

Distribution of Income or Consumption by Percentage Share: Australia

Lowest 10%	2.0
Lowest 20%	5.9
Second 20%	12.0
Third 20%	17.2
Fourth 20%	23.6
Highest 20%	41.3
Highest 10%	25.4

Survey year: 1994

Note: This information refers to income shares by percentiles of the population and is ranked by per capita income.

SOURCE: *2000 World Development Indicators* [CD-ROM].

is growing. The poorest 20 percent of households earned 1 percent of private income, while the richest 20 percent earned 50 percent. For a small minority of the population (nearly all Aboriginal), levels of education and health are very low, and these people are often at or below the poverty line. Australia has been internationally criticized for this situation. The richest minority in Australia are very wealthy and play key roles in international finance. On the whole, the majority of Australia's population would probably be defined as middle class.

Poorer families in Australia are generally characterized by financial struggle and limited opportunities. The national government has an obligation to provide basic services to such families. Australia, like many developed western economies, is partly a **welfare state**. The poorest citizens, and those on low wages or dependant upon care, receive social security and are granted access to free or reduced price health services, education, transportation, and housing. A poorer family in Australia will most likely live in a cheaply constructed, and often highly subsidized public housing area. Many of the basic family services provided by the Commonwealth government, such as rent assistance, childcare assistance, health care, and legal aid, are often busy and run on stretched resources. This situation is more extreme in the country's rural areas. General health levels among such families are low, primarily from inferior housing, poor diet, and increased susceptibility to the abuse of alcohol and drugs. While free education has been the hallmark of the Australian school system, budget cuts have increased the actual cost of sending children to school, with poor families having to pay for many extracurricular activities. The lifestyle of a poor family in Australia is characterized by the need to work to live and support a family in the short term. Rarely, even if members of a family are employed full time, is there the financial ability to take time off work for vacations. Access to higher education, the Internet and even basic computer knowledge, and inclusion in political decision-making are all limited.

The typical family in the higher income brackets of Australian society enjoys many more opportunities, choices, and luxuries than do poorer families. Many richer families have the choice of living outside busy urban centers in rural areas within commuting distance of the cities. Those who choose to live in the major metropolitan areas enjoy spacious, well built, modern or traditional heritage housing. Education has traditionally been a priority for the richer families, and children will often be sent to private schools where the educational standards are usually far better and more inclusive of physical and personal development programs. It is not uncommon for such children to attend boarding schools in another state or region. Almost universally, higher-income families take advantage of a well-developed private health care system, with education being a key factor in better levels of health among such families. While domestic violence, drug abuse, and support services are commonly associated with poorer families in Australia, such abuses transcend socio-economic boundaries and can also occur among the richer families. Richer families have ease of access to private vehicles, typically 1 per person in the family, and the ability to take time off work for domestic and international vacations. In contrast to poorer families, substantial and self-funded retirement plans are

Household Consumption in PPP Terms

Country	All food	Clothing and footwear	Fuel and power[a]	Health care[b]	Education[b]	Transport & Communications	Other
Australia	24	5	9	2	16	9	36
United States	13	9	9	4	6	8	51
India	N/A	N/A	N/A	N/A	N/A	N/A	N/A
Indonesia	47	3	6	5	14	3	22

Data represent percentage of consumption in PPP terms.

[a]Excludes energy used for transport.

[b]Includes government and private expenditures.

SOURCE: World Bank. *World Development Indicators 2000.*

universal among richer families. Such families easily access personal or home information and entertainment technology. Personal computers, reliable and private access to the Internet, cellular telephones, and entertainment technologies are common and form the basis of better connections to news, information, and public opinion. Richer families have a considerable political voice through their ability to make contributions to political parties, to be informed about current affairs, and to participate in debate.

WORKING CONDITIONS

In world terms, Australian working conditions are of a high standard. Australian industrial relations are characterized by fairly high union membership and a federally driven, but state determined, compulsory arbitration and conciliation system. Industrial relations practices are specified in the Conciliation and Arbitration Act (1904), which encouraged employer associations to recognize unions and empowered these unions to make working condition claims on behalf of employees. In Australia there are 7 distinct systems of industrial regulation and relations: the national system is supplemented by those of the 6 states, each having its own distinct industrial relations legislation and arbitration processes. As a result, there has long been a high degree of state intervention in the labor market. There is now only 1 main central union confederation, the Australian Council of Trade Unions (ACTU). "Awards" are the legal decisions made by independent industrial organizations, and they specify minimum standards of pay and working conditions that an employer must meet or otherwise face legal penalties. Working conditions are regulated by legislation and industrial awards.

While Australia carries no social restrictions on employment opportunities for women, the percentage of women in the formal workforce has traditionally been smaller than that of men. Female participation in the workforce has been increasing steadily since the early 1960s, when women comprised 25 percent of the workforce. In 1993, women's participation in the workforce was still increasing at 42 percent. The national Affirmative Action (Equal Employment Opportunity for Women) Act (1986) obliges employers to take steps specifically designed to remove discrimination towards women and promote equality in employment. Despite this act and award conditions for equal pay for equal work being well established, women's earnings on average remain slightly less their male counterparts. This inequity is partially due to the fact that women remain concentrated in industries where pay and working conditions remain relatively less favorable than other occupations and professions. More recent trends in equal opportunity employment address factors such as childcare, maternity and paternity leave, affirmative action, and sexual harassment, and sees them as significant industrial relations issues rather than exclusively women's issues.

Unemployment in Australia has been between 6 and 8 percent since the early 1980s and continues to remain in this range. Many Australian employers have readily employed immigrant workers, especially in times of labor shortages.

COUNTRY HISTORY AND ECONOMIC DEVELOPMENT

1770. Captain James Cook claims Australia for Great Britain.

1788. Australia is settled as a British penal colony.

1793. The first free settlers arrive.

1817. Australia's first bank, the Bank of New South Wales, is established.

1851. Gold is discovered in New South Wales and Victoria.

1883. Silver is discovered at Broken Hill, New South Wales.

1901. The Commonwealth of Australia, a federation of the colonies, is proclaimed. Australia adopts a federal system similar to the United States.

1914–18. Australia sends troops to fight for Great Britain in World War I.

1917. Transcontinental railroad opens.

1920. Qantas, the national airline, is founded.

1927. The national capital is moved from Melbourne to Canberra.

1940–45. Australian troops serve in World War II.

1942. Japanese planes bomb the Northern Territory capital of Darwin. Japanese midget submarines penetrate Sydney harbor.

1952. Uranium is discovered in the Northern Territory.

1960. Aboriginal people are granted Australian citizenship. The Reserve Bank of Australia is established.

1961. Iron ore deposits are discovered in Western Australia.

1966. Australia changes its currency from the British pound to the Australian dollar.

1992. The *Mabo* decision in the High Court allows Aboriginal people to claim title to their traditional lands.

1997. The Asian financial crisis weakens Australia's economy.

1999. A referendum to change Australia from a constitutional monarchy to an independent republic is defeated.

2000. The Summer Olympics in Sydney lead to a boom in tourism.

FUTURE TRENDS

Australia's well rounded economy is likely to see continued growth in both the near and distant future. The country's importance as a leading supplier of minerals and agricultural products, its increasing presence in financial services and specialized technology industries, and its growing appeal as a tourism destination all hold great promise. The diversity of the Australian economy, its many trading partners, and its peaceful democratic political system all help stabilize economic conditions and encourage new investment. The Asian financial crisis of the late 1990s slowed Australia's exports, particularly of minerals, but is unlikely to have any long-term effects on the overall economy. Australia's economy is a careful balance of free market policies with close regulation of key economic sectors, combined with extensive social services programs. Australia's standard of living is assured of remaining one of the world's highest.

The Australian economy will have to increasingly address environmental and Aboriginal issues. Environmental damage caused by mining and agriculture, especially, have come under frequent media attack. Current issues include soil erosion caused by overgrazing, urbanization, and poor farming practices; increases in soil salinity largely due to farming practices; depletion of fresh water supplies, again largely due to farming and urbanization; and coastal damage, especially around the Great Barrier Reef on the Queensland coast, caused by shipping and extensive tourism. Mining impacts on the environment, such as the release of toxic substances, tend to be more localized. Mining and agricultural enterprises are becoming more responsive to environmental issues, but there is still room for improvement. Australia only recognized the potential land claims of its Aboriginal population in the 1990s, placing it far behind the political history of indigenous-settler relations in other countries such as New Zealand, Canada, and the United States. The *Mabo* and *Wik* High Court decisions of the 1990s recognized that Aboriginal title to land may still exist and that it can overlap with pastoral and mining leases. The implications of these decisions have not yet been worked out. They will probably have no major impact on the Australian economy as a whole but will give Aboriginal people a greater voice in managing natural resources on their traditional lands.

DEPENDENCIES

Australia has no territories or colonies.

BIBLIOGRAPHY

Australian Tourist Commission. *ATC Online: Tourism Industry Essentials.* <http://www.atc.net.au>. Accessed April 2001.

Economist Intelligence Unit. *Country Profile: Australia.* London: Economist Intelligence Unit, 2001.

Gruen, Peter, and Sona Shrestha, editors. *The Australian Economy in the 1990s.* Canberra: Economic Group, Reserve Bank of Australia, 2000.

Kriesler, Peter, editor. *The Australian Economy: The Essential Guide.* Sydney: Allen and Unwin, 1995.

Kriesler, Peter, editor. *The Australian Economy.* 2nd Edition. Sydney: Allen and Unwin, 1997.

Lewis, John, et al. *A Guide to the Australian Economy: Structure, Performance, Policy.* Melbourne: Longman Cheshire, 1994.

Nicholson, Margaret. *The Little Aussie Fact Book.* Melbourne: Penguin, 2000.

U.S. Central Intelligence Agency. *World Factbook 2001.* <http://www.odci.gov/cia/publications/factbook/index.html>. Accessed September 2001.

U.S. Department of State. *FY 2001 Country Commercial Guide: Australia.* <http://www.state.gov/www/about_state/business/com_guides/2001/eap/index.html>. Accessed October 2001.

U.S. Geological Survey. "The Mineral Industry of Australia." *Minerals Information, International: Asia and the Pacific.* <http://minerals.usgs.gov/minerals/pubs/country/asia.html#af>. Accessed October 2001.

—Michael Pretes and Rory Eames

AZERBAIJAN

Azerbaijani Republic
Azarbaichan Respublikasy

CAPITAL: Baku.

MONETARY UNIT: Manat. One manat equals 100 gopiks; however, there are no gopiks in circulation due to inflation in the early 1990s. The currency comes in denominations of 50, 100, 250, 500, 1,000, 10,000, 50,000, and 100,000. Some coins may still be found of 10, 20 and 50 gopik.

CHIEF EXPORTS: Oil, gas, machinery, cotton and foodstuffs.

CHIEF IMPORTS: Machinery and equipment, foodstuffs, metals and chemicals.

GROSS DOMESTIC PRODUCT: US$14 billion (purchasing power parity, 1999 est.).

BALANCE OF TRADE: **Exports:** US$885 million (1999 est.). **Imports:** US$1.62 billion (1999 est.).

COUNTRY OVERVIEW

LOCATION AND SIZE. Azerbaijan, a country of eastern Transcaucasia, is located on the western border of the Caspian Sea, between Iran and Russia. It is bounded by Russia to the north, Georgia to the northwest, Armenia to the west, Turkey to the southwest by the border of Nakhichevan, and Iran to the south. Azerbaijan has an area of 86,600 square kilometers (33,436 square miles), of which 86,100 square kilometers (33,243 square miles) is land and 500 square kilometers (193 square miles) is water. The area is slightly smaller than Maine. The total area includes the exclave (portion of the country separated from the main part) of Nakhichevan Autonomous Republic and the enclave (a distinct territorial, cultural, or social unit enclosed within foreign territory) of Nagorno-Karabakh, a region whose autonomy was abolished by the Azerbaijani Supreme Soviet on 26 November 1991. The coastline on the Caspian Sea is about 800 kilometers (497 miles). The total borderline of the country is 2,013 kilometers (1251 miles) long. The capital, Baku, is located on the Caspian Sea border and the other major cities, Ganja and Sumgait, are located to the west and just to the north of Baku, respectively.

POPULATION. The population of Azerbaijan was estimated at 7.75 million as of 2000, an increase of 10.6 percent from the 1990 population of 7 million. The population growth rate declined from 3 percent between 1959–1970, to 1.3 percent in the late 1980s, and 0.27 percent in 2000. The population is expected to reach 8.6 million in 2010. Approximately 63 percent of the population is between the ages of 15 and 64, whereas people of ages 0–14 account for 30 percent of the population, while those of ages 65 and over account for 7 percent. The most populous city of Azerbaijan is the capital, Baku, with over 1.7 million inhabitants. As of 1999 the urban and rural population rates were 51.7 percent and 48.3 percent respectively.

The Azerbaijani population consists of different ethnic groups: Azeris are the majority with 90 percent share in the total population. The rest is made up of Dagestani (3.2 percent), Russian (2.5 percent), and Armenian (2 percent) groups.

OVERVIEW OF ECONOMY

Azerbaijan is a nation of Turkic Muslims. It became an independent republic following the collapse of the Soviet Union in 1991. The country has come into conflict with Armenia over the Azerbaijani Nagorno-Karabakh enclave, when almost 20 percent of total land in Azerbaijan was occupied by Armenia. In comparison to Armenia and Georgia, the industrial sector in Azerbaijan is less developed, with its main focus on the oil industry. There is high **structural unemployment**, and a low standard of living.

Following the break-up of the Soviet Union in 1991, Azerbaijan's economy suffered from serious problems. **Real gross domestic product** (GDP) declined by 60 percent between 1991 and 1995, by which time high **inflation**

had eroded real incomes, the **exchange rate** had weakened, and monetary reserves were nearly depleted. This sudden economic decline had a disastrous effect on the people's living standards. Per capita GDP declined from US$5,841 in 1988 to US$1,770 in 1999, the **inflation rate** rose as high as 1,664 percent in 1994, and from 1988–1998 food prices multiplied as much as 28,750 times. Economic recovery started only after 1996, mostly driven by investment from abroad in the oil, construction, and communications industries. Foreign companies, primarily from the United States, were eager to control Azerbaijan's oil-rich lands.

The main products of the economy are oil, natural gas, and cotton. In order to improve industrial development, Azerbaijan signed arrangements with foreign firms, which have already committed US$60 billion to oil field development. The conflict with Armenia over the Nagorno-Karabakh region, however, stands as an obstacle to economic progress, including stepped-up foreign investment. Due to the fact that old Soviet ties have been broken in the transformation to a market economy, trade with Russia and the former Soviet republics has decreased, while the country has involved itself with other regions like Turkey, Iran, the United Arab Emirates, and Europe. Oil is a very important product of the country, and economic success will depend on world oil prices and the agreements over a pipeline project in the region. In 2000 the construction of a prospective oil pipeline, originating in Baku, passing through the Republic of Georgia, and terminating at Ceyhan, a Turkish port on the Mediterranean coast, was still considered a high cost project. Increasing oil prices will likely make the project more affordable in the near future.

The **external debt** of the country increased steadily from 1991 onward due to economic **restructuring**, and was recorded at US$684 million in 1998. Though economic stabilization measures improved the economic climate considerably during the second half of the 1990s, and inflation improved (exceeding 1,000 percent in both 1993 and 1994, but thoroughly contained in 2000) Azerbaijan needed increasing amounts of International Monetary Fund (IMF) credits. As a result of successful restructuring with the aid of the IMF, Azerbaijan started to repay its debts after 1999.

POLITICS, GOVERNMENT, AND TAXATION

After the declaration of the independence of the republic in 1991, severe political and economic instability lasted until 1994. Heydar Aliyev seized power in June 1993 through a military coup, toppling the democratically elected Abulfaz Elchibey. In October 1993, however, Aliyev legitimized his rule by winning presidential elections. In 1998 the incumbent president was reelected to office for a second term which continues through October 2003.

In the executive branch of the government, there is a president, a prime minister, and a Council of Ministers appointed by the president and confirmed by the National Assembly. The president is elected by popular vote for a 5-year term. The prime minister and cabinet members are appointed by the president and confirmed by the National Assembly. The National Assembly is **unicameral** (one-chambered), has 125 seats, and the members are elected by popular vote for a 5-year term. Parties in the Assembly from 1998 were: the New Azerbaijan Party (center party) chaired by the president Aliyev, the Party of the Popular Front of Azerbaijan (nationalist) chaired by Abulfaz Elchibey, the Party for National Independence of Azerbaijan (nationalist) chaired by Etibar Mammadov, and the Musavat Party (liberal) chaired by Isa Gambar.

Azerbaijan's government consumes about 11 percent of the GDP. However, in 1998 Azerbaijan received only 1.28 percent of its revenue from state-owned enterprises and from government ownership of property. The **privatization** program following independence was poorly thought out and was derailed by poor administration and corruption. It was thought necessary to privatize state-owned companies so that they could perform better in the market. However, the government mostly sold small firms rather than the large-scale companies that were poor performers. What made this process worse was that the opportunities for foreign participation were never properly defined. As a result of these major problems with the privatization program, the **public sector** remains large in the country's economic life. For example, 75 percent of outstanding loans in the banking system were from publicly owned enterprises in 2000, many of which chronically record operating losses. As high as that debt is, it represented some improvement from a 90 percent ratio of such loans in 1995.

The main revenue generators for the government are an **income tax** (levied on the employee's income at progressive rates ranging from 12 percent to 35 percent), a profit tax (0.5 percent), a **value-added tax**, and a **social security tax** (the employer is required to pay an amount equal to 33 percent of the gross salary of the employee). The contribution of these taxes reached 2.6 percent, 2.1 percent, 4.5 percent, and 3.7 percent of GDP in 1998, respectively.

INFRASTRUCTURE, POWER, AND COMMUNICATIONS

Azerbaijan's **infrastructure** of roads and railways is poorly maintained and needs investment. Important transport links with Russia were periodically cut off due to the war in Chechnya (an autonomous Muslim republic in southwestern Russia) that disrupted much of the road and rail links. The total length of the railways is 2,125 kilometers (1,320 miles) in common carrier service, excluding industrial lines. Much of these rails need an overhaul; however, Azerbaijan does not own repair facilities. The 24,981 kilometers (15,523 miles) of roads are also in poor condition. The European Union has sponsored a project to provide new transit routes. The number of passenger cars was 35.5 per 1000 people in 1998.

There are 69 airports in Azerbaijan, 29 of which have paved runways. There are flights to other former Soviet republics, Germany, the Netherlands, Switzerland, Israel, Iran, Turkey, the United Kingdom, and the United Arab Emirates. Baku, Ganja, and Nakhichevan have international airports that are in need of reconstruction and repair. Turkish Airlines, Lufthansa, and British Airways have offices in Baku.

Azerbaijan has maritime connection to the high seas only through the Volga-Don canal, a Russian waterway. Baku has the largest port on the Caspian Sea, but it needs repair. Azerbaijan has a 55-ship marine fleet (1000 GRT or over) and a total of 3000 kilometers of pipelines for crude oil, petroleum products, and natural gas, which are also main sources of export income.

Azerbaijan has an 18.9 billion kilowatt electricity generating capacity (1998), which is sufficient for domestic consumption. Hydroelectric power stations account for 18 percent of the total generation capacity. The generation technology is in need of replacement. The government subsidizes the household consumption of electricity, yet the collection of charges from the consumers is a persistent problem due to the fact that for many consumers the cost is still high considering the low income levels.

As a result of heavy investment during the Soviet era, Azerbaijan has an extensive natural gas distribution and use system. Its gas distribution network extends to over 80 percent of the population and comprises 4,500 kilometers (2,797 miles) of high-pressure transmission lines, 7 compressor stations, and over 31,000 kilometers (19,263 miles) of medium and slow pressure distribution lines. While the country was at one time self-sufficient in gas, declining oil and gas production in recent years has led to a need for substantial gas imports to meet increasing supply shortfalls. The gas sector recovered in 1998, after Azerbaijan managed to eliminate gas imports from suppliers such as Turkmenistan. Azerbaijan is likely to become a gas supplier to Turkey within 10 years.

Communications

Country	Newspapers	Radios	TV Sets[a]	Cable subscribers[a]	Mobile Phones[a]	Fax Machines[a]	Personal Computers[a]	Internet Hosts[b]	Internet Users[b]
	1996	1997	1998	1998	1998	1998	1998	1999	1999
Azerbaijan	27	23	254	0.1	8	N/A	N/A	0.23	8
United States	215	2,146	847	244.3	256	78.4	458.6	1,508.77	74,100
Russia	105	418	420	78.5	5	0.4	40.6	13.06	2,700
Armenia	23	224	218	0.4	2	0.1	4.2	1.85	30

[a]Data are from International Telecommunication Union, *World Telecommunication Development Report 1999* and are per 1,000 people.

[b]Data are from the Internet Software Consortium (http://www.isc.org) and are per 10,000 people.

SOURCE: World Bank. *World Development Indicators 2000.*

Azerbaijan's telecommunications system is poorly developed. Baku has the most telephones, whereas about 700 villages still do not have public telephone service. Although fixed telephone users are very small in number, mobile phone use is increasing, especially among a growing middle class, large commercial ventures, international companies, and most government officials. The Ministry of Communications (Azertel) handles international telephone requirements through the old Soviet system of cable and microwave which is still serviceable, and the satellite service between Baku and Turkey, which provides access to 200 countries. Azerbaijan is a signatory of the Trans-Asia-Europe Fiber-Optic Line (TAE) that is hoped to improve international communication; however, the lines are not yet laid.

Though Internet and e-mail services are available only in Baku, it is strictly controlled by the government. As of January 2001, Internet service cost was about US$0.62 per hour; however, given the relatively high cost of this service for many Azerbaijanis, the poor conditions of phone lines, and the high costs of imported personal computers and modems, the average number of Internet hosts was only 20 per 100,000 residents in January 2001. The number of television sets was estimated to be around 2 million in 1998.

ECONOMIC SECTORS

The main economic sectors are agriculture, industry, and construction, which have shown much improvement from foreign investment. Agriculture, about 90 percent privatized, represented 21.7 percent of GDP in 1999. Cotton was the leading crop; however, caviar production was world famous. Industry accounted for 23.6 percent of GDP in 1999, the main contributors to which were the metallurgy and fuel industries. It was widely estimated that about 10 percent of the world's oil reserves were located in Azerbaijan and the Caspian Basin. In 1999, construction accounted for 9.4 percent of GDP.

Azerbaijan
GDP–COMPOSITION BY SECTOR–1997 est.

Services 60%
Agriculture 22%
Industry 18%

SOURCE: *CIA World Factbook 2000* [Online].

AGRICULTURE

Agriculture is the largest employer in Azerbaijan. In 1999, it had 32 percent of the total workforce and a 22 percent share of the total GDP. The primary products are grains, cotton, tobacco, potatoes, other vegetables, grapes, melons and gourds, fruits, and tea. The sector meets most of Azerbaijan's grain needs. Farming is concentrated in central Azerbaijan along the Kura and Araxes rivers, where the land is fertile. The collective and state farms that were common in the Soviet times have been dismantled, leaving room for smaller farms. Cotton, an important export crop, experienced sharp declines in production in 1999 due to shortages and price increases of fertilizers, defoliants, and spare parts of harvesting machinery.

The total value of agricultural exports decreased from US$168.2 million in 1994 to US$96 million in 1998, representing a decrease of 43 percent. Agricultural exports accounted for 26.2 percent of total exports in 1994, decreasing to 15.8 percent in 1998. Fishing also is an important sector, with 90 percent of the world's caviar production coming from the Caspian Sea.

INDUSTRY

MINING. The main mining product of Azerbaijan is oil. At the beginning of the 20th century, Azerbaijan ac-

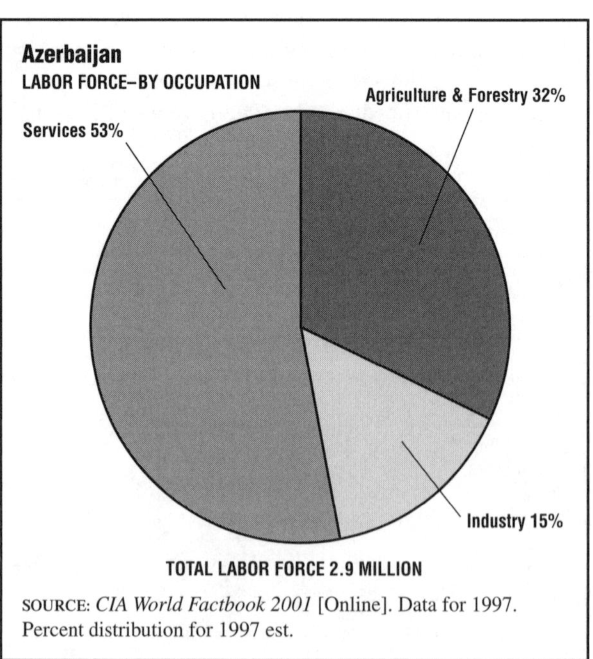

SOURCE: *CIA World Factbook 2001* [Online]. Data for 1997. Percent distribution for 1997 est.

counted for nearly half of the world's total oil production. Although at the end of the century it lost this place to Middle Eastern countries, Azerbaijan is still the most geopolitically important country among the former Soviet republics, being relatively the closest to the high seas and possessing an open investment environment, which is crucial in terms of oil transportation. The State Oil Company of the Azerbaijan Republic (SOCAR) is the largest employer of the country, with 78,000 workers. The revenues from exports of oil products accounted for US$434 million in 1998, 64 percent of total exports. In addition, the expenses for imports of the oil sector accounted for US$355.7 million in 1998, or 20.6 percent of total imports.

Other mineral sources of Azerbaijan include iron, bauxite, zinc, copper, arsenic, molybdenum, marble, and fire clay. There are also small reserves of gold. Large reserves of iron and aluminum are located in the Dashkesen Mountains. Since the only buyer of the iron, Georgia, stopped purchases after the dissolution of the Soviet Union, iron production has been suspended. The mining industry is in need of modernization due to the aging technology and equipment employed in the sector.

MANUFACTURING. Oil equipment manufacturing and related sectors such as instrument-making, electrical engineering, and radio electronics sectors produce almost 20 percent of the total manufacturing sector. The government considers the oil engineering sector of strategic importance and the sector is not included in privatization plans. After independence, the manufacturing sector experienced a decrease in non-oil-related production. The majority of heavy industry is located in Sumgait, just north of Baku. However, much of this capacity is declining, due to a lack of government incentives, foreign capital, and infrastructure. Other important sectors include textile, food, and beverages. However, these sectors, too, have experienced a sharp decline and lost their competitiveness against imported goods for the same reasons.

CONSTRUCTION. The share of construction in total GDP increased from 8.1 percent in 1990 to 9.4 percent in 1999. Construction work related to the oil industry accelerated after 1995. Turkish companies are also active in the construction of homes and businesses.

SERVICES

BANKING. The Azerbaijan National Bank (ANB), responsible for **monetary policy** and the supervision of the financial sector, was established in 1992 and privatized in 1995. There are many commercial banks, but most of them are small and undercapitalized. After a consolidation in the number of the banks, as of July 2000, Azerbaijan had 66 commercial banks, the central bank, the state-managed International Bank of Azerbaijan, and the United State Industrial Bank. The ANB informally protects the state-owned banks from foreign competition by allowing only 30 percent of capital to be foreign-owned in the national banking system.

INTERNATIONAL TRADE

During the late 1980s, exports and imports accounted for 37 percent and 46 percent of GDP, respectively. In 1999, exports stood at US$885 million, and imports totaled US$1.62 billion. After a brief **trade surplus** was achieved in 1992, a deficit occurred again in 1993. Due to increases in the purchase of machinery and equipment for the oil industry and increased imports of **consumer goods**, there was a rapid increase in imports. Accordingly, there was a chronic current account deficit, which was expected to shrink with the increase of oil exports by 2001.

Azerbaijan relies heavily on crude oil exports. Oil export figures reached 68.9 percent of total exports in 1998. Turkey was the main trading partner of Azerbaijan for both exports and imports, accounting for 22.4 percent and 20.4 percent of total exports and imports in 1998, respectively. This high rate is mainly due to the special relationship between the countries (Azerbaijan citizens speak a dialect of modern Turkish and have the same religious and cultural background as Turkey). Other major trading partners include Russia, Georgia, Ukraine, Italy, the United Arab Emirates, and Iran.

MONEY

After independence Azerbaijan suffered from the mismanagement of the economy by the former Soviet Union. The country applied severe monetary and **fiscal policies** in order to stabilize the economy. Inflation was reduced from upwards of 1000 percent to single digit rates. The fiscal system, banking services, and exchange system were entirely overhauled. Azerbaijan remained in the Russian ruble zone (a monetary system used by the former Soviet countries) until 1993. Leaving the zone

Trade (expressed in millions of US$): Azerbaijan

	Exports	Imports
1994	637	777
1995	637	667
1996	631	960
1997	781	794
1998	606	1077
1999	N/A	N/A

SOURCE: United Nations. *Monthly Bulletin of Statistics* (September 2000).

Exchange rates: Azerbaijan

manats per US$1	
Feb 2001	4,579
Oct 1999	4,342
1999	4,373
1998	3,869
1997	3,985.38
1996	4,301.26

SOURCE: CIA *World Factbook 2001* [ONLINE].

GDP per Capita (US$)

Country	1975	1980	1985	1990	1998
Azerbaijan	N/A	N/A	N/A	1,067	431
United States	19,364	21,529	23,200	25,363	29,683
Russia	2,555	3,654	3,463	3,668	2,138
Armenia	N/A	N/A	N/A	1,541	892

SOURCE: United Nations. *Human Development Report 2000; Trends in human development and per capita income.*

marked the beginning of effective economic policy making. The manat became the only legal currency after January 1994.

The first 2 years of stabilization included tight monetary and fiscal policies, overseen by the central bank, the Azerbaijan National Bank. The gradual **liberalization** of prices caused interest rates and the exchange rates to become more realistic and led to a more stable financial situation. In order to prevent the currency from over appreciation due to high oil-related capital inflows, the exchange rate was also managed by the state. Oil-related foreign capital inflows increased the amount of foreign currency in the Azerbaijani money markets. These inflows, and the sharp decrease in inflation, caused the appreciation of the manat over foreign currencies. Therefore, to control the **balance of payments** and make the country's export-driven sectors more competitive, the government chose to depreciate the national currency by launching a managed float policy.

With the drop in oil prices during 1998 and 1999 and the tight monetary policies of the previous decade, the annual average inflation rate slowed to -8.5 percent in 1999, compared to 1,664 percent in 1994. Since then, basic foods such as bread, vegetables, meat, and dairy products have become more accessible to Azerbaijanis. There are no stock exchanging facilities in Azerbaijan.

POVERTY AND WEALTH

The level of poverty in Azerbaijan was officially estimated to be 34 percent of the population in 1989. However, with **subsidies** for employment, food, housing, and social services, poverty rarely meant severe deprivation. After independence, on the other hand, poverty increased dramatically. Average food prices multiplied as much as 28,750 times from 1988 to 1998. According to the Azerbaijan Survey of Living Conditions that was conducted in 1995, over 61 percent of the population was poor. Poverty was substantially higher among internally displaced people (due to Armenian occupation in the Nagorno-Karabakh region).

The gap between the rich and the poor widened after independence, especially when the oil-related sector began surging while the other industries (manufacturing, mining) deteriorated. The country consists of an upper class (2–4 percent) living in extraordinary luxury, while the majority of the population (80–85 percent) suffers from very low wages and poor living conditions.

Although poverty is high, human development indicators such as school enrollment, literacy levels, and infant mortality rates are positive. However, public spending on education declined by three-quarters from 1992 to 1996. The health system also suffers from mismanagement, deteriorating quality, excess capacities, and access problems. In 1998, the number of hospital beds was 9.6 per 1000 people. Bribes from patients were

Household Consumption in PPP Terms

Country	All food	Clothing and footwear	Fuel and power[a]	Health care[b]	Education[b]	Transport & Communications	Other
Azerbaijan	51	5	16	9	2	4	14
United States	13	9	9	4	6	8	51
Russia	28	11	16	7	15	8	16
Armenia	52	3	8	3	18	9	23

Data represent percentage of consumption in PPP terms.
[a]Excludes energy used for transport.
[b]Includes government and private expenditures.

SOURCE: World Bank. *World Development Indicators 2000.*

a major form of financing adequate health care. During the 1990s, public health spending decreased. In 1999, the government's health spending was only about 20 percent of its 1990 level.

WORKING CONDITIONS

High incomes are mostly seen in the oil-related sectors and especially in foreign companies. The legal workweek is 40 hours. In order to ensure that citizens enjoy healthy and safe working conditions, a Labor Protection Law was passed in Azerbaijan on 19 September 1992. According to the law, labor protection is defined as a system of socioeconomic, organizational, technical, sanitary, and hygienic measures and means designed to ensure the safety, health, and working capacity of persons engaged in work activities. However, these regulations are not strictly applied.

Azerbaijan is a participant of the International Labor Organization. A minimum wage, which is about US$3 per month, exists. This wage is not sufficient to provide a decent standard of living for a worker and family. The recommended monthly wage level to meet basic subsistence needs was estimated to be US$50 per person as of 1999. Since practically all persons who work earn more than the minimum wage, enforcing its low level is not a major issue in labor or political debate. According to the European Commission, the average monthly wage rate was about US$44 in September 2000.

The largest labor organization is the Azerbaijan Confederation of Trade Unions (or the Azerbaijan Labor Federation), which depends on government support. Its main functions are to promote employment, develop the labor market, support social insurance, ensure employee health and safety, enforce the legal regulation of labor relations, and provide social partnership. The constitution provides the right to strike. Unions are free to form federations and to affiliate with international bodies; but none have done so.

COUNTRY HISTORY AND ECONOMIC DEVELOPMENT

1918. The first Republic of Azerbaijan is established.

1919. The Soviet Union conquers Azerbaijan, absorbing it back into the country.

1989. Azerbaijan calls for withdrawal from the Soviet Union. The conflict in Nagorno-Karabakh begins.

1990. Soviet military intervenes. Moscow appoints Ayaz Muttalibov as the leader of Azerbaijan.

1991. Azerbaijan declares independence in October.

1992. The war with Armenia dominates Azerbaijani politics.

1992. Abulfaz Elchibey wins the presidential election in June.

1993. Heydar Aliyev is elected president in October, with 98.9 percent of the votes.

1994. A ceasefire is signed with Armenia.

1995. A new constitution is adopted by referendum.

1998. Aliyev wins reelection as president.

2000. Aliyev's party wins parliamentary elections in November.

FUTURE TRENDS

Azerbaijan still has to go through a severe democratization process (including proper representation of the people, free elections, and the improvement of human rights), as observed in the parliamentary elections in November 2000, which proved to be a failure in the election mechanism.

Economically, Azerbaijan is improving, with some reservations in the non-oil sectors, which have deteriorated sharply due to the focus on oil. There has been a significant fall in the agricultural, mining (excluding oil), and manufacturing sectors' production levels, decreasing the export levels at the same time. Between 1994 and 1998, agricultural exports decreased by 43 percent, metals by 87.3 percent, chemicals and petrochemicals by 50.4 percent, and machinery and equipment by 62.6 percent.

Energy remains the keystone of Azerbaijan's economic future. In the oil sector, pipeline projects and the gains from production are estimated to reach substantial levels in 2010–2015, giving Azerbaijan political and economic leverage in the region. The production of oil and the supplementary sectors in the oil industry are of importance. In addition, recent discoveries of gas deposits will help supply both Azerbaijan's energy needs and provide exports to Turkey and Eastern Europe. Privatization is another important task. Renovation of the infrastructure, including roads, railways, communications, power generation and distribution, will gain importance as trade relations improve.

The resolution of the Armenian conflict over Nagorno-Karabakh will also affect economic and social conditions in the region and will help improve the international relations of Azerbaijan.

DEPENDENCIES

Azerbaijan has no territories or colonies.

BIBLIOGRAPHY

Economist Intelligence Unit. *Country Profile: Azerbaijan, 2000.* London: Economist Intelligence Unit, 2000.

"National Food Security Information System (Summary Report)." *European Commission Food Security Network.* <http://www.resal.org/geo/nei/index>. Accessed February 2001.

Population Reference Bureau. <http://www.prb.org/pubs/wpds99/wpds99_asia.htm>. Accessed January 2001.

U.S. Central Intelligence Agency. *World Facbook 2000.* <http://www.odci.gov/cia/publications/factbook>. Accessed July 2001.

U.S. Department of State. *FY 2000 Country Commercial Guide Azerbaijan.* <http://www.state.gov/www/about_state/business/com_guides/2000/europe/index.html>. Accessed July 2001.

World Bank Poverty Monitoring Database. <http://wbln0018.worldbank.org/dg/povertys.nsf>. Accessed January 2001.

—Yüksel Sezgin

BAHRAIN

State of Bahrain
Dawlat al-Bahrayn

CAPITAL: Manama (Al-Manamah).

MONETARY UNIT: Bahrain dinar (BD). One dinar equals 1000 fils. There are coins of 5, 10, 25, 50, and 100 fils. There are notes of 500 fils, and 1, 5, 10, and 20 dinars.

CHIEF EXPORTS: Petroleum and petroleum products (61 percent), aluminum (7 percent).

CHIEF IMPORTS: Non-oil imports (59 percent, including machinery and transport equipment, manufactured goods, chemicals, food, and live animals), crude oil (41 percent).

GROSS DOMESTIC PRODUCT: US$10.1 billion (purchasing power parity, 2000 est.).

BALANCE OF TRADE: **Exports:** US$5.8 billion (f.o.b., 2000). **Imports:** US$4.2 billion (f.o.b., 2000).

COUNTRY OVERVIEW

LOCATION AND SIZE. Bahrain is the smallest country and the only island-state in the Persian Gulf and the wider Middle East. It covers an area of 620 square kilometers (385 square miles), about 3.5 times the size of Washington, D.C. Bahrain consists of 33 islands, of which only 3 are inhabited. The capital, Manama, is on the main island of Bahrain, which contains most of the population and is linked to Saudi Arabia by a causeway. A southern portion of the main island is a restricted zone where the U.S. Middle East Operations Force is based.

POPULATION. With an estimated 645,361 inhabitants in 2001, Bahrain has the smallest population of all Gulf States, but its annual population growth of 3 percent (1990–98) was among the highest in the world, with an equally high fertility rate (3.2 percent). According to UN figures, it is estimated that the population will double by 2017. Approximately one-third of the population is under 14 years of age. Bahrain's population is highly urbanized: 91.06 percent of Bahrainis lived in cities in 1998.

As much as one-third of the people are non-nationals, mainly foreign workers from Asia (19 percent) or other Arab countries (10 percent). Some 8 percent of the population is of Iranian descent, and the majority of the people (85 percent) are Muslims, 75 percent of whom are members of the Shi'a branch of Islam and 25 percent of the Sunni branch. Half of the Shi'a population is under 15 years old. The remaining 15 percent of the population is made up of Christian, Jewish, Hindu, and Parsee minorities.

OVERVIEW OF ECONOMY

Bahrain was the first country on the Arabian side of the Persian Gulf to discover oil in 1932. Oil wealth dramatically improved education and health care, but the country's oil reserves are relatively limited in comparison to most of its neighbors. Bahrain has therefore developed a more diversified economy than most of the Gulf States.

During the 1960s and 1970s, Bahrain emerged as the principal financial and communications center of the Gulf region. Oil and gas, however, still play a dominant role in the country's economy, providing about half of the government's income and accounting for two-thirds of exports. An undersea pipeline pumps oil from Saudi Arabia to Bahrain's large refinery, Sitrah. An estimated 70 percent of Bahrain's oil revenues come from the sale of products refined from crude oil extracted from an oilfield that is shared with Saudi Arabia, but from which Bahrain takes all the income. In effect, therefore, Saudi Arabia supplies Bahrain with financial aid. In addition, it enjoys grants from Abu Dhabi and Kuwait, which contribute considerably to the government budget. Most of the budget (60 percent) is used to pay salaries to Bahrainis and foreigners working in the **public sector**.

Until very recently, wholly or partially government-owned enterprises dominated much of the Bahraini

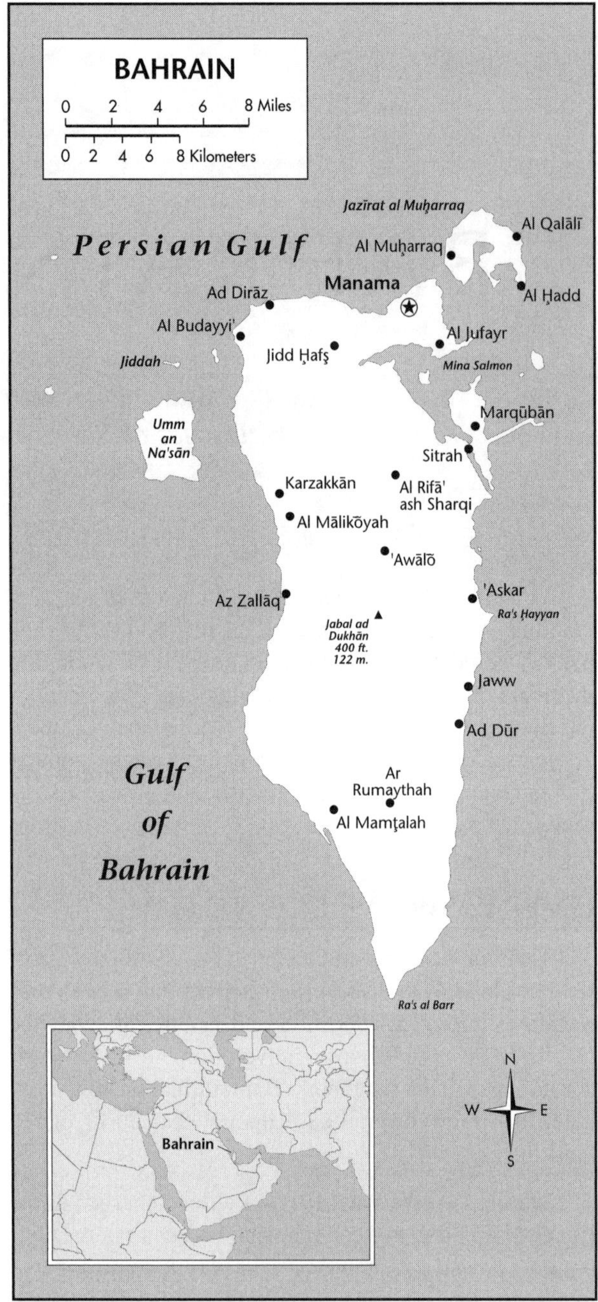

economy, but there has been an increase in **private sector** activity in recent years. This situation stems from the general decline in oil prices during the 1980s, which resulted in decreasing revenues. This financial downturn made an increase in free enterprise and foreign investment necessary in order to maintain the country's high standard of living and to guarantee its economic welfare. Bahrain became a member of the World Trade Organization (WTO) in 1992 and has since overhauled many laws and regulations. Nevertheless, the government has been slow to implement required measures. For example, it has only partially **privatized** 14 government-owned companies, and only one of these is an important industrial enterprise.

POLITICS, GOVERNMENT, AND TAXATION

Bahrain is characterized by autocratic tribal rule, with authority invested in a single family. The al-Khalifa family, minority Sunni Muslims in a majority Shi'a country, hold 11 of the 20 cabinet posts, while the rest are controlled by the prime minister, Sheikh Khalifa, who is the uncle of the ruler, Sheikh Hamad Bin Isa al-Khalifa. The present emir (prince) succeeded to the throne in March 1999, on the death of his father, and depends to a large degree on his much more experienced uncle, the prime minister, for the running of everyday government affairs. While Sheikh Hamad himself, and his son, Crown Prince Sheikh Salman bin Hamad, are in favor of implementing cautious political reforms, the prime minister is seen as the vanguard of the old order.

In 1899, the al-Khalifa family became the first of the ruling families in the Gulf to sign a so-called "exclusive agreement" by which local rulers granted control of foreign affairs to Britain in exchange for military protection. On August 14, 1971, during the reign of Sheikh Isa bin Salman, which lasted from 1961 until his death in 1999, Bahrain became independent, and a constitution was issued in May 1973. The elected National Assembly convened in December 1973 but was dissolved only 20 months later when the emir decided that radical assembly members were making it impossible for the executive to function properly. For 20 years, the country functioned without a representative body.

Since 1993, there has been a Consultative Shura Council, which is wholly appointive and does not possess any legislative power. There are no political parties and no elections for government positions. In many ways, Bahrain is a typical rentier state, i.e., a state whose political system benefits from large revenues from the sale of natural resources, in this case oil. The government distributes the state income to its citizens by providing them with jobs and a generous welfare system; in addition, the level of taxation is very low. In return, these citizens are tied to the state and remain loyal to undemocratic regimes. Such a relationship is often encapsulated in the phrase, "no taxation, no representation."

During the mid-1990s, the country experienced civil unrest directed against the regime, during which several people were killed. Protests, mainly orchestrated by the underprivileged Shi'a majority, have since continued, although on a lesser scale. The new emir, Sheikh Hamad, has promised municipal elections in the near future and has made new appointments to the Shura Council, including a woman and a Jewish representative. In addition, a Supreme Council for Economic Development, chaired by the prime minister, was created in 2000 with the aim of identifying, developing, and promoting foreign investment opportunities. In February 2001 Bahrainis voted to approve a new constitution that would institute a partially elected parliament and grant political rights to women.

INFRASTRUCTURE, POWER, AND COMMUNICATIONS

Bahrain's **infrastructure** is modern, and the government is currently forging ahead with several major projects. These include constructing a new water distribution network, upgrading the Sitrah power and water station, and expanding other water, power, and waste-treatment facilities. Bahrain invested heavily in its infrastructure during the years of the oil boom, but the demand for water and electricity already taxes available capacity, and the expansion of the present facilities is a major priority.

The country's road network, with 2,433 kilometers (1,511 miles) of paved roads, is excellent. The low fees of Bahrain International Airport, located on Al-Muharraq Island, have turned it into a regional hub. The principal port, Mina' Salman, handles most of the country's general cargo, and petroleum products are loaded at the Sitrah jetty. A national bus company provides public transport throughout the populated areas of the country. There are no railways in Bahrain.

POWER. There are 3 main power stations. Rifaa, with a capacity of 700 Megawatts (mw), is the largest. Domestic demand for electricity was estimated to have reached 5.752 billion kilowatt-hours (kWh) in 1999, and this demand is more than exceeded by production of 6.185 billion kWh in 1999.

TELECOMMUNICATIONS. Bahrain is the communications center of the Gulf and has invested heavily in the sector since the late 1960s. There are excellent cable and satellite services using the latest digital exchange technology. The Bahrain Telecommunications Company (BATELCO) owns a 60 percent stake in the telecommunications network, which is operated by the United Kingdom's Cable & Wireless company. BATELCO is also the country's **monopoly** Internet service provider (ISP) and has recently begun to cut its relatively high access rates in an effort to boost subscriptions. Bahrain's cellular phone network has about 170,000 subscribers, according to the U.S. Department of State's *Country Commercial Guide* for 2001.

ECONOMIC SECTORS

Due to its small size and shortage of natural resources other than oil, Bahrain has developed a relatively diversified economy in comparison with the other Gulf states, which are almost exclusively dependent on oil. Oil, gas, and related products still dominate the economy, but finance, banking, industrial production (mainly in aluminum), and tourism are also important sectors in the country's economy and are becoming increasingly significant.

AGRICULTURE

The agricultural sector accounted for only 1 percent of **gross domestic product** (GDP) in 1998 and employed 2 percent of the workforce. The development of agriculture is limited by lack of water and the strong salinity (saltiness) of the soil. Over a period of 30 years since 1971, Bahrain's cultivated area has been reduced from around 6,000 hectares to less than 1,500 hectares. The major crop is alfalfa for animal fodder, although farmers also grow dates, figs, mangos, pomegranates, melons, papayas, water turnips, potatoes, and tomatoes, and produce poultry and dairy products for the local market.

Communications

Country	Telephones[a]	Telephones, Mobile/Cellular[a]	Radio Stations[b]	Radios[a]	TV Stations[a]	Televisions[a]	Internet Service Providers[c]	Internet Users[c]
Bahrain	152,000	58,543	AM 2; FM 3; shortwave 0	338,000	4	275,000	1	37,500
United States	194 M	69.209 M (1998)	AM 4,762; FM 5,542; shortwave 18	575 M	1,500	219 M	7,800	148 M
Saudi Arabia	3.1 M (1998)	1 M (1998)	AM 43; FM 31; shortwave 2	6.25 M	117	5.1 M	42 (2001)	400,000 (2001)
Qatar	142,000	43,476	AM 6; FM 5; shortwave 1	256,000	2	230,000	1	45,000

[a]Data is for 1997 unless otherwise noted.
[b]Data is for 1998 unless otherwise noted.
[c]Data is for 2000 unless otherwise noted.

SOURCE: CIA *World Factbook 2001* [Online].

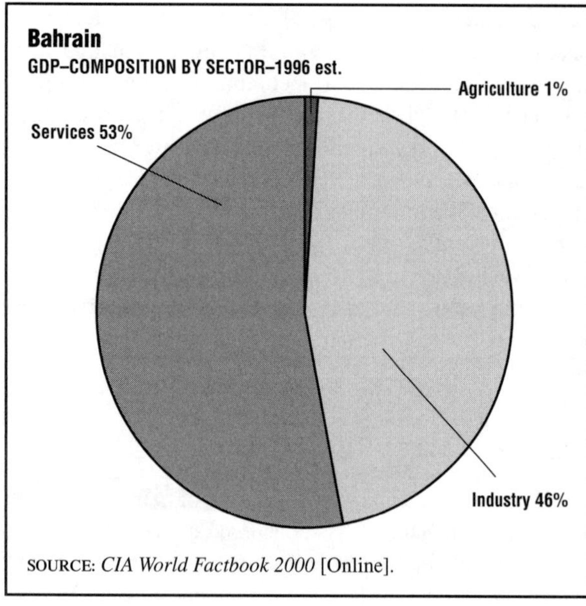

SOURCE: *CIA World Factbook 2000* [Online].

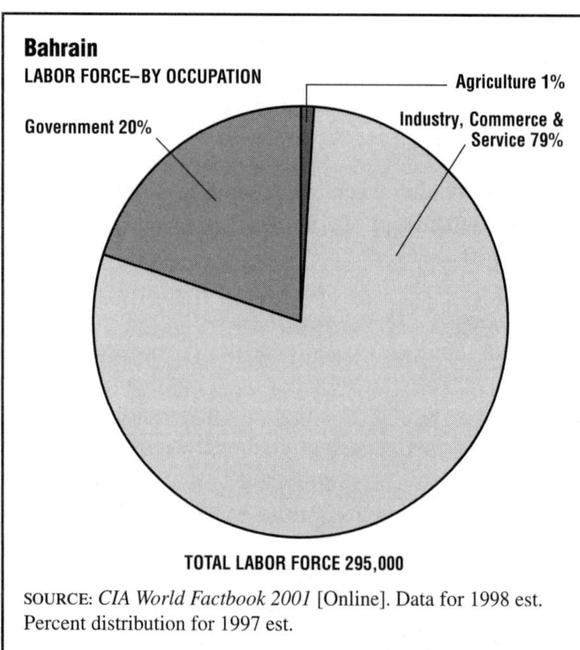

SOURCE: *CIA World Factbook 2001* [Online]. Data for 1998 est. Percent distribution for 1997 est.

Bahrain's fishing industry is small and only serves the domestic market. In the 1970s, the fishing industry declined, largely as a result of pollution and over-fishing in the Gulf. Since 1993, the government has been releasing young fish into local waters in order to boost stocks. Since 1997, trawlers have been banned from operating during the breeding season.

INDUSTRY

The industrial sector contributed 19 percent to GDP in 1996 and employed 34 percent of the **labor force**. Bahrain's aluminum industry was launched some 30 years ago as a measure to diversify the economy and take advantage of the country's low energy costs. The government-owned Aluminum Bahrain (ALBA) is one of the largest single-site aluminum smelters in the world and the biggest aluminum producer in the Middle East. Aluminum exports are one of Bahrain's biggest earners, particularly in light of increasing world prices. ALBA dominates the manufacturing sector with a production capacity of 500,000 metric tons per year.

Iron and steel production is increasing, and various free industrial zones have attracted export-oriented light and medium industries. These include plastics, paper, steel wool and wire-mesh producers; marine service industries; aluminum extrusion, assembly, and asphalt plants; cable manufacturing; prefabricated building; and furniture. In 1997, it was announced that the government was investing US$2.8 billion in the construction of a new seaport and a new industrial area in the eastern part of the country, and work was underway by 2000.

MINING/HYDROCARBONS. The mining and hydrocarbons (oil and related products) sector contributed 20.8 percent to GDP in 1998 but employed only 1 percent of the workforce. Bahrain is not a member of Organization of Petroleum-Exporting Countries (OPEC) and is thus not faced with production quotas but is a member of the Organization of Arab Petroleum Exporting Countries (OAPEC). Total oil reserves are estimated at between 150–200 million barrels, a minimal quantity in comparison with neighboring Arab monarchies.

SERVICES

Services contributed 53 percent of GDP in 1996. Tourism is Bahrain's fastest-growing industry and a heavily-promoted sector. It already accounts for over 10 percent of GDP and employs 16.7 percent of the workforce. Most visitors (3.3 million in 1999) come from the states of the Gulf Cooperation Council (GCC), especially Saudi Arabia, to enjoy the beaches and the comparatively liberal atmosphere in Bahrain, where alcohol is served and Muslim women are not forced to cover their heads. As of July 2000, the government has allowed citizens from member states of the GCC to visit the country using their local identity cards, and the number of tourists is expected to increase substantially over the next few years.

FINANCIAL SERVICES. Bahrain's banking sector has shown consistent growth, particularly since the outbreak of the Lebanese civil war in 1975, when many foreign banks began searching for an alternative regional base. There are now more than 200 financial institutions present in Bahrain. Assets of the country's **offshore banking** units have risen by more than 50 percent in the past decade. Bahrain also has the largest concentration of Islamic banking operations in the Middle East. Islam prohibits interest rates, and Islamic banking thus employs other methods of creating financial gains from investments.

INTERNATIONAL TRADE

Over the course of the last 30 years, Bahrain has maintained a relatively even **balance of trade**, with imports usually slightly exceeding exports. In 2000, however, the situation was reversed, with imports of US$4.2 billion trailing exports of US$5.8 billion. Bahrain's main export destinations are India (14 percent), Saudi Arabia (5 percent), the United States (5 percent), the United Arab Emirates (5 percent), Japan (4 percent), and South Korea (4 percent). All these countries import mainly processed and refined oil and oil-related products, which have the largest share in Bahrain's exports. Another important export for Bahrain is aluminum, accounting for about 7 percent. Bahrain's total exports rose by nearly 63 percent from 1998 to 2000, while oil-related exports increased from 52 percent of total exports in 1998, to 66 percent in 1999, and back down to 61 percent in 2000.

Bahrain's imports come from a similarly large range of countries. France supplies the majority of imports, with 20 percent, followed by the United States (14 percent), the United Kingdom (8 percent), Saudi Arabia (7 percent), and Japan (5 percent). The heavy trade volume between Bahrain and Saudi Arabia stems from the undersea pipeline between the 2 countries and the shared oilfield located in Saudi Arabia. Bahrain's imports, mainly machinery, manufactured goods, chemicals and food, come from developed industrial states.

MONEY

The **exchange rate** of the Bahraini dinar is fixed to the U.S. dollar, which means that developments in the American economy have repercussions for Bahrain. Bahrain's central bank is the Bahrain Monetary Agency (BMA), an independent organization praised for its adherence to international standards.

Trade (expressed in billions of US$): Bahrain

	Exports	Imports
1975	1.107	1.189
1980	3.606	3.483
1985	2.897	3.107
1990	3.761	3.712
1995	4.113	3.716
1998	N/A	3.463

SOURCE: International Monetary Fund. *International Financial Statistics Yearbook 1999.*

Exchange rates: Bahrain

Bahraini dinars (BD) per US$1	
2001	0.3760
2000	0.3760
1999	0.3760
1998	0.3760
1997	0.3760
1996	0.3760

Note: Fixed rate pegged to the US dollar.

SOURCE: CIA *World Factbook 2001* [ONLINE].

The Bahrain Stock Exchange (BSE) opened in 1989, and in 1995 Bahrain and Oman signed an agreement linking their stock exchanges. The link-up allows cross-listing of companies on both exchanges, which between them have 110 listed companies with a total **market capitalization** of US$8.1 billion. In 1996, the Bahraini and Jordanian stock exchanges linked up, and the BSE also has links with the Sri Lankan and Bangladeshi exchanges and plans to link up with the Bombay Stock Exchange.

POVERTY AND WEALTH

Although Bahrain is generally a wealthy country, there is a considerable gap between the rich and the poor. Wealthy families shop for the latest fashions in spacious new malls, young Saudi Arabians cruise the broad highways and enjoy the relaxed atmosphere of the island state, and foreign employees of the national oil company take advantage of huge leisure centers built for their exclusive use. The poor live only a short drive away from the cities, in many villages all over the island. Shiites, who make up 75 percent of the Muslim population, are often excluded from government jobs and form the poorest segment of Bahraini society. The ruling al-Khalifa family is Sunni Muslim and has "imported" many Sunnis from other Arab countries, and it is they who form the backbone of the widely resented security forces.

Most members of the ruling political elite are Sunni Muslims, and Bahrain's wealth is heavily concentrated

GDP per Capita (US$)

Country	1975	1980	1985	1990	1998
Bahrain	N/A	12,022	8,797	8,551	9,260
United States	19,364	21,529	23,200	25,363	29,683
Saudi Arabia	9,658	11,553	7,437	7,100	6,516
Qatar	N/A	N/A	N/A	N/A	N/A

SOURCE: United Nations. *Human Development Report 2000; Trends in human development and per capita income.*

Household Consumption in PPP Terms

Country	All food	Clothing and footwear	Fuel and power[a]	Health care[b]	Education[b]	Transport & Communications	Other
Bahrain	32	7	8	1	6	9	37
United States	13	9	9	4	6	8	51
Saudi Arabia	N/A	N/A	N/A	N/A	N/A	N/A	N/A
Qatar	22	12	11	5	13	8	29

Data represent percentage of consumption in PPP terms.
[a]Excludes energy used for transport.
[b]Includes government and private expenditures.

SOURCE: World Bank. *World Development Indicators 2000.*

among them, while there are only a few wealthy Shiites in the country. Many Shiites have charged that there has been a systematic process of discrimination against them. Their dissatisfaction with the political and economic situation came to the fore in demonstrations and protests that turned violent in 1994 and 1995, triggering the first change of cabinet for more than 20 years in 1995.

For decades, the country has seen an influx of foreign workers who can earn good salaries in the oil industry or as domestic servants and in other jobs locals do not want to do, further exacerbating the plight of the Shi'a community. **Immigration** to Bahrain began in the early years of the oil boom and resulted in the employment of foreigners rather than Bahraini Shiites, who are often less educated and treated with suspicion by the ruling Sunni minority.

WORKING CONDITIONS

Due to the sharp rise in the growth of the local population since the 1980s and the increasing levels of education, the government, as in many other states in the Gulf region, needs to provide young Bahrainis entering the job market with employment. It plans to gradually reduce dependence on foreign labor by training the local workforce and by insisting that expatriates coming to Bahrain to work must have better expertise and skills and be willing to train their local counterparts. After decades of importing foreign labor, foreigners comprised about 44 percent of the workforce of 295,000 in 1998.

Population growth has been proportionately higher among foreigners and Shiites than among Sunni Muslims, who have enjoyed relative job security in government positions. Foreign workers and Shiites have increasingly had to compete for both skilled and unskilled jobs. Since Bahraini Shiites are not allowed to join the armed forces and are discriminated against for senior positions in the civil service, an increasing number of young Shiites try to enter the job market with few qualifications and few opportunities for work.

Officially, unemployment stands at only 2.4 percent, but the United States embassy in Bahrain estimates that the actual rate is closer to 18 percent. Among the Shi'a community in Bahrain, especially those under the age of 30, unemployment may be as high as about 30 percent. In rural areas, agricultural laborers represent about 25 percent of the population. Women are traditionally confined to the household and cannot participate freely in the labor market. Thus, only about 19 percent of the labor force is female, equaling figures in other Middle Eastern countries.

COUNTRY HISTORY AND ECONOMIC DEVELOPMENT

1820. Bahrain becomes a British protectorate with the signing of the General Treaty of Peace but is ruled by the al-Khalifa family. Treaties of protection with Britain are re-signed in 1861, 1892, and 1951.

1928. Iran claims ownership of Bahrain. The dispute is not resolved until 1970 when Iran accepts a United Nations report stating that the vast majority of Bahrainis want to retain complete independence.

1932. Oil is first discovered in Bahrain, to be followed shortly thereafter by discoveries in Saudi Arabia and Kuwait.

1968. Bahrain joins Qatar and the Trucial States (now the United Arab Emirates) in the Federation of Arab Emirates. These countries had all enjoyed the protection of Great Britain up until this point.

1971. Bahrain gains complete independence on August 15, leaving the Federation of Arab Emirates.

1973. A constitution is adopted and elections held for the National Assembly. The Assembly is disbanded in 1975 and indefinitely suspended in 1976.

1981. Bahrain is one of the six founding members of the Gulf Cooperation Council (GCC).

1990. Bahrain actively supports the allied forces against Iraq in the Gulf military conflict, and is the target of an Iraqi missile attack.

1994–97. Civil unrest breaks out following the decline of the economy and expectations of more political rights for the mainly Shiite population after the Gulf war.

1999. Sheikh Isa Bin-Sulman al-Khalifa dies and is succeeded by his son Sheikh Hamad Bin Isa al-Khalifa in March.

2001. In February Bahrainis vote to approve a new constitution that would institute a partially elected parliament and grant political rights to women.

FUTURE TRENDS

With high oil prices in 2000 and 2001, the pressure on the Bahraini government to reform the economy has recently eased a little. But given that the country cannot sustain its dependence on oil for much longer, economic reform remains necessary. The government is expected to push for limited privatization, starting with public transport, although the major state revenue-generating organizations such as the Bahraini Petroleum Company (BAPCO) and Aluminum Bahrain (ALBA) will remain off limits.

At the end of 2000, a new corporate law was introduced, aimed at streamlining regulations and enticing foreign investment. In addition, the establishment of a new international Islamic banking system in Bahrain in October 2001 suggests that there will be further progress in developing the offshore financial services sector. Unemployment among locals remains the government's main economic and social problem. The government will continue to emphasize training to enhance the skills of existing workers and the 6,500 new entrants into the job market each year. But where government policy clashes with the interests of foreign firms—for example, over efforts to encourage companies to replace foreign workers with locals (the so-called "Bahrainization" of the workforce)—the development of a welcoming business environment will take precedence.

Politically, there are several challenges ahead. The emir has signaled his will to broaden political participation but is still struggling with the prime minister over the pace of reform. In the long run, however, both political and economic **liberalization** will prove unavoidable, with one reinforcing the other to the benefit of the country.

DEPENDENCIES

Bahrain has no territories or colonies.

BIBLIOGRAPHY

Allen, Robin. "Survey: Bahrain." *Financial Times.* 20 November 2000.

Cordesman, Anthony H. *Bahrain, Oman, Qatar, and the UAE: Challenges of Security.* Boulder, CO: Westview Press, 1997.

Embassy of the State of Bahrain. <http://www.bahrainembassy.org>. Accessed September 2001.

U.S. Central Intelligence Agency. *World Factbook 2001.* <http://www.odci.gov/cia/publications/factbook/index.html>. Accessed August 2001.

U.S. Department of State. *FY 2001 Country Commercial Guide: Bahrain.* <http://www.state.gov/www/about_state/business/com_guides/2001/nea/index.html>. Accessed September 2001.

Zahlan, Rosemarie Said. *The Making of the Modern Gulf States: Kuwait, Bahrain, Qatar, the United Arab Emirates and Oman.* Reading, UK: Ithaca Press, 1998.

—Ralph Stobwasser and Markus R. Bouillon

BANGLADESH

People's Republic of Bangladesh
Gana-Prajatantri Bangladesh

CAPITAL: Dhaka.

MONETARY UNIT: Taka (Tk). One Bangladeshi taka equals 100 paisa. Notes are in denominations of 1, 2, 5, 10, 20, 50, 100, and 500 taka. There are coins of 1, 5, 10, 25, 50, and 100 paisa.

CHIEF EXPORTS: Garments, jute and jute goods, tea, leather and leather products, frozen fish, and seafood.

CHIEF IMPORTS: Machinery and equipment, chemicals, fertilizers, iron and steel, textiles, raw cotton, food (mainly rice and wheat), crude oil and petroleum products, and cement.

GROSS DOMESTIC PRODUCT: US$187 billion (purchasing power parity, 1999 est.).

BALANCE OF TRADE: **Exports:** US$5.523 billion (1999). **Imports:** US$8.381 billion (1999).

COUNTRY OVERVIEW

LOCATION AND SIZE. Bangladesh is situated in southern Asia, on the delta of the 2 largest rivers on the Indian subcontinent—the Ganges and Jamuna (Brahmaputra). It borders with India in the west, north, and east, with Burma (also known as Myanmar) in the southeast, and with the Bay of Bengal in the south. The country's area is 144,000 square kilometers (55,598 square miles), and it is divided into 6 administrative divisions (Dhaka, Chittagong, Khulna, Barisal, Rajshai and Sylhet) and 4 major municipal corporations (Dhaka, Chittagong, Khulna and Rajshahi). Comparatively, the territory of Bangladesh is slightly greater than the state of New York. Bangladesh's capital city, Dhaka, is located in the central part of the country. Bangladesh occupies the eastern part of the Bengal region (the western part of the region is occupied by the Indian state of West Bengal), which historically was part of the great civilizations in the northeast of the Indian subcontinent.

POPULATION. The population of Bangladesh was estimated at 129,194,224 in July of 2000, making Bangladesh the tenth-most populous state in the world. Having a total area the size of New York state, the country has a population equal to half that of the United States or 8 times the population of New York State. It has almost doubled since the 1960s, due to improved health, medical facilities, and longer life expectancy. In 2000 the birth rate stood at 25.44 per 1,000 (slightly higher than the world average), adding around 190,000 people every month. Meanwhile the death rate stood at 8.73 per 1,000. The estimated population growth rate is 1.59 percent, and if the current trend remains unchanged, the population could double within the next 45 years.

The Bangladesh population is relatively homogeneous, with Bengalis making up 98 percent of the population and other ethnic groups, including various tribal groups, making up the remaining 2 percent. Religion plays a very important role in this country, and the main division is between Islam and Hinduism. Almost 88.3 percent of the population are Muslims, 10.5 percent are Hindus, and 1.2 percent are Buddhists, Christians, or animists. The Bangladesh population is very young, with 36 percent below age 14 and just 4 percent of the population older than 65. In 1998 over 80 percent of Bangladeshis were living in rural areas, although during the last decade the growth of the population in the urban areas was twice as fast as in rural areas (due to both the migration of the rural population and the high birth rate). The rapid growth of the urban population is especially noticeable in the urban centers of Dhaka, Chittagong, Khulna, and Rajshahi.

In 1970, the population of Bangladesh was about 66 million, and the country at one time had one of the highest birth rates in Asia. The country's population doubled between 1950 and 1977 and almost doubled again between 1977 and 2001, putting severe pressure on the natural resources and leading to land shortages. In the 1970s the government introduced population control and family

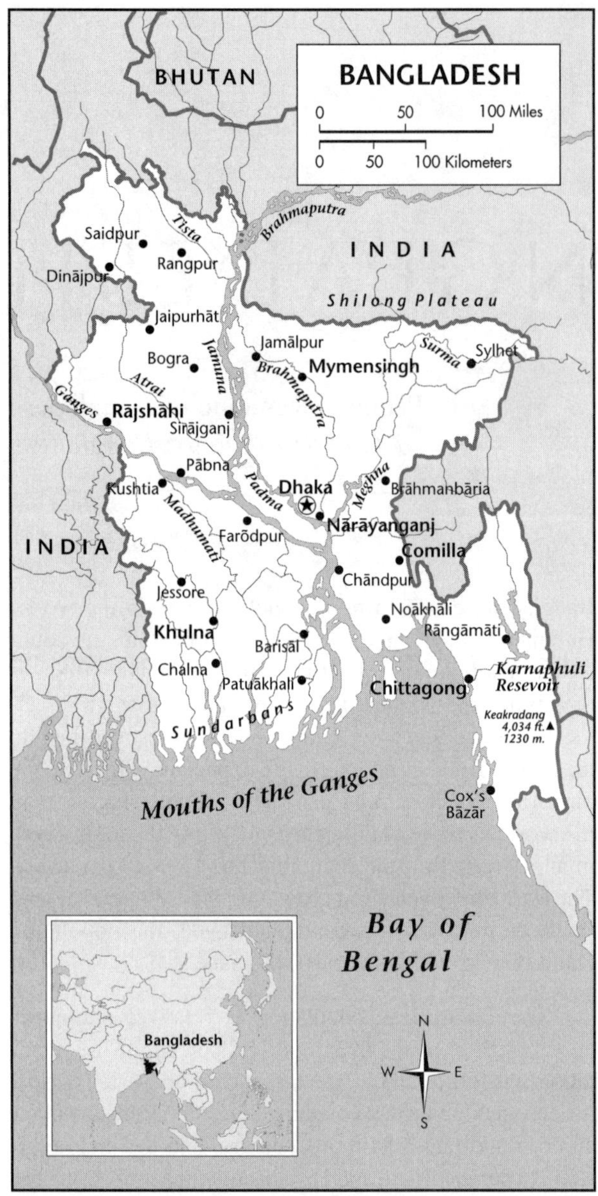

planning initiatives, aided by various international organizations, including United Nations Children's Fund (UNICEF), United Nations Population Fund (UNFPA), and the World Bank. The fertility rate (the average number of children born to a woman) in Bangladesh declined from 6.8 babies per woman in 1965 to around 3 per woman in 1999. However, these population control initiatives were undermined by the fact that two-thirds of the population still lives in rural areas, where historically population growth was very high, and by the fact that almost two-thirds of the people in the country are illiterate. A number of issues still need to be addressed, including the supply of safe drinking water, malnutrition among children (which remains the highest in the world), early and forced marriages, and illiteracy among the population in general and women in particular.

The population growth in the country was offset by rapidly rising **emigration** of people, both permanent and temporary, in the 1980s and 1990s. The major destinations for Bangladeshi workers seeking temporary jobs are Kuwait, Malaysia, Qatar, Saudi Arabia, Oman, and the United Arab Emirates, where they are employed mainly in the low-skill and low-wage construction and service sectors and in agricultural plantations. Other popular destinations for emigration are Western Europe, the Americas and Australia, where large Bangladeshi communities formed during the last 3 decades. According to the *CIA World Factbook,* the emigration rate stood at the 0.77 migrant(s) per 1,000 population in 2000, or around 1 million a year.

OVERVIEW OF ECONOMY

Agriculture and labor-intensive manufacturing remain the 2 major pillars of the Bangladeshi national economy. Historically, a tropical climate and warm temperatures throughout the year made it possible to grow 2 or 3 crops of rice each year, although floods and cyclones regularly damaged crop yield. Flourishing trade, manufacturing—traditionally in light manufacturing and agricultural processing—along with the wealth of the region's nobility, attracted English, French, and Dutch traders. The British East India Company had slowly but steadily advanced into the region in the 17th and 18th centuries, acquiring trade privileges from the Mogul emperors and exploiting rivalries between local rulers, and gradually established control over the trade between India and Europe. The company and its often corrupt administration had greatly benefited from the trade between India and Europe. The British East India Company established control over administration of the Bengal province in 1765. However, in 1858 the company was abolished, and the British crown assumed direct control over British India, in response to the local uprising of 1857 to 1858 and to growing evidence of the company's inefficiency. Throughout the colonial era, East Bengal (the territory of modern Bangladesh) received very limited investments in its industrial sector or toward development of its transportation system, and largely relied on the production and export of its agricultural goods, including jute, rice, and tea. The British colonial rule in India was accompanied by uprisings, greater polarization of society, and a decline in the traditional values and institutions of the society; nevertheless, it included India in the global trade of the early capitalist era and introduced the British legal and political systems and the technological innovations of that era.

In August 1947, India was granted independence within the British Commonwealth and was divided into the dominions of India and Pakistan. Pakistan, which included the areas populated predominantly by the Muslims, was itself divided with the West Pakistan comprising the area now known as Pakistan, and East Pakistan, occupying what had been Eastern Bengal. Powerful West Pakistan was politically and economically dominant over East Pakistan, giving rise to a secessionist movement in the eastern province. Despite attempts to ease the tensions, these factions gradually grew into open hostility and in 1971 a brief but bloody civil war flared up that lasted for 2 weeks and ended with the intervention of Indian troops. On 17 December 1971 a new government in Dhaka declared the independence of the new state, Bangladesh.

After achieving independence in 1971, Bangladesh confronted the challenging task of developing and diversifying its economy, as the country had very limited natural resources and arable land with which to support its rapidly growing population. The task was complicated by years of political turbulence and military coups (in 1975, 1981, and 1982) that did little to attract international investors and by devastating natural disasters that regularly visited Bangladesh in the 1970s and 1980s. By the beginning of the 21st century, according to the World Bank, Bangladesh had become one of the poorest and least-developed economies in Asia.

During the 1970s and 1980s the government of Bangladesh promoted economic development based on heavy state involvement both in economic management and economic planning. In fact, after achieving independence, the government led by the Awami League, **nationalized** large and medium-sized enterprises in jute, cotton textile, sugar processing, banking and insurances. Its economic policies were centered on 5-year plans (the first 5-year plan was launched in 1973), which aimed at development and public resource allocation modeled on the Soviet 5-year experience. However, the Bangladeshi experiment with **socialism** did not last long, and the government eschewed radical changes. The country's average **gross domestic product** (GDP) growth of around 3.3 percent in the 1970s and 4.4 percent in the 1980s (World Bank calculation) were very impressive, but this growth was offset by even more rapid growth of the population.

In 1991 the first free and fair election was held in Bangladesh and the Bangladesh National Party (BNP) won the election. The new civilian government considerably revised the economic policies of the previous government, introducing elements of free market economy, limiting state intervention, downsizing the government, launching **privatization** and attempting to attract **foreign direct investments** (FDIs) and technologies. The political stability of the 1990s and the new economic policies attracted international investors and greatly contributed to the economic growth of around 5 percent throughout the 1990s. However, Bangladesh still depends heavily on international assistance and loans, as well as **remittances** from Bangladeshis working abroad. According to the International Monetary Fund's (IMF) *Country Report,* in 1999 the country's **external debt** stood at US$15.145 billion, or 35 percent of GDP. This amount is relatively small according to international standards and mainly due to past capital account restrictions. According to the IMF, one of the peculiarities of the Bangladeshi **foreign debt** that makes it different from that of Indonesia or Malaysia is that it is almost entirely public, with private debt accounting for a low 5 percent of the total country's debt. Bangladeshi official reserves stood at a level of US$1.522 billion in 1999.

The structure of the Bangladeshi economy changed gradually over the last 3 decades. According to the World Bank, the contribution of agriculture to the country's GDP has been steadily declining from 55 percent in 1970 to 31.6 in 1999, although it still provides employment to large numbers of people. Bangladesh remains one of the world's leading producers of jute and rice, although most of the rice is for domestic consumption rather than export. The proportion of manufactured production grew from 9 percent of GDP in 1970 to 19.3 percent of GDP in 1999. Manufactured products accounted for around 60 percent of gross export earnings in 1999, with clothing goods becoming the single most important product. Tourism is a very small but rapidly growing sector of the economy that increased by around 42 percent between 1993 and 1998. Approximately 171,000 tourists visited the country in 1999, contributing Tk2.4 billion to the national economy. By comparison, tiny Singapore attracts a similar number of tourists every week.

For a long time Bangladesh struggled to diversify its economy. Large and medium state-owned enterprises dominate the manufacturing sector, although a number of private enterprises were established during the 1990s. Medium and small farms dominate the agricultural sector, and many farmers are still engaged in subsistence agriculture. Meanwhile, a number of medium and small, usually family-owned, enterprises dominate the service sector, especially **retail**. Bangladesh tried to catch up with the information technologies boom in the 1990s, but unlike neighboring India, it failed to promote this sector of its economy on a similar scale.

Economic growth and stability failed to bring economic prosperity to a large proportion of the population, especially in rural areas. Since the 1970s there has been an outflow of large numbers of the young and the most talented people from the country through various legal and illegal channels. Allegedly, organized criminal groups connected to drug trafficking control this outflow. Drugs are another important issue, as Bangladesh shares a border with Burma (Myanmar), which is a part of the world's largest opium producing region called the "Golden Triangle" (an area between Burma, Laos, and

Thailand). The **shadow economy** is believed to be very large due to incomplete economic activities data collection, tax evasion, and a strong tradition of cash economy, although this shadow economy is not necessarily related to organized criminal activities. In 1996 a national account task force was formed to upgrade the outdated and inefficient system of national accounting, having among other goals to deal with the problem of calculating and capturing shadow economy activities.

POLITICS, GOVERNMENT, AND TAXATION

Bangladesh is a parliamentary democracy largely influenced by the British parliamentary system. Executive power is in the hands of the prime minister, who is the head of the cabinet, and who must be a member of the 300-seat Jatiya Sangsad (**unicameral** parliament). She/he recommends the council of ministers to the president. The president is the constitutional head of state and is elected for a 5-year term by the parliament, but plays a largely ceremonial role. The president can act only on the advice of the prime minister, as the presidential power was significantly reduced in accordance with constitutional changes in 1991.

All adult citizens (18 years old and over) are eligible to vote, including women and ethnic minorities. One of the unique features of the political system in Bangladesh is that 30 seats (10 percent) in the parliament are reserved for female members, and they are elected by the members of the parliament.

Bangladesh experienced a number of military coups after achieving independence in 1971, and several military governments tried to restrict activities of political parties. However, after the return to civil rule in 1990, all political parties may openly function in the country. There are a number of political organizations in Bangladesh. Most prominent of them are: the Awami League (a coalition of 8 parties); the Bangladesh Nationalist Party; the Jatiya Party; and the Jamaat-e-Islami Party. The Awami League (AL), which led the country to independence in 1971, generally supports more government interventionist policies and has a very cautious attitude towards **liberalization** or opening of the national economy to international competition; in fact, in the early 1970s the party had strong pro-socialist elements in its economic policy. The Bangladesh Nationalist Party (BNP), which was the ruling party from 1991 until its defeat in the parliamentary election of 1996, is more free-market oriented. The BNP introduced the policy of economic liberalization and privatized some state-owned enterprises. It opened the national economy to international competition in an attempt to attract foreign investors.

Once Bangladesh had achieved independence, political stability, the creation of a viable national economy, and the elimination of poverty became the major political issues shaping political debate and conflict in the state. The political process in the country was complicated by the hostility and often violent confrontations between the 2 leading parties, AL and BNP. The Awami League won the first post-independence general elections while promulgating ideas of nationalism, socialism, democracy and secularism. In economic areas, this government took a strongly interventionist role in the development and industrialization of the national economy. The party, however, could not overcome the economic and political divisions within Bangladeshi society and lost its power in a military coup in August 1975. The coup pushed the country towards even greater political instability, which continued until 1990, when charismatic General Hossain Ershad was forced to resign. Military rule failed to bring stability to the country because it did not stop the rivalry between the 2 major parties, the AL and BNP. In fact, the army was drawn into the groups' political confrontations.

In 1991, the first free and fair election was held in Bangladesh. Begum Khaleda Zia (widow of General Ziaur Rahman, the president from 1978 until his assassination in 1981) and her party (BNP) won the election. The new government brought radical changes to the economic policy, promoting private entrepreneurship, especially among representatives of poor communities, and supporting small- and medium-size businesses and privatization. This program was successful, and Bangladesh experienced economic growth throughout the 1990s. According to the World Bank, between 1989 and 1999 the average annual GDP growth was around 4.8 percent, with industrial production growing at an annual average of 7.3 percent and exports of goods and services at an annual average of 14.2 percent, albeit from a very low base. For the first time in decades the Bangladeshi government had brought a sense of stability to the country.

The 1996 parliamentary election, however, was again accompanied by irregularities and almost pushed the country into chaos again. The BNP won the February 1996 parliamentary election, which was boycotted by the AL-led opposition. The confrontation escalated in violence, and the BNP handed power over to a caretaker government. After 2 decades in opposition, the Awami League won the June 1996 parliamentary election, with support from the Jatiya Party. This time the Awami Party significantly moderated its position, supporting a gradual liberalization of the national economy, encouraging private entrepreneurship, and advocating the secular state; it had largely abandoned socialist ideas. One of the most important achievements of the 1990s was the diminishing role of the army in the political life of the state, although the army threatened to take matters into its own hands during the period of political conflict in 1996.

According to the IMF *Country Report,* the major source of government revenue comes from taxes, although the tax ratio of 7.6 percent of GDP remains one of the lowest in the world. Total government revenue was Tk210 billion in the 1997/1998 financial year. Tk51 billion came from **value-added tax** (VAT), Tk43.5 billion from customs **duties**, Tk20.0 billion from income and profit taxes, Tk21 billion from supplementary duties, and the rest from other sources. According to the U.S. Department of State, the maximum customs duty rate has been reduced from 350 percent in 1991 to around 37 percent in 2000.

INFRASTRUCTURE, POWER, AND COMMUNICATIONS

Bangladesh is a country of a thousand rivers, large and small, and most of its territory is regularly flooded during the monsoon season. This fact makes it extremely difficult and expensive to build modern transportation and communication networks. The river boats and ferries traditionally used for transportation are cheap, but slow and inefficient. The situation is further complicated by the fact that the Bangladeshi government has sharply limited resources not only for building new **infrastructure** but also for maintaining the existing one. From the colonial era Bangladesh inherited underdeveloped and unevenly distributed infrastructure and transportation networks. Poor and inefficient infrastructure undermined the economic development in the country, and only recently has the government been able to address the problem systematically and channel investments towards expanding its highways, railroads, seaports, and airports. More recently, with international assistance the government has also started to modernize its telecommunications infrastructure and introduce the Internet.

According to the *CIA World Factbook,* Bangladesh is served by a network of 201,182 kilometers (125,014 miles) of primary and secondary roads, but only around 10 percent of them, or 19,112 kilometers (11,876 miles) are paved. In June 1998 the huge US$1 billion Jamuna Multipurpose Bridge was completed, becoming the 12th-longest bridge in the world. The bridge connected for the first time the eastern and western parts of Bangladesh. The completion of this project made an important contribution to the development of the country's transportation network and significantly boosted the quality and speed of passenger and freight transportation. The number of privately-owned cars grew throughout the 1990s, albeit from a very low level (there were 40,000 private cars in 1994). Many cars are very old and in poor repair and produce high levels of pollution on the congested roads of the capital and other major cities. Despite all the problems with the roads and the often-outdated equipment, 66 percent of all freight and 73 percent of all passengers are carried by roads; however, animal-driven carts are still a part of the national landscape, as they provide the cheapest and most reliable transportation for people and goods in most of the country's rural areas.

Bangladesh has a railway system of about 2,745 kilometers (1,706 miles), of which only 923 kilometers (573.5 miles) is a broad gauge (1.676 meter gauge) and the remaining 1,822 kilometers (1,132 miles) is narrow gauge (1.000 meter gauge), according to CIA estimates for 1998. Major links run from the largest Bangladeshi port, Chittagong, to Dhaka and further to the north of the country; other links connect such centers as Khulna and Rajshahi. Historically, the railway was built by the British colonial administration in 1884, running between Calcutta (now India) and Khulna (now Bangladesh). Rail services were halted following the Indo-Pakistan war in 1965. In the 1970s cargo trains resumed their services between the 2 countries. According to a BBC report on 26 January 2001, the government of Bangladesh has expressed its interest in "seriously studying the potential of linking the national railways with the proposed Trans-Asian Railway Network." The Bangladeshi railway system remains a state-owned **monopoly** requiring large

Communications

Country	Newspapers	Radios	TV Sets[a]	Cable subscribers[a]	Mobile Phones[a]	Fax Machines[a]	Personal Computers[a]	Internet Hosts[b]	Internet Users[b]
	1996	1997	1998	1998	1998	1998	1998	1999	1999
Bangladesh	9	50	6	N/A	1	N/A	N/A	0.00	50
United States	215	2,146	847	244.3	256	78.4	458.6	1,508.77	74,100
India	N/A	121	69	18.8	1	0.2	2.7	0.18	2,800
Burma	10	95	7	N/A	0	0.1	N/A	0.00	1

[a]Data are from International Telecommunication Union, *World Telecommunication Development Report 1999* and are per 1,000 people.
[b]Data are from the Internet Software Consortium (http://www.isc.org) and are per 10,000 people.

SOURCE: World Bank. *World Development Indicators 2000.*

subsidies, as it is notorious for its poor management and a long-established tradition of ticketless travel among the local population. In recent moves, the government began the privatization of some railway services, including ticket reservation and in-service catering. Despite all shortcomings, the railway remained an important mode of transportation, operating 3.7 billion passenger-kilometers and carrying 3.76 million metric tons of goods in the 1998–99 financial year.

The waterways are an important mode of transportation, especially to some remote areas of the country, as no other mode of transportation is available during monsoon season. Bangladesh has 3 major seaports, at Chittagong, Dhaka, and Mongla, and several smaller ports. The largest and most important port is Chittagong, situated around 200 kilometers (124 miles) southeast of Dhaka. According to the *EIU Country Report,* in 2000 the Chittagong seaport handled around 80 percent of country's imports and 75 percent of exports, or 14.6 million metric tons of cargo and 420,850 containers. There have been several plans backed by private investors to set up 2 modern container terminals (in Chittagong and in Dhaka), but these plans have met opposition from the labor unions. According to the U.S. Department of State, in 1998 the U.S.-based company Stevedoring Services of America (SSA) signed a US$440 million contract to develop a private container project, which includes the construction of 2 container terminals.

Currently, Bangladesh is putting considerable efforts into developing its aviation industry to serve growing tourism and business needs. According to the *CIA World Factbook,* the country has 16 airports with paved runways, including 2 international airports (Chittagong and Dhaka). The largest, Zia International Airport at Dhaka, is capable of handling 25 million passengers and 1.2 million tons of cargo annually. Bangladeshi Biman Airline, the national air carrier, operates a fleet of about 15 aircraft, including 3 Airbus 310–300s, flying to 25 international destinations and serving several domestic routes. In the 1998–99 financial year it carried 1.22 million passengers and 30,869 metric tons of cargo.

Bangladesh belongs to the group of countries with the lowest commercial energy consumption per head in the world. The CIA estimated that in 1999 the country produced 12.5 billion kWh, 85 percent of which was produced using gas, 7.0 percent was produced at hydroelectric power plants, and around 8 percent by using liquid fuel. According to the *EIU Country Profile,* 85 percent of households in Bangladesh have no electricity and in these places where it is delivered, 40 percent of the electricity generated is not paid for. The country experiences regular electricity blackouts and shortages, and its poor reliability is often cited among factors driving away foreign investors. The Bangladeshi government is willing to address the problem but in general has not had enough resources to build new electric power generating plants. In a recent trend, the Asian Bank of Development (ABD) approved a US$140 million loan to construct a 450-mw gas-fired power station near Dhaka, scheduled for completion in 2003.

Telecommunication services in Bangladesh are underdeveloped and provide one of the lowest rates of telephone ownership per 1,000 inhabitants in the world. The largest company is the Bangladesh Telegraph and Telephone Board (BTTB), which enjoyed a state monopoly until 1972, when private operators were allowed. As most of the telephone service uses outdated analogue technology, the quality of telecommunication services is often poor and in need of upgrades. In 2000 the country had a mere 490,000 telephone lines and 52,000 mobile phones serving 129 million people. The government is aiming to provide telephone coverage of remote towns and villages that until now have had no telephone connections. With international assistance and increasing private investments, Bangladesh is upgrading its telecommunication system, replacing analogue technology with digital, introducing the Internet and e-mail services, and expanding cellular mobile services.

ECONOMIC SECTORS

According to the *World Bank Development Indicators,* Bangladesh is the 50th-largest economy in the world, judged by its gross national income, although it is the 10th-largest state in the world if judged by its population. Although it has a good environment and climate for the production of various crops and huge potential for developing a tourist industry, the country suffers from

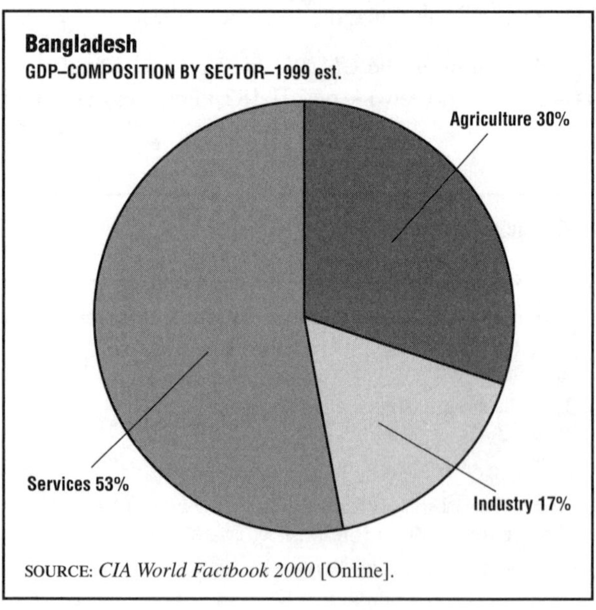

SOURCE: *CIA World Factbook 2000* [Online].

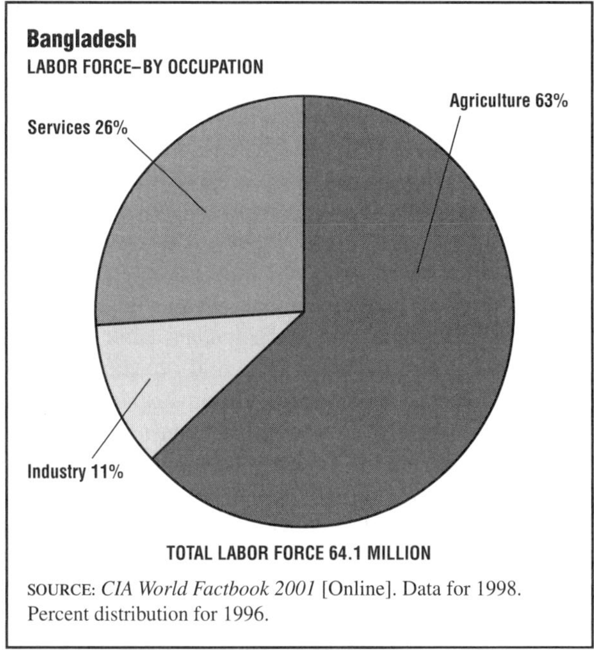

SOURCE: *CIA World Factbook 2001* [Online]. Data for 1998. Percent distribution for 1996.

scarcity of natural resources, shortage of arable land, regular natural disasters (flooding and cyclones), and a lack of investment.

For decades after independence, political instability, low demand in the local market, and economic stagnation hindered the economic development of the country. Since establishing a civil government in 1991, Bangladesh has been struggling to diversify its economy, to reform its agricultural sector, and to expand its industrial sector, as it needs average annual economic growth of at least 7 percent in order to eliminate widespread poverty. In the 1990s while Bangladesh was unable to solve its economic difficulties and eliminate poverty, it achieved impressive growth in many areas, including manufacturing and agriculture. Recognizing the difficulties, the Bangladeshi government was willing to accept the IMF's recommendations and to conduct structural changes, which included relinquishing its socialist orientation and state control over the economy, decentralization of economic management, and privatization, although many of these changes were painful and implemented only slowly.

Agriculture is still the single most important sector of economy. Between 1989 and 1999, it experienced stagnation with an average annual growth of only 1.6 percent, which was not enough to support a rapidly growing population. Throughout the 1980s and 1990s, Bangladesh tried with some success to achieve politically and economically important self-sufficiency in food production, increasing productivity and diversifying the crop base. Nevertheless, the share of agriculture in the GDP declined from 55 percent in 1970 to 19.6 percent in 1999.

The role of the manufacturing sector is growing, but the growth is painfully slow due to a lack of foreign investment, small demand in the local market, and red tape and inefficiency in the local bureaucracy. According to the World Bank, the industrial sector in Bangladesh grew at an average annual rate of around 4.1 percent between 1979 and 1989 and around 7.3 percent between 1989 and 1999. Bangladesh has a relatively large reserve of gas, which has become increasingly important as a source of energy and has potential to become a source of export revenue.

Bangladesh tries to promote its service sector, especially tourism and the information technologies sector. However, in doing so it has to compete with neighboring India. Local trade, tourism, and other services currently make important contributions to the country's GDP, providing employment for 26 percent of the **labor force** in the country.

AGRICULTURE

Agriculture remains the most important sector of Bangladeshi economy, contributing 19.6 percent to the national GDP and providing employment for 63 percent of the population. Agriculture in Bangladesh is heavily dependent on the weather, and the entire harvest can be wiped out in a matter of hours when cyclones hit the country. According to the World Bank, the total arable land in Bangladesh is 61.2 percent of the total land area (down from 68.3 percent in 1980). Farms are usually very small due to heavily increasing population, unwieldy land ownership, and inheritance regulations. The 3 main crops—rice, jute, and tea—have dominated agricultural exports for decades, although the rice is grown almost entirely for domestic consumption, while jute and tea are the main export earners. In addition to these products, Bangladeshi farmers produce sugarcane, tobacco, cotton, and various fruits and vegetables (sweet potatoes, bananas, pineapples, etc.) for the domestic market.

Rice is the staple food in the everyday diet of Bangladeshis. The production of rice, which can be harvested 2 or even 3 times a year, reached 19.9 million metric tons in 1998–99. The production of wheat reached about 2 million metric tons in 1998–99. Both crops play an important role in achieving self-sufficiency in food production. However, due to weather conditions the production of rice and wheat fluctuate greatly, forcing Bangladesh to import food from the international market or turn to international aid. Bangladesh imported 1.6 million tons of wheat (mainly from the United States) in 2000 in order to meet the demand in the local market.

Jute, often called the "golden fibre" of Bengal, is the main export-earner for Bangladeshi agriculture, as Bangladesh remains the world's second-largest producer of jute (after India) and the world's largest exporter of fiber. Jute is traditionally used for the fiber of carpet backing, burlap bags, cheap paper, and various other purposes. Its importance for the Bangladeshi economy comes from the fact that almost 3 million farms are involved in jute production. In 1999 Bangladeshi export earnings from jute amounted to US$55 million, with the country producing 720,000 metric tons of jute, although this is about one-third of the jute production of the middle of the 1980s. The decline in jute production is attributed to declining world prices for this crop and to farmers switching to other crops.

Bangladesh also produces tea leaves, mainly for export, although the export of this product contributes only 1 percent of the country's **hard currency** earnings. In 1998–99 the country produced 56,000 metric tons of tea leaves, but it could produce twice that amount. The main obstacle to increasing production is in falling prices for tea in the international market and in management and regulation problems in the industry in the country.

Tropical rainforest is important for maintaining the ecological balance in Bangladesh, and forestry contributes 1.9 percent to the GDP (1999–2000). The forest covers around 17 percent of the country's territory, or 2.5 million hectares (6.18 million acres). The timber is used by the construction industry as a source of building materials, by the printing industry as a source of materials to produce paper, and in the agricultural sector as a source of firewood. Commercial logging is limited to around 6.1 million cubic feet, and the government plans to plant more trees within the next 15 years.

Fishing is another important activity in the country, contributing 4.9 percent to the GDP (1999–2000) and providing 6 percent of the total export income. The overall fish production was around 1.6 million metric tons (1999–2000). Bangladesh mainly exports its shrimp to the international market.

INDUSTRY

MINING. The main commercially viable natural resource in Bangladesh is gas, although there are reports of the existence of moderate-sized reserves of coal. Total gas reserves are estimated at 21,000 billion cubic feet. In 2000 Bangladesh utilized 370 billion cubic feet, mainly for domestic consumption. The major gas fields are situated in Greater Sylhet district, the Bay of Bengal, and Greater Chittagong district. Transnational corporations are keen to be involved in gas exploration in Bangladesh and its exportation to the huge Indian market, however the Bangladeshi government is resistant to the idea of exporting the gas, as according to local experts' estimates the proven reserves could run out within the next 30 to 40 years.

MANUFACTURING. During the 20th century Bangladesh, like neighboring Burma (Myanmar) and Nepal, largely missed the industrialization wave that changed the economies of many countries in the Asian region, such as Malaysia, Singapore, and Taiwan. At the beginning of 2001, manufacturing contributed about 24.3 percent of the GDP, providing employment to 6.2 million people or 11 percent of the workforce. Between 1989 and 1999, the manufacturing sector in Bangladesh grew at an average annual rate of around 7.2 percent, albeit from a very low base. The cheap, reliable, and abundant labor available in Bangladesh is attractive to the world's leading transnational corporations, but they have been very slow to move into the country, as they face regular industrial unrest led by radical trade unions, poorly developed infrastructure, red tape, and a very small local market. As in neighboring India, the Bangladeshi government promoted the idea of state-led industrialization combined with heavy state involvement in and state control of enterprise activities.

The manufacturing sector in Bangladesh comprises mainly small, privately-owned, often unmechanized enterprises or large, state-owned, often loss-making enterprises. The main industrial centers are Dhaka, Chittagong, Khulna, and Rajshahi, which have (by local standards) well-developed transport infrastructure, including access to seaports and railways and the sizeable and very cheap unskilled and skilled labor force. The industrial enterprises concentrate mainly on the production of jute goods, ready-made garments, foodstuff processing, and chemical production.

Most of Bangladeshi jute goods are produced in large state-controlled enterprises for export to the United States, Europe, and other markets, contributing Tk13.3 billion in 1997–98 to the country's export earnings and Tk11.7 billion in 1998–99. According to the *EIU Country Profile,* Bangladesh accounts for 90 percent of world jute fiber exports. The jute processing enterprises are vulnerable to downturns in the regional and international market and experienced some **recession** in 1998–99. Additionally, during the last few years the demand for jute in the international market has been in decline due to increasing use of synthetic materials in the areas where jute was previously used. However, these jute processing businesses still have plenty of the cheap local supply of raw materials and, if they continue to improve the quality of their products, with efficient management and marketing they may expand their export potential.

During the last 2 decades Bangladesh has found a strong niche in ready-made garments (RMG), becoming one of the world's leading exporters of these products. There are around 2,600 small and medium-size garment-manufacturing enterprises, providing employment for about 1.4 million local workers, mainly women. Access to cheap and reliable local labor makes Bangladeshi

RMG manufacturers very competitive in the international market, although most of the fabrics and machinery must be imported (in 2000 Bangladesh imported 160,000 metric tons of cotton from the United States). According to the U.S. Department of State, total clothing exports reached about US$5 billion in 1999–2000, mainly to the United States, Europe, and Canada. Bangladesh especially benefited from the multi-fiber arrangement with the United States and the generalized system of preferences with the European Union, which set special quotas for the RMG imports from Bangladesh. The RMG sector experienced rapid growth during the last 5 years, but with the rise of free trade and elimination of the quota system at the end of 2004, Bangladesh will face very tough competition from other Asian countries such as China, India, Indonesia, Thailand, and Vietnam.

Bangladesh has a well-established food processing sector, which relies on domestic agricultural production and is oriented mainly to domestic needs. It includes sugar refining and milling, production of edible oils, processing and preserving of fruits and fruit juices as well as fish processing, especially shrimp and prawns. As a tropical country Bangladesh has a plentiful domestic supply of exotic fruits and sea species.

In the 1990s 2 major changes affected the development of the industrial sector in Bangladesh. First, the end of the numerous military coups and the establishment of civil government brought in political stabilization, which attracted direct international investments and encouraged the inflow of foreign aid. Secondly, the policy of economic liberalization, structural adjustment, and privatization helped to increase the competitiveness of the local industries and encouraged them to search for new overseas markets. In order to promote the attractiveness of the Bangladesh economy, the government established special export-processing zones (EPZ). They are situated in Chittagong, Dhaka, Chalna (near Mongla port in Khulna) and in Commila, where investors are given access to well-developed infrastructure and enjoy tax breaks and other privileges. By the year 2000, the EPZs had attracted around US$415 million worth of foreign investments and more than 150 firms had moved there. According to the U.S. State Department, the United States is the single largest foreign investor in Bangladesh with total fixed direct investment of about $750 million. The major investment projects were in the chemical, electronics, and electrical industries. The United States is followed by Malaysia, Japan, and the United Kingdom, and the next tier of investors are Singapore, India, Hong Kong, China, and South Korea. The U.S. State Department estimates U.S. investment in Bangladesh will be about $2.5 billion in 2 to 4 years.

SERVICES

TOURISM. Tourism is a small but rapidly growing sector of Bangladeshi economy. According to the International Labor Organization, together with the wholesale and retail sector it provides employment for almost 6.0 million people (1996), or around 10.8 percent of the labor force. Government statistics state that 171,000 tourists visited the country in 1998, contributing Tk2.4 billion to the national economy. Most visitors were from India, Australia, Germany, the United Kingdom, and the United States.

Tourism could only take off in the 1990s, after the stabilization of the political situation in the country and the end of the tribal insurgency in the Chittagong Hill Tracts area (southeast of the country). Bangladesh has huge potential for attracting foreign tourists as it has a deep cultural heritage, a number of ancient monuments and temples, and a rich natural heritage, including tropical forests, beautiful hills, rivers, and national parks. The country offers bargain-shopping and exotic souvenirs, as well as a wide variety of activities, from eco-friendly to adventure tourism. However, it needs to renovate and expand its hotels' infrastructure and other services, which are still underdeveloped.

FINANCIAL SERVICES. The financial service industry remains underdeveloped in spite of a decade of major reforms conducted under the Financial Sector Reforms Program. According to the International Labor Organization, this sector provides employment for 213,000 people (1996). Since independence it has been under state control, as the major commercial banks were nationalized soon after independence. The local banks are often accused of providing poor financial services and being beset by corruption, inefficient management and capital inadequacies. Bangladesh lags behind in the introduction of computerized banking payment systems, the development of electronic payment systems, and electronic banking. The Agrani Bank, Janata Bank, Rupali Bank and Sonali Bank are the main financial institutions still under state control. They account for almost half of all deposits.

In 1999 the government launched a Commercial Bank Reform Project intended to improve the functioning of the private commercial banks. One bank has provided a success story: the Grameen Bank, which was founded by university professor Mohammad Yunus, pioneered in providing small credits to local communities in need. At present the IMF and the World Bank, which are often notoriously ineffective in the poor countries of Asia and Africa, have carefully studied the Grameen Bank's **microcredit** model with a view to applying it in other developing countries.

RETAIL. In Bangladesh, as in many other Asian countries, many small- and medium-sized businesses have been built around the retail sector and are often associated with small shops and restaurants. The retail sector provides employment for a large number of people, but it still remains relatively underdeveloped, due to a generally low level of income among the population. There are still a number of small family-run traditional shops and cafes, selling mainly locally-made products.

The United States has found that the enforcement of intellectual property rights is "weak" and that "intellectual property infringement is common." The Bangladeshi government has begun to address this problem seriously, introducing a new Copyright Act in 2000 in order to bring the country's copyright laws into compliance with the WTO. This act updated the Patents and Design Act of 1911, and some other outdated regulations.

INTERNATIONAL TRADE

Bangladeshi international trade is extremely small relative to the size of its population, although it experienced accelerated growth during the last decade. It is not very diversified and depends on the fluctuations of the international market. The Bangladeshi government struggles to attract export-oriented industries, removing red tape and introducing various financial and tax initiatives. Between 1990 and 1995 Bangladesh doubled its exports from US$1.671 billion in 1990 to US$3.173 billion in 1995 and then almost doubled them again from US$3.173 billion in 1995 to US$5.523 billion in 1999.

During the 1990s, the United States has been the largest trading partner for Bangladesh, with its exports to the United States reaching 35.7 percent in 1998–99. This percentage consisted mainly of Ready-Made Garments (RMG). Germany is the second-largest export market, with the proportion of goods reaching 10.4 percent; and the United Kingdom is in third place at 8.3 percent. Other export destinations are France, Italy, the Netherlands, Belgium, and Japan.

India, China, and Singapore are the 3 largest sources of imports. Most Bangladeshi imports originate from neighboring India, reaching 20.8 percent in 1998–99. The second most important source is China, totaling 9.3 percent, third is Singapore with 8.6 percent, with Hong Kong fourth at 7.6 percent.

During the last decade, Bangladeshi exports shifted from the sale of agricultural products and raw and processed natural resources to labor-intensive manufactured goods (including clothing, footwear, and textiles), but the country, unlike neighboring India, could not catch up with the exporters of skill-intensive products. While India is becoming an important international player in the field of software and applications development, Bangladesh lags far behind, despite the government's efforts to promote this area.

Bangladesh has a long history of maintaining a negative trade balance, importing more goods than it exports. In the 1970s and 1980s it imported goods and services twice and sometimes 3 times as much as it exported. Even during the relatively successful 1999 financial year, the country exported just US$5.523 billion worth of products while it imported US$8.381 billion worth of products, leaving a large trade shortfall of US$2.858 billion.

At present, Bangladesh faces growing economic competition from India, Pakistan, and Indonesia, countries which could offer better infrastructure and larger and growing domestic markets. A border conflict between Bangladesh and India, the worst in the last 30 years erupted in April 2001, bringing political and economic uncertainty to the region and undermining international investor confidence in the Bangladeshi market. If the investors move out, they could cause further social polarization and increased poverty in the country.

MONEY

The Bangladeshi government tightly controls the **exchange rate** of the taka against the U.S. dollar and major regional currencies. During the last decade the value of the currency showed a steady decline, mainly due to the **devaluation** of many of the neighboring currencies

Trade (expressed in billions of US$): Bangladesh

	Exports	Imports
1975	.327	1.321
1980	.793	2.599
1985	.999	2.772
1990	1.671	3.598
1995	3.173	6.497
1998	3.831	7.042

SOURCE: International Monetary Fund. *International Financial Statistics Yearbook 1999.*

Exchange rates: Bangladesh

taka (Tk) per US$1	
Jan 2001	54.000
2000	52.142
1999	49.085
1998	46.906
1997	43.892
1996	41.794

SOURCE: CIA *World Factbook 2001* [ONLINE].

(especially the Indian and Pakistani rupees). In 1995 the Bangladeshi taka was valued at 40.278 taka per US$1; in January 2000 the value of the taka declined to 51.000 taka per US$1. According to the IMF, the Bangladesh Central Bank has followed a policy of gradual depreciation of the taka against the U.S. dollar since the middle of the 1990s, devaluing the taka in gradual steps of 1 to 2 percent 2 or 3 times a year. The taka's market value has been protected by the large sums of foreign currencies Bangladesh receives every year through aid transfers and through remittances from overseas workers. The taka is still not fully convertible. The government periodically revises its exchange control regulations, introducing further liberalization of the controls. The government lifted restrictions on the **repatriation** of the profit and dividends from foreign direct investments (in the industrial sector); however, non-residents are not allowed to buy money market instruments or **treasury bills**.

During the period between 1970 and 1980 inflationary pressure was relatively small, as the country's economy was closed to outside influences and was tightly controlled by the government. In the 1990s consumer prices became more volatile, fluctuating between a low of 2.9 percent and a high of 8.9 percent a year, due to the liberalization and gradual opening up of the national economy to international competition.

The Bangladeshi banking system suffers from a lack of capital and poor management. Other problems include banks' exposure to corruption and to **bad loans** allegedly made to politically well-connected businessmen. There are 43 private banks in the country, including 29 domestic and 14 foreign banks, but most of them are active in major urban areas (Dhaka and Chittagong). The foreign banks are represented by such names as the Scotiabank of Canada and Societe Generale of France.

The 1997 Asian financial crisis did not bring damages in the scale of the economic and financial downturn in Indonesia, although it did negatively affect Bangladeshi exports. This escape was mainly due to the limited size of the Bangladeshi market, existing currency exchange controls and the relatively closed nature of its economy. Nevertheless, the Bangladeshi taka depreciated between 1997 and 1999 at a faster rate, declining from Tk43.892 in 1997 to Tk49.085 in 1999.

Bangladesh has 2 stock exchanges, the Dhaka Stock Exchange (DSE) and the Chittagong Stock Exchange (CSE; opened in 1995). Share prices shot up after the 1996 parliamentary election and **market capitalization** reached US$6.0 billion in November 1999; however, share prices fell dramatically the following year, with some shares losing up to 60 or 70 percent of their value. The all share indexes both in the DSE and the CSE still remain far below those of the 1996 levels.

POVERTY AND WEALTH

Bangladesh belongs to the poorest group of countries in the world; during the last 3 decades its **GDP per capita** income barely increased from US$203 in 1975 to US$348 per capita in 1998. The World Bank's *World Development Indicators* puts Bangladesh in 170th place (out of 207 countries) in the global ranking of gross national income per capita. Despite considerable international assistance, Bangladesh has been unable to eliminate extreme poverty and hunger. There is a huge disparity between standards of living in urban and rural areas of the country. The urban areas, especially the capital Dhaka, and major industrial cities such as Chittagong, Khulna, and Rajshahi, enjoy a better quality of living, with electricity, gas, and clean water supplies. Still, even in the major cities a significant proportion of Bangladeshis live in squalor in dwellings that fall apart during the monsoon season and have no regular electricity. These Bangladeshis have limited access to health care and to clean drinking water. The rural population, meanwhile, often lives in traditional houses in villages with no facilities associated with even the most modest standards of living.

Disparities encompass 3 dimensions that define considerable differences: geographic, educational, and gender. There is still considerable inequality in the distribution of income between rural and urban populations. In general, the urban population, in the areas around Dhaka, Chittagong, and other large cities, has long been involved in small- and medium-sized businesses or employed in various industries. They benefited from the recent growth and have higher incomes. Meanwhile, the rural population experience chronic shortages of land and regular floods and cyclones, which often a within matter of hours sweep away the results of months of hard work. The 1998 flood, for example, affected two-thirds of the country, wiping out the entire winter crop and displacing millions of people.

Education is another problem, as the adult literacy rate reached just 60 percent in 2000, despite the fact that primary education is universal, compulsory and free. The illiterate section of the population is generally much

GDP per Capita (US$)

Country	1975	1980	1985	1990	1998
Bangladesh	203	220	253	274	348
United States	19,364	21,529	23,200	25,363	29,683
India	222	231	270	331	444
Burma	N/A	N/A	N/A	N/A	N/A

SOURCE: United Nations. *Human Development Report 2000; Trends in human development and per capita income.*

Distribution of Income or Consumption by Percentage Share: Bangladesh

Lowest 10%	3.9
Lowest 20%	8.7
Second 20%	12.0
Third 20%	15.7
Fourth 20%	20.8
Highest 20%	42.8
Highest 10%	28.6

Survey year: 1995–96

Note: This information refers to expenditure shares by percentiles of the population and is ranked by per capita expenditure.

SOURCE: *2000 World Development Indicators* [CD-ROM].

poorer as they are missing employment opportunities in the industrial sector as well as government and international assistance in form of micro-credits, and awareness of better cultivation methods and other market skills. Also, women in Bangladesh, especially those with large families, have heavier workloads and often fewer skills than the male population; the illiteracy rate is much higher among women than men. These differences may be seen in the statistical data. The wealthiest 20 percent of Bangladeshis control 42.8 percent of the wealth. The poorest 20 percent of the population control only 3.9 percent of the wealth. In fact, the poorest 40 percent of the population controls just 20.7 percent of the wealth.

Since the 1970s, the Bangladeshi government has implemented a social policy aimed at the elimination of poverty and social inequality, and largely funded by international organizations and individual donors. This policy aims at increasing the literacy rate, providing access to safe drinking water, family planning, and micro-crediting the poorest and most disadvantaged groups of society.

Throughout the 1990s the Bangladeshi government achieved some positive results, although the 1998 floods put pressure on scarce government resources, brought hunger to some areas of the country, and made food prices higher. These difficulties particularly affected the most vulnerable social groups of society, both in rural areas and in major urban centers. The chronic poverty, **underemployment** and unemployment forced large numbers of people to migrate from the country, using all possible legal and illegal channels. Bangladesh's quality of life remains much lower than in neighboring India, Pakistan, or Sri Lanka. According to the *CIA World Factbook,* in 1996 around 35.6 percent of the population lived below the poverty line, most of them in rural areas of the country.

WORKING CONDITIONS

Due to rapid growth of the population in the last few decades the Bangladeshi labor force has grown rapidly, as there was a large proportion of young people born in the 1960s and 1970s. According to the *EIU Country Profile* the Bangladeshi labor force almost doubled in a matter of a decade, growing from 30.9 million people in 1985–86 to 56.0 million people in 1995–96. Although all sectors of the national economy experienced significant growth, they were far below the speed of the labor force growth. According to Bangladeshi national statistics, in 1995–96 only 12.4 percent of the labor force had formal employment, while 40 percent were considered "employed in family-based" businesses, 29.6 percent were considered "self-employed," and 17.9 percent had their jobs on a "daily basis." In general, the competition for working positions in the country is intense, and the working conditions are very harsh, especially in rural areas, where 63 percent of the labor force are employed.

The Bangladeshi government pays special attention to improving education at all levels, as it wants to attract labor-intensive manufacturing and services to the country. Primary education is compulsory. Various initiatives have been tried, including direct special stipends, designed to increase the proportion of female students at school. However, as the government admits, the country's education system suffers from poor quality education, chronic shortages of trained teachers, and a shortage of books. Secondary education is not accessible for

Household Consumption in PPP Terms

Country	All food	Clothing and footwear	Fuel and power[a]	Health care[b]	Education[b]	Transport & Communications	Other
Bangladesh	49	4	18	8	9	4	8
United States	13	9	9	4	6	8	51
India	N/A	N/A	N/A	N/A	N/A	N/A	N/A
Myanmar	N/A	N/A	N/A	N/A	N/A	N/A	N/A

Data represent percentage of consumption in PPP terms.
[a]Excludes energy used for transport.
[b]Includes government and private expenditures.

SOURCE: World Bank. *World Development Indicators 2000.*

children from many poor families. The government channels considerable funds into tertiary education, and the quality of teaching in some areas, particularly in technical subjects, is relatively strong. Nevertheless, the overall quality of the Bangladeshi universities' graduates often does not match the demands of modern technological developments in many areas, including information technologies and engineering. A number of Bangladeshis, receive their education overseas, many with state or international organizations' support, although in the past many of the students have opted not to return home after graduating from overseas universities. Bangladesh suffers shortages of medical doctors, information technology specialists, qualified teachers, and professionals in various other areas.

The very low wages, starting from Tk1,500, and harsh working conditions drive large numbers of people to seek jobs as temporary workers in Kuwait, Malaysia, Qatar, Saudi Arabia, Oman, and the United Arab Emirates. According to some unofficial estimates there are as many as 20 million Bangladeshi illegal immigrants in neighboring India. Many are hired to work in the low-skill and low-wages construction and service sectors and on agricultural plantations. The workers' remittances, sent home regularly, are one of the most important sources of hard currency not only for the extended families of these workers, but also for the national economy as well, totaling, according to the IMF's figures, US$1.706 billion (1998–99) or equivalent to the Bangladeshi gross official currency reserves in 1998–99.

The trade unions are very strong in Bangladesh, although only 3.5 percent of the workforce is unionized, but most of the unions are limited to the **public sector** or state-controlled enterprises. According to the International Confederation of Free Trade Unions (ICFTU), there are a total of 23 national trade union centers in Bangladesh and approximately 5,450 trade unions. The largest of these are the Bangladesh Jatio Sramik League (BJSL); the Bangladesh Jatiyatabadi Sramik Dal (BJSD); the Jatiya Sramik Party (JSP); the Bangladesh Free Trade Union Congress (BFTUC); and the Jatio Sramik League (JSL). These bodies are organized together in the ICFTU Bangladesh Council. About 1.8 million of the country's workers belong to unions, out of a total workforce of approximately 58 million. The unions tend to have strong links to major political parties or are controlled by political figures, and they often lead political action and strikes in the country. The power of the trade unions is exemplified in the fact that their continuous general strikes (hartals) forced the BNP government to resign in 1996, and their support led to the victory of the Awami League in the 1996 parliamentary election. Strikes are extremely common in Bangladesh and can paralyze business activities for weeks. The **private sector** is less unionized and trade unions are practically banned from the Export Processing Zones (EPZ), as the EPZ is exempted from certain labor laws. In case of industrial dispute the problems are supposed to be solved through the Labor Tribunal.

Unlike many Middle Eastern countries, women in Bangladesh enjoy considerable freedom and are generally involved in education and labor, although the employment and literacy rates among them generally are lower than among men. Recent surges in the garment industry brought new employment opportunities for women, as around 95 percent of people employed in this sector are women. However, in the rural areas the women very often are disadvantaged and among the poorer members of the communities. Currently, more than 37 percent of the labor force is women. However, unionization among women, and hence the protection of their rights, is generally lower than among men.

Despite the presence of strong trade unions, the use of child labor was quite common until recently. Not until 1995 did the Bangladeshi garment exporters' association agree to eliminate children from the industry. However, according to the International Confederation of Free Trade Unions, included in export sectors such as garments and leather production, there are over 6 million child laborers between the ages of 5 and 14 years who work for pay and are not enrolled in school. About 1.9 million working children are below the age of 10. In addition to remunerated employment, children often have to work alongside other family members in small-scale and subsistence agriculture. Bangladesh has not ratified either of the ILO core conventions on child labor, although there are various laws and regulations protecting children.

COUNTRY HISTORY AND ECONOMIC DEVELOPMENT

1500 B.C. Hinduism, the system of beliefs, practices, and socio-religious institutions of the Hindus, is introduced in the Indian subcontinent.

327 B.C. Alexander the Great invades the province of Gandhara, in northwest Indian subcontinent.

800s A.D. The first Muslim Arabs appear in the north of the Indian subcontinent, and the first Muslim trading communities are established in various parts of the region.

1192. Muhammad of Ghur wins the battles of Taraori, which leads to the establishment of the Delhi sultanate, principal Muslim sultanate in North India from the 13th to the 16th century.

1341. Most of Bengal becomes independent of Delhi.

1498. Vasco da Gama, Portuguese traveler and adventurer, lands at Calcutta.

1576. Akbar, the great Mogul emperor, conquers the territory of modern Bangladesh.

1608. Dhaka becomes the Mogul's capital of Bengal province.

1757. The nawab (ruler) of Bengal is defeated by Robert Clive's British force at Plassey.

1765. The British East India Company establishes control over the administration of the territory of Bengal.

1857. Indian Sepoys (soldiers) in the Bengal army of the British East India Company rebel against British rule in India (known as the Sepoy Rebellion).

1858. The East India Company is abolished, and the British crown assumes direct control over British India.

1885. The Indian National Congress is founded.

1905. The British colonial administration introduces division into West Bengal and East Bengal, with East Bengal being more or less within the territory of modern Bangladesh, although the partition is withdrawn in 1911.

1947. Bangladesh becomes independent as a part of Pakistan under the name "East Pakistan."

1970. In November, a powerful cyclone hits Bangladesh, causing great damage and more than 500,000 deaths, one of the worst natural disasters of the 20th century.

1970. In December, Sheikh Mujibur Rahman (popularly known as Sheikh Mujib) and his political party, Awami League (AL), win both national and provincial elections and demand greater autonomy for East Pakistan.

1970. The AL declares its intention to achieve independence from West Pakistan.

1971. With the help of Indian forces, the Bangladeshi pro-independence movement wins independence.

1974. A state of emergency is declared in Bangladesh.

1975. Sheikh Mujibur Rahman becomes president and assumes absolute power.

1975. President Sheikh Mujib is assassinated in a military coup in August.

1975. Abusadat Muhammad Sayem becomes president but resigns 2 years later.

1978. General Ziaur Rahman wins the presidential election.

1981. President General Ziaur Rahman is assassinated in a military coup.

1981. Abdus Sattar wins the presidential election in November.

1982. General Hossain Ershad takes power in a military coup.

1985. General Hossain Ershad wins the presidential election and bans all active political opposition.

1988. Devastating floods hit three-quarters of the country, leaving 30 million people homeless and causing food shortages.

1990. General Hossain Ershad resigns.

1991. The first free and fair election is held in Bangladesh. Begum Khaleda Zia (widow of General Ziaur Rahman) and her party, Bangladesh Nationalist Party (BNP), win the election.

1991. A powerful cyclone hits Bangladesh, causing the deaths of more than 120,000 people and great damage to the economy.

1996. Begum Khaleda Zia wins the April parliamentary election, which is accompanied by violence and a low turnout, but is forced to resign shortly after.

1996. Hasina Wajed, daughter of Sheikh Mujib, and her Awami League (AL) win the June parliamentary election.

1996. An important 30-year agreement is reached with India on the sharing of the Ganges River's water.

1997. A peace treaty is signed between the government and Chakma rebels, ending a 20-year uprising.

1998. Another powerful cyclone hits the country, causing extensive damage to the national economy.

2001. Indian and Bangladeshi forces clash on the border between their 2 countries.

FUTURE TRENDS

For decades after 1971 the development of the Bangladeshi national economy has been hindered by political instability, poor economic performance, pressure on scarce natural resources by the rapidly growing population, and an ineffective bureaucracy. The major changes introduced during the 1990s included more flexible economic policies, export-oriented industrialization, and inflow of foreign direct investments. **Inflation** remains low and is under control. The Bangladeshi currency exchange managed to avoid any spectacular failures similar to Indonesia or South Korea during the Asian financial crisis of 1997, and it is still stable, tightly regulated and pegged to the basket of the regional currencies. In 1999 and 2000 Bangladesh achieved strong economic recovery after the devastating floods of 1998, and if the regional and global economic environment remains positive, the Bangladeshi economic annual growth rate of 5 to 6 percent might continue. This development may ease the poverty, low standards of living, underemployment, and unemployment problems.

Nevertheless, there are several issues to be addressed. There is strong potential for all the problems, including political instability and recession, to return if the government fails to improve the economic situation in the country or if global recession or global competition negatively affect the country's exports. Both the border clashes with Indian border guards in early 2001, which led to heavy casualties, and confrontations along the border with Burma (Myanmar) show how fragile regional stability is. Meanwhile, although the changes brought some positive results to the national economy and some level of prosperity to some groups of the population (often limited to the educated urban population of the large metropolitan areas), they also brought new social ills such as growing criminality and drug usage among youth. The government has often been criticized for its intervention in economic development and its inability to improve economic management or to conduct further reforms, including privatization. There is also a serious problem with widespread corruption, with some political groups accused of wasting public resources. The experience of Indonesia shows how dangerous corruption and political instability are. It remains to be seen whether economic liberalization combined with the force of globalization measures will strengthen the performance of the national economy.

In the longer term, Bangladesh will need to maintain its international competitiveness, since the current globalization trend eliminates borders for international trade and brings growing competition from **emerging markets** for FDIs and for the transfer of modern technologies. Political and social unrest in neighboring Burma might affect Bangladesh, threatening and undermining regional stability and thus scaring off potential investors. Environmental issues are also very important for Bangladesh in the longer term, as global climate change and the rise of the surface level in the world's seas may undermine the country's agriculture, which still plays a dominant role in the national economy. In fact, a warmer Earth could well witness sizeable areas of the country covered by water, or it might increase salinization of the currently arable land, making it impossible to continue agricultural activities.

DEPENDENCIES

Bangladesh has no territories or colonies.

BIBLIOGRAPHY

Alauddin, M., and Samiul Hasan, editors. *Development, Governance and the Environment in South Asia: A Focus on Bangladesh.* New York: St. Martin's Press, 1999.

Caf, Dowlah. *Privatization Experience in Bangladesh, 1991–1996.* Washington D.C.: World Bank, 1997.

Economist Intelligence Unit. *Bangladesh: EIU Country Profile 2000.* London: Economist Intelligence Unit, 2000.

Economist Intelligence Unit. *Bangladesh: EIU Country Report.* London: Economist Intelligence Unit, February 2000.

Government of the People's Republic of Bangladesh. <http://www.bangladeshgov.org>. Accessed August 2001.

Government of the People's Republic of Bangladesh. *Ministry of Planning Statistics Division.* <http://www.bangladeshgov.org/mop/ndb/index.htm>. Accessed August 2001.

The Independent (newspaper). <http://www.independent-bangladesh.com>. Accessed August 2001.

Moon, P. *The British Conquest and Dominion of India.* London: Duckworth, 1989.

Spear, Thomas. *The Oxford History of Modern India.* 2nd edition. Delhi: Oxford University Press, 1978.

Statistical Pocketbook of Bangladesh. Dhaka: Bangladesh Bureau of Statistics, 1998.

World Bank. *Bangladesh: from Stabilization to Growth.* Washington D.C.: World Bank, 1995.

World Bank Group. *The World Bank Dhaka Office.* <http://www.worldbank-bangladesh.org>. Accessed August 2001.

—Rafis Abazov

BHUTAN

Kingdom of Bhutan
Druk-Yul

CAPITAL: Thimpu.

MONETARY UNIT: Ngultrum (Nu). One ngultrum equals 100 chetrum. Notes in circulation are Nu1, 2, 5, 10, 100, and 500. Indian currency (rupees) is also legal tender and at par value with Bhutanese currency.

CHIEF EXPORTS: Cardamom, gypsum, timber, handicrafts, cement, fruit, electricity, precious stones, and spices.

CHIEF IMPORTS: Fuel and lubricants, grain, machinery and parts, vehicles, fabrics, and rice.

GROSS DOMESTIC PRODUCT: US$0.44 billion (1999). [CIA reports GDP at purchasing power parity to be US$2.1 billion (1999 est.).]

BALANCE OF TRADE: **Exports:** US$146 million (1999). **Imports:** US$243 million (1999). [The *CIA World Factbook* reports exports to be US$111 million (f.o.b., 1998) and imports to be US$136 million (c.i.f., 1998).]

COUNTRY OVERVIEW

LOCATION AND SIZE. A landlocked country located in South Asia, north of India and south of China, Bhutan has an area of 47,000 square kilometers (18,1467 square miles). Comparatively, the area occupied by Bhutan is about half the size of Indiana. Bhutan's capital city, Thimpu, is centrally located towards the country's western border with India. Bhutan shares a 605-kilometer (376-mile) border with India and a 470-kilometer (292-mile) border with China.

POPULATION. In 2000 the population of Bhutan was estimated at 2,005,222 by the *CIA World Factbook.* The UN *Statistical Yearbook* gave the population as 1,034,774. Giving a third figure, the World Bank *World Development Report 2000/1* estimated the population at 782,000. The disparity between population estimates is caused by 2 different ways of counting people: the government of Bhutan's population estimate, the World Bank figure, is based upon those who have "official" citizenship, and the CIA estimate seems to account for those who claim such status or live in the country and may not be recognized by the government. Uncertainty in population figures is also connected to Bhutan's ongoing problem with the Lhotshampa people (Bhutanese of Nepalese origin), who have lost their citizenship or are simply not recognized due to a series of nationality-specific laws enacted in the 1980s. The government claims that a large number of the Lhotshampa are illegal immigrants who threaten the cohesion of traditional Bhutanese society, while the Lhotshampa argue that they are rightful citizens. Another problem with such estimates is the limited number of statistical gathering mechanisms in Bhutan, partly due to the country's limited financial resources and **infrastructure**. As a result, statistical indicators such as **gross domestic product** (GDP) or the quantity of telephones per capita are difficult to estimate. Clearly, the formulation of statistical averages depends upon which population estimate is used. To encourage comparative consistency, this entry indicates what population estimates are used to express particular statistical data.

In 2000 the birth rate stood at 36.22 per 1,000, while the death rate was 14.32 per 1,000. The overall population density is very low at 12.5 people per square kilometer, but this figure does not take account for the fact that, with 92.9 percent of the population living in rural areas, access to arable land is primary in any estimate of population density. Therefore, if the ratio of population to arable land is taken into account then density rises to 100 people per square kilometer. Bhutan has a very young population with almost 50 percent aged 17 years or younger. Given the continuation of Bhutan's current annual population growth of 2.19 percent, the United Nations Development Programme (UNDP) in Bhutan projects that there will be 3.64 million people living in Bhutan by 2025, from a 1998 level of 1.91 million. The

UNDP also estimates that 31,000 people live in Thimpu city (the capital and administrative center) and another 25,000 in Phuentsholing (the primary commercial center on the Indo-Bhutanese border).

OVERVIEW OF ECONOMY

In 2001 Bhutan's economy remained one of the smallest and least developed in the world, almost entirely dependent upon basic agricultural production, forestry, and hydroelectricity. In 2000 rural inhabitants constituted 92.9 percent of the total population, a slight decline from the 1990 level of 94.8 percent. A large majority of agricultural activity is subsistence-based and takes place outside of the **monetized economy**. In other words, **subsistence farmers** do not use the ngultrum (the national currency) in their day-to-day lives; they trade and **barter** goods for the few basic manufactured essentials that they might need. However, in 2000 the government cited indications that the monetized economy was experiencing substantial growth.

Bhutan is a very poor country with a **GDP per capita** of only US$197 (based upon a population of 1.03 million), although it is important to note that because the majority of subsistence farmers are outside of the monetized economy this figure is not an adequate representation of actual living standards.

After the serious attacks upon Buddhism in Tibet by the **communist** government in China during the late 1950s, Bhutan began to develop more links with India in order to counter the possibility of a similar fate. In 1960, Bhutan closed its borders with Tibet and, with considerable Indian financial and technical assistance, began to construct roads to link India with Bhutan. This action constituted a key turning point for Bhutan's economic development, and by 2001 the national economy was highly dependent upon Indian trade, aid, and investment.

It must be stressed that the government emphasizes the concept of "Gross National Happiness" (GNH) as an essential indicator and factor in Bhutan's development, a very specific approach to developmental ideology. The GNH idea stresses the importance of cultural heritage, the stability and protection of the natural environment, greater self-sufficiency, and human development. This approach, with its roots in the traditional Buddhist principles of compassion, compromise, and pragmatism, is in direct contrast to the globally dominant view of the primacy of economic and material development. As the government maintains in a policy document for the UNDP in 2000 that GNH "means that development is only valuable if it is an 'efficient means' to happiness and human development."

National debt in Bhutan is relatively stable and controllable in amount. The government has actually been able to reduce total **public sector** debt from US$139.5 million in 1993–94 to US$115.8 million by 1997–98. Consequently, over the same period **debt service** payments declined from US$17.6 million to US$9.6 million. Official development assistance from both individual governments and international financial institutions in 1997 consisted of US$59.9 million in grants and US$10.1 million in loans. The Asian Development Bank (ADB) made 2 loans to Bhutan in 2000. The first, of US$10 million, was to assist Bhutan in setting out a health reform program, The Bhutan Health Trust Fund, which has the aim of maintaining the free supply of medicines to the public. The second, of US$9.6 million, was for the regeneration of the country's primary road, the east-west highway. The ADB had made another loan of US$10 million in 1999 for a Sustainable Rural Electrification Project to provide electricity to the poorer and more remote areas of Bhutan.

POLITICS, GOVERNMENT, AND TAXATION

Bhutan is the world's only Buddhist kingdom. The Bhutanese name for their country is *Druk Yul* which means "Land of the Thunder Dragon." Ruled by a hereditary monarchy since 1907, Bhutan received full independence from India in 1949 after the British colonial administration withdrew from India. Bhutan's political system is unlike historical precedents in the West and is most appropriately categorized as a "Buddhist monarchy."

The third hereditary monarch, Jigme Dorji Wangchuck, ruled Bhutan from 1952 to 1972. He is generally considered the "architect of modern Bhutan." In 1953 he established the National Assembly. Consisting of representatives of the people, the civil service, and the Buddhist monastic order, the National Assembly meets once a year to debate aspects of public policy and development. The Royal Advisory Council was formed by the king in 1965 to constantly monitor the progress of National Assembly resolutions and advise the king on day-to-day policy matters.

In a similar vein, his son King Jigme Singye Wangchuk (who acceded to the throne in 1972 and continued to reign in mid-2001) has also followed a reformist approach to rule. In 1999 an analyst of Bhutanese affairs, Thierry Mathou, maintained: "Many Bhutanese . . . were stunned by the suddenness and amplitude of the changes introduced by the king. . . . [c]ontrary to most countries with monarchies where royals have resisted democratic politics, Bhutan's has always been the leading force of change." For example, in 1998 the king pushed a political reform that reduced his authority through the devolution of executive powers to the cabinet. Nonetheless, the king continued to have final say on matters relating to security and sovereignty as well direct administration of the Royal Bhutan Army.

Even though Bhutan's governmental system of monarchy is justified on the grounds of maintaining traditional values and national identity by the country's ruling elite, it has received considerable criticism both domestically and internationally. For example, Freedom House (a U.S.-based political liberties and civil rights organization) classified Bhutan in 2000 as "Not Free." Freedom House measured this conclusion upon the lack of democratic representation of the people and the apparent mistreatment of critics of the regime. In its report for 2000, Amnesty International (a London-based human rights organization) maintained that individuals in Nepali-speaking communities faced police discrimination when they attempted to get permission to open a bank account, when attempting to travel abroad for training, for work, or to send their children to school.

In fact, discrimination against Lhotshampa is rife. A series of laws passed in the 1980s revealed tough remits for the acquisition of citizenship, even if an individual were married to a Bhutanese national, and the fact that naturalized citizenship can be terminated if a person criticizes the government. Still, there is some justification for this policy because militant Lhotshampa movements have called for a merging of Bhutan into a greater Nepal. Some of these militants, whom the government calls "anti-nationals," have been involved in campaigns of violence and have done damage to some infrastructure and development projects.

Nationalism and tradition are actively promoted in Bhutan. In part due to the economic and military-political weakness of the country in international relations and also due to the perceived threat from the Lhotshampa community's tendency to reduce Bhutanese identity, the government emphasizes rules of national dress, the code of etiquette (driglam namzha), and the national language (Dzongkha).

A serious ongoing security problem for the government is the presence of the communist guerrilla group, the United Liberation Front of Assam (ULFA) and the Assamese (Bodo) guerrilla insurgency in east and south Bhutan. These groups are fighting for independence for Assam. Although there has been vocal engagement between the ULFA and the Bhutanese government, a solution to their presence has yet to be reached. The existence of these anti-Indian government forces on Bhutanese territory could led to a deterioration in the special friendship between India and Bhutan.

Non-tax revenue constituted 61 percent of total revenue in 1998–99. The Chukha Hydro Power Corporation, the Department of Power, and the Department of Telecommunications are some of the key sources of this revenue. Government revenue from the power sector provided 42 percent of total national revenue in 1998–99. **Direct tax** collection improved in the late 1990s from Nu831 million in 1997–98 to Nu914 million in 1998–99. Of this direct tax 65 percent was from corporate **income tax**. Taxation on rural areas is very low, around 0.02 percent of total revenue in 1998–99, in order to encourage the population to remain on their farms and thus reduce the strain of uncontrolled urbanization. However, it should be noted that rural inhabitants contribute via the application of their labor to the construction and maintenance of local schools, water supplies, and health centers.

INFRASTRUCTURE, POWER, AND COMMUNICATIONS

Bhutan's infrastructure is limited although the government is actively attempting to open the more isolated areas of the country by improving the road network. Around 14,000 passenger vehicles were in use on Bhutan's 3,285 kilometers (2,041 miles) of roads in 1999. In 1997 the Road Surface Transport Authority was established to improve the efficiency and quality of the road infrastructure and to enforce the observation of transport regulations. There are no railways in Bhutan. In accordance with the government policy of allowing a restricted opening-up of Bhutan for both citizens and foreigners, total passengers on scheduled flights rose from 8,000 in

Communications

Country	Telephones[a]	Telephones, Mobile/Cellular[a]	Radio Stations[b]	Radios[a]	TV Stations[a]	Televisions[a]	Internet Service Providers[c]	Internet Users[c]
Bhutan	6,000	N/A	AM 0; FM 1; shortwave 1	37,000	0	11,000	N/A	500
United States	194 M	69.209 M (1998)	AM 4,762; FM 5,542; shortwave 18	575 M	1,500	219 M	7,800	148 M
China	135 M (2000)	65 M (2001)	AM 369; FM 259; shortwave 45	417 M	3,240	400 M	3	22 M (2001)
Nepal	236,816 (2000)	N/A	AM 6; FM 5; shortwave 1 (2000)	840,000	1 (1998)	130,000	6	35,000

[a]Data is for 1997 unless otherwise noted.
[b]Data is for 1998 unless otherwise noted.
[c]Data is for 2000 unless otherwise noted.

SOURCE: CIA *World Factbook 2001* [Online].

1990 to 36,000 in 1997. The national airline, Druk Air, owns 2 planes which fly to and from Paro International Airport which opened a new terminal building in the late 1990s. Bhutan is landlocked; the nearest seaport is 435 miles away in Calcutta.

Electricity, gas, and water provided 11.8 percent of **value-added** activity to the economy in 1997. In 2000, Bhutan's electricity-generating capacity was 3530 megawatts, 97 percent of which is hydro power and the rest thermal. The central role of electricity production to Bhutan's economy is likely to expand in the early 21st century. New large-scale hydro power stations were under construction by 2001 which are expected to provide considerable government revenue. However, over 95 percent of domestic energy consumption in Bhutan consists of biological mass, predominantly firewood.

Bhutan was cut off from the outside world for centuries. Television only began to be provided by the state-run Bhutan Broadcasting Service (BBS) Corporation in 1999 and was limited to a small number of hours a day of programming (consisting solely of national news and documentaries about Bhutan). Nonetheless, (based upon a population of 1.03 million) there were already 5.5 televisions per 1,000 population in 1997, which by 2000 received 25 channels from 2 cable television companies. By 1997, there were 19 radios per 1,000 inhabitants. According to UN estimates there is only 1 telephone per 100 inhabitants. In 1999, a Japanese-funded project to provide domestic digital telecommunications was completed. The Internet became operational in Bhutan in 1999.

ECONOMIC SECTORS

Bhutan's economic sectors are small like the country; the country has limited population, domestic markets, and natural resources. Geographical isolation caused by highly mountainous terrain and political isolation due to a formerly inward-looking society means that the economy's integration into the world economy is minimum. Isolation in combination with previously low levels of education means that a medium and large-scale **private sector** is almost non-existent. The majority of the monetized economy is dominated by **parastatals**.

Bhutan's economy is primarily agricultural, mostly subsistence farming, although some export-oriented commercial farming of fruit and spices does exist. Industry is limited to the production of hydro power and basic manufactures. Services to support these sectors are basic. Tourism, whilst small in size, provides a high proportion of the country's foreign exchange.

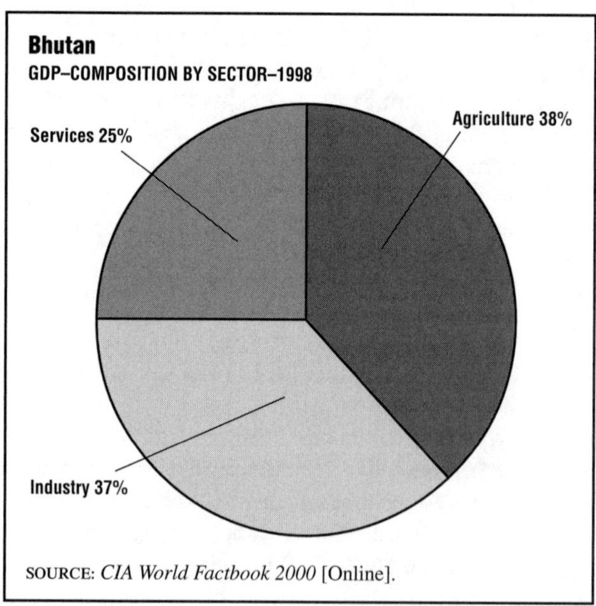

SOURCE: *CIA World Factbook 2000* [Online].

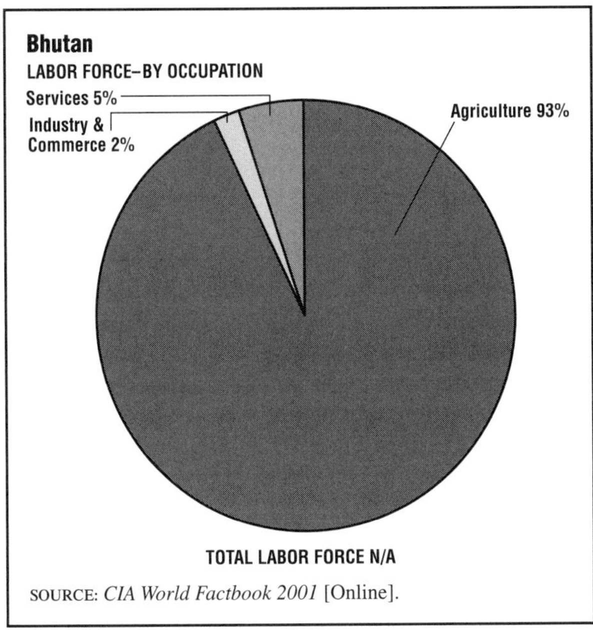

SOURCE: *CIA World Factbook 2001* [Online].

AGRICULTURE

The agricultural sector provided 38.5 percent of GDP in 1997, a significant decline from the 55 percent in 1985. The 1997 GDP consisted of a total production of 18.1 percent crops, 11.4 percent of economic activity in the forestry sector, and 9 percent livestock production. Of the 970,000 people who were employed in Bhutan in 1998 (using a population estimate of 2 million) 93.8 percent were engaged in agricultural activities. There were 160,000 hectares of arable land under permanent crops in 1998, compared to the 1980 level of 122,000. In 1998 only 40,000 hectares of this land was irrigated, an improvement upon the 1980 level of 26,000 hectares.

Cereal production increased from 95,000 metric tons in 1989 to a consistent level of 112,000 tons per annum in the period 1995 to 1998. While self-sufficient in maize, barley, millet, and buckwheat, Bhutan is only 50 percent self-sufficient in rice and 30 percent in wheat. In total the country is around 60 percent self-sufficient in cereals. Other key crops which are actually exported are potatoes, spices (mainly cardamom and nutmeg), and fruit which in 1997 consisted mainly of oranges (54,000 metric tons) and apples (13,600 metric tons). In total, agricultural goods provided 13.7 percent of Bhutan's total exports in 1997.

Bhutan continues to import substantial amounts of essential food items. The Food Corporation of Bhutan imports subsidized food items from India, among which are rice, wheat, edible oils, sugar, and salt. Between 1994–98 an annual average of 12,500 metric tons of rice, 12,500 tons of wheat, and 3,600 tons of sugar were imported. It is important to note that 58 percent of farming households own less than 2 hectares. This small level of landholding makes some households susceptible to seasonal shortages of food, to poor health, and even to malnutrition.

FORESTRY. The government is actively trying to maintain the economic exploitation of Bhutan's extensive forestry resources at sustainable levels. In keeping with the GNH concept, plans by the Forest Services Division of the Ministry of Agriculture for improved harvesting of forests are being undertaken to assure environmental balance. For example, 60 percent of Bhutan's total land area is required to have good tree cover; by 2000 72 percent was covered. In 1997–98, 27,770 cubic meters of trees were felled for commercial logging and an additional 22,884 cubic meters for housing construction and public works. The gross sales of Bhutan Board Products in 1998 were Nu383.8 million.

INDUSTRY

HYDRO POWER. The electricity sector showed an average growth of 48.2 percent in the period 1985–1995. In 1998–99 hydro power contributed 30 percent to total exports. This rate will increase considerably in the early 21st century when new hydro power stations being built in Tala, Kurichhu, and Basochhu are completed. Hydro power has also acted to stimulate the growth of the manufacturing and services sectors.

MANUFACTURING. Manufacturing provided 12.8 percent of value added activity to the economy in 1997. The production of cement is one of the principal enterprises in Bhutan's industrial sector. In 1998, Penden Cement Authority had gross estimated sales of Nu564.7 million, a substantial increase from the 1997 level of Nu265.5 million. Another cement plant was due to be completed by 2002, but due to disturbances related to Assam insurgents this project was suspended. The processing of Bhutan's agricultural produce is another significant dynamic factor in the manufacturing sector. For example, Bhutan Fruit Products enjoyed gross sales of Nu112.3 million in 1998; these sales were mainly of juices and canned fruit.

SERVICES

TOURISM. Bhutan is one of the safest countries in the world. Crime rates are minimal and foreign visitors are treated politely and with respect. The country's history, culture, and isolation offer a great deal to the more adventurous tourists who have been visiting Bhutan since 1974. The **privatization** of the tourism sector in 1991 led to fast-paced growth in hotels and travel agencies. This growth was so rapid that by 2001 there was excess capacity in tourism services. The failure to fully exploit this capacity is primarily due to government restrictions on the number of tourists admitted into Bhutan, a policy devised to reduce outside influence upon national traditions. Consequently, only 6,203 tourists entered Bhutan in 1998, and these people provided US$7.8 million in much-needed foreign currency. Around 40 percent of these tourists came from EU countries, 24 percent from the United States, and 17 percent from Japan. Nonetheless, this is a significant rise from the 1993 level of 2,984 where only US$3 million in tourism receipts were recorded. The high level of foreign exchange earnings from tourism is partly due to a compulsory government charge on tourists of US$200 a day.

Exchange rates: Bhutan

ngultrum (Nu) per US$1	
Jan 2001	46.540
2000	44.942
1999	43.055
1998	41.259
1997	36.313
1996	35.433

Note: The Bhutanese ngultrum is at par with the Indian rupee which is also legal tender.

SOURCE: CIA *World Factbook 2001* [ONLINE].

INTERNATIONAL TRADE

Bhutan's engagement with international trade is highly dependent upon its neighbor and ally, India. In 1997, US$114.2 million of Bhutan's exports were purchased by India, which constituted 94.6 percent of the total. Bangladesh received US$5.1 million of Bhutanese goods. In the same year, the direction of the flow of Bhutan's imports consisted of US$97.6 million from India, 69.4 percent of the national total. In addition, Bhutan imported US$23.8 million of goods from Japan, US$4 million from Singapore, and US$1.8 million from Germany.

Bhutan is a founding member of the South Asian Association for Regional Co-operation (SAARC), whose other members are Bangladesh, India, Nepal, Pakistan, and Sri Lanka. Bhutan will host the 2002 SAARC summit meeting. As part of its policy of engagement with the world economy, Bhutan is preparing to join the World Trade Organization.

MONEY

The widespread use of money in Bhutan only began in the early 1960s with the growth of trade with India and the initiation of bilateral development aid from India to Bhutan. Even though Bhutan's economy is highly underdeveloped the price of **consumer goods** has remained fairly stable. The average percentage change of prices each year was only 10 percent between 1990 and 1998. Total international currency reserves by major Bhutanese holders (mainly the Royal Monetary Authority, Bank of Bhutan, and Bhutan National Bank) rose dramatically in value from US$106.9 million in 1993–94 to US$218.2 million in 1997–98.

Two banks operate in the country: the Bhutan National Bank has offices in Thimpu and a branch in Phuentsholing, and the Bank of Bhutan has branches in the country's main centers. No restrictions are placed on the quantity of currencies that can be taken into Bhutan although they are limited to the main international currencies. In the late 1990s Bhutan National Bank was partly privatized when the government sold 40 percent of its shares to Citibank and the Asian Development Bank; the government now owns only 27 percent of the bank. Bhutan has a stock exchange but it is not open to external investment.

POVERTY AND WEALTH

From the 1960s free basic health services began to be provided by the government across most of Bhutan where populations were concentrated. Nonetheless, by 2000 the UNDP estimated that 20 percent of the population still lacked sufficient access to health services.

Trade (expressed in billions of US$): Bhutan

	Exports	Imports
1975	N/A	N/A
1980	.017	.050
1985	.022	.084
1990	.068	.078
1995	.103	.112
1998	N/A	N/A

SOURCE: International Monetary Fund. *International Financial Statistics Yearbook 1999.*

GDP per Capita (US$)

Country	1975	1980	1985	1990	1998
Bhutan	N/A	232	292	387	493
United States	19,364	21,529	23,200	25,363	29,683
China	138	168	261	349	727
Nepal	149	148	165	182	217

SOURCE: United Nations. *Human Development Report 2000; Trends in human development and per capita income.*

Lack of health care is a serious drawback because the general diet lacks sufficient fruits and vegetables. Consequently, over half of the country's children 6 and younger suffer from stunting, and over 30 percent are underweight. Poor nutrition is not nation wide, however, but determined by regional, urban-rural, and socio-economic factors. For example, in Pemagatshel average calorie consumption per day is 1,647 whereas in Punakha it is 3,227.

The incidence of rural poverty is as high as 90 percent. Unhygienic conditions are prevalent in Bhutan with 42 percent of the population lacking access to safe water and 30 percent of the people living in conditions of poor sanitation. Nonetheless, poverty in Bhutan has declined as indicated by the rise of average life expectancy from 37 years in 1960 to 66 years in 1994. The increased longevity suggests that the consistent government policy of providing a socially oriented infrastructure, in accordance with the GNH concept, is effective even though much work remains to be done.

WORKING CONDITIONS

Bhutan is yet to ratify the key International Labour Organization Conventions Number 87 (Freedom of Association and Protection of the Right to Organize, 1948) or Number 98 (Right to Organize and Collective Bargaining). Trade unionism is not permitted in Bhutan, nor does it exist in practice. In fact, terms and conditions as well as salaries are generally fixed by the government, which requires employees and employers (at least in the formal economy) to engage in formal written contracts of agreement. The population employed in Bhutan is estimated at 970,000 (based upon a population of 2 million).

Education has received considerable emphasis by the government of Bhutan, and primary schooling is available in even the remotest areas. The Bhutanese government spent 7 percent of total expenditure on education in 1997. Mainly due to government initiatives in its drive to reduce illiteracy, levels fell from 71.9 percent in 1980 to 52.7 percent in 2000. The Bhutanese workforce is becoming more skilled, although this is problematic because there are serious limits upon the amount of educated workers required in what is essentially an agricultural economy. Consequently, while there are rising employment expectations amongst the literate population the labor market cannot provide sufficiently skilled work.

COUNTRY HISTORY AND ECONOMIC DEVELOPMENT

1616. Bhutan is unified by Zhabdrung Ngawang Namgyal who makes comprehensive laws and local administrations.

1907. The hereditary monarchy is created.

1949. The Indo-Bhutan Treaty of friendship is signed, and Bhutan receives full independence.

1952. Jigme Dorji Wangchuck (the "architect of modern Bhutan") becomes king.

1953. The National Assembly is established.

1960. Trading is entirely oriented toward India.

1965. The king forms the Royal Advisory Council.

1972. Jigme Singye Wangchuk becomes king.

1974. Bhutan begins to encourage tourism.

1983. The South Asian Association for Regional Cooperation is established.

1998. The king devolves some of his executive powers to the cabinet.

FUTURE TRENDS

Problems with the Lhotshampa population seem likely to continue into the 21st century. Unless the Bhutanese government finds an amicable solution to this problem, Lhotshampa militancy is likely to intensify. Similarly, the security issue of the presence of Assam independence insurgencies on Bhutanese territory needs to be addressed in order to avoid embittering relations with militarily powerful India. This point is all the more important due to the ongoing flow of free trade with India. Bhutan is highly dependent upon developments within India's economy. As a result, levels of integration with the world economy will closely follow those of India. Planned membership of the WTO will exacerbate Bhutan's economic openness.

In 2001, Bhutan's excellent environmental conservation and balance meant that the economy had greater ability to use its forestry and hydroelectricity resources. For example, while the government insists that 60 percent of the country remain forested, the 2000 coverage of 72 percent indicated room for increased use without compromising governmental policy. Similarly, the 3 hydroelectricity plants to be completed early in the 21st century are projected to contribute vast amounts of government revenue without significantly damaging the environment. This revenue is intended to support human-centered development. If the government remains true to these policies and continues to widen political freedoms, Bhutan has a bright political, social, and economic future.

DEPENDENCIES

Bhutan has no territories or colonies.

BIBLIOGRAPHY

Amnesty International. *Amnesty International: Report 2000.* London: Amnesty International, 2000

British Broadcasting Corporation (BBC). *Country Profile: Bhutan.* <http://news.bbc.co.uk//hi/english/world/south_asia/country_profiles/newsid_11660000/1166513.stm>. Accessed June 2001.

Central Intelligence Agency. *CIA World Factbook.* <http://www.odci.gov/cia/publications/ factbook/index.html>. Accessed June 2001.

Ciment, J. and I. Ness. *The Encyclopaedia of Global Population and Demographics.* Chicago: Fitzroy Dearborn, 1999.

Europa. *The Far East and Australasia 2001.* 32nd edition. London: Europa, 2001.

Food and Agriculture Organization. *FAO Yearbook: Trade, Vol. 52, 1998.* Rome: FAO, 1999.

Food and Agriculture Organization. *Nutrition Country Profile—Bhutan.* Rome: FAO, December 1999. <http://www.fao.org/es/ESN/ncp/BHU.pdf>. Accessed July 2001.

Freedom House. *Freedom in the World: The Annual Survey of Political Rights and Civil Liberties 1999–2000.* New York: Freedom House, 2000.

International Monetary Fund. *Bhutan: Statistical Annex.* No. 99/63. Washington, D.C.: IMF, July 1999.

International Monetary Fund. *International Financial Statistics Yearbook 2000.* Washington D.C.: IMF, 2000.

Mathou, T. "Bhutan in 2000: Challenges Ahead." *Asian Survey.* Vol. 41, No. 1, 2001.

Mathou, T. "Political Reform in Bhutan: Change in a Buddhist Monarchy." *Asian Survey.* Vol. 39, No. 4, 1999.

Pattanaik, S. S. "Ethnic Identity, Conflict and Nation Building in Bhutan." *Strategic Analysis.* Vol. 22, No. 4, 1998. <http://www.idsa-india.org/an-jul8–10.html>. Accessed June 2001.

Pommaret, F. *Bhutan,* translated by E. B. Booz. London: Hodder and Stoughton, 1991.

Royal Government of Bhutan. *Background Document to the Seventh Round Table Meeting for Bhutan, Thimpu 7–9 November 2000.* <http://www.undp.org.bt/RTM2000/Final%20RTM%20Documents.pdf>. Accessed July 2001.

United Nations. *International Trade Statistics Yearbook 1998.* New York: United Nations, 1999.

United Nations. *Statistical Yearbook Forty-Fourth Issue.* New York: United Nations, 2000.

United Nations Development Programme. <http://www.undp.org>. Accessed June 2001.

United Nations Development Programme. *Human Development Report 2000.* New York: UNDP, 2000.

United Nations Development Programme in Bhutan. *Briefing Report: Bhutan.* Thimpu: UNDP, July 1999. <http://www.undp.org.bt/BHUTAN/Brieflc99.PDF>. Accessed June 2001.

United Nations Economic and Social Commission for Asia and the Pacific. *Asia-Pacific in Figures.* 14th edition. New York: United Nations, February 2001.

Upham, M. *Trade Unions of the World.* 4th edition. London: Cartermill, 1996.

U.S. Energy Information Administration. <http://www.eia.doe.gov/emeu/cabs/bhutan2.html>. Accessed June 2001.

World Bank. "Bhutan Data Profile" and "Bhutan at a Glance." <http://www.worldbank.org>. Accessed June 2001.

World Bank. *World Development Report 2000/2001: Attacking Poverty.* Oxford: Oxford University Press, 2001.

—Liam Campling

BRUNEI DARUSSALAM

Nation of Brunei, Abode of Peace
Negara Brunei Darussalam

CAPITAL: Bandar Seri Begawan.

MONETARY UNIT: Brunei dollar (B$). One Brunei dollar equals 100 cents. The Brunei dollar is at par with the Singapore dollar, and the currencies are interchangeable. There are coins of 1, 5, 10, 20, and 50 cents, and bills of 1, 5, 10, 50, 100, 500, 1,000, and 10,000 dollars.

CHIEF EXPORTS: Crude oil, liquefied natural gas, and petroleum products.

CHIEF IMPORTS: Machinery and transport equipment, manufactured goods, food, and chemicals.

GROSS DOMESTIC PRODUCT: US$5.9 billion (purchasing power parity, 2000 est.).

BALANCE OF TRADE: **Exports:** US$2.55 billion (f.o.b., 1999). **Imports:** US$1.3 billion (c.i.f., 1999).

COUNTRY OVERVIEW

LOCATION AND SIZE. Located in Southeast Asia, bordering the South China Sea and Malaysia, Brunei is geographically divided by Malaysia into 2 unconnected parts. Brunei has an area of 5,770 square kilometers (2,228 square miles) and a total coastline of 161 kilometers (100 miles). Comparatively, the area of Brunei is slightly smaller than the state of Delaware. Brunei's capital city, Bandar Seri Begawan, is located on the northeastern coast of the country.

POPULATION. The population of Brunei was estimated at 336,376 in July of 2000, with a growth rate estimated at 2.17 percent. In 2000 the birth rate stood at 20.81 per 1,000, and the death rate stood at 3.39 per 1,000.

The population is generally young, with 31 percent below the age of 14 and just 3 percent over the age of 65. In 2000, male life expectancy was estimated at 71.23 years and female at 76.06, and that of the population as a whole at 73.58 years. By 1995, the literacy rate of the total population was relatively high at 88.2 percent, with 92.6 percent of males and 83.4 percent of females over the age of 15 able to read and write.

The Malay people comprise 62 percent of Brunei's population, with Chinese accounting for 15 percent, indigenous people 6 percent, and other groups 17 percent. Islam is Brunei's official religion and Muslims account for 67 percent of the population. About 13 percent are Buddhist, Christians make up 10 percent, and those with indigenous beliefs make up the remaining 10 percent.

OVERVIEW OF ECONOMY

Brunei is a wealthy oil-rich country in Southeast Asia. Oil and natural gas have been the basis of the country's wealth. Dependency on this single valuable commodity has made it vulnerable to international market fluctuations, however, and the government has been making efforts to diversify the economy. The economy is dominated by the oil and gas sector, but large-scale government expenditure on **infrastructure** programs has made the construction sector the second largest economic sector in Brunei. The country's main exports are oil and gas products, but it must import most of its food.

Brunei has a limited **labor force**. Most ethnic Malays work in the **public sector** administration and government departments and enjoy substantial benefits, but the Malay labor force is limited in number. The country hosts a large number of foreign skilled and unskilled workers, especially in the construction sector. In order to maintain the leadership of Brunei Malays, government policies protect and promote Malays involved in industry and commerce.

The government of Brunei has very large foreign reserves from oil, no **foreign debt**, and is a significant international investor. The Brunei Investment Agency (BIA) manages foreign reserves for the government

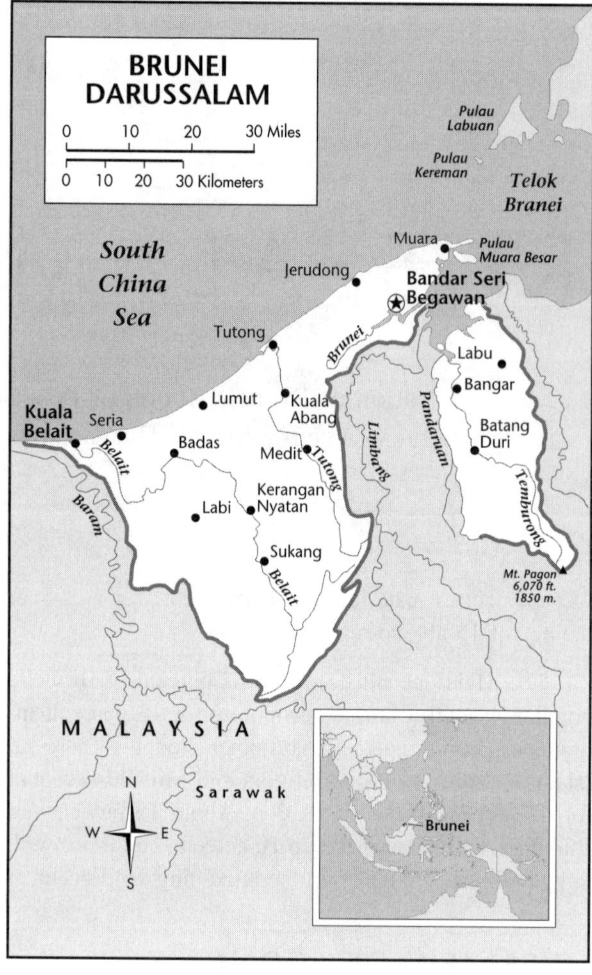

(excluding the ruling sultan and other members of the royal family). The BIA tries to increase the value of Brunei's foreign reserves by spreading its investments across the United States, Japan, Western Europe, and the countries of the Association of South East Asian Nations (ASEAN).

POLITICS, GOVERNMENT, AND TAXATION

Brunei has long been ruled by sultans (kings), though for much of its modern history those sultans have ruled in cooperation with European colonial powers. Spanish and Dutch colonists began arriving in Brunei in the 16th century. English colonists came during the 17th century, and the country was made a British protectorate in 1888, which meant that Britain provided military and economic assistance. During World War II (1941), the Japanese occupied the country. The British returned after the war, and negotiations began for Brunei's eventual independence. In 1959 a written constitution was introduced granting Brunei internal self-rule under British protection. In 1984 Brunei achieved full independence and became an independent sovereign sultanate governed on the basis of a written constitution.

The 1959 constitution granted the sultan full executive authority, but called for an elected legislative council. A limited effort to meet this requirement with a partially elected legislative body was tried but quickly abandoned. In 1962 the Partai Rakyat Brunei (Brunei People's Party, PRB) won the election for the legislative council but was denied access to office. The party's ensuing uprising was rapidly crushed by the ruling sultan and the PRB was then banned. Since that time the legislative council has been an appointed body. Currently, the Brunei Solidarity National Party (PPKB), with closer allegiance to the government, is the only legal political party. In 1995, for the first time in 10 years, the PPKB was permitted to hold its national assembly, but its activities were circumscribed, and the party has had little influence.

Brunei is an Islamic sultanate. The hereditary sultan is the head of state and holds ultimate authority. He is also the country's prime minister, minister of finance, and minister of defense, and presides over a council of ministers, a religious council, a privy council, and a council of succession, all of whose members he appoints. There are no popular elections and the Legislative Council functions in a purely consultative capacity. The concept of Melayu Islam Beraja (Malay Muslim Monarchy, MIB) was introduced as a state ideology, invoking Brunei's history of monarchy, Brunei Malay culture, and Islamic values, in order to justify absolute monarchy.

The government plays a large role in the economy. In the 1990s the government has made concerted efforts to diversify the economy from oil and gas. Industries promoted by the government are agriculture, manufacturing, tourism, commerce, and banking. In the Seventh National Development Plan (1996–2000), the government allocated more than B$7.2 billion for the implementation of various projects and programs. Thanks to such commitments, the non-oil sector's contribution to the GDP rose from 24.3 percent in 1991 to 66 percent in 1998. The government actively encourages more foreign investment. It extends "pioneer status" to aircraft catering services as well as the cement, textile, furniture, glass, plastics, and synthetic rubber industries. Pioneer status companies can get exemption from the 30 percent corporate tax.

One of the government's most important priorities is to encourage Brunei Malays to move into the **private sector** from the public sector where most are employed. The government policy of "Bruneisation" of the workforce encourages Brunei Malays to work in the private sector. The Brunei Shell Petroleum (BSP) company and the 2 largest foreign banks, the Hong Kong and Shanghai Banking Corporation and Standard Chartered Bank, have had to increase the number of Brunei Malays on their staffs under this policy. The Bruneian government also boosts private business to nurture Brunei Malay leaders in industry and commerce.

The sole tax levied by the government of Brunei is the corporate tax, generally 30 percent. Otherwise, everything that is normally taxed in other countries—capital, gains, import and export, sales, manufacturing—is free of tax, and there is no personal **income tax**. The huge government revenues from oil and gas are sufficient to finance government expenditures, and Brunei is the least taxed country in the region and perhaps in the world.

INFRASTRUCTURE, POWER, AND COMMUNICATIONS

Brunei's infrastructure is well developed. The road network serving the entire country is being expanded and modernized and totaled 2,525 kilometers (1,569 miles) in 1998. A 1,150-kilometer (715-mile) main highway, of which 399 kilometers (248 miles) are paved, runs the entire length of the country's coastline. It conveniently links Muara, the port at the eastern end, to Belait, the oil-production center at the western end of the state. Per capita car ownership in Brunei is one of the highest in the world. In 1995 there were 167,786 cars, of which 139,658 were private cars. Since 1996 the Brunei government has attempted to improve public transit by expanding taxi and bus services in Bandar Seri Begawan and its vicinity. Bus services to other districts are infrequent and irregular. Other than a 13-kilometer (8-mile) private railway line, there are no rail services in Brunei.

Brunei has 2 major ports: a large, deepwater harbor at Muara and a smaller port at Kuala Belait. They offer direct shipping to Hong Kong, Singapore, and several other Asian destinations. An expanded international airport is located at Bandar Seri Begawan. Royal Brunei Airlines (RBA) serves long-distance destinations in Asia, Australia, the Middle East, and Europe, as well as several short-haul destinations to East Malaysia and Indonesia, and Brunei Shell Petroleum (BSP) owns a small airport in the oil field at Seria.

Brunei has one of the best telecommunication systems in Southeast Asia. The rate of telephone availability is currently 1 telephone for every 3 persons. There are 2 earth satellite stations providing direct telephone, telex, and facsimile links to most parts of the world. There are 2 television broadcast stations and, by 1997, there were 196,009 TV sets. Brunei was connected to the Internet in September 1995 through Brunet. By the end of 1999 there were 15,000 registered Internet users in the country. Keen to develop **e-commerce**, the government is investing B$55 million in installing a countrywide multimedia highway called RAGAM 21 to serve both the private and public sectors.

According to the CIA *World Factbook 2000*, 2.56 billion kilowatt-hours (kWh) of electricity were generated and 2.381 billion kWh consumed in Brunei in 1998. There were no exports or imports of electricity. All the electricity is produced from fossil fuels (oil and gas). The country has no nuclear or hydro-power plants.

ECONOMIC SECTORS

Brunei's status as a major oil and natural gas producer and its political goal of promoting **full employment** for ethnic Bruneian Malays are the 2 forces most responsible for the shape of the Bruneian economy. Because it is the third largest oil producer in Southeast Asia, and the fourth largest producer of liquified natural gas in the world, the oil and gas sector dominates the private

Communications

Country	Telephones[a]	Telephones, Mobile/Cellular[a]	Radio Stations[b]	Radios[a]	TV Stations[a]	Televisions[a]	Internet Service Providers[c]	Internet Users[c]
Brunei Darussalam	79,000 (1996)	43,524 (1996)	AM 3; FM 10; shortwave 0	329,000 (1998)	2	201,900 (1998)	2	28,000 (2001)
United States	194 M	69.209 M (1998)	AM 4,762; FM 5,542; shortwave 18	575 M	1,500	219 M	7,800	148 M
Philippines	1.9 M	1.959 M (1998)	AM 366; FM 290; shortwave 3 (1999)	11.5 M	31	3.7M	33	500,000
Malaysia	4.5 M (1999)	2.698 M (1999)	AM 56; FM 31; shortwave 5 (1999)	10.9 M (1999)	27 (1999)	10.8 M (1999)	7	1.5 M

[a]Data is for 1997 unless otherwise noted.
[b]Data is for 1998 unless otherwise noted.
[c]Data is for 2000 unless otherwise noted.

SOURCE: CIA *World Factbook 2001* [Online].

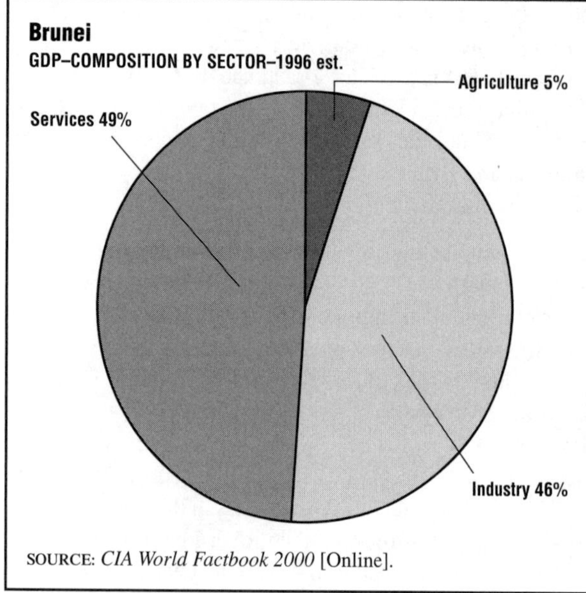

SOURCE: *CIA World Factbook 2000* [Online].

economy. Along with the construction which is heavily funded by the Bruneian government, oil and gas contributed some 46 percent of GDP in 1996. The construction industry was greatly affected by the Asian financial crisis in 1997–98, but the industrial sector as a whole was expected to thrive with rising world oil prices in 2000. Services, including finances, accounted for 49 percent of GDP in 1996. Within the service sector, community, social, and personal services contributed a large percentage of GDP. The government has made consistent efforts to diversify its economy to boost non-oil sectors.

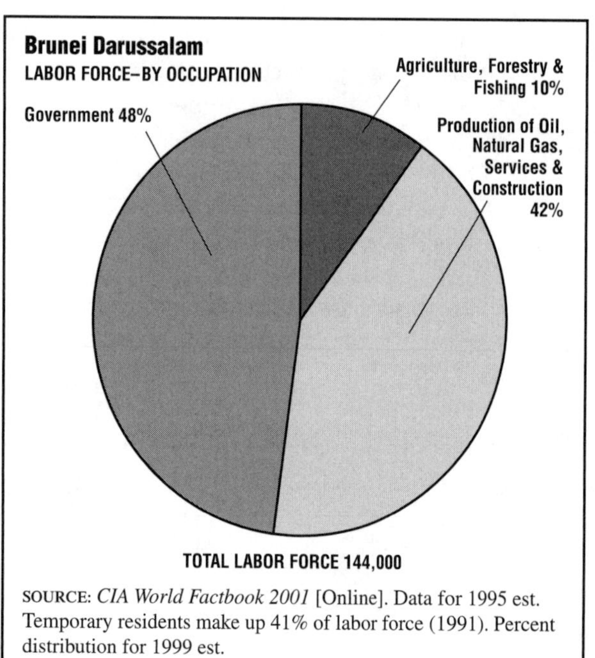

SOURCE: *CIA World Factbook 2001* [Online]. Data for 1995 est. Temporary residents make up 41% of labor force (1991). Percent distribution for 1999 est.

Government estimates, which do not divide employment according to agriculture, industry, and services, indicate that 48 percent of the population is employed by the government and 42 percent in the oil, gas, services, and construction industries. Only an estimated 10 percent of the workforce are employed in Brunei's agricultural sector, which contributed about 5 percent of GDP in 1996.

AGRICULTURE

Agricultural activity in Brunei is not high. The government has attempted to increase agricultural production in order to achieve self-sufficiency in food, but results have been unsatisfactory. Agriculture made up only 5 percent of the GDP in 1996, and the country has had to import 80 percent of its food needs. While land, finance, and irrigation facilities are available, agricultural activities lack manpower resources. The gap between wages in farming and the public sector is large, and most Bruneians have little interest in agricultural production.

Brunei is nearly self-sufficient in vegetables, but only 1 percent of the nation's rice is produced locally. The production of tropical fruits is being encouraged. Cattle—both beef and dairy—buffalo, and goat rearing are also being promoted. Pig farming has been banned since 1993, but the country is self-sufficient in egg production and nearly self-sufficient in poultry.

FISHING. Fish is an important part of the local diet. The fishing sector, comprising catch, aquaculture, and seafood processing, contributed about 0.5 percent to the total GDP in 1998. In 1996 more than 60 percent of fish and prawns sold in Brunei were imported. The government hopes to develop the fishing industry, including fishing fleets and fish-processing factories, and sees foreign **joint ventures** as the way to obtain finance and expertise. The government believes the sector could become an important export revenue earner and employer. Brunei declared a 200-nautical mile fisheries limit in 1983.

FORESTRY. Because of Brunei's mostly urban population and the wealth deriving from oil and gas, forest use has been limited. Currently about 80 percent of Brunei's total land is covered by forests, nearly 60 percent of it virgin. Forestry accounted for only 0.3 percent of the total economic output in 1998. The government is committed to preserving the important environmental, biotechnological, and other economic and social functions of its forests and hopes to develop their potential as a tourist attraction. Consequently, logging, limited to 100,000 cubic meters annually, is confined to meeting local needs only, and timber extraction for export is strictly prohibited.

INDUSTRY

PETROLEUM PRODUCTS. Oil and natural gas mining is the backbone of Brunei's economy. In 1998 the oil and gas sector contributed an estimated 34 percent to GDP and dominated exports. In 1998 crude oil and partly refined petroleum accounted for an estimated 39 percent of total exports and natural gas for 49 percent. Brunei is the third largest oil producer in Southeast Asia and the fourteenth largest in the world; it ranks fourth in production of natural gas. Oil and gas mining is a capital-intensive industry and employs only a small percentage of the total labor force (5.2 percent in 1995). At the beginning of 1993 reserves were estimated at 1.4 billion barrels of oil and 320 billion cubic meters of gas. The government has pursued a national depletion policy since 1988 aimed at preserving resources and continuing exploration of new fields.

Brunei Shell Petroleum (BSP) is the biggest oil mining company. It has 7 offshore and 2 onshore oil fields in Brunei. The Brunei government is an equal shareholder with the Royal Dutch Shell Group in the company. Another important oil-exploration company is Jasra-Elf, a joint venture that has been actively exploring for hydrocarbons offshore and has made some discoveries.

Brunei's annual sales of liquefied natural gas (LNG) sales are currently nearly 6 million metric tons. LNG is as important a revenue earner as oil exports, and the bulk of it is purchased by 3 Japanese utility companies: Tokyo Electric, Tokyo Gas, and Osaka Gas. About 10 percent of LNG is used for domestic consumption.

Following the regional economic crisis in 1997, combined with concerns about falling oil prices throughout 1998, the Brunei government realized that the oil and gas industry can no longer limit itself just to exploration, drilling, and export. It is now aiming at developing a hydrocarbon products industry in Brunei.

CONSTRUCTION. The construction sector is the second most important industry in Brunei, contributing 6.6 percent of GDP in 1998. The sector's performance depends heavily on government spending. Indeed, the development of this sector is the direct result of increased government investment in developing infrastructure projects such as government offices, hospitals, schools, mosques, housing, fire stations, and sporting facilities.

Hit by the regional economic crisis in 1997–98, private sector construction projects almost collapsed. The government cut development spending on infrastructure projects by 50 percent from B$950 million in 1999 to B$550 million in 2000. Thus, growth in this sector is expected to be sluggish.

MANUFACTURING. Manufacturing contributes only a small portion of Brunei's economic output. Its contribution to GDP has increased from 0.8 percent in 1980 to an estimated 3 percent in 1998. The major large-scale industries include food and beverage processing, garment making, cement production, and the production of precast concrete structures. According to International Monetary Fund (IMF) data for the year 2000, 23 industrial sites are being established in Brunei. Food processing and furniture manufacture are designated for further development, while ceramic tiles, cement, chemicals, plywood, and glass are considered to have development potential by the government.

SERVICES

TOURISM. Before the mid-1990s the only tourists visiting Brunei were relatives and friends of expatriates who were working there. Several factors have held back the development of tourism: access to alcohol is limited; the cost of accommodation in the capital is high; accommodation and transport outside the capital is not available; and the general perception about the country is that there is little of interest to see. However, Brunei does offer both natural and cultural attractions, and the government is now actively promoting tourism as an important part of economic diversification.

The capital, Bandar Seri Begawan, is a neat, clean, and modern city. The cultural attractions there include the sultan's magnificent palace, the Brunei Museum, the Malay Technology Museum, and the Omar Ali Mosque. Kampung Ayer is a centuries-old collection of 28 water villages built on stilts in the Brunei River, and Jerudong Park is a recreational center located close to Tutong. The large tropical rain forest areas have been earmarked for **ecotourism** in sites such as Temburong National Park. However, the underdeveloped transport and accommodation facilities remain an obstacle to the expansion of the tourism sector.

In 1996 Brunei had 703,300 foreign visitors, most of them from the neighboring Sabah and Sarawak regions of Malaysia. Passengers on RBA flights to and from Australia are stopping over in the capital in increasing numbers. With 2000 designated as "Visit Brunei Year," the Asia-Pacific Economic Co-operation (APEC) meetings were held in Brunei and proved a boost for Brunei tourism.

FINANCIAL SERVICES. The contribution of financial services to the GDP was 6.4 percent in 1998. There are 9 banks operating in Brunei. The 2 largest foreign banks in the country are the Hong Kong and Shanghai Banking Corporation (HSBC) and Standard Chartered Bank. There are a number of Malaysian banks and 3 locally incorporated banks: the Islamic Bank of Brunei (IBB), Baiduri Bank, and the Development Bank of Brunei (DBB). The IBB offers savings and loan facilities in accordance with Islamic principles. The other Islamic financial institution is the Tabung Amanah Islam Brunei (Brunei Islamic Trust Fund, TAIB). The financial sector also includes a number of locally incorporated and international finance and insurance companies. The authorities have been preparing to implement a comprehensive financial regulatory system via the proposed new Banking Act.

RETAIL. Until the late 1980s the **retail** sector in Brunei was not particularly sophisticated. Aside from the local market, there were only coffee shops, general provision shops, Chinese supermarkets, and a few Chinese restaurants. In 1986 a Japanese store group, Yaohan, opened its first department store in Brunei. Since 1995 a more international range of shops has come to Brunei, including the Body Shop, and the fast food chains McDonald's, Pizza Hut, and Kentucky Fried Chicken. The new Sultan Foundation complex of shops now stands in the center of Bandar Seri Begawan.

INTERNATIONAL TRADE

In 1999 the value of Brunei's exports reached US$2.55 billion, while imports were valued at US$1.3 billion. The country's export trade is dominated by petroleum products. In 1998 crude oil and partly refined petroleum accounted for an estimated 39 percent of total exports and natural gas for 49 percent. By far the most important export market is Japan, which took 42 percent of Brunei's exports in 1999, followed by the United States (17 percent), South Korea (14 percent), and Thailand (3 percent).

Since only a few non-oil products are produced locally, Brunei has to rely exclusively on imports for nearly all of its manufactured goods and most of its food. Singapore is the largest supplier of imported goods, accounting for 34 percent in 1999. The United Kingdom and Malaysia both provided 15 percent of imports, while the United States provided 5 percent. As in many other countries, Japanese products such as motor vehicles, construction equipment, electronic goods, and household appliances dominate Brunei's local markets.

Trade (expressed in millions of US$): Brunei Darussalam

	Exports	Imports
1994	3290	2760
1995	3402	2959
1996	3498	3516
1997	3648	3258
1998	3443	2598
1999	N/A	N/A

SOURCE: United Nations. *Monthly Bulletin of Statistics* (September 2000).

Exchange rates: Brunei Darussalam

Bruneian dollars (B$) per US$1	
Jan 2001	1.7365
2000	1.7240
1999	1.6950
1998	1.6736
1997	1.4848
1996	1.4100

Note: The Bruneian dollar is at par with the Singapore dollar.

SOURCE: CIA *World Factbook 2001* [ONLINE].

Although Brunei enjoyed a positive trade balance (a **trade surplus**) throughout the late 1990s, that surplus has been shrinking. This phenomenon was caused by reduced earnings from petroleum and an increase in imports due to a demand for higher living standards.

MONEY

Brunei's financial system is operated by a **currency board** which regulates the issue and management of the currency. There are laws that govern and regulate the activities of banks and financial institutions, designed to ensure a stable and fiscally sound business environment.

The Brunei dollar is at par with the Singapore dollar and both are freely traded in their respective countries. The trend of interest rates follows that of Singapore. The peg to the Singapore dollar has helped maintain a stable **macroeconomic** environment. There are currently no exchange controls in Brunei.

The Brunei dollar appreciated (grew in value) steadily for years until the beginning of the Asian economic crisis in 1997, when the depreciation of currencies in neighboring countries caused the Brunei dollar to weaken in 1997 and 1998. The Brunei dollar continued to appreciate against these neighboring currencies but was offset by its depreciation against the U.S. dollar, Japanese yen, and major European currencies. This combined effect helped moderate imported inflationary pressures since ASEAN members account for 45 percent of Brunei's total imports, while the United States, Japan, and Europe account for 39 percent.

POVERTY AND WEALTH

As the monarch of a rich state, Brunei's ruler, Sultan Hassanal Bolkiah, has been named as one of the richest men in the world. His wealth mainly comes from oil,

GDP per Capita (US$)

Country	1975	1980	1985	1990	1998
Brunei Darussalam	21,758	29,442	21,152	18,716	18,038
United States	19,364	21,529	23,200	25,363	29,683
Philippines	974	1,166	967	1,064	1,092
Malaysia	1,750	2,348	2,644	3,164	4,251

SOURCE: United Nations. *Human Development Report 2000; Trends in human development and per capita income.*

and he has attracted international attention by purchasing luxury hotels in Singapore, Britain, and the United States, while making generous donations in the United Kingdom. All members of the Bruneian royal family are engaged in business transactions such as property purchasing and rental.

Wage and benefit packages in Brunei tend to be generous and the labor shortage ensures that most citizens command good salaries. There are nonetheless unemployed and poor members of society, but most of these live under the protection of an extended family system, where idle youth can find shelter and the aged and infirm are cared for. The citizens enjoyed a per capita GDP of US$17,600 in 2000.

Oil-rich Brunei has a wealth that enables the sultanate to maintain a **welfare state**. All Brunei citizens receive free education (through university for those who qualify), free health care, and various other **subsidies** such as subsidized housing, food, fuel, and low-interest loans for government employees. Brunei's health care system is one of the best in Asia. Every citizen of Brunei pays only a nominal fee for medical and dental services. Medical treatment unavailable in Brunei will be conducted overseas (usually in Singapore) at government expense.

WORKING CONDITIONS

Brunei suffers a serious shortage of both skilled and unskilled labor and has to recruit large numbers of these from abroad. It was estimated in 1997 that 60,000 out of the total workforce of 130,000 were foreigners. Many unskilled and manual workers from neighboring Malaysia, Thailand, the Philippines, and Bangladesh work mainly in the construction industry. The government is concerned that too large a number of foreigners in the country might disrupt Brunei's society and thus only issues work permits for short periods. Despite the need for foreign workers, there are still unemployed Bruneians, since they are reluctant to accept manual work (e.g. in the construction sector) and are not qualified to fill other vacancies. The unemployment rate in 2000 was 5 percent.

Brunei's dependence upon foreign labor stems from a cultural predisposition for public sector employment. Most Brunei Malays prefer to work in well-paid government jobs or for large companies such as Brunei Shell Petroleum (BSP), Royal Brunei Airlines (RBA), and the banks. In the private sector, which is subject to chronic labor shortage in both professional and unskilled fields, Chinese and other foreign nationals make up the bulk of the workforce.

Women's participation in the labor force has increased significantly from 29.5 percent in 1986 to 52.3 percent in 1999, partly offsetting the labor shortage. Brunei law protects women and children. Women under age 18 are not allowed to work at night or on offshore oil platforms, and the employment of children below the age of 16 is prohibited. The government has continued to set up a number of technical and vocational training institutions to improve the abilities of job seekers. Occupational health and safety standards apply, but enforcement is lax in the unskilled labor sectors, especially where foreign laborers work.

Trade unions in Brunei are legal but must be registered. Conditions, however, are not conducive to the development of trade unions: the cultural tradition favors consensus over confrontation and workers have little interest in participating. There are only 3 trade unions, all in the oil sector, and they are not particularly active.

COUNTRY HISTORY AND ECONOMIC DEVELOPMENT

1847. Brunei signs a trade relations treaty with Britain.

1888. Brunei becomes a British-protected state.

1906. A treaty is established with Britain, introducing a representative of the British government, known as a British resident, to advise the sultan on all matters with the exception of local customs and religious matters.

1929. Oil is discovered and explored at Seria.

1941–45. Brunei is occupied by the Japanese during World War II.

1950–67. Sultan Omar Ali reigns.

1959. An agreement is signed with Britain replacing the 1906 treaty and giving Brunei self-governance under a new constitution. The British remain responsible for both internal and international security.

1962. The Brunei People's Party wins election to the recently established legislature but is denied access to office. Its ensuing armed uprising is crushed, and the sultan claims full executive authority.

1967. Brunei issues its own currency.

1967. The 28th sultan, Omar Ali, voluntarily abdicates in favor of his eldest son, Hassanal Bolkiah.

1970. The state capital, Brunei Town, is renamed Bandar Seri Begawan.

1971. The 1959 agreement with Britain is amended to give Brunei responsibility for its own internal security.

1972. A deep-water port is opened in Muara.

1973. The world's largest liquefied natural gas (LNG) plant opens.

1974. The Brunei International Airport is opened, followed a year later by the creation of the Royal Brunei Airlines.

1979. Brunei and Britain sign The Treaty of Friendship and Co-operation laying down a timetable for complete Bruneian independence some 5 years later.

1984. Brunei resumes full independent political sovereignty. Brunei joins the Association of Southeast Asian Nations (ASEAN), the Organization of the Islamic Conference (OIC), and the United Nations.

1997. The Asian financial crisis brings a **recession** to Brunei and hits the construction sector especially hard.

FUTURE TRENDS

In 1998, hit by the Asian financial crisis and falling world oil prices, the Brunei economy slipped into a mild recession with a 1 percent growth rate. Rising oil prices in late 1999 increased Brunei's economic growth, estimated at between 3 and 3.5 percent in 2000. Despite the beneficial rise in oil prices, Brunei has continued with plans to **restructure** its economy away from over-reliance on oil and gas. The Brunei Darussalam Economic Council (BDEC) will oversee this development. The government will continue with its short-term economic stimulus plan, boosting manufacturing and tourism and attempting to create an offshore financial center. However, the diversification effort remains impeded by high public sector remuneration, restrictions on activities open to foreign participation, and cumbersome foreign investment approval procedures.

Whether Brunei can achieve sustained economic growth and maintain high living standards depends heavily on the world economy, especially on world oil prices, and on the government's ability to formulate and implement successful economic measures to bring economic diversity.

DEPENDENCIES

Brunei Darussalam has no territories or colonies.

BIBLIOGRAPHY

Brunei Darussalam: Brunet Homepage. <http://www.brunet.bn>. Accessed September 2001.

Clear, Mark, and Shuang Yann Wong. *Oil, Development and Diversification in Brunei Darussalam.* New York: St. Martin's Press, 1994.

Economist Intelligence Unit. *Country Profile: Brunei.* London: Economist Intelligence Unit, 2001.

"Economy Report - Brunei Darussalam." *Asia Pacific Economic Cooperation.* <http://www.apecsec.org.sg>. Accessed March 2001.

The Government of Brunei Darussalam Official Website. <http://www.brunei.gov.bn/index.htm>. Accessed September 2001.

Gunn, Geoffrey C. *New World Hegemony in the Malay World.* Lawrenceville, NJ, and Asmara, Eritrea: The Red Sea Press, 2000.

International Monetary Fund. "Brunei Darussalam and the IMF." *International Monetary Fund.* <http://www.img/org/external/country/BRN/index.htm>. Accessed September 2001.

Saunders, Graham. *A History of Brunei.* Kuala Lumpur, Oxford, Singapore and New York: Oxford University Press, 1994.

U.S. Central Intelligence Agency. *World Factbook 2001.* <http://www.odci.gov/cia/publications/factbook/index.html>. Accessed September 2001.

U.S. Department of State, Bureau of East Asian and Pacific Affairs. *Background Notes: Brunei, October 2000.* <http://www.state.gov/www/background_notes/brunei_0010_bgn.html> Accessed January 2001.

—Xingli Zhang

BURMA (MYANMAR)

CAPITAL: Rangoon (Yangon).

MONETARY UNIT: Kyat (Kt). One kyat is equal to 100 pyas. There are coins of 1, 5, 10, 25 and 50 pyas and 1 kyat, and notes of 1, 5, 10, 15, 20, 40, 90, 100, 200, 500, and 1,000 kyat.

CHIEF EXPORTS: Pulses and beans, prawns, fish, rice, teak, and opiates.

CHIEF IMPORTS: Machinery, transport equipment, construction materials, and food products.

GROSS DOMESTIC PRODUCT: US$59.4 billion (purchasing power parity, 1999 est.).

BALANCE OF TRADE: **Exports:** US$1.2 billion (1998). **Imports:** US$2.5 billion (1998).

Union of Burma
Pyidaungzu Myanma Naingngandaw

COUNTRY OVERVIEW

LOCATION AND SIZE. Situated between Indian and Thailand, Burma is a southeast Asian nation. From the borders of India and China in the north, the country extends into the Andaman Sea and the Bay of Bengal in the south. The country also shares borders with Laos and Bangladesh. Slightly smaller than the state of Texas, Burma has an area of 678,500 square kilometers (261,969 square miles). Its land borders are 5,876 kilometers (3,651 miles) long and its coastline, home to many excellent natural harbors, is 1,930 kilometers (1,199 miles) long. Burma's capital, Rangoon (also known as Yangon), is in the south. Mandalay, Moulmein, Pegu, Bassein, Taunggyi, Sittwe, and Myanwa are the other most important cities in the country.

POPULATION. The population of Burma, according to July 2000 estimates, was 41,734,853. A high mortality rate caused by AIDS is factored into this estimate; it is estimated that at least 1 million people are infected with HIV, the virus that causes AIDS. This high mortality rate from AIDS has slowed population growth to a projected rate of growth of 0.64 percent. The country registered a birth rate of 20.61 per 1000 population and a death rate of 12.35 per 1000; consequently, the population of Burma in 2015 is expected to be 45,925,967.

In the past, the government of Burma sought to restrict **emigration** (people leaving the country) and **immigration** (people settling there from outside the country). Burmese authorities negotiated with India to reduce the number of people of Indian origin in the country. As a result, Burma **repatriated** about 100,000 people to India between 1963 and 1965. Thousands of Burmese also fled to neighboring countries to escape military repression and armed conflicts in the ethnic minority areas.

Ethnic diversity is an interesting feature of the Burmese population. Burmans, an ethnic group related to the Tibetans, constitute the majority at 68 percent of the population. Shan (9 percent), Karen (7 percent), Rakhine (4 percent), Chinese (3 percent), Mon (2 percent), Indian (2 percent), and other ethnic groups account for the rest of the population mix. Buddhism is the major religion, with 89 percent of the population; there are minorities of Christians and Muslims. A majority of the people, 65 percent, are between the ages of 15 and 64. Only 5 percent of the population is older than 65, while 30 percent of the population is under 14 years of age. This is in sharp contrast to Japan, west European countries, and the United States where the number of older people in the population is much higher. The density of population is about 65.2 per square kilometer (169 per square mile). With agriculture as the most important occupation, a majority of the people live in the rural areas and only an estimated 27.3 percent (1999) reside in cities.

OVERVIEW OF ECONOMY

Despite many attempts to industrialize and modernize, Burma remains an essentially agricultural economy. Attempts in the 1990s to encourage foreign investments,

revitalize the economy, and promote the tourism industry as a source of income and employment have been only moderately successful. Agriculture remains the most dominant sector of the economy, generating 59 percent of the **gross domestic product** (GDP) in 1997 and employing more than 65 percent of the workforce in 1999.

Only 10,680 square kilometers (4,123 square miles) of the country's arable land was irrigated in 1993. Agriculture, for the most part, depends on the monsoon rains. Periodic droughts are a major problem. Similarly, natural disasters such as cyclones, earthquakes, floods, and landslides, especially during the long monsoon season, can have an adverse impact on agricultural production.

Until it became independent in 1948, Burma was a British colony. The colonial authorities promoted agriculture by encouraging the settlement of people in the delta regions. Roads, bridges, and ports were built to facilitate the movement of agricultural products. This development led to an internal migration from the dry northern regions to south of the country. The delta produced large quantities of rice. The British were not interested in encouraging industries in Burma. Foreign domination of the economy was complete.

During the 1950s, the capital of Rangoon was one of the commercial centers of Southeast Asia. At the time, the World Bank estimated that Burma would become one of the most prosperous countries of the region. But independence, democracy, and a free market economy failed to produce political stability or economic prosperity. In 1962, a military takeover of the government led to **socialism** and central economic planning. Foreign businesspeople—especially those from India, China, and Pakistan—were expelled and foreign investment in Burma stopped. The new rulers adopted a "Burmese road to socialism"—a policy of state socialism and isolationism (a policy of keeping foreign influence and involvement to a minimum so that a country can develop on its own). Economic conditions did not improve under the harsh rule of the generals; rather, they worsened. In 1987, the United Nations declared the country a "Least Developed Nation."

Many people in Burma remained antagonistic toward the military rule and the state-controlled economy. This opposition finally led to mass protests and violence in March 1988, which the government sought to suppress. The army chief of staff took control of the government, abandoned the 3-decade-old period of state socialism, and freed the market from most of the state controls.

Burma now has a mixed economy with a private, state, and a joint private-state sector. Agriculture, light industries, and other businesses are in the **private sector**. Heavy industries that require huge capital investment are in the state sector. The economic reforms of the last decade sought to promote **joint ventures** between private Burmese and foreign firms. Therefore, foreign investments were once again encouraged with modest success. The state sector continues to be inefficient, and attempts to **privatize** at least a portion of it remain on the books. **External debt** amounts to 10 percent of the GDP, and imports exceed exports by 2 to 1, causing a serious trade imbalance.

Burma is a top producer of illicit drugs and contributes 80 percent of all Southeast Asian production of opium. Most of the heroin available in the United States originates from Burma. The trafficking in drugs is illegal; thus, an accurate assessment of its contribution to the economy is impossible to gauge. A parallel **black market**, perhaps bigger than the state's economy, continues to pose problems for the authorities.

During the 1998–99 **fiscal year**, Burma received an estimated US$99 million in economic aid. In 1995, the figure was about US$157 million. Economic **sanctions** imposed by the United States, the European Community, and other nations have contributed to this decline. These sanctions are in response to continued political repression and human rights violations by the military regime. In 1990, the opposition National League for Democracy (NLD) had won a clear victory in the elections, but the generals refused to transfer power to the duly-elected representatives of the people. Moreover, the leaders of the NLD were harassed, detained, tortured, and even murdered by the regime.

Politically and economically, Burma remains a pariah (outcast) nation. Except for its membership in the Association of Southeast Asian Nations (ASEAN), the country is not befriended by most nations. In May 2000, U.S. president Bill Clinton imposed new sanctions on the military junta (a group of military personnel who overthrow a government) making it difficult for the Burmese authorities to get foreign loans, economic assistance, and foreign investments. Many American companies such as Apple Computer, Oshkosh B'Gosh, Eddie Bauer, Reebok, Levi Strauss, Pepsi Cola, and Liz Claiborne have withdrawn from the country. Therefore, the attempts of the military junta to revitalize the economy have been only partly successful.

Despite the introduction of banking and trade regulations in the late 1990s, Burma failed to achieve fiscal or monetary stability. **Inflation** continues to be high. Although poor and undeveloped, Burma is rich in natural resources. Nevertheless, the decline of the agricultural sector, regional economic crises, international sanctions, and shortages of electricity have all contributed to a slowdown in the economy since 1997.

POLITICS, GOVERNMENT, AND TAXATION

Burma fought for independence from Great Britain in the late 1940s under the Anti-Fascist People's Freedom League led by Aung San, U Nu, and Ne Win. The independence movement was a pro-Burman, anti-British, and anti-foreign movement that emphasized Burmese values, symbols, and experiences. This movement had very strong socialist leanings in response to Chinese and Indian domination of the Burmese economy during the British rule. In 1948, the country became independent under the leadership of U Nu because his political opponents had already killed Aung San, the father of Burmese nationalism. In 1962 the army, under the leadership of Ne Win, overthrew the democratic government and set up the Burmese Socialist Party, **nationalized** schools, banks, and factories, and followed a policy of socialist central planning and international isolationism. Later on, the party of the generals changed its name to the Burma Socialist Program Party. In 1974, all political parties were abolished.

In September of 1988, amid massive demonstrations against the government, a new regime seized power in a military coup. Calling themselves the State Law and Order Restoration Council (SLORC), the new regime also changed the name of the country from Burma to Myanmar, something that opposition groups still object to. Following the anti-government protests, riots, and bloodshed in 1988, the opposition parties coalesced into the National League for Democracy (NLD) under the leadership Aung San Suu Kyi, the daughter of the martyred national hero, Aung San.

Responding to nationwide protests, the SLORC allowed national elections in May of 1990. The NLD dominated the elections, winning 80 percent of the seats in the National Assembly, but the ruling SLORC refused to concede power and imprisoned NLD leader Aung San Suu Kyi. Since that time the SLORC has exercised complete control over all branches of government. The National Assembly elected in 1990 has in fact never convened, the judicial system is bankrupt, and all executive positions are held by military representatives of the SLORC.

In 1997 the ruling SLORC was reorganized as the State Peace and Development Council (SPDC) amid a shakeup that saw several high officials dismissed for corruption. Five top generals, including Secretary Khin Nyunt, consolidated their power but showed no signs of ceding control of the government to the opposition, most of which was banned from any official forms of organization. Like the SLORC, the SPDC is primarily concerned with cracking down on opposition and not on improving the economic fortunes of the country.

The government's mounting deficit financing, resulting mostly from declining tax revenue and escalating military expenditures, has had a negative impact on the economy. The regime's policies led to the growth in the money supply and accelerated inflation. Mounting **foreign debt** and depleting **foreign exchange reserves** also affected the health of the economy. Military expenditures increased while the funding for health and education declined. The government's oppressive attitude towards the opposition has caused international censure, prompting foreign firms to pull out or cut back on their activities. Because of foreign economic sanctions, Burma is unable to get assistance from other countries or loans from international funding sources.

The country's tax base shrank in the last years of the 20th century, due to the government's inability to collect taxes because of a corrupt bureaucracy and a black market perhaps as large as the legitimate market. The sources of government revenue include general sales and **value-added taxes**, income from state enterprises, taxes on international trade, fees, and grants from donor nations and international agencies. The government also collects customs at its border posts, but most of the border trade is unrecorded.

The judicial system that Burma inherited from its British colonial masters was abolished in 1974. The new constitution calls for a council of People's Justices. In addition, there are lower courts at the state, town, village and ward level. The courts settle both civil and criminal cases. The armed forces—controlling most aspects of the country's politics and government—also exert influence over Burma's judicial system.

INFRASTRUCTURE, POWER, AND COMMUNICATIONS

In most developing countries of the world including Burma, inadequate **infrastructure**—roads, bridges, canals, railways, ports and communication facilities—impedes economic growth. Burma's long coastline is home to many excellent natural harbors such as Bassein, Bhamo, Mandalay, Rangoon, and Tavoy. The government has taken steps to develop new ports and maintain the existing ones, although all the ports are not used to their maximum capacity. A salient geographic feature of Burma is its many rivers, especially the Irrawaddy. The country's waterways remain the most important traditional mode of transportation to many remote areas of the country. Of more than 12,800 kilometers (7,954 miles) of waterways, 3200 kilometers (1,988 miles) are navigable by large commercial vessels.

Since the economic **liberalization** in 1989, the government started many public works programs. Early in the 1990s the government used forced rural labor to work on these projects. However, due to international criticism, the government began to engage the armed forces on these construction projects starting in mid-1990s. These projects did not bring about major improvement in the infrastructure needs of the country. The result has been that economic expansion was made difficult because in the absence of adequate transportation facilities, distribution of goods and services has been extremely difficult and costly.

In 1996, Burma had a total of 28,200 kilometers (17,523 miles) of roads, of which only 3,440 kilometers (2,138 miles) were paved. Although the government attempted to improve many major roadways during the final years of the 20th century, most remain in poor repair and are not passable during the monsoon season. A major effort in this regard was to reconstruct the Old Burma Road from Mandalay to the borders of China. As of late 2000, the work on the project was still incomplete.

Rail services remain poor despite attempts in the 1990s to renovate the existing lines, add new ones, and upgrade railway services on the main routes. Burma has a total of 3,991 kilometers (2,480 miles) of railways, over 320 locomotives, and more than 4,000 rail cars. The recent efforts include upgrading Rangoon-Mandalay rail line and beginning a new 162-kilometer Ye-Dawai Rail track project. In the 1995–96 fiscal year the railways carried 53,400,000 passengers and 3,280,000 tons of freight.

Burma has 80 airports and 1 heliport. Only 10 airports have paved runways. Both the private sector and the state sector are active in air transportation. The Department of Civil Aviation is responsible for the airports and the state-run airline. Air Mandalay, Myanma Airways, and Myanma Airways International are the chief airlines of the country. Burma's chief airports at Rangoon, Mandalay, and Bago were upgraded in the late

Communications

Country	Newspapers	Radios	TV Sets[a]	Cable subscribers[a]	Mobile Phones[a]	Fax Machines[a]	Personal Computers[a]	Internet Hosts[b]	Internet Users[b]
	1996	1997	1998	1998	1998	1998	1998	1999	1999
Burma	10	95	7	N/A	0	0.1	N/A	0.00	1
United States	215	2,146	847	244.3	256	78.4	458.6	1,508.77	74,100
China	N/A	333	272	40.0	19	1.6	8.9	0.50	8,900
Thailand	63	232	236	10.1	32	2.5	21.6	4.49	800

[a]Data are from International Telecommunication Union, *World Telecommunication Development Report 1999* and are per 1,000 people.
[b]Data are from the Internet Software Consortium (http://www.isc.org) and are per 10,000 people.

SOURCE: World Bank. *World Development Indicators 2000.*

1990s. During the 1995–96 fiscal year state-run airlines carried a total of 719,000 domestic passengers and 138,000 international passengers.

Light transportation such as buses and cars are a private sector activity in Burma. As of March 31, 1996, Burma had 151,934 passenger cars, 42,828 trucks, 15,639 buses, 88,521 motorcycles, and another 6,611 registered vehicles.

Also during 1996, state-owned maritime vessels carried 24,491,000 passengers and 3,158,000 tons of freight. These numbers show an increase over the same period of the previous fiscal year.

Industrial production and expansion are limited due to inadequate production and intermittent supply of electric power. Electricity production of 4.38 billion kilowatt-hours (kWh) in 1998 was far below demand. Around 38 percent of the electricity is generated by hydroelectric projects while the remaining 62 percent comes from fossil fuels. Chronic shortages and frequent disruptions of supply exist. Therefore, state and private enterprises operate far below their capacity. Moreover, very often they have to depend on their own diesel-run power generators to meet their electrical needs.

As of 1995, there were 158,000 main telephone lines. In 1997, there were 500 exchanges with a capacity to reach 320 of the 324 townships in the nation. The number of mobile cellular phones was only 2,007 in 1995. Although the telephone system is capable of providing basic services, it is inefficient and outdated. Attempts in the 1990s to upgrade the system yielded only minimal results. Cellular and wireless phones function more efficiently than the traditional lines. The switching system is incapable of meeting current demands, and people have to wait for a long time for a telephone connection to their homes and factories. International service powered by a satellite earth station is relatively good.

The 2 television stations in Burma service 260,000 (1997) television sets. TV Burma is able to transmit 82 percent of its broadcasts to 267 of the 324 townships in the country with the help of 120 TV relay stations. These are in addition to Burma's 2 AM, 3 FM, and 3 short-wave radio stations. In 1997 the country had a total of 4.2 million radio sets. Radio and television stations are state-owned and operated. In 1996, there were 5 newspapers with an estimated circulation of 449,000, a significant decline from 1994 circulation figures.

There are about 50,000 computers in all of Burma. Public access to the Internet is prohibited for fear that it could encourage and widen political dissent and protest. Unauthorized ownership of modems is punishable by up to 15 years in jail. E-mail is restricted to foreigners and businesspeople with close ties to the administration. Private e-mail providers are prohibited, and only the Ministry of Post and Telegraph is allowed to provide e-mail service.

Improvements in the infrastructure were partly funded by deficit spending. In the absence of adequate funds, the government is unable to fully develop the country's transportation and communication systems and facilities. This situation had a negative impact on modernization and economic growth of the country for many decades.

ECONOMIC SECTORS

Agriculture, industries, energy and tourism are the main sectors of the Burma economy. Agriculture, however, is the dominant sector and accounts for almost 60 percent of the GDP. The heavy industries are owned and operated by the state. Agriculture is mostly a private activity, although rice exports are a state **monopoly**. Recent government initiatives to improve agricultural production failed because drought and flooding diminished in rice production. The cultivation of pulses and beans, however, has increased significantly.

Industrial manufacturing is still undeveloped. Government attempts to privatize some industries have stalled, even though government-owned concerns continue to lose large sums of money. Foreign investments, although encouraged, have failed to generate enough international interest due to sanctions and boycotts protesting the military regime's human rights violations. All told, industry contributed just 11 percent of GDP in 1997.

The energy sector grew considerably during the late 1990s. The exploration and discovery of petroleum and

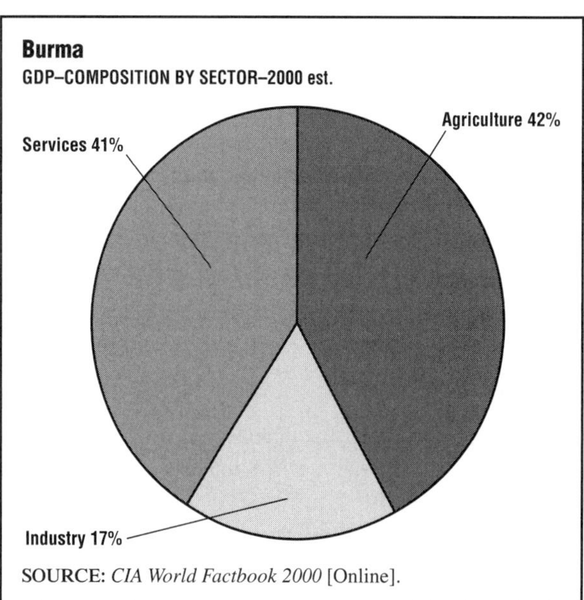

SOURCE: *CIA World Factbook 2000* [Online].

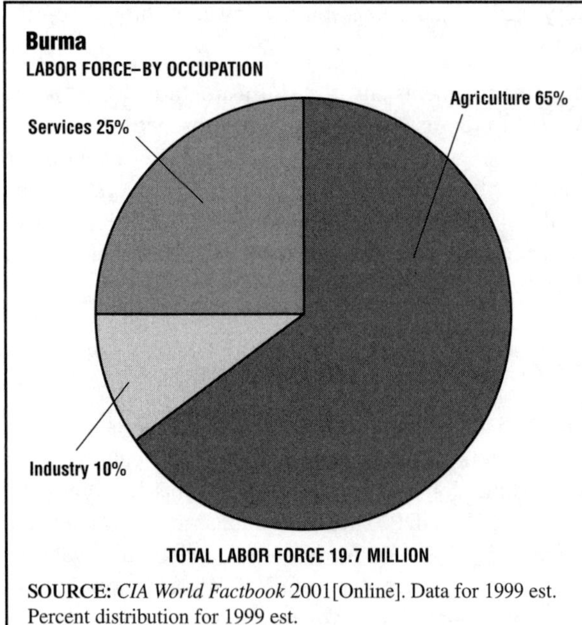

SOURCE: *CIA World Factbook* 2001[Online]. Data for 1999 est. Percent distribution for 1999 est.

natural gas deposits continued during this period. The construction of the Yadna gas pipeline to Thailand was a major development and is expected to be a major source of revenue. The lack of sufficient electrical power contributes to the country's poor economic growth.

Following the military crackdown on the pro-democracy movement in 1988, there was a sharp decline in the number of foreign tourists visiting the country. Early in the 1990s the government placed great emphasis on tourism development. The government's attempt to turn tourism into a "cash cow" has not materialized, although the number of people visiting Burma has certainly increased in the last several years.

Realizing the difficulties on the road to rapid industrialization, the government of Burma, while not giving up on industrialization, is hoping to make the agricultural sector the centerpiece of its plans for economic revitalization of the country. This sector, however, has seen declining financial returns. Burma is caught in a vicious circle of inflation, deficit financing, unemployment, and poverty. In an age of increasing international interdependence, Burma cannot expect to develop without the cooperation of the international community.

AGRICULTURE

Agriculture, which includes crop production, hunting, fishing, and forestry, is the mainstay of the Burma economy. This sector is responsible for much of the income and employment in the country. About 60 percent of the GDP comes from agriculture, and as much as 65 percent of the **labor force** is employed in this sector alone. Burma produces enough food to feed its entire population. In the absence of purchasing power, however, many people go hungry. Further, about a third of the rural households do not have any land or livestock. Only half of the arable 45 million acres is under cultivation.

Rice is the most important agricultural commodity of Burma. Rice production increased from 5,200,000 metric tons in 1950 to 16,760,000 metric tons in 1993. The crop is cultivated along the river valleys, coastal areas, and in the Irrawaddy River delta. A wide variety of crops are cultivated in the northern dry zone. Rubber and other commercially useful products are cultivated in the Irrawaddy and Tenasserim regions. Agricultural products form the bulk of the export trade and include rice, teak, prawns, beans and pulses, and opiates.

Burma's agriculture is heavily dependent on the monsoon rains. While some areas suffer from too much rain, other regions receive too little. Government efforts in the 1990s increased the amount of irrigated land to 2.2 million acres. Many agricultural products like tobacco, sugar, groundnut, sunflower, maize, jute and wheat, however, have not reached their pre-1985 production levels. This reduction is offset by higher production in rice, pulses and beans. Rice production increased due to supportive government policies as well as favorable market forces. According to Asian Development Bank estimates, however, real annual growth in agriculture declined from 5.0 percent in 1996–97 to 3.7 percent in 1997–98 and to 2.8 in the 1998–99 fiscal years. Further, per-acre yield of the crops has not increased because of inadequate application of fertilizers and pesticides. One factor that helped to improve production was the removal of government controls over the agricultural sector.

Deforestation has been a major concern in Burma. The slash-and-burn method of agriculture is destroying the forests of the country, causing soil erosion and depletion of fertility. Periodic droughts, floods, landslides, and cyclones sometimes have devastating effect on agriculture. For example, flooding in Pegu and Irrawaddy during the 1997–98 growing season did considerable damage to rice production. Consequently, Burma exported only 28.4 thousand metric tons of rice in the 1997–98 season as opposed to 93.1 thousand metric tons in the previous year.

The heavy reliance on monsoons is a major handicap for Burmese agriculture. The authorities have recently renovated dams and reservoirs, built new ones, pumped water from rivers and streams and taken other measures to improve irrigation. More remains to be done in this regard. Another impediment to agricultural improvement is the inability of farmers to secure adequate loans to enhance cultivation. Private lenders charge exorbitant rates, and there are not enough banking institutions to serve people in the rural areas. As a result, farmers are not able to buy fertilizers and pesticides for their crops. Financial services need to be improved to make funds available to the cultivators.

The economic liberalization policies of the military junta have transformed the agricultural sector. Under the new economic system, the government distributed land among the landless, improved irrigation facilities, and increased the **floor price** of paddy that the government procures from the farmers. Some private activity in the export sector has been allowed since economic liberalization began in 1989. Consequently, the share of the agricultural sector in the GDP has gone up.

LIVESTOCK. Burmese farmers raise a variety of animals including cattle, water buffalo, goats, sheep, chickens, and pigs. Oxen and water buffalo serve as draught animals in agriculture and for rural transportation. The GDP share of the livestock has increased slightly during the past decade. Most of the cattle are raised in the dry zone in the north.

FORESTRY. Burma is rich in forests and woodland. While its neighbors, India, China and Thailand, have already depleted their forests, Burma is still regarded as the "last frontier of biodiversity in Asia." (Biodiversity refers to ecosystems that are rich, varied, and largely unpolluted or tampered with by human development.) Most of the timbers, especially teakwood, consumed in these Asian countries come from Burma, although most of these exports are illegal. In their search for precious foreign exchange, the military junta is engaged in indiscriminate destruction of forests. Deforestation increases erosion and landslides and threatens the lives of many already endangered species in the rain forests.

Burma is the leading supplier of teak in the international market. In addition to hardwoods, Burma also produces large quantities of bamboo in the delta regions and in the areas of heavy rainfall. Elephants and water buffalo play a key role in hauling teak and other hardwoods.

FISHING. Burma is blessed with some of the world's most bountiful fishing grounds that extend from the Bay of Bengal to the Gulf of Martaban. Fish, often dried and salted, is part of Burmese cooking and is the most important source of protein in the diet. The government took many steps to encourage deep-sea fishing although the people prefer fresh-water fish. There has been a steady increase in the catch since the 1980s. Since 1989, Thai companies have been given permission to fish in the Burma waters. They use a modernized trawler fleet to harvest fish. The government also encourages fresh-water fish farms with a view to increasing fish production. Moreover, the Tenasserim area is home to some of world's finest pearls. As a result, the export value of fish and fish products alone has gone up from 159.4 million kyats in 1995–1996 to 227.8 million in 1996–97.

INDUSTRY

Primarily an agricultural country, Burma has always lagged behind in industrial production. The colonial authorities discouraged industrialization and encouraged only the production of raw materials, although there were some industrial developments towards the end of the colonial period.

World War II caused serious damage to the country's infant industries. It took a long time for production to catch up to pre-war levels, and in 1952, the government established the Industrial Development Corporation to stimulate industrial production. The country's effort to industrialize without foreign assistance was successful to a certain extent in areas such as petroleum and natural gas production. In the 1960s, under military rule, many industries were nationalized. Since the 1970s, there has been a steady growth in industrial production. In 1988, the government liberalized the economy, abandoned state socialism, and encouraged foreign investment.

Much of the industrial sector, especially heavy industries, is controlled by the government, although the share of private enterprise in this area is steadily growing. Industry accounts for only about 11 percent of the GDP and employs only 10 percent of the total labor force. Most of the industries center around agricultural processing, textiles, footwear, wood and wood products, copper, tin, tungsten, iron, construction materials, petroleum and natural gas, pharmaceuticals, and fertilizers. Cars and television sets are also assembled in the country. In 1999, the annual rate of growth of industries was estimated at 4 percent. The heavy losses of the **public sector** factories and industries are in part responsible for slow industrial growth.

Pegu is the seat of most industrial activity. In addition, the government has opened 17 special industrial zones all over the country, 5 of which are in the Rangoon area. Foreign investment is encouraged in 2 of the zones. While these zones are not fully developed, several factories and plants manufacturing clothing, **consumer goods**, and iron and steel materials are already operating there.

MINING. Although their GDP contribution is not very significant, mineral products are important in earning foreign exchange. Burma has large amounts of mineral deposits. They include tin, zinc, copper, tungsten, lead, silver, gold, iron and antimony. Coal, natural gas, and crude oil are also extracted. Jade, rubies, sapphires, and gold are also found in Burma. Should the country ever open to foreign investment there may be significant opportunities for development in this sector.

OIL AND NATURAL GAS. Burma's petroleum industry dates back to pre-independence days. During 1963–1964, the government took complete control of petroleum exploration, extraction, and purification. Petroleum is found in the Irrawaddy basin, the delta region, and at offshore sites. Burma is self-sufficient in oil.

The discovery of natural gas reserves in the Gulf of Martaban added to Burma's energy reserve. In 1986 the country produced 32,600 million cubic feet of natural gas. Burma also has large deposits of natural gas in the Andaman off-shore fields. In its efforts to facilitate the growth of its energy sector, the government built the Yadana natural gas pipeline, connecting natural gas stores off the Andaman Islands and Thailand, with the help of Unocal and Total, 2 international petroleum companies. According to government estimates, the energy sector grew approximately 88 percent in 1998. Government projections showed a 77 percent growth for the year 1999.

SERVICES

With just 30 percent of GDP and 25 percent of the workforce, the services sector is not a dominant part of the economy as it often is in developed countries.

TOURISM. Like the cash-strapped countries of Jamaica and Cuba, Burma is also actively promoting itself as an island paradise to increase tourism. Both the government and private enterprises are heavily engaged in the tourism industry. In order to attract tourists, the country has improved roads, built international standard hotels, and other facilities. In 1988, roughly 40,000 foreigners visited the country, although following the suppression of the democracy movement that same year, tourism decreased. Between 1993 and 1996, tourism once again revived. The government proclaimed 1996 as "Visit Burma Year" and hoped to attract 500,000 tourists. However, only 180,000 people showed up. In the 1997–98 fiscal year 191,000 tourists visited the country. Both the government and the private sector, having invested heavily in new tourist facilities, were disappointed.

Nevertheless, Burma—the land of Buddhist pagodas—has great tourism potential. Rangoon, Mandalay, Pagan, Pegu, and Tawnggys, with their palaces and shrines and pagodas, are the centers of tourism. However, the tense political situation, human rights violations, and boycotts by the international community have deterred many people from visiting. Tourism, so far, makes up only a small percentage of the GDP.

FINANCE. During the post-independence days, most financial institutions were private. In 1964, the military junta nationalized all of the country's 24 banks. In their place, the government created 4 state banks. In 1990, the financial sector was revamped under the provisions of the Central Bank of Myanmar Law. Since then the financial institutions are the Central Bank of Myanmar, the Myanmar Agricultural and Rural Development Bank, the Myanma Economic Bank, the Myanma Foreign Trade Bank, the Myanma Industrial and Commercial Bank, the Myanma Small Loans Enterprise, and Myanmar Insurance. The 1990 law also allowed for both private and foreign banks. As a result, by February 1996, 16 private banks were formed, most of them in Rangoon. During the same period, more than 20 foreign banks opened branches or offices in Myanmar.

The banking sector is still underdeveloped. The people have yet to maintain regular banking habits. The **inflation rate** is so high that the real rate of interest does not encourage deposits. But without deposits, banks cannot provide credit. In contrast, during the 1970s, when the interest rate was raised, people deposited more money in the banks.

The Burma Securities Exchange was founded in 1996 as a joint venture between Japan's Daiwa Institute of Research and Myanma Economic Bank. The financial sector contributes only a small percentage of the GDP.

INTERNATIONAL TRADE

Historically, most of Burma's export-import trade was with Asian countries. In 1999, more than 80 percent of the country's export-import trade was with Asian nations, including about half with ASEAN countries. Japan, Singapore, Malaysia, and China are its major trading partners. Singapore is the single most important partner both in terms of imports and exports, providing 31 percent of imports and taking 10 percent of exports. There has been a decline in trade with Europe and the United States since the 1988 military crackdown on the democracy movement. Burma's export-import trade with the United States constitutes about 5 percent of the total foreign trade.

The country's exports are mostly agricultural products. They include pulses and beans, teak, prawns, rubber, rice and other agricultural products. There is a large black market that smuggles live animals, gems, minerals, teak, and rice into the neighboring countries. Burma

Trade (expressed in billions of US$): Burma

	Exports	Imports
1975	.173	.197
1980	.472	.353
1985	.303	.283
1990	.325	.270
1995	.846	1.335
1998	1.067	2.666

SOURCE: International Monetary Fund. *International Financial Statistics Yearbook 1999.*

also conducts brisk trade in narcotics. During the 1997–98 fiscal year, imports included raw materials, transport equipment, construction materials, and food items. While priority was given to the importation of materials needed for the Yadana natural gas pipeline, the government took measures to control importation of non-essential goods.

In 1998 the country exported $1.2 billion in goods and services while importing $2.5 billion, reflecting a steady increase of imports over exports during the 1993–98 period. In fact, the trade imbalance has been a chronic problem for the country for well over 2 decades. During the 1965–75 period, rice exports fell, and Burma cut back on imports. During the 1976–80 period, although exports increased, there was a corresponding increase in imports. By the mid-1980s, exports declined, but imports continued to soar. The adverse **balance of payment** situation continues to plague Burma.

This imbalance has a negative impact on the economy as a whole, forcing Burma to spend its precious foreign exchange reserves. To compensate for this situation, the government has printed currency to buy foreign exchange, thereby accelerating the inflationary tendencies of the economy. This inflation has wiped out many of the gains the country made as a result of economic liberalization in the 1990s. Making matters worse, the government had to buy foreign exchange from foreign sources at commercial rates. Consequently, Burma was unable to service its debt payment, prompting the World Bank to sever ties with the country. The net effect for Burma's people is that their purchasing power and standard of living declined.

The regime, while continuing to increase military spending, was forced to cut back on education, health, and other essential services. Growing international concern about human rights abuses and the regime's inability to tackle narcotics trafficking have led many countries, including the United States, and international financial institutions, to refuse aid or loans to the country. The government's use of forced labor has also led to boycotts of Burmese goods.

MONEY

Adverse balance of payments, decreasing tax revenues, high defense spending, and deficit financing all have led to the printing of more currency and price inflation. The official **exchange rate** of the kyat to dollar, however, remains unchanged. There are 4 different rates for currency exchange: the official exchange rate, the customs rate, the official market rate, and the black market rate. Officially, US$1 equals 6.73 kyats, whereas in the black market the dollar may fetch 375 or more kyats.

Exchange rates: Burma

kyats per US$1	
Jan 2001	6.5972
2000	6.5167
1999	6.2858
1998	6.3432
1997	6.2418
1996	5.9176

SOURCE: CIA *World Factbook 2001* [ONLINE].

The Asian currency crisis of 1997 added to Burma's currency woes. The sharp decline in the Thai bhat had a negative impact on the kyat. During the 1997–98 fiscal year, according to U.S. embassy estimates, the kyat lost 54 percent of its value. Between April and December 1997, the kyat declined from 167/dollar to 257/dollar. In 1997 and 1998, when the kyat fell, the government intervened to prop up the value of the kyat and took strong measures to keep foreign exchange from leaving the country. It put a monthly cap of $50,000 on **remittances**, cut the number of banks allowed to handle foreign exchange transactions, and placed stiff controls on trade.

The Asian economic crisis prompted foreign investors to either withhold investments or stay out of the Burmese market. Crises in the neighboring countries, Burma's principal trading partners, cost the country its export markets. The resultant ballooning of the **trade deficit** prompted the country to expand its money supply and draw down on foreign exchange reserves. According to the U.S. State Department *Commercial Guide* for 1999, the country was "virtually bankrupt."

POVERTY AND WEALTH

Like most countries of the world, Burma has extremes of wealth and poverty. Once prosperous, Burma was, in 2001, one of the poorest countries of the world.

GDP per Capita (US$)

Country	1996	1997	1998	1999	2000
Burma	1,120	1,190	1,200	1,200	1,500
United States	28,600	30,200	31,500	33,900	36,200
China	2,800	3,460	3,600	3,800	3,600
Thailand	7,700	8,800	6,100	6,400	6,700

Data are estimates.

SOURCE: *Handbook of the Nations*, 17th, 18th, 19th and 20th editions for 1996, 1997, 1998 and 1999 data; CIA *World Factbook 2001* [Online] for 2000 data.

Most people live in the 40,000-odd villages of the country, while the majority of the urban population resides in the capital city of Rangoon. Among the population engaged in agriculture, 37 percent of the people do not have any land or livestock. Poverty and misery have increased in the past 3 decades. In 1997 the CIA *World Factbook* estimated that 23 percent of the Burmese population had incomes that placed them below the poverty line.

The economic crisis of 1997 added to the problem. Inflation as of 1999 was at an all-time high of 50 percent on domestic goods and 104 percent on imported items. The government's policies have not helped to diminish inflation, which has eroded the purchasing power of Burma's citizens. The gap between rich and poor and rural and urban areas has increased. According to the International Monetary Fund (IMF), per capita income registered only a minimal increase in the 1990s. Many poor people are forced to send their children to work. Many women reportedly are sent to work in Thailand. The number of street children has also increased, and malnutrition among children is widespread. Sanitary conditions are far from satisfactory. Malaria, diarrhea, dysentery, tuberculosis, and more recently HIV/AIDS (due to drugs and prostitution) are the major health hazards of the country.

In the countryside, a bullock cart (a 2-wheeled cart drawn by 2 castrated bulls) is the most popular means of transportation. Most farmers own a pair of oxen or water buffalo, a hoe, and a bullock cart for agricultural purposes. The rural houses (actually huts without running water or toilets) are made of bamboo. One portion is used for cooking and the other for sleeping. In the major towns and cities, there are houses made of brick and concrete. They are usually small and overcrowded.

The government's socio-economic policies have not helped the people. Large outlays of money have been spent on the military, while only meager funds have gone to education and health issues. The numbers of children who do not attend school or who have dropped out reportedly increased in the 1990s. According to World Bank estimates, only 46.9 percent of the secondary school-age children were enrolled in schools during 1995. Education beyond the primary age is not compulsory. Burmese authorities boast a literacy rate of 83 percent, though independent observers have suggested that the rate may be as low as 30 percent. Most universities have been closed since December 1996.

Health care in the rural areas was marginal until the 1960s. The government has opened more rural health centers and directed more doctors to the rural areas. As a result, the doctor-patient ratio has decreased considerably, from 1 per 15,560 to 1 per 3,578 in 1986. Health care is provided free of charge.

WORKING CONDITIONS

The Burmese labor force is estimated to be 19.7 million strong and consists of people between the ages of 15 and 59. About 65 percent of the labor force is employed in the agriculture sector. Of the remaining 35 percent, 10 percent is employed in the industrial sector while the remaining 25 percent is employed in a variety of service sectors. The official government unemployment rate for the fiscal year 1997–98 was reported as 7.1 percent.

One serious concern about the Burma labor situation is the reported use of forced labor on public works projects. In November 2000, the International Labor Organization (ILO) concluded that Burmese authorities had not discontinued the practice and advised member nations to review their relations with Burma. In response, Burmese authorities said that they would stop cooperating with the ILO. The government has maintained that the ILO action represented an effort by its member states to exert improper influence on Burma's internal affairs.

According to U.S. sources in Rangoon, the government lessened its dependence on forced labor. Instead, it was using military personnel on some of these projects. Military authorities, however, continue to force civilians to work for them. Many women and children, for instance, have to work as porters for the army.

There are reports of the continued prevalence of child labor in the country. Legally, children must be 13 or above before they can be employed. This and the compulsory education law, however, are not fully enforced. Consequently, a large number of children never enroll in school and many do not complete the primary school course. Therefore, children are frequently employed in many areas, especially in the arts and crafts industries.

Since the military takeover in 1962, the authorities have consistently denied the people their freedom of speech, press, assembly, and association. Also in 1964, the government abolished all trade union organizations. Substituting for independent unions are government-sponsored Regional Workers Councils. In 1985, there were 1.8 million members. Coordinating the work of the regional councils is the central workers organization in Rangoon, formed in 1968. The Central Arbitration Board is given the responsibility to settle major labor disputes but is inactive. Minor labor concerns are addressed by the township level agencies. One labor organization, the Federation of Trade Unions-Burma (FTUB), is an anti-government group that was formed in 1991 by Burmese living in exile.

Working conditions were set forth in a 1964 law called The Law on Fundamental Workers' Rights and the Factories Act of 1951. An abundance of labor and the failure of the government to protect the workers have led to substandard working conditions. The public sector employees follow a 5-day, 35-hour workweek. Employees in the private sector and state enterprises have a 6-day, 44-hour workweek. The law provides for overtime pay. However, these laws cover only a small percentage of the workers. Moreover, the workers are not allowed to organize in unions and bargain collectively. In the public sector industries, the government sets the wages and benefits. The **joint sector** companies are discouraged from paying their employees more than their counterparts in the public sector.

As of March 2000, all institutions of higher education, with the exception of a military academy and a medical school affiliated with the army, were closed. The middle class is frustrated that their children are not able to get an education. Many Burmese of all classes have fled the country for fear of oppression. Thousands of Burmese refugees remain in camps in Thailand and Bangladesh.

COUNTRY HISTORY AND ECONOMIC DEVELOPMENT

1044. Pagan empire is founded on the banks of Irrawaddy.

1824. First Anglo-Burmese war leads to Burmese defeat and loss of territory.

1886. Burma is defeated in the Second Anglo-Burmese war, and Britain annexes the remainder of the country's territory.

1941–45. Japanese forces invade Burma and occupy much of the country during World War II.

1948. Burma becomes an independent, democratic country with a free market economy.

1962. The military under General Ne Win overthrows democracy, establishing the "Burmese way to socialism" and nationalizing banks and other private industries.

1974. The government establishes a new constitution and announces the formation of the Socialist Republic of the Union of Burma.

1988. Amid widespread protests and riots, a military junta headed by Generals Ne Win and Saw Maung replaces the civilian president with a new government called the State Law and Order Restoration Council (SLORC). The SLORC renames the nation the Union of Myanmar, dropping the name "Burma," and liberalizes the economy.

1990. Elections are held, and the opposition National League for Democracy wins a clear majority. The SLORC refuses to cede power and opposition leaders are jailed.

1997. The Asian economic crisis damages Burma's economy.

2000. The International Labor Organization concludes that Burma is in violation of rules regarding forced labor and advises member nations to review their relations with Burma.

FUTURE TRENDS

Burma is a resource-rich, naturally beautiful, and culturally significant country. Its potential for growth and prosperity is tremendous. Yet Burma can never reach its potential until the military regime negotiates with the opposition and transfers power to the elected representatives of the people. The regime, however, has been trying to eradicate the opposition. Most international observers agree that the government must end human rights violations, release political prisoners, establish sound **monetary policies**, increase the tax base and revenue, enhance the infrastructure, and further liberalize the public sector if the country has any hopes of taking its place in international commerce. Despite announcing plans for such improvements, however, the ruling SPDC seems most concerned with retaining its grip on power through violence and intimidation of internal opposition and disengagement with the international community. In the absence of a change in this program, economic stagnation, poverty, disease, and illiteracy will remain Burma's most notable features.

DEPENDENCIES

Burma (Myanmar) has no territories or colonies.

BIBLIOGRAPHY

"Amnesty International Report 2000-Country Reports, Myanmar." *Amnesty International.* <http://www.web.amnesty.org/web/ar2000web.nsf/ebbd3384655495f2802568f500615e2f/3a9085ff93e50f80802568f200552950!OpenDocument>. Accessed December 2000.

Cady, John Frank. *Southeast Asia: Its Historical Development.* New York: McGraw Hill, 1964.

Cady, John Frank. *The United States and Burma.* Cambridge, MA: Harvard University Press, 1976.

Soe, Maung Maung. "Economic Reforms and Agricultural Development in Myanmar." *ASEAN Economic Bulletin.* Vol. 15, No. 1, April 1998.

U.S. Central Intelligence Agency. *World Factbook 2000.* <http://www.odci.gov/cia/publications/factbook/index.html>. Accessed July 2001.

U.S. Department of State. *Country Commercial Guides FY 1999: Burma.* <http://www.state.gov/www/about_state/business/com_guides/1999/eastasia/burma99.html>. Accessed December 2000.

—George Thadathil

CAMBODIA

Kingdom of Cambodia
Preahreacheanachakr Kampuchea

CAPITAL: Phnom Penh.

MONETARY UNIT: Cambodian riel (KHR). One riel equals 100 sen. There are no coins in use, but there are notes of 100, 200, 500, and 1,000 riel. The 1,000 riel note (worth about a quarter in U.S. currency) is the most commonly used. In recent years Cambodia has basically become a dollarized economy. People often pay for goods and services in dollars, but receive small change in riel banknotes.

CHIEF EXPORTS: Timber, garments, rubber, rice, and fish.

CHIEF IMPORTS: Cigarettes, gold, construction materials, petroleum products, machinery, and motor vehicles.

GROSS DOMESTIC PRODUCT: US$16.1 billion (purchasing power parity, 2000 est.).

BALANCE OF TRADE: **Exports:** US$942 million (f.o.b., 2000). **Imports:** US$1.3 billion (f.o.b., 2000).

COUNTRY OVERVIEW

LOCATION AND SIZE. Cambodia is one of the ten nations of Southeast Asia and part of mainland Southeast Asia. It is bordered on the north by Laos and Thailand, on the west by Thailand, and on the east by Vietnam. Its geographic area is 181,040 square kilometers (69,900 square miles), making it slightly smaller than the state of Oklahoma. Its total land boundaries are 2,572 kilometers (1,598 miles), and it has a coastline on the Gulf of Thailand of 443 kilometers (275 miles). The Mekong River flows directly through the country from north to south, eventually flowing into the Mekong Delta of Vietnam. Cambodia's largest city and capital, Phnom Penh, is on the Mekong River. The other major cities in Cambodia are Battambang, Siem Reap (the gateway to Angkor Wat), and Kampong Saom (Sihanoukville), Cambodia's major port.

POPULATION. Cambodia's population was 12,491,501 in July of 2001, according to the CIA *World Factbook*. This compares with a population of 5,728,772 in 1962; 6,682,200 in 1981; and 11,426,223 in 1998. The current population growth rate is a relatively high 2.25 percent. If this population rate were to continue, the country's population would double to approximately 25 million by the year 2033. The major cause of this high population growth rate is the high fertility rate of Cambodian women. The average Cambodian woman has 4.74 children.

With such a high fertility rate and the loss of much of the adult population through the prolonged civil war (1970–75, 1979–98), the Cambodian population is extremely young. Around 41.25 percent of the population is less than 15 years of age, and only 3.47 percent of the population is over 65. Unfortunately, Cambodia has a serious AIDS problem, which will have a negative effect on its future population growth. In 1999, it was estimated that the HIV/AIDS incidence among adults was 4.04 percent.

Unlike many other Southeast Asian countries such as Laos, Burma, Indonesia, and the Philippines, the Cambodian population is relatively homogenous. Approximately 90 percent of the population is Khmer, with 5 percent Vietnamese, 1 percent Chinese, and 4 percent other (Cham, Lao, Tai, and various hill peoples in northeastern areas such as Ratanakiri and Mondulkiri). Khmer is also the official language. Theravada Buddhists are the dominant religious group, claiming 95 percent of the population.

OVERVIEW OF ECONOMY

Cambodia is one of the world's poorest economies, and, thus, economic development is its highest priority. Much of its population is involved in **subsistence**

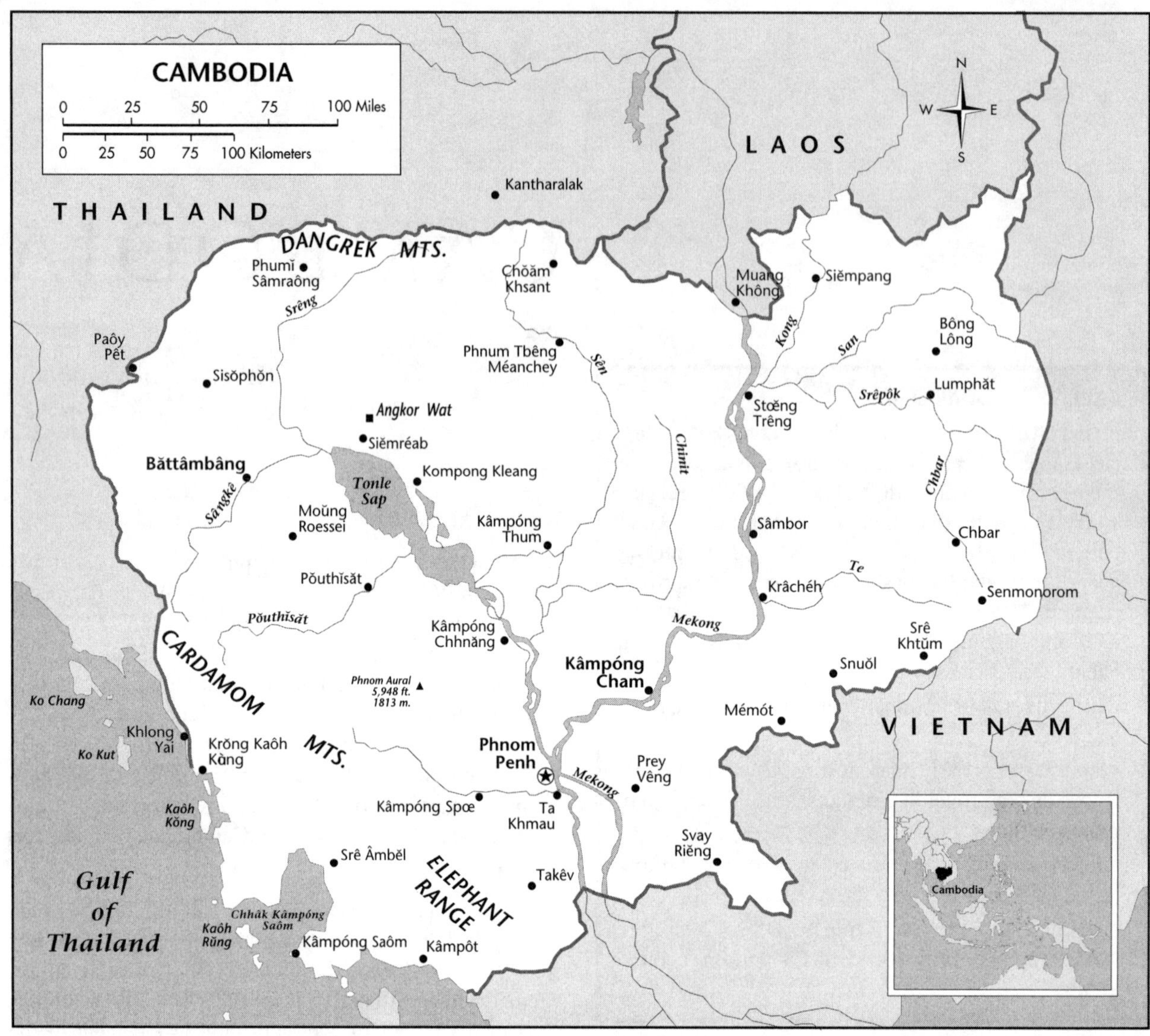

farming (families producing what is needed for daily living). About 66 percent of the country is forested or woodlands, with only 13 percent of the land arable.

Another major disadvantage has been Cambodia's long period of turmoil and civil strife, which began in 1970 with the overthrow of the government of Prince Sihanouk. That strife and instability lasted 28 years and severely and adversely affected the Cambodian economy, its human resource base, and its physical **infrastructure**.

With respect to its economic history, Cambodia is an excellent example of pre-development (advanced development centuries before the European Renaissance). Its prehistory dates back to the fourth millennium B.C. By 500 B.C., the use of metal had become widespread. As early as the 3rd century there was an Indianized trading state named Funan with Mon-Khmer inhabitants. In the last half of the 6th century, a new state Chenla emerged.

The years from 802 to 1432 mark the period of the great Angkor Khmer civilization. This Khmer civilization produced the largest religious monument in the world, the Angkor Wat complex. The Chinese sailor, Chou Ta-kuan, visited Angkor and described vividly the Khmer Empire at that time. The dynamic leadership of King Jayavarman VII produced an impressive network of hospitals, royal roads, rest houses, and advanced hydraulic irrigation schemes which allowed for as many as 3 crops of rice each year. During the reign of Jayavarman VII the Khmer Empire encompassed what is currently Cambodia and much of what is Thailand, Laos, and the southern part of Vietnam. After Jayavarman VII's death, Khmer power declined at the hands of the Siamese and later the Vietnamese. After the Siamese sacked Angkor several times the capital moved to Phnom Penh, which became a center for maritime trade. During the 19th century, Cambodia fell under Siamese and Vietnamese domination.

In 1863 the French then established a protectorate over Cambodia, and in the early 1900s Cambodia became part of colonial French Indochina. Under its colonial rule, the French established plantations to exploit Cambodian natural resources such as rubber. In 1953 Cambodia achieved its independence from France. Under the leadership of Prince Sihanouk, Cambodia enjoyed peace and stability. In terms of its economy, the country was poor, but most of the population enjoyed affluent subsistence. Farmers, for the most part, had their own land and there was adequate fish, rice, fruit, and vegetables for much of the population.

In 1970, Cambodia became a war-plagued economy. With a coup against Prince Sihanouk in March of that year, Cambodia was drawn into the vortex of the Cold War and the U.S. war in Vietnam. For the next 5 years there was civil war between the Khmer Rouge (the Cambodian communists) and the U.S.-backed rightist government of General Lon Nol. The United States provided both military and economic assistance to the Lon Nol government. The secret bombing of the Cambodian countryside by the United States and the civil war drove hundreds of thousands of rural people into the capital of Phnom Penh and devastated the economy.

On 17 April 1975, the Khmer Rouge captured the capital and immediately evacuated the population to the countryside. There then ensued the most radical **socialist** experiment in the history of the world, in which basically the entire population became a huge work camp engaged in various agricultural activities. As a result, as many as possibly 2 million Cambodians may have died between 1975 and 1978, due to starvation, overwork, disease, and executions (of those who were part of the old elite, those perceived to be a threat to the state, or those who were uncooperative).

In December 1978, the Vietnamese intervened to drive the Khmer Rouge to the remote countryside in the west and northwest and installed a new Vietnamese-oriented Cambodian government, which was called the People's Republic of Kampuchea (PRK). Then Cambodia became a normal economy, though it still suffered from continued conflict with the Khmer Rouge. During this period, it also suffered from an economic boycott by the United States and other countries who would not recognize the legitimacy of the new government. In 1991, **communism** came to an end with the establishment of the State of Cambodia and the 2-year presence of the United Nations Transition Authority in Cambodia (UNTAC) to oversee the transition to a multi-party democracy and free market economy. UN-supervised national elections were held in 1993. However, real political stability came to Cambodia only in 1998 with new national elections and the death of Khmer Rouge leader Pol Pot in April 1998.

With this new stability, the Cambodian economy shows signs of recovering. Its being a dollarized economy (an economy which uses the U.S. dollar) gave it some immunity from the currency **devaluations** suffered by its close neighbors, such as Thailand and Laos. Cambodia achieved impressive economic growth of 4.5 percent in 1999 and 5 to 5.5 percent in 2000.

Two industries which have greatly helped the recovery of the Cambodian economy have been the garment industry and tourism. Output from the garment industry in 1993 was only US$4 million, but by 1999 it had increased dramatically to US$600 million. Cambodia is extremely fortunate to be home to the great Angkor Wat complex, recently publicized in the popular adventure feature film *Tomb Raider*. Cambodia wisely decided to allow direct international flights to Siem Reap, the gateway to Angkor Wat, and is one of the few countries in the world (if any) to allow international airlines to fly domestic flights within Cambodia. This flexibility has been a boon to Cambodian tourism, which was up 34 percent in 2000. A 3-day pass to visit Angkor Wat costs US$60. Thus, tourism is a major new source of significant foreign exchange earnings. Cambodia also benefits from considerable international aid, constituting 61 percent of its public funds.

POLITICS, GOVERNMENT, AND TAXATION

Prior to 1991, Cambodia had long been dominated by authoritarian regimes. Since 1993, however, Cambodia has had a multi-party democracy. During its first phase of democracy, Cambodia actually had 2 prime ministers, 1 from each of the 2 major political parties, as a kind of political compromise. In 1993, Cambodia became a constitutional democracy with the popular Norodom Sihanouk serving as the king. Sihanouk has been an important force in contributing to compromise among competing political factions. The system of having 2 prime ministers, however, became unworkable and was highly inefficient. It also created a particularly complex environment for international investors or others pursuing economic or development activities in Cambodia. New national elections in 26 July 1998, resulted in a new government with only 1 prime minister.

Cambodia has a **bicameral** legislature, consisting of a popularly elected National Assembly (122 seats) and a Senate (61 seats). The members of both bodies serve 5-year terms. The king chooses the prime minister after a vote of confidence by the National Assembly. Since 1998, the prime minister has been Hun Sen. There is also a judicial branch led by the Supreme Court.

Taxation and the ability to collect revenues by the government remain weak, though government revenues increased 40 percent between 1998 and 1999. Such revenues represented only 11 percent of the GDP and **direct taxes** accounted for only 6 percent of total domestic revenue. Corruption and an inability to collect taxes plagued the government throughout the 1990s.

INFRASTRUCTURE, POWER, AND COMMUNICATIONS

As the result of decades of conflict and civil war, Cambodia's infrastructure is extremely weak. There is a limited train system which runs to the southern seaport of Kampong Saom and to the northwest (Poipet) on the Thai border. There are plans to rehabilitate the railway to Poipet and to build a new railway linking Phnom Penh and Ho Chi Minh City in Vietnam as part of the trans-Asia railway. These railways cover a total of 603 kilometers (375 miles). The country has 35,769 kilometers (22,227 miles) of highways, of which only 11.6 percent are paved. The best road is from the capital to the seaport of Kampong Saom. Past U.S. aid facilitated the renovation of that important road. Many factories are locating along that road because of its excellent access to a major Pacific seaport. Travel to many remote provinces is often done by plane. The country has 19 airports. The country also has 3,700 kilometers (2,299 miles) of navigable waterways, and it is possible to travel to the famous Angkor Wat complex by jetboat using the Tonle Sap River and the great Tonle Sap Lake.

In Cambodia's agricultural sector traditional forms of power such as waterwheels are still being used. Much of the population, especially in rural areas, does not have access to electricity. In 1999, Cambodia's electricity production was 147 million kilowatt-hours (kWh), of which 40.8 percent were derived from hydroelectric power; the rest was from fossil fuels.

Communications in urban areas has greatly improved in recent years. The number of mobile phones (which were estimated at 80,000 in 2000) are now 4 times greater than the number of conventional phone lines. Few rural areas have access to conventional phone lines. There are 10 radio and 5 television stations. In the capital of Phnom Penh, inexpensive cable television is available with a great number of diverse channels in many languages such as Thai, Japanese, Chinese, English, and French. The country had an estimated 97,000 televisions in 1997.

Cambodia has joined the Internet and has a .kh suffix. However, Internet access in Cambodia is extremely expensive relative to local income levels, which greatly restricts the use of the Internet by non-wealthy Cambodians.

With respect to print media, there has been a rapid expansion in recent years. There are currently 3 English language papers, a French language paper, 88 Khmer language newspapers, 19 Khmer language magazines, and 6 Khmer language bulletins.

ECONOMIC SECTORS

During the decade of the 1990s, Cambodia's agricultural sector grew at an average of 2.1 percent, its industrial sector grew at an annual rate of 9.6 percent, and its service sector grew at a rate of 6.9 percent, resulting in shifts in the economic structure of Cambodia. In 1998, agriculture contributed 43 percent of GDP, industry contributed 20 percent, and services contributed 37 percent.

Based on the 1998 census, the active **labor force** in Cambodia was 4,909,100. Around 76.8 percent of these individuals were engaged in agriculture; only 3.4 percent in industry; and 19.8 percent in services.

Though most Cambodians are still involved in agricultural work, the country's industrial and service sectors are both growing rapidly. With Cambodia's excellent tourism potential and its low cost labor in close proximity to a major seaport, the economy will continue to shift in the direction of greater industry and services. Nike, for example, is now sourcing apparel production in Cambodia.

Communications

Country	Newspapers	Radios	TV Sets[a]	Cable subscribers[a]	Mobile Phones[a]	Fax Machines[a]	Personal Computers[a]	Internet Hosts[b]	Internet Users[b]
	1996	1997	1998	1998	1998	1998	1998	1999	1999
Cambodia	2	127	123	N/A	6	0.3	0.9	0.12	4
United States	215	2,146	847	244.3	256	78.4	458.6	1,508.77	74,100
China	N/A	333	272	40.0	19	1.6	8.9	0.50	8,900
Vietnam	4	107	47	N/A	2	0.3	6.4	0.00	100

[a]Data are from International Telecommunication Union, *World Telecommunication Development Report 1999* and are per 1,000 people.
[b]Data are from the Internet Software Consortium (http://www.isc.org) and are per 10,000 people.

SOURCE: World Bank. *World Development Indicators 2000.*

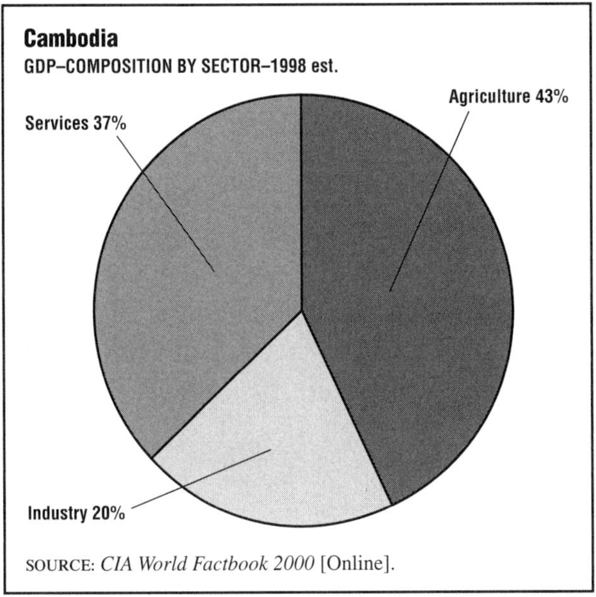

SOURCE: *CIA World Factbook 2000* [Online].

AGRICULTURE

With a population density of just 263 persons per square kilometer (681 per square mile) of arable land, Cambodia has special advantages compared to much more densely populated rural areas such as Bangladesh, Vietnam, or Indonesia, whose densities are 3 or 4 times as great. However, the sector is far below its potential. The 80 percent of the workforce engaged in agriculture account for only 43 percent of GDP in 1998. Average rice paddy yield in 1997 was 1.8 tons per hectare, compared to an average of 2.7 tons per hectare achieved by neighboring countries. Among numerous problems affecting agricultural productivity are a lack of irrigation, shortage of male manpower, and the continued presence of land mines in the northwest region of the country, a major rice-growing area. At present only 16 percent of rice land is irrigated, though the government has the goal to increase this figure to 20 percent by the year 2003. Important secondary food crops are maize, cassava, sweet potatoes, beans, vegetables, and fruit. Among industrial agricultural crops are cotton, soybeans, sesame, jute, sugar cane, and rubber. Principal crops in 1999 in order of magnitude of production were rice, cassava, vegetables, sugar cane, maize, soybeans, sweet potatoes, and mung beans.

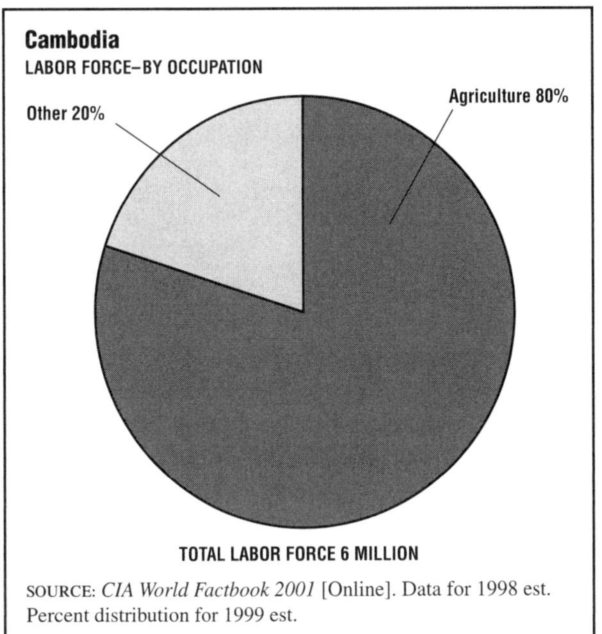

SOURCE: *CIA World Factbook 2001* [Online]. Data for 1998 est. Percent distribution for 1999 est.

FORESTRY AND LOGGING. In 1969, 73 percent of Cambodia was forested. By 1997, only 58 percent of the country was forested. Much of this deforestation has resulted from illegal logging activities, with logs destined for Thailand, which has had a long-standing ban on logging. Illegal logging seriously threatens the long-term viability of Cambodia's timber resources. With sustainable forestry, the government could earn an estimated US$40 million to US$80 million in government revenue per year according to some estimates.

FISHING. Major sources of freshwater fish are the great Tonle Sap Lake in the center of Cambodia and the Mekong and Tonle Sap Rivers. However, deforestation represents a serious threat to freshwater fishing because of increased runoff into rivers and lakes. In 1999 Cambodia produced 124,000 metric tons of fish, of which 57.3 percent were freshwater fish.

INDUSTRY

Industry now employs approximately 250,000 people, 5 percent of the labor force. Until the mid-1990s, Cambodia's industry was dominated by rice mills (of which there were approximately 1,500) and 80 to 100 state-owned enterprises, a legacy from the communist period. The major new development in the latter half of the 1990s is the rapid development of Cambodia's garment industry, facilitated by the achievement of political stability, an abundant supply of cheap labor, good road access to Cambodia's major seaport, and having Most Favored Nation trading status since 1997 for exports to the large U.S. market. By the end of 1999, there were approximately 200 garment factories employing about 100,000 workers. In 1995, by comparison, there were only 13 such factories. Another major growth area associated with the need to build and rebuild Cambodia's infrastructure has been construction, which is expected to increase in importance as more investment is made in infrastructure.

MINING. Mining contributed only 0.3 percent of the GDP in 1999 and the country has few commercially viable mineral resources. However, in western Cambodia in the Pailin area near Thailand, there is an abundance of high-quality gems, primarily sapphires and rubies. The trade in such gems was a major source of revenue for the Khmer Rouge in support of their guerilla warfare. Even currently the trade in gems is largely part of the **informal economy** and does not provide benefit to the central government.

SERVICES

BANKING AND FINANCE. Under the new capitalist system, the former socialist state bank became the National Bank of Cambodia (NBC) in 1992. The new system allows for private commercial banks, of which there are now approximately 30. Use of such banking services is limited, since much of the population has a preference for keeping their savings in either gold or U.S. dollars.

GOVERNMENT EMPLOYMENT. With the shift from a socialist to a capitalist system, the **public sector** has been downsized. Nearly all of the former state enterprises have been **privatized**. Many individuals lost jobs through this process. Major efforts have also been initiated to reduce the size of the military and police forces, including the elimination of "ghost soldiers" and "ghost police" who were listed only for budgetary purposes.

TOURISM. Cambodia has excellent potential to develop its tourism sector, which has grown significantly since the achievement of political stability in 1998. In 1999 tourism revenues increased 41 percent, and tourist arrivals have been growing 20 to 30 percent annually since 1998. In 1999, the number of visitors was 271,100. The largest number of tourists are from the United States, followed by China, France, and Taiwan.

Cambodia's major tourist attractions are the great Angkor Wat complex, attractive beaches with related tourist infrastructure at Kompong Saom (Sihanoukville), and **ecotourism** in pristine Ratanakiri Province in Cambodia's remote northeast. The capital Phnom Penh also is a charming city with numerous attractions. Its famous Royal Hotel has been totally remodeled. In the Angkor Wat area the Grand Hotel d'Angkor has been remodeled by the Raffles Group. At one point, 1 cabinet minister even proposed to have all of Cambodia become a national park as part of an effort to make Cambodia unique and attractive. This proposal was not approved, though Cambodia has developed an extensive system of national parks.

The operation of direct international flights to Siem Reap, gateway to the Angkor Wat area, has significantly improved Cambodian tourism, while adversely affecting tourism to the capital, Phnom Penh, which is no longer the sole gateway to Angkor Wat.

Primarily as the result of the presence of many UN military forces in the 1991–93 period and the shift to a free market capitalist system, a commercial sex industry has emerged which has contributed to international tourism, especially to Phnom Penh. Numerous Vietnamese prostitutes are guestworkers in this industry.

RETAIL AND THE INFORMAL ECONOMY. With a high level of unemployment and **underemployment**, an informal **retail** economy provides employment to large numbers, especially in urban areas. In Phnom Penh there are a number of local markets and 2 large markets popular with tourists (the Central and Russian Markets).

INTERNATIONAL TRADE

For years Cambodia has been running a negative trade balance, meaning that the value of its imports exceeds that of its exports. In 1997 the deficit was US$328 million; in 1998, US$391.4 million; and US$215.7 million in 1999. Contributing to an improved trade balance was the dramatic growth in the export of garments, now the country's major export. The export of garments more than doubled in value between 1997 and 1999. Cambodia's major exports in 1999 (in order of value) were garments, logs and sawn timber, and crude rubber. Its major imports (in order of value) were petroleum products, cigarettes, motorcycles, gold, and other vehicles. In 2000, Cambodia had exports of US$942 million and imports of US$1.3 billion.

Cambodia's leading export markets (in order of importance) in 1999 were Singapore, Hong Kong, Thailand, Vietnam, Taiwan, Japan, and Malaysia. Its imports were primarily from (in order of importance) Thailand, Hong Kong, Singapore, Vietnam, Japan, Indonesia, and France. Its greatest **trade deficit** is with Thailand followed by Vietnam and Hong Kong. It has a trade surplus with Singapore, Malaysia, and Taiwan. With the collapse of the Soviet Union and its shift to **capitalism**, Cambodia's trade with Russia has declined dramatically.

MONEY

Since Cambodia is basically a dollarized economy, the National Bank of Cambodia has only limited influ-

Exchange rates: Cambodia

new riels per US$1	
Jan 2001	3,909.0
2000	3,840.8
1999	3,807.8
1998	3,744.4
1997	2,946.3
1996	2,624.1

SOURCE: CIA *World Factbook 2001* [ONLINE].

ence with respect to **monetary policy**. Given the strength of the dollar and, thus, Cambodia's relative immunity to currency devaluation problems, the country has done well in avoiding **inflation**, which was virtually nil in 2000, 4 percent in 1999, and only 12 percent in 1998, despite the Asian economic crisis. In fact, inflation has been extremely low since 1994.

POVERTY AND WEALTH

Cambodia is currently one of the poorest countries in the world. Its per-capita income is only US$260. However, if adjusted for **purchasing power parity** (which takes into account the low prices for goods in Cambodia), its per-capita income jumps rather dramatically to US$1300. Approximately 36 percent of the population is living below the poverty line. Because of the years of civil war and strife, more than 25 percent of households in Phnom Penh are headed by a single mother. The existence of poverty and unemployment among less-educated women has contributed to the emergence of a commercial sex industry. This industry is part of a large informal economy in Cambodia that is not reflected in the official statistics reported in this entry.

Distribution of Income or Consumption by Percentage Share: Cambodia

Lowest 10%	2.9
Lowest 20%	6.9
Second 20%	10.7
Third 20%	14.7
Fourth 20%	20.1
Highest 20%	47.6
Highest 10%	33.8

Survey year: 1997

Note: This information refers to expenditure shares by percentiles of the population and is ranked by per capita expenditure.

SOURCE: *2000 World Development Indicators* [CD-ROM].

WORKING CONDITIONS

Working conditions in Cambodia are best for those with good education who can find modern sector employment, particularly in the rapidly growing service sector such as in tourism or banking. There are also now in Cambodia a large number of both international and local non-governmental organizations (NGOs) which hire more educated Cambodians for work on diverse development projects.

Those working in the public sector, such as public school teachers, face the problem of receiving extremely low wages. Thus, they often are forced to take other part-time work to pay for their expenses.

Farmers possessing their own adequate land can enjoy a certain degree of affluent subsistence, if they can grow adequate rice, fruit, and vegetables and have access to fish resources. Recently, however, farmers, especially from western Cambodia, have complained about losing their land to business interests planning various kinds of development or **agribusiness**.

For those working in the rapidly expanding garment industry, there is concern about working conditions and low wages, though these jobs are desperately needed. Conditions are likely to vary considerably depending on the sub-contractors involved. Also, it is not appropriate to look simply at salaries of such workers in dollar terms. People with modern sector jobs tend to pool their "low" salaries in extended family situations. Also costs are much lower in Cambodia than in many other countries, particularly more advanced industrial countries.

GDP per Capita (US$)

Country	1975	1980	1985	1990	1998
Cambodia	N/A	N/A	N/A	240	279
United States	19,364	21,529	23,200	25,363	29,683
China	138	168	261	349	727
Nepal	149	148	165	182	217

SOURCE: United Nations. *Human Development Report 2000; Trends in human development and per capita income.*

COUNTRY HISTORY AND ECONOMIC DEVELOPMENT

2ND-6TH CENTURIES. The state of Funan, predecessor to Cambodia, is established in the Mekong Delta.

9TH-15TH CENTURIES. The glorious Angkor Empire reigns in present-day Cambodia.

1863. France establishes a protectorate over Cambodia.

1953. On 8 November, Cambodia claims its independence from France.

1955–70. The reign of Prince Sihanouk as ruler of the Kingdom of Cambodia; Cambodia remains neutral and peaceful in a sea of political turmoil.

1970. Neutral Prince Sihanouk is ousted by General Lon Nol and Prince Sirik Matak, who abolish the monarchy and rename the country the Khmer Republic (KR). Subsequently U.S. and South Vietnamese armies invade eastern Cambodia and the economy is totally disrupted by the civil war that ensues.

1973. The United States carries out an intensive campaign of bombing rural Cambodia, forcing a tremendous influx of people into Phnom Penh and other cities and disrupting Cambodian agriculture.

1975. In April, Phnom Penh is overtaken by the radical Khmer Rouge, who are led by Pol Pot. The urban population is forced into the countryside and over the next 3 years, the country—renamed Democratic Kampuchea (DK)—becomes a massive work camp, with up to 2 million dying from overwork, starvation, poor health, and executions.

1978. Vietnam invades Cambodia and overthrows the Pol Pot regime.

1979–89. The Vietnamese-backed government (People's Republic of Kampuchea, PRK) wages a long civil war against the Khmer Rouge. Though the economy returns to near normalcy, it is boycotted economically by the United States, the Association of Southeast Asian Nations (ASEAN), and many other nations because of its ties to Vietnam and the former USSR.

1993. United Nations-supervised elections are won by Prince Sihanouk's party, FUNCINPEC; as a compromise, a new 2-headed government is formed with 2 prime ministers, 1 representing FUNCINPEC and the other representing the Cambodia People's Party (CPP), the former communist party.

1997. The 2-headed government ends with military action by CPP Prime Minister Hun Sen.

1998. New national elections won by CPP and Hun Sen. Following the death of Khmer Rouge leader Pol Pot in April, peace and stability return to Cambodia for the first time in 3 decades, and tourism begins to grow rapidly.

2001. The consultative group of international donors pledge US$560 million of international aid to Cambodia, primarily for infrastructure development.

FUTURE TRENDS

With its debilitated infrastructure resulting from 3 decades of civil war and strife, Cambodia faces tremendous economic challenges in the years ahead. Major disparities between rural and urban areas remain a persistent problem. Reform implementation, particularly in the area of governance, also remains a major issue. There is considerable debate about the government and its commitment to reforms. In June, 2001, the International Monetary Fund representative in Cambodia stated "that the donors generally recognize that Cambodia, more than many other countries, has shown a high level of commitment to reform." The 2001 increase in aid pledges by the consultative group reflects such underlying confidence.

With its great Angkor Wat complex, Cambodia has tremendous tourism potential. The 11 September 2001 attacks on the United States will adversely affect Cambodian tourism in the short term, but in the long term, its tourist industry will provide substantial revenues to the government, which can be used for both physical and human infrastructure improvements. This special resource is not seen in many other developing countries. The country is also fortunate to have a deep seaport at Sihanoukville, which is being upgraded. With its great Tonle Sap Lake and with little of its agricultural land currently irrigated, it has considerable potential for improvements in agriculture as well. Finally, Cambodia has a special "wild card" that has been ignored. A good portion of its current population are survivors of the Khmer Rouge tragedy and, thus, represent a special genre of individuals with unusual capacities for survival, perseverance, and flexibility. Such a special human resource base augurs well for the economic future of Cambodia.

DEPENDENCIES

Cambodia has no territories or colonies.

BIBLIOGRAPHY

Ayres, David. *Anatomy of a Crisis: Education, Development, and the State in Cambodia, 1953–1998.* Honolulu: University of Hawaii Press, 2000.

Cambodia at a Glance. Washington, D.C.: The World Bank, August 29, 2000.

Chandler, David. *A History of Cambodia.* 2nd ed. Boulder, CO: Westview Press, 1996.

"China and Cambodia: Bearer of Gifts." *The Economist.* 23 June 2001.

Eckardt, James. *The Year of Living Stupidly: Boom, Bust and Cambodia.* Bangkok: Asia Books, 2001.

Economist Intelligence Unit. *Country Profile: Cambodia.* London: Economist Intelligence Unit, 2001.

Embassy of Cambodia in Washington, D.C. <http://www.embassy.org/cambodia>. Accessed October 2001.

Export-Import Bank of Thailand. *Kingdom of Cambodia Economic Indicators.* <http://www.exim.go.th/main_econmic_cambodia_emerging.htm>. Accessed October 2001.

Livingston, Carol. *Gecko Tails: A Journey Through Cambodia.* London: Phoenix, 1997.

Osborne, Milton. *The Mekong: Turbulent Past, Uncertain Future.* New York: Atlantic Monthly Press, 2000.

Rooney, Dawn F. *Angkor: Temples of Cambodia's Kings.* Lincolnwood, Illinois: Passport Books, 1994.

Summers, Laura, and Sok Hach. "Economy of Cambodia." *The Far East and Australasia 2001.* London: Europa Publications, 2001.

U.S. Central Intelligence Agency. *World Factbook 2001.* <http://www.odci.gov/cia/publications/factbook/index.html>. Accessed September 2001.

U.S. Department of State. *Background Notes: Cambodia, January 1996.* <http://www.state.gov/www/background_notes/cambodia_0196_bgn.html>. Accessed October 2001.

Westlake, Michael, editor. "Cambodia." In *Asia 2001 Yearbook.* Hong Kong: Far Eastern Economic Review, 2000.

—Gerald Fry

CHINA

People's Republic of China
Zhonghua Renmin Gongheguo

CAPITAL: Beijing (Peking).

MONETARY UNIT: Chinese Renminbi (in Chinese "Renminbi" means "People's Currency") Yuan (RMB). One yuan equals ten jiao; one jiao equals ten fen. Paper bills include 1, 2, 5, 10, 20, 50, and 100 yuan; 1 jiao, 2 jiao, 5 jiao; 1 fen, 2 fen, 5 fen. There are coins of 1 yuan; 1 jiao, 2 jiao, 5 jiao; 1 fen, 2 fen, and 5 fen.

CHIEF EXPORTS: Crude oil, textile yarn, fabrics, chemicals, coal, soybeans, vegetable oil, rice, and small machinery.

CHIEF IMPORTS: Machinery, steel and other metals, wheat, chemicals, and fertilizers.

GROSS DOMESTIC PRODUCT: US$4.8 trillion (purchasing power parity, 1999 est).

BALANCE OF TRADE: **Exports:** US$194.9 billion (f.o.b., 1999). **Imports:** US$165.8 billion (c.i.f., 1999).

COUNTRY OVERVIEW

LOCATION AND SIZE. China is situated in the eastern part of Asia, on the west coast of the Pacific Ocean, in the southeastern part of the Eurasian continent, bordering the East China Sea, Korea Bay, Yellow Sea, and South China Sea, between North Korea and Vietnam. Its border countries include Afghanistan, Bhutan, Burma, (Hong Kong), India, Kazakhstan, North Korea, Kyrgyzstan, Laos, (Macau), Mongolia, Nepal, Pakistan, Russia, Tajikistan, and Vietnam. The land area consists of 9,596,960 square kilometers (3,696,000 square miles), the third largest in the world after Russia and Canada. The country's coastline is 14,500 kilometers (9,010 miles) long. China is divided into 22 provinces, 4 municipalities, 5 autonomous regions, and 2 special administration regions (Hong Kong and Macau). Beijing, the capital, is also the cultural and educational center of China. The city has an area of 65 square kilometers (25 square miles) and is partially surrounded by walls that were built in the 15th century.

POPULATION. The population of China was estimated at 1,262 million in July of 2000, an increase of 10.36 percent from the 1990 population of 1,143 million. In 2000 the population growth rate was estimated at 0.9 percent, the birth rate was 16.12 per 1,000, and the death rate was 6.73 per 1,000. With a projected annual population growth rate of 0.9 percent between 2000 and 2010, the population is expected to reach 1,392.5 million in 2010. A simulation study conducted by the China State Statistics Bureau indicates that country's total population will peak at 1,402 to 1,550 million in the 2030s or 2040s.

The population of China consists of 56 ethnic groups. Han Chinese make up 91.9 percent while Zhuang, Uygur, Hui, Yi, Tibetan, Miao, Manchu, Mongol, Buyi, Korean, and other ethnic minorities make up 8.1 percent. The great majority, 68 percent of the population, is between ages 15 and 64; while 25 percent is at the age of 14 or below, 7 percent is at 65 or older. The life expectancy at birth in 2000 is estimated at 71.4 years (total population), 69.6 years (male) and 73.3 years (female). The country's high life expectancy and low infant mortality rates are envied by much richer nations.

In 1949, when China became a **communist** nation, the population was about 541 million. Over the following 10 years, it increased by another 118 million. It continued to rise through the 1960s. The government encouraged this increase so China could develop water control and communication infrastructures. The government also thought increased production could help produce more food and strengthen the nation's defense. Twenty years later, the millions born during that period contributed to another baby boom. By 1970, there were roughly 830 million Chinese. The over-growing population had generated serious problems and negatively affected the national economy.

To slow the population growth the government introduced a one-child-per-family policy in the late 1970s.

The policy was created not only to deal with the huge population problem but as a prerequisite for the social and financial planning necessary in a **socialist** system. The policy is more strictly enforced in urban areas and is unpopular in the rural areas where male children are more important. However, it is enforced enough to make most couples obey it. With the introduction of the one-child policy, the population growth has slowed, with probably 250 million fewer births since 1979. Two types of obvious changes in population have taken place. First, the people are aging. The number of people 65 or older is estimated at 87.8 million in 2000 and is expected to be 167 million by 2020, compared with an elderly population of 66 million in 1990. Second, the population is becoming more urban. For instance, the urban population was at 297 million in 1990, up 90 million from 1982. During the same period, the populations of the 2 largest cities, Beijing and Shanghai, have increased 17 percent and 13 percent respectively.

Overpopulation is the number-one global problem. Many people question controlling population through legislation. Even after the 20 years that the Chinese civilization has trusted this solution to solve their problem, some still violate the policy. However, this does not imply that legislative control is wrong, especially when dealing with the extremes facing China. Backers of China's population policy say that such state-mandated birth control and family planning is necessary not only for the well-being of China but for that of the whole world.

OVERVIEW OF ECONOMY

China's economy has grown increasingly faster since the 1978 introduction of economic reforms. The Chinese official statistics show that **real gross domestic product** (GDP) from 1979 to 1999 was growing at an average annual rate of 9.7 percent, making China one the world's fastest growing economies. According to the World Bank, China's rapid development has raised nearly 200 million people out of extreme poverty.

Since its establishment in 1949 and until the end of 1978, China maintained a centrally planned, or command, economy. The state directed and controlled a large share of the country's economic output; the state set production goals, controlled prices, and allocated resources throughout most of the economy. By 1978, nearly three-fourths of the country's industrial production was produced by centrally controlled state-owned enterprises (SOEs) according to centrally planned output targets. There were almost no private enterprises or foreign invested firms in China. It was estimated that China's real GDP grew at an average annual rate of about 5.3 percent from 1960 to 1978. Because the central planning economic systems and government economic policies put little emphasis on profitability or competition, the country's economy was relatively stagnant and inefficient. As a result the Chinese living standards were substantially lower than those of many other developing countries. The Chinese government took steps to improve economic growth and raise living standards in the late 1970s.

The first of China's economic reforms started in 1978 when Den Xiaoping came into power again. The reforms concentrated on the agricultural production system in rural areas. The central government initiated price and ownership incentives for farmers; for the first time, farmers were able to sell a portion of their crops on the free market. In addition, the reforms tried to attract foreign investment, boost exports, and begin the importation of high technology products into the country. To do this, the government established 4 special economic zones (SEZs). Additional reforms followed in stages that sought to decentralize economic policymaking in several economic sectors, especially trade. As a part of the decentralization of economic policymaking, provincial and local governments took economic control of various enterprises, allowing them to operate and compete on free market principles.

The economic reforms had produced such promising economic growth that by the middle of 1980s the government selected additional coastal regions and cities as open cities and development zones to test more free market reforms and to offer tax and trade incentives to attract investment from overseas. Moreover, the state gradually eliminated the **price controls** on a wide range of products. Agricultural output doubled in the 1980s, and industry also demonstrated major gains, especially in coastal areas close to Hong Kong and opposite Taiwan, where foreign investment helped stimulate output of both domestic and export goods. Even more reforms were initiated in late 1993 when China's leadership approved additional long-term reforms which would allow the state enterprises to continue to dominate many key industries in what was now termed "a socialist market economy."

The transition of the country's economic system from a command to a market-based economy helped fuel a strong average growth. Between the start of an economic reform program in 1978 and 1995, the GDP growth was 8.0 percent a year. The growth remained strong from 1996 to 2000. In 1999 China became the second largest economy in the world, after the United States. But China's **GDP per capita** of US$3,800 was much less than the United States.

China's trade and investment reforms as well as its incentives led to a surge in **foreign direct investment** (FDI), which has served as a major source of China's capital growth. Annual utilized FDI in China grew from US$636 million in 1983 to US$45.6 billion in 1998 (but dropped to an estimated level of US$40.5 billion in 1999), making China, in the late 1990s, the second largest destination of FDI (after the United States). About two-thirds of FDI in China comes from Hong Kong and Taiwan. The United States is the third largest investor in China, accounting for 8.0 percent (US$24.6 billion) of total FDI in China from 1979 to 1999.

Since the reforms, China has made great strides in improving its social welfare. Both consumption and saving have more than doubled, and the poverty rate has declined. According to the World Bank, about 200 million Chinese who used to live in absolute poverty have been raised above the minimum poverty line. And only 10 percent of the country's population of 1.25 billion were illiterate.

Although the reforms were encouraging, the Chinese government experienced various difficulties. It struggled to collect revenues due from provinces, businesses, and individuals; to reduce corruption and other economic crimes coinciding with the reforms; and to maintain daily operations of the large state-owned enterprises. Many of the state-owned enterprises had not participated in the vigorous expansion of the economy, and some of them had lost the ability to pay full wages and pensions.

POLITICS, GOVERNMENT, AND TAXATION

China's form of government is a communist state known as a People's Republic. The Chinese Communist Party (CCP) is the leading political party in China. Unlike parties in Western democracies, CCP is a tightly organized political force that controls and leads society at all levels. The party sets policy and controls its execution through government officials who are required to be CCP members. It is organized as a hierarchy, with power concentrated at the top. Above the local units, or cells, is a pyramid-like structure of party congresses and committees at various levels, culminating in the National Party Congress.

Generally, CCP's national congress is supposed to meet every 5 years, though this has not always been the case. When it is not in session, direction of the party is in the hands of a Central Committee of about 200 members, which is symbolically elected by the congress according to the name list distributed by the congress board. The symbolically elected Central Committee, in turn, elects the Political Bureau. It is within the Political Bureau and its elite Standing Committee that power is concentrated, which make the state's highest-level decisions. There is also a secretariat, which carries on the day-to-day business of the party.

Theoretically, party membership is open to anyone over 18 years of age who accepts the party program and is willing to work actively in one of its organizations. In reality, only those who are deemed to be fellows of local CCP branch leaders will have the chance to be recruited into the party. Members are expected to abide by the party's discipline and to serve as model citizens. The backbone of the party consists of full-time paid workers known as **cadres** (Chinese, *ganbu*). The term *cadre* is also used for public officials holding responsible positions, who may or may not be members of the party.

The People's Republic was first governed according to the "Common Program" and organic laws adopted in 1949. Since 1954, 4 constitutions followed, each reflecting shifts in policy and the balance of power among factions of the top leadership. The government structure forms a pyramid, ranging from local units such as residents' (urban) and villagers' committees through counties, prefectures, and then to the 22 provinces, 5 autonomous regions, and 4 special status municipalities (Beijing, Shanghai, Tianjin, and Chongqing), each with its own people's congress and administrative organs, and 2 special administration regions (Hong Kong, Macau). At the top of the government structure is the national government in Beijing.

The chief of state is President Jiang Zemin, who has served as president since 1993. The president and vice-president are elected to 5-year terms by the National People's Congress. The head of government is Premier Zhu Rongji, who has served in his position since 1998. The president nominates the premier who is confirmed by the Congress.

The National People's Congress is the legislature of China and serves annual sessions with 5-year terms. The Standing Committee of the Congress exercises its functions between sessions. The highest administrative organ is the State Council (similar to the United States Cabinet), headed by the premier. The court system parallels the administrative system. However, the Chinese have traditionally tended to resolve conflicts through social rather than legal or judicial mediation, and the rule of law as it is known in Western countries is currently not well-known. The number of lawyers is very small compared with many Western countries, and legal methods are not familiar to most Chinese.

The judiciary is headed by the Supreme People's Court, which consists of 1 president and 1 vice president, who each serve 4-year terms. Other courts include Special People's Courts and Local People's Courts. Supreme People's Procuratorates and Local People's Procuratorates enforce laws.

Tax policies are administered by the Ministry of Finance (MOF) and the State Administration of Taxation (SAT). The SAT is the central tax authority at ministerial level. Tax policy is the exclusive domain of the central government although the local government may input some efforts in taxation. With the adoption of a new tax system in 1994, the country adopted a tax revenue-sharing system. This means that some taxes, mostly **direct taxes**, are assigned to local government, while other taxes, such as **value-added tax** (VAT), are shared between the central government (75 percent) and local government (25 percent). Shared taxes are levied on the same tax base and then allocated between different levels of governments at pre-determined ratios.

The ratio of the total tax revenue to GDP has declined over the 1990s, although the total tax revenue has increased substantially. The main reason for the decline is the rapid growth of the service sector, whose tax burden is lower than that of manufacturing, and an increase in foreign investment, mostly in special zones where very generous tax incentives have been granted. The 1994 tax reform emphasized taxation on consumption, and currently efforts are being made to fine tune these **indirect taxes**, particularly the administration and collection of VAT. The abuse of invoices is a serious, continuing tax fraud problem. The main tax types for business, citizens, foreign enterprises, and foreigners in China are value-added tax (VAT); consumption tax; business tax; foreign enterprises **income tax**; individual income tax; customs **duties**; urban **estate tax**; vehicle and vessel usage and license plate tax; land appreciation tax; stamp duties; resources tax; and deed tax.

INFRASTRUCTURE, POWER, AND COMMUNICATIONS

Infrastructure in China varies from fairly good to very poor. Resources for industry are currently heavily constrained by infrastructure shortages. The government

Communications

Country	Newspapers	Radios	TV Sets[a]	Cable subscribers[a]	Mobile Phones[a]	Fax Machines[a]	Personal Computers[a]	Internet Hosts[b]	Internet Users[b]
	1996	1997	1998	1998	1998	1998	1998	1999	1999
China	N/A	333	272	40.0	19	1.6	8.9	0.50	8,900
United States	215	2,146	847	244.3	256	78.4	458.6	1,508.77	74,100
Japan	578	955	707	114.8	374	126.8	237.2	163.75	27,060
Russia	105	418	420	78.5	5	0.4	40.6	13.06	2,700

[a]Data are from International Telecommunication Union, *World Telecommunication Development Report 1999* and are per 1,000 people.
[b]Data are from the Internet Software Consortium (http://www.isc.org) and are per 10,000 people.

SOURCE: World Bank. *World Development Indicators 2000.*

recognizes infrastructure as the key to achieving full-industrialized status and to offsetting a diminishing cheap labor advantage. Energy and transportation needs in particular have stalled growth and fueled **inflation**, while telecommunications is acknowledged as a requirement for further economic growth.

RAILWAYS. China has an estimated 69,412 kilometers (43,131 miles) of railroad. Every province-level administrative unit except Tibet was served by rail, and plans were being made to extend a line south from the Lanzhou-Urumqi line to Lhasa, in Xizang (Tibet). Railways have been the most important tools for transportation in China. For example, more than 50 percent of the country's traffic is moved by the railroad system. China's railway network consists of a series of north-south trunk lines, crossed by a few major east-west lines. Most of the large cities are served by these trunk lines, forming a nationwide network, with Beijing as its hub.

ROADS AND HIGHWAYS. China has 1,209,800 kilometers (751,894 miles) of highway in total, among which 271,300 kilometers (168,586 miles) are paved (with at least 24,474 kilometers or 15,200 miles of expressways). The network of all-weather roads and highways is not a unified national system with consistent standards; the conditions of many of the roads are poor. Despite its shortcomings, the road network is probably adequate to meet the country's current needs. China has a small number of cars, trucks, and buses as compared with the United States or Japan. In the early 1990s there were about 7 million motor vehicles, two-thirds of which were trucks and buses. It produces about 200,000 trucks annually and limited automobiles. An increasing number of cars are owned privately, which will lead fast demand for qualified highways. The highway network accounts for only about 2 percent of total freight traffic.

AIR TRANSPORTATION. China set up the General Administration of Civil Aviation of China (GACAC) after 1949, which has continued to serve as the nation's domestic and international air carrier. Most major cities are served by domestic flights, and a few large cities like Guangzhou, Shanghai, and Beijing have international service. GACAC planes fly to Europe, Japan, the United States, and South Asia. Some provincial and urban authorities operate intercity airlines that carry passengers and freight. There are 206 airports (1996 est.), among which 192 have paved runways.

SHIPPING. China has 110,000 kilometers (68,354 miles) of navigable waterways and 1,746 ships (merchant marine). It has 9,070 kilometers (5,636 miles) of crude oil pipelines, 560 kilometers (348 miles) of petroleum products pipelines and 9,383 kilometers (5,830 miles) of natural gas pipelines (1999 est.).

POWER. China's power sector has performed impressively in support of economic growth during the past twenty years. Faced with the need to expand its power capacity, the state is investing heavily in the construction of new power plants and self-financing capability. Equally significant in the development of the national power sector are the establishment of regional power grids and the implementation of an electricity **tariff** reform to tackle the problems of inefficient power distribution and usage. Electrical power is supplied mainly by the state-owned enterprises. China has effectively **restructured** its power industry by closing a large number of small thermal power plants with high coal consumption, heavy pollution, and poor economic efficiency. According to the official statistics, the country generated 1.16 trillion kilowatt hours (kWh) of electricity in 2000, a 6 percent increase from the previous year; the country has made headway in building and renovating 87 urban power grid projects and 1,590 rural ones. China has also developed its enormous hydroelectric potential so that a larger share of its domestic demand for electric power can be met with renewable hydropower. Renewable hydropower is tapped from moving water such as waterfalls and fast-moving streams.

The reform and opening up policies have brought great leaps and bounds to the development of the country's nuclear power industry. Meanwhile, China attracts foreign funds to supplement the domestic shortage of funds in power construction and to upgrade the technological equipment of the power industry. According to the statistic communiqué of the PRC on the 1998 national economic and social development issued in February of 1999, the newly-increased annual production capacity in 1998 through capital construction projects included 16.9 million kilowatts of power generation by large and medium-sized generators and 47.26 million kilovolt-amperes of power transformer equipment (including 7.79 million kilovolt-amperes of updated power grid in urban and rural areas). China is the country to deliberate the biggest nuclear power station construction plan in the world. According to the central government's plan, by year 2020, China will possess 40,000,000 KM of nuclear power installed capacity.

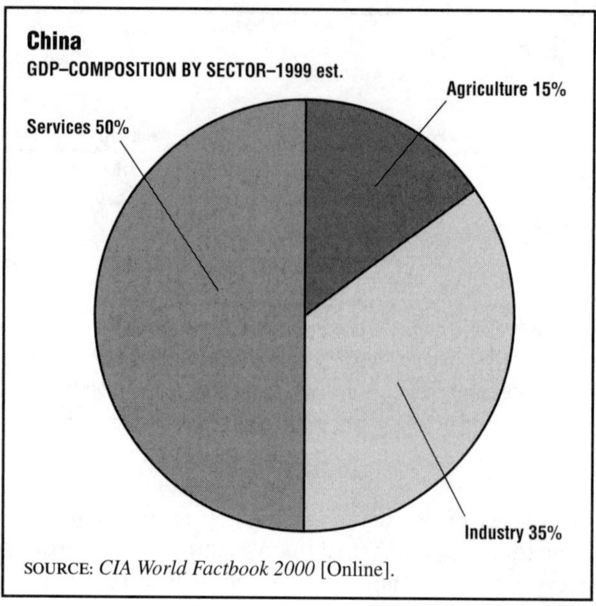

SOURCE: *CIA World Factbook 2000* [Online].

COMMUNICATION. Considerable effort has been expended on the postal and telecommunications systems in China since 1949, but they are still far from meeting Western standards of speed and efficiency. The mail is mainly carried by the nation's railroad. As is the case with transportation, the telecommunications system is sufficient enough to meet the needs of a growing economy. There were 110 million main lines in use (1999 est.) and 23.4 million mobile cellular phones in use (1998). Domestic and international services are increasingly available for private use; an unevenly distributed domestic system serves principal cities, industrial centers, and most small and middle-sized towns. Domestically, inter-provincial fiber-optic trunk lines and cellular telephone systems have been installed; a domestic satellite system with 55 earth stations is in place. Internationally, China has 5 Intelsat (4 Pacific Ocean and 1 Indian Ocean), 1 Intersputnik (Indian Ocean region), and 1 Inmarsat (Pacific and Indian Ocean regions), as well as several international fiber-optic links to Japan, South Korea, Hong Kong, Russia, and Germany. The country had 673 radio broadcast stations—369 AM, 259 FM, 45 shortwave—and 417 million radios. In 1997, the country had 3,240 television broadcast stations, (of which 209 are operated by China Central Television, 31 are provincial TV stations and nearly 3,000 are local city stations), and 400 million televisions. In 1999, the country had 3 Internet service providers (ISPs).

ECONOMIC SECTORS

Over the years, China has become gradually more industrialized. Like other modernizing countries, for instance, the contribution of China's agricultural sector to its GDP has kept decreasing, from 37.9 percent in 1965 to 28.4 percent in 1985 and then to 18.4 percent in 1998—a net decrease of 19.5 percent in the 3-decade period. At the same time, the contribution of the industrial sector to GDP has kept increasing, from 35.1 percent in 1965 to 43.1 percent in 1985 and then to 48.7 percent in 1998, a net increase of 14.6 percent in the 3-decade period. The contribution of tertiary industry (service) to the GDP has increased from 27.0 percent in 1965 to 28.5 percent in 1985 and then to 32.9 per cent in 1998, a total increase of only 5.9 percent in the same period.

The world's economic development history indicates that as a country heads toward modernization, the ratio of agriculture to its GDP is set to drop, the ratio of service to its GDP will go up, while the ratio of industry to its GDP will first go up and then drop. China's economic

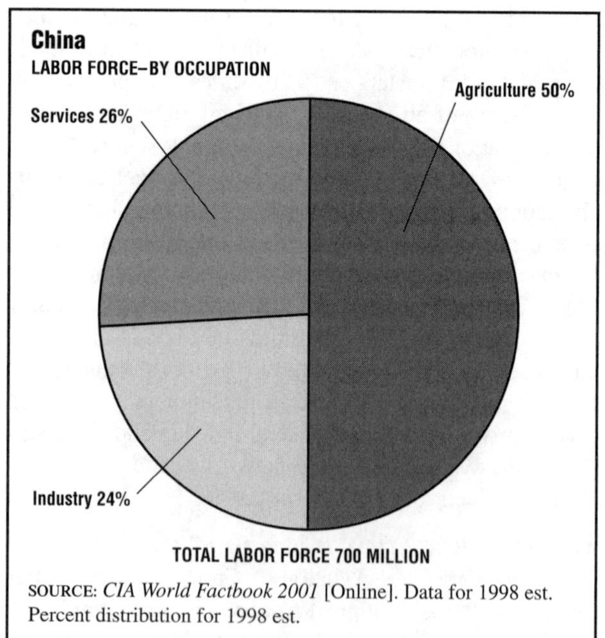

SOURCE: *CIA World Factbook 2001* [Online]. Data for 1998 est. Percent distribution for 1998 est.

development followed the same patterns. For instance, the ratio of agriculture's **value added** to the world's GDP was 7 percent in 1980 and fell to 5 percent in 1998. The ratio of agriculture's value added to the GDP of developed countries is normally 2 to 3 percent. The popular development model also demonstrates that when the GDP annual per capita income stood between US$300 and US$500, the proportions of agricultural and industrial sectors were virtually similar in the GDP while the employment proportion was higher in agricultural sector; when the annual per capita income reached US$1,500, the proportions of the industrial sector and service sector were basically similar in the GDP while the employment proportion in agricultural sector fell to the lowest proportion. However, China's situation varies somewhat from the traditional development model. For instance, in 1999, the per capita income in China exceeded US$1,000 (using the **purchasing power parity** method), while the proportion of the employment in the agricultural sector was still as high as 50 percent.

As shown above, non-agricultural industries' value amounts to the main body of the national economy, but the proportion of employees in the agricultural sector dominates the workforce at present and will do so in the future. The conflict of a dual economic structure is still obvious. It is reflected in the enlarged income gap between industry and agriculture, rising from 2.12 in 1991 to 5.25 in 1995, and its estimated value will reach 5.62 in 2005. Obviously, the changes of the industrial structure and employment structures are not consistent with other developing countries. The Chinese government and scholars have noticed this phenomenon, and many efforts have been made to reshape the structure more properly.

AGRICULTURE

In the thousands of years that farming has been practiced in China, the Chinese have refined and perfected their agricultural techniques. Traditional Chinese agriculture is labor intensive; the emphasis is on using many workers to increase the crop yield per unit of land rather than on increasing the productivity of the individual worker. Chinese agricultural practices have been shaped by the a shortage of farmland in the country, at least relative to the population.

Agriculture and rural activities are important in China for many reasons. First, farming provides the food and fiber needed for the sustenance of China's people. At the same time, nearly 65 percent of the people depend on agriculture or other rural economic activities for their livelihood. Second, agriculture has always provided the means of employment for most new workers entering the **labor force**. With between 12 and 16 million new workers entering the labor force annually since the 1980s, agriculture must continue to absorb tremendous numbers of new workers while continuing to find ways to use these workers productively. Finally, the agricultural sector has been an important source of investment money. If, through hard work, good management, and the application of sound, scientific farming, Chinese agriculture can be more productive, capital surpluses can be created and invested in other sectors of the economy, which could accelerate the rate of economic growth and ultimately benefit all of China's people.

China's grain output hit over 500 million tons in recent years, while current annual consumption is 463.5 million tons. Grain reserves now stand at historically high levels. However, it is true that the weak and fragile foundations of the agricultural system remain basically unchanged. Grain supply is still threatened by a series of unfavorable factors in production, circulation, consumption and foreign trade. A recent detailed estimate forecasts that the country's grain consumption requirements in the year 2030 would be between 632.8 and 725.8 million tons, with projected production at that time of 662.5 million tons. So even faced with the maximum shortfall of 63.3 million tons, the country would still be able to satisfy 90 percent of its own needs. Over the past decades, China has imported about 12 million tons annually, or 3 to 4 percent of consumption. Considering the trend of grain shortages in the medium and long term, China might need to import about 5 percent of its grain demand, or 20 million tons, in regular years.

CROPS AND LIVESTOCK. China's principal food crops are rice, wheat, corn, *gaoliang* (Chinese sorghum), millet, barley, and sunflower seeds. China is the world's largest producer of rice, and rice accounts for almost half of the country's total food-crop output. Rice, wheat, and corn together make up more than 90 percent of China's total food grain production, and these crops occupy about 85 percent of the land under cultivation. Grain production has risen steadily since rural economic system reform started in 1978. There has also been a steady rise in the output of industrial crops, the most important of which are cotton, oil-bearing crops (such as peanuts and rapeseed), sugar (both cane sugar and beet sugar), tobacco, baste fiber (for cordage, matting, and similar uses), tea, and fruits. Poultry and livestock production, though rising, remains the weakest sector of Chinese agriculture. Livestock numbers are high, but the amount of meat produced per animal is low. Thus, China has 15 percent of the world's livestock and about 40 percent of its pigs, but it provides only 7 percent of the meat products and 15 percent of the pork.

FORESTRY. Despite China's large land area, its forest resources are modest. Much of the western interior is too high or too dry to support dense forest stands. In the humid east, the forests were harvested for centuries for building material and firewood; limited effort was made to regenerate them. In 1949, it was estimated that about 8 percent of the total surface of the country was covered with forests. Since then, an active program of forestation has been undertaken, and it is estimated that the forested area has been increased to 12 to 13 percent. In recent years about 2.5 million acres (1 million hectares) of forestland have been added annually. The state is aiming to have 20 percent of the country's surface in forest. In contrast, more than 30 percent of the United States is forested.

FISHING. China has a long tradition of ocean and freshwater fishing and of aquaculture. Pond raising has always played an important role and has been increasingly emphasized to supplement coastal and inland fisheries threatened by over-fishing. China produces about 17.6 million tons yearly, first among the world's nations. More than 57 percent of the total catch is from the ocean. The remainder comes from rivers, canals, lakes, and ponds. China's coastal zone is rich in fish. All the coastal seas have extensive areas of shallow water over the continental shelf. In these seas, especially the Yellow River and East China River, cold and warm ocean currents mix, creating an environment that is particularly suitable for many species of ocean fish, including croakers, mackerels, tuna, herring, and sharks. Several varieties of shellfish and specialties such as squid and octopus are also produced.

INDUSTRY

Since 1949 when the People's Republic of China was established, and especially since 1978, China's transformation from a traditional agricultural society to a modern industrial society has been greatly accelerated by a rapid industrial restructuring. China's industrial structure developed according to the objective of industrialization, which aimed at the proportion of agriculture being declined ceaselessly, the proportion of the industrial sector being ascended continually, and the proportion of the services sector being ascended greatly. The industrial goods produced in China all range from **capital goods** to consumption goods currently, though certain consumer products remain in short supply.

China's factory outputs extend from textiles to railway locomotives, jet planes, and computers. China is the largest producer of inexpensive cotton textiles in the world and exports large quantities of textiles and garments. Food processing is very important, and many agricultural goods are exported. China is one of the leaders of cement production in the world. Iron- and steel-making has declined recently, the production having dropped somewhat to about 44 million tons annually. Other industrial products include television sets, bicycles, cars, trucks, and washing machines. The product quality and production technology lag behind those made in Japan, the United States, and the European countries. The processing and manufacture of chemicals, including fertilizers, petroleum products, and pharmaceuticals, is another large and expanding segment of Chinese industry.

China has become an industrialized country to some extent. The pillar industries, such as the auto industry and the housing industry, in the interim of industrialization have developed by leaps and bounds. Iron and steel manufacturing are also major industries in China. The most important export products are machinery and electric equipment; while the most important import products are raw materials. In recent years, due to economic extroversion, China's industry has competed internationally, and as a result, the country's industrial development is increasingly influenced by international economic environments. On one hand, exporting becomes more difficult and export prices keep declining; on the other hand, market share of foreign products and foreign-invested enterprises' products keeps growing. The above 2 factors increase the difficulties for the country's domestic industry in terms of producing and selling; the state-owned enterprises are impacted particularly. In fact, textile and other light industries have slowed their growth since 1985. Since 1989, the production capability of durable consumption goods has become idle; after the mid-1990s, bottleneck sectors including steel, oil, and raw material began to fall into market saturation. Large-scale IC chips account for only 40 percent of all IC chips made in China; 80 percent of the Chinese telecom equipment and instrument market is taken by foreign enterprises.

Generally, China's industrial system has a low level of technology; the high-tech industries are simply in their starting periods. The technologies of major industrial sectors are poor and lack self-equipment capability. Average life cycle for more than 2000 kinds of Chinese leading products is 10.5 years, 3.5 times that of the same products in America. And fewer Chinese work in the information sector than do U.S. citizens, for example. About 45 percent of the American workforce is involved in information technology, but only 10 percent of the Chinese workforce is. Chinese technological level of industries needs to be raised, particularly high-tech oriented industries, so that the country's industries can be advanced toward a knowledge economy in the 21st century.

MINING. With one of the largest and richest stocks of minerals of any country, China has enough minerals to support a modern industrial state. Mining of all types of minerals is expanding rapidly. The most significant minerals are coal, iron, tin, copper, lead, zinc, molybdenum, tungsten, mercury, antimony, and fluorspar. China has the world's largest coal reserves, which are estimated at more than 600 billion tons. These reserves would keep the country supplied with coal for about 500 years, if usage were to continue at its present level.

PETROLEUM. The country also has substantial petroleum reserves, both on land and offshore. Offshore prospecting is under way in several locations, with a number of Western and Japanese petroleum companies assisting China. Such minerals as tungsten, aluminum, titanium, and copper have export possibilities. Extensive deposits and promising sites were located in 1960s. The main production centers are in the North China Plain and in the Northeast. For instance, Daqing petroleum production basis in Heilongjiang Province is one of the largest petroleum producers in the country. Since the mid-1970s, China has been ranked as one of the ten largest oil-producing countries in the world, with the capacity to produce more than 1 billion barrels yearly. A small quantity of this output has been exported for earning foreign currency.

MANUFACTURING. Chief manufactured products include cement, rolled steel, chemical fertilizer, paper and paperboard, sulfuric acid, sugar, cotton yarn, cotton fabrics, cigarettes, television sets, and washing machines. Generally, the Chinese industrial structure has a higher level of manufacturing although it is far from high manufacturing in terms of productivity. Since 1978, the proportion has decreased, largely of output of low-level manufacturing sectors in light industry with agricultural products as raw material and mining sectors in heavy industry, but low-level expansion and repetitious construction in these sectors are still very serious. Product quality upgrade is still behind the demand of structures' upgrade, which in turn leads to the dependence on import of high-level manufactured goods for economic growth. The proportion of the 2 preceding sectors dropped from 34.1 percent and 8.19 percent in 1985 to 27.16 percent and 5.97 percent in 1998, dropping in total by 7.03 percent and 2.22 percent respectively. Compared with the United States and other developed countries, the horizontal industrial expansion with low levels of manufacturing causes low-level malignant competition in the domestic manufacturing sector. The same effects can be found in high-level consumption of energy and raw materials. For this reason inflated demands bring about a large increase of sectors with low technology content and delay upgrade of industrial structures.

SERVICES

According to a State Development Planning Commission (SDPC) document entitled *Report on China's National Economic Growth and Social Development for the Year 2000,* China's fast growing service sector has become the country's key employer. Preliminary statistics indicate that the service sector created 5.71 million new jobs in 1999, making up 70 percent of China's total new employment in the year. The service sector employed the majority of the country's urban new labor force and at the same time rehired the redundant labor force from the other 2 sectors. The SDPC data show that employment in the service industry by the end of 1999 rose 0.6 percent from 1998 to 192.5 million people, accounting for 27.3 percent of the total national workforce.

The service industry has become a major factor in boosting national economic growth. The key growth areas for the service industry in recent years include community services, domestic tourism, higher and non-compulsory education, information, culture and other intermediary services. In the first 4 years of China's 9th 5-Year Plan (1996 to 2000), the average contribution of the service industry to the GDP was 40.8 percent, a 10.4 percentage point increase over the 8th 5-Year Plan (1990–95). The state aimed at encouraging more involvement by the **private sector** in the development of the service industry by channeling more private investment into the industry.

FOOD SERVICE. Dining out is one of the most important social activities for both personal and business reasons in China. The food service can be categorized as fine dining, family restaurants, neighborhood restaurants, quick-serve restaurants, street vendors, food courts, and cafeterias operated by the institutions or corporations. Since the 1980s, Western-style chain restaurants have been the driving force for the development of service, quality, value and distribution in the Chinese food service industry. A recent survey indicates that China has approximately 2.2 million restaurants and cafeterias. With the growth of China's economy, the changing life styles, and increased **disposable incomes** for the potentially largest group of middle-income families in the world, China is expected to be the new leader in the growth of the food service industry in the 21st century.

TOURISM. China is a world-class destination that offers several thousand years of history and brilliant cultural achievements. Tourism has been designated as an important growth area under the current national restructuring. Remarkable progress has been made in China's tourism since 1978, when it barely existed as an industry. In 1978, on the eve of the open-door policy, China received a mere 760,000 tourists and US$260 million in tourism-related foreign exchange earnings.

During the 1980s, the state council strengthened its management over tourism and adopted a policy of enlisting support from all quarters—the state, the collectives, related ministries or departments, individuals and foreign investors. China began the construction of a large number of tourist hotels by using foreign capital and also improved the ability of its travel agencies to solicit tourists. In 1988, the national tourism industry earned

US$2.24 billion in foreign exchange, or 10 times the figure in 1978. Meanwhile, efforts have continued to open up new scenic spots, tap new visitor sources and improve tourism-related rules and laws. Drawing experience from developed countries, China improved its management skills and the overall quality of employees to optimize the environment for tourism expansion.

In the 1990s, the country began to design special tourism projects. The Visit China '97 program was a big success, with overseas visitors hitting 57.6 million and foreign exchange earnings reaching US$12.074 billion, thus catapulting China's place in world tourism earnings from 41st to 11th. At the same time domestic tourism also reached a new record with the number of tourists jumping to 644 million and earnings reaching US$27 billion. As a result, tourism income in the year totaled over US$38 billion, or 4.1 percent of the GDP. Massive infrastructure investments and rising living standards helped to stabilize the basic tourism market and improve the overall environment for tourism expansion. China's tourism earnings in the year 2000 were estimated as US$43.9 billion, or 5 percent of the GDP, with US$14 billion in foreign exchange earnings from overseas.

RETAIL. **Retail** was one of the fastest growing sectors in China in the earlier 1990s. Since retail industry reforms began in 1992, the government has adopted some new policies highlighted by the proclamation of the Provisional Rules on Retailing and Wholesaling in June 1999. These policies have propelled the retail industry through a process of fundamental transformation. While shopping in the past meant visiting a run-down department store and choosing from a limited range of low-quality products, currently the Chinese consumer is exposed to a growing number of sophisticated retail formats and wooed by a wide range of foreign and domestic products. The existing retail formats in China are warehouse/discount stores, supermarkets, department stores, convenience stores, franchised service or chain-store outlets, specialty stores, shopping centers, catalogue sales, TV home shopping, and recently developed **e-commerce**.

One eye-catching development is that local governments, in spite of central regulations, approved a large number of joint commercial ventures. Some Chinese retail stores in large cities are even beginning to hire foreign managers or are being contracted to a foreign management team. Large **multinational corporations** have made considerable inroads into China's consumer markets. They do so by forming **joint ventures** with domestic manufacturers to produce and sell their own brand-name products. By doing so they effectively take over the well-developed distribution channels of the domestic firms, and consequently their market shares improve steadily. In this area, Asian businesses (especially overseas Chinese ones) again enjoy an edge because of their familiarity with the Chinese consumption culture. They are not deterred by the lack of policy transparency and inadequate legal infrastructure. They thrive on personal connections cultivated with state officials and often regard these as a better guarantee for security. In 2000, the activities of foreign-invested retailers remained subject to tight regulation although the government took its first steps towards opening the retail sector to real foreign participation in 1992. A pilot program restricted Sino-foreign retail joint ventures to 11 cities, with only 2 such ventures allowed in each pilot site.

INTERNATIONAL TRADE

International trade has been used to bring in new equipment and technologies and to meet scarcities in the domestic economy since China has sought to modernize its economy. Exports have been used as a means of producing foreign earnings to pay for the imports. The state has sought to maintain an even **balance of trade** so that the country can pay for imports rather than buying on credit. With 1.2 billion people and the world's fastest growing major economy, China is hailed as potentially the "market of all markets," which has helped to attract investments from around the world at such a magnitude that China is now the second largest recipient of foreign capital (next only to the United States). However, it has also given the government more reasons to carefully guard its market. The issue of market entry has been a contentious one, bogging down its negotiations to join the General Agreement on Tariffs and Trade and the World Trade Organization for over a decade.

The total volume of China's exports was US$232 billion (**f.o.b.**, 2000), according to the CIA *World Factbook.* The country's principal commodities are machinery and equipment, textiles and clothing, footwear, toys and sporting goods, and mineral fuels. The United States bought 21 percent of China's exports, Hong Kong 18 percent, and Japan 17 percent; Germany, South Korea, the Netherlands, the United Kingdom, Singapore, and Taiwan are other main export partners.

Trade (expressed in billions of US$): China

	Exports	Imports
1975	7.689	7.926
1980	18.099	19.941
1985	27.350	42.252
1990	62.091	53.345
1995	148.797	129.113
1998	183.589	140.305

SOURCE: International Monetary Fund. *International Financial Statistics Yearbook 1999.*

China exports agricultural commodities and goods (about one-third of total exports) and manufactured goods (about half), as well as mineral products such as oil and coal. Foodstuffs account for about 6 percent of total imports, and industrial supplies and materials such as crude steel and chemicals account for about 50 percent. The remainder consists chiefly of expensive capital goods such as machinery, precision instruments, and transportation equipment.

In 1998, machinery and transport equipment took the first place among the exports, amounting to 50.2 billion dollars. The proportion of it is 48.4 percent, much higher than the proportion of light and textile industrial products (26.5 percent). On the other hand, export structure of machinery and transport equipment is changing for the better. The proportion of more technologically-intensive products is growing up, and labor-intensive products are slowing down. Also, the interim structure of traditional export products, such as light and textile industrial products, changed tremendously. Resource and labor-intensive, low value-added, low-technological products declined, lower labor-extensive but higher technological and value-added products increased.

China imports a total volume of US$197 billion (2000). The principal commodities China imports are machinery and equipment, mineral fuels, plastics, iron and steel, and chemicals. Japan provides the main source (20 percent) of China's imports. The United States provides 12 percent, Taiwan 12 percent, and South Korea 10 percent. Other trading partners include Germany, Hong Kong, Russia, and Singapore.

The 5 top import products of China during the first semester in 1999 included mechanical and electrical products at US$35 billion (up 28 percent from 1998); plastics in primary form at US$4.1 billion (up 3.9 percent from 1998); steel products at US$3.4 billion (up 14.6 percent from 1998); computer parts at US$1.8 billion (up 18.7 percent from 1998); and crude petroleum oil at US$1.6 billion (down 23.6 percent from 1998). The commodities China imports are materials essential to modernizing China's economy and increasing export-oriented industries.

MONEY

China embarked on its open-door economic policy in 1979 by reforming the agricultural sector and establishing several special economic zones (SEZs). The high export-led growth rates in the SEZs contributed to an annual **inflation rate** of over 10 percent in the 1980s. As a result the economy was overheating. The monetary authorities were ineffective in dealing with inflation. Fiscal revenues declined during the reform period and pressed the Ministry of Finance (MOF) to sell bonds to the central bank in exchange for currency to cover its **budget deficit** and to release aggravating inflationary pressures. By 1994, laws were passed to create a more consistent and more transparent tax system, which would reverse the steady decline in fiscal revenues. The new laws also banned fiscal overdrafts on the financial system. In reflecting tighter **monetary policies** and stronger measures to control food prices, inflation dropped sharply between 1995 and 1999.

Exchange rates: China

yuan per US$1	
Jan 2001	8.2776
2000	8.2785
1999	8.2783
1998	8.2790
1997	8.2898
1996	8.3142

Note: Beginning January 1, 1994, the People's Bank of China quotes the midpoint rate against the US dollar based on the previous day's prevailing rate in the interbank foreign exchange market.

SOURCE: CIA *World Factbook 2001* [ONLINE].

Financial reform first appeared in 1984, when the People's Bank (monobank) discarded its commercial banking functions to become a central bank. The 3 specialized banks were reformed as commercial banks, passing on their policy lending to newly established policy banks. The banking system was decentralized, and inter-bank competition was allowed. Urban and rural credit cooperatives were established as alternative banking institutions. Interest rates remained under government control; preferential lending rates have been removed in certain sectors but continue in many others. Although lending rates are a highly political issue for the impact on state-owned enterprise (SOE) **debt-servicing** obligations, **deregulating** lending rates and deposit will be on the official agenda. Various ministries, including the monobank and the State Planning Commission, are in charge of a credit plan that involves a multi-step, highly negotiated process in which lending quotas are allocated to the state banks (lenders) based on their balance of deposits against borrowings. A re-lending facility allows the central bank to reallocate deposits from surplus to deficit ones at bank levels or regional levels. The mechanism is funded by reserves set at 20 percent of deposits; thus, deposit-poor lenders are assured that their allocated funding requirements will be covered by monobank loans.

Under the re-lending facility the loans are generally rolled over, which make up 30 percent of state banks' liabilities and are estimated to equal 3 to 4 percent of the GDP. The continuing injection of funds to SOEs under the credit plan allowed many profitless SOEs to remain in business, some SOEs even staying while making a net loss. Many of the loans to SOEs could not be called back and eventually became the bank's liabilities, which suggests that any financial sector reform and resolution of the SOE debt problem are intricately linked. Moreover, the continued reliance on state bank loans to support SOEs has also exacerbated the government's fiscal weakness, as it causes the lack of funds for much-needed enterprise and welfare reforms.

China used 2 systems of currency between 1979 and 1994: Renminbi and Foreign Exchange Certificates (FEC). Foreign exchange could be obtained through either FEC exchange centers (FECs) or foreign exchange adjustment centers (FEACs) until the 1994 currency unification. There were over 100 FEACs, or swap centers, where foreign currency was exchanged at a floating rate that varied widely among the centers in the 1980s. By 1993, 80 percent of all foreign exchange transactions were handled by FEACs. With the currency unification of 1994 came the gradual, complete withdrawal of FECs altogether from foreign exchange. The yuan's **exchange rate** is determined by the swap centers. It is noticeable that the movements toward convertibility of the current account have allowed foreign firms to make their transactions through designated foreign exchange banks and through FEACs. However, the domestic firms must sell all of their foreign exchange holdings to designated banks.

BANKING. The financial sector's main regulatory authority is the People's Bank of China (PBOC), the country's central bank. The PBOC controls the money supply, determines interest and deposit rates, and handles **foreign exchange reserves** through its division, the State Administration of Exchange Control. The PBOC also supervises banks' operations, uses the credit plan to administratively control overall lending, and oversees the People's Insurance Company of China as well as through its branches, trust and investment companies (TICs).

China has 4 state banks and eleven commercial banks. The state banks were created in 1984, when specialized banks and part of the monobank were transformed into commercial banks. The Agricultural Bank of China provides finance services in rural areas. The People's Construction Bank of China is responsible for medium- and long-term finance for capital construction. The Bank of China functions as the main international and foreign exchange bank, and the Industrial and Commercial Bank of China, the largest state bank, extends working capital loans to SOEs for fixed-asset investment. State banks with a network of branches, newly created affiliates, and special departments are responsible for implementing the credit plan.

More than 60,000 urban and rural credit cooperatives were established as an alternative to banks by 1999. Urban cooperative banks, small and manageable, are structured in a 2-tier system: the upper tier interfaces with capital markets and acts as a supervisor for the system, while the lower tier, a number of small-scale banks, handles deposits and loans. The rural or agricultural cooperative banks, acting under the guidance of the Agricultural Development Bank, have limited autonomy in management and lending decisions. Their clients are mainly rural townships and enterprises.

The state-owned People's Insurance Company of China (PICC) used to be a **monopoly** insurer. In 1993, it still handled over 95 percent of China's total insurance business. The new insurance law of 1995 limited the PICC to commercial insurance business and transferred its social insurance business to the Ministry of Labor. Currently, although the PICC and several government financial authorities own 17 regional life insurers, there are 3 other regional insurers and 2 independent national insurers. The market for life insurance and household casualty insurance is still small in China, and corporate customers purchase most casualty insurance. Most assets have to be deposited with domestic banks in interest-bearing accounts, while other investments need to be spread among safe investments and are limited to short-run commitments.

STOCK EXCHANGES. The Shanghai and Shenzhen Stock Exchanges, China's only 2 stock exchanges currently, were established in 1990 and 1991, respectively. No cross listing exists between these 2 exchanges. Since their founding, securities markets have grown rapidly, especially in the later 1990s. Securities exchange centers, limited to government and corporate bond trading only, exist in 18 larger cities. Securities exchange centers were established in the mid-1980s when SOEs were allowed to sell bonds to employees, other companies, and, to some extent, to the public. Securities exchange centers are linked to the stock exchanges through electronic trading networks.

Chinese companies offer 2 types of shares: A shares, which are exclusively sold to Chinese nationals, and B shares, denominated in Renminbi but traded and purchased in foreign currency exclusively by foreigners originally. By March 2001, B shares could also be purchased by Chinese citizens using foreign currency. B shares are restricted to limited liability shareholding companies. To be qualified, companies must have been profitable for at least 2 consecutive years; must possess sufficient foreign exchange revenues to pay dividends and cash bonuses; must be able to provide financial statements and earning forecasts for 3 consecutive years and at the time of listing; and must have a price-earning ratio of less than 15.

The state planning commission formulates quotas for stock and debt listings, which sets a figure for the aggregate offering price of issuances in a given year. The formulated quotas are then allocated on a provincial level. This process generates some problems, such as politicized selection and approval process, lowered quality of issuer with a large number of small issuers, the lack of predictability in the schedule of announcements of annual quotas, and the fact that announced quotas change yearly according to market conditions. Furthermore, the quota system pushes non-quota activity into unofficial and semi-official channels such as the securities exchange centers. Because of these problems, it is widely agreed that the Chinese stock markets are far from formal and mature and, thus, are full of myth and risks.

FOREIGN PARTICIPATION. Foreign banks are generally restricted to **hard currency** operations, although the government has announced its intention to partially open a local currency business to foreign banks in its bid to join the WTO. Foreign banks are allowed to set up branches and local subsidiaries and to establish joint venture banks with Chinese partners in selected cities and SEZs. However, their activities must be limited to wholesale banking and only a limited number of foreign exchange transactions such as foreign exchange deposits and loans for joint ventures, foreign exchange investments and guarantees, and the settlement of import and export accounts. Foreign non-bank financial institutions consist of 6 finance companies and 6 fully-licensed insurance companies. Generally, it takes about 3 years for foreign insurance companies to obtain a PBOC-issued insurance license.

POVERTY AND WEALTH

In the early decades after the communist state was founded in 1949, incomes were low and roughly the same. However, according to a newly conducted investigation, economic reforms over the past 20 years have created a substantial class of very wealthy Chinese, with more than 5.3 million families boasting annual incomes of US$6,000 or more. The average annual urban income is about US$600, and the average earned by rural residents is about US$230. Private businessmen and managers make up the core of the newly affluent. Others include scientists who own patents, teachers who tutor privately, consultants, securities traders, entertainers or advertising executives. There are roughly 30 million Chinese considered to be well off, which makes only a small fraction of China's population of 1.2 billion. Heavily concentrated in major cities such as Beijing and Shanghai, the affluent Chinese represent a newly **emerging market** for all sorts of luxuries. China is counting on the desire of the well-to-do for better housing and **consumer goods** to help keep the economy growing.

GDP per Capita (US$)

Country	1975	1980	1985	1990	1998
China	138	168	261	349	727
United States	19,364	21,529	23,200	25,363	29,683
Japan	23,296	27,672	31,588	38,713	42,081
Russia	2,555	3,654	3,463	3,668	2,138

SOURCE: United Nations. *Human Development Report 2000; Trends in human development and per capita income.*

Distribution of Income or Consumption by Percentage Share: China

Lowest 10%	2.4
Lowest 20%	5.9
Second 20%	10.2
Third 20%	15.1
Fourth 20%	22.2
Highest 20%	46.6
Highest 10%	30.4

Survey year: 1998

Note: This information refers to income shares by percentiles of the population and is ranked by per capita income.

SOURCE: *2000 World Development Indicators* [CD-ROM].

URBAN-RURAL INCOME INEQUALITY. Economic reforms have made substantial improvements in the living standards of rural residents. Since 1978, the farmers boosted their incomes by engaging in specialized agricultural activities such as animal husbandry, agriculture, and orchard production, in addition to raising traditional crops. Furthermore, township and village enterprises (TVEs) accounted for the bulk of increased wage income earned by the rural residents. As the result, the disposable income among rural residents has increased dramatically since the early 1980s. However, in spite of these improvements, the rise in income of rural residents is markedly small when compared to that of urban areas. The total rural incomes are only 40 percent of urban incomes in China when in most countries rural incomes are 66 percent or more of urban income. The gap in income between rural and urban residents has grown at an increasing rate since the late 1980s. In fact, such disparity has been the most important contributor to the problem of social **equity** in China, followed by interregional disparity.

REGIONAL INCOME INEQUALITY. Decades of strict central planning created serious disparities in incomes among citizens in different regions. The average annual income is high, for example, in Jiangsu province located in the eastern region, but Guizhou, located in the western region, has a low income level. The difference is quite enormous. For instance, in 1996, per capita annual income of Jiangsu was 2613.54 yuan while in Guizhou it was 609.80 yuan; the ratio between the two was 4.3:1. In the same year, per capita GDP and the total GDP of the eastern region were 1.9 times and 5.5 times larger, respectively, than those of the western region.

INTRA-URBAN INCOME INEQUALITY. In addition to the gap between urban and rural areas, city dwellers also feel the income inequality among themselves. According to the Urban Socio-Economic Survey Organization of the State Statistics Bureau, in the middle 1990s the per capita income of the top 20 percent income earners was 4.2 times greater than the bottom 20 percent, worsened from 2.9 times in the later 1980s. Although many enterprises in urban areas have either stopped working or closed down, many of the idle employees who have been laid off are waiting for future employment that would provide them the minimum incomes to maintain the basic standard of living in the urban areas. Currently, many idle workers are either receiving low incomes or no incomes at all. The wage level of retired employees is also quite low, and, considering the effects of inflation, their living standard is falling.

POVERTY REDUCTION. About 10 percent of the Chinese population lives below the poverty line. One of the largest challenges in China is poverty alleviation and elimination. According to the World Bank, due to aggressive measures, China has achieved great success in its anti-poverty struggle in the past 2 decades. The impoverished population dropped from about 250 million in 1978 to 125 million in 1985 because rural areas experienced economic growth. The Chinese government has been planning and organizing a number of large-scale anti-poverty programs all over the country since 1986. By the end of 1992, the poverty population of rural China was reduced to 80 million, reducing the poverty rate to 8.8 percent.

In 1994, in order to accelerate the poverty alleviation and ultimately eliminate poverty by the end of last century, the Chinese government launched the "8–7 Plan," the main point of which was to eliminate absolute poverty in 7 years through the tax favorite policy, financial support, and social-economic development program. For the convenience of implementing the "8–7 Plan," the central government selected the 592 poorest counties from the more than 2000 counties nationwide and designated them as "national poor counties." It was estimated that more than 70 percent of the 80 million poor concentrated in these 592 counties had very bad natural environments and under-developed social-economic conditions.

After 4 years, the poor population of rural China was reduced to 42.1 million, and the poverty rate was 4.6 percent by the end of 1998. The Chinese government spent 24.8 billion yuan (US$3 billion) on poverty alleviation in 1999, 30 times more than in 1980. Rural per capita income among China's 870 million rural residents in 1999 was 2,210 yuan. Only 3 percent of the rural population remained impoverished or living below the 635-yuan standard, making China's rural poverty rate the lowest among developing nations. In 2000, China announced that it had eliminated "absolute poverty."

WORKING CONDITIONS

China has the largest labor force in the world. According to Chinese official data, over 700 million people were employed by the end of 1990s. More than half of its labor force is engaged in agriculture, although that sector accounts for less than 20 percent of China's GDP. In other words, China's agricultural labor force is over 100 times as large as its U.S. counterpart. By the middle of the 1990s, most of China's urban workers were employed in state-owned enterprises (SOEs). In the 1990s, China's increasingly dynamic service sector employed more workers than industrial enterprises for each of the last 3 years. Latest sources from the State Statistics Bureau show that 6.4 percent of labor force in rural China shifted to the country's secondary and tertiary industries in 1999. With 0.5 percent of its rural labor force having made a change in their life from agricultural to non-agricultural labor, the net shifting amount of rural labor force was placed at 5.9 percent of the rural total, up 0.4 percent over the same period in 1998. According to one official survey, as many as 50 million people leave rural areas in search of urban jobs every year. Of this number, approximately 30 million people leave their home provinces.

Shifting labor forces experienced a big rise in proportion on a provincial, regional, or municipal scale. About 79 percent of surplus labor force became locally employed in the industrial and service sectors in the country in 1999, up 11 percentage points over 1998. East China remains the hottest destination for drawing rural laborers, although more people began to focus on west China. Among the rural laborers leaving their native place to seek employment in other provinces, 79.8 percent headed for the East in 1999, down 2.5 percentage points compared with the same period of 1998. About 10 percent chose central China for employment, up 0.6 percentage points. More than 10.2 percent went to the country's west, up 1.9 percentage points over 1998. Most of the laborers are young or people in their prime. People ages 18 to 40 accounted for 77.3 percent. Of these, 57.9 percent were between 18 and 30 years of age.

EMPLOYMENT PROBLEMS. Chinese labor has benefitted significantly from economic reforms. During the 8th 5-Year Plan (1991–95), real incomes increased by 7.7 percent annually in urban areas and 4.5 percent annually in the countryside. However some serious problems existed in the labor market, which threatened to impede economic reforms and to disrupt social stability. Increased lay-offs (officially labeled as "temporarily losing a job"), placing workers "off post" (*xiagang*), as well as delayed wage and pension payments, resulted in a number of demonstrations by workers and retirees in several Chinese cities. Within a certain period, typically 1 year, these "laid off" workers are usually encouraged to take other types of jobs, generally with less pay and/or status than their original positions. Many workers also take second jobs. Some continue to draw a basic salary and benefits from their previous employer for whom they do little or no real work. By 2001, the problems caused by the increasing lay-offs from SOEs, along with several other issues, became the first worries of the nation's leaders.

The official unemployment rate was officially reported to be 6 percent by the end of 1990s. Labor officials readily admitted that the official unemployment rate did not include 2 large and important groups that are effectively unemployed, redundant state sector workers and rural surplus laborers. By official estimate, the **underemployed** population in the countryside, defined as those with productive employment less than half of the year, exceeds 200 million people. Some probably more accurate estimates of urban unemployment vary anywhere between 10 and 23 percent. Even according to the official unemployment criteria, a report completed by China's State Commission for economic restructuring in early 1997 projected that China could have 15 to 20 million unemployed urban workers by 2000. Meanwhile, it is estimated that between the years 2000 and 2010 over 40 million new entrants will be brought into the urban workforce.

LABOR LAW. A national labor law effective 1 January 1995 codified earlier regulations and provides a framework for labor reform. New provisions in the law require workers at all types of businesses to sign labor contracts with the employers; establish arbitration and inspection divisions at all levels of government; set out a preliminary framework for collective bargaining at all types of enterprises; and empower managers to dismiss workers for economic reasons. However, the local governments are less effective in enforcing strict worker safety and overtime provisions of the Labor Law. As the result, industrial accidents, particularly in the mining sector, claim a high number of lives every year.

The Labor Law also requires localities to establish local minimum wages. For instance, the monthly minimum wage in Beijing at the end of 1996 was RMB 270 (approximately US$33); RMB 300 (approximately US$36) in Shanghai; RMB 398 (approximately US$48) in Shenzhen; and RMB 140 (approximately US$17) in Guizhou province. Other parts of China, including Guangdong, Jiangsu, and Shandong provinces, have created a sliding scale of minimum rates for different trades and localities. The minimum wage level determinations are generally higher than the local poverty relief ceiling but lower than the current wage level of the average worker.

Labor disputes, including delayed wages and strikes, have been increasing over the last several years in China. The upward trend has made some labor and union officials become defensive. The official media continuously pay attention to worker abuse, invariably at small, export-oriented foreign ventures with Asian (Hong Kong, Taiwan, South Korea) investment. However, many unofficial observers indicate that working conditions are generally worse in private Chinese enterprises and in domestic small town and village enterprises, which are often owned by local government. Most labor disputes are solved through arbitration and recently some cases reached the courts. According to official statistics, based on National Mediation Center and Labor Bureau records, 48,121 labor disputes occurred nationwide in China during 1996.

ALL-CHINA FEDERATION OF TRADE UNIONS (ACFTU). For the most part, unions in China maintain their primary function of enhancing production and sustaining labor discipline, rather than supporting worker rights. Local unions also perform a variety of social and welfare functions, such as handling disability benefits and housing funds and operating clubs, eating facilities, nurseries, and schools. The All-China Federation of Trade Unions (ACFTU), the country's only officially recognized workers' organization, remains focused on the state sector. There is still little evidence to suggest that ACFTU is being positioned to assume the new role of worker advocate mandated by article seven of the labor law, although some union officials at the working level may be increasingly interested in representing the interests of workers, particularly on safety issues.

For the ACFTU, improving labor discipline and mobilizing workers to achieve party and government goals are their primary objectives. However, since the early 1980s, additional objectives have been to increase productivity and encourage participation in, and support for, economic reforms. Generally, the membership is limited to the workers in SOEs. Over half of the country's non-agricultural workers are not members of the ACFTU, those who are outside the state industrial structure in collectives, private and individual enterprises, foreign-invested enterprises, and township and village enterprises.

WORKING CONDITIONS. The working conditions are generally poor in China, especially in the rural areas. The rate of industrial accidents had remained high until 1996 when, according to Ministry of Labor statistics, for the first time in many years the number of industrial accidents actually dropped. Total accidents stood at 18,181, 13.5 percent less than in 1995, with total fatalities at 17,231, a 13.9 percent drop from 1995. By 2001, there was no evidence to confirm whether this decline represents a permanent trend. The official media continue to criticize the overall high number of work-related accidents and fatalities. The majority of industrial accidents in China occur in mines, particularly in poorly regulated small-scale private, township, and village mines. For instance, in 1996 there were 7,695 mining accidents and 9,974 workers were killed.

Work safety issues attracted the attention of senior government leaders; occupational safety and health became the subject of constant campaigns. All work units are required to designate a safety officer. Since 1991, the Ministry of Labor has conducted an annual "industrial safety week" during May, to promote safety consciousness among managers and workers. As of mid-1997, the Ministry of Labor fulfilled new National Occupational Safety and Health legislation. Labor Ministry officials have also indicated that they have the responsibility of drafting improved National Mine Safety legislation. However, much evidence demonstrates that enforcement of existing regulations, rather than the drafting of new legislation, is what is needed most. Moreover, pressures for increased output, lack of financial resources to maintain equipment, lack of concern by management, poor enforcement of existing regulations, and a traditionally poor understanding of safety issues by workers, all make it difficult, if not impossible, to lower the high rate of accidents.

On 1 May 1995 China reduced the national standard workweek from 44 to 40 hours, excluding overtime. The Labor Law mandates a 24-hour rest period weekly and does not allow overtime work in excess of 3 hours a day or 36 hours a month. The Labor Law also sets forth a required scale of remuneration for overtime work that is set at no less than 150 percent of normal wages. Enforcement of these regulations varies according to region and type of enterprise. The official media regularly report cases of workers required to work long overtime hours at small-scale foreign-invested enterprises, particularly in special economic zones and other areas of Southeast China. Similar abuses in non-state sector enterprises are also widely acknowledged to occur.

WOMEN IN THE WORKFORCE. Economic reforms have increased employment opportunities for both men and women in China. The growth of the less regulated non-state sector and the declining role of the government in job assignments has also increased the likelihood that women will face employment discrimination in China. In 1995 while hosting the U.N. Fourth World Conference on Women (FWCW), China pledged to pay more attention to the problems faced by women in the workforce. The state council promulgated the national program for Chinese Women's Development in August 1995 with the goal of increasing enforcement of the right to education and employment and asserting the status of women. Responding to the hesitancy demonstrated by government ministries to hire women at a Beijing job fair in early 1996, the All-China Women's Federation (ACWF) called for stricter safeguards of women's rights.

In SOEs, women are more likely to be forced into early retirement or placed "off-post." A joint study of sample enterprises in 5 cities performed by the Ministry of Labor and the ILO in early 1995 indicated that 70 percent of workers described as "surplus" were women. According to an official survey completed in Shanghai in August 1996, women were the first to be affected by unemployment in the city because of their overall lower level of skills. The 1988 Women's Protection Law provides a minimum of 3 months of maternity leave and additional childcare benefits for women. The law also provides exclusion for breastfeeding mothers from certain categories of physical labor and night shifts. However, the regulations are designed to provide additional incentives to women workers of childbearing age to abide by family planning policies, which do not affect rural workers.

AGE DISCRIMINATION. China perhaps is one of few countries that discriminates against middle aged and older workers in terms of re-entering employment after being laid off. Many employers will state openly in their job advertisements that they would not hire those who are over 45 years old. Older workers are also finding it increasingly difficult to compete. Some managers complain that older workers do not have the skills needed for the current marketplace; others note that older workers are in poor health. Older workers are likely to be the first to be affected by downsizing in the state sector. By all accounts, older women have an especially difficult time maintaining their employment. Many older women are poorly educated upon entry into the job force and receive little opportunity to upgrade their skills thereafter. While managers may want to keep on a certain number of experienced men, most view older women simply as a burden. Older women find the differences in China's statutory retirement age especially rankling. The retirement age for men is 60, while for women it is 50 in industry and 55 elsewhere. Although traditional views hold that women want to retire early to take care of grandchildren, women today, especially educated women, prefer to make this decision themselves and not be forced out of the workforce before they are ready.

CHILD LABOR. In theory, child labor is forbidden in China. For instance, the 1995 National Labor Law specifies, "No employing unit shall be allowed to recruit juveniles under the age of 16." Administrative review, fines, and revocation of business licenses of those businesses that hire minors are specified in article 94 of the Labor Law. Chinese children are entitled to receive 9 years of compulsory education and to receive their subsistence from parents or guardians. Laborers between the ages of 16 and 18 are referred to as "juvenile workers" and are prohibited from engaging in certain forms of physical work including labor in mines. The Labor Law mandates the establishment of labor inspection corps at all administrative levels above county government. The rapid growth of China's non-state sector has outpaced the evolution of government inspection and enforcement regimes. However, in poorer, isolated areas, child labor in agriculture is widespread given the few options available to minors who have completed their primary school education at approximately 13 years of age. According to official statistics, 10 million children between the ages of 6 and 14, two-thirds of whom were girls, dropped out of Chinese primary schools during 1996. Presumably they ended up performing some type of labor to help the family's financial well-being.

COUNTRY HISTORY AND ECONOMIC DEVELOPMENT

2205–1783 B.C. Early Bronze Age occurs, as does use of metal.

1783–1134 B.C. Economy is based on agriculture, with some hunting and animal husbandry. More advanced bronze metallurgy appears. Silk fabric appears.

1134–770 B.C. Feudalistic society appears. Routine taxation on agriculture begins. Systematic irrigation, fertilization, and animal-drawn plows are used in farming. Iron tools appear in farming and mining. Cowry shells, silk, jade, pearls, leather, and pieces of silver are used in trading.

770–246 B.C. Commerce improves through coinage and technology.

246–206 B.C. Standardization of legal codes, bureaucratic procedures, coinage, writing, philosophical thought, and scholarship take place. Walls from warring states are combined to make a Great Wall. Public works projects begin, including an imperial road.

206–1 B.C. Merchant class grows wealthy due to agricultural enterprises (cereals and rice), cattle, fish farming, cloth mills, private foundries, lacquer factories, shops, and money lending. State foundries appear in most areas. Technological advances occur, noticeably in paper and porcelain.

1–88. Government supports free, no-interest loans to curb usury. Regional commissions set prices on staple goods. Granaries hold surplus food in case of famine. State Wine Monopoly is formed. State monopolies in iron and salt are abolished.

89–166. Embassies from various nations are established.

220–265. Advances in medicine, astronomy and cartography occur. State supports silk weaving workshops, each with thousands of workers. Gunpowder is introduced in fireworks.

300–399. Oil wick lamps and umbrellas appear. Coal is used in lieu of wood in making cart iron.

400–499. Harness with paddle-horse collar is invented. Fusion process is used in making steel. First true porcelain is made in China.

552. Byzantine emperor, Justinian, sends missionaries to China to smuggle out silk worms and mulberry leaves.

600. Man-powered paddle-wheel boat appears. Merchants from 27 different lands meet at Zhang-ye on silk road to discuss trade.

618–907. Tang Dynasty adopts function of state affairs over public administration, finances, rites, army, justice, and public works. A censorate ensures compliance of governmental performance with plans. Use of receipts of deposit, for exchange of commercial transactions, begins. Earlier restrictions on business activities are ignored. Tang dynasty recognizes middle class over peasants.

894–1300. Japan severs all relations with China; however, it allows informal commercial visits by private traders with luxury goods.

960–1126. K'ai-feng becomes a major city, under the Northern Song Dynasty, with broad roads, wide canals, all-day markets, eateries, and restaurants, merchants, vendors, and entertainers. Invention of navigational compasses, astronomical instruments, celestial globes, water-driven mechanical clocks, blast furnace using coke, and spinning wheel occurs. Government prints promissory notes. Civil servants manage state monopolies. The government recognizes association of merchants and artisans and "chambers of commerce." Silk working machinery aids production. Specialization in pottery occurs. Tea and cotton are major cultivated crops.

1000–99. Large-scale iron and steel complexes are built in the north using blast furnaces and employing some 3,000 workers. An industrial complex is built to mass-produce ceramic for imperial court.

1068–85. Under emperor Shen Tsung, provincial money taxes are substituted for labor obligation to reduce peasant's dependence on moneylenders. A financial bureau reduces budget by 40 percent. Government loans cash or grain to poor to protect usury on crop loans.

1100–99. Intaglio printing is used in money printing to prevent counterfeiting.

1260–94. Kublai Khan rules over the Mongol empire, Central Asia, Persia, North China, and Mongolia. He retains the salt and iron monopolies. Discrimination against the Huns begins. Three types of paper money are established: one based on silk and two based on silver. Fixed taxes are adopted and large **levies** of Song Dynasty are abolished. Government is reorganized to include a bureau of imperial manufactures (industrial matters), a secretariat (civilian matters), a privy council (military matters), a censorate (evaluating officials), and offices of personnel, revenue, rites, war, justice, and public works. Banners are used to advertise wine. Pawnshops are first seen.

1277. Marco Polo is appointed agent to the imperial council.

1287. Kublai Khan replaces paper money with new currency to fight against rapid inflation.

1295. Marco Polo returns to Italy, incites interest in trade with China.

1342. Weapons, fans, screens, laquerware, and books are traded during Japanese trading expeditions.

1368–1644. Ming Dynasty begins, and government is re-organized. Silk is reserved for imperial use. Nationwide tax system is implemented, and corrupt Mongols are replaced. Slavery is abolished. Large estates are confiscated and poor peasants rent land. The wealthy are taxed heavily. Contact with foreigners is restricted. Elementary school system is established.

1420. Ming navy produces combat vessels. More than 250 are capable of long-range voyages.

1421. Beijing becomes the capital. The imperial workshop employs more than 27,000 craftsmen in trade and foreign relations.

1557–97. Chinese allow Portuguese colonization and development on Macau.

1637. First English factory is established in Canton.

1644–1912. Manchu overthrow Ming Dynasty, and China enters Qing Dynasty.

1800. China produces 33.3 percent of the world manufacturing output. Foreign merchants exchange opium for goods.

1842. Treaty of Nanking is signed; Britain gets control of Hong Kong. Shanghai and other coastline cities are open to foreign settlements.

1873–90. Modern non-military enterprises begin to form, owned and operated by Chinese compradors and merchant middlemen.

1900–01. Boxer Rebellion tries to force foreigners out, suppressed by Britain, United States, France, and Japan. China pays US$330 million in restitution.

1916–31. Japanese receive commercial rights to Inner Mongolia and Southern Manchuria and create the puppet state of Manchuria.

1937. Japanese forces invade and eventually occupy Beijing.

1949. People's Republic of China is formed when Communists take over the government. A mass exodus of entrepreneurs to Hong Kong and nationalists to Taiwan occurs.

1958. Great Leap Forward begins by creating communes to increase production and increase collectivism. However, it fails to increase economic growth.

1966. Great Cultural Revolution is launched, attacking bourgeoisie ideology and capitalist thought, which leads to rioting and instability. These events have a devastating impact on the economy.

1976. The death of Mao Zedong and arrest of Gang of Four end Great Cultural Revolution.

1980. Special Economic Zones are extended for capitalist enterprises north of Hong Kong. The country's first management program is established and forms the Chinese National Center for Industrial Science and Technology at Dalian Institute of Technology.

1985. The development of consumer-based industry occurs. The first stockbroker in Shanghai trades with 10 corporations.

1989. The first Beijing International Fair opens, which is the first and the biggest international fair held independently by China. Growing student objections to official corruption lead to violence after a demonstration in Tiananmen Square.

1990. The 4th Asian Trade Promoting Meeting is held in Beijing. Official census counts 1 billion people. China is granted observer status in GATT.

1991. China Stock Association announces its establishment in Beijing.

1992. China announces that the goal of the economic reform is to set up a socialist market system.

1993. Electric power groups (North, East, Middle, Easter-North, and West-North) were permitted to be set up by the State Council.

1994. The launching ceremony of Yangtzi River Three Gorges is held and its construction started.

1995. The China Investment Association announces its establishment in Beijing.

1996. With sharp economic growth and controlled inflation under control, China achieves the goal of macro economic control.

1997. China decreases tariffs and promises to reduce the average tariff of the industrial products to 10 percent.

1998. In order to protect China's growing economy from the Asian economic crisis, Chinese government issues 1,000 billion **national debts** for the construction of domestic infrastructure and civil services.

1999. China resumes the collection of tax on the interest of personal savings.

2000. China successfully completes the 9th 5-Year Plan for economic growth; and the country's GDP reaches US$10,000 billion.

FUTURE TRENDS

Since 1978, China's economic system has undergone a market-oriented reform and begun its open-door policy. In more than 20 years, although system devolvement and structural transformation were mostly driven by domestic factors, China has been increasingly influenced by economic globalization and worldwide industrial upgrade. In the 21st century, it is estimated that Chinese economic development will be influenced by world economy, especially the economy of the Asian area. The Chinese economy will depend on the attitude and strategy China will take toward being involved in the globalization process.

OUTLOOK FOR CHINA'S ECONOMY. The long-term outlook for the Chinese economy remains unclear. China's commitment to join the WTO appears to represent a major commitment on the part of the Chinese government to significant economic reform and greater access to its domestic markets. Some observers believe that the Chinese government views accession to the WTO as an important, though painful, step towards making Chinese firms more efficient and competitive in the world market. In addition, the government hopes that **liberalized** trade rules will attract more foreign investment to China. It is expected that over the long run a more open market system would boost competition, improve productivity, and lower costs for consumers, as well as for firms using imported goods as inputs for production. Economic resources would be redirected towards more profitable ventures, especially those in China's growing private sector. As a result, China would likely experience more rapid economic growth than would occur under current economic policies. It is estimated that WTO membership would double China's trade and foreign investment levels by the year 2005 and raise real GDP growth by an additional 0.5 percent per year.

In the short run, due to increased foreign competition, widespread economic reforms (if implemented) could result in disruptions in certain industries, especially unprofitable SOEs. As a result, many firms would likely go bankrupt and many workers could lose their jobs. How the government handles these disruptions will greatly determine the extent and pace of future reforms. The central government appears to be counting on trade liberalization to boost foreign investment and spur overall economic growth; doing so would enable laid-off workers to be employed in higher growth sectors, especially in the growing private sector. However, the Chinese government is deeply concerned about maintaining social stability. If trade liberalization were followed by a severe economic slowdown, leading to widespread bankruptcies and layoffs, the central government might choose to halt certain economic reforms rather than risk possible political upheaval.

In February 1998 the officials announced their intentions to spend US$750 billion on infrastructure development over the next 3 years, although many analysts have questioned China's ability to obtain funding for such a massive financial undertaking in such a short period of time. It is likely that China intends to attract foreign investment for much of its infrastructure needs.

However, Chinese restrictions on ownership, profits, and operational control of major projects, China's demands for subsidized financing and sharing of technology, and uncertainties regarding obtaining approval from Chinese officials at the central and local levels have made foreign investors reluctant to invest in major Chinese infrastructure projects.

WEST REGION DEVELOPMENT. The central government has decided to accelerate the economic development in its west regions over the next few decades. China will build more highways in its western region, including 2 linking the heartland with the Tibet Autonomous Region, over the next 5 to 10 years. There are already 3 highways linking the inland areas with Tibet. China will also build another 14 main highways in the western region in the coming 10 years. China will have completed a modern highway network in the west by 2030. At the moment, roads in the western region are poor and insufficient. There are only 7.8 kilometers of highways per 100 square kilometers in the region, only half the national average. China has made the improvement of infrastructure the priority in its program to develop the vast western region. This development is expected to become one of the most dynamic forces in the country's economic growth.

ENVIRONMENTAL PROTECTION. The last 2 decades of rapid economic growth, urbanization, and industrialization have been accompanied by steady deterioration of the environment in China. The concentration of both air and water pollutants are among the highest in the world, causing damage to human health and lost agricultural productivity. Some major Chinese cities have particulate and sulfur levels from 2 to 5 times World Health Organization and Chinese standards. Soil erosion, deforestation, and damage to wetlands and grasslands have resulted in deterioration of the national ecosystems and pose a threat to future agricultural sustainability.

China has already taken some steps to reduce pollution and deforestation and has staved off an abrupt worsening of environmental conditions in general. A system of pollution control programs and institutional networks for environmental protection is being constructed at the national and local levels. As part of the recent government reorganization, China's environmental agency, the State Environmental Protection Agency (SEPA), has been upgraded to full ministerial rank and its coverage expanded to include the "green" issues. For better urban and industrial pollution control, China has focused increasingly on river basin management, greater use of economic incentives, and increased use of public information campaigns. Issues of vehicle emissions in urban areas are being tackled through improved traffic management, public transport initiatives, changes in transport fees, and phasing out of leaded gas, which has already been implemented in the largest city centers. Coastal zone management has been introduced, and energy conservation efforts and the development of renewable sources of energy have been expanded.

DEPENDENCIES

China has no territories or colonies.

BIBLIOGRAPHY

Cao Yuanzheng. "World Economic Restructuring and China's Economic Transformation." Paper Presented at 6th Meeting of the Trilateral Forum, Sponsored by Berkeley Roundtable on International Economy. Berkeley, California, 28–29 January 2000.

Economist Intelligence Unit. *Country Profile: China.* London: Economist Intelligence Unit, 2001.

Economist Intelligence Unit. *Financing Foreign Operation: China.* London: Economist Intelligence Unit, 1992.

Embassy of the People's Republic of China in the United States of America. <http://www.china-embassy.org/eng/index.html>. Accessed October 2001.

Han, Taejoon. "China: A Shared Poverty to Uneven Wealth?" *The George Washington University.* <http://www.hfni.gsehd.gwu.edu/~econ270/Taejoon.html>. Accessed February 2001.

Holmes, William D. "China's Financial Reforms in the Global Market." Paper presented at the Conference on Regulation of Capital Markets and Financial Services in the Pacific Rim, Washington. Georgetown University Law Center, 11–13 November 1996.

Hong Kong Christian Industrial Committee. "Working Conditions in Chinese Factories Making Disney Products." *Global Exchange.* <http://www.globalexchange.org/economy/corporations/china/HongKongReport.html>. Accessed February 2001.

Hu, Angang. "Employment and Deployment: China's Employment Problem and Employment Strategy." *World Economy & China.* Vol. 7, No. 1, January, 1999.

Khan, Azizur Rahman. "Issues in Development Discussion Paper 22: Poverty in China in the Period of Globalization: New Evidence on Trend and Pattern." *International Labor Organization.* <http://www.ilo.org/public/english/employment/strat/publ/iddp22.htm>. Accessed February 2001.

Lamble, Peter, and Robin Low. *The Asia Pacific Insurance Handbook.* Sydney, NWT: Coopers & Lybrand, 1995.

Liu Jintang, and Lin Fude. "Zero Growth: Long-Term Effect of China's Family Planning Program." <http://www.cpirc.org.cn/e-view1.htm>. Accessed February 2001.

Liu Yingqiu. "Changes in China's Economic Growth Pattern and Domestic Demand Stimulation." *World Economy & China.* Vol. 7, No. 3–4, 5–6, 1999.

Maurice, Beryl. "Working Conditions in Chinese Factories Making Disney Products." *Global Exchange.* <http://www.globalexchange.org/economy/corporations/china/HongKongReport.html>. Accessed February 2001.

Morrison, Wayne M. "IB98014: China's Economic Conditions." *The National Council for Science and the Environment.* <http://www.cnie.org/nle/inter-10.html>. Accessed February 2001.

Rojas, Róbinson. "The Other Side of China Economic Miracle: Unemployment and Inequality." *The Róbinson Rojas Archive.* <http://www.rrojasdatabank.org/chinaemp.htm>. Accessed February 2001.

U.S. Central Intelligence Agency. *World Factbook 2001.* <http://www.odci.gov/cia/publications/factbook/index.html>. Accessed September 2001.

U.S. Department of the Treasury. *National Treatment Study.* Washington: Government Printing Office, 1994.

—Robert Guang Tian and Camilla Hong Wang

CYPRUS

Republic of Cyprus
Kypriaki Dimokratia

CAPITAL: Republic of Cyprus: Nicosia. **Turkish Republic of Northern Cyprus:** Lefkosia.

MONETARY UNIT: Greek zone: Cypriot pound (CP). One Cypriot pound equals 100 cents. There are coins of 1, 2, 5, 10, 20, and 50 cents and 1 pound. Paper notes include a 50 cent note, and 1, 5, 10, and 20 pound notes. **Turkish zone:** Turkish lira (TL). One Turkish lira equals 100 kurus. This zone uses the same currency as used in Turkey. The smallest unit in circulation in the TRNC is TL50,000. The kuru is no longer in circulation due to high rates of inflation and the devaluation of the currency. Paper money comes in bills of 50,000, 100,000, 250,000, 500,000, 1 million, 5 million, and 10 million lira. There are coins of 5,000, 10,000, 25,000, 50,000, and 100,000 lira.

CHIEF EXPORTS: Both Greek and Turkish zones: Citrus, potatoes, and textiles. **Additional exports from the Greek zone:** Grapes, wine, cement and shoes.

CHIEF IMPORTS: Greek zone: Consumer goods, petroleum and lubricants, food and feed grains, machinery. **Turkish zone:** Food, minerals, chemicals, machinery.

GROSS DOMESTIC PRODUCT: Greek zone: US$9 billion (1998 est.). **Turkish zone:** US$820 million (1998 est.).

BALANCE OF TRADE: Exports: *Greek zone,* US$1 billion (1999); *Turkish zone,* US$63.9 million (1998). **Imports:** *Greek zone,* US$3.309 billion (1999); *Turkish zone,* US$421 million (1998).

COUNTRY OVERVIEW

LOCATION AND SIZE. The Republic of Cyprus is the internationally recognized government on the island. In 1983, a separate Turkish administration declared the northern territory an independent state and calls itself the Turkish Republic of Northern Cyprus (TRNC). Unless otherwise indicated, the "Republic of Cyprus" or "the government of Cyprus" mentioned in this entry refers to the internationally recognized government administered by the Greek Cypriots. For practical purposes, the terms "Greek zone" and "Turkish zone" are used to describe the 2 parts of the island.

The third largest Mediterranean island after Sicily and Sardinia, Cyprus is located in the East Mediterranean Basin 75 kilometers (47 miles) south of Turkey. The island has an area of 9,251 square kilometers (3,571 square

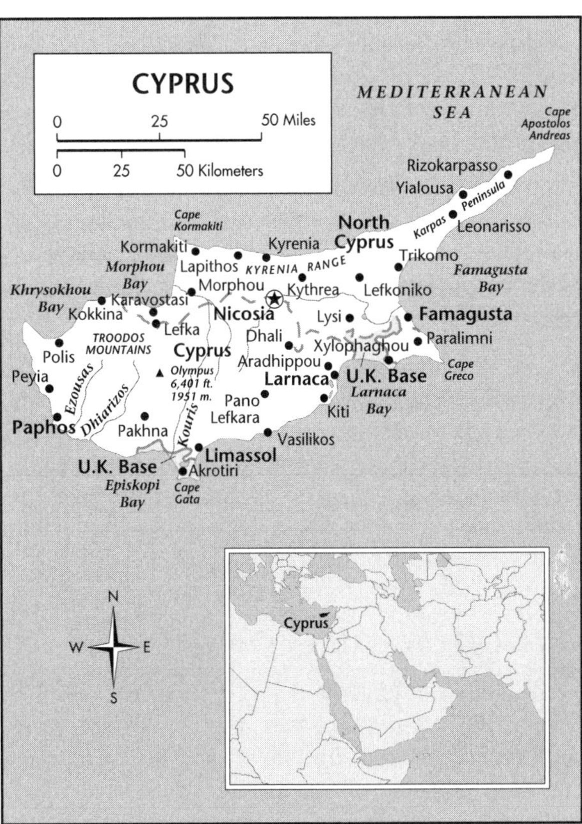

miles) and a coastline of 648 kilometers (402 miles). Comparatively the island is only about half the size of the state of Connecticut. The capital, Nicosia, is located in the central part of the island. It is a militarily-divided capital, with the Greek Cypriots controlling the southern portion of the city (called Nicosia) and the Turkish Cypriots controlling the northern portion of the city (called Lefkosia).

POPULATION. The population of the entire Republic of Cyprus in 2000 was 758,363. The predicted growth rate for the population is 0.6 percent, according to 2000 estimates. The country is relatively young, with the age group between 0 and 14 making up about 23 percent of the total population. The life expectancy is 72 years for women and 70 for men in the Turkish zone, but 80 and 75, respectively, in the Greek zone.

The population of the Turkish Republic of Northern Cyprus, according to the revisions of the 1996 census, was 200,587. Of this number, 164,460 were Turkish Cypriot citizens, 30,702 Turkish citizens, and 5,425 people with citizenship in other countries. The natural rate of population growth in the Turkish zone is 0.9 percent.

The Greek Cypriots make up slightly more than three-fourths of the island's population, with 99.5 percent of them living in the Greek zone and the remaining 0.5 percent in the Turkish zone. Turkish Cypriots make up nearly all of the remaining population, with 98.7 percent of them living in the Turkish zone and 1.3 percent in the Greek zone. Other ethnic minorities make up less than 5 percent of the island's total population, and they live mainly in the Greek zone. Turkish nationals can enter the Turkish zone without passport formalities. However, entry is restricted from the Turkish to the Greek zones.

Three languages are spoken on the island: Greek, Turkish, and English. Greek is the dominant language in the south; Turkish predominates in the north. A majority of the population can also speak English. More than 90 percent of the population is literate.

The religious structure of the island is divided, like its people. Members of Greek Orthodox churches comprise 78 percent of the island's total population and live mainly in the Republic of Cyprus. The Turks in the TRNC are mainly Muslims. Other religious groups like Maronites and Armenian Apostolics together account for less than 5 percent of the total population.

OVERVIEW OF ECONOMY

The division of Cyprus into 2 areas, controlled by Greek and Turkish authorities respectively, shapes the economic affairs and structure of the island. The economy of the Republic of Cyprus experienced rapid growth in the 1970s after the island's division into 2 zones. The government financed investment to replace housing for the Greek Cypriots who moved to the Greek zone after the division. That explains why the **real gross domestic product** (GDP) growth rates were over 6 percent annually in the 1980s. However, the GDP growth rate fell back to an average of 4.3 percent between 1994 and 1999.

Both the Greek and Turkish zones face severe water shortages. The island has no natural reservoir and experiences seasonal inequalities in rainfall. Although there is an aquifer (underground water supply) on the island, it is subject to seawater intrusion, which increases salt content, especially in the Turkish zone. Both administrations have sought ways to overcome the issue; several desalination (salt removal) plants are planned for construction in the near future.

GREEK ZONE: The economy of the Greek zone is prosperous but can easily be affected by external shocks, since it is heavily dependent on the tourism industry. For instance, in the 1990s the region's economy attained inconsistent growth rates due to swings in tourist arrivals, caused by political instability on the island and changes in economic conditions in Western Europe. Being a candidate for membership in the European Union (EU), economic policies in the Greek zone are focused on meeting the criteria for admission. On the other hand, the attractiveness of the island has led to a concentration of investment and labor in the tourism sector, thus reducing the Greek zone's competitiveness in manufacturing and other sectors.

Inflation rates in the Greek zone have been moderate. The average was 4.8 percent between 1982 and 1990, and had dropped to 1.6 percent by 1999 as a result of economic slowdown. The government uses a wage determination system called COLA (cost-of-living-allowance), which automatically adjusts wages and salaries for **inflation**. The country's unemployment rate stood at 3.6 percent in 1999, below the levels of many EU countries. **Immigration** helps the Cypriot economy maintain its economic growth rate even in times of economic slowdown. Unskilled immigrant labor usually takes agricultural and domestic jobs.

TURKISH ZONE: The economy of the Turkish zone (US$820 million) is much smaller compared to that of the Greek zone (US$9 billion). The northern region has about one-fifth the population and only one-third of the per capita GDP of the south. The GDP growth rates in the north averaged around 4.7 percent in the 1980s, slowing down to an average of 2.8 percent in the 1990–98 period. In 1991 real GDP actually fell by 4.3 percent, and then by 4.1 percent in 1994 as a result of the economic crisis in Turkey. The "Turkish Republic of Northern Cyprus" is recognized only by Turkey, which means the rest of the world still considers the southern Greek administration as the sole administrator of the whole island.

This has created problems for the Turkish Republic of Northern Cyprus' government and its economy. Foreign firms and investors cannot do business in the Turkish zone, as they cannot transfer funds or goods from a country that is not recognized as an independent state. As a result, the economy of the Turkish zone remains heavily dependent on agriculture and government service, which together employ about half of the workforce. The economy also has a small tourism sector, with legalized gambling, serving especially tourists from Turkey, where all forms of gambling have recently been banned. The economy of the Turkish zone is more vulnerable to outside shocks not only because of its small size and its legitimacy (diplomatic recognition), but also because it uses Turkish lira as the legal tender, which has **devaluated** (decreased in value) greatly over the past decade. To compensate for the economy's weakness, Turkey provides direct and indirect aid to tourism, education, and industries located in the Turkish part of the island.

POLITICS, GOVERNMENT, AND TAXATION

Cyprus gained its independence from the United Kingdom in August 1960. Three years later, clashes between the Greek and Turkish communities on the island began, and the island started to disintegrate politically. A junta-based (a small military ruling group) coup attempt backed by Greece in July 1974 led to a Turkish intervention that divided the island in two, creating the de facto (existing if not officially recognized) Turkish Republic of Northern Cyprus. The Greek Cypriots took full control of the internationally recognized government of Cyprus while the Turkish Cypriot administration declared independence for its zone in November 1983. "The Turkish Republic of Northern Cyprus" (TRNC), however, has been recognized only by Turkey. The period from 1983 until 2001 has been characterized mainly by international efforts, under the leadership of the United Nations and the United States, to resolve the conflict between the 2 sides and to create a new type of government. The Greek Cypriot position on the issue has been towards a new federal system (with stronger power for the national government) while the Turkish Cypriots prefer a confederate system (with more power-sharing between Greeks and Turks).

The island has different constitutions and sets of governing bodies for each side. The Greek Cypriots are still using the constitution that took effect in 1960 following independence, while the Turkish Cypriots created their own constitution and governing bodies in 1975 following the 1974 break-up. The TNRC adopted a new constitution passed by a referendum (popular vote) in May 1985. Talks to find a peaceful resolution between the 2 Cypriot zones resumed in 1999.

Glafcos Clerides has served as the president of the Republic of Cyprus since February 1993. He serves as both the head of state and the head of government. According to the 1960 constitution, the post of the vice president is reserved for a Turkish Cypriot, but the office has not been filled since the 1974 separation.

The Turkish Republic of Northern Cyprus also elects a president by a popular vote, although he is only recognized as a head of state by Turkey. Rauf R. Denktash has served as president of the TRNC since February 1975. Dervis Eroglu has been the TRNC's de facto prime minister since August 1996, heading the Turkish zone's Council of Ministers (cabinet).

As there are 2 different heads of state and 2 separate sets of governing bodies on the island, political parties for the 2 zones are different. In the Greek Cypriot political system, the following parties have dominated: Democratic Party (DIKO), Democratic Rally (DISY), Ecologists, New Horizons, Restorative Party of the Working People (AKEL or Communist Party), United Democratic Union of Cyprus (EDEK), United Democrats Movement (EDI, formerly Free Democrats Movement or KED). In the Turkish Cypriot area the main parties have been: Communal Liberation Party (TKP), Democratic Party (DP), National Birth Party (UDP), National Unity Party (UBP), Our Party (BP), Patriotic Unity Movement (YBH), Republican Turkish Party (CTP).

Taxes and foreign economic aid provide the main sources of income for both the Greek Cypriot and Turkish Cypriot governments. In both zones, the government plays an important role in the island's economy. The Turkish zone relies heavily on financial aid from Turkey. Until recently, the Republic of Cyprus government has controlled key sectors of the economy by means of semi-governmental organizations such as those that oversee the telecommunications and power industries. The Republic of Cyprus government has been moving toward a more liberal role in the economy. The country's candidacy for EU membership supports efforts to loosen government control over the economy. For instance, the **liberalization** of air transportation in Europe has forced Cyprus Airways, the island's government-owned airline, to become more efficient. The traditional regulations that restricted retailers' hours of operations and limited special sales to certain times of the year have been recently liberalized so that the island's economy can be more competitive and productive.

INFRASTRUCTURE, POWER, AND COMMUNICATIONS

Cyprus has an efficient power and communications **infrastructure** according to European standards. The state-run enterprises handle most of the island's needs in

Communications

Country	Telephones[a]	Telephones, Mobile/Cellular[a]	Radio Stations[b]	Radios[a]	TV Stations[a]	Televisions[a]	Internet Service Providers[c]	Internet Users[c]
Cyprus	488,162 (1998)	138,000 (1999)	AM 10; FM 71; shortwave 2	366,450	8 (1995)	300,300	6	80,000
United States	194 M	69.209 M (1998)	AM 4,762; FM 5,542; shortwave 18	575 M	1,500	219 M	7,800	148 M
Turkey	19.5 M (1999)	12.1 M (1999)	AM 16; FM 72; shortwave 6	11.3 M	635 (1995)	20.9 M	22	2 M
Lebanon	700,000 (1999)	580,000 (1999)	AM 20; FM 22; shortwave 4	2.85 M	15 (1995)	1.18 M	22	227,500

Note: Totals are combined for Greek and Turkish Cypriot areas.
[a]Data is for 1997 unless otherwise noted.
[b]Data is for 1998 unless otherwise noted.
[c]Data is for 2000 unless otherwise noted.

SOURCE: CIA *World Factbook 2001* [Online].

the way of power generation, harbors, airports, and telecommunications. The island does not have a railroad system; instead the country is covered by highways, of which 10,663 kilometers (approximately 6,626 miles) are within the Greek Cypriot zone and 2,350 kilometers (approximately 1,460 miles) within the Turkish zone. Most of these highways are double-lane highways. There is a limited bus system that connects the cities with the inland, and a convenient taxi service. The island also has 12 airports with paved runways (15 total), which benefits the growing tourist industry. Its main harbors are Famagusta, Kyrenia, Larnaca, Limassol, Paphos, and Vasilikos. Despite its small size, Cyprus maintains the sixth largest ship registry in the world with about 2,700 ships and 27 million gross registered tons. Power generation in the Greek Cypriot zone was 2.675 billion kilowatt hours in 1998, all derived from fossil fuels. Power details on the Turkish zone were unavailable.

The Cyprus Telecommunications Authority handles the communications services in the Greek Cypriot zone, while another state-run enterprise provides this service in the Turkish zone. The Greek zone has 405,000 main telephone lines and 68,000 mobile lines in use; the Turkish zone has 70,845 and 70,000, respectively. Direct international dialing is also available on the island, and postal and courier services are also efficient. There are 4 main TV broadcasting stations in both the Greek and Turkish zones. As of 1999, the island had 5 Internet service providers.

ECONOMIC SECTORS

GREEK ZONE: The Greek Cypriots are among the most prosperous people in the Mediterranean region, and the Greek zone has enjoyed a high level of economic development, especially from the tourism industry. The inflation rate was 2.3 percent in 1998 and declined to 1.6 percent in 1999. The unemployment rate remains around 3.6 percent. The Greek zone has an open, free-market, service-based economy with some light manufacturing. Agriculture and natural resources make up only about 6 percent of its economy, according to 1998 figures. The industrial and construction sectors, on the other hand, accounted for nearly 25 percent of economic activity in that year, with most of the production for domestic need. The remainder of the economy is based on tourism and other services. Included in this category are restaurants and hotels, with 21.6 percent of the GDP; and banking, insurance, real estate, and business sectors with 17.5 percent. Transport, communication, government services, and social and personal services make up the remainder.

Cyprus-*Greek Cypriot area*
GDP–COMPOSITION BY SECTOR–1998

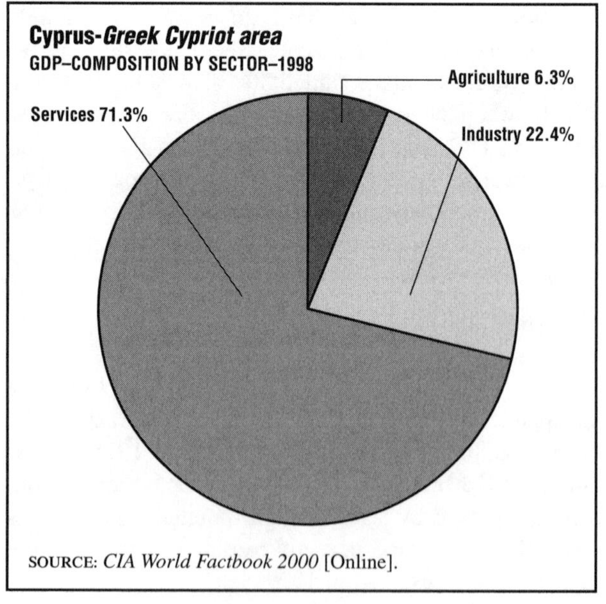

SOURCE: *CIA World Factbook 2000* [Online].

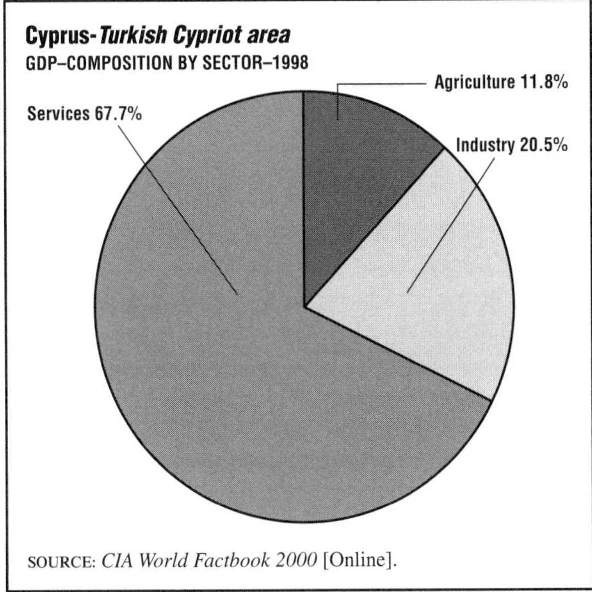

SOURCE: *CIA World Factbook 2000* [Online].

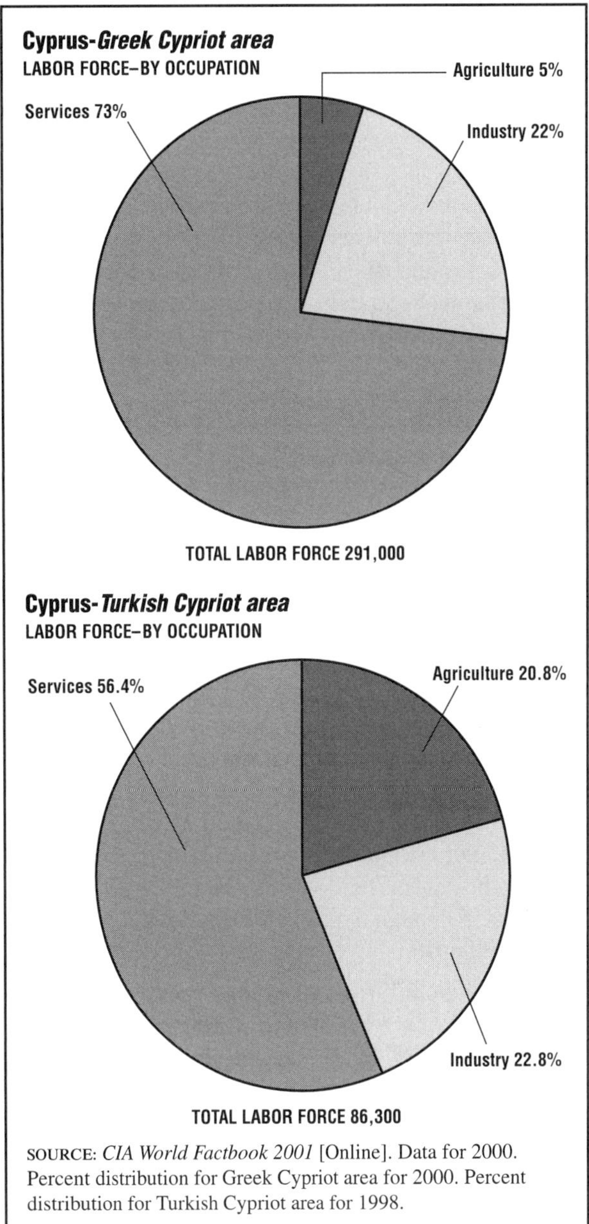

SOURCE: *CIA World Factbook 2001* [Online]. Data for 2000. Percent distribution for Greek Cypriot area for 2000. Percent distribution for Turkish Cypriot area for 1998.

The island receives approximately US$3 billion from service-related exports led by tourism. Compared to only US$1.2 billion from merchandise exports, this is a fairly high proportion in the total economy. The service sector, including tourism, employs about 62 percent of the **labor force**. Consequently, the economy's growth rate is quite vulnerable to swings in tourist arrivals that are in turn affected by economic and political conditions in Cyprus, Western Europe, and the Middle East. According to the U.S. State Department's *Country Background Notes* on Cyprus, the real GDP growth was 9.7 percent in 1992, 1.7 percent in 1993, 6.0 percent in 1994, 6.0 percent in 1995, 1.9 percent in 1996, and 2.3 percent in 1997. Such a volatile pattern shows the effect of tourist arrivals on the overall economy.

Agriculture, on the other hand, employs only 12 percent of the population. Potatoes and citrus are the principal export crops. The island is not self-sufficient in agricultural products and must import other agricultural products for survival. More than 50 percent of Cyprus's trade is with the European Union. Cyprus signed an Association Agreement with the European Union in 1972, which established a Customs Union between the 2 zones. It applied for full EU membership in 1990 and since then the Cyprus pound has been pegged to the euro. The economic agenda in the Republic of Cyprus is geared towards joining the EU.

Trade is vital both to the Greek and Turkish Cypriot economies as the island is not self-sufficient. That explains why both zones have had structural **trade deficits**, which continue to grow. The Republic of Cyprus has a very important ship registry, and currently more than 2,700 ships are registered in Cyprus. As an open registry, it can include foreign ships and vessels. By 2001, more than 43 countries, including the United States, have registered ships with Cyprus. To encourage ship registrations, the Republic of Cyprus has enacted laws that provide incentives to Cypriot ships, including tax exemptions.

TURKISH ZONE: The Turkish Republic of Northern Cyprus does almost all of its trade with Turkey and uses Turkish lira, the currency used in the republic of Turkey, as its legal tender. Assistance from Turkey is the mainstay of this zone's economy, thus making it very vulnerable to shocks coming from Turkey. For instance, the TRNC experiences the same rate of inflation that exists in mainland Turkey. As the value of Turkish lira falls against other currencies such as the dollar or the euro, so does the purchasing power of Turkish Cypriots against imported goods from the United States or Europe. In 1998, the Turkish zone experienced an inflation rate of 66 percent, which was the same as in Turkey. The unemployment rate in the Turkish zone reached 6.4 percent in 1997, almost double the rate in the Greek zone. According to an economic protocol signed in January 1997, Turkey has undertaken the provision of loans to the TRNC totaling $250 million for public finance, tourism, banking, and **privatization**.

AGRICULTURE

GREEK ZONE: Agriculture accounted for 6 percent of the GDP in 1997, and it employed about 12 percent of the labor force. Agricultural products accounted for 21 percent of total domestic imports in 1997. In 1998 revenue from agricultural products was US$531 million. Citrus fruits and potatoes are the main export commodities, followed by grapes, barley, and vegetables. In 1996 the area under field crops was 93,000 hectares. Vineyards covered 15 percent of this acreage, while permanent orchards accounted for 11 percent, and olive vineyards and nut trees an additional 6.2 percent. Agricultural production is dependent on the island's temperate Mediterranean climate with hot dry summers and cool winters. In terms of value, 56 percent of the 1996 gross harvest was consumed in Cyprus. Although domestic markets are important for agriculture, processing of agricultural products for other uses is becoming more important. Per capita consumption levels of fruits and citrus are exceptionally high in Cyprus, with 55 kg per person for citrus and 146 kg for other fruits.

In Cyprus, farm processing is important, with production of halloumi cheese, raisins, and wine being the most important. Such processed farm products have higher export values than unprocessed food products and are easier to sell abroad, especially since closer integration with the European Union has made more of Cyprus's farm products available to consumers in Europe.

Fishing is an expanding sub-sector of agriculture. Fish farms have been installed on the south coast, and local and tourist fish markets provide a continuous demand. In recent years, the catch from inshore and trawler fisheries has increased, while marine aquaculture (sea fishing) has stagnated. The Cyprus government reported that the Cyprus Fisheries produced more than 3 tons of fish in 1997.

Agriculture in the Greek zone has an uncertain future, because the sector is declining in importance against other sectors like tourism. It is also affected by rainfall fluctuations and by the water-shortage problem on the island as a whole.

TURKISH ZONE: The northern Turkish zone relies more heavily on agriculture than the southern Greek zone. Although only one-third of the island's area is under Turkish control, its agricultural sector accounts for 46 percent of Cyprus's total crop production and 47 percent of its livestock population. Agriculture employs more than 25 percent of the Turkish zone labor force. Its agriculture sector experienced a severe blow in 1995 when the region lost nearly 10 percent of its forests in a major fire. The sector has also been hurt by regulatory difficulties surrounding the export of agricultural products. The European Court of Justice has ruled that agricultural products must have phytosanitary (certifying that plants are disease-free) certificates from the legally recognized authorities of the Republic of Cyprus. As a result, many agricultural products from the Turkish zone must first be exported to Turkey before getting into European markets. Another disadvantage is that the Turkish Cypriots have to accept payments for their exports in Turkish liras instead of **hard currency** such as the dollar or the euro.

INDUSTRY

MINING. Information about mining in the separate zones is not available. Mining has long played an important role in Cyprus's economy. For several thousand years, the island has been an important source of copper ores. It also produces pyrites, asbestos, gypsum, salt, marble, clay, and earth pigment. In the 1950s, minerals accounted for almost 60 percent of all exports and employed more than 6,000 people. After independence in 1960, however, the share of mineral exports had fallen to 34 percent. The 1974 Turkish intervention further disrupted the mining sector. In 1981 its share in total exports fell below 5 percent and by the end of the 1980s to less than 1 percent. The contribution of the sector to the GDP also declined, to 0.5 percent in 1985 and 0.4 percent in 1987 and 1988. Most of the deposits on the southern part of the island are nearly gone today. The asbestos mines were closed in 1988, thus further reducing the share of the mining sector in the economy. By the 1990s, the main mining products were pyrites and copper. The mining of sand and other construction minerals fluctuates with demand. By the late 1990s, 250 quarries were operating in the Republic of Cyprus. Though the mining industry had declined since the Turkish invasion, the Hellenic Copper Mine's 1996 establishment of a mine at Skouriotissa was encouraging.

MANUFACTURING. According to the U.S. State Department's *Background Notes* on Cyprus, manufactured goods accounted for approximately 69 percent of the Greek zone's domestic exports in 1997. Before the partition of the island, most of the manufacturing goods were produced in what is now the Turkish zone by small, owner-operated plants. Most of the production was for the domestic market. After 1974, the industries were reoriented for export, and large factories were built in the southern Greek-controlled zone. Output grew rapidly there through the 1980s. The manufacturing sector's contribution to the economy of the Greek zone declined from 17.3 percent in 1983 to 10.9 percent in 1999. During the same period, the total employment in the manufacturing sector has also declined, from 21 percent of the overall labor force to around 13 percent. The heavy industries include petroleum refining and cement while the light industries include clothing, footwear, and machinery and transport equipment. High **tariffs** put on imports to protect domestic manufacturing industries were lifted under the membership agreement with the European Union. This fact, plus the rise of tourism and the service economy, has hurt the competitiveness of the manufacturing sector in the Greek zone. In 2000, the Republic of Cyprus was actively trying to attract high-technology businesses to the country.

In the Turkish zone, industry in 1998 accounted for about 11.8 percent of the GDP and 55.4 percent of the total employment in its region, according to the *World Factbook 2000*. Manufacturing is almost entirely based on light industry, with textiles and clothing being the most important products. The only example of heavy industry is a cement factory at Boghaz. In the late 1980s, clothing accounted for over 30 percent of all exports in the Turkish region, exceeded only by citrus exports. In 1989, for the first time, manufacturing surpassed agriculture's contribution to the GDP and has grown since then. However, compared to the situation in the Greek zone, the Turkish-zone manufacturing sector is small.

SERVICES

TOURISM. Tourism is very important to the functioning of the Cypriot economy both in the south and the north. Revenue from tourism contributed approximately US$1.7 billion to the economy of the Greek zone in 1998. The reduced airfares resulting from the liberalization of the airline industry in Europe helped make Cyprus a major tourist destination during the 1970s. The tourist industry on the island was hurt during that decade because of the ongoing disputes between the Turkish and Greek populations, but since the 1980s, it has grown dramatically, especially in the Greek zone. By 2001, Cyprus, especially the southern side, had become a popular holiday spot for many Europeans. Offering natural beaches, warm climate, and unspoiled nature, the island attracts many vacationers from nearby countries. The Greek zone is also more easily accessible via its international airports and cruise-ship ports.

Tourism in the Turkish zone is hampered by legitimacy problems. Since the TRNC is not recognized as an independent and sovereign state by any other nation except Turkey, it does not have consular offices (official offices to represent a country's commercial interests abroad) in other countries where visitors or tourism agencies can easily arrange travel. There are few international flights to the Turkish zone. The TRNC's official airline, Cyprus Turkish Airlines (KHTY), circumvents such problems by making brief stops on the Turkish mainland prior to its final destination in Turkish Cyprus. Tourists from Turkey make up more than 80 percent of all tourists coming to the Turkish zone. Despite these limitations, tourism continues to be the driving force behind the TRNC's economy. In 1999, earnings from tourism were estimated at around US$405 million, equivalent to 43 percent of the region's GDP. Since gambling is permitted, the TRNC serves as an important holiday destination for tourists coming from Turkey, where casinos are banned. The Turkish zone is also a popular shopping destination for mainland Turks who take advantage of the region's lower taxes.

Both the Greek and Turkish zones have a good tourism infrastructure with sufficient, quality lodging and other facilities. As of 1998, the Greek zone had a capacity of 86,151 beds, according to the Cyprus Statistical Service. In 1999, 2.4 million foreign tourists arrived in the southern zone. U.S. State Department surveys forecast even higher revenues from tourism in coming years, though the political dispute between the 2 sides on the island remains a potential barrier.

FINANCIAL SERVICES. According to the U.S. State Department's *Country Commercial Guide* on Cyprus, finance, insurance, real estate, and business services recorded gains recently (from 16.6 percent of GDP in 1992 to 19.8 percent in 1998).

The banking system in Cyprus consists of the Central Bank of Cyprus and 9 local commercial banks, as well as several specialized financial institutions, leasing companies, and co-operatives. There is also an established foreign banking community, which includes 30 international banking units. Commercial banking arrangements and practices follow the British system. In 1996, the Central Bank of Cyprus achieved substantial progress in its campaign to liberalize and reform Cyprus's financial sector. **Monetary policy** is now conducted through the use of market-based instruments. Repurchase transactions between the Central Bank and financial institutions are the main tool of **liquidity** management, and the use of the minimum liquidity requirement has been abandoned. The new procedures are fully in line with EU practices.

In the Greek zone, a law that came into effect on 1 January 2001 abolished the 9 percent ceiling on interest rates that had existed since 1944, enabling depositors to receive higher returns on their savings. In addition, previous restrictions on Cypriots' ability to own foreign currency and make overseas investments are being loosened as part of a 3-stage plan to harmonize the country's financial industry with EU standards. The Greek zone is now an open country for foreign investment, whereas prior to 1997 there were restrictions on the participation of foreigners in Cypriot firms. In preparation for EU membership, all foreign-investment restrictions for EU investors have been abolished since January 2000. Foreigners can own up to 100 percent of companies in the manufacturing and services sectors and up to 49 percent of businesses in the agriculture, media, press, and travel sectors. Cyprus also has a stock exchange, where foreigners are permitted to own up to 49 percent of publicly traded companies. Foreign investment makes the economy stronger by bringing new capital and technologies to existing industries, helping to modernize them, and creating jobs.

Businesses in the Turkish zone cannot attract foreign investment because of the legitimacy problem mentioned earlier.

INTERNATIONAL TRADE

GREEK ZONE: In 1998 the Greek zone recorded a **balance of payments** deficit of US$342.8 million compared to a deficit of US$229.9 million in 1997. The trade deficit reached a record of US$2.5 billion in 1998, due in part to a decline in tourism revenues in 1996 and 1997. Also, the volume of imports did not decrease as much as the decline in the country's export revenues, helping to make the deficit even higher.

Middle Eastern countries receive 20 percent of exports from Cyprus. Cyprus **re-exports** cigarettes from the United States to 2 major markets for tobacco products: Russia and Bulgaria. The economic crisis in these countries has hurt consumer purchasing power, thus lowering Cyprus's revenues from these exports.

The amount of total imports increased in 1998 to a total of US$3.5 billion. Most of these imports were **intermediate goods** and **capital goods**. While Cyprus faced difficulty in selling its products or re-selling U.S. products abroad, it bought more from abroad, making its trade deficit higher. Cyprus must import fuels, most raw materials, heavy machinery, and transportation equipment. More than 50 percent of the country's trade is with the European Union, especially with England.

Cyprus has recently attempted to liberalize its trade policies by eliminating import quotas and licenses. It has also lowered tariffs on most products as a result of its obligations to the EU for the Customs Union Agreement. The country's entry into the Customs Union with the EU has also made trade conditions more competitive (restrictive) for U.S. exporters doing business in Cyprus.

Trade (expressed in billions of US$): Cyprus

	Exports	Imports
1975	.150	.308
1980	.532	1.202
1985	.476	1.247
1990	.957	2.568
1995	1.229	3.694
1998	1.061	3.685

SOURCE: International Monetary Fund. *International Financial Statistics Yearbook 1999.*

However, according to the U.S. State Department's analysis, the United States has a competitive edge over its European allies in the sales of computer-assisted design systems, medical equipment, environmental products, and new capital equipment for production of textiles, clothing, and footwear. Compared to those of European origin, U.S. software products are in higher demand in Cyprus. U.S. pressure resulted in new copyright (1994) and patent (1998) laws that helped protect U.S. software products, thus increasing the sales of those products.

TURKISH ZONE: The TNRC does most of its trade with Turkey (around 47 percent in 1998), followed by England (slightly more than 25 percent) and other EU countries (15 percent). The Turkish zone's trading account continues to be in deficit, but is offset by earnings from tourism and development programs, which come largely from Turkey, and also from income by United Nations personnel stationed in the zone.

MONEY

GREEK ZONE: The Cyprus pound is printed and circulated through the Central Bank of Cyprus, which aims to keep it stable in relation to the euro. Cyprus does most of its trade with the European Union. As a result, the Cyprus pound has been linked to the European Monetary Union system of currencies (EMU). As of 1 January 1999, the Cyprus pound has been linked to the euro.

TURKISH ZONE: Following the 1974 separation, the Turkish Cypriot zone adopted the Turkish lira as the legal tender, but the Cyprus pound was used until 1983. The Cyprus pound is now considered a foreign currency in this region and is subject to foreign exchange regulations. Still, the Cyprus pound is used by businesses, along with the British pound and the U.S. dollar in the Turkish zone to assess export and import prices or in trading. There is also a central bank in the Turkish zone, but its functions and powers are limited. Since the Turkish lira is the legal tender and is printed in mainland Turkey, the central bank can neither print money nor decide on mon-

Exchange rates: Cyprus

	Cypriot pounds per US$1	Turkish liras per US$
Jan 2001	0.6146	N/A
2000	0.6208	625,219
1999	0.5423	418,783
1998	0.5170	260,724
1997	0.5135	151,865
1996	0.4663	81,405

SOURCE: CIA *World Factbook 2001* [ONLINE].

GDP per Capita (US$)

Country	1975	1980	1985	1990	1998
Cyprus	3,619	6,334	7,818	10,405	12,857
United States	19,364	21,529	23,200	25,363	29,683
Turkey	1,898	1,959	2,197	2,589	3,167
Lebanon	N/A	N/A	N/A	1,721	2,999

Note: Totals are combined for Greek and Turkish Cypriot areas.

SOURCE: United Nations. *Human Development Report 2000; Trends in human development and per capita income.*

etary policy. It receives daily **exchange rates** from Turkey and passes them on to commercial banks operating in the northern zone, but it has no control over the interest rates. Since it has such strong links to Turkey, the economy in the TNRC is affected by the same high inflation as in mainland Turkey, where the consumer-price inflation rate was 99.1 percent in 1997 and 69.7 percent in 1998. The economy of the Turkish zone also suffered in 1994 when Turkey experienced a severe economic crisis and devalued its currency. To compensate for these problems, Turkey has long provided direct and indirect aid to nearly every sector. Today, financial support from mainland Turkey accounts for about one-third of the zone's total GDP.

POVERTY AND WEALTH

The people of the Greek zone are among the most affluent in the world. According to the World Bank's Development Report, Cyprus is ranked 16th in terms of per capita income adjusted for purchasing power. In 1988 per capita income was US$15,500, according to the CIA *World Factbook.*

The Republic of Cyprus reported that 97 percent of the houses in Cyprus are in good or average condition and that 69 percent of those houses have facilities like electricity and plumbing. No information is available regarding the percentage of the population below the poverty line. A May 2000 editorial in the *Sunday Mail*, a Greek Cypriot newspaper, estimated that 70,000 people in the Greek zone (about 10 percent of the population) live below the poverty line and receive welfare from the government. When the Turkish invasion of 1974 displaced about 25,000 people, the Republic of Cyprus responded with policies to provide housing to low and middle-income people. By 1995, the government reported that 14,000 housing units had been constructed, including schools, shopping centers, and playgrounds, and that 12,000 people had taken advantage of **subsidies** available to build their own homes.

In the Turkish zone, the per capita income decreased to around US$5,000. The Republic of Cyprus estimated that nearly one-third of the Turkish Cypriots have **emigrated** since 1974. Turkish nationals began moving to Cyprus in 1974 and by 1995 outnumbered Turkish Cypriots. In addition to the Turkish nationals, the TRNC maintains 35,000 Turkish military personnel who guard the area.

WORKING CONDITIONS

GREEK ZONE: The Republic of Cyprus had a 3.3 percent unemployment rate in 1999 and a workforce of about 314,000 people. Workers are protected by laws regulating their health and safety on the job. In addition to legislation, trade unions also play an important role in workers' lives. The initial attempt to form trade unions in Cyprus took place in 1915, when the country was under British rule, but the first of them, the Nicosia Footwear Union, was not recognized until 1932, a year after it was established. After labor unrest in 1944, Cyprus adopted a cost-of-living allowance (COLA) for its workers. The 8-hour workday was accepted only after independence.

TURKISH ZONE: The Turkish zone labor force was estimated at 80,200 people in 1998, and the unemployment rate was 6.4 percent. Almost one-third of the labor force in the Turkish zone is unionized. Minimum wages are untaxed and are fixed annually by law according to inflation indexing, the so-called "cost of living allowance" (COLA) standard.

COUNTRY HISTORY AND ECONOMIC DEVELOPMENT

1500–1450 B.C. First traces of settlement on Cyprus. Some evidence suggests that the settlers were related to the peoples of Asia Minor (present-day Turkey).

1450–1000 B.C. Beginning of the Egyptian domination of the island.

1200–1000 B.C. Establishment of the city-states of Salamis, Soli, Marion, Paphos, Kurium, and Kyrenna; arrival of Greek colonists.

850–750 B.C. Phoenicians settle in several areas and share political control with the Greeks.

750–612 B.C. Period of Assyrian rule. The Assyrian king Sargon II conquers the 7 independent kingdoms on the island.

568–525 B.C. Period of Egyptian rule.

525–333 B.C. Period of Persian rule.

333–58 B.C. Period of Hellenistic rule by the heirs of the Alexander the Great.

58 B.C.-395 A.D. Period of Roman Empire rule.

395–1191. Period of Byzantine Empire rule.

1191–1192. Briefly ruled by Richard the Lionheart of England.

1192–1489. Period of Lusignan rule. Tensions between the Greek Orthodox Church and the Roman Catholic Church increase. The Cypriots remain loyal to their Orthodox heritage and by the middle of the 14th century the Latin clergy become less determined to convert the islanders.

1489–1570. Island is dominated by the Italian city-state of Venice.

1571–1878. Period of Ottoman Empire rule. The Ottomans grant land to Turkish soldiers and peasants who then become the nucleus of the island's Turkish community.

1878–1914. Cyprus is administered by Great Britain according to an agreement with the Ottoman Empire.

1914. Cyprus is annexed by Great Britain at the start of World War I.

1925. Cyprus becomes a British Crown colony.

1960. Foundation of the Independent Republic of Cyprus.

1963. Inter-communal strife in Cyprus between Greek and Turkish sectors leads to establishment of United Nations peacekeeping mission.

1974. Greek army officers stage coup d'état and overthrow President Makarios with the aim of uniting the island with Greece. Turkey intervenes and lands its forces on the northern part of the island, where they have remained ever since. The island is divided into a Turkish Cypriot northern zone and a Greek Cypriot southern zone.

1983. Turkish Cypriots proclaim the Turkish Republic of Northern Cyprus (TRNC). Rauf Denktash is elected the president.

1987. The Republic of Cyprus signs a new association agreement with the European Union establishing a full customs union by 2002.

1996. Greece lifts its veto on Turkey's customs union with the European Union in exchange for a date for the commencement of negotiations to allow for Cyprus's membership.

1998. EU accession talks begin.

FUTURE TRENDS

Cyprus entered the 21st century as a separated island of 2 nations and 2 religions. The division between the two will be the main focus of debate and discussion in the international arena in the years to come. The division between the 2 economies also affects the level of development of the nation. The Greek zone (Republic of Cyprus) enjoys the benefits of international recognition and has attained high levels of development and per capita income, but the Turkish zone (TRNC) has suffered economically and politically from the international **embargo**.

Cyprus's application for full EU membership is also a critical step that will have further consequences for the island's political economy and development. It is unclear whether the Turkish Cypriots will abandon their claims for a confederation in favor of the Greek Cypriot proposal of a federated state. Although TRNC president Denktash has called for further integration with mainland Turkey, which would mean the annexation of the island's Turkish zone into the homeland, the likelihood of this scenario is still unclear. EU officials project that Cyprus will be a full member of the European Union by 2010.

As the Republic of Cyprus prepares for full EU membership, it will continue to harmonize its economy and institutional framework with EU standards. As indicated by the World Trade Organization (WTO) in its 1997 policy review, financial openness is one of the cornerstones of policy reform for Cyprus. The WTO also notes the growing importance of the nation's services sector. This sector accounts for roughly 70 percent of the country's foreign exchange receipts as well as its GDP. Although the economy of the Greek zone is a prosperous one, the fact that the country suffers from a structural deficit and that it must rely on imports is not likely to change, even after a possible EU membership.

DEPENDENCIES

Cyprus has no territories or colonies.

BIBLIOGRAPHY

Agribusiness Online. "World Agricultural Trade Import and Export of Agricultural Products including Fish." <http://www

.agribusiness.asn.au/Statistics/International/world_agricultural_trade1.htm#Total Exports>. Accessed February 2001.

Central Bank of Cyprus. "Cyprus in Brief; Banking and Finance." <http://www.centralbank.gov.cy/cyprus/bank-fin.html>. Accessed February 2001.

Economist Intelligence Unit. <http://dataservices.bvdep.com>. Accessed March 2001.

———. *Country Profile: Cyprus and Malta.* London: Economist Intelligence Unit, 2001.

———. *Country Report: Cyprus and Malta.* London: Economist Intelligence Unit, December, 2000.

Federal Research Division/Library of Congress. "Cyprus, A Country Study." <http://lcweb2.loc.gov/frd/cs/cytoc.html>. Accessed February 2001.

"'In Your Face,' Wealth, 'Below the Line,' Poverty." *The Sunday Mail* (Nicosia, Cyprus), 14 May 2000.

The Republic of Cyprus. "The Official Web Site of the Republic of Cyprus." <http://www.pio.gov.cy/index.html>. Accessed February 2001.

Smith, Bamijoko S., editor. "International Development Options. USA." *Global Development Studies.* Winter-Spring 1999.

U.S. Central Intelligence Agency. *The World Factbook.* <http://www.cia.gov/cia/publications/factbook>. Accessed January 2001.

U.S. Department of State. *FY2001 Country Commercial Guide: 2001.* <http://www.state.gov/www/about_state/business/com_guides/2001/europe/cyprus_ccg2001.pdf>. Accessed February 2001.

World Trade Organization. "WTO: Trade Policy Reviews; Cyprus, June 1997." <http://www.wto.org/english/tratop_e/tpr_e/tp55_e.htm>. Accessed February 2001.

—Emre Ozsoz

FIJI

Republic of Fiji

CAPITAL: Suva.

MONETARY UNIT: Fijian dollar (F$). One Fijian dollar equals 100 cents. Coins are in amounts of 1, 2, 5, 10, 20, and 50 cents. Notes come in denominations of F$1, 2, 5, 10, and 20.

CHIEF EXPORTS: Sugar, garments, gold, timber, silver, fish.

CHIEF IMPORTS: Machinery and transport equipment, petroleum products, food, chemicals.

GROSS DOMESTIC PRODUCT: US$5.9 billion (purchasing power parity, 1999 est.).

BALANCE OF TRADE: **Exports:** US$537.7 million (f.o.b., 1999). **Imports:** US$653 million (f.o.b., 1999).

COUNTRY OVERVIEW

LOCATION AND SIZE. Fiji is a Melanesian island group located in the South Pacific at 175 degrees east longitude and 18 degrees south latitude. The islands are about 1,770 kilometers (1,100 miles) north of New Zealand. The group comprises 332 volcanic islands scattered in a horseshoe across an area of ocean some 595 kilometers (370 miles) across. Fiji has a total land area of 18,270 square kilometers (7,054 square miles), of which 87 percent is made up by its 2 largest islands, Vanua Levu and Viti Levu. Comparable in size to New Jersey, with a coastline of 1,129 kilometers (702 miles), Fiji has more land mass and people than all the other Melanesian islands put together. The capital of Fiji is Suva (pop. 77,366), on the southeast shore of the island of Viti Levu. The country's highest point, also on Viti Levu, is Mt. Victoria (Tomanivi) at 1,324 meters (4,344 feet).

POPULATION. Fiji's population was estimated in 2000 at 832,494, up from 775,077 in 1996, and 715,375 in 1986. If its annual growth rate of 1.41 percent continues, Fiji's population will have passed the million mark by 2014. Relatively high standards of health care have given Fijians a life expectancy at birth of 67.94 years, with an infant mortality rate of 14.45 per 1,000. The population remains young, with a median age of 21; about 34 percent of the population is clustered between the ages of 5 and 20.

Only a third of Fiji's 332 islands are inhabited, and three-quarters of Fijians live on Viti Levu, the largest of them. In 1996 53.6 percent of the population lived in rural areas and 46.4 percent in cities. Of the latter group, 46.7 percent, or a little less than a quarter of the total population, live in the greater Suva district. The other

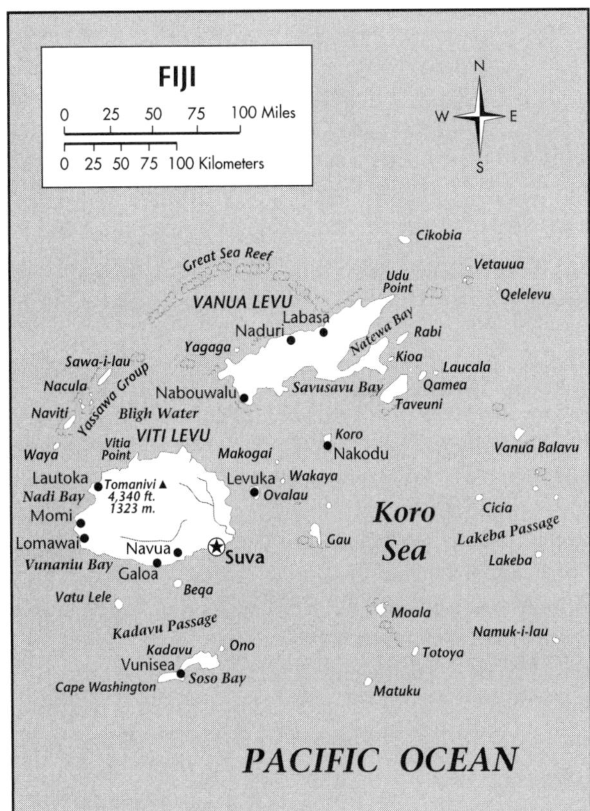

main urban center is Lautoka (pop. 36,083), on the northwest shore of the island of Viti Levu.

Fiji's ethnic composition is largely split between indigenous Melanesian Fijians, who constitute a narrow majority (51 percent), and those of Indian descent (44 percent); the remaining 5 percent is comprised of Europeans, Chinese, and other Melanesians. Fiji's religious situation reflects this division: 52 percent are Christian (including 37 percent Methodist and 9 percent Roman Catholic), 38 percent Hindu, and 8 percent Muslim. The proportion of Fijian Indians in the population has been decreasing since 1987, when army forces allied with indigenous Fijians staged a coup against the Fijian Indian-led government. (Fijian Indians are primarily the descendents of Indian indentured laborers brought to Fiji by British colonizers between 1879 and 1916.) As recently as the 1986 census, Fijian Indians made up a slight majority in population, with 48.7 percent as compared to 46 percent for the indigenous Fijians. But a slightly higher indigenous birthrate—27.3 per 1,000, compared to 17.2 for the Fijian Indian population—and heavy rates of Indian out-migration (the large-scale departure of persons from one region to another) have changed the population balance. The out-migration rate for 2000 is estimated at 3.6 per 1,000 per year, with most people moving to the United States, Australia, and New Zealand. Ongoing interethnic disputes threaten to further change population distribution.

OVERVIEW OF ECONOMY

As the largest and most resource-rich nation in the central South Pacific, Fiji also enjoys the region's largest and most developed economy. Still, its reliance on a single resource—sugar—makes it economically vulnerable, exposed both to an unpredictable tropical climate and an unstable world market. Attempts to expand and diversify the economy are being seriously undercut by Fiji's ethnic tensions and ongoing political uncertainty.

Since its introduction by Fiji's British colonizers in the 1870s, sugar production has been the mainstay of the Fijian economy. While the country has had some significant success in developing supplementary industries in mining, fishery, timber, clothing, and especially tourism, sugar continues to account for nearly a quarter of its export earnings. The industry's fragility was painfully demonstrated in late 1998 when an unusually severe drought, followed by widespread cyclonic flooding, saw sugar exports drop by almost 30 percent and earnings by more than US$100 million. Similarly, upsets in the world sugar cane price can be sudden and sharp. If pressure from the World Trade Organization (WTO) erodes the special, fixed prices (well above world market levels) that Fijian sugar enjoys in the European sugar market, the industry will face even further strain.

Recent ethnic strife between indigenous Fijians and the nation's East Indian population continues to threaten the stability of the nation's government. From 1879 to 1916, Britain imported tens of thousands of contract laborers from India to work on the sugar plantations, and their descendants remain an ethnically and culturally distinct community. In 1987 hostility erupted during the first of a series of coups designed to preserve and formalize indigenous Fijian political power. Subsequent efforts at reconciliation have failed to achieve a workable solution. In early 2000 there was a fresh outbreak of violence and rioting against Indian businesses, and Fiji's government buildings were seized by armed indigenous dissidents. Such unrest has had a devastating effect on Fiji's economy, paralyzing its tourist industry, and frightening away much of the foreign investment the country needs to develop its **infrastructure** and expand its economic base. The Reserve Bank of Fiji, its central bank, forecast an economic contraction of 8 percent in 2000 (down from its original estimates of 13–15 percent, however). Growth since 1987 has averaged less than 2 percent—well below half that of the average for developing nations.

Ethnic tensions also have a direct impact on the sugar industry. Indian planters control some 90 percent of Fiji's commercial sugar cane production, but 80 percent of plantations are on land leased from indigenous Fijian property owners. Given the country's volatile ethnic politics, it is expected that many of these 18,000 leases will be ceded to indigenous growers, thus threatening widespread displacement of Fijian Indian farmers. This is a problem for which the government has not yet found an adequate solution.

POLITICS, GOVERNMENT, AND TAXATION

Annexed as a colony of the British Empire on 10 October 1874, Fiji gained its independence exactly 96 years later, on 10 October 1970. For the next 17 years Fiji remained a British-style parliamentary democracy within the British Commonwealth.

In April 1987, the Alliance Party (AP), which had ruled Fiji since independence, was defeated at the polls by a coalition headed by the Fijian Labor Party (FLP) and the National Federation Party (NFP). The defeat represented a momentous shift in Fijian politics by introducing for the first time a substantial Fijian Indian presence in the government (although the coalition's leader and new prime minister was an indigenous Fijian, Dr. Timoci Bavadra). The new coalition moved power away from Fiji's traditional rural oligarchy and towards its long under-represented urban small-business and working class. Seeing its position threatened, the old order turned to racial politics, and the eruption of ethnic tension that resulted provided the pretext for a coup a month later led by Lieutenant-Colonel Sitiveni Rabuka. Four months later, fearing foreign intervention, Fiji's parliamentary leaders brokered a power-sharing accord between the AP and FLP-NFP coalition. But the newly promoted Brigadier Rabuka, feeling the accord had sacrificed the coup's central aim of securing indigenous domination, staged a second coup that revoked Fiji's 1970 constitution and declared the country a republic.

Two months later civilian government was restored, though it excluded the FLP-NFP, and a new constitution was drafted. In the first election under the new constitution in May 1992, a coalition led by now-Major General Rabuka won office, and he became prime minister. A series of crises over budgetary matters forced an early election in February 1994. Although Rabuka survived, dissatisfaction mounted at his government's failure to address the country's political divisions and its economic crises. Heavy out-migration by Fijian Indians resulted in a crippling flight of capital and expertise.

In June 1997 a new and more equitable constitution was adopted. In the first election under it in May 1999, the Rabuka government was overwhelmingly defeated, and a new FLP-led coalition took office under Fijian Indian prime minister Mahendra Chaudhry. While Chaudhry won the election on a promise of better economic management, his victory also re-kindled fears of a Fijian Indian "takeover." Protests by indigenous groups led to widespread civil violence and rioting against Fijian Indian businesses, culminating on 19 May 2000 with the seizure of the government buildings by armed extremists. After holding the cabinet at gunpoint in a 2-month long hostage drama, the extremists managed to have the president and new government dismissed by the military on July 5. Although the military subsequently restored the civilian government on July 18, and discussed the drafting of a new constitution, Fiji's political stability and international credibility remain grievously damaged. Prime Minister Laisenia Qarase was given a second title—Minister for National Reconciliation—to highlight the job that lay ahead of him in the coming years.

Fiji's revenue base is taxation. In 1998, according to the Fiji Islands Statistics Bureau, 58.4 percent of its revenue (US$251.7 million) came from **income tax**, estate and gift **duties**, and 27.0 percent (US$116.1 million) from customs duties and port dues. Its revenue shortfall for that year was US$917.8 million. Quarterly indicators from 2000 suggest that the imbalance is likely to worsen. Economic reforms by the government in 1992 designed to stimulate business saw the top individual and corporate tax rate drop to 35 percent, and a new 10 percent **value-added tax** (VAT) was introduced on goods and services, replacing previous sales and **excise taxes**. Attempts by the government to re-ignite the economy after the 2000 coup have followed a similar tack: the 10 percent VAT (removed by the previous coalition) was reinstated, and the corporate tax rate was reduced to 34 percent, with similar cuts scheduled for 2002 and 2003. With these measures, government revenues will be reduced and lower-income families will have to shoulder a proportionally larger tax burden.

INFRASTRUCTURE, POWER, AND COMMUNICATIONS

Fiji has a fairly well-developed infrastructure, with a reasonably comprehensive system of bridges and highways. The islands have 2,137 miles (3,438 kilometers) of roadway, nearly half of which is paved, and 371 miles (597 kilometers) of rail lines. In 1998 Fijians registered 2,265

Communications

Country	Telephones[a]	Telephones, Mobile/Cellular[a]	Radio Stations[b]	Radios[a]	TV Stations[a]	Televisions[a]	Internet Service Providers[c]	Internet Users[c]
Fiji	72,000	5,200	AM 13; FM 40; shortwave 0	500,000	N/A	21,000	2	7,500
United States	194 M	69.209 M (1998)	AM 4,762; FM 5,542; shortwave 18	575 M	1,500	219 M	7,800	148 M
Philippines	1.9 M	1.959 M (1998)	AM 366; FM 290; shortwave 3 (1999)	11.5 M	31	3.7 M	33	500,000
Solomon Islands	8,000	658	AM 3; FM 0; shortwave 0	57,000	0	3,000	1	3,000

[a]Data is for 1997 unless otherwise noted.
[b]Data is for 1998 unless otherwise noted.
[c]Data is for 2000 unless otherwise noted.

SOURCE: CIA *World Factbook 2001* [Online].

new motor vehicles, 1,424 being private cars. The country also has 5 commercial ports and 25 airports, 3 with paved runways. An international airport, the hub for most trans-Pacific air traffic, is located in Nandi, outside Suva.

Telecommunication systems are also expanding, with full inter-island and international telephone and teleprinter connections, cable links, and satellite access. In 1997 Fiji had 71,403 subscriber telephone lines, or about 1 for every 10 Fijians. A Fijian-British **joint venture** has attracted the investment of US$7.1 million in a cellular telephone network. As of 1998, there were 4,300 cellular phones in the country. The government intends to further its **deregulation** of telecommunications by **privatizing** all or part of Telecom Fiji and opening the market to new Internet service providers (ISP). As of 1999, there were 2 ISPs in Fiji.

Fiji's mountainous terrain is favorable to the development of hydroelectric generation, which supplies 80 percent of its electricity; the remaining 20 percent is produced from imported fossil fuels.

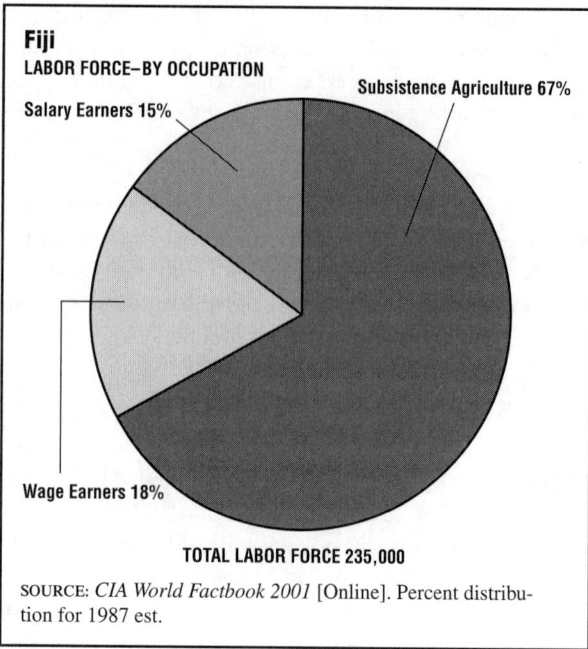

SOURCE: *CIA World Factbook 2001* [Online]. Percent distribution for 1987 est.

ECONOMIC SECTORS

Despite government attempts to diversify the economy, the relative profile of Fiji's different economic sectors has changed little since 1992. Agriculture is still dominant and, along with forestry and fishing, accounted for 16.5 percent of **gross domestic product** (GDP) in 1999. But the manufacturing sector, especially the garment industry, and the **retail** and service sector, especially those businesses related to tourism, are also vitally important. Industry and services contribute 25.5 percent and 58 percent of GDP, respectively. The government has actively encouraged both the manufacturing and tourism sectors in an attempt to broaden the country's economic base, increase foreign exchange receipts, and expand the number of wage and salary earners. Fiji's political strife, however, has seriously undermined the effectiveness of these attempts.

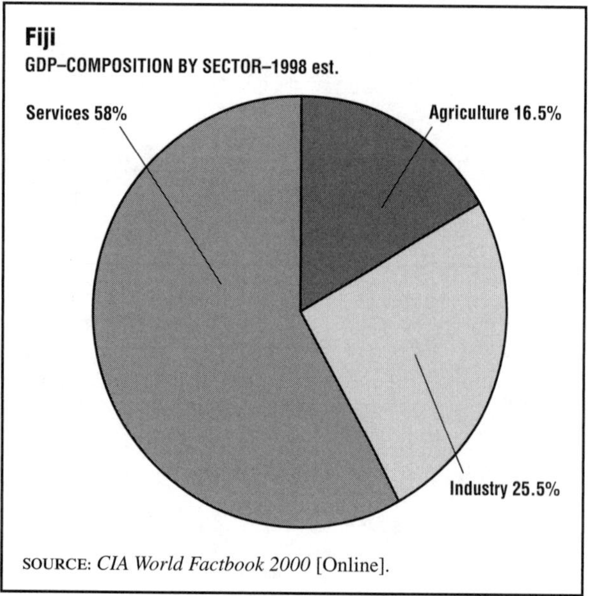

SOURCE: *CIA World Factbook 2000* [Online].

AGRICULTURE

Agriculture continues to be the bedrock of the Fijian economy, accounting in 1999 for some 16 percent of its GDP and two-thirds of its 310,000-strong workforce. Sugar, the most important agricultural product, generated almost 30 percent of Fiji's agricultural GDP in 1998, and 15 percent (through sugar processing) of its manufacturing GDP. The 364,000 tons of sugar that Fiji produced that year earned the country some US$122.9 million. The commercial future of this industry depends on the resolution of the property system that has been in place since 1909, when the British colonial government froze landownership titles in an attempt to protect indigenous (Fijian) property owners. As a result, only 8 percent of a total of 607,982 acres (1,519,956 hectares) is freehold (privately-owned); the remainder is either tribal- (83 percent) or government-owned (8 percent) land. As of 1993, only 9.9 percent of that total acreage was arable, with most of it in tribal hands or leased to Fijian Indian farmers, who produce 90 percent of Fiji's sugar-cane. As these leases expire and the land is returned to indigenous growers, major disruptions in sugar-cane production can be expected.

With 64.9 percent of Fiji's land area being forest and woodland, timber is also economically important, especially pine and mahogany. Attempts since the mid-1980s to bolster the industry, and offset Fiji's dependence on sugar, have encouraged significant strides in timber production. In 1999 timber provided US$27.6 million in export revenue, a 45 percent increase over 1994 levels.

The fishing industry, especially tuna harvesting, also shows significant promise. Fiji controls a 200-nautical mile (370.4-kilometer) economic exclusion zone around its shoreline. In 1998 fishing brought Fiji US$24.9 million in overseas earnings, and tuna is Fiji's fourth largest export earner.

Fiji also exports copra (dried coconut meat), ginger, and coconut oil, as well as bananas, rice (a product for which Fiji is aiming at self-sufficiency), cereals and vegetables, pineapples and other tropical fruit. Copra, in particular, has benefitted from the removal in 1998 of the ban on its export; since the licensing of a second copra-buying company, prices for producers have increased considerably. The discovery of kava's (a shrubby pepper) medicinal qualities and its potential as a pharmaceutical ingredient have also fueled the growth of a small but promising export industry.

INDUSTRY

MINING. Although Fiji lacks a heavy industrial base, it has made significant progress in mining and manufacturing. Mining and quarrying account for around 2.7 percent of Fiji's total GDP (1999). Most of this revenue is generated by gold, which in 1998 made up 6.9 percent (US$35 million) of Fiji's foreign exports. Although production capacity has increased, the low price of gold has depressed earnings. The dip in prices saw growth in production tumble from 30.9 percent in 1996 to 2.9 percent in 1997. In 1998 mining in 2 gold mines was suspended and further exploration discontinued. Fiji's uncertain political climate has also made it difficult to attract the foreign financing it needs to sustain the industry. In September 2000 the government was forced to issue tax concessions worth nearly US$2 million to rescue one its largest mining companies and preserve its 2,000 jobs. Fiji also produces silver and copper. When the copper mining venture launched at Namosi in 1997 hits full production, earnings of as much as US$178 million per annum are possible.

MANUFACTURING. Responsible for 14.5 percent of GDP in 1999, this sector is one of Fiji's diversification success stories. Whereas it once comprised largely the processing of agricultural products, especially sugar and timber, the introduction in 1987 of tax exemptions for factories exporting more than 70 percent of their annual production has seen the rapid emergence of a vibrant garment industry. Since 1986 the volume of garment production has grown twelve-fold, and in 1998 it provided 30 percent of Fijian exports, valued at US$152.4 million. However, the Australian government's refusal in September 2000 to renew its highly favorable **tariff** concessions for Fijian imports (a reaction to the coup) has clouded the future of this industry.

SERVICES

TOURISM. Fiji's beaches, climate, and relative proximity to Australia and New Zealand have helped tourism become one its most important revenue earners; in 1997 hotels, restaurants, and cafés made up 3 percent of GDP, accounting for 40,000 jobs. But tourism has been one of the biggest casualties of Fiji's political upheavals. In 1999, according to the Fiji Islands Statistics Bureau, 409,995 tourists visited Fiji, bringing with them US$274 million in foreign exchange. This represented an increase over the previous year of 38,000 visitors and US$30 million, a growth rate that showed every sign of continuing. But after the 2000 coup, visitor numbers dropped drastically, forcing some of Fiji's biggest resorts to close. Despite an energetic campaign by the industry to restore visitor confidence, and government tax incentives for investors, this sector has not recovered.

FINANCIAL SERVICES. Fiji's commercial banking sector is served by 6 banks, including the Bank of Hawaii and several other merchant banking providers and insurance companies, as well as the Fiji National Provident Fund (NPF, Fiji's national pension scheme), and Fiji Development Bank. The government-owned banking sector, on the other hand, is less stable. Mismanagement of the National Bank of Fiji led to its near-collapse in the mid-1990s and forced the government in 1997 into a US$105 million bailout. The relationship between government and commercial banking sectors has yet to be properly defined. As part of its economic stimulation program, the Fijian government is working to strengthen the financial system by expanding the Fijian Stock Exchange, decentralizing the NPF, and allowing greater investment flexibility for insurance companies.

RETAIL. With more than half of Fiji's population living in rural areas, and a large proportion of these outside the wage and salary economy, Fiji's retail sector is understandably small. Fiji's isolation makes imported goods expensive, further inhibiting its consumer culture, and leaving most retailing at the level of basic foods, clothing, and essential merchandise. The capital, Suva, has a variety of stores, including specialty stores that cater to tourists. The larger retail sector, taking into account wholesale suppliers, hotels, and restaurants, accounted for 15.2 percent of Fijian GDP in 1999.

INTERNATIONAL TRADE

With Fiji's own limited resources and industrial base, the country relies on imports for many of its basic

Trade (expressed in billions of US$): Fiji

	Exports	Imports
1975	.202	.268
1980	.470	.562
1985	.307	.442
1990	.615	.743
1995	.607	.864
1998	N/A	N/A

SOURCE: International Monetary Fund. *International Financial Statistics Yearbook 1999.*

Exchange rates: Fiji

Fijian dollars (F$) per US$1	
Jan 2001	2.1814
2000	2.1286
1999	1.9696
1998	1.9868
1997	1.4437
1996	1.4033

SOURCE: CIA *World Factbook 2001* [ONLINE].

goods, making international trade essential. As Fiji's political woes have worsened, however, its **balance of trade** has become less favorable. In 1999 Fiji ran a US$115.6 million trade deficit, or about 7.37 percent of GDP. In 1998 it had exports of $393 million and imports of $612 million. While the post-coup **devaluation** of the Fijian dollar will help Fijian exporters, it will also make Fiji's imports more expensive.

Fiji's main trading partners are its Commonwealth neighbors (Australia, New Zealand, other Pacific islands) and old and new regional powers (United Kingdom, United States). The chief importer of Fijian wares is Australia, which in 1999 bought 33.1 percent of all Fijian exports. Other important partners include the United States (14.8 percent of exports) and the United Kingdom (13.8 percent). Penetration into Asia has been limited and variable, and only significant with Japan and Singapore. Fiji's imports come primarily from Australia, whose dominance in the Fijian market (41.9 percent) continues to rise. Other suppliers include the United States (14.1 percent of imports) and New Zealand (13.3 percent). The main imports are manufactured goods (27.3 percent), machinery and transport equipment (26.3 percent), food (14.4 percent), and mineral fuels (11.1 percent).

MONEY

Since 1995 the Fijian dollar has been in steady decline. During the Asian financial crisis of the late 1990s, the government announced a 20 percent devaluation in 1997, when it was valued at around US$0.69. Further depreciation followed, accelerated by the 2000 coup. In 2001 the dollar stood at around US$0.44. **Fiscal policy** is now focused on controlling the deficit and reducing Fiji's large **national debt**, both of which are long-standing problems made worse by the costs of political crisis. A target deficit of 1.9 percent of GDP in the 1999 budget was found to be unattainable; 2000–01 targets stood at 4 percent, the equivalent of a debt level of around 45 percent of GDP.

POVERTY AND WEALTH

Fiji's traditional tribal structure creates wide status differentials, and there are wide gaps between the income levels of rich and poor. Although much of the land in Fiji is collectively owned, it is controlled by tribal chiefs who derive most of the economic benefit. Traditionally, Fiji's political leaders come from the eastern part of the country, from Vanua Levu and the Lau Group, where the feudal structure is best preserved. Fiji's cities and industry, on the other hand, are concentrated in the west, on Viti Levu in and around Suva, where most of the population lives. The result is a very unequal distribution of wealth and political power, which has survived because it has become connected with racial issues. Despite a very small Fijian Indian entrepreneurial class, many members of which have left the country, most Fijian Indians are no better off than indigenous Fijians since both groups suffer under a political system that concentrates power in the hands of the ruling class. The burden of Fiji's economic difficulties falls heaviest on its poorer citizens, who are obliged to commit a greater proportion of their incomes to basic essentials.

WORKING CONDITIONS

Fiji's workforce numbers around 310,000 people, and the official unemployment rate hovers at a low 6 percent. This figure is misleading since only a third of this workforce is in paid employment; the remaining two-thirds are

GDP per Capita (US$)

Country	1975	1980	1985	1990	1998
Fiji	2,086	2,319	2,102	2,356	2,416
United States	19,364	21,529	23,200	25,363	29,683
Philippines	974	1,166	967	1,064	1,092
Solomon Islands	419	583	666	784	753

SOURCE: United Nations. *Human Development Report 2000; Trends in human development and per capita income.*

Household Consumption in PPP Terms

Country	All food	Clothing and footwear	Fuel and power[a]	Health care[b]	Education[b]	Transport & Communications	Other
Fiji	35	5	19	2	13	4	23
United States	13	9	9	4	6	8	51
Philippines	37	3	11	1	14	1	32
Solomon Islands	N/A	N/A	N/A	N/A	N/A	N/A	N/A

Data represent percentage of consumption in PPP terms.
[a]Excludes energy used for transport.
[b]Includes government and private expenditures.

SOURCE: World Bank. *World Development Indicators 2000.*

subsistence farmers and fishermen (subsistence workers produce just enough goods to support their own subsistence, with rarely any surplus to sell and generate additional income). There are 4 times as many young people in the workforce as there are available jobs. The unemployment rate also conceals large-scale under-employment such as seasonal workers in agriculture and casual laborers in the construction industry. While the numbers of wage and salary workers have been rising (8.5 percent over the period from 1993 to 1998), Fiji's economic crisis threatens to offset these gains. The loss of tens of thousands of professionals and skilled workers through out-migration has also produced a skills deficit, which poses a further obstacle to future growth. Labor disputes are another symptom of tension, and in 1999, an average of 19.7 worker-days were lost due to strikes, though this figure was atypically high. Part of the government's recovery program is to deregulate the workforce and shrink the **public sector**.

COUNTRY HISTORY AND ECONOMIC DEVELOPMENT

1643. Abel Tasman, the Dutch navigator, sites the Fiji island group.

1774. Captain Cook visits southern Lau.

1835. The first Methodist missionaries arrive.

1854. King Cakobau renounces his traditional gods and accepts Christianity.

1857. First British consul appointed at Levuka.

1862. King Cakobau invites the British to annex Fiji; Britain refuses.

1874. Britain, fearing Fiji will fall to another power, accepts Fiji as a colony.

1879–1916. Indentured laborers are imported from India.

1904. First elected Legislative Council.

1909. System of property leases instituted.

1966. Internal self-government achieved.

1970. Fiji becomes independent.

1973. Sugar industry **nationalized**.

1987. Defeat of Alliance Party by Fijian Indian-backed opposition coalition; the first Fijian coup by Sitiveni Rabuka removes Prime Minister Bavadra from power; Fiji declared a republic.

1994. New constitution enacted; Rabuka becomes prime minister.

1997. Fiji rejoins Commonwealth.

1999. Landslide victory by the Fijian Indian-led opposition coalition.

2000. Armed forces led by George Speight seize Parliament; dismissal of the Mahendra government by the military. Ratu Josepha Iloilovatu Uluivuda becomes president, and Laisenia Qarase prime minister.

FUTURE TRENDS

Before the return of the political problems that gripped Fiji in late 1999 and 2000, Fiji was believed by many observers to have, in the words of the *Wall Street Journal,* "the South Pacific's most promising economy." It was widely believed that Fiji was capable of increasing its production of every major exportable product, and capable of reducing its debt load accordingly. But the recent problems leave the growth of Fiji's economy in doubt. Striking problems remain: rising unemployment; declining investor confidence; a drastic fall in tourist visits, which reverberates throughout the economy; and the lack of any long-term solution to the political conflict between Fijian Indians, who control most of the sugar production companies, and indigenous Fijians, who own most of the land and provide most of the labor. Fiji's problems have left the country both politically and economically isolated, as former allies, potential investors, and tourists have all withdrawn their support from the country. The government's attempts to re-stimulate the economy will continue to fail unless the root causes of Fiji's ethnic tension can be adequately addressed and substantive cooperation achieved, an unlikely prospect in the near future. However, if the potential mediation of outside entities returns Fiji to political stability, the island nation should be well-equipped for further growth.

DEPENDENCIES

Fiji has no territories or colonies.

BIBLIOGRAPHY

Bank of Hawaii. *Pacific Economic Reports.* <http://www.boh.com/econ>. Accessed July 2001.

Economist Intelligence Unit. *Country Profile: Fiji, 2000.* London: Economist Intelligence Unit, 2000.

Economist Intelligence Unit. *Country Report: Fiji, December 2000.* London: Economist Intelligence Unit, 2000.

Fiji Islands Statistics Bureau. <http://www.statsfiji.gov.fj>. Accessed February 2001.

Lal, Brij V. *Broken Waves: A History of Fiji in the Twentieth Century.* Honolulu: University of Hawaii Press, 1992.

U.S. Central Intelligence Agency. *The World Factbook, 2000.* <http://www.cia.gov/cia/publications/factbook>. Accessed January 2001.

U.S. Department of State. *Country Commercial Guide, FY 1999: Fiji.* <http://www.state.gov/www/about_state/business/com_guides/1999/eastasia/fiji99.html>. Accessed February 2001.

—Alexander Schubert

FRENCH POLYNESIA

CAPITAL: Papeete.

MONETARY UNIT: Comptoirs Français du Pacifique franc (CFPF), also known as the Pacific Financial Community franc or Pacific French franc. One CFPF has 100 centimes. There are notes of CFPF500, 1,000, 5,000, and 10,000, and coins of CFPF1, 2, 5, 10, 20, 50, and 100.

CHIEF EXPORTS: Cultured pearls, coconut products, mother-of-pearl, vanilla, shark meat.

CHIEF IMPORTS: Coconuts, fuels, foodstuffs, equipment.

GROSS DOMESTIC PRODUCT: US$2.6 billion (1997 est.).

BALANCE OF TRADE: **Exports:** US$212 million (1996 est.). **Imports:** US$860 million (1996 est.).

Territory of French Polynesia
Territoire de la Polynésie Française

COUNTRY OVERVIEW

LOCATION AND SIZE. An overseas territory of France, French Polynesia's 118 islands and atolls are grouped into 5 archipelagos (group of islands) scattered across some 3,200 kilometers (2,000 miles) in the South Pacific Ocean midway between South America and Australia. The islands have a total land area of 4,167 square kilometers (1,609 square miles), slightly less than one-third the size of Connecticut. The 5 archipelagos include the Society Islands (which include Tahiti and Bora-Bora); the Tuamotu Archipelago; the Gambier Archipelago; the Marquesas Islands; and the Austral Islands. Together they have 2,525 kilometers (1,569 miles) of coastline. Only 65 of the islands are inhabited, and the overwhelming majority of French Polynesians live along the coastlines. The most inhabited island by far, with about 70 percent of the total population, is Tahiti, which also accounts for a quarter of the islands' total land area. Half of Tahiti's population lives in its major urban center, the capital city of Papeete (population, including surroundings, 69,000, 1996 est.). Tahiti is also the largest island, with a land mass equal to 1,041 square kilometers (402 square miles).

The islands represent a wide variety of topographies (land surfaces), from the plunging waterfalls and extinct volcanoes of Tahiti or Moorea to the low-lying, white-sand lagoon coral-reef atolls of the Tuamotu and Gambier groups. One of French Polynesia's most serious long-term problems is the threat presented by global warming and the rising of the world's water level, estimated by the United Nations Environment Program in 1993 to rise by more than 25 inches by 2100. If this proves correct, entire archipelagoes like the Tuamotus may eventually disappear. In the meantime, pressure from the ocean is eroding the available cultivatable land and contaminating the groundwater.

POPULATION. French Polynesia's population was estimated in 2000 at 249,110, with an annual growth rate of 1.78 percent. Comprehensive public health care has secured a long life expectancy—74.79 years at birth—and a low infant mortality rate—9.3 per 1,000 live births. The annual rate of **immigration**—3.14 per 1,000 of population—is accounted for mostly by French government officials and retirees. Those under 15 years of age make up 30 percent of the population, with 65 percent between 15 and 64 years of age. The remaining 5 percent are over 65 years of age.

The majority of the population (78 percent) is of Eastern Polynesian descent. They are closely related to the New Zealand Maoris, but quite distinct from the closer Western Polynesian Samoans and Tongans. Another 12 percent are of Chinese descent, and 10 percent French, of whom 6 percent are local French and 4 percent from France itself. These figures, however, conceal a considerable degree of racial mixture. Europeans, the majority of whom are French, are concentrated in Papeete. The Chinese, descendants of laborers imported in the 1860s to work Tahiti's short-lived cotton plantations, are scattered throughout the islands and run much of the

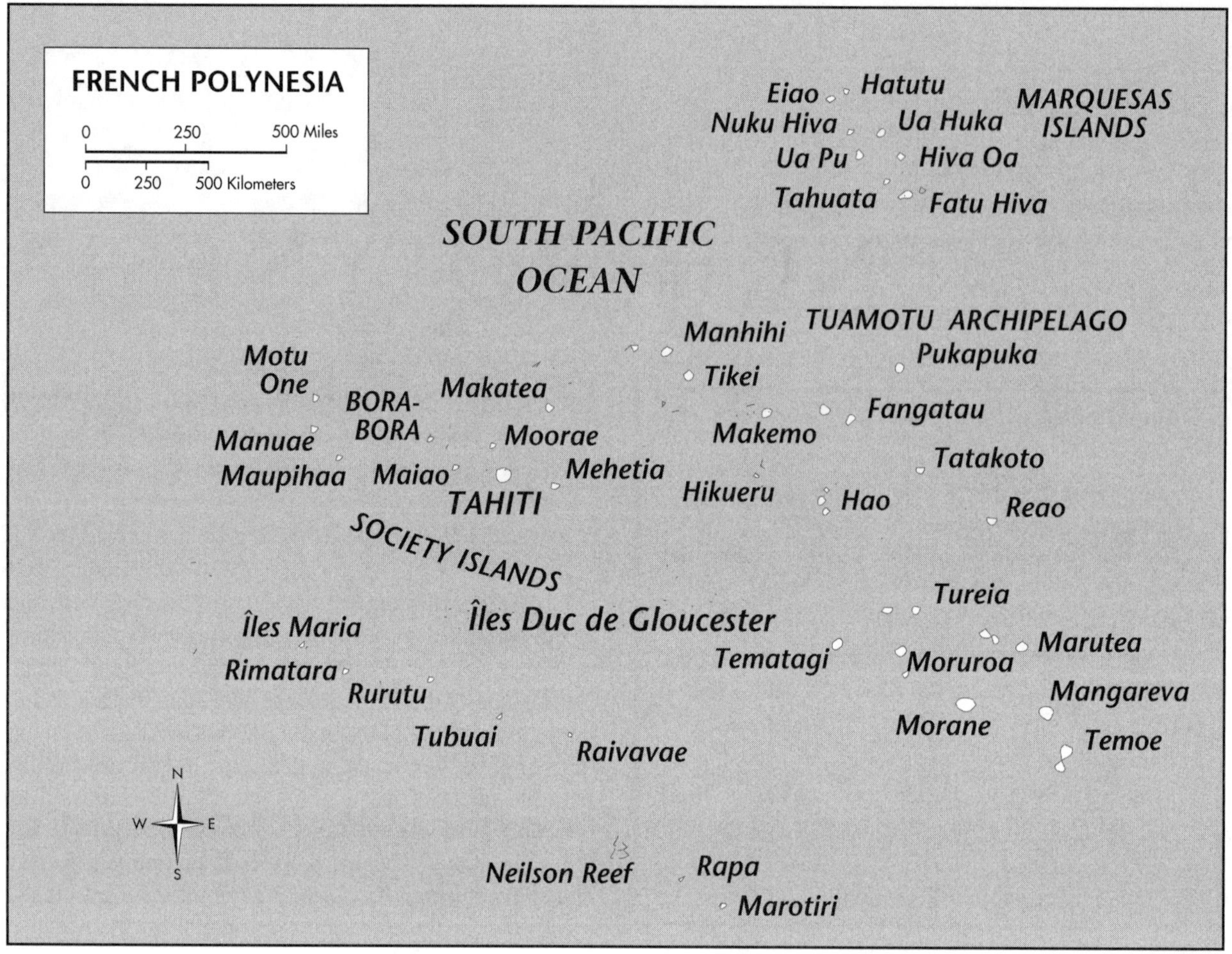

territory's **retail** trade. French Polynesians are 54 percent Protestant, 30 percent Roman Catholic, with 16 percent belonging to other religions. The official languages are French and Tahitian.

OVERVIEW OF ECONOMY

Until the 1960s, the French Polynesian economy was largely based on subsistence agriculture (raising enough to survive), but in 1962 France began nuclear testing in the islands. This attracted some 30,000 settlers to work in the Centre d'Expérimentations du Pacifique (CEP), a facility that changed the islands' economy forever. By 2000, only 1 in 8 French Polynesians was involved in agriculture. The rest were wage and salary earners in the territory's extensive service sector and various industries. The territory has the highest **GDP per capita** ($10,800, 1997 est.) in the South Pacific region.

Such progress can be credited to 2 factors: the strength of French Polynesia's tourist potential and continuing economic support from France. Both of these assets look secure for the immediate future. Tourism continues to climb, and new developments, such as the expansion of cruise ship facilities and the opening of isolated islands, have enhanced the industry's **infrastructure** and ensured its ongoing growth. French subsidization shows no signs of stopping; the French economy is one of the healthiest and fastest-growing in Europe, and both of its main political parties are committed to continued union.

Nevertheless, French Polynesia's overwhelming dependence on a single overseas patron leaves it highly vulnerable in the long term. France's long-range goal is for a more self-sustaining economy for the territory, and within the islands the independence movement is vocal. In the 1996 elections the Independent Front for the Liberation of Polynesia gained 10 of the Territorial Assembly's 41 seats. If this party should ever win a majority, it is highly likely to push for full independence. How the islands would adapt to such a change is unclear, but for it to achieve complete economic self-sufficiency, radical economic reorganization would be required.

A narrow economic base also makes the islands vulnerable. While tourism receipts continue to climb, and French Polynesia enjoys well-established "brand recognition" as a vacation destination, tropical storms are a recurring threat, and competition from other international beach resorts is increasingly sharp. Other industries are being developed, such as cultured pearls (already an important export earner) and coconut products (especially palm oil), mother-of-pearl, vanilla, handicrafts, and fish. But these too are niche industries, susceptible to shifting world prices, and may not be strong enough to be the basis of real diversification.

POLITICS, GOVERNMENT, AND TAXATION

France began to take over the French Polynesian islands in the late 18th century, and formed them into the group as it exists today in 1903. In 1958, the islands were granted overseas territory status, acquiring further control over their internal government in 1975 and 1984. The territory enjoys considerable latitude over its domestic administration, with its 41-member Territorial Assembly responsible for public works, sports, health, social services, primary education, and the election of the president. However, the military, justice system, and **monetary policy** are directed by France, and the French constitution remains the supreme law. The high commissioner is France's chief representative in the islands and retains considerable control, with the power to dissolve the Territorial Assembly and take personal control of the budget (as was done in 1992). There is consequently a vibrant independence movement, provoked especially by France's resumption of nuclear testing in the territory in 1995. Protests against the testing led to extensive rioting in Papeete, which caused France to tighten its control.

French Polynesia is essential to France's perception of itself as a world power, even though such aspirations cost France around $300 million a year. The transfer of payments from France to the islands reached a high of 27.5 percent of French Polynesian GDP in 1997 and was estimated to be around 20.6 percent in 2000. These **subsidies** constitute the territory's primary source of income and are critical to its economic survival. The focus of the subsidies, beyond the maintenance of French facilities and personnel in the territory, is especially for projects designed to build a more self-sustaining economy. While full self-sufficiency is recognized as unfeasible except as a very long-term goal—and for which no specific timetable has so far been set—the immediate target is to slowly increase the islands' domestic contribution to national production. This has risen on average around 5 percent per year from 1989 to 1999, increasing the domestic share of production to 43.7 percent in 1999. The plan is to raise it to 60 percent by 2003.

In 1993, in return for the 5-year, US$118 million Pacte de Progrès subsidy program, France demanded the institution of an **income tax** in order to make the territory more self-supporting. A 3 percent tax on earnings over $1,600 was introduced. The government, however, continues to rely heavily on **indirect taxes**, which make up around half of the territory's tax revenues. **Levies** and excises on imported goods and licensing fees are thus among the highest in the Pacific islands.

INFRASTRUCTURE, POWER, AND COMMUNICATIONS

French Polynesia's infrastructure is in good condition. It undergoes ongoing improvement as a result of French development programs, including tax incentives for businesses who invest in infrastructure. The islands have 792 kilometers (492 miles) of roads, all of them paved. There are 30 paved-runway airports, with 15 more unpaved airstrips, and an international airport at Faa'a outside Papeete. The 4 seaports are Mataura, Papeete,

Communications

Country	Telephones[a]	Telephones, Mobile/Cellular[a]	Radio Stations[b]	Radios[a]	TV Stations[a]	Televisions[a]	Internet Service Providers[c]	Internet Users[c]
French Polynesia	52,000	5,427	AM 2; FM 14; shortwave 2	128,000	7	40,000	2	5,000
United States	194 M	69.209 M (1998)	AM 4,762; FM 5,542; shortwave 18	575 M	1,500	219 M	7,800	148 M
Philippines	1.9 M	1.959 M (1998)	AM 366; FM 290; shortwave 3 (1999)	11.5 M	31	3.7 M	33	500,000
Solomon Islands	8,000	658	AM 3; FM 0; shortwave 0	57,000	0	3,000	1	3,000

[a]Data is for 1997 unless otherwise noted.
[b]Data is for 1998 unless otherwise noted.
[c]Data is for 2000 unless otherwise noted.

SOURCE: CIA *World Factbook 2001* [Online].

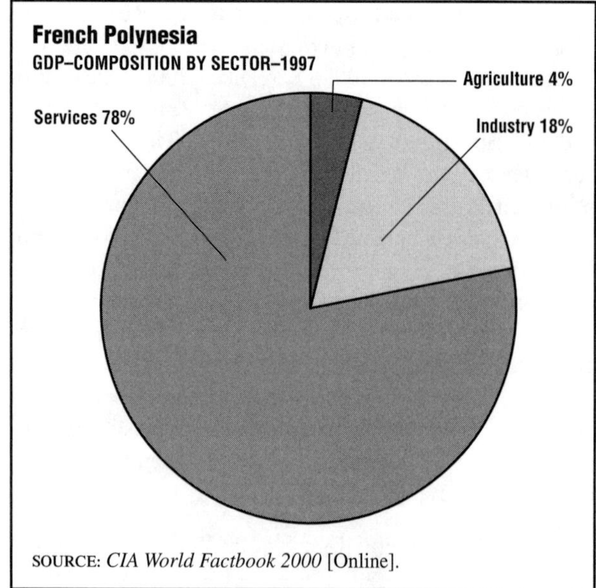

SOURCE: *CIA World Factbook 2000* [Online].

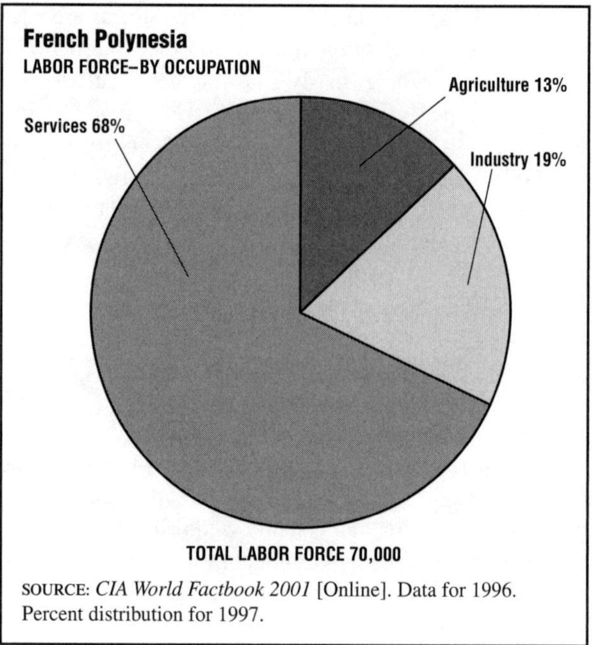

SOURCE: *CIA World Factbook 2001* [Online]. Data for 1996. Percent distribution for 1997.

Rikitea, and Uturoa. Most of the islands' fuel needs (60 percent in 1998) are supplied by imported fossil fuels. The remaining 40 percent is provided by hydroelectric power stations. A comprehensive and reliable telephone network also exists, with 32,000 main lines and 4,000 cellular lines in use in 1995.

ECONOMIC SECTORS

With its large tourism industry and **public sector**, the economy of French Polynesia is heavily service-oriented, with services accounting for 78 percent of GDP (1997). Industry, especially pearl cultivation, is also important, making up 18 percent of GDP. Workforce figures reflect this division, with around 40 percent working for the government, 40 percent in services, and 10 percent each in industry and in agriculture.

AGRICULTURE

Farming was once the primary means of survival for most French Polynesians. The development of the French nuclear program in the 1960s lured thousands of workers away from farming, however, and the sector nearly collapsed. By 1965, exports of coffee and vanilla had ended, and coconut production had dropped by 40 percent. In 1997, agriculture made up only 4 percent of GDP and employed 11 percent of the population. In that year, 80 percent of the islands' food had to be imported. The islands have fairly good agricultural resources, however, with 6 percent of available land under crops, 1 percent arable, and a further 5 percent used for pasturage. Local production supplies about half of the islands' vegetables and three-quarters of its fruit. Other products include vanilla and coffee, especially on Tahiti; poultry, beef and dairy products, especially in the Marquesas; and coconuts in the outer islands. Aquaculture is also being developed, with cultivation of shrimp, prawns, live bait, and green mussels.

INDUSTRY

After tourism, French Polynesia's primary money-earning industry and export product is cultured pearls. Founded in 1963, the industry has shown buoyant growth. In 1990, pearl exports brought the islands $38 million, a figure that had risen to $184.9 million by 2000. Although production has steadily increased from 599 kilograms (1,318 pounds) in 1990 to 7,116 kilograms (15,655 pounds) in 2000, the price per kilogram has been dropping, from US$27.67 in 1997 to $20.84 in 1999. The fall can be blamed on the large quantities of pearls being harvested, which has depressed the price, and to the weakness of the Japanese market, the largest consumer of Tahitian pearls. Producers have tried to address these trends through brand differentiation, by promoting the uniqueness of Tahitian pearls, and by turning their attention to the U.S. market. But the failure of producers in the territory to form an effective marketing cartel, and pressure from other Pacific producers (such as the Cook Islands), have slowed the impact of these efforts.

Other manufactured goods include beer, sandalwood oil, sandals, and handicrafts. Food processing is also important, especially the refining of dried coconut flesh (or copra) into oil for use in vegetable oil, margarine, candles, soap, and cosmetics. French Polynesia's extensive waters also show signs of rich deposits of nickel, cobalt, manganese, and copper. Though plans exist for their extraction, mining will prove expensive.

SERVICES

TOURISM. French Polynesia's tourist appeal is legendary. Even before the paintings of French artist Paul Gauguin gave form to the islands' paradise-like mystique, the islands held a special place in the Western imagination. Tourism proper, however, is relatively recent, largely a consequence of the opening of Tahiti's Faa'a Airport in 1961. Tourist numbers are still only a tiny fraction of those of Hawaii, which gets more visitors in 10 days than French Polynesia gets in an entire year. Still, tourist arrivals have continued to increase, bolstered by new hotel construction and renovation in the mid-1990s, which increased the number of hotel beds by 29 percent between 1990 and 2000. From 139,705 arrivals in 1989, numbers have climbed to 210,800 in 1999, an increase of more than 50 percent (with a 16.8 percent rise from 1997 to 1999 alone). Arrivals are estimated at 240,000 for 2000. Growth has been particularly brisk in terms of North American visitors, with an increase of 48.9 percent from 1997 to 1999. Some 85 percent of these are from the United States. There has also been an increase in cruise-ship traffic, whose generally older and more affluent tourists are especially valuable sources of revenue. Other important markets are Europe (40.1 percent of visitors in 2000, with two-thirds of these from France) and Asia (16.8 percent, with about two-fifths of these from Japan and two-fifths from Australia and New Zealand).

In 1997, tourism generated US$340.2 million in foreign exchange, and accounted for 4,000 jobs and 9.5 percent of GDP. In 2000, receipts of $396.2 million were expected, and a total GDP share of 10.1 percent. The tourism industry is dominated by **multinational corporations**, as most facilities are foreign-owned and managed—a situation that has tended to cause unease among the indigenous Polynesians. Some 80 percent of tourist spending, however, is for goods imported to the islands, and so brings little real gain to the territory's economy. In the long term, though, the hope is that tourist revenue will replace **transfer payments** from France.

FINANCIAL SERVICES. French Polynesia is served by 4 main banks: the Banque Socredo, Banque de Tahiti, Banque de Polynésie, and Australia's Westpac Bank. Offices are only on the main islands of Tahiti, Bora Bora, and Moorea.

RETAIL. Retail services vary widely. Papeete, with its long-established French presence, high standards of living, and extensive tourist trade, is a cosmopolitan city of expensive hotels, restaurants, cafés, cinemas, bars, and nightclubs. Papeete features a range of shops and markets selling jewelry, designer clothes, souvenir handicrafts, books, and art. This is also true to a lesser extent for the other major islands, Moorea and Bora-Bora. On remoter and more sparsely populated islands, where agriculture may still be the main form of livelihood, retailing becomes much simpler, with local food markets and general stores predominating.

Trade (expressed in billions of US$): French Polynesia

	Exports	Imports
1975	.025	.286
1980	.030	.547
1985	.040	.549
1990	.111	.928
1995	.193	1.008
1998	N/A	N/A

SOURCE: International Monetary Fund. *International Financial Statistics Yearbook 1999.*

INTERNATIONAL TRADE

French Polynesia's narrow economic base leaves it dependent on imports for many of its basic goods, and its **trade deficit** has traditionally been a heavy one. In 1996, the country imported $860 million in goods while exporting only $212 million. The consumer culture that French subsidies have tended to encourage has given the islands one of the largest import-export imbalances in the world. In 2000 imports exceeded exports by a factor of around 5 and accounted for 19.3 percent of GDP, but the gap has been slowly closing. In 1991 the territory's imports had been worth nearly 40 times their exports. The largest supplier of goods to the islands is France, which provided 44.7 percent of the islands' imports (1994); a further 13.9 percent comes from the United States. Exports go to the United States (11 percent, 1994) and France (6 percent). Imports include food, fuel, building materials, **consumer goods** and automobiles; exports include copra, cultured pearls, vanilla, and perfume.

MONEY

The currency of French Polynesia is the Pacific Financial Community franc, known in French as the Comptoirs Français du Pacifique franc (CFPF). The CFPF is pegged at a fixed rate to the French franc (18.18 CFPFs = 1 French franc), and, through it, to the euro. Initiated in 1945, the CFPF is also used by France's 2 other Pacific possessions, New Caledonia and Wallis and Futuna. In 1967, responsibility for issuing and circulating this currency was transferred from the Banque d'Indochine to the French government. **Exchange rates** have affected the tourism sector most; prices have generally been high in the islands, and during periods in which currencies

Exchange rates: French Polynesia

Comptoirs Français du Pacifique francs per US$1	
Jan 2001	127.11
2000	129.44
1999	111.93
1998	107.25
1997	106.11
1996	93.00

Note: Pegged at the rate of 119.25 CFPF to the euro.

SOURCE: CIA *World Factbook 2001* [ONLINE].

such as the U.S. dollar have weakened, so has tourism. The reverse is true as well, with tourism increasing as foreign currencies grew stronger against the CFPF.

POVERTY AND WEALTH

In French Polynesia, where unemployment and **underemployment** are growing problems, the inequalities in wealth are sharp. At one end of the scale is the large ring of slums around Papeete, home to 20,000 dispossessed Polynesians; at the other end are the luxury holiday homes of French Polynesia's seasonal migrants, like actor Marlon Brando, owner of the island of Tetiaroa, just north of Tahiti. The 2,200 expatriate French administrators and advisors, who make up around 4 percent of the islands' population, earn 84 percent more than their metropolitan French counterparts, and are the country's economic elite. Such disparities are made worse by the division of haves and have-nots along racial lines, with French at the top, mixed races in business and minor government posts in the middle, and the indigenous Polynesians at the bottom. The result has been serious social tensions, which have also put a strain on the traditionally relaxed and egalitarian tenor of indigenous life. The public education system has not helped, although it has created a 98 percent literacy rate. With the curriculum entirely French, the indigenous failure rate is high, ranging from 40 to 60 percent. This, combined with unemployment, is threatening to produce a Polynesian underclass.

GDP per Capita (US$)

Country	1996	1997	1998	1999	2000
French Polynesia	N/A	10,800	N/A	N/A	N/A
United States	28,600	30,200	31,500	33,900	36,200
Philippines	2,600	3,200	3,500	3,600	3,800
Solomon Islands	3,000	3,000	2,600	2,650	2,000

Note: Data are estimates.

SOURCE: *Handbook of the Nations*, 17th, 18th, 19th and 20th editions for 1996, 1997, 1998 and 1999 data; CIA *World Factbook 2001* [Online] for 2000 data.

WORKING CONDITIONS

The massive influx of French personnel that accompanied the creation of the Centre d'Expérimentations du Pacifique (CEP) in the early 1960s radically altered the basis of the islands' economy. The nature of their labor conditions changed the economy as well, shifting the workforce away from fishing and farming and into services and industry. This set in motion a migratory drift toward Papeete that still continues. Whereas in 1962 46 percent of French Polynesians were employed in agriculture and fishing, in 1996 only 11 percent were so occupied. The trend has been supported by France's development subsidies, an aim of which has been job creation. From 1997 to 2000, the numbers of those in wage and salary employment increased by 4.2 percent per year, against a 1.6 percent annual increase in the general population over the same period. As a result, there were 20 percent more wage and salary earners in 2000 than there had been in 1995. The gains have been in industry and services, which employ 19 percent and 68 percent of the workforce, respectively. The single largest employer is the government, which accounts for around 40 percent of the workforce. The workforce was most recently estimated at 118,744 in 1988, and unemployment was estimated at 15 percent in 1992.

COUNTRY HISTORY AND ECONOMIC DEVELOPMENT

c. 300. Polynesians reach the Marquesas Islands.

1521. Portuguese explorer Ferdinand Magellan sights Pukapuka in the Tuamotus.

1595. Spanish explorer Mendaña lands on the Marquesas Islands.

1767. British navigator Captain Samuel Wallis discovers Tahiti for Europe.

1768. French navigator Louis-Antoine de Bougainville visits Tahiti and claims it for France.

1797. Protestant missionaries arrive on Tahiti.

1842. French protectorate declared over Tahiti and the Marquesas.

1880. Protectorate becomes a colony.

1903. Islands organized into a single colony.

1945. French Polynesians become French citizens.

1958. French Polynesia becomes a French overseas territory.

1962. The French establish the nuclear test program Centre d'Expérimentations du Pacifique (CEP).

1966. French begin nuclear testing on Mururoa.

1975. Worldwide opposition forces French to move nuclear testing underground on Fangataufa.

1984. Partial local autonomy granted.

1995. French president Jacques Chirac resumes nuclear tests after their suspension by President François Mitterand in 1992.

FUTURE TRENDS

After the end of French nuclear testing in 1996 and the subsequent winding down of the French military presence, the role of French subsidies in the economy has decreased. French Polynesia has been encouraged, with the help of considerable French assistance, to develop alternative sources of income. The territory has had some considerable success in doing so, and economic indicators suggest a positive forecast for French Polynesia. After sluggish growth in the mid-1990s, the economy has climbed from 0.3 percent annual growth in 1996 to 4.0 percent in 2000, while keeping **inflation** at around 1 percent. But French aid is a mixed blessing. If French support falters, or if not enough is done to address the condition of indigenous and economically excluded Polynesians, this progress could be quickly undermined. In the longer term, global warming and rising sea levels are expected to have an adverse effect.

DEPENDENCIES

French Polynesia has no territories or colonies.

BIBLIOGRAPHY

Stanley, David. *Tahiti-Polynesia Handbook* (3rd ed.). Chico, California: Moon Publications, Inc., 1996.

"An Update on French Polynesia." Honolulu: Bank of Hawaii, August 2000. <http://www.boh.com/econ/pacific>. Accessed March 2001.

U.S. Central Intelligence Agency. *The World Factbook 2000.* <http://www.cia.gov/cia/publications/factbook>. Accessed June 2001.

—Alexander Schubert

HONG KONG

Hong Kong Special Administrative Region (SAR) of the People's Republic of China

CAPITAL: Hong Kong.

MONETARY UNIT: Hong Kong dollar (HK$). One Hong Kong dollar is equal to 100 cents. There are coins of 10, 20, and 50 cents, and HK$1, 2, 5, and 10. Paper currency comes in denominations of HK$20, 50, 100, 500, and 1,000.

CHIEF EXPORTS: Clothing, textiles, footwear, electrical appliances, watches and clocks, toys.

CHIEF IMPORTS: Foodstuffs, transport equipment, raw materials, semi-manufactures, petroleum.

GROSS DOMESTIC PRODUCT: US$158.2 billion (1999 est.).

BALANCE OF TRADE: **Exports:** US$169.98 billion (including re-exports, 1999 est.). **Imports:** US$174.4 billion (1999 est.).

COUNTRY OVERVIEW

LOCATION AND SIZE. Hong Kong is located in eastern Asia. It borders the South China Sea to the south, west, and east, and shares a land border with mainland China to the north. It consists of 4 main areas: Hong Kong Island, Kowloon, the New Territories, and the Outlying Islands. Kowloon and the New Territories are on a peninsula, accounting for the bulk of Hong Kong's land. The New Territories link Hong Kong to mainland China. The Outlying Islands are made up of 234 islands in the proximity of Hong Kong, excluding Hong Kong Island where the capital city (Hong Kong) is located; the island is in the southern part of the territory. Lantau Island and Hong Kong Island are the largest islands. The entire territory, including its islands, has an area of 1,092 square kilometers (421 square miles), which makes it 6 times larger than Washington, D.C. The length of its land border and coastline are 30 kilometers (18 miles) and 733 kilometers (455 miles), respectively.

POPULATION. Hong Kong's population was estimated to be 7,116,302 in July 2000. Its population increased from 4.4 million in 1975 to 6.7 million in 1998, indicating a growth rate of 1.8 percent. With an estimated growth rate of 0.8 percent, the population will increase to 7.7 million by 2015. In the year 2000 the estimated birth rate was 11.29 births per 1,000 people while the estimated death rate was 5.93 deaths per 1,000 people.

The majority of Hong Kong's population is of Chinese ethnicity, but non-Chinese constitute more than 8 percent of the population. Out of 595,000 foreigners residing in Hong Kong in 1999, 274,100 were from Asian countries (Philippines, Indonesia, Thailand, India, Japan, and Nepal) and the rest from Western countries (United

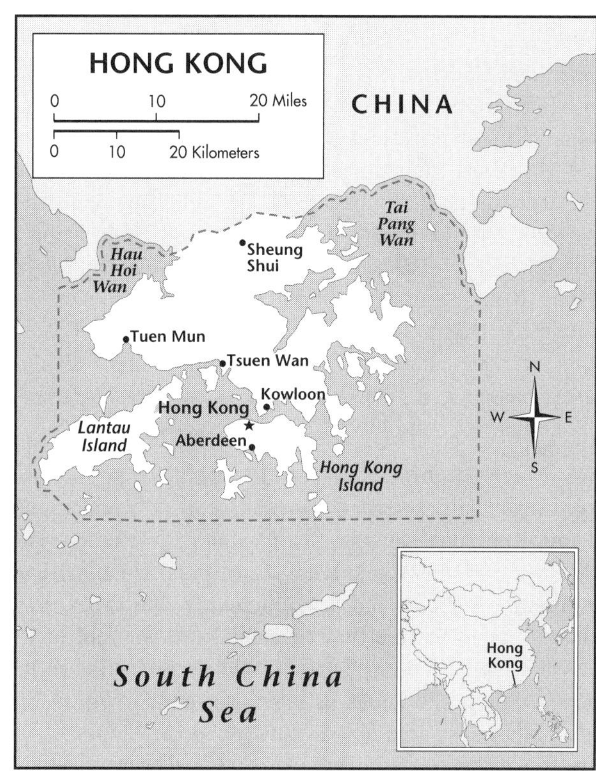

States, Canada, United Kingdom, and Australia). The number of expatriates grew from 320,700 in December 1993 to 485,880 in December 1998.

The population of Hong Kong is old, with 18 percent of the population age 14 or younger and 71 percent between the ages of 15 and 64. This leaves 11 percent of Hong Kong's people 65 years old and up. Given the estimated low growth rate for the 1998–2015 period, the population will be even older by 2015 when 13.7 percent of the population will be over 65 years of age.

Hong Kong is a highly urbanized society. About 95.4 percent of its population lived in urban areas in 1998, an increase of 5.7 percent since 1975. The urban population is estimated to reach 96.7 percent by 2015. The capital city of Hong Kong and the Kowloon peninsula house the majority of the population.

OVERVIEW OF ECONOMY

During the first Opium War (1839–43), the British government colonized Hong Kong in 1841. Over time it established a free-enterprise economy in the colony and turned it into a trading center in Asia. Hong Kong has retained these characteristics since its hand-over to China in 1997, as stipulated in the 1984 Sino-British Joint Declaration on the transfer of Hong Kong's sovereignty to China. Accordingly, the Chinese government guaranteed that it would preserve Hong Kong's capitalist economy and its political and social systems for at least 50 years. This commitment was justified under the Chinese formula of "one country, two systems," which allowed for the coexistence of a capitalist Hong Kong with the **socialist** mainland China as 2 parts of 1 single country. The Chinese government also guaranteed that it would not intervene in the internal affairs of Hong Kong, and would let its government function independently in all its internal affairs, including economic policies. The Chinese central government in Beijing is in charge only of Hong Kong's foreign and defense issues. China's official acceptance of Hong Kong's mini constitution, the Basic Law of the Hong Kong Special Administrative Region, consolidated this arrangement when China's National People's Congress passed it in 1990. The latter guarantees free trade, free enterprise, and low taxes for at least 50 years.

Much of the anxiety of the pre-1997 period has proven to be baseless. China has kept its promise and Hong Kong continues to be a bastion of free enterprise. The territory has retained all its colonial financial and **monetary policies** and laws, including those regarding its currency, the free flow of capital into and out of its territory, and taxation. It uses its own currency, the Hong Kong dollar, and keeps its revenues for its own needs. Its government does not pay any tax to the Chinese central government. The hand-over has not changed Hong Kong's economy, but the post-1997 period has had at least 2 major impacts on it. First, this period has consolidated a change in the economy that began in the early 1980s. This was the transfer of large, sophisticated, and labor-intensive industries from Hong Kong to mainland China where there is no scarcity of land and raw material and where labor is significantly cheaper. As a result, existing manufacturing in Hong Kong mainly focuses on the necessary activities for the **re-export** of goods produced by Hong Kong enterprises in China. Being the largest economic sector even prior to 1997, Hong Kong's service sector has since grown significantly in the fields of trade and transportation. This was done to meet the increasing demand for re-exporting and to absorb the loss of jobs in the manufacturing sector. Second, there has been a growing interest in 2 new industries: high-tech and information technology (IT). This is a positive move towards the broadening of the service-dominated economy of Hong Kong. IT activities have also created new types of employment opportunities, most of which cannot be filled immediately due to a lack of skilled workers. Consequently, there were 18,400 vacant IT positions in 2000. The root cause of this problem is that those who have lost their jobs in other sectors (e.g. manufacturing) are either unskilled or have skills that are not in demand. The Hong Kong government has addressed this issue by increasing its spending on retraining programs by 5.4 percent in 1997–98, 11.8 percent in 1999–2000, and 42.8 percent in 2000–01.

Like many other Asian economies, the Hong Kong economy suffered from the financial crisis of the late 1990s. However, unlike most of them, it was able to cope with the crisis with tolerable losses and begin recovery in 1999. Its large service sector has been given credit for the economy's ability to recover. This sector has been the reason for a constant **balance-of-payment** surplus since 1997. In that year, Hong Kong had a balance-of-payment deficit of US$6.159 billion (equal to 3.6 percent of its GDP). However, it enjoyed 2 consecutive balance-of-payment surplus years of US$2.902 billion (equal to 1.8 percent of its GDP) and US$9.285 billion (equal to 5.8 percent of GDP) in 1998 and 1999, respectively. Figures for 2000 are not yet available, but there are indications of a surplus for that year as well. Unlike other Asian countries fallen victim to the 1997–98 financial crisis, Hong Kong's **external debt** has remained small in comparison to its available finances. For example, its total **foreign debt** was US$48.7 billion in 1998, US$53.5 billion in 1999, and US$56.5 billion in 2000 while its **foreign exchange reserves** were US$89.601 billion, US$92.236 billion, and US$97.218 billion, respectively. The crisis slowed down the economy temporarily, as reflected in a large drop in its GDP growth rate from 5 percent in 1997 to -5.1 percent in 1998. However, it did not lead to widespread closures of industries and companies or massive unemployment as experienced in Indonesia and Malaysia, for instance. The economy began to recover in 1999 and 2000 when the GDP growth rates jumped to 3 percent and 9.7 percent, respectively. Additionally, its unemployment rate reached the record high of 6.2 percent in 1999, only to drop to about 5 percent in 2000 despite the continued relocation of the manufacturing jobs to mainland China.

Geography and size impose certain limits on the economic activities that Hong Kong can undertake, but they also open opportunities for its economic growth. Maintaining extensive ties with China has been an imperative for the survival of this small territory, which has no mineral and water resources and lacks an adequate agriculture sector to meet its essential private and commercial needs. Being connected to China via land, Hong Kong has depended on its only neighbor for raw materials, food, and water. Its small size and acute scarcity of land also lead Hong Kong to look to China for the establishment of large and labor-intensive manufacturing establishments. This has been a blessing in disguise as China's low wages significantly reduce the cost of production of its exports and make them more competitive in international markets. Reliance on China has also helped Hong Kong penetrate the huge and growing Chinese market, the largest in the world and to which many developed economies are trying so hard to gain access. Not only are Hong Kong businesses interested in China, but the Chinese government also encourages extensive ties with Hong Kong, its reunified territory. Expanding economic ties with China also helps Hong Kong tolerate losses in its economic transactions elsewhere.

The service sector dominates Hong Kong's economy. This is the result of the territory's limited opportunities for agricultural and industrial activities on the one hand, and the interest of the British colonizers to develop it as a trading center on the other. Being the engine of economic growth, the service sector is the largest employer and the largest contributor to Hong Kong's GDP (84.7 percent in 1998). The major services are trade, financial services (e.g., banking and insurance), tourism, **retail**, and real estate. Trade has been the heart of Hong Kong's economy. The service sector has been growing steadily over the last few decades under British and Chinese rule alike.

Agriculture is negligible as a source of employment or revenue and makes only a miniscule contribution to GDP (0.1 percent in 1998). The scarcity of arable land leaves very limited opportunity for agricultural activities. Hong Kong is heavily dependent on agricultural imports.

Industry is a significant sector, but is mainly geared to the re-export of goods produced in China. This sector is small, accounting for 15.2 percent of GDP in 1998. Thanks to a lack of minerals, there is no mining industry of any significance. There is a small utility (water, gas, and electricity) industry, a relatively significant construction industry, and a more important export-oriented manufacturing sector. As a small territory with limited land and a very large population, Hong Kong cannot support heavy industries, which are land-intensive by nature. Nor can it have large labor-intensive industries. Besides low wages and an abundance of resources in China, space has been the main reason for the relocation of Hong Kong's large and labor-intensive industries to that country. The remaining industries of Hong Kong are small-scale establishments, which employ small numbers of workers. Garment production has been the leading component of the manufacturing sector for decades, but Hong Kong has other marketable products—mainly light and **consumer goods** such as footwear, toys, and plastics. Manufacturing lacks a significant high-tech segment, but has a viable electronics branch in need of development.

POLITICS, GOVERNMENT, AND TAXATION

The political parties of Hong Kong are at the initial stage of their development and do not represent a long tradition of political activities. Political parties were illegal until 1990. Being a British colony directly ruled by a British-appointed governor, the territory did not need active political parties. They seemed to be irrelevant to a political system whose executive branch, the Executive Council (Exco), and the legislative branch, the Legislative Council (Legco), were simply advisory bodies. The latter was run by appointed or selected businesspeople and professionals and not by elected politicians.

As part of the preparation for the hand-over of Hong Kong to China, efforts to democratize the Hong Kong political system led to the introduction of an elected Legco and the gradual elimination of legislative seats occupied by the British governor's appointees. These developments justified the creation of political parties. Yet, the Basic Law of Hong Kong provides for an election process, which undermines the status of the Legco as a truly democratic and representative body. Out of its 60 members, only 20 members are directly elected by popular votes. Functional constituencies (created by professional, business, and labor groups) elect 30 members, and an electoral committee (formed mainly by functional constituencies' chosen delegates) elect the remaining 10 members. Consequently, big business dominates Legco, which reflects the pre-eminence of business-oriented groups and the irrelevance of political parties in the running of Hong Kong and overseeing its economy.

In such a situation, the emerging political parties, which suffer from internal weaknesses, are practically out of the decision-making process and are therefore unable to have a major impact on the economy. Major politicians, including Chief Executive Tung Chee-hwa, do not have party affiliations and are prominent business figures.

The Hong Kong political parties are divided into 3 major groups: pro-democracy, pro-business, and pro-China. None of these groups advocate any economic policy to undermine the free-enterprise nature of the economy or the status of the territory as a center for free trade. The merger of 2 pro-democracy groups (the United Democrats of Hong Kong and the Meeting Point) formed the Democratic Party of Hong Kong in 1994, the largest pro-democracy party. It suffers from infighting on various issues, including economic issues. Pro-business parties include the Association for Democracy and People's Livelihood, the Hong Kong Democratic Foundation, the Frontier Party, the Citizens Party, and the Liberal Party. All these parties tend to advocate close ties with China and cooperate with pro-China groups. The major pro-China groups include the DAB (Democratic Alliance for the Betterment of Hong Kong). Not surprisingly, it also advocates close economic ties with China. The 3 largest parties in Legco are the Democratic Party of Hong Kong, the Liberal Party, and the DAB.

The Hong Kong government has a very limited role in economic affairs. This is in keeping with the proclaimed status of Hong Kong as a haven for unfettered free enterprise and free trade, in which the task of creating a viable economy is granted to the **private sector**. The intervention of the government in the economy is limited only to providing the essential services for its normal functioning and for creating an environment conducive to its growth. Therefore, government must ensure the existence of the required **infrastructure** for the daily life of the population and the economy—for instance, education, health care, communications, and telecommunications—with or without the involvement of the private sector. It must also ensure the absence of barriers to free economic activities. Such barriers include laws and regulations which complicate, impede, or prohibit economic activities such as difficult and lengthy processes for registration of economic establishments, various licenses for their activities, restrictions on the transfer of funds from and to Hong Kong, and the imposition of **tariffs** and restrictive export/import regulations.

To create a suitable environment for economic growth, the Hong Kong government imposes very few laws and regulations on economic activities. It continues the British policy of "positive non-intervention," meaning it **levies** low taxes to encourage economic activities and limits government expenditures as well as its role in providing essential services (e.g. education, health care, and housing). Apart from these functions, the government's role in the economy is limited to the extent justified for the well-being of the economy. In this regard, its first and foremost duty is to ensure the stability of the Hong Kong dollar, which demands the stability of the economy. To that end, in August 1998 it purchased US$15.3 billion worth of stocks to prevent the fall of the Hong Kong stock market and put it back in a healthy position. That move also prevented huge losses which could have seriously damaged the economy and weakened its currency.

Hong Kong's government gives a free hand to the private sector in practically all economic affairs pertaining to the 3 main economic sectors (agriculture, industry, and services), including investment, production, trade, and transfer of capital. For example, there is no need for a business to acquire a license in Hong Kong. Regardless of the nature of their activities, the only requirement for setting up businesses is to register them as companies; the registration process is not complicated. Nor is there any restriction on investments or on financial transactions regardless of size, including the transfer of funds from and to Hong Kong or the **repatriation** of profits and investments. Finally, tariffs do not exist in Hong Kong.

The private sector has been the main engine of growth before and after 1997. This sector also includes foreign businesses, which are treated practically like local ones. The only major restriction on foreign investors checks their involvement in television broadcasting concerns. These investors can buy up to 10 percent of the concerns' shares individually and cannot own more than 49 percent of the voting shares as a group. While there is no systematic restriction on the operation of foreign investors in Hong Kong, there is not any specific program to attract them either. The Hong Kong government believes that its territory's geographical location, its good infrastructure, its low taxes and absence of tariffs, and its very limited and simple business regulations make investment in Hong Kong attractive enough for local and foreign entrepreneurs.

TAXES. The Hong Kong government imposes tax on salaries, employment-generated incomes, pensions, property incomes, and on revenues of economic establishments. The simple tax system is characterized by low tax rates, varying between 15 and 16 percent. All individuals who receive salaries, wages, or pensions are liable for **income taxes**, which are not more than 15 percent of their income. As an **equity** measure provided by law, 61 percent of the workforce does not pay tax on salaries. All corporations or individuals involved in any type of trade, business, or profession are liable for taxes on their profits, excluding those generated from the sale of capital assets. There is a flat rate of 16 percent for the business profit tax.

The Chinese government cannot tax Hong Kong in any manner, as stipulated in the Basic Law and the Sino-British Joint Declaration. The Hong Kong government keeps all revenues, including taxes, for its own use. In February 1998, Hong Kong signed a treaty with China to eliminate double taxation of their respective businesses operating in each other's territory.

Taxes account for more than 50 percent of government revenues. The amount of direct and **indirect taxes** (personal and corporate) collected in the **fiscal years** 1998 and 1999 was US$9.7 billion and US$4.9 billion, respectively. The total amount accounted for 52.5 percent of the total government revenue of US$27.8 billion. This showed a drop in both the absolute amount of collected taxes and in the percentage of their contribution to the government revenue in 1997–98. In that fiscal year, the government collected US$11.7 billion in **direct taxes** and US$8.39 billion in indirect taxes. The total collected taxes contributed to 55.4 percent of the government revenue of US$36.2 billion. The financial crisis of 1997–98 caused a slowdown in the economy and lowered the amount of collected taxes in the fiscal year of 1998–99. Transportation services, including those related to seaports and airport, and capital revenues (i.e. revenues generated from investments by the Hong Kong government) are 2 other major sources of government revenues. They accounted for 44.6 percent (US$16.11 billion) and 47.5 percent (US$13.2 billion) of such revenues in the fiscal years of 1997–98 and 1998–99, respectively. In the same years, the government's share of capital revenues fell from 29.4 percent (US$10.6 billion) to 22.8 percent (US$6.3 billion), while the share of transportation services rose from 15.2 percent (US$5.3 billion) to 24.7 percent (US$6.7 billion). A growth in the use of port facilities by China-based enterprises was the main factor for the rise.

The judicial system of Hong Kong plays a major role in the economy. It is an independent body in charge of ensuring the continuation of the rule of law in all fields, including in the economy as set prior to the hand-over of Hong Kong to China and as stipulated by the Basic Law. This is essential for the free enterprise economy of Hong Kong, as it guarantees the right of its people to private property and to engage in legitimate economic activities. It also guarantees the unrestricted economic environment of Hong Kong and prevents government intervention in Hong Kong's economic affairs, which would have a negative impact on the status of the territory as a bastion of free enterprise. This status has been the major factor for the phenomenal economic growth of Hong Kong and its continued attractiveness to local and international investors. Finally, the continuation of rule of law is a guarantee against any attempt on the part of the Chinese government to intervene in the internal affairs of Hong Kong and to impose its laws and regulation on that territory.

The Hong Kong courts are in charge of upholding laws, rights, and freedoms, including respect for private property and all rights and laws necessary for the continuation of economic activities. These courts are independent and exercise jurisdiction over all cases except those falling under the jurisdiction of China's central authority, namely defense and foreign affairs.

INFRASTRUCTURE, POWER, AND COMMUNICATIONS

Hong Kong has a superb infrastructure, which meets its population's needs and contributes to the efficiency and growth of the economy. Hong Kong has an advanced land, sea, and air transport and communications system, including 1,831 kilometers (1,138 miles) of paved roads (1997 est.) and 34 kilometers (21 miles) of electrified railways (1996 est.). The railway system is one of the most efficient systems of the world and is connected to Chinese railways via the Kowloon peninsula. The construction of 3 new lines was begun in 1998. In 2000, the Hong Kong government hinted at a huge project to construct 6 more lines to facilitate (make easier) rail traffic between Hong Kong Island and the rest of the territory and also to improve freight links with mainland China to meet the expected future needs.

Hong Kong's land transportation services are very efficient. To decrease the level of air pollution, its government encourages the use of public transportation

Communications

Country	Newspapers	Radios	TV Sets[a]	Cable subscribers[a]	Mobile Phones[a]	Fax Machines[a]	Personal Computers[a]	Internet Hosts[b]	Internet Users[b]
	1996	1997	1998	1998	1998	1998	1998	1999	1999
Hong Kong	792	684	431	61.8	475	54.3	254.2	142.77	2,430
United States	215	2,146	847	244.3	256	78.4	458.6	1,508.77	74,100
China	N/A	333	272	40.0	19	1.6	8.9	0.50	8,900
South Korea	393	1,033	346	138.3	302	N/A	156.8	55.53	10,860

[a]Data are from International Telecommunication Union, *World Telecommunication Development Report 1999* and are per 1,000 people.
[b]Data are from the Internet Software Consortium (http://www.isc.org) and are per 10,000 people.

SOURCE: World Bank. *World Development Indicators 2000.*

services and discourages the use of private cars in its small territory. It therefore keeps improving public transportation services while increasing the cost of maintaining private cars through various measures such as high car-registration fees, a compulsory inspection for cars over 6 years old, and a point system to disqualify offending drivers. Public transport facilities include the mainly underground Mass Transit Railway, which provided services to 2.2 million passengers every working day in 1999. It also includes very efficient bus services run by 4 private companies, supplemented by public and private light minibus services. A line of streetcars, about 18,000 taxis, 113,770 cargo vehicles, and 321,617 private cars further facilitated passenger movements in 1999.

Sea communications are vital for Hong Kong, both for trade and daily life. There are at least 5 major ferry companies providing daily service between the islands where its population lives and works. Hong Kong is a major port in Asia and one of the busiest container ports in the world. It handled 6.2 million twenty-foot containers in 1999. To meet future increases in cargo handling, an expansion of its container terminal facilities began in the same year.

Hong Kong's eminent status as a major international port could be undermined in 2 ways. First, Taiwan and Singapore rival Hong Kong by improving their port facilities regularly. Second, a major portion of Hong Kong's cargo handling is shipping of re-exports to and from China, which will decrease as China develops its mainland ports. Besides its good port facilities, Hong Kong has a very advanced commercial fleet, which operated 38,000 vessel departures in 1999. In the same year the capacity of its cargo fleet was 215,226 metric tons.

Hong Kong has high-quality private airlines and was home to 3 modern airports with paved runways and 2 heliports as of 1999. A new Hong Kong international airport, Chek Lap Kok Airport, replaced the old international airport (Kai Kak airport) in 1998. Kai Kak Airport handled 30 million passengers and 1.6 million tons of cargo in 1997. Located on Lantau Island, the new airport is one of the world's best airports, and is capable of handling up to 460 flights a day. Its annual passenger and cargo capability is 87 million passengers and 9 million metric tons of cargo, respectively.

Hong Kong's utility services are excellent even though they are highly dependent on imports for their daily operations. The territory has no source of fresh water, which makes it dependent on China for all its water needs to run its efficient water system.

Hong Kong has the highest rate of energy consumption per capita in Asia. For example, in 1998 its electricity consumption per capita was 5,569 kilowatt hours (kWh) compared to mainland China's 922 kWh. Hong Kong imports all its needs in fuel for private and commercial consumption, and power generation amounted to 18 million metric tons of oil in 1998. Hong Kong also imports gas from China and liquified gas through oil companies such as Shell, Mobil, Esso, Caltex, and China Resources, while producing gas from naphtha (a mixture of liquid hydrocarbons made from distilling petroleum, coal tar, and natural gas) at home. The value of its energy imports increased from about US$3 billion in 1998 to US$3.5 billion in 1999.

Two private companies supply electricity to Hong Kong and each has a **monopolized** area. In addition to the generated electricity in its 3 fossil-fuel power stations, Hong Kong imports electricity from China, including from the Daya Bay atomic power station, a Chinese government-Hong Kong **joint venture**. The power generation capacity of the 2 private companies (9,590 megawatts [mw] in 1998) is well above the demand (8,620 mw in 1998). This guarantees a continuous supply of uninterrupted power.

The telecommunications system of Hong Kong is excellent, consisting of fixed-line and cellular services. In 1998, there were 3.7 million fixed-line telephones and 2.4 million cellular phones in use. Hong Kong has one of the highest rates of usage of cellular phones in the world. In 2000, for instance, 55.6 percent of its population (3.9 million people) owned cellular telephones, an increase of 1.5 million from 1998. Personal computers are widely used and their availability is high (254 computers per 1,000 people in the same year). Internet services were provided by 49 Internet service providers in 1999.

Cable & Wireless HKT, a private company, dominates the telecommunications market. It had a 100 percent monopoly until 1997, when the Hong Kong government began to end its monopoly by encouraging competition. Through licensing of 3 new companies, the government reduced the market share of Cable & Wireless HKT to 97 percent in 2000. In that year it announced the licensing of 5 more companies.

Radio and television services are also advanced. In addition to foreign cable and satellite TV programs, 20 AM and FM radio stations and 4 television networks were operating in 1997. The number of televisions and radios in use in that year were estimated to be 1.84 million and 4.45 million, respectively.

ECONOMIC SECTORS

The economy of Hong Kong survived the financial crisis of 1997–98. This service-dominated economy began its recovery in 1999 and continued it in 2000 thanks to its viable service sector. To a varying extent, the 3 eco-

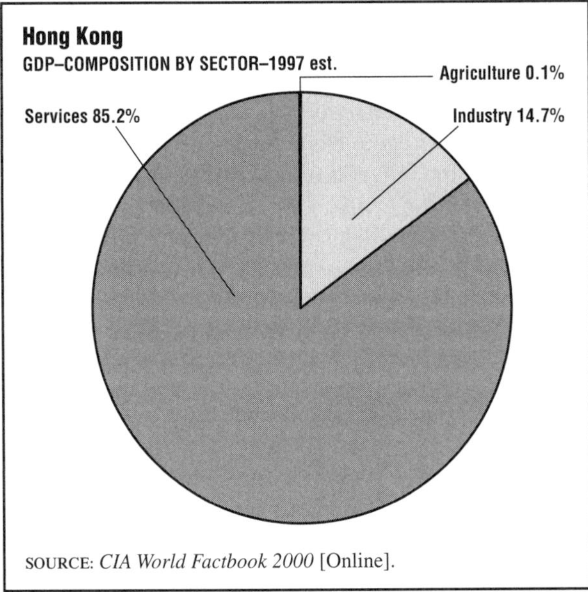

SOURCE: *CIA World Factbook 2000* [Online].

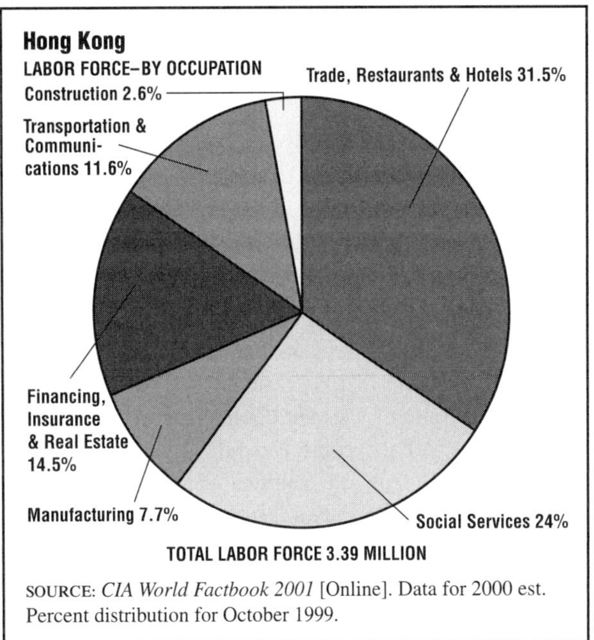

SOURCE: *CIA World Factbook 2001* [Online]. Data for 2000 est. Percent distribution for October 1999.

nomic sectors suffered from the crisis. The impact of the crisis on agriculture, the smallest sector with a very small contribution to the Hong Kong economy, was negligible. However, the industry and particularly the service sectors suffered considerably and experienced contraction during the crisis period. The CIA *World Factbook* reported the percentages of each sector's contribution to GDP in 1997 to be agriculture, 0.1 percent; industry, 14.7 percent; and services, 85.2 percent. As the largest and dominant economic sector, the service sector has always been the engine of growth and includes international trade, financial services, tourism, retail, and real estate. These service industries are the largest employers and taxpayers.

The industry and service sectors have undergone structural changes over the last decades. The catalyst has been the gradual relocation of large and labor-intensive manufacturing to mainland China, which began in the early 1980s. This trend has been reinforced since the 1997 hand-over of Hong Kong to China. As a result, the industry's manufacturing branch has been shrinking. The service sector has been expanding to re-orient itself towards functions pertaining to China's international trade.

The reunification with China has not changed the business-friendly environment of Hong Kong. As promised, China has respected the autonomy of the territory in its internal affairs, including its economic policies. China's approach has bolstered the confidence of the local and international business community in the stability and predictability of Hong Kong, which became somewhat shaky on the eve of the 1997 hand-over. Hong Kong is as friendly as ever to local and foreign investors, including Western (American, British, French, Swiss, and Dutch) and non-Western (Japanese and South Korean) **multinational corporations** (MNCs).

AGRICULTURE

Hong Kong has a small agricultural sector, including fisheries, with a very limited productivity and insignificant role in the economy. Its contribution to GDP and share of the workforce was about 0.1 percent in 1998. The available arable land is extremely limited in Hong Kong, where land is generally scarce. Less than 7 percent of Hong Kong's land is used for agricultural activities, i.e., farming and fish farming. As the available farming land cannot produce enough food for the Hong Kong population of more than 7 million, the population survives on large imports of agricultural products valued at US$8.32 billion in 1998, which fell to US$7.335 billion in 1999 as a result of the financial crisis. China is the main exporter of these products.

The scarcity of land has determined the nature of agricultural activities. Instead of land-intensive and low-priced rice and grain production, 2 lucrative activities (vegetable farming and flower growing) have become the dominant activities, accounting for 93 percent of the total value of crops grown in 1998. The scarcity of pastoral land sets limits on animal husbandry, and has led to the rearing of only poultry and pigs. Domestic production accounted for 10 percent of live poultry and 16 percent of live pigs in 2000.

Fishing is a very small source of employment, but its products meet a significant portion of demands for seafood. They amounted to 75 percent of the fresh marine consumption and 11 percent of the freshwater fish consumption in 2000. Fish ponds produced 4,900 metric tons of freshwater fish in 1998, and the fresh marine catch was 188,000 metric tons. In 2000, the fishery fleet consisted of 4,460 vessels of various sizes, of which 3,820 were motorized.

INDUSTRY

Industry has experienced a slow decline over the last 2 decades. Its contribution to GDP was 15.2 percent (equal to US$23 billion) in 1998, a significant decrease from its 1990 contribution of 17.7 percent. Its share of the workforce, which was 28 percent in 1990, dropped to about 15 percent in 1998. The decline of industry has been the outcome of a steady contraction in manufacturing, the result of the continued relocation of manufacturing establishments to mainland China. Manufacturing's share of GDP sharply fell from 24.3 percent in 1984 to 6.2 percent in 1998. The constant expansion of the service sector has also contributed to the process of decline. Other activities, such as construction, energy, and mining, are not significant enough to stop the steady decline of the industrial sector.

The largest sector of industry is manufacturing. It is a major contributor to GDP (6.5 percent in 1998) and the workforce (7.3 percent in 1998, or 245,457 employees). Manufacturing's contribution to the workforce dropped to 7 percent (244,720 employees) in 1999, and the value of manufacturing exports also fell from US$10.31 billion in 1998 to US$9.42 billion in 1999, suggesting that the sector was beginning to contract.

There were 23,553 manufacturing establishments in Hong Kong in 1998. Known as "flatted factories," these establishments are mostly very small and located on 1 or 2 floors of a high-rise building. The average number of employees per establishment is 10. The migration of many large and labor-intensive industries to mainland China resulted in the loss of more than 500,000 industrial jobs in the 1990s.

Certain factors have created "natural" barriers to the growth of the manufacturing sector and have forced a peculiar pattern of development on it. Scarcity of land, the absence of mineral resources, the high cost of labor, and the close proximity to China have ruled out the establishment of heavy industry or other land- and labor-intensive industries in Hong Kong. Prior to the 1980s, Hong Kong produced mainly labor-intensive consumer products, including food, beverages, clothing, textiles, printed products, and fabricated metal products. Being a resource- and land-rich country with a very low-wage **labor force**, China became a "natural" place for Hong Kong's manufacturing in the 1980s. Improved relations between the 2 sides made the relocation of major industries to China feasible. China's growing interest in foreign investment facilitated the process.

The result was a re-structuring of Hong Kong's manufacturing sector. Labor-intensive and sophisticated industries were moved to China, mainly to the neighboring Guangdong Province, while light and capital-intensive industries were kept in Hong Kong. This trend is continuing. Given the removal of all political barriers and the willingness of the Chinese government, it is simply logical for Hong Kong industrialists to continue their establishment of the labor- and land-intensive industries in China where they have access to minerals, low-cost labor, and abundance of land. Their products are exported via the very modern and efficient port of Hong Kong.

The existing Hong Kong industries are small-scale operations. They are involved mainly in certain manufacturing processes pertaining to re-exporting goods produced in China by Hong Kong-owned establishments. These processes can involve the packaging of goods produced on the mainland, for instance. However, there are still export-oriented industries that produce textiles, electronics, plastics, and watches and clocks. The textile industry is the largest industrial employer and accounts for the bulk of annual domestic industrial exports, accounting for 45 percent (US$11.3 billion) and 49 percent (US$10.79 billion) of those exports in 1998 and 1999, respectively.

The electronics industry, including telecommunications, is the second largest export earner, but it is small and underdeveloped. The value of its exports was US$4.24 billion in 1998 and US$3.55 billion in 1999. Its products are generally of lower quality compared to other Asian products such as those of Singapore and Taiwan. Its rapid growth over the last 3 decades is owed to large foreign investments and transfer of technology. This situation makes it highly dependent on foreign sources for investments and parts; local industries can produce only 20 percent of the necessary parts. The electronics industry produces various sophisticated products, including semiconductors, computers, televisions and telecommunications equipment. The Hong Kong government has sought to help expand this industry, especially in the fields of computer products, in order to diversify the economy, now heavily dependent on services.

The plastics industry has been shrinking in Hong Kong, with most of its manufacturing establishments being moved to China. Nevertheless, Hong Kong is one of world's largest toy exporters. The exports of plastic goods generated about US$210 million in 1998 and US$163 million in 1999.

A major component of the industrial sector is the construction industry. It accounted for 6.1 percent of GDP and employed 2.2 percent of the workforce (72,253 employees) in 1998. In the aftermath of the Asian financial crisis, a decline in construction activities lowered its share of the workforce to 2.1 percent (71,789 workers) in 1999, but government-financed infrastructure projects increased its share to 79,300 employees in June 2000. The constant government investment in infrastructure and private sector investments in related fields (such as housing and commercial establishments, which total more than 50 percent of investments in the sector) make construction a viable industry.

The industry has gone through periods of expansion and contraction for political and economic reasons since the 1980s. Politically, the smooth hand-over of Hong Kong to China encouraged investment in private and commercial construction projects in 1998 and 1999. Recent economic factors include a 1994 government policy on buying and selling unfinished apartments. That policy made those transactions more difficult and therefore lowered property prices, resulting in a reduction in investment in apartment building projects. Thanks to a wide range of road and railway expansion projects, the construction industry is expected to experience a period of growth in the first half of the decade (2000–10).

The utility industry is a vital sector in Hong Kong, which lacks freshwater and fossil energy resources. As discussed earlier, several companies ensure uninterrupted supplies of water and energy (electricity and fossil fuel) for private and commercial purposes through imports of water and both limited local production and large imports of energy. Despite its importance, the utility industry is small and employs an insignificant portion of the workforce, but its contribution to GDP is significant (2.4 percent in 1998).

There is no mining industry of any significance in Hong Kong, as the territory lacks mineral resources. The share of mining and quarrying activities of GDP was about 0.02 percent in 2000. Cement production is the most important activity of this sector.

SERVICES

The service sector dominates the Hong Kong economy. In the absence of a significant agriculture and a large and growing industrial base, it has become the largest economic sector in terms of income-generation, employment, and contribution to GDP. The contraction of the manufacturing sector has contributed to further enlargement of the service sector to absorb the growing number of those laid off from manufacturing jobs, a continuing trend since the 1980s. So far, this strategy has been successful, but there are concerns about the future ability of the service sector to absorb manufacturing job losses, especially because many of the affected workers are middle-aged and/or unskilled or poorly skilled. The contribution of services to GDP was 84.7 percent (equal to US$129 billion) in 1998, when they employed roughly the same proportion of the workforce.

The service sector consists of a wide range of companies of various sizes—local and foreign, including multinational corporations (MNCs)—interested in Hong Kong for its many opportunities for service activities. The major services are financial, trade, tourism, retail, real estate, and transportation.

Finance, insurance, real estate, and investment services are the most viable economic activities, which have made Hong Kong a major global financial center. These services accounted for 26.2 percent of GDP and employed 390,454 people (11.6 percent of the workforce) in 1998. The number of employees rose to 415,326 (11.9 percent of the workforce) in 1999, and to 429,300 (about 12 percent) in June 2000.

Banking is the heart of Hong Kong's financial services. In terms of the volume of external transactions, Hong Kong is the ninth-largest international banking center in the world. It is home to many local and foreign-owned banks. Banking makes a major contribution to the growth of the Hong Kong economy, and the huge revenues generated in this sector help the territory to tolerate fluctuations in its manufacturing exports and pay its foreign debt.

Hong Kong does not have a central bank, but the Hong Kong Monetary Authority (HKMA) assumes some of the functions of a central bank, namely monetary management, supervision of the banking sector, and regulating financial institutions. However, the issuance of banknotes is the task of 3 banks: the Hong Kong and Shanghai Banking Corporation (HSBC), the Standard Chartered Bank, and the Bank of China. In 2000, Hong Kong's banking system consisted of 285 authorized banks and 127 representative offices of other financial institutions. Of Hong Kong's 158 licensed (full-service) banks, 125 were registered outside Hong Kong.

Most major American, Japanese, and European banks operate in Hong Kong. There are also Thai and Taiwanese banks as well as 3 major state-owned banks from mainland China. In general, foreign banks concentrate mainly on large business clients (such as MNCs), unlike local banks, which tend to be more interested in small- and medium-size clients. Apart from its importance as an international trading center, Hong Kong's access to the growing market of China is the major reason for its attractiveness to foreign banks, through which they can enter the Chinese market. Foreign banks have a free hand for banking operations. The only restriction on their activities is a limit on their branch operations, meaning that in 2000 they could have only 3 branches.

The large and efficient insurance industry of Hong Kong is among the best such industries in Asia. This growing segment of the economy consists of 204 authorized insurers, of which 148 are general insurers, 43 long-term insurers (mostly life insurers), and 19 combined life and non-life insurers. The insurance companies include foreign ones, e.g., American (22) and British (18). In general, the industry has experienced growth over the last decade, excluding the year 1999, when the economy was not performing well. Its average annual growth rate was 10.7 percent during the period 1993 to 1998.

Hong Kong's retail sector is well developed. The total value of retail sales was about US$25 billion in 1998, equal to 15 percent of GDP. The industry includes a wide range of establishments, including small privately-owned stores, foreign department store chains (e.g., British and Japanese), supermarkets, and domestic retail chains. There are also many large shopping malls housing a wide range of stores. The retail industry includes a large network of restaurants, including international franchises.

Hong Kong's transportation industry, including storage and communications, has developed over the last few decades to meet growing demand in international trade and internal movement of goods and people. As mentioned previously, the territory has an advanced land, sea, and air transportation infrastructure. This industry is a major contributor to GDP, accounting for 9.1 percent in 1998 (equal to US$14.88 billion), and a large employer with 175,000 employees in the same year. The number of employees jumped to 180,600 in June 2000, which indicated 3.2 percent growth from 1998.

The vivid night-life of Hong Kong, including its numerous night clubs and restaurants, and its low-priced imported goods (thanks to the absence of tariffs) attracts millions of tourists to this small territory every year. To host and entertain them, Hong Kong's tourist industry has become extensive and highly developed. The industry makes a significant contribution to GDP (4.15 percent in 1998 and 4.09 percent in 1999) and generates employment for a large portion of the workforce. Restaurants and hotels are major employers of this industry. Together with trade, they accounted for 27.2 percent (equal to 913,070 jobs) and 28.8 percent (equal to 1,002,263 jobs) of the workforce in 1998 and 1999, respectively. There are many hotels, including local and foreign five-star hotels, with 35,420 total rooms in 1999, which are fully capable of providing high-quality services to tourists. In the same year, 10,678,000 tourists visited Hong Kong and generated US$6.5 billion in revenues. In comparison to 1998, this showed an increase of 1,103,000 tourists, but a decrease of US$300 million in revenue. The major factors responsible for this phenomenon were an increase in the number of low-income Chinese visitors at the expense of high-income non-Chinese visitors that led to an overall fall in spending per head from US$715 in 1998 to US$615 in 1999.

A decline in the number of non-Chinese tourists and in the average amount of tourists' spending has created a concern about the declining interest in Hong Kong as a tourist destination. Apart from short-term reasons, 2 major factors endanger the industry in the long run. One factor is the existence of less expensive destinations in Asia offering the same quality of services (such as Singapore). Another is the expected easing of travel restrictions between China and Taiwan. This development may diminish the attractiveness of Hong Kong for the Chinese and especially for high-spending Taiwanese who have had to go through points such as Hong Kong to get to each other's countries, because of the current travel restrictions between China and Taiwan. To address this concern and to ensure a significant increase in tourism, the Hong Kong government has sought to attract more tourists through a joint venture with an American company, Walt Disney, to establish a theme park. It is expected to bring 5 million visitors in its first year of operation (2005) and 10 million by 2020.

INTERNATIONAL TRADE

International trade is Hong Kong's most important economic activity. Its government policy towards trade reflects Hong Kong's status as a center of free trade. This policy contains minimum restrictions and allows the market forces to regulate exports and imports. It therefore proscribes protective measures (e.g., tariffs and quotas) and **subsidies** as a means for avoiding **balance-of-trade** deficits.

Hong Kong is a major exporter and importer of goods and services in Asia. It exported US$175.8 billion in goods and US$34 billion in services in 1998. In the same year the value of its imports was US$183.7 billion for goods and US$11.7 billion for services. As a result of the financial crisis of 1997–98, the value of its international trade decreased in 1999 when it exported US$174.7 billion worth of goods and US$35.7 billion worth of services while importing US$177.9 billion in goods and US$13.2 billion in services.

Exports consist of goods produced in Hong Kong (domestic exports) and those produced in Hong Kong-owned industries in China (re-exports). Re-exporting has become the largest component of Hong Kong's trade since the early 1980s, when its large and labor-intensive industries began to move to mainland China. For example, between 1986 and 1996, the volume of re-exports and domestic exports rose by about 700 percent and 17.3 percent, respectively. The small contribution of domestic exports to total exports was evident in 1999, for instance, when the total value of exports of goods was US$174.7 billion, of which the share of domestic exports was only US$21.9 billion. Because of the growing value of re-exports, Hong Kong has experienced a constant balance-of-trade deficit since the 1980s. As recent examples, the deficit was

Trade (expressed in billions of US$): Hong Kong

	Exports	Imports
1975	6.026	6.766
1980	19.752	22.447
1985	30.187	29.703
1990	82.160	82.490
1995	173.750	192.751
1998	173.990	184.503

SOURCE: International Monetary Fund. *International Financial Statistics Yearbook 1999.*

Exchange rates: Hong Kong

Hong Kong dollars (HK$) per US$1	
Jan 2001	7.7990
2000	7.7912
1999	7.7575
1998	7.7453
1997	7.7421
1996	7.7343

Note: Hong Kong became a special administrative region of China on July 1, 1997; before then, the Hong Kong dollar was linked to the US dollar at the rate of about 7.8 Hong Kong dollars per US dollar.

SOURCE: CIA *World Factbook 2001* [ONLINE].

US$17.298 billion in 1997, US$7.833 billion in 1998, and US$3.158 billion in 1999.

Consumer goods and light manufactures are the major exports of Hong Kong. In order of importance, they include apparel and clothing, electrical machinery and apparatus, textile yarn and fabric, office machinery and data processing equipment, watches and clocks, telecommunications equipment, jewelry, printed matter, plastics, toys, games, and sports goods. The major re-exports consist of consumer goods, raw materials, metals (iron and steel), semi-manufactures, **capital goods**, foodstuffs, and fuels. Hong Kong's major imports include consumer goods, raw materials, semi-manufactures, capital goods, foodstuffs, and fuels.

Hong Kong has lost most of its manufacturing capability since reunification with mainland China. Its most important domestic export industries are garments, textiles, and clothing, which accounted for 49 percent of its 1999 domestic exports. The Hong Kong government has tried to diversify this sector by encouraging the high-tech industry, which has expanded over the last decade, but its share of domestic exports is still small. For example, telecommunications equipment accounted for 2.2 percent of the domestic exports in 1999, valued at US$486 million.

The major trading partners of Hong Kong are China, the United States, Japan, the United Kingdom, and Taiwan. Its main export destinations in 1999 were China (33.4 percent), the United States (23.8 percent), Japan (5.4 percent), and the UK (4.1 percent). In the same year, its main sources of import were China (43.6 percent), Japan (11.7 percent), Taiwan (7.2 percent), and the United States (7.1 percent). Because of re-exports, China has become the largest trading partner of Hong Kong.

MONEY

The government of Hong Kong pegged the Hong Kong dollar to the U.S. dollar in October 1983 at a **fixed exchange rate** of HK$7.8 against US$1, and has continued this relationship as of 2001. Meant to ensure the stability of the Hong Kong dollar, this policy has been implemented under the Linked Exchange Rate System. This system subjects any change in the size and flow of the money in circulation to a corresponding change in the foreign exchange reserves of Hong Kong. This occurs whether as a result of Hong Kong's domestic resources or as a result of an inflow of foreign capital. Accordingly, the 3 banks in charge of issuing bank notes can do so only if they deposit an equivalent amount of U.S. dollars in an exchange fund kept by the Hong Kong Monetary Authority (HKMA) for any amount of HK dollars that they want to issue. The equivalent amount of these foreign currencies is determined at the fixed exchange rate of HK$7.8/US$1. Apart from this official **exchange rate**, there is also a free-**floating exchange rate**. This exchange rate has remained around 7.7 since 1995. While the official exchange rate of the HK dollar against the U.S. dollar is fixed and determined by the HKMA, the exchange rate of the HK dollar against any other major currency follows the U.S. dollar exchange rate against that currency, which makes it a free-floating rate.

The HKMA maintains the stability of the HK dollar-U.S. dollar exchange rate through an automatic interest-rate adjustment mechanism. This requires the control of local **liquidity** and interest rates. Through this mechanism, Hong Kong has managed to have monetary stability and avoid high **inflation rates** and sharp fluctuations in the value of the national currency. This has made a major contribution to the stability and growth of its economy, which has not experienced long and sudden periods of economic declines with their destructive impacts on employment and prices. The Hong Kong monetary policy has also helped its economy cope better with the financial crisis of the late 1990s, which devastated many Asian economies. However, this policy has a negative side since it links the HK dollar to the U.S. dollar and leaves little room for independent monetary policy of Hong Kong since it has to follow that of the United States.

Consistent with its status as a strong base for free enterprise, there is no official control on foreign currency exchange transactions in Hong Kong. Regardless of their size, there is no restriction on transfers to and from Hong Kong of funds in any currency, including the HK dollar.

The Stock Exchange of Hong Kong (SEHK) was established in 1986 as a result of the merger of 4 stock exchanges. Having a **market capitalization** of US$616.3 billion (June 2000), the SEHK is one of the world's major stock markets, and the second largest stock market in Asia after Japan.

GDP per Capita (US$)

Country	1975	1980	1985	1990	1998
Hong Kong	7,404	11,290	13,690	18,813	21,726
United States	19,364	21,529	23,200	25,363	29,683
China	138	168	261	349	727
South Korea	2,894	3,766	5,190	7,967	11,123

SOURCE: United Nations. *Human Development Report 2000; Trends in human development and per capita income.*

POVERTY AND WEALTH

Hong Kong is a prosperous territory with a high **GDP per capita** (US$18,813 in 1998). However, the distribution of income is uneven and there is a wide gap between social groups in terms of wealth and income. Large parts of the economy are dominated by a small group of tycoons who are among the richest people in the world and whose wealth is increasing. At the same time, there is a growing number of unemployed with practically no chance for rejoining the workforce. They are the victims of the migration of manufacturing establishments to mainland China who are middle-aged and unskilled or whose skills are not in demand. The service sector has absorbed a large portion of manufacturing unemployed since the 1980s, but the continuation of this trend is unlikely, since the skills of the unemployed often do not match those of the available positions.

The role of the Hong Kong government in the economy is minimal, but it has an extensive role in providing essential services, including health care, education, and housing. The health-care system, which provides high-quality standard services, is accessible by the entire population. Government-run hospitals dominate the medical institutions and provided 85 percent of hospital beds in 1996, but there are also private medical clinics and hospitals. Government-provided health-care services are not free, but their fees are low, as these services are subsidized. Costs of medical services can be waived if patients cannot afford them. Government spending on the health-care system receives a large percentage of its total annual spending, increasing from 11.1 percent in 1989–90 to 14.3 percent in 1996–97. The government has considered reforming the health-care system since the cost has been increasing. If the current situation continues, this cost will absorb 21 to 23 percent of total government spending in 2016. Government spending on health-care services amounted to US$3.4 billion in 1998–99. Hong Kong's high life expectancy (78.6 years in 1998) ranks the territory fifth among the top developed economies after Japan (80 years), Canada (79.1), and Sweden and Switzerland (78.7 years). This rank puts it far ahead of China with its life expectancy of 70.1 years in 1998. In addition to the absence of widespread malnutrition and the availability of safe water and adequate sanitation, Hong Kong's impressive high life expectancy indicates the efficiency of its health-care system.

Hong Kong has a very good system for basic education, thanks to significant government spending. Total public funds spent on education were equal to 4.2 percent of GDP (US$4.6 billion) in 1998–99, an increase of about US$500 million from the previous year. About 92.9 percent of its population was literate in 1998. The government provides free and compulsory education for children between the ages of 6 and 15. Children over the age

Household Consumption in PPP Terms

Country	All food	Clothing and footwear	Fuel and power[a]	Health care[b]	Education[b]	Transport & Communications	Other
Hong Kong	10	17	4	2	8	6	54
United States	13	9	9	4	6	8	51
China	N/A	N/A	N/A	N/A	N/A	N/A	N/A
South Korea	18	3	7	5	14	6	48

Data represent percentage of consumption in PPP terms.
[a]Excludes energy used for transport.
[b]Includes government and private expenditures.

SOURCE: World Bank. *World Development Indicators 2000.*

of 14 who wish to continue their studies at the high-school level must pay for their education, but there are government subsidies for those who cannot afford it. In 1998, for example, the government subsidized the education of 84 percent of children of school age. Hong Kong's post-secondary educational system includes 7 universities, which offer degree programs to 18 percent of the 17–to–20 age group who wish to enter university programs. There were 65,800 university students in 1998, an increase of 11,800 from 1994.

Despite its merits, the education system has certain problems. Its inability to train people with the skills required for the economy is the main problem. This has resulted in a vacancy of thousands of jobs in the high-tech industry, for instance, while there is a large number of unemployed with skills irrelevant to the changing economy. Another significant problem is discrimination against the physically and mentally disabled in education, despite the existence of anti-discrimination laws. Finally, some primary schools operate 2 sessions a day at the expense of lowering educational standards.

WORKING CONDITIONS

Hong Kong has a large and growing labor force. Its numeric strength has increased steadily from 3,000,700 in 1995 to 3,476,600 in 1999, in spite of the 1997–98 financial crisis. Over the last 3 decades, Hong Kong's unemployment rate has usually been small. The average unemployment rate during from 1985 to 1997 was 3.5 percent, as the growing service sector could easily absorb many of those who had lost their manufacturing jobs. During the 2 years prior to the financial crisis, the unemployment rate declined from 3.2 percent in 1995 to 2.6 percent in 1996, and to 2.2 percent in 1997. The crisis and its aftermath pushed the rate up to 4.7 percent in 1998 and 6.2 percent in 1999 (equal to 217,100 people). The latter was a record high for Hong Kong. The rate fell to about 5 percent in 2000.

The overwhelming majority of Hong Kong's workforce is employed in urban economic establishments, due to the insignificance of agriculture. The workforce is a mixture of skilled and unskilled workers. The old and middle-aged manufacturing workers tend to be unskilled or low-skilled, whereas those employed with the growing service industries are more likely to be better educated and possess more advanced skills, including those related to high-tech and information technology. There was a shortage of skilled workers for the service sector as well as for the growing high-tech manufacturing sector in 2000.

In keeping with its emphasis on free enterprise, Hong Kong gives the market the authority to determine wages. Apart from a small number of professions with a uniform wage structure, wages are determined by supply and demand. Individual agreements between employees and employers set wages. Thus, there is no minimum wage except for foreign domestic workers, which was set at about US$500 per month in 1998. Employers of such workers are required by law to provide a decent standard of living for their employees, including housing and food, but the law is not widely observed. Two-income households are common in Hong Kong, although the average wage is usually adequate for most workers and their households. In addition to wages, some employers provide their employees with various kinds of allowances (e.g. free medical services and daycare centers), but employers are not obliged by law to do so. As part of the social safety net, employees are entitled to benefits such as pensions, disability insurance, and food assistance.

Hong Kong is a member of the International Labor Organization (ILO), and has laws and regulations on working conditions. These include laws on safety and health conditions at the workplace verified by government inspections. Workers' safety has improved over the last 2 decades, partly because of such inspections and partly because of the transfer of many high-risk manufacturing jobs to China. Nevertheless, there are still many serious safety problems.

Labor laws also include workers' rights, in accordance with international agreements. For example, the right of association is recognized, and trade unions are legal. There were 558 employee unions in 1998, but they represented only 22 percent of the 3.1 million salaried employees and wage earners. Unions are not strong and are unable to impose collective bargaining on management. Consequently, collective bargaining is not widely practiced as a means of settling labor disputes. Generally speaking, work stoppages and strikes are permitted, but there are some restrictions on civil servants' involvement in such activities. In practice, these activities could lead to loss of employment since most workers must include an article in their employment contracts that their refusal to work is a breach of their contracts. This gives the right to employers to dismiss workers involved in strikes or stoppages. There have not been major strikes or similar labor activities over the last 2 decades.

Hong Kong's labor laws also include provisions to ensure the rights of certain social groups and prevent their exploitation. In general, forced labor is prohibited. Employment of children under the age of 15 in industrial establishments is also prohibited. Nevertheless, children between 13 and 14 years of age with a minimum of 9 years of education can work in certain non-industrial establishments if their employers can ensure their safety, health, and welfare. These children are not allowed to work overtime and cannot work for more than 8 hours a day and 48 hours a week. With the exception of male workers of 16 and 17 years of age, children are not allowed to work in dangerous trades. There is also an anti-discrimination law to protect women in the labor market. Women are well-represented in government and in the civil service (46 percent of senior civil servants are women), but they are not nearly as numerous in other prestigious areas. This includes the judiciary, where only 18 percent of senior employees (judicial officers and judges) are women. The physically and mentally disabled are discriminated against in employment and education in spite of the existence of anti-discriminatory laws.

COUNTRY HISTORY AND ECONOMIC DEVELOPMENT

1841. Hong Kong is seized by the British navy at the height of the first opium war (1839–42). The Chinese government is forced to accept Britain's sovereignty over the island by signing the Convention of Chuenpi.

1842. The British Royal Charter formally establishes Hong Kong as "a separate colony." The British government proclaims Hong Kong a free port, which encourages **immigration** from mainland China to Hong Kong. The United States government establishes the first foreign consulate in the colony.

1844. To control the Chinese population, the Hong Kong Legislative Council (Legco) passes a restrictive law which leads to a general strike, the return of many workers to China, and the paralysis of businesses. The Legco amends the law to restore normalcy.

1856. The Second Opium War (1856–58) begins. The Chinese workers of Hong Kong go on a strike and boycott British businesses.

1860. Britain expands its holdings in China by occupying Kowloon and Stonecutters Island. The Treaty of Beijing legalizes the occupation by leasing these lands to Britain in perpetuity.

1860s. Hong Kong's population grows significantly as a result of migration from mainland China. Its economy begins to flourish. Hong Kong's infrastructure emerges, including telegraph systems, street gas lighting, and secular schools.

1898. In the aftermath of the Sino-Japanese war (1894–95), the British government forces the weakened Chinese government to cede to Britain the New Territories and 235 islands in the proximity of Hong Kong on a 99-year lease to expire in June 1997.

1911. The Wuhan Uprising in Canton overthrows the Chinese Empire and makes its leader, Dr. Sun Yat-sen, the first president of China.

1920. Around 9,000 Hong Kong mechanics go on strike and leave for Canton. The subsequent paralysis of commerce leads to a wage increase and the settlement of the labor dispute.

1921. The Hong Kong government has to accept a wage increase for seamen similar to the one given to the mechanics in 1922 to end a general workers' strike.

1926. In October, the long general strike of Hong Kong's workers, in which 30 percent of the workforce participates, ends when the British Foreign Office agrees to change some of its unequal economic treaties with China.

1937. The Sino-Japanese War begins. The Japanese navy lands at Bias Bay in the New Territories.

1939. Japanese military forces occupy Hong Kong's Hainan Island.

1941. On 8 December, Japan invades Hong Kong. Governor Young accepts defeat and surrenders to the Japanese commander on 25 December.

1949. The Chinese Communist Party wins the civil war in China and declares the establishment of the People's Republic of China (PRC) on 1 October.

1950s. Hong Kong's population increases to 2.5 million as a result of the flight of hundreds of thousands of refugees from mainland China.

1961. Hong Kong's population increases to 3.1 million.

1970. Hong Kong's population grows to 4 million.

1979. As part of improving ties between China and Britain, China invites Hong Kong governor MacLehose for an official visit to discuss certain issues, especially the expiration of the New Territories lease in 1997.

1980. Hong Kong's population increases to 5.2 million. Hong Kong governor MacLehose announces the "Touch Base" policy to stop illegal immigration from China, which provides for the return of illegal immigrants to China.

1982. In September, British prime minister Margaret Thatcher visits Beijing to begin negotiations about the future status of Hong Kong.

1983. In July, the first official round of Sino-British talks over the future status of Hong Kong begins. In October, the Hong Kong dollar is pegged to the U.S. dollar at a rate of HK7.8 against US$1.

1984. The British and Chinese governments sign the Sino-British Joint Declaration regarding the peaceful hand-over of Hong Kong to China on 1 July 1997.

1985. In September, the Hong Kong government holds the first elections for Hong Kong's legislative body, the Legco.

1990. China's National People's Congress passes the Basic Law to serve as its mini-constitution based on the principle of "one country, two systems."

1991. In June, the Bill of Rights of Hong Kong is enacted with the power to override all other laws.

1994. Hong Kong holds its first fully democratic elections, and pro-democracy parties win a majority in the Legco. Selecting from among Hong Kong nationals, China appoints a 150-strong Preparatory Committee to lead Hong Kong's transfer to China. Over half of the committee are from Hong Kong's business elite.

1996. In December, China selects a Hong Kong tycoon, Tung Chee-hwa, to be Hong Kong's first chief executive after the 1997 hand-over.

1997. On 1 July, the British government returns Hong Kong to China, which is renamed as the Hong Kong Special Administrative Region (SAR) of the People's Republic of China. Its Basic Law guarantees legal, judicial, and legislative systems independent from those of China and full economic autonomy.

1998. Hong Kong signs a treaty with China to eliminate double taxation of their respective businesses operating in each other's territory. In May, a Legco is formed by elections, which replaces the Provisional Legislative Council (PLC).

2000. In September, a new Legco is formed by elections.

FUTURE TRENDS

Hong Kong has a very strong economic base, which has enabled it to tolerate periods of economic hardship. Its economic strength helped it survive the severe financial crisis of the late 1990s with minor damage, compared to the extensive devastation of many Asian economies. This strong economic base will help Hong Kong to regain its losses and expand its economy to play a more significant role in global markets. Hong Kong's access to China will make a large contribution to the expansion of its economy and will elevate its international status. The migration of the manufacturing industry to mainland China has weakened the local industrial base and created unemployment, but it has also opened a very promising economic opportunity for Hong Kong. China's abundance of land and raw materials and its low cost of labor have addressed the major limitations of the Hong Kong manufacturing sector. These limitations have prevented it from growing in light and consumer industries and from establishing labor- and land-intensive industries, including heavy industry. Mainland China has thus offered to Hong Kong an opportunity for industrial growth and expansion of exports of manufactures. It has also offered its huge 1.3-billion strong market, the world's largest, for investment and exports. This has put the Hong Kong economy well ahead of many other developed economies, which have been trying to gain extensive access to China. Hong Kong's manufacturing will surely expand, and its role in its economy will become more prominent, but the service sector will remain the largest and most dominant sector and the engine of growth. This is partly because of the strength and the phenomenal size of that sector, which have enabled it to grow and will ensure its continuity. It is also partly because of its crucial role in the re-export of goods produced in China, including their packaging, shipping, handling, and marketing, as well as financing their production.

Hong Kong's high-tech and IT industries have a great potential for growth. The territory's private sector has taken steps towards that end while its government has encouraged private initiatives. The high-tech and IT industries should have a stronger presence in international markets over the next few years, even though they face a challenge from the more developed industries of Taiwan, Singapore, and South Korea.

The service industry has absorbed most of the unemployed workers of the manufacturing sectors, but it has been unable to find jobs for a growing number of them. Given the continued migration of manufacturing industries to mainland China, the number of these unskilled or low-skilled middle-aged unemployed workers will continue to grow. Unless the Hong Kong government or the service sector retrains them to find jobs in emergent industries, most of them will become permanently unemployed. Their frustration will likely contribute to social and political disorder in Hong Kong, which has not experienced such phenomena in its contemporary history.

DEPENDENCIES

Hong Kong has no territories or colonies.

BIBLIOGRAPHY

Economist Intelligence Unit. *Country Finance: Hong Kong, 2001.* London: Economist Intelligence Unit, January 2000.

Economist Intelligence Unit. *Country Profile: Hong Kong.* London: The Economist Intelligence Unit, 2001.

International Labor Office. *Yearbook of Labor Statistics 1999.* Geneva, Switzerland: International Labor Organization, 1999.

International Monetary Fund. *International Financial Statistics Yearbook.* Washington, D.C.: International Monetary Fund, 1999.

Lonely Planet. *Hong Kong.* <http://www.lonelyplanet.com/destinations/north_east_asia/hong_kong/index.htm>. Accessed February 2001.

United Nations Development Project. *Human Development Report 2000.* New York: Oxford University Press, 2000.

U.S. Central Intelligence Agency. *World Factbook 2000: Hong Kong (Special Administrative Region of China).* <http://www.odci.gov/cia/publications/factbook/geos/er.html>. Accessed January 2001.

U.S. Department of State. *1999 Country Reports on Human Rights Practices: Hong Kong.* <http://www.state.gov/www/global/human_rights/1999/eritrea.htm>. Accessed January 2001.

U.S. Department of State. *FY 2000 Country Commercial Guide: Hong Kong.* <http://www.state.gov/www/about_state/business/com_guides/index.html>. Accessed January 2001.

Welsh, Frank: *A History of Hong Kong.* London: Harper Collins, 1993.

The World Bank. *The Emerging Asian Bond Market (Background Paper), Hong Kong. The World Bank East Asia & Pacific Region.* Washington, D.C.: World Bank, June 1995.

Yan-Ki Ho, Richard, Robert Haney Scott, and Kie Ann Wong, editors. *The Hong Kong Financial System.* Hong Kong: Oxford University Press, 1991.

—Dr. Hooman Peimani

INDIA

Republic of India
Bharat Ganarajya

CAPITAL: New Delhi.

MONETARY UNIT: Rupee (Rs). Rs1 equals 100 paise. Coins are in denominations of Rs1, 2, and 5, and 10, 25, and 50 paise. Paper currency is in denominations of Rs5, 10, 20, and 50.

CHIEF EXPORTS: Clothing, engineering goods, chemicals, leather products, gems and jewelry, cotton fiber, yarn, fabrics.

CHIEF IMPORTS: Chief imports of India are crude oil and petroleum products, machinery, gems, fertilizer, chemicals.

GROSS DOMESTIC PRODUCT: US$497 billion (2001 est. of real GDP at market exchange rates). [The CIA *World Factbook* estimated the GDP at PPP to be US$2.2 trillion in 2000.]

BALANCE OF TRADE: **Exports:** US$46.0 billion (2001 est.). **Imports:** US$54.9 billion (2001 est.). [The CIA *World Factbook* estimated exports at US$43.1 billion in 2000 (f.o.b.) and imports at US$60.8 billion (f.o.b.).]

COUNTRY OVERVIEW

LOCATION AND SIZE. India is located in the south of the Asian continent, bordering the Arabian Sea and the Bay of Bengal. The country is slightly more than one-third the size of the United States. The country's territory is measured at nearly 3.3 million square kilometers (1.3 million square miles) extending from the snow-capped Himalayan Mountains in the north to tropical forests in the south. India shares more than 14,000 kilometers (8,800 miles) of borders with 7 neighboring countries. To the northwest are Afghanistan and Pakistan; to the north are China, Bhutan, and Nepal; and to the east are Burma (also known as Myanmar) and Bangladesh. A narrow channel of sea formed by the Palk Strait and the Gulf of Mannar separates another neighbor, Sri Lanka, an island nation with which southeast India shares strong cultural ties. The Indian mainland consists of 4 regions, namely the Himalayan Mountains, the plains of the Ganges and the Indus, and the southern desert. The Himalayas, which contains the highest peaks in the world, consists of 3 almost parallel ranges dotted with large plateaus and valleys, some of which, like Kashmir and Kullu valleys, are vast, fertile, and of great natural beauty. The plains of the Ganges and the Indus, about 2,400 kilometers (1500 miles) long and on average about 280 kilometers (175 miles) wide, are formed by the basins of 3 river systems of the Indus, the Ganges and the Brahmaputra Rivers. These fertile basins are among the most densely populated areas in the world. India is composed of 25 states and 7 union territories. The top 5 most populated states are Uttar Pradesh (140 million people), Bihar (86 million), Maharashtra (79 million), West Bengal (68 million), and Andhra Pradesh (67 million). The top 3 most populated union territories are New Delhi (10 million), Pondichery (800,000), and Chandigarh (650,000).

POPULATION. The population of India is estimated to have passed the 1 billion mark in May 2000 (1,014,000,000; July 2000 estimate). For centuries, India has been a land of startling contrasts. Maharajahs and millionaires, snake charmers and poor farmers, beauty queens and burnt brides, and a population explosion juxtaposed with high child and maternal mortality. The billionth citizen of this ancient land entered a country with 40 political parties and 24 official languages, each spoken by at least a million people. A cultural preference for male children (who are thought to bring prosperity to a household) has resulted in a significant gender disparity with 927 females to every 1,000 males. The 2 relatively prosperous northern states of Haryana and Punjab have the largest gender disparities. Only Kerala—the **socialist**-run state—has a gender balance of 1 to 1. Feticide (the killing of a fetus), infanticide (the killing of an infant) or, later in life, forced suicide are still the lot of some Indian girls and young women. Though India was

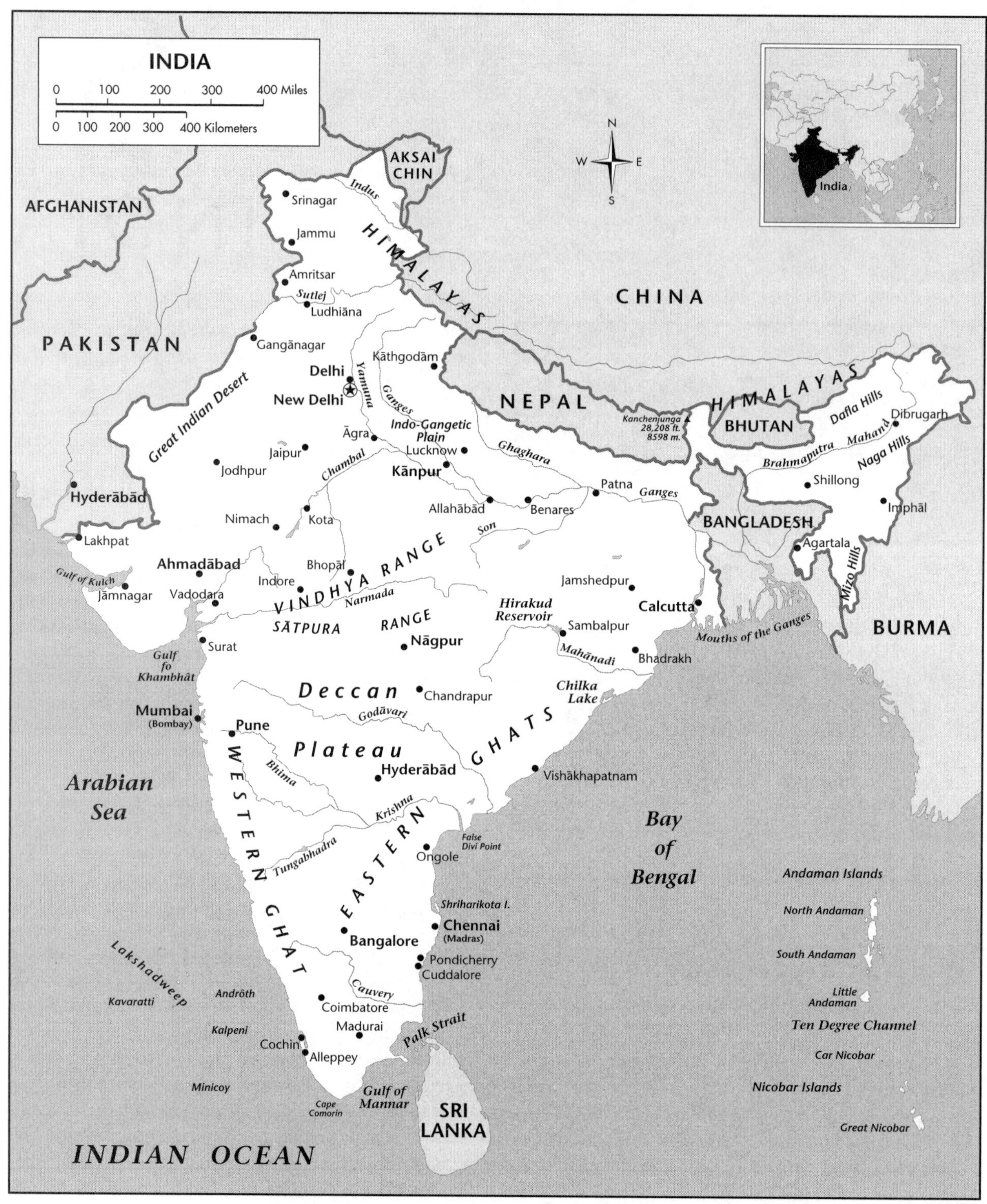

among the first countries to adopt population-control policies, those efforts have largely failed. The population continues to grow at the rate of 1.8 percent per year, and by 2025 India will likely overtake China as the world's most populated country, with a projected population of 1.42 billion. A newly established National Population Policy may lead to a reduction in the rate of population growth and to a stabilized population of slightly more than 1.5 billion by 2045. The immediate aims of the policy are to address the unmet needs of the health-care **infrastructure**, including the family-planning services, and to integrate delivery of basic reproductive and child health care. Special emphasis will be put in containing population growth in the states of Bihar, Madhya

Pradesh, Orissa, Rajasthan, and Uttar Pradesh, which currently constitute about 45 percent of the total population of India.

CASTE SYSTEM. The caste system (a centuries-old traditionally rigid social hierarchy which allows little social mobility), though not officially sanctioned today, continues to divide Indian society. The caste system has a historical basis in the economic organization of Indian society, with different peoples or castes allocated to various occupations. Many Hindus believe that people are born into a particular social status based on their experiences in past lives and that good deeds can help a person scale the rungs of caste, allowing movement up to a higher caste upon reincarnation in the next life. The caste system continues to be a strong force, especially in rural India. In many Indian villages, for example, one's caste influences what food one cooks or what sari one wears (the garment worn primarily by women in southern Asia made up of several yards of lightweight cloth). The *dalits* or "untouchables" are people of traditionally poor households who may be peasants, laborers, or servants (and their ancestors as well). Up to this day, many *dalits* are forced into menial and undesired occupations, such as cleaning restrooms, sweeping streets, and disposing of the dead—all considered "unclean" by orthodox Hindus. In the urban areas, the caste system is less obvious, though it is still defended by many as a way to uphold social order. In recent years, the government has taken serious measures to stamp out such age-old discriminatory practices. It has, for example, enacted affirmative action measures that recognize that some groups in society, such as the *dalits,* have been left far behind and have suffered on account of the practice and custom of caste differentiation.

OVERVIEW OF ECONOMY

India's economy encompasses a wide range of activities, anywhere from traditional village farming to the production of modern military hardware such as tanks. A full two-thirds (67 percent) of India's **labor force** of more than 450 million people is employed in agriculture, which accounts for about 23 percent of the country's **gross domestic product** (GDP). Another 26 percent of the GDP is accounted for by industry and 47 percent by services. The CIA *World Factbook* estimated the division of the GDP to be slightly different, indicating agriculture at 25 percent, industry at 24 percent, and services at 51 percent in 2000. Although India's human development indicators are among the worst in the world, the country has also a large number of highly qualified professionals, as well as several internationally established industrial groups. Reforms since 1991 in production, trade, and investment have provided new jobs and opportunities for Indian businesspersons. An estimated 300 million consumers are considered to be middle class. In past decades, India attempted to develop its industry as part of an effort to attain self-sufficiency, and as a result, the economy had remained closed to foreign investors. Recent liberal reforms, however, have opened some sectors to interested foreign investors. Currently, cars, motor scooters, electronic goods, and computers are manufactured by foreign firms and **joint ventures**.

During the 6-year period from 1996 to 2001, services have had the highest growth rate among the various sectors of the economy with an average of 8 percent growth rate per year, while the overall economy during the same period grew by an average rate of 6 percent per year. Despite the impressive economic performance of the past few years, however, several factors have hindered an even more impressive performance. The repercussion of the 1997 Asian financial crisis, the falling of world commodity prices, and the effects of **sanctions** after India conducted its first nuclear weapons tests in the late 1990s have all dampened further increases in the GDP. Other factors negatively affecting the GDP are the still slow process of market **liberalization**, limited access to investment capital, and reduced demand for manufactured goods. Infrastructure weaknesses such as poor transportation networks and erratic and insufficient power supplies have also limited increased growth and investment. Furthermore, for the past 2 decades, India's economy has been facing continuous problems of national **budget deficits**, much of it as a result of **subsidies** to inefficient state-owned industries. The majority of these state sector enterprises are debt-ridden and overstaffed.

There has, nevertheless, been a slow but steady trend in favor of market liberalization. As a result of the government's efforts and its membership obligations in the World Trade Organization (WTO), sectors of the economy such as power, steel, oil refining and exploration, road construction, air transport, telecommunications, ports, mining, pharmaceuticals, and banking have to a variety of degrees been liberalized. Since 1991, the **exchange-rate regime** has also been liberalized. This initially led to a 22 percent **devaluation** of the Indian rupee against the U.S. dollar. Furthermore, the leading political party, the Bharatiya Janata Party (BJP), has promoted the **restructuring** of state industry in favor of foreign and domestic competition. Despite these reforms, however, India's economy is still mostly closed. Foreign firms, due to historically disappointing experiences with India's bureaucracy and high taxes and **tariffs**, have been relatively reluctant to invest in the country. On the whole, there remains strong resistance to further market liberalization and globalization (increasing integration of the national economy and culture with the rest of the world, especially Western Europe and the United States) on the part of much of the population, such as the followers of the Hindu nationalist movement. Yet the fundamentals of the economy, including the savings rate (household savings is estimated at 19 percent of income), national reserves (about US$24 billion in 1997), **inflation rate**, and **foreign debt** (about US$94 billion in 2001) are considered to be healthy and improving.

POLITICS, GOVERNMENT, AND TAXATION

India is considered by many to be the largest democracy in the world. Inspired by Mahatma Gandhi and his Satyagraha (a unique non-violent campaign), India declared independence from British rule on 15 August 1947. Free India's first prime minister, Pandit Jawaharlal Nehru who founded the Indian National Congress, described the moment as a "tryst with destiny." Since independence, India has developed as a multiparty democracy. The Indian National Congress that led India to independence in 1947 was the largest party, governing in coalition with minor centrist parties. It was later known as the Congress Party and ruled the nation until the 1990s—to some extent through the use of corruption and intimidation. Over the years, a number of parties were formed, and the major opposition to the Congress Party comes from the BJP, which among its followers has some strong Hindu nationalists, who believe that India should not be a multiethnic state.

India has a federal system with 25 states and various territories. The constitution separates the powers of the government into 3 branches: legislative, executive, and judicial. The relationship between the legislative and executive branches follows the parliamentary model of Great Britain. The initiative and responsibility for executive leadership rests with the office of the prime minister, not with the president. Neither of these offices is gained by direct popular vote, however. The president is the head of state for a 5-year term and is elected by an electoral college composed of members of parliament and state legislatures. The president's role is so limited by the constitution that he or she has rare opportunities to determine national policy. The president can, however, upon the advice of the prime minister, declare a state of emergency and suspend both national and state governments, an executive tool that has been used far more frequently than the framers of India's constitution envisioned. In general, the president serves as more of a symbolic head of state. The prime minister has the primary responsibility to lead the country and is officially invited by the president to form a government and lead it. In order to remain in power, the prime minister must enjoy the support of a majority of the 545-member Lok Sabha (People's House). The president normally looks first to the leadership of the majority party to nominate its candidate for prime minister. Legislative power is vested in the **bicameral** (2-chamber) parliament, which consists of a 245-member of Rajya Sabha (Council of States) and the Lok Sabha. The majority of the members of the Rajya Sabha are chosen by the state legislatures; the president selects the remainder. The members of the Lok Sabha are directly elected and serve for 5 years. According to the constitution, a new election must be held at least every 5 years. If none is called before that time, parliament is automatically dissolved. India has an independent judiciary, which is headed by a Supreme Court, the highest court in the land. The president appoints its chief justice and justices. The Supreme Court acts as the court of final appeal.

The Union (federal) government of India is responsible for developing and implementing various domestic and foreign policies and sets its economic policies in consultation with representatives of the states and various other representative bodies of businesses, farmers, and labor.

The government generates most of its revenues from taxes. For the **fiscal year** ending 31 March 2000, the total revenue generated through taxes for the central government came to about Rs3.28 trillion (US$73 billion). The main sources of Union tax revenues are customs **duties**, **excise taxes**, corporate taxes, and **income taxes**. Non-tax revenues largely comprise interest receipts, including interest paid by the railways and telecommunications, dividends and profits. The main sources of revenue for state governments are also taxes and duties, in addition to grants received from the central government. Property taxes are the mainstay of local finance. In recent years, tax rates imposed by the government have been cut. The current peak income tax rate of 30 percent and corporate tax rate of 35 percent, for example, are low compared to most industrial countries. Furthermore, the peak customs duty rate has been cut to 35 percent with a promise to move towards the East Asian average rate of 20 percent.

INFRASTRUCTURE, POWER, AND COMMUNICATIONS

INFRASTRUCTURE. Infrastructure covers a wide spectrum in India and includes transportation, power generation and distribution, telecommunications, postal facilities, and urban infrastructure. Historically, the responsibility for providing infrastructure services has been vested with the Indian government. This has been due to a number of reasons including high capital requirements, long gestation periods, high financial risks, and low rates of return. Fiscal shortages and technological innovations have challenged the old paradigm of a government **monopoly** in infrastructure development. Some amount of private involvement in the maintenance and formation of infrastructure, therefore, has been taking place.

Communications

Country	Newspapers	Radios	TV Sets[a]	Cable subscribers[a]	Mobile Phones[a]	Fax Machines[a]	Personal Computers[a]	Internet Hosts[b]	Internet Users[b]
	1996	1997	1998	1998	1998	1998	1998	1999	1999
India	N/A	121	69	18.8	1	0.2	2.7	0.18	2,800
United States	215	2,146	847	244.3	256	78.4	458.6	1,508.77	74,100
China	N/A	333	272	40.0	19	1.6	8.9	0.50	8,900
Pakistan	23	98	88	0.1	1	1.9	3.9	0.22	80

[a]Data are from International Telecommunication Union, *World Telecommunication Development Report 1999* and are per 1,000 people.
[b]Data are from the Internet Software Consortium (http://www.isc.org) and are per 10,000 people.

SOURCE: World Bank. *World Development Indicators 2000.*

Transportation in India includes roads, railways, aviation, and coastal shipping. The road network of India totals 2.7 million kilometers (1.3 million miles), making it one of the largest national networks in the world. Only 40 percent of the road system is paved, however. Nearly 63,000 kilometers (39,000 miles) of railroads are in operation in India, transporting millions of passengers and millions of tons of freight daily. Nearly 13,000 kilometers (8,000 miles) of Indian railroads function by electricity. Coastal shipping is an energy efficient and comparatively cheaper means of transportation, especially for bulk cargo. The country has the largest merchant shipping fleet among the developing countries. India has 14,500 kilometers (9,000 miles) of navigable waterways, which includes rivers, canals, backwaters, and creeks. Only about one-quarter of those waterways are navigable by large vessels, however. There are 11 major ports and 139 minor ports along the Indian coastline. The civil aviation sector is comprised of both private and public lines. Air India, Indian Airlines, Alliance Air (a subsidiary of Indian Airlines), and various private air taxis provide domestic and international air services. There are 343 airports, with two-thirds having paved runways.

POWER. With respect to energy, India is a net importer. Among other fuels, it imports nearly US$8 billion worth of petroleum annually. Though India constitutes nearly 17 percent of the world population, it consumes only about 3 percent of the world's total energy, or 12.2 quadrillion BTUs (British Thermal Units, a common means of expressing energy as the production of heat) per year. On a per capita basis (12 million BTUs), Indians consume more than 5 times less energy per year than the average world citizen (65 million BTUs) and 28 times less than the average American (352 million BTUs). With increasing economic development, however, these figures are likely to rise significantly in the near future. Some 75 percent of India's electricity comes from thermal power plants, which use coal or atomic energy to boil water and in turn produce electricity. India has large domestic coal reserves and is the third largest coal-producing country in the world, behind China and the United States. More than half (55 percent) of all energy consumption in India is produced by coal. Another third (31 percent) of energy needs is met by petroleum, and 7 percent by natural gas (the country consumes about 8 billion cubic feet per year). Some 4 percent of energy needs are met by renewable and traditional fuels (wood, for instance), 3 percent by hydropower, and a mere 1 percent by atomic power (India operates 14 atomic reactors with a combined annual generating capacity of about 2,700 megawatts). The consumption of natural gas is expected to more than triple by 2010, reaching 2.7 trillion cubic feet per year. Despite increased reliance on natural gas, coal will continue to be the dominant fuel for power generation in India. The country's consumption of nearly 350 million tons in 1999 will likely increase by more than 40 percent by 2010, reaching just short of half a billion tons. Proven coal reserves are estimated to be more than 80 billion tons. Much of India's coal reserves, however, are not anthracite (which is clean-burning coal), forcing the government to import some anthracite coal from Australia and New Zealand, much of it for use in the steel industry.

Various government agencies oversee energy policy in India, including the Ministry of Petroleum and Natural Gas, the Ministry of Coal, the Ministry of Non-conventional Energy Sources, and the Ministry of Power. The Directorate General of Hydrocarbons (DGH) was set up in 1993 to oversee petroleum exploration programs, develop plans for the state-owned oil enterprises and private companies, and oversee efficient utilization of gas fields. Continued economic development and population growth are driving energy demand faster than India's capacity for energy supply. Electricity in India reaches about 80 percent of the country. The country faces an electricity shortage conservatively estimated at 11 percent and as high as 18 percent during peak demand. As a result, electricity blackouts are common. Furthermore, industry cites power supply as 1 of the biggest limitations on progress. One estimate projects 8 to 10 percent annual growth in energy demand over the next 15 years. Most of this energy will probably be imported via ship and pipeline. Oil consumption, for example, may increase by 60 percent by 2010, climbing to approximately 3.1 million barrels per day (b/d). Currently, as little as 750,000 b/d of oil is produced domestically, the majority of which is from the Bombay High, Upper Assam, Cambay, Krishna-Godavari, and Cauvery basins. The Bombay High Field is India's largest producing field, generating an average of about 230,000 b/d. The potential for discoveries of offshore oil reserves, particularly in deep water, is high. So far, exploration has taken place in only one-quarter of India's 26 sedimentary basins. India's offshore basins cover approximately 380,000 square kilometers (147,000 square miles). India's off- and onshore basins are estimated to contain as much as 30 billion tons of hydrocarbon reserves. To satisfy the growth in energy consumption, the country is also increasing its nuclear power capability via the construction of new reactors. Although India is trying to encourage greater foreign participation in its atomic power program, its failure to sign the Comprehensive Test Ban Treaty (CTBT, an international treaty that prohibits signatories from testing nuclear weapons) has inhibited investment and technical support from Western firms. Russia has taken advantage of this scenario and has been awarded permission to construct two 1,000 megawatt (MW) reactors at Kudankulam in southern India scheduled to begin service in 2006 and 2008. India would like to increase its atomic power capability by 2.7 times to 7,300 MW by 2007.

The country also has vast hydroelectric potential. Estimates place India's hydroelectric potential at 86,000 MW, a mere one-quarter of which is being utilized. India plans to build the world's largest hydroelectric plant on the Brahmaputra River. The dam is expected to have a capacity of 21,000 MW and cost US$23 billion and be operational by 2012. Furthermore, special attention is being paid to alternative energy sources such as wind, solar photo-voltaic (PV) technologies, and biomass. India has abundant wind resources, ranking fifth in the world in the number of wind power installations; wind power installed capacity as of June 2000 was 1,175 MW. The Ministry of Non-Conventional Energy Sources has identified 192 potential sites for wind stations with a total estimated potential of 20,000 MW. The ministry also estimates India's energy potential from biomass at nearly 20,000 MW, 3,500 MW being from co-generation plants using bagasse (a fibrous plant residue left over after the extraction of juice from sugarcane) from sugar mills. Plans are also in the works to create a national electricity grid, which would provide for easy power sharing among regions and even neighboring countries. An impediment to the construction of large power plants has been scrutiny by public interest groups, which have rightly cited the potential damage to the environment caused by large hydroelectric dams.

COMMUNICATIONS. India has probably the least adequate telephone system among industrializing countries. In 1996, for instance, it had only 12 million telephones. The equivalent of 3 out of every 4 villages have no telephone service and only 5 percent of Indian villages have long-distance service. Poor telephone service significantly impedes India's commercial and industrial growth and penalizes the country in global markets. Recently, several satellite earth stations (including 8 Intelsat and 1 Inmarsat) and submarine cables to Malaysia and the United Arab Emirates (UAE) were put into service for long-distance communications.

ECONOMIC SECTORS

The Indian economy presents a mixture of the traditional and modern. Prior to 1947, the major sectors were agriculture, forestry, fishing, and textile manufacturing. Currently, village farming, state agriculture, energy, manufacturing, mining, services, and a flourishing information technology are the chief economic sectors of India. Though agriculture employs the most people (186 million), the service sector, with a labor force of 57 million, contributes the most to the country's income, accounting for nearly half of India's GDP. Industry and manufacturing expanded rapidly during the 1990s, and information technology is a sector with very high expectations. The information technology sub-sector of software experienced 70 percent growth in 1999. The CIA *World Factbook* estimated that agriculture accounted for 25 per-

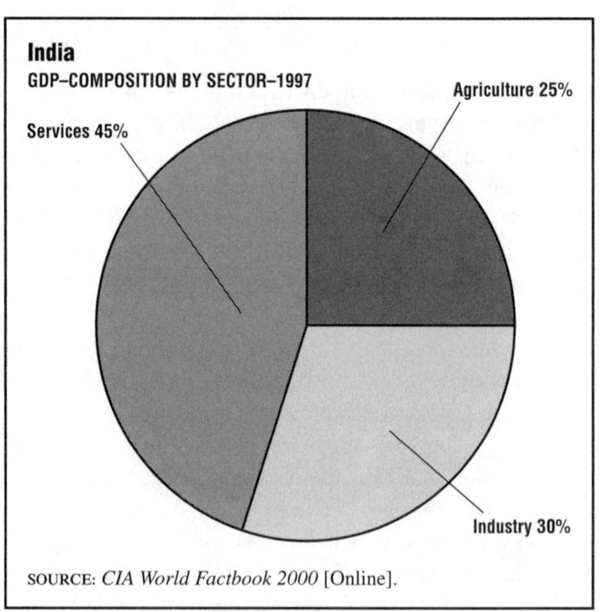

SOURCE: *CIA World Factbook 2000* [Online].

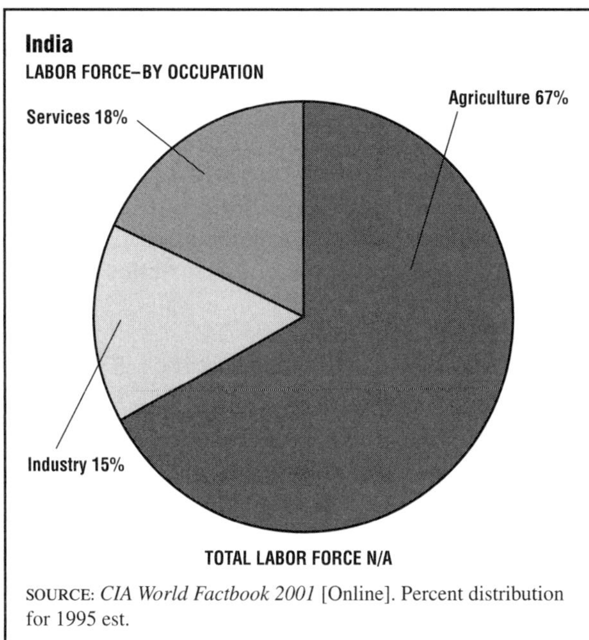

SOURCE: *CIA World Factbook 2001* [Online]. Percent distribution for 1995 est.

cent, industry for 24 percent, and services for 51 percent of GDP in 2000.

The Indian economy is currently at a difficult stage. Despite the initiatives taken by the government in deepening structural reforms and accelerating the **privatization** process, some problems of growth will likely be faced in the near future. Because of irregular rainfall for the second successive year, for example, agricultural growth was low or absent in 2000. Industrial growth also slowed, and despite some efforts to open the economy to private and foreign businesses, the sentiment for new investment has not improved. The persistence of high international oil prices and the slowdown of the global economy have compounded the problem. Although the major industries of Gujarat have fortunately escaped the worst effects of the recent massive earthquake, the impact of dislocations on the various sectors of the economy cannot be ignored.

AGRICULTURE

India's agriculture is composed of many crops, with the foremost food staples being rice and wheat. Indian farmers also grow pulses, potatoes, sugarcane, oilseeds, and such non-food items as cotton, tea, coffee, rubber, and jute (a glossy fiber used to make burlap and twine). India is a fisheries giant as well. A total catch of about 3 million metric tons annually ranks India among the world's top 10 fishing nations. Despite the overwhelming size of the agricultural sector, however, yields per hectare of crops in India are generally low compared to international standards. Improper water management is another problem affecting India's agriculture. At a time of increasing water shortages and environmental crises, for example, the rice crop in India is allocated disproportionately high amounts of water. One result of the inefficient use of water is that water tables in regions of rice cultivation, such as Punjab, are on the rise, while soil fertility is on the decline. Aggravating the agricultural situation is an ongoing Asian drought and inclement weather. Although during 2000–01 a monsoon with average rainfall had been expected, prospects of agricultural production during that period were not considered bright. This has partially been due to relatively unfavorable distribution of rainfall, leading to floods in certain parts of the country and droughts in some others.

Despite the fact that agriculture accounts for as much as a quarter of the Indian economy and employs an estimated 60 percent of the labor force, it is considered highly inefficient, wasteful, and incapable of solving the hunger and malnutrition problems. Despite progress in this area, these problems have continued to frustrate India for decades. It is estimated that as much as one-fifth of the total agricultural output is lost due to inefficiencies in harvesting, transport, and storage of government-subsidized crops.

INDUSTRY

India's policy of economic self-reliance after independence led to a surge in industrial activity, although much of it was inefficient. Indian industry currently, which includes the sectors of manufacturing, textiles, chemicals, food processing, construction, mining, energy, and IT, contributes about 30 percent of the country's GDP and employs 18 percent of the whole labor force. Among the Indian industry's successes are electronics and software manufacturing. Software engineering has been growing by around 50 percent per year, with as much as 80 percent of software production being exported, earning an estimated US$4 billion in 2000 out of a total export earnings of US$37.5 billion.

MANUFACTURING. According to the Central Statistical Organization of India, the manufacturing sector was expected to grow by 6.4 percent in 2001, slightly down from the 6.8 percent growth a year earlier. A combination of higher oil prices, a weak national currency, and an easing of import restrictions—in compliance with India's membership in the WTO—is thought to be having some initially negative effects on domestic manufacturing.

ENERGY. Indian consumption of natural gas grew from 17 billion cubic meters in 1995 to 34 billion cubic meters in 2000 and is projected to reach nearly 85 billion cubic meters in 2020. This is one of the fastest-ever increases in fuel demand by Indian customers. Most of the increase is due to a projected increase in the demand for natural gas for power generation. Almost 70 percent of India's limited natural gas reserves are found in the Bombay High basin and the state of Gujarat. The Indian government has been avidly encouraging the construction of gas-fired electric power plants, especially in coastal regions where they can be easily supplied with liquefied natural gas (LNG) by sea. Given that domestic gas supply is not likely to keep pace with demand, India will have to import most of its gas requirements, either via pipeline or LNG tankers, making it potentially one of the world's largest gas importers. The dominant commercial fuel in India, however, continues to be coal. Coal accounts for more than half of India's energy demand, and 70 percent of coal consumption is used for power generation. Coal consumption is projected to increase to 465 million short tons in 2010, a 26 percent increase from 1998. India's coal industry is the world's third largest, and most of the country's coal demand is satisfied by domestic supplies.

MINING. The mining industry has grown substantially since independence, with the value of minerals mined exceeding US$10 billion today. Still, mining accounts for only about 2 percent of India's GDP. India has been extracting a range of minerals. Among others, it produces significant amounts of coal, iron ore, bauxite, copper, gold, diamonds, limestone, and chromite. India has among the world's largest reserves of iron ore (more than 19 billion tons) and is one of the world's lowest-cost sources. Most of India's iron ore—the largest being in the privately owned mines in the state of Goa—is exported to South Korea and Japan. India's bauxite reserve is approximately 2.7 billion tons or 8 percent of the world total. Given this, and bauxite's critical role in the production of aluminum, India has tentative plans to expand its aluminum production. Copper reserves are estimated at more than 410 million tons, yet India has been importing copper as well. Reserves of lead and zinc are estimated at 360 million tons. Foreign investors have shown interest in mining gold in partnership with the government at a mine in Kolar. The main mining industry remains, however, the production of steaming coal for power generation.

SERVICES

Services play a significant role in the economy of India, accounting for nearly 40 percent of the GDP or about US$200 billion per year. Services include the sectors of telecommunications, airlines, banking, construction, and small-scale enterprises. Some components of the services sector are also in the **public sector**.

FINANCIAL SERVICES. Although some form of banking, mainly of the money-lending type, has been in existence in India for thousands of years, it was only a little over a century ago that Western-style banking was introduced to the country. Indian households account for nearly 90 percent of the national savings. Whereas in 1980, as little as 10 percent of all savings of Indian households were held in financial form (as in bank deposits, shares, and insurance policies) rather than physical form (as in money under mattresses). As of 2001, that figure has surpassed 50 percent. In addition, although the percentage of people who own company shares or have invested in mutual funds is still low as compared to more affluent and Western countries, those numbers are also on the rise. Government banks still play an important role and own more than four-fifths of the banking business. However, private (especially foreign) banks are gradually taking up an increasing share of the financial market. There are an estimated US$400 billion worth of private savings in India, some 44 percent of which is in bank deposits, another 5 percent in mutual funds, and less than 25 percent in postal savings and pension funds. Despite considerable openness in the Indian economy, increasing liberalization of the financial sector is hindered by that fact that nearly 30 percent of assets are considered to be non-performing. This is due to an excessive number of loans having been extended to businesses and individuals through political pressure rather than economic merit. As a result, the rate of bankruptcy of financial institutions has been high, which in turn has forced interest rates to be high as well. As a result of these and other factors, Indian industry's access to proper credit has been limited.

Market liberalization in India has led to the sale of shares of private and some public companies to domestic and international bidders. Currently, there are more than 6,000 companies listed on India's largest stock market, the Bombay Stock Exchange, but only about 8 percent of them are actively traded. The stock market has attracted a good amount of international institutional **equity** investment, such as foreign pension schemes and mutual funds. However, the Indian stock market, not unlike others worldwide, has had periods of intense volatility. In 2000, for example, **market capitalization** fell by 62 percent in 6 months, from US$265 billion in February to US$100 billion in August.

TOURISM. Due to its wealth of cultural and recreational facilities, India has had a large tourism industry. Tourism is India's fourth largest foreign currency earner. The top states for tourist attractions are Kerala, Delhi, and Assam. The state of Kashmir used to have a thriving tourism industry; however, the number of tourists has sharply declined due to political unrest and extremist activities over the border dispute with Pakistan. Overall, India's tourism in the past decade has been growing at an average rate of about 7 percent yearly. With about 2.25 million people per year, India's international visitors constitute less than 0.5 percent of world's total number of international tourists. (Top world tourism countries such as France and Spain receive as many as 50 million visitors and generate tens of billions of dollars from tourism annually.) The income generated from tourism in India is estimated to be a mere 1 percent of total world spending of international tourists or US$3 billion per year. Indeed, more Indians travel abroad (3 million per year) than tourists visit India. India's tourism industry is hampered by an international perception of India as being very poor, politically unstable, and requiring precautions against epidemic diseases, despite the attractions of its beautiful historic sites, rich and varied cultures, and appetizing cuisine. The Taj Mahal, for instance, is regarded as one of the architectural marvels of the world. The country also attracts backpackers and adventurers who come for the local festivals, to ride on India's famous railroads, or to see the holy Ganges River.

INTERNATIONAL TRADE

For decades after independence in 1947, India embarked on a program of autarky (national economic self-sufficiency) which included **import substitution** policies. By 1991, however, a sluggish economy combined with the forces of globalization led to a more open Indian economy. There was simultaneously a gradual rise in exports, imports, **foreign direct investment** (FDI), and overall economic growth. In the 1990s, exports of goods and services rose from 6.2 percent to 8.2 percent of total output. By the end of the decade, however, growth in exports began to level off due to reduced international demand, especially with India's main economic partners, the United States and the European Union (EU). Indian exports were further hit by serious competition from east Asian countries, which had recently experienced depreciated domestic currencies, which led to a decline in global prices for their manufactured goods. As a result, exports of Indian textiles, chemicals, machinery, electronic goods, and automotive parts all began to decline.

As compared to a couple of decades earlier, however, the size of India's foreign trade has noticeably expanded, both in absolute terms and relative to the country's GDP. Exports have again picked up since 1999, when they showed a 13 percent growth. Imports have also ballooned, showing an average of 20 percent growth per year during 1992–2000. Total exports in 2001 are expected to be near US$46 billion and total imports at US$51 billion. Petroleum constitutes the largest import item at more than US$6 billion and accounts for 14 percent of total imports in 1999. Petroleum imports may be as high as US$17 billion in 2001. Gems and jewelry constitute the single largest export item, accounting for 16 percent of exports and earning about US$4.5 billion in 1999. The top 3 export destinations of Indian goods were the United States, Britain, and Germany, which together constituted one-third of total Indian exports in 1999. In turn, the top 3 import sources were the United States, Britain, and Belgium, together constituting 21 percent of total imported items.

Trade (expressed in billions of US$): India

	Exports	Imports
1975	4.355	6.381
1980	8.586	14.864
1985	9.140	15.928
1990	17.975	23.642
1995	30.764	34.522
1998	32.881	42.201

SOURCE: International Monetary Fund. *International Financial Statistics Yearbook 1999.*

In 2001, FDI in India was expected to near US$4 billion. To further seek buyers for Indian products, Indian companies have also major plans for investing abroad. Several Indian information technology companies, for example, have plans to outsource some of their production to China, where labor is as much as 20 percent cheaper. Furthermore, India's largest car manufacturer, Mahindra and Mahindra, may soon be entering the European market via the production of tractors in the Czech Republic. One Indian investment that is already operating abroad is a US$180 million fertilizer plant in the Persian Gulf nation of Dubai.

MONEY

India has pursued a conservative policy in the expansion of its money supply during the past 2 decades. Money was thought to have grown by a relatively high rate of 15 percent during 2000–01, however. The reserve bank of India is the sole authority for issuing the national currency. It formulates and administers **monetary policy** with a view to ensuring stability in prices while promoting increased production of goods and services via the deployment of credit. The reserve bank's monetary policy

Exchange rates: India

Indian rupees (Rs) per US$1	
Jan 2001	46.540
2000	44.942
1999	43.055
1998	41.259
1997	36.313
1996	35.433

SOURCE: CIA *World Factbook 2001* [ONLINE].

also plays an important role in maintaining the stability of the exchange value of the Indian rupee. Furthermore, the reserve bank is in charge of the borrowing program of the government from both domestic and international lenders. High levels of exports have led to a comfortable **balance of payments** situation in recent years, which in turn has put at the disposal of the reserve bank, aside from the nation's gold reserves, as much as US$38 billion of cash reserves in 2001. The total money supply in India (which includes the various deposits in commercial banks, the reserve bank, and the currency in the hands of the public) is estimated to have grown by 60 percent since 1995 and to have been a bit more than Rs3 trillion (US$66 billion) in 2000.

Distribution of Income or Consumption by Percentage Share: India

Lowest 10%	3.5
Lowest 20%	8.1
Second 20%	11.6
Third 20%	15.0
Fourth 20%	19.3
Highest 20%	46.1
Highest 10%	33.5

Survey year: 1997

Note: This information refers to expenditure shares by percentiles of the population and is ranked by per capita expenditure.

SOURCE: *2000 World Development Indicators* [CD-ROM].

POVERTY AND WEALTH

At the time of India's independence famine and severe malnutrition were periodic occurrences, and life expectancy was only about 30 years. Due to improvements in health care and agriculture, by 1970 life expectancy had reached 50 years, and by 1993 it was 61 years. Infant mortality fell from 137 per 1,000 live births in 1970 to 71 in 1993. In agriculture and food production, India has also made great progress. While it was a nation dependent on food imports to feed its population after independence, it is now largely self-sufficient in food production. It has done so, to an extent, by enacting policies that have favored impoverished working-class citizens and farmers.

Despite improvements, by 1994 it was still estimated that 1 in every 3 Indians lived in what could be categorized as absolute poverty—a total of 310 million people. In essence, more Indians were estimated to be poor than the whole of sub-Saharan Africa. Currently, though starvation is something of a distant memory, a large part of the Indian population remains too poor to afford an adequate diet. According to the Indian Institute of Population Sciences, more than half of all children under the age of 4 suffer from different degrees of malnourishment. Diseases such as diarrhea, diphtheria (caused by bacteria leading to inflammation of the heart and nervous system), pertussis (whooping cough), tetanus (also known as lockjaw), and measles, long done away with in many countries, can still be found among some poor communities in India. Furthermore, due to iron deficiency, as much as 87 percent of all pregnant women are thought to be anemic.

GDP per Capita (US$)

Country	1975	1980	1985	1990	1998
India	222	231	270	331	444
United States	19,364	21,529	23,200	25,363	29,683
China	138	168	261	349	727
Pakistan	274	318	385	448	511

SOURCE: United Nations. *Human Development Report 2000; Trends in human development and per capita income.*

Inter- and intra-state discrepancies in terms of education and overall well-being also remains large. The poorest quintile (one-fifth or 20 percent) of the population is estimated to have 2.5 times more incidence of infant mortality, double the fertility rate, and a 75 percent higher rate of child malnutrition than the average figures for India. The south and west of India have traditionally been better off relative to the north and east. Furthermore, irrigated plains are richer than primarily rain-fed regions. For a variety of reasons, some states such as Maharashtra, Goa, Delhi, and Gujarat have been able both to provide better infrastructure, such as power supply and telecommunications, to their peoples and likewise attract a significantly higher FDI than other states. Kerala has a high literacy rate and access to health care even though its **GDP per capita** is less than the Indian average. Kerala's fertility rate dropped to 1.8 children per woman in 1991, which is below the replacement level; in the same year, literacy in Kerala was over 90 percent, compared to India's average of 51 percent. Kerala's infant mortality in 1996 was 13 deaths per 1,000 live births; in all of India the number was 72 per 1,000 births. Schools and health clinics are available throughout the state, and newspapers are also available in most villages. There is also a strong commitment to equal rights for women in Kerala, where women occupy significant government positions. Kerala's elected **communist** government, together with an emphasis on local control, participation in government, and investment projects are all thought to be important factors for Kerala's better quality of life. Those especially vulnerable throughout India continue to be rural women, the disabled, and people of lower castes.

Poverty in many developing countries is more predominant in rural areas. Though that has also been true in India, the gap between rural and urban India was closing during the 1980s due to the continuing effects of state-sponsored expansion of irrigated agriculture and the green revolution. (This was the substantial increase in the production of food grains—such as rice and wheat—begun in the 1960s as a result of the introduction of improved plant varieties, better farming, and the application of newly-developed pesticides and herbicides.) By the early 1990s, however, India began to show signs of "Malthusian overload": Thomas R. Malthus (1766–1834) theorized that population tends to grow faster than its means of subsistence—food and other resources—and unless population growth is checked, it will inevitably lead to widespread poverty. The increases in food production brought about by the green revolution were not able to keep pace with the rate of population growth. This discrepancy was especially evident in the rural areas, where the majority of the people are farmers living off the land. The gap between rural and urban India since the early 1990s, therefore, began to widen again. Poverty, however, is not purely a phenomenon of rural areas. In recent years, for example, as a result of the population increase and the lack of sufficient waste disposal infrastructure, the city of Calcutta has seen an increase in the waterborne and communicable diseases such as tuberculosis, a problem exacerbated during the rainy season.

Illiteracy remains a major problem as well. The number of illiterate Indians actually rose in the 1980s. In the 1990s, successful government programs began once again to reduce illiteracy. Progress has been very slow, though. If India continues to reduce illiteracy by its current rate of approximately 2.8 percent per year, it is estimated that it would still take 16 years for it to reach the literacy rate of 90 percent, a rate which neighboring Sri Lanka currently holds. Even then, there would still remain 120 million illiterate Indians. Likewise, while fertility dropped from 6.0 children per child-bearing woman in the early 1980s to 3.8 in 1992, maternal mortality is a high of 430 per 100,000 live births, 23 percent more than the average of 350 for low and middle income countries.

Overall, though the per capita income in India is higher than in some of its neighbors, it remains very low compared to economically developed countries. India's per capita income of US$2,077 per year is 121 percent that of neighboring Pakistan. Yet, India's per capita income is still 67 percent that of China's, 9 percent that of Canada's, and only 7 percent that of the United States'.

WORKING CONDITIONS

The liberalization policies of the Indian government, begun in 1991, assisted in opening up the economy to domestic and international competition. Autarkic policies of the past decades had limited foreign investment and prioritized the growth of domestic industry through import substitution and public ownership of much of the means of production. Emphasis on self-reliance had eventually led to an economic crisis, which did not help to improve working conditions for the majority of the Indian labor force. During this period, many skilled and unskilled workers among the population had opted for better employment opportunities in other countries.

Despite the benefits of economic liberalization, it has not quickly solved the problem of unemployment and other social and economic ills. Short- and long-term job losses as a result of competition, for example, have been common, especially among the unprofitable firms. One of the main areas of employment for many of the poor has been the cotton textile industry with its traditional concentration of mills in the cities of Bombay, Ahmedabad, and Coimbatore. Along with mills that use the most advanced technology to process raw cotton and form cotton fiber, there also have existed a large number of small-scale workshops and households that use traditional handlooms (the type used by Mahatma Ghandi) and rely on manual labor for the processing of cotton. India's market liberalization led to the foreclosure of much of the traditional handloom cotton industry and resulted in nearly 2.3 million workers losing their jobs. Many of these workers have remained unemployed. Managers of the modern mills attribute this to the older age of handloom workers and their inflexibility or inability to adjust to the mechanized cotton mills.

As opposed to neighboring China, trade unions in India play a very prominent role in the business community. Every industry has a trade union that advocates the rights and employment opportunities of its members. Trade unions strive to obtain the best deal for their members in terms of wages, working conditions, acceptable remuneration, and welfare packages. As much as 92 percent of the labor force in India is unionized. Some of the laborers of the cotton industry have gained employment in the textile industry, which with its labor force of 39 million is among the largest unionized industries.

Women constitute an important segment of the Indian labor force whose working conditions have not made significant progress. Despite some noticeable advances for a small percentage of women, women as a whole have been relegated largely to agricultural and menial pursuits that pay the lowest wages. In some ways, as the overall economy has grown, the situation of working women in India has even deteriorated. In 1911, for example, three-quarters of the working women of India were agricultural workers; in 1991, the proportion was over 80 percent. Nearly 70 percent of the population as a whole derives its livelihood from land resources, and women contribute an estimated 55 to 66 percent of the total farm labor force.

COUNTRY HISTORY AND ECONOMIC DEVELOPMENT

2500 B.C. Inhabitants of the Indus River Valley develop an urban culture based on commerce and sustained by agricultural trade. This new activity leads to some ecological changes in the region.

1000–600 B.C. The caste system is established.

400–500. Northern India is unified under the Gupta dynasty which leads to new heights for the Hindu culture and politics.

1100s. Indian subcontinent is invaded by the Turks and Persians who establish their empires at Delhi. The descendants of Genghis Khan sweep across the Khyber pass and established the Moghul empire which lasts for 2 centuries.

1619. The first British outpost is established in Surat. Later, the East India Company opens trading stations at Madras, Bombay, and Calcutta.

1850. Great Britain expands its influence and controls most of the provinces of India (present-day India, Pakistan and Bangladesh) through direct rule and treaties established with local rulers.

1920. Indian leader Mohandas K. Gandhi transforms the Indian National Congress Party into a mass movement to campaign against British colonial rule. This change is achieved through parliamentary acts, non-violence, and non-cooperation.

1947. India achieves independence from the UK and is divided into 2 nations: India and Pakistan. The new Commonwealth nation of India is led by Jawaharlal Nehru as prime minister.

1961. India becomes a founding member of the Non-Aligned Movement, which among other tasks, seeks solutions for global economic problems.

1966. Indira Gandhi, daughter of Jawaharlal Nehru, becomes India's first female prime minister.

1975. Citing political and economic turmoil, Prime Minister Gandhi declares a state of emergency and the suspension of civil liberties in India. She loses power in the election of 1977 to Moraji Desai of the Janata Party.

1979. After the downfall of the Desai government, Charan Singh forms the interim government followed by a return of Indira Gandhi to power in 1980.

1984. Indira Gandhi is assassinated on 31 October. Rajiv Gandhi, her son, is chosen by the Indian congress as her successor.

1991. Rajiv Gandhi is assassinated by Tamil extremists which results in a sympathy vote for the Congress Party. P. V. Narashima Rao becomes prime minister. Under his leadership, the government serves a full 5-year term and initiates various economic liberalization reforms opening the Indian economy to global trade and investment.

1998. The president approves of a BJP-led coalition government. India conducts a series of underground nuclear tests in May, leading to United States-led economic sanctions in an attempt to force India to sign and abide by the Nuclear Non-Proliferation Treaty.

1999. The BJP-led coalition government falls apart, leading to fresh elections. The BJP forms a coalition with the National Democratic Alliance Party, with Atal Bihari Vajpayee as prime minister.

2001. On 13 December, Kashmiri separatists attack the Indian parliament building. Thirteen people are killed in the attack, including the five separatists. The separatists' ties to Pakistan lead India to accuse Pakistan of being behind the attack, which brings hostile relations between the two countries to a boiling point.

FUTURE TRENDS

There are many future challenges that India will need to address in order for it to be a more prosperous country. Government corruption, the population explosion, the issue of Kashmir and other potentially vigorous separatist movements, relations with Pakistan, nuclear arms, the growing gap between the rich and poor, and last but not least, ecological devastation are among the issues that the Indian government will need to address seriously.

The government sector in India is known to be among the most bloated and overstaffed in the world. Furthermore, nearly all transactions with government agencies, from acquiring one's passport to obtaining a birth certificate, often require some amount of bribe. Stealing and skimming services, such as electricity, is common. In New Delhi, for example, as much as 51 percent of electricity is "lost" in transmission, much of it stolen by relatively prosperous urban households. Increasing efforts by the government to minimize waste, corruption, and grand and petty theft would be beneficial.

Population growth will likely not subside for several more decades. The high rate of growth of the population has negative effects on the well-being of people. The number of Indians consuming diets with fewer than 1,900 kilocalories (kcal) per day, for example, has quadrupled since the early 1970s. (Many nutritionists assert that a diet of at least 2,600 kcal per day is necessary to maintain body weight.) During the same period, total food grain production in India has doubled. High rates of fertility are thought to be indirectly proportional to economic well-being of households, as well as the level of education of parents—especially mothers. In essence, the more prosperous a household and the more educated the mothers, the fewer children couples have.

The success of government education and public health programs, however, depends not only on more spending but also on improving the quality of services. There is a need to phase out a number of anti-poverty programs and direct some of the savings to ensure quality education, which is more effective in reducing poverty over the long-term. For the poor to take advantage of the new educational opportunities, however, their health status needs to improve. Targeting government spending to primary education, reducing communicable diseases, improving water and sanitation, and reducing household insecurity through public works programs would do much to reduce poverty. The government should invest in health care and education, especially for children in grades 1 though 8. According to the United Nations, current spending on education takes up about 13.4 percent of the central and local government budget as compared to an average of 17.5 percent for all low-income countries. Without substantial increases in spending on education and health care, the gap between the rich and poor is likely to remain and intensify.

Improving relations with neighboring Pakistan is also a determinant of improvement of people's lives in India. Much of the dispute between the 2 countries is over Kashmir. Both India and Pakistan claim ownership to the entire Kashmir region. India is thought to have stationed nearly half a million troops in the state of Jammu-Kashmir along the Pakistani border. According to human rights reports, as many as 60,000 people have died in Jammu-Kashmir due to fighting between Indian troops and Kashmiri nationalists. Relations with Pakistan could also improve if a pipeline agreement that envisions pumping natural gas from Iran to India through Pakistan goes through. The proposed deal would allow India to increase its consumption of natural gas to as much as 85 billion cubic meters (3 trillion cubic feet) by 2020 and for Pakistan to collect up to US$600 million of transit fees. However, the 2001 attack on the Indian parliament by Kashmir separatists based in Pakistan placed the pipeline and future relations with Pakistan in serious jeopardy.

DEPENDENCIES

India has no territories or colonies.

BIBLIOGRAPHY

Abram, David et al. *India: The Rough Guide.* London: Rough Guides Ltd., 1996.

Bradnock, Robert. *India Handbook.* Chicago: Passport Books, 1996.

Economist Intelligence Unit. *Country Finance: India.* London: Economist Intelligence Unit, February 2001.

———. *Country Forecast: India.* London: Economist Intelligence Unit, May 2001.

———. *Country Profile: India.* London: Economist Intelligence Unit, 2000.

———. *Country Report: India.* London: Economist Intelligence Unit May 2001.

"Environmental Clean-up For Calcutta." *Asian Development Bank.* <http://www.adb.org/Documents/News/2000/nr2000156.asp>. Accessed June 2001.

"Family Planning Success Based on Equity: Human Development, Health and Governance in the Indian State of Kerala." *Harvard School of Public Health.* <http://www.hsph.harvard.edu/grhf/SAsia/suchana/1299/h027.html>. Accessed October 2001.

Government of India. *India 1996: A Reference Annual.* New Delhi: Ministry of Information and Broadcasting, Government of India, 1997.

International Telecommunication Union. *World Telecommunication Development Report: Mobile Cellular 1999.* Geneva: ITU, 1999.

Ministry of Finance. Government of India. "The Economic Survey of India, 1997." *The Indian Economy Overview.* <http://ieo.org/es009.html>. Accessed June 2001.

Office of Fossil Energy. "An Energy Overview of India." *U.S. Department of Energy.* <http://www.fe.doe.gov/international/indiover.html>. Accessed June 2001.

"Sustainable Development Information Service: Global Trends." *World Resources Institute.* <http://www.wri.org/wri/trends/rx4healt.html>. Accessed October 2001.

United Nations Development Program. "Human Development Report 2000." <http://www.undp.org/hdro/HDR2000.html>. Accessed June 2001.

U.S. Central Intelligence Agency. *World Factbook 2001.* <http://www.cia.gov/cia/publications/factbook/geos/in.html>. Accessed October 2001.

Wolpert, Stanley. *India.* Berkley: University of California Press, 1991.

World Bank Group. *India: Policies to Reduce Poverty and Accelerate Sustainable Development.* Washington: The World Bank, 2000.

World Bank Group. *World Development Indicators 2000.* Washington: The World Bank, 2000.

—Payam Foroughi, Raissa Muhutdinova-Foroughi, and Sujatha Naidu

INDONESIA

Republic of Indonesia
Republik Indonesia

CAPITAL: Jakarta.

MONETARY UNIT: Indonesian rupiah (Rp). One rupiah equals 100 sen. There are coins of 1, 2, 5, 10, 25, 50, and 100 rupiahs, and notes of 100, 500, 1,000, 5,000, and 10,000 rupiahs.

CHIEF EXPORTS: Oil and gas, plywood, textiles, rubber.

CHIEF IMPORTS: Machinery and equipment, chemicals, fuels, foodstuffs.

GROSS DOMESTIC PRODUCT: US$610 billion (purchasing power parity, 1999 est.).

BALANCE OF TRADE: **Exports:** US$48 billion (f.o.b., 1999 est.). **Imports:** US$24 billion (c.i.f., 1999 est.).

COUNTRY OVERVIEW

LOCATION AND SIZE. Indonesia is an archipelago (a group of islands) stretching along the equator between the Southeast Asian mainland and Papua New Guinea, with which it shares an island. The country has a total land area of 1,919,440 square kilometers (741,096 square miles), or about 3 times the size of Texas. An additional 3.2 million square kilometers (1,235,520 square miles) of ocean is within Indonesia's borders.

With 17,000 islands (11,000 of them inhabited), Indonesia's coastline stretches 54,716 kilometers (34,000 miles). The country controls important shipping lanes from the Indian Ocean to the Pacific Ocean, in particular the Strait of Malacca lying between the western Indonesian island of Sumatra and Malaysia. Indonesia has territory on some of the world's largest islands, such as New Guinea, Borneo, Sumatra, and Sulawesi.

POPULATION. The 2000 official census found 203,456,005 Indonesians (though most outside sources estimate 210 million), making Indonesia the world's fourth most populous country. An estimated birth rate of 22.6 per 1,000 people and death rate of 6.31 per 1,000 people means that the population is growing at an annual rate of 1.63 percent. The **United Nations Development Program** predicts that the population will reach 250.4 million by 2015. Like many developing countries, Indonesia has a young population, with 30.6 percent of its people under the age of 15. In 1998 almost two-fifths of the population lived in urban areas, double the 1975 level.

Indonesia has hundreds of ethnic groups, with the 2 largest—Javanese (45 percent) and Sundanese (14 percent)—living on the island of Java. One of the most densely populated places in the world, Java is about the size of New York State and is home to more than 110 million people. Other ethnic groups include Madurese and coastal Malays, who each make up 7.5 percent of the population, and numerous other ethnic groups accounting for 26 percent. Indonesian Chinese, whose ancestors mostly came to the Dutch East Indies as workers, are a small but economically important minority with 2 percent of the population but a majority of the wealth.

Java and Bali are often referred to as the Inner Islands, with the other less densely populated ones known as the Outer Islands. Starting in 1969, the government pursued a policy of transmigration (a program to shift inhabitants from more crowded to less crowded areas). Millions of people have joined this official migration program based on the promise of land and support. After years of criticism for damage to the environment, failure to live up to promises to the transmigrants, and conflicts with local inhabitants, the government announced an end to the program in 2000. Many Indonesians also migrate on their own from one part of the country to another in search of farmland or jobs.

Indonesia has 5 officially recognized religions: Muslim (88 percent), Protestant (5 percent), Roman Catholic (3 percent), Hindu (2 percent), and Buddhist (1 percent), as well as numerous traditional religions. More Muslims live in Indonesia than in any other country. The official

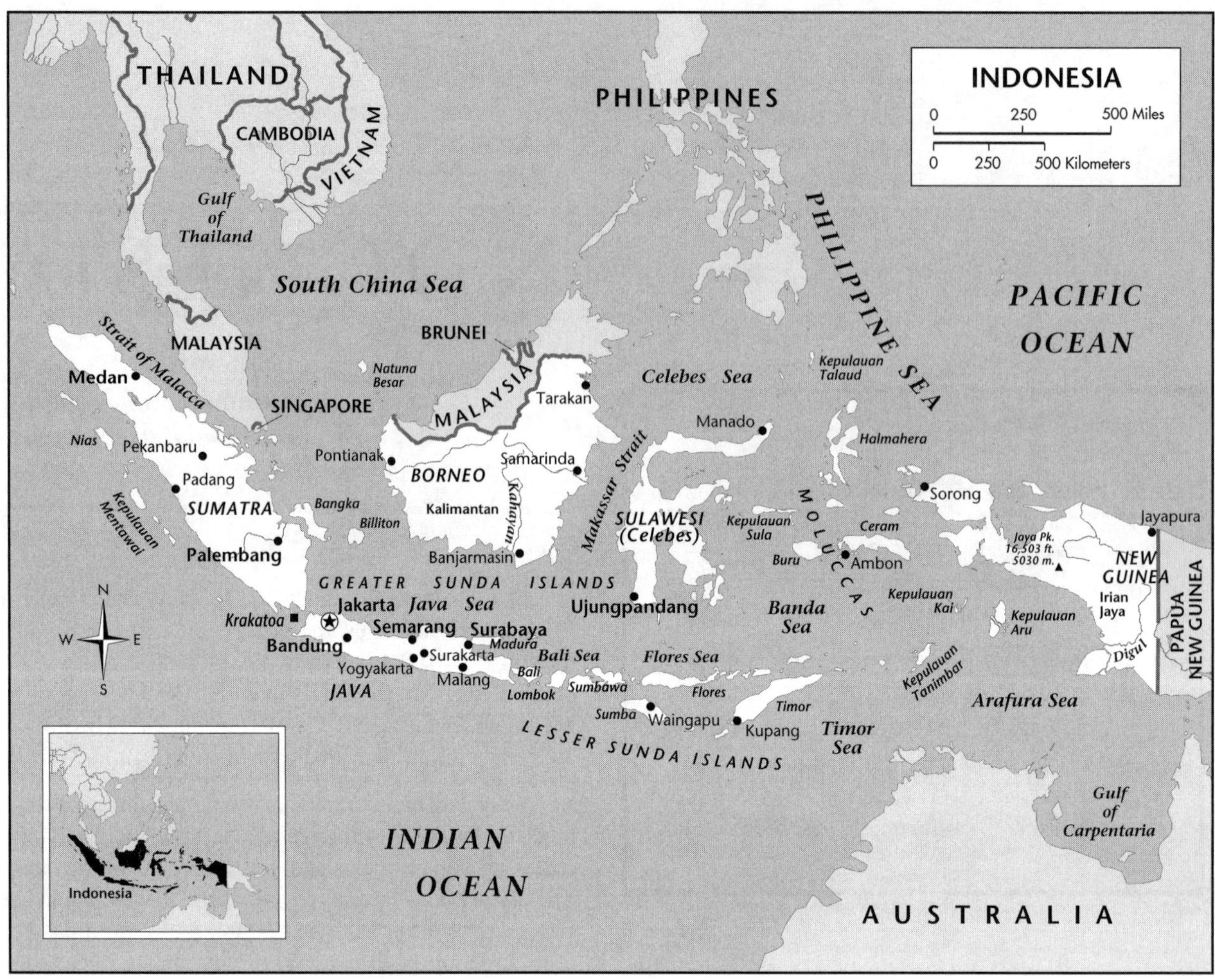

language is Bahasa Indonesia, a modified form of Malay adopted as a national language and taught in all schools. Most Indonesians, except some raised in Jakarta or by parents from different ethnic groups, speak Bahasa Indonesia as a second language after their native tongue, one of some 250 local languages and many more dialects.

Indonesia's family planning program was formally established in 1970 after years in which rapid population growth was not seen as a problem and even at times encouraged. The Indonesian family planning program has involved thousands of village-level volunteers, grassroots organizations, and religious leaders and a multifaceted approach that brings together agencies and organizations. The phrase "dua anak cukup" (2 children are enough) appears on T-shirts, statues, and television broadcasts, and family planning and reproductive health program services are made available in over 10,000 clinics, hospitals, and community health centers. The National Family Planning Coordinating Board (BKKBN) coordinates efforts but does not implement activities by itself.

Indonesia has a significant challenge in implementing a population policy, given the size of the population, the geographic distribution, and occasional cultural and religious objections. Despite this, Indonesia has achieved what the World Bank has called "one of the most impressive demographic transitions anywhere in the world." The growth rate has fallen from 2.5–2.7 percent in 1970 to 1.63 percent, and the total fertility rate fell from 5.5 births per women between 1967–70 to 2.6 births per woman in 1995–2000. Indonesia is often held up as a model for developing countries.

As a result of various conflicts, Indonesia has over 1 million internally displaced people (IDPs) who have fled their homes to avoid ethnic, religious, or political violence and military repression, most notably involving populations in Maluku, West Kalimantan, and East Timor.

OVERVIEW OF ECONOMY

Indonesia is made up of the islands of the former Dutch East Indies, a colony established by the Netherlands to control the important spice trade and take advantage of the fertile tropical soil. Indonesia's first 15 years after gaining independence in 1949 were marked by high **inflation** and very little development beyond the economy inherited from the colonial system, which was heavily dependent on agriculture. The economy grew quickly after that, however, fueled first by oil and gas exports and then by the export of manufactured goods, such as shoes, clothing, and textiles. Agriculture remains important, including both small farmers producing crops for internal consumption and export, and large plantations producing products such as palm oil and rubber.

Indonesia has gone through 6 5-Year Development Plans, known by the Indonesian acronym Repelita. The first 5-Year Development Plan (Repelita I) started in 1969 and emphasized rebuilding the economy by improving agriculture, irrigation, and transportation. Repelita II, starting in **fiscal year** 1973–74, tried to increase the standard of living through better food, clothing, and housing, **infrastructure**, social-welfare benefits, and employment opportunities. Repelita III, beginning in fiscal year 1978–79, introduced the "trilogy of development" of high economic growth, national stability, and equitable distribution. Self-sufficiency in food and the promotion of industries processing basic materials into finished goods were also objectives. Starting in fiscal year 1984–85 Repelita IV continued to emphasize self-sufficiency in rice and industrial machinery. Repelita V, from fiscal year 1989–90, stressed rapid development with emphasis on the industrial and agricultural sectors. The sixth 5-Year Development Plan (Repelita VI) began to encourage foreign investment and abandoned policies of high **tariff** barriers, heavy regulation, and **import substitution** (manufacturing **consumer goods** domestically to reduce imports). The greatest success in attracting investment has been in textiles, tourism, shoes, food processing, and timber products.

Indonesia was hit hard by the Asian financial crisis that swept the region in 1997. Following problems with the currency in Thailand, the rupiah fell, causing investors to panic, debts to soar, and the banking sector to collapse. After growing throughout the 1990s, **real gross domestic product** (GDP) fell by 13 percent in 1998. The GDP was stagnant the next year, and increased slightly in 2000, but investment remained low, and many of the underlying problems still have not been dealt with: banks are weak, large companies are technically bankrupt, the government controls many assets acquired after bailouts, and reform of the corrupt judicial system has been delayed. While other countries in the region, such as Thailand and South Korea, began to rebound, Indonesia's failure to deal decisively with deep-seated problems and continued political uncertainty slowed recovery.

Before the crisis, Indonesia borrowed about US$5 billion annually from foreign countries and international financial institutions such as the World Bank and the International Monetary Fund (IMF) to finance its budget. The government debt slowly increased from US$55.5 billion in 1992 to US$59.9 billion in 1997, but the economy seemed strong and there was little domestic debt. However, in the same period, debt resulting from borrowing by private companies increased from US$28.2 billion to US$78.1 billion, making the economy vulnerable to a fall in the **exchange rate**. After the crisis, government debt soared as the government bailed out bankrupt companies and banks, and borrowed heavily from the IMF. The total cost of the bailout quickly reached US$69.6 billion. Due to the crisis, Indonesia borrowed US$43 billion from an IMF program and other outside financing from 1997 to 2000. Government debt is estimated by the World Bank to be equal to 80 percent of the GDP, and debt repayments eat up 27 percent of government allocations, more than the entire development budget.

Surveys of business travelers in Asia regularly rank Indonesia as one of the most corrupt places to do business. Corruption has interfered with recovery as well, as the IMF and the World Bank stopped payments in 1999 after a private bank was discovered to have funneled payments from the government to the former ruling political party. In September 2000, the Supreme Court convicted the son of former president Suharto for corruption in a real estate deal, but he vanished before he could be jailed. It is believed that Indonesia is becoming increasingly involved in the shipment of heroin from the Golden Triangle in mainland Southeast Asia.

POLITICS, GOVERNMENT, AND TAXATION

The Republic of Indonesia consists of 23 provinces, 2 special regions, and the capital-city district. In August of 1999, a referendum approved independence for East Timor, the area formerly known as Propinsi Timor Timur, but its status remains in transition. The president, who is both chief of state and head of government, is elected by the People's Consultative Assembly for a 5-year term, as is the vice president. Legislative power is vested in a **unicameral** House of Representatives of 500 seats, 462 of whom are elected by popular vote and 38 are appointed from the military. The People's Consultative Assembly, which meets every 5 years to elect the president and vice president and broadly approve national policy, is comprised of the House of Representatives plus 200 members chosen indirectly. Judicial power is vested in a Supreme Court, whose judges are appointed by the president. Major political parties include the Crescent Moon and Star Party (PDB), the Development Union Party (PPP), the Indonesia Democratic Party (PDI), the Indonesia Democracy Party-Struggle (PDI-P), the National Awakening Party (PKB), and the National Mandate Party (PAN).

The former Dutch East Indies proclaimed independence on 17 August 1945, and fought a lengthy war with the Dutch, who were not ready to give up their colony. After 4 years of fighting and negotiations, the territory was formally recognized as the independent nation of Indonesia. Under Indonesia's first president Sukarno (who like many Indonesians used only one name), Indonesia experimented with **socialism**, and the government controlled most markets, foreign trade, and banking. A violent change in government in 1965 brought General Suharto to power. He presided over the extermination of what had been the world's third largest **communist** party, a process that killed at least half a million suspected communists and arrested a million more. Most of those arrested were deprived of their civil rights for decades. Suharto's "New Order" government also appointed a group of U.S.-trained economists (sometimes known as the Berkeley Mafia) to guide economic policy in a more **technocratic** and non-political way. The government directed state investment and protected favored industries from competition, but the system was decidedly capitalist. At the same time, state corporations and private conglomerates, mostly owned by Suharto's family and supporters (many of them ethnic Chinese), were built through government-granted **monopolies** and preferential access to credit, licenses, and products.

The New Order adopted as its slogan a "trilogy of development" consisting of stability, growth, and equitable distribution. Stability was enforced by the harsh repression of dissent from students, journalists, workers, or politicians. Elections were scheduled every 5 years, but no meaningful opposition was allowed. Suharto maintained power through the support of the military and control of the bureaucracy but also in part through the perceived legitimacy that came with significant economic growth.

That legitimacy fell with the onset of the Asian financial crisis in 1997, which also revealed the deep-seated corruption, cronyism (favoritism shown by public officials to their political supporters) and nepotism (favoritism shown by public officials to their relatives) that had left the economy so vulnerable. The economic crisis led to massive student protests that forced Suharto to step down. His vice-president assumed power and announced the first democratic elections in 44 years, which took place in June 1999. After years of restrictions on parties and campaigning, 45 new parties participated in the elections. Despite fears of instability and corruption, the vote was considered a fair representation of the electorate, 93 percent of whom participated. The party winning the most votes (37.4 percent) was the Indonesian Democratic Party (PDI). Led by Megawati Sukarnoputri, the daughter of Indonesia's first president, this nationalist party was unable to form a coalition in the People's Consultative Assembly, where the president is selected. Abdurrahman Wahid, the moderate head of the National Awakening Party (PKB) party, was sworn in for a 5-year term in October 1999, with Megawati as vice-president. Wahid, usually known by the nickname "Gus Dur," is nearly blind and has suffered a stroke, but he is a shrewd politician who led the largest Muslim organization in Indonesia. Wahid's policies have generally supported foreign investment but have also been erratic, sparking fears of instability and economic uncertainty.

The Wahid administration reversed some of the Suharto-era restrictions on free expression: it released political prisoners, eliminated the feared security coordination body BAKORSTANAS, and increased freedom of the press. There is still very weak commitment to investigating and prosecuting human rights violations, which continue to be a problem, particularly in conflict areas such as Aceh, at the northern tip of the island of Sumatra and in East Timor. Moreover, Wahid failed to put a stop to the economic slide that began in 1998. By 2001 the legislature, responding to popular protests, proceeded with impeachment proceedings against Wahid. Ignoring Wahid's threats to dissolve the parliament, the legislature impeached Wahid and replaced him on 26 July 2001, with vice-president Megawati Sukarnoputri.

Although Indonesia has generally pursued a free-market approach to economic development, the government has kept state control over enterprises in sectors such as oil, plantations, and some areas of technology. The role of state-owned enterprises increased during the first decades of the New Order, contributing 30 percent of the GDP by 1990 and remaining dominant players in banking, plantations, transportation, and some areas of manufacturing. The bankruptcy of nearly all the major conglomerates and the subsequent bailout has left the government officially owning major segments of the economy at the dawn of the 21st century. There is pressure from the IMF to sell off assets and **privatize** the state-owned companies, but movement in this direction has been slow.

Wahid's policies aimed to encourage foreign investment and, in accord with IMF agreements, to take steps to strengthen the weak banking and corporate sectors. But President Wahid was distracted in pursuing these goals by such factors as the ongoing violence in certain regions, allegations of government corruption, the difficult problem of reforming the political role of the military, and battles with parliament. It is uncertain how Megawati, as the new president is known, will solve these problems, but it is clear that she will do so with the backing of the military, long the prop for political power in Indonesia. Indonesian voters will have a chance to voice their approval of Megawati's measures in elections in 2003.

Government revenues in fiscal year 1999–2000 were estimated at US$25.4 billion (including US$6 billion from international financial institutions such as the IMF). Tax revenues have historically been small, with revenues from the personal **income tax** falling from 6.5 percent of total revenues in 1968 to 2.9 percent in 1984. To boost revenue, the government changed the personal and corporate tax system in 1983 and introduced a **value-added tax** (VAT) in 1985. The 2000 budget called for the government to broaden the tax base, end most VAT exemptions, and review **tax holidays**, which guarantee some businesses a period of several years of tax-free operations.

New decentralization laws scheduled to take effect in 2001 will shift most functions from the capital to the provincial and district levels and redistribute a much higher share of profits from oil, gas, forestry, mining, and fishing to local governments. This process has significantly slowed down, however, due to concerns from Indonesian authorities and foreign investors that the local governments were not ready to assume control.

The legal system is based on Roman-Dutch law, modified by indigenous concepts and recent reforms. The court system is extremely corrupt and vulnerable to political influence. Weak courts make it even harder to reform the economic system, as influence and corruption block attempts to resolve the crisis.

Under the New Order, the military was given "dwifungsi," or "dual function," in which it played a social and political role as well as a military one. Active-duty officers occupied important positions in the executive branch, including serving as governors and ministers. The military was also given appointed seats in the national assembly. In their self-described roles as "guardians of development," the military participated in such activities as reforestation and family planning, which led to some charges of coercion or other human-rights abuses. The military also played a pervasive but unofficial role in the economy by placing officers on the boards of private and state-owned enterprises. In exchange for political protection for the businesses, the military was given access to funds for personal and official uses. Military-owned companies also operated in the open market. For example, a **holding company** tied to the important Army Strategic Reserve Command owned a film company, an airline, and an automobile assembly plant. While its political function has been much reduced since the end of the New Order, the military still has 38 out of 500 seats in the National Assembly, although this may be reduced in the future. Military expenditures in fiscal year 1998–99 were estimated at $1 billion, or 1.3 percent of the GDP. The police force was only recently separated from the armed forces and are not yet seen as an effective or accountable agent of law enforcement.

INFRASTRUCTURE, POWER, AND COMMUNICATIONS

Indonesia has fairly effective telecommunications and infrastructure, especially roads. From 1969 to 1988, the first 3 Repelitas allocated 55 percent of expenditures on transportation infrastructure to road building and maintenance, with the rest for marine transportation, railroads, and air and river transportation. This trend has continued in the 1990s. As a result, Indonesia had 342,700 kilometers (212,954) miles of roads in 1997, although fewer than half of that number were paved. Railway lines totaled 6,458 kilometers (4,013 miles) in 1995. In 1998 there were more than 16 million vehicles on the road, but only 2.6 million were cars, with most of the rest (11.7 million) being motorcycles.

There are 446 airports throughout Indonesia, but only 127 of them have paved runways. As an archipelago, Indonesia relies on a huge fleet of ships for transporting both passengers and goods. Important ports include Cirebon, Jakarta, Kupang, Palembang, Semarang, Surabaya, and Ujungpandang. Once highly restricted and bureaucratic, inter-island shipping was **deregulated** as part of the economic reform packages of the 1980s. Traditional shipping still plays an important role, with an estimated 10,000 two-masted sailing ships shuttling around the islands, though many have been motorized.

Communications

Country	Newspapers	Radios	TV Sets[a]	Cable subscribers[a]	Mobile Phones[a]	Fax Machines[a]	Personal Computers[a]	Internet Hosts[b]	Internet Users[b]
	1996	1997	1998	1998	1998	1998	1998	1999	1999
Indonesia	24	156	136	N/A	5	0.9	8.2	0.76	900
United States	215	2,146	847	244.3	256	78.4	458.6	1,508.77	74,100
China	N/A	333	272	40.0	19	1.6	8.9	0.50	8,900
Malaysia	158	420	166	5.2	99	6.9	58.6	23.53	1,500

[a]Data are from International Telecommunication Union, *World Telecommunication Development Report 1999* and are per 1,000 people.
[b]Data are from the Internet Software Consortium (http://www.isc.org) and are per 10,000 people.

SOURCE: World Bank. *World Development Indicators 2000.*

Electricity production in 1998 was estimated at 73.13 billion kilowatt hours (kWh), mostly from fossil fuels (88 percent), with most of the rest from hydroelectric plants (8 percent). An August 1998 **restructuring** policy for the power sector included plans to restore profitability, improve efficiency, and attract private investment.

There were 4.8 million telephone lines in use in 1997, and an estimated 1.2 million cell phones, as well as 31.5 million radios and 13.75 million television sets. By 1999, Indonesia had 24 Internet service providers for an estimated 1 million users, a figure expected to grow by 50 percent by 2000, despite a shortage of phone lines and limited access to computers.

There are 2 state-owned telephone companies. Indosat provides international telecommunications while Telkom provides service domestically. Both are economically healthy, and Indosat is listed on the New York Stock Exchange. Indonesia is under pressure to privatize its telecommunications sector.

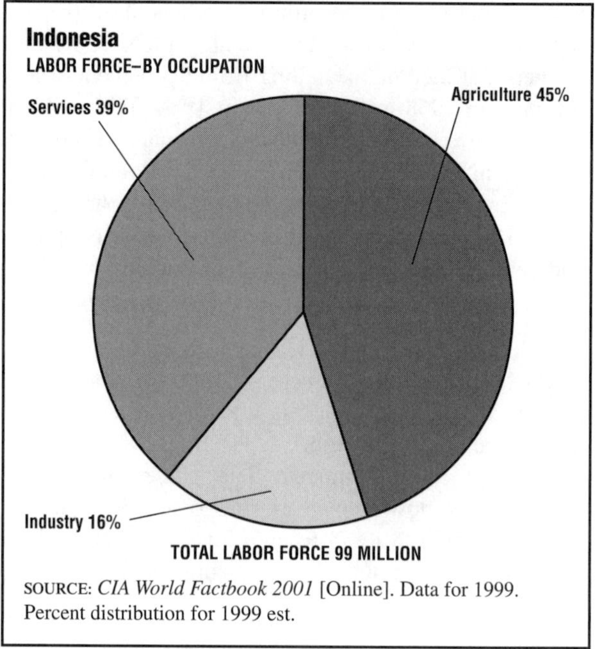

SOURCE: *CIA World Factbook 2001* [Online]. Data for 1999. Percent distribution for 1999 est.

ECONOMIC SECTORS

In 1998, agriculture accounted for 19.5 percent of Indonesia's total GDP, industry for 45.3 percent, and services for 35.2 percent, a quite different scenario than in decades past. For the first 20 years after independence in 1945, the agricultural sector contributed more than 50 percent of the nation's GDP from independence. There was little development of industry, and production per capita was no more than it had been when Indonesia was a Dutch colony. From 1965–74 there were few major industrial projects due to the still weak economy and a strategy of import substitution, which created more jobs.

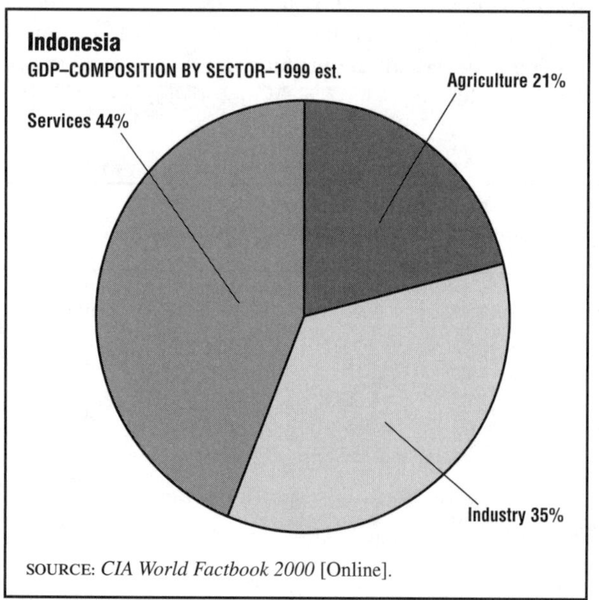

SOURCE: *CIA World Factbook 2000* [Online].

In the early 1970s the Organization of the Petroleum Exporting Countries (OPEC) raised oil prices, greatly increasing Indonesia's export income. Indonesia used this windfall, as well as profits from high prices for tropical agricultural products in the 1970s, to build heavy industries, such as steel, and advanced technologies, such as aeronautics. By the 1980s this industrialization process allowed growing industries such as steel, aluminum, and cement production to reduce the dependence of the economy on agriculture.

These industries, especially the high-tech ones, met with only mixed success, and none of them generated the significant employment required by such a populous country. Agriculture and natural resources were still important to the economy, and Indonesia's economy was vulnerable to frequent changes in the prices of these commodities, as well as of oil and gas. Oil earnings dropped in 1982–83 from US$18.825 billion to US$14.744 billion and kept falling over the next 2 years. Non-oil exports grew but not enough to make up for the fall in earnings. As Indonesia's **balance of payments** became negative, the World Bank pushed Indonesia to open its markets, and beginning in the mid-1980s the government initiated reforms to boost manufactured exports in order to strengthen the economy. These measures included a currency **devaluation** to help make exports competitive, export incentives, the relaxation of rules on foreign investment and trade, and an end to some monopolies, such as plastics.

AGRICULTURE

In 1998 agriculture accounted for 19.5 percent of Indonesia's GDP. The agricultural sector is crucial to the economy not just for the portion of the GDP it produces, but also because it employs almost half the total workforce. Agriculture was hit hard by drought in 1997–98 but has recovered somewhat since then. Although the drop in the value of the rupiah resulted in much higher prices for fertilizer, pesticides, and other inputs, it did benefit some producers of export commodities, who could now get a higher price for their goods in the international markets. In January 2000, Indonesia told the IMF that the focus of its policy would be "to maintain food security and promote efficient production, processing, and marketing of agricultural products."

FARMING. In much of the nation, the primary crop is rice, sometimes grown in extensive rice terraces with complex irrigation systems. Secondary crops, known as palawija, grown outside of the rice-growing season, include soybeans, corn, peanuts, and mung beans. In mountainous areas highland vegetables are grown, including potatoes, cabbage, carrots, and asparagus. Major fruit crops include bananas, mangos, papaya, oranges, and pineapples. In drier areas root crops such as cassava are an important product.

In the 1970s the set of agricultural innovations known as the Green Revolution introduced new seed varieties that responded well to fertilizers and pesticides, dramatically boosting rice production. Indonesia went from being the world's largest importer of rice in the 1970s to being self-sufficient in 1985. However, the increased dependence on these costly chemicals also carried negative environmental and economic impacts, and the benefits did not reach farmers in dry, mountainous, and other marginal areas.

FORESTRY. Forests and woodlands cover 62 percent of the country, making Indonesia the most heavily forested region in the world after the Amazon. Tropical rainforests make up the vast majority of this acreage, particularly in Kalimantan, Sumatra, and Papua (Irian Jaya). The colonial authorities found the climate and rich volcanic soil perfect for commercial crops such as coffee, rubber, and palm oil. Large private European and American plantations were crucial to the colonial economy in the late 19th century. Many of these estates were **nationalized** and are now operated by state-owned enterprises. Large private plantations remained as well, such as the Goodyear rubber plantation in North Sumatra.

The 1967 Basic Forestry Law gives the government sweeping control over 143 million hectares (357.5 million acres) classified as public forest land. State interest takes precedence over customary ownership of forests, despite the frequent presence of communities who have used the forests for generations. The 1967 law sparked a boom in the timber industry, and in 1978 timber exports reached half the world's total. Exports dropped after the government issued new regulations on the export of unprocessed timber, forcing logging firms to build plywood plants to capture more of the value of the lumber. In 1999 there were some 442 concessions (rights to forest lands given to logging companies) covering 51 million hectares (127.5 million acres), nearly a third of the country. These concessions generally last for 20 years and average 98,000 hectares (245,000 acres) in size. The government promotion of timber processing, the transmigration program, and population pressures on traditional shifting cultivation systems led to annual deforestation of 1 percent in the 1990s, much higher than the world average.

In the last few years, the combination of drought and human activity has led to massive forest fires, on the island of Borneo in particular, covering parts of Southeast Asia in haze. Although the fires were at first blamed on small farmers, a major cause was determined to be illegal clearing of land for large plantations. In 2000 the attorney general's office carried out investigations into the misuse of Rp1.6 trillion (US$216 million) in funds intended for reforestation. The 5 suspects were all linked to Suharto, including 1 daughter and a half-brother. The Ministry of Forestry and Estate Crops recently suspended 46 forest concessions due to documentation errors and improper logging operations.

FISHERIES. Fish is a main source of animal protein in the typical Indonesian diet. The fishing industry continues to rely on traditional methods and equipment, although the government has been promoting the motorization of traditional fishing boats. Foreign fishing boats contribute to growing exports, mostly shrimp and tuna caught for sale in the Japanese market. However, the supply of fish is threatened by illegal fishing from foreign boats and severe environmental degradation.

Prawns are an important export and are increasingly raised on massive coastal farms capable of bringing in large amounts of export earnings. Indonesian prawn exports exceeded US$1 billion in 1998, a significant portion of total agriculture exports. These operations often destroy coastal mangrove forests and have been involved in the exploitation of workers in Sumatra who raise the shrimp on a contract basis and are unable to get out of debt to the shrimp farm companies.

INDUSTRY

MANUFACTURING. Manufactured goods such as textiles, clothing, footwear, cement, and chemical fertilizers are an important part of Indonesia's international trade, with textiles being the largest export, as well as other labor-intensive products such as garments, furniture, and shoes. Indonesia has been unable to move to high-technology exports like computer equipment but has had growing success with basic machinery and electronics. In 2000, electronics increased to 10 percent of total exports (not including oil and gas), still much less than other developed Southeast Asian economies such as Malaysia, Philippines, and Thailand.

Government policies of the 1970s helped move industry toward heavy industries such as petroleum processing, steel, and cement. The sector shifted again in the mid-1980s towards manufacturing of goods for exports, this time mostly through private rather than government investment. Manufactured exports grew in value from under US$1 billion in 1982 to more than US$9 billion in 1990. As a share of exports, manufactures grew from only 4 percent in 1965 to 35 percent in 1990. After a long period of growth, industrial production fell during the financial crisis that hit the region in 1997.

Following the government bailout of bankrupt companies, the Indonesian Bank Restructuring Agency (IBRA) officially owned most of the manufacturing sector in 2000, although the original owners may retain control of their businesses in the end. Small and medium businesses were less affected by the crisis because they borrowed less. However, they also suffered from the sudden disappearance of credit and were not eligible for bailout programs as the big companies were. The government, recognizing the historical failure to reach Small and Medium Enterprises (SMEs) with government assistance, established a task force to develop an SME strategy with support from the World Bank and the Asian Development Bank. The strategy, under preparation in 2000, aims to make businesses development services more responsive to SMEs, expand access to credit, and simplify regulations.

MINING. Important minerals and metals include tin, nickel, bauxite, copper, coal, gold, and silver. As in the oil and gas industry, foreign companies carry out mining operations, assume all risks, and share revenues with the government. The world's largest copper and gold mine is in Papua (formerly Irian Jaya); it has brought in tremendous revenues, but there have been charges of environmental damage and human rights abuses of local inhabitants.

OIL AND GAS. The role of oil and gas in Indonesia's economy is extremely important, especially following the OPEC oil price hikes in 1974. As a result, the share of government revenues derived from this sector grew from 19.7 percent in 1969 to 48.4 percent in 1975. As a share of export earnings, oil and gas hovered around two-thirds of the total over the next decade and even reached 80 percent in 1981. During the 1970s, these revenues were a major source of the country's development budget. By 1999 the economy was more diverse and had a strong manufacturing sector, with oil and gas accounting for just 20 percent of total exports of US$48 billion.

Indonesia is the world's largest exporter of liquefied natural gas, much of it from the strife-torn area of Aceh, where resentment of the government's failure to share the benefits of the windfall is one factor in the separatist movement. Most oil exploration and drilling is done by foreign contractors under agreements with Pertamina, the state-owned oil and gas company. Pertamina grew in the 1970s to be a colossal conglomerate active in many sectors, but it was later discovered to be deeply indebted and in need of restructuring. During this time it was an important source of unofficial funds for military and political factions.

SERVICES

The service sector, including stores, food vendors, and banks, is an important part of Indonesia's economy, accounting for 35 percent of the GDP in recent years. While more people work in agriculture, the service sector is an important source of wage labor, accounting for 12.4 million jobs in 1996. However, there is low productivity in the service sector, much of which lies within the **informal economy** (small businesses such as street vendors that are outside the formal system of registration and taxes).

FINANCIAL SERVICES. The Indonesian financial sector was long burdened by heavy debt and by numerous **bad loans** made on the basis of corruption and cronyism. In the aftermath of the financial crisis of the 1990s, more than two-thirds of bank loans were thought to be impossible to recover, and the number of banks fell from 238 to 162. Many surviving banks are technically bankrupt or limited by very low amounts of capital. Following the collapse of the banking system, the government formed the Indonesian Bank Restructuring Agency to restructure banks, collect on bad loans taken over from banks, and, unlike similar agencies in other countries, even sell assets pledged to it in return for the bailouts. IBRA reported US$52 billion in assets in 2000. The agency has been slow to carry out its duties, and has also been accused of cronyism.

By 2000 banks had slowly begun lending again, but mostly to consumers rather than companies. Businesses were forced to try to raise money in other ways, such as through their business activities, by borrowing overseas, or by issuing bonds. Deregulation in 1998 opened the banking, securities, and insurance industries to more foreign investment. In 1999, the central bank, Bank Indonesia, was given full autonomy from government interference. Bank Indonesia still works to maintain the value of the rupiah and keep inflation under control.

TOURISM. Given Indonesia's beaches, temples, and rich spectrum of cultural events, tourism remains an important source of foreign exchange. Bali is one of the most visited spots in the world. Fears of political instability and conflict have hurt tourism, though, in recent years, but there is a good potential for recovery and growth, as facilities and infrastructure are intact, and the exchange rate is favorable to visitors.

In 1983 Indonesia discovered that tourism had fallen by a third in just 1 year and took measures to increase visits, including issuing visas on arrival, creating better airline connections, and appointing a minister of Tourism, Post and Telecommunications. The strategy worked, and tourist arrivals peaked at more than 5 million just before the financial crisis. Tourism has slowed since then, but in 2000 the government recorded a small increase, to 4.15 million foreign tourists. The airport on the small island of Bali accounts for 1.47 million arrivals alone. Continued increases in tourist arrivals are likely, but some tourists may be scared off by violence, ethnic unrest, and labor stoppages.

RETAIL. The **retail** market was badly affected by the financial crisis, as increased unemployment and poverty reduced consumer demand for goods. Retailers selling imported goods were forced to charge much higher prices. There has been some recovery since 1998, partially due to wealthier Indonesians' bringing money back from overseas where they tried to shelter it from the effects of the financial crisis. The retail food sector is dominated by traditional outlets such as small restaurants and the omnipresent street stalls, known as warungs. Modern supermarkets and retail outlets make up only 20 percent of retail food outlets even in Jakarta, which has the most advanced economy in the country.

INTERNATIONAL TRADE

In 1999, Indonesia exported $48 billion worth of goods and services and imported $24 billion. Exports are mainly low-tech goods and natural resource-based products, including sport shoes, textiles, basic electronics, plywood, furniture, paper, palm oil, rubber, and spices. Imports are primarily machinery and equipment, chemicals, fuels, and foodstuffs.

Japan is the main destination for Indonesian goods, with 18 percent of total 1999 exports, followed by the European Union (15 percent), the United States (14 percent), Singapore (13 percent), South Korea (5 percent), Hong Kong (4 percent), China (4 percent), and Taiwan (3 percent). Japan also is the main source of imports (17 percent), followed by the United States (13 percent), Singapore (10 percent), Germany (9 percent), Australia (6 percent), South Korea (5 percent), Taiwan (3 percent), and China (3 percent).

The crisis of the late 1990s ended a period of rising levels of trade, with exports increasing an average of 11 percent annually from 1993 to 1996. After the onset of the crisis, fluctuating exchange rates and the sudden absence of credit made it difficult for Indonesian companies to trade. Inflation and unemployment also reduced consumer demand for the increasingly expensive imports. Initial reports estimated that imports of **capital goods** (goods used to produce other goods), such as manufacturing equipment, fell 70 percent from 1997 to 1999. High levels of debt continue to restrict the ability of firms to borrow to finance trade deals.

The beginning of 2000 saw export growth resume to pre-crisis levels, although some of that was due to the rise in oil prices. Imports also rose, but by early 2000 they were still at only 60 percent of what they had been before the crisis. Further growth in imports is likely, especially in educational and training services, computers, telecommunications equipment, life insurance, and food supplements, as well industrial and agricultural chemicals, pulp and, paperboard, and equipment for forestry, mining, oil and gas exploitation, and food processing. There is still a need for reforms to reduce corruption and cronyism and promote the rule of law. Fears of political instability have also compounded the economic problems, scaring off foreign investors and trading partners.

MONEY

The first decades after independence were marked by rampant inflation, as Sukarno's government printed money as needed. After Suharto's New Order government took power in 1965, the so-called Berkeley Mafia of U.S.-trained economists was able to bring inflation un-

Trade (expressed in billions of US$): Indonesia

	Exports	Imports
1975	7.102	4.770
1980	21.909	10.834
1985	18.587	10.259
1990	25.675	21.837
1995	45.417	40.630
1998	48.847	27.337

SOURCE: International Monetary Fund. *International Financial Statistics Yearbook 1999.*

Exchange rates: Indonesia

Indonesian rupiahs (Rp) per US$1	
Jan 2001	10,000
2000	8,421.8
1999	7,855.2
1998	10,013.6
1997	2,909.4
1996	2,342.3

SOURCE: CIA *World Factbook 2001* [ONLINE].

der control through tight control of fiscal and **monetary policy**. An exception was the sudden surge of oil wealth that sent inflation soaring to 40 percent. Inflation was brought back under 10 percent by 1978, but in the meantime exports fell due to the combination of inflation and a **fixed exchange rate**.

To facilitate the exporting of goods at competitive prices, the government lowered the value of the rupiah 50 percent in 1978, and again in 1983 and 1986. After that devaluations of about 5 percent a year were allowed. Until the crisis of 1997, the government tried to limit exchange rate fluctuations to within this range (a policy called a "managed float"). Between 1990 and 1996 the rupiah depreciated by an average of 3.9 percent. This stability encouraged investment, as investors knew that their profits would not be eaten up by inflation. It also encouraged domestic businesses to borrow money in foreign currencies such as the dollar (reaching almost US$80 billion), which would prove disastrous for them once the rupiah crashed. In August 1997, after seeing neighboring countries try and fail to keep their currencies stable, the government announced it could no longer pursue the managed float policy. Exchange rates fell from Rp2,500=US$1 in July 1997 to Rp17,000=US$1 in June 1998, before improving to Rp8,000=US$1 later that year. Indonesia does not maintain capital controls, and foreign exchange may be freely converted and can flow in and out of the country unrestricted. As part of the recovery strategy, the International Monetary Fund required Indonesia to raise interest rates to bring back foreign investment.

The first stock exchange was set up in Jakarta (then known as Batavia) in 1912, though it was closed during World War II. After independence an exchange was established in 1952, only to be shut down by a program of nationalization in which the government took over private companies. In 1977 the modern Jakarta Stock Exchange was opened, first under government control and later privatized. Growth was slow at first, with only 24 traded companies by 1987. By 2000, only 278 companies have been listed, most of them owned by the company founders with small amounts of public ownership.

GDP per Capita (US$)

Country	1975	1980	1985	1990	1998
Indonesia	385	504	603	778	972
United States	19,364	21,529	23,200	25,363	29,683
China	138	168	261	349	727
Malaysia	1,750	2,348	2,644	3,164	4,251

SOURCE: United Nations. *Human Development Report 2000; Trends in human development and per capita income.*

POVERTY AND WEALTH

At independence, Indonesia was an extremely poor country, and it was not until after the change in governments in 1965 that any progress was made in lowering the rate of poverty. In the 2 decades prior to 1996, Indonesia saw consistent growth, with the official poverty rate falling from 60 percent to 15 percent. However, not all groups and regions have benefitted equally, and Indonesia has a highly uneven distribution of income. The poorest fifth account for just 8 percent of consumption, while the richest fifth account for 45 percent. Average income today is about US$650 a year.

Poverty rates have always been higher in the outer islands. The rise of manufacturing disproportionately benefitted Java, Bali, and Sumatra due to the better infrastructure of the inner islands. Economic disparity and the flow of natural resource profits to Jakarta has led to dissatisfaction and even contributed to separatist movements in areas such as Aceh and Papua (Irian Jaya). While the new laws on decentralization (moving more economic and political decision-making to the outer islands) may partially address the problem of unequal growth and satisfaction, there are many obstacles to putting this new policy into practice.

The financial crisis of 1997 had social ramifications by reversing many of the income-distribution gains made over the previous decades. Though the enormous informal economy and family-support networks helped soften the impact of higher unemployment rates, social effects were nonetheless profound. In a few parts of the outer islands, the devaluation meant higher prices abroad for export crops such as cloves, nutmeg, cocoa, and vanilla, but overall, Indonesians suffered from rising poverty, surging unemployment, reduced schooling and public services, worsening health and nutrition, more crime and violence, and increased social stress and fragmentation. While some 15 percent of the population was below the poverty line before the crisis, an additional 40 million

Distribution of Income or Consumption by Percentage Share: Indonesia

Lowest 10%	3.6
Lowest 20%	8.0
Second 20%	11.3
Third 20%	15.1
Fourth 20%	20.8
Highest 20%	44.9
Highest 10%	30.3

Survey year: 1996

Note: This information refers to income shares by percentiles of the population and is ranked by per capita income.

SOURCE: *2000 World Development Indicators* [CD-ROM].

Household Consumption in PPP Terms

Country	All food	Clothing and footwear	Fuel and power[a]	Health care[b]	Education[b]	Transport & Communications	Other
Indonesia	47	3	6	5	14	3	22
United States	13	9	9	4	6	8	51
China	N/A	N/A	N/A	N/A	N/A	N/A	N/A
Malaysia	N/A	N/A	N/A	N/A	N/A	N/A	N/A

Data represent percentage of consumption in PPP terms.
[a]Excludes energy used for transport.
[b]Includes government and private expenditures.

SOURCE: World Bank. *World Development Indicators 2000.*

people (20 percent of the population) may have since fallen into poverty.

Inflation has been a particular burden to Indonesia's poorest citizens. During the late 1990s, the price of rice, the staple food for most people, leapt from Rp1,000 per kilogram to Rp5,000. In 1998 the Ministry for Food and Horticulture estimated that about 80 million individuals were facing food shortages. In Central and East Java alone over 30 million people were able to afford only 1 meal per day. Eastern Indonesia, hard hit by drought as well as economic problems, experienced widespread famine. Due to the rising costs of imports, medicine ran short and prices doubled or tripled. The International Labor Organization estimated that the number of Indonesians using public health services would double in 1998, to 68 percent of the population, even as the government was under pressure to spend less money on such health-related public services. It was reported in the press that the number of women dying in childbirth shot up from 22,000 per million to 35,000 per million in the space of 1 year, due to the lack of money to transport women to health facilities and to increased anemia levels in pregnant women.

In 1998 education accounted for 14 percent of household expenditures. Rising school costs and falling family incomes forced many poor students to drop out of school. Roughly 5 percent of students did so in 1999 alone, according to official estimates. Enrollments in junior high schools in Jakarta declined disproportionately in the case of girls (19 percent), as did enrollment in poorer rural areas. In July 1998 the government launched a scholarship program for the poorest students. However, to help pay for this program it had to cut funding for high schools and colleges.

WORKING CONDITIONS

The Indonesian **labor force** is estimated at about 95 million, two-thirds of which is between the ages of 15 and 34, and two-fifths of which is made up of women. Even during the period of significant GDP growth from 1985 to 1995, the rise in employment failed to keep up with the rise in population. More than 4 million people (nearly 5 percent of the labor force) were looking for jobs even before the crisis of 1997. The government's August 1999 Labor Force Survey found 6 million people over age 15 unemployed, and a much higher number **underemployed** (34 million workers, or 39 percent), working less than 35 hours a week in 1998. Some economists question the reliability of these figures, and suggest that more than half the population is underemployed.

In 1998, the labor force was distributed approximately as follows: agriculture (45 percent); trade, restaurant, and hotel (19 percent); manufacturing (11 percent); transport and communications (5 percent); and construction (4 percent). The manufacturing workforce is skilled in the basics but undereducated. While many light manufacturing companies, such as sneakers and clothing plants, opened factories in Indonesia to take advantage of a mostly young, female labor pool of migrants to the cities, high-tech manufacturers have been slow to move in. As competition increases from China, Vietnam, and India, these unskilled workers are starting to lose out. There have been well-documented charges of sweatshop conditions (forced overtime, unsafe workplaces, and inadequate pay) in many of these export-oriented factories.

The government sets minimum wages in each region; in Jakarta it was set at Rp286,000 (US$33) per month in April 2000. While workers were allowed to join a single union established by the government under the Suharto regime, new regulations put forth in 1998 have allowed the formation of more than 2 dozen new labor unions. Strikes have increased in recent years, with the return of economic activity. According to the International Labor Organization, "women are likely to be more adversely affected by the [economic] crisis than men. They are concentrated in the most precarious forms of wage employment and are thus more vulnerable to lay-offs."

Indonesia has also traditionally sent large numbers of workers overseas, both legally and illegally. As countries such as Malaysia and Thailand suffered the effects of the crisis, nearly all of these Indonesian workers were sent home, worsening the problems of unemployment and poverty.

COUNTRY HISTORY AND ECONOMIC DEVELOPMENT

1300s. Islam begins to take hold in Indonesia.

1500. Fall of Majapahit marks the last Hindu-Buddhist empire.

1511. Portuguese explorers arrive in the islands seeking trade in spices.

1596. The first Dutch ships arrive.

1602. The Dutch East India Company is formed as a private stock company to trade, make treaties, and maintain troops in the Indies.

1799. The Dutch East India Company declares bankruptcy and is replaced by Dutch government bureaucracy.

1830. The Dutch institute the Culture System, a forced cultivation system to produce coffee, sugar, indigo, pepper, tea and cotton, resulting in rice shortages and famines.

1927. Sukarno, a university student who later becomes president, founds the Indonesian National Party.

1942. The Japanese invade Indonesia during World War II, driving out the Dutch.

1945. The Dutch return, only to find Indonesians declaring independence on 17 August.

1949. Indonesia's independence is recognized, and Sukarno is elected as the first president.

1965. Suharto takes power in a military coup.

1974. Oil revenues rise due to price hikes by OPEC.

1975. Indonesia invades East Timor.

1978. First major devaluation (50 percent) of the rupiah occurs following inflation.

1980s. Oil prices fall, leading to shocks in the economy.

1988. Economic reform packages begin to open up trade, investment, and banking and reduce monopolies.

1997. The Asian financial crisis hits Indonesia, leading to the crash of the rupiah, bank and business failures, and unemployment.

1998. Suharto steps down in the face of massive protests.

1999. President Abdurrahman Wahid is sworn in.

2001. Wahid is impeached in July, and vice president Megawati Sukarnoputri is installed as president.

FUTURE TRENDS

In 2001, Indonesia stood at a crossroads. Just 3 years after the removal of the autocratic Suharto, only the country's second leader since independence, the country had gone through 3 presidents, with the second, Abdurrahman Wahid, removed by impeachment. The biggest question on the political horizon is whether the newly-installed President Megawati Sukarnoputri can secure the stability of the presidency and lead the way to peaceful elections in 2003. Her critics worry that she will lead the country back to the days of military control. Foreign investment and economic stability in the coming years may well depend on her success.

If all goes well politically, Indonesia should be able to build on its strengths to restore the confidence of foreign investors. It has a large domestic market and labor force, a well-functioning telecommunications and infrastructure, extensive natural resources, a strategic location, and experience with market economics. Many obstacles remain to economic recovery, however: Indonesia's huge public and private debt, private assets under government control that must be restructured or sold, its ineffectual legal system, and cronyism. Despite the need for social programs, the much higher debt that followed the crisis will pressure the government to keep expenditures down. While more investment is needed, a forecast by the National Development Planning Agency in May 2000 found that even with optimistic assumptions about successful reforms, foreign investment would not return until 2002.

Reform is progressing slowly. At the end of 2000, the IMF was threatening to delay new loans unless Indonesia fulfilled previous promises to take action to reduce risks in its decentralization plan, use higher oil revenues to pay down debt, and set a timetable for selling assets obtained through the bailout.

The economy will also be affected by whether the decentralization process is able to increase the fair development of the regions while still reassuring investors of stability. It is hoped that better sharing of revenues with the provinces will reduce some tensions, but unrest is likely to continue in some of the most conflict-torn areas, such as Maluku, Aceh, and Papua (Irian Jaya).

DEPENDENCIES

Indonesia has no territories or colonies.

BIBLIOGRAPHY

"But What Will Megawati Do?" *Economist.* 26 July 2001.

"Chaos Rebuffed." *Far Eastern Economic Review.* 18 January 2001.

Djiwandono, J. Soedradjad. "A New Development Paradigm For Indonesia: Challenges After The Crisis." *Pacific Link.* <http://www.pacific.net.id/pakar/sj/towards_a_new_development_paradigm.html>. Accessed August 2001.

Economist Intelligence Unit. *Country Profile: Indonesia.* London: Economist Intelligence Unit, 2001.

Fox, James, J. "Managing the Ecology of Rice Production in Indonesia." In Hardjono, Joan, editor, *Indonesia: Resources, Ecology, and Environment.* Singapore: Oxford University Press, 1991.

"Indonesia Signs New Letter of Intent with IMF." *Jakarta Post.* 22 January 2000.

"Industry Profile: Prawn Agroindustry Still Promising; Part 1 of 2." *Indonesian Commercial Newsletter.* 11 May 1999.

Lawyers Committee for Human Rights and the Institute for Policy Research and Advocacy. *In the Name of Development.* New York: Lawyers Committee for Human Rights, 1995.

"A Restless People." *Far Eastern Economic Review.* 18 January 2001.

Robison, Richard. *Power and Economy in Suharto's Indonesia.* Manila: The Journal of Contemporary Asia Publishers, 1990.

U.S. Central Intelligence Agency. *World Factbook 2000.* <http://www.odci.gov/cia/publications/factbook/index.html>. Accessed August 2001.

U.S. Department of Commerce, National Trade Data Bank. "Economic Highs and Lows, February 2000." *Tradeport.* <http://www.tradeport.org/ts/countries/indonesia/mrr/mark0057.html>. Accessed August 2001 (report prepared 3 November 2000).

U.S. Department of State. *FY 2000 Country Commercial Guide: Indonesia.* <http://www.state.gov/www/about_state/business/com_guides/index.html>. Accessed August 2001.

World Bank. *Indonesia: Family Planning Perspectives for the 1990s.* Washington: World Bank, 1990.

Yue, Chia Siow, and Shamira Bhanu. "The Asian Financial Crisis: Human Security Dimensions." *Japan Center for International Exchange.* <http://www.jcie.or.jp/thinknet/tomorrow/chia1.html>. Accessed August 2001.

—Matthew Easton

IRAN

Islamic Republic of Iran
Jomhuri-ye Eslami-ye Iran

CAPITAL: Tehran.

MONETARY UNIT: Iranian rial (IR). One Iranian rial equals 100 dinars. There are coins of 1, 5, 10, 20, and 50 rials and notes of 100, 200, 500, 1,000, 2,000, 5,000, and 10,000 rials.

CHIEF EXPORTS: Petroleum (80 percent), carpets, fruits, nuts, hides, steel.

CHIEF IMPORTS: Machinery, military supplies, metal works, foodstuffs, pharmaceuticals, technical services, refined oil products.

GROSS DOMESTIC PRODUCT: US$347.6 billion (purchasing power parity, 1999 est.).

BALANCE OF TRADE: **Exports:** US$12.2 billion (f.o.b., 1998). **Imports:** US$13.8 billion (f.o.b., 1998).

COUNTRY OVERVIEW

LOCATION AND SIZE. Iran, a country slightly larger than Alaska, is located in the Middle East, bordering the Gulf of Oman and the Persian Gulf in the south and the Caspian Sea in the north. It covers an area of 1.648 million square kilometers (636,296 square miles) and is edged between Iraq, with which it shares a border of 1,458 kilometers (906 miles), and Pakistan and Afghanistan in the east, with which Iran has 909 kilometers (565 miles) and 936 kilometers (582 miles), respectively, of common borderline. Iran also shares 499 kilometers (310 miles) of borderline with Turkey, 992 kilometers (616 miles) with Turkmenistan, 432 kilometers (268 miles) with Azerbaijan, and some 35 kilometers (22 miles) with Armenia, the latter 3 states formerly being part of the USSR.

Most of the 2,440 kilometers (1516 miles) of coastline are on the Persian Gulf and the Gulf of Oman. The 2 gulfs are connected by the strategic strait of Hormuz. Iran has dozens of islands in the Persian Gulf, many of which are uninhabited but used as bases for oil exploration. Those that are inhabited—notably Qeshm and Kish—are being developed, attracting investors and tourists. The Iranian coast of the Caspian Sea is some 740 kilometers (460 miles) long. Apart from being home to the sturgeon that provides for the world's best caviar, the Caspian Sea is the world's largest lake, with an area of some 370,000 square kilometers, and is co-owned by Azerbaijan, Russia, Kazakhstan, and Turkmenistan.

In general, Iran consists of an interior plateau, 1,000 meters to 1,500 meters (3,000 feet to 3,500 feet) above sea level, ringed on almost all sides by mountain zones. The Elburz range with the Iranian capital, Tehran, at its feet, features the country's highest peak, the snowcapped volcanic cone of Mt. Damavand, at 5,604 meters (18,386 feet). To the north of the range there is a sudden drop to a flat plain occupied by the Caspian Sea, which lies about 27 meters (89 feet) below sea-level and is shrinking alarmingly in size. The larger Zagros mountain range runs from north-west Iran down to the eastern shores of the Persian Gulf, and then eastward, fronting the Arabian Sea, and continuing into Pakistan.

The interior plateau of Iran is mostly desert, and the settled areas are generally confined to the foothills of mountains, though oasis towns, such as Kerman, are growing in size. Major towns and historical centers are spread all over the country, such as the country's largest cities of Tabriz (1.2 million) in the far northwestern corner; Mashhad (1.9 million) in the far northeastern corner; Esfahan (1.3 million) to the south; and Shiraz (1.1 million) to the distant south of the capital, Tehran (6.8 million).

POPULATION. Iran's population was estimated to total 65.6 million in July 2000 according to CIA figures. Almost two-thirds of Iran's people are of Aryan origin—their ancestors migrated from Central Asia. The major groups in this category include Persians, Kurds, Lurs, and Baluchi. The remainder are primarily Turkic but also include Arabs, Armenians, Jews, and Assyrians. Iran's

ethnic diversity is reflected in the variety of languages Iranians speak, with 58 percent speaking Persian and Persian dialects, 26 percent speaking Turkic dialects, 9 percent Kurdish, and 7 percent other languages. Persian—an Indo-European language almost unchanged since ancient times with a share of Arabic, Turkic, and European words—is now spoken by the majority of Iranians as their first language and operates as a lingua franca for minority groups. Although granted equal rights by the constitution, ethnic minorities are second-class citizens.

Iran's population is approximately 99 percent Muslim, of which 89 percent are followers of the state religion, Shi'a Islam. Some 10 percent are followers of the Sunni branch of Islam (mostly Turkomen, Arabs, Baluchs, and Kurds living in the southwest, southeast, and northwest). Sufi Brotherhoods (mystical religious orders) are popular, but there are no reliable figures available to judge their true size. Baha'is, Christians, Zoroastrians, and Jews constitute less than 1 percent of the population. The largest non-Muslim minority is the Baha'i faith, estimated at about 300,000 to 350,000 adherents throughout the country. Estimates on the size of the Jewish community vary from 25,000 to 30,000. These figures represent a substantial reduction from the estimated 75,000 to 80,000 Jews who resided in the country prior to the 1979 Revolution. The Christian community is estimated at approximately 117,000 persons. According to government figures the size of the Zoroastrian community was estimated at approximately 35,000 adherents. Zoroastrian groups cite a larger figure of approximately 60,000. Zoroastrianism was the official religion of the pre-Islamic Sassanid Empire and thus has played a central role in Iranian history. Zoroastrians are mainly ethnic Persians concentrated in the cities of Tehran, Kerman, and Yazd. In general, society is accustomed to the presence of Iran's pre-Islamic, non-Muslim communities. However, the government restricts freedom of religion, creating a threatening atmosphere for some religious minorities, especially Baha'is, Jews, and evangelical Christians.

Iran has a relatively young population, with 34 percent of the population under the age of 14 and 61 percent between 15 and 64 years of age. Thanks to a family planning program, population growth decreased from 3.2 percent in 1984 to 1.7 percent in 1998 and further to 0.83 percent in 2000. Of the population, an estimated 38 million Iranians (or 60 percent) live in urban areas, while approximately 27 million live in rural areas. The population density was 37.6 inhabitants per square kilometer (97 per square mile) in 1998, though many people are concentrated in the Tehran region, and other parts of the country (especially deserts) are basically uninhabited. Basic literacy rates are above the regional average, although uncertain reporting standards give a wide margin for error. In 1997–98 the central bank estimated literacy at 80.5 percent in those over 6 years old, with 75.6 percent of women and 85.3 percent of men judged to be functionally literate, i.e. they were taught to read and write at some point.

Between 1920 and 1960 Iran's population doubled to 23 million, and by 1979 the equivalent to the entire population of the country in 1920 had been added. Most of the increase in population migrated to urban centers and found jobs in industry and services, as opposed to agriculture. In 1960, about one-third of the population lived in towns; by 1979 nearly half the population was urban. Tehran became the center of government, higher education, and industry; in 1976, it contained two-thirds of all university students, and nearly one-third of high school students; about half of all factories were in or around Tehran. After the Islamic revolution of 1979, this trend continued. Currently, around 60 percent of the Iranian population lives in towns. Tehran remains the principal political, economic, and industrial center, with a population of 6.8 million, according to a 1996 census, although it is very likely that the metropolitan area accommodates some 11–12 million people, or 20 percent, of the country's overall population.

The civil war in Afghanistan, the Iran-Iraq war of the 1980s, and Iraqi policies in the aftermath of the Gulf War in 1990–91 have caused a constant influx of refugees to Iran. The country hosts the largest refugee population in the world. According to the government, the total refugee population counts 2 million—1.4 million Afghans and 580,000 Iraqis—while a smaller number have been driven into Iran by the conflict in the Nagorny Karabakh region in Azerbaijan. The Iraqis include Kurds from the north and Arab Shiites from the south. Only 5 percent of refugees live in 30 designated camps, while others are scattered among cities and villages throughout the country. The increase in unemployment and deteriorating economic conditions have somewhat eroded the Iranians' so far rather tolerant and welcoming attitude toward refugees, and more pressure is being exerted for refugees to return to their countries of origin. The Iranian government feels it bears a heavy social and economic burden and believes the international community should share more of this burden.

OVERVIEW OF ECONOMY

Iran has a mixed economy that is heavily dependent on export earnings from the country's extensive petroleum reserves. Oil exports account for nearly 80 percent of foreign exchange earnings. The constitution mandates that all large-scale industries, including petroleum, minerals, banking, foreign exchange, insurance, power generation, communications, aviation, and road and rail transport, be owned publicly and administered by the state. Basic foodstuffs and energy costs are heavily subsidized by the government. Although economic performance improved somewhat during 1999 and 2000 due to the worldwide increase in oil prices, performance is affected adversely by government mismanagement and corruption. Unemployment was estimated to be as high as 25 percent, and **inflation** was an estimated 22 percent. Iran's **gross national product** (GNP) is the highest in the Middle East, although its GNP per capita is comparatively low because of Iran's large and growing population.

From medieval times until the 20th century, the socioeconomic structure of Iran remained almost unaltered. Only half of the population was settled; the remainder were tribal nomads, mainly engaged in the herding of grazing animals. A system of land assignment was in place, similar to the medieval European system of feudalism, under which the ruler, the shah, granted land to loyal subjects who became absentee landowners, collecting taxes from the peasants on their land. Economic activity further suffered from the handicaps of topography and climate, as well as prolonged political and social insecurity (with constant pressure by foreign powers). Things began to change when Reza Shah Pahlavi, a colonel in the Persian army and founder of the Pahlavi dynasty, seized the throne in 1925 and initiated a modernization of Iran's political and economic system, while also changing the country's name from Persia to Iran.

Following World War II the new shah, Mohammed Reza, guided the economy through public planning, urbanization, industrialization, and investment in the **infrastructure**, and achieved sustained growth, all supported by substantial oil revenues. Compared with other third world countries during the period from 1960–77, Iran's annual real growth rate of nearly 9.6 percent was about double the average. Therefore, one explanation for the Islamic revolution of 1979 is that the modernization program imposed by the shah was too rapid for the Iranian people, who wished to hold on to their traditional values and ways. Another view suggests that in fact, the shah failed to modernize rapidly enough. The Iranian economic and social infrastructure was found increasingly inadequate to meet expectations, despite rising oil revenues that produced a superficial modernism. The standard of living did increase in Iran during the early 1970s, when per capita income rose from US$180 per year just before the massive oil price increase to US$810 in 1973–74, and up to an estimated US$1,521 just one year later. During the last years of the shah's reign, per capita income rose less rapidly and living costs soared. By 1978, the typical rent for a house in Esfahan had risen from about US$70 per month in 1973 to over US$500 a month, while a typical salary was still below US$2 per hour. In addition, corruption had become widespread.

In 1979 an Islamic revolution ousted Shah Mohammed Reza Pahlavi from power and placed the Shiite clergy in control of the government of the country. The revolution was followed by trade **sanctions** and the freezing of Iranian assets in the United States after radical Iranian students stormed the American embassy in Tehran and held embassy staff as hostages. These measures and the war which broke out between Iran and Iraq in September 1980 and lasted for 8 years harmed the development of the Iranian economy considerably. Since that conflict, efforts to resume broad economic development and diversification have been hindered by volatile world oil prices, by internal structural weaknesses and rampant inflation, and by persistent political tensions with the West, especially with the United States, which still considers Iran to be the most active state sponsor of terrorism, supporting extremist groups such as Lebanon-based Hezbullah and the Palestinian Hamas.

The most remarkable features of the post-revolutionary Iranian political and economic scene are the influence of the so-called *bazaar* and the *bonyad.* The bazaar refers to Iran's traditional import-export markets, the leaders of which wield considerable influence over economic policy. These leaders, known as bazaaris, showed their power in 1978 by calling a series of strikes, paralyzing Iran's economy and speeding up the departure of the shah. Since the revolution the bazaaris have enjoyed a close relationship with the Islamic regime, benefiting from lucrative business contracts in exchange for funding individual mosques and conservative parliamentary and presidential candidates. The bazaar also provides an informal banking service to the **private sector** and is responsible for much of the **black-market** trade in currency; as a result, bazaaris tend to oppose **exchange-rate** reunification. In broad terms, they also oppose wider economic reform, the reduction of **tariff** barriers, and the greater participation of foreign investors in the economy.

The bonyad (religious foundations) were created after the revolution to safeguard the Islamic Republic's revolutionary principles and to attend to the plight of the poor. While providing much-needed welfare support for the families of those killed or wounded in the Iran-Iraq war, the bonyad have exploited their position to become multi-billion dollar conglomerates controlling large portions of the Iranian economy, especially properties and businesses taken from the Pahlavi family and individuals associated with the monarchy. The larger bonyad, such as the Bonyad-e Mostazafan (Foundation of the Oppressed) and Bonyad-e Shahid (Foundation of the Martyrs), oppose better relations with the West and the **liberalization** of the economy, fearing that foreign investment in Iran could threaten their economic empires.

In the early 1990s, Iran faced a huge **foreign debt** and other serious economic dislocations stemming from the nearly decade-long Iran-Iraq war (1980–88), while its population continued to grow at a rapid pace. Most of the economic resources were allocated through the vast **public sector**, widespread **price controls**, extensive trade and exchange restrictions, heavily subsidized energy and petroleum products, and protective labor and business practices. With oil prices changing considerably during the 1980s, planning became difficult and resulted in inflation, since the government did not want to borrow on international markets, but financed war-related and other expenses through the central bank. Between 1981–82 and 1984–85, the **real GDP** had grown by about 8 percent annually, which reflected oil production and export recovery after the low-point during and in the immediate aftermath of the revolution. But when oil prices fell to a historic low in 1987–88, this drop was also reflected in the economy at large, and Iran witnessed a negative growth rate of 10 percent.

After the war, efforts were made to revive oil exports and to shift the economy onto a peacetime basis. Through the 1990s, attempts at **privatizing** public enterprises, liberalizing prices and the exchange system, removing tariff barriers, and lowering **income taxes** to encourage investment were made. During the First 5 Year Development Plan (1989–94), these measures worked well and the economy grew in real GDP terms at an average annual rate of 7 percent. While the First 5 Year Development Plan focused on infrastructure development and reconstruction programs, the Second 5 Year Development Plan (1994–99) concentrated on Iran's financial problems. The sharp drop of oil prices in 1998–99 forced the government to abandon structural reforms and brought about a **budget deficit** of US$2.1 billion, which was financed by monetary expansion, thus accelerating inflation from 17 percent in 1997–98 to 25 percent in 1998–99.

The reformist president Khatami, elected in 1997, has continued to follow the market reform plans of his predecessor, President Rafsanjani, and has indicated that he will pursue diversification of Iran's oil-reliant economy, although he has made little progress toward that goal so far, mainly because of Iran's dependence on oil and the decline in oil prices in the first 2 years of his government. A broad program of economic adjustment and reform was issued in August 1998 to form the Third 5 Year Development Plan (2000–05). It involves restoring market-based prices, reducing the size of the public sector and encouraging private sector investment. As a result, domestic petroleum prices were raised by 70 percent in 1999, and a more market-based official exchange rate was introduced on the Tehran Stock Exchange (TSE).

The recovery of oil prices during 1999–2000 significantly strengthened Iran's external and financial position. Although annual GDP growth remained weak at 2.4 percent and the **inflation rate** remained almost unchanged at 20 percent, the government incurred a large **budget surplus** of about US$4.7 billion and hurried to pay **external debt**, reducing outstanding debt to about 10 percent of the GDP. The Third 5 Year Development Plan aims at accelerating growth to an average annual rate of 6 percent in order to create sufficient employment opportunities for the rapidly growing **labor force**, which currently increases by an estimated 5 percent every year.

POLITICS, GOVERNMENT, AND TAXATION

The Islamic revolution of 1979, during which the monarch, Shah Mohammed Reza Pahlavi, was driven out of the country, brought the Shiite clergy to power with Ayatollah Ruhollah Khomeini as its charismatic leader. Following the revolution, Iran adopted a constitution based on Ayatollah Khomeini's theory of Islamic government. The constitution ratified by popular referendum established a theocratic (from ancient Greek, literally meaning "the rule of God") republic and declared as its purpose the establishment of institutions and a society based on Islamic principles and norms, adopting the shari'a (Islamic law) as the basis for the country's legal system. The Constitution of the Islamic Republic provided for a *Vali-ye Faqih*, a Supreme Leader of the Islamic Revolution. Since the death of Ayatollah Khomeini, in 1989, this office has been held by Ayatollah Ali Khamenei. The Supreme Leader still enjoys primary control of many organs of the state and has the right to appoint key officials such as heads of the judiciary, the broadcast media, the armed forces, and various revolutionary bodies, as well as the power to supervise the overall policies of the regime.

The 1979 constitution created an Islamic Consultative Assembly called the Majlis, Iran's most democratic legislature in its history. Its 290 members are elected by universal adult suffrage—men and women from the age of 16 are eligible to vote—and serve for 4-year terms. The Majlis develops and passes legislation that is reviewed for adherence to Islamic and constitutional principles by a Council of Guardians, which consists of 6 clerical members. These are appointed by the Supreme Leader and 6 jurists, who in turn are appointed by the head of the judiciary and approved by the Majlis. The constitution provides the Council of Guardians with the power to disqualify candidates for elective offices based on a set of requirements, including the candidates' ideological beliefs.

The country's president is elected by popular vote to a 4-year term and has the power to appoint a cabinet known as the Council of Ministers, with the approval of the legislature. Mohammad Khatami was elected in elections held on 3 August 1997.

Political parties, legalized in 1998 after a 13-year ban, are still at an early stage of development. Nevertheless, factions within the ruling hierarchy, particularly in the Majlis, are increasingly visible. While these are most often defined broadly as "reformist" or "conservative," political allegiances do exist based on patronage, loyalties, specific interests, and the exchange of favors.

Several agencies share responsibility for internal security, including the Ministry of Intelligence and Security, the Ministry of Interior, and the Revolutionary Guards, a military force that was established after the revolution. Paramilitary volunteer forces known as Basijis, and groupings, known as the Ansar-e Hezbollah (Helpers of the Party of God), who often are aligned with specific members of the leadership, act as watchdogs, intimidating and physically threatening demonstrators, journalists, and individuals suspected of counterrevolutionary activities. According to Amnesty International and Human Rights Watch, both regular and paramilitary security forces committed numerous serious human rights abuses. Iranians also suffer from violations of freedom of expression. Iran's conservative-dominated judiciary waged an extensive campaign against the local reformist press, closing newspapers and prosecuting critical journalists throughout 2000.

HISTORICAL BACKGROUND. Although briefly occupied during World War II by Soviet and British troops, Iran is 1 of only 2 countries in the Middle East that were never colonized (the other being Saudi Arabia). However, the country's geopolitical significance—Iran has the longest Gulf shoreline and is a vital link between Asia, the Middle East and Europe—has made it of central concern to the world's most powerful empires and a target for frequent political manipulation. Following the occupation of Iran by allied forces during World War II, Iran's Pahlavi ruler, Reza Shah, was forced to abdicate in favor of his son, Mohammed Reza.

Mohammed Reza Pahlavi sought to ally Iran closely with Western powers and particularly with the United States. However, growing nationalist sentiment in Iran forced him to appoint the nationalist Mohammed Mossadeq as prime minister in 1951. Prime Minister Mossadeq **nationalized** the Anglo-Iranian Oil Company (AIOC) the same year, sidelining the shah politically. Alarmed at the threat the nationalist leader posed to their position in the Gulf and the broader Middle East, the Western powers imposed an oil **embargo** on Iranian exports, crippling the government. This was followed in 1953 by support from the U.S. Central Intelligence Agency (CIA) and the British counter-intelligence agency, MI6, for a successful coup, which overthrew Mossadeq and returned authority to the shah. Mohammed Reza subsequently initiated a massive modernization program, known as the "white revolution," accompanied by a greater centralization of power and increased use of repression to subdue political dissent. In 1964 the government exiled the cleric Ayatollah Khomeini after a series of his speeches led to widespread rioting.

The oil price explosion of 1973–74 fueled rapid economic growth, but at the cost of increased volatility in the Iranian economy and high levels of inflation. Economic hardship, the growing dominance of Western culture—which traditional Iranians found offensive—and the government's repressive security methods brought about an increasingly determined collection of opposition groups. Unifying into an anti-monarchist coalition with Ayatollah Khomeini as their figurehead, these activists organized nation-wide demonstrations and strikes, culminating in the overthrow of the Pahlavi dynasty in February 1979 and the return of Khomeini from exile. Following a popular vote, Iran became a self-styled "Islamic Republic" in March 1979.

International opinion turned strongly against the new government in November 1979, when militant students seized the U.S. embassy in Tehran and held 52 people hostage for more than a year. In September 1980, Iraqi forces invaded Iran, hoping for an easy victory that would allow the annexation of Iranian territory around the strategically important Shatt al-Arab waterway. While remaining neutral, the Western powers, together with many Arab states, assisted Iraq in order to suppress Khomeini's Islamic state. Until August 1988, when Iran finally accepted a U.N. cease-fire resolution, the 2 countries engaged in one of the bloodiest wars of the century, suffering widespread human and economic losses. Ayatollah Khomeini died in June 1989, and the Council of Experts, a clerical body empowered to choose the next Supreme Leader, selected Hojatoleslam Seyyed Ali Khamenei as Khomeini's successor, rapidly promoting him to the clerical rank of Ayatollah (literally: Sign of God). Hojatoleslam Ali Rafsanjani won the presidential election in August of the same year.

Since the amendment of the constitution in 1989 the president has appointed the government, though all ministers must be approved by the parliament before taking office. Iran's domestic politics have since evolved into an increasingly bitter power struggle between conservatives and reformers within the regime. From 1989 to 1997, President Rafsanjani sought to implement a program of gradual economic and political reform, but his more conservative rivals frequently blocked his policies. In 1997, the reform-orientated cleric, Mohammad Khatami, was elected to a 4-year term as president in a landslide victory and is set to stand a second term in June 2001 after winning the election with a great majority, almost 77 percent of the votes cast. Though with a turnout at the polls of only 65 percent of eligible voters, after 90 percent in the 1997 election, people seem to be disillusioned by politics and the pace of reform. Mohammed Khatami's reform-orientated supporters also defeated the conservatives in the parliamentary election held in February 2000, gaining majority control. Nevertheless, the power struggle with the conservatives continues. Through their control of various oversight institutions, the judiciary and state-run broadcasting, they manage to contain power.

INFRASTRUCTURE, POWER, AND COMMUNICATIONS

Iran's infrastructure is relatively poor and inadequate. Part of this stems from the fact that the vast country was never fully developed, but it also experienced considerable setbacks during the Iran-Iraq war of the 1980s, and restoration since then has been slow.

TRANSPORTATION. Iran has a network of 140,200 kilometers (87,120 miles) of roads, of which 49,440 kilometers (30,722 miles) are paved. The 2,500-kilometer (1,553-mile) A1 highway runs from Bazargan on the Turkish border across Iran to the Afghan border in the east. The A2 runs from the Iraqi border to Mirjaveh on the Pakistani frontier. Tehran is linked to major cities in the vicinity by 470 kilometers (292 miles) of expressways. A heavy expansion of car use has led to increased demand for fuel, severe overcrowding of roads in metropolitan areas, and mounting pollution problems. Government estimates put the average annual increase in domestic fuel consumption at 5.5 percent, well above the real economic growth rate. The government has sought to limit motor use by raising domestic fuel prices, but petroleum products in Iran remain heavily subsidized and among the cheapest in the world.

An important transportation link is the railway constructed with great effort before World War II between the Caspian Sea, Tehran, and the Persian Gulf. Other rail links with neighboring countries already exist or are un-

Communications

Country	Newspapers	Radios	TV Sets[a]	Cable subscribers[a]	Mobile Phones[a]	Fax Machines[a]	Personal Computers[a]	Internet Hosts[b]	Internet Users[b]
	1996	1997	1998	1998	1998	1998	1998	1999	1999
Iran	28	265	157	0.0	6	N/A	31.9	0.05	100
United States	215	2,146	847	244.3	256	78.4	458.6	1,508.77	74,100
Saudi Arabia	57	321	262	N/A	31	N/A	49.6	1.17	300
Iraq	19	229	83	N/A	0	N/A	N/A	0.00	N/A

[a]Data are from International Telecommunication Union, *World Telecommunication Development Report 1999* and are per 1,000 people.

[b]Data are from the Internet Software Consortium (http://www.isc.org) and are per 10,000 people.

SOURCE: World Bank. *World Development Indicators 2000.*

der construction. Recently the long-closed link to Van in Eastern Turkey reopened, enabling passengers and goods to travel from Tehran to Istanbul and on to Europe. Overall, the Iranian railway network covers 5,600 kilometers (3,480 miles).

The Shatt al-Arab, the main waterway shared by Iran and Iraq on the Persian Gulf, is navigable by maritime traffic for about 130 kilometers (81 miles). Ports include Abadan/Khorramshahr, which was largely destroyed in fighting during the Iran-Iraq war, and has been overtaken by Bandar Abbas as the country's major port. About 12 million tons of cargo pass through Iran's Gulf ports each year. Smaller ports at Bushehr, Bandar Lengeh, and Chah Bahar have also assumed new importance. The 1998 Lloyd's Register of Shipping lists 382 Iranian merchant vessels.

The 3 major international airports of Tehran, Bandar Abbas, and Abadan, have recently been joined by the international airports on the free-trade islands of Qeshm and Kish. Most domestic and international flights go through Mehrabad international airport in Tehran. The huge Imam Khomeini international airport to the south of Tehran, currently under construction, is going to take over operations in a few years with a projected capacity of 30 million passengers a year. The state-owned national carrier, Iran Air, serves 15 Iranian cities and runs scheduled routes in the Gulf, Asia, and Europe. In 1997 it carried 907,000 international and 6,240,000 domestic passengers.

POWER. Electricity generation was severely restricted by Iraqi attacks on power stations during the Iran-Iraq War, reducing available capacity from 8,000 MW to 5,000 MW, according to estimates. In December 1988, the Ministry of Energy stated that the general capacity of the national grid was deficient by at least 2,500 MW, owing to war damage, lack of fuel, and inadequate rainfall. At the beginning of the 1990s, residential consumption accounted for about 40 percent of total consumption, and industry for about one-quarter. However, industrial demand rose dramatically and accounted for almost half of total consumption in 1998. Overall consumption reached 90 billion kilowatt hours (kWh) in 1998, up from 73.4 billion kWh in 1994. Installed power production capacity had reached about 24,000 MW, with another 4,600 MW coming from private generators.

Iran plans to increase this capacity to 96,000 MW by 2022. Power plants currently under construction, and due for completion by 2002, will add about 13,000 MW to the national grid. Some 8,000 MW of this will come from hydroelectric (turbines powered by water that generate electricity) dams, although the proportion of hydroelectricity will fall in subsequent years. The balance of 5,000 MW under construction comes from gas-fuelled plants and other facilities. Currently, some 89.5 percent of electricity is produced by thermal power plants (using fossil fuels like coal, oil, or gas) and the rest by hydroelectric stations. Recent years have seen Iran advancing on a nuclear power program of 3,000–5,000 MW. The United States stated that nuclear cooperation and the transfer of technology to Iran was dangerous, as it would accelerate a secret program to develop nuclear weapons. Nevertheless, Chinese and Russian officials have expressed their determination to proceed with deals aimed at selling nuclear reactors to Iran.

TELECOMMUNICATIONS. As a result of heavy investment in the telephone services since 1994, the number of long-distance channels has grown substantially; many villages have been brought into the net. The number of main lines in the urban systems has approximately doubled since 1994, and the technical level of the system has been raised by the installation of thousands of digital switches. Countrywide, there were some 7 million lines in 1998. There is now also a mobile cellular system in place that was serving 265,000 subscribers in August 1998. This figure is up from under 60,000 in 1996 and has grown rapidly since.

Iran has radio relays to Turkey, Azerbaijan, Pakistan, Afghanistan, Turkmenistan, Syria, Kuwait, Tajikistan, and Uzbekistan. The fiber-optic Trans Asia Europe line runs through northern Iran, and the country is also connected to the Fiber-optic Link Around the Globe (FLAG) through a submarine fiber-optic cable link to the United Arab Emirates.

Internet access is increasing. However, price rather than official censorship remains the greatest hindrance to wider use. The state remains in control of terrestrial radio and television broadcasts, but the illegal use of satellite television receivers in urban areas continues to be widespread. There were 82 radio stations in 1998, and Iranians had 17 million radios. Television receivers numbered 4.9 million.

ECONOMIC SECTORS

Iran's economy clearly relies on its natural resources, and most importantly, oil. Agriculture still contributed 21 percent to the GDP in 1999, while industry accounted for 34 percent, and services for 45 percent. About one-third of the labor force is engaged in agriculture (33 percent); industry employs 25 percent of the workforce and 42 percent are occupied in services. Except for petroleum and petrochemical industries, Iran also has industrial production in steel, textiles, cement and other construction materials, food processing (especially sugar refining and vegetable oil production), metal fabricating, and armaments.

After the Islamic revolution in 1979, Iran nationalized all major industries, banks, and insurance companies. It committed itself to heavy investment in both the agricultural sector and selected industries, with the ultimate goal of economic independence, but unstable internal conditions and the war with Iraq made economic growth almost unattainable until the mid-1990s. The revival of oil production helped stabilize national finances, and free-market initiatives and reforms sparked a rise in domestic agricultural and industrial production.

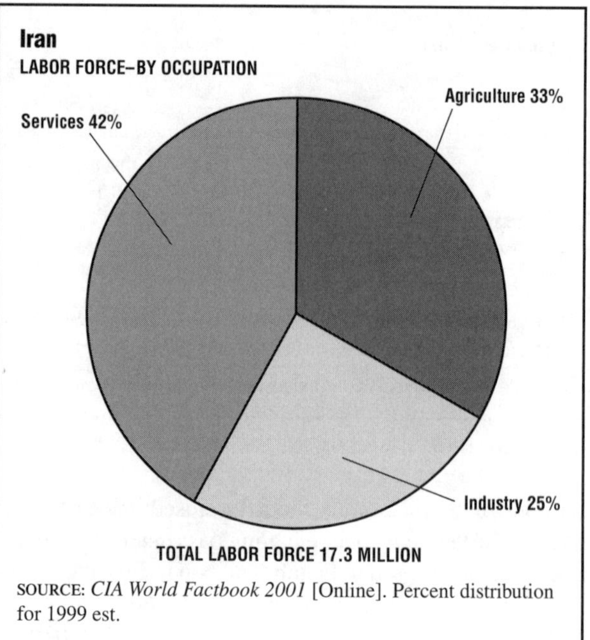

SOURCE: *CIA World Factbook 2001* [Online]. Percent distribution for 1999 est.

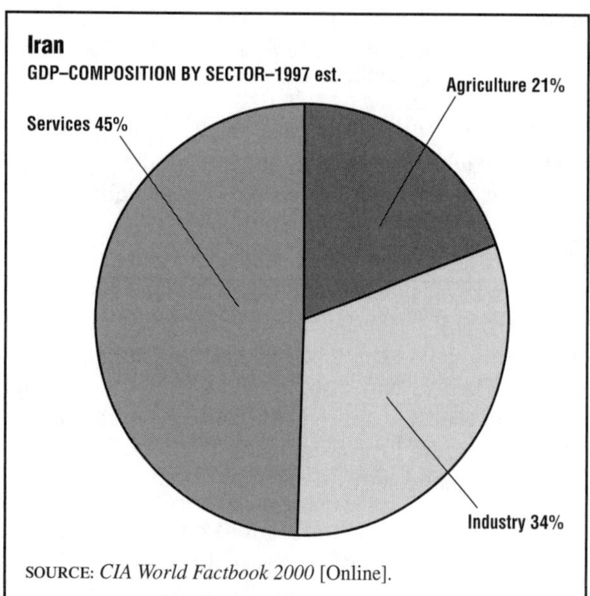

SOURCE: *CIA World Factbook 2000* [Online].

AGRICULTURE

Iran is a mostly arid or semi-arid country, with a subtropical climate along the Caspian coast. Deforestation, **desertification**, overgrazing, and pollution from vehicle emissions and industrial operations have harmed the land over the last few decades and hampered production. Other significant problems include poor cultivation methods, lack of water, and limited access to markets. Iran's agricultural sector is especially dependent on changes in rainfall, and although the government has attempted to reduce this dependence through the construction of dams, irrigation and drainage networks, agriculture remains highly sensitive to climate developments. Still, the agricultural sector accounts for about one-fifth of the GDP and employs one-third of the workforce. The country's most important crops are wheat, rice, other grains, sugar beets, fruits, nuts, cotton, and tobacco. Iran also produces dairy products, wool, and a large amount of timber. Irrigated areas are fed from modern water-storage systems or from the ancient system of qanat. Qanat are underground water channels stretching up to 40 kilometers (26 mi) and first used at least 2000 years ago. Unfortunately, many of them have fallen into disrepair in recent years.

The centerpiece of the "white revolution," during which the shah pressed the modernization of Iran during the 1960s, was land reform. Until the 1950s, only about 5 percent of peasants owned sufficient land to maintain themselves. The dominant figures in rural areas were the landowners; it is estimated that about half of Iran's cultivated land was held by big landowners, those who controlled one or more villages, a typical holding being between 20 and 40 villages (there were some 70,000 villages altogether). These landowners were absentees and included members of the royal family, military officers, tribal shaykhs, religious dignitaries, and big merchants. The land reform, which began in 1961 and was not completed until 1971, had dramatic effects. The power and influence of large landowners was extinguished; smaller absentee landowners survived and in 1971 still owned half of all cultivated land. Seemingly, the benefits went to those 50 percent of peasants who had cultivation rights. By 1971, 90 percent of them were owners of land, though it turned out that for most of them acquired holdings were too small to support a family. Farm laborers remained without rights and holdings.

The traditional dominance of agriculture was eroded by oil and gas exploitation, which became the country's major source of export revenues as population growth made Iran a net importer of foodstuffs. The agricultural sector has nevertheless usually been the largest contributor to the GDP, its share falling only slightly in the 1990s, from 23.9 percent in 1992–93 to 19.7 percent in 1997–98, when it was overtaken by the industrial sector. In 1999–2000, real growth in the sector declined by 0.3 percent, production of cotton fell by 9 percent, and wheat and barley outputs declined by 27 percent and 39 percent, respectively. This came after the successful year of 1998–99, when a rise in rainfall led to sharp overall growth in the sector, achieving 9.5 percent growth. The government continues to gear efforts toward reducing its role in agriculture and encouraging private sector activities and the growth of cooperatives, while restricting itself to the provision of infrastructure. **Subsidies** have been reduced over the last few years, but agriculture remains favored with price guarantees and persisting subsidies, in particular for wheat.

The offshore fishing industry is important in Iran both for domestic consumption and for export, mainly of caviar. The total Iranian fish catch rose from 327,727 metric tons in the year 1991–92 to 385,200 tons in 1997–98, of which 244,000 tons came from the Persian Gulf and the Gulf of Oman, 76,200 tons from the Caspian Sea, and 65,000 tons from inland waters. The government remains committed to increasing the annual catch to at least 700,000 tons, principally by the development of fisheries in southern waters. The caviar industry, which enjoys a worldwide market, is by far the most developed field within Iran's fisheries sector. Iran, Russia, Azerbaijan, Kazakhstan, and Turkmenistan form a cartel to protect caviar prices and sturgeon stocks in the Caspian Sea, but over-fishing has begun to threaten the industry. Caviar exports averaged around US$30 million per year in the 1990s.

INDUSTRY

Petroleum and natural gas clearly dominate Iranian industry, which is mostly controlled by the state or run by one of the religious foundations, the bonyad. With the revolution came nationalization, and by the end of 1982, 130 nationalized industries were under the direct control of the 3 ministries that were authorized to conduct industrial policies, and 450 industrial units were placed under the control of the National Iranian Industrial Organization.

MINING/HYDROCARBONS. Iranians became involved with oil before most of the rest of the world, granting their first exploration concession to British prospectors in 1901. After the discovery of commercially viable deposits at Masjid-e Suleiman in 1908, the reserves were worked by the newly formed Anglo-Persian Oil Company, which changed its name to the Anglo-Iranian Oil Company (AIOC) in 1935 and is now known as BP Amoco. The oil industry's pivotal position in modern Iranian society was demonstrated during the 1979 revolution, when a series of strikes at oil installations culminated in the strikers' refusal to resume exports until the shah left the country. Iran's petroleum industry suffered extensive damage to wells, refineries, and export terminals with the outbreak of the Iran-Iraq war in 1980. Crude oil production recovered to 3.2 million barrels per day (bpd) in 1990 and since 1994 has averaged around 3.6–3.7 million bpd. Proven oil reserves at the end of 1998 totaled 90 billion barrels, representing 8.7 percent of world reserves, and were expected to last about 70 years at current production rates. As of January 2000, Iran possessed 9 operational refineries with an aggregate capacity of 1.5 million bpd, the government's aim being to boost refining capacity to 2 million bpd during its Third 5 Year Development Plan (until 2005).

The dramatic decrease in world oil prices from late 1997, to below early 1973 levels in real terms, prompted the Organization of Petroleum Exporting Countries (OPEC, a cartel grouping together most significant oil producing countries to fix production quotas and attempt to stabilize prices) to decree that its members should reduce production from April 1998 in an effort to boost prices. In March 1999 Iran agreed to cut its output from the benchmark of an average production of 3.6 million bpd by 7.3 percent, to 3.36 million bpd. In their September meeting OPEC countries decided to retain reduced quotas despite the sharp rise in world oil prices. When in March 2000 OPEC responded to what was seen as a dangerously high world oil price of US$30 per barrel by increasing aggregate production quotas by 1.7 million bpd, only Iran declined to accept the plan proposed by Saudi Arabia, on the grounds that OPEC was buckling to U.S. pressure for lower oil prices. However, resistance was short, and the new Iranian production quota had increased to 3.84 million bpd by September 2000. As a result of the production cuts in 1999, exports fell by 10 percent from 1998–99 to 1999–2000, to 2.1 million bpd. Thanks to higher prices, however, oil export revenues increased by 63 percent to US$16.3 billion and are expected to hit the US$20 billion in 2000–01.

Iran's petroleum industry basically works as an extension of the government. The Minister of Petroleum serves as chairman of the 3 main companies, the National Iranian Oil Co. (NIOC), the National Iranian Gas Co. (NIGC), and the National Petrochemical Co. (NPC). The NIOC handles oil and gas exploration, production, refining, and oil transportation; NIGC manages gathering, processing, transmission, distribution, and exports of gas and gas liquids; and NPC handles petrochemical production, distribution, and exports. The majority of Iran's oilfields are concentrated in the southwest of the country, where 90 percent of Iran's total production of crude oil is produced. The state-owned gathering and distributing system for natural gas from Iran's enormous reserves—second in the world only to Russia's—is one of the largest in the Middle East. Other mineral resources are largely underdeveloped.

With proven natural gas reserves of 23 trillion cubic meters (at the end of 1999), Iran is the world's second richest country in gas resources after Russia, with some 15.7 percent of the global total and 46.4 percent of the Middle East regional total. Production increased from 12.2 billion cubic meters in 1989 to 29.5 billion cubic meters in 1993 and to 54 billion cubic meters in 1998, the bulk of which was consumed domestically in line with the government's policy of substituting gas for petroleum. Currently, natural gas accounts for about 40 percent of total domestic energy consumption. Iran plans to construct a 1000-kilometer (621-mile) onshore and 1200-kilometer (746-mile) offshore gas pipeline to India. In 1996, Iran signed an agreement worth US$20 billion to supply gas to Turkey over a 22-year period. With pipeline construction in its final stage, deliveries should begin in mid-2001. In April 2000, the discovery of the country's biggest onshore gas field to date, north of the city of Bushehr, was announced. It is estimated to contain 445,000 million cubic meters of gas not needing to be refined, as well as 240 million barrels of liquid gas. The field is to be brought to production by 2002 and is expected to yield revenue of US$16.5 billion over 20 years.

In addition to the enormous hydrocarbon reserves, Iran has considerable mineral resources. Around 80 million tons of minerals are quarried each year from some 1,500 non-metallic and 50 metallic mines in Iran, with the bulk coming from mines owned by the Bonyad-e Mostazafan (Foundation of the Oppressed). Minerals currently being worked include copper, lead-zinc, iron ore, bauxite, coal, strontium, gold, chromium, uranium, red oxide, turquoise, sulphur, and salt. Foreign investors have concentrated most on Iran's copper-extraction industry, which has taken the lead in moves towards privatization.

MANUFACTURING. Iran's industrial sector is dominated by relatively few but large public enterprises accounting for approximately 70 percent of **value added** in manufacturing. Steel, petrochemicals, and copper remain the country's 3 basic industries. Other important branches are automobile manufacturing (mainly assembled under license from Western or Japanese manufacturers), construction material, textiles (mainly woven carpets, for which Iran has traditionally been famous), food processing, and pharmaceuticals. Despite large investments in the 1970s, problems persist to this day, including a shortage of skilled labor, insufficient raw materials and spare parts, and an inadequate infrastructure.

After the revolution in 1979, no clear policy was formulated for the industrial sector. Subsequently, then-president Bani-Sadr estimated a drop of at least 34 percent in industrial output in the first post-revolutionary year alone. The manufacturing industries' poor performance continued throughout the 1980s with many factories still operating at only 30 percent of their capacity at the end of the decade. Much of this downturn had to do with the **emigration** of industrial owners and a resulting shortage of managerial skills. The high degree of Iran's dependency on imports for raw materials, along with the economic sanctions imposed against the Islamic Republic, further increased the vulnerability of the manufacturing sector. Taken together, these factors resulted in inefficiency and low productivity.

The steel industry is one of the few exceptions to Iran's disappointing manufacturing scene. Development began late—Iran's first steel mill was a **joint venture** with the Soviet Union in the 1960s—and proceeded slowly, with output standing at just 1 million tons per year in 1979. Since the end of the Iran-Iraq war, however, a huge expansion has taken place. New plants have been commissioned in Khuzestan, Khorasan, and Azerbaijan provinces, and Iran has become the world's third largest steel producer, with an output of 6.7 million tons in 1997–98.

In recent years the government has placed great emphasis on expanding the petrochemical industry to generate products of higher value added and higher export earnings. In the medium term the petrochemical industry represents Iran's only chance of diversifying away from crude oil exports. Iranian petrochemical production has more than doubled in the last 5 years, making it the second largest producer in the region, after Saudi Arabia. Total petrochemical output was estimated at about 12 million tons in 1998, compared to 2.4 million tons in 1989. The government plans to triple the annual output to 30 million tons within 20 years, which requires investments of US$20 billion. Government predictions were that Iran's share of the world's petrochemical production would reach 2 percent by 2005 and that the value of exports would rise from US$500 million in 1999 to US$2 billion in 2005. Main petrochemical products are fertilizers, methanol, aromatics, and olefins.

The automotive sector is underdeveloped. The most common vehicle on Iran's roads is the Paykan, the locally produced version of a 1960s British model. The car's old-fashioned engineering makes it inefficient and one of the worst polluters in the country. Since 1989, the industry has enjoyed a modest recovery, as local plants have contracted to assemble Nissan, Peugeot, and Kia models under license. Some manufacturers, such as Iran Khodro, which held the rights to assemble General Motors vehicles until 1985, have begun to modernize and **restructure**. Local production of cars reached 245,556 units in 2000–01, compared to some 80,000 units in 1995–96, and up 23 percent from the previous year. However, poor access to finance and a shallow inventory suggest that there is further need for improvement.

In 1995, the Chamber of Commerce and Industry reported that Iran's textile mills were operating at an average of 56 percent of their capacity, owing to shortage of foreign exchange and raw material. The textiles industry is partly based on domestic supply of cotton. During the 1970s, European manufacturers purchased Iranian cotton, but as profits fell in the 1980s, most cotton was absorbed domestically. The government hopes to promote textile exports, and some public investment has been devoted to improving production quality. However, the results have been visible only in niche areas, and export earnings in 1997–98 remained below US$100 million per year. Revenues from exporting carpets dropped severely in the 1990s from US$2 billion in 1990 to US$570 million in 1998, rendering it a shaky business.

SERVICES

The services sector is the largest in the Iranian economy and contributed approximately 40 percent to the GDP during 1999–2000. The sector has seen the greatest long-term growth in terms of its share of the GDP, but currency-exchange restrictions, excessive bureaucracy, and the uncertainty of long-term planning have hindered further development.

FINANCIAL SERVICES. The Iranian banking sector is dominated by 10 state-owned banks, including the 6 full-service commercial banks, and 4 sectorally specialized ones. In addition, 4 small private non-bank credit institutions have recently been licensed. The total number of state-owned bank branches was 14,518 in 1999, compared with 11,634 in 1995. Commercial banks engage mainly in short-term lending, primarily to the private sector and public non-bank financial enterprises, and act as agents of depositors in the investment of funds. The profits and losses from these investments are then distributed to depositors based on the duration and amount of their investment. Specialized banks lend mainly on a long-term basis (5 years or more) and have investments in various sectors of the economy.

After the revolution, 2 major changes were made in the banking system: one was nationalization and restructuring in the year immediately after the revolution, the other was the introduction of Islamic banking in 1983–84. Islamic banking is characterized by the prohibition of interest on loans, according to Islamic law. Interest on loans, or *riba*, was replaced by a commission of 4 percent a year compared with the traditional 14 percent, whereas interest on deposits was replaced with profits, estimated at a minimum of 7–8 percent a year. The banks would become temporary shareholders in major industrial enterprises to which they lent money. Unfortunately, the changes to the banking sector were made just when the public sector was relying heavily on the banking system to finance the large deficit, due to low oil revenues. Consequently, the inflation rate accelerated rapidly. While it amounted to only 4 percent in 1985–86, it surged to 21 percent the following year, and increased to 28 percent and 29 percent, respectively, during 1987–88 and 1988–89 and has since remained at a high level.

The Tehran Stock Exchange (TSE) benefitted from a wave of privatization during the early 1990s. Stock **market capitalization** of IR38 trillion at the end of 1999 corresponded to about 9 percent of the GDP, although relatively few of the shares are routinely available for purchase by the general public. The ownership of stocks is highly concentrated. The largest 5 shareholders account, together, for more than 82 percent of company shareholdings. A small handful of institutional investors dominate the market as a whole. These are all either government institutions or state-owned banks or their subsidiaries, but nevertheless operating on a market-oriented basis.

COMMERCE. Iran has traditionally been an agricultural nation populated by traders. With the exception of the carpet industry and a tiny jewelry industry, the Iranian economy was essentially agrarian until the time of Reza Shah Pahlavi. Despite the crash industrialization program launched by the Pahlavi regime in the 1960s and 1970s and the necessity for self-sufficiency during Iran's 8-year war with Iraq, the country retains its preference for trade over production.

The merchant, or bazaar, classes had profited from the economic boom Iran experienced under the shah in the 1970s. Many had amassed fortunes in these years. Yet, the bazaar provided valuable support to the revolutionary movement, contributing generously to the clerical cause in the lead-up to the revolution. The bazaar merchants had several grievances against the shah, whose policies favored a new industrial and entrepreneurial elite, and import licenses made life difficult for the smaller merchants. The bazaar was relegated to secondary status, especially after some of the major industrial families started combining interests in industry with interests in banking, insurance, and trade by the mid-1970s; several of the largest trading companies developed alongside major industrial enterprises. These new trading companies threatened to drive the bazaar merchants out of wholesale trade, and then, by establishing new **retail** networks and outlets, out of retail trade as well.

After the revolution, the trading sector achieved positive growth, and this sector absorbed most of the new entrants into the job market. In the absence of a properly functioning banking system, demand for capital has been frequently met from moneylenders in the bazaar. Indeed, currency exchange and money lending has become a major source of business for the bazaar's traders in Iran's distorted economy. This further intensified a tendency among Iranians to invest in businesses with a cash-based return, such as constructing homes for the rental market or the import of **consumer goods**.

TOURISM. Before the revolution Iran had begun to build a reputation as an exotic holiday destination; its ski resorts at Shemshak and Dizin, north of Tehran, attracted international celebrities. After 1979, the Islamic government discouraged tourism, leaving many renowned archaeological and historical sites, including Persepolis, Pasargard, and Esfahan, barely visited by foreigners. Although hardly a booming sector, visitor rates are beginning to rise. The government has begun to issue visas more freely to non-Muslim individuals and groups, and the country is appearing with greater frequency in tourism brochures, but still only around 320,000 foreign tourists actually visit, bringing in revenue of US$170 million. The bulk of tourism remains to be founded on Shia pilgrimage centers such as Mashhad and Qom. The Bonyad-e Mostazafan (Foundation of the Oppressed), which owns most of Iran's large hotels, plans to increase the number of hotel beds from the current 34,500 to 59,500 by 2002.

INTERNATIONAL TRADE

Following a strong **balance of payments** performance in 1996–97, mainly due to high oil prices, the period 1997–99 witnessed the deterioration of Iran's external accounts, triggered by tumbling oil prices and stagnant non-oil exports. Imports went down due to the resulting scarcity of foreign exchange, and Iran negotiated re-phasing part of its external debt in 1998 in order to alleviate financial pressure. When oil prices recovered during 1999–2000, and non-oil exports also grew by 9 percent, the Islamic Republic's external position was enhanced considerably. Iran's trade balance had dropped from a surplus of US$2.8 billion in 1996–97 to a deficit of US$4 billion in 1997–98, although this was reversed again into a US$2 billion surplus in 1999–2000. The International Monetary Fund (IMF) in its 2000 country report on Iran estimated that exports during 1999–2000 totaled US$19.726 billion, while total imports that year amounted to US$13.511 billion. Changes in Iran's external balance are mainly dependent on oil prices. Thus, in 1999–2000, proceeds from crude oil exports rose by 60 percent, despite a decline in the export volume, reflecting the 77 percent increase in the average export price of Iranian crude oil.

Trade (expressed in billions of US$): Iran

	Exports	Imports
1975	7.963	10.343
1980	7.109	12.246
1985	13.328	11.635
1990	19.305	20.322
1995	18.360	13.882
1998	N/A	N/A

SOURCE: International Monetary Fund. *International Financial Statistics Yearbook 1999.*

Non-oil exports consist mainly of consumer goods (55 percent on average during 1997–2000), followed by raw materials and **intermediate goods** (about 38 percent). Carpets remain the single most exported Iranian non-oil product. Such exports have declined significantly over the second half of the 1990s, from US$2 billion in 1994 to US$570 million in 1998, which is attributed to competition from low-priced carpet-producing countries. Exports of fresh and dried fruits, at about US$600 million in 1998–99 (of which $416 million came from pistachios alone), have captured a larger share of the total. Chemicals are the most prominent export of raw materials and intermediate goods, hovering at about US$500 million during 1997–2000.

The direction of exports has also remained unchanged since the mid-1990s. While Japan and the United Kingdom are the largest importers of Iranian goods (absorbing about 16 percent and 17 percent of total exports, respectively), Germany and the United Arab Emirates (UAE) are the main destinations for non-oil exports, capturing 13 percent and 16 percent of these exports, respectively. Other important destinations for Iranian exports are Italy (6 percent of non-oil exports and 9 percent of total exports), Greece and South Korea (5 percent of total exports), and Turkey (5 percent of non-oil exports).

Iran imports mainly raw materials and intermediate and **capital goods**. Imports of consumer goods, at about US$2 billion per year, represent only 14 percent of total imports. Imports of machinery and tools average about US$4–5 billion, which cover the bulk of capital goods imports. Iran's imports of grains and derivatives fell drastically in 1998–99 from about US$1.8 billion the previous years to below US$900 million. Iran also imports a large quantity of chemical products, totaling about US$1.8–2 billion per annum. The most important sources of Iranian imports are Germany (12 percent), Japan (7 percent), and Italy (6 percent).

Since Iran's first application to join the World Trade Organization (WTO) in 1996, it has been constantly blocked by the United States. The application was blocked again in May of 2001, but the administration of U.S. President George W. Bush is thought to be considering dropping its objection now that Egypt has sponsored Iran's application. Iran is a founding member of the Asian Clearing Union (ACU), established in 1974 to provide a mechanism for the settlement of transactions among countries in the Asia-Pacific region. Members are Bangladesh, Burma, India, Nepal, Pakistan, Sri Lanka, and Bhutan. Iran undertakes only about 3 percent of its total trade within the ACU, with Bangladesh, India, Pakistan, and Sri Lanka importing oil and oil products, handicrafts, and machinery equipment. Iran's imports from these countries include machinery, spare parts, and spices from India, jute from Bangladesh, and rice and cotton from Pakistan.

MONEY

The Bank-e Merkazi-ye Jomhuri-ye Eslami-ye Iran, or Central Bank of the Islamic Republic of Iran, is the highest monetary authority in the country. Each year after the approval of the government's annual budget, the Central Bank presents a detailed monetary and credit policy. Short-term credit policies need to be approved by the government and long-term credit policies have to be incorporated into the 5 Year Development Plan with Parliament's consent.

After the introduction of the Tehran Stock Exchange (TSE) rate in July 1997 and until March 2000, 2 officially recognized exchange rates coexisted in Iran. The official rate of the Iranian rial—1,750 per U.S. dollar—applies to oil and gas export receipts, imports of essential goods and services, and repayment of external debt. The "export" rate, fixed at 3,000 rials per dollar since May 1995, applied to all other trade transactions, but mainly to capital goods imports of public enterprises. In order to ease pressure on exporters, the bank introduced a currency certificate system allowing exporters to trade certificates for **hard currency** on the Tehran Stock Exchange (TSE). This method finally replaced the fixed export rate in March 2000, and has since held steady at some IR8,500:US$1. There is an active black market in foreign exchange, but the development of the TSE rate and the ready availability of foreign exchange over 2000 narrowed the differential to as little as IR100 in mid-2000. The reunification of Iran's multi-tiered exchange-rate system, which has plagued Iran's non-oil exports and frustrated potential investors since the revolution, had been under discussion since a failed attempt in 1993 to operate a single, **floating exchange rate**. At the same time, as a step toward further liberalization and integration of foreign exchange markets, banks were allowed to deal relatively freely with foreign exchange. Despite this, foreign currency is still hard to get and even harder to keep for ordinary Iranians.

Given recent government decisions to allow banks to sell currency at free-market rates, together with the positive outlook for oil earnings, and the apparent willingness of new lenders, particularly European banks, to extend new credit lines to Iran, an attempt at reunification is likely to be made in 2001–02, at a rate of around IR9,000=US$1.

Exchange rates: Iran

Iranian rials (IR) per US$1	
Jan 2001	1,754.71
2000	1,764.43
1999	1,725.93
1998	1,751.86
1997	1,752.92
1996	1,750.76

Note: Iran has three officially recognized exchange rates; the averages for 1999 are as follows: the official floating rate of 1,750 rials per US dollar, the "export" rate of 3,000 rials per US dollar, and the variable Tehran Stock Exchange rate, which averages 7,863 rials per US dollar; the market rate averages 8,615 rials per US dollar.

SOURCE: CIA *World Factbook 2001* [ONLINE].

POVERTY AND WEALTH

Before the Islamic revolution, Iran had gradually been transformed from a largely farm-based economy to a modern society by ways of major changes in the traditional

GDP per Capita (US$)

Country	1975	1980	1985	1990	1998
Iran	1,611	1,129	1,208	1,056	1,275
United States	19,364	21,529	23,200	25,363	29,683
Saudi Arabia	9,658	11,553	7,437	7,100	6,516
Qatar	N/A	N/A	N/A	N/A	N/A

SOURCE: United Nations. *Human Development Report 2000; Trends in human development and per capita income.*

socioeconomic order between 1946 and 1979. Under the shah, thanks to considerable outlays allocated to education and health, great strides were made in improving social welfare. Infant mortality, malnutrition, endemic diseases, and illiteracy were greatly reduced. Caloric intake, life expectancy, and school enrollment were all markedly increased. While rural-income gaps and income inequalities within the respective areas did not narrow, indicators showed that absolute poverty was reduced. Although elementary school enrollment during the 1970s quadrupled to more than 9 million, this was achieved in many cases only by running students through in 3 shifts and having teachers in the classroom 60 to 80 hours a week. About 90 percent of high school graduates were denied admission to college because of inadequate facilities. About 20 percent of Iran's institutions of higher education had no library facilities, nor were they likely to obtain them because, while the state budget set aside 5 percent for sports, it did not have any reserves for books and libraries.

It was thought and hoped that the new regime would remedy these faults. The Islamic government declared a policy of improving the lot of the poor for whom, after all, the revolution itself had been launched, but there has been little evidence of success. Nominal wages and salaries lagged behind inflation throughout the 1980s, which according to one Majlis deputy left more than 90 percent of public servants below the poverty line. According to the official line, the poor were better off after, rather than before, the revolution. This was undoubtedly true for certain groups of people who have been especially well positioned within the regime, such as members of the Revolutionary Guards, many families of the war dead, some among the subsidized urban proletariat, and others from extremely low-income households. It does not hold true, however, for the majority of the population. In 1972, some 44 percent of the population were living below the subsistence poverty line. During the 1979–85 period, absolute poverty increased by 40 percent; some reports indicated that absolute poverty had spread among as many as 65–75 percent of the population in 1988. According to the IMF, 53 percent of Iranians still live below the poverty line.

Health conditions outside major cities are poor. Many small towns and rural areas suffer from unsanitary conditions and a shortage of medical personnel and facilities. The infant mortality rate remains a serious problem; it is very high by world and Middle Eastern standards, although it has been reduced significantly (26 deaths per 1,000 live births in 1998, down from 91.6 during 1980–85 and 50 during 1991–95). Although primary education is compulsory for 5 years, many rural children never attend school because of either parental objection or a lack of facilities. The secondary-school system in Iran is relatively underdeveloped, and it serves for the most part to prepare small numbers of students for university-level education. In order to improve the situation for the poorest segments of Iranian society, the government is considering an anti-poverty program comprising expanded provision of food, clothing, health care, education, social security, and bank credits to these people.

WORKING CONDITIONS

The highly fluid nature of Iran's labor market and the large size of the informal services sector make accurate estimates of employment levels difficult. A census, conducted in 1991, recorded 25.2 percent of the 57.8 million population as economically active, and 22.3 percent as in employment, suggesting that around 11 percent of the workforce was unemployed. However, the census ignored the fact that most Iranian adults must hold 2 or even 3 jobs in order to provide for the rest of their family. The government put unemployment at 2 million in 1997–98, equivalent to 12.1 percent of the workforce and up sharply from the previous year's estimate of 9.1 percent. Given the rapid population growth experienced over the past 20 years, together with a real reduction of government resources aimed at job creation, it is likely that even this estimate is too conservative. According to the Economist Intelligence Unit (EIU), an accurate estimate for unemployment figures lies between 14 percent and 18 percent, while the IMF suggests it may be as high as 25 percent.

High inflation has been another characteristic of the Iranian economy since the early 1970s and played a crucial role in the industrial action that presaged the 1979 revolution. In recent years changes in the exchange rate, the gradual removal of subsidies, and the suppression of imports have all contributed to rising prices and eroded **real wages**. Some evidence indicates that inflation has dropped steadily since 1995, settling in a range of 22–30 percent, according to sources from the International Monetary Fund (IMF).

The Labor Code empowers the Supreme Labor Council to establish annual minimum wage levels for each sector and region. The minimum wage has been inadequate for some years by the government's own admission. Officially the minimum wage should be sufficient to meet the living expenses of a family and should take inflation into account. The daily minimum wage was raised in March 1997 to US$2.80 (8,500 rials). This wage apparently is not sufficient to provide a decent standard of living for a worker and family. Information on the percentage of the working population covered by minimum wage legislation is not available. Private-sector personnel in contrast are better off.

Formally, workers are granted the right to establish unions; however, the government does not allow independent unions to exist. A national organization known as the Worker's House, founded in 1982, is the sole authorized national labor organization. The leadership of the Worker's House coordinates activities with Islamic labor councils, which are made up of representatives of the workers and 1 representative of management in industrial, agricultural, and service organizations of more than 35 employees. These councils also function as instruments of government control, although they frequently have been able to block layoffs and dismissals. In 1993, the parliament passed a law that prohibits strikes by government workers. Nevertheless, strikes occur, apparently in increasing numbers. Reports over the last 2 years included strikes and protests by oil, textile, electrical manufacturing, and metal workers, and by the unemployed.

One unforeseen result of the revolutionary government's drive for gender segregation has been the improvement in women's education. As men and woman are expected to work separately, the demand for female professionals has risen markedly, boosting the number of female graduates. The war effort contributed to this process, as women took the places of men required for military service. In 2000, there were more women enrolled in universities than men. In tertiary education, vocational subjects such as computer studies and engineering are becoming increasingly popular, while the quality of language tuition is improving. These trends will undoubtedly improve the qualifications of the local population from the point of view of foreign investors, but they also present the government with higher demands for skilled job-creation and increase the pressure to cut bureaucratic and ideological obstacles to a free labor market.

COUNTRY HISTORY AND ECONOMIC DEVELOPMENT

4000 B.C. Ancient settlements develop in the Caspian region and on the Iranian plateau.

2000 B.C. Aryans arrive and split into the Medes and the Persians.

550 B.C. Cyrus the Great founds the Persian Empire.

200 A.D. After periods of Greek and Parthian rule, the Sassanids take power and rule until the Arab final victory in 641.

1502. The Safavid dynasty is established and continues to rule until 1736.

1904. The Qajar dynasty, founded by Fath Ali Shah, comes to an end.

1906–08. Iran's modern history begins when the Constitutional Movement achieves the declaration of a constitution and the establishment of a parliament in 1906 and when oil is discovered in 1908.

1919. The country is occupied by Russia and Great Britain during World War I; it signs a trade agreement with Great Britain in 1919, in which Britain formally re-affirms Iran's independence.

1921. After Iranian recognition of the USSR, the Soviet Union withdraws occupation forces from Iranian territory; Reza Khan, an army officer, establishes military rule and subsequently becomes shah in 1925 and founder of the new Pahlevi dynasty.

1941. Iran is occupied by British and Soviet forces at the start of World War II, prompting the shah to abdicate in favor of his son, Muhammad Reza Shah Pahlevi.

1943–46. Iran is formally guaranteed independence by the United States, Great Britain, and the Soviet Union in 1943; however, political instability delays the withdrawal of troops until 1946.

1951–53. The National Front Movement under Prime Minister Mossadeq nationalizes the oil business and forms the National Iranian Oil Company (NIOC); Mossadeq is subsequently ousted from power with the help of U.S. covert activity, and an international consortium operates Iran's oil facilities, with profits shared equally between Iran and the consortium.

1960–73. The shah's modernization program—named the "white revolution"—transforms the country and its economy, with a dramatic land reform, huge investments in infrastructure, and continued economic growth.

1973. The shah gives the NIOC full control over Iran's oil industry, placing the international consortium in an advisory capacity. Iran does not participate in the Arab oil embargo in September.

1979. After years of political repression and with a growing divide between rich and poor, popular protests oust the shah in the Islamic Revolution of 1979. Ayatollah Khomeini becomes the figurehead of the revolution and subsequently the Supreme Leader of the country until his death in 1989.

1980. On 22 September, Iraqi troops invade Iran, triggering a prolonged and devastating war that lasts until Khomeini accepts a UN-brokered cease-fire in July 1988.

1989. The Ayatollah Khomeini is succeeded by Iran's president, Ali Khamenei. Ali Akbar Rafsanjani becomes president and is re-elected in 1993. Iran begins to re-build its economy.

1997. Mohammed Khatami, a moderately liberal Muslim cleric, is elected president and becomes the figurehead for the country's reformist movement; economic reforms begun under Rafsanjani continue.

FUTURE TRENDS

The Iranian government has set itself the priority of achieving political reform, believing that its victory over conservative forces in the February 2000 parliamentary elections gives it the authority to deal with what President Khatami has described as Iran's "sick economy." Despite good intentions, President Mohammed Khatami has done little to change the overall pattern of Iran's **macroeconomic** policy. While many observers hoped that the new president would speed up the reform process, he has been bothered by entrenched political opposition in the Majlis (parliament) and pressure from the powerful bonyad (religious foundations) and by external debt repayments. Pending the outcome of the political battle, the government has to deal in the short term with a chronically weak currency, high unemployment, and the arrival of 800,000 young people on the job market every year. The lack of economic opportunities and social freedom has led to growing discontent, especially among young Iranians, and may result in extended civil unrest and an increase in emigration. Returns in the June 2001 presidential election gave President Khatami the thumping victory which is needed to revive the economic, political, and social reform process.

A key factor in Iran's economic prospects is whether the country will be able to break its international isolation which will have to be overcome in order to integrate the country into the world economy and to bring much-needed foreign investment into the Islamic Republic. This depends in particular on the lifting of U.S. sanctions. Signals show that Iran's rehabilitation is a desired U.S. objective if the reformists carry out their agenda. Iran's further international and domestic economic progress, therefore, depends in large part on the outcome of the political contest between reformers and conservatives in Tehran. Economic development will also depend on the success of privatizing enterprises in the inefficient state sector, to which about 60 percent of the current budget expenditure is allocated in subsidies and other support. Finally, to have the financial means to cope with needed reforms Iran will try to keep oil prices stable on a high level.

DEPENDENCIES

Iran has no territories or colonies.

BIBLIOGRAPHY

Amid, Mohammad Javad. *Poverty, Agriculture, and Reform in Iran.* London: Routledge, 1990.

Ansari, Sarah. *Women, Religion and Culture in Iran.* Richmond, Virginia: Curzon, 2001.

Daniel, Elton L. *The History of Iran.* Westport, CT: Greenwood Press, 2001.

Economist Intelligence Unit. *Country Profile: Iran.* London: Economist Intelligence Unit, 2001.

Esposito, John L., and R. K. Ramazani. *Iran at the Crossroads.* Basingstoke: Palgrave, 2001.

Iqbal, Zubair, et al. *Iran: Recent Economic Developments.* IMF Staff Country Report 00/120, September 2000.

Parsa, Misagh. *Social Origins of the Iranian Revolution.* New Brunswick, NJ: Rutgers Univ. Press, 1989.

Parvin, Alizadeh. *The Economy of Iran.* London: I.B. Tauris, 2000.

U.S. Central Intelligence Agency. *World Factbook 2000.* <http://www.odci.gov/cia/publications/factbook/index.html>. Accessed August 2001.

—Markus R. Bouillon and Ralph Stobwasser

IRAQ

Republic of Iraq
Al-Jumhuriyah al-'Iraqiyah

CAPITAL: Baghdad.

MONETARY UNIT: Iraqi dinar (ID). One Iraqi dinar equals 20 dirhams, or 1,000 fils. Coins of ID1, and 1, 5, 10, 25, 50, and 100 fils. Notes are in denominations of 5, 10, 50, and 100 dinars.

CHIEF EXPORTS: Crude oil.

CHIEF IMPORTS: Food, medicine, manufactures.

GROSS DOMESTIC PRODUCT: US$59.9 billion (purchasing power parity, 1999 est.).

BALANCE OF TRADE: **Exports:** US$12.7 billion (1999 est.). **Imports:** US$8.9 billion (1999 est.).

COUNTRY OVERVIEW

LOCATION AND SIZE. Iraq is located in the Middle East, between Iran and Saudi Arabia. Iraq is also bordered by Jordan and Syria to the west, Kuwait to the south, and Turkey to the north. A very small sliver of the Persian Gulf (58 kilometers, or 36.04 miles) abuts Iraq on its southeast border. With an area of 437,072 square kilometers (168,753 square miles), Iraq is slightly more than twice the size of Idaho. Iraq's capital city, Baghdad, is located in the center of the country. Other major cities include al-Basra in the south and Mosul in the north.

POPULATION. The population of Iraq is the fifth largest in the Middle East and North Africa. The population was estimated at 22,675,617 in July of 2000, an increase of 4.675 million from the 1980 population of 18 million. In 2000, Iraq's birth rate stood at 35.04 per 1,000, while the death rate was reported at 6.4 per 1,000. With a projected growth rate of 2 percent between 2000 and 2015, the population is expected to reach 38 million by the year 2030.

Some 97 percent of the population are Muslims. Shi'ite Muslims make up the majority (60–65 percent), while Sunnis comprise 32–37 percent of Muslims in the country. The remaining 3 percent is made up of Christians and other religious groups. The Kurds, descendants of Indo-European tribes who settled in Iraq in the 2nd century B.C., make up 15–20 percent of the population. Arabic is the official language, but Kurdish, Assyrian, and Armenian are also spoken.

Iraq's population growth has increased since 1993, despite the exodus of the middle class as a result of the Gulf War and the adverse effects of the United Nations (UN) economic **sanctions** imposed since 1991. Population growth before the 1991 Gulf War was as high as 3.6 percent annually. The government has strongly encouraged population growth. With a high fertility rate and a relatively young population, 45 percent of which is under 15 years of age, population growth is expected to remain high. Population growth dropped significantly to 1.9 percent in 1993 but resumed in recent years, with the growth rate reaching 2.98 percent in 1998. This rate suggests that the **emigration** of the middle class has slowed. The International Monetary Fund (IMF) also estimates that the effects of the UN sanctions have begun to fade. An estimated 1 to 2 million Iraqis live abroad, many as political exiles. The large majority of these are concentrated in Iran, after having been forced to leave in the wake of the 1990–91 Gulf War.

As in many developing countries, a majority of Iraqis live in urban areas. The population of urban areas has grown significantly since the 1960s at a rate of 5.2 percent annually. Baghdad and its suburbs are home to some 31 percent of the population. Rural-urban migration has eroded some of the ethno-religious and linguistic differences between regions, with the exception of the Kurdish minority, which is concentrated in the north. Iraqi society is dominated by tribal and familial affiliations.

OVERVIEW OF ECONOMY

Iraq's economy has suffered greatly as a result of the United Nations sanctions, imposed following Iraq's military defeat at the hands of a U.S.-led coalition that freed

Kuwait after it was invaded by Iraq in 1990. The sanctions were imposed to contain militarily the regime of Saddam Hussein by ensuring that all weapons of mass destruction (such as nuclear, chemical, and biological weapons capable of killing large numbers of people indiscriminately) at its disposal are destroyed by a UN-appointed inspections committee. However, Iraq's incomplete compliance with UN resolutions pertaining to the destruction of its weapons has precluded the removal of the trade sanctions more than a decade after the war.

Iraq entered the 20th century as part of an enfeebled Ottoman Empire (a 700-year empire that spanned much of the Middle East and centered in what is now Turkey). By 1915, Iraq became a British mandate area administered by a civil government headed by a British high commissioner. In 1921, the British replaced their direct rule with a monarchy headed by King Faisal. Iraq became a sovereign independent state in 1932 after the British finally acceded to local demands for full independence. Iraq was proclaimed a republic in 1958, after the monarchy was overthrown by a military coup executed by officers under the leadership of General Abdul Karim Qasim, who became Iraq's first president. In fact, Iraq has been controlled by a series of strongmen, the latest of which is Saddam Hussein, who took power in 1979.

Oil, discovered in Iraq in the early 1950s, has made Iraq one of the world's largest oil producers. Its economy is largely dependent on the oil sector, which has traditionally accounted for about 95 percent of foreign exchange. Iraq's economy has, however, been on a downward trend since the early 1980s. Gains achieved during the initial years of the Ba'ath party (Iraq's only political party and the center of power in the country) rule were reversed as the Hussein regime sought to finance the 10-year war with Iran that broke out in 1980. As a result of the war, Iraq's oil production capabilities were curtailed, and the government's debts to Western nations for the purchase of military matériel grew considerably throughout the 1980s. Iraq sustained heavy debts as a result of its war with Iran. Accurate figures regarding Iraq's total external liabilities are hard to establish because the Iraqi government did not publish official information on its debt. In 1986, Iraq's total debt was estimated to be between US$50 billion and US$80 billion. Of this total, Iraq owed about US$30 billion to Saudi Arabia, Kuwait, and the other Gulf states. Most of this debt resulted from the sale of crude oil on Iraq's behalf. Iraq's total **foreign debt** today is estimated to be in the range of US$130 billion. Iraq has not made any debt payments since the United Nations' sale of its overseas assets to compensate the Kuwaiti victims of the invasion and to pay creditors.

Since 1996, Iraq has been allowed to export only a limited quantity of oil, worth US$2.14 billion every 6 months, in return for food and medical supplies to address the country's deteriorating humanitarian conditions after the war, which include a lack of clean water supplies and basic services. Of revenues accruing from the sale of oil, some 53 percent is used to finance the import of food and medicine for the Iraqi people, while 13 percent is being diverted by UN agencies to the Kurdish provinces in the north. The effects of the sanctions have led to a sharp increase in poverty and infant mortality, especially in the south, and much of the country's **infrastructure** is not functioning.

POLITICS, GOVERNMENT, AND TAXATION

A complex web of social, economic, ethnic, religious, and ideological conflicts has hindered the process of state formation in Iraq since it gained independence from Britain in 1932. Festering socioeconomic problems—such as widespread poverty and deep divisions between the Sunnis and the Shi'ites in the post-World War II period—were compounded by an enduring leadership crisis that continued to afflict Iraqi politics and society for more than 5 decades after independence. The political process has been characterized by deep social and political divisions that have meant that no single political group was able to gain enough support to rule the country without resorting to violence. As a result, Iraq's deep-rooted fragmentation has allowed the armed forces to exercise great control over politics since the 1930s. A total of 11 coups took place between 1936 and 1968. The Ba'ath party, which came to power in 1968, also through a military coup, has greatly shaped the country's modern history and its economic system. The party espouses the goals of **socialism**, freedom, and unity, and has attempted to redress widespread social inequality through the redistribution of wealth.

According to the constitution, Iraq is a republic with an elected legislature and an independent judiciary. Executive power is concentrated in the hands of the president and Council of Ministers. In reality, and owing to the revolutionary nature of Iraqi politics, all executive and legislative powers rest with the Revolutionary Command Council president (RCC). The RCC elects the president, who, in addition to being the chairman of the RCC, also serves as prime minister and commander of the armed forces. The president and the Council of Ministers are accountable to the RCC.

Since the late 1960s, the ruling Ba'ath Party has used vast oil revenues to build a modern state, although it is also one of the most highly militarized countries in the world. The Ba'ath party adopted a centralized socialist welfare system, which regulated every aspect of the economy, with the exception of the agriculture and personal services sectors. Much of Ba'ath party's ambitious plans to develop Iraq and exploit its vast oil resources were done with Soviet technical assistance. Since taking office in 1979, President Saddam Hussein pursued a state-sponsored industrial modernization program that led to a more equitable distribution of wealth, greater social mobility, improved education and health-care standards, as well as the redistribution of land. The government experimented with economic **liberalization** in the 1980s, which sought to ease state control of the economy and to increase commercialization in the state sector. These efforts, however, were largely unsuccessful, mainly due to a long legacy of state control and a bloated state bureaucracy that was unable to meet the challenges of reform.

Iraq's spending on defense has traditionally accounted for 25–33 percent of the state budget, even when the country was not at war with any of its neighbors. Since the early 1970s, the government has dedicated huge resources to thwart efforts by the Kurdish people to establish their own state in the northern Kurdistan region. After efforts to reach an agreement to establish a politically and culturally autonomous area in the north failed in 1975, the government waged in 1976 a costly campaign to forcibly evacuate 800 Kurdish villages along the border with Iran. This campaign to replace the Kurdish population with Arabs resumed after an 8-year hiatus during the Iraq-Iran war. At least 300,000 Kurds were deported from their villages in the north, and chemical weapons were used against Kurdish civilians at Halabjah in 1988 in which more than 5,000 Kurds were killed. Following Iraq's military defeat in 1991, U.S.-led allied forces carved out an autonomous region for the Kurds in the north, effectively separating the region from the rest of the country. Since 1991, the Iraqi Kurds have enjoyed a large degree of autonomy from the central government in Baghdad under the protection of allied forces. Nevertheless, the Kurds live in primitive conditions, often in large "tent cities," with only the barest necessities (such as food, medicine and clean water) supplied by aid agencies.

In the wake of the Gulf War and its aftermath, the Iraqi government's role in the economy is bigger than ever, as it continues to control the vast majority of imports and foreign exchange flowing into the country from the limited sale of oil allowed under the sanctions. The government, however, lacks a clear economic objective, given its primary goal since the 1990 Gulf War has been to ensure the survival of the regime in the face of international political and economic isolation. Instead of using its limited resources from oil sales to benefit the economy and expand its base, the state has redirected its efforts toward guaranteeing the continued support of the regime's chief domestic allies, mainly the merchant class and the military. This class has been both paid off and allowed to accumulate wealth illegally to ensure its continued allegiance to the state.

Taxation is not and has never been a major source of government income. Iraq's relative prosperity in the years preceding the Iran-Iraq war enabled the government to adopt a welfare system that exempted the population from paying taxes. After the 1990 Gulf War, however, the government has attempted to impose taxes to increase its revenue, but collection enforcement has been rather poor. **Private sector** employees are required to pay **income tax**, although the tax is rarely collected. State employees continue to be exempt from taxation.

INFRASTRUCTURE, POWER, AND COMMUNICATIONS

Prior to the Gulf War, Iraq's infrastructure was one of the most highly developed and extensive in the region. The government has been largely successful in its efforts to repair the severe damage the infrastructure sustained as a result of the 1990 Gulf War. The lack of resources available to the government, however, has meant that most of the repair work is substandard. In 1996, the country was serviced by a network of over 45,550 kilometers (28,304 miles) of primary and secondary roads, 38,400 kilometers (23,862 miles) of which were paved. The nation's 2,032-kilometer (1,263-mile) railway system is in good condition and connects Iraq to its neighbors to the north, Syria and Turkey.

Iraq has 2 major airports, located in Baghdad and Basra. Both airports are in fairly good condition. There are 3 smaller civil airfields at Haditha, Kirkuk and Mosul. All commercial airlines stopped service to Iraq in 1991 under the United Nations sanctions. A number of countries, mainly France, Russia, and Jordan, began sending humanitarian flights carrying food and medicine to Baghdad in mid-2000, in violation of the sanctions. These flights were sent as an expression of opposition to the continuation of the UN sanctions against Iraq. The country has 3 ports at Umm Qasr, Khawr az-Zubayr, and al-Basra, which currently have limited functionality because of the damage sustained during the Gulf War and the subsequent trade sanctions. Since 1997, most of Iraq's needs are serviced at Umm Qasr, the main point of entry for most food imports.

Communications

Country	Newspapers	Radios	TV Sets[a]	Cable subscribers[a]	Mobile Phones[a]	Fax Machines[a]	Personal Computers[a]	Internet Hosts[b]	Internet Users[b]
	1996	1997	1998	1998	1998	1998	1998	1999	1999
Iraq	19	229	83	N/A	0	N/A	N/A	0.00	N/A
United States	215	2,146	847	244.3	256	78.4	458.6	1,508.77	74,100
Saudi Arabia	57	321	262	N/A	31	N/A	49.6	1.17	300
Iran	28	265	157	0.0	6	N/A	31.9	0.05	100

[a]Data are from International Telecommunication Union, *World Telecommunication Development Report 1999* and are per 1,000 people.
[b]Data are from the Internet Software Consortium (http://www.isc.org) and are per 10,000 people.

SOURCE: World Bank. *World Development Indicators 2000.*

Electric power is supplied to Iraqis by state-owned power stations throughout the country, which have a total capacity of 17,000 megawatts of power. As a result of repeated bombings during the Iran-Iraq war and the Gulf War, power stations today can barely meet local demand, and it is estimated that in 2000, capacity in the central and southern regions supplied only 50 percent of demand. Despite the construction of 4 new power stations after the Gulf War, blackouts are common, and at least 14 central and southern provinces experience an average of 12 hours of power cuts daily. In Baghdad, 4-hour power outages are routine.

Telecommunications services in Iraq are in poor condition and are quite unreliable, mainly as a result of repeated air strikes by allied forces during and after the war. The country had 675,000 working lines in 1995. Mobile cellular service is unavailable. Internet service is available but is both costly and unreliable.

ECONOMIC SECTORS

Iraq's economic sectors reflect the state of devastation that the country has endured as a result of war. The economy has traditionally been heavily dependent on the oil sector, which accounted for more than 60 percent of the GDP before the Gulf War. The oil sector's contribution to the GDP, however, greatly diminished in the immediate years after the war, but its contribution to GDP has increased since the 1996 introduction of the United Nations oil-for-food program, which allows limited oil exports in return for food and medicine. Iraq in 1991 exported less than 10 percent of its pre-war oil export levels. By 2001, Iraq had regained three-quarters of the pre-war oil export levels. However, the UN's control of oil exports removed these revenues as a source of the GDP.

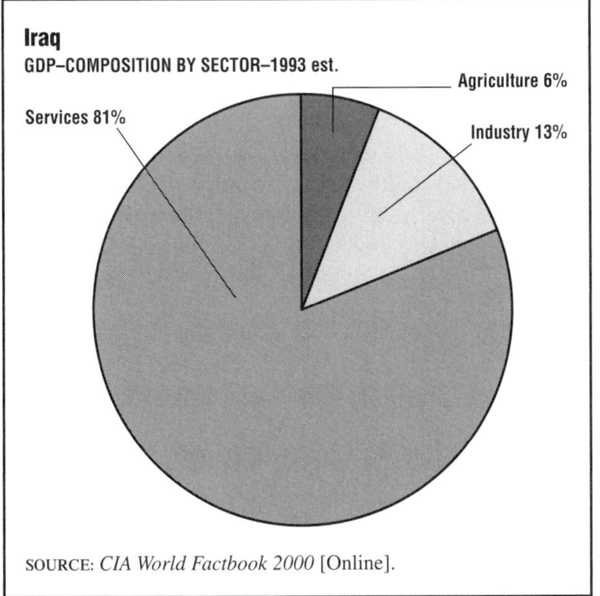

SOURCE: *CIA World Factbook 2000* [Online].

In the post-Gulf War era, services was the largest contributor to the GDP at 81 percent in 1993. Industry contributed 13 percent in the GDP, while agriculture accounted for 6 percent of the GDP. **Real GDP** was cut by around 63 percent in 1991, a direct result of the war and subsequent sanctions. The GDP was estimated in 1999 to be equivalent to US$59.9 billion. The country's major economic sectors witnessed a serious decline in 1990–91 because of the Gulf War, and continued allied bombardment of key Iraqi infrastructure facilities, including power generators and communications equipment. The manufacturing sector was hit by the shortage of imported raw materials and spare parts, while the collapse of the country's irrigation system in the aftermath of the war has left the agricultural sector in dire straits.

AGRICULTURE

Despite intermittent government efforts to develop the sector, agricultural production has always been a modest contributor to Iraq's economy, accounting for 7 percent of GDP prior to the 1980 Iran-Iraq war and 6 percent in 1993. Despite declining performance, however, the sector continues to employ almost one-third of the country's **labor force**. The agricultural sector employed 30 percent of the labor force in 1989, and although the number is believed to have declined as a result of the sector's declining performance, no hard figures are available to support this contention.

Iraq's arable land is estimated at 8 million hectares, comprising less than 15 percent of the country's total area. However, only 4 to 5 million hectares of this land is being cultivated. Arable land is mostly concentrated in the north and northeast, where winter crops—mainly wheat and barley—are grown, and in the valleys of the Tigris and Euphrates rivers.

The sector's contribution to the GDP has steadily declined since the early 1980s, despite repeated government efforts to boost agricultural production. Until the late 1980s, cultivable land was under the control of the state, the direct result of the land reforms begun in 1958. In 1988–89, in an effort to boost agricultural production, the state **privatized** agriculture, but the sector's weakness persisted. Further, the government continued to control the price of agricultural products, mainly to protect the urban consumer. Despite government efforts to encourage agricultural production after the Gulf War by raising the price of staple foods—especially of wheat, barley and rice—the labor-intensive sector remains in 2001 underdeveloped and inefficient, as a result of the high costs of energy, credit, and land and lack of investment. The problem is further aggravated by the lack of pesticides, fertilizers, and machinery. Further, competition from produce and agriculture products imported under the UN food-for-oil program, which allows the sale of a given amount of oil in return for basic foodstuffs and medicine, has also hurt the sector. In 2000, Iraq's farmers were also hit hard by the worst drought in a century. This drought devastated output and forced many farmers to ask the government to loan them the money to pay local banks back for funds they had borrowed to plant their crops, which in the summer of 2000 were failing.

Major agricultural products are cereals, including wheat and barley. Iraq is also a producer of dates, sheep and goat meat, chicken meat, and milk. Most agricultural activity is concentrated in the fertile lowlands in the Mesopotamian plains irrigated from the Tigris and the Euphrates. The Kurdish areas in the north, which have received minimal attention due to the conflict between the central government and the Kurds, remain underdeveloped and mostly dependent on rainwater. Agricultural production in Kurdish areas has improved under the UN sanctions regime, due to the distribution of fertilizers and spare parts by international agencies in those areas.

INDUSTRY

MINING. Oil dominates the country's mining activity, and accounted for more than 60 percent of the GDP before the 1990 Gulf War. Iraq has 112,500 billion barrels in proven reserves—the second largest known reserves in the world. Prior to its war with Iran, which began in 1980, Iraq was also the second-largest exporter of oil in the world.

Oil production is concentrated in the north in Kirkuk, Jambur, Bai Hassam, Ain Zalah, Butman, and Baiji. Oil fields in the south include Rumaila and Zubeir, and until the Gulf War, oil was exported via the Gulf port at Khor al-Amaya. In addition, smaller fields can be found at Luhais, Nahr Umr, Buzurgan, Abu Ghuraib, and Jabal Fauqi. Iraqi oil exports consist of 2 types of crude. The "Kirkuk Crude," which forms the majority of exported oil, is extracted from the northern oil fields and exported via Turkey. The "Basra Light" comes from the fields in the south and is exported via the Mina al-Bakr terminal on the Persian Gulf.

Oil production and output has more than once been interrupted as a result of armed conflict, first with Iran and then with the allied forces during the Gulf War. Production before the Iran-Iraq war reached as high 3.5 million barrels a day (b/d) in 1979 but declined to 700,000–870,000 b/d with the start of the war in 1980. Although most damage to Iraq's facilities was repaired, and production was restored to 3.07 million b/d by the end of the 1980s, the Gulf War and subsequent UN sanctions imposed once more severely depressed both production and output capacity. Until 1996, Iraqi exports were forbidden under the terms of the UN sanctions, with the exception of 65,000 b/d exported to Jordan as part as a special deal worked out with the United Nations. As a result, oil production averaged only 500,000–600,000 b/d between 1990 and 1996, with the majority used for domestic consumption.

Iraq was allowed to resume partial exports in 1996, as part of the food-for-oil program designed to provide for the humanitarian needs of the Iraqi people. Oil production was estimated at 2.52 million b/d in 1999, 1.76 million of which are exported under the food-for-oil program. Local consumption accounts for 500,000 million b/d, while an estimated 166,000 million b/d are believed to be smuggled through Turkey and Iran. In June 1998, Iraq was permitted to import spare parts in the amount of $300 million every 6 months to repair its oil facilities. In December 1999, the value of imports was doubled to $600 million per 6 months, but Iraq was allowed to purchase parts only from a list of parts drawn up by the United Nations. Despite an increase in production, which reached 2.49 million b/d in July 2000, the oil sector continues to suffer from the lack of adequate investment and of the kind of Western expertise that was once available to Iraq before the war.

Before 1972, a consortium of British, U.S., French and Dutch companies virtually dominated the oil industry through the Iraqi Petroleum Company and its associates. This company was **nationalized** by the Iraqi government in 1972, and the U.S. and Dutch interests in the last remaining foreign oil firm—the Basra Petroleum Company—were confiscated because of their governments' pro-Israel stance during the 1973 Arab-Israeli war. The entire oil sector was nationalized in December 1975 and placed under the control of the state-owned Iraqi National Oil Company. In the late 1990s, however, and as a direct result of the sanctions, the Iraqi government has once again allowed production-sharing agreements with foreign companies, mainly Russian and Chinese, to develop the oil sector and increase production to 3.4 million b/d in the short-term and 6 million b/d in the medium-term. These agreements, however, are contingent upon the lifting of the UN sanctions, and it remains to be seen whether the United States will allow the Russian and Chinese firms to benefit from the development of the Iraqi oil sector.

In addition to oil, Iraq ranks tenth in the world in terms of proven reserves of natural gas, which are estimated at 3.1 trillion cubic meters. In 1998, Iraq's production of natural gas reached 2.9 billion cubic meters, most of which was used for domestic consumption. Natural gas is currently not being exported, although the government has recently signed agreements with Turkish companies to export 10 billion cubic meters worth of gas annually from its northern field.

Iraq also has phosphate deposits located at Akashat near its border with Syria, which are used to produce fertilizers. Sulphur deposits can also be found in Mishraq. European companies were involved in the mining of sulphur before the Iran-Iraq war, but these efforts came to a standstill during the war and have not resumed. The mining of both phosphates and sulphur has largely remained limited in scope due to the dominance of the oil sector.

MANUFACTURING. The manufacturing sector is the second largest non-oil sector, accounting in 1993 for 13 percent of the GDP. The sector's contribution to the GDP in 2001 is hard to assess in the absence of government data about manufacturing activity in the country. Total employment in manufacturing in 1989 stood at 968,000 or 22 percent of the labor force.

Historically, the sector has been dominated by oil refining and natural gas processing industries. Refineries are situated in Baghdad, Basra, al-Hadithah, Khanaqin, Kirkuk, and Qayyarah, and by the late 1980s were producing a total of 743.3 million barrels of petroleum and 3.7 billion cubic meters (131 billion cubic feet) of natural gas per year. Since the 1970s, Iraqi companies have processed iron and steel at plants located at Khawr az-Zubayr. Other manufacturing activities include the production of advanced military hardware, tractors, electrical goods, car assembly, truck manufacture, aluminum smelting, detergents, and fertilizers.

Since the mid-1970s, Iraqi industries have been under the control of the state. The government experimented with privatization in late 1988, right after the end of its war with Iran, in an effort to boost manufacturing production. The state, however, continues to control all heavy industry, the oil sector, power production, and the infrastructure, while private investment is restricted to light industry. An important reason for the failure of the privatization program was the **price controls** that the government was forced to introduce following the outbreak of popular unrest over rising prices in 1989.

Overall, the sector has been characterized by mismanagement and constant policy shifts, which severely hindered its development. In the 1970s, the government encouraged the development of local food processing and building supplies industries to substitute for imports, but by the late 1970s, the government shifted its focus toward the development of heavy industries, such as iron and steel. The initiative, however, never took off. Efforts to expand the manufacturing sector came to a standstill during the Iran-Iraq war, as resources had to be reallocated to finance the war, and greater emphasis was placed on increasing the output of existing industries.

In the 1990s, the manufacturing sector has also been severely hurt by the UN sanctions and has shrunk considerably as a result. The UN closely monitors the import of industrial raw materials to ensure that implements necessary for the production of weapons of mass destruction do not enter the country. The sector has also been hurt by the lack of the foreign currency needed to purchase imported parts.

CONSTRUCTION. The construction sector has been a major contributor to the economy for most of the last 3 decades. The sector's growth can be attributed to the government's continuous involvement since the 1970s in reconstructing war-damaged facilities or in expanding the military infrastructure. Spending on construction dropped significantly in 1991, reaching ID578 million, down from ID1.7 billion in 1990. Spending on construction, however, has been on an upward trend since 1991, reaching some ID20 billion in 1994.

SERVICES

FINANCIAL SERVICES. Financial services in Iraq are fairly outdated. As a result of the nationalization of banks and insurance companies in 1964, all financial transactions are controlled by the government through the Central Bank of Iraq, which is responsible for issuing and monitoring all aspects of the Iraqi dinar. **Black market** currency dealings are prohibited but continue to take place. International banking transactions are undertaken by the Rafidain Bank, which represents the government in all transactions not undertaken by the Central Bank. The Rasheed Bank, established in 1989, deals with domestic transactions. The banking sector was liberalized in 1991, paving the way for the establishment of 6 new banks.

RETAIL. Iraq has a poor **retail** sector. Baghdad's once well-developed commercial centers have been severely hurt by the UN sanctions, and the lack of imported goods has forced many of them to close in the last 10 years. The majority of shops in major cities, including Baghdad, consist of small family-owned and -run businesses. Small shops and temporary road stands also characterize the majority of towns in the interior of the country.

INTERNATIONAL TRADE

Iraq's imports have declined dramatically in the last decade, as a direct result of the UN sanctions. In 2001, Iraq's total imports were estimated at US$8.9 billion, almost 40 percent lower than their 1989 levels of US$22 billion. Iraq was not allowed to import any goods until 1997. After the conclusion of the food-for-oil agreement, Iraq's imports have been regulated by the UN, which approves all goods entering the country.

Exchange rates: Iraq

Iraqi dinars (ID) per US$1	
2000	N/A
Dec 1999	1,910
Dec 1998	1,815
Dec 1997	1,530
Dec 1996	910
Dec 1995	3,000

Note: Rates are black market rates and are subject to wide fluctuations; Iraqi dinars have been officially fixed at 0.3109 since 1982.

SOURCE: CIA *World Factbook 2001* [ONLINE].

GDP per Capita (US$)

Country	1996	1997	1998	1999	2000
Iraq	2,000	2,000	2,400	2,700	2,500
United States	28,600	30,200	31,500	33,900	36,200
Saudi Arabia	10,600	10,300	9,000	9,000	10,500
Iran	5,200	5,500	5,000	5,300	6,300

Note: Data are estimates.

SOURCE: *Handbook of the Nations*, 17th, 18th, 19th and 20th editions for 1996, 1997, 1998 and 1999 data; CIA *World Factbook 2001* [Online] for 2000 data.

Iraq imports a variety of goods, but food imports (wheat, rice, barley, sugar and meat) and medicine are by far the largest component of the import bill. However, the Iraqi government and its agencies control the purchase and marketing of imported goods. Before the Gulf War, Iraq imported the majority of its goods from the United States, Japan, the United Kingdom, Germany, France, Italy, Brazil and Turkey. By the late 1990s, France (19.2 percent of total imports), Australia (18 percent), China (12.5 percent), Russia (8.2 percent), and the United States (2.1 percent) are the largest exporters of goods to Iraq.

The majority of exports are dominated by oil, which accounted for about 95 percent of total sales abroad before the Gulf War. Iraq in 2000 had restored three-quarters of its pre-war oil export levels, which means that oil sales in 2001 account for around 70 percent of total exports. Other non-oil exports included fertilizers and dates. Sales of liquefied natural gas are expected to surge, but the prospects for that eventuality are far from certain. In 1999, Iraq exported the majority of its oil to the United States (US$3,879 million), the Netherlands (US$848 million), Japan (US$644 million), France (US$521 million), and Spain (US$402 million). Given its weak industrial base and the unlikely removal of the UN sanctions, oil is expected to continue to be the country's major export. Total exports in 1999 reached US$12.7 billion, with the vast majority of export earnings coming from the sale of oil.

MONEY

The value of the Iraqi dinar has declined steadily on the world market over a period of 20 years, making it increasingly harder for the average Iraqi to afford imported goods. The value of the dinar held steady until the beginning of the Iran-Iraq war, but that trend was reversed with the collapse of oil prices in mid-1980s. The dinar, which sold at ID0.3109=US$1 in 1982 (which is still the official rate set by the Iraqi government), was further weakened in the aftermath of the Gulf War, reaching a low of ID2,660:US$1 in December 1995. Despite occasional peaks, the value of the dinar against the U.S. dollar has held steady in the last 2 years at ID2,000:US$1 on the black market, the same rate sold by state banks since June 1999. However, the dinar's instability is likely to persist as a result of the uncertain political and the continuation of the UN sanctions.

Iraq has a single stock market, established in Baghdad in March 1992 in the wake of the privatization of state enterprises. Trading, however, remains thin due to the uncertain political conditions prevailing in the country.

POVERTY AND WEALTH

The UN sanctions imposed on Iraq since 1990 have severely affected the social fabric and living conditions in the country. As a result of the severe deterioration of services—including water and sanitation, health care, and education—the living standards of all Iraqis have declined. Rising unemployment and **inflation**, which was estimated at around 250 percent in 1995 and 135 percent in 1999, coupled with the falling purchasing power of salaries and rising prices, have deepened social divisions and inequalities, with all sectors of the society growing more impoverished. Wealth as of 2001 is concentrated in the hands of a small privileged group of regime supporters, mainly from among the military and the business community who have been allowed to benefit from the sanctions. This group is heavily involved in black market currency dealing and the smuggling of food and merchandise on a regional scale.

The economic **embargo** has also had an uneven impact on different Iraqi regions. Ethnic, religious, and tribal rivalries have always been the dominant feature of Iraqi society. The Sunni-dominated central government in Baghdad has historically discriminated against the Shi'ites in the south and the Kurds in the north. Systematic efforts to "Arabize" the predominantly Kurdish region in the north resulted in a rebellion in the 1970s that brought the Kurds further retribution. Under the sanctions regime, living conditions in the northern provinces that are under Kurdish control have improved, partly because the UN, rather than the government of Iraq, is administering the oil-for-food program there, and partly as a result of the infusion of higher per capita international humanitarian assistance to this region between 1991–96. The future social and economic prospects of this region, however, remain uncertain, given that the status of the region is yet to be determined.

The predominantly Shi'ite south, which witnessed an uprising against the Sunni-controlled Baghdad government in the wake of the 1991 war, has been less fortunate. The military continued its water-diversion and other projects in the south designed to displace the Shi'ite community there, known as the "marsh Arabs." Since the 1980s, the government has drained most of the southern areas by either drying up or diverting the streams and rivers, effectively cutting off water supplies to the Shi'ite community inhabiting those areas for thousands of years.

The government also limited the delivery of food, medical supplies, drinking water, and transportation to the region. The regime has used food rations allowed under the oil-for-food program to reward regime supporters and silence opponents. As a result of this policy, the humanitarian conditions of Shi'ites in the south continued to deteriorate, despite a significant expansion of the oil-for-food program after 1997.

WORKING CONDITIONS

Iraq's labor force has increased steadily since the 1970s, reaching over 6 million workers in 1998. No official statistics are available for the unemployment rate in the country, but it is widely believed that the unemployment rate has increased dramatically as a result of the war and the subsequent sanctions. Iraq suffered labor shortages in the 1980s as result of the conscription of thousands of Iraqi men in the military. Declining economic conditions forced thousands of foreign workers who migrated to Iraq for work opportunities during the war to leave after the war ended. This problem was further aggravated by the exodus of thousands of Iraqi professionals at the outset of the Gulf War. The majority of the labor force (67 percent) is concentrated in the services sector, which is dominated by the military, in comparison to only 14 percent in the agricultural sector and 19 percent in the industrial sector.

Iraq's trade unions were legalized in 1936, and although more than a dozen are in existence today, the labor movement has been largely ineffective due to the domination of the government and Ba'ath Party. In 1987, the government established the Iraqi General Federation of Trade Unions (IGFTU) as the sole legal trade federation, which is used to promote the principles and policies of the Ba'ath party among union members. Iraqi employees work a 6-day, 48-hour week, but working hours in the **public sector** are set by the head of each ministry. Child labor is prohibited, although children under the age of 14 can work in the agricultural sector and are encouraged to help support their families.

Although labor laws protecting the right of workers have been in place since 1958 and subsequently amended in 1964, working conditions in Iraq are not ideal. Workers do not enjoy the right to strike, as mandated by the 1987 Labor Law; do not have the right to bargain collectively; and are often arbitrarily moved from their positions for political considerations. Salaries in the public sector are set by the government, but no information is available on minimum wages. Declining economic conditions in the 1990s have forced many government employees to take second and third jobs to support themselves.

Since the 1970s, the ruling Ba'ath party has encouraged the participation of women in the labor force and much effort was exerted to improve their level of education. The percentage of women in the labor force has, however, remained rather steady in the 2 decades between 1970 and 1990, hovering at around 16.8 percent. According to World Bank figures, Iraqi women's participation in the labor force has risen consistently since the 1990/91 Gulf War, jumping from 16.6 percent in 1991 to a high of 19 percent in 1998. This increase can be best explained in terms of the harsh economic conditions that Iraqis have had to endure as a result of the war, which have forced many women to seek employment opportunities outside their homes to earn a living.

COUNTRY HISTORY AND ECONOMIC DEVELOPMENT

1917. As the Ottoman Empire collapses, Iraq comes under the control of the British.

1921. The British declare Faisal king of Iraq.

1932. Modern Iraq gains independence. A new government headed by General Nouri al-Said is formed.

1933. Ghazi, the son of King Faisal, becomes king.

1941. The Ba'ath Party is founded by 2 Syrian students, espousing the goals of socialism, freedom, and unity.

1939. King Ghazi is killed in a car accident and is succeeded by his son Faisal II.

1958. Hashemite monarchy is overthrown by officers of the Nineteenth Brigade under the leadership of

Brigadier Abdul-Karim Qassem and Colonel Abdul Salam Arif. Iraq is declared a republic.

1963. President Abdul-Karim Qassem is overthrown by Abdul Salam Arif and a coterie of military officers in a bloodless coup.

1970. The government signs a 15-article peace plan with the Kurds after years of rebellion and conflict.

1972. Iraq and the Soviet Union sign a treaty of friendship for political and economic cooperation. Iraqi Petroleum Company is nationalized and Iraq National Oil Company is established to exploit new oil concessions.

1979. President Bakr resigns, and Saddam Hussein officially replaces him as president of the republic, secretary general of the Ba'ath Party Regional Command, chairman of the RCC, and commander in chief of the armed forces.

1979. Shah of Iran is overthrown.

1980. Iran-Iraq War begins.

1988. Iran-Iraq War ends.

1988. Government launches privatization program to spur economy.

1990. Iraq invades Kuwait.

1991. Iraq is defeated by allied forces. United Nations sanctions are imposed.

1997. Iraq is permitted to export limited amounts of oil in return for food and medicine.

FUTURE TRENDS

Iraq entered the 21st century under a cloud of great uncertainty. Despite the large sums of money that have entered the government's coffers from the sale of oil in the last 50 years, Saddam Hussein's legacy of war, first with Iran and then as a result of the invasion of Kuwait, has left the economy in ruins. The country's economic and social achievements during the 1970s and 1980s have been completely lost. Despite the food-for-oil program approved by the United Nations in 1997, the Iraqi economy will continue to suffer as a result of the sanctions.

Further, the prospects for the lifting of the United Nations sanctions remain uncertain, given that their termination has been made conditional upon the removal of President Saddam Hussein from power. Even after the sanctions are lifted, it is estimated that Iraq will have to pay US$12 billion in **debt-servicing** annually and to pay for food imports, medicine, and reconstruction. The problem will be further aggravated by the massive reparations payments that Iraq will be forced to pay. Unless forgiven, Iraq's debts will continue to greatly hinder its ability to undertake large-scale reconstruction and repair needed to restore the civilian infrastructure.

Internally, the social and ethnic divisions that have long characterized Iraq are stronger than ever. Despite being greatly weakened by the Gulf War and the sanctions, the repressive Saddam Hussein regime continues to rule the country unchallenged. The country itself has been divided into 3 zones, with the center and the south remaining under the control of the Iraqi government. Meanwhile, the north, where the Kurdish minority is concentrated, has been granted, at least temporarily, the right to administer its own affairs. For the last 10 years, the Kurds have enjoyed the protection of U.S. and British forces against potential military attacks by the Iraqi government. However, it remains uncertain whether such an arrangement can be sustained after the U.N. sanctions are lifted.

DEPENDENCIES

Iraq has no territories or colonies.

BIBLIOGRAPHY

"Another Dry Year Means Bad Harvest For Iraq." *Arabia.com/Iraq.* <http://www.arabia.com/iraq/business/article/english/0,5508,24836,00.html>. Accessed June 2001.

Arnove, Anthony, editor. *Iraq Under Siege: The Deadly Impact of Sanctions and War.* Cambridge, Mass.: South End Press, 2000.

Batatu, Hanna. *The Old Social Classes and the Revolutionary Movements of Iraq: A Study of Iraq's Old Landed and Commercial Classes and of Its Communists, Bathists, and Free Officers.* Princeton, NJ: Princeton University Press, 1978.

Clawson, Patrick. *How Has Saddam Hussein Survived?: Economic Sanctions, 1990–93.* Washington, D.C.: Institute for National Strategic Studies, 1993.

Economist Intelligence Unit. *Country Profile Iraq, 2000/2001.* London: Economist Intelligence Unit, 2000.

Helms, Christine Moss. *Iraq, Eastern Flank of the Arab World.* Washington, D.C.: Brookings Institution, 1984.

"Kurds Despair Under West's Leaky Umbrella." *Guardian Unlimited.* <http://www.guardian.co.uk/The_Kurds/Story/0,2763,440396,00.html>. Accessed June 2001.

U.S. Central Intelligence Agency. *World Factbook 2000.* <http://www.odci.gov/cia/publications/factbook/index.html>. Accessed July 2001.

—Reem Nuseibeh

ISRAEL

State of Israel
Medinat Yisrael
Dawlat Israel

CAPITAL: Tel Aviv/Jerusalem. Israel proclaimed Jerusalem as its capital in 1950, but most countries, including the United States, have not recognized this internationally disputed move and maintain their embassies in Tel Aviv.

MONETARY UNIT: New Israeli Shekel (NIS, named after the currency in use in biblical Israel, was introduced in the late 1980s). Bills include 10, 20, 50, 100, and 200 shekels, and there are coins worth ½, 1, 5, and 10 shekels. The New Israeli shekel is divided into 100 agorots, of which there are 5, 10, and 20 agorot coins.

CHIEF EXPORTS: Machinery and equipment, software, cut and polished diamonds, chemicals, textiles and apparel, agricultural products.

CHIEF IMPORTS: Raw materials, military equipment, investment goods, rough diamonds, fuels, consumer goods.

GROSS DOMESTIC PRODUCT: US$110.2 billion (purchasing power parity, 2000 est.).

BALANCE OF TRADE: **Exports:** US$35.1 billion (f.o.b., 2000). **Imports:** US$31.5 billion (f.o.b., 2000).

COUNTRY OVERVIEW

LOCATION AND SIZE. Israel, a country slightly smaller than the U.S. state of New Jersey, is located in the Middle East, bordering the Mediterranean Sea for a length of 273 kilometers (168 miles). In the south and southwest, it borders the Gulf of Aqaba and the Sinai Peninsula, occupied in the war of June 1967 and returned to Egypt in April 1982. To the east, it shares a 238-kilometer (147-mile) borderline with the Hashemite Kingdom of Jordan and 307 kilometers (189 miles) with the Palestinian Autonomous Area on the western shore of the Jordan river. In the north, Israel shares 79 kilometers (49 miles) of borders with Lebanon, and with Syria for 76 kilometers (47 miles) on the disputed Golan Heights.

The "Gaza Strip," a small piece of territory running some 40 kilometers (25 miles) along the Mediterranean coast, has been under limited jurisdiction of the Palestinian National Authority (PNA) since 1994 and may eventually form a part of a single Palestinian entity, together with the Palestinian Autonomous Area in the West Bank. The territories which were occupied after the war of June 1967 are not recognized as forming part of the State of Israel, although it seems unlikely that Israel will reverse its annexation of East Jerusalem. Control over the Old City, which is the Jews' principle holy site, the Wailing Wall, and the Muslims' holy mount, the Haram al-Sharif with the al-Aqsa mosque, is heavily disputed.

POPULATION. Israel's population was estimated to total 5.85 million in July 2000. This number includes about 171,000 Jewish settlers in the West Bank; about 20,000 in the Israeli-occupied Golan Heights; about 6,500 in the Gaza Strip; and about 172,000 in East Jerusalem. The country's population is heavily concentrated along the coastal strip, with about 75 percent of the Jewish inhabitants and around 60 percent of the non-Jewish population located between Ashkelon and Nahariya. In 1997, the Tel Aviv district had almost 1.2 million inhabitants, accounting for some 20 percent of total population. Jerusalem (Yerushalayim in Hebrew and al-Quds in Arabic) counted 633,700 inhabitants, in 1998. Haifa (Hefa) is the largest city in the north with some 265,000 inhabitants. Of the total population, 91 percent are defined as urban, that is resident in localities with more than 2,000 inhabitants. Around 80 percent of Israel's population is Jewish of which 40 percent were born abroad, mostly European or American-born (1.2 million citizens), and 60 percent (2.8 million citizens) were Israeli-born Jews. The 20 percent of non-Jewish Israeli citizens are mostly of Arab origin.

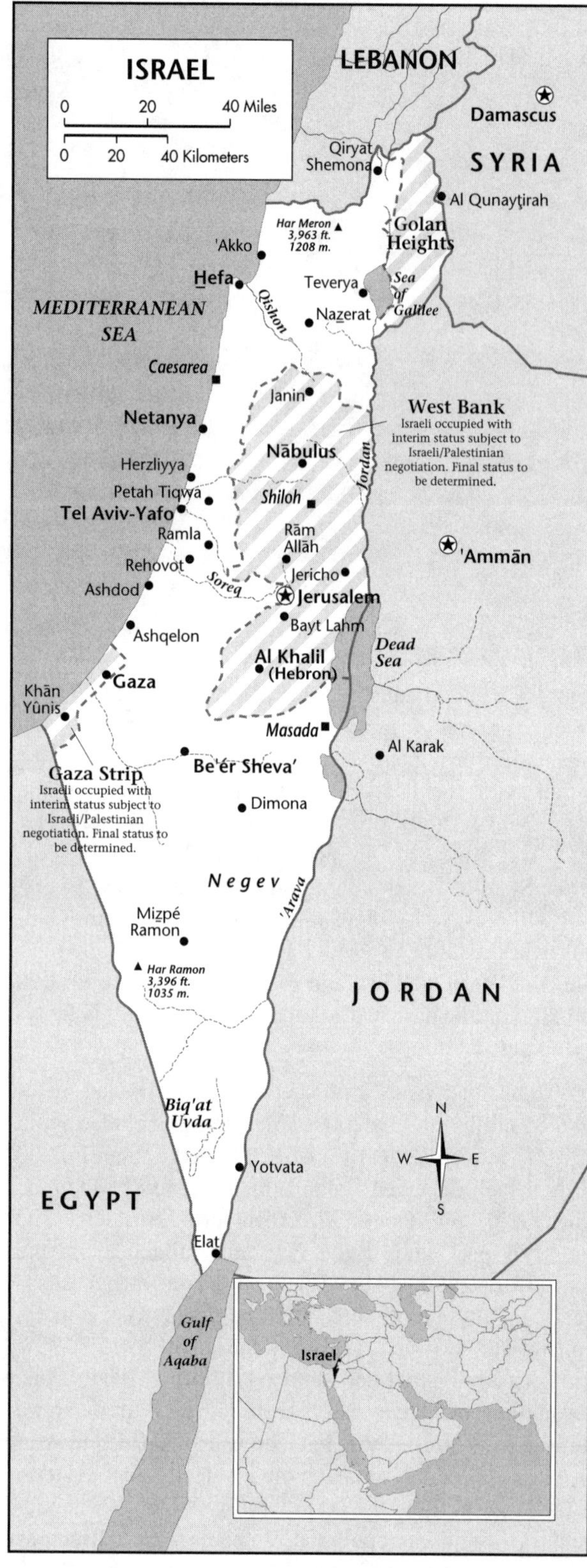

There are 2 main Jewish communities, the Ashkenazim and the Sephardim. The former are the Jews from Eastern, Central, and Northern Europe, while the latter originate from the Balkan countries, North Africa, and the Middle East. There are around 15 percent Muslims and some 2 percent Christians and 2 percent Druze. Israel is also home to the Bahai community's principal sanctuary in Haifa.

Hebrew is the official language and Arabic is officially used for the Arab minority. English is the most commonly used foreign language. Ultra-orthodox Jews, who refuse to converse in the holy language of Hebrew, and elder Eastern European immigrants speak Yiddish. Due to the diversity of the immigrant population, most Israelis are multilingual.

After the Diaspora (the dispersion of Jews from their homeland) for nearly 2000 years, *aliyas* or waves of **immigration** started bringing Jews to what had once been Israel in the last decades of the 19th century, driven by the idea of establishing a Jewish national homestead in their biblical land. From the early 1920s, the Jewish population in Palestine increased more than sevenfold, from only 80,000 to 600,000 in 1948, when the State of Israel was declared. In the first 20 years of the state's existence, between 1948 and 1972, the country's population quadrupled.

OVERVIEW OF ECONOMY

Once a traditional economy based mainly on agriculture, light industry and labor intensive production, Israel was until the 1990s described as the "most **socialist** economy of any nation outside of the Eastern bloc". High growth, second only to Japan in the period 1922–73, was achieved through a highly centralized, state-driven economic policy, making Israel a world record-holder in high taxes, **foreign debt**, and finally **inflation**, which reached triple digit levels from 1977 to 1984.

Since a national unity government first began implementing measures of stabilization and reform in 1985, Israel's economy has been transformed from a highly state-centered one to a mixed economy focused on high-tech and exports. The influx of Jewish immigrants from the former Soviet Union topped 750,000 between 1989 and 1999, bringing the population of Israel from the former Soviet Union to 1 million, one-sixth of the total population, and adding scientific and professional expertise of substantial value for the economy's future. The influx, coupled with the opening of new markets at the end of the Cold War, and the onset of the Middle East peace process, energized Israel's economy, which grew rapidly in the 1990s, despite a slight setback during 1997 to 1999. Capitalizing on the country's human resource potential, the government instituted economic reforms and new policies that have created a global high technology powerhouse in such industries as semiconductors, computer software, telecommunications, and biomedical equipment. The dramatic growth of Israel's high tech sector in recent years has led to a shortage of qualified workers and a significant rise in salaries for these positions.

In the 1990s, Israel enjoyed a remarkable economic expansion that brought new levels of prosperity and a significant increase in purchasing power. With economic growth averaging nearly 6 percent between 1990 and 1996, Israel's economy expanded by some 40 percent in real terms, and per capita income jumped from US$11,000 to almost US$17,000. The slowdown in economic growth between 1997 and 1999 was generally attributed to the waning of the stimulative effects of the immigration waves, such as for residential construction and new business investment, high interest rates, and much tighter **fiscal policy** in this period. A further reason was increased political and security uncertainty due to a lack of progress in the peace process. In 2000, Israel's **GDP per capita** was US$17,500—higher than in Spain or New Zealand.

Both major parties, the currently ruling Likud under Ariel Sharon and the Labor party, are committed to further **liberalizing** the economy, strengthening exports and attracting further foreign investments, mainly in the high-tech sectors, and to keeping the **macroeconomic** environment stable. Despite moving gradually toward a more open, competitive, and market-orientated economy over the past decade, the level of government involvement in the economy remains high, as do the public's expectations for government assistance. The country's **infrastructure** network remains publicly owned, as does much of the banking system. However, the pace of **privatization** has quickened in recent years.

POLITICS, GOVERNMENT, AND TAXATION

Israel is a parliamentary democracy. The president, who has ceremonial function, is elected by the Knesset, a **unicameral** parliament, for a 5-year term. Moshe Katzav, member of the Likud party and of Persian origin, was elected president in 2000. Since the May 1996 election, the prime minister is elected directly by a separate universal vote. The minimum voting age is 18. The prime minister since 2001 is Ariel Sharon, who took over from Ehud Barak. The latter had failed to achieve an agreement with the Palestinian National Authority at Camp David and could not meet the Israeli public security expectations in the early phase of the second intifada or uprising. Apart from Ehud Barak, the 1990s saw a number of prime ministers come and go. Benyamin Netanyahu, Shimon Peres, Yitzhak Shamir, and the much-loved Yitzhak Rabin, who was assassinated in 1995 by an ultra-orthodox Jew frustrated by rapprochements with the Palestinians, have held the office in the last decade.

The State of Israel was declared on 14 May 1948, its political leadership emerging from the Jewish Agency. Its chairman, David Ben Gurion, became the first prime minister and is considered the father figure of the state. For decades the country was dominated by the Labor Party (though under changing names) first under Ben Gurion, then under other leaders, and the Histadrut, Israel's General Federation of Labor. The 2 institutions formed a quasi-socialist system with large state welfare provisions. The first change of the ruling party came as a surprise in 1977, when the Likud Party, under Menachem Begin, won the largest share of seats.

With 5 wars fought since the inception of Israel with its Arab neighbors the Israeli Defence Forces (IDF) have at any stage played an important role. Virtually all leading statesmen in Israel had senior positions in the IDF before coming to office. A permanent peace settlement seemed possible for the first time when President Sadat of Egypt visited Jerusalem in 1977 and addressed the Israeli parliament. A year later at Camp David under the guidance of President Carter, Begin and Sadat agreed on a peace treaty that was finally signed in March 1979. Until today, though, a comprehensive peace agreement with all Arab neighbors has not been struck and the problem of a Palestinian entity has not been resolved.

The Israeli Parliament, known as the Knesset, consists of 120 members elected to 4-year terms, although the prime minister has the option to call for new elections before the end of the term, or the prime minister's government can fall on a vote of no-confidence in the Knesset. A total of 11 political parties are currently represented in the 16th Knesset. The political spectrum includes the Hadash Party, a left-wing umbrella group, including the Communist Party and other **Marxist** factions that is made up of both Arab and Jewish citizens; the left-wing Meretz Party; the center-left and chief opposition Labor Party; the new centrist Third Way Party; the ruling right-center Likud Party; the religious parties (National Religious Party, Shas, and United Torah Judaism); and the rightist Moledet. Yisrael B'Aliya is a centrist party focused on the rights of Russian immigrants. The United Arab List, a combination of the Democratic Arab Party and representatives of Israel's Islamic Movement, is a defender of the rights of Arab citizens.

After the failed talks between Palestinians and Israelis at Camp David the ongoing second intifada began in September 2000. The Israeli-Palestinian conflict over land and the status of Jerusalem remains a crucial issue. Israel had benefitted considerably from the onset of the Middle East peace process, and its economic success depends at least to some degree on political stability. Since the 1993 signing of the Declaration of Principles on Palestinian self-rule, the future status of Jerusalem and the continuing expansion of Jewish settlements in East Jerusalem and the West Bank have emerged as 2 of the most critical issues affecting the peace process. The ongoing intifada was triggered when Ariel Sharon, as prime minister, paid a highly disputed visit to the Muslim holy site in the Old City of Jerusalem. The Old City, within the walls of which are found the ancient quarters of Jews, Christians, Muslims, and Armenians, has a population of some 25,500 Arabs and 2,600 Jews. In addition there are some 600 recent Jewish settlers in the Arab quarter. It is highly unlikely, though, that any Israeli government will give up control, gained in 1967, over East Jerusalem and the Old City, in particular.

INFRASTRUCTURE, POWER, AND COMMUNICATIONS

Israel's infrastructure is modern and well developed. To cope with its growing population and to improve the functioning of the economy, Israel is making large investments to upgrade its infrastructure. Major projects include the construction of a new terminal at Ben Gurion International Airport; a tunnel through Mt. Carmel to provide a bypass route around Haifa; the Cross-Israel Highway, a major north-south artery; and mass transit systems planned for Jerusalem, Beer Sheva, and the Tel Aviv region.

TRANSPORTATION. Israel has a total of almost 16,000 kilometers (9,942 miles) of paved roads, including 56 kilometers (35 miles) of expressways. The main highway runs along the Mediterranean coast, linking the north (Haifa) and the center (Tel Aviv). The second major link between Tel Aviv-Jerusalem causes major problems. Due to little space for the construction of new roads, the 45-minute-drive from Tel Aviv to Jerusalem takes about 3 hours during rush hours. Part of the old Beirut-Jerusalem railway connection runs from Nahariya via Haifa to Tel Aviv. The route from Tel Aviv to Jerusalem is not in use anymore. The importance of trains especially in passenger transportation is overshadowed by the government-owned Egged bus company, which operates the second largest bus system in the world after Greyhound. Freight traffic consists of grain, phosphates, potash, containers, petroleum, and building materials. Rail service serves Haifa and Ashdod ports and extends to Eilat port. Haifa and Ashdod on the Mediterranean Sea coast are the main ports in Israel. The port of Eilat is Israel's gateway to the Red Sea. In 1997, Israel's merchant fleet consisted of 55 vessels. There are 2 international airports in Israel, Tel Aviv's Ben-Gurion airport and Eilat airport. Plans to merge the airports of Eilat and of the neighboring Jordanian city of Aqaba did not materialize. An international airport in the Gaza strip in operation since 2000 but currently largely dysfunctional due to security problems.

POWER. The Israel Electric Corporation (IEC) has completed a US$10 billion investment program in 2000, which has boosted the country's generating capacity from 8,000 megawatts to about 12,000 megawatts. The country's plants almost entirely run on fossil fuels; no nuclear power plants are in operation. Israel is preparing for the availability of natural gas by planning a natural gas distribution network. Local authorities are searching for solutions to environmental problems related to municipal solid waste and wastewater treatment. The first international tender for a waste-to-energy plant was issued in January 1998. Development of regional sanitary landfills, a national air pollution monitoring system, and municipal wastewater treatment plants, even in outlying regions of the country, are indicative of a growing awareness of environmental issues.

TELECOMMUNICATIONS. Israel is one of the world leaders in mobile communications. There are currently 3 major Israeli cellular mobile network providers, as well as a Palestinian company and almost as many cell phones in use as main lines. In 1999, there were 2.8 million land-lines and 2.5 million mobile users. The Israeli telephone

Communications

Country	Telephones[a]	Telephones, Mobile/Cellular[a]	Radio Stations[b]	Radios[a]	TV Stations[a]	Televisions[a]	Internet Service Providers[c]	Internet Users[c]
Israel	2.8 M (1999)	2.5 M (1999)	AM 23; FM 15; shortwave 2	3.07 M	17 (1995)	1.69 M	21	1 M
United States	194 M	69.209 M (1998)	AM 4,762; FM 5,542; shortwave 18	575 M	1,500	219 M	7,800	148 M
Saudi Arabia	3.1 M (1998)	1 M (1998)	AM 43; FM 31; shortwave 2	6.25 M	117	5.1 M	42 (2001)	400,000 (2001)
Jordan	403,000	11,500 (1995)	AM 6; FM 5; shortwave 1 (1999)	1.66 M	20 (1995)	500,000	5	87,500

[a]Data is for 1997 unless otherwise noted.
[b]Data is for 1998 unless otherwise noted.
[c]Data is for 2000 unless otherwise noted.

SOURCE: CIA *World Factbook 2001* [Online].

system, no longer **monopolized** by the government-owned Bezek company but open to competition, is the most highly developed system in the Middle East, with a good system of coaxial cable and microwave radio delay. All systems are digital. In addition to telephony providers, Israel has now at least 21 ISPs, a figure constantly increasing.

Israelis are radio listeners: There were 3.07 million radios in the country in 1997, compared to 1.69 million televisions. Given the importance of news and information, people commonly listen to the news at work; bus drivers usually turn up the volume to allow passengers to listen to the news. Since 1999, there has been a digital TV station in operation, which has also drawn a large number of subscribers.

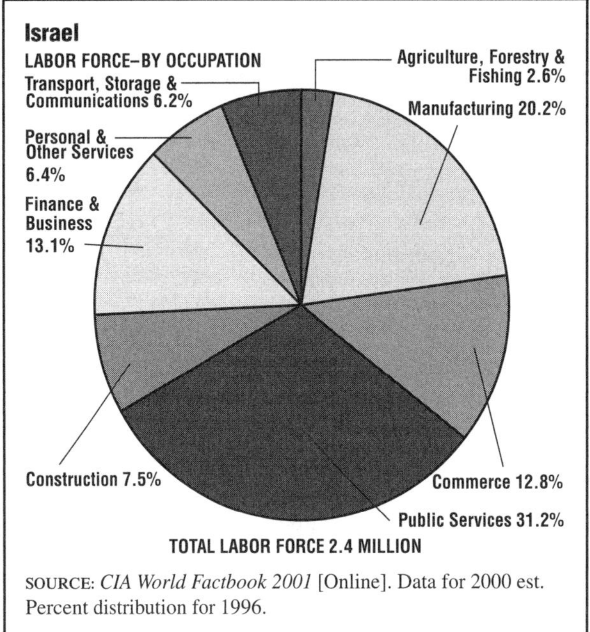

SOURCE: *CIA World Factbook 2001* [Online]. Data for 2000 est. Percent distribution for 1996.

ECONOMIC SECTORS

Once strongly based on agriculture and low-cost industrial production for the domestic market, the country has undergone major structural changes, shifting to a modern export-oriented economy. In recent years, it has been the high-tech sector that has grown most substantially. Agriculture contributed 4 percent to the GDP in 1999, while industry accounted for 37 percent, and services for 59 percent.

AGRICULTURE

The agricultural sector is fairly small, accounting for 3.5 percent of the GDP in 2000 and employing 2.6 percent of the **labor force**. Nonetheless, Israel is largely self-sufficient in foodstuffs lacking only in grains, oils, and fats. Since the establishment of the State of Israel, the area under cultivation has increased. Currently, the cultivated area totals 4.2 million dunams (4 dunams equal 1 acre) about 50 percent of which are irrigated crops. The main factor limiting agricultural development is not land but the availability of water. With several years of water shortages in summer the further development of Israel's agriculture will involve raising the yield of existing land and recycling wastewater. Revenues in the agricultural sector amounted to around US$4 billion in recent years. The main categories are livestock and poultry, vegetables, fruits, flowers and field products.

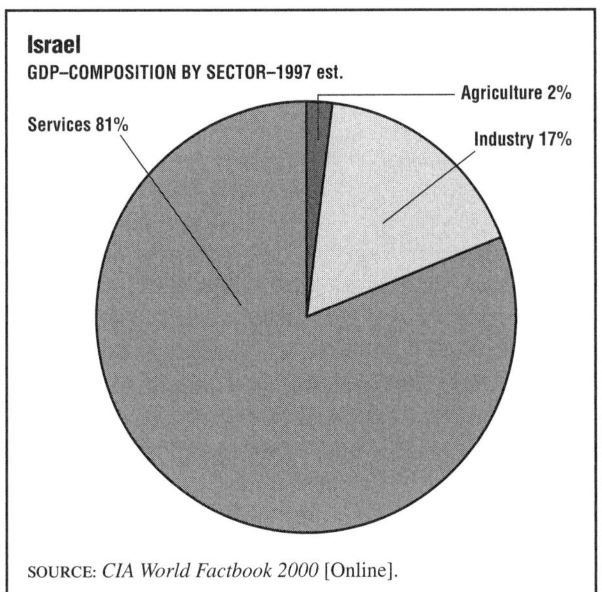

SOURCE: *CIA World Factbook 2000* [Online].

A special feature of Israel's agriculture that has gained a great deal of international attention is its cooperative settlements. For centuries, Jews in the Diaspora were barred from owning land; therefore, the Zionist movement saw land settlement as one of the chief objectives of Jewish colonization. There are 2 basic forms of settlements, the *moshav* and the *kibbutz,* both developed to meet the needs and challenges encountered by a farming community new to its professions and its sometimes hostile surroundings. The *moshav* works on the principal of a co-operative with individual farms of equal size with every farmer working his own land to the best of his ability. The farmer's economic and social security is ensured by the cooperative structure of the village which handles marketing his products, purchasing farm equipment, and providing credit and other services. In 1998, a total of 455 *moshavim* existed, inhabited by 180,000 people. The *kibbutz* is a collective settlement of a unique form, based on common ownership of resources and the pooling of labor, income, and expenditure. Every member is to work to the best of his ability. He is not paid any wage but is supplied with all the goods and services he needs. The *kibbutz* is, therefore, based on voluntary action and mutual liability, equal rights for all members, and it assumes for them full material responsibility. In 1998, the 268 *kibbutzim* were inhabited by around 120,000 people.

INDUSTRY

Israel's industry was originally designed to cater to a domestic market. It was to supply such basic commodities as soap, vegetable oil and margarine, bread, ice, printing, and electricity. It used raw materials available locally to produce goods as canned vegetables and fruit, cement, glass, and bricks. In order to save foreign exchange, imports of processed goods were curtailed, giving the local industry the opportunity of adding local value to the manufacturing process of products imported from abroad. Although most of Israel's industrial production is still for domestic consumption, the country's economy is far more export-oriented. Higher valued processed goods (excluding diamonds), especially electronics and high-tech related, currently constitute 90 percent of total exports. There has been a heavy expansion in export-oriented industries as a result of government tax and investment incentive schemes.

MINING/HYDROCARBONS. The Dead Sea area, a land depression bordering Jordan, which contains potash, bromides, magnesium, and other salts in high concentration, is the country's chief source of mineral wealth. The large potash works on the southern shore of the Dead Sea are linked by road to Beer Sheva from which a railway runs northward.

Lacking large-scale resources of fuel and power, Israel is forced to import more than 90 percent of its energy requirements. Petroleum constitutes around 8 percent of all goods imports. The main sources of the annual crude oil requirements of around 50 million barrels are Egypt, Mexico, and Norway. Around 30 percent of requirements are purchased on the spot market. Most imported crude oil is refined at the Haifa oil refinery, which has a capacity of more than 6 million tons a year. Output of natural gas from the Dead Sea area is transported through a pipeline to the Dead Sea potash works and to towns in the Negev desert and a large phosphate plant. Production totaled 21.5 million cubic meters in 1994.

MANUFACTURING. The total value of Israeli exports has risen: US$18 million in 1950, US$780 million in 1971, and almost US$21 billion by 2000. The greatest expansion has taken place in the electronics industry with Israel specializing in defense-related and communication equipment, software, and network equipment. The value of exports of this sector and of metals and machinery has grown from US$12.8 million in 1970 to US$9.5 billion in 1999 and by an incredible 40 percent to US$13.3 billion in the strong export year of 2000.

Israel's single most important industrial export product is cut and polished diamonds. The diamond trading and processing industry has traditionally been a Jewish stronghold. Expertise and trading contacts were brought to Israel by immigrants from the Netherlands and Belgium, home to the world's largest diamond trading center, Antwerp. Israel's specialty is medium-sized diamonds which controls approximately 75 percent of the world market in this segment. Annual exports grew from US$4.6 billion in 1995 to US$5.7 billion in 1999 and jumped to US$6.8 billion in 2000.

SERVICES

TOURISM. Israel and the surrounding countries, also known as the Holy Land, are the sites of biblical history. David's mountaintop capital, Jerusalem, is holy to the world's 3 monotheistic religions. Nearby in the West Bank lies Bethlehem, birthplace of Jesus. But Israel is also an attractive destination for hiking, desert trips, diving, or relaxing in one of the Dead Sea spas.

Tourism is the industry most severely affected by the security downslide caused by the ongoing Palestinian uprising. Since October 2000 tourism has declined by 45 percent in comparison to the peak in the quarter immediately preceding the intifada. Experience has shown that tourists take many months to return after the end of unrest. With no improvement of the security situation in sight the sector is unlikely to recover in 2002. Since the end of the Gulf War visitor numbers had been on the rise. While in 1990 only 1.1 million tourist visas were issued, this number continuously increased to 2.3 million in 1999, according to Israel's Ministry of Tourism. Tourist receipts totaled US$2.77 billion in 1996 and reached US$3 billion in 1999.

FINANCIAL SERVICES. Israel possesses a highly developed banking system, consisting of a central bank, the Bank of Israel, 14 commercial banks, 5 mortgage banks, and other financial institutions. Bank groups, namely Bank Leumi group, Bank Hapoalim, and Israel Discount Bank, are at the core of the industrial complex and hold 92 percent of the total assets of the banking system. Once owned by the Histadrut, the all-powerful General Federation of Labor, they had to be bailed out by the government during an economic crisis in the early 1980s. Since then, they have been quasi-government owned, but there are plans for privatization. A law inhibiting banks to own more than 10 percent of industrial **holding companies**, introduced to prevent another structural crisis, has not been enforced strictly.

In 1997, the Tel-Aviv Stock Exchange (TASE) adopted an automated trading system leading to lower transaction costs. The then ongoing peace process and flourishing high-tech industries have since strongly attracted foreign investors. The real value of stocks traded in TASE increased by 59 percent during 1999. In 2000, 681 companies were listed on the TASE. The **turnover** was US$58.7 billion in 2000. In October 2000, Israel's Securities Authority adopted a dual listing regulation, allowing for Israeli companies that are traded on the New York Stock Exchange (NYSE) and Nasdaq to trade on the TASE without additional regulatory requirements. This measure enables Israeli and foreign investors to trade in these shares at convenient hours, and at low costs. Nevertheless, the general slump, especially in the high-tech shares, has affected the TASE, too. The combined effects of the economic downturn and security uncertainties will have to be monitored. Investment in the Tel Aviv Stock Exchange, acquisitions of Israeli companies, and **equity** flotation by Israeli companies on foreign stock markets, principally New York, have brought billions of dollars in new capital to Israel in recent years, primarily though not exclusively to its high technology industries.

INTERNATIONAL TRADE

Until the 1990s, high **tariffs** and strong non-tariff barriers characterized Israel's trade policy, and several barriers are still in place in particular with regard to processed food and agricultural products. Israel has free trade agreements with the European Union (since 1975), the United States (signed in 1985, fully effective since 1995), the European Free Trade Association (EFTA, effective since 1993), Canada (1997), and Turkey and has concluded bilateral agreements with a number of other states. Israel is the sole country in the world to have both European Union and U.S. free trade agreements. In June 2000 an association agreement between the EU and Israel came into force. In line with WTO regulations, Israel gradually began exposing the domestic market to foreign imports since September 1991. This process allowed administrative limitations on imports from third countries to be canceled, imposed higher rates of customs tariffs that since have been reduced, according to their degree of influence on local production, and allowed Israeli industry time to adjust to competition. The final stage of this process came to an end in September 2000, when tariff rates reached a maximum range of 8 percent to 12 percent.

Trade (expressed in billions of US$): Israel

	Exports	Imports
1975	1.941	5.997
1980	5.540	9.784
1985	6.267	9.875
1990	11.576	16.791
1995	19.046	29.579
1998	23.286	29.342

SOURCE: International Monetary Fund. *International Financial Statistics Yearbook 1999.*

Israel's main exports are manufactured goods and software, which accounted for 97 percent of total exports (excluding diamonds, ships and aircraft) in 2000. Agricultural exports accounted for 3 percent in 2000, compared to 16.5 percent in 1970, illustrating the depth of Israel's structural changes. The share of Israel's information communication technology exports as a percentage of exports of services is substantially high. In 1997, this share (20.1 percent) was second only to Japan (24 percent), and much higher than the OECD average, which was 12.5 percent. The United States alone absorbs more than a third (41.2 percent) of Israel's exports. Other important destinations include the European Union (27.3 percent), of which Belgium (6 percent), Germany (4.8 percent), and United Kingdom (4.3 percent) dominate; and Asia (18.5 percent), of which Japan (2.7 percent) dominates, according to Central Bureau of Statistics 2000 figures. The change in Israel's exports between 1999 and 2000 indicate that the growth rate of traditional manufacturing exports increased slightly, whereas it increased dramatically in the high-tech industries.

The geopolitical situation that has prevailed in the Middle East, since the inception of Israel, has prevented trade between Israel and its neighbors. Furthermore, the difference in the level of development and production structure between Israel and its neighbors made Europe and the United States her main trading partner. In 2000, the United States and the EU accounted for 32 percent and 30 percent, respectively, of Israel's exports and for 22 percent and 41 percent of its imports. In 2000, exports for the United States (excluding diamonds) totaled US$21.7 billion, constituting an increase of 23.3 percent in Israel's exports. Within the EU, Israel's largest export markets were Germany (21 percent), the United Kingdom (18 percent), The Netherlands and Italy (both 11 percent), and France (10 percent). Exports to Asia (excluding diamonds) increased from 12 percent in 1998 to 16 percent in 1999.

Israel has traditionally run a large external **trade deficit**, meaning that imports exceeded exports. Israel's imports have always exceeded its exports because of the Jewish state's dependence on raw materials. In addition, Israel imports military equipment, investment goods, rough diamonds, fuels, and **consumer goods**, mainly from the United States (18.6 percent), Belgium (9.9 percent), Germany (7.5 percent), the United Kingdom (7.6 percent), Italy (4.8 percent), and Japan (3.3 percent), according to 2000 figures. The cost of Israel's imports has largely been offset by cash grants from the U.S. government and charitable organizations and individuals abroad. The EU accounted for 67 percent of Israel's 2000 trade deficit, and Asia accounted for 15 percent. The trade balance with the United States was positive.

MONEY

Israel's fiscal policy has focused on reducing the state's intervention in the economy and improving Israel's fiscal stance, namely, reducing the budgetary deficit as a percentage of the GDP and the government's debt relative to the GDP. The reduction of the deficit law was drafted in 1991 for the **fiscal year** 1992 and for the years to come. The law sets a maximum level for the **budget deficit**. Indeed, the budget deficit as a percentage of the GDP decreased from 4.9 percent in 1990 to 0.6 percent in 2000. However, Israel's ratio of government debt to the GDP still remains high compared to European countries. The internal debt, as a percentage of the GDP was reduced from 104 percent in 1989 to 70 percent in 2000; the **external debt** decreased from 39 percent in 1990 to 24 percent in 2000. Both the political right and the political left are committed to a sound fiscal policy. Since 1985 the Israeli government has not been allowed to borrow from the Bank of Israel and has had to finance its debt by issuing bonds. The Israeli government issues bonds in Israel, as well as in the United States, Europe, and the Far East.

The end of the disinflation process in Israel, which began with the 1985 Economic Stabilization Program, is aimed for 2003. Israel's **inflation rate** was cut from a worrying 444.9 percent annual inflation in 1984 to 18 percent in the late 1980s. Currently, the country has virtually reached price stability with inflation down to 1 percent in 2000. The inflation rate in the past 2 years has been consistently under the inflation target and is one of the lowest in the developed world.

POVERTY AND WEALTH

Though Israel has a strong social record, as in most societies, inequality exists in different guises. In 1988, families in the upper 10 percent of household income received 8.4 times the share of the bottom 10 percent; in 1997, the share of the uppermost 10 percent increased to 10.6 times that of the lowest 10 percent. The 20 percent of households with the highest income increased their share of the national wealth while the share of the lower income households decreased. Nevertheless, the economic boom in the early 1990s has left the average Israeli better off. The GDP per capita has increased from US$5,600 in 1980 to US$17,500 in 2000, an increase only exceeded by Singapore and Hong Kong.

However, inequality between Israelis of different ethnic origins is deeply entrenched. The average incomes of Arab citizens of Israel are the lowest and have hardly changed over the last decade. The average income of Israel-born Mizrahi Jews (originating from Africa or Asia) are somewhat higher, increasing over the last decade, but the gaps between their incomes and those of Ashkenazi Jews (originating from Europe or America) did not change. The average incomes of Israel-born Ashkenazis are the highest and increase steadily. In 1997, Israel-born Ashkenazi salaried employees earned 1.6 times more than Israel-born Mizrahi employees and 1.9 times more than Arab employees, according the Central Bureau of Statistics. Israeli society also faces gender inequality, which are stronger among Oriental Jews and Arab Israelis. In 1997, women's monthly wages were, on average, 63 percent those of men. Women's hourly wages were, on average, 83 percent those of men. These figures show an

GDP per Capita (US$)

Country	1975	1980	1985	1990	1998
Israel	10,620	11,412	12,093	13,566	15,978
United States	19,364	21,529	23,200	25,363	29,683
Saudi Arabia	9,658	11,553	7,437	7,100	6,516
Jordan	993	1,715	1,824	1,436	1,491

SOURCE: United Nations. *Human Development Report 2000; Trends in human development and per capita income.*

Exchange rates: Israel

new Israeli shekels (NIS) per US$1	
Dec 2000	4.0810
2000	4.0773
1999	4.1397
1998	3.8001
1997	3.4494
1996	3.1917

SOURCE: CIA *World Factbook 2001* [ONLINE].

Distribution of Income or Consumption by Percentage Share: Israel

Lowest 10%	2.8
Lowest 20%	6.9
Second 20%	11.4
Third 20%	16.3
Fourth 20%	22.9
Highest 20%	42.5
Highest 10%	26.9

Survey year: 1992

Note: This information refers to income shares by percentiles of the population and is ranked by per capita income.

SOURCE: *2000 World Development Indicators* [CD-ROM].

Household Consumption in PPP Terms

Country	All food	Clothing and footwear	Fuel and power[a]	Health care[b]	Education[b]	Transport & Communications	Other
Israel	23	6	11	2	6	8	44
United States	13	9	9	4	6	8	51
Saudi Arabia	N/A	N/A	N/A	N/A	N/A	N/A	N/A
Jordan	32	6	17	5	8	8	23

Data represent percentage of consumption in PPP terms.
[a]Excludes energy used for transport.
[b]Includes government and private expenditures.

SOURCE: World Bank. *World Development Indicators 2000.*

improvement over 1993 when women's earnings as a percent of men's was still 58 percent. The fact that many women only work part-time explains some of the gap in monthly earnings. Most salaried Israelis make less than the average wage; in 1996, 62 percent made less than 75 percent of average income. For about one-third of Israelis the labor market does not provide a decent living. Between 1979 and 1990, the proportion of Israeli families with poverty-level wages increased from 27.9 percent to 34.3 percent, according to the National Insurance Institute. This figure remained stable throughout the 1990s.

WORKING CONDITIONS

The Israeli civilian labor force were 2.435 million, or 54 percent of the 4.487 million population aged 15 years and over, in 2000. In Israel the rate of participation in the labor force is low compared to other developed economies. Women's rate of participation in the civilian labor force was 48.2 percent in 2000, as opposed to 60.8 percent for men. In 2 segments of the Israeli society, among Arab Israelis and ultra-orthodox Jews, the rate of participation in the labor force is rather low, especially for women. About 11.5 percent of the labor force in the business sector are foreign workers, of which 46 percent are Palestinians, and the rest are from other countries. Except for the Dead Sea minerals, Israel has almost no natural resources, making human capital the country's catalyst for economic growth and competitiveness. In 1999, about 13 percent of those employed were academic professionals, and 14.6 percent were professionals and technicians. In 1999 about 15 percent of the civilian labor force had 16 years of schooling or more, compared to 1 percent in 1979, indicating a sharp rise in qualified Israeli professionals.

The General Federation of Labor in Israel, usually known as the Histadrut, is the largest voluntary organization in Israel and an important economic body. It is open to all workers, including the self-employed, members of co-operatives and of the liberal professions, as well as housewives, students, **pensioners**, and the unemployed. The reach of the Histadrut extends to approximately 85 percent of all workers. Dues are between 3.6 and 5.8 percent of wages and cover all its trade union, health insurance, and social service activities. The federation engages in 4 main fields of activity: trade union organization, social services, educational and cultural activities, and economic development.

Israel's labor standards are in line with international regulations and norms. There is a minimum monthly wage, and employees are entitled to social benefits under the comprehensive national insurance, Bituah Le'umi. There is also a state-provided health-care system in place, the so called Kupat Holim. Every male conscript has to serve up to 30 days of army reserve duty every year; employers continue paying their employees' salaries during this time. Israel has a minimum wage law, which is 47.5 percent of the average wage. Sometimes questionable is the enforcement of labor standards with regard to foreign workers, mainly from Eastern Europe and South Asia, as well as Palestinian workers employed in Israel.

COUNTRY HISTORY AND ECONOMIC DEVELOPMENT

70 A.D. After a Jewish uprising against Roman occupation, the Diaspora begins, and Jews **emigrate** to Europe, the Balkans, the Middle East, and North Africa.

1882–1903. First Aliya (large-scale immigration) occurs, mainly from Russia.

1897. First Zionist Congress is convened by Theodor Herzl in Basel, Switzerland; Zionist Organization is founded.

1904–14. Second Aliya occurs, mainly from Russia and Poland.

1909. First kibbutz, Degania, and first modern all-Jewish city, Tel Aviv, are founded.

1917. The Ottoman rule, which has lasted for 400 years, is ended by British conquest; British Foreign Minister Balfour pledges support for establishment of a "Jewish national home in Palestine." (This statement is called the Balfour declaration).

1919–23. Third Aliya occurs, mainly from Russia.

1924–32. Fourth Aliya occurs, mainly from Poland.

1933–39. Fifth Aliya occurs, mainly from Germany.

1936–39. Arab revolt against Jewish immigration.

1947. After World War II and the Holocaust, the UN proposes the establishment of an Arab and a Jewish state in Palestine. The British pledge to end their mandate in 1948.

1948. On 14 May, David Ben Gurion, chairman of the Jewish Agency in the mandate of Palestine, declares the State of Israel. The following day, the armies of Lebanon, Syria, Iraq, Jordan, and Egypt attack the newborn Jewish State. The War of Independence (Israel) or the "Nakba" (catastrophe) begins and continues in 3 phases until 1949. Israel not only defends itself but increases its territory far beyond the original division plan. To Israelis, this is the miracle of David defeating Goliath; for the Arabs, it means escape and expulsion and the beginning of the refugee Odyssey of the Palestinians, the "Nakba." Peace talks in Cyprus fail.

1956. England, France, and Israel collaborate in a plot to remove Egyptian president Nasser, the hero of the Arab world and one of the leaders of the Non-Alignment movement, and attack Egypt. Under U.S. and Soviet pressure, Israeli troops withdraw, and Nasser claims victory

1967. On 6 June, following misinformation from Soviet observers, tensions suddenly build up and lead to an Israeli "pre-emptive" strike against its Arab neighbors. Within 6 days, Israel defeats all its enemies, among them the entire Egyptian air force before it can even take off, and occupies large amounts of land: in the South, Israel "frees" the Negev and occupies the Sinai peninsula; in the North, the Jewish state captures the strategic Golan Heights; and to the East, Israel occupies the Jordanian West Bank, including Jerusalem. The historic town is immediately declared the "eternal and undivided capital" of the Jewish state. At the same time, Israel becomes an occupation force controlling a large population of Palestinian Arabs in the West Bank and Gaza Strip.

1973. A surprise attack by Egypt and Syria gives the Arab states a face-saving "victory" that, in fact, is another defeat in the Yom-Kippur or October War.

1977. The Likud wins the general elections in 1977, introducing a new era in Israeli politics. Egyptian president Anwar Sadat visits Jerusalem and speaks to the Knesset, paving the way for ensuing peace negotiations at Camp David. A peace agreement between Egypt and Israel is signed in 1979.

1982. Israel invades Lebanon and manages to drive the PLO leadership from Beirut to Tunis. Ariel Sharon, the minister of defense and former war hero, single-handedly and somewhat illegally masterminds the invasion as far as Beirut. He has to resign after the invasion and later faces a court charge over a massacre of Palestinian refugees in the camps of Sabra and Shatilla by Israeli-allied Christian militias. In the midst of a deepening economic crisis, a national unity government and reform measures are implemented. Economic deprivation and general dissatisfaction with the Israeli military occupation trigger a Palestinian uprising, the Intifada.

1990. The downfall of the Soviet Union brings almost 1 million new immigrants to Israel. During the Gulf War and the liberation of Kuwait from Iraqi occupation, Iraq fires missiles on Tel Aviv and Haifa.

1992–93. The elections are won by war hero and ex-prime minister, Yitzak Rabin, in 1992. A secret channel leads to direct negotiations between PLO and Israel, resulting in mutual recognition and a Declaration of Principles for the assumption of peace talks, known as the Oslo Accord, presented to the public in Washington, D.C., on 23 September 1993.

1994–95. Israel concludes a peace treaty with Jordan and the Gaza-Jericho (Oslo II) agreement with the Palestinians. After a series of suicide bomb attacks within Israel, Rabin is assassinated on 4 November 1995. Shimon Peres becomes prime minister but loses the elections to Benyamin Netanyahu ("Bibi") who becomes prime minister in May 1996 and opens his reign with the tunnel under Al-Aqsa, leading to violent riots.

2000. Having won the elections against Bibi Netanyahu in June 1999 on a pro-peace platform, Israel's highest-decorated soldier, Ehud Barak, realizes his promise to pull Israeli troops out of South Lebanon within a year. Peace talks with the Palestinians at Camp David fail and the so-called Al-Aqsa Intifada breaks out in September, after a highly controversial visit of the new Likud leader, Ariel Sharon, to the holy sites in the Old City of Jerusalem.

2001. Ariel Sharon becomes prime minister.

FUTURE TRENDS

The real key to Israel's economic take-off will be its ability to come to some peaceful accommodation with its immediate Palestinian neighbors and the other countries of the region. As the Peace Process has stalled, so have the bright prospects for economic integration which were supposed to boost the regional demand for Israeli products and services. With a genuine peace in this region, Israel is easily poised to be a significant "engine of growth" for the whole Middle East.

Israel remains well positioned to compete in the knowledge-intensive industries of the 21st century, and its economy has the potential to grow at some 4 to 5 percent per year. Israel's proportion of scientists, engineers, and other skilled personnel in the labor force is high by international standards, and Israeli companies are rapidly developing experience in the business aspects of transforming technology into marketable products and services. Further, the ongoing structural transformation of the economy, especially its shift from traditional to higher-value goods and services, should add to Israel's growth potential in the near future. Finally, structural reforms that will increase the level of competition and reduce the role of the state should add to overall efficiency and productivity.

DEPENDENCIES

THE WEST BANK AND GAZA STRIP. Since the Oslo Accords in 1993 between the Palestine Liberation Organization (PLO) and the State of Israel, a Palestinian National Authority has been established and autonomously rules over parts of the West Bank and Gaza Strip. Those territories are Israel's largest market and most important trade partner, with a total population of 2.9 million, of which 1.9 million lived in the West Bank and 1 million in the Gaza Strip in 1997.

With the occupation of the West Bank and Gaza Strip by Israel in the 1967 war, both territories became economically dependent on Israel. By 1987, almost 50 percent of the Gaza Strip's total labor force was employed in Israel. About 90 percent of imports came from Israel, in an involuntary and one-sided customs union. Local trade was concentrated in the hands of a few large-scale wholesalers. As a result, indigenous development did not occur. The Palestinians became increasingly dependent on Israeli wages, imports, and technologies. Industry remained weak, contributing only a small percentage of GDP, employing only a small fraction of the total labor force and remaining limited to small firms that were mainly engaged in subcontracting for Israeli firms of the textiles and clothing industry.

Until 1989, the combined level of the GNP in the Palestinian territories was only 6 percent of Israel's; the combined GDP of the territories was only 5 percent of Israel's, thus indicating the massive inequalities implied in the relationship. The outbreak of the first intifada, or uprising, in 1987, itself the result of the oppressive conditions of life under occupation, worsened the economic situation. The 1991 Gulf War effectively stopped vital **remittances**, direct aid, and income from wages in Israel, with frequent closures and curfews imposed on the territories. The repeated closures in the context of a deteriorating security situation in 1992 and 1993 led to mass unemployment and impoverishment.

The 1993 beginning of the peace process was hoped to bring remedy. But despite the peace process, employment of Palestinian workers in Israel steadily decreased, and as a result, unemployment soared to 20 percent to 30 percent on average and up to about 50 percent in Gaza. Closures have also contributed to a decline in the GDP, which fell by about 14 percent during 1992–96, while private investment declined by about 60 percent. Poverty has risen substantially. Trade relations have barely changed. Israel has remained Palestine's most important partner, still accounting for about 90 percent of trade. The current second intifada, an expression of the population's dissatisfaction with the peace process, has had devastating effects so far. Unemployment has soared to more than 50 percent, in the case of the Gaza Strip estimates reach figures as high as 80 percent. Billions of dollars of investments have been destroyed, and the little business infrastructure that has existed has been disrupted or destroyed.

BIBLIOGRAPHY

Aharoni, Yair. *The Israeli Economy: Dreams and Realities.* London: Routledge, 1991.

BDO Shlomo Ziv. *Doing Business in Israel.* <http://www.bdo-israel.co.il/db2001–2.html>. Accessed September 2001.

Economist Intelligence Unit. *Country Profile: Israel.* London: Economist Intelligence Unit, 2001.

Israeli Ministry of Finance. <http://www.mof.gov.il>. Accessed September 2001.

Rivlin, Paul. *The Israeli Economy.* Boulder: Westview Press, 1992.

U.S. Central Intelligence Agency. *World Factbook 2001.* <http://www.odci.gov/cia/publications/factbook/index.html>. Accessed October 2001.

U.S. Department of State. *Commercial Guide, FY 1999: Israel.* <http://www.state.gov>. Accessed September 2001.

—Ralph Stobwasser and Markus R. Bouillon

JAPAN

Nippon

CAPITAL: Tokyo.

MONETARY UNIT: Yen (¥). One yen equals 100 sen. There are coins of 1, 5, 10, 50, 100, and 500 yen. There are notes of 500, 1,000, 5,000, and 10,000 yen.

CHIEF EXPORTS: Motor vehicles, semiconductors, office machinery, chemicals.

CHIEF IMPORTS: Fuels, foodstuffs, chemicals, textiles, office machinery.

GROSS DOMESTIC PRODUCT: US$3.15 trillion (2000 est.).

BALANCE OF TRADE: **Exports:** US$450 billion (2000 est.). **Imports:** US$355 billion (2000 est.).

COUNTRY OVERVIEW

LOCATION AND SIZE. Japan, an island nation in east Asia, is an archipelago (large group of islands) located east of the Korean peninsula. It has an area of 377,835 square kilometers (145,882 square miles), which makes it slightly smaller than the state of California. Japan is bordered by the Pacific Ocean on the north and east, by the Philippine Sea and the East China Sea to the south, and by the Sea of Japan on the west. It has a coastline of 29,751 kilometers (18,487 miles). Japan's major cities, including Tokyo, its capital, and Yokohama, its major port, are located in the southeastern part of the country, on the main island of Honshu. Kyoto, Nagoya, and Osaka are in the southern part of Honshu. Sapporo is located on the northern island of Hokkaido. The other 2 main islands in the Japanese archipelago are Kyushu and Shikoku, to the southwest.

POPULATION. Japan's population was estimated at 126,549,976 in July 2000. The population grew from 115,000,000 in 1975 to 126,300,000 in 1998, indicating a growth rate of 0.5 percent. With Japan in a state of near zero population growth, this total is expected to decline to 126,000,000 by 2015. In 2000, the estimated birth rate was 9.96 per 1,000 population, and the estimated death rate was 8.15 per 1,000. In the same year, the net migration rate was 0 percent.

The Japanese population is very old. According to the 2000 estimation, 17 percent of the population is 65 years old and over, a proportion that is expected to rise to 24.6 percent by 2015. In 2000, 15 percent of the population was under 14, and 68 percent was between 15 and 64.

Japan's population is very homogenous, with ethnic Japanese constituting 99.4 percent of the total. Ethnic minorities, which account for 0.6 percent of the total population, include about 24,000 indigenous Ainu people in Hokkaido and about 690,000 Koreans, mostly citizens of North or South Korea. There are much smaller groups of Chinese and Caucasians.

The population is highly urbanized, with about 78.5 percent of the population living in urban areas in 1998, a very small increase from 1975, when they accounted for 75.7 percent. The urban population is expected to increase to 82 percent by 2015. Based on 1999 statistics, Tokyo, the capital, is the largest urban center, with a population of 8,049,000. Other major urban areas are Yokohama (3,393,000), Osaka (2,594,000), Nagoya (2,167,000), Sapporo (1,811,000), and Kyoto (1,460,000).

OVERVIEW OF ECONOMY

Once a predominantly agrarian society, Japan began its industrialization in the second half of the 19th century by adopting Western technology, and developed itself into a major industrial power by the first decade of the 20th century. Its economic and military power continued to grow in the following decades, enabling it to emerge as an expanding global power in the 1930s. The Japanese entry into World War II (1939–45) led to a devastating defeat marked by the U.S. atomic bombing of the cities of Hiroshima and Nagasaki. Apart from the destruction caused by the atomic bombs, the war devastated

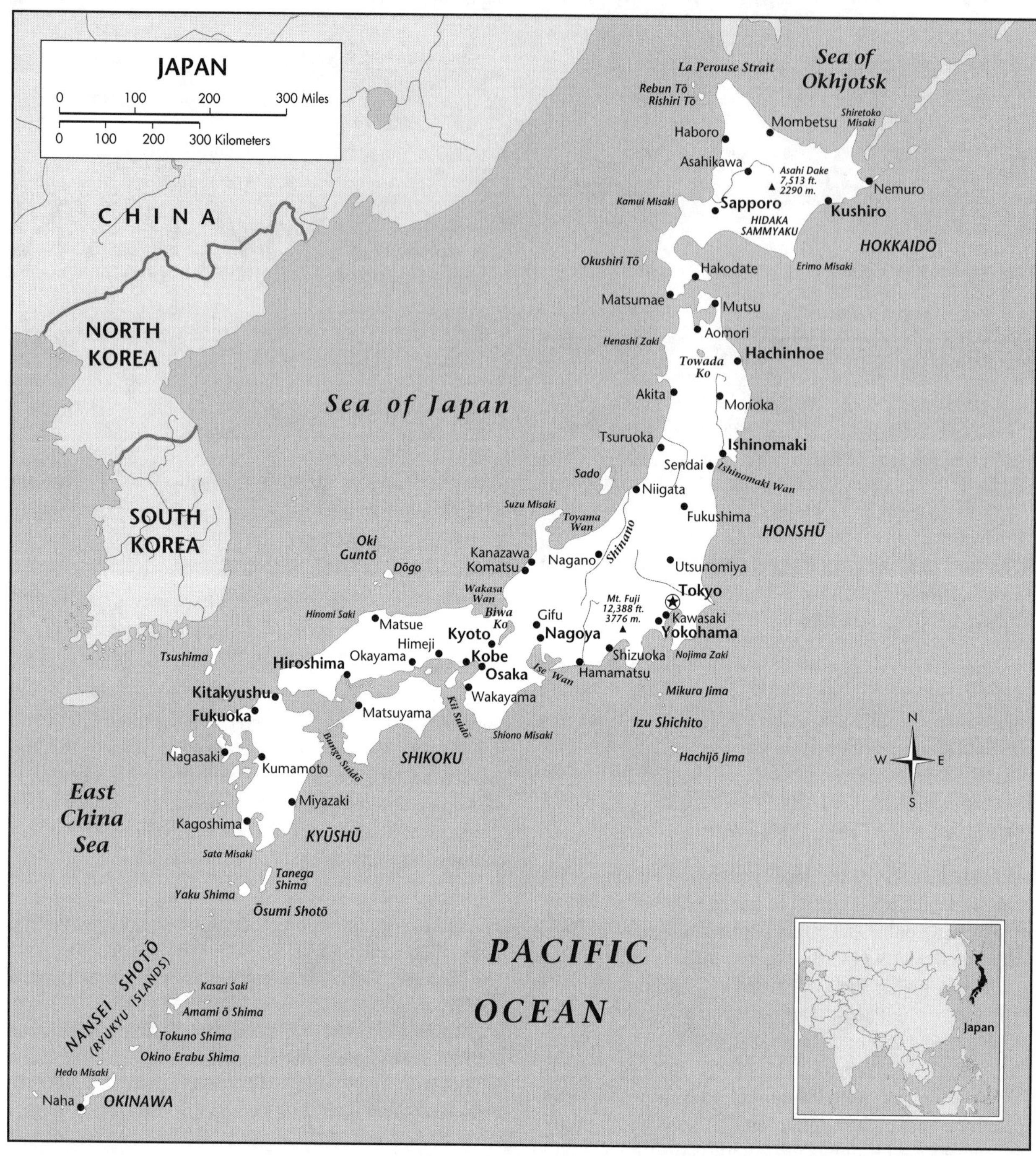

the Japanese economy and destroyed most of its industrial base and **infrastructure**.

Thanks in part to U.S. support during the postwar occupation, Japan began restoring its free-enterprise economy and industries in the 1940s. The Japanese economy began to expand in the 1950s and continued its impressive growth as a highly modern mature industrial economy until the early 1990s, when it slowed considerably. By the 1980s, it ranked as the world's second largest economic power after the United States. In 1999, Japan's GDP was 45 percent of that of the United States, but larger than the combined GDP of France and Germany. By the first decade of the 21st century, Japan had established itself as a major exporter of industrial products.

On average, Japan's annual GDP growth was about 10 percent from the 1950s until the 1970s. The growth rate began to fall in the 1970s for external and internal reasons. The first "oil shock" in the early 1970s pushed up oil prices and significantly increased imported fuel costs. Since Japan's economy depends heavily on imported fuel, this development slowed economic growth.

In 1974, the economy contracted by about 1.2 percent of total GDP. The second oil crisis of the late 1970s and the early 1980s slowed the economy to a smaller extent, causing a 0.4 percent annual shrinkage of GDP from 1980 to 1985. The situation worsened in the mid-1980s when an increase in the value of the yen increased the price of Japanese exports, leading to a decrease in global market demand. As a result, GDP growth dropped from 4.4 percent in 1985 to 2.9 percent in 1986. The damaged export industries sought to regain their competitiveness in international markets through massive relocation of their production to facilities abroad, notably in southeast Asian countries, where the cost of production was much lower than in Japan.

To offset the negative impact of the stronger yen on the economy and to stimulate growth in the domestic market, the Japanese government adopted a financial policy in the late 1980s to bolster the real estate and financial sectors. During this period, which came to be known as the "bubble economy," the Bank of Japan reduced its lending interest rate and the government increased its spending dramatically, which raised the value of stocks and inflated the price of land. This in turn stimulated spending and investment by both businesses and consumers. By 1991, stock speculation and large investments in real estate pushed prices up so much that the Bank of Japan was forced to intervene. This burst the bubble economy, and contributed to a decline in the Japanese economy during the 1990s. During that decade, Japanese products became less competitive in domestic and international markets because of higher prices.

The end of the bubble era initiated a period of sluggish growth and a loss of public confidence in the economy, both of which have continued into 2001. Although the government's **deflationary** measures (policies to reduce prices) triggered a decline in the Japanese economy in the 1990s, they did succeed in keeping **inflation** very low throughout the decade; annual rates were 1.8 percent in 1997, -0.3 percent in 1999, and -0.6 percent in 2000. The declines in the financial sector have resulted in higher unemployment through layoffs, once considered unthinkable in Japan. From its near-zero levels before 1991, the unemployment rate jumped to 2.2 percent in 1992, 3.2 percent in 1995, and 4.7 percent in 1999. The rate reached a record high of 4.9 percent in March 2000. Compared with many other developed economies such as Canada's, with an average unemployment rate of about 10 percent in the 1990s, Japan's unemployment rates since 1991 have not been very high. Yet they have been very high for a country which long prided itself on its traditions of "lifetime employment" for selected workers and strong employee loyalty. To avoid massive layoffs, many companies initiated a policy of reducing salaries, wages, and bonuses, thus lowering the living standards of many employees and decreasing spending, which, in turn, has prolonged the economic decline. Aimed at boosting the declining economy, Japan tried to **restructure** the financial sector in 1996 by introducing the so-called "Big Bang" reform measures. Its near zero-percent interest rate contributed to a short-lived increase in GDP (5.1 percent), but it failed to make growth sustainable.

The 1997 Asian financial crisis (which affected South Korea, Hong Kong, Thailand, Indonesia, Malaysia, and Singapore) was the major external factor responsible for Japan's economic downturn. It affected many markets of importance to Japan and worsened the Japanese economy by reducing export demand. The collapse of 3 major Japanese banks and a decrease in consumption further damaged the Japanese economy, which registered a 2.5 percent GDP decline in 1998, though it increased slightly, by 0.2 percent, in 1999 and about 1 percent in 2000.

Japan has benefited from continuous **trade surpluses** since the 1980s, amounting to $107 billion in 1999 and $95 billion in 2000. As a result, it has the world's largest foreign reserves, equal to $288 billion that same year. Four factors are responsible for these trade surpluses. First, Japan has a highly diversified advanced manufacturing sector capable of producing high-quality exportable products, and total cxports were valued at $450 billion in 2000. Second, Japan's protected economy puts restrictions on foreign competition, including barriers to large-scale imports of foreign products. This situation has been gradually changing since the early 1990s, and the main barriers to foreign **consumer goods**, for instance, have been removed. Nevertheless, many restrictions have limited the flow of imports, which totaled $355 billion in 2000. Third, Japan's poor economic performance since the early 1990s has decreased demands for the import of various products, including fuel and raw material for commercial purposes, while also decreasing demand for many consumer products by a public concerned about unemployment and wage/salary cuts. Finally, Japan's aging population has, since the 1980s, gradually been spending less money on consumer products. If the population decreases as predicted, the shrinkage of the domestic market will have a severe economic impact on the Japanese economy.

Still, Japan is the world's second largest economic power and the second most technologically advanced economy after the United States. The most important sector of the Japanese economy is industry, which includes manufacturing, construction, and mining. Manufacturing is highly diversified and includes light industry, heavy industry, and high-tech. Manufacturing is the largest contributor to exports, but it is heavily dependent on imported raw materials and fuels. Industry is the second largest sector in terms of contribution to GDP (35 percent in 1999) and to the workforce (30 percent in 1999). Like other mature industrial economies, services form the largest economic sector, accounting for the largest contribution to GDP (63 percent in 1999) and to the workforce (65 percent in 1999). The growing service sector consists of many services such as financial, **retail**, and tourism. At the beginning of the 21st century, agriculture, including fishing and forestry, is its smallest sector, accounting for the smallest share of GDP (2 percent in 1999) and of the workforce (5 percent in 1999). However, this sector is highly developed and produces all of Japan's rice, but it does not supply all its agricultural needs, which makes Japan dependent on large imports of agricultural products, including foodstuffs. Being a major industry, fishing has expanded into the world's most highly modernized and efficient fishing industry, accounting for 15 percent of the globe's annual catch. Nevertheless, its products meet only a portion of domestic needs, making large imports of fishery products a necessity. Japan is also dependent on large forestry product imports, because its forestry industry can only satisfy a fraction of needs.

The Japanese economy consists of a large **private sector** and a small **public sector**. The economy benefits from a very dedicated and disciplined workforce whose members are known for their strong work ethic and loyalty to their corporations. It also enjoys advanced technology, which makes it capable of producing state-of-the-art products. Close cooperation among suppliers, manufacturers, and distributors in close-knit groups called *keiretsu* also helps the economy grow fast. Such cooperation has received credit for the rapid rebuilding of the devastated Japanese economy in the post-World War II period. However, the economy lacks adequate domestic production of raw materials, fuel, and agricultural products; consequently, it is extremely sensitive to fluctuations in world prices for these items.

The Japanese economy is highly regulated. In the postwar period, this turned it into a well-protected economy practically closed to foreign competition by **tariffs**, restrictions, and quotas. Pressures by its trading partners and competitors (mainly the United States and the European Union) forced it to begin opening its market to foreign competition (goods and investments) in the 1980s. The economic decline of the 1990s inclined the Japanese government to encourage foreign investment by further **liberalizing** the economy. Since the early 1990s, the government has sought to reduce its role in the economy by initiating **deregulation** reforms that removed an enormous number of restrictive government regulations.

The Japanese government has not implemented the deregulation reforms evenly. The consumer-goods market is now open to foreign imports, while many restrictions on the financial sector have been removed. Deregulation in the air transport industry has increased foreign flights to Japan, especially from the United States, which now has an "open skies" pact with Japan. However, the reforms have been quite limited in the manufacturing sector due to a fear of massive unemployment caused by an extensive foreign presence in this sector. The increased competition will likely force domestic manufacturers to downsize their operations while bankrupting others, resulting in layoffs and unemployment. In short, the ongoing deregulation reforms have gradually contributed to a more open Japanese economy, although there are still many restrictions on economic activities.

History and geography have made an impact on the shaping of the Japanese economy. Japan's close proximity to the Asian Pacific countries (South Korea, Taiwan, Hong Kong, China, Singapore, Thailand, and Malaysia), all among the world's fastest-developing economies, has helped it expand its trade with them. These countries have been emerging as Japan's largest group of trading partners, accounting for 37.2 percent of its exports and 39.6 percent of its imports in 1999. These economies address some of Japan's major needs for fuel, minerals, and agricultural products, for example, while being large markets for its industrial products. Japan recognizes South Korea as the only legitimate Korean government, and its growing economic ties with South Korea have worsened Japan's relations with North Korea. North Korea's strong military force remains a security threat to Japan, a justification for spending $42.9 billion on defense (0.9 percent of its GDP) in the **fiscal year** of 1998–99. This is a small amount, with no major negative impact on Japan, but symbolically reflects concern about North Korea's military power. Russia's continued occupation of the Kurile Islands, captured by the Soviet Union in 1945, has prevented the conclusion of an official peace treaty between the 2 countries, and has limited their economic relations.

POLITICS, GOVERNMENT, AND TAXATION

Defeated in World War II, Japan began its postwar political life as an occupied country. The Allied military occupation, which aimed to democratize the nation, continued until 1952 when Japan regained its full sovereignty. Japan began political, economic, and social reforms in the second half of the 1940s, which paved the way for its future economic growth. In 1947, its new constitution provided for a democratic multi-party political system based on a free-enterprise economy. The emperor remains as a ceremonial head of state, but political power rests with the prime minister as head of government. The parliament consists of a 480-seat House of Representatives (Shugi-in) and a 252-seat House of Councilors (Sangi-in). Members of parliament are elected through regular free and fair parliamentary elections held every 4 years. In practice, the leader of a party, or coalition of parties, with the majority of seats in the House of Representatives becomes the prime minister. The central government in Tokyo makes all major policies and decisions, which are implemented by the regional and municipal governments.

The Liberal Democratic Party (LDP) has dominated the Japanese political system for most of the postwar era, either as the ruling party or as the leading member of a coalition government. In the June 2000 parliamentary elections, the ruling coalition of the LDP, the New Komeito, and the Conservative Party maintained its parliamentary majority and remained in power. These 3 parties favor a free-enterprise economy with a strong private sector in which the state also plays a role.

The Japanese government has a great influence in the economy. It is extensively involved in the development and operation of the nation's infrastructure (roads, airports, power generation, and telecommunications services). The government's regulatory power enables it to exert control over economic sectors and activities. It uses its resources and power to develop domestic industries through direct financial assistance to emerging or ailing industries and by setting various regulations to protect industries from foreign competition. The worsening of the economic situation in 1991 resulted in a demand by business for the deregulation of the Japanese economy to enable it to cope with the economic downturn. Deregulation reforms have resulted in a smaller state role in the economy, although it still exercises great influence.

With the exception of the Japan Communist Party, the opposition political parties of Japan support a free-enterprise economy led by a strong private sector with a varying degree of state involvement. Among them, the most important ones are the Democratic Party of Japan, the Liberal Party, the Reform Club, and the Social Democratic Party.

TAXATION. Japan has a relatively complicated tax system. There are a variety of tax rates for corporations depending on their size, revenue, and location, and for individuals based on their income, location, and personal status. In 1999, tax rates ranged between 5 percent and 30 percent. Tax rates for Japanese and foreign corporations are the same. Foreign corporations operating in Japan are only liable for their income generated in that country. There are various tax breaks for businesses to stimulate economic activities. Corporate taxes accounted for 40.87 percent of total collected taxes in 1999, while other taxes, including personal **income taxes** and **indirect taxes**, accounted for the rest.

Taxes and stamp revenues form the bulk of government revenues (92.6 percent in 1999). Non-tax revenues (e.g., tariffs and various government fees) account for the remainder of government revenues (7.4 percent in 1999). **Budget deficits** are common, since government expenditures are always much larger than government revenues. There are 3 major reasons for this: tax rates are generally low; the aging Japanese population provides limited tax revenues, especially from the growing retired population, and consequently requires more government spending on health-care services; and the government spends large sums to stimulate economic growth. In the 1999–2000 fiscal year, total government revenues from tax and non-tax sources were about $446 billion while expenditures were $718 billion. The government finances budget deficits by issuing bonds, equal to $272 billion in 1999–2000. This reflects a substantial increase in budget deficit from the fiscal year of 1996–97. The Japanese government has tried to avoid raising taxes because of the reductions in consumer purchasing power caused by the economic decline of the 1990s.

The Japanese government's annual issuance of bonds to finance its deficits has created a huge debt. In 2000, the outstanding government bonds were estimated at about $3.5 trillion. The government also engages in off-budget spending (equal to 70 percent of its annual spending) under its Fiscal Investment and Loan Program (FILP), which funds large projects such as housing and road building. The source of this spending is the savings of individuals deposited in the state-run postal savings system. In 1999, the government paid $174 billion in service charges on its debt. This is a huge financial burden on the economy, though it has not yet created a crisis. Still, if the economy does not grow significantly in the next few years and the debt continues to increase, the debt burden will have a major negative impact on the Japanese economy between 2005 and 2010.

INFRASTRUCTURE, POWER, AND COMMUNICATIONS

Japan has a very advanced and well-maintained infrastructure, which undergoes regular upgrading and expansion. Both the private and public sectors undertake various infrastructural projects and operate their respective services.

Japan has a very extensive and modern road network. It consists of 1,152,207 kilometers (715,981 miles) of highways, of which 863,003 kilometers (536,270 miles) are paved. They include 6,114 kilometers (3,799 miles) of expressways. The number of motor vehicles increased from 70,106,536 in 1995 to 73,688,389 in 1999. Major development projects to expand the Japanese highway network include a $32-billion project for the construction of a second Tomei-Meishin Expressway, connecting Tokyo and Kobe via Nagoya. The length of Japan's railways is 23,670 kilometers (14,708 miles), more than half of which is electrified. Japan is famous for its high-speed trains.

Communications

Country	Newspapers	Radios	TV Sets[a]	Cable subscribers[a]	Mobile Phones[a]	Fax Machines[a]	Personal Computers[a]	Internet Hosts[b]	Internet Users[b]
	1996	1997	1998	1998	1998	1998	1998	1999	1999
Japan	578	955	707	114.8	374	126.8	237.2	163.75	27,060
United States	215	2,146	847	244.3	256	78.4	458.6	1,508.77	74,100
China	N/A	333	272	40.0	19	1.6	8.9	0.50	8,900
South Korea	393	1,033	346	138.3	302	N/A	156.8	55.53	10,860

[a]Data are from International Telecommunication Union, *World Telecommunication Development Report 1999* and are per 1,000 people.
[b]Data are from the Internet Software Consortium (http://www.isc.org) and are per 10,000 people.

SOURCE: World Bank. *World Development Indicators 2000.*

As a country surrounded by water, Japan has developed a very extensive and modern sea transportation system. It includes many ports and harbors such as Akita, Amagasaki, Chiba, Hachinohe, Hakodate, Higashi-Harima, Himeji, Hiroshima, Kawasaki, Kinuura, Kobe, Kushiro, Mizushima, Moji, Nagoya, Osaka, Saki, Sakaide, Shimizu, Tokyo, Tomakomai, and Yokohama. Japan has a very large merchant-marine fleet, which is a necessity for its international trade and for ensuring an uninterrupted arrival of raw material, fuel, foodstuffs, and other necessary products. The fleet comprises 662 ships with a total capacity of 13,039,488 tons.

Japan benefits from a modern and extensive air transportation system. In 1999, there were 171 airports, of which 140 have paved runways, and 14 heliports. Airports in Tokyo, Kagoshima, Osaka, and Kansai provide international services. The major international airports are Narita, which serves Tokyo; Kansai, which serves Kobe, Kyoto, and Osaka; and Chitose (Sapporo) and Sendai in Northern Japan, which serve many northern cities. Major airport construction projects include a second runway for Kansai International Airport, a $7.2 billion-project for Central Japan International Airport in Ise Bay, and the New Kitakyushu Airport in the Kyushu region located in the western part of Japan. Japan has a large air passenger fleet consisting of private and public airlines.

Japan's telecommunication system is very advanced. It consists of private and public service providers, but a public company, Nippon Telephone and Telegraph (NTT), is the largest provider, controlling about 95 percent of fixed telephone lines. In 1997 there were 60.3 million fixed telephone lines in use. By 1999, there were 30.6 million cellular phones in operation, a 260 percent increase in 2 years, and 6.3 million personal handphone systems (PHS), cheaper versions of cellular phones with limited signal coverage. Personal computer ownership is high: 237 PCs per 1,000 population, in 1998, compared to 459 per 1,000 population in the United States, which has the world's highest rate of PC use. In 1999, there were 357 Internet service providers in Japan. The rate of Internet use is low: 13.34 per 1,000 population in 1999, as compared with 112.77 in the United States. Japan has a very large television and radio industry operated by private and public sectors. In 1997, there were 86.5 million television sets and 120.5 million radios in use.

The Japanese power-generation industry includes both private and public companies, though in 1999, only 5 percent of the nation's power was created by the private sector, a proportion that is expected to increase with industry deregulation (a lessening of government controls). Japan's electricity is derived from 4 major methods: thermal (using oil, liquefied natural gas, and coal), nuclear, hydro (water power), and non-conventional (geothermal, solar, and wind). In 1998, the proportion of electricity generated from these sources was 57 percent, 32 percent, 9 percent, and 2 percent, respectively. In that year, total electricity produced amounted to 995.982 billion kWh, well above the consumption of 926.263 billion kWh. In anticipation of large increases in consumption in the 21st century, Japan is planning to increase its output to 1,280 billion kWh by 2020.

Since its thermal generators depend heavily on large imports of fuel, Japan is planning to decrease its dependency on this method and increase its dependence on nuclear power, although that method is more costly. Accordingly, 9 new nuclear reactors are planned to become operational by 2008, providing an additional 11.3 gigawatts (GW) of electricity. Japan is also encouraging the expansion of generators using renewable energy, such as hydropower and geothermal energy.

ECONOMIC SECTORS

Japan rebuilt its economy in the late 1940s and the 1950s to establish itself as the world's second largest economy in the 1980s, a position it still holds as it enters the 21st century. As a result, its 3 main economic

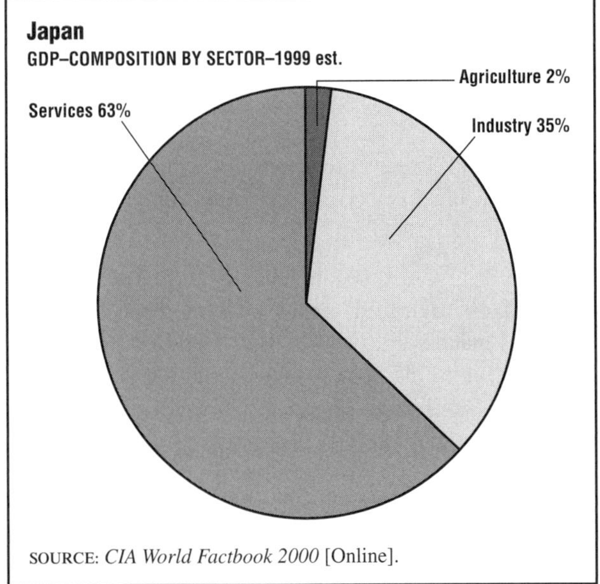

SOURCE: *CIA World Factbook 2000* [Online].

sectors are technologically advanced. Agriculture, the smallest sector, is capable of meeting some domestic needs, though most foodstuffs must be imported. Industry, the second largest sector, has a highly advanced and efficient manufacturing branch that has been the engine of growth for Japan since the 1960s. Its state-of-the art products have captured many markets to ensure healthy annual trade surpluses for Japan. As in all matured industrial economies, services constitute Japan's largest economic sector, and this sector has been growing since the 1980s.

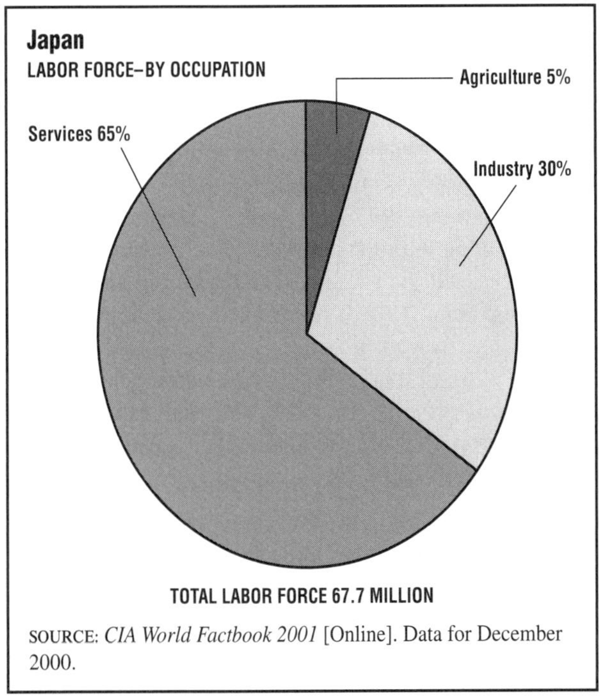

SOURCE: *CIA World Factbook 2001* [Online]. Data for December 2000.

AGRICULTURE

Agriculture, including fishery and forestry, is Japan's smallest economic sector. Its contribution to GDP has decreased substantially since 1945. It represented 6.1 percent of GDP in the 1970s, but fell to about 2 percent in 1999. Its share of the workforce has remained stable since the 1980s; totaling 5 percent (about 3.38 million workers) in 1999.

FARMING. Production of agricultural products, including rice for domestic consumption, is declining due to the scarcity of farming land, which makes large-scale and efficient cultivation rather difficult. High input costs push up the prices of domestic products, as do restrictions on production, pricing, and marketing imposed by the government and agricultural cooperatives. As a result, expensive domestic products are less attractive to consumers than cheaper imported goods.

As an indicator of its declining economic importance, the growth rate of agriculture has been mainly negative over the last 2 decades, even with direct government support, such as heavy tariffs on imported rice (300 percent in 2000). In 1999, the growth rate was 1 percent, a slight improvement from 1996 and 1998 when the growth rates were -6.8 percent and -4.5 percent, respectively.

The agriculture sector is technologically advanced and completely mechanized, but it does not satisfy the essential agricultural needs of the country. Major agricultural products include foodstuffs (wheat, barley, maize, potatoes, rice, soybeans, sugar beets, and sugar cane), fruits, meat products (beef, veal, chicken, horse, lamb, pork, and turkey), fishery products, and forestry products (timber). Export items include fish, prepared foods, cigarettes, crude organic materials, and husked rice. Major imports are fish products, grains, and fruits. In 1998, for example, the values of agricultural exports and imports were about $2.2678 billion and $51.7805 billion, respectively, revealing Japan's dependency on agricultural imports.

In 1999, total agricultural production was 21,177,737 tons, down from 23,016,800 tons in 1995. Rice production met domestic needs, but total output fell from 13,435,000 tons in 1995 to 11,468,800 tons in 1999. Production of potatoes and wheat showed slight increases during this period.

FORESTRY. Forests cover about 70 percent of Japan, of which 40 percent are human-made. Reforestation is a necessity in a land that is endangered by systematic soil erosion caused by heavy rainfalls. Forestry products meet only a small portion of domestic needs (about 20 percent in 2000), while the rest has to be imported, mainly from such sources as the United States and Indonesia. The value of forestry imports was $5.7 billion in 1999, a sharp decrease from 1995 when it was $10 billion. Japan's economic downturn was responsible for this decline.

FISHERIES. Japan has a large fishing industry. Despite the fact that its large annual catch accounted for 15 percent of the world's total for 1999, the industry is unable to meet Japan's domestic needs. Japan is therefore the world's largest importer of fishery products, consuming 30 percent of such imports in 1996. In 1999, 2,924,000 tons of fishery products were imported, a relatively large increase from the 1995 levels of 2,803,000 tons. The annual catch in the post-World War II era, which had always been above 10 million tons before 1990, dropped to 7.4 million in 1997. This decline is attributed to several factors, notably coastal-water pollution and disputes over fishing in international waters.

INDUSTRY

Industry, including manufacturing, construction, and mining, has been the engine of growth for Japan since the end of World War II. As happens in all mature industrial economies, the expansion of the service sector has surpassed that of industry, which has been reduced to the second largest sector. In 1999, industry's contribution to GDP was about 35 percent, a decrease from the 1970s when it was more than 40 percent. In 1999, industry employed about 30 percent of the **labor force** (20.34 million workers), a decrease from 1995 when it accounted for 31.7 percent (21.2 million).

MANUFACTURING. Japan has a highly advanced and diversified manufacturing branch that has been the heart of the Japanese economy in the postwar era. It helped the Japanese rebuild their shattered industrial sector after the end of World War II while enabling them to emerge as a global exporter of a variety of products. It is the reason for the high-value of exports from Japan ($450 billion in 2000). Manufacturing is the most important reason for its constant trade surpluses ($95 billion in 2000), despite the poor performance of the Japanese economy since the early 1990s. Its share of GDP increased from 24.5 percent in 1995 to 25 percent in 1999, registering a limited growth. Its share of workforce dropped from 14.6 percent to 13.4 percent in the same period.

The high cost of labor and the high value of the yen encouraged the relocation of manufacturing to other countries, especially in Southeast Asia and the Pacific region, since the 1980s. This trend has continued through 2001. Japan's direct investment abroad increased from $40.8 billion in 1998 to $66.7 billion in 1999.

Manufacturing consists of light industry (textiles and processed foods), heavy industry (chemicals, automobiles, shipbuilding, machine tools, steel, and nonferrous metals) and high-tech industry (electronics, telecommunications, and computers). Japan is one of the world's largest and most technologically advanced producers of a wide range of light and consumer products such as semiconductors and electronic devices, as well as cars, ships, and steel. Manufacturing includes small, medium, and large enterprises, of which the first 2 groups account for the overwhelming majority, 99 percent in 1997.

The 3 largest contributors to exports are industries involved in high-tech transport equipment and nonelectrical machinery. In 1999, the value of high-tech exports, including computer devices and semiconductors, was $101.5 billion, a decline from the 1995 figure of $113.5 billion but a significant increase from 1998, when it was $89.7 billion. The transport-equipment industry had 1999 exports valued at $94.8 billion, a substantial increase from the 1995 figure of $89.7 billion. Exports of motor vehicles were the largest segment of this industry, totaling $54.7 billion in 1999, an increase from 1995 and 1998 levels, when they totaled $53.1 billion and $50 billion, respectively. In 1999, the non-electrical machinery industry exported $89.1 billion in various products, such as office machinery, a decline from its 1995 exports of $106.5 billion.

A major weakness of the Japanese manufacturing sector is its heavy dependency on imported raw materials and fuel. For example, its iron and steel industry needs to import almost all of its iron ore requirements, which totaled 119.2 million tons in 1996.

CONSTRUCTION. The construction industry accounted for about 9 percent of Japan's GDP in 1999, against a 10.8 percent share in 1995. It employed 9.7 percent of the Japanese workforce (6.57 million workers) in 1999, a small decrease from 1995, when its share was 9.8 percent (6.6 million).

The deflationary policies of the Japanese government since the 1990s had a negative impact on the construction industry, as demonstrated in a 1.8 percent loss in GDP between 1995 and 1999. Construction projects declined along with the economy. These economic policies accelerated the process of relocation of many manufacturing units abroad, resulting in a decline in large construction projects at home. The Japanese government has tried to assist this industry by implementing large infrastructural projects. In 1999, the total value of construction projects was $136.3 billion, a sharp decline from its 1995 level of $206.8 billion.

Many new, major projects after 2000 will help the industry survive until the economy begins to grow again. There is a $400-billion project by the Kansai local government to build complexes for commercial, industrial, and research facilities. There are also 2 multibillion dollar airport projects: one to construct a second runway at

Kansai International Airport, and another to build a new airport in Ise Bay; as well as road projects such as the $32-billion Tomei-Meishin Expressway, connecting Tokyo and Kobe via Nagoya.

MINING. Japan's lack of adequate minerals and fossil energy (oil, gas, and coal) forces it to rely extensively on imports. For example, domestic production of copper ore, lead ore, zinc ore, and iron ore met only 0.1 percent, 4.8 percent, 2.2 percent, and almost 0 percent of annual needs in 1999, respectively. This greatly handicaps the Japanese economy, since this situation makes it highly sensitive to any interruption of imported supplies. The mining industry makes a very insignificant contribution to Japan's GDP, 0.2 percent in the period 1995 to 1999, with about the same contribution to the workforce.

Japan's small mining industry is in decline because of the depletion of the country's small mineral and fossil energy resources. The production of copper ore dropped from 6,043,000 tons in 1994 to 1,070,000 tons in 1998. Likewise, lead-ore production fell from 9,946,000 tons in 1994 to 6,198,000 tons in 1998, and coal production declined from 6,932,000 tons in 1994 to 3,663,000 tons in 1998. Iron-ore output dropped from 3,000 tons in 1994 to 2,000 tons in 1998, and zinc from 101,000 to 68,000 tons during the same period.

Japan has no significant energy reserves other than a small deposit of coal equal to 865 million tons. Most of its major deposits were consumed in the 1960s during the period of rapid economic growth, at which time the annual production was about 61 million tons. The existing deposits are not economically viable because of high labor costs and strict environmental regulations. In 2000, there were only 2 operating mines with a total annual production of 3 million tons. These mines operated with government **subsidies**, and the Japanese government will end these subsidies in 2003. This will make their continued operation unprofitable, since domestic coal is priced 3 times higher than imported coal. Domestic production accounted for only 2.8 percent of supplies in 1998 and 1999, a drastic decrease from 1960, when it accounted for 86 percent. In 1999, coal imports totaled 109,263,000 tons, while domestic production totaled 3,286,999 tons. This marked a decline from 1995 levels of 128,978,000 tons and 6,263,000 tons, respectively.

Consuming 5.5 million barrels of oil per day in 1999, Japan is the world's second largest oil consumer after the United States, but has practically no oil reserves, as its proven stock is equal to only 59 million barrels. This consumption will likely increase significantly when the Japanese economy begins to grow again. Japan's oil consumption has declined since 1996 because of poor economic performance. In 1999, Japan imported over 228,927,000 tons of crude oil, while producing only 604,000 tons, a decline from 1996 when their respective shares were 266,921,000 tons and 861,000 tons.

Japan's natural gas reserves are about 1.4 trillion cubic feet. Its domestic production is limited, which makes it rely on large imports of liquefied natural gas (LNG), mostly from Indonesia and Malaysia. In 1999, such imports equaled about 97 percent of its needs and reflected a 200-percent increase from 1991 levels, while domestic production remained almost the same.

SERVICES

The service sector (financial, retail, tourism, and transportation) has been growing since the 1970s and now forms Japan's largest economic sector. In 1999, services accounted for 63 percent of GDP and 65 percent of the workforce (44.07 million workers). Both figures indicate a significant growth from 1995, when they accounted for 54 percent and 63.2 percent, respectively.

FINANCIAL SERVICES: BANKS. Japan has one of the world's largest financial sectors, a necessity for its large economy. Among the most important are banks, securities companies, the postal savings system, and insurance companies. Financial services contributed 18.9 percent of GDP in 1999, an increase from its share of 17.9 percent in 1995. The entire financial system is highly regulated, making financial activities more difficult in Japan than in other mature industrial economies. The system is controlled and regulated by the Ministry of Treasury (formerly known as the Ministry of Finance), the Bank of Japan, which is the central bank, the Financial Supervisory Agency (FSA), and the Financial Reconstruction Commission (FRC). The Japanese financial system includes other institutions such as venture-capital firms, financial leasing, and asset-management firms.

Despite the deregulating reforms of the Japanese government since the 1990s, the financial system is still extensively regulated. Of these, the "Big Bang" reform has been the most comprehensive one. Launched in 1996, it was aimed at liberalizing the financial system to address the demand of domestic institutions for the removal of various government restrictions and also to open the financial sector to foreign competition. A new governmental entity, the Financial Supervisory Agency, was created to oversee the reforms. A major beneficiary has been foreign financial institutions, which are now faced with less restrictive regulations, and can extend their operations in areas previously closed to them, such as the mutual-fund business. They can also engage in alliances with Japanese firms or take them over. In 2000, for instance, Ripplewood Holdings, an American firm, took over the Long-Term Credit Bank of Japan.

Based on 1999 statistics, the Japanese banking system consists of 9 city banks, 1 long-term credit bank, 7 trust banks, 121 regional banks, 396 credit associations, and 322 credit cooperatives, with total assets valued at $6.74 trillion. City banks are large financial institutions that provide nationwide services while having extensive operations abroad. The largest of these have their headquarters in major cities such as Tokyo, Osaka, and Nagoya, where their principal activity is in serving large corporations, though they are gradually undertaking other types of activities including serving small corporations. Smaller regional banks, with total assets of $1.7 trillion in 2001, operate mainly in a particular region and provide services to small and medium-size companies. Credit banks, with 2000 assets valued at $570 billion, supply long-term industrial capital to large and small firms. Except for the Industrial Bank of Japan, all credit banks collapsed in the late 1990s. Credit associations, with estimated assets of $900 billion in 2000, function like credit unions in that they receive deposits from the general public and lend only to their members. Credit cooperatives, which provide financing to small- and medium-size businesses in urban areas, had assets of $172 billion in 2000. Like the credit associations, they receive deposits from, and lend to, their members only.

The Japanese banking system also includes public banks, such as the Development Bank of Japan (DBJ), the Japan Bank for International Cooperation (JBIC), and the National Life Finance Corporation (NLFC). Their mandate is to supplement the activities of commercial banks. The JBIC is mainly involved in international financial operations such as export/import and overseas investment loans. The DBJ provides Japanese and foreign companies operating in Japan with services such as long-term financing. The NLFC provides financial assistance to small businesses such as retailers, restaurants, and small construction companies.

There are also 89 foreign banks in Japan, of which 14 are American, 30 Asian, and 35 European. Owing to the financial reforms of the late 1990s, these banks can be involved in all types of banking operations, such as retail and investment banking and international business. They are also permitted to have branches and provide services to large corporations. As a matter of practice, they provide services mostly to foreign firms and **joint ventures**, while offering banking services to individuals.

OTHER FINANCIAL SERVICES. Securities companies, which are active in investment services, have the combined role of underwriters, dealers, and brokers. In 2000, there were 291 securities companies, of which the 3 largest—Nomura Securities, Daiwa Securities, and Nikko Securities—controlled most of the industry. Some 59 are foreign companies, such as 2 American giants, Merrill Lynch and Salomon Smith Barney.

With assets valued at $2.27 trillion in 1999, the Japanese postal savings system is the world's largest. It consists of about 24,000 post office branches that accept savings deposits and offer insurance activities and annuities. The system provides an inexpensive source of funds for government projects.

As part of Japan's financial system, the insurance industry has reformed many of its restricted activities since the late 1990s, such as non-life premiums. The industry consists of 46 life and 34 non-life insurance companies with total assets of $1.9 trillion, making it the world's largest insurance industry. Foreign insurance companies are small (44 life and non-life companies), but they are growing. Joint ventures between foreign and domestic firms are also increasing.

RETAIL. The Japanese retail industry is very large, consisting of a wide range of retailers capable of distributing goods and services throughout the country. In 1999, its share of GDP was 14.4 percent, an increase from its 12.7 percent share in 1995. The industry includes restaurants of various sizes, which also includes franchised restaurants of Japanese and foreign origin. Most retail stores are small (less than 500 square meters), although there are large supermarkets and department stores. High land prices and various regulations restrict the number of large stores, while regulatory laws seeking to protect small businesses from competition create a major barrier to the expansion of large stores. Regulations such as those limiting store space and business hours have contributed to high retail prices, though these have recently been relaxed to some extent. Laws also discourage the establishment of discount retailers and shopping malls.

The distribution system in Japan is complex, tightly controlled, and labor-intensive, making the sector difficult for foreign retailers to enter. As a rule, imported products are usually sold at large stores, department stores, and discount stores, while about half of all consumer purchases are made at small neighborhood stores with fewer than 5 employees.

TOURISM. Japan has a very large and well-developed tourist industry, which generated $4.3 billion in 1997. It provides an insignificant contribution to GDP, equal to 0.1 percent in 1997, no change from its share in 1993. The country's mild temperatures and long coastlines, together with its numerous historical sites, make the country an attractive destination. Foreign tourists mostly visit Tokyo and Kyoto on the main island of Honshu, while domestic tourists are also attracted to the northern island of Hokkaido and the southern islands of Okinawa, Miyako, and Ishigaki. Still, only 4.2 million tourists visited Japan in 1997, a significant increase of 24 percent from 1993, but still far below other Asia-Pacific tourist destinations, such as the 9 million who visited Hong

Kong in 1997, bringing $9 billion in revenues. This is mainly due to the high cost of living in Japan, one of the highest among the industrialized economies, and to its remote location. Events such as the 2002 soccer World Cup, which will be co-hosted by Japan and South Korea, will uplift the Japanese tourist industry. If successful, Japan's efforts to host the 2008 Olympics in Osaka will be a major boost for its tourist industry. In anticipation of an increase in tourism, many hotel projects are underway all over the country, including a 780-room Marriott hotel in Nagoya.

INTERNATIONAL TRADE

Japan has amassed large trade surpluses since the early 1980s because of 2 factors. Its diversified manufacturing sector has produced high-quality products such as electronics and cars, which are much in demand in many international markets. Also, the post-war Japanese economy was largely closed to foreign competition through restrictive regulations and high tariffs aimed at protecting domestic industries. Under heavy pressure of its trading partners and competitors such as the United States, Japan began to open its economy to foreign competition late in the 1980s. That resulted in a higher rate of imports, which lowered trade surpluses until early in the 1990s. The economic decline following the bubble economy era significantly reduced demands for imports, resulting in the return of large trade surpluses in the 1990s, which reached $144.2 billion in 1994 before falling to $131.8 billion in 1995 and $83.6 billion in 1996. By 1998, with the economic slowdown, the trade surplus had risen to $122.4 billion, but it declined again to $95 billion in 2000.

The return of large trade surpluses in the 1990s has restarted trade disputes between Japan and its main trading partners, including the United States and the European Union (EU). Two major trading partners of Japan—the United States and the EU—have negotiated with Japan since the 1980s to remove barriers preventing their extensive access to the Japanese market. These negotiations have resulted in relaxed regulations on the imports of foreign consumer goods, like foodstuffs, by Japan, but they have failed to remove barriers in many other areas. Nevertheless, the Japanese government's economic deregulation policy has made the Japanese market more open to foreign imports, especially in the field of consumer goods.

Trade (expressed in billions of US$): Japan

	Exports	Imports
1975	55.819	57.860
1980	130.441	141.296
1985	177.164	130.488
1990	287.581	235.368
1995	443.116	335.882
1998	387.927	280.484

SOURCE: International Monetary Fund. *International Financial Statistics Yearbook 1999.*

In 2000, the values of Japan's exports and imports were $450 billion and $355 billion, respectively. This registered a significant increase in both exports and imports from 1998, when their respective values were $374 billion and $251 billion.

Major exports of Japan include electrical equipment and machinery, electronics, telecommunication and computer devices and parts, transport equipment and motor vehicles, non-electrical machinery, chemicals, and metals. Its imports are mainly machinery and equipment, raw materials, including minerals and fuel (oil, liquefied natural gas, and coal), agricultural products, and fishery products.

Japan's major trading partners are the Asian Pacific countries, the United States, the EU, and the Persian Gulf countries. The United States is Japan's largest single trading partner. In 1999, it accounted for 30.7 percent of Japan's exports, an increase from its share of 27.3 percent in 1995, and 21.7 percent of its imports, a decrease from its 1995 share of 22.4 percent. As a group of countries, the Asian Pacific countries (South Korea, Taiwan, Hong Kong, China, Singapore, Thailand, and Malaysia) form the largest collective trading partner of Japan. In 1999, they accounted for 37.2 percent of its exports, a decrease from their 1995 share of 43.2 percent, and 39.6 percent of its imports, an increase from their 1995 share of 36 percent. The Asian financial crisis of the 1990s resulted in a decline in Japan's exports to these countries. The slowdown in the Japanese economy was the main factor in lowering the share of imports from the United States and the EU. The EU (especially Germany and the United Kingdom) is Japan's third largest trading partner, accounting for a 17.8 percent share of Japan's exports and 13.8 percent of its imports in 1999, compared to its 1995 shares of 15.9 percent and 14.5 percent, respectively. As the main oil suppliers to Japan, the United Arab Emirates and Saudi Arabia accounted for 5.5 percent of Japan's imports in 1999, a small decrease from their share of 5.9 percent in 1995. Japan's economic slowdown of the 1990s reduced its fuel requirements and therefore lowered its imports.

MONEY

Japan has a free-**floating exchange rate** system against foreign currencies (one in which the exchange market determines **exchange rates**). The rates fluctuate with the Japanese economy and those of its major trading partners, though the Bank of Japan intervenes in the

Exchange rates: Japan

yen per US$1	
Jan 2001	117.10
2000	107.77
1999	113.91
1998	130.91
1997	120.99
1996	108.78

SOURCE: CIA *World Factbook 2001* [ONLINE].

GDP per Capita (US$)

Country	1975	1980	1985	1990	1998
Japan	23,296	27,672	31,588	38,713	42,081
United States	19,364	21,529	23,200	25,363	29,683
China	138	168	261	349	727
South Korea	2,894	3,766	5,190	7,967	11,123

SOURCE: United Nations. *Human Development Report 2000; Trends in human development and per capita income.*

market to ensure that fluctuations do not damage the Japanese economy. Tokyo is the Japanese main foreign-exchange market where about 99 percent of all foreign-exchange transactions are conducted.

Japan has not experienced sharp and sudden fluctuations in its exchange rates since the late 1970s, even with the economic decline of the early 1990s. The rate of exchange of the yen against the U.S. dollar was ¥94.06:$1 in 1995; it rose to ¥130.91 in 1998, and then began to decrease, to ¥113.91 in 1999 and to ¥108 in 2000. As a result of the foreign-exchange liberalization program, which began in the 1980s, and the deregulatory reforms in the 1990s, various restrictions on foreign-exchange transactions have been removed. The 1998 Foreign Exchange and Foreign Trade Law eliminated almost all remaining government restrictions and controls over foreign-exchange transactions. Consequently, companies are now allowed to trade foreign currencies and individuals can open bank accounts in foreign countries without requiring government authorization.

Japan has a stock market of global significance. The **market capitalization** of the Tokyo Stock Exchange, the largest in Asia, was $4 trillion in 1999, an increase from the 1995 level of $3.2 trillion.

POVERTY AND WEALTH

Since the end of World War II, Japan has developed a highly efficient infrastructure capable of meeting the essential needs of its population in various services. This capability ensures the availability of safe water, sanitation, and health services to all citizens in urban and rural areas alike.

Japan spends a significant amount of its GDP on a modern and efficient health-care service. Spending equaled 7.3 percent of GDP in 1997, about half the level in the United States. The health insurance system introduced in 1961 ensures the availability of health-care services to everyone. Coverage is provided by 2 major insurers: the national health insurance scheme (NHIS) and the employee health insurance scheme (EHIS). Since all Japanese must take part in a public or a semi-public heath insurance plan, there are few private insurance plans. Depending on the case, the insurance programs cover 70 to 80 percent of the cost services, while the insured covers the rest. The health-care system has contributed to Japan's achievement of the world's highest life expectancy, which was 80 years in 1998.

Japan also has one of the world's highest literacy rates, 99 percent. The Japanese government provides free public schooling for 6 years of primary school and 3 years of junior-high school. In 2000, about 95.9 percent of eligible students attended 3-year senior-high schools, a huge increase from 1960 when only 57.7 percent of the students did so. In 1999, almost 90 percent of the Japanese population completed high school. The quality of the schooling up to grade 12 is very high. The schooling system has been given credit for training an educated and highly disciplined workforce. In 1998, about 45 percent of the population between the ages of 18 and 22 participated in post-secondary education.

Japan is an affluent society where extreme poverty does not exist, although extreme wealth does. High wages and salaries guarantee high living standards, reflected in the high percentage of ownership of electronic devices and home appliances, for instance. In 1999, a color TV, washing machine, vacuum cleaner, and re-

Distribution of Income or Consumption by Percentage Share: Japan

Lowest 10%	4.8
Lowest 20%	10.6
Second 20%	14.2
Third 20%	17.6
Fourth 20%	22.0
Highest 20%	35.7
Highest 10%	21.7

Survey year: 1993

Note: This information refers to income shares by percentiles of the population and is ranked by per capita income.

SOURCE: *2000 World Development Indicators* [CD-ROM].

Household Consumption in PPP Terms

Country	All food	Clothing and footwear	Fuel and power[a]	Health care[b]	Education[b]	Transport & Communications	Other
Japan	12	7	7	2	22	13	37
United States	13	9	9	4	6	8	51
China	N/A	N/A	N/A	N/A	N/A	N/A	N/A
South Korea	18	3	7	5	14	6	48

Data represent percentage of consumption in PPP terms.
[a]Excludes energy used for transport.
[b]Includes government and private expenditures.

SOURCE: World Bank. *World Development Indicators 2000.*

frigerator were found in 98 percent of Japan's households. The standard of living has fallen somewhat due to rising unemployment and reductions in wages, salaries, and bonuses in the 1990s. Heavy government spending on Japan's social safety net, including its unemployment and welfare benefits, prevents extreme poverty. Such spending accounted for $141 billion in 1999, equal to 8.4 percent of GDP.

WORKING CONDITIONS

The Japanese workforce is well-educated and mostly skilled, thanks to the Japanese educational system. It grew from 66.7 million workers in 1995 to 67.8 million in 1999, of whom about 95 percent worked in urban enterprises. The rural workforce involved in farming, fishing, and forestry forms only 5 percent of the total workforce, or about 3.39 million workers. In 1999, 4.7 percent of the workforce (3.18 million workers) was unemployed, a significant increase from its 1995 rate of 3.2 percent (2.13 million).

Japan is a signatory to the International Labor Organization's conventions on workers' rights and freedoms. The Japanese Constitution also guarantees the right to form and join trade unions. Its labor laws recognize the right to organize and bargain collectively. With the exception of the military, police officers, and firefighters, all employees have the right to join unions, to bargain collectively, and to strike. Public employees may join unions, but do not have the right to strike, and their collective bargaining rights are also limited. The government determines their pay according to the recommendations of an independent body called the National Personnel Authority.

There are many unions in Japan, which operate freely. The largest is the Japanese Trade Union Confederation (JTUC), formed when several trade unions merged in 1989. In 2000, it had a membership of about 7.6 million. In 2000, about 22 percent of the workforce (12 million workers) were union members.

Japanese labor law provides for a 40-hour workweek, but the law is not usually enforced in small enterprises. It also prohibits forced or compulsory labor as well as child labor. Children under the age of 15 may not work; children over the age of 15 may be employed for non-hazardous jobs only.

Based on the recommendation of tripartite advisory councils (formed by workers, employers, and public authorities), minimum wages are set that vary from region to region and from industry to industry. On average, minimum wages range between $46 and $53 per day, which are adequate for a decent living standard for a worker and family. Generally speaking, employers usually consult with their respective unions on wage-related issues.

The labor law forbids discrimination in the workforce, though it exists in practice. The Burakumin, who are ethnically Japanese but are the offspring of the so-called outcasts of the feudal era, experience both social and employment discrimination. The labor law provides for equal pay for equal work and the right of women to work. Still, women receive less compensation than men in the same age and work groups. They are also poorly represented in managerial positions, accounting for about 9.2 percent of such jobs in 2000. Also, they form a very small portion of local government positions. Unemployment is disproportionately higher among women and foreign workers, especially undocumented ones coming from the Asian Pacific countries like China, South Korea, and Thailand, who are usually denied their labor rights and are subject to abuses. Work-related safety and health regulations are enforced by government inspectors.

COUNTRY HISTORY AND ECONOMIC DEVELOPMENT

300 B.C. Jomon, an ancient hunting and fishing culture, begins to be displaced by Yayoi migration. Rice cultivation begins.

300 A.D. The Yamato state consolidates its power.

592. Prince Shotoku encourages the adoption of Chinese political and religious practices.

1543. First Europeans visit Japan in the form of Portuguese traders and Jesuit missionaries.

1573–1603. The Momoyama period begins as Oda Nobunaga assumes power.

1603–1867. The Edo period begins as Ieyasu establishes the Tokugawa shogunate, which closes Japan to foreign contact and expels European traders and missionaries. Rise of the merchant class in Osaka and Edo (Tokyo).

1853. Arrival of U.S. Commodore Matthew Perry in Japan leads to "opening" of Japan to the West after 2 centuries of relative isolation.

1868–1912. The Meiji period begins, initiating a period of Westernization. The power of the shoguns is curbed and the emperor is restored as a constitutional monarch.

1894–1895. Japan and China engage in Sino-Japanese War; Japan wins many decisive military victories.

1904–1905. Japan and Russia engage in Russo-Japanese War; Japan wins many decisive military victories.

1910. Japan annexes Korea and retains it as a colony until the end of World War II in 1945.

1912–1926. The Taisho period begins with accession of Emperor Yoshihito.

1923. The Great Kanto Earthquake levels much of Tokyo.

1926–1989. The Showa period begins with accession of Emperor Hirohito.

1931–1932. Japan invades Manchuria and annexes it to its empire as Manchukuo.

1937. Japan and China go to war.

1938. Military leaders in Japan call for "new order" in Asia, which leads to the Pacific War.

1941–1945. During World War II, Japan engages U.S., British, and other Allied troops in the Pacific, Philippines, and throughout Southeast Asia. The war ends with the American atomic bombings of Hiroshima and Nagasaki, forcing Japan's surrender. U.S. occupation continues through 1951.

1947. Japan adopts a postwar Constitution largely drafted by U.S. legal experts during the occupation period.

LATE 1940s. Japan begins the reconstruction of its industry and infrastructure, which were devastated during World War II.

1952. Japan regains full sovereignty upon signing a peace treaty with the United States and 45 other Allied nations.

1955. The Liberal Democratic Party (LDP) is formed by the merger of Japan's 2 main conservative parties, the Democratic Party and the Liberal Party.

1960s. Japan becomes a major global producer of electronics.

1973. The first oil crisis damages the Japanese economy and reduces GDP growth.

1979. The second oil crisis has a less drastic impact on Japan's economy than the first, in 1973.

1985. The yen appreciates against foreign currencies, increasing the cost of Japanese exports, and leading to the relocations of some manufacturing activities abroad.

1980s. Japan emerges as the world's second largest economy, and this era sees the beginning of the "bubble economy." Under foreign pressure, the Japanese government begins its economic liberalization program.

1989. Death of Showa Emperor (Hirohito). The Heisei period begins with the accession of Emperor Akihito.

1990s. The bubble economy ends with the intervention of the Japanese government, whose deflationary policy contributes to a period of economic decline and rising unemployment which lasts throughout the decade.

1995. In January, an earthquake kills more than 5,000 people in the Kobe area; in March, the Aum Shinrikyo cult attacks Tokyo's subway system with nerve gas.

1996. Prime Minister Murayama resigns and is succeeded by Ryutaro Hashimoto. Japan's economy experiences a significant growth rate (5.1 percent) after years of sluggish growth.

1998. Prime Minister Hashimoto resigns and is succeeded by Keizo Obuchi. The Financial Supervisory Agency is established.

2000. Prime Minister Obuchi suffers a fatal stroke and is succeeded by Yoshiro Mori.

2001. Prime Minister Mori resigns and is succeeded by Junichiro Koizumi.

FUTURE TRENDS

At the beginning of the 21st century, Japan has a very technologically advanced and mature industrialized economy. Even after a long period of sluggish and negative growth in the 1990s, its economy is still the world's second largest and most technologically advanced one. While the prospect for long-term growth is assured, certain internal and external factors will impede or slow down its growth in the short run.

The external factors include the poor economic performance of the major trading partners of Japan. After about a decade of healthy growth, the American economy is entering a period of low growth and quite possibly decline and **recession**. With the exception of Taiwan, all other Asian Pacific countries are still suffering from the devastating blow of the 1997 financial crisis. Some of them, such as South Korea, are showing recovery, but their heavy **foreign debt** could easily prevent their full recovery and growth. As the major trading partners of Japan, the poor economic performance of these countries will damage the Japanese recovery and prolong its economic stagnation. External barriers also include the toughening competition among and between Japan, the United States, and the Asian Pacific countries over world markets, especially for motor vehicles and high-tech products like personal computers and semiconductors. More intensive competition will reduce Japan's share of these markets and negatively affect its economic recovery.

Internally, Japan will be faced with continued pressure to liberalize its economy and make it open to foreign competition. Economic liberalization carried out under the deregulation reforms has encouraged foreign investment in Japan, which is a positive stimulus to the economy in the short run. However, in the long run, extensive foreign competition will likely lead to downsizing, bankruptcies, and takeovers. The Japanese government has restricted much deregulation in the manufacturing sector, but it is not clear how long it can resist foreign pressure to do so, mainly from the United States and the European Union. Japan faces a dilemma here: its refusal to comply with their demands could lead to restrictions on Japanese exports to other markets, while its full compliance could damage its manufacturing industry.

Japan's aging population is another major long-term factor. Any future economic recovery will encourage spending by the Japanese, which will further contribute to the recovery, but an aging population has a lower demand for goods and services than a young one and tends to spend less and more cautiously even when the economy is booming. The gradual shrinkage of the domestic market will hamper Japan's economic growth in the short run, and could create major problems in the long run as Japanese enterprises face tough competition in foreign markets while suffering a decline in domestic demand. With an aging population, Japan will face a reduction in tax revenues and an increase in spending for health care and other components of the social safety net.

If the post-war history of Japan is of any indication, the Liberal Democratic Party will remain a leading political party in the foreseeable future. Though a reduction in its popularity has denied it a majority of parliamentary seats necessary for its forming governments on its own, it has proven quite capable of forging coalition governments and will likely remain a determining factor in future elections.

DEPENDENCIES

Japan has no territories or colonies.

BIBLIOGRAPHY

Economist Intelligence Unit. *Country Profile: Japan.* London: Economist Intelligence Unit, 2001.

Embassy of Japan, Washington, D.C. <http://www.embjapan.org>. Accessed October 2001.

Farrell, William Regis. *Crisis and Opportunity in a Changing Japan.* Westport, CT: Quorum, 1999.

Flath, David. *The Japanese Economy.* Oxford and New York: Oxford University Press, 2000.

Japan Information Network Statistics. <http://www.jinjapan.org/stat/index.html>. Accessed October 2001.

JETRO: Japan External Trade Organization. <http://www.jetro.go.jp>. Accessed October 2001.

Katz, Richard. *Japan, the System that Soured: The Rise and Fall of the Japanese Economic Miracle.* Armonk, NY: M.E. Sharpe, 1998.

Posen, Adam. *Restoring Japan's Economic Growth.* Washington, DC: Institute for International Economics, 1993.

Richardson, Bradley. *Japanese Democracy.* London: Yale University Press, 1997.

Statistics Bureau & Statistics Center: Ministry of Public Management, Home Affairs, Posts and Telecommunications. <http://www.stat.go.jp/english/1.htm>. Accessed October 2001.

UNDP. *Human Development Report 2000.* New York: Oxford University Press, 2000.

U.S. Central Intelligence Agency. *World Factbook 2001.* <http://www.odci.gov/cia/publications/factbook/index.html>. Accessed September 2001.

U.S. Department of State. *FY 2001 Country Commercial Guide: Japan.* <http://www.state.gov/www/about_state/business/com_guides/2001/eap/index.html>. Accessed October 2001.

Wood, Christopher. *The Bubble Economy: Japan's Extraordinary Speculative Boom of the 1980s and the Dramatic Bust of the 1990s.* New York: Atlantic Monthly Press, 1992.

—Hooman Peimani

JORDAN

The Hashemite Kingdom of Jordan
Al-Mamlaka al-Urdunniyya al-Hashimiyya

CAPITAL: Amman.

MONETARY UNIT: Jordanian Dinar (JD). One dinar equals 1000 fils. There are coins of 1, 5, 10, 20, 25, 50, 100, and 250 fils. There are notes of 1, 5, 10, and 20 dinars.

CHIEF EXPORTS: Phosphates, fertilizers, potash, agricultural products, manufactures.

CHIEF IMPORTS: Crude oil, machinery, transport equipment, food, live animals, manufactured goods.

GROSS DOMESTIC PRODUCT: US$17.3 billion (purchasing power parity, 2000 est.).

BALANCE OF TRADE: **Exports:** US$2 billion (f.o.b., 2000 est.). **Imports:** US$4 billion (f.o.b., 2000 est.).

COUNTRY OVERVIEW

LOCATION AND SIZE. Jordan, a Middle Eastern kingdom, is sandwiched between Saudi Arabia in the south and east, Syria and Iraq in the north, and Israel (including the West Bank of the Jordan River) in the west. The country has an area of 89,213 square kilometers (34,445 square miles) and a coastline of only 26 kilometers (16 miles) along the Gulf of Aqaba in the south. Jordan shares its longest border with Saudi Arabia, some 728 kilometers (452 miles). Amman, Jordan's capital, is located in the northwest of the country. Jordan occupies an area slightly smaller than Indiana.

POPULATION. In July 2000 the population of Jordan was estimated to be 4,998,564, increasing on average by 3.1 percent a year. The country has a very young population, of which 41 percent are under the age of 20. Only 3 percent of Jordanians are over the age of 65. In 2000 the birth rate stood at 26.24 births per 1,000 while the death rate stood at 2.63 per 1,000. With a projected annual population growth rate of 3 percent, the population is expected to reach approximately 7.5 million by the year 2015.

The Jordanian population is almost entirely Arab except for pockets of people from Armenia, Chechnya, and a very small community of Circassians (the oldest indigenous people of North Caucasus). Although there are no accurate figures to date, it is estimated that up to 75 percent of the Jordanian population is Palestinian. The Palestinian people have been flooding into Jordan since the creation of the state of Israel in 1948, when they were either forced to leave their homes or subjected to such economic, cultural, and political hardship that they felt compelled to leave. There are existing tensions between the Jordanians who inhabited the country before 1948 and the refugees and immigrants who have since settled. The former group are known as the "East Bankers" and the latter group known as "West Bankers." Despite these tensions, the 2 communities are deeply inter-linked socially and economically. Many Palestinians living in Jordan refer to themselves as Jordanians, and it is hard to generalize about the loyalty and identity of the Palestinian population. In addition, there are 1 million foreign workers in the kingdom mainly from Egypt, Syria, and Iraq who perform menial, physical, and in some cases managerial jobs.

OVERVIEW OF ECONOMY

Jordan is a small Arab country with inadequate supplies of water and other natural resources such as oil and coal. Until the 1950s the economy was underwritten mostly by Britain, and in 1967 foreign aid still represented 60 percent of government revenues. The most important event for the Jordanian economy since the end of the World War II was the quadrupling of world oil prices in October 1973. Although Jordan possessed virtually no oil itself, it became inextricably linked to the other economies in the region. Between 1973 and 1981 the Arab budget (the sum of all Arab governments' budgets) rose more than 16-fold, from US$71.8 million to US$1.179 billion, and during the same period Jordanian exports rose almost 13-fold from US$57.6 million to US$734.9 million. In addition, Jordan

sent hoards of doctors, scientists, engineers, construction workers, and teachers to the Persian Gulf who sent home **remittances** of more than $US1 billion between 1973 and 1981. Even after deducting the dinars flowing out of the country from the 125,000 foreigners working in unskilled jobs, the net remittances rose from US$15 million in 1970 to US$900 million in 1981. During this oil boom, Jordan's annual **real GDP** growth averaged 10 percent.

This rapid economic growth combined with the increase in oil prices also caused prices and import bills to rise. Then when world oil prices crashed in the early 1980s, reductions in both Arab aid and worker remittances slowed real economic growth to an average of roughly 2 percent per year. Imports—mainly oil, **capital goods**, consumer durables, and food—outstripped exports with the difference mostly covered by aid and borrowing. The Jordanian government was immediately forced to downsize the **public sector**, stop construction projects, and cut **subsidies**.

In mid-1989 the Jordanian government embarked upon debt rescheduling negotiations and agreed to accept an International Monetary Fund (IMF) **structural adjustment program**, a lending program designed to correct an economies problems. Such programs usually involve devaluing the currency, reducing government spending, lowering the **budget deficit**, and implementing broad structural reforms. The Gulf War crisis, begun in August 1990, however, aggravated Jordan's already serious economic problems, forcing the government to shelve the IMF program, stop most debt payments, and suspend rescheduling negotiations. Aid from Gulf Arab states, worker remittances, and trade all contracted while refugees flooded into the country, producing serious **balance of payments** problems. (Jordan had to increase its imports, which pushed the trade imbalance further into deficit.) This action stunted GDP growth and strained government resources. The economy rebounded in 1992, largely due to the influx of capital **repatriated** by workers returning from the Gulf, but the recovery was uneven throughout 1994 and 1995. The government is currently implementing the reform program adopted in 1992 and continues to secure rescheduling and write-offs of its heavy **foreign debt**, which amounted to US$8.4 billion in 2000. A new IMF package was approved in April 1999 that entitles Jordan to funds worth US$174 million over 3 years. The U.S. Agency for International Development (USAID) agreed to an economic assistance program for Jordan in 1999 that amounted to $150 million. However, debt, poverty, and unemployment (which stood officially at 15.5 percent in 1999) remain Jordan's biggest on-going problems.

POLITICS, GOVERNMENT, AND TAXATION

Transjordan was created in 1921 by the British, who brought over Hashemite Prince Adbullah from Saudi Arabia to be head of state. The Hashemite clan claims to descend from the Muslim prophet Mohammed and have enjoyed very close ties to the West since the creation of the country. Transjordan achieved independence from Britain in 1946 and was renamed The Hashemite Kingdom of Jordan. Jordan is a constitutional monarchy based on the constitution promulgated in 1952. The king and his cabinet ministers hold the executive authority, and the king signs and executes all laws, however, his veto power may be overridden by a two-thirds vote of both houses of the National Assembly. He appoints and may dismiss all judges by royal decree, approves amendments to the constitution, can declare war, and holds the title of commander-in-chief of the armed forces. Cabinet decisions, court judgments, and the national currency are also all issued in his name. The cabinet is led by a prime minister who is appointed by the king. Legislative power rests in the **bicameral** (2-chamber) Majlis al-Umma (National Assembly). The 80-member Majlis al-Nuwaab (Assembly of Deputies or House of Representatives) is subject to dissolution by the king and of the 80 seats, 71 must go to Muslims and 9 to Christians. The 40 members of the Senate are appointed by the monarch for 4-year terms.

From 1953 until 1999 all this authority resided in Jordan's beloved King Hussein, who was one of the most famous and internationally respected Middle Eastern heads of state. King Hussein was instrumental in designing the framework for the "Peace Process" (the aim of which was to settle the historical conflict between the Palestinians and the Israeli government). His indefatigable commitment to a just and lasting peace accorded him the honor of being a guest speaker at the funeral of assassinated Israeli Prime Minister Yitzhak Rabin (prime minister of Israel [1974–77, 1992–95]). A strong proponent of democratization, King Hussein brought an end to martial law in 1991 and legalized political parties in 1992. He survived many assassination attempts, relying on the loyalty of his military. After King Hussein died of cancer, his son Abdullah II was crowned king on 9 June 1999. King Abdullah, along with Bashar Assad of Syria, belongs to a new generation of Arab leaders who have been educated in the West and whose priorities lie in the realm of economic **liberalization**, political accountability, societal justice, greater equality, and international status. Jordan's new politically accountable setting combined with its economic liberalization and its fast-growing population have led to the appearance of several political parties including the **Communist** Party and the Muslim Brotherhood. (The latter is a Sunni Islamic movement founded in Egypt in 1928 and active throughout the Arab world, although banned in most countries. It aims at the establishment of a Muslim state governed by Islamic law.) Several Arab nationalist parties are also active.

INFRASTRUCTURE, POWER, AND COMMUNICATIONS

Prior to 1950, Jordan had a very undeveloped **infrastructure** and the remarkable improvements that have

Communications

Country	Newspapers	Radios	TV Sets[a]	Cable subscribers[a]	Mobile Phones[a]	Fax Machines[a]	Personal Computers[a]	Internet Hosts[b]	Internet Users[b]
	1996	1997	1998	1998	1998	1998	1998	1999	1999
Jordan	58	287	52	0.1	12	8.6	8.7	1.17	120
United States	215	2,146	847	244.3	256	78.4	458.6	1,508.77	74,100
Egypt	40	324	122	N/A	1	0.5	9.1	0.28	200
Israel	290	520	318	184.0	359	24.9	217.2	187.41	800

[a]Data are from International Telecommunication Union, *World Telecommunication Development Report 1999* and are per 1,000 people.

[b]Data are from the Internet Software Consortium (http://www.isc.org) and are per 10,000 people.

SOURCE: World Bank. *World Development Indicators 2000.*

been made over the last 50 years have largely been shaped by the ever-changing politics and geography of the Middle East. Before 1948, Jordan's trade was almost entirely dependent on the port of Haifa, which was in Palestine at the time. However, Haifa was captured by the Israelis in 1948, and Jordan was forced to develop its own port at Aqaba. The peace treaty signed between Jordan and Israel in 1994 made Jordan a main route linking the Middle East to the Mediterranean and, therefore, a major trading hub. There are 2 major roads in Jordan, the north-south Desert Highway from Amman to Al Aqabah and the east-west highway from Al Mafraq to the Iraqi border. Jordan is a very small country that can be driven across in 5 hours, but in spite of its size, the country has a 6,200 kilometer (3,852 mile) road network. In addition, Jordan has a very small rail system that is used only for transporting raw materials to the southern port of Aqaba. There are 3 main airports, Queen Alia International Airport, 30 kilometers (18.6 miles) south of Amman; the old international airport at Marka; and King Abdullah Airport in Amman, used primarily by the Royal Jordanian Air Force.

The telecommunications sector was partially **privatized** in 1995 and currently Jordan enjoys a thoroughly modern communications system. Many people use cellular phones and pagers, and Internet access is widespread. In 1999, roughly 60,000 Jordanians owned mobile phones. In 2000 this number increased to 100,000. Forecasters have predicted that by the end of 2002 there will be 800,000 users. There were 403,000 main telephone lines in use in 1997.

Over 98 percent of the Jordanian population has access to electricity, and the demand for it has been growing at a rate of 10 percent in recent years. In 1999 total electrical energy production was 6.9 million kilowatt hours (kWh), and over 90 percent of this energy is supplied by the state-owned National Electric Power Company. Industry is the largest consumer at 34 percent of total production, and domestic consumption is the second largest consumer at 31 percent. Jordan has entered into a multilateral agreement with Egypt, Syria, Turkey, and Lebanon whereby electricity supplies will be taken from neighboring countries when domestic demand rises above domestic supply.

ECONOMIC SECTORS

The small size of Jordan is mirrored in the relatively small size of its economic sectors. Given that there are few natural resources in the country, the Jordanian economy is heavily dependent on imports from other countries, notably from the European Union. The largest economic sector is manufacturing and the smallest is agriculture. Unfortunately the agricultural sector is vulnerable to changes in climatic conditions, and droughts

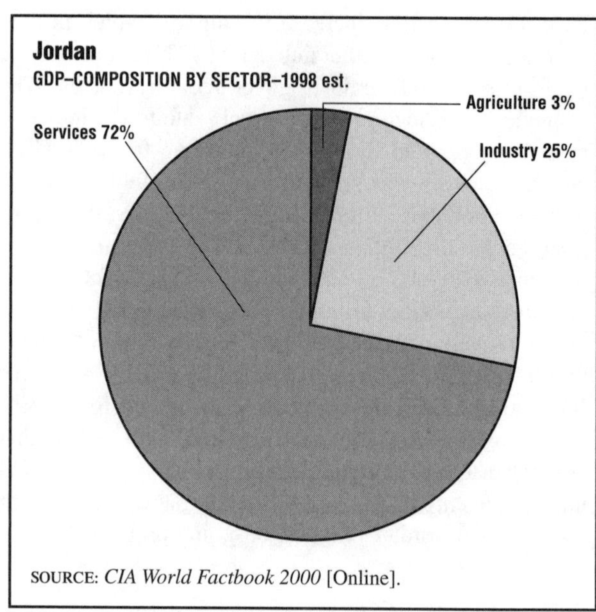

SOURCE: *CIA World Factbook 2000* [Online].

that plagued the country since 1998 seriously undermined the sector's productivity.

AGRICULTURE

In 2000, Jordanian farms accounted for just 500,000 of the country's 8.9 million hectares of land. The agricultural sector employed 7.4 percent of the Jordanian **labor force** in 1998 and contributed 3 percent to the GDP. Jordan experienced 2 serious consecutive droughts in 1998–99 and 1999–2000, which highlighted the agricultural sector's troublesome dependence on rainfall. Three-

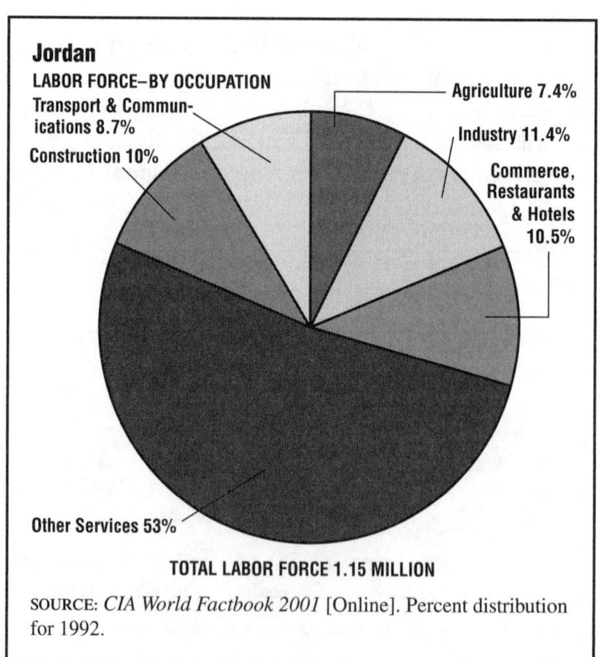

SOURCE: *CIA World Factbook 2001* [Online]. Percent distribution for 1992.

quarters of the country's cultivable land is rain-fed territory to the north producing wheat, barley, lentils, and chickpeas. The remaining quarter of agricultural land in the Jordan Valley and the highlands is irrigated and produces eggplants, bananas, potatoes, cucumbers, citrus fruits, tomatoes, and onions. In 1999 tomatoes were the main crop with production reaching 293,000 tons, followed by 142,000 tons of melons. Agricultural products are mostly exported to the Gulf countries such as Bahrain, Kuwait, the United Arab Emirates, Saudi Arabia, and Lebanon. Some farmers, however, have tried to sell their produce to European markets. They have been largely unsuccessful because of their poor packaging, inadequate quality control, and the high transportation costs involved.

MEAT AND LIVESTOCK. There is very little land for grazing because 90 percent of the country is classified as desert, but Jordan is usually able to supply its people with 30 percent of domestic demand for red meat and milk, with the remaining 70 percent needing to be imported. However, regular outbreaks of foot and mouth disease (a destructive disease that infects cattle and sheep) associated with very dry climatic conditions have pushed the production of red meat and milk 40 percent below the normal levels. In 1999 only 21,000 tons of red meat was produced, along with 171 tons of milk. In addition to this problem, the structural adjustment program adopted by the government has cut subsidies on water and fodder, which has forced 30 percent of breeders to close.

The drought was so severe in 1998–99 that the cereal harvest met only 1.2 percent of domestic needs instead of the usual 10 percent. The reduction in cereal supply was coupled with soaring demand for wheat, which reached 650,000 tons in 1999–2000 when the country was producing only between 40,000–50,000 tons a year. The agricultural sector's problems have caused the food gap (the difference between the amount of food a country produces and the amount of food it has to import) to widen and the import bill to appreciate. In 1995 Jordan imported US$61 million worth of fruits and nuts, and in 1999 this figure amounted to US$82 million, an increase of US$19 million. This trend has shaken the Ministry of Agriculture into reviving talks with the Sudanese government over the use of their spare land and water. Jordan currently has use of 24,200 hectares of land to the north of Khartoum given by the Sudanese government in thanks for the medical aid provided by Jordan in the 1980s.

INDUSTRY

Jordan's industry can be divided into 2 sub-sectors: mining/quarrying and manufacturing. In 1998 the industrial sector employed approximately 14 percent of the country's labor force and contributed 25 percent to Jordan's GDP. This sector is the much-needed provider of foreign exchange because it accounts for 68 percent of domestic exports.

MINING AND QUARRYING. Phosphates and potash are Jordan's main natural resources, and both of these minerals are used in the production of fertilizers. In 2000 Jordan was the second largest supplier of phosphates in the world after Morocco, producing 7 million tons and announcing proven reserves of 1.5 billion tons. The bulk of the phosphate industry is located in the south of the country near the Saudi Arabian border and is dominated by the Jordan Phosphate Mines Company, which is mostly owned by the government. Mining is certainly one of the strongest **emerging markets** in Jordan, and the government has made significant investments in the sector. The sector's output has been growing steadily with profits increasing from US$27 million in 1997 to US$35 million in 1998. The Jordan Phosphate Mines Company has been very successful in attracting international capital especially through contracts with Indian and Japanese firms.

Jordan has impressive proven shale oil reserves that have been estimated to amount to the equivalent of 29.5 billion barrels of oil. This oil has not been exploited yet because shale oil is difficult and costly to extract. However, in 1999 a Canadian firm, Suncor, entered into talks with the Jordanian government and hopes to produce 17,000 barrels per day (b/d), 67,000 b/d after 2004, and 210,000 b/d after the year 2008. This project would be a great boost for the Jordanian economy because it would make Jordan self-sufficient in energy production. Currently, Jordan imports 100,000 b/d of oil from Iraq.

MANUFACTURING. Jordan has never had a large heavy industry base because it does not have the purchasing power to import the necessary and costly machinery. Second, the regional instability makes it an unattractive place for potential investors. The principal heavy industries, such as cement and fertilizer production, have developed only through heavy government intervention. Most private investment is concentrated in light industry such as **consumer goods**, textiles, food processing, and construction materials. In order to spur growth in the industrial sector, the Jordanian government has set up a series of **free trade zones**. Light industry has largely been driven by the growth of Jordan's pharmaceutical industry, which has been very rapid since 1998. In 2000, Jordan was exporting pharmaceutical products to over 30 countries. In 1995, US$125 million worth of pharmaceutical products were exported, and in 1999 this figure had increased to US$143 million.

CONSTRUCTION. The construction industry has been growing steadily since the oil boom in the 1970s, helped by the economy through the remittances flowing into the country from Jordanian workers in the Gulf. The fast-growing Jordanian population has led to growing urban communities, and the capital Amman has almost doubled in size over the last 30 years. Major construction contracts are usually held by foreign companies because they hold the large amounts of required capital. However, these companies have been sensitive to the needs of Jordan and have often used Jordanian architects and engineers in major projects. Local companies have nevertheless been instrumental in building more schools, roads, and waterways.

SERVICES

Jordan tends to attract more tourists on average than other Arab countries because of its central geographic position in the region. Jerusalem is merely 1 hour away from the capital Amman, as are Jericho, Nazareth, and Bethlehem. Syria is a 2-hour drive to the north, as is Lebanon, and Egypt is only a ferry ride from the Gulf of Aqaba. Jordan itself has much to offer the adventurous traveler, including the magnificent "rose-red" city of Petra where the movie *Indiana Jones and the Temple of Doom* was filmed, the Roman city of Jerash, and the Dead Sea, where one can float on top of the water because of its heavy salt content. Jordan is also home to the Jordan river, beautiful deserts, and the Gulf of Aqaba, which boasts some of the best diving in the world.

The Jordanian tourism sector has certainly not been developed to its full potential because of the continuous problems with regional security. When the peace treaty was signed between Jordan and Israel in 1994, tourism grew as more and more Israelis visited the country. However, the sector did not achieve the growth targets that were hoped for. Following the Gulf War in 1991, there was a slowdown in the number of tourists from Saudi Arabia and the other Gulf countries, but recently the deepening of ties between all the countries in the region has led to an increase in the number of Arab visitors to Jordan. In 1999 over 50 percent of tourists were Arab. The number of tourists from Europe and the United States fluctuates in response to the regional political situation. In 1995 roughly 84,000 U.S. tourists visited Jordan, and in 1999 this number increased to 100,000. Since the beginning of 2001 many tourists have canceled their holidays to the country due to the violence that erupted in Israel and the West Bank and Gaza Strip in September 2000 between the Palestinians and the Israeli authorities.

Despite the daily uncertainties faced by the tourism sector, the government has continued to encourage hotel development in all parts of the country. Since 1995 many 5-star hotels have been built including the Holiday Inn, the Grand Hyatt, the Four Seasons, and the exclusive Movenpick Hotel on the Dead Sea coast, which boasts a luxurious health resort.

FINANCIAL SERVICES. Jordan has a modern and well-functioning financial services sector. The banking sector is regulated entirely by the Central Bank and includes 21 banks of which 5 are foreign, 5 are Islamic, and 9 are commercial. The Central Bank of Jordan has encouraged smaller banks to merge by offering incentives and raising minimum capital requirements to 20 million dinars (US$28.2 million). This is being done in part to offset the overwhelming national presence of the Arab Bank, which holds 60 percent of the country's financial assets. The Jordanian government has also historically encouraged the setting up of **microcredit** institutions and, unlike many other Arab countries, Jordan is well-served by 5 highly accessible organizations that provide substantial funds to people in the agricultural, industrial, and housing sectors. In 1996 the first mortgage company was set up allowing Jordanians to reorganize the loans they had taken from the Housing Bank and reschedule their payments in a manageable way.

Jordan has long been dependent on outside capital to sustain its development programs. In the 1980s, the kingdom sought to develop its internal financial base by establishing a stock exchange, the Amman Financial Market (AFM). The establishment of the stock market was an important step in enabling the country to use its financial resources in a more efficient way by allowing both Jordanians and foreigners to invest in the **private sector**, thus helping the economy to grow.

INTERNATIONAL TRADE

Given that Jordan does not posses a wealth of natural resources like the oil-rich countries in the Gulf and does not have a very wide industrial base, it has been plagued with **trade deficits** since its creation. The situation has worsened as the food gap in the country widens, and more and more food has to be imported. The past 4 governments have attempted to address this issue by promoting exports and tightening imports. The dinar was devalued in 1991, which made Jordanian products cheaper on the international markets and foreign imports more expensive. The Gulf War also helped to boost exports as regional demand exploded in the aftermath of the war,

Trade (expressed in billions of US$): Jordan

	Exports	Imports
1975	.153	.732
1980	.574	2.402
1985	.789	2.733
1990	1.064	2.600
1995	1.769	3.698
1998	N/A	N/A

SOURCE: International Monetary Fund. *International Financial Statistics Yearbook 1999.*

notably in the pharmaceutical industry. Jordan's principal export markets are Saudi Arabia and Iraq, the former an important market for pharmaceuticals and consumer goods and the latter an important market for out-of-season vegetables and fruit. Jordan's phosphates, potash, and fertilizers are bought by the Indians, the Chinese, and the Indonesians. As the Asian economies recover from their devastating 1997 financial crisis, demand is growing rapidly again. In spite of this positive growth, however, average annual imports cost twice as much as the revenues from exports. In 2000 Jordan exported US$2 billion worth of goods, but imported US$4 billion worth of goods, producing a trade deficit of US$2 billion.

In 1999, about 21.6 percent of Jordanian imports originated from Iraq (mostly oil), 9.9 percent from the United States, 9.7 percent from Germany, and 4.7 from the United Kingdom. The country imports most of its consumer goods from South Korea, Turkey, and China, and Saudi Arabia provides it with the bulk of its processed food.

FREE TRADE AGREEMENTS. An important free trade agreement was signed between Jordan and the European Union, which took effect in January 1999. It aims to eliminate **tariffs** on nearly 500 industrial goods over 5 years and to spur local industrial activity. Essentially, Jordan's products will be eased onto the European market as **duties** and taxes on European products are removed. Another significant part of the agreement will lift the ban on majority foreign ownership of Jordanian firms. Jordan also became a member of the World Trade Organization (WTO) in December 1999 and is currently in talks with the European Union regarding a free-trade agreement with the European Free Trade Association (EFTA). Jordan has been actively involved in promoting inter-regional free-trade zones, signing an agreement with Saudi Arabia that provides for a free-trade zone before 2005, and it is involved in similar talks with the Egyptians. In October 2000 Jordan also signed a free trade agreement with the United States, and as a result exports to the United States have risen rapidly. In 1999, Jordan provided US$13.1 million worth of exports to the United States, and in 2000 this figure had jumped to US$27 million.

MONEY

The aim of the Central Bank is to maintain a stable dinar so as to enable the economy to function competitively abroad. The Jordanian Central Bank controls foreign exchange transactions as well as the **exchange rate**. The dinar was devalued in 1991 against the French franc, the U.S. dollar, the British pound, and the German mark in order boost exports. In an effort to maintain exchange rate stability in 1995, the dinar was pegged to a **fixed exchange rate** to the dollar. In mid-2001, US$1 is equal to 0.7090 JD, which means that 1 JD is equal to US$1.41.

Exchange rates: Jordan

Jordanian dinars (JD) per US$1	
2001	0.7090
2000	0.7090
1999	0.7090
1998	0.7090
1997	0.7090
1996	0.7090

Note: Rate has been set since 1996; since May 1989, the Jordanian dinar has been pegged to a group of currencies.

SOURCE: CIA *World Factbook 2001* [ONLINE].

POVERTY AND WEALTH

Amman is a capital in which the foreigner neither marvels at the numbers of homeless on the sidewalks nor remarks on the number of flashy Mercedes Benzes on the roads. Jordan is simply not a rich country like Saudi Arabia, and those families that do possess fortunes tend to be discreet about it. Of course, there are exclusive neighborhoods in Amman but, on the whole, wealth is not flashed around. Poverty, on the other hand, does exist in Jordan, especially in cities.

Approximately 15 percent of the Jordanian population of 4,998,564 live below the poverty line and up to two-thirds of these poor people are concentrated in urban areas. According to the World Bank, 17 percent of Jordanian children are malnourished, the infant mortality rate per 1,000 live births is high at 31, and 11 percent of the population does not have access to safe drinking water. In addressing these issues, the Jordanian government in 1997 set up a poverty reduction initiative called the Social Productivity Program. Not only did this ambitious scheme aim to reduce poverty and educate the poor but it also targets members of underprivileged groups who are typically more vulnerable to poverty such

GDP per Capita (US$)

Country	1975	1980	1985	1990	1998
Jordan	993	1,715	1,824	1,436	1,491
United States	19,364	21,529	23,200	25,363	29,683
Israel	10,620	11,412	12,093	13,566	15,978
Egypt	516	731	890	971	1,146

SOURCE: United Nations. *Human Development Report 2000; Trends in human development and per capita income.*

Distribution of Income or Consumption by Percentage Share: Jordan

Lowest 10%	3.3
Lowest 20%	7.6
Second 20%	11.4
Third 20%	15.5
Fourth 20%	21.1
Highest 20%	44.4
Highest 10%	29.8

Survey year: 1997

Note: This information refers to expenditure shares by percentiles of the population and is ranked by per capita expenditure.

SOURCE: *2000 World Development Indicators* [CD-ROM].

as female-headed households, widows, divorced women, and mothers of disabled children. The fund has received money from the World Bank and the **United Nations Development Program** and has been very successful in reducing the percentage of those below the poverty line from 30 percent in 1998 to 15 percent in 2001.

WORKING CONDITIONS

Jordan has a mushrooming labor force. In 1997 the labor force stood at 1.2 million, a substantial increase from the 1991 figure of 525,000. The official unemployment rate stood at 15.5 percent in 1999. Half of the unemployed are under the age of 25, and many of these young people are unskilled. The country has a national literacy rate of 86.6 percent, and about 95 percent of the workforce under the age of 35 is literate. Many young graduates sadly find themselves without jobs, and those who do find employment are often very badly paid. It is likely that the real rate of unemployment is significantly higher than the official rate, and some estimates put it as high as 20 or 25 percent. According to the *EIU Country Profile 2000,* the largest percentage of the labor force, at 18 percent, work in crafts, only 14 percent of the labor force are professionals, and 14 percent of the labor force are plant and machine operators. In 1997, 158,097 people were employed by the public sector and their average monthly wage was US$310. There is also a substantial **underground economy** whose production is estimated at 3 percent of the GDP.

The Jordanian workforce is protected under labor laws enforced by Ministry of Labor inspectors. There is no minimum wage in Jordan, however, the government often assigns a minimum wage to certain trades based on recommendations made by unions. The maximum work week is 48 hours except in hotels, bars, and restaurants where employees can work up to 54 hours. Employment of foreign workers in Jordan is not permitted unless the employer is in need of the expertise and qualifications of a foreign employee. Arab technicians and experts are given priority over their foreign counterparts.

COUNTRY HISTORY AND ECONOMIC DEVELOPMENT

1920. The League of Nations places Palestine and Transjordan under a British mandate following the collapse of the Ottoman Empire at the end of World War I.

1946. Britain's mandate over Transjordan comes to an end, and Emir Abdullah is declared king.

1948. The state of Israel is created under the British mandate in Palestine. Thousands of Palestinians flee Arab-Israeli fighting to the West Bank and Jordan.

1950. Jordan annexes the West Bank of the Jordan River.

1951. King Abdullah is assassinated by a Palestinian gunman in Jerusalem.

1952. Hussein is proclaimed king after his father, Talal, is declared mentally unfit to rule.

1957. British troops complete their withdrawal from Jordan.

1963. Political parties are banned.

Household Consumption in PPP Terms

Country	All food	Clothing and footwear	Fuel and power[a]	Health care[b]	Education[b]	Transport & Communications	Other
Jordan	32	6	17	5	8	8	23
United States	13	9	9	4	6	8	51
Egypt	44	9	7	3	17	3	17
Israel	23	6	11	2	6	8	44

Data represent percentage of consumption in PPP terms.

[a]Excludes energy used for transport.

[b]Includes government and private expenditures.

SOURCE: World Bank. *World Development Indicators 2000.*

1967. Israel takes control of Jerusalem and the West Bank during the Six-Day War, and there is a large influx of refugees into Jordan.

1970. Major clashes break out between government forces and Palestinian guerrillas resulting in thousands of casualties in a civil war remembered as Black September.

1976. The Amman Financial Market opens for business. Non-Jordanian Arabs are permitted to buy shares in Jordanian firms without limit.

1989. First general election since 1967 is contested only by independent candidates because of the ban on political parties in 1963.

1991. The Gulf War begins. Jordan comes under severe economic and diplomatic strain as a result of the Gulf crisis following Iraq's invasion of Kuwait.

1992. Political parties are legalized.

1993. The World Bank agrees to restructure Jordan's debt.

1994. Jordan signs a peace treaty with Israel ending the 46-year official state of war.

1996. Food price riots occur after subsidies are removed under the economic plan supervised by the International Monetary Fund.

1997. Jordan signs an association agreement with the European Union that aims to establish a free trade zone over the next 12 years. Iraq agrees to supply Jordan with 4.8 million tons of crude oil at a considerable discount from market price.

1998. King Hussein is treated for lymphatic cancer in the United States.

1999. King Hussein returns home and is put on a life support machine. He is pronounced dead on 7 February. More than 50 heads of state attend his funeral. Hussein's son, Crown Prince Abdullah ibn al-Hussein, is sworn in as king.

1999. Jordan joins the World Trade Organization.

2000. The government bans public protests following clashes between demonstrators and police during anti-Israeli protests.

FUTURE TRENDS

The change in leadership following the death of King Hussein concerned the international community because many countries were unsure as to whether the young king would be capable of successfully taking a fragile economy into the 21st century. However, King Abdullah has shown the international community that he is committed to continuing the economic liberalization of Jordan. If **macroeconomic** policy continues to be well managed, the Jordanian people will enjoy increased foreign investment, increased privatization, and steady growth over the next few years. Forecasters put the future annual GDP growth as high as 4 or 5 percent.

Following the adoption of the IMF structural adjustment program, the government also hopes to expand the tourism industry, increase exports, and reduce interest rates in order to boost the economy. Nevertheless, the extent to which the Jordanian economy can grow is somewhat dependent on the events that will take place in neighboring Israel and the Occupied Territories during the course of 2001. If the violence continues in the West Bank and Gaza Strip and indeed if a war were to break out between the Palestinians and Israelis, Jordan's tourism industry would come to a halt. In addition, potential investors would be very unwilling to risk putting their money into a region that might possibly be on the brink of war.

DEPENDENCIES

Jordan has no territories or colonies.

BIBLIOGRAPHY

Day, Arthur R. *East Bank/West Bank: Jordan and the Prospects for Peace.* New York: Council on Foreign Relations, 1986.

Economist Intelligence Unit. *Country Profile: Jordan.* London Economist Intelligence Unit, 2001.

Embassy of the Hashemite Kingdom of Jordan, Washington, D.C. <http://www.jordanembassyus.org/new/index.html>. Accessed October 2001.

"Keys to the Kingdom: Economy." *The Hashemite Kingdom of Jordan.* <http://www.kinghussein.gov.jo/economy.html>. Accessed February 2001.

King Abdullah II Official Website. <http://www.kingabdullah.jo/about_jordan/about_jordan.html>. Accessed October 2001.

International Monetary Fund. *International Financial Statistics Yearbook 1999.* Washington, DC: International Monetary Fund, 1999.

Salibi, Kamal. *The Modern History of Jordan.* London: IB Tauris, 1993.

U.S. Central Intelligence Agency. *World Factbook 2001.* <http://www.odci.gov/cia/publications/factbook/index.html>. Accessed September 2001.

U.S. Department of State. *FY 2001 Country Commercial Guide: Jordan.* <http://www.state.gov/www/about_state/business/com_guides/2001/nea/index.html>. Accessed October 2001.

Wilson, Rodney, editor. *Politics and the Economy in Jordan.* New York: Routledge, 1990.

—Salamander Davoudi

KAZAKHSTAN

Republic of Kazakhstan
Kazakstan Respublikasy

CAPITAL: Astana.

MONETARY UNIT: Tenge (T). One tenge equals 100 tiyin. No coins exist. Paper currency comes in denominations of 1, 2, 5, 10, 20, 50, 100, 200, 500, and 1000 tenge as well as 1, 3, 5, 10 and 20 tiyin.

CHIEF EXPORTS: Oil, ferrous and nonferrous metals, machinery, chemicals, grain, wool, meat, coal.

CHIEF IMPORTS: Machinery and parts, industrial materials, oil and gas, vehicles.

GROSS DOMESTIC PRODUCT: US$54.5 billion (in purchasing power parity, 1999 est.).

BALANCE OF TRADE: **Exports:** US$5.2 billion (1999 est.). **Imports:** US$4.8 billion (1999 est.).

COUNTRY OVERVIEW

LOCATION AND SIZE. Kazakhstan is located in the center of the Eurasian landmass in what is known as Central Asia. Kazakhstan is bordered on the east by China, on the south by Kyrgyzstan and Uzbekistan, on the west by the Caspian Sea, and on the north by Russia. The capital city of Astana is located 1,300 kilometers (808 miles) north of Almaty (the former capital), roughly in the center of the country. With a total surface area of 2,717,300 square kilometers (1,049,150 square miles), Kazakhstan is the ninth-largest country in the world, slightly less than 4 times the size of the U.S. state of Texas. The northern border with Russia, which spans 6,846 kilometers (4,030 miles), is the longest continuous bi-national border in the world.

In physical respects, Kazakhstan is a country of superlatives. It sweeps from the high mountain border regions near China across the mineral rich regions of Eastern Kazakhstan, then further west across broad expanses of plains to the oil-rich regions of Western Kazakhstan near the shore of the Caspian Sea. To the north, Kazakhstan is bordered by the taigas of southern Siberia (taigas are subarctic forests that border on the harsher arctic tundra); to the south, Kazakhstan is bordered by the Aral Sea and the deserts of Central Asia. Kazakhstan is rich in oil, gas, and other mineral resources including gold, iron ore, coal, copper, chrome, and zinc. Large oil deposits are located in the western regions of Kazakhstan and in the Caspian coastal region. Massive Soviet Union-era mining and mineral processing complexes are located at various points around the country. Kazakhstan is home to the Baikonur Soviet Cosmodrome, still used as the launching pad for Russian space flights. Kazakhstan is also home to the main Soviet nuclear weapons testing range, not used since 1992, located near the city of Semipalatinsk in the northeastern part of the country.

POPULATION. The population of Kazakhstan was estimated at 16,733,227 in July 2000, a slight decrease from the 1990 population. In 2000 the birth rate stood at 16.78 births per 1,000 while the death rate was 10.56 deaths per 1,000 persons. Migration out of the country, estimated at 6.7 persons per 1,000, has been a major source of the country's population decline. The population was estimated to be shrinking at a rate of .05 percent a year in 2000.

Kazakhstan is the second largest state in terms of territory to emerge from the former Union of Soviet Socialist Republics (USSR). In December 1991, when Kazakhstan declared national independence from the USSR, the government and economy were still closely tied to the Soviet centralized economic and managerial systems. Kazakhstan's politically moderate, multi-national population was divided roughly in half between indigenous ethnic Kazakhs and other peoples—Russians, Germans, Ukrainians, Chinese, Uygurs, Koreans—as well as dozens of other smaller national and ethnic groups. In 2000 the population was roughly 46 percent Kazakh, 35 percent Russian, 5 percent Ukrainian, 3 percent German, 3 percent Uzbek, 2 percent Tatar. In terms of religious identification, roughly 47 percent of the

population professed Islam, while 46 percent was Russian Orthodox or Protestant.

The Kazakh language belongs to the family of Turkic languages. Turkic languages are far removed in structure and derivation from Indo-European languages. Russian shares many structural features and linguistic roots with other European languages. The Turkic languages, in contrast, have few links with major European languages. Soon after national independence, the Kazakh language was adopted as the official state language of Kazakhstan. Roughly 40 percent of the population of the country lists Kazakh at their principal language, about while 40 percent of the population lists Russian as their principal language. In practice, most government and commerce is conducted in Russian.

Kazakhstan's multicultural composition is a source of both tension and cooperation. Given the roughly equal balance of numbers among the largest ethnic groups, there is a widespread recognition of the need for equal treatment under the law.

OVERVIEW OF ECONOMY

Kazakhstan is a new state, established as an independent country in 1991 as a result of the breakup of the USSR. In the first decade of national independence, the Kazakh government demonstrated a commitment to establishing the foundation for an open, market-based economy. As a legacy of decades of Soviet-style centralized economic planning, Kazakhstan inherited a physical **infrastructure** designed to serve the Soviet economy by providing **primary commodities**, particularly energy and minerals, to industrial markets in the north, particularly in the Ural and central Siberian industrial regions of Russia. Kazakhstan's population of roughly 16.5 million makes it a relatively small country compared to international standards, but it is the world's ninth largest country. Kazakhstan is rightly considered to be the world's "largest small country."

The transition from a **communist** system of government and economy to a market-based system has been difficult for Kazakhstan. The transition began in 1991, but the economy contracted sharply in the first years, with 1994 a particularly difficult year. Kazakhstan was shaken by the economic instability that hit Asian financial markets in 1997 and swept across Russia in 1998. After recovering from the setbacks caused by the 1998 financial market crash, Kazakhstan began to make significant progress in 1999. Economic growth surged ahead in 2000, reaching a level of 8 percent. The government pursued prudent **fiscal policies**, avoiding overspending despite the fact that government revenues—taxes and other forms of income—exceeded original expectations. The economic recovery was led by strong growth in exports, particularly gas and oil, and was helped by high prices for fuel products in international markets.

Many areas of macro-economic reform have been highly successful, even providing a model for other post-communist countries to follow. The government established a legal foundation and regulatory system for a private economy. It moved quickly to establish sound and fiscal **monetary policies** and actively encouraged international trade and foreign investment. The government adopted sound taxation and spending policies. The government introduced a national currency, the tenge, which has been quite stable. The government established a regulatory structure for the private banking and financial sector and **privatized** major enterprises, including the majority of power generation facilities and coal mines. The government passed environmentally sound oil and gas legislation that meets international standards.

Yet Kazakhstan's reform has made less headway in other areas. Kazakhstan's agriculture remains without adequate investment in infrastructure such as roads, processing equipment, and farm inputs. Moreover, the banking system has virtually ignored agriculture, failing to provide much needed credit for farm expansion. Kazakhstan adopted a private pension system, moving ahead of other former communist countries, but the social safety net has worn thin in many areas. With a per capita income of US$1,300, most citizens of Kazakhstan have yet to see the benefits of macro-economic reform and the resurgence of world prices for the country's significant oil, gas, and gold deposits. The social safety net has been weakened with declines in health status, benefits for senior citizens, and education opportunities. Dramatic increases in infectious diseases, such as drug-resistant tuberculosis, pose serious social threats.

POLITICS, GOVERNMENT, AND TAXATION

The dominant feature of Kazakhstan's government is the transition from communism. As a part of the Soviet Union until 1991, Kazakhstan was a testing ground for many important communist policies of the USSR. The communist system was distinguished by a powerful central government, an official state ideology of **Marxism**, and a centralized, planned economy. The communist government took control of the means of production (farms, factories, and natural resources) in the early 1920s through a process of **nationalization**. The changes in the Soviet Union began in 1988 with the introduction of open and relatively free elections. Kazakhstan's first open election was held in February 1990. Nursultan Nazarbaev—then the first secretary of the Kazakhstan Communist Party—was elected chairman of the Kazakhstan parliament. A short time later the parliament passed the Kazakhstan Declaration of Sovereignty. The true meaning of the declaration was somewhat obscure. Kazakhstan became a sovereign government but remained within the larger government of the Union of Soviet Socialist Republics, the Soviet Union. As the Soviet Union began to unravel in the autumn 1991, President Nazarbaev scheduled popular elections. Running without opposition, he won the election and became Kazakhstan's first popularly-elected president. Just 2 weeks later the Kazakhstan parliament adopted the Kazakhstan Declaration of Independence, and Kazakhstan became truly independent.

In the first 2 years following the disintegration of the USSR, Kazakhstan began to define its strategy for the transition from communism to a market-based economy. One of the most important elements in this transition is the transfer of property rights from the government to the **private sector**. If property belongs to everyone—as is the case under communism—it is often treated as if it belongs to no one. Establishing private property rights is, therefore, a first step in the transition to the economically rational use of resources. In 1993 the Kazakhstan government adopted a privatization program to return control of economic assets to the people themselves.

The most important stage of privatization in Kazakhstan took place between 1994 and 1997. Sales and public auctions were held to distribute the country's 4 categories of properties: the country's major industries, mines, and oil fields; large factories; small shops, stores, and apartments; and agricultural enterprises. The "case-by-case privatization program" sold most of the country's major industries, mines, and oil fields. The "mass privatization program" held auctions for most of the country's large factories. Most small shops and stores were sold in the country's "small scale privatization program." Agricultural enterprises were privatized, although agricultural land itself was not. Residents were also allowed to privatize the apartments and houses in which they were living at the time. Residents were required to pay a nominal sum for their property, but there were few cases of people who were left without hearth and home by the privatization program.

In December of 1991, Communist Party chiefs of 11 of the former 15 Communist Party organizations of the USSR gathered in the Kazakh capital (then called Alma-Ata) in a dramatic meeting to decide what to do about the collapsing Soviet Union. The outcome of this meeting was the Alma-Ata Declaration, announcing that the Union of Soviet Socialist Republics would "henceforth cease to exist." The Alma-Ata Declaration also established a loose coordinating structure called the **Commonwealth of Independent States** (CIS) and **sanctioned** the emergence of 15 new and independent states from the former Soviet Union. Kazakhstan was one of these states.

In its first decade of independence Kazakhstan made great progress in the transition to a modern, democratically governed state with a market-based economy. The steps the Kazakh government has taken over these years of independence follow a textbook description for the establishment of a civil society—a constitutionally organized, secular society based on the rule of law, the protection of human and civil rights, and the limited role of popularly elected, accountable government. The Kazakh government established the fundamental institutions of civil development, such as a constitutional form of limited government based on a separation of powers, open electoral process, a professional judiciary, a deliberative parliament, free press, and the rights of speech, assembly, and religion. The government also initiated and carried through the process of selling the state's assets to the public through privatization.

The Kazakh government carried out **macroeconomic** reforms including true price **liberalization**, freeing the markets from government controls. It also established the legal and regulatory structure of a private economy, including a modern civil code and tax, banking, and investment laws that accord with international standards. The Kazakhstan government relinquished control of the nuclear weapons on its territory in accordance with international treaty agreements. And, although it is not entirely unblemished, Kazakhstan's record of protection of human and civil rights compares favorably with that of its former Soviet neighbors.

Kazakhstan enacted its first post-communist tax code in April 1995. The Kazakhstan tax code is based on international standards and stresses **equity**, economic neutrality, and simplicity. Taxation takes place at the 3 levels of government: central, provincial (called an "oblast" in the Russian language), and local. The 3 most important taxes are the enterprise profits tax, the individual **income tax**, and the **value-added tax** (VAT). Profits for most private firms are taxed at a rate of 30 percent. Most business expenses are deductible, including wages. The individual income tax ranges from 5 to 30 percent. The VAT is applicable to all goods, work, and services, including imports into Kazakhstan. The VAT on imports is usually 20 percent of the **value added**, or the difference between the purchase and resale price. In addition to these basic taxes, there are a number of other, less common taxes such as the natural resource tax paid for the right to explore for oil and other mineral resources. Land is taxed annually. Business assets are taxed at .50 percent yearly. And individually owned land is taxed at .10 percent of the assessed value. Automobiles and trucks are taxed on their value.

INFRASTRUCTURE, POWER, AND COMMUNICATIONS

With a highway system that includes some 103,272 kilometers (64,123 miles) of paved highways, Kazakhstan ranks favorably in terms of miles of road per inhabitant. Many quite developed countries in the world have much less roadway per inhabitant. Kazakhstan's main form of transport infrastructure for haulage and

Communications

Country	Newspapers	Radios	TV Sets[a]	Cable subscribers[a]	Mobile Phones[a]	Fax Machines[a]	Personal Computers[a]	Internet Hosts[b]	Internet Users[b]
	1996	1997	1998	1998	1998	1998	1998	1999	1999
Kazakhstan	N/A	384	231	N/A	2	0.1	N/A	1.42	70
United States	215	2,146	847	244.3	256	78.4	458.6	1,508.77	74,100
Russia	105	418	420	78.5	5	0.4	40.6	13.06	2,700
Uzbekistan	3	465	275	N/A	1	N/A	N/A	0.05	8

[a]Data are from International Telecommunication Union, *World Telecommunication Development Report 1999* and are per 1,000 people.
[b]Data are from the Internet Software Consortium (http://www.isc.org) and are per 10,000 people.

SOURCE: World Bank. *World Development Indicators 2000.*

freight is rail. Kazakhstan's main railway system includes 14,400 kilometers (8,948 miles) of track. Kazakhstan's transport infrastructure also includes oil and gas pipelines. Kazakhstan has 2,850 kilometers (1,770 miles) of crude oil pipelines, 1,500 kilometers (932 miles) for refined oil products, and 3,480 kilometers (2,162 miles) of natural gas pipelines. In early 2001 a new pipeline was opened to carry crude oil from Kazakhstan's northwestern oil fields through Russia to western markets. Kazakhstan has major port facilities at the Caspian harbors of Aqtau and Atyrau, as well as ports on the navigable Irtysh River at Oskemen, Pavlodar, and Semey. There are 10 major airports in the country, with international airports at Astana and Almaty.

Kazakhstan's railway system was integrated into the Soviet system. Connections allowed for shipment of freight throughout the Eurasian landmass. However, the access to markets in Europe, the Middle East, and the Far East is through rail connections that now pass through the territory of Russia. Kazakhstan's highway system is in a poor state of maintenance but otherwise is adequately developed. The highway system allows for truck freight traffic through all bordering countries.

Kazakhstan is the largest of the 5 post-Soviet Central Asian countries (in addition to Kyrgyzstan, Tajikistan, Turkmenistan, and Uzbekistan). All the Central Asian countries are highly interdependent with respect to energy resources, transportation infrastructure, and markets. The greatest source of wealth in the region is natural resources, particularly gas and oil. The Caspian region's major oil and gas reserves are located in Azerbaijan, Kazakhstan, Turkmenistan, and Uzbekistan. Much of the oil wealth is located in the shallow coastal regions of the Caspian Sea or in the remote regions of western Kazakhstan. The potential for increasing oil and gas production in the region is great. Oil industry analysts expect that the region could be exporting as much as 2 million barrels a day by 2010. But because all the region's oil-producing countries are landlocked, routes to the market invariably involve shipment through third party countries. As a consequence, the complexities of the region's geography and the differing national interests of the countries make access to market a matter of mutual agreement.

Kazakhstan inherited from the Soviet period a telecommunications system that was exceptionally poor. In 1995 Kazakhstan had slightly fewer than 2 million phone lines in use. The number of mobile cellular lines in the country was quite small (4,600 according to U.S. government official estimates). Most cities and small towns rely on deteriorating fixed copper wire phone systems that are comparable to what was used in the United States in the 1940s. Inter-city communications take place through landline and microwave radio relay. However, the system is being modernized. The cities of Almaty and Astana have had recent telecommunications upgrades.

In 1999 the cellular and digital phone revolution arrived in Kazakhstan. Like many developing countries with aging fixed copper wire systems, a steep drop in the cost of cellular services made it possible to bypass over the existing copper service. Statistics are not available concerning the extent to which cellular phones are in common use, but observations on the street would suggest that soon the copper wire fixed system may be replaced by reliance upon new mobile phones. International phone connections are possible with other countries by satellite and by the Trans-Asia-Europe (TAE) fiber-optic cable, as well as by earth-to-satellite-to-earth stations.

ECONOMIC SECTORS

Kazakhstan's economy is export-oriented. Gas, oil, and metals make up 72 percent of Kazakhstan's exports. Since a rise in world market prices for oil in 1999, Kazakhstan's oil and gas sector has benefitted from strong foreign demand, comparatively strong domestic demand, a crossroads geographic location, a favorable foreign investment climate, and multiple **joint ventures** with Western and Eastern oil companies. Agriculture, while accounting for 23 percent of employment in Kazakhstan, accounted in 1999 for just slightly over 10 percent of the GDP. Industry, with 27 percent of the country's employment, accounted for 30 percent of Kazakhstan's GDP. Kazakhstan's industrial sector rests on the extraction and processing of natural resources and also on a relatively small machine building sector. This sector specializes in construction equipment, tractors, agricultural machinery, and transportation equipment such as small

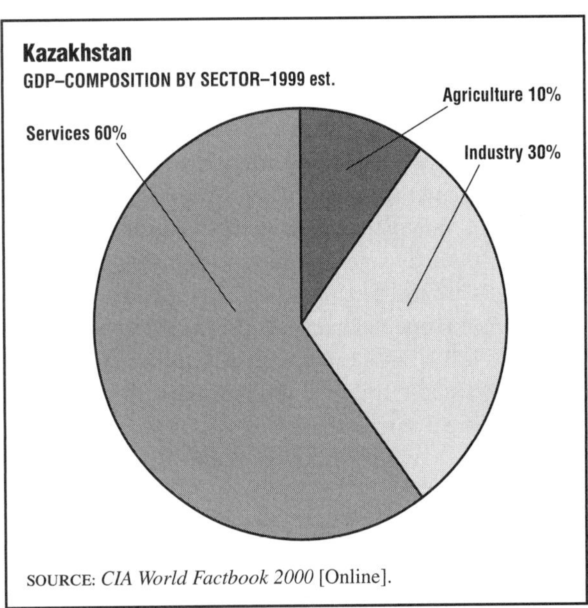

SOURCE: *CIA World Factbook 2000* [Online].

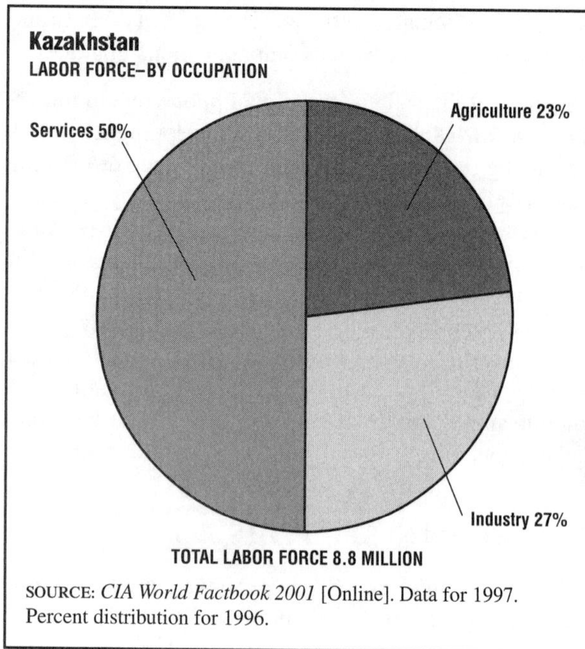

SOURCE: *CIA World Factbook 2001* [Online]. Data for 1997. Percent distribution for 1996.

buses and railroad cars. The country has considerable agricultural potential with its vast lands accommodating both livestock and grain production.

The breakup of the USSR and the collapse of demand for Kazakhstan's traditional heavy industry products have resulted in a sharp contraction of the economy since 1991, with the steepest annual decline occurring in 1994. In the period 1995–97 the pace of the government program of economic reform and privatization quickened, resulting in a substantial shifting of assets into the private sector.

The December 1996 signing of the Caspian Pipeline Consortium agreement to build a new pipeline from western Kazakhstan's Tengiz oil field to the Black Sea increased prospects for substantially larger oil exports in the years ahead. Kazakhstan's economy turned downward, however, in 1998 with a 2.5 percent decline in the GDP growth due to slumping oil prices and the August financial crisis in Russia. A bright spot in 1999 was the recovery of international oil prices, which, combined with a well-timed tenge **devaluation** and a bumper grain harvest, pulled the economy out of **recession**. If initial reports of the production capacity of the new Kashagan field on Kazakhstan's Caspian shelf turn out to be accurate, Kazakhstan's ability to produce oil will far outstrip its ability to get it to market.

AGRICULTURE

Kazakhstan has substantial untapped agricultural potential, yet its agricultural sector is underdeveloped and under-financed. The country's capital, Astana (previously known as Tselinograd), was the epicenter of a major Soviet agricultural expansion program—the "Virgin Lands" program—of the 1950s and 1960s. During this period, tens of thousands of households moved to central Kazakhstan to assist in the expansion of agriculture. Currently agriculture is the country's major employer. Yet it comes in a distant second to the industrial sector in attracting government attention for investment and support.

Kazakhstan produced about 8 million tons of wheat in the 2000–01 growing season, down from 11.2 million tons produced the previous year. Total grain production was about 10.5 million tons, down from over 14 million the year before. Area under cultivation increased approximately 4 percent in 2000 from the previous year, to 9.0 million hectares of wheat and 11.4 million total hectares of grain. Conditions were generally favorable for wheat in Kazakhstan's key north-central oblasts since the beginning of the growing season, with adequate precipitation in the form of frequent light-to-moderate showers. Vegetation indices from late July indicate that crop conditions in Kazakhstan in 2000 were not as good as in 1999, when near-ideal conditions prevailed, but they were better than during the drought of 1998 when wheat output dropped to 4.7 million tons.

One constraint that some economists see on Kazakhstan's agricultural development is the failure of the country to develop firm private property rights for agriculture. Economists maintain that private property rights play a critical role in providing the incentives necessary for investment and careful use of resources. During the Soviet period, large-scale agriculture was carried out on state farms (Sovkhozes) and collective farms (kolkhozes). With the end of the Soviet period, these farms were reorganized into large agricultural cooperatives with the understanding that they would eventually become private farms. However, the Kazakhstan government has postponed the adoption of true private property in agricultural land for cultural and political reasons. The lower chamber of Kazakhstan's parliament decided in June 2000 to postpone debate on a proposed law on land ownership. The Kazakhstan government originally submitted the draft bill to the parliament for passage in 1999, but the law was withdrawn after widespread public protests against land privatization. An amended version was resubmitted for debate in 2000. The year 2000 version stipulated that only land adjacent to rural dwellings, but not all the country's agricultural land, could be privately-owned. The amended draft also triggered public protests, including a hunger strike by opposition members of the Alash party organization. Members of the Alash fear that if agricultural land is privatized there will be little public support for defending the interests of small farmers against the interests of large farm owners. Kazakhstan, they fear, will witness the development of large plantation-style farms that derive profits for multinational companies while small farmers are increasingly pushed into subsistence-level farming.

INDUSTRY

The country is rich in mineral resources, including chrome, coal, copper, gold, iron ore, wolfram, and zinc. The economy is still closely linked with the other economies of the former Soviet Union and especially with the Russian Federation. However, since independence in 1991, foreign trade has been redirected toward markets outside the former Soviet Union.

Prior to the breakup of the USSR, Kazakhstan's electrical grid was a single component within the unified Soviet electrical system. When independence came, Kazakhstan underwent a wrenching withdrawal from the physical infrastructure of the Soviet system. Dozens of independent power grids appeared, fragmenting energy markets. The reliability of energy supplies fell sharply. Cases of forced restrictions of power supplies and disconnections rose. Many small towns in northern Kazakhstan were forced to suffer the severe Siberian winters without gas and electricity supplies in the early years of the transition. During this period the Kazakh government sought to develop independent electrical and natural gas supply systems for the purposes of self-sufficiency. Ultimately, the country came to see the wisdom of reintegrating regional Eurasian energy markets. In summer 2000 Kazakhstan began the steps to create a single power system stretching across the states of Russia, Kazakhstan, Kyrgyzstan, Uzbekistan, Tajikistan, and Turkmenistan.

In 1991 the Kazakh government began negotiating with international oil firms to develop Kazakhstan's Tengiz oil fields. The Kazakhstan government joined the large multinational oil firm Chevron to form a joint venture called Tengizchevroil. The agreement committed Chevron to spend about US$20 billion over 20 years to develop the Tengiz field's 6 billion barrels of proven reserves. The agreement anticipated that eventually Kazakhstan would be exporting as much as 700,000 barrels a day from the field. Other major international petroleum firms, including Birlesmis Muhendisler Burosu, British Gas, and Agip also committed investment in the country's oil fields.

Beginning in 1992, Kazakhstan's northern neighbor Russia **restructured** the management of its state-owned oil and gas companies. Large, powerful, and politically well-connected private oil companies emerged from the reorganization in Russia. These new firms and the Russian government cooperated to restrict the access of the Caspian states to the Russian pipeline system and its connections to western markets. Russia first imposed high taxes and surcharges on the movement of gas and oil and then, in order to block economic development that might run contrary to the interests of Russian energy firms, sought to blockade its southern neighbors by cutting off access to foreign markets entirely.

In response to the Russian measures, the Caspian oil and gas producing countries (principally Kazakhstan, Azerbaijan, and Turkmenistan) began seeking ways to bring energy supplies to market without having to pass through Russian territory. Russia lobbied for a continued reliance on the Soviet-era pipeline system, the so-called northern option. European and North American countries favored the idea of shipment across the Caucasus and on to world markets through the Bosporos, the narrow strait that leads from the Black Sea to the Mediterranean Sea. The Economic Cooperation Organization (ECO), based in the countries of the Middle East, urged pursuit of a southern option. Thus, 4 routes for the Caspian oil eventually gained attention. First was a pipeline from Baku (Azerbaijan) to Ceyhan (Turkey), the Baku-Ceyhan line. Another was a pipeline that originated in Kazakhstan, went through Turkmenistan and Afghanistan before going to Pakistan and the Indian Ocean. Yet another pipeline discussed would go from Turkmenistan through Iran, Turkey, and then onward toward Europe. Finally there was discussion of a pipeline that would supply Uzbek and Turkmen gas to Pakistan through Afghanistan.

In 1995 negotiations among the oil and gas producing countries resulted in the Caspian Littoral Agreement. The agreement, which included Azerbaijan, Iran, Kazakhstan, Russia, and Turkmenistan, was designed to coordinate trade routes, regulate the access to natural and mineral resources, and unite efforts at environmental protection. The agreement also established a Caspian Council, consisting of a secretariat and 4 specialists' committees. The council was to be politically controlled by an intergovernmental council representing the Caspian states. The Caspian Pipeline Consortium (CPC) was founded by Russia, Kazakhstan, and Oman in 1995. The goal of the consortium was originally to deliver oil from the Tengiz field in Kazakhstan to a Russian port on the Black Sea for shipment to western markets. In the summer of 1997, Kazakhstan and China concluded an over US$10 billion agreement for the extraction and transportation of Kazakh oil. In 1998 the 2 countries began to develop and operate the Uzen oil field and the Aktyubinsk oil and gas field in northwestern Kazakhstan. The Chinese National Petroleum Corporation (CNPC) bought a 60 percent stake in Kazakhstan's large Aktobemunaigaz oil field for US$325 million and pledged to invest another US$4 billion in it over the next 20 years. Kazakhstan and China began exploring the possibility of jointly laying an oil pipeline from Western Kazakhstan to China. The project would cost an estimated at US$3 to US$3.5 billion and be the largest pipeline construction project in history. The pipeline, if constructed, would be about 3,000 kilometers long and its annual handling capacity would be at least 20 million tons.

In some categories of mining Kazakhstan is among world leaders. The country has about one-third of the world's chromium and manganese deposits. It has substantial tungsten, lead, zinc, copper, bauxite, silver, and phosphorus. Kazakhstan is also a major producer of beryllium, tantalum, barite, uranium, cadmium, and arsenic. Major iron mines are located in the north of the country. There are reserves of goethite and limonite, but these are generally considered to be low grade. The capacity of these mines has been listed as 25 million tons/year. Large reserves of coal are generally found in the central and northern parts of the country. Kazakhstan has large reserves of phosphorus ores in the Zhambyl region in the south. The government privatized state mining companies in 1994.

Kazakhstan has major aluminum, copper, steel, uranium, and zinc factories. The country's major steel producer, Karaganda Metals (or Karmet), was privatized in 1994 and sold to the international firm Ispat-Karmet. Production dropped for several years but in 2000 began to increase, reaching 300,000 tons. The major aluminum producer, Aluminum of Kazakhstan, is engaged in a major expansion of output. The country's chief zinc complex, Kazzinc, announced in 2000 that it would expand production to 250,000 tons. Kazakhstan also has a growing precious metals sector, with production increases in recent years in gold and silver in particular. The majority of gold and silver output comes as a by-product from base metal production, but there are also separate deposits. There are 23 gold-bearing regions in Kazakhstan. The Vasilkovskoye mine in north Kazakhstan is considered to be the fourth largest gold mine in the world.

SERVICES

Kazakhstan's consumer markets are small by comparison with the markets of Europe and Asia. Consequently, most manufacturing focuses on primary commodities for export rather than on the production of **consumer goods** to meet domestic demand. The service sector in Kazakhstan is large and growing in the major municipal areas. However, the service sector is limited by the relatively small size of the markets and the fact that Kazakhstan's urban population is concentrated in only 10 major towns that are located at great distances from one another.

Kazakhstan's **retail** sales and service markets have been underdeveloped for many years. As a result of the heavy emphasis on primary commodities, little attention was paid during the Soviet period to consumer goods and services. After Kazakhstan became independent, new laws and regulations made it possible to open private businesses offering consumer goods and services. The small service sector surged ahead as business people began offering services, such as car repair, housing construction and improvement, real estate services, legal services, beauty shop services, and other small businesses that did not require substantial investment.

Because few consumer goods, such as processed foods, small appliances, clothing, and beauty products were produced in Kazakhstan, people had to import them. For a brief period of 2 or 3 years after independence there was a remarkable amount of growth in the import of clothing and household consumer goods that was conducted by shopping tours. These were trips made by individuals either by car, plane, or train to foreign countries such as the United Arab Emirates, China, or Turkey in order to purchase and bring back to Kazakhstan for resale large quantities of goods which are imported as luggage. In 1997 government customs agents began to apply import taxes to these goods, thereby discouraging much of this activity. In addition, because the transaction costs of such economic activity is very high, the market for these goods was eventually taken over by shipping and hauling companies that could import large volumes of foreign-made consumer goods.

While Kazakhstan is a country possessing many areas of great natural beauty and potential, the tourist industry is still underdeveloped but growing rapidly. Kazakhstan's new capital, the city of Astana, has several recently constructed world-class hotels. Kazakhstan's other major city, Almaty, has numerous major hotels that cater to international travelers. But the majority of cities in Kazakhstan have few hotels that can offer tourists accommodations and travel services that are in accordance with international standards.

Kazakhstan's banking sector has undergone substantial restructuring during the decade of independence. During the period between 1997 and 2001 the number of banks in Kazakhstan went from 129 to 48 as many small and non-competitive banks went out of business, merged, or were acquired by larger banks. During this period of restructuring, Kazakhstan's banking sector won high marks from international institutions for its rapid adoption of international standards of policy and practice. But these standards have not yet succeeded in convincing international investors and Kazakhstan's citizens that the financial services that are offered by Kazakhstan's major banks are critical to business success and personal finance. The major banks have still not managed to attract major foreign investment. According to banking industry estimates, fewer than 3 percent of Kazakhstan citizens regularly use personal banking services such as checking and consumer credit cards. As a result, most small business transactions in Kazakhstan continue to be cash transactions.

Financial markets are those in which stocks, bonds, and other forms of investment and savings can be bought and sold. In the transition from a **centrally-planned economy** to a **liberal economy**, the growth of the financial markets is critical to success. Financial markets facilitate capital formation for businesses and governments and provide a means of profitable utilization of assets for investors. Efficient financial markets also encourage a lot of otherwise idle financial resources to circulate more freely in the economy, what economists refer to as high **liquidity**. A well functioning financial market is an engine of savings and investment for any free-market economy.

There was great expectation that Kazakhstan would be able to rapidly develop active and vital financial markets immediately after independence. A decade after independence, however, those expectations have not proved well-founded. Kazakhstan's capital markets and stock markets have not proved attractive to foreign investors. **Foreign direct investment** has been concentrated in a few sectors, particularly oil, gas, and minerals development. Kazakhstan's offering of government bonds has met with interest from investors primarily because investors have confidence that the Kazakhstan government, with its long-term expected revenues from the oil, gas, and mineral sectors, will continue to make good on its promise to pay off its state debt.

INTERNATIONAL TRADE

Kazakhstan has become a relatively open economy. In 1999 the shares of export and imports in terms of GDP stood at 38 percent and 35 percent, respectively, reflecting a favorable trade balance. In that same year exports stood at US$5.2 billion while imports were US$4.8 billion. The country has the trade structure of a primary commodity supplier. In 1999 oil, gas, and minerals accounted for 78 percent of exports. In contrast, in this same year consumer products dominated imports.

Kazakhstan's largest trading partner is Russia. In 1999 Kazakh exports to Russia accounted for 20 percent of all exports, followed by China accounting for 8 percent, Italy for 7 percent, Germany for 6 percent, and Switzerland for 6 percent. The United States accounted for less than 2 percent of Kazakhstan's exports. Russia was also the largest importer to Kazakhstan, accounting for 37 percent of total imports. Russia was followed by the United States, which accounted for 9 percent of imports, the United Kingdom for over 6 percent, and Italy for about 3 percent. Other trading partners accounted for less than 2 percent each.

Before independence 90 percent of Kazakhstan's trade was with Russia. After independence, the government committed itself to establishing the conditions for integration into the international market. These steps included price liberalization, through the reduction of **subsidies** and the **deregulation** of prices, as well as a balanced government budget through increases in taxes and cuts in government spending. The government also instituted a tight monetary policy through an increase in the Central Bank interest rate and encouraged foreign trade liberalization by lifting export and import licenses, granting permission to all firms to engage in foreign trade, and lifting **tariffs**. Kazakhstan also devalued the domestic currency to bring it down to the domestic market rate, and privatized and restructured state **monopolies**. The government sought to create a market environment through the legislative and regulatory reform of banking, capital markets, civil and contract law, and dispute adjudication. In order to cushion the social impact of these sweeping economic structural transformations, the government developed a social safety net. The Kazakh government has also pushed ahead with plans to join the World Trade Organization (WTO) in 2002.

MONEY

For a period after national independence, Kazakhstan chose to rely upon the Russian ruble as its currency. None of the successor states of the USSR was in a position at independence to rapidly introduce its own currency, yet none of the countries wanted to be dependent upon monetary decisions taken by Russian financial authorities. Each of the states considered the idea of introducing

Trade (expressed in millions of US$): Kazakhstan

	Exports	Imports
1994	3230	3561
1995	5250	3806
1996	5910	4241
1997	6496	4300
1998	5403	4256
1999	5592	3682

SOURCE: United Nations. *Monthly Bulletin of Statistics* (September 2000).

Exchange rates: Kazakhstan

tenges per US$1	
Jan 2001	145.09
2000	142.13
1999	119.52
1998	78.30
1997	75.44
1996	67.30

SOURCE: CIA *World Factbook 2001* [ONLINE].

separate currencies during the first months of independence. Estonia introduced the first post-Soviet currency, the Kroon, in June 1992. Throughout 1992 most of the states, however, stayed in the ruble zone—those countries that used Russia's currency. Russia announced that it would make the ruble a **fully convertible currency** in the summer of 1992. After the ruble floated on the international market as a tradable currency, it immediately plunged in value, falling from 130 to over 450 rubles to the U.S. dollar. The fall of the ruble motivated the movement of huge amounts of old rubles to post-Soviet countries, particularly Kazakhstan where the ruble was still the only legal currency. As a result, the Kazakh money supply quadrupled in just a few months. To insulate itself from such disruptions, Kazakhstan introduced a new national currency, the tenge, in November 1993.

The purpose of a national currency is to allow the central economic planners and bank managers a measure of control over the economic activity of the country and to provide a medium of exchange to promote domestic commerce and foreign trade. To be an effective medium for commerce, the currency must be tradable so that buyers and sellers can exchange their goods and services with knowledge that the currency is a reliable medium for exchanging things of value. The marketability of the currency depends upon a system that allows purchasers of the currency to buy it and sell it in accordance with their currency needs. This, in turn, requires that the banking system is arranged in such a way that banks may settle their accounts among themselves and foreign banks on a regular basis, moving the currency of the country and of other countries in response to the demands of the currency users. The Kazakhstan government has taken key steps to assure that the tenge is a tradable currency with adequate provisions for clearing and settlements among banking institutions.

The Kazakhstan National Bank, the government agency responsible for maintaining the stability of the currency, has sought over the past years to maintain a stable but flexible **exchange rate** for the tenge. The value of the tenge fluctuated in a narrow band at about T138–143 per U.S. dollar in late 1999 and early 2000, settling at about T142.5 per U.S. dollar in late 2000. Given the strong growth in deposits and the confidence of market participants in a stable exchange rate, interest rates declined. Rates on 3-month **treasury bills** declined by about one-half in late 2000, reaching about 8 percent per annum.

Kazakhstan's central bank has sought to avoid many of the problems associated with the "boom and bust" syndrome of economies that are dependent upon the sale of natural resources, minerals, and other primary commodities. During 2000 the government recorded a substantial surplus. Exports grew strongly, resulting in a current account surplus as a percentage of the GDP. During 2000 the Kazakh government borrowed money on the international market by issuing Eurobonds of US$350 million. These bonds are basically treasury bills that the government issues with a promise to pay at a later date. They are called "Eurobonds" simply because they can also be purchased by investors in European markets. In May 2000 the Central Bank (the National Bank of Kazakhstan, or NBK) repaid outstanding obligations of roughly US$385 million to the International Monetary Fund, substantially reducing the public **external debt** .

POVERTY AND WEALTH

Poverty is a major concern in Kazakhstan. More than a third of the population of the country was estimated by the World Bank to live below the subsistence minimum in 1996. Some 6 percent of the population was estimated to live on less than US$2.15 per day. Almost two-thirds of the poor live in the southern and eastern regions of the country, the areas that are largely agrarian and rural. Certain groups are most affected by poverty: the young, households with many children, households with one parent, and the retired.

Under the Soviet system, industrial facilities based in cities and regions were largely responsible for the welfare of the local citizens. The farms, factories, offices, and enterprises in which virtually every Soviet citizen worked were responsible for providing everything from road maintenance to health care to childcare. When Kazakhstan ended state ownership of industry and agriculture, these large enterprises ceased to provide social services. However, few programs came into being to rapidly assume the responsibility for providing these public services. Many Kazakh citizens who were unable to find employment in the new, rapidly changing circumstances of a market economy found their incomes lost or dramatically diminished and social services almost non-existent.

In the Soviet Union, most people lived at a roughly equal socio-economic level. The Soviet personnel system and the system of distribution of state resources such as

GDP per Capita (US$)

Country	1975	1980	1985	1990	1998
Kazakhstan	N/A	N/A	N/A	2,073	1,281
United States	19,364	21,529	23,200	25,363	29,683
Russia	2,555	3,654	3,463	3,668	2,138
Uzbekistan	N/A	N/A	N/A	1,338	1,007

SOURCE: United Nations. *Human Development Report 2000; Trends in human development and per capita income.*

Distribution of Income or Consumption by Percentage Share: Kazakhstan

Lowest 10%	2.7
Lowest 20%	6.7
Second 20%	11.5
Third 20%	16.4
Fourth 20%	23.1
Highest 20%	42.3
Highest 10%	26.3

Survey year: 1996

Note: This information refers to expenditure shares by percentiles of the population and is ranked by per capita expenditure.

SOURCE: *2000 World Development Indicators* [CD-ROM].

housing and access to education was highly standardized. Such systems are inherently wasteful because the scarcity of goods and services is not efficiently or accurately represented. The end of communism and the advent of market economics introduced new efficiencies. At the same time, the transition period introduced the possibility of using government positions or control over resources to amass great personal wealth. New extremes of rich and poor arose quickly. Some townspeople with access to wealth benefitted greatly from the first stages of the post-communist transition. Many rural dwellers, such as herdsmen and farmers, suffered terribly as government subsidies came to an end and health, education, and other social services ended abruptly. Many small towns that had been organized during the Soviet period were essentially "company towns," that is, towns in which virtually all the population worked in one large factory. After the Soviet era, many of these communities turned into ghost towns as unprofitable factories teetered on the edge of bankruptcy, released workers, and were unwilling to support the social services for the towns and villages.

Some analysts estimate that as much as 30 percent of the economic activity in the Kazakh service sector takes place in the **informal economy** and is thus not visible to tax collectors. In transition economies people often seek to conceal their earnings out of fear that conspicuous wealth may attract outlaws or the tax collectors. Payments for services are often made in cash; many kinds of government control over the economy allow bureaucrats to pad their modest incomes through bribes, that is secure payments for government licenses, approvals, or support. As a consequence, many business people find that they often have to make bribes or other payments to advance their business deals or assure that they will not be harassed by officials.

A step the Kazakhstan government has taken to address this situation is the strengthening of the funded pension system that was introduced 1 January 1998. This fully-funded pension system was designed to help the government improve the marketability of financial assets held by the pension funds. Pension funds are now compelled to use internationally-accepted accounting and valuation standards, and they have greater freedom to invest in high-quality foreign assets. In the long run, workers in Kazakhstan can be assured that their earnings over their productive years will grow and pay them dividends in retirement. However, the new system amasses money as new entrants into the **workforce** begin regularly paying a portion of their incomes into the pension funds. Those workers already on pension or close to pension will receive little benefit from the funds. A great social injustice of the transition period is the large number of **pensioners** who worked their entire productive lives and only to receive monthly pensions amounting to no more than US$15 per month.

The government has taken steps to focus public assistance programs on providing critical services to the truly needy. In 1998 the Kazakhstan government adopted a system of needs tests to ensure that social assistance is provided to those who need it and not provided to those who are not entitled to it. In addition, the government discontinued reliance on unemployment registration as a means of identifying eligibility for social assistance. Overall, public assistance in such areas as medical care,

Household Consumption in PPP Terms

Country	All food	Clothing and footwear	Fuel and power[a]	Health care[b]	Education[b]	Transport & Communications	Other
Kazakhstan	37	10	20	9	6	6	12
United States	13	9	9	4	6	8	51
Russia	28	11	16	7	15	8	16
Uzbekistan	34	3	13	4	7	9	30

Data represent percentage of consumption in PPP terms.

[a]Excludes energy used for transport.

[b]Includes government and private expenditures.

SOURCE: World Bank. *World Development Indicators 2000.*

assistance to children and the elderly, however, has fallen far below the level needed.

WORKING CONDITIONS

Kazakhstan has a workforce of roughly 8.8 million people. Some 27 percent of the labor force is occupied in industry, 23 percent in agriculture and forestry, 20 percent in education, and the remaining 30 percent in the service sector and other sectors such as government and military. The unemployment rate was estimated to be 14 percent in 1998. Unemployment is much higher in rural areas than in urban areas, where the service sector has enjoyed robust growth in recent years. Employment by women in urban areas lags behind that of men by a considerable margin, reaching 20 percent.

Kazakhstan has paid a high social price for its rapid progress in the transition from communism. Under communism, economic growth was restrained but there was a very low level of inequality. Most workers made roughly the same income. Extremes of high and low incomes were rare. Since independence, Kazakhstan's success in rapid macroeconomic and political reforms created anxiety among the country's southern neighbors, particularly Uzbekistan, where government-regulated prices and subsidized production were still the norm. Kazakhstan's abandonment of subsidies for Soviet-era industries permitted a steep industrial decline, throwing hundreds of thousands of Kazakh citizens out of work. Kazakhstan's success in privatization led to charges in the press and among many industrial workers that the Kazakhstan government had sold out to large **multinational corporations**, abandoning social principles in favor of rapid income gains for the few. Kazakhstan's efforts to court a few large multinational enterprises—particularly in the gas, oil, and minerals sectors—led to the widespread perception of growing corruption, bribery, and cronyism.

The socio-economic consequences of the transition are immediately visible in Kazakhstan. High unemployment, deteriorating or even non-existent social services, unpaid salaries, social security and pension payments, unheated apartments, and unavoidable confrontations with dishonest or corrupt local officials: these are everyday features of life in Kazakhstan.

Kazakhstan's industrial workers have sought to use collective bargaining to promote their common welfare. However, trade unionism has weak traditions in the country. The Confederation of Free Trade Unions claims a membership of about 250,000 workers. In fact, the number of independent trade union members is much lower. Other unions have had even less success. To obtain legal status, an independent union must apply for registration with local judicial authorities and with the Ministry of Justice. Registration is generally lengthy, difficult, and expensive. Independent unions gravitated towards opposition political candidates but turned more pro-government in 1999 when the government authorities introduced protectionist trade policies aimed at supporting domestic industries. Kazakhstan law does little to protect workers who join independent unions from threats and harassment by enterprise management or state-run unions. Members of independent unions have been dismissed, transferred to lower-paying jobs, threatened, and intimidated.

COUNTRY HISTORY AND ECONOMIC DEVELOPMENT

650–750. A tribal alliance of herders and nomads known as the Kaganate moves into the area that is now Kazakhstan.

750. Arabs invade the area, spreading the influence of the Islamic culture and religion.

1700. The people divide into 3 Kazakh tribes (called "Juz"), which become known as the senior, middle, and junior tribes.

1731. The junior tribe joins the Russian empire, while the senior and middle tribes remain independent.

1820. The khan of Kokand, ruling from the ancient city of Kokand located far to the south, extends its political influence northward, capturing and taking control of areas of southern Kazakhstan.

1850. Major Russian **emigration** occurs. Russians arrive in Kazakhstan in search of new agricultural lands.

1867. The Russian tsar decrees the establishment of the Turkestan general-governorship, extending official Russian rule into Kazakhstan and Central Asia, making Kazakhstan part of the Russian Empire.

1917. The Bolshevik Revolution in Russia toward the end of World War I leads to the establishment of a communist government and the creation, in 1918, of the Russian Socialist Republic (which includes the territory of present-day Kazakhstan).

1925. Ethnic Kazakhs in the southern region gain recognition as the separate Karakalpak Autonomous Province. The province is included in the new republic of Uzbekistan, not in Kazakhstan, thereby dividing the ethnic Kazakhs.

1929. The capital of Kazakhstan is moved from the city of Kzyl Orda to Alma-Ata (later known as Almaty).

1929–33. The Russian government embarks upon the collectivization of agriculture to reorganize agriculture along the lines of industrial management. The disastrous agricultural policies lead to widespread opposition, farmers' uprisings, and famine.

1936. The province of the territories of modern day Kazakhstan is proclaimed to be a Soviet Socialist Republic, called the Kazakh Soviet Socialist Republic. During the rule of Soviet leader Joseph Stalin, the communist government conducts campaigns against political opposition. Thousands of Kazakhs are imprisoned for crimes against the state, the political crime of disagreement with state policy.

1957–61. Under the leadership of Soviet leader Nikita Khrushchev a new agricultural initiative called the Virgin Lands Campaign relocates tens of thousands of people from the European parts of the USSR to Kazakhstan. Kazakhstan is identified as the new bread basket of the USSR.

1986. After a decision by Soviet leaders to appoint an ethnic Russian as the head of the Kazakhstan Communist Party, widespread nationalist opposition to the dominance of the Communist Party results in public protests and riots.

1990. Demands for greater political autonomy on the part of the Socialist Republics of the USSR lead to a movement for republican sovereignty. The Kazakhstan Soviet-era parliament passes the Declaration of Sovereignty, asserting that the natural resources of the country belong to Kazakhstan and not the Soviet Union.

1991. An unsuccessful attempt to take over the Russian government by Communist Party hard-liners precipitates a crisis in Moscow. Many rank and file communists join opponents of Moscow's long-standing domination of the rest of the country. Kazakhstan, like all of the 15 republics that made up the USSR, declares national independence.

1991. In December, 11 high Communist Party officials gather in Almaty (then known as "Alma-Ata") to sign a document announcing the end of the USSR and the establishment of the Commonwealth of Independent States (CIS).

1992. Kazakhstan joins major international organizations such as the United Nations, the World Bank, the Asian Development Bank, and the European Bank for Reconstruction and Development.

1993. The Kazakhstan Constitution is adopted.

1995. A new version of the Kazakhstan Constitution, assigning greater powers to the executive branch, is adopted.

1995. The first Kazakhstan tax code is introduced.

2000. Kazakhstan joins the Eurasian Economic Community, an international organization designed to create a common economic market throughout much of the former USSR.

FUTURE TRENDS

Kazakhstan's government has made substantial progress in the transition to a modern, globally integrated economy. Following independence, Kazakhstan quickly carried out macroeconomic reforms and established the legal and regulatory structure of a private economy. The country has adopted a tradable currency, liberalized prices, and privatized major sectors of the economy including industry, telecommunications, and energy. Kazakhstan lifted virtually all subsidies on consumer goods in 1994. State industrial subsidies were abandoned in 1994, and small-scale privatization has also taken place. Kazakhstan established the fundamental institutions of a civil society—a constitution recognizing a separation of powers, an electoral process, a professional judiciary, a deliberative parliament, a free press, and rights of speech, assembly, and religious freedom. Kazakhstan's record of protection of human and civil rights compares favorably with that of its former Soviet neighbors. Given these facts, it can be argued that Kazakhstan has gone further than many of the former Soviet states in the establishment of a modern state. Yet serious challenges remain.

Kazakhstan inherited a physical infrastructure designed to serve the Soviet economy by providing primary commodities such as energy and minerals to industrial markets in the north, particularly in the Ural and central Siberian industrial regions of Russia. Kazakhstan's industry was previously tightly connected to these regions of Russia because its industrial suppliers and consumers were primarily in these regions. The country's rail and road transportation systems were designed to connect its primary commodity industries with the northern manufacturing markets. These are the realities of Kazakhstan's contemporary situation: primarily commodity-based industries, a sparse population, previous economic specialization under Soviet-style **socialism**, and a legacy of centralized planning.

In terms of Kazakhstan's political future, the stakes are obviously big. Kazakhstan is potentially one of the richer countries of the region, and perhaps one of the richer countries of the world if it can succeed in negotiating access to world markets for its oil, gas, and mineral riches. But an oil-led economic development strategy has potential drawbacks for Kazakhstan. A strategy that relies exclusively on the export of primary commodities and raw materials is likely to make Kazakhstan susceptible to fluctuations in international markets. Like the other post-communist countries, Kazakhstan will very likely continue to be influenced by economic trends that it cannot control. Private international investors, with the exception of the major oil companies, have been reluctant to make major commitments to Kazakhstan. Those foreign companies that have moved into the Kazakhstan market, such as Tractabel, the large European energy company, have found the Kazakh domestic market to be more challenging than they anticipated. There is a consensus that the Kazakh government needs to strengthen the institutional and legal underpinnings of a market economy, balance its public and private sectors, and make a more substantial commitment to strengthening the social safety net. The Kazakh government has made substantial progress in developing a market-based policy framework, at least in theory. Making this framework function in practice is one of the main challenges facing the country's economic managers.

DEPENDENCIES

Kazakhstan has no territories or colonies.

BIBLIOGRAPHY

Cummings, Sally N. *Kazakhstan: Centre-Periphery Relations.* London: Royal Institute of International Affairs, 2000.

Economist Intelligence Unit. *Country Profile: Kazakhstan.* London: Economist Intelligence Unit, 2001.

Hopkirk, Peter. *The Great Game: The Struggle for Empire in Central Asia.* London: Kodansha International, 1994.

Kalyuzhnova, Yelena. *Kazakstani Economy: Independence and Transition.* New York: St. Martin's Press, 1998.

Kaser, Michael Charles. *The Economies of Kazakstan and Uzbekistan.* London; Royal Institute of International Affairs, and Washington, DC: Brookings Institution, 1997.

Kazakhstan: The Transition to a Market Economy. Washington, D.C.: World Bank, 1993.

Kazecon. <http://www.kazecon.kz/>. Accessed February 2001.

Kazhegeldin, Akezhan. "Shattered Image: Misconceptions of Democracy and Capitalism in Kazakhstan," *Harvard International Review.* Vol. 22, Winter/Spring 2000.

International Monetary Fund. *Republic of Kazakhstan and the IMF.* <http://www.imf.org/external/country/KAZ/index.htm>. Accessed February 2001.

The National Bank of Kazakhstan. <http://www.nationalbank.kz/eng/>. Accessed February 2001.

President's Office of the Kazakhstan Government. *Welcome to the Official Kazakhstan.* <http://www.president.kz/>. Accessed February 2001.

U.S. Central Intelligence Agency. *World Factbook 2000.* <http://www.odci.gov/cia/publications/factbook/index.html>. Accessed September 2001.

U.S. Department of State. *FY 2000 Country Commercial Guide: Kazakhstan.* <http://www.state.gov/www/about_state/business/com_guides/2000/Europe/index.html>. Accessed September 2001.

—Gregory Gleason

KIRIBATI

Republic of Kiribati

CAPITAL: Tarawa.

MONETARY UNIT: Australian dollar (A$). One Australian dollar equals 100 cents. There are notes of A$5, 10, 20, 50, and 100. There are coins of A$1 and 2, and 1, 2, 5, 10, 20, and 50 cents.

CHIEF EXPORTS: Copra, seaweed, fish.

CHIEF IMPORTS: Food, machinery and equipment, miscellaneous manufactured goods, fuels.

GROSS DOMESTIC PRODUCT: US$74 million (1999 est.).

BALANCE OF TRADE: **Exports:** US$6 million (1998 est.). **Imports:** US$37 million (1998 est.).

COUNTRY OVERVIEW

LOCATION AND SIZE. The Republic of Kiribati comprises 33 atolls in 3 principal island groups, scattered within an area of about 5 million square kilometers (2 million square miles) in the mid-Pacific Ocean. The 3 island groups are the Gilbert Islands, the Line Islands, and the Phoenix Islands. The country extends about 3,870 kilometers (2,400 miles) from east to west and about 2,050 kilometers (1,275 miles) from north to south and has a coastline of 1,143 kilometers (710 miles). The total land area is 717 square kilometers (277 square miles). The nearest neighbors are Nauru to the west, and Tuvalu and Tokelau to the south. The capital, Tarawa, is on the island of Bairiki. Bairiki is the most populous island with around 65,000 inhabitants. The nation's largest atoll is Kiritimati (Christmas Island)—in the Line Islands group at the eastern extremity—at 388 square kilometers (150 square miles). The smallest is Banaba Island in the west at 6 square kilometers (2.3 square miles).

POPULATION. The population of Kiribati was estimated at 91,985 in July 2000. The current annual population growth rate is 2.34 percent, which will result in a population of 113,509 by 2010. The birth rate is 32.43 births per 1,000 population, and the fertility rate is 4.4 births per woman. The death rate is 9.01 deaths per 1,000 population. There is little or no migration to or from Kiribati. Partly because of sanitation problems caused by the lack of fresh water, as well as heavy pollution in the lagoon of South Tarawa, Kiribati has a high infant morality rate of 55.36 deaths per 1,000 live births (compared to the U.S. rate of 7 deaths per 1,000 live births).

The people are known locally as I-Kiribati. The population structure is biased toward the younger age groups, with some 41 percent of the population aged less than 15, while just 3 percent are over the age of 64. Most Kiribati are ethnically Micronesian (78 percent). The population is mainly urban and more than two-thirds (65,000) live on Tarawa atoll.

OVERVIEW OF ECONOMY

The Gilbert Islands were granted self-rule by the United Kingdom in 1971 and complete independence in 1979 under a new name, Kiribati. The United States relinquished all claims to the sparsely inhabited Phoenix and Line Island groups in a 1979 treaty of friendship with Kiribati, thus giving the island nation its present geographic composition.

The economy of Kiribati is small, and growth prospects are limited by the nation's remote location, poor **infrastructure**, poor soil, unskilled **labor force**, and lack of natural resources. Marine resources offer the greatest potential for the development of an independent, sustainable economy. Interest earned from the phosphate reserve fund is the nation's main source of foreign exchange. Prior to independence, it was realized that the phosphate resources of Kiribati were limited, and instead of using the royalty revenues from phosphate mining for immediate expenditures, they were placed in a trust fund, the Revenue Equalization Reserve Fund (RERF). The interest income from the investment of this trust fund has

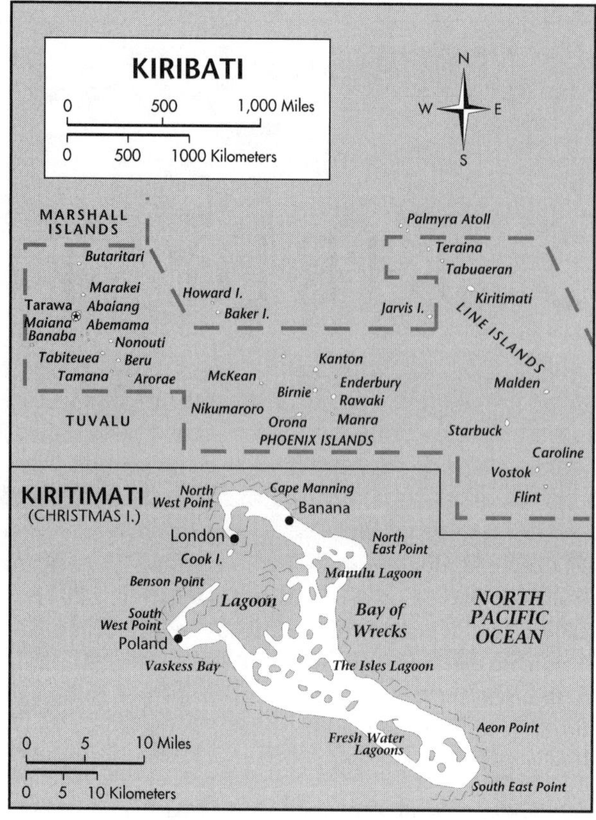

been available for expenditure by the Kiribati government since independence in 1979. Commercially viable phosphate deposits were exhausted by the time of independence. Other sources of foreign exchange include some commodity exports (copra [coconut meat], seaweed, and fish), licensing income from fishing, and **remittances** from Kiribati citizens working for international shipping lines. The financial sector is at an early stage of development, as are private initiatives in other sectors. Economic development is constrained by a shortage of skilled workers, weak infrastructure, and remoteness from international markets.

Kiribati has a modest income level that places it among the poorer countries in the world's lower middle-income group. The agricultural base, including subsistence production, is narrow and generated 14 percent of GDP in 1996. Copra is the only important **cash crop**, and commercial fishing (mainly tuna) is undertaken by the small fleet of the national fishing company. The agriculture sector (including fishing) is the occupation of the majority of the working population and accounted for 71 percent of employment in 1990, though most of this employment was self-employment on small family farms. The industrial sector contributed 7 percent of GDP in 1996 (of which manufacturing was 1 percent) and the services sector contributed 79 percent. The main service activity is the government sector, with trade and hotels accounting for 14 percent of GDP. Tourism remains underdeveloped, although it has the potential to become the second largest sector after fisheries. Kiribati's extremely limited export base and dependence on imports for almost all essential commodities result in a permanent (and widening) **trade deficit**, which is in most years only partially offset by revenues from fishing license fees, interest earned on the RERF, and remittances from Kiribati working overseas.

The government has earmarked Christmas and Fanning islands in the Line group and Canton Island in the Phoenix group as prime areas for future development. There is little open unemployment in the sense of people being unable to find some gainful employment if they so wish, and unemployment is estimated at around 2 percent of the workforce. However, there is evidence of **underemployment**, with the workforce engaged for perhaps only 30 percent of the hours that might be considered normal in a working week.

Foreign financial aid is a critical supplement to GDP, equal to 25 to 50 percent of GDP since independence in 1979. Initially the United Kingdom was the largest aid donor, but has now been overtaken by some of Kiribati's Pacific Ocean neighbors. Grants from principal donors amounted to an estimated US$20.7 million in 1998, of which US$5.7 million was from Japan, US$4.5 million from Australia, and US$4.3 million from New Zealand. The country is particularly reliant on foreign assistance for its development budget. Remittances from workers abroad account for more than US$5 million each year.

The government is involved in all aspects of the economy—its spending accounts for 71.5 percent of GDP—and it is taking measures to expand the **private sector** and develop the fledgling industrial sector. The poor performance of most public enterprises burdens the budget and adversely effects economic efficiency. Unfortunately, little progress has been made in implementing the government's Medium Term Strategy, which focuses on reducing the role of the **public sector** by freezing civil service recruitment, reducing government spending, improving the accountability of public enterprises, and introducing **privatization**.

The sale of fishing licenses to foreign fleets provides an important source of income. Revenues from the sale of fishing licenses amounted to more than half of GDP in 1998. Mining of phosphate rock on the island of Banaba (which ceased in 1979) formerly provided some 80 percent of earnings. As well as providing foreign exchange, interest from the phosphate reserve fund, RERF, continues to be an important source of budgetary income. The value of the fund was put at US$380 million at the end of 1998, and generates around US$20 million a year in revenues from interest.

POLITICS, GOVERNMENT, AND TAXATION

Kiribati is an independent republic and a member of the British Commonwealth. The president is head of state and chief executive, and leads a cabinet made up of a vice-president, attorney-general, and 8 ministers. The president appoints the ministers, while the president is elected nationally from several candidates nominated by the House of Assembly (Maneaba-ni-Maungatabu). The House of Assembly consists of 41 members, elected every 4 years. Local councils have considerable autonomy in the management of local affairs.

Kiribati is governed by a constitution adopted in 1979. The first general election since independence took place in March-April 1982. The current president is Teburoro Tito, who was first elected in 1994 and re-elected in November 1998.

The Kiribati government aims to improve the growth performance of the country by encouraging new businesses and attracting new foreign companies through designation of "pioneer status." Any company that wishes to establish a business in Kiribati may apply to the Internal Revenue Board for "pioneer status". This allows for a reduced company tax rate of 10 percent for 5 years with the exceptions of business operations on South Tarawa and Christmas Islands. In addition, the government hopes to encourage diversification of the economy and is introducing reforms (such as privatization) to improve the efficiency of the economy.

There is personal **income tax**, which is set at 25 percent of gross income for the first US$36,000 and at 35 percent for amounts in excess of this. Normal company tax is based on a flat rate of 25 percent of net profit for the first US$36,000 and 35 percent for amounts above this. Tax on dividends paid to overseas investors is 30 percent, except for dividends paid to an Australian resident, where the rate is 15 percent.

Because of the high population density on South Tarawa was giving rise to social and economic problems, it was announced in 1988 that nearly 5,000 inhabitants were to be resettled on outlying atolls, mainly in the Line Islands. A further resettlement program from South Tarawa to 5 islands in the Phoenix group was initiated in 1995. Another important issue is a 1989 UN report on the "greenhouse effect" (the heating of the earth's atmosphere, and a resultant rise in the sea-level), which listed Kiribati as one of the countries that would completely disappear beneath the sea in the 21st century unless drastic measures are taken. None of the land on the islands is more than 2 meters above sea level, making the country extremely vulnerable to the effects of climate change.

The current president, Teburoro Tito, declared that reducing Kiribati's dependence on foreign aid would be a major objective for his government. He also announced his intention to pursue civil and criminal action against members of the previous administration for alleged misuse of public funds while in office.

INFRASTRUCTURE, POWER, AND COMMUNICATIONS

The infrastructure of Kiribati is quite rudimentary. Whenever practicable, roads are built on all atolls, and connecting causeways between islets are also being built as funds and labor permit. A program to construct causeways between North and South Tarawa was completed in the mid-1990s. Kiribati has about 640 kilometers (398

Communications

Country	Telephones[a]	Telephones, Mobile/Cellular[a]	Radio Stations[b]	Radios[a]	TV Stations[a]	Televisions[a]	Internet Service Providers[c]	Internet Users[c]
Kiribati	2,000	N/A	AM 1; FM 1; shortwave 1	17,000	1	1,000	1	1,000
United States	194 M	69.209 M (1998)	AM 4,762; FM 5,542; shortwave 18	575 M	1,500	219 M	7,800	148 M
Philippines	1.9 M	1.959 M (1998)	AM 366; FM 290; shortwave 3 (1999)	11.5 M	31	3.7 M	33	500,000
Solomon Islands	8,000	658	AM 3; FM 0; shortwave 0	57,000	0	3,000	1	3,000

[a]Data is for 1997 unless otherwise noted.
[b]Data is for 1998 unless otherwise noted.
[c]Data is for 2000 unless otherwise noted.

SOURCE: CIA *World Factbook 2001* [Online].

miles) of roads that are suitable for motor vehicles. All-weather roads exist in Tarawa and Kiritimati. In 1998, there were some 2,000 motor vehicles registered in the islands, of which some 75 percent were motorcycles.

In early 1998, work began on a major project to rehabilitate the port terminal and facilities at Betio. Financing for the project, with expected completion by mid-2000, was funded by a grant from Japan of US$22 million. There is a small network of canals, totaling 5 kilometers (3.1 miles), in Line Islands as well as ports and harbors such as Banaba, Betio, English Harbor, and Kanton. There are 21 airports, 4 of them with paved runways. Only Tarawa and Christmas Island are served by international flights.

Electricity production and consumption was equal to 7 million kilowatt-hours (kWh) in 1998, 100 percent of which is produced from imported fossil fuels.

Kiribati has an earth satellite station, 1 Intelsat (Pacific Ocean). Kiribati is being linked to the Pacific Ocean Cooperative Telecommunications Network, which should improve the telephone service. In 1995, it was estimated that there were 2,600 main telephone lines in use. There is 1 short-wave radio station, 1 AM station, and 1 FM station broadcasting to 17,000 radios, according to 1997 estimates. There is 1 television broadcast station and 1,000 televisions.

ECONOMIC SECTORS

The majority of the population—an estimated 79 percent—depends on subsistence fishing and agriculture for its livelihood. Fishing and agriculture together contributed only 14 percent of GDP in 1996, however. The private sector of the economy is small, and there are few manufacturing activities. Industry contributed just 7 percent of GDP in 1996. Government services are the biggest portion of the services sector, which contributed a total of 79 percent of GDP in 1996. The country is heavily reliant on overseas aid for government administration, education, health, and the development of infrastructure. One of the government's main priorities is to reduce reliance on foreign aid through developing a more efficient economy.

Kiribati
GDP–COMPOSITION BY SECTOR–1996 est.

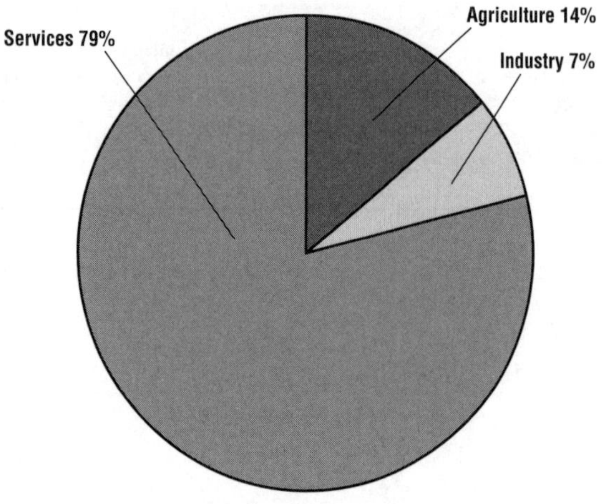

SOURCE: *CIA World Factbook 2000* [Online].

AGRICULTURE

Agriculture (including fishing) employed 79 percent of the working population and contributed an estimated 14 percent of GDP in 1996. Much agricultural production goes to provide food for the families producing it. The major agricultural products are copra, taro, breadfruit, sweet potatoes, and vegetables; fishing is another major source of food for I-Kiribati. The principal cash crop is coconuts yielding copra, which accounted for an estimated 60 percent of merchandise export earnings in 1998. Bananas, screw-pine, breadfruit (a round seedless fruit from the mulberry family whose texture resembles bread when cooked), and papaya are also cultivated as food crops. Seaweed provided an estimated 8 percent of domestic export earnings in 1998. Pigs, chickens, and cattle are the most common agricultural livestock. Most of the land is farmed, and agriculture accounts for 51 percent of land-usage.

Average annual rainfall varies greatly, from 3,000 millimeters (118 inches) in the northern islands to 1,500 millimeters (59 inches) in Tarawa and 700 millimeters (28 inches) in the Line Islands, but the rains are reliable and sufficient to provide stable agricultural conditions.

The closure of the state fishing company was announced in 1991, as a result of a dramatic decline in the fish catch. Fish provided only 2 percent of export earnings in 1996 (compared with 32 percent in 1990). However, earnings from exports of fish had recovered to an estimated 12 percent of domestic export earnings by 1998. Agricultural GDP grew at an average annual rate of 4.1 percent in 1990–98, comfortably faster than the rate of increase of the population. Kiribati allows other nations such as South Korea, Japan, Taiwan, and the United States to fish in its territorial waters in exchange for license fees that amounted to US$28.3 million in 1998.

INDUSTRY

Industry (including manufacturing, construction, and power) contributed an estimated 7 percent of GDP in 1996. Industrial GDP increased by an average of 4.2 percent per year in the period 1990–98. Kiribati's industry is quite limited and mainly consists of fishing processing and handicrafts for tourists and for export.

INTRODUCTION TO WORLD CURRENCY

The following insert contains color photographs of paper currency from around the world. Where possible, the most recent issue and lowest denomination was selected to show the bank notes of the countries represented in this encyclopedia. As of the year 2002, approximately 169 countries issued their own paper money.

Bank notes are more than a measuring system for value to be used as payment for goods and services. In many instances a banknote is a graphic reflection of a country's history, politics, economy, environment, and its people. For example, many bank notes depict plant life such as flowers and trees, as well as birds and other animals native to that geographic region. The 5-lats note of Latvia has a giant oak tree on the front, while the 25-rupee note of Seychelles and the 5-guilder note of Suriname both show flowers from the homeland. Birds adorn notes from São Tomé and Príncipe, Papua New Guinea, and Zambia. Large animals such as the mountain gorillas on the 500-franc note from Rwanda, the white rhinoceros on the 10-rand note from South Africa, and the bull elephant on the 500-shilling note of Uganda are commonplace.

Famous rulers and political figures from history are prevalent. Sir Henry Parkes, a famous 19th-century statesman, graces the front of the 5-dollar note from Australia; and Canada's Sir John Alexander MacDonald, a noted Canadian prime minister from the same time period, appears on the front of the 10-dollar Canadian note. Mieszko I, a medieval prince credited with being the founder of Poland in 966, is on the 10-zloty note from that country. Bank notes also reflect the power of more contemporary rulers, as exemplified by the image of Iraq's current president, Saddam Hussein, on that country's 50-dinar note, issued in 1994. Malaysia's paramount ruler and first chief of state, Tunku Abdul Rahman, is on the front of that country's 1-ringgit note and all notes of all denominations issued since 1967.

Architectural vignettes are common on world notes. Islamic mosques with minarets can be found on the 5000-afghani note from Afghanistan, as well as the 25-piaster note from Egypt, indicating the prevalent Islamic religious influence in those 2 countries. The 5-pound 1994 regular issue note from Ireland shows the famous Mater Misericordiae Hospital in Ireland, where Sister Catherine McAuley, founder of the Sisters of Mercy religious order, served in the area of health care. The depiction of religious figures is common on European notes. Examples include St. Agnes of Bohemia on the 50-koruna note of the Czech Republic, St. John of Rila on the 1-lev note of Bulgaria, and the Archangel Gabriel on the 50-denar note of Macedonia.

Artists, authors, scientists, and musicians are also honored on many bank notes. James Ensor (1860–1949), an innovative painter and etcher, is shown on the 100-franc note from Belgium, while Baroness Karen Blixen (pen name Isak Dinesen), the famed Danish author of *Out of Africa* is found on the 50-krone note of Denmark.

Several notes commemorate the new millenium, significant local events, or anniversaries. The front of the 2000-leu commemorative note from Romania has an imaginative reproduction of the solar system as a reference to the total solar eclipse of 11 August 1999. Another example of a commemorative note is the 200-rupee note from Sri Lanka. The note was issued 4 February 1998 to commemorate the 50th anniversary of independence as a self-governing Dominion of the British Commonwealth.

As of 2002, 15 countries did not issue or use their own paper currency, but allowed the bank notes of neighboring countries as well as U.S. currency to circulate freely in their local economies. Many of these countries are relatively small in size with economies to match. Countries such as San Marino, Monaco, Liechtenstein, and Vatican City are tourist-oriented and do not see a need to issue their own homeland currency. Five of these fifteen countries—namely Marshall Islands, Micronesia, Palau, Panama, and Puerto Rico—all use the U.S. dollar as their monetary unit of exchange. As of March 2001, Ecuador and El Salvador had joined the above-mentioned countries in adopting the U.S. dollar. Countries struggling with hyperinflation (uncontrolled inflation marked by the sharp devaluation of the homeland currency) may choose to use the U.S. dollar in place of their own currencies in an attempt to stabilize their economy by linking it directly to the strength and stability of the

U.S. economy. Countries that use U.S. dollars in conjunction with sound economic policies can usually expect to control and/or minimize inflation. The complete adoption of the U.S. currency has been more successful than the practice of pegging the value of local currency to the U.S. dollar according to a fixed ratio, an approach attempted recently by Argentina to disastrous effect. Even those countries that have not completely adopted the U.S. dollar as their currency often have economies operating freely with both their own national and the U.S. currencies. The strength of the U.S. dollar has also made it the currency of choice in the global black market.

Another trend that will probably continue into the future is the joining together of several neighboring countries to form a central bank issuing a common currency. The primary objective of these economic and monetary unions is to eliminate obstacles to free trade, creating a single unified marketplace. This grouping together tends to strengthen the economy and currency of the member countries as well as providing a cost savings in currency production. While such economic partnerships have occurred throughout history, more recent examples began in the early 1950s with the union of the East Caribbean States, followed by the Central African States, French Pacific Territories, and West African States. The most recent and highly publicized example is the European Monetary Union (EMU), composed of 12 European member countries—namely Austria, Belgium, Finland, France, Germany, Greece, Ireland, Italy, Luxembourg, the Netherlands, Portugal, and Spain. On 1 January 2002, the EMU, through its newly formed central bank, replaced the participating countries' homeland currencies with a new common currency called the *euro*. An example of the 10-euro note is shown on the following currency insert pages. Those countries that had pegged their currencies to an EU member's currency prior to the euro's adoption (as several Francophone countries in Africa did with the French franc) now peg their currency to the euro.

It should be mentioned that, in contrast to this recurring trend of country unification for economic and monetary purposes, there are several countries with isolationist governments that have done just the opposite in order to limit the influence of the international community on their economies and populations. For example, Iraq and Syria have made it illegal to use or export their currency outside of their homelands. Several other nations embraced this isolationist attitude through the use of trade voucher and tourist certificates in place of currency, thus keeping their national circulating bank notes from being used or exported by visitors to their country. China, Bulgaria, and Poland are examples of countries that issued what they termed "foreign exchange certificates" for this specific purpose. However, this practice has largely been discontinued, with the exception of Cuba, which still uses a similar certificate first issued in the mid-1980s.

So what does the future have in store for the economies of the world? Trends indicate most countries in the world want free, open, and balanced trade with a strong, stable, and growing economy, free of hyperinflation. More countries are achieving this goal by unifying in regional economic partnerships such as the European Union, or by clearing the barriers to free trade through agreements such as NAFTA (North American Free Trade Agreement). As the use of the U.S. dollar increases throughout the Americas, some economists predict that this region will follow in the footsteps of Europe in terms of establishing a common currency under a central bank. The Asian and Middle-Eastern regions are also likely candidates for similar regional economic partnerships given the prevalence of established trade agreements already in existence among those countries. As the globalization of trade necessitates closer economic ties between countries, it is not inconceivable that a single central bank and common currency will eventually unite the countries of the world. While that development is still only a remote possibility at this point, there is little doubt that nations' increased dependence on international trade for economic prosperity will promote a currency policy conducive to closer trade ties and cross-border partnerships.

—Keith S. Bauman, professional numismatist
International Bank Note Society
American Numismatic Association
Professional Currency Dealers Association

Afghanistan

Albania

Algeria

Andorra
(used both Spanish and French currency until the adoption of the euro in January of 2002)

Angola

Antigua and Barbuda
(shares currency with other East Caribbean States)

Argentina

Armenia

Aruba

Australia

Austria
(adopted the euro as of January 2002)

Azerbaijan

The Bahamas

Bahrain

Bangladesh

Barbados

Belarus

Belgium
(adopted the euro as of January 2002)

Belize

Benin
(shares currency with other West African States)

Bhutan

Bolivia

Bosnia and Herzegovina

Botswana

Brazil

Brunei Darussalam

Bulgaria

Burkina Faso
(shares currency with other West African States)

Burma (Myanmar)

Burundi

Cambodia

Cameroon
(shares currency with other Central African States)

Canada

Cape Verde

Central African Republic
(shares currency with other Central African States)

Chad
(shares currency with other Central African States)

Chile

China

Colombia

Comoros

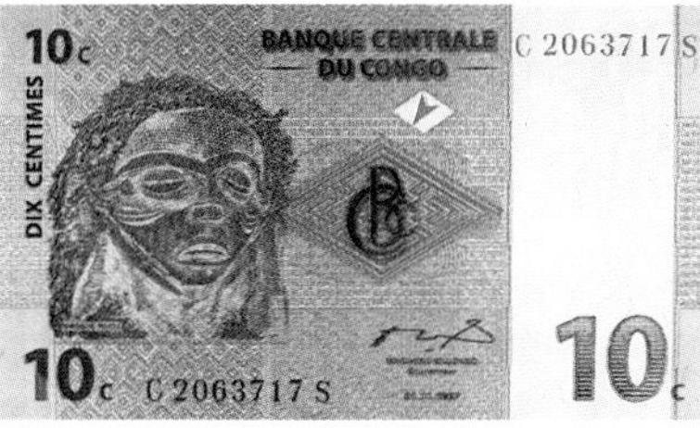

Democratic Republic of the Congo

Republic of the Congo
(shares currency with other Central African States)

Costa Rica

Côte d'Ivoire
(shares currency with other West African States)

Croatia

Cuba

Cyprus

Czech Republic

Denmark

Djibouti

Dominica
(shares currency with other East Caribbean States)

Dominican Republic

Ecuador

Egypt

El Salvador

Equatorial Guinea
(shares currency with other Central African States)

Eritrea

Estonia

Ethiopia

European Union (EU)

Fiji

Finland
(adopted the euro as of January 2002)

France
(adopted the euro as of January 2002)

French Guiana, Martinique, and Guadeloupe
(used the Fench currency until the adoption of the euro in January 2002)

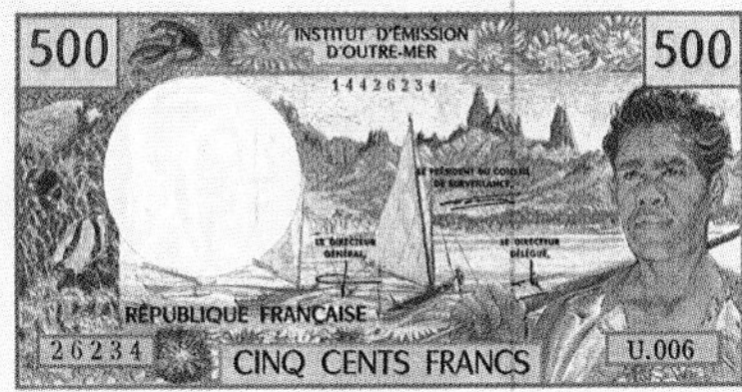

French Polynesia

Gabon
(shares currency with other Central African States)

The Gambia

Georgia

Germany
(adopted the euro as of January 2002)

Ghana

Greece
(adopted the euro as of January 2002)

Grenada
(shares currency with other East Carribbean States)

Guatemala

Guinea

Guinea-Bissau
(shares currency with other West African States)

Guyana

Haiti

Honduras

Hong Kong

Hungary

Iceland

India

Indonesia

Iran

Iraq

Ireland
(adopted the euro as of January 2002)

Israel

Italy
(adopted the euro as of January 2002)

Jamaica

Japan

Jordan

Kazakhstan

Kenya

Kiribati
(uses the Australian currency)

North Korea

South Korea

Kuwait

Kyrgyzstan

Laos

Latvia

Lebanon

Lesotho

Liberia

Libya

Liechtenstein
(uses the Swiss currency)

Lithuania

Luxembourg
(adopted the euro as of January 2002)

Macau

Macedonia

Madagascar

Malawi

Malaysia

Maldives

Mali
(shares currency with other West African States)

Malta

Marshall Islands
(uses the U.S. currency)

Mauritania

Mauritius

Mexico

Micronesia
(uses the U.S. currency)

Moldova

Monaco
(used the Frency currency until the adoption of the euro in January 2002)

Mongolia

Morocco

Mozambique

Namibia

Nauru
(uses the Australian currency)

Nepal

The Netherlands
(adopted the euro as of January 2002)

Netherlands Antilles

New Zealand

Nicaragua

Niger
(shares currency with other West African States)

Nigeria

Norway

Oman

Pakistan

Palau
(uses the U.S. currency)

Panama
(uses the U.S. currency)

Papua New Guinea

Paraguay

Peru

Philippines

Poland

Portugal
(adopted the euro as of January 2002)

Puerto Rico
(uses the U.S. currency)

Qatar

Romania

Russia

Rwanda

San Marino
(used the Italian currency until the adoption of the euro in January of 2002)

São Tomé and Príncipe

Saudi Arabia

Senegal
(shares currency with other West African States)

Seychelles

Sierra Leone

Singapore

Slovakia

Slovenia

Solomon Islands

Somalia

South Africa

Spain
(adopted the euro as of January 2002)

Sri Lanka

St. Kitts and Nevis
(shares currency with other East Caribbean States)

St. Lucia
(shares currency with other East Caribbean States)

St. Vincent and the Grenadines
(shares currency with other East Caribbean States)

Sudan

Suriname

Swaziland

Sweden

Switzerland

Syria

Taiwan

Tajikistan

Tanzania

Thailand

Togo
(shares currency with other West African States)

Tonga

Trinidad and Tobago

Tunisia

Turkey

Turkmenistan

Tuvalu
(uses Australian currency)

Uganda

Ukraine

United Arab Emirates

United Kingdom

United States

Uruguay

Uzbekistan

Vanuatu

Vatican City
(used the Italian currency until the adoption of the euro in January of 2002)

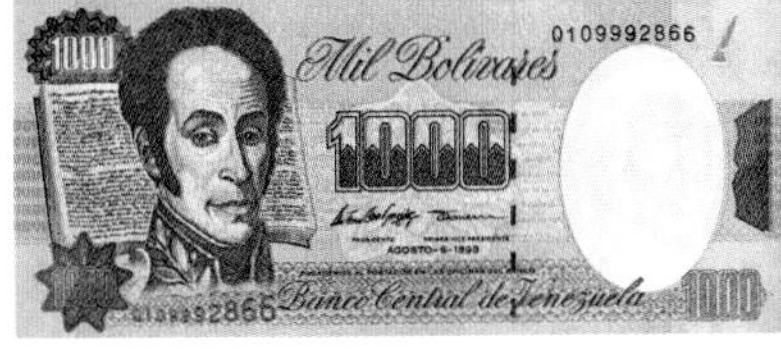

Venezuela

Vietnam

Yemen

Yugoslavia

Zambia

Zimbabwe

SERVICES

Services provided 79 percent of GDP in 1996. The GDP of the services sector increased at an annual average rate of 4.2 percent between 1990 and 1998. Tourism makes a significant contribution to the economy, with the trade and hotels sector providing an estimated 15 percent of GDP in 1998. Between 3,000 and 4,000 visitors per year provide US$5 to US$10 million in revenues. Attractions include World War II battle sites, game fishing, **ecotourism**, and the Millennium Islands, situated just inside the International Date Line and the first place on earth to celebrate each New Year.

The financial sector is heavily reliant on 1 commercial bank, the Bank of Kiribati. Modern expertise is provided by the majority shareholder, the Westpac Banking Corporation of Australia, which owns 51 percent, while the government of Kiribati owns 49 percent. The bank has 3 branches and provides checking and savings accounts, makes loans to individuals and businesses, provides financial facilities for international trade (such as letters of credit), and undertakes foreign exchange dealings. However, the bank provides no credit card facilities. The only other bank is the Kiribati Development Bank, which lends to small-scale businesses.

The **retail** sector consists mainly of small outlets, with a few supermarkets and department stores, mostly owned by Australian companies, in the capital, Tarawa.

INTERNATIONAL TRADE

As a result of its small size and its negligible manufacturing sector, Kiribati relies heavily upon products produced in other countries. The main imports include foodstuffs, machinery and equipment, miscellaneous manufactured goods, and fuel. The main exports of Kiribati are copra (62 percent of the total), seaweed, and fish. Kiribati's main export destinations are the United States, Australia, and New Zealand, while the main origins of imports are Australia (46 percent), Fiji, Japan, New Zealand, and the United States. In 1998, the country had exports of US$6 million and imports of US$37 million.

MONEY

The Australian dollar (A$) is the legal currency of Kiribati. The value of the A$ fluctuates against the value of other world currencies. The Bank of Kiribati is responsible for the majority of the available financial services. In December 1997, its total assets amounted to US$26.1 million, of which deposits were US$23.3 million and reserves amounted to US$0.9 million. The Development Bank of Kiribati identifies, promotes, and finances small-scale projects, and its capital amounts to US$1.33 million. There is also a network of small-scale lending agencies known as "village banks" operating throughout the islands.

Exchange rates: Kiribati

Australian dollars (A$) per US$1	
Jan 2001	1.7995
2000	1.7173
1999	1.5497
1998	1.5888
1997	1.3439
1996	1.2773

SOURCE: CIA *World Factbook 2001* [ONLINE].

POVERTY AND WEALTH

Only 2 percent of the working population is registered as unemployed, and poverty (as defined by the US$1 a day poverty line) is virtually unknown. Using the **purchasing power parity** conversion (which takes into account the low prices of many basic commodities in Kiribati, and which is the best indication of living standards) annual income per capita was US$860 in 1999 (in the United States, by way of comparison, it was US$33,900).

Education is free and compulsory for children between the ages of 6 and 15. Every atoll is provided with at least 1 primary school. The adult literacy rate was estimated at 90 percent in 1993–95. There are about 200 seamen trained each year by the Marine Training Center for employment by overseas shipping companies. In 1998, education was allocated US$7.8 million (22.5 percent of total budgetary expenditures).

The government maintains a free medical service. Each atoll has a dispensary, with a medical assistant in charge. In 1982, Kiribati had 34 government-controlled hospital establishments, with a total of 308 hospital beds. Life expectancy is 60 years (in the United States, by way

GDP per Capita (US$)

Country	1996	1997	1998	1999	2000
Kiribati	800	N/A	N/A	860	850
United States	28,600	30,200	31,500	33,900	36,200
Philippines	2,600	3,200	3,500	3,600	3,800
Solomon Islands	3,000	3,000	2,600	2,650	2,000

Note: Data are estimates.

SOURCE: *Handbook of the Nations*, 17th, 18th, 19th and 20th editions for 1996, 1997, 1998 and 1999 data; CIA *World Factbook 2001* [Online] for 2000 data.

of comparison, it is 76). In 1999, a major public health project, involving the improvement of water supply and sanitation, was undertaken with a loan of some US$10 million from the Asian Development Bank.

WORKING CONDITIONS

The society of Kiribati is egalitarian, democratic, and respectful of human rights. There have been no reports of human rights abuses. However, in the traditional culture, women occupy a subordinate role and have limited job opportunities.

The Kiribati Trades Union Congress (KTUC) was formed in 1998 and includes 2,500 members affiliated with other unions, of which the most important are the Fishermen's Union, the Seamen's Union, and the Teachers' Union. Workers are free to organize unions and choose their own representatives. The government does not control or restrict unions. More than 80 percent of the workforce is occupied in fishing or **subsistence farming**, but the small wage sector has a relatively strong and effective trade union movement.

The Constitution prohibits forced or compulsory labor, and it is not practiced. The prohibition does not specifically mention children, but the practice of forced and bonded labor by children does not occur. The law prohibits the employment of children under the age of 14. Children through the age of 15 are prohibited from industrial employment and employment aboard ships. Women may not work at night except under specified circumstances. Labor officers from the Ministry of Commerce, Industry, and Employment normally enforce these laws effectively, given the rudimentary conditions of the economy and its industrial relations system.

The government has taken no concrete action to implement longstanding legislation authorizing the establishment of minimum wages. There is no legislatively prescribed length to the working week. The government is the major employer in the cash economy. Employment laws provide rudimentary health and safety standards for the workplace. Employers must, for example, provide an adequate supply of clean water for workers and ensure the existence of sanitary toilet facilities. Employers are liable for the expenses of workers injured on the job. The government's ability to enforce employment laws is hampered by a lack of qualified personnel.

COUNTRY HISTORY AND ECONOMIC DEVELOPMENT

0–100 A.D. Kiribati begins to be settled by Austronesian-speaking peoples.

1300. Fijians and Tongans arrive during the 14th century and subsequently merge with the already established groups to form the traditional I-Kiribati Micronesian society and culture.

1837. First British settlers arrive.

1892. British protectorate is established.

1915–16. Gilbert and Ellice Islands become a Crown Colony of Great Britain.

1919. Kiritimati (Christmas) Atoll becomes a part of the Crown Colony.

1937. Phoenix Islands becomes a part of the Crown Colony.

1941–45. Tarawa and other islands of the Gilbert group occupied by Japan during World War II. Tarawa is the site of one of the bloodiest battles in U.S. Marine Corps history when Marines land in November 1943 to dislodge Japanese defenders.

1975. The Gilbert Islands and Ellice Islands separate and the Ellice Islands are granted internal self-government (as Tuvalu) by Britain.

1979. Kiribati becomes independent on 12 July.

1995. Kiribati unilaterally moves the international date line to the east, so that all of Kiribati's islands are in the same date zone.

1999. Kiribati gains United Nations membership.

FUTURE TRENDS

Kiribati's economic prospects are limited by its small size in terms of both geographical area and population, its remote location, and the absence of any valuable mineral resources now that the phosphate deposits are exhausted. The population size not only means that there is not a domestic market of sufficient size to support any serious manufacturing, but that there is limited provision of services. There is only 1 bank, and as a **monopoly**, its services will tend to be expensive and the range of services limited.

On the positive side, Kiribati has a tropical location with good facilities for an expansion of tourism. Moreover, the marine fishing resources are excellent and can provide for expanded local production and employment and even be the basis of some manufacturing, such as fish processing and canning. Finally, the national revenue from the phosphate fund remains a vital, and secure, source of foreign exchange.

However, to make the most of its tourism and fishing grounds, it is important that Kiribati attract foreign investment into these sectors. The fishing is large-scale and requires expensive fishing fleets together with equipment and installations for storage. Tourism needs high-quality hotels and international marketing. The current development plan recognizes these needs, but it remains to be seen how successful Kiribati will be in implementing the plan. A recent initiative is the agreement to lease land on Christmas Island to the Japanese National Space Agency, who will build a space shuttle launch facility there. Under the arrangement Kiribati will be paid just under $1 million a year in leasing fees. A research project is under way to use coconut oil to power internal combustion engines for electricity generation, and this may well contribute to energy self-sufficiency, as will the expansion of solar power on the outlying islands.

Overall, Kiribati can be expected to maintain its lower middle-income status in the immediate future, but its long-term growth prospects depend on its ability to expand tourism and undertake more of the exploitation of its fishing grounds rather than licensing foreign fleets.

DEPENDENCIES

Kiribati has no territories or colonies.

BIBLIOGRAPHY

Asian Development Bank. *Kiribati: 1997 Economic Report.* Manila: Asian Development Bank, 1998.

Economist Intelligence Unit. *Country Profile: Kiribati.* London: Economist Intelligence Unit, 2001.

"Kiribati and the IMF." *International Monetary Fund.* <http://www.imf.org/external/country/KIR/index.htm>. Accessed September 2001.

Pacific Island Business Network. *Kiribati: Country Profile.* <http://pidp.ewc.hawaii.edu/pibn/countries/Kiribati.htm>. Accessed September 2001.

U.S. Central Intelligence Agency. *World Factbook 2000.* <http://www.odci.gov/cia/publications/factbook/index.html>. Accessed August 2001.

U.S. Department of State. *Country Reports on Human Rights Practices: Kiribati.* <http://www.state.gov/www/global/human_rights/1998_hrp_report/kiribati.html>. Accessed September 2001.

—Oygal Musakhanova

KOREA, NORTH

CAPITAL: P'yongyang.

MONETARY UNIT: North Korean won (KPW). One won equals 100 ch'on (or jeon). There are coins of 1, 5, 10, and 50 ch'on. There are notes of 1, 5, 10, 50, and 100 won.

CHIEF EXPORTS: Minerals, metallurgical products, manufactures (including armaments), agricultural, fishery products.

CHIEF IMPORTS: Petroleum, coal, machinery and equipment, consumer goods, grain.

GROSS DOMESTIC PRODUCT: US$22 billion (purchasing power parity, 2000 est.).

BALANCE OF TRADE: **Exports:** US$520 million (f.o.b., 2000). **Imports:** US$960 million (c.i.f., 2000).

Democratic People's Republic of Korea
Choson Minjujuui Inmin Konghwa-guk

COUNTRY OVERVIEW

LOCATION AND SIZE. North Korea is in eastern Asia and occupies the northern half of the Korean Peninsula. It borders China to the north, Russia to the far northeast, the Sea of Japan to the east, South Korea to the south, and the Korean Bay and Yellow Sea to the west. The country covers an area of 120,549 square kilometers (46,543 square miles), making it slightly smaller than the state of Mississippi. It has 1,673 kilometers (1,039 miles) of land borders and 2,495 kilometers (1,550 miles) of coastline. The capital city, P'yongyang, is situated in the western part of the country, while the other major cities of Hungnam, Ch'ongjin, and Namp'o are in the east, northeast, and west, respectively.

POPULATION. Data on North Korea's population is scarce and unreliable. Because of serious famine in the late 1990s, it is thought that between a half million and 3 million North Koreans may have died of hunger and about 100,000 might have fled to China in search of food. In July 2000 the population was estimated at 21,687,550, with a growth rate of about 1.35 percent. The birth rate in 2000 was 20.43 births per 1,000 population and the death rate 6.88 deaths per 1,000 population.

The population is ethnically homogenous, consisting primarily of ethnic Koreans plus small communities of Chinese and Japanese. About 68 percent of the people are aged between 15 and 64 years and 6 percent over 65 years. The literacy rate, estimated at 99 percent in 1990, is high. The majority of North Koreans (about 70 percent in 1993) live in urban areas. Based on 1987 statistics, P'yongyang is the largest city with a population of 2,355,000, followed by Hungnam (701,000), Ch'ongjin (520,000), and Namp'o (370,000).

Most of the population follows the Buddhist faith. There are a handful of Christians, but freedom of religion is illusory, religious practice—like all else in North Korea—being manipulated and controlled by the state.

OVERVIEW OF ECONOMY

The crippled economy of North Korea is the direct product of its political system, a **communist** dictatorship. Severe economic problems are the legacy of years of Soviet-style development and controls that have ceased to function efficiently in a free market oriented world. Korea was annexed by Japan in 1910. In 1945, at the end of World War II when the Japanese surrendered to the Western allies, Korea was divided into North and South under the control of the Soviet Union and United States, respectively. The division, marked at the 38th parallel, was made permanent in 1948. North Korea, under the dictatorship of President Kim Il Sung, emerged as an autocratic, state-controlled nation. Despite the establishment of an extensive **infrastructure** and the introduction of mechanized agriculture, the government's emphasis on heavy industry at the expense of light manufacturing, service, and agriculture, and the isolationist nature of the regime, have cost the country dearly. North Korea has accumulated many economic problems, experiencing years of negative growth in its **gross domestic product**

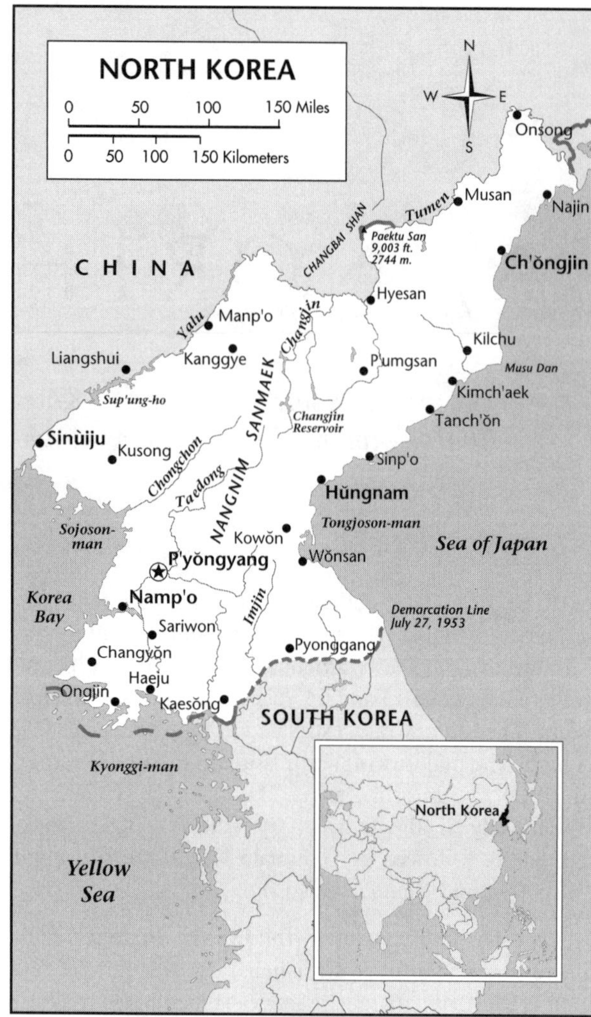

(GDP), which sank to -6.3 percent in 1997. The economy improved in 1999 and 2000 thanks to extensive foreign aid and better agricultural performance, but the reported growth rate of 6.2 percent for 1999 seems unrealistic. The estimated growth rate in 2000 was a more realistic -3.0 percent. Production in 1999 was 75 percent of the 1989 level.

The North Korean economy remains in decline, and the country is unable to meet its basic needs in food and **consumer goods**. It produces little for export, and its international isolation has limited its opportunities for trade or financial assistance, resulting in a **trade deficit** of US$440 million in 2000 and a growing dependency on foreign aid. High expenditures on defense (estimated at between 25 and 33 percent of GDP in 1998) has worsened the situation, while floods and drought between 1995 and 1997 devastated the country's agriculture and led to famine.

North Korea established its economy with assistance from the major communist powers, the Soviet Union and China. Until 1991, both regimes provided assistance in funds, equipment, training, and technology, enabling North Korea to advance more rapidly than South Korea during the 1970s. The government has also received loans from Japan, France, West Germany, Sweden, and Austria. By 1997, the country's **foreign debt** amounted to US$11.9 billion, of which US$7.4 billion was owed to China and Russia. Although hampered by financial problems in paying its debts, the government has refused to pay back loans even when it has been able to do so. It has acquired poor status in the international community, depriving the country of foreign loans. This is a serious situation for a country that requires substantial investment to modernize and expand its crumbling infrastructure, heavy industry, agriculture, light industry, and services.

The deteriorating economy has inclined the North Korean leadership to consider shifting to the Chinese model of **socialism**, which leaves room for a degree of free enterprise (though not a corresponding political and social openness). In 2000 President Kim Jong Il (who replaced his father upon his death in 1994) indicated a shift, reflecting constitutional revisions made in 1998. These revisions allow increased scope for private property ownership and the establishment of farmers' markets. By tolerating the expansion of these markets and increasing trade with China, North Korea's government has sanctioned the creation of a **private sector**. With its politically conciliatory hosting of official visits from South Korean President Kim Dae-jung and U.S. Secretary of State Madeline Albright to P'yongyang in 2000, North Korea hoped to create ties that would help in **restructuring** its economy. South Korea has offered to rebuild infrastructure in the North and to invest in its economy.

POLITICS, GOVERNMENT, AND TAXATION

The Korean Workers' Party (KWP) has dominated the North Korean political system since 1948. As a communist party opposed to free enterprise, it controls the economy with little room for private initiative. The state is the country's only economic actor, its only economic planner, and its sole employer. The suppression of any form of political dissent has not allowed opposition parties to advance an alternative economic model.

The constitution, created in 1948 and revised in 1972, 1992, and 1998, calls for a single legislative body called the Supreme People's Assembly, with 687 seats. Though Assembly members are "elected," in fact the KWP supplies a single list of candidates who are elected without opposition. The Assembly members similarly elect the premier, but true executive power lies with the president, Kim Jong Il. There is also a judicial branch whose members are selected by the Supreme People's Assembly.

The state's ideology and autocracy are responsible for North Korea's economic problems. The North Korean economy proved unstable because it relied on outside financing and socialist ideology, rather than private enterprise. In the absence of a viable private sector, the economy was forced to survive on foreign assistance and trade with the Soviet Union. The Soviet collapse in 1991 brought an end to its aid to North Korea. China's ideological "betrayal" of North Korea in establishing ties with South Korea in 1992 also deprived the North of much financial support. The North Korean government has since then found itself unable to solve its economic problems on its own. Despite the massive national deficit, the country spends vast sums of money (estimated at between US$3.7 and US$4.9 billion in 1998) on the armed services, maintaining one of the world's largest armies while requiring international food aid for the survival of its starving population.

Taxes and exports are the main sources of government revenues. In 1996 taxes accounted for 83 percent of revenue and exports for about 9 percent (US$9.4 billion). Additional funds come from the association of pro-P'yongyang Koreans residing in Japan, known as Chongryun, but the exact amount of their contribution is unknown. Income from rights leased to Japanese fishing boats operating in North Korean waters is another source of money. Allegations have been levied against the North Korean government about earning income from counterfeit money, heroin trafficking, and smuggling used cars.

INFRASTRUCTURE, POWER, AND COMMUNICATIONS

Although North Korea's infrastructure is extensive, it is crumbling and in need of expansion and modernization. The country's road system, estimated at 20,000 to 31,200 kilometers (between 12,400 and 19,344 miles), is limited and unpaved. Private cars are scarce and the number of trucks is limited. The 5,000-kilometer (3,100-mile) railway network, originally built by the Japanese, provides 70 percent of passenger transport and carries about 90 percent of the annual freight traffic.

Most of the country's ports and airports need modernization. Of North Korea's 12 ports, only a few can handle large ships, while only 22 of its 49 airports have paved runways. P'yongyang's Sunan airport operates 20 weekly flights, servicing only 6 destinations.

North Korea suffers from a shortage of oil and gas. The oil shortage came after the country was deprived of its access to low-priced Soviet oil and saw a significant decrease in oil shipments from China. The country produces electricity from fossil fuel (34.4 percent) and hydroelectric power generators (65.6 percent). Over the next several years, North Korea will approve funds to construct over 100 new power generating plants. The state-owned oil and gas facilities are being **privatized** and provide excellent opportunities for investment. In 1999 it was estimated that the country produced 28.6 billion kilowatt-hours (kWh) of electricity.

The telecommunication system is undeveloped. In 1995 there were 1.1 million telephone lines in use. Based on 1998 statistics, North Korea has 12 radio stations (AM, FM and short wave) and 38 television stations. There are 3.36 million radios and 1.2 million television sets in use. The country has 1 Internet service provider and no cellular telephone system.

ECONOMIC SECTORS

North Korea's economy is in ruins. The disintegration of the Soviet Union, government mismanagement, and natural disasters have been partly responsible for the poor performance of the country's economic sectors. Industry is the dominant sector but is unable to generate revenue, jobs, and consumer goods to meet the country's demands. While agriculture is mechanized, the equipment is outmoded and fertilizers are in short supply. The service sector is both limited and underdeveloped. The overhaul and development of these sectors is essential for

Communications

Country	Newspapers	Radios	TV Sets[a]	Cable subscribers[a]	Mobile Phones[a]	Fax Machines[a]	Personal Computers[a]	Internet Hosts[b]	Internet Users[b]
	1996	1997	1998	1998	1998	1998	1998	1999	1999
North Korea	199	147	53	N/A	0	N/A	N/A	N/A	N/A
United States	215	2,146	847	244.3	256	78.4	458.6	1,508.77	74,100
Japan	578	955	707	114.8	374	126.8	237.2	163.75	27,060
South Korea	393	1,033	346	138.3	302	N/A	156.8	55.53	10,860

[a]Data are from International Telecommunication Union, *World Telecommunication Development Report 1999* and are per 1,000 people.

[b]Data are from the Internet Software Consortium (http://www.isc.org) and are per 10,000 people.

SOURCE: World Bank. *World Development Indicators 2000.*

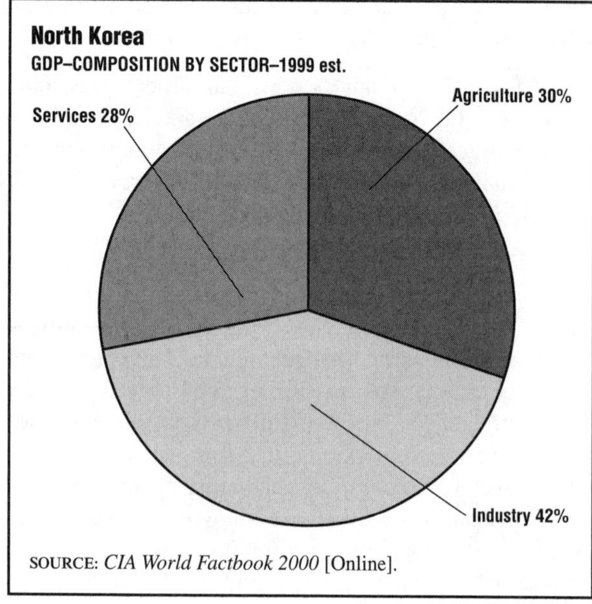

SOURCE: *CIA World Factbook 2000* [Online].

recovery and growth, as is the adoption of a new economic model.

AGRICULTURE

Despite the occurrence of drought in late spring, often followed by floods, the North Korean climate is temperate. Only 14 percent of the land is arable, however. North Korea has never been agriculturally self-sufficient. Agriculture is nevertheless a major contributor to the economy. In 1999, the sector accounted for 30 percent of GDP and employed 36 percent of the workforce (3.5 million workers). Rice, corn, potatoes, soybeans, pulses, eggs, and pork make up the bulk of agricultural production.

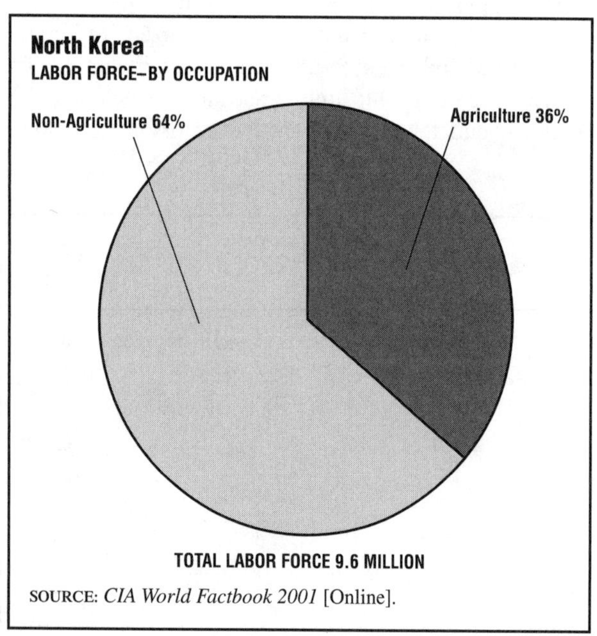

SOURCE: *CIA World Factbook 2001* [Online].

North Korea's agriculture was collectivized in the 1950s and was fairly successful until the early 1990s. Modern techniques more than doubled the total harvest from 3.85 million tons in 1966 to 8.47 million tons in 1984. However, the sector's annual growth rate fell from 2.8 percent in 1991 to 1.5 percent in 1995. A misguided emphasis on rice and maize production led to over-cultivation and exhausted the soil. Ill-conceived terracing, a shortage of fertilizers, floods, and a drought contributed to a steep decline in yield during the 1990s, leading to widespread famine and deaths. Massive foreign aid halted the death rate and helped increase the land under cultivation in 1998 and 1999. Crop production rose to 4.62 million tons in 1999, but remained 1.1 million tons short of the minimum needed. The country survived on foreign assistance, which included 550,000 tons of rice from Japan in 2000.

North Korea needs large investments for the revival of its agriculture. Recent initiatives include aid from the **United Nations Development Program** for Agricultural Recovery and Environmental Protection, and the expansion of farmers' markets, which might stimulate growth by creating financial incentives for farmers. However, these measures still fall short of what is required.

There is little data on 2 important contributors to the North Korean economy: forestry and fishing. Such data as there is suggests that these activities are sufficient to satisfy domestic demand for lumber and fish and to supply exports. Fish products are exported to Japan and lumber to Russia. However, North Korea's annual catch declined in 2000 when fuel shortages grounded much of its fishing fleet.

INDUSTRY

Accounting for 42 percent of GDP in 1999, industry is the largest sector of the North Korean economy. Along with services, it employs 64 percent of the North Korean workforce.

MINING. North Korea has significant mineral resources, including the world's largest deposits of magnesite. However, the rest of its resources (brown and lignite coal, iron ore, cement, copper, lead, zinc, gold, tungsten, graphite, salt, and silver) are not sizeable enough to make the country a major world producer, though it may be able to engage in some production should these sectors receive some investment. Precious and non-ferrous metals are the country's most important exports. Aging equipment and flood damage in the mid-1990s led to a fall in North Korea's mineral output. Mining recorded negative growth between 1991 (-6.8 percent) and 1995 (-2.3 percent), when its share of GDP was 8 percent. As with other industries, only significant investment will allow the mining industry to become a vital source of economic growth.

MANUFACTURING. Manufacturing is the largest contributor to North Korea's GDP, accounting for the bulk of industry's share of GDP. Manufacturing produces metallurgical products, armaments, and textiles for export to China, Japan, South Korea, Germany, and Russia. North Korea's heavy industrial base was developed originally by the Japanese and later expanded by the Soviets. However, while the country expanded heavy industry and the production of military hardware, little was invested in light industry or the manufacture of consumer goods. The heavy dependency on the Soviet Union for financing, technology, equipment, spare parts, and energy caused a major decline in manufacturing once the Soviet Union ceased to be a source of assistance. Many industrial units work at a fraction of their original output following the cut in Soviet aid in 1991.

The country's manufacturing facilities need modernization and the expansion of its light and consumer industries. An improved relationship between North and South Korea has brought the North limited investment by 2 South Korean companies, Samsung and LG, who manufacture electronics in North Korea. These companies take advantage of the country's low labor costs. The South Korea-based car company Hyundai has also been negotiating with the North Koreans about the possible creation of an export-oriented industrial complex.

CONSTRUCTION. The construction industry has also suffered from the country's economic decline. Since the 1990s, a decline in industrial construction, housing, and building of infrastructure has reduced activity in the sector. The construction industry's share of GDP fell from 9.1 percent in 1992 to 6.1 percent in 1999.

SERVICES

Services are the least developed sector in the North Korean economy, contributing just 28 percent of GDP in 1999. There is no precise record of employment figures for the services sector, but the little available evidence indicates that only a small percentage of the **labor force** is involved.

TOURISM. Since the 1990s, some tourists have begun to visit North Korea from Taiwan, Singapore, and the West. The country's scenic landscape and mountains offer much potential for the growth of tourism. The government built new hotels in the 1990s, and there is a casino for the use of foreigners, which accepts **hard currencies** only. Improved relations between the 2 Koreas have made short trips to the North possible for tourists from South Korea. The South Korean Hyundai company took a total of 80,000 South Koreans to Mount Kumgang between November 1998 and June 1999, but the South Korean government suspended such trips after a South Korean tourist was arrested on spy charges. North Korea claims that the number of tourists doubled in 2000 compared to 1999, but no actual figures are available for either year.

RETAIL. The **retail** sector is also state-dominated, although there is now a little room for limited private initiatives. The sector consists of state-run stores and direct factory outlets for average citizens, farmers' markets, and special shops for the elite where luxury products are sold. There is a chain of hard-currency stores in large cities that were established as a **joint venture** between the state and the Chongryun. As a general rule, the range of consumer goods is limited and their quality is low.

FINANCIAL SERVICES. North Korea's financial sector is state-dominated. Two state banks control the entire industry: the Central Bank of North Korea, which has 227 local branches, and Changgwang Credit Bank, with 172 branches. The Foreign Trade Bank handles most international trade affairs. Two state companies, the State Insurance Bureau and the Korea Foreign Insurance Company, **monopolize** the insurance industry.

INTERNATIONAL TRADE

North Korea's international trade is characterized by its ongoing deficit, which varied from US$570 million in 1995, US$320 million in 1998, and US$440 million in 1999. This chronic disparity between import expenditure and export income reflects the low level of the country's exportable products as well as its international isolation, which limits the number of its trade partners. The loss of large-scale trade with Russia in 1991 was a blow that worsened the trade deficit. Soviet-North Korean trade dropped from US$2.7 billion in 1990 to US$100 million in 1999. The loss increased North Korea's growing foreign debt.

North Korea exports minerals, metallurgical products, manufactures, armaments, timbers, and fish products, and imports energy products, grain, machinery, equipment, and consumer goods. Its 2 largest trading partners are China and Japan, with South Korea, Germany, and Russia making up its other markets. In 1995, Japan purchased 28 percent of North Korea's exports, followed by South Korea (21 percent), China (5 percent), Germany (4 percent), and Russia (1 percent.) The largest suppliers of imports to North Korea were China (33 percent), Japan (17 percent), Russia (5 percent), South Korea (4 percent), and Germany (3 percent).

Better relations between North and South Korea might well turn the South into the North's largest trading partner. Inter-Korean trade increased by 24 percent during the first 5 months of 2000, with more than a third of this sum contributed in aid from South Korea.

MONEY

North Korea used to have multiple **exchange rates**, but now has a single, fixed rate set by the Central Bank of North Korea. A free-**floating exchange rate**, determined by supply and demand, exists in the Rajin-Sonbong Free Economic and Trade Zone only (a zone in the north of Korea in which state control has been relaxed and free-market interactions flourish). This rate, and that of the **black market**, reveal the lack of worth of the North Korean currency. In 1999, floating and black market rates revealed an exchange rate of 200 won to US$1, while the official rate was 2.20 won to US$1. The economic upheavals of the 1990s had no impact on the official fixed rate, which has been kept just higher than 2 won against the U.S. dollar since 1989. The artificial rate and the low value of the North Korean won on the open market have made it very difficult for the country to trade with most modernized economies. North Koreans and foreigners are subject to exchange restrictions, with certain exceptions in the Rajin-Sonbong zone.

GDP per Capita (US$)

Country	1996	1997	1998	1999	2000
North Korea	900	900	1,000	1,000	1,000
United States	28,600	30,200	31,500	33,900	36,200
Japan	22,700	24,500	23,100	23,400	24,900
South Korea	14,200	13,700	12,600	13,300	16,100

Note: Data are estimates.

SOURCE: *Handbook of the Nations*, 17th, 18th, 19th and 20th editions for 1996, 1997, 1998 and 1999 data; CIA *World Factbook 2001* [Online] for 2000 data.

POVERTY AND WEALTH

Neither extreme poverty nor wealth exists in North Korea, though in general the inhabitants live under conditions that do not match those of people in more modern countries, including their prosperous neighbors in South Korea. The government is committed to providing necessities to every person, but the ruling elite enjoys a more prosperous life than the general population. They are entitled to privileges such as quality housing, access to select shops with quality imported goods, and foreign travel.

Until the famine of 1995, North Korea's education, health-care, and nutrition systems were thought to operate efficiently. Education is free and compulsory to age 15, which may explain the 99 percent literacy rate. A kindergarten system is available to all children. Higher education is serviced by over 200 institutions, which specialize in science and technology. In 1998 college graduates made up 13.7 percent of the adult population, compared to 9.2 percent in South Korea. Health care is free in North Korea. The health system provides a large number of hospitals and clinics staffed by skilled professionals.

The natural disasters of the late 1990s caused phenomenal human casualties, however. Although little information is available about survivors in the affected areas, the worsening economic situation and famine have lowered the living standard of the entire population. Attendance has fallen at all educational institutions, and there have been reports of severe shortages of medicines and equipment. Malnutrition among children has been increasing since 1995. A system of food rationing designed to provide an adequate diet collapsed in various parts of the country during the late 1990s. In 1998 about 16 percent of children were malnourished, and another 62 percent suffered from illnesses related to undernourishment.

Exchange rates: North Korea

North Korean won (KPW) per US$1	
1995–2001	N/A
May 1994	2.15
May 1992	2.13
Sep 1991	2.14
Jan 1990	2.1
Dec 1989	2.3

Note: Latest data available.

SOURCE: CIA *World Factbook 2001* [ONLINE].

WORKING CONDITIONS

Although North Korea has labor laws, it is not a member of the International Labor Organization. All working-age North Koreans are expected to work for the good of the nation. Women have equal rights, and are well represented in the workforce, except at senior party or government levels. Forced labor is not prohibited and is often used as punishment for political offenses; in addition, people are often mobilized for construction projects. Child labor for children under the age of 16 is prohibited, but school children are sent for short periods to factories or farms to help production. The law provides for an 8-hour working day, but some reports claim that the hours are longer.

The country's union, the General Federation of Trade Unions of Korea, is run by the state. It encourages workers to meet production goals and also provides health, education, cultural, and welfare services to its members. Workers do not have the right to organize, bargain collectively, or strike. The formation of independent unions is prohibited.

The government sets wages and assigns all jobs. Besides free medical care and education, it provides other benefits such as subsidized housing. No data exists on the minimum wage paid by the state-owned enterprises, but it fluctuates between US$80 and US$110 per month in North Korea's free economic zone, and in foreign-owned businesses and joint ventures.

COUNTRY HISTORY AND ECONOMIC DEVELOPMENT

1910. Japan annexes Korea following wars on the Asian continent with China and Russia, ruling Korea as a colony until the end of World War II in 1945.

1945. At the end of World War II, Japan surrenders to the Western allies and ends its colonial rule of Korea. The Korean Peninsula is "temporarily" divided between the Soviet Union and the United States.

1948. Led by Kim Il Sung, the Democratic People's Republic of Korea was established in the northern half of the Korean Peninsula.

1950–53. The Korean War pits the communist North, backed by Russia and China, against the capitalist South, backed by the United States. The war is fought to a standstill, and ends with the 2 countries divided by a demilitarized zone along the 38th parallel.

1950s. Agriculture is collectivized .

1980. Kim Il Sung's son, Kim Jong Il, is announced as his father's successor.

1991. The Soviet Union collapses and the Russian government stops economic assistance to North Korea.

1993. In December, North Korea's government admits the failure of its 7-year economic plan.

1994. Kim Il Sung dies and is replaced by his son, Kim Jong Il, as the country's supreme leader.

1995. A flood devastates North Korea's agriculture, sparking widespread famine.

1996. Another flood further damages agriculture and mining.

1997. A drought paralyzes the North Korean agricultural sector and worsens the famine.

1998. North Korea amends its constitution to make room for the growth of a small private sector.

2000. South Korean President Kim Dae-jung and U.S. Secretary of State Madeline Albright pay an official visit to P'yongyang, marking the end of North Korean isolation.

FUTURE TRENDS

Economic realities should soon force the North Korean government to loosen its constraints on free enterprise while keeping its socialist framework in place. The country needs foreign assistance in various forms to address its many economic problems, which should push it towards the cementing of improved relations and the forging of closer ties with South Korea. A better relationship with the United States would also help North Korea engage more actively in international trade. However, unless North Korea provides a suitable environment for economic growth, dissolves its isolationism, and improves relations with South Korea, the United States, and the major economies in its geographical region (e.g. Japan), the economic situation will continue to deteriorate and cause more social and political problems. The reclusive leader of the country, Kim Jong Il, has not yet given clear indications that he is capable of leading his country in the direction of improved economic conditions.

DEPENDENCIES

North Korea has no territories or colonies.

BIBLIOGRAPHY

Eberstadt, Nicholas. *The End of North Korea.* Washington, D.C.: AEI Press, 1999.

Economist Intelligence Unit. *Country Profile: North Korea.* London: Economist Intelligence Unit, 2001.

Eui-Gak, Hwang. *The Korean Economies: A Comparison of North and South.* London, UK: Oxford University Press, 1993.

Hunter, Helen-Louise. *Kim Il-song's North Korea.* Westport, CT: Praeger, 1999.

Reese, David. *The Prospects for North Korea's Survival.* Oxford and New York: Oxford University Press, 1998.

U.S. Central Intelligence Agency. *World Factbook 2001.* <http://www.odci.gov/cia/publications/factbook/index.html>. Accessed September 2001.

U.S. Department of State. *Background Notes: North Korea, October 2000.* <http://www.state.gov/www/background_notes/n-korea_0010_bgn.html>. Accessed October 2001.

—Hooman Peimani

KOREA, SOUTH

Republic of Korea
Taehan Min-guk

CAPITAL: Seoul.

MONETARY UNIT: South Korean won (W). A won is equal to 100 chun. There are notes of W1,000, 5,000, and 10,000, as well as coins in denominations of W10, 50, 100, and 500.

CHIEF EXPORTS: Electronic products, machinery and equipment, motor vehicles, steel, ships, textiles, clothing, footwear, fish.

CHIEF IMPORTS: Machinery, electronics and electronic equipment, oil, steel, transport equipment, textiles, organic chemicals, grains.

GROSS DOMESTIC PRODUCT: US$764.6 billion (purchasing power parity, 2000 est.).

BALANCE OF TRADE: **Exports:** US$172.6 billion (f.o.b., 2000). **Imports:** US$160.5 billion (f.o.b., 2000).

COUNTRY OVERVIEW

LOCATION AND SIZE. South Korea occupies the southern half of the Korean Peninsula in eastern Asia. It is bordered by North Korea to the north, the Sea of Japan to the south and to the east, and the Yellow Sea to the west. South Korea has an area of 98,480 square kilometers (38,023 square miles), which makes it slightly larger than the state of Indiana. It has 238 kilometers (148 miles) of land borders with North Korea and 2,413 kilometers (1,499 miles) of coastline. Among its major cities, Seoul, the capital city, and Inchon are located in the northwestern part of the country, while Kwangju and Pusan are in the south, Taegu is in the southeast, and Taejon is in the center.

POPULATION. The population of South Korea was estimated at 47,470,969 in July 2000. It increased from 35.3 million in 1975 to 46.1 million in 1998, indicating a growth rate of 1.2 percent. At the current estimated growth rate of 0.6 percent, the population will increase to 51.1 million by 2015. In 2000 the estimated birth rate was 15.12 per 1,000 population while the estimated death rate was 5.85 per 1,000 population. The estimated migration rate was 0 percent.

South Korea's population is ethnically homogeneous. With the exception of a small Chinese community of about 20,000, the rest of the population are ethnic Koreans. Some 78 percent of the population falls within the age groups of 15–64 (71 percent) and 65 or older (7 percent). By 2015, 10.6 percent of the population will be older than 65.

South Korea is a highly urbanized society. In 1998, about 84.5 percent of its population lived in urban areas, a significant increase from 1975 when the urban population accounted for 48 percent of the total. The urban population is estimated to reach 92.2 percent by 2015. Seoul, the capital city, is the largest urban area, with a population of 10.4 million, followed by Pusan (3.9 million), Taegu (2.5 million), Inchon (2.5 million), Kwangju (1.3 million), and Taejon (1.3 million).

OVERVIEW OF ECONOMY

The 1945 surrender of Japan in World War II ended about half a century of the Japanese colonization of Korea. In its aftermath, the "temporary" division of Korea led to the creation, in 1948, of the Republic of Korea (South Korea) in the southern half of the Korean Peninsula and the Democratic People's Republic of Korea (North Korea) in its northern half.

South Korea opted for a free-enterprise economy at the time of independence and has since sought to consolidate it with a great deal of success. The mainly agrarian nation began to industrialize in the 1950s, after the Korean War (1950–1953). Its relatively insignificant industries mainly served its domestic market until the early 1960s, when the South Korean government encouraged

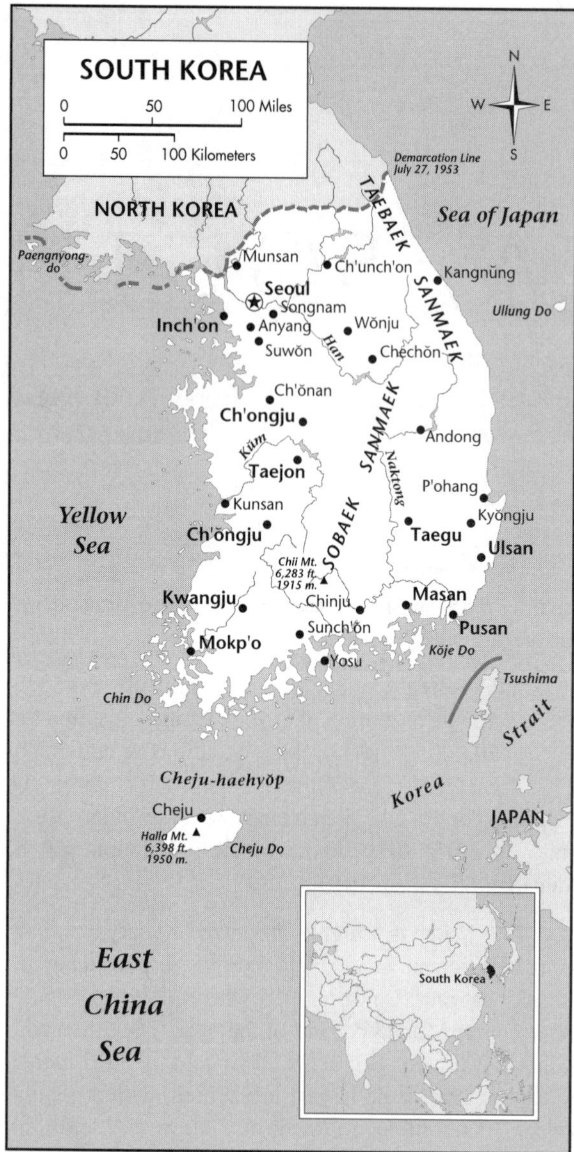

massive industrialization. Unlike many developing countries, South Korea chose an export-led industrialization strategy to produce labor-intensive products that could be produced more cheaply than in North America and Western Europe and therefore competitive and exportable to those markets. Initially, the emphasis was on light industry products such as fabric and clothing, later supplemented by assembly-line production of electronic products like radios or black-and-white television sets. By the late 1960s, South Korea became a major producer of telecommunication devices and computer parts.

The service sector, consisting of growing industries like **retail**, tourism, and finance is now South Korea's largest economic sector, accounting for 51.5 percent of **gross domestic product** (GDP) in 1999, while industry, including construction and mining, claimed a 43.5 percent share. Construction, though still a major industry, is in the process of decline. The industrial sector meets most of the needs of the country, but its manufacturing branch cannot produce without heavy imports of **capital goods**. Agriculture, which was the main economic activity in the 1960s, accounted for only about 5 percent of GDP in 1999. This sector, including forestry and fishery, was expanded and modernized in the 1950s and 1960s, a process that has continued to this date. The South Korean government has encouraged and generously supported its growth, while protecting it from foreign competition. The agricultural sector produces basic domestic needs in rice, vegetables, and fruits, though South Korea is still dependent on large imports of grains, fish, and forestry products (timber). The *World Factbook* reported similar, but not the same estimates of each sector's contributions for the same year, noting that services contributed 53 percent, industry 41.4 percent, and agriculture 5.6 percent of GDP.

Trade plays a major role in South Korea's export-oriented economy. In 1999, exports accounted for 45 percent of GDP, a phenomenal increase from the 1970s when it accounted for about 6 percent on average. Apart from a limited trade in fishery products, manufactured goods, including light- and heavy-industry products and high-tech devices and parts, are the major exports.

South Korea's economy grew rapidly from the 1960s through the 1980s, with an average annual GDP growth rate of 8.4 percent during that period. The growth rate fell to about 6.9 percent annually during the 1993–97 period. GDP contracted by 6.7 percent in 1998 alone as a result of the financial crisis, which pushed the unemployment rate to 6.8 percent (1,461,000 workers), a large increase from the 1997 rate of 2.6 percent (556,000). **Inflation** jumped from 4.5 percent in 1997 to 7.8 percent in 1998. Two factors helped economic recovery in 1999: the growth of the U.S. economy, which is South Korea's largest export market, and large direct foreign investments, made possible by economic **liberalization**. The latter rose to US$8.9 billion in 1998 and soon soared to US$15.5 billion, exceeding the total foreign investment over the previous 35 years. Data for the first 4 months of 2000 indicate such investment totaled US$3.7 billion, about 33 percent higher than the same period in 1999. South Korea's GDP grew by 10.7 percent in 1999, and continued its growth in the first quarter of 2000. The estimated growth rate for the entire year is about 8 percent. The recovery pushed the unemployment rate down to 4.8 percent (1,353,000 workers) in 1999, and it fell to 3.7 percent (about 800,000) in May 2000. It also brought the **inflation rate** down to 0.8 percent in 1999, a record low rate over the previous 3 decades. Inflation in 2000 was expected to be about 3 percent, far lower than during the 1980s, when the average inflation rate in the 1980s was 8.4 percent.

The South Korean government has helped the industrialization of its country via protectionist measures (the imposition of import quotas and **tariffs** aimed at limiting foreign competition in South Korea) as well as generous government financing for emerging industries and subsidization to make their products competitive in international markets. These government measures continued until the 1990s when they provoked criticism on the part of South Korea's competitors and trading partners, including the United States, Japan, and the European Union. Their growing pressure on the South Korean government to open its market to foreign competition and to stop subsidizing South Korean exports forced it to begin addressing these demands. Nevertheless, the South Korean market remained highly protected until 1997 when the financial crisis hit many Asian countries, including South Korea. Heavy borrowing by the public and **private sector**, especially from foreign banks, created the crisis, as most of the borrowers were unable to repay their large debts. Devastated by the crisis, the South Korean government, which desperately needed foreign financial assistance to stop the wave of bankruptcies and closures of large enterprises, had to accept the conditions outlined by the International Monetary Fund (IMF) in its rescue package: to liberalize its closed and highly protective economy through reforms and make it accessible to foreign competition.

Liberalization has sought to change South Korea's economy from one where the state directs and controls economic activities into one where the private sector, including foreign enterprises, operate with minimum government regulation. This required the nation to embark on a program of **privatization** designed to minimize the role of the **public sector** in the economy. This unfinished process has resulted in the sale of government assets in some large corporations to foreign investors, and the privatization of all state-owned banks, except for 2 development banks. By 2000, the government still owns about 108 non-financial enterprises, most of which are planned to be sold. Liberalization has also resulted in the removal of government regulations that restrict the economic activities of domestic and foreign enterprises in favor of a less-regulated economic system. Liberalization has also involved the **restructuring** of financial institutions and big corporations, most of which have long survived on heavy borrowing from public and private financial institutions, including foreign banks.

By and large, the reform of the financial system has been more successful than that of big corporations known as *chaebols* (conglomerates). The financial system's reform has justified the closure or merger of many non-viable private and public banks that formerly survived on government assistance, as well as the privatization of most public banks. The government's tight control on fiscal and monetary activities has been loosened in order to facilitate domestic and foreign private investments. In 1998, a Foreign Investment Protection Act was ratified to encourage and to ensure the safety of foreign investments. However, the 1998 corporate reform program called the "Big Deal" has been, so far, less successful. The program aims at turning the weak chaebols into strong corporations capable of offsetting the destructive impact of the financial crisis so that they might grow and compete with large foreign corporations inside and outside the South Korean market. To that end, the South Korean government has tried to reduce excessive competition between big corporations and to encourage their merger to create viable enterprises. It has also sought to encourage them to eliminate economic activities that are not of crucial significance to their main operations. For the most part, the chaebols' reform program is yet to be implemented.

South Korea has a very large **foreign debt**, which in 1999 was equal to more than 25 percent of its GDP. The debt burden emerged as a major economic problem in the 1990s. Encouraged and facilitated by the South Korean government, banks and large corporations borrowed heavily to finance industrialization, creating a debt that amounted to US$163.5 billion in 1996, a 5-fold increase from 1990. The heavy burden of this debt, most of which was borrowed on floating rates by major private enterprises, created the 1997 financial crisis, which resulted in a series of bankruptcies and closures of major enterprises. This situation also undermined the credit-worthiness of most surviving enterprises and forced the South Korean government to seek IMF assistance to prevent the total collapse of the economy. The IMF arranged a rescue package of about US$60 billion. It also facilitated an agreement between the South Korean government and the foreign banks for rescheduling debts held by South Korean private and public debtors. The IMF-led rescue package prevented the worsening of the situation and contributed to a gradual economic recovery. The recovery and the economic reform with its tough regulations on borrowing by large enterprises have reduced the debt from US$159.2 billion in 1997 to US$148.7 billion in 1998 and to US$136.4 billion in 1999. Statistics from the first 4 months of 2000 indicated a small increase in debt (US$4 billion), pushing its total to US$140.4 billion. Financing of a short-term **trade deficit** caused by an increase in the prices of imported oil products seems to be the reason for this increase. However, a predictably poor economic performance of South Korea's main trading partners (the United States and Japan) in 2001, which could reduce its exports and create a trade deficit, would likely increase its foreign debt substantially. South Korea's **foreign exchange reserves** are significant (US$86.8 billion in early 2000), but are still much smaller than its foreign debt.

History and geography have shaped the development of the South Korean economy to a great extent. The division of the Korean Peninsula into 2 different political and economic systems has been a major factor. The Cold War rivalry between the United States and the Soviet Union made them the protectors of South Korea and North Korea, respectively. Each helped its protegé establish a peculiar economic system: free-enterprise in South Korea and a planned economy in North Korea. For South Korea, this situation led to a lack of ties with the 2 major supporters of North Korea: Russia and China, which lasted until the early 1990s when both sides began to normalize relations; South Korea established ties with Russia in 1990 and China in 1992. These ties have since expanded to the point where South Korea now produces some of its labor-intensive export products in China.

Threat of a North Korean military invasion forced the South Koreans to spend a significant amount on defense (US$9.9 billion in 1999, equal to 3.2 percent of GDP). However, South Korea's relations with North Korea have been improving since 1998 when President Kim Dae-jung initiated his "Sunshine Policy" to improve bilateral relations with the north. This policy led to a limited investment of South Korean corporations in North Korea, where local cheap labor is used to produce electronics for exports. South Korea's Hyundai group began tourist cruises to North Korea in 1998, but the trips were suspended after a South Korean tourist was arrested on spy charges. During that period, 80,000 South Koreans visited North Korea.

The South Koreans have backed the idea of peaceful unification of the 2 Koreas. Given the depth of North Korea's economic problems, they are not interested in an immediate unification, which would force them to spend an estimated US$1.2 trillion to rescue the North Korean economy. Instead, South Korea prefers a gradual process of unification in which it would help the economy of North Korea through modernization of **infrastructure** and by production of labor-intensive export goods in that country.

The bitter memory of the Japanese colonial era has also affected South Korean-Japanese economic relations. Japan has been a major source of equipment, machinery, and technology for South Korea, and has provided its largest source of tourism. Public resentment of the Japanese has limited their official and cultural ties. The situation has been improving since 1998 when President Kim Dae-jung took office. The heavy pressure of the 1997 financial crisis required Japanese economic aid and facilitated better official ties. The 1998 visit of President Kim to Japan broke the diplomatic ice between the 2 countries, and by mid-1999 a ban on Japanese cultural imports was lifted.

The South Korean economy has 2 major weaknesses. First is its heavy reliance on imported fossil fuels (oil and natural gas). South Korea is the second largest importer of liquefied natural gas (LNG), mostly from Malaysia and Indonesia. In 1999, it imported 874 million barrels of oil, 184.4 million barrels of petroleum products, and nearly 16.9 metric tons of LNG. These fuel imports accounted for 97.1 percent of its energy consumption in 1999, a significant increase from 1979 when fuel imports accounted for 73.4 percent of such consumption. Second, the South Korean economy depends heavily on imported capital goods and technology for its industries. Despite its emergence as a major exporter of light and heavy industrial products, its export industries require foreign machinery and equipment for production. While South Korea has surpassed Japan and the United States in selling memory chips, it still needs imported chip machinery to produce them. Another example is its automobile industry's reliance on imported parts and technology. Japan and the United States have been the major source of technology and capital goods for South Korea, constituting 40.5 percent of its annual imports in 1999.

POLITICS, GOVERNMENT, AND TAXATION

South Korea has a presidential system governed by a directly-elected president and a **unicameral** legislature, the National Assembly, in which various political parties are represented. Cabinet members are accountable only to the president. Parliamentary elections take place every 4 years, in which 227 candidates are elected, while an additional 46 parliamentary seats are distributed among political parties in proportion to their share of the popular vote.

Until 1995, the political system was a unitary one (the central government appointed all governors of provinces and mayors, who acted as its representatives). In 1995, the first elections for these provincial and local offices took place. A year later, there were local elections for councils at all levels: provincial, county, and ward. Still, the central government maintains enormous power at all levels by controlling appointments and by using its economic power, as in the allocation of construction projects.

Democratic regimes are very recent phenomena in South Korea's history, which has been ruled mainly by civilian and military authoritarian regimes. From 1948 to 1988, the country was governed by 1 civilian president (Syngman Rhee, 1948–60) and by 2 consecutive military rulers (Park Chung-hee from 1961–79 and Chun Doo-hwan from 1980–88). The first semi-democratic transfer of power happened in 1989 when Roh Tae-woo, a military nominee of President Chun Doo-hwan, was elected president in a relatively fair election. In 1993, he agreed to a peaceful transfer of power to a civilian, Kim Young-sam, who had been elected president in another relatively free election. The election of an opposition leader as president, Kim Dae-jung in December 1997, was of great significance for the South Korean political system in that it marked the first transfer of power by an elected president to an opposition leader. Coming to power in the midst of the 1997 Asian financial crisis, President Kim Dae-jung has since presided over the restructuring of the economy.

The South Korean government has had a major role in the economy since the foundation of the nation in 1948. Through its direct involvement in the economy, it has sought the economic growth and industrialization by which it has turned South Korea from an agrarian society into a highly industrialized one. Various government measures and financial assistance have helped establish enterprises and protect them from foreign competition while helping them expand at home and abroad. The government has also been actively involved in industrial and financial activities through its industries and banks. Due to the IMF and other factors, its role in the economy has been limited since the mid-1990s, but it still plays a significant part in economic affairs as the mastermind of South Korea's economic reform, the director of its large infrastructure projects, and as the entity in charge of paying the country's foreign debt.

Despite the existence of political parties in South Korea, they had no major influence until recently. In practice, the military was the power base of the political system, and directly or indirectly ran the country—a situation that lasted until 1993. In that year, the election of a civilian, Kim Young-sam, as president laid the groundwork for meaningful participation by political parties, which led to the 1997 election of Kim Dae-jung, an opposition leader. Under his leadership, the Millennium Democratic Party (MDP) runs the country in coalition with the United Liberal Democrats (ULD). The opposition includes the Grand National Party (GNP) and the Democratic People's Party (DPP). However, the South Korean political parties have yet to establish themselves as the vehicles of representation of different political and economic interests. Generally speaking, they all lack internal cohesion, reflected in the constant defection of party members and their leaders from one party to another and the frequent formation, renaming, and merger of political parties.

All parties advocate a free-enterprise economy within which the state and the private sector both play a role. However, they also advocate a strong role for the government in economic growth through its policies and regulations. Under IMF pressure, the ruling coalition has significantly reduced the public sector by privatizing many state-owned financial and industrial enterprises and also by removing many economic regulations. Nevertheless, the government still has a major impact on the economy because its economic reforms and the payment of its foreign debt have incurred many new governmental regulations. Until the South Korean government privatizes all its enterprises, it will also remain a large economic player.

The South Korean constitution provides for an independent judiciary, though it is still trying to move toward that goal and away from manipulation by influential individuals. Absence of trial by jury gives judges the power of rendering verdicts in all cases, which makes the system more prone to abuse. Hence, in addition to political and economic liberalization, judicial reform is also necessary for creating a safe business environment. The judiciary provides for the defense of property and contractual rights through laws on economic activities. Commercial disputes can be adjudicated (settled) in a civil court, or may be presented to the Korean Commercial Arbitration Board. South Korea's membership in various international conventions obliges it to observe international commercial laws.

TAXATION. South Korea's tax system relies heavily on **indirect taxes**, which account for about 50 percent of tax revenue. Resident and non-resident individuals and corporations are liable for taxation. Real-estate rental income, business income, earned income, temporary property income, and miscellaneous income attributed to a resident are taxed progressively. Interests and dividends are subject to withholding tax. Non-residents are also taxed on income from sources in Korea. Tax rates on individual income range from 10 percent to 40 percent. Taxation applies to all corporations operating in South Korea, whether domestic or foreign. Companies that have been incorporated in Korea are considered to be domestic corporations and are liable for taxation on their worldwide income, whereas foreign corporations pay taxes on their Korean-generated income only. The corporate **income-tax** rates range between 16 percent and 28 percent.

Taxes, customs **duties**, and other government-generated revenues (assorted fees, social security contributions, and the income of public enterprises) are the main sources of government revenue. **Budget deficits** are financed through borrowing, either directly from domestic and foreign banks or through the issuance of bonds. In 1999, total government revenue was US$90.78 billion, of which all taxes and custom duties accounted for 70.1 percent of the revenue. Other government revenues accounted for 29.9 percent of the total revenue. The government spent a total of US$101.77 billion that year and incurred a deficit of US$10.99 billion. Better economic performance in 2000 resulted in a small surplus (about US$11 billion). Of the total revenue of US$118.18 billion, all taxes and customs duties accounted for 69.48 percent (US$82.12 billion) of the revenue, while other government revenues accounted for 30.52 percent (US$36.06 billion).

INFRASTRUCTURE, POWER, AND COMMUNICATIONS

South Korea has a very advanced and modern infrastructure, which has been expanding since the 1960s. Both the South Korean government and the private sector are involved in the financing, construction, and operation of various infrastructure projects and services. Over the first 20 years of the 21st century, the government will spend more than US$300 billion on airports, roads, railways, and mega-resorts. Additionally, it will spend US$60 billion on the construction of more than 100 new power-generation facilities.

South Korea has an extensive and well-kept system of roads. In 1998, it boasted 64,808 kilometers (40,272 miles) of paved roads, including 1,996 kilometers (1,240 miles) of expressways, and 22,182 kilometers (13,784 miles) of unpaved roads. There are several major north-south and east-west highways, but the growing number of vehicles in use puts heavy pressure on the land transport network. The number of private cars rose from fewer than 500,000 in the early 1980s to 7.581 million in 1999 when there were also 2.1 million trucks and 749,000 buses in use. To deal with the growing pressure on roads, the South Korean government has initiated a multibillion dollar project to expand the highways. Land transportation also includes regular train and bus services around the country. The railways consist of 6,240 kilometers (3,878 miles) of standard gauge tracks of which 525 kilometers (326 miles) are electrified.

In 1999, South Korea's air transportation system was served by 103 airports, of which 67 have paved runways. Major international airports are in Seoul (Kimpo), Pusan, and on Cheju Island. A new international airport, Inchon, is scheduled to open in 2001, after which Kimpo will function as a domestic airport for Seoul.

South Korea's sea transportation network includes various ports and harbors, the most important of which are in Chinhae, Inchon, Kunsan, Masan, Mokpo, Pohang, Pusan, Tonghaehang, Ulsan, and Yosu. To meet the needs of its growing economy, the South Korean government is planning billions of dollars' worth of port/harbor expansion projects. In 1999, South Korea's merchant fleet consisted of 461 ships of various size and functions (bulk, cargo, container, passenger, vehicle carrier, and fuel tanker) with a net cargo capacity of 5 million metric tons.

South Korea has a growing power-generation system that provides electricity for private and commercial needs. Originally a state-owned sector, the power system is being privatized. During the 1990s, total production increased from 184,660 gigawatt-hours (gWh) in 1995 to 239,325 gWh in 1999, outpacing demand by a comfortable level. Over time, South Korea's dependency on thermal and hydroelectric generators has been reduced in favor of nuclear-powered generators. The country lacks domestic fossil-energy resources, so the growing cost of imported oil and natural gas has encouraged this shift. Still, thermal generators account for the bulk of generated electricity. In 1998, the percentage of electricity generated by various methods was as follows: fossil fuel generators (59.56 percent), nuclear-powered generators (38.51 percent), hydroelectric generators (1.91 percent), and other (0.02 percent). The share contributed by nuclear-power generators rose to 42.8 percent in 1999.

The South Korean telecommunications system is among the best, the most modern, and the fastest growing in the world. The number of fixed telephone lines increased from 763,200 in 1973 to 20,963,000 in 1999, while the number of cellular telephone lines jumped from 1,641,000 in 1995 to 12,019,000 in 1999, an eightfold increase over a 5-year period. In 1999, there were at least 11 Internet providers. With 14 million Internet users in 2000, South Korea ranked third in the world after the United States and the United Kingdom. Also in 1999, there were at least 106 AM, 97 FM, and 6 shortwave radio stations, and 121 television stations apart from the 8 stations operated by the U.S. Armed Forces in South Korea. In 1997, there were at least 47.5 million radios and 15.9 million television sets in use.

Communications

Country	Newspapers	Radios	TV Sets[a]	Cable subscribers[a]	Mobile Phones[a]	Fax Machines[a]	Personal Computers[a]	Internet Hosts[b]	Internet Users[b]
	1996	1997	1998	1998	1998	1998	1998	1999	1999
South Korea	393	1,033	346	138.3	302	N/A	156.8	55.53	10,860
United States	215	2,146	847	244.3	256	78.4	458.6	1,508.77	74,100
Japan	578	955	707	114.8	374	126.8	237.2	163.75	27,060
North Korea	199	147	53	N/A	0	N/A	N/A	N/A	N/A

[a]Data are from International Telecommunication Union, *World Telecommunication Development Report 1999* and are per 1,000 people.
[b]Data are from the Internet Software Consortium (http://www.isc.org) and are per 10,000 people.

SOURCE: World Bank. *World Development Indicators 2000.*

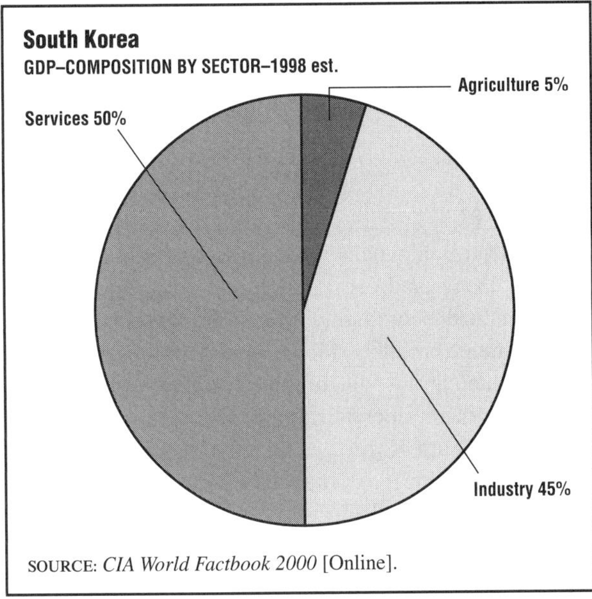

SOURCE: *CIA World Factbook 2000* [Online].

ECONOMIC SECTORS

South Korea's economy has undergone a very impressive development experience. Through economic planning, its government modernized the agricultural sector, established a large industrial sector, and helped create a service sector. Its extensive regulations have largely protected domestic enterprises from foreign competition and helped them grow and consolidate over time. Government polices and practices, including generous loans, have stimulated economic growth. The 1997 financial crisis damaged the South Korean economy as a whole and forced it to contract in 1998, but the economy began its recovery in 1999 and continued it in 2000, an indicator of the strength of its sectors. At the beginning of the 21st century, South Korea's smallest economic sector, in terms of contribution to GDP, is agriculture, including forestry and fisheries. Second largest is the industrial sector, which consists of manufacturing, construction, and mining, a vital sector of which manufacturing accounts for the bulk of South Korea's expanding exports. As with agriculture, industry's share of GDP is declining while the service sector is growing, a phenomenon consistent with the maturity of the South Korean economy. The service sector is now the largest and the fastest growing economic sector, accounting for the largest share of GDP.

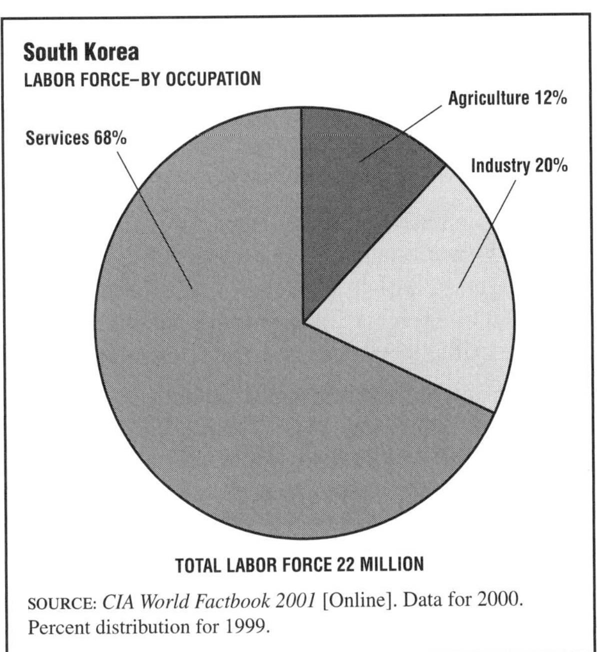

SOURCE: *CIA World Factbook 2001* [Online]. Data for 2000. Percent distribution for 1999.

AGRICULTURE

FARMING. Arable land is limited in South Korea. It accounts for 21 percent of the total land (20.7 million hectares), a decrease from its share of 21.8 percent (21.6 million hectares) in the early 1950s. Growing urbanization and road building are the 2 major factors responsible for the decrease. Agriculture's share of GDP, including forestry and fishery, has declined from 6.2 percent in 1995 to 5 percent in 1999. The total output of the sector, including forestry and fishery, grew 4.7 percent in 1999, after a contraction of 6.6 percent in 1998 as a result of the 1997 financial crisis. In 1999, its share of the workforce was 10.09 percent (2,349,000 workers), a decrease from 1995 when its share was about 12.2 percent (2,534,000).

Since the 1950s, South Korea has a well-developed and highly productive agricultural sector, thanks to several factors: government financial assistance (US$8.3 billion in 2000), mechanization, and extensive use of fertilizers. To encourage growth and make the country self-sufficient in its major food item, rice, the government has prohibited rice imports under normal circumstances. It has also paid farmers higher than the world price for their rice while subsidizing consumers to make rice affordable for all. As a result, South Korea is now self-sufficient in rice production and the production of many kinds of fruit and vegetables. In 1999, rice production was 5,975,000 metric tons, a large increase from 1995 (5,060,000 metric tons). South Korea also produces significant amounts of other major items such as barley and wheat (189,000 metric tons in 1999), but it is not self-sufficient in grains. Therefore, it imports agricultural products, mainly cereals and preparations, equal to US$1.716 billion in 1998.

FORESTRY. Although forests account for 65.7 percent of its total land, the topography makes commercial forestry difficult, so South Korea imports most of its forestry products (timber), mainly from Indonesia and Malaysia. Beginning in the 1950s, the reforestation policy of the government, combined with the rural development program of the 1970s known as the Saemaul Movement, has restored forests, which were massively destroyed during World War II. This resulted in a large increase in the production of timber from 30.8 million cubic meters in 1954 to 363.6 million cubic meters in 1998, mostly used by rural inhabitants as fuel. For its various needs, the country relies heavily on imported timber, which amounted to US$1.886 billion in 1998.

FISHERIES. The fishing industry has been declining over the last 2 decades, with only 315,000 people so employed in 1999, down from 750,000 in the 1970s. Its role in the economy has declined along with that of agriculture in general as a result of industrialization and the growth of the service sector. In 1999, fishery products accounted for about 1 percent of exports (about US$1.4 billion), a sharp decline from its share of 5 percent in the 1970s. South Korea relies on large imports of fishery products for domestic consumption, although catches increased from 2.4 million metric tons in the late 1970s to 3 million metric tons in the late 1990s. The value of imported fishery products was about US$1 billion in 1996–97, a huge jump from the mid-1970s when they were less than US$20 million annually.

INDUSTRY

The industrial sector, including mining, manufacturing, and construction, has been growing in South Korea since the 1960s. Its share of GDP has remained around 43 percent since 1995. The sector contracted by 6.1 percent in 1998 as a result of the 1997 financial crisis, but it expanded by 11 percent in 1999 when the South Korean economy began to recover. Despite its significant expansion, the overall economic growth pushed its share of GDP a little lower than 1998. In 1999, it accounted for about 25.61 percent (4,026,000 workers) of the workforce, a decrease from 1995 when it accounted for about 23 percent (4,824,000).

MINING. Mining and quarrying are very insignificant economic activities, accounting for only 0.4 percent of GDP (US$1.47 billion) in 1999. South Korea has few significant mineral resources, and no oil or natural gas. Its available minerals are lead, zinc, and copper, which supply only a fraction of its needs. As a result, it imports all its needs in fuel and almost all its needed minerals, accounting for 50.8 percent of its total imports in 1999. South Korea was once a major exporter of tungsten concentrate, but its output of tungsten ore stopped completely in 1993 when China flooded the world markets with tungsten, sharply decreasing its world prices. The mining industry, including quarrying, grew by 5.2 percent in 1999, a negligible growth for an industry that experienced a 24 percent contraction in 1998.

MANUFACTURING. Manufacturing has been the engine of growth and development for South Korea, which has emerged as a major supplier of various manufactured products. The sector's contribution to GDP was 31.8 percent in 1999, an increase from 30.9 percent in 1998 and an improvement over the levels during the economic slowdown of 1996 and 1997.

South Korea's manufacturing sector produces a wide range of labor- and capital-intensive products to satisfy domestic needs, but mainly for export. They include light and consumer products (fabrics and clothing); electronic, telecommunication, and computer devices; and heavy industrial products (metals, automobiles, and ships). Since the 1970s, South Korea has become one of the world's major steel producers. The automobile industry began growing in the 1980s for export purposes only, but it eventually expanded to meet domestic demands too. Annual production of automobiles grew from 935,271 in 1990 to 2.2 million in 1999.

The value of South Korea's manufactured goods was US$129.5 billion in 1999, as compared to US$97.9 billion in 1998 during the economic crisis. The best-performing sectors included telecommunications, electronics, industrial machinery, and transport equipment, which grew by more than 30 percent. Heavy industry and chemicals grew by 25.9 percent, and light industry (textile, footwear and food products) by 7.2 percent.

During the financial crisis of 1997, many manufacturers, including large conglomerates, went bankrupt. Corporate restructuring, as part of the conditions for receiving IMF aid, has changed the ownership structure of manufacturing to some extent. This previously closed sector is now open to unlimited investment and acquisition by foreign investors. In 1998 Hyundai Motor, the largest South Korean automaker, acquired the troubled Kia Motors, South Korea's third largest carmaker and its affiliate, Asia Motors. In 2000, Renault, a French automaker, purchased the bankrupt Samsung Motors while Ford, a U.S. company, bought the bankrupt Daewoo Motors.

The manufacturing sector employed 4,006,000 people in 1999, a substantial increase from 1998 (2,324,000 people). The 1999 figure indicates a large increase since the 1980s (15.3 percent), but a phenomenal increase since the early 1970s (169.9 percent). As has happened in most developed economies, the growing cost of labor has forced many South Korean manufacturers to relocate large industries and/or labor-intensive ones to countries with much cheaper wages, such as Thailand, Malaysia, Indonesia, the Philippines, Vietnam, and China. Thanks to better ties between the 2 Koreas since 1998, some South Korean manufacturers have established a few electronics factories in North Korea, but extensive relocation of South Korean industries to North Korea will not be a real option until the 2 countries have further improved their relations.

CONSTRUCTION. Despite its decades of growth resulting from massive infrastructure projects, the construction industry has experienced a decline since 1995 when its share of GDP was 11.3 percent. With the financial crisis, its share fell to 10.1 percent in 1998 and 8.8 percent in 1999.

In the 1960s and the 1970s, construction prospered as South Korea was entering its industrialization phase. This continued until the housing boom of the late 1980s. The number of residences (houses and apartments) built averaged 196,000 annually from 1973 to 1982 and reached 750,000 in 1990. The boom continued until 1996 when the economic slowdown began. The 1997 financial crisis saw a sharp drop in construction-industry revenues from US$32.4 billion in 1997 to US$9.9 billion in 1998. The limited recovery of 1999 increased the revenues to US$16.7 billion.

Overseas projects have helped the construction industry over time, but their importance has declined since the early 1990s. Taking advantage of cheap labor, South Korean construction companies won contracts in the 1980s for road-building projects, mainly in the rich oil-producing nations of the Middle East.

SERVICES

The service sector has developed substantially over time, accounting for 51.5 percent of GDP in 1999, surpassing agriculture and industry. It is the largest employer, with 64.3 percent share of total workforce in 1999 (13,906,000 workers), a small increase from 1995.

FINANCIAL AND BUSINESS SERVICES. These services accounted for 19.7 percent of GDP in 1999, an increase of 5.7 percent since 1989. A major reason for its modest growth was the collapse of the Daewoo group with more than US$80 billion of unpaid loans. The collapse damaged the bond market and led to a loss of confidence in the investment trust industry.

Under the directive of the central bank (Bank of Korea), the government-owned banks have manipulated economic activities by providing credits to those enterprises who follow the government's development strategy, while punishing others by denying them credit. The 1997 crisis forced the government to reform the financial system to receive an IMF-led rescue package conditioned on economic restructuring. To minimize its intervention in the financial sector, the government has privatized all public banks with the exception of 2 development banks: the Korea Development Bank and the Export-Import Bank of Korea. They provide medium- and long-term credit for both export industries and the heavy-equipment and chemical industries funded by the South Korean government and foreign investors. In compliance with the IMF demand for the opening of South Korea's financial sector to foreign competition, it has sold one of its privatized banks to foreign bidders, while considering the sale of some others. Banks and insurance companies are still underdeveloped and suffer from various problems, a consequence of years of government mismanagement and especially the continued tight government control of financial services. Years of continued reform will therefore be required to address its underdevelopment.

The 1997 financial crisis forced many financial and business services to consolidate. Between 1997 and 2000, government regulators closed down about 498 financial institutions, including 11 banks, 21 merchant banking corporations, 13 insurers, 16 securities firms and investment trust companies, and 437 other non-banking institutions. In 2000, the financial system consisted of 22 banks and thousands of non-bank institutions, including 5 merchant banking corporations, 43 securities firms, 36 insurers, 28 investment-trust companies, 15 leasing companies, and 7 credit-card issuers. Non-bank institutions consist of several mutual savings and finance companies, credit unions, community credit cooperatives, postal savings plans, and insurance, installment-credit, and venture-capital companies. Assets held by all domestic banks totaled US$440.8 billion in 2000.

In January 2001, there were 44 foreign banks doing business in Korea, and some Korean banks have been taken over by foreign banks. Assets held by foreign banks are estimated at US$36 billion. Foreign banks work under regulatory conditions almost identical to those of domestic banks, but they are exempted from direct control by the South Korean government. However, they are not allowed to have a branch network, and therefore their retail operations are small.

Investment trust companies (ITCs) constitute another component of South Korea's financial and business services sector. The bankruptcy of the Daewoo group in late 1999 inflicted heavy damage on the ITCs, which had purchased a large share of its bonds. This drastic event caused panicked investors to transfer about US$84.2 billion of their investments from ITCs into banks. To restore confidence, the South Korean government has injected large sums (US$25.3 billion in 2000) into the worst-hit ITCs. It has also promised another rescue package of US$41.3 billion for 2001.

The South Korean life-insurance market is the world's sixth largest in terms of premium income. The insurance industry has also suffered from the weaknesses of the financial sector, and some companies have closed as a result. The government now supervises the insurance industry, which has been opened to foreign investors. In 2000, the insurance industry included 23 life-insurance companies, including 7 foreign ones and 3 **joint ventures**, and 13 non-life insurance companies. In 1999, their assets were estimated at about US$47.2 billion.

TOURISM. With its ancient historical sites, many Buddhist temples, various opportunities for summer and winter sports, and natural beauty, South Korea has become an important tourist attraction. Government support and private investments have helped the tourist industry grow impressively in the 1990s, after it had been an insignificant industry in previous decades. The number of tourists grew on average by 7.2 percent per year between 1995 and 1999 to reach 3,921,000 in 1999, a large increase over the 2,294,000 visitors in 1995. In 1999, tourist-generated revenue was US$4.615 billion, a significant drop from 1998's figure of US$6.924 billion. The **devaluation** of the South Korean currency and a sharp decline in the price of many goods and services pushed down the tourist-generated revenues despite an increase in the number of tourists.

Tourists are mainly from the Pacific region. Japan has been the largest source of tourism, followed by the United States and Taiwan, with 1999 figures of 2,174,000, 473,000, and 146,000, respectively. South Koreans residing abroad form a large segment of tourists as well, sending 1,128,000 tourists that year. The tourist industry has a large and expanding infrastructure. In 1998, it included 446 hotels (nearly half of them 5-star) with 46,360 hotel rooms. The hotel industry received a boost in the 1980s with the 1986 Asian Games and the 1988 Summer Olympics. The 2002 World Cup soccer tournament, which will be co-hosted by Japan and South Korea, will give another major boost to the South Korean tourist industry.

TRANSPORTATION. South Korea's economic growth has contributed to the expansion of land, sea, and air transportation. The transportation industry grew significantly in the 1990s when South Korea began to emerge as a major trading nation. The industry accounted for 7 percent of GDP in 1999, a little more than its share in 1995 (6.6 percent). The South Korean marine commercial fleet has a large cargo capacity, (5,093,620 metric tons in 1999), and is expected to grow in the first decade of the 21st century. Its commercial air fleet grew rapidly in the 1990s, carrying 74,375,000 international passengers and 9,052,000 domestic ones in 1997. The slowdown in South Korea's economy in 1998 sharply reduced passengers to 55,736,000 and 6,877,000, respectively, but a likely recovery is suggested as the economy recovers.

RETAIL. South Korea has a very large and growing retail sector, whose share of GDP in 1999 was 10.9 percent. The retail industry, which had been dominated mainly by small-scale traditional shops and restaurants, began to diversify and include larger and modern establishments as well as various foreign retailing networks in the 1980s. Nevertheless, most retail units are still small family-run stores, stalls in markets, or street vendors, though this traditional retail network is giving way rapidly to large discount stores. Discount-store chains, including the domestic E-mart, the U.S. Wal-Mart and Price Costco, and the French Carrefour, are growing. The retail sector also includes a growing food service sector with estimated revenue of US$22.7 billion in 1999. Franchise restaurants, including American ones, accounted for about 5 percent of this sector's revenue in 1999. Like all other types of economic activities, the 1997 financial crisis damaged the retail sector in general and slowed growth of the franchised restaurants in particular, but the economic recovery has improved the situation. Retail and wholesale trade recovered 13 percent in 1999, offsetting a similar decline in 1998. Partial statistics for 2000 reflect about 6.9 percent growth of the retail industry and a sharp jump in retail sales of an estimated US$98 billion.

INTERNATIONAL TRADE

South Korea's international trade began in the 1960s when it started its export-led growth development strategy, exporting mainly light and **consumer goods** and labor-intensive products (toys, footwear, and clothing). Since the 1990s, it has reduced the exports of such items in favor of heavy-industry, capital-intensive, and high-tech products. This has come about for 2 reasons: light and labor-intensive products have lost their competitiveness in international markets where they now face cheaper products from the other Asian nations; and South Korea's industrial growth has enabled it to produce competitive heavy-industry products like automobiles and ships and high-tech products like memory chips and computer products. It is now a major exporter of telecommunications and computer equipment and devices. South Korea's shipbuilding industry now sells ships to Japan, a major global shipbuilder in its own right.

Since the early 1960s, South Korea has targeted developed markets (the United States, Japan, and Europe) for its exports. Since the 1990s, it has also added the growing Pacific market (China, including Hong Kong and Taiwan) to its target list.

South Korea's exports totaled US$143.7 billion in 1999, a growth of 8.6 percent from 1998 (US$132.3 billion) and of about 11 percent from 1995 (US$125.1 billion). An increasing demand for South Korea's semiconductors and telecommunication products pushed the share of semiconductors in total 1999 exports to 13.1 percent, slightly higher than its 1998 share of 12.8 percent. Vehicle exports also rose by 12.3 percent to US$11.1 billion, but textile exports increased only by 6.8 percent to US$5.8 billion. However, its labor-intensive steel exports declined by 13.4 percent to US$7 billion. In 1999, South Korea's major export destinations were the United States

(20.5 percent), the European Union (14.1 percent), Japan (11 percent), China (9.5 percent), and Hong Kong (6.3 percent).

South Korea's imports in 1999 totaled US$119.8 billion, a 28.4 percent rise over the 1998 levels of US$93.3 billion. South Korean export industries heavily depend on foreign capital goods (machinery and equipment) for their production. In 1999, South Korea's main sources of imports were the United States (20.8 percent), Japan (20.2 percent), the European Union (10.5 percent), China (7.4 percent), Saudi Arabia (4.7 percent), and Australia (3.9 percent). In the 1990s, its largest trade deficit was in 1996 (US$20.6 billion), while its largest trade surplus was in 1998 (US$39 billion).

Exchange rates: South Korea

South Korean won (W) per US$1	
Jan 2001	1,271.89
2000	1,130.96
1999	1,188.82
1998	1,401.44
1997	951.29
1996	804.45

SOURCE: CIA *World Factbook 2001* [ONLINE].

MONEY

Four government entities are in charge of foreign exchange activities in South Korea: the Ministry of Finance and Economy (MOFE), the Bank of Korea (BOK), the Financial Supervisory Service (FSS), and the Korea Customs Service (KSS). The ministry sets the overall foreign exchange policy, and the Bank of Korea holds and manages the foreign reserves, while managing all transactions pertaining to foreign trade and capital movements. It also supervises money-changers and foreign-exchange brokers, and provides foreign-exchange banks with foreign currency loans. The FSS supervises financial institutions that are involved in foreign-exchange activities. The KSS has some foreign-exchange regulatory responsibilities towards international trade. Apart from these government regulatory and supervisory institutions, banks involved in foreign exchange have the authority to engage in such financial transactions, including international banking.

South Korea has a free-**floating exchange rate** (a rate determined by supply and demand). This type of fluctuating **exchange rate** limits the MOFE's ability to prevent or to minimize the negative impacts of sudden changes of exchange rates. In 1997, for instance, the MOFE temporarily prohibited South Koreans from purchasing foreign currencies for holding purposes.

The rate of exchange of the South Korean won against the U.S. dollar remained more or less stable in the early 1990s. As the economy began to experience problems in the second half of the 1990s, it began to depreciate gradually against the dollar from 771.27 in 1995, to 804.45 in 1996, and to 951.29 in 1997. This relatively small fluctuation did not have a major impact on the pace of economic activities and the purchasing power of the population until the financial crisis of 1997. In early 1998, the exchange rate jumped to 2,000 and gradually fell to average at about 1,401.44. As the economic recovery began, the rate fell to 1,188.82 in 1999 and to 1,130.96 in 2000. Reflecting the depreciation of the won against the U.S. dollar, the sharp and sudden increase in the exchange rate had a major negative impact on the South Korean economy, which is heavily dependent on large imports of capital goods and energy. The lowering of the exchange rate in 1999 and 2000, which was the result of a gradual economic recovery, contributed to the recovery itself by decreasing the cost of imported goods and fuel.

There have been various restrictions and regulations on foreign-exchange operations since the 1960s. These government-imposed measures were designed to ensure the availability of foreign currencies to South Korean enterprises and to prevent the flight of capital from South Korea. Under foreign pressure, the South Korean government began to liberalize the foreign exchange market in mid-1992. The 1997 IMF-led rescue package required the country to commit itself to liberalizing all aspects of the foreign-exchange system by the end of 2001. In reality, the system has yet to become fully liberalized as the South Korean government has introduced many new direct and indirect regulations in various forms, including restrictions on certain transactions, tax rules, and monitoring regulations, to ensure its control over the financial system.

The Korea Stock Exchange (KSE) in Seoul is the only stock market in South Korea for trading bonds and stocks. It was opened in 1992 to direct portfolio investment from abroad. The reform of the South Korean economy since 1997 has removed restrictions on foreign ownership of South Korean enterprises, and the KSE is now authorized to sell their stocks to foreign buyers without any limit.

POVERTY AND WEALTH

Since the 1960s, South Korea has greatly improved the living standards of its entire population, especially in infrastructures that ensure access to safe water, sanitation, medical services, and adequate diet. According to 1998 statistics, all South Koreans have access to health services and adequate sanitation, while only 7 percent has no access to safe water. The expansion and modernization of

GDP per Capita (US$)

Country	1975	1980	1985	1990	1998
South Korea	2,894	3,766	5,190	7,967	11,123
United States	19,364	21,529	23,200	25,363	29,683
Japan	23,296	27,672	31,588	38,713	42,081
China	138	168	261	349	727

SOURCE: United Nations. *Human Development Report 2000; Trends in human development and per capita income.*

Distribution of Income or Consumption by Percentage Share: South Korea

Lowest 10%	2.9
Lowest 20%	7.5
Second 20%	12.9
Third 20%	17.4
Fourth 20%	22.9
Highest 20%	39.3
Highest 10%	24.3

Survey year: 1993

Note: This information refers to expenditure shares by percentiles of the population and is ranked by per capita expenditure.

SOURCE: *2000 World Development Indicators* [CD-ROM].

the health-care system has been particularly effective: between 1963 and 1998, the number of doctors rose from 9,052 (1 for every 2,981 people) to 65,431 (1 per 710 people), and the number of hospital beds from 10,477 (38 beds per 100,000 population) to 236,187 (509 beds per 100,000). There has been universal health-care insurance since 1989. Infant mortality decreased from 43 per 1,000 live births in 1970 to 5 per 1,000 in 1998. Life expectancy increased from 62.6 years in the period 1970–75 to 72.4 years during 1995–2000. It is significantly higher than other Pacific nations such as Thailand (68.8 years), but much lower than Japan, which has the world's highest life expectancy (80 years), and the United States (76.7 years).

Education, which is compulsory until the age of 14, has been a priority for the South Korean government since 1948. During the period 1995–97, it accounted for 17.5 percent of government annual spending, which is higher than most countries including Japan and the United States. The literacy rate has risen from 22 percent in 1945 to 87.6 percent in 1970 and to 97.5 percent in 1998, but is a little lower than North Korea's rate of 100 percent. South Korea has surpassed certain major industrialized countries in college-level enrollments in science (34 percent in South Korea, 23 percent in Japan, 29 percent in the United Kingdom, and 31 percent in Germany). Nevertheless, it is still lags behind North Korea in the percentage of the population with post-secondary education; in 1998, post-secondary graduates equaled 9.2 percent of the adult population compared to 13.7 percent in North Korea.

Economic development has improved the standards of living of the South Koreans over time. As a result, only 4.2 percent of them lived below the poverty line in 1999. However, the rapid economic development has created extremes of wealth and poverty. The 1997 financial crisis worsened the situation as many people lost their employment while many others faced wage cuts and declining purchasing power. To address the situation, the government spends large amounts on the social safety net (welfare and unemployment insurance), which amounted to 7 percent of government expenditure in 2000.

WORKING CONDITIONS

South Korea joined the International Labor Organization (ILO) in 1991, but has not yet ratified the ILO conventions on Workers Rights (agreements on the freedom of association, on the right to organize and collective bargaining, and on the right of public-service employees to organize). South Korea's constitution provides for the right of workers to associate freely, excluding public-sector employees. According to 1998 legislation, white-collar public workers are allowed to form work-

Household Consumption in PPP Terms

Country	All food	Clothing and footwear	Fuel and power[a]	Health care[b]	Education[b]	Transport & Communications	Other
South Korea	18	3	7	5	14	6	48
United States	13	9	9	4	6	8	51
Japan	12	7	7	2	22	13	37
North Korea	N/A	N/A	N/A	N/A	N/A	N/A	N/A

Data represent percentage of consumption in PPP terms.

[a]Excludes energy used for transport.

[b]Includes government and private expenditures.

SOURCE: World Bank. *World Development Indicators 2000.*

place councils, but blue-collar workers in the postal services, railways, telecommunications, and the National Medical Center are allowed to have unions. In 1997, South Korea amended its labor laws to permit competing unions from 2002 onward, and also to permit more than 1 national labor federation. In 2000, there were 3 such federations: the Korean Confederation of Trade Unions, the Federation of Korean Trade Unions, and the Independent Korean Federation of Clerical and Financial Workers, in addition to 1,600 district labor unions.

The constitution and the Trade Union Law provide for the right of workers to collective bargaining and collective action. There are provisions for workers to seek retribution in case of unfair practices by employers. The 1997 revision of the labor law removed a ban on third-party intervention (union intervention) in labor disputes. In South Korea, labor disputes tend to escalate to work slowdowns and confrontational interruption of businesses through rallies, sit-ins, and occupation of company offices or factories.

Workers have the right to strike, but strikes in government agencies, state-run enterprises, and defense industries are prohibited. The government has the power to end labor disputes by compulsory arbitration in enterprises that are considered to be of "essential public interest" such as public transportation, public health, and utilities. Wage cuts and layoffs since the 1997 crisis have contributed to the rise of labor disputes, which had dropped to 80 cases in 1995 from the 1980s, when they numbered in the thousands.

The South Korean government implemented a minimum wage in 1998 for companies with more than 10 employees. The rate is subject to annual reviews. In 1999, the minimum wage was US$1.45 per hour. As a rule, it is not adequate for a typical blue-collar worker who must supplement his/her salary with overtime payments and bonuses that most companies usually offer to their employees.

The 1989 amendment to the labor law provides for a 44-hour workweek, but its 1997 revisions enable employers to require some 48-hour weeks without overtime. A reduction in the workweek to 40 hours has become a major goal of the labor movement.

Forced labor and child labor are prohibited, but children under the age of 18 may work under certain conditions. To do so, they require a special employment certificate from the Labor Ministry, which is rarely issued because education is compulsory until the age of 14. Children under the age of 18 who wish to work require written approval from their parents or guardians. There are several laws concerning child labor, which are usually enforced, but regular inspections are not done due to lack of human resources. The government sets safety and health standards at work, but accident rates are high because of the lack of regular inspections.

The 1987 Equal Employment Act provides for the equality of men and women in the workplace. Despite improvement in their hiring and promotion, women are still discriminated against, and many women have been sexually abused. The government has enacted laws to punish abusers and provide redress for the abused, but abuses still continue. Foreign workers, most of whom are undocumented, are subject to various physical and financial abuses. Although the government has legalized the status of some of them and sought to ensure their better treatment by employers, they are still vulnerable to various forms of abuse, including withholding wages and passports.

South Korea has a highly educated workforce of 22 million (1998 est.), a growing segment of which is skilled. Unemployment more than doubled during the 1997 financial crisis, from 2.6 percent (556,000) in 1997 to 6.8 percent (1,461,000) in 1998. Economic recovery reduced it to 4.8 percent (1,353,000) in 1999. In May 2000, the unemployment rate was 3.7 percent.

COUNTRY HISTORY AND ECONOMIC DEVELOPMENT

c. 100 A.D. Emergence of the Kingdom of Koguryo, the first truly Korean state.

668–892. Silla Unification Period marked by cultural borrowings from China.

914–1392. Koryo Dynasty marked by Mongol invasion and decline of Buddhism in favor of Confucianism.

1392. Yi Dynasty moves capital to Seoul.

1590s. Japan invades Korea under Hideyoshi and occupies Seoul.

1884. U.S. Presbyterian missionaries arrive in Korea.

1910–45. Japan colonizes the Korean Peninsula.

1919. Samil (1 March) Independence Movement suppressed by the Japanese.

1945. Japan surrenders in World War II and ends its colonization of Korea. The Korean Peninsula is "temporarily" divided between Soviet and U.S. spheres of influence.

1948. The Republic of Korea is established in the southern half of the Korean Peninsula. Syngman Rhee, a civilian, becomes the first president of South Korea.

1950–53. The Korean War is fought between United Nations (mostly U.S.) and **Communist** forces.

1950s. South Korea mechanizes and expands its agricultural sector.

1961. Park Chung-hee, a military person, becomes the second president of South Korea.

1960s. South Korea begins its export-driven strategy of industrial growth by producing and exporting light consumer and labor-intensive products as well as some electronics (radios and black-and-white televisions).

1970s. Production and export of more sophisticated electronics, such as color televisions and calculators.

1974. Assassination attempt on President Park; his wife is killed.

1976. Opposition leaders are purged by President Park's increasingly authoritarian regime.

1979. President Park is assassinated a year after his re-election; martial law follows for 15 months.

1979. Major General Chun Doo-hwan becomes South Korea's third president and tightens military rule.

1980s. South Korea begins its production and export of more advanced electronics, such as VCRs, microwave ovens, and cameras. Heavy industry (steel, automobiles, and shipbuilding) emerges as an important sector.

1988. South Korea hosts the Summer Olympics, which also help expand its tourism industry.

1989. Roh Tae-woo, a former military person, becomes South Korea's fourth president.

1990s. South Korea's high-tech industry emerges, which turns South Korea into a major supplier of telecommunication and computer devices and parts.

1990. South Korea normalizes relations with the Soviet Union.

1992. South Korea normalizes relations with China.

1993. Kim Young-sam, a civilian, becomes the fifth president of South Korea.

1996. South Korea joins the OECD, for which it begins liberalizing its economy.

1997. After labor unrest in the early part of the year, a financial crisis emerges, resulting in a series of bankruptcies and collapse of major enterprises. The government negotiates a bail-out package with the IMF for about US$60 billion. Kim Dae-jung, an opposition leader, is elected as the sixth president of South Korea.

1998. Kim Dae-jung takes office as president and announces his "sunshine policy" of seeking better ties with North Korea. Financial crisis eases with private and public initiatives to reduce long-term debt.

1999. The South Korean government establishes the Financial Supervisory Service, and announces a fiscal plan to balance the budget by 2006. Curbs on foreign investments are eased.

2000. Foreign automakers take control of some troubled South Korean firms. President Kim Dae-jung pays an official visit to P'yongyang, the first such visit since the creation of the 2 Koreas.

FUTURE TRENDS

South Korea went through a very difficult economic period in the late 1990s. Its gradual recovery has shown the resilience of its economy and its capability to grow further. The major factor for its success has been the strength of its export industries, the engine of growth since the 1960s. The diversification of this sector, which also includes high-tech industries, will ensure a position for South Korea as a major economic power and a major global exporter.

The high domestic labor costs have led to the relocation of some labor-intensive industries to other Asian countries like China and Vietnam. This process will likely be accelerated, especially because it can speed up recovery of the South Korean economy and help it grow faster by making its products more competitive in world markets.

If the current process of reconciliation between the 2 Koreas continues, better ties will likely lead to extensive production of South Korean goods-for-export in North Korea, where labor costs are much lower. Better ties will also provide a big opportunity for South Korean industries as their government has agreed to expand and modernize North Korea's crumbling infrastructure pending the settlement of major security concerns. The unification of the 2 Koreas could also turn a united Korea into a stronger economic and military power. Despite its current difficulties, South Korea has a large military force and is an economic power with a growing high-tech sector. North Korea suffers from major economic problems and requires heavy investments to repair its aging industries, devastated agriculture, and crumbling infrastructure. However, it has a very extensive industrial sector with an advanced military branch, a relatively significant mining sector, and a highly educated population. It is linked via land to China and Russia, which are South Korea's targeted markets. The combined economic and military capabilities of the 2 Koreas will likely help a united Korea to establish itself as a regional power in the Pacific.

The restructuring of South Korea's economy and the growing presence of foreign investors and enterprises in the previously protected South Korean market will impose bankruptcies and mergers on weak and small firms to make the larger firms strong enough to withstand foreign competition. Unless the economy grows fast enough to generate employment for the jobless, this situation could contribute to a growing unemployment rate with negative economic, social, and political consequences on South Korea. The role of foreign firms in its economy will significantly increase as its closed and highly-protected markets are opened.

DEPENDENCIES

South Korea has no territories or colonies.

BIBLIOGRAPHY

Economist Intelligence Unit (EIU). *Country Commerce: South Korea.* London: EIU, 29 January 2001.

———. *Country Finance: South Korea.* London: EIU, February 2001.

———. *Country Profile: South Korea, 2000–01.* London: EIU, June 2000.

———. *Country Report: South Korea, 2001–02.* London: EIU, February 2001.

———. *Country Report: South Korea, 2001–02.* London, EIU, November 2000.

———. *Country Risk Service: South Korea.* London, UK: EIU, March 2001.

Eui-Gak, Hwang. *The Korean Economies: A Comparison of North and South.* London: Oxford University Press, 1993.

Kie-Chiang Oh, John. *Korean Politics: The Quest for Democratization and Development, 1960–1990.* Ithaca: Cornell University Press, 1999.

UNDP. *Human Development Report 2000.* New York: Oxford University Press, 2000.

U.S. Central Intelligence Agency. *The World Factbook 2001.* <http://www.cia.gov/cia/publications/factbook>. Accessed May 2001.

U.S. Department of State. *1999 Country Reports on Human Rights Practices: Korea, Republic of.* <http://www.state.gov/www/global/human_rights/1999/korea.html>. Accessed April 2001.

U.S. Department of State. *FY 2001 Country Commercial Guide: Korea.* <http://www.state.gov/www/about_state/business/com_guides/index.html>. Accessed April 2001.

—Dr. Hooman Peimani

KUWAIT

State of Kuwait
Dawlat al-Kuwayt

CAPITAL: Kuwait City.

MONETARY UNIT: Kuwaiti dinar (KD). One Kuwaiti dinar is divided into 1000 fils. Bills come in denominations of ¼, ½, 1, 5, 10, and 20KD. There are coins of 5, 10, 20, 50, and 100 fils.

CHIEF EXPORTS: Oil and oil-related products and fertilizers.

CHIEF IMPORTS: Food and livestock, construction materials, vehicles and parts, clothing.

GROSS DOMESTIC PRODUCT: US$29.3 billion (purchasing power parity, 2000 est.).

BALANCE OF TRADE: **Exports:** US$23.2 billion (f.o.b., 2000). **Imports:** US$7.6 billion (f.o.b., 2000).

COUNTRY OVERVIEW

LOCATION AND SIZE. Kuwait lies at the northwestern corner of the Persian Gulf. With a total area of 17,820 square kilometers (11,073 square miles), it covers an area slightly smaller than the state of New Jersey. To the south and southwest, it shares a 222-kilometer (138-mile) border with Saudi Arabia. To the north and west, there is a 242-kilometer (150-mile) borderline with Iraq. Most major towns, including the capital, Kuwait City, are located along the Gulf, toward the south.

POPULATION. Kuwait's population totaled 2,041,961 in July 2001, of which almost 60 percent were foreign residents. The population increased 1.6 percent per year between 1980 and 1997. The population growth rate was estimated by the CIA to be 3.38 percent in 2001. Most of the growth stems from the arrival of foreign immigrants who come to Kuwait looking for jobs, rather than from a high birth rate. Nevertheless, an estimated 70 percent of the population is under the age of 24.

In 1998, the population density of Kuwait was 102 inhabitants per square kilometers (264 per square mile), with most people living in towns; the urbanization rate is 97 percent. The majority is Muslim (85 percent), with an almost equal split between Sunni Muslims (45 percent) and Shiites (40 percent). Christian, Hindu, Parsee, and other religious minorities make up the remaining 15 percent.

OVERVIEW OF ECONOMY

Kuwait is a small, open economy that depends to a large extent on oil. Worldwide, Kuwait's oil reserves are second only to those of Saudi Arabia, representing about 10 percent of total global reserves. Oil accounts for nearly half of the **gross domestic product** (GDP), more than 90 percent of exports, and 75 percent of government income. Over the last 20 years, the government has tried to broaden the country's importance as a player at all levels of the oil industry by purchasing petroleum distribution networks and gas stations in other parts of the world.

In 1990, Iraq invaded and annexed Kuwait and was then driven out by United Nations (UN) forces under the leadership of the United States. A decade later, Kuwait has fully recovered: the economy is on the upswing and the **infrastructure** has been restored. Kuwait operates the world's most generous state welfare system for its indigenous population. Nationals enjoy access to a free (local) telephone service, electricity at 10 percent of production cost, and water supplies at a third of cost. In addition, as the constitution stipulates, nationals are provided with lifetime guaranteed employment in the civil service, with subsidized housing for married employees.

Like many other Gulf states, Kuwait is heavily dependent on international oil prices. Therefore, it needs to develop a viable non-oil related industrial base and is pressed hard to create jobs for the growing number of young nationals entering the job market every year. The government is, in principle, committed to economic reform. It presented a package of structural reforms to the National Assembly in 1999, which are designed to

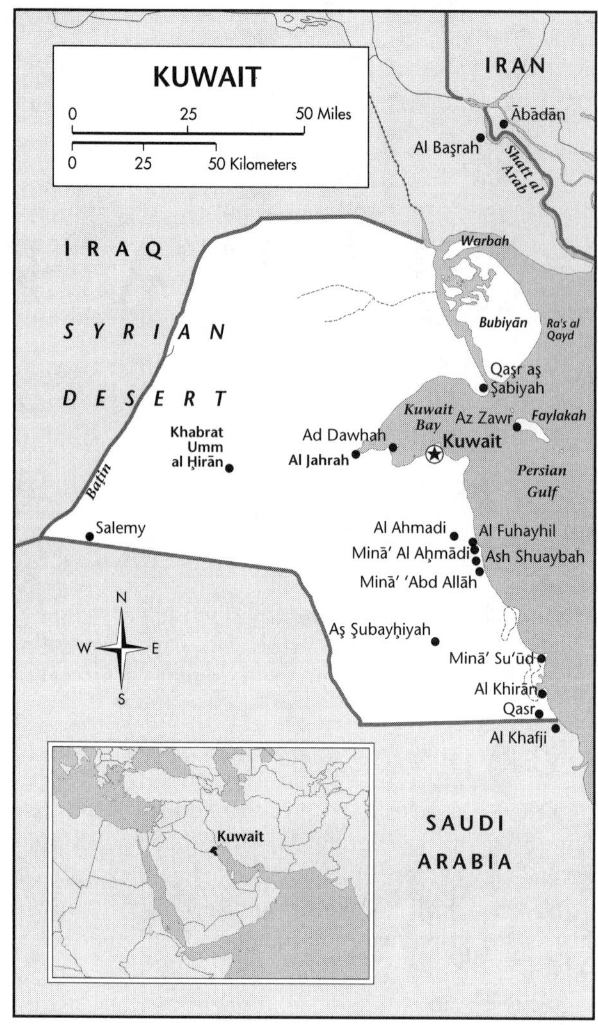

enhance overall efficiency and growth potential. However, implementation has been slow, and **privatization** programs have met stiff resistance because of fears over job losses between nationals and the possible elimination of consumer **subsidies**.

POLITICS, GOVERNMENT, AND TAXATION

The State of Kuwait is a hereditary constitutional monarchy, headed by an emir chosen from the Al-Sabah family. The current emir is Sheikh Jaber al-Ahmed al-Jaber al-Sabah, who acceded to the throne in 1977. Sheikh Jaber al-Sabah is head of state and head of the executive council of ministers, and he rules by decrees agreed to by the council of ministers and, in theory at least, approved by the 50-member National Assembly.

Kuwait can be considered a typical rentier state, that is, a state benefitting from large revenues from the sale of natural resources, in this case oil. As in another oil-dependent sheikhdom, Bahrain, the government distributes the income to its citizens by providing them with jobs and welfare and keeping taxation low. In return, Kuwait's citizens are tied to the state and remain loyal to an undemocratic regime. The concept may be captured in the phrase, "no taxation, no representation."

No political parties are allowed in Kuwait although informal groupings do exist. The largest are the religiously motivated Islamic Patriotic Coalition, the Islamic Constitutional Movement, and the Islamic Popular Grouping, also called the Salafi. The Kuwait Democratic Forum is the largest secular political group and is the voice of liberal and Arab nationalist opinions. The legislature, Majlis Al-Umma, is a **unicameral** National Assembly of 50 elected members, plus appointed cabinet ministers, serving for a 4-year period. The Assembly's legislative power is restricted, since the emir can simply dissolve it at will and rules by decree. In fact, the National Assembly was temporarily dissolved by decree of the emir in 1976, 1986, and 1999. Kuwaitis under the age of 21 and women cannot vote. Though the issue of women's suffrage (right to vote) is heavily debated, in January 2001, Kuwait's constitutional court followed a lower-court ruling refusing to grant women their voting rights.

The Kuwaiti emir also has ultimate authority over major decisions relating to oil. In December 1975, the country **nationalized** its domestic and foreign oil assets and created the Kuwait Petroleum Company (KPC), which is an umbrella company for subsidiaries handling oil production and marketing. The economy is heavily dominated by state-owned enterprises.

INFRASTRUCTURE, POWER, AND COMMUNICATIONS

Kuwait's infrastructure is modern and well developed. Within a few years after liberation from the Iraqi occupation, Kuwait managed to restore facilities and services to pre-war standards.

TRANSPORTATION. A network of 3,800 kilometers (2,361 miles) of good paved roads and modern multi-lane expressways link all areas of the country, extending south and west from Kuwait City to neighboring cities and to Iraq and Saudi Arabia. The ports—Shuwaykh, Shuaybah, and Mina Al-Ahmadi—handle commercial shipping and petroleum exports.

POWER. Kuwait has several major electric power-generating plants. These incorporate desalination operations, which remove salt from seawater to provide the country with drinking water. Currently, the country has enough electric capacity from plants fired by natural gas or oil, but with demand rapidly rising as the population increases, expansion projects are already underway to increase capacity. To meet demand, the *Middle East Eco-*

Communications

Country	Newspapers	Radios	TV Sets[a]	Cable subscribers[a]	Mobile Phones[a]	Fax Machines[a]	Personal Computers[a]	Internet Hosts[b]	Internet Users[b]
	1996	1997	1998	1998	1998	1998	1998	1999	1999
Kuwait	374	660	491	N/A	138	27.6	104.9	23.76	100
United States	215	2,146	847	244.3	256	78.4	458.6	1,508.77	74,100
Saudi Arabia	57	321	262	N/A	31	N/A	49.6	1.17	300
Iraq	19	229	83	N/A	0	N/A	N/A	0.00	N/A

[a]Data are from International Telecommunication Union, *World Telecommunication Development Report 1999* and are per 1,000 people.
[b]Data are from the Internet Software Consortium (http://www.isc.org) and are per 10,000 people.

SOURCE: World Bank. *World Development Indicators 2000.*

nomic Digest (MEED) estimates that Kuwait will need to spend US$3.6 billion over the next 10 years to install 5,000 megawatts (MW) of generating capacity to add to the 6,900 MW that was already available at end-1999.

TELECOMMUNICATIONS. Before 1990–91, the telephone system had more than 250,000 subscribers, with work under way to increase this number to more than 500,000. Since demand is running at only 400,000 lines, the emphasis is on upgrading rather than expanding the system. There is a mobile cellular system in operation, which had 150,000 subscribers in 1996. By 2000, Kuwait had 3 Internet service providers and 5,000 hosts registered under their own domain. The Ministry of Communications retains control over these services and access is expensive, but the Internet is hugely popular and, according to the U.S. State Department's *Country Commercial Guide for 2001*, the number of individual users is expected to jump to 300,000 by 2003.

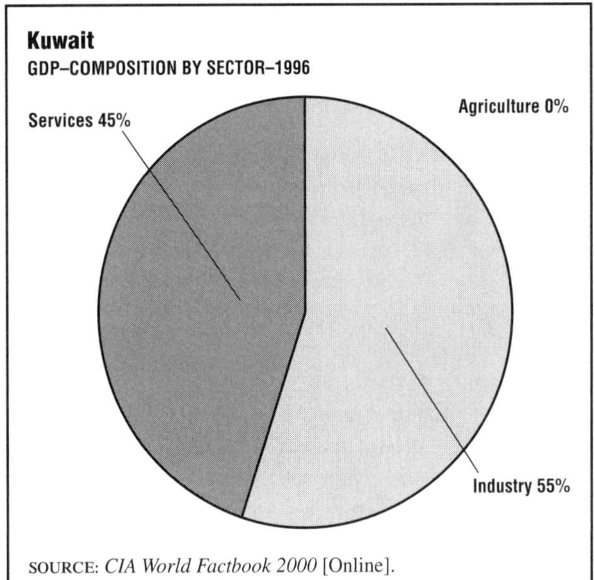

SOURCE: *CIA World Factbook 2000* [Online].

ECONOMIC SECTORS

The economy of Kuwait relies heavily on industry and services. In 1996, agriculture accounted for none of the country's GDP, while industry accounted for 55 percent and services accounted for 45 percent. Agriculture only contributed 0.4 percent to the GDP in 1999, while industry accounted for 51.4 percent, and services for 48.2 percent. These figures, however, can be misleading, since oil dominates the Kuwaiti economy. Except for petroleum industries, Kuwait's only other industrial enterprises are desalination, salt production, food processing, and construction.

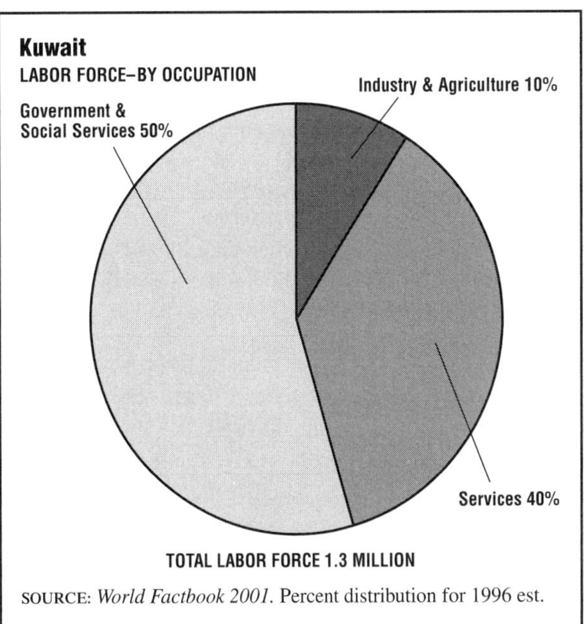

SOURCE: *World Factbook 2001.* Percent distribution for 1996 est.

AGRICULTURE

Because Kuwait is desert and has almost no water, agriculture has seen minimal development. As a result, Kuwait imports over 96 percent of its food, while over 75 percent of its drinking water has to be distilled or imported.

Pollution, dating from the deliberate oil spillage and torching of wells under Iraqi occupation, has further hindered agricultural development in the aftermath of the war.

In the 1970s, over-fishing by many states in the Gulf considerably reduced catches of fish and shrimp. In the late 1980s, war and environmental damage, including oil spills, also harmed the fishing industry. Large-scale commercial fishing takes place as far afield as the Indian Ocean and the Red Sea but serves domestic demand.

INDUSTRY

Industrial development in Kuwait has faced formidable obstacles. The country, so rich in oil, is poor in most other resources. The small domestic market restricts production for local consumption to small-scale operations, while the small Kuwaiti **labor force**, possessing limited skills, and high labor costs are further constraints.

MINING/HYDROCARBONS. Kuwait's oil production of 2.095 million barrels per day (bpd) in 1998 accounted for 3 percent of total world output. Although Iraqi forces set fire to over 60 percent of Kuwaiti oil wells and thus destroyed about 2 percent of Kuwait's total reserves, the country holds about 10 percent of known world reserves. The U.S. Department of Energy estimates that Kuwait's importance as a world oil producer will steadily increase. Kuwait and Saudi Arabia hold about 80 percent of the world's excess production capacity, which means that the 2 countries can easily produce more or less oil at will, thus influencing the prices in the world markets. The emirate plans to invest US$15 billion over the period 1995–2005 to increase its output capacity to 3.5 million bpd. There are also plans to modernize 3 refineries to increase total domestic processing capacity from 800,000 barrels per day (bpd) to 1 million bpd and to allow for environmentally cleaner products. At present, Kuwait produces about 2 million barrels of crude oil per day. With oil prices remaining high throughout 2000, earnings amounted to an estimated KD5.4 billion (US$17.5 billion).

The emirate also ranks among the nations with the world's largest natural gas reserves. Most of its gas is used for domestic needs rather than export, but Kuwait estimates that it has 1.5 trillion cubic meters, or 1.1 percent of global reserves.

MANUFACTURING. Most industry is concentrated in petrochemicals and production of fertilizers. The Petrochemical Industries Company (PIC), a subsidiary of the Kuwait Petroleum Company (KPC) and the leading industrial enterprise, is involved in the production of petroleum-based fertilizers. Kuwait's capacity to produce fertilizer stands at approximately 1.65 million tons per year. In recent years, however, the market has been hit by technical problems, weak prices, and the imposition of European Union (EU) **tariffs**. Other light industries include chemicals, food processing, textiles, furniture, paper, mineral and metallic products, cement, sulphur processing, detergents, and construction materials.

SERVICES

Aside from oil, services dominate the Kuwaiti economy. Most people are employed by the government, whose over-staffed bureaucracy and generous welfare system provides most Kuwaitis with their income. Since there is hardly any tourism, banks and financial services are the only commercial services involving the **private sector**.

FINANCIAL SERVICES. By the 1980s, Kuwait's banks were among the Gulf region's largest financial institutions. Because of the high oil revenue in the 1970s, many private individuals with money to dispose began to speculate. This action prompted a small crash in the official stock market in 1977 and a much larger crash in the alternative stock market, the *Souq al-Manakh* in 1986. The debts from the crash (US$64 billion) left all but one bank in Kuwait technically insolvent and held up only by support from the Central Bank. A government imposed reform program for the banking sector was still incomplete in 1990 when the Iraqi invasion changed the entire financial picture.

After liberation, new plans were announced for reform, which involved the government purchase of the banks' outstanding debts, but the reform has not yet been completed. Only the National Bank of Kuwait (NBK), the largest commercial bank, which handled the exiled government's finances during the crisis, survived both crises intact. The NBK, with current assets of over US$12 billion, is one of the 5 biggest banks in the Arab world and ranks in the top 250 banks worldwide. the jointly owned Bank of Bahrain and Kuwait and 6 other Kuwaiti banks are also in the top 1,000.

INTERNATIONAL TRADE

Ever since the era of oil began after World War II, the priceless mineral has been Kuwait's main export product. Thanks to the huge revenue from oil sales, the government accumulated surplus money and invested abroad. Many of these reserve investments were cashed in during the Iraqi occupation and the liberation period to meet the expenses of Kuwait and the allied coalition. By the mid-1990s the value of exports exceeded the costs of imports by US$4 billion. **Trade surplus** hit a low in 1998, due to declining oil prices but began rising again in 1999. Figures show a US$2.7 billion increase to US$13.5 billion in the value of exports, and a US$1 billion drop in imports, which totaled US$8.1 billion, compared to 1998. By 2000, the *World Factbook* estimated

Trade (expressed in billions of US$): Kuwait

	Exports	Imports
1975	9.184	2.390
1980	19.663	6.529
1985	10.487	6.005
1990	7.042	3.972
1995	12.931	7.784
1998	9.529	6.130

SOURCE: International Monetary Fund. *International Financial Statistics Yearbook 1999.*

that exports totaled US$23.2 billion and imports totaled US$7.6 billion.

Because of Kuwait's small domestic manufacturing sector, the country's imports for its high-income economy are finished products, which come primarily from the United States and Japan. In 1999, according to the *Economist Intelligence Unit*, 15.4 percent of imports came from the United States, 10.2 percent from Japan, 7.3 percent from Germany, and 7.1 percent from the United Kingdom. Japan, however, led Kuwait's export markets, absorbing 22.8 percent, followed by the United States at 11.5 percent, Singapore 8.2 percent, and the Netherlands 7.3 percent.

MONEY

The Kuwaiti dinar's **exchange rate** is pegged to the U.S. dollar and has remained stable throughout the last few decades. The International Monetary Fund (IMF) has praised the Central Bank of Kuwait, established in 1959, for its successful policies in keeping the Kuwaiti currency stable. One dinar roughly equals 3 dollars.

Kuwait is one of the few major capital-exporting countries, that is, the state has more income at its disposal than it spends, and this surplus money is invested overseas or lent to the international banking sector. The Kuwait Investment Authority (KIA) controls 2 portfolios, the Reserve Fund for Future Generations and the State General Reserve Fund. The combined value of these funds is estimated at between US$60billion and US$90 billion; although impressive, these figures are well below the pre-1990 Gulf War peak of US$117 billion. KIA's investments include bonds and international stocks listed on the New York and London stock exchanges, as well as real estate property, in Europe and North America. The (official) Kuwait Stock Exchange is small and is characterized by intensive trading, of only a limited number of stocks, among local investors.

POVERTY AND WEALTH

In a state such as Kuwait, class based on private property and wealth becomes less important than the power of access to the state that distributes the large (oil) revenues. Although Kuwait is a wealthy country and poverty is almost non-existent, there are still important divisions within society. There are divisions between long-settled tribal families and those who only settled in the last 3 decades and do not benefit from long established ties to the powerful. Some of the latter have not even been granted Kuwaiti citizenship and are usually called *Bidoon*, meaning "without" (nationality) and thus face grave disadvantages. Another important determinant of proximity to the state apparatus is the sectarian division between Sunni Muslims and Shiites. The Shi'a community (immigrants from neighboring countries) has often been excluded from the government bureaucracy that provides Kuwaiti Sunnis with work and social security.

The provision of social services to Kuwaiti citizens, compared with most Western countries, is extensive. The state welfare system especially cares for the needy, providing direct transfers to widows and students, and aiding families in need because of divorce, old age, disability, parental death, illness, or financial difficulty. Educational and marital status are taken into account in granting aid.

WORKING CONDITIONS

Kuwait's vast wealth has attracted many immigrants from poorer countries who come looking for work. Thus,

Exchange rates: Kuwait

Kuwaiti dinars (KD) per US$1	
Jan 2001	0.3057
2000	0.3067
1999	0.3044
1998	0.3047
1997	0.3033
1996	0.2994

SOURCE: CIA *World Factbook 2001* [ONLINE].

GDP per Capita (US$)

Country	1975	1980	1985	1990	1998
Kuwait	21,838	16,922	10,736	N/A	N/A
United States	19,364	21,529	23,200	25,363	29,683
Saudi Arabia	9,658	11,553	7,437	7,100	6,516
Qatar	N/A	N/A	N/A	N/A	N/A

SOURCE: United Nations. *Human Development Report 2000; Trends in human development and per capita income.*

after decades of **immigration**, at least 55 percent of the total population of Kuwait are foreign, and the rate within the workforce is even higher (84 percent). In the private sector, 94 percent of employees are expatriates, working in shops, services and, frequently, as domestic servants. Only about 26 percent of Kuwaitis participate in the workforce, as opposed to 70 percent for expatriates. The Kuwaiti **participation rate**, although still low, has been gradually increasing (it was 22 percent in 1989) owing to a rise in female participation in the workforce. For cultural and social reasons this rate is still low, and, because of Kuwait's oil wealth, many women do not need to work.

Kuwaiti citizen workers—95 percent are government employees—are entitled to join unions. However, according to the U.S. State Department's *Country Commercial Guide for 2001*, in June 1998, there were only 50,000 union members. There is a legal minimum wage in the government sector, but none in the private sector. Public health care is free to citizens, but a health insurance charge is levied on employers to cover expatriates (most workers in the private sector). Foreigners thus do not benefit equally from the state social services, which favor Kuwaiti nationals.

About 40 percent of Kuwaitis are under the age of 14, and young Kuwaitis are seeking jobs in steadily increasing numbers. These factors are a cause for growing government concern, and the government will at some point have to abandon its guarantee of a **public sector** job for every university-educated citizen. One recent measure is the "Kuwaitization" of the economy, promoting the employment of Kuwaitis over foreign labor in the private sector and limiting immigration. It has been nearly impossible for foreign workers to obtain Kuwaiti citizenship; those who do achieve it are not entitled to vote for another 20 years.

COUNTRY HISTORY AND ECONOMIC DEVELOPMENT

1756. Part of the Ottoman Empire since the 16th century, Kuwait gains semi-autonomy under the Sheikh of the Sabah family.

1899. The ruling Sabah family accepts British protection to counter the spread of Turkish influence and grants control of external relations to Britain.

1918. The end of World War I ends what is already nominal Turkish control over Kuwait.

1938. Oil is discovered in Kuwait, but World War II interrupts further exploration. Drilling resumes after the war and Kuwait soon develops into a thriving commercial center. The government begins to use oil revenue to develop the country's infrastructure and a modern and comprehensive welfare system.

1960. Kuwait becomes a founding member of the Organization of Petroleum-Exporting Countries (OPEC) on 14 September.

1961. Kuwait's status as a British protectorate ends, and the country assumes independence on 19 June. The ruling sheikh becomes the emir and assumes full executive power.

1961–63. Iraq moves troops to the border, threatening to annex Kuwait but draws back due to international pressure and a coup within Iraq.

1974–75. The Supreme Petroleum Council is created, followed by the nationalization of domestic and foreign oil assets and the creation of the Kuwait Petroleum Company (KPC).

1977. Sheikh Jaber Al-Ahmad Al-Sabah becomes emir, succeeding Sheikh Sabah Al-Salem Al-Sabah.

1990–91. Iraq invades Kuwait. The international community condemns the invasion and, led by the United States, deploys armed forces to Saudi Arabia. The allied forces launch an aerial bombing campaign against Iraqi forces in Kuwait and Iraq on 17 January 1991. On 24 February 1991, American-led ground forces enter Kuwait, and on 28 February Iraq agrees to accept UN resolutions concerning Kuwait.

1999. A draft law granting women full political rights is narrowly rejected in December.

FUTURE TRENDS

At the beginning of the 21st century, Kuwait is facing major challenges. Political reform, including women's right to vote, is under debate and cannot be put off in the long run. Economic reform is even more pressing. Kuwait's oil reserves will last for another 100 years, but the country has to **restructure** its economy and reduce its dependence on oil. Many young Kuwaitis will demand their share in the country's wealth and need to be provided with work opportunities and prospects if they are not to challenge the country's political power structures. The government is currently debating various reform packages in both the economic and political arenas. And, however much resistance there may currently be to economic reform, privatization and **liberalization** might prove to be the only way to sustain the country's wealth in a post-oil era.

DEPENDENCIES

Kuwait has no territories or colonies.

BIBLIOGRAPHY

Chalk, Nigel Andrew, and others. *Kuwait: From Reconstruction to Accumulation for Future Generations*, Washington, D.C.: IMF Occasional Papers No. 150, April 1997.

Cordesman, Anthony H. *Kuwait: Recovery and Security after the Gulf War.* Boulder, CO: Westview Press, 1997.

Crystal, Jill. *Kuwait: The Transformation of an Oil State.* Boulder, CO: Westview Press, 1992.

Economist Intelligence Unit. *Country Profile: Kuwait.* London: Economist Intelligence Unit, 2001.

U.S. Central Intelligence Agency. *World Factbook 2001.* <http://www.odci.gov/cia/publications/factbook/index.html>. Accessed October 2001.

U.S. Department of State. *FY 2001 Country Commercial Guide: Kuwait.* <http://www.state.gov>. Accessed August 2001.

U.S. Library of Congress, Federal Research Division. *Kuwait: A Country Study.* >http://lcweb2.loc.gov/frd/cs/kwtoc.html>. Accessed January 2001.

—Markus R. Bouillon and Ralph Stobwasser

KYRGYZSTAN

Kyrgyz Republic
Kyrgyz Respublikasy

CAPITAL: Bishkek (formerly known as Frunze).

MONETARY UNIT: Som (KS). One som equals 100 tyiyn. Som are circulated in denominations of 1, 3, 5, 10, 50, 100, 500, 1,000, 2,000, and 5,000.

CHIEF EXPORTS: Cotton, wool, meat, tobacco, gold, mercury, uranium, hydropower machinery, shoes.

CHIEF IMPORTS: Consumer durables, oil and gas, machinery and equipment, foodstuffs.

GROSS DOMESTIC PRODUCT: US$10.3 billion (purchasing power parity, 1999 est.).

BALANCE OF TRADE: **Exports:** US$515 million (1999 est.). **Imports:** US$590 million (1999 est.).

COUNTRY OVERVIEW

LOCATION AND SIZE. Located in the central region of Asia, bordered by China on the east, Kazakhstan on the north, and Uzbekistan and Tajikistan on the west and south, Kyrgyzstan is a remote, landlocked, mountainous country with a total area of 198,500 square kilometers (76,641 square miles). It is a bit smaller than the U.S. state of South Dakota. Kyrgyzstan's capital, Bishkek, is located near the northern border of the country close to the border with Kazakhstan and Kazakhstan's largest city, Almaty.

POPULATION. The population of Kyrgyzstan was estimated at 4,685,230 in July 2000. In 2000 the birth rate stood at 26.29 births per 1,000 while the death rate was 9.15 deaths per 1,000 persons. The population growth rate was estimated at 1.43 percent in 2000. Migration out of the country was estimated at 2.8 per 1,000.

The vast majority of Kyrgyzstanis live in rural areas. The World Bank reported that only 33.6 percent of the population lived in urban areas in 1999. The population density for the entire country was 25 per square kilometer (65 per square mile) that same year, according to the World Bank.

At the beginning of the 21st century, roughly 50 percent of Kyrgyzstan's multinational population was ethnic Kyrgyz; 20 percent was ethnic Slavic (Russian, Ukrainian, and other Slavic groups); 13 percent was Uzbek; about 2 percent was German; and other groups comprised the remaining 12 percent. The Kyrgyz (also spelled Kirghiz) language is a Turkic language. Russian and Kyrgyz are the principal languages spoken in Kyrgyzstan, but Uzbek, Tajik, and Uigur are also widely spoken outside the major towns. In practice, most government and commerce is conducted in the Russian language in the large cities. Many Kyrgyz government officials and professional and technical workers use Russian as their principal language. Most rural areas use Kyrgyz or one of the other indigenous languages of the region as their principal language.

OVERVIEW OF ECONOMY

Kyrgyzstan is a remote, landlocked country with inadequate trade and transportation **infrastructure**. Kyrgyzstan's economy heavily emphasizes agriculture and animal husbandry, but there is a growing service sector in the urban areas. In 1999 agriculture accounted for 45 percent of the economy, while services comprised 35 percent. Industry made up the remaining 20 percent. Oil and gas, machinery and equipment, and foodstuffs are Kyrgyzstan's main imports. Kyrgyzstan's principal trading partners are Germany, Russia, Kazakhstan, and Uzbekistan. Cotton, wool, hides and meat are the main agricultural products and exports. Industrial exports include gold, mercury, uranium, and electricity. Kyrgyzstan is a mountainous country with significant hydroelectric power generating potential.

While it was part of the Union of Soviet Socialist Republics (USSR) from 1917 to 1991, Kyrgyzstan had a highly specialized economic niche in the **communist** economic system. Kyrgyzstan served primarily as a provider

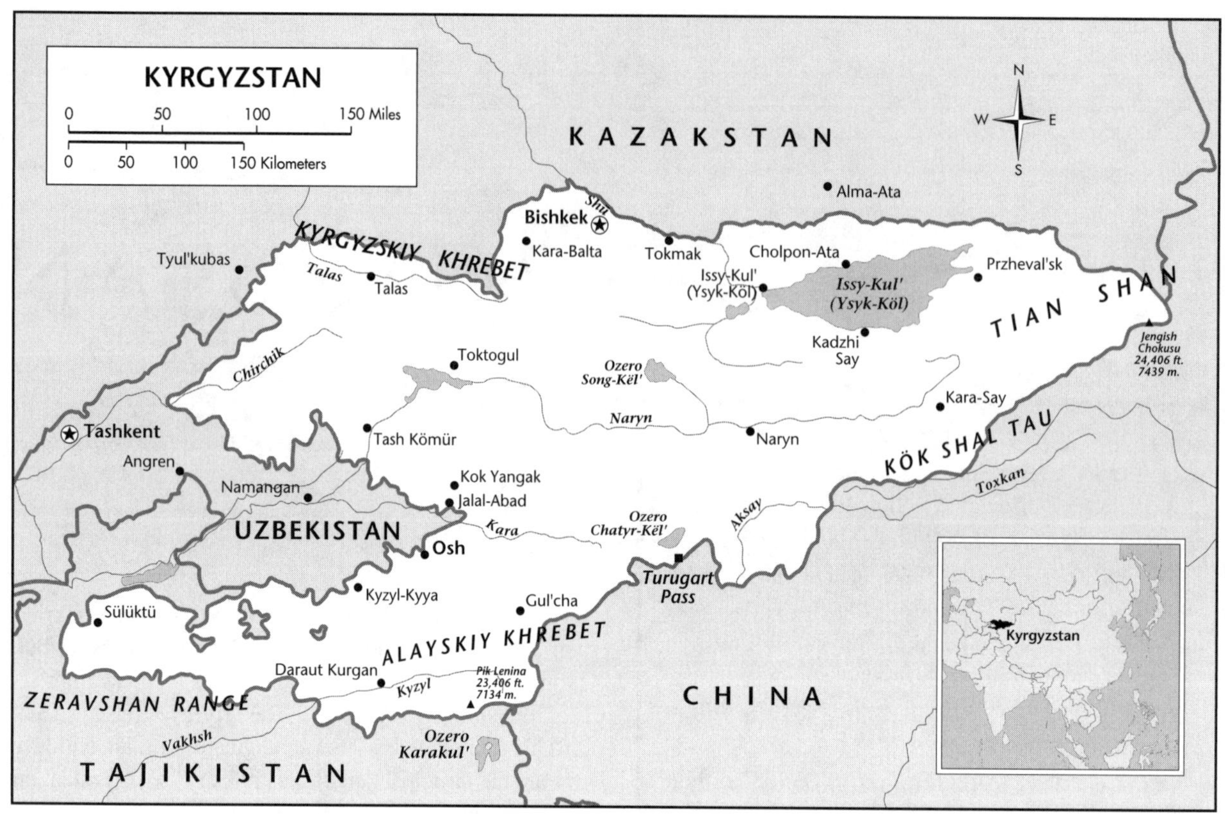

of **primary commodities** such as gold, mercury, and uranium, and unprocessed agricultural goods such as foodstuffs, cotton, wool, and meat. After the USSR collapsed in 1991, Kyrgyzstan's mining and industrial enterprises underwent rapid contraction due to the loss of orders from buyers and the inability of the existing transportation infrastructure to make possible a rapid entrance into other markets. Kyrgyzstan's military industrial enterprises soon lost their financing. Production at Kyrgyzstan's gold, mercury, and uranium mines fell sharply.

After national independence on 31 August 1991, the newly established Kyrgyz government planned to create a market-based economy and to integrate into the world economy. Among the former communist countries, Kyrgyzstan became a leader in the movement of the post-Soviet states toward an open market economy. But the transition to an open economy has been difficult for this small country with few manufactured goods. The economy underwent severe contraction between 1990 and 1995. However, the Kyrgyzstan economy began to rebound in 1996 as new, post-communist practices began to take effect. The **budget deficit** as a proportion of the GDP was cut in half during the period 1995 through 1997.

With assistance from international organizations, such as the World Bank and the International Monetary Fund, the Kyrgyzstan government has made good headway in establishing the legal and regulatory foundation for a market economy. Kyrgyzstan carried out **privatization** of small enterprises and overhauled the country's banking and financial systems. In 1998 the Kyrgyzstan constitution was amended to allow for private ownership of land. Kyrgyzstan was the first country of the CIS to join the World Trade Organization (December 1998). At the urging of international financial institutions, the Kyrgyzstan government took steps to **liberalize** its foreign trade relations. These steps included eliminating some **tariff** restrictions (1991–92), eliminating certain highly bureaucratic export registration requirements (1998), and eliminating export **duties** (1999).

But Kyrgyzstan's enthusiastic pro-market posture has not met with the anticipated level of economic success. Basic economic indicators plunged between 1991 and 1995 when Soviet-era government **subsidies** for industry, farming, and public services were eliminated. Rapid **restructuring** of the economy led to sharp drops in farm and industrial output. From 1996 to 1997, the declines in output were reversed and the economic picture for Kyrgyzstan brightened considerably. A large increase in government revenue from the newly opened Kumotr gold mine, the largest single industrial enterprise in the country, combined with favorable weather that helped boost agricultural production. Economic growth in 1996 registered 7 percent and climbed to 10 percent in 1997. **Inflation** declined, and the government's current account deficit, an indicator of the government's fiscal responsibility, dropped to its lowest level since independence.

This picture changed when Kyrgyzstan was hit hard by the 1998 financial collapse in its major trading partner, Russia. The financial collapse in Russia led to a sudden drop in orders for Kyrgyzstan goods from Russia. The contraction in output led also to a deterioration in Kyrgyzstan's **balance of payments** at the same time as the country's indebtedness to foreign lenders increased substantially.

POLITICS, GOVERNMENT, AND TAXATION

The Republic of Kyrgyzstan was an early leader in the post-communist transition. The country's pro-reform leader, Askar Akaev, a scientist and former president of the republic's Academy of Sciences, quickly established an impressive record of encouraging political and economic liberalization. The Kyrgyz government liberalized most prices, established a national currency, began privatization and financial sector reform, and introduced the legal and regulatory framework for open trade with its neighbors. Non-tariff barriers were removed, and export taxes were eliminated on all goods between 1994 and 1997. In December 1998, the Kyrgyz Republic became the first former communist country to qualify for entrance to the World Trade Organization.

Kyrgyzstan's legal system is based on the continental legal system. Kyrgyzstan's constitution was adopted in 1993. The constitution recognizes a separation of powers among 3 branches of government: an accountable executive, a deliberative legislative, and an independent judiciary. The constitution has provisions to ensure checks and balances, competitive elections, and judicial independence. The judiciary consists of Constitutional Court (to decide issues of constitutional import), the Supreme Court, an arbitration court to resolve commercial disputes. There is a system of lower courts. The constitution was amended in February 1996 by a popular referendum that substantially expanded the powers of the president.

The Kyrgyzstan political system is formally a competitive system. Officials are popularly elected in multi-candidate elections. The country's president is elected by popular vote for a 5-year term. Kyrgyzstan president Askar Akaev was first elected in October 1990 and re-elected in December 1995 and December 2000. High officials such as the prime minister and other top cabinet officials are appointed by the president and submitted for approval to the Kyrgyzstan legislature, the Zhogorku Kenesh. There are numerous parties and political movements. The officially registered political parties are the Agrarian Party, the Agrarian Party of Kyrgyzstan, the ASABA party, the Communist Party of Kyrgyzstan, the Democratic Movement of Kyrgyzstan, the Dignity Party, the Fatherland Party, the Justice Party, Kyrgyzstan Erkin Party, the Movement for the People's Salvation, the Ashar Party, the National Unity Democratic Movement, the Peasant Party, the Republican Popular Party of Kyrgyzstan, and the Social Democratic Party.

The Kyrgyzstan government has sought to limit the size of the **public sector** to enable greater opportunities for the growth of private industry and services. Accordingly the government has sought to reduce the total government revenue as a percentage of the GDP. However, after the 1998 economic crisis, tax collection fell behind anticipated levels. Tax revenue collection relies heavily on industry. Poor industrial performance contributed to the shortfall in tax revenue. Yet during the economic crisis total government expenditures were higher than anticipated in recent years due to the increased costs of social protection programs. International financial institutions urged the Kyrgyzstan government to maintain a tight **monetary policy**, reduce government spending, and increase revenue collection. Yet the Kyrgyzstan government was reluctant to adopt these politically unpopular measures.

INFRASTRUCTURE, POWER, AND COMMUNICATIONS

The main components of Kyrgyzstan's physical infrastructure include roads, rail, electric grids, gas pipelines, and a telecommunications system. The country's road system consists 16,854 kilometers (10,467 miles) of paved roads. The rail system consists of 1 major rail line of a length of 370 kilometers (299 miles) linking the Kyrgyz capital, Bishkek, with Kazakhstan. The fixed (copper wire) telephone system and microwave relay stations dating from the Soviet period (consisting of 357,000 lines) are rapidly being overtaken by new, decentralized mobile phone services. Of the country's 14 airports, only the capital airport is capable of accommodating international flights.

Mountainous Kyrgyzstan has abundant low-cost hydropower but only very limited amounts of oil, gas, and coal. Consequently, Kyrgyzstan is dependent upon the other Central Asian countries for much of its gas and petroleum. Kyrgyzstan trades hydroelectric energy for natural gas with both Uzbekistan and Kazakhstan. With the urging of international donors, Kyrgyzstan is seeking to adopt an energy policy that will reduce the role of the state, increase **private sector** involvement, and explore the potential for energy exports, particularly to China. China's recently adopted "Go West" policy has opened a potentially rich market for hydroelectric energy in the adjoining Xinjiang-Uigur Autonomous Province of China.

Communications

Country	Newspapers	Radios	TV Sets[a]	Cable subscribers[a]	Mobile Phones[a]	Fax Machines[a]	Personal Computers[a]	Internet Hosts[b]	Internet Users[b]
	1996	1997	1998	1998	1998	1998	1998	1999	1999
Kyrgyzstan	N/A	384	231	N/A	2	0.1	N/A	1.42	10
United States	215	2,146	847	244.3	256	78.4	458.6	1,508.77	74,100
Russia	105	418	420	78.5	5	0.4	40.6	13.06	2,700
Tajikistan	20	142	285	N/A	0	0.3	N/A	0.24	2

[a]Data are from International Telecommunication Union, *World Telecommunication Development Report 1999* and are per 1,000 people.
[b]Data are from the Internet Software Consortium (http://www.isc.org) and are per 10,000 people.
SOURCE: World Bank. *World Development Indicators 2000.*

Since being corporatized (that is, separated from the previous unified Soviet system and turned into a Kyrgyzstan state-owned corporation) in 1994, the Kyrgyz state power company, Kyrgyzenergo, has operated 22 hydroelectric power stations with a combined capacity of over 30 billion kilowatt hours (kWh) annually. Electricity production averaged roughly 12 billion kWh per year. The expansion of electricity output was held back, though, by inadequate transmission equipment and inadequate pricing and cost recovery. Given these factors, Kyrgyzstan commenced the privatization of its energy utility in 1998. The process came to a conclusion in early 2001. The goal of the privatization was to separate regulatory functions from energy production and sales. As a result of the strategy to separate the various energy functions and shift to a cost-recovery basis for energy production, there have been significant increases in electricity and district heating costs. Loans and credits with the World Bank and other multilateral development banks are earmarked to reduce the social costs of the transition to a privatized energy sector.

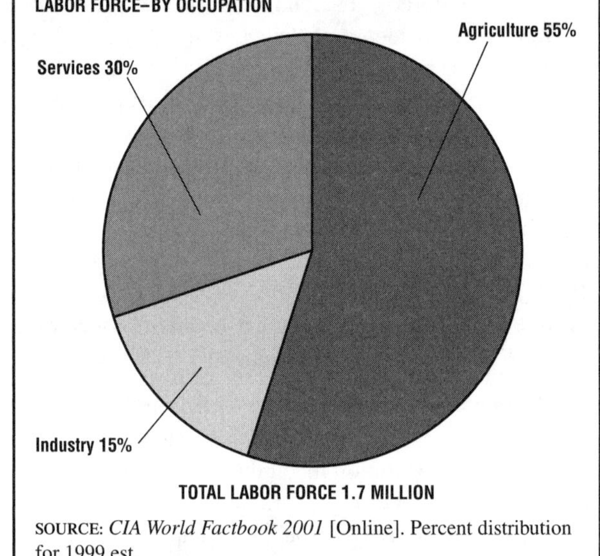

SOURCE: *CIA World Factbook 2001* [Online]. Percent distribution for 1999 est.

ECONOMIC SECTORS

The 3 most important sectors of Kyrgyzstan's economy are: agriculture, accounting for about 45 percent of the GDP (US$52.8 million in 1999); industry, accounting for about 20 percent of the GDP; and services, accounting for the remaining 35 percent in 1999. The most significant economic sector, agriculture, is the largest employer in the country, employing over half of the country's **labor force**. In 1999 the International Monetary Fund estimated that 886,000 workers were employed in Kyrgyzstan's agriculture and forestry sectors. Agriculture accounted for about 22 percent of the country's exports in 1999. Other important sectors are hydroelectric energy production, mining, particularly gold mining, and service. Small industries and processing plants are located in Kyrgyzstan's larger cities, particularly Jalalabod, Osh, and Talas in addition to the capital, Bishkek.

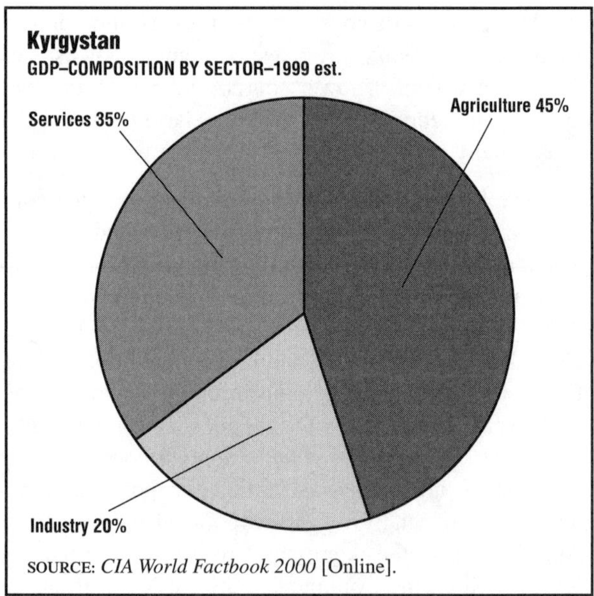

SOURCE: *CIA World Factbook 2000* [Online].

AGRICULTURE

Kyrgyzstan produces cotton, sugar beets, vegetables, potatoes, grapes, melons, tobacco, fruits and berries, grain, wool, and meat. Total agricultural production dropped in 1992 from earlier levels and then began to rise. The disruption in farm inputs such as seeds, farm machinery, and agricultural extension services, along with transportation difficulties and weak consumer demand, led to the drop in output. After the effects of the market transition from communism began to be felt, overall agricultural production began to increase after 1996. However, livestock and wool production, 2 of the traditional mainstays of the Kyrgyzstan rural economy, continued to decline due to slack demand for products such as hides and wool and new competition from Turkish, Chinese, and other suppliers.

In connection with the Kyrgyzstan government's goal of maintaining an open market and **liberal economic** order, the government has avoided intervention in the agricultural economy through price supports and targeted subsidies. This policy contrasts sharply with that of neighboring Uzbekistan, where the government has continued to maintain a major presence in the agricultural economy. Kyrgyzstan instituted a land reform program to transfer use rights to land from the Soviet-era large state farm cooperatives to individual farmers. By 1999 over 90 percent of Kyrgyz farms were held in private hands with long term (99 years) use rights. Farm land may be bought and sold and transferred through inheritance. The CIA *World Factbook* reported that 55 percent of the Kyrgyzstan workforce was engaged in agriculture in 1999.

INDUSTRY

Since the collapse of the USSR, the industrial and manufacturing sector has undergone considerable contraction. Between 1990 and 1995 production declined in all sectors of the power industry, engineering and metalwork, and fuel, light, chemicals, and petrochemicals sectors. By 1999, the industry sector accounted for 20 percent of the country's GDP and employed 15 percent of the labor force, according to the CIA *World Factbook.*

Kyrgyzstan's manufacturing plants are concentrated in and around the capital, Bishkek. Many of these enterprises were not competitive on international markets and thus have been shuttered and closed since they lost subsidies from the government. The enterprises that remain tend to operate well below capacity.

Unlike other developing countries faced with transferring workers from low productivity subsistence agriculture to higher productivity industry, Kyrgyzstan faces the opposite problem. The government seeks to spur industrial restructuring to cut employment in formerly subsidized, inefficient industries, and to encourage the emergence of new lower tech enterprises in the agricultural and service sector.

The only industrial sector that experienced significant growth recently was gold mining. In May 1997 the Kumtor Operating Company, which is two-thirds owned by the Kyrgyzstan Republic and one-third by a Canadian company, began gold mining operations. The construction of the mine cost US$450 million. The initial estimate of recoverable gold was 16.5 million troy ounces of gold, and gold was expected to average around 485,000 ounces a year over the life of the project. In late 1999 the company revised its estimates of recoverable gold downward, taking into account the changes in the price of gold and a revision of the geological expectations of the mining work. Accordingly, the amount of recoverable gold was revised downward to 4.27 million troy ounces. Company officials announced that the mine would be closed in 2008. This represents a major setback for the Kyrgyz government's development plans, given that revenue from the gold mine constituted a major portion of the government's income (40 percent in 1999).

SERVICES

The service sector is the second largest sector after agriculture. An estimated 566,000 workers were employed in the Kyrgyzstan service sector in 1999, according to the International Monetary Fund. This sector was under developed during the Soviet period when the government put most emphasis on heavy industry and agriculture. After independence, the service sector expanded rapidly. New laws and regulations made it possible to open private businesses offering **consumer goods** and services. The small service sector surged ahead as business people began offering services, such as car repair, housing construction and improvement, real estate services, legal services, beauty shop services, and other small business that did not require substantial investment.

The banking and financial services industry expanded rapidly, although during the first decade of independence (1990–2000) this financial sector continued to be heavily oriented toward foreign economic activity rather than local financial services. The government adopted a program in 2000 to support micro-credit lending to put more emphasis on local financial services.

TOURISM. The year 2001 was declared the "year of the tourist." Since Kyrgyzstan is the "Switzerland of Asia," the government has sought to take advantage of the beauty of Kyrgyzstan's spectacular mountains and lakes to encourage greater tourism. The tourism sector is a priority area for economic development in Kyrgyzstan. The country, with major mountain ranges and some of the highest peaks in the world, possesses breathtaking natural features. The towering mountains of Peak Pobeda (7,439 meters), Peak Lenin (7,134 meters), and Peak Khan-Tengri (6,995 meters) exist in what is called the "realm of eternal ice and snow." The country offers white water rafting, pony trekking, hiking, mountaineering, skiing, mountain biking, and many other possibilities.

INTERNATIONAL TRADE

Very nearly one-half of Kyrgyzstan's foreign trade is with former Soviet countries. Kyrgyzstan's largest trading partner is Russia, comprising almost 40 percent of foreign trade. Behind Russia is Ukraine, the United States, Uzbekistan, Turkey, the United Kingdom, Germany, South Korea, and other countries. Kyrgyzstan exported to Germany goods worth US$148 million in 1999. Russia imported goods worth US$70 million, Kazakhstan imported goods worth US$50 million, Uzbekistan imported US$46 million, and China imported goods worth US$25 million. In the same year, Kyrgyzstan imported from Russia goods worth US$110 million, from Kazakhstan US$73 million, from Uzbekistan US$50 million, from the United States US$56 million, from Germany US$47 million, from China US$36 million, and from Canada US$26 million.

Kyrgyzstan's main exports are processing industry products (67 percent) and agricultural goods (17 percent), while the main imports were machine-building products (21 percent), coal and petroleum products (11 percent), food and tobacco (7 percent) and textiles (6 percent).

Kyrgyzstan is heavily dependent on the outside world for fuel imports. In 1999 Kyrgyzstan imported 576 million metric meters of natural gas, 1,075,000 tons of coal and 368 tons of high grade petroleum fuels (diesel and gasoline). Kyrgyzstan sustains this level of fuel imports primarily through exporting electricity. The country exported, primarily to Kazakhstan and Uzbekistan, 2,001 million kilowatt hours in 1999.

Trade (expressed in millions of US$): Kyrgyzstan

	Exports	Imports
1994	340	522
1995	408	837
1996	505	709
1997	603	841
1998	513	599
1999	453	201

SOURCE: United Nations. *Monthly Bulletin of Statistics* (September 2000).

The Kyrgyzstan government has taken measures to improve the trade environment. Customs procedures and non-tariff barriers have been reduced in recent years in anticipation of the country's joining the World Trade Organization (1998). However, Kyrgyzstan's trade potential is complicated by the fact that Kyrgyzstan is landlocked. Few goods and services move from Uzbekistan into Kyrgyzstan. The borders with Tajikistan and China have been subject to heavy security regulation. But Kyrgyzstan's border with Kazakhstan is a long and relatively open border. The Kazakh and Kyrgyz languages are closely related and mutually comprehensible. However, Kazakhstan produces few of the manufactured goods that Kyrgyzstan requires. Consequently, Kazakhstan serves mainly as a transshipment point for goods from outside Central Asia, particularly Russia and Europe.

The Kyrgyzstan government has taken steps to improve the foreign investment climate in the country. A new foreign investment law was adopted in September 1997. The law was adopted to bring the country into conformance with the standards of the World Trade Organization. The law provides protection against expropriation, that is, **nationalization** of property by the government. According to the law, foreign investors have the same legal status and conditions as Kyrgyz investors and can do business as wholly-owned foreign businesses in Kyrgyzstan or as **joint ventures** either with Kyrgyz partners or other foreign partners. Foreigners can buy stocks and securities in Kyrgyz companies and participate in privatization programs. Foreign investors can **repatriate** capital, that is bring earnings from foreign investments and foreign trade back into the country. They can also freely export profits as foreign currency or as goods produced or as commodities or services bought. Local currency is freely convertible into foreign currency, including for import purposes or payment against project expenses. Investors may retain earned foreign currency, without having to convert it into local currency.

MONEY

Kyrgyzstan was the first country in Central Asia to introduce its own currency (May 1993) following the collapse of the USSR. When first introduced, 4 som were equal to US$1. However, over the years since the som was introduced inflation reduced the value of the som relative to the dollar. Kyrgyzstan experienced hyperinflation in the early 1990s, with inflation reaching 1,400 percent, but economic measures have since brought inflation down.

Between 1995 and 1997, positive developments in the economy reinforced the government's intention to restrict the supply of money. A scarce currency will tend to be valuable, but as the currency becomes more available, its value declines. Accordingly, as the money sup-

Exchange rates: Kyrgyzstan

soms (KS) per US$1	
Jan 2001	48.701
2000	47.704
1999	39.008
1998	20.838
1997	17.362
1996	12.810

SOURCE: CIA *World Factbook 2001* [ONLINE].

GDP per Capita (US$)

Country	1975	1980	1985	1990	1998
Kyrgyzstan	N/A	N/A	N/A	1,562	863
United States	19,364	21,529	23,200	25,363	29,683
Russia	2,555	3,654	3,463	3,668	2,138
Tajikistan	N/A	N/A	N/A	718	345

SOURCE: United Nations. *Human Development Report 2000; Trends in human development and per capita income.*

ply increased, the value of the Kyrgyz som declined. Following the 1997 crisis in the Asian financial markets and, in particular, following the collapse of financial markets in Russia in August 1998, the Kyrgyz economy suffered dramatically. Kyrgyzstan's money supply rose in 1998 and 1999. During this period inflation, which had been brought under control, rebounded in 1998 and reached nearly 40 percent in 1999. During 1999, the som lost 35 percent of its value to the U.S. dollar. Public confidence in the currency was further shaken by a major financial fraud involving some of the country's largest commercial banks.

In 1998 the Kyrgyzstan banking system suffered a major financial crisis which led to closing half of Kyrgyzstan's 26 commercial banks in 1999. The Soviet-era banking system had been expanded and slightly modified during the period between 1992 and 1995 but had not adopted standards of bank operations in accordance with international practice. As a result, in 1995, according to a World Bank study, over half of the commercial banks had a negative net worth. The study also concluded that 60 percent of all the banking sector's loans were considered unrecoverable, that is, these loans would never be paid back by the borrowers, according to the IMF. The public lost confidence in the banking system, and many people withdrew their funds, leading many of the banks to go out of business.

Kyrgyzstan is a relatively heavily indebted country. Outstanding debt in the first quarter of 2000 amounted to US$1,409 billion, according to the IMF. Much of the Kyrgyzstan republic's debt is concessional; that is, it has been loaned by public entities as special assistance at better-than-market terms by international financial institutions such as multilateral development banks. But a considerable portion is non-concessional; that is, it is money that was loaned by private lenders such as commercial banks. Even if Kyrgyzstan is granted special repayment terms, delays, or postponements in the repayment schedule, the burden of future debt will remain high. The Kyrgyzstan government will need to bolster its fiscal position through reducing government expenditures and increasing revenue. More competent debt management and limits on contracting debt will help. More emphasis on government reforms may also improve the overall economic pictures by improving the investment climate and enhancing the productive and export potential of the country.

POVERTY AND WEALTH

Poverty in Kyrgyzstan increased between 1994 and 2000. IMF estimates of the consumer **price index** rose in 1995 to 143 percent, in 1996 to 189 percent, in 1997 to 233 percent, in 1998 to 252 percent, and in 1999 to 343 percent, and in 2000 to over 400 percent. At the same time, the index of **real wages** (adjusted for inflation and other factors) climbed only gradually from 100 percent in 1994, to 117 percent in 1995, to 112 percent in 1996, to 116 percent in 1997, to 139 percent in 1998, dropping to 128 percent in 1999 and further to 105 percent in 2000. Thus, while the cost of living increased fourfold between 1994 and 2000, wages remained approximately at the same level.

In 2000 Kyrgyzstan ranked 98 out of 174 countries listed on the UNDP Human Development Index. Income distribution and social indicators for Kyrgyzstan fell considerably behind other countries at comparable stages of

Distribution of Income or Consumption by Percentage Share: Kyrgyzstan

Lowest 10%	2.7
Lowest 20%	6.3
Second 20%	10.2
Third 20%	14.7
Fourth 20%	21.4
Highest 20%	47.4
Highest 10%	31.7

Survey year: 1997

Note: This information refers to income shares by percentiles of the population and is ranked by per capita income.

SOURCE: *2000 World Development Indicators* [CD-ROM].

Household Consumption in PPP Terms

Country	All food	Clothing and footwear	Fuel and power[a]	Health care[b]	Education[b]	Transport & Communications	Other
Kyrgyzstan	33	11	11	3	22	6	14
United States	13	9	9	4	6	8	51
Russia	28	11	16	7	15	8	16
Tajikistan	48	7	10	0	14	5	18

Data represent percentage of consumption in PPP terms.
[a]Excludes energy used for transport.
[b]Includes government and private expenditures.

SOURCE: World Bank. *World Development Indicators 2000.*

development. For instance, nearly a quarter of the population was not expected to reach age 60. The proportion of young people enrolled in schools dropped. The rates of infectious diseases, particularly tuberculosis, increased. By 1997 an estimated one-half of the population had fallen below the official poverty line, living on the equivalent of less than US$0.75 per day. The average monthly pension payment was among the lowest in the former Soviet states, amounting to less than US$10 in 1999.

Although on national average only 1 in 2 persons in Kyrgyzstan is categorized as poor, 80 percent of the poor live in rural areas. During the 1990s, despite substantial recovery in agricultural production, rural incomes per capita fell substantially. The degree of poverty in rural areas has also become more severe relative to urban areas. While extreme poverty decreased from 19.1 percent of the population in 1996 to 14.8 percent in 1997, most of this resulted from a targeted poverty reduction program in urban areas only. Poverty is also distributed unevenly in the population, affecting more women than men. The Kyrgyzstan government has initiated a national poverty reduction program, the Arakat program. Moreover, the government is waging major efforts to revamp its poverty-fighting strategy in coordination with major donors, including the Asian Development Bank and the World Bank.

WORKING CONDITIONS

Kyrgyzstan had a working population in 1999 of 1,854,000 people, but the total number of people within working age (16 to 60) was 2,542,000. An estimated 1,718,000 of these were employed, and 54,000 people were estimated as unemployed in 1999, only 5,400 of whom received unemployment benefits.

The decline in Kyrgyzstan industrial sector has pushed many people out of technical and professional positions. Most of this movement has been in the direction of the service sector. A large proportion has also moved to agricultural employment. While the legal system and social security systems traditionally provide for fewer protections for these sectors, in fact working conditions in Kyrgyzstan's declining industry deteriorated significantly in the post-Soviet years as workers' unions and collective bargaining was unsuccessful in promoting the health and safety of working conditions in such declining industries. The international donor organizations, such as the World Bank and the multilateral development banks, have identified social protection as one of the highest priorities of future assistance to Kyrgyzstan.

COUNTRY HISTORY AND ECONOMIC DEVELOPMENT

552. Formation of the first Turkic khanate, uniting Turkic-speaking regions under one political leadership.

750. Arabs conquer the area that is now Kazakhstan, spreading the influence of the Islamic culture and religion.

840. Formation of the Kyrgyz khanate.

1240–1440. The Mongol Horde—armies originating from what is now Mongolia—overwhelm the Kipchak nomads. The Mongol Horde sweeps westward and southward, extending Mongol influence over much of modern-day Central Asia.

1850. Major Russian **emigration** to Kyrgyzstan occurs as emigrants search for new agricultural lands.

1867. The Russian tsar decrees the establishment of the Turkestan general-governorship, extending official Russian rule into Kyrgyzstan, making the country part of the Russian Empire.

1917. The Russian provisional government, unable to rule a country exhausted by World War I, falls to the Bolshevik Revolution. Bolshevik revolutionaries (communists) in St. Petersburg proclaim the establishment of a communist government.

1918. The communists announce the establishment of the Russian Socialist Republic (which includes the territory of present-day Kyrgyzstan). Opponents of the communists rally to restore the monarchy. Civil war ensues and continues for 2 years.

1924. The Kyrgyz Autonomous District is formed within Russia.

1936. The Kyrgyz Autonomous District is transformed into the Kyrgyz Socialist Republic.

1957–61. Under Soviet leader, Nikita Khrushchev, a new agricultural initiative called the "Virgin Lands Campaign" relocates tens of thousands of people from the European parts of the USSR to Central Asia, including Kyrgyzstan.

1991. An unsuccessful attempt to take over the Soviet government by Communist Party hard-liners precipitates a crisis in Moscow. Kyrgyzstan declares independence from the USSR on 31 August. A group of 11 high Communist Party officials gather in Almaty (then known as Alma-Ata) to sign a document announcing the end of the USSR and the establishment of the **Commonwealth of Independent States** (CIS) on 21 December.

1992. Kyrgyzstan joins major international organizations: the UN, World Bank, the Asian Development Bank, and the European Bank for Reconstruction and Development.

1993. The Kyrgyzstan constitution is adopted.

1995. A new version of the Kazakhstan constitution, assigning greater powers to the executive branch, is adopted.

1998. Kyrgyzstan is the first post-Soviet state to be admitted as a member of the World Trade Organization.

2000. Kyrgyzstan joins the Eurasian Economic Community, an international organization designed to create a common economic market throughout much of the former USSR.

FUTURE TRENDS

Kyrgyzstan faces major challenges. The country has liberal trade orders in the former Soviet Union. However, as a small, landlocked country with only limited trade potential, the latitude for development through globalization is limited. The most urgent issue is reducing poverty. Changes in the way that the government treats foreign investors, tourists, and foreign companies may lead to an improvement in the country's ability to promote investment and create new jobs.

DEPENDENCIES

Kyrgyzstan has no territories or colonies.

BIBLIOGRAPHY

Anderson, John. *Kyrgyzstan: Central Asia's Island of Democracy?* London: Harwood Academic Publishers, 1999.

Brinton, William M. *An Abridged History of Central Asia, 1998.* <http://www.asian-history.com/choose.html>. Accessed September 2001.

Child, Greg. "Fear of Falling." *Outside Magazine.* November 2000. <http://www.outsidemag.com/magazine/200011/200011hostages1.html>. Accessed September 2001.

Haghayeghi, Mehrdad. *Islam and Politics in Central Asia,* New York: St. Martin's Press, 1995.

Hopkirk, Peter. *The Great Game: The Struggle for Empire in Central Asia* London: Kodansha International, 1994.

International Monetary Fund. "Kyrgyz Republic: Selected Issues and Statistical Appendix." IMF Staff Country Report No. 00/131, October 2000.

Pomfret, Richard. *The Economies of Central Asia.* Princeton: Princeton University Press, 1995.

Rashid, Ahmed. *The Resurgence of Central Asia: Islam or Nationalism?* Karachi [Pakistan]: Oxford University Press, 1994.

Roy, Olivier. *The New Central Asia: The Creation of Nations* London: Tauris, 1998.

United Nations Development Programme. *Human Development Report 2000.* <http://www.undp.org/hdro/>. Accessed September 2001.

—Gregory Gleason

LAOS

Lao People's Democratic Republic
Sathalanalat Paxathipatai Paxaxon Lao

CAPITAL: Vientiane (Viangchan).

MONETARY UNIT: Lao kip (K). There are no coins, and there are notes of 1, 5, 10, 20, 50, 100, 500, 1,000, 2,000, and 5,000 kip. With considerable inflation over the last several decades, kip notes under 500 are rarely seen or used now. The Thai baht and U.S. dollar are also commonly used, especially in larger transactions, though official policy calls for the exclusive use of the kip.

CHIEF EXPORTS: Wood products, garments and textiles, electricity, coffee, tin.

CHIEF IMPORTS: Machinery and equipment, vehicles, fuel.

GROSS DOMESTIC PRODUCT: US$7 billion (purchasing power parity, 1999 est.).

BALANCE OF TRADE: **Exports:** US$271 million (1999 est.). **Imports:** US$497 million (1999 est.).

COUNTRY OVERVIEW

LOCATION AND SIZE. The Lao People's Democratic Republic, or Lao PDR, is a land-locked nation bordered on the north by China, the east by Vietnam, the west by Burma (Myanmar), and the south by Thailand and Cambodia. The Mekong River forms much of the boundary between Laos and Thailand. The country's total land boundaries are 5,083 kilometers (3,159 miles). Its geographic area is 236,800 square kilometers (91,428 square miles), making it just slightly larger than the state of Minnesota. Its capital, Vientiane, the largest city in central Laos, is located on the Mekong River. The other 3 major cities are Luang Prabang, Savannakhet, and Pakxé.

POPULATION. The Lao PDR differs from many other Asian countries in that it has an extremely low population density of only 23.2 persons per square kilometer (60 per square mile). Its population density is almost the same as the state of Minnesota. In July of 2000 its population was estimated as 5,497,459. This compares with a population of 3,586,083 in 1985; 2,886,000 in 1976; and 1,789,000 in 1953. The current population growth rate is a relatively high 2.5 percent. If this rate were to continue, the country's population would double to over 10 million by the year 2028. The major cause of this high population growth is the high fertility rate of Lao women. The Lao women on average currently have 5.21 children.

Thus, it is not uncommon to find families of 4 to 10 children, even in urban areas.

The ethnically diverse Lao PDR population is comprised of 3 major ethnic groups: Lao Lum, lowland; Lao Theung, upland; and Lao Sung, highland. Among prominent highland groups are the Hmong and Yao. Ethnic minorities comprise 47.5 percent of the total population, according to the 1995 census, which distinguished 47 main ethnic groups and 149 sub-groups. Thus, the Lao PDR is one of the most ethnically diverse countries in Asia.

With the country's low population density and the need to import labor (often Vietnamese **guest workers**), the government has been reluctant to adopt a strict birth control or family planning policy. Instead the policy has been the more moderate one of birth spacing (delaying natural pregnancies so that women have fewer children than the biological maximum).

With such high fertility, the Lao PDR has a very young population. Roughly 54.2 percent of the population is under the age of 20. With poor health conditions, particularly in rural areas and related high mortality rates, only 2.2 percent of the population is over 70 years of age.

OVERVIEW OF ECONOMY

Laos is one of the world's poorest countries, and thus its primary policy goal is to strengthen its economy and develop its own means to earn foreign exchange. Much of its population is involved in a subsistence economy, in which families produce by themselves what is needed for daily basic living. Laos' major economic disadvantage has been that it is a landlocked nation with weak **infrastructure**. Nearly 80 percent of the country is mountainous and/or forested with only 21 percent of the land cultivable and less than 4 percent actually cultivated. Laos perhaps has the highest ratio of forest cover to land area in all of Asia: 47 percent of the country is forested.

Laos' long history dates back to the founding of its first kingdom in 1353. It was then known as Lan Xang (the land of a million elephants). It reached its period of greatest glory and influence during the years 1633–90. Later succession struggles led Lan Xang to break into 3 smaller kingdoms. These weakened kingdoms then came initially under the Siamese orbit and later French colonialism. Under French colonialism, Laos suffered neglect.

After achieving complete independence from the French in 1953, the royalist Lao regime was gradually drawn into the vortex of the U.S. war in Vietnam. The economy became war-torn, suffering from extreme dependence on foreign aid. Extensive U.S. bombing of northern, northeastern, and eastern Laos from 1965 to 1973 seriously disrupted the rural economy. The U.S. dropped 33 percent more bombs on Laos than on Nazi Germany.

On 2 December 1975, the Lao People's Democratic Republic was established, representing the culmination of a long extended revolutionary war. This event brought peace and independence to the country. The economy was transformed into a Soviet-style state planned economy and received economic and technical assistance from other **communist** nations. The attempt to collectivize agriculture was rather quickly abandoned, however. In 1986, a new policy termed the New Economic Mechanism (NEM) was introduced to transform the economic system from a state-planned one to that of free market forces and prices. The major goal of this reform was to provide greater incentives to increase economic performance and productivity. With the collapse of the USSR in 1991, the Lao PDR opened its doors to active economic involvement with the West, both in terms of international aid and investment. The Lao PDR became a favorite of diverse donors, and foreign aid currently represents some 20 percent of the GDP. From 1991 to 1997, the Lao PDR enjoyed considerable **macroeconomic** success under the NEM system, with annual economic growth averaging 6.5 percent

During the 1990s, the Lao economy became increasingly interconnected with the Thai economy. Laos imports many basic modern consumer products from Thailand. On weekends, it is common to find many Lao families from Vientiane visiting Thailand via the Friendship Bridge, shopping for basic household items such as various packaged foods.

Initially, it appeared that the Lao economy (with no stock market and a currency not traded internationally) would be immune to the Asian economic crisis of 1997 which shook so many Asian economies. In a somewhat delayed effect, the Lao currency went into a free fall far greater than that of any other Asian country. Given Lao's dependence on imports, this had a serious, adverse effect on nearly all Lao, except a small number of elite individuals connected to the dollarized economy. The Asian economic crisis also adversely affected the Lao economy by reducing **foreign direct investment** from other Asian countries and reducing the demand for Lao electricity exports, a major source of foreign exchange.

Since it received foreign aid earlier from the Eastern block countries and in the past decade from multilateral agencies (primarily the World Bank and Asian Development Bank) and other countries, the country does have a debt burden. Total **external debt** in 1997 was estimated to be US$2.32 billion, and debt payments represented 4 percent of government expenditures in 1995–98. Many Lao loans are granted at highly concessional terms, meaning that the interest rates are quite low over a long payment period and thus are almost like grants.

The major challenge facing the Lao PDR currently is to restore the sound macroeconomic performance of the early and mid-1990s and develop its own sources of foreign exchange earnings. Hydroelectric power development on the tributaries of the Mekong, the development of light industries such as garments and textiles, marketing of natural resources such as gypsum, tin, and wood products, and tourism development are the primary economic sectors being promoted.

The government plays an active role in evaluating and assessing potential international investments coming into the country. The government, with the strong support of the Lao Women's Union, has been active in preventing the development of a commercial sex industry. At this point, there is absolutely no standardized fast food industry in the country, such as KFC or McDonald's. Interestingly, in terms of the cola wars, Laos is a Pepsi country. Coke must be imported from Singapore or Thailand.

POLITICS, GOVERNMENT, AND TAXATION

The Lao PDR remains a 1-party state with complete dominance by the Lao People's Revolutionary Party (LPRP). The president since 1998 has been Khamtain Siphandon and the prime minister has been Sisavat Keobounphan. The National Assembly, last elected in 1997, has 99 members. Basic economic policies are determined in major Party Congresses which are held every 5 years. The LPRP is strongly supportive of the current mixed policy of having a **privatized** economy with a reduced role for state-owned enterprises but with a 1-party political system.

As part of the reform policies introduced in 1986, the government has attempted to reduce the size of the **public sector**, including the military. They have done this, however, in humanistic ways by avoiding the direct firing of people. International donors and agencies have been concerned that such reforms have slowed in the late 1990s.

The government's ability to tax is limited. Tax revenue is only 10 percent of the GDP, and major capital outlays are financed by external assistance, according to Bourdet. Major sources of revenues are business taxes, import/export taxes, and various fees (such as visa fees and fly-over fees). For smaller businesses, flat fixed taxes are used, which discourages tax evasion. In 1995–98, tax on foreign trade represented 27.1 percent of government tax revenues. The **income tax** represents only 6.3 percent of all revenues.

INFRASTRUCTURE, POWER, AND COMMUNICATIONS

Overall, the Lao PDR has a weak physical infrastructure. As yet, there is no train system. Travel to remote provinces requires a plane. During the rainy season, roads to remote areas may be impassable. At other times, inexpensive bus transportation is available for ordinary people to travel through the country.

The country is served by a network of 21,534 kilometers (13,381 miles) of roads, of which 16.5 percent are paved. As part of the 1996–2000 National Plan, major work has been undertaken to improve the country's limited road infrastructure. A key project is the reconstruction of Highway 13 which links China in the north and Pakxé in the south.

The Lao PDR is receiving considerable international assistance to develop its infrastructure. The Japanese, for example, provided assistance in building a new international airport in Vientiane, and the Thais assisted with a new airport in Luang Prabang. The country's weak road infrastructure adversely affects the development of its rich natural resources, such as minerals and wood products

In April 1994, the Friendship Bridge, the first ever across the lower parts of the Mekong River, was completed with a US$40 million grant from Australia. Upon completion of the bridge, the Lao government issued a regulation not allowing private cars to use the bridge. The government feared a wave of private cars from Thailand

Communications

Country	Newspapers	Radios	TV Sets[a]	Cable subscribers[a]	Mobile Phones[a]	Fax Machines[a]	Personal Computers[a]	Internet Hosts[b]	Internet Users[b]
	1996	1997	1998	1998	1998	1998	1998	1999	1999
Laos	4	143	4	N/A	1	N/A	1.1	0.00	2
United States	215	2,146	847	244.3	256	78.4	458.6	1,508.77	74,100
China	N/A	333	272	40.0	19	1.6	8.9	0.50	8,900
Thailand	63	232	236	10.1	32	2.5	21.6	4.49	800

[a]Data are from International Telecommunication Union, *World Telecommunication Development Report 1999* and are per 1,000 people.
[b]Data are from the Internet Software Consortium (http://www.isc.org) and are per 10,000 people.

SOURCE: World Bank. *World Development Indicators 2000.*

which would cause accidents, congestion, and pollution. Thus, the bridge is used mainly commercially by trucks and buses and has helped landlocked Laos connect economically with its neighbors in the region. A second new bridge over the Mekong, the Lao-Nippon Bridge, was completed in the south near Pakxé in August 2000 and was financed primarily by the Japanese. A third bridge across the Mekong at Savannakhet is scheduled for completion in 2003. This bridge connected to Route 9 will connect both central Laos and northeast Thailand to the Vietnamese port of Da Nang. These bridges, as well as better road infrastructure, will improve Lao links with major ports in Thailand and Vietnam.

With its many mountains and tributaries of the Mekong River, the Lao PDR has excellent hydroelectric power potential. The country's total hydropower potential is estimated to be 25,000 megawatts (MW). Laos has even been referred to as the potential battery of Southeast Asia. Currently the country has 10 major electric power plants with a total capacity of 1329.5 MW. In 1998, the nation consumed just over one-third of the 1.34 billion kilowatt hours (kWh) of electricity generated. The Lao PDR plans to construct a total of 12 dams on the Mekong's tributaries over the next decade. The decision has caused considerable controversy in the international environmental community. Major concerns include effects on displaced rural populations in Laos itself, the fish populations of the Mekong and its tributaries, and unintended effects on downstream communities in Cambodia and Vietnam, which are highly dependent on the natural flows of the Mekong River.

Only those of higher socioeconomic status have telephones in their homes, though cell phones are increasingly popular among those of higher socioeconomic status. The country has only a total of 18,139 conventional phone lines, of which 71.8 percent are in the capital. Phone cards are also now available. It is the goal of Lao Télécommunications to have 49,000 telephone lines installed by 2001. Televisions are widely used wherever there is access to electricity. About 72 percent of urban households and 22 percent of rural households have televisions. Much of the Lao population lives in the lowlands in close proximity to Thailand. Thus, they have access to popular Thai TV programming with related advertisements for a variety of popular Thai **consumer goods**. Shinawatra (a Thai telecommunications conglomerate) has been active in assisting the Lao PDR develop its telecommunications infrastructure.

Though Laos has not officially joined the World Wide Web (there is not yet a .lao suffix), some Lao people, especially in urban areas, are using the Internet. There are now a number of private cyber shops in Vientiane offering public Internet service.

ECONOMIC SECTORS

Like many undeveloped countries, Laos generates a majority of its GDP from the agricultural sector. Agriculture accounted for 51 percent of the GDP in 1999 and employs about 80 percent of the total **workforce** of 2,220,000. In most areas of the country, 90 percent of the people work in agriculture. Industry accounted for 22 percent of the GDP but employed only 3.3 percent of the people (though this figure was 20 percent in the capital). The services sector accounts for 27 percent of the GDP and roughly 10.3 percent of the workforce.

Traditionally, Laos has been a subsistence agricultural economy. That remains true today, though other economic sectors are growing in the Lao PDR. While the Lao PDR has no intention to develop heavy industry, it is developing its light industry, particularly the production of garments and textiles. The Lao PDR has excellent capability in producing attractive traditional textiles and handicrafts. Lao silk and cotton textiles are becoming known for their quality around the world.

The Lao PDR is also developing an important service sector, which has 2 new components: banking and tourism. There are now many newly established foreign banks located in the Vientiane area, most of which were established in the 1990s. Among 6 such Thai banks are the Bangkok Bank and Siam Commercial Bank. The 1999–2000 year was called the "Visit Laos Year" to promote tourism. In the late 1990s travel to Laos was dramatically **liberalized** with visas available on arrival. The tourist infrastructure was also improved substantially. Tourism has expanded dramatically in the 1990s from only 14,400 visitors in 1990 to 500,200 in 1998. In 1997 tourism contributed US$73.3 million to the economy,

Lao People's Democratic Republic
GDP–COMPOSITION BY SECTOR–1999 est.

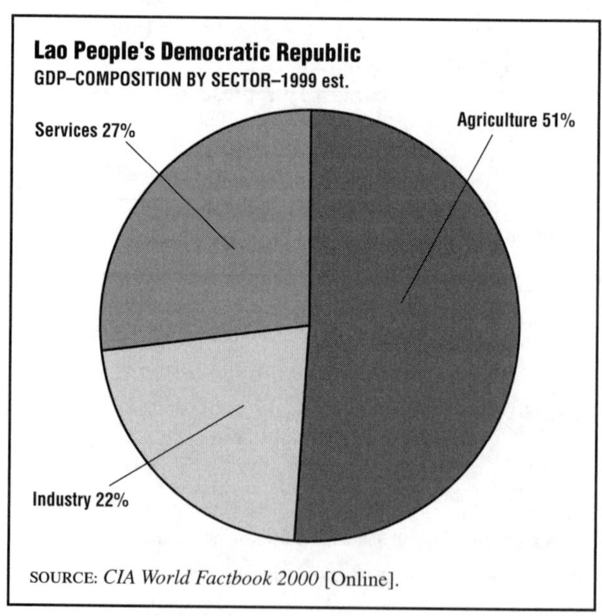

SOURCE: *CIA World Factbook 2000* [Online].

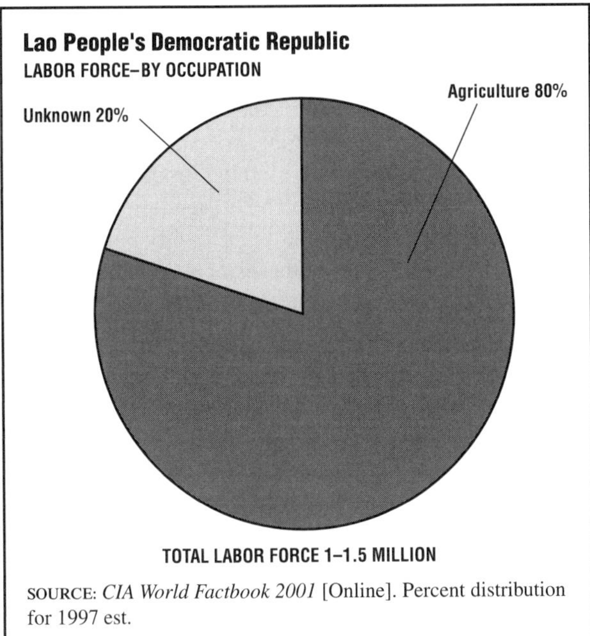

SOURCE: *CIA World Factbook 2001* [Online]. Percent distribution for 1997 est.

representing 23 percent of export earnings. The designation of Luang Prabang, perhaps the best preserved traditional Southeast Asian city, as a world heritage site was definitely a positive development for Lao tourism. Other important tourist attractions in Laos are the Wat Phu ancient Khmer ruins in southern Laos, the Khon waterfalls in the same region, and the Plain of Jars in Xiengkuang Province. The latter area was heavily bombed during the U.S. War in Vietnam. In fact, as of 2001 Laos is the most heavily bombed country in the history of the world.

AGRICULTURE

The Lao PDR is primarily an agricultural economy, with this sector contributing 51 percent of the GDP. Approximately 1,880,000 individuals are involved in agricultural work. Recently the Lao PDR conducted a major agricultural census which provides an excellent overview of the basic nature of Laos' agricultural system. The results of this survey indicate that 79.7 percent of the total population is engaged in farming. The average land holding is 1.62 hectares with 27 percent of households having 2 hectares or more and 36 percent having less than 1 hectare. An impressive 97 percent of farmers own their own land. About 93 percent of the area devoted to rice production is for the production of sticky rice, a subsistence crop used primarily for home consumption. Tree farming is another important part of Lao agricultural life. About 23 percent of such farms have mango trees, 17 percent coconut trees, 17 percent banana trees, 11 percent jackfruit trees, and 11 percent tamarind trees. Also 8 percent of farmers are engaged in aquaculture, and 71 percent do other fishing. Roughly 31 percent of farmers have cattle, 48 percent water buffaloes, 49 percent pigs (73 percent in the case of Hmong people), and 73 percent chickens.

Only 6 percent of farmers sell their total output, while 35 percent sell some of their farm output. This means that the majority of farmers (59 percent) are engaged solely in subsistence agriculture. The basic staple of such farmers is the production of sticky rice for local consumption. Unlike its neighbors Thailand and Vietnam, the Lao PDR is not a rice exporting country. Their goal is simply to attain self-sufficiency in rice production, which is possible in good weather years. The production of sticky rice may be supplemented by vegetable gardens; animal raising (goats, chickens, ducks, turkeys, pigs); and mango, coconut, or banana trees. Some maize is also grown. In the tropical forests of Laos, there are also many edible wild plants and foods that are gathered, primarily by women. Hunting and fishing also supplement the subsistence diet and provide valuable protein. Lao greatly enjoy fishing.

In terms of tons of agricultural production, the top 5 crops in Laos in order of importance are rice, vegetables and beans, sugarcane, starchy roots, and tobacco. Since 1990, among these 5 leading crops, production of vegetables and beans has grown the fastest in percentage terms, followed by sugarcane. In the decade since 1990 rice production has increased 47.9 percent. Among agricultural products often produced as **cash crops** are mungbeans, soybeans, peanuts, tobacco, cotton, sugarcane, coffee, and tea.

Given its subsistence nature, Lao agriculture has not played a major role in the country's foreign trade. The major export products from Laos' agricultural sector are timber, lumber, plywood, and coffee. The major agricultural imports are sugar, condensed milk, and long-grain rice.

Numerous city dwellers have rural roots and the Lao love gardening. Thus, some urban dwellers supplement limited cash incomes by having gardens, small fish ponds, or raising animals. They also may engage in fishing in the Mekong River, hunting, and the gathering wild foods. Some urban dwellers in the capital of Vientiane cultivate gardens along the Mekong River during the dry season.

FORESTRY AND LOGGING. The Lao PDR has extensive tropical forests containing many valuable hardwoods such as teak. With a total ban on logging in Thailand, there is considerable demand for Lao wood products from other Asian countries such as Thailand, Malaysia, and Japan. Malaysia has projects for teak cultivation in southern Laos. The Lao military is involved in timber exploitation. In 1991, timber and furniture exports totaled 39.2 percent of all exports, while in 1996 such exports dropped to 28 percent. In 1998, export of all types of wood products brought in US$115.4 million to the Lao economy.

Deforestation and the need for sustainable forestry are major environmental issues facing the Lao PDR and its agricultural/rural sector. The Lao are very conscious that much of Thailand's northeast was deforested as the result of expanded rice field acreage. Also, upland agricultural production can result in serious deforestation. The reduction of upland rice production and the expansion of irrigated rice lands to allow more crops on a given piece of land should help preserve Lao forests by reducing the need to expand acreage at the expense of forests.

IRRIGATION PROJECTS. A major recent policy is an ambitious irrigation project. Given the spread of the contagion of the Asian economic crisis to Laos, organizations such as the IMF strongly urged restrictive monetary and **fiscal policies**. The Lao PDR ignored the policy dictates of the IMF and instead they moved boldly ahead with a major rural irrigation infrastructure project. For doing this they were severely criticized by the international financial community, and no doubt this expansionary program contributed to both **inflation** and the **devaluation** of the Lao kip. In continuing their agricultural irrigation program, the Lao government was both demonstrating its economic sovereignty and also clearly putting the interests of the Lao agricultural sector ahead of those in urban communities which are most severely affected by inflation.

The French scholar Catherine Aubertin argues that Lao agricultural policy favors the lowland Lao over the upland Lao because of its resettlement schemes to decrease slash and burn agriculture in mountainous areas. The Lao government feels such policies are essential for forest conservation.

INDUSTRY

The Lao PDR has relatively little industry. This sector employed only 3.3 percent of the workforce in 1995. There is no heavy industry and much of the country's industry is comprised of smaller companies. In 1999, there were only 108 establishments in the whole country with more than 100 employees. However, there were 19,797 establishments with fewer than 9 employees. These small establishments are involved primarily in the production of textiles and handicrafts. Laos is well known for the high quality of its aesthetically attractive textiles. Even though industry plays a small role in the Lao economy, its importance has increased significantly. In 1987, industry represented only 11 percent of the GDP of the Lao PDR, while in 1999, it represented 22 percent, doubling since the introduction of the New Economic Mechanism policy.

MANUFACTURING. The following are the principal products manufactured in the Lao PDR: oxygen-acetylene, battery acid, industrial alcohol, detergent powder, soap, shoes made of animal skin, leather, medical drugs, fans, vaccines, plastic goods, timber, lumber, plywood, flood lumber, rattan furniture, books, fabrics, clothing, bricks, blocks, cement, tiles, chalk, lime, electric poles, agricultural tools, tin plates, nails, electric wire, and barbed wire. For the economy, the most significant of these are clothing/fabrics and rattan furniture. Manufacturing represented 16.5 percent of the GDP in 1999, up from 13.9 percent in 1995. Except for fabrics and clothing, most of these manufactured products are for local consumption. Laos' manufacturing export potential is currently limited by its status as a "non-market economy" restricting its access to U.S. and other developed country markets. Admission to the WTO and completion of a trade agreement with the United States are essential to enable Laos to have more secure access for its exports.

ELECTRICITY AND WATER. Electric power generation is one of Lao's most significant industries. In 1998, the country produced 1.34 billion kWh of electric power. About 43 million cubic meters of water were produced and distributed, primarily in the 4 major urban areas for household and industrial use. Electricity and water production represented 2.3 percent of the GDP in 1999. As of the mid-1990s, only 1 percent of the country's vast electric potential had been exploited.

MINING. The Lao PDR has an abundant supply of minerals. Gypsum, for example, is exported to Vietnam. Tin, coal, lignite, and limestone are also mined. In the Vanvieng area, there is a major cement works, established with the assistance of the Chinese. Mining and quarrying, however, represented only .051 percent of the GDP in 1999, and minerals are not yet a significant export. The major problem in exploiting Lao mineral resources is their inaccessibility.

CONSTRUCTION. In recent years there have been a number of new construction projects mainly in the capital of Vientiane. International funding has assisted many of these projects. Among notable recent projects have been the Lao-Nippon Bridge, the new International Airport, the Lao Plaza Hotel, and the National Cultural Hall (with funding provided by the PRC). Construction in 1999 represented 2.6 percent of the GDP.

SERVICES

Services represented 27 percent of the Lao economy in 1999 and employed roughly 10 percent of the workforce. The largest component (37.2 percent) of the service sector is wholesale and **retail** trade. Perhaps the largest entities in this arena are Honda and Shell. Honda retails a wide variety of products, particularly motorcycles. With Laos' rapid economic development in the 1990s, many Lao in urban areas have up-graded from bicycles to motorcycles or scooters, or among elites from motorcycles to private cars or SUVs. Toyota, Pepsi Cola, and Bier Lao are also active retailers. In urban areas there are a large number of formal retail shops as well as a large **informal economy**. Those in the formal retail sector market a wide range of consumer goods. A large number of small family-owned stores sell a variety of low cost products for basic everyday needs. Those selling goods in the large informal economy are often selling agricultural products.

The next largest component of the service sector is represented by transportation, communications, and postal services (23 percent), followed by ownership and rental of dwellings (12.1 percent). The latter grew significantly in the 1990s with the presence of a growing expatriate community associated with diverse development aid activities who are in need of modern housing.

The public service still represents an important element of the service sector (11.6 percent), though the government, with assistance from organizations such as the World Bank has sought to reduce the size of the public sector. For the most part, the Lao government has used non-draconian methods to reduce the size of this sector. Considerable success has been achieved in reducing the size of the military, for example. The next most important component of the service sector is represented by hotels and restaurants (7.6 percent), reflective of the growing importance of tourism in the Lao economy.

TOURISM. In the Lao service economy, tourism has been a major growth area. Between 1991 and 1995, tourism grew approximately 60-fold, and from 1995 to 2000 it has more than doubled. On a per capita basis, Laos has even more tourists than Thailand. The major tourist attractions of the country are its rich culture and many Buddhist temples; Luang Prabang, the former royal capital in the north and a world cultural heritage site; the majestic Mekong River which flows through the country; and shopping for Lao textiles and handicrafts in Vientiane. Laos is also noted for its genuinely friendly people who warmly welcome tourists. By April 1999, tourism was the country's highest revenue earner, contributing US$79.9 million to the Lao economy. Despite such economic contributions, tourism employs at most only 3 percent of the non-farm workforce. Tourist facilities have improved significantly in recent years. There are now large numbers of hotels, guesthouses, and restaurants in major cities. Both Vientiane and Luang Prabang now offer some up-scale tourist facilities.

BANKING. In the early 1990s banking reforms were introduced which diversified Laos' banking system. These reforms led to the National Bank being separated from 7 state-owned commercial banks such as the Lao Foreign Trade Bank (BCEL) and 5 regional banks. The reforms also opened the sector to international banks from Thailand, Vietnam, and Malaysia. In 1999, 6 of the 8 state-run commercial banks were merged into just 2 entities. Thus, the Bank of the Lao People's Democratic Republic (the national bank) now monitors a total of 14 banks consisting of 4 government banks, 3 joint banks (for example, the Lao-Viet Bank), and 7 foreign banks (6 Thai and 1 Malaysian). This network of local and international banks provides standard banking and financial services for both the average citizen and the commercial community. This banking component represents 5 percent of Laos' service sector. A major current issue facing the industry relates to questions about the **solvency** of the banking system as a result of the Asian regional economic crisis.

INTERNATIONAL TRADE

In the 1990s there were considerable diversification of Lao exports. Laos' largest export earner is timber and furniture (28 percent of exports), followed by garments (19.9 percent), raw logs (10.6 percent), electricity (9.2 percent), manufactured products (8.6 percent), coffee (7.7 percent), agricultural products (5.5 percent), gold **re-export** (4.7 percent), and motorcycle assembly (3.9 percent). With respect to garment exports, Nike, for example, is now sourcing some apparel production in Laos. Imports are comprised primarily of consumer goods (44.6 percent), **capital goods** (40.2 percent), and industrial inputs (11.9 percent).

Approximately 52 percent of Laos' imports are from neighboring Thailand, while only 22 percent of its exports go to Thailand, reflecting a strong negative trade balance with that country. In contrast, 42.7 percent of Laos' exports go to Vietnam, while only 3.9 percent of its imports are from that country. Thus, Laos has an extremely favorable trade balance with Vietnam. Other leading export destinations for Laos are in order of importance (after Vietnam and Thailand): France (6.3 percent), Germany (5.1 percent), and the U.K. (4.7 percent). Since the Lao PDR does not have most favored nation

Trade (expressed in billions of US$): Laos

	Exports	Imports
1975	.012	.045
1980	.028	.092
1985	.054	.193
1990	.079	.185
1995	.311	.589
1998	.370	.553

SOURCE: International Monetary Fund. *International Financial Statistics Yearbook 1999.*

status with the United States, it is difficult to export to the U.S. market. Major sources of imports (after Thailand and Vietnam) are Japan (1.6 percent) and Hong Kong (1.5 percent).

Prior to the communist revolution, Laos had a severe trade imbalance with exports being only a tiny fraction of imports. While Laos still imports much more than it exports, the ratio of exports to imports has steadily improved. In 1975, the first year of the current communist regime, Lao exports were only adequate to cover 12 percent of imports. In 1999, exports of US$271 million were sufficient to cover 55 percent of imports, which stood at US$497 million. Also, the total of exports plus imports divided by the GDP has also steadily increased, reflecting the internationalization of the Lao economy. By 1998 this ratio had reached 72 percent. To decrease its dependence on international aid and to alleviate poverty, the Lao government seeks to expand its exports. That is the primary rationale for its long-term plan to build more dams to produce electricity exports, an area in which Laos has a clear comparative advantage. Laos also has a comparative advantage in the export of textiles such as clothing and garments.

Laos' current **trade deficit** is financed by 2 primary sources: international aid, primarily provided by Japan, Australia, and Sweden; and growing financial **remittances** from Lao living overseas. The State Planning Committee in a December 1999 report indicated that the latter was the single most important source of income in the Vientiane Valley. Given the recent economic crisis, the government has also turned to both China and Vietnam for important economic assistance.

MONEY

Since the establishment of the Lao PDR in 1975, the country has experienced periods of both currency stability and instability with related fluctuations in inflation. As part of the New Economic Mechanism introduced in 1986, the policy was to have a single **exchange rate** determined by market forces. During the early and mid-1990s the Lao PDR achieved impressive macroeconomic stability. However, contagion from the Asian economic crisis, especially in neighboring Thailand, eventually affected the Lao PDR dramatically in 1998 and 1999. The Lao currency at one point was worth only one-tenth of its previous value. It has since improved to be worth about one-seventh of its previous value. This led to 87.4 percent inflation in 1998 and 134 percent inflation in 1999.

In the year 2000 the currency stabilized and inflation fell to 33 percent. **Monetary policy** is implemented by the Bank of the Lao PDR, but it is certainly directly influenced by economic policies of the Party and Government.

Exchange rates: Laos

new kips (K) per US$1	
2001	N/A
Dec 2000	7,578.00
1999	7,102.03
1998	3,298.33
1997	1,259.98
1996	921.02

SOURCE: CIA *World Factbook 2001* [ONLINE].

POVERTY AND WEALTH

Though Laos is an extremely poor country with 46.1 percent living below the material poverty line in 1993, the country does not have the gross economic inequalities typical of many developing countries. Rural farmers generally have their own land and are engaged in subsistence agriculture which provides for certain basic needs. Major problems for the rural poor are access to quality health care and education.

There are also serious regional income disparities primarily between urban centers and remote rural areas, often mountainous areas with a large proportion of ethnic nationalities. An average person in the richest province, Vientiane, has approximately 2 and a half times more income than the average individual in the poorest province, Huaphanh. The incidence of poverty in rural areas (53 percent) is double that of urban areas (24 percent). The areas most economically disadvantaged tend to be those more remote areas inhabited by diverse ethnic communities.

WORKING CONDITIONS

Because of the country's low population density and its former **socialist** economic system, unemployment has not been a serious problem in the Lao PDR. The visible urban unemployment rate in Laos was 3.5 percent overall in 1994. The large informal sector also provides opportunities for those who cannot find meaningful em-

GDP per Capita (US$)

Country	1975	1980	1985	1990	1998
Laos	N/A	N/A	N/A	321	421
United States	19,364	21,529	23,200	25,363	29,683
China	138	168	261	349	727
Thailand	863	1,121	1,335	2,006	2,593

SOURCE: United Nations. *Human Development Report 2000; Trends in human development and per capita income.*

Distribution of Income or Consumption by Percentage Share: Laos

Lowest 10%	4.2
Lowest 20%	9.6
Second 20%	12.9
Third 20%	16.3
Fourth 20%	21.0
Highest 20%	40.2
Highest 10%	26.4

Survey year: 1992

Note: This information refers to expenditure shares by percentiles of the population and is ranked by per capita expenditure.

SOURCE: *2000 World Development Indicators* [CD-ROM].

ployment in the formal sector. The Lao PDR has a progressive labor law, which is extremely specific related to working age, minimum wage, and overtime payments, for example. This labor law primarily covers those employees working in the modern formal sector. Women and children are active in the labor force, particularly in the agricultural sector and informal economy. Those able to attain higher levels of education can gain access to work in the public sector, the modern **private sector**, or with various international agencies and organizations present in the Lao PDR. Those with superior English language skills are particularly advantaged in the modern, urban labor market.

COUNTRY HISTORY AND ECONOMIC DEVELOPMENT

1353–73. Reign of Fa Ngum, king of Lan Xang (the land of a million elephants), marks the beginning of recorded Lao history.

1633–90. The height of the Lan Xang kingdom occurs.

18TH CENTURY. Lan Xang breaks into 3 independent kingdoms.

19TH CENTURY. Lao kingdoms fall under the Siamese orbit, and many Lao people are repopulated to Siam as slave labor.

1890. French colonial rule in Laos begins.

1953. On 22 October, Laos achieves its independence from France.

1975. Declaration of the Lao People's Democratic Republic occurs on 2 December.

1981. First 5 Year Plan begins.

1986. New Economic Mechanism approved at Fourth Lao People's Revolutionary Party (LPRP) Congress paves the way for major economic reforms.

1994. Completion of Friendship Bridge across the Mekong River connects Laos and Thailand.

1997. Lao PDR becomes the eighth member of the Association of Southeast Asian Nations (ASEAN).

1998–99. Asian economic crisis contagion spreads to the Lao PDR, leading to free fall of the Lao kip and triple digit inflation.

2000. The Lao-Nippon Bridge across the Mekong River is completed.

2000–01. Macroeconomic stability is restored.

FUTURE TRENDS

With its low population density and favorable natural resources/people ratio, the Lao PDR has a potentially bright economic future. Assuming recovery from the Asian economic crisis, there should be growing demand in the long term for Laos' valuable energy exports, which will enable the country to become more economically self-sufficient and less dependent on international aid. There are many in the West who would like Laos to adopt a multi-party system similar to that in liberal democracies. Given the problems of money politics and instability in such systems, however, the Lao PDR is more oriented toward a single party political system to ensure stability and avoid policy gridlock often associated with unstable multiple party systems. Given the past economic performance of areas such as Hong Kong, Singapore, South Korea, Taiwan, and Malaysia, the Lao are confident that their current political system is compatible with dynamic economic growth and reaching its goal to liberate the country from underdevelopment and mass poverty by the year 2020.

DEPENDENCIES

Laos has no territories or colonies.

BIBLIOGRAPHY

Anderson, Kym. *Lao Economic Reform & WTO Accession: Implications for Agriculture and Rural Development.* Adelaide: Center for International Economic Studies, 1999.

Annual Report 1999. Vientiane: Bank of the Lao PDR, 1999.

Aubertin, Catherine. "Institutionalizing Duality: Lowlands and Uplands in the Lao PDR." *IIAS Newsletter.* Vol. 24, February 2001.

Basic Statistics of the Lao P.D.R. 1975–2000. Vientiane: State Planning Committee, National Statistics Center, 2000.

Bounthavy, Sisouphanthong, and Christian Taillard. *Atlas of Laos: Spatial Structures of the Economic and Social Development of the Lao People's Democratic Republic.* Copenhagen, Denmark: Nordic Institute of Asian Studies, 2000.

Bourdet, Yves. *The Economics of Transition in Laos: From Socialism to ASEAN Integration.* Northampton, MA: Edward Elgar Publishing, 2000.

Chazée, Laurent. *The Peoples of Laos: Rural and Ethnic Diversities.* Bangkok: White Lotus Press, 1999.

Economist Intelligence Unit. *Country Profile: Laos.* London: Economist Intelligence Unit, 2001.

Freeman, Nick. "Laos: Economy." *Far East and Australasia 2001.* 32nd ed. London: Europa Publications, 2001.

Fry, Gerald W. "The Future of the Lao PDR: Relations with Thailand and Alternative Paths to Internationalization." *New Laos, New Challenges,* edited by Jacqueline Butler-Diaz. Tempe, AZ: Program for Southeast Asian Studies Monograph Series, Arizona State University, 1998.

Fry, Gerald W., and Manynooch Nitnoi Faming. "Laos." *The Southeast Asia Handbook,* edited by Patrick Heenan and Monique Lamontagne. London: Fitzroy Dearborn Publishers, 2001.

Hopkins, Susanna. "The Economy." *Laos: A Country Study,* edited by Andrea Matlas Savada. Washington, D.C.: Library of Congress, 1995.

"Laos." *Asia 2001 Yearbook.* Hong Kong: Far Eastern Economic Review, 2000.

Murphy, Dervla. *One Foot in Laos.* London: John Murray, 1999.

National Human Development Report 1998. Vientiane: State Planning Committee, National Statistics Center, UNDP, 1998.

Osborne, Milton. *The Mekong: Turbulent Past, Uncertain Future.* New York: Atlantic Monthly Press, 2000.

Pham, Chi Do, editor. *Economic Development in Lao P.D.R.: Horizon 2000.* Vientiane: IMF and Bank of the Lao People's Democratic Republic, 1994.

U.S. Central Intelligence Agency. *World Factbook 2000.* <http://www.odci.gov/cia/publications/factbook/index.html>. Accessed August 2001.

—Gerald W. Fry

LEBANON

Republic of Lebanon
Al-Jumhuriyah al-Lubnaniyah

CAPITAL: Beirut.

MONETARY UNIT: Lebanese pound. One Lebanese pound (known locally as the lira) equals 100 piasters. There are notes of 50, 100, 250, 500, 1,000, 10,000 and 50,000 liras. There are no coins.

CHIEF EXPORTS: Foodstuffs, tobacco, textiles, chemicals, metal and metal products, electrical equipment and products, jewelry, paper and paper products.

CHIEF IMPORTS: Machinery and transport equipment, foodstuffs, chemicals, consumer goods, textiles, metals, fuels, agricultural products.

GROSS DOMESTIC PRODUCT: US$16.2 billion (purchasing power parity, 1999 est.).

BALANCE OF TRADE: **Exports:** US$866 million (f.o.b., 1999 est.). **Imports:** US$5.7 billion (f.o.b., 1999 est.).

COUNTRY OVERVIEW

LOCATION AND SIZE. Situated in the Middle East, Lebanon is a small country on the eastern shore of the Mediterranean Sea. Lebanon has a narrow coastal plain along the Mediterranean Sea, which is 225 kilometers (139.8 miles) long and is bordered by Syria on the north and east and by Israel on the south. A small country, Lebanon's total area is only 10,400 square kilometers (4,014 square miles), roughly two-thirds the size of the state of Connecticut in the United States. Beirut, the capital, is located in the center and overlooks the Mediterranean Sea. Other major cities include Tripoli in the north and Sidon in the south.

POPULATION. The population of Lebanon is estimated at 3,578,037, according to July 2000 estimates, an increase of 578,037 from 1980. In 2000, Lebanon's birth rate stood at 20.26 per 1,000, while the death rate was reported at 6.42 per 1,000. With a projected growth rate of 1.2 percent between 2000 and 2015, the population is expected to reach 6 million by the year 2029.

Lebanon's population is highly divided along both religious and confessional lines (the presence of groups of different faiths within the same religion). Muslims in 2001 were believed to have accounted for 60 percent of the population. Christians form the second largest group in the country. Lebanon is also home to some 200,000 Palestinian refugees, mostly Sunni Muslims, many of whom have lived in refugee camps since arriving in the country in 1948. For political reasons, no official census has been conducted since 1932. Muslim and Christian factions in Lebanon were engaged in a devastating civil war that began in 1975 and ended in 1990, when stability was restored to the country.

As in many developing countries, a majority of Lebanese (around 90 percent) live in urban areas. The population is unevenly distributed, with the vast majority of the population concentrated in the coastal cities of Beirut, Sidon, and Tyre, while other parts of the country, namely the Bekáa Valley, remain sparsely populated. The uneven population distribution has given rise to regional disparities. The coastal cities continue to receive much government attention, while the rest of the country has remained largely neglected. The population of urban areas has grown significantly since the 1960s, mostly because the cities have received more government funding and attention. In 2000, the capital Beirut and its suburbs was home to 1.3 million people. The northern city of Tripoli is the second largest in the country, with an estimated population of 450,000.

Lebanon's population is generally young, with 50.7 percent below the age 24, and is one of the most highly educated in the region. The adult literacy rate in Lebanon is estimated at 90 percent. Primary education in Lebanon is mandatory, and private education is prevalent. Lebanon's university system is also highly developed. The health-care system is one of the most

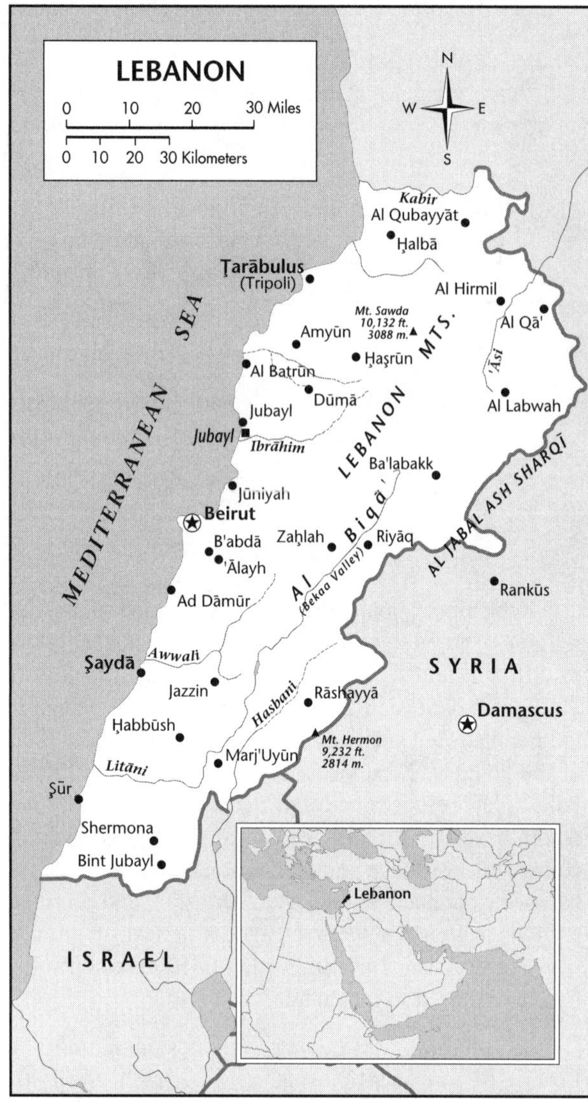

developed in the region. As a result, Lebanon also has one of the highest average life expectancies in the region, at 68.5 years. Infant mortality in Lebanon is also low by regional standards.

OVERVIEW OF ECONOMY

Lebanon's relatively small economy is based mainly on services, which have traditionally accounted for approximately 68 percent of the GDP. The sector is mainly comprised of a thriving regional banking market, tourism, and trade. Most economic activity is concentrated in the coastal cities. Other economic activity includes quarrying for the cement industry and small-scale farming, largely concentrated in the coastal plain and the Bekáa Valley in the south. Agriculture has traditionally accounted for only 13 percent of the GDP, which explains why the country is heavily dependent on the import of foodstuffs. The industrial sector is also relatively small, mostly because of the small domestic market. Jewelry, cement, processed food, and beverages are among the country's chief exports.

Lebanon entered the 20th century as a French protectorate heavily dependent on trade, especially along the coastal cities of Tyre, Sidon, Beirut, and Tripoli. Most of Lebanon's present-day problems can be traced to 1920, when the French incorporated Beirut and other coastal towns, the Bekáa Valley, and certain other districts in Mount Lebanon to form Greater Lebanon. The establishment of Greater Lebanon meant that the Maronites, concentrated largely in the Mount Lebanon area, were no longer the majority, and the population became equally divided between Muslims and Christians. In 1926, the French drew up a constitution that provided a formula for power-sharing among the various religious groups, making it mandatory for the president of the republic to be a Maronite, the prime minister a Sunni Muslim, and the speaker of the chamber a Shi'ite Muslim. This formula ensured that the pro-France Maronites exercised more control than any other religious group, allowing France to continue to control Lebanon through its close relations with the Maronites long after its full withdrawal from Lebanon in 1946.

The 1926 constitution, coupled with an unwritten power-sharing agreement known as the National Pact drawn up between Christians and Muslims in 1943, allowed Lebanon to maintain parliamentary democracy until the mid-1970s. However, rising tensions between Christians and Muslims, who by the mid-1970s became a majority and began demanding more political power, led to the outbreak of the civil war in 1975. In the immediate years before the outbreak of the war, Maronite Christians, feeling threatened by Muslim demands, resorted to violence to crush Lebanese Muslim opposition. They also wanted to oust the Palestinian Liberation Organization (PLO), which had a strong presence in Lebanon in the 1970s and was seen as an ally of the Muslims. The civil war intensified and broadened during the 1980s, with Palestinian refugees and their allies launching attacks into Israel from Lebanon, and the taking of Western hostages in Beirut by various Arab guerilla groups (guerilla groups practice non-conventional warfare in an effort to wear down the resistance of their adversaries). Syria was also involved, stepping in to fill the vacuum left by the weak Lebanese government and army. In an effort to stop the attacks and destroy the PLO, Israel invaded southern Lebanon in 1982, and it required major efforts by the United States and other powers to stop the fighting—at least temporarily—and escort the PLO out of the country. But Lebanon's war dragged on and did not end until 1990, with the adoption of the U.S./Arab-brokered Ta'if accords, which essentially recognized Syria's continued involvement in Lebanon's affairs and slightly adjusted the power-sharing formula among the various religious groups designed by the French in 1926.

Until 1975, Lebanon's economy was characterized by minimal state intervention in private enterprise. In those years, the country managed to transform itself into a major banking center by avoiding restrictions on foreign exchange or capital movement and enforcing strict bank secrecy regulations. Lebanon's economic **infrastructure**, however, was severely damaged by the 1975–90 civil war. International organizations estimated the cost of physical destruction to be between US$25 billion and US$30 billion. Since the end of the civil war, the country has been engaged in an economic reconstruction process and has made significant progress toward the restoration of democracy. As a result, **inflation** fell from more than 100 percent to 5 percent between 1992 and 1998, and **foreign exchange reserves** jumped to more than US$6 billion from US$1.4 billion in the same period. The Lebanese pound has been relatively stable. Much of the physical and financial infrastructure damaged during the war has been rebuilt.

Lebanon's economic policy after the war has been largely shaped by Rafik al-Hariri, who served as prime minister between 1991 and 1998 and returned to power in August 2000. Hariri's economic policies have focused on reconstructing the country's war-damaged economy through the infusion of huge capital into the construction sector. Much of this capital has come from Lebanese expatriates and Arab investors from the Persian Gulf region. As a result, the period between 1991 and mid-1996 witnessed high levels of growth. This growth, however, slowed in 1996, mainly as investor confidence began to weaken in the wake of Israel's 2-week bombardment of the country in April 1996. The resulting economic slowdown has affected the country since, and attempts by the government to curb inflation by raising interest rates has caused the economy to slow even further. The Lebanese economy has been in **recession** since 1999, and the country's **real GDP** has experienced a decline of 0.5 percent, mainly the result of the drop in private demand, consumption, and investment. The government's huge spending bill has fueled a large **budget deficit**, which was equivalent to 53.5 percent of expenditure in the first 7 months of the year 2000.

Lebanon in 2001 continues to be primarily a free-market economy and is by far the most liberal among Arab economies. Since the end of the civil war in 1991, the country has had a fairly stable multiparty system and is strongly supported by the United States and the European Union. The main challenge facing the economy is the large budget deficit, which is fueled by a substantial government debt, mostly spent on reconstruction and a large government bureaucracy. A hike in public spending has thus far failed to stimulate economic growth. Further, the government's **privatization** program, launched in the first half of 2000, has thus far not been successful; in May 2000, the Lebanese parliament adopted a new law that sets the general framework for privatization. However, privatizing state-owned companies is going very slowly and hinders true economic reform.

Corruption is widespread in Lebanon. Officially, several anti-corruption regulations are in place, but they are rarely enforced. According to the U.S. State Department, corruption is more pervasive in the **public sector** than in private businesses, and is especially evident in **procurement** and public works contracts. A 1998 study by the World Bank estimated that at least US$45 million is spent annually in bribes to brokers and government officials. Between 1998 and mid-2000, the cabinet of Prime Minister Salim al-Hoss made it a priority to fight corruption, which it mostly blamed on Prime Minister Rafiq al-Hariri's economic reconstruction drive while he was in office. The government's initial efforts to enforce anti-corruption measures led to the dismissal of hundreds of public servants, but the general verdict has been that corruption continues to be pervasive in the country.

POLITICS, GOVERNMENT, AND TAXATION

The country's political system in 2001 is derived from the 1989 Ta'if Accords, which put an end to the 16-year civil war. Lebanon is now a parliamentary republic with a president and a **unicameral** (single chamber) National Assembly. The president of the republic is elected by the parliament for a 6-year term. The speaker of parliament is elected by parliament every 4 years, which is also the length of time between parliamentary elections. The president appoints the prime minister, who forms the Cabinet of Ministers. Under the new constitution drafted after the conclusion of the Ta'if Accords, Muslims now have an overall numerical advantage in the National Assembly, since representation is based along sectarian lines. Further, the power of the president has been somewhat diminished, although by custom, the president of the republic must still be Maronite Christian, while the prime minister must be a Sunni Muslim and the speaker of the parliament a Shi'ite Muslim.

The major political parties are arranged, although not explicitly, along religious lines. The Hizballah and Nabih Berri's Amal movement represents the Shi'ite Muslim community, while the Sunni Muslims are divided between pro-government parties and marginal leftist parties. The Druze, a community concentrated around Mount Lebanon, are represented by Walid Jumblatt's Progressive Socialist Party. The Christian-Maronite community controlled the country before the war. The Ta'if Accords attempted to correct this bias but left the Christian community feeling relatively powerless. This impression was especially intensified when the accords resulted in the expulsion of a generation of Maronite leaders, including former president Amin Gemayyel and former Christian warlords Michel Aoun and Samir Jaja.

Parliamentary elections were held in August 1992 for the first time in 20 years. Prime Minister Rafiq al-Hariri's coalition won the majority of seats in those elections and in subsequent parliamentary elections in 1996 and 1998. Turnout by Christians was very low, and there were charges of irregularities. Municipal elections were held for the first time in 35 years in May and June 1998.

As of 2001, at least 35,000 Syrian troops still remain in northern, central, and eastern Lebanon, where they have been stationed since October 1990. Syria's deployment into Lebanon was legitimized by the Arab League a few years after the civil war started and then reaffirmed in the Ta'if Accords. Only with Syrian military power could Maronite-Christian leader Gen. Michel Aoun, who rejected the Ta'if Accords and maintained that he was the legitimate head of the government, be expelled from the country in 1991 and Lebanon reunited under one government. While Syria remains the dominant player in Lebanon, it began to withdraw its troops from central Beirut in 2000 and abandoned many checkpoints. It is gradually ceding more control to Lebanese security forces, which now control most strategic points in Beirut as well as the main highway to the airport, but Syria still exercises de facto control over Lebanese politics. Syria continues to cast a shadow on Lebanese politics because of the Syrian-Israeli conflict in the area, which makes Lebanon strategically important to Syria.

Since the end of the civil war, Lebanon has been engaged in a massive reconstruction process to repair the damage inflicted during the war. In 1993, Hariri launched "Horizon 2000," an US$18 billion program to rebuild Lebanon and transform the country into a regional center of finance and services. Under this national reconstruction plan, a huge investment has been made in various sectors focused on rebuilding the country. Large infrastructure projects, including a coastal highway, a new airport, and a highway to the Syrian border are being built as part of "Horizon 2000." The program also seeks to rehabilitate Beirut's city center and the telecommunications network. The financing for the project has come from a growing budget deficit and foreign investors, particularly Saudi Arabia and Kuwait. The expansion was coupled with a **fiscal policy** that aimed to raise interest rates in order to curb inflation. Hariri's reconstruction program was hampered by increased government spending in the 1990s, mainly as a result of the government's hiring policies, which sought to expand the civil service by hiring employees of various religious backgrounds as a means to ease friction between the various religious groups. As a result, the Lebanese government's debt, considered one of the highest in the region, soared to 140 percent of the GDP by the end of 2000.

The budget deficit has also proven difficult to tackle for the administration of Salim al-Hoss, which came to power following Hariri's resignation in 1998. The Hoss government focused on **restructuring** the public-sector debt and other fiscal reforms. For instance, the government improved tax collection methods, increased income and corporate taxes, and increased customs **duties**. Customs duties and property transaction fees are the two most important sources of revenue for the government. Custom duties account for 40 percent of the government's revenue, mostly from Beirut port. The government's efforts were seen as half-hearted and ineffective, primarily due to its weakness in the face of opposition from the legislature and its inability to institute a **value-added tax** (VAT). Perceptions that the Hoss government had not followed through in its efforts to reform the economy led to the resignation of the prime minister in August 2000.

With the return of Prime Minister Hariri to office in August 2000, the government once more focused on resuming reconstruction efforts by securing foreign aid, mainly from European and Arab countries. In October 2000, the Kuwaiti government agreed to deposit US$100 million at the Lebanese Central Bank to help stabilize the Lebanese pound. Hariri is also expected to proceed with economic reforms, especially the privatization of state-owned enterprises. In mid-January 2001, the government announced plans to introduce a sales tax on consumer products rather than the VAT, previously planned by the government of Prime Minister Salim al-Hoss. The government, however, has no plans to slash the budget deficit and has argued that it can be maintained for years without affecting economic growth.

INFRASTRUCTURE, POWER, AND COMMUNICATIONS

Lebanon enjoys an extensive, though aging, infrastructure that was severely damaged during the civil war. The country is served by a network of over 7,000 kilometers (4,350 miles) of primary and secondary roads, 6,200 kilometers (3,853 miles) of which are paved. Since 1991, the government has given much attention to rebuilding the infrastructure. The road system, however, especially within Beirut and in remote areas, remains in poor condition. With growing numbers of licensed automobiles in the 1990s, the road system, especially in Beirut, has become congested. The country's railway system is mostly unusable, due largely to damage sustained during the civil war.

Lebanon has 9 airports, 2 of which have unpaved runways. Beirut International Airport, the country's ma-

Communications

Country	Newspapers	Radios	TV Sets[a]	Cable subscribers[a]	Mobile Phones[a]	Fax Machines[a]	Personal Computers[a]	Internet Hosts[b]	Internet Users[b]
	1996	1997	1998	1998	1998	1998	1998	1999	1999
Lebanon	107	906	352	1.4	157	N/A	39.2	7.02	200
United States	215	2,146	847	244.3	256	78.4	458.6	1,508.77	74,100
Egypt	40	324	122	N/A	1	0.5	9.1	0.28	200
Israel	290	520	318	184.0	359	24.9	217.2	187.41	800

[a]Data are from International Telecommunication Union, *World Telecommunication Development Report 1999* and are per 1,000 people.
[b]Data are from the Internet Software Consortium (http://www.isc.org) and are per 10,000 people.

SOURCE: World Bank. *World Development Indicators 2000.*

jor airport, handles 2 million passengers a year. In fact, 35 airlines service Beirut and bring in most of the country's tourists. Lebanon has 12 ports, the most notable of which are Beirut, Tyre, Sidon, and Tripoli. The ports of Beirut and Tripoli are currently being rehabilitated and modernized.

Electrical power is supplied to Lebanon by the state-owned Electricite du Liban (EDL), which has the capacity to produce 1,500 megawatts (mw) of power. Plans are underway to expand power production to 2,700 mw by 2006. Total annual electricity production came to 9.7 billion kilowatt hours (kWh) in 1998, with the majority produced from fossil fuels. Power production falls short of actual demand, however, and the 220-volt power system is subject to repeated shortages and blackouts. Furthermore, several Israeli raids on Lebanon's power stations since 1996 have led to severe power cuts.

Telecommunications services, damaged during the civil war, have been largely restored. The government has been expanding the public telephone network to reach some 698,000 customers. Cellular telephone service is widely available with some 750,000 subscribers. In 1999, the country had 19 Internet service providers.

ECONOMIC SECTORS

Lebanon's economic sectors reflect the small size of the economy, which places limits on the availability of natural resources, population, and domestic markets. Before the civil war, the services sector was by far the largest contributor to the economy and employed the largest proportion of the **labor force**. The industrial sector was the second largest contributor to the economy, while agriculture accounted for a smaller proportion of national income.

As of 2001, Lebanon's economy continues to rely heavily on the services sector. Services—mainly banking, tourism and trade—account for 68 percent of the GDP. Lebanon's agricultural and manufacturing base continue to be small and has yet to regain its pre-war competitiveness. Economic slowdowns in Lebanon began in 1996, with a drop in construction activity, and the economy was in recession during the 2000–01 period. The greatest obstacles to growth in all of Lebanon's economic sectors are their vulnerability to regional instability and international trade opportunity.

Recognizing these obstacles, Lebanon has moved to form a series of trade alliances, including a customs union concluded with Syria in 2000, an Arab free trade agreement, and a Euro-Mediterranean Association Agreement with the European Union. Lebanon is also planning to join the World Trade Organization. Lebanon's domestic political environment has improved since the Israeli withdrawal from south Lebanon in May 2000. Although some elements of instability still remain (mainly the occasional exchanges of gunfire between guerrillas belonging to the Shi'ite Hizballah group and Israeli soldiers), the Israeli withdrawal is expected to enhance international confidence in Lebanon's investment potential. The tourism

Lebanon
GDP–COMPOSITION BY SECTOR–1998 est.

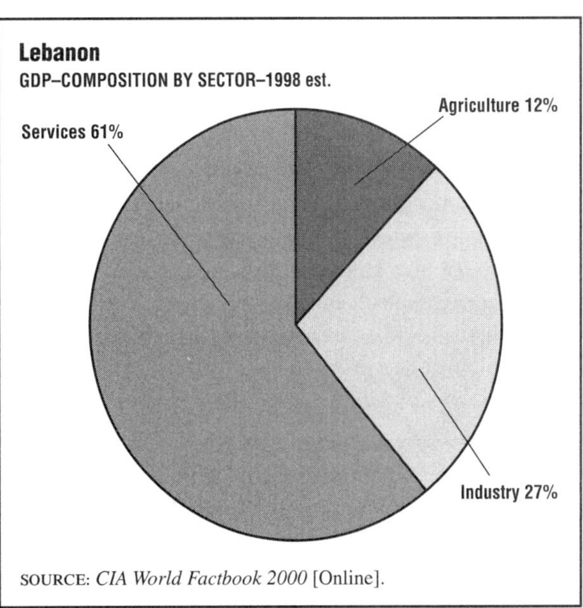

SOURCE: *CIA World Factbook 2000* [Online].

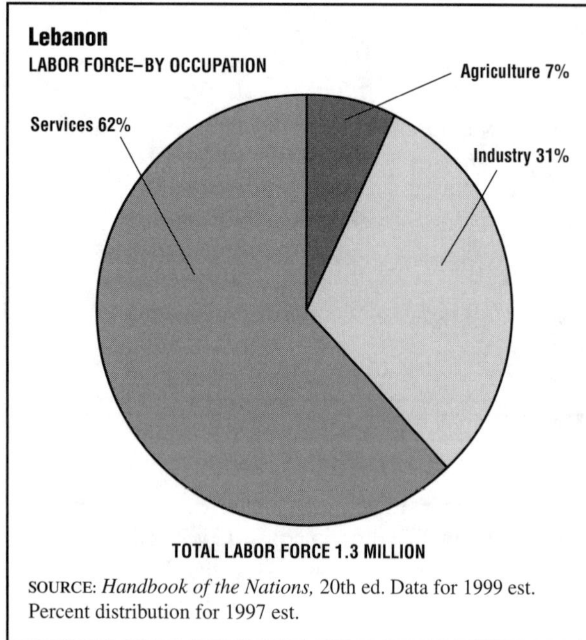

SOURCE: *Handbook of the Nations,* 20th ed. Data for 1999 est. Percent distribution for 1997 est.

sector stands to benefit most. Since 1997, the government has attempted to tackle seriously the budget deficit, raising custom duties by 2 percent in 1998 and introducing an entertainment tax on restaurant, bar, and hotel bills. However, spending continues to be high, and the budget deficit in 2000 was equivalent to 53.5 percent of expenditures.

AGRICULTURE

Lebanon's agricultural sector is underdeveloped and has yet to realize its potential. The sector's development is hindered by the large number of small un-irrigated land holdings and the lack of modern equipment and efficient production techniques. The sector also suffers from a lack of funding and inaccessibility to loans. In 1999, the government allocated only US$11 million, or 0.4 percent of the state budget, to agriculture.

There are 207,060 hectares of arable land in Lebanon, 60,047 hectares of which are irrigated. Most agricultural activity is concentrated in the High Bekáa Valley and the coastal plains, which combined account for more than two-thirds of the cultivated land. Bekáa Valley crops mostly consist of vegetables and some cereals. Fruits, such as bananas, melons, and apples, are cultivated in the coastal plains. The production of certain crops, such as tobacco, is subsidized by the government. During the civil war, Lebanon was a major producer and exporter of heroin and hashish. In 1992—pressured by the United States, Interpol, and the United Nations—the Lebanese government officially banned poppy and cannabis cultivation, a ban effectively enforced by the Syrian and Lebanese armies.

Agricultural production is a moderate contributor to Lebanon's economy, traditionally accounting for 13 percent of the GDP and employing approximately 13 percent of the labor force. Most of Lebanon's agricultural products are consumed locally and a small percentage is exported to the Gulf region, primarily to Saudi Arabia and the United Arab Emirates.

INDUSTRY

MANUFACTURING. The manufacturing sector is an important contributor to the economy, accounting for 17 percent of the GDP in 1998 and employing 15 percent of the labor force. In 1999, the sector accounted for 40 percent of exports. Total employment in the manufacturing sector in 1998 stood at 180,000 people.

Historically, and unlike neighboring Arab countries, Lebanon has never gone through a state-led industrial growth phase, and the governments have generally adopted an open policy that has encouraged free competition in the sector without government interference. Lebanon's industrial base is by all means modest, mostly comprised of family-based small firms. Most finished and semi-finished goods are imported. Much of Lebanon's local manufacturing consists of producing goods for local consumption—mainly food, furniture, and clothing manufacturing. The most important industrial activity is focused on food, beverages, and chemical products, which receive the highest level of investment. Manufacturing activity is concentrated in the population centers of Beirut and Mount Lebanon, where an estimated 60 percent of the firms are located. Some 19 percent of manufacturing firms are located in the north.

Since the end of the civil war in 1991, the manufacturing sector has had to struggle to regain its pre-war competitiveness and invest heavily in new equipment. During the war, several factories were forced to close as a result of the armed hostilities, declining consumer spending, and lack of funding. Major barriers facing the sector in 2001 are rising customs duties and political instability, 2 difficulties which have prevented many multinational companies from establishing subsidiaries in Lebanon. The U.S. State Department stated that "the sector's outlook remains bleak, as high operating costs, low productivity, obsolete equipment and limited access to medium and long term credit impede the performance of the sector."

MINING. With no commercially exploitable mineral deposits, Lebanon has no significant mining base. Quarrying for marble, sand, and limestone for cement production, however, has accelerated in recent years. The output is mostly consumed locally for construction, and only a tiny fraction is now being exported.

SERVICES

TOURISM. Tourism was once a very important contributor to Lebanon's economy, accounting for almost 20 percent of the GDP in the 2 decades before the start of the civil war. Since the end of the war, the sector has managed to revive somewhat, but tourism has yet to return to its pre-war levels. Tourism in 1999 accounted for 9 percent of the GDP. In 2001, the tourism sector was one of the fastest growing sectors of the economy, with the number of tourists visiting Lebanon between 1996 and 2000 growing at the rate of 14 percent annually. Lebanon's rich archeological and cultural heritage, coupled with a mild climate and diverse terrain, has been a major attraction to tourists.

Successive governments have invested heavily in the sector, and there has been substantial investment in building luxury hotels and upscale restaurants, in response to the return of tourists (mainly Gulf Arabs) to Lebanon, especially in summer. It is estimated that there are 12,000 hotel beds, with 90 percent located in Beirut and Mount Lebanon. Some 860 additional hotel rooms will be built in 2001 and another 1,200 will be added in 2002. Despite continued political instability, growth in the tourism sector is expected to pick up in the coming years, especially after the Israeli withdrawal from south Lebanon in May 2000.

FINANCIAL SERVICES. The most important sector of Lebanon's service industry is the financial services industry. The sector lost most of its importance during the civil war with the flight of the majority of foreign firms, but there has been a concerted effort to renew the sector since 1991. As a result, the sector grew rapidly in the 1990s, mostly the result of investment in government debt and reconstruction and reported double-digit growth throughout the 1990s.

Financial services continue to undergo expansion and consolidation, especially of small family-owned banks. Several international banks now have offices in Beirut. In an effort to present Lebanon as an international financial center, the government announced in 1995 a series of financial laws aimed at preventing **money laundering**. In particular, one of the passed laws gives international investigators access to the accounts of Lebanese banks.

Banking, by far the most profitable sector, employs some 15,000 people. Before the civil war, Lebanon was the banking center of the Middle East, owing to its liberal banking regime, one of the most liberal in the Arab world. Several Arab and foreign banks pulled out of Lebanon during the war, but by 2001 several of these banks had returned. However, most of them have only small branches in Beirut, and the pre-war interest in Lebanon's banking sector is yet to return.

There are some 67 active commercial banks in the country, in addition to small family-owned enterprises. Most of these banks are up to international standards, largely due to concerted government efforts to tighten regulations and increase **capital adequacy** requirements.

The Beirut Stock Exchange, closed in 1975 with the outbreak of the civil war, re-opened in 1995. Trading, which began in January 1996, has been thin, and the number of listed companies has been relatively small. There is a total of 12 listed companies, including 4 financial institutions, 1 car retailer, and a supermarket chain. Weekly trading in 2000 rarely exceeded US$2 million.

CONSTRUCTION. The construction sector grew at a very fast pace between 1991 and 1996, contributing to an average of 6.5 percent growth in the GDP. The sector's growth was in response to the influx of huge sums of private investments, mostly from Lebanese expatriates and Gulf Arabs who were devoted to the reconstruction of residential and commercial buildings destroyed during the war. These investments were coupled with large-scale government projects to rebuild the country's infrastructure, including the US$400 million project to rebuild Beirut International Airport and the complete renovation of downtown Beirut by the quasi-government company, Solidere.

Since 1996, the sector's contribution to GDP has dropped, as private investments and government spending began to dwindle. The slowdown was partly brought about by the oversupply in some areas of the construction market, especially in housing. International and domestic confidence in Lebanon's stability also dropped significantly in the aftermath of Israel's military operations in Lebanon in the summer of 1996.

RETAIL. Lacking many large commercial centers other than Beirut and its suburbs, Lebanon has a poorly-developed **retail** sector. While Beirut is home to a variety of retail stores, including fast food franchises such as McDonald's, Burger King, and Starbuck's, the majority of towns in the interior of the country have small family-owned shops, farmers' markets, and temporary roadside stands.

ADVERTISING. Lebanon has a booming advertising industry that ranks second in the region in terms of size and profitability after Dubai. Some 150 national and international advertising agencies are based in Lebanon, employing some 8,000 people. In the absence of reliable statistics, the sector's revenue is believed to be in the range of US$150 million annually. The largely unregulated sector is dominated by the country's 4 television stations and the print media, which account for 55 percent and 34 percent of the sector's revenue, respectively.

Trade (expressed in billions of US$): Lebanon

	Exports	Imports
1975	1.233	2.048
1980	.955	3.650
1985	.530	2.203
1990	.494	2.525
1995	.825	7.278
1998	N/A	N/A

SOURCE: International Monetary Fund. *International Financial Statistics Yearbook 1999.*

Exchange rates: Lebanon

Lebanese pounds per US$1	
Jan 2001	1,507.5
2000	1,507.5
1999	1,507.8
1998	1,516.1
1997	1,539.5
1996	1,571.4

SOURCE: CIA *World Factbook 2001* [ONLINE].

INTERNATIONAL TRADE

With few natural resources, over the past several decades, Lebanon has relied heavily on imports. The value of imports in 1999 was US$5.7 billion, while exports totaled just US$866 million. Lebanon imports the majority of its goods from Europe—mostly Italy (12 percent), France (10 percent), and Germany (9 percent)—followed by the United States (9 percent). On the other hand, the majority of Lebanon's exports are sent to neighboring Arab Gulf countries, especially Saudi Arabia (12 percent) and the United Arab Emirates (10 percent), which are Lebanon's largest trade partners. Major exports are food, vegetables and fruits, followed by chemical products and jewelry.

Imports of foreign goods have usually amounted to 40–65 percent of the GDP. Lebanon's imports consist of fuel, electrical goods, and vehicles. Expenditures on imports rose dramatically in the post-civil war period, largely due to the need to import **capital goods** and high consumer spending on food, cars, and luxury items. The trend has reversed since 1999 due to the economic slowdown but is expected to rise again as the economy recovers.

Although the value of exports increased from US$544 million in 1994 to US$866 million in 1999, the substantial trade imbalance that Lebanon has endured over the years has meant that the country will continue to run a **trade deficit** which forces it to borrow heavily to pay for its consumption.

MONEY

The value of the Lebanese pound has slowly improved on the world market since 1992, thanks to a wise monitory policy that has sought to restore its value. As a result, the value of the pound to the dollar has improved from 1,800 Lebanese pounds for every U.S. dollar at the end of 1992 to 1,508 pounds to 1 U.S. dollar at the end of 1999, and has remained at roughly this value in the years since. The U.S. dollar was widely used throughout the civil war, and although its use has decreased since 1991, more than 60 percent of transactions in 2001 are still conducted using the U.S. dollar, which is available at many Lebanese banks. The nation's central bank, the Central Bank of Lebanon, is highly respected by the international banking community and has done a good job of maintaining the value of the currency and keeping low inflation.

POVERTY AND WEALTH

Wealth and income are unevenly distributed in Lebanon. Despite the absence of reliable statistics, income disparity in Lebanon is believed to have increased in the last 10 years since the end of the civil war. According to a recent study, the income of the upper and middle classes has risen since 1991, but most Lebanese have not seen a significant appreciation in their income. A minority of Lebanese have in fact seen their incomes drop below the poverty line. Farmers in the Bekáa Valley, for example, have been affected by the ban on the cultivation of hashish, which during the civil war constituted a major source of income for the region.

Income disparity also is manifested along regional lines. According to the UN Economic and Social Council for Western Asia (ESCWA), the average **GDP per capita** in 1999 reached US$5,148 (the CIA World Factbook places the figure at US$4500). However, average GDP per capita in areas such as the Bekáa Valley is only US$620 per year. Almost one-third of the population live

GDP per Capita (US$)

Country	1975	1980	1985	1990	1998
Lebanon	N/A	N/A	N/A	1,721	2,999
United States	19,364	21,529	23,200	25,363	29,683
Israel	10,620	11,412	12,093	13,566	15,978
Egypt	516	731	890	971	1,146

SOURCE: United Nations. *Human Development Report 2000; Trends in human development and per capita income.*

Household Consumption in PPP Terms

Country	All food	Clothing and footwear	Fuel and power[a]	Health care[b]	Education[b]	Transport & Communications	Other
Lebanon	31	13	10	7	9	7	22
United States	13	9	9	4	6	8	51
Egypt	44	9	7	3	17	3	17
Israel	23	6	11	2	6	8	44

Data represent percentage of consumption in PPP terms.
[a]Excludes energy used for transport.
[b]Includes government and private expenditures.

SOURCE: World Bank. *World Development Indicators 2000.*

below the poverty line, with one-quarter of families subsisting on less than US$620 per year. Unemployment in 1997 was estimated to have reached 18 percent.

As a result of declining economic conditions, public-sector strikes have become commonplace. To prevent mass protest against its economic and social policies and to preclude opposition forces from exploiting discontent, the government uses the army to guard public security. As a result, the army has been privileged and strengthened, becoming assertive in its demands for salaries and promotions.

The government has generally adopted a hands off policy toward social inequality and has not attempted to redress differences between the poor and the rich. Lebanon's dependence on imports, especially food and fuel, has made it increasingly more difficult for the poor to spend a high amount of their relatively small incomes on the necessities of life. As a result, many Lebanese have opted to seek job opportunities in neighboring Arab countries, especially in the Gulf region.

WORKING CONDITIONS

Reliable official data about Lebanon's labor force are unavailable, but it is estimated that the country's labor force in 1999 was 1.3 million. A 1996 Ministry of Social Affairs survey estimated that there were some 944,282 foreign workers in the country as well. Foreign workers are mostly unskilled laborers from Syria, Asia, India, and Africa, and they are employed mostly in construction, agriculture, industry, and households. Unemployment in the country is high, with official estimates in 1999 set at 10 percent and unofficial estimates reaching as high as 25 percent; the CIA World Factbook reported 1999 unemployment of 18 percent.

Trade unions are allowed in Lebanon and are supported by the government with membership restricted to Lebanese workers. Trade unions operate under the umbrella of the Federation of Labor Unions, which negotiates cost of living adjustments and other social benefits on behalf of the workers. The 48-hour work week is the standard.

Although labor laws protecting the right of workers have been in place since 1964, regulations are rarely enforced, and working conditions in Lebanon are far from ideal. Labor actions, strikes, slow downs, and protests frequently disturb work life, and wages remain relatively low. The largest proportion of the labor force, some 15,000 people, is employed by the financial sector, working in banks and other financial institutions, followed by the manufacturing industry, which employs 15 percent of the labor force.

COUNTRY HISTORY AND ECONOMIC DEVELOPMENT

1516. Lebanon becomes part of the Ottoman Empire.

1920. French General Gouraud establishes Greater Lebanon with its present boundaries and with Beirut as its capital.

1926. First Lebanese constitution is promulgated.

1932. The first and only complete census is taken in Lebanon. Charles Dabbas, a Greek Orthodox, is elected the first president of Lebanon.

1936. Emile Iddi elected president.

1941. Lebanon gains independence from the French.

1943. General elections take place; Bishara al Khuri is elected president.

1945. Lebanon becomes a member of the Arab League and the United Nations (UN). French troops completely withdraw from the country, with the signing of the Franco-Lebanese Treaty.

1975. Civil war breaks out.

1978. The Riyadh Conference formally ends the Lebanese Civil War; Syria intervenes militarily in Lebanon.

1981. Fighting resumes.

1982. Israel invades Lebanon.

1989. Ta'if Accords officially ends civil war and sets power-sharing formula between Lebanon's religious groups.

1992. Prime Minister Hariri launches "Horizon 2000" reconstruction program.

1997. Entertainment tax is introduced. Custom duties are raised.

1998. Prime Minister Hariri resigns. Salim al-Hoss takes office.

2000. Israel withdraws its troops from South Lebanon. Prime Minister Hariri returns to office.

FUTURE TRENDS

After nearly 2 decades of civil conflict, Lebanon entered the 21tst century on a positive note. Most of the country's infrastructure has been restored, and despite occasional violence, Lebanon's political system has been fairly stable. The 1989 Ta'if Accords, which brought an end to the civil war and set the terms for power-sharing among the various religious groups, has thus far been successful in creating a functional government in Beirut that is increasingly spreading its control over the rest of the country. Parliamentary elections have been held periodically since 1992. After almost 2 decades of occupation, Israel withdrew its military forces from southern Lebanon in May 2000.

Despite these positive developments, the government is faced with serious challenges, mainly lowering the budget deficit by focusing on tax reform and modernization, expenditure rationalizing, and reducing of the burden of servicing its debt. The government is also under pressure from the IMF to proceed with plans to adopt a privatization program of state-owned enterprises. Having lost its status as a regional banking and trade center and lacking a solid agricultural and industrial base, Lebanon must develop alternative plans to define its new role in the Middle East region. So far, beyond rhetorical official statements, no steps have been taken in that direction.

DEPENDENCIES

Lebanon has no territories or colonies.

BIBLIOGRAPHY

Banque du Liban: Central Bank of Lebanon. <http://www.bdl.gov.lb>. Accessed July 2001.

Economist Intelligence Unit. *Country Profile: Lebanon.* London: Economist Intelligence Unit, 2000.

Khalaf, Samir. Lebanon's Predicament. New York: Columbia University Press, 1987.

"Lebanon: Economy" and "Lebanon: History." *CNN Countrywatch.* <http://cnn.countrywatch.com>. Accessed June 2001.

Republic of Lebanon, Ministry of Economy and Trade. <http://www.economy.gov.lb>. Accessed July 2001.

U.S. Department of State. *FY 2001 Country Commercial Guide: Lebanon.* <http://www.usembassy.com.lb/wwwhcom.htm>. Accessed February 2001.

—Reem Nuseibeh

MACAU

Macau Special Administrative Region
Macao

CAPITAL: Macau.

MONETARY UNIT: Pataca (MOP). One Macau pataca equals 100 avos. Coins include denominations of 1, 5, 10, 20 and 50 avos, as well as MOP1 and MOP5. Paper currency comes in denominations of MOP5, 10, 50, 100, and 500.

CHIEF EXPORTS: Textiles, clothing, toys, electronics, cement, footwear, machinery.

CHIEF IMPORTS: Raw materials, foodstuffs, capital goods, mineral fuel, consumer goods.

GROSS DOMESTIC PRODUCT: US$7.65 billion (1999 est).

BALANCE OF TRADE: **Exports:** US$1.7 billion (1999 est.). **Imports:** US$1.5 billion (1999 est.).

COUNTRY OVERVIEW

LOCATION AND SIZE. Macau is located in Southeast Asia, approximately 60 kilometers (37 miles) southwest of Hong Kong, bordering China. Made up of Macau city and the islands of Taipa and Coloane, Macau has a land area of 21 square kilometers (8.3 square miles). Comparatively, the territory of Macau is 4 times smaller than the Manhattan area of New York City. Macau is joined to the Chinese province of Guangdong by a narrow land corridor. Because of land reclamation efforts, Macau has enlarged its territory by 50 percent since 1912.

POPULATION. The population of Macau, which is virtually all urban-based, was estimated at 445,594 in July 2000. In 2000, the birth rate stood at 12.54 per 1,000 and this low level is mainly attributed to the effect of urbanization. The death rate stood at 3.64 per 1,000. The estimated population growth rate is 1.83 percent, although unofficial estimates show higher figures due to a high net migration rate, which has been estimated at 9.41 migrants per 1,000. Macau has one of the highest population densities in the world, standing at a level of around 21,218 people per square kilometer (or 54,954 per square mile).

The Macau population represents 2 major ethnic groups, with ethnic Chinese making up almost 95 percent of the population, and Macanese (mixed Portuguese and Asian ancestry) and other ethnic groups making up the remaining 5 percent. Around 100,000 inhabitants of Macau hold Portuguese passports that give them the right to settle in Portugal. Approximately 23 percent of the population is below the age of 15, and just 8 percent of the population is older than 65. The current ethnic structure was formed in the 19th century and remains practically unchanged. Buddhism is the primary religion, with 50 percent of the population practicing; Roman Catholicism follows with 15 percent, and the remainder is made up of numerous other faiths.

The government is keen to limit the inflow of illegal immigrants from China. Between 20 and 25 illegal immigrants are deported daily, although foreigners may legally buy residential permits for US$250,000. New chronic diseases such as AIDS are also of great concern to the Macau government, since the country is a busy tourist destination.

OVERVIEW OF ECONOMY

Manufacturing and services are the 2 main pillars of the modern Macau economy. Macau, like Hong Kong and Singapore, has an export-oriented economy, which benefits from growing trade with Western Europe and the United States. Throughout the 20th century, Macau specialized in manufacturing for the export market and servicing international merchants and bankers.

Macau was established as a Portuguese colony in 1557, becoming one of the most important trade distribution centers in the region for the next 3 centuries. Its significance as a trading center rose as the Chinese government maintained a policy of voluntary isolation from

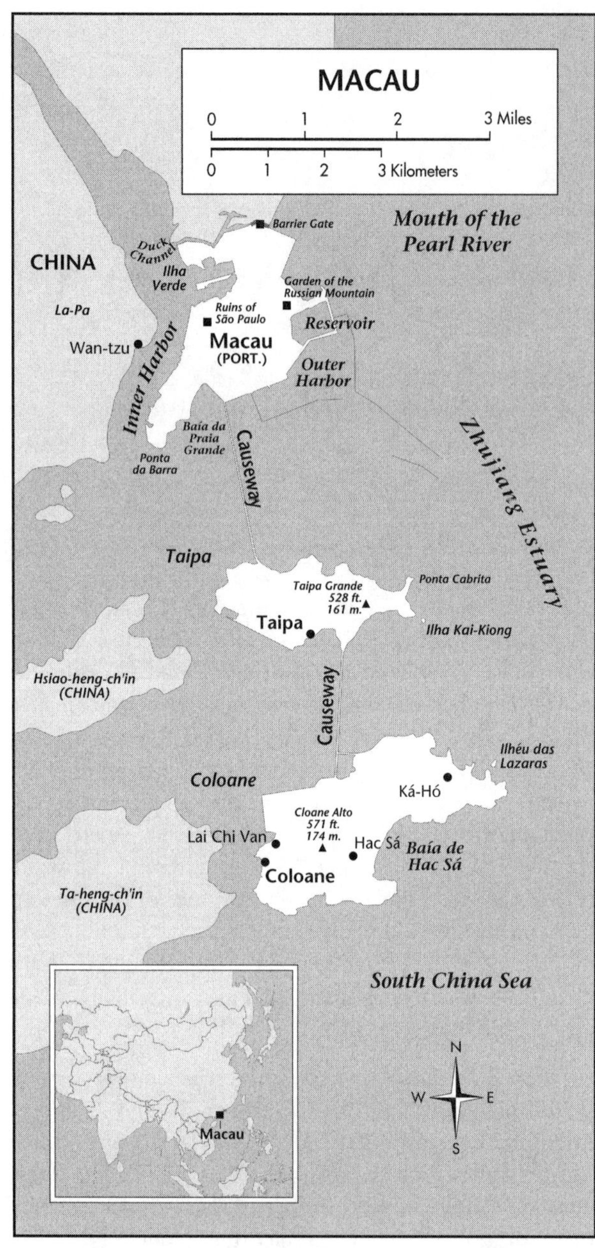

the world, allowing international trade only in few assigned ports. Portugal proclaimed Macau a free port (such ports were set up in Asia by the European colonial powers in the 19th century in an effort to promote international trade with a minimum of **tariffs** and other barriers) in 1849. However, in the 19th century Macau's importance declined with the rise of the British colony in Hong Kong.

The Macau administration has maintained a free-market economy, which in combination with the entrepreneurial skills of the local population and the region's political stability, has contributed to growth of wealth and prosperity. Macau's main exports are textiles, clothing, and services, though it lags behind Hong Kong and Singapore in the proportion of **value-added** production. Tourism also plays a significant role in Macau's economy. However, it has been the gambling industry that has contributed so much to the image of Macau as a tourist destination. The gambling industry also has attracted organized criminal syndicates, called "triads," which are involved in gambling, illegal people trafficking, prostitution, and pirated production of various goods, including music and computer CDs. During the 1990s, the government made considerable efforts to restrain and eliminate the power of these criminal groups.

The territory depends heavily on imports of foodstuffs and raw materials from neighboring China because it has no agriculture, due to its very small size. Nonetheless, it maintains a relatively high standard of living due to its sound **infrastructure**, promotion of economic balance, low **inflation**, stable currency, and foreign **trade surplus**.

POLITICS, GOVERNMENT, AND TAXATION

Throughout the 20th century, Macau remained a remote outpost of the Portuguese colonial empire. The situation changed, however, after the 1974 revolution in Portugal. The new democratic Portuguese government offered Macau back to China, although it took more than a decade before Portugal and China formally agreed on the future of Macau in 1987. This agreement was very similar to the one struck between the British government and China on the future of Hong Kong. On 20 December 1999, the administration of the territory was formally handed over to China. Macau became a Special Administrative Region (SAR) of the People's Republic of China with a "high degree of autonomy" (self-government) in domestic affairs for a period of 50 years under the principle of "one country, two systems." In 1999, Edmund Ho Hau-Wah became the first governor appointed by China's central government, replacing General de Rocha Vieira, the last Portuguese governor of the territory. According to the Macau's Basic Law (the territory's constitution), the governor has strong policy-making and executive powers, which are limited only by the central government in Beijing and by the Macau legislature. The Legislative Assembly is comprised of 8 directly elected members, 8 indirectly elected members, and 7 members appointed by the governor, totaling 23 members. After establishing its control over Macau, Beijing stationed its army on the territory. However, the military does not play any active role in Macau's economic development.

The Macau authorities traditionally did not attempt to establish control over the territory's economy and, unlike the **communist** Chinese, they always supported free-market institutions. Nevertheless, since the early 1980s, the Macau government has begun to adopt a more active role in the economic development, encouraging economic variety, promoting large infrastructure projects, and introducing attractive fiscal initiatives for local and foreign investors.

In order to compete with neighboring Hong Kong, Macau established very low **direct taxes** and abolished currency exchange controls. The property tax ranges up to 15 percent and the wage tax up to 10 percent; this is a very low rate compared to countries in Europe or North America. There are also profit and business taxes on industrial enterprises. Nevertheless, the web of various fiscal initiatives reduces business and other taxes considerably. Imports are free of **duty**, but they are subject to a consumption tax. The main source of revenue in Macau is taxes on gambling, accounting for 44 percent of total revenue (1999). The pataca, the Macau currency, is pegged to the Hong Kong dollar at the rate of 1.03 patacas per Hong Kong dollar. Unlike South Korea, Thailand, or Indonesia, the pataca remained stable despite the Asian financial crisis in 1997 and the Russian **foreign debt** default in 1998.

INFRASTRUCTURE, POWER, AND COMMUNICATIONS

Macau's infrastructure and well-developed transportation network were established mainly during the colonial era. Visitors can reach Macau by ferry, hydrofoils, or helicopters from Hong Kong, or by cars or buses from China. The territory's international profile was boosted by opening the US$1 billion international airport built on reclaimed land on Taipa island. It is capable of carrying 6 million passengers and 180,000 metric tons of cargo per year. Macau was eclipsed long ago by Hong Kong as the area's leading port, because its surrounding waters were not deep enough for large ocean cargo vessels. Nevertheless, the Macau authorities made considerable efforts to develop its seaport as an alternative to Hong Kong, and Macau's port is currently able to handle container cargo vessels and oil tankers. In 1993, a new ferry terminal capable of carrying 30 million passengers a year was opened.

Macau is served by a network of 50 kilometers (31 miles) of highways, all of them paved. In the 1990s, there was a steep increase in private car ownership, leading to traffic congestion and rising air pollution. In 1999, there was a total of 55,144 registered motor vehicles or 123 cars per 1,000 inhabitants, an increase of almost 30 percent from the 40,600 cars in 1995.

Macau is totally reliant on imports of mineral fuel for domestic consumption, and these imports accounted for almost 6 percent of merchandise imports in 1999. This makes Macau particularly vulnerable to world oil prices. Electrical power plants, which use imported fossil fuel, have a total capacity of 351.6 megawatts (mw). In 1999 electricity net supply stood at 1.53 billion kilowatt hours (kWh) and imports stood at 194.4 million kWh.

Macau had 70,403 new telephone lines installed in 1999, bringing the number of telephones up to 300,000, or 686 telephones per 1,000 people. The number of mobile cellular telephones was growing rapidly, reaching 55,000 in 1998. Macau has only 2 radio stations—both FM—and no television stations, receiving their television signals from Hong Kong. Macau's Internet service was to be opened to applicants in October 2000, having formerly been a **monopoly** owned by Macau Telecom.

ECONOMIC SECTORS

Macau has the advantage of being an entry point to the huge China market, although its economic development has been held back by its small territory, small pop-

Communications

Country	Telephones[a]	Telephones, Mobile/Cellular[a]	Radio Stations[b]	Radios[a]	TV Stations[a]	Televisions[a]	Internet Service Providers[c]	Internet Users[c]
Macau	176,837 (2000)	120,957 (2000)	AM 0; FM 2; shortwave 0	160,000	0	49,000	1	40,000
United States	194 M	69.209 M (1998)	AM 4,762; FM 5,542; shortwave 18	575 M	1,500	219 M	7,800	148 M
China	135 M (2000)	65 M (2001)	AM 369; FM 259; shortwave 45	417 M	3,240	400 M	3	22 M (2001)
Hong Kong	3.839 M (1999)	3.7 M (1999)	AM 7; FM 13; shortwave 0	4.45 M	4	1.84 M	17	1.85 M

[a]Data is for 1997 unless otherwise noted.
[b]Data is for 1998 unless otherwise noted.
[c]Data is for 2000 unless otherwise noted.

SOURCE: CIA *World Factbook 2001* [Online].

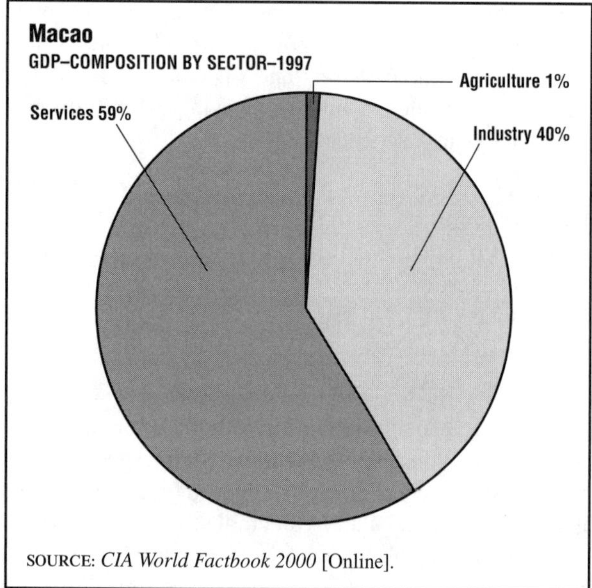

SOURCE: *CIA World Factbook 2000* [Online].

ulation, and extremely limited natural resources, as well as competition from neighboring Hong Kong. The policy of encouraging private entrepreneurship, giving priority to the development of export-oriented sectors and capital intensive industries—combined with a relatively cheap **labor force**—has contributed to the rise of Macau's prosperity. By 2000, manufacturing (textiles, clothing, toys, and electronics), gambling, and tourism became the largest sectors of Macau's economy.

The 1997 Asian financial crisis contributed to the slowing of economic growth in all sectors of the economy, although Macau managed to avoid an economic decline on the scale of Indonesia or Thailand. The crisis also indicated the need for a further broadening of the economy. Throughout the 1990s, the Macau government struggled to attract value-added manufacturing on the same scale as Hong Kong or Singapore, especially in such important sectors as computer hardware and information technologies (IT). Due to the small size of Macau's market, it lags behind neighboring Hong Kong in providing business and banking services. Macau tries to compete with Hong Kong by offering good infrastructure, cheaper business property rent and labor, and efficient administrative services.

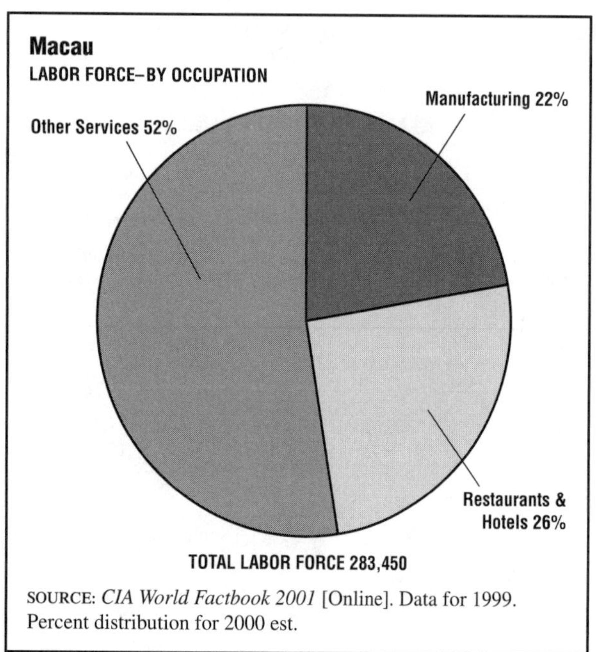

SOURCE: *CIA World Factbook 2001* [Online]. Data for 1999. Percent distribution for 2000 est.

AGRICULTURE

Agriculture and fishing play a negligible role in Macau's economy, accounting for just 1 percent of the GDP and employing less than 1 percent of the workforce. For a long time, Macau has been fully reliant on imports of foodstuffs, mainly from neighboring China. The territory has a very small fishing industry, consisting of a small fishing fleet, which supplies local restaurants and the fish market with fresh catch. There is a small land area under cultivation mainly for fresh vegetables. A very small livestock industry supplies chickens and ducks to the restaurants specializing in traditional Asian cuisine.

INDUSTRY

MANUFACTURING. Macau has a well-established manufacturing sector that plays an important economic role. Manufacturing contributes 40 percent of the GDP, providing employment to 87,141 people or 31 percent of the workforce (1998). In the 1960s and 1970s, Macau attracted investment and technologies to its manufacturing industry (mainly textiles, clothing, toys, and electronics) through low cost and efficiency, producing a range of exports to Europe and the United States. However, Macau fell behind Hong Kong and Singapore in attracting electronic assembling and computer technologies in the 1980s and 1990s. Since the early 1990s, however, the manufacturing sector's share in the GDP has been steadily declining because of strong competition from China's Special Economic zone of Zhuhai. The manufacturing sector is dominated by small- and medium-size enterprises, which specialize in small-volume and high-quality garments, toys, leather goods, and artificial flowers. It also produces optical goods, electronics, and machinery.

Manufacturing was negatively affected by the 1997 Asian financial crisis. However, Macau escaped a large-scale **recession** because the local business community switched quickly between markets and products, and because most of the goods were produced by small private enterprises for export to the United States, Europe, and East Asia. Macau benefited from the existence of U.S.-imposed quotas for goods made in China. Such restrictions can provide an initiative for **re-export** of goods manufactured in China and labeled as Macau-made products. During recent years, Macau reportedly became heavily involved in producing pirated computer software, CD-ROMs, and DVDs, which have been distributed in Southeast Asia, Eastern Europe, and even in the United States.

SERVICES

TOURISM. Tourism is the most important sector of Macau economy, providing direct employment (such as in hotels and restaurants) for 28 percent of the labor force or 78,708 people. Macau has long been a tourist destination for business people and other travelers due to its famous gambling facilities. Macau promotes itself as a "dream come true," offering 24-hour gambling services, a multicultural environment, exotic festivals, and tax-free shopping (most items are 50 percent cheaper than in Hong Kong). According to the national authorities, Macau had a total room capacity of 8,886 in 1999, although most of the hotels report an occupancy rate below 60 percent. Most visitors come for a short stay, arriving from Hong Kong, China, Taiwan, and Japan. The number of tourists visiting the territory rose steadily throughout the 1980s and 1990s, reaching a peak in 1996 with 8.1 million tourists. There was, however, a sharp decline of around 15 percent in 1997 and a further 3 percent in 1998, because of economic turmoil in the region and the outbreak of gangster-style killings and bombings on Macau's streets. In 1999 and 2000, tourism was helped by the economic recovery in Hong Kong and Taiwan.

GAMBLING. Gambling, together with tourism, is one of the most important sectors of Macau's economy. Macau's casinos and its facilities for horse and greyhound racing have attracted visitors to the region for decades. The government has benefited from the gambling industry by imposing direct taxes, which accounted for 44 percent of its revenue in 1999. However, the dark side of the industry is gambling addiction and criminal activities. In fact, the outbreak of violence in hotels, restaurants, and casinos in 1997 and 1998 was largely attributed to feuds between powerful organized crime syndicates.

FINANCIAL SERVICES. Macau has a small but vibrant financial services sector, which provided employment for 8 percent of the labor force, or 22,488 people, in 1999. It is built around banking, insurance, and business services. The banking sector was opened for international competition in 1992, and there were 9 local and 13 foreign incorporated banks in 1998. The largest banks are Banco Comercial Portugues and Bank of China. The 1997 Asian financial crisis hurt the financial services sector, although there were no major bank collapses or bankruptcies.

RETAIL. The **retail** sector is well-established in Macau, providing inexpensive products to the local population and foreign tourists. Large supermarkets are complemented by thousands of small retail shops where tourists and local consumers can buy a wide variety of duty-free products much cheaper than in Hong Kong. Thousands of small- and medium-size restaurants serve exotic Asian cuisine, attracting gourmands (sophisticated diners) from across the region.

INTERNATIONAL TRADE

Macau was declared a "free port" in 1849, establishing very few barriers against the import of goods and services and promoting export to the international market. Historically, the United States has remained one of Macau's major trading partners, with exports to the United States reaching US$1 billion dollars in 1999 or 46.9 percent of all exports, consisting mainly of textiles, garments, and manufactured electronics. The European Union is the second-largest trading export market, accounting for US$663 million or 30.2 percent of total exports. China and Hong Kong were also important destinations for Macau exports, accounting for 9.2 percent and 6.8 percent of exports, respectively.

Imports originating from China accounted for US$725 million, or 35.6 percent of its total imports in 1999, so Macau was running a considerable trade deficit with this country. Hong Kong was the second largest source of import accounting for US$368 million or 18.1 percent of total imports. The European Union, Japan, and the United States were other major sources of imports.

Macau's economic vulnerabilities were exposed during the sharp oil price increases in 2000 and 2001. It also faces increasing competition from low-cost, mass-production enterprises in neighboring China and is vulnerable to changes in the U.S. and EU markets.

MONEY

Macau's currency, the pataca, is pegged to the Hong Kong dollar and remains stable. The territory managed to avoid high inflation or economic recession during last

Trade (expressed in billions of US$): Macau

	Exports	Imports
1975	.133	.161
1980	.538	.544
1985	.905	.778
1990	1.694	1.532
1995	1.977	2.021
1998	2.122	1.937

SOURCE: International Monetary Fund. *International Financial Statistics Yearbook 1999.*

Exchange rates: Macau

patacas (MOP) per US$1	
Jan 2001	8.033
2000	8.025
1999	7.990
1998	7.978
1997	7.974
1996	7.966

Note: Linked to the Hong Kong dollar at the rate of 1.03 patacas per Hong Kong dollar.

SOURCE: CIA *World Factbook 2001* [ONLINE].

2 decades, although the Asian financial crisis of 1997 did hurt its economy. There was an economic slow-down in 1997 and 1998, affecting all sectors and bringing a small rise in inflation. However, in 1999 and 2000 the economy overcame these difficulties and began to grow again. One of the unique features of Macau's economy was that in 1998 it experienced **deflation** of 4 percent.

Due to the regional economic downturn, the value of the Macau patacas declined slightly against the U.S. dollar from 7.962 in 1996 to 8.1 in January 2000.

POVERTY AND WEALTH

Macau has no official poverty line, so the number of citizens living at that level is difficult to determine. Also, many foreign workers illegally enter Macau looking for jobs, and these individuals cannot be accounted for in official statistics. Their presence in Macau ebbs and flows, as the government fights a continuing battle to deport illegal entrants into the region.

Macau's gap between poor and rich is wide. Macau's per capita GDP was listed in 2000 at US$17,500, placing it 37th in the world. While impressive considering Macau's small size, such wealth does not get equally passed among all strata of society. Gambling, which provides more than 40 percent of Macau's income, benefits the poor very little.

GDP per Capita (US$)

Country	1996	1997	1998	1999	2000
Macau	13,600	15,600	16,000	17,500	17,500
United States	28,600	30,200	31,500	33,900	36,200
China	2,800	3,460	3,600	3,800	3,600
Hong Kong	26,000	26,800	25,100	23,100	25,400

Note: Data are estimates.

SOURCE: *Handbook of the Nations*, 17th, 18th, 19th and 20th editions for 1996, 1997, 1998 and 1999 data; CIA *World Factbook 2001* [Online] for 2000 data.

WORKING CONDITIONS

In 1998, Macau's labor force stood at 281,117 people, with an unemployment rate of around 6.9 percent. Macau's economy experienced 2 difficult years in 1997 and 1998, when the unemployment rate was on the rise. However, since the beginning of the economic recovery in 1999 and 2000, there has been some improvement in the labor market. Wages are generally below those in neighboring Hong Kong, but much higher than in China, although there is no regulation of minimum wages or unemployment compensations.

The Macau government encourages women to work, and women made up around 40 percent of the workforce in 1999. In 1984 child labor was banned in Macau, but the law has never been strongly enforced.

Trade unions are allowed in Macau, within the framework of its labor law and other regulations. Labor actions, such as strikes, slow downs, and other protests, are very rare in Macau.

COUNTRY HISTORY AND ECONOMIC DEVELOPMENT

1513. First Portuguese ship anchors in the Pearl River estuary.

1557. Portuguese establish a trading post on the islands.

1849. Portugal proclaims Macau a free port.

1949. Communist party comes to power in China.

1951. Portugal officially makes Macau an overseas province.

1974. A military coup takes place in Portugal. The new democratic Portuguese government offers to return Macau to China.

1979. Portugal and China establish diplomatic relations.

1987. Portugal and China reach a formal agreement on future status of Macau.

1989. People demonstrate in Macau in support of the pro-democracy demonstrations in Beijing.

1989. Chinese language is made an official language along with Portuguese.

1992. A new banking ordinance is introduced, opening the banking sector for international competition.

1997. Outbreak of contract killings and bombings indicate the beginning of the war between organized criminal groups.

1999. Macau officially returns to Chinese jurisdiction.

FUTURE TRENDS

Macau has experienced 2 decades of economic growth, benefiting from the rise of international trade and the dismantling of barriers to free movement of goods and services in the global market. This has elevated standards of living and brought prosperity to Macau's people. However, globalization also made the territory's economy vulnerable to downturns in the international market and to increasing competition from other Asian economies. Still, Macau has been able to find its economic niche in services and manufacturing.

On the eve of the 21st century, the territory was finally returned to Chinese sovereignty, but was given a high degree of economic autonomy. In the longer term, Macau will depend on economic and political developments in China and Hong Kong. Future economic development depends fully on the capability of the government to maintain the country's economic position and to promote economic growth based on capital- and skill-intensive technologies.

DEPENDENCIES

Macau has no territories or colonies.

BIBLIOGRAPHY

Economist Intelligence Unit. *Country Report: Macau.* London: Economist Intelligence Unit, December 2000.

International Financial Statistics Yearbook, 1999. Washington, DC: International Monetary Fund, 2000.

Macau Economic Services. <http://www.economia.gov.mo>. Accessed February 2001.

Macau Statistics and Census Service. <http://www.dsec.gov.mo>. Accessed February 2001.

Macau Statistics and Census Service, Macau. *Yearbook of Statistics.* Macau Special Administrative Region, People's Republic of China: DSEC, 1995.

Macau Trade and Investment Promotion Institute. <http://www.ipim.gov.mo/pageen/home.asp>. Accessed February 2001.

Monetary Authority of Macau. <http://www.amcm.gov.mo>. Accessed February 2001.

Porter, Jonathan. *Macau, The Imaginary City: Culture and Society, 1557 to the Present.* New Perspectives in Asian Studies. Boulder, Colorado: Westview Press, 2000.

U.S. Central Intelligence Agency. *World Factbook 2000: Macau.* <http://www.cia.gov/cia/publications/factbook/geos/mc.html>. Accessed February 2001.

—Rafis Abazov

MALAYSIA

CAPITAL: Kuala Lumpur.

MONETARY UNIT: Malaysian ringgit (also known as the Malaysian dollar). One Malaysian ringgit (RM1) equals 100 sens. There are coins of 1, 5, 10, 20, and 50 sens. Paper currency is in denominations of RM2, 5, 20, 50, and 100.

CHIEF EXPORTS: Electronic equipment, petroleum and liquefied natural gas, chemicals, palm oil, wood and wood products, rubber, textiles.

CHIEF IMPORTS: Machinery and equipment, chemicals, food, fuel, lubricants.

GROSS DOMESTIC PRODUCT: US$229.1 billion (at purchasing power parity, 1999 est.).

BALANCE OF TRADE: **Exports:** US$83.5 billion (1999 est.). **Imports:** US$61.5 billion (1999 est.).

COUNTRY OVERVIEW

LOCATION AND SIZE. Malaysia is situated in Southeast Asia, bordered by Thailand in the north, Indonesia in the south, and the Philippines in the east. The country has an area of 329,758 square kilometers (127,320 square miles). Comparatively, the territory of Malaysia is slightly greater than that of the state of New Mexico, the fourth-largest state in the United States. The Federation of Malaysia consists of 13 states, and is divided into 2 parts: 11 states are located in Peninsular Malaysia (also called West Malaysia) and 2 comprise East Malaysia, which is situated on the island of Borneo (see map). Peninsular and East Malaysia are separated by 640 kilometers (400 miles) of the South China Sea. Malaysia's capital city, Kuala Lumpur, is located in southeast Peninsular Malaysia, just 300 kilometers (187 miles) from Singapore. However, a new capital, Putrajaya, is being developed outside the overcrowded metropolitan area as the new administrative center. The strategic importance of Malaysia is in its location along the Strait of Malacca, which is a major sea-route connecting the Far East to Asia, Europe, and the Middle East.

POPULATION. The population of Malaysia was estimated at 21,793,000 in July 2000. It has almost doubled since the 1960s due to improved health, medical facilities, and longer life expectancy. In 2000, the birth rate stood at 25.3 per 1,000, while the death rate stood at 5.25 per 1,000. The estimated population growth rate is 2.01 percent and if the current trend remains unchanged, the population could reach 31 million by 2020. The population is very unevenly distributed, with almost 81 percent, or 17.5 million, living in Peninsular Malaysia, and 19 percent, or 4.2 million, living in East Malaysia. The population density is about 129 people per square kilometer (334 people per square mile) in Peninsular Malaysia and about 20 people per square kilometer (52 people per square mile) in East Malaysia.

Malaysia is a multinational and multicultural country with a very diverse population. Malays and several indigenous groups make up 58 percent of the population. Ethnic Chinese, the second-largest ethnic group, make up 26 percent of the population; Indian descendants make up 7 percent, and various other groups together account for the remaining 9 percent. The current ethnic structure was formed during the colonial era in the 19th and 20th centuries, when the British administration encouraged migration from India and especially from China. The Malaysian population is very young, with 35 percent below age 14 and just 4 percent of the population older than 65. Urbanization came to Malaysia relatively late. In 1970, just over 28.8 percent of Malaysians lived in urban areas. In 1999 over half of Malaysians—57 percent—were living in urban areas. It is expected that within the next 10 to 15 years more than 70 percent of the population will live in urban areas, mainly in the Peninsular Malaysia.

Religion plays a very important role in the country. Islam is the official national religion and nearly all Malays are Muslims. Most ethnic Chinese are Buddhist. The majority of Indians (comprising the descendants of migrants from what became India, Pakistan, and Bangladesh) are Hindu, although there are many Muslims among members of this community. The largest proportion of the Chinese community has traditionally lived in the urban areas, while Malays have often lived in the country's rural regions.

In 1960, the Malaysian population was about 8 million, and the country at one time had one of the highest

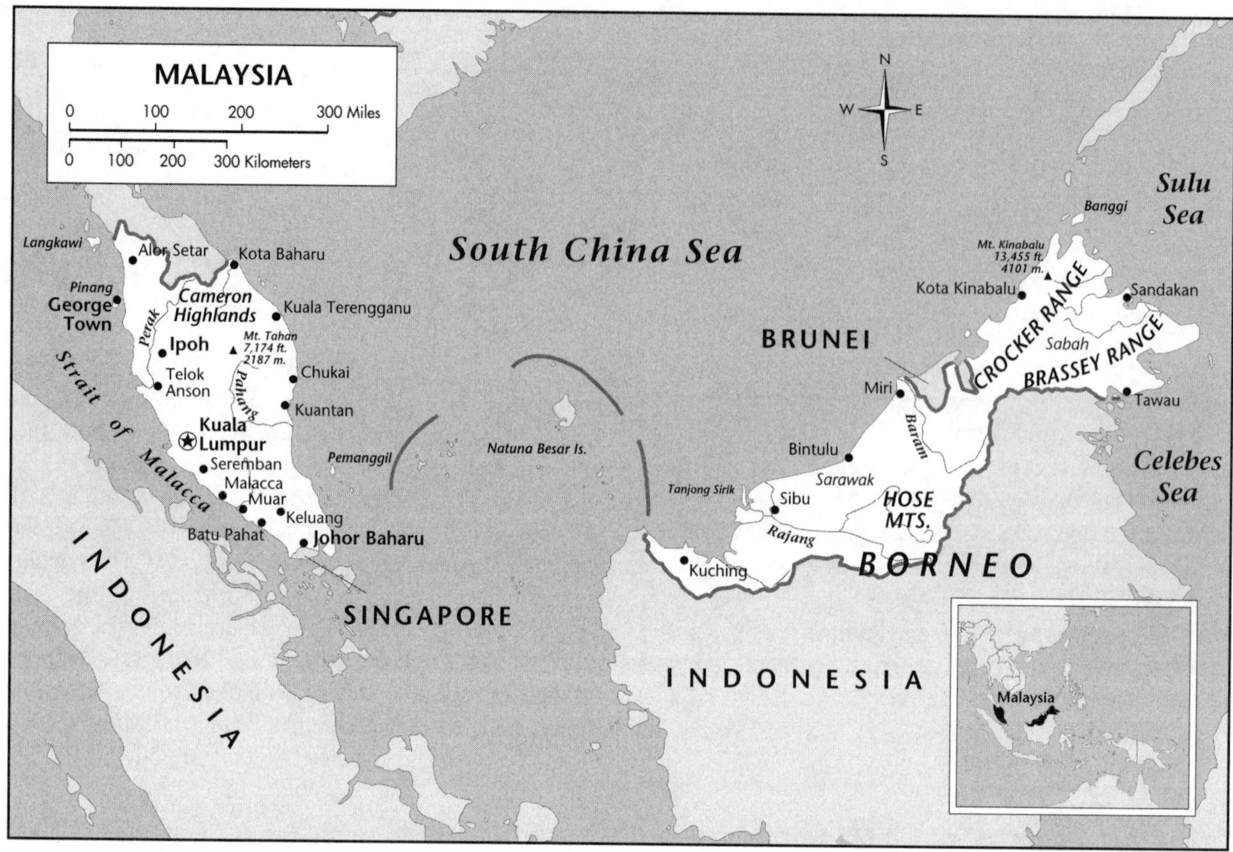

birth rates in Asia. The population doubled between 1960 and 1990, although population growth began to decline in the 1990s. The decline in population rates could be linked to the socio-economic changes in the economy that tightened the labor market and increased the number of women in the workforce, and the better education of women. Malaysia experienced an inflow of foreign workers employed mainly in the low-skill and low-wage construction and services sectors and in agricultural plantations. The Malaysian government would like to regulate the inflow of illegal migrants, who arrive mainly from neighboring Indonesia, as well as from Bangladesh and Burma, attracted by the geographical proximity and higher wages.

OVERVIEW OF ECONOMY

At present, Malaysia's industrial and service sectors are the 2 major pillars of the national economy. However, agriculture and mining were the 2 dominant sectors during its early history. Britain had slowly but steadily advanced into the region in the 18th and 19th centuries, establishing control over the territory of what would become present-day Malaysia. The British were attracted by the rich natural resources of this region and its convenient location along the Strait of Malacca, which was the main sea route connecting the Far East with British India and Europe. The British established large-scale plantations and introduced new commercial crops (rubber in 1876, palm oil in 1917, and cocoa in the 1950s). They also developed a large mining sector and encouraged migration of Chinese and Indian workers to these plantations and mines.

In August 1957, the Federation of Malaya was granted independence within the Commonwealth of Nations. In 1963, the Malaysian Federation was founded, comprising the Federation of Malaya, Sabah, Sarawak, and the State of Singapore. Singapore, however, left in 1965.

Since achieving independence, the Federation of Malaysia faced a need to develop and to diversify its economy, having a rapidly growing population. The country abandoned reliance on the export of primary natural resources and agricultural products and established itself as a rapidly industrializing country with a diversified export base. By the beginning of the 21st century Malaysia had become one of the fastest growing economies in Southeast Asia and third-richest state (after Brunei and Singapore) in the regional grouping known as the Association of South East Asian Nations (ASEAN).

The Malaysian government promoted the free market with limited state intervention and export-oriented industrialization. Its exports to the international market were used to promote efficient use of the country's resources and generate **hard currency**, which was necessary for catching up and further developing into areas of technological and industrial innovation. In the mid-1960s, Malaysia established 5-year planning, targeting certain areas of economic growth and social changes, and allocating public resources for priority sectors of the economy and for **infrastructure** development. Despite these efforts, the government was reluctant to institute centralized control over the state's economy. The 5-year plans became a basis for official development strategies. For example, the recently completed "Seventh Plan" (1996–2000) targeted productivity growth and moved the country towards capital-intensive, high-technology industries. The political and inter-communal violence that had undermined the country's stability and security in the 1960s and 1970s gave way to a period of remarkable stability. This has attracted international investors and greatly contributed to the rapid economic growth of the 1980s and 1990s, especially in the manufacturing and service sectors of the Malaysian economy. Unlike the government of neighboring Indonesia, the Malaysian government has managed to keep its **external debt** at a relatively moderate level. In 1998, external debt stood at US$42 billion, or 59 percent of GDP with **debt service** payments of about US$6.0 billion. Estimates for the year 2000 estimated that Malaysian official reserves stood at US$29.6 billion. However, the **repatriation** of the profits by foreign investors may cause a problem for the Malaysian economy in the future.

The structure of the Malaysian economy has changed during the last 2 decades. According to the World Bank, the proportion of manufactured production grew from roughly 20 percent of GDP in the early 1980s to 31.5 percent of GDP in the late 1990s. Manufactured products accounted for around 85 percent of gross export earnings in 1999, with electronic goods becoming one of the most important products. The role of mining has steadily declined during the last few decades (Malaysia was one of the world's largest exporters of tin in the 1970s), now contributing just 7 percent of GDP. Malaysia continues, however, to export tin, gold, bauxite, ilmenite (a titanium ore), oil, and gas. Meanwhile, the role of agriculture in the country's economy has also been declining, although it provides employment to large numbers of Malaysians. Nevertheless, Malaysia remains one of the world's leading exporters of rubber and timber and produces almost half the world's palm oil. Tourism is another important and rapidly growing sector of the economy, with about 7.5 million tourists visiting the country in 1999 and contributing RM10 billion to the national economy.

Malaysia has a very diverse economy. The manufacturing sector is dominated by large **multinational corporations**, with a heavy Japanese presence among the largest companies. Meanwhile, the agricultural sector is dominated by medium and small firms. In East Malaysia, Sabah, and Sarawak, and in some northern states, many farmers are still engaged in subsistence agriculture. In the service sector, especially in **retail** trade, large international superstores such as Marks and Spencer, SOGO, and Yaohan are complemented by a number of medium and small enterprises.

Rapid economic growth and stability brought economic prosperity to a large proportion of the population, especially in urban areas. It also helped to keep unemployment at a very low 3 percent (for comparison, unemployment in the United States was 4.2 percent in 1999). In some sectors, Malaysia has begun to experience a shortage of labor. In the late 1990s, there was an inflow of large numbers of foreign workers through legal and illegal channels from neighboring Indonesia, with whom Malaysia shares some linguistic and cultural similarities, and from Bangladesh, the Philippines, and Burma (Myanmar). This inflow is sometimes blamed for existing criminal activities and **black market** operations.

Drugs are another important issue; Malaysia is situated very close to the so-called "Golden Triangle" (an area between Burma, Laos, and Thailand) that is the world's largest producer of illicit drugs such as opium. Malaysia is among the few countries in the world to have adopted the death penalty for possession and sale of drugs. However, neither organized crime nor the black market have had a significant impact on the national economy.

Due to the tremendous economic growth and its ability to preserve stability and promote its multicultural environment, Malaysia has become an increasingly popular destination for tourists from Europe, Japan, and North America. Malaysian tropical forests and beaches, colorful festivals in major cities, and luxurious hotels provide a vibrant environment for the development of hospitality businesses.

POLITICS, GOVERNMENT, AND TAXATION

Malaysia is a federal constitutional monarchy with a parliamentary democracy largely influenced by the British parliamentary system. The country consists of 13 states and 2 federal territories. The heads of 9 of the states are hereditary rulers, and the heads of the remaining 4 states are governors appointed by the sovereign, on the advice of the federal parliament. One of the unique features of the political system in Malaysia is that the sovereign (Paramount Ruler or *Yang di-Pertuan Agang* in Malay) is elected every 5 years by and from the 9 hereditary rulers of 9 states of Peninsular Malaysia. The sovereign is the supreme head of Malaysia and supreme commander of the armed forces, but his power significantly diminished in the 1990s due to the constitutional changes initiated by the parliament; at present he plays a visible but mostly ceremonial role in the political process in the country. The prime minister, who has considerable executive power, must be a member of the 192-seat House of Representatives, and he chooses the cabinet with approval from the sovereign.

There are a number of political organizations in Malaysia. Most prominent of them are the *Barisan Nasional* (National Front); the governing coalition of 14 parties that forms the United Malays National Organization (UMNO); the Malaysian Chinese Association (MCA); and the Malaysian Indian Congress (MIC). Of the opposition parties, the most influential is the *Barisan Alternatif* (Alternative Front), which brings together the *Parti Islam sa-Malaysia* (Islamic Party of Malaysia), the Democratic Action Party, and some others. The governing coalition of the UMNO, MCA, and MIC was formed on the eve of independence, on a platform of achieving independence by peaceful means. It was transformed into the National Front after bloody inter-communal riots between Malays and Chinese in 1969. The Malayan Communist Party (MCP), which had gained much of its influence through its leading role in the resistance to Japanese occupation during World War II, ran a militant campaign for independence that did not get mass support and led to the Malayan Emergency (1948–1960), a period of social and political unrest. The MCP was banned and has never played an active political role in independent Malaysia.

Since Malaysia achieved independence, preservation of the balance between the main ethnic groups, political stability, and equal access to the national wealth were the major issues that shaped political debate and fueled conflict in the state. The coalition between the 3 main political parties and later the National Front, which represent the biggest ethnic communities in Malaysia, came to power on a platform of national consolidation and state paternalism (where the state makes decisions in social and economic affairs that in other countries would have been left to individuals and the market). This coalition was able to overcome deep divisions in Malaysian society and implement a successful policy of economic reforms, and it has remained in power ever since. In economic areas, the government has taken a very active role in the development and industrialization of the national economy. This has included significant investment in the state sector, a close alliance between government and private businesses, and the gradual **privatization** of state enterprises under a major privatization program launched in 1986.

In response to growing discontent between ethnic communities and the resultant rising social polarization, in 1970 the Malaysian government introduced a 20-year program called the New Economic Policy (NEP). The program was intended to encourage rapid economic growth in all sectors of the national economy, promote private entrepreneurship—especially among representatives of poor communities—and support small and medium-sized businesses. It was also intended to attract foreign investments, especially in modern technologies, by offering cheap and well-trained labor. At the same time, however, the government made major efforts to redistribute wealth. The NEP recognized the need for radical social changes and aimed to improve living conditions, economic power, and access to education and social benefits for Malays and indigenous people. These groups, who were called *Bumiputera* (sons of the soil), received privileged access to public services, were granted land rights and preferences in education and training, and benefited from job quotas in the **public sector**. This program was successful, and Malaysia achieved impressive economic growth, especially during the late 1970s, and throughout the 1980s. Between 1979 and 1989, the average annual GDP growth rate was around 5.2 percent, with manufacturing growing at an annual average of 8.2 percent and exports of goods and services at an annual average of 9.3 percent. In 1990, the NEP was replaced by the National Development Policy (NDP), which continued to promote economic growth, but relaxed some of the social requirements and privileges institutionalized under the NEP. Between 1989 and 1999, the average annual growth of GDP was around 7.6 percent, with manufacturing growing at an even more impressive 10.2 percent.

However, in 1997 Malaysia was affected heavily by the Asian financial crisis that started with the currency collapse in neighboring Thailand. Unlike Indonesia and Thailand, Malaysia became the only country in Southeast Asia to reject the International Monetary Fund's package of conditions and financial assistance, blaming international speculators for creating the crisis. The government, led by Prime Minister Dr. Mahathir bin Muhammad, opted for direct state intervention, imposing temporary restrictions on the currency exchange market and introducing various other measures, while his deputy called for further **liberalization** and economic **restructuring**. Against the recommendations of the International Monetary Fund (IMF), the Malaysian government temporarily established tough capital-control measures to contain **capital outflow**. The Malaysian currency, the Malaysian ringgit, was pegged to the U.S. dollar at a fixed rate of RM3.8 per U.S. dollar (according to the IMF, out of 16 larger **emerging market** economies, only China and Malaysia have fixed pegs). Although the IMF initially criticized the Malaysian government's imposition of capital control and other restrictive measures, it later recognized their effectiveness.

Allegedly, disagreement over the handling of the crisis led to the dismissal of Anwar Ibrahim, finance minister and deputy prime minister, who was also expelled from the UMNO, effectively ending his career. In 1998, Anwar was arrested on charges of corruption and homosexual activity and allegedly beaten while in custody. The trial consolidated Anwar's supporters and sparked protests across Malaysia in 1998 and 1999. Nevertheless, he was convicted on controversial charges of obstruction of justice. This trial undermined Mahathir's popularity at home and his standing internationally. The irregularities during the trial and police actions against demonstrations were condemned by human rights activists around the world.

The major proportion of government revenue comes from taxes, totaling 76 percent of revenue in 1999 (46 percent from **direct taxes** and 30 percent from **indirect taxes**). In 1999, the **income tax** rate was 28 percent for both resident and non-resident companies; however, companies resident in Malaysia have tax exemption on income brought in from abroad. The Malaysian government has introduced a number of initiatives for manufacturing activities, tourism, the agricultural sector, transportation, and communication.

INFRASTRUCTURE, POWER, AND COMMUNICATIONS

From the colonial era, Malaysia inherited relatively well-developed but unevenly distributed infrastructure and transportation networks. After achieving independence, the Malaysian government made considerable efforts and large investments in expanding its highways, railroads, seaports, and airports. More recently, the government played an active role in encouraging development of modern modes of communications such as satellite telecommunications and the Internet. In the late 1990s, the government launched a privatization program in the transportation and communication sector, which brought private investments, allowed more flexibility, and provided initiatives for managers to increase profitability and production efficiency.

Malaysia is served by a network of 94,500 kilometers (58,721 miles) of primary and secondary roads, 70,970 kilometers (44,100 miles) of which are paved. This includes 580 kilometers (360 miles) of superior quality expressways, which connect Kuala Lumpur with Singapore and with major seaports and other destinations. However, the road transportation system is still underdeveloped in East Malaysia (Sabah and Sarawak), with most of the roads in Peninsular Malaysia. In the 1990s, with the rapidly growing number of privately-owned cars (840,000 new registrations in 1997 alone), the roads in the capital and other major cities became highly congested. This also brought air pollution in Kuala Lumpur to a very high level, which combined with pollution from forest fires in the Indonesian part of Borneo to create hazardous smog in 1997 and 1998. In 1996, there was a total of almost 7 million motor vehicles registered in Malaysia, including 2.8 million passenger cars, 3.4 million motorcycles and mopeds, 37,000 buses and coaches, and 400,000 trucks and vans. In response to the growing number of cars on the national roads, the government invested in development of the public transport system, including modernization of the country's railways and the construction of a light rapid-transit system in Kuala Lumpur.

Malaysia has a railway system of about 1,800 kilometers (1,120 miles), part of which was planned for privatization in 1998–99. In 2000, only 148 kilometers (92 miles) of railways were electrified. The major tracks run from Singapore to Kuala Lumpur, and further to Pinang and Bangkok (Thailand). However, the railways are unevenly distributed. There is only 1 railway track of about 134 kilometers (83 miles) in East Malaysia (in Sabah). Malaysia intends to invest heavily in development of a monorail system in Kuala Lumpur and into building new railways. The biggest project is the US$632 million (RM2.4 billion) Express Rail Link (ERL), which will connect Kuala Lumpur Central (the main railway station in the Kuala Lumpur City) with Kuala Lumpur International Airport (KLIA). In 1996–97, the 8.6-kilometer Kuala Lumpur People Rapid Transit (monorail) was built at a cost of US$300 million (RM1.14 billion). The U.S.-based Parsons Transportation Group provided design and engineering services to the local Malaysian firm build-

Communications

Country	Newspapers	Radios	TV Sets[a]	Cable subscribers[a]	Mobile Phones[a]	Fax Machines[a]	Personal Computers[a]	Internet Hosts[b]	Internet Users[b]
	1996	1997	1998	1998	1998	1998	1998	1999	1999
Malaysia	158	420	166	5.2	99	6.9	58.6	23.53	1,500
United States	215	2,146	847	244.3	256	78.4	458.6	1,508.77	74,100
China	N/A	333	272	40.0	19	1.6	8.9	0.50	8,900
Indonesia	24	156	136	N/A	5	0.9	8.2	0.76	900

[a]Data are from International Telecommunication Union, *World Telecommunication Development Report 1999* and are per 1,000 people.
[b]Data are from the Internet Software Consortium (http://www.isc.org) and are per 10,000 people.

SOURCE: World Bank. *World Development Indicators 2000.*

ing Kuala Lumpur's light rail transit systems. Several other multi-multimillion dollar railway projects have been initiated, but some were put on hold due to the difficulties caused by the Asian financial crisis.

Malaysia's seaports were established during the colonial era and served as merchant ports as well as British naval bases. The major ports are Kelang, George Town, Pinang, and Kuantan on the Peninsula, and Kota Kinabalu and Kuching in East Malaysia. During the last few decades, these ports were expanded to serve rapidly-growing Malaysian exports and imports. The West Port of Port Kelang has seen RM2.2 billion worth of combined (private and government) investments, while there has been RM2.8 billion worth of investment in the Tanjung Pelepas Port. Competition has grown between Malaysia and Singapore for servicing international ships and handling containers, although 40 percent of Malaysia's international trade was handled through Singapore until recently. In 1998 Malaysia's seaports handled 83 million metric tons of cargo. In late 2000, there was an announcement that the world's largest container line, Maersk-Sealand, intends to move its regional trans-shipment operations from Singapore to the Malaysian port in Johor.

Malaysia has also promoted development of aviation in order to serve growing tourism and business needs. The country has 32 airports with paved runways, and 83 airports with unpaved runways. The largest of them, the US$3.2 billion state-of-the-art Kuala Lumpur International Airport, was opened in 1998. It is capable of handling 25 million passengers and 1.2 million tons of cargo annually. U.S. firms, including Harris, FMC, Adtranz, and Honeywell, have been awarded contracts to supply passenger trams, jetways, and information systems for this new airport. Malaysia transformed its national partly-privatized air carrier, Malaysian Airlines, into a world-class company, operating a fleet of about 100 aircraft.

In Peninsular Malaysia, electrical power is supplied by the predominantly state-controlled *Tenaga Nasional* company. Due to the rapid industrial development and growing demand for electricity, considerable efforts were made to privatize the national utility company and develop private initiatives to build and operate new power generating plants. To this end, a private consortium, the Independent Power Providers (IPPs), was established. Malaysia has sufficient reserves of oil, gas, and coal to meet its energy needs. Additionally, in East Malaysia there is huge potential for building hydroelectric power plants, but their development will require considerable investments. In the mid-1990s, the Malaysian government considered building the Bakun Hydro-electric Dam, which would have been one of the world's largest dams, in Sarawak; the controversial plan was abandoned, however, due to financial difficulties. In 1998, Malaysia produced 57.45 billion kilowatt hours (kWh), 94 percent of which was produced using fossil fuel and 5.22 percent by hydroelectric power plants.

Telecommunications services in Malaysia are provided by several competing companies. The largest is Telecom Malaysia, which formerly had a state **monopoly** in the sector. The quality of telecommunication services is up to international standards, thanks to an inflow of private investments and the government's initiatives in developing this sector. In 1998, the country had 4.4 million telephone lines and 2.17 million mobile phones. In 1999 there were 8 major Internet service providers (including Telecom Malaysia, MIMOS Ltd., and Maxis Ltd.), with a number of new companies announcing their intention to enter the market. In 1998, the Malaysian government announced the development of the multi-billion-dollar Multimedia Super Corridor (MSC). This ambitious project, 15 kilometers wide and 50 kilometers long, and stretching from Kuala Lumpur to the new international airport, is planned to become a Malaysian "Silicon Valley." The MSC will include 2 "smart cities," employing a high-technology environment, high-capacity telecommunications, sophisticated infrastructure, and even "electronic government."

ECONOMIC SECTORS

By international standards, Malaysia has a medium-sized, but rapidly growing economy. It is self-sufficient in important natural resources, including gas and oil, and has a good environment and climate for the production of various crops. Its location, on a crossroads of major sea routes that connect the Far East to South Asia, the Middle East and Europe, provides some additional advantages for the development of its international trade.

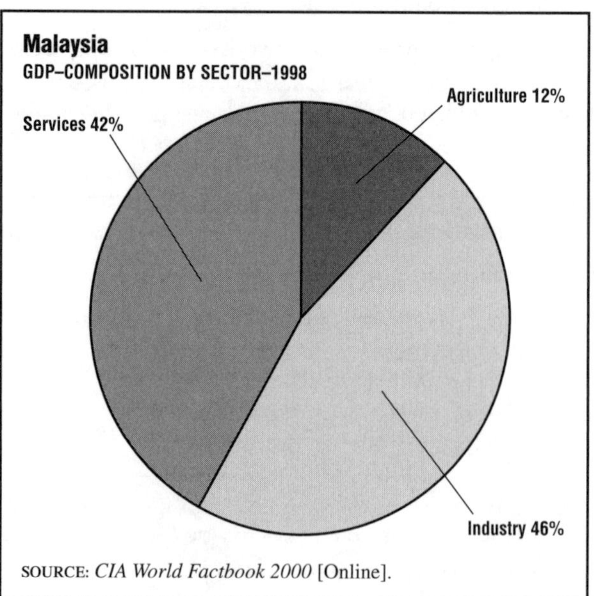

SOURCE: *CIA World Factbook 2000* [Online].

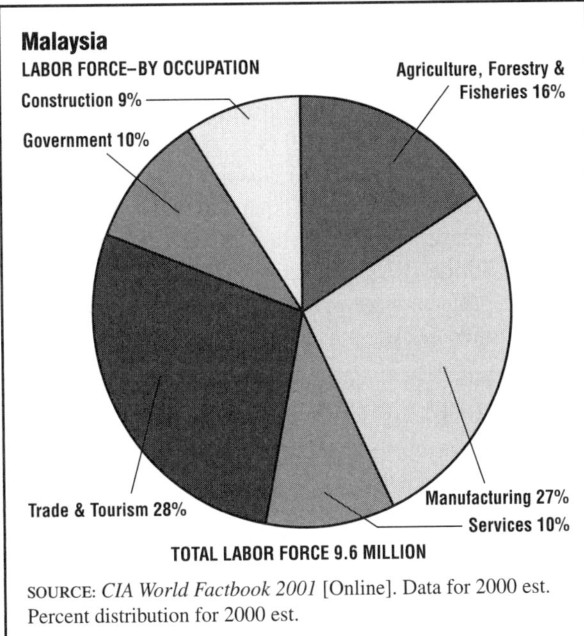

SOURCE: *CIA World Factbook 2001* [Online]. Data for 2000 est. Percent distribution for 2000 est.

Malaysia has a diversified and rapidly expanding manufacturing sector, which between 1989 and 1999 grew at an annual average of 10 percent. Although in many areas of manufacturing, it relies on imported technologies and foreign investments, Malaysia was able to join the world's leaders in some fields. In the 1990s, it became the world's third-largest producer of integrated circuits and one of the leading producers of domestic appliances. Some of the world's largest corporations, such as Dell and Microsoft of the United States, NEC and Mitsubishi of Japan, and others, have opened branches in Malaysia.

Agriculture is still an important export earner, although it experienced stagnation with an average annual growth of only 0.2 percent between 1989 and 1999. Malaysia is the world's largest producer of palm oil, accounting for almost half of the world's production. In the past, the country also was the world's largest producer of rubber, but in the early 1990s it was overtaken by Thailand and Indonesia. Malaysia remains the world's fourth-largest producer of cocoa. Nevertheless, the share of agriculture in the GDP declined from 29 percent in 1970 to 12 percent in 1998.

The role of the mining sector, which once played a very important role in Malaysian exports, is also declining. For a long time, Malaysia was the world's largest producer of tin, but in the early 1990s was overtaken by Brazil and neighboring Indonesia. Malaysia has relatively large reserves of gas and oil. The country is ranked 13th in terms of the world's gas reserves and 22nd in oil reserves.

Malaysia also tries to promote its service sector, which has grown steadily over the last 2 decades, becoming the second-largest sector of the Malaysian economy. However, in doing so, Malaysia has to compete with neighboring Singapore. Local trade, tourism, and other services currently make important contributions to the country's GDP, providing employment for 32 percent of the Malaysian **labor force**.

AGRICULTURE

Agriculture remains an important sector of Malaysia's economy, contributing 12 percent to the national GDP and providing employment for 16 percent of the population. The British established large-scale plantations and introduced new commercial crops (rubber in 1876, palm oil in 1917, and cocoa in the 1950s). The 3 main crops—rubber, palm oil, and cocoa—have dominated agricultural exports ever since, although the Malaysian share of the world's production of these crops declined steadily during the last 2 decades. In addition to these products, Malaysian farmers produce a number of fruits and vegetables for the domestic market, including bananas, coconuts, durian, pineapples, rice, rambutan (a red, oval fruit grown on a tree of the same name in Southeast Asia), and others. The Malaysian tropical climate is very favorable for the production of various exotic fruits and vegetables, especially since Peninsular Malaysia seldom experiences hurricanes or droughts.

As rice is a staple foodstuff in the everyday diet of Malaysians and is a symbol of traditional Malay culture, the production of rice, which stood at 1.94 million metric tons in 1998, plays an important part in the country's agriculture. However, the overall production of rice does not satisfy the country's needs, and Malaysia imports rice from neighboring Thailand and Vietnam.

In 1999, Malaysia produced 10.55 million metric tons of palm oil, remaining one of the world's largest producers. Almost 85 percent or 8.8 million metric tons of this was exported to international market. Malaysia is one of the world's leading suppliers of rubber, producing 767,000 metric tons of rubber in 1999. However, in the 1990s, large plantation companies began to turn to the more profitable palm oil production. Malaysia also is the world's fourth-largest producer of cocoa, producing 84,000 metric tons in 1999.

Logging in the tropical rainforest is an important export revenue earner in East Malaysia and in the northern states of Peninsular Malaysia. In 2000, Malaysia produced 21.94 million cubic meters of sawed logs, earning RM1.7 billion (US$450 million) from exports. Malaysia sells more tropical logs and sawed tropical timber abroad than any other country, and is one of the biggest exporters of hardwood. Despite attempts at administrative control and strict requirements regarding reforestation in the early 1990s, logging companies often damage the fragile tropical environment. Sharp criticism from local and international environmentalist groups gradually led to bans on the direct export of timber from almost all states, except Sarawak and Sabah. In December 2000, the government and representatives of indigenous and environmentalist groups agreed that there is a need to adopt standards set by the international Forest Stewardship Council (FSC), which certifies that timber comes from well-managed forests and logging companies have to be responsible for reforestation.

INDUSTRY

MINING. Tin, oil, and gas are the major natural resources of export significance produced by the mining sector in Malaysia. The mining of tin was introduced during the colonial era and until the 1980s the country was the world's largest producer of tin, being overtaken in the early 1990s by Brazil and neighboring Indonesia. The major mines are situated in Peninsular Malaysia, making it easy to transport their products to the nearest seaports. Malaysia's exports of tin declined from 36,812 metric tons in 1994 to 22,376 metric tons in 1998, affected by fluctuations in the world market.

During recent decades, Malaysia has increased production of crude petroleum and natural gas. In 1999, it produced 693,000 barrels of crude oil per day and 3.8 billion cubic feet of liquefied natural gas (LNG). The high-quality oil is extracted mainly from offshore platforms in the states of Terengganu, Sabah, and Sarawak, with a total of about 40 oilfields in operation (1999). There are 5 oil refineries situated in Malaysia. The production of gas increased steadily in the 1990s to meet the rising demand in the domestic and international markets, with exports mainly going to Taiwan, South Korea, and Singapore. Malaysia was ranked thirteenth in the world in terms of gas reserves and twenty-second in oil reserves in 1999. The state-controlled petroleum corporation, Petronas, has been seeking a greater role in the international market, investing in promising new projects in the Middle East and Southeast Asia.

Overall, mining plays a declining role in the national economy of the country, contributing just under 7.3 percent of GDP and providing employment for 39,000 people or under 1 percent of the labor force (1998). However, there is great potential for development of this sector, since Malaysia has various relatively under-exploited mineral resources in East Malaysia (Sabah and Sarawak), including bauxite, iron ore, copper, ilmenite, and gold. Additionally, there are large offshore reserves of high-quality oil and gas.

MANUFACTURING. Malaysia has established a diverse and quickly-growing manufacturing sector that plays an increasing role in the Malaysian economy. Manufacturing contributes about 29 percent of the GDP, providing employment to 2.3 million people or 27 percent of the workforce (1999). From the late 1970s, the proportion of GDP provided by the manufacturing sector in Malaysia grew from 20.2 percent in 1979 to around 29 percent in 1999. The United States continues to be the single largest foreign investor in Malaysia's manufacturing sector, with approved new manufacturing investments totaling US$1.37 billion (RM5.2 billion) in 1999. The major investment projects were in the chemical, electronics, and electrical industries.

Malaysia built up its manufacturing sector mainly in the 1970s and 1980s, utilizing its long-established industrial centers on the island of Pinang and the Kelang Valley, its well-developed transportation infrastructure (including seaports and railways), and the entrepreneurial skills of its small and medium-sized businesses. The industrial sector initially consisted of oil refining, machinery assembly, and light industries (including foodstuff processing and textile manufacturing). However, as in neighboring Singapore, the Malaysian manufacturing sector was boosted in the 1970s and 1980s by the extensive growth of the electric assembly and electronics sectors. Malaysia became an important producer of radios, television sets, stereo equipment, and other related products. In the 1980s, the Malaysian government launched its national automobile project, the locally produced Proton car (in cooperation with Mitsubishi of Japan), and in the late 1980s, it started exporting the Proton to the international market. In the 1990s, there was further growth in the manufacturing sector, especially in export-oriented electronics production, including semiconductors, silicon wafers, and other items. Malaysia has become the world's third-largest producer, and one of the world's largest exporters, of semiconductors.

As in neighboring Singapore, the Malaysian government has played an active role in industrialization and economic development. In this regard, the Malaysian Industrial Development Agency (MIDA) has been instrumental in promoting the rapid development of targeted sectors of industries (especially knowledge- and technology-intensive sectors), since all industrial projects that involve **foreign direct investments** (FDIs) must be approved by the MIDA. The government also used direct investments and encouraged the inflow of FDIs, establishing special export-processing zones where investors were given access to well-developed infrastructure and enjoyed tax breaks and other privileges. Since the 1980s, the government has actively promoted the electronics, information technology, and multimedia sectors, and has encouraged the relocation of labor-intensive industries to Indonesia and Thailand.

Most of Malaysia's electrical and electronic products are produced for export to the United States, Europe, and other markets. This makes its manufacturing economy vulnerable to downturns in the regional and international market. Despite some restrictive measures and financial initiatives, Malaysia was negatively affected by the 1997 Asian financial crisis. In 1997 and 1998, its manufacturing sector experienced serious contraction; dozens of plants were closed and thousands of workers lost their jobs. In 1998 alone, the sector was reduced by about 10.9 percent across the board. However, in 1999 and 2000, Malaysia managed to reverse the **recession** in manufacturing, and this sector experienced an impressive growth of 12 percent per annum.

Malaysia is one of ASEAN's leading exporters of furniture, with total exports reaching about US$1.02 billion (RM3.9 billion) in 1999. Access to cheap local wood makes Malaysian furniture manufactures very competitive in the international market. In 1999, the United States was the largest single market for Malaysian wooden furniture (37 percent), followed by Japan (14 percent), Singapore (9 percent), and the United Kingdom (9 percent). If the rapid growth in this sector remains unchanged, by 2005 Malaysia could become one of the top ten furniture exporters in the world.

SERVICES

TOURISM. Tourism is becoming an increasingly important sector of Malaysia economy. Together with the retail sector, it provides employment for almost 1.57 million people, or around 17 percent of the labor force. Roughly 7.5 million tourists visited the country in 1999, contributing RM10 billion to the national economy. This makes tourism one of Malaysia's top foreign exchange earners. According to the national authorities, the country has 1,426 hotels, the total room capacity of which almost doubled during the 1990s to about 110,000 in 2000. Most visitors have been from Singapore, Thailand, Indonesia, Japan, China, the United Kingdom, and Australia.

In order to develop tourism, Malaysia has promoted its diverse cultural environment, hosting a number of cultural festivals and performances. It has also publicized its rich natural heritage, which includes tropical forests, coral reefs, unspoiled mountain ranges, rivers, and national parks. The country offers tax-free bargain shopping and excellent service, with top-class hotels such as Sheraton, Hilton, Intercontinental, and other well-established international chains opening branches. It offers a wide variety of activities, from eco-friendly and adventure tourism to scuba diving and relaxed family holidays on the numerous Malaysian islands and beaches. Additionally, Malaysia has signed visa-free regimes with most countries in Asia, the Americas, and Europe, enabling international tourists to travel to Malaysia without obtaining entry visas. In 1997, however, tourism suffered from the regional financial crisis and by the smog caused by several months of forest fires in Indonesia. The number of tourist arrivals declined significantly in 1997 and 1998; however, there was a strong recovery in arrivals in 1999 and 2000.

FINANCIAL SERVICES. The financial service industry is another rapidly growing sector of Malaysia's economy. In terms of employment, it almost doubled from 230,900 people in 1988 to 447,200 people in 1998. Traditionally, this sector was built around the banking system, investments, insurance, and some other activities. For more than a decade until 1997, the financial service sector experienced rapid expansion fuelled by the inflow of Foreign Direct Investments (FDIs), reasonably cheap credits, and overall rapid economic growth in all sectors of the economy. Malaysia developed a sophisticated computerized banking payment system, encouraging development of electronic payment systems and electronic banking. The U.S.-based Motorola and Unisys have taken part in these projects as members of consortia that included local companies. Malaysia's government considered developing Kuala Lumpur into a regional financial center, competing with Singapore for this role, although it was slow to allow foreign brokers to operate at the Kuala Lumpur Stock Exchange (KLSE).

The 1997 regional financial crisis started with the collapse of the Thai currency (the Baht), which severely affected the Malaysian financial sector. Share and property prices declined significantly, provoking panic among local and international investors. Within a short time, the Malaysian ringgit had depreciated against major international currencies, especially the U.S. dollar. This inflicted considerable damage on local businesses, as a significant number of credits were in U.S. dollars and local companies faced extreme difficulties repaying those credits. The Kuala Lumpur Stock Exchange (KLSE) lost more than half its value, plunging from RM807 billion in the middle of 1996 to RM376 billion in the middle of 1997. In response to this crisis, the Malaysian government imposed currency and capital controls, locked in foreign investors' share holdings for 1 year, and initiated a share-buying scheme with the government-controlled funds. In 1999 and 2000, financial services began their recovery, and the government slowly eased various restrictions and state control in this sector.

RETAIL. Traditionally, in Malaysia many small and medium-sized businesses were built around the retail sector and were often associated with small shops and cafés run by Chinese merchants. The retail sector grew, in terms of its size and quality of service, due to a general rise in income among the population and an increase in tourism arrivals. In the 1990s, major international retail chains such as Yaohan and SOGO of Japan, Marks and Spencer of the United Kingdom, MAKRO of France and fast-food franchises such as McDonald's, Kentucky Fried Chicken (KFC), and others opened outlets in Malaysia. However, there are still a number of small family-run traditional shops and cafés, selling both imported and locally-made products.

Tourists can also buy pirated products, including footwear, optical disks (CDs), and computer software. According to one study, piracy may have accounted for losses of US$84.2 million (RM320 million) in market value in 1999. In April 2000, the United States Trade Representative (USTR) placed Malaysia on the special Priority Watch List for its failure to reduce pirated optical disc production and export. In response to this, the Malaysian police regularly launch crackdowns on unlicensed software businesses.

INTERNATIONAL TRADE

Malaysia's international trade experienced tremendous growth throughout the last 3 decades. The Malaysian government welcomed export-oriented industries, created a very positive investment environment in the country, and fostered close relations between government and private businesses. The government established a few barriers on the importation of goods and services, although it often opted for selective intervention and for protecting some sectors of the national economy. Over 5 years, Malaysia more than doubled its exports from US$29.416 billion in 1990 to US$74.037 billion in 1995. After the 1997 regional financial turmoil, Malaysia experienced economic recession, although this recession was much smaller and less destructive than that in South Korea or in Indonesia. Due to tough economic measures, Malaysia's exports recovered and reached US$83.5 billion in 1999.

Historically, the United States has long been one of Malaysia's largest trading partners, its exports to the United States reaching 21.9 percent in 1999, a year in which it was the United States' 12th largest trading partner. Trade between these 2 countries consisted mainly of assembled electrical goods and manufactured electronic products. Neighboring Singapore is traditionally the second-largest export market, with the proportion of goods to Singapore reaching 16.5 percent and dominated by electrical and electronic equipment, machinery, metals, and mineral fuels. Japan is in third place at 11.6 percent, and, once again, exports are dominated by electrical and electronic equipment, machinery and mineral fuels. Other export destinations are the Netherlands, Taiwan, and Hong Kong.

Trade (expressed in billions of US$): Malaysia

	Exports	Imports
1975	3.843	3.566
1980	12.958	10.820
1985	15.442	12.301
1990	29.416	29.258
1995	74.037	77.751
1998	73.304	58.326

SOURCE: International Monetary Fund. *International Financial Statistics Yearbook 1999.*

Japan, the United States, and Singapore are also the 3 largest sources of imports. Most Malaysian imports originate from Japan, with the Japanese share of imported products reaching 20.8 percent in 1999, and consisting mainly of electrical and electronic equipment and machinery. The second most important source of imports is the United States, totaling 17.4 percent and dominated by electrical and electronic equipment and transportation equipment. Malaysia was the United States' 17th largest export market in 1999. Malaysia's third most important source of imports is Singapore, totaling 14.0 percent.

During the last 3 decades, Malaysian exports shifted from the sale of agricultural products, raw and processed natural resources, and labor-intensive manufactured goods (including clothing, footwear, and textiles) to the sale of skill-intensive products, including electrical and electronic equipment and parts, and services. The proportion of exported electrical machinery, appliances, and parts—including semiconductors, electronic equipment, and electrical appliances—reached almost 56 percent in 1998. The other important export products were commodities, chemicals and chemical products, manufactured metal products, and textiles, clothing, and footwear.

Malaysia has managed to maintain a positive trade balance, exporting more goods than it imports. Even during the recession of 1997 and 1998, the country had a large **trade surplus** of US$4.0 billion in 1997 and US$17.7 billion in 1998.

In the mid-1990s Malaysia faced growing competition from neighboring Indonesia, the Philippines, and Thailand, which could offer cheaper labor and larger and growing domestic markets. However, recent political and economic uncertainty in the region, especially military conflicts and terrorist activities in Indonesia and the Philippines has undermined the attractiveness of those markets. This has given an advantage to politically and economically stable Malaysia, although its government has often been criticized for the undemocratic measures used to maintain stability and political balance within the country.

Although Malaysia's industrialization and economic growth is highly dependent on international trade, the Malaysian government was less supportive of full economic liberalization than neighboring Singapore.

Malaysia's leadership was quite reluctant to support free trade within the Asia Pacific Economic Co-operation (APEC) region, arguing that developing countries need more time to prepare for lifting all trade barriers. Additionally, the Malaysian prime minister, Dr. Mahathir, suggested setting up a new regional body, the East Asian Economic Caucus (EAEC), in order to strengthen the negotiating power of East-Asian countries with regard to the North American Free-Trade Agreement (NAFTA) and the European Union.

MONEY

During the last 2 decades the value of Malaysian currency has shown remarkable stability, mainly due to the country's steady economic growth and regular state intervention into the currency **exchange rate**. The Malaysian dollar was floated in 1973, and in that year its exchange rate stood at around RM2.45 per US$1. At the same time, the Malaysian dollar became the sole unit of legal tender, as Singapore and Brunei currencies were excluded from free circulation in the country. The government periodically revised its exchange control regulations, introducing further liberalization of the controls. In 1985, the Malaysian ringgit was valued at RM2.48 per US$1, and this exchange rate remained practically unchanged until the 1997 Asian financial crisis.

During the period between 1973 and 1997, inflationary pressure was relatively small, with a peak **inflation rate** of around 17 percent in 1974. Remarkable stability was supported by a very high rate of savings. Malaysia has one of the highest savings rates in the world, at a level of around 40 percent of GDP. However, Malaysians also borrow rampantly, with a large proportion of investments directed to the booming property market and stock market. Outstanding loans were equivalent to 170 percent of GDP by the end of 1997, one of the highest such ratios in the world.

The Malaysian banking system is well established, with 38 commercial banks operating in the country in 1996, including 14 foreign banks and 12 merchant banks. The foreign banks were represented by the biggest names, such as ABN AMRO Bank of the Netherlands, Mitsubishi and Tokyo banks of Japan, Citibank of the United States, Standard Chartered Bank of the United Kingdom, and others. However, the fundamental problem of the banking system in Malaysia, as in other emerging markets in Asia, was its exposure to **bad loans**, allegedly made to politically well-connected businessmen and to overheated property and share markets. This was an important factor that eventually led to a financial downturn.

Exchange rates: Malaysia

ringgits (RM) per US$1	
Jan 2001	3.8000
2000	3.8000
1999	3.8000
1998	3.9244
1997	2.8133
1996	2.5159

SOURCE: CIA *World Factbook 2001* [ONLINE].

The 1997 Asian financial crisis affected all regional currencies, dragging them downwards. The property and share markets also dwindled, putting additional pressure on the currencies. The Malaysian ringgit had plummeted from about RM2.55 per U.S. dollar in early 1997 to about RM3.75 in April 1998, and further to RM4.2 in August 1998 (speculations against the Malaysian ringgit on the currency exchange market largely contributed to this downturn). In response to this pressure, in September of 1998 the Malaysian government introduced a range of capital and currency-exchange control measures. A key component of this unprecedented move was pegging the Malaysian ringgit at RM3.80 per US$1. The Malaysian government also closed all legal channels for the transfer of Malaysian ringgit abroad and froze the repatriation of stock assets abroad held by non-residents in Malaysia for a period of 12 months. It even limited its own tourists headed abroad from taking more than RM500 in cash.

Such tough measures reduced the impact of the financial turmoil of 1997 and 1998, although they were sharply criticized by the IMF and other international organizations. In August 1998, Russia defaulted on its international obligations, while Malaysia was slowly achieving economic recovery. Malaysia rejected financial assistance from the IMF and kept its external debt at the relatively moderate level of US$42 billion, or 59 percent of GDP, with debt service payments of about US$6.0 billion (1998). In order to rehabilitate **non-performing loans** (NPLs), the Malaysian government established the *Danaharta,* an asset-managing company with the task of buying and rehabilitating NPLs, and the Corporate Debt Restructuring Committee, which facilitated voluntary debt restructuring between creditors and debtors. By May 2000, the *Danaharta* had acquired about 42 percent of NPLs, with a total value of US$9.63 billion. The government also injected US$1.9 billion into 10 banking institutions. In 1999 and 2000, Malaysia's economy was recovering, prompting the government to ease many of the restrictive measures, although it will take time for international investors to revive their confidence in the Malaysian market.

Malaysia has a single stock exchange, the Kuala Lumpur Stock Exchange (KLSE). During the period of expansion in the 1980s and 1990s, the KLSE was among the fastest growing stock exchanges in the region, with ambitions to become one of the region's leading financial centers. However, the KLSE lost ground after the stock market collapse in 1997, with some shares losing up to 80 percent of their value. With the strong economic recovery, there was a return of investors and the KLSE strengthened in late 1999 and 2000.

POVERTY AND WEALTH

Malaysia experienced extraordinary economic growth during the last 3 decades, which brought prosperity and higher standards of living to the majority of the people. One of the most important achievements in Malaysia has been the elimination of extreme poverty and hunger. The urban areas—especially the capital Kuala Lumpur, and major tourist destinations and industrial cities such as George Town, Malacca, and Petaling Jaya—enjoy a quality of living very similar to that in developed countries. The major cities have first-class shopping centers, condominiums with air-conditioning and swimming pools, expensive private schools, and elite clubs. The rural population, meanwhile, often lives in traditional wooden houses in *kampungs* (villages) with limited facilities.

The monthly gross household income nearly doubled from MR1,167 in 1990 to MR2,007 in 1995. There has emerged a fairly strong middle class. However, incomes are still distributed unevenly. For instance, the wealthiest 20 percent of Malaysians control 53.8 percent of the wealth, while the poorest 60 percent of the population controls just 21.3 percent of wealth. At the very bottom of the income range, the poorest 20 percent of the population controls only 4.5 percent of wealth. Disparities exist along both geographic and ethnic lines. In general, the Chinese population, which has traditionally lived in urban areas and been involved in small and medium-sized businesses or employed in various industries, has had higher incomes than the Malays, who often live in small towns and villages and were traditionally engaged in agriculture. Secondly, there are considerable differences in standards of living, incomes, and access to medical and other social benefits in different parts of the country. Peninsular Malaysia, where the majority of the population lives, has much higher standards of living compared to East Malaysia.

GDP per Capita (US$)

Country	1975	1980	1985	1990	1998
Malaysia	1,750	2,348	2,644	3,164	4,251
United States	19,364	21,529	23,200	25,363	29,683
China	138	168	261	349	727
Indonesia	385	504	603	778	972

SOURCE: United Nations. *Human Development Report 2000; Trends in human development and per capita income.*

Distribution of Income or Consumption by Percentage Share: Malaysia

Lowest 10%	1.8
Lowest 20%	4.5
Second 20%	8.3
Third 20%	13.0
Fourth 20%	20.4
Highest 20%	53.8
Highest 10%	37.9

Survey year: 1995

Note: This information refers to income shares by percentiles of the population and is ranked by per capita income.

SOURCE: *2000 World Development Indicators* [CD-ROM].

Since 1970, the Malaysian government has actively implemented social policies aimed at the elimination of poverty and social inequality, and the development of a **social welfare system**. The communal unrest of 1969 prompted the Malaysian government to introduce the New Economic Policy (NEP). This 20-year program established state support of poor communities and access to education and social benefits for Malays and indigenous people (the *Bumiputera*). This latter aspect included the establishment of privileged access to public services, the granting of land rights, preference in education and training, and job quotas in the public sector. In the 1980s, Malaysia's leadership envisioned the formation of the *Malay Baru* (New Malays), a better-educated, politically and socially active people able to live in harmony with other communities. In the early 1990s the government relaxed some privileges and reduced some quotas for *Bumiputera,* making the social welfare system more inclusive and accessible to a wider range of people than it had been before.

The recent economic turbulence of 1997 and 1998 brought higher unemployment, higher prices, and lower incomes. This particularly affected the most vulnerable social groups of society, not only in rural areas, but also in major urban centers. Nevertheless, there were no large groups of people migrating from the country, and Malaysia's quality of life remained much better than in neighboring Indonesia, the Philippines, or Thailand. Around 6.8 percent of the population lived below the poverty line in 1997, most of them in East Malaysia (for comparison, in the neighboring Philippines 32 percent of the population lived below the poverty line in 1997). The economic recovery of 1999 and 2000 reversed the decline in incomes and standards of living.

WORKING CONDITIONS

During the last decade the Malaysian labor force has grown rapidly, due to robust economic growth and the large proportion of young people born in the 1970s. In

1999, the Malaysian labor force was 9.3 million people, with an unemployment rate of 3 percent, or around 270,000. Due to rapid expansion of all sectors of the national economy, there has been a high demand for all types of workers, especially skilled labor in the manufacturing sector and well-trained professionals in the services sector. This led in turn to better wages and rapidly improving working conditions.

The Malaysian government is trying to develop better education at all levels, as it wants to attract skill-intensive industries and services to the country. Primary education is compulsory, and young people may choose between a large number of both public and private schools and colleges. There is an established system of vocational and technical training. A number of Malaysians receive their education overseas, many of them with state support, although during 1997 and 1998, many students returned home. The most popular destinations for overseas education are the United States, England, Canada, and Australia. However, even the rapidly growing numbers of educated and trained Malaysians cannot meet market demand. In the late 1990s, Malaysia experienced shortages of medical doctors, information technology specialists, and professionals in various other areas. In order to meet growing demand of university-trained professionals, in 1994 Malaysia allowed foreign universities to establish campuses in the country.

The higher wages and better working conditions attract large numbers of temporary workers from neighboring Indonesia, Bangladesh, Thailand, and the Philippines. Many of them are hired to work in the low-skill and low-wage construction and service sectors and on agricultural plantations. However, Malaysia has also experienced an inflow of illegal foreign workers, prompting the government to implement harsh detention measures and mass deportation of unauthorized arrivals. Malaysian law does not allow foreign workers to join trade unions. The working conditions of illegal workers are generally inferior to those enjoyed by legally contracted workers. However, labor contractors may be prosecuted if workers complain about abuses or other problems.

The first trade unions appeared in Malaysia before World War II. There are currently 544 trade unions in Malaysia, engaging in the union activities of just over 11 percent of the workforce. Most of the **private-sector** trade unions are members of the Malaysian Trade Union Congress (MTUC), which was established in 1951. Around 90 unions of public- and civil-sector employees are members of the Congress of Unions of Employees in the Public and Civil Services (CUEPACS). Unions maintain their independence from the government and from political parties; by law, union officers may not hold principal positions in political organizations. However, some individual trade union leaders have been elected to the parliament, and the leader of MTUC joined the ruling party in 1997. The Malaysian Trade Union Act guarantees the right to form or participate in trade union activities, but it restricts the right to strike, calling for "socially responsible behavior." Strikes are extremely rare in Malaysia for several reasons, including strong demand in the labor market and the government's promotion of "industrial harmony." In case of labor disputes, the Ministry of Human Resources may intervene in conciliation procedures; in extreme cases, disputants may refer their case to the Industrial Court. The Industrial Relations Act prohibits employers from taking actions against workers for participating in lawful trade-union activities. There is no national minimum wage, although there have been calls recently from trade unions for its introduction. The Employment Act of 1955 established a maximum 48-hour working week.

The Malaysian Constitution prohibits forced and bonded labor by children, and the government claims that it rigorously enforces child-labor provisions. However, the International Confederation of Free Trade Unions estimates that 75,000 children are engaged as laborers. Faced with the shortages in the workforce, the Malaysian government encourages women to work, providing various initiatives. Currently, more than 35 percent of the labor force are women. However, unionization among women is generally lower than among men.

COUNTRY HISTORY AND ECONOMIC DEVELOPMENT

1400s. The Kingdom of Malacca is founded.

1511. Malacca is conquered by the Portuguese under Afonso de Albuquerque.

1641. The Dutch establish control in the region.

1786. The Sultan of Kedah leases the island of Pinang to the British East India Company.

1819. Singapore is founded by Sir Thomas Raffles.

1824. Malacca falls to Britain.

1888. British North Borneo and Sarawak become British protectorates.

1896. The British form a federation, comprised of Perak, Selangor, Negri Sembilan, and Pahang.

1909. British acquire control over Kedah, Kelantan, Perak, and Terengannu—the 4 northern states in Peninsular Malaysia—from Siam (now Thailand).

1921. Port Singapore becomes the principal base for British Navy in East Asia.

1942. Malay Peninsula is occupied by Japanese Army.

1945. Malaya is liberated from Japanese occupation.

1946. British impose a system known as the Malayan Union and grant political rights to immigrants.

1948. The Federation of Malaya is established.

1948. State of Emergency is declared in response to armed campaign by the Malayan Communist Party.

1957. Malaya is granted independence within the British Commonwealth.

1963. Malaysia is expanded to form the Federation of Malaysia; Singapore joins the federation.

1965. Singapore leaves the federation.

1967. Malaysia becomes a founding member of the Association of South East Asian Nations (ASEAN).

1969. Serious rioting breaks out in the capital city, Kuala Lumpur; more than 200 people killed.

1970. The Malaysian government introduces the New Economic Policy (NEP).

1981. Dr. Mahathir bin Muhammad becomes prime minister of Malaysia.

1983. Prime minister imposes restrictions on the power of the *Yang di-Pertuan Agang* and the Council of Rulers.

1995. The ruling political coalition *Barisan Nasional* wins parliamentary elections in landslide victory.

1997. In response to the Asian financial crisis, the government imposes restrictions on currency trading and announces public spending cuts.

1998. National Economic Action Council is established to advise the Malaysian Cabinet on the economic crisis.

1998. Prime Minister Mahathir bin Muhammad dismisses his apparent successor, Finance Minister and Deputy Prime Minister Anwar Ibrahim.

1999. The ruling political coalition *Barisan Nasional* wins parliamentary elections while losing 14 seats in the parliament.

FUTURE TRENDS

Malaysia's economy has benefited from several factors, including a stable political environment, an effective bureaucracy, flexible economic policies, export-oriented industrialization, and inflow of foreign direct investments (FDIs). This has brought prosperity and a high level of confidence to the majority of the population. The country has a healthy, rapidly growing economy, although its government has often been criticized for state intervention into economic development and the imposition of capital and currency exchange controls in 1998. However, subsequent events have shown that these were temporary measures, and the government is considering re-liberalization of its economy. **Inflation** remains low and is under control. Malaysian currency exchange is still tightly regulated and pegged to the U.S. dollar; with the economic recovery, the Malaysian ringgit might be floated again within the next few years. In 1999 and 2000, Malaysia achieved strong economic recovery and, if economic growth at an annual rate of 7.4 percent continues, within the next 20–30 years Malaysia may join the international club of developed nations. In 1998, as if to announce that it had arrived on the world stage, Kuala Lumpur saw the completion of the stunning Petronas Towers, the world's tallest skyscraper complex.

Nevertheless, there are several issues to be addressed. Malaysia's government has developed close relations with its private businesses. These "special relations" with some business groups have allegedly led to the emergence of political cronies with unlimited access to public resources. The experience of neighboring Indonesia shows that this is a dangerous trend that could negatively affect economic development in the future. In 1998–99, Malaysia was widely criticized for establishing increasingly tough political control of the country, and for some harsh measures against the opposition. It remains to be seen whether these measures have in the long term strengthened political stability or undermined it. The political succession of the current leadership will also be a problem. In neighboring Indonesia and Thailand, changes in the political leadership have led to destabilization of the political environment.

In the longer term, Malaysia will need to maintain its international competitiveness, since there is growing competition from other emerging markets for FDIs and for the transfer of modern technologies. Although political and social unrest in neighboring Indonesia and the Philippines has no direct effect on Malaysia, it threatens social stability by causing influxes of refugees and by undermining regional stability. Environmental issues are also important for Malaysia in the longer term as deforestation and global climate change may undermine the country's agriculture, which still plays an important role in the national economy. The recent forest fires in the Indonesian part of Borneo affected not only East Malaysia, but Peninsular Malaysia as well, by injecting hazardous air pollution. This sort of thing, if repeated, may undermine tourism, another important sector of the Malaysian economy. The forecast global economic slowdown may also negatively effect the export-oriented Malaysian economy.

DEPENDENCIES

Malaysia has no territories or colonies.

BIBLIOGRAPHY

Bank Negara Malaysia (Central Bank of Malaysia). "Current Highlights." <http://www.bnm.gov.my>. Accessed March 2001.

Department of Statistics, Malaysia. <http://www.statistics.gov.my>. Accessed March 2001.

Economist Intelligence Unit. *Country Profile: Malaysia.* London: Economist Intelligence Unit, 2000.

Economist Intelligence Unit. *Country Report: Malaysia.* London: Economist Intelligence Unit, November 2000.

Gomez, Terence E., and K.S. Jomo. *Malaysia's Political Economy: Politics, Patronage and Profits*, New York: Cambridge University Press, 1997.

The Government of Malaysia. *Prime Minister's Office.* <http://www.smpke.jpm.my>. Accessed March 2001.

Grouch, H. *Government and Society in Malaysia.* Singapore: Cornell University Press, 1996.

International Financial Statistics Yearbook, 1999. International Monetary Fund, 1999.

Jomo, K. S., and Greg Felker. *Technology, Competitiveness, and the State: Malaysia's Industrial Technology Policies.* London: Routledge, 1999.

Khoo, B. T. *Paradoxes of Mahathirism.* New York: Oxford University Press, 1995.

Kuala Lumpur Stock Exchange. <http://www.klse-ris.com.my>. Accessed March 2001.

Lucas, Robert E. B., and Donald Verry. *Restructuring the Malaysian Economy: Development and Human Resources.* London: MacMillan Press, 1999.

Malaysian External Trade Development Corporation. <http://www.matrade.gov.my>. Accessed March 2001.

The New Straits Times. <http://www.nstp.com.my>. Accessed March 2001.

U.S. Central Intelligence Agency. *CIA World Factbook 2000: Malaysia.* <http://www.cia.gov/cia/publications/factbook/geos/my.html>. Accessed March 2001.

—Rafis Abazov

MALDIVES

Republic of Maldives
Dhivehi Raajjeyge Jumhooriyyaa

CAPITAL: Malé.

MONETARY UNIT: Rufiyaa (Rf). One rufiyaa equals 100 laari. There are coins of 1, 2, 5, 10, 25, and 50 laari, and 1 and 2 rufiyaa. There are notes of 2, 5, 10, 20, 50, 100, and 500 rufiyaa.

CHIEF EXPORTS: Fish products, clothing.

CHIEF IMPORTS: Consumer goods, intermediate and capital goods, petroleum products.

GROSS DOMESTIC PRODUCT: US$540 million (1999 est.).

BALANCE OF TRADE: **Exports:** US$92 million (1999 est.). **Imports:** US$402 million (1999 est.). [*CIA World Factbook* indicates exports at US$98 million (1998) and imports at US$312 million (1998).]

COUNTRY OVERVIEW

LOCATION AND SIZE. A series of 1,190 coral islands grouped into 26 atolls (a ring-shaped coral reef enclosing a lagoon) located in the Indian Ocean, the Maldives has an area of less than 300 square kilometers (115 square miles) and a total coastline of 644 kilometers (400 miles). The islands form a narrow chain 820 kilometers (510 miles) in length and 130 kilometers (81 miles) in width within an area of 90,000 square kilometers (34,749 square miles) of ocean. Of these islands, around 200 are inhabited and 85 are tourist resorts. Comparatively, the area occupied by the Maldives is about 1.7 times the size of Washington, D.C. The capital city island, Malé, is located within Malé atoll, which is in the center of the strip of islands that makes up the Maldives. The Maldives is the smallest country in Asia.

POPULATION. From a 1980 level of 155,300, the population of the Maldives was estimated at 301,475 in July 2000. With the 2000 population growth rate at 3.06 percent per annum (one of the highest population growth rates in the world), by 2010 the Maldives population is expected to have almost doubled. In 2000, the birth rate stood at 38.96 per 1,000, while the death rate was 8.32 deaths per 1,000. With the continuation of a similar population growth rate, the population of the Maldives will fail to stabilize for at least another 50 years.

More than 200 of the 1,190 islands in the Maldives are inhabited, of which only 5 islands have a population of more than 3,000. The majority have a population of 500 or less. Nonetheless, the country has a very high population density of 916 people per square kilometer. Twenty-six percent of Maldivians live on the overcrowded capital island of Malé, with an average of 10 persons per household compared with a national average of 6.5. The implications of the country's high population growth and density are severe. The traditional construction material, coral, is near its point of full depletion. More importantly, the fresh water held beneath the soil surface is in rapid decline. This means that the Maldives faces the prospect of importing a large percentage of its water needs to support the growing population, unless there are fast developments in desalination services on the islands.

OVERVIEW OF ECONOMY

The Maldives government has followed a policy of free market economy, making it one of the most liberal in the developing world. This has had considerable benefits. The promotion of a favorable economic climate has assisted the economy's inflow of **foreign direct investment**. This doubled from an annual average inflow of $5 million between 1988 and 1993 to $10 million in 1999. But with the economy's high level of dependence on just 2 economic sectors—fisheries and tourism—it is highly susceptible to constant fluctuations on world markets. Total dependence on imports to supply a number of its sectors, such as textile manufactures and tourist supplies, means that the rise and fall of the rufiyaa on international money markets can significantly affect the competitive-

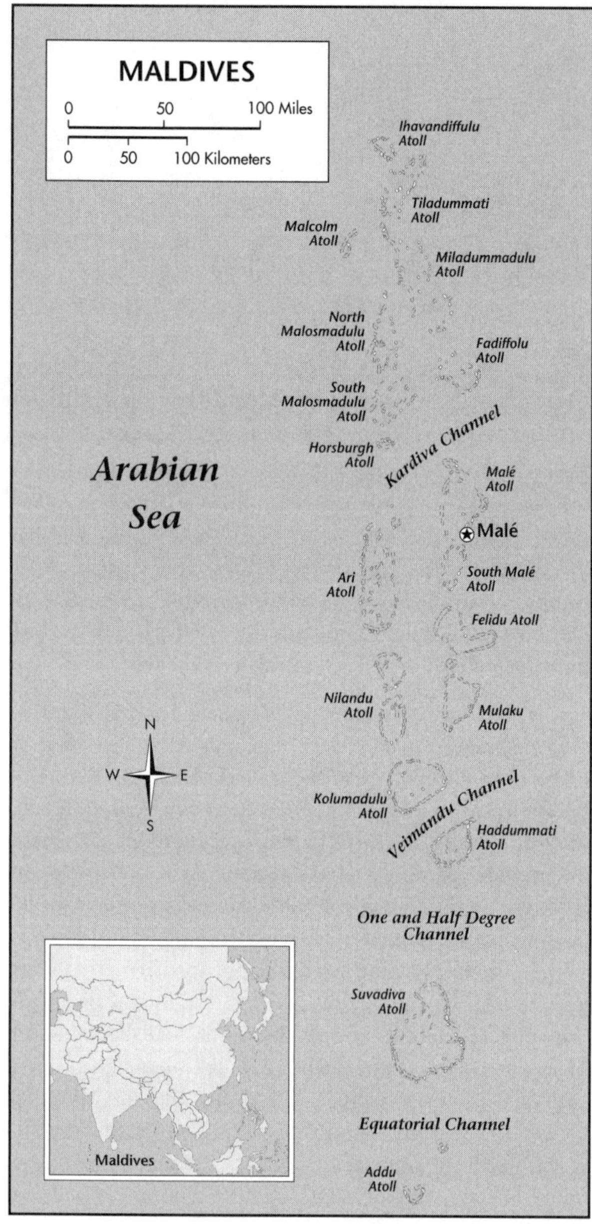

ness of exports and cost of imports. The simultaneous decline of fisheries exports and influx of tourists in the early 1990s led to a serious deficit in the national **balance of payments** that required the government to introduce unpopular cuts in public spending.

Compared to the other Maldives, Malé is highly developed. Some of the other islands have benefited from the carry-over effects of the tourism sector, the availability of arable land, or from the collection service for fish catches provided by the government. However, the geographical isolation of a significant number of islands means that their access to the productive sectors of the economy and to social services is very limited. The government has initiated a set of policies to address these disparities and spent 28.7 percent of its 1999 budget on atoll development. This was done in part to take the strain off the high population density in Malé and also to allow more of the outlying population access to the strategic economic situation of the capital. One example is Villingili, a nearby former resort island, which was transformed into a residential island with a commercial harbor. It now supports around 15,000 Maldivians. A similar government policy is to provide **infrastructure** and facilities to regional centers throughout the atolls to encourage people to move from isolated islands to local commercial focal points and develop the economy in a more unified trajectory.

Although the Maldives has benefited considerably from growth over the past 20 years, there are a number of factors that act as considerable limitations on the continued sustainable development of the economy. For example, the exploitation of coral for construction purposes is at such a level that it is estimated that all of the reefs in the north Malé atoll will be depleted by 2014. **National debt** has risen considerably, from $13 million in 1979 to $203 million in 1999. Rising population growth and such factors as the rise of tourism and the mechanization of the fishing fleet has meant that imports have risen significantly, especially for such commodities as petroleum products. Consequently, whereas exports only rose from $8 million in 1980 to $64 million in 1999, imports expanded from $29 million to $402 million. Although the total national balance of payments remained at an annual average of $7 million in credit between 1994 and 1999, the serious drain of imported goods limits the potential of reinvestment and development on the islands.

The Maldives Ministry of Planning and National development emphasizes the government's "international reputation for its high-level commitment to environmental protection, demonstrating its readiness to subordinate short-term economic gain to environmental conservation." This progressive policy-orientation entails a number of factors of self-interest ranging from the desire to maintain the country's natural beauty to continue enticing tourists, to the more serious issue of 80 percent of the land elevation being less than 1 meter above sea level. This means that the islands will be even more susceptible to storms and rising sea levels if the projected consequences of the "greenhouse effect" are realized.

POLITICS, GOVERNMENT, AND TAXATION

The formation of the Maldives as a political entity is generally dated from the period of conversion to Islam in the 1100s. This makes the Maldives one of the oldest surviving small states in the world. Unlike most other countries in the region, the Maldives was not subject to the overt domination of foreign powers. This is most likely due to the problems of navigating the sea around and within the islands as, without a high level of knowledge of the dangers of the reefs and shallow lagoons, ships would often be smashed or grounded. The Portuguese managed to rule the Maldives for a period of 17 years in the mid-1500s. They were soon thwarted in their dominance by a guerrilla war assisted by the Rajah of Cannanore in what is now India. Various sultans then ruled the Maldives unhindered, until Sultan Muhammad Muenuddin entered into an agreement with the British in 1887. The British, whose empire extended throughout South Asia, made the Maldives a British protectorate in return for the payment of tribute.

After a gradual rise in its level of sovereignty, the Maldives became fully independent of Britain on 26 July 1965. Three years after, a national referendum saw 80 percent of votes cast call for the abolition of the hereditary sultanate in favor of a republic, although the country's status as an Islamic state remained. This included civil law being subject to Sharia (Islamic law) which remained in place by mid-2001. Although the executive position of sultan was abolished, the office of the president wields similarly large powers. (The president is required to be a male Sunni Muslim.) The president is the head of state, the supreme authority defending the national faith of Islam, the chief executive, and commander-in-chief of the military. And not only does he have the power to appoint the prime minister and cabinet of ministers, but he can dismiss them too. Amir Ibrahim Nasir, formerly the prime minister under the sultan, was elected president in 1968. Nasir ruled until the 1978 elections, when he cited poor health and did not stand for office. He instead left for Singapore after the new president, Maumoon Abdul Gayoom, initiated investigations into Nasir's alleged misappropriation of government revenues.

President Gayoom was re-elected in 1998 for a fifth consecutive 5-year term with the support of 90.9 percent of votes cast. In each election, he ran unopposed—presidential candidates are selected by the Citizens' Majlis (parliament) and posed to the people in a simple "for" or "against" referendum. The Majlis itself consists of 48 members, 8 of whom are selected by the president, while voters in the Maldives' 20 administrative atoll districts elect the rest (2 members per district). In November 1988, Tamil mercenaries from Sri Lanka, in collusion with some Maldivian nationals, attempted to overthrow the government. However, President Gayoom appealed to India for military assistance, which swiftly foiled the rebels.

The Maldives electoral system has received criticism for being limited, unfair, and unrepresentative. For example, Freedom House (the U.S. political liberties and civil rights advocacy group) classified the Maldives in 2000 as "Not Free." Amnesty International (a London-based human rights organization) has reported the detention of a number of politically motivated prisoners. Gayoom himself is often cited as authoritarian. In a country profile on the Maldives, the British Broadcasting Corporation (BBC) suggested that Gayoom "has been accused of heading a small heredity elite which holds decisive power and which uses intimidation to discourage political activity." However, the government addresses these criticisms by maintaining that this limited style of democracy provides a stable and consistent form of rule that also acts to protect the basic tenets of the nation's Muslim faith. Maldives' brand of Islam is among the most emancipated of current Islamic states. This is exemplified by the Maldives' comparatively high rating in the Gender-related Development Index.

The Maldives government receives the majority of its revenues through **direct taxation** and the earnings of state-owned enterprise and property. There is no **income tax**. Import **duties** provided 63 percent of government tax revenues in 1997, while various taxes on the lucrative tourism sector accounted for 27 percent of tax revenues. Key non-tax revenue sources are government-owned property, such as resort islands which are leased to tour operators, and the profits from public enterprise, such as the regular collection of fisheries produce, which provided 46 percent of total government revenues in 1997.

INFRASTRUCTURE, POWER, AND COMMUNICATIONS

The Maldives transportation infrastructure is very limited. The capital city island, Malé, has 9.6 kilometers (6 miles) of coral highways. Due to their small size and the tiny amount of cars throughout the rest of the islands, the total quantity of roads is not known. There are no railways in the Maldives. Since the tourism boom of the 1970s, the availability and frequency of inter-island transportation has considerably improved. While the cheapest and most common mode of transport used by Maldivians are *dhonis* (wooden all-purpose water taxis/fishing boats), tourists and the wealthy have the option of using private seaplanes, helicopters, and speedboats. When travelling on an island, the majority of people use bicycles or motorbikes, although there are a limited number of cars and taxis in use on the more populated and larger islands.

When Malé International Airport on Hulhule Island (2.5 miles from Malé) was opened in 1981, it caused a considerable rise in tourist arrivals. While improved air transportation has benefited the tourism sector, international sea cargo remains very important. Malé's port can intake around 200,000 tons of cargo per year and offers shipping services to and from Europe and a large portion of Asia. With its fleet of 7 cargo boats and 1 container vessel, Maldives National Shipping Ltd. handles about 60 percent of the country's imports.

Communications

Country	Telephones[a]	Telephones, Mobile/Cellular[a]	Radio Stations[b]	Radios[a]	TV Stations[a]	Televisions[a]	Internet Service Providers[c]	Internet Users[c]
Maldives	21,000 (1999)	1,290	AM 1; FM 1; shortwave 1	35,000 (1999)	1	10,000 (1999)	1	2,000
United States	194 M	69.209 M (1998)	AM 4,762; FM 5,542; shortwave 18	575 M	1,500	219 M	7,800	148 M
India	27.7 M (October 2000)	2.93 M (2000)	AM 153; FM 91; shortwave 68	116 M	562	63 M	43	4.5 M
Sri Lanka	494,509 (1998)	228,604 (1999)	AM 26; FM 45; shortwave 1	3.85 M	21	1.53 M	5	65,000

[a]Data is for 1997 unless otherwise noted.
[b]Data is for 1998 unless otherwise noted.
[c]Data is for 2000 unless otherwise noted.

SOURCE: CIA *World Factbook 2001* [Online].

The **parastatals** the Maldives Electricity Bureau and the State Electricity Company (STELCO) provide power throughout over 95 percent of the Maldives inhabited islands. Tourist resort islands are required by the government to supply independent energy supplies, this is generally via oil-fuelled generators. However, wood accounts for 55 percent of total domestic energy consumption and is mainly used in households for cooking purposes.

Telecommunications facilities are of an excellent quality in Malé and throughout most of the tourist islands. By 2001, the government had successfully extended the availability of telephones throughout the vast majority of inhabited islands. Telecommunications are provided through a **joint venture** between the government and the British company, Cable and Wireless. By 1999, there were 8.1 Internet hosts per 100,000 people.

ECONOMIC SECTORS

The Republic of Maldives' economic sectors reflect the very small size of the population, a limited infrastructure principally caused by the country's division across hundreds of tiny islands, a low level of skilled labor, and the very limited level of agricultural potential and mineral resources. Consequently there are severe limits on domestic markets and the availability of land on those islands that are inhabited. Nonetheless, the country's situation as a series of small isolated islands works

Maldives
GDP–COMPOSITION BY SECTOR–1999 est.

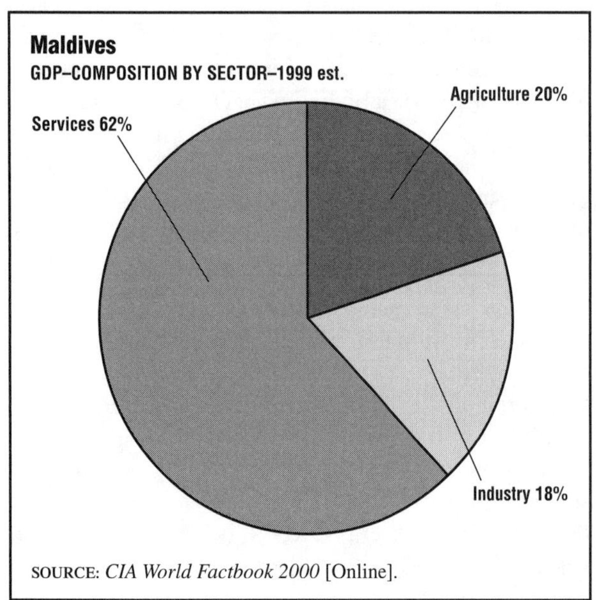

SOURCE: *CIA World Factbook 2000* [Online].

Maldives
LABOR FORCE–BY OCCUPATION

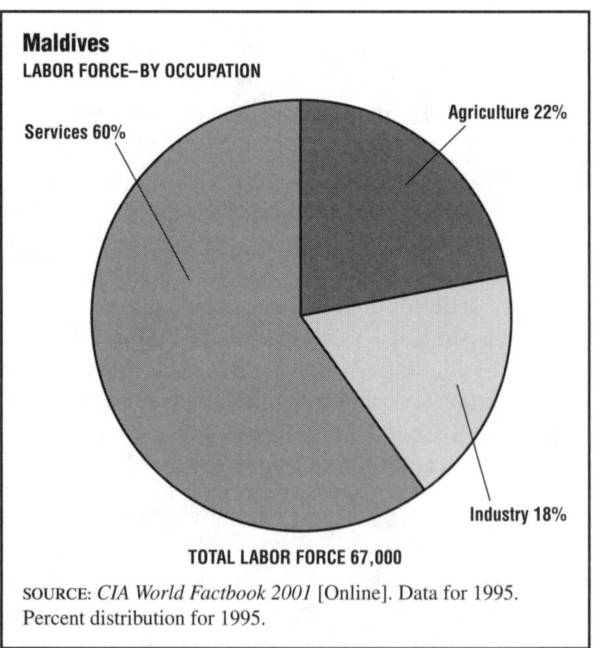

TOTAL LABOR FORCE 67,000

SOURCE: *CIA World Factbook 2001* [Online]. Data for 1995. Percent distribution for 1995.

more positively as a strategic trading point, a tourist destination, and as an excellent base for tapping the Indian Ocean's abundant fish stocks.

The Maldives economy consists of 3 main sectors—trade, tourism, and fisheries. Although the fisheries sector was historically the primary source of national employment and economic activity, the rise of tourism in the 1970s caused it to become the third most important economic sector by 2001.

AGRICULTURE

Traditional agricultural production in the Maldives is limited by poor soil, a low level of arable land, and a geographically split landmass which disallows large-scale commercial farming. In 1995, only 3,000 hectares of arable land was under permanent crops. There are, however, a number of crops grown for domestic consumption. These include coconuts, bananas, breadfruit, other exotic fruits, betel, chiles, sweet potatoes, and onions.

FISHERIES. Until the development of the tourist industry, the fisheries sector was the Maldives principle economic activity and source of export earnings. In 2000, the sector employed about 20 percent of the national workforce and acted as the main source of livelihood for a majority of Maldivians. In addition, it is the second largest source of foreign exchange and provides more than 10 percent of GDP. The government established the Maldives Fishing Corporation in 1979 to exploit the country's vast fisheries resource.

The use of fishing nets is illegal, and as a result, the more labor intensive traditional method of fishing by line and pole dominates. Nonetheless, the productivity of the fisheries sector has improved considerably during the 1990s. Although traditional small boats made of coconut wood remain in use, most are used in conjunction with outboard motors. The mechanization of the fishing fleet has been combined with the introduction of Fish Aggregating Devices (which allow the detection of shoals of fish). This meant that the nominal catch of fish in the Maldives expanded from 71,245 metric tons in 1989 to 118,183 tons in 1998. The opening of the Maldives **Exclusive Economic Zone** in the early 1990s meant that more Maldivian vessels were fishing in the sea around the islands. In fact, this zone allowed Maldivian fishermen to tap into a range of around 330 kilometers (200 miles). With the decline of fish stocks in the Atlantic Ocean, the price of fish on international markets seems likely to continue rising into the 21st century, although the subsequent increased pressure on Indian Ocean fish stocks threatens one of the foundations of the Maldives economy.

INDUSTRY

The Maldives industrial sector is small. Traditional industries are still in place. For example, women collect cowrie shells (the former national currency) for export. They weave the labor-intensive coir rope from coconut husks, which is a very strong, flexible and waterproof rope. Male carpenters build the traditional fishing boats (dhonis) from coconut trees, which can last up to 20 years. However, more modern developments have occurred in the Maldives industrial sector.

CANNING. The Maldives' primary industry is the canning and processing of fish. In 1998, $19.06 million of canned fish, predominantly tuna, was exported. The development of the Felivaru Tuna Fish Cannery in the early 1990s was a key factor in the modernization of this industry. The export of dried, smoked, and salted fish constituted an additional $9.07 million of exports in 1998. This constitutes a significant enterprise for levels of employment and national income, although it remains a more traditional industry. The canning industry is expected to continue to thrive and replace more traditional fish exports with the opening of the Kooddoo Fisheries Complex, which included large refrigeration facilities.

MANUFACTURING. The development of manufacturing is limited by the low level of domestic demand, limited skilled labor, and the lack of national resources. This means that many material and labor inputs into domestic goods rely heavily on imports. The economy has diversified into the production of clothing, both for domestic consumption and for export. In 1989, garment exports amounted to $10 million. Because of government initiatives, this had more than doubled to $25 million by 1999.

However, garment factories (some with U.S. investment) rely almost exclusively on the import of materials for the manufacture of their goods. The competitiveness of finished products is reduced due to the costs of passing through multiple **tariff** boundaries. In an attempt to address this problem, the government has granted duty-free status on the import of fabrics and similar materials essential in the production of clothing and apparel. The government is keen to follow this policy, as it wishes to improve the amount of foreign exchange earnings and, in a similar vein, to create jobs for an ever-expanding and very young population. Other low-level manufactures that have developed in the Maldives through the 1990s are the production of PVC piping, soap, and food products. Between 1989–2000, the average annual growth of the manufacturing sector was 9.4 percent.

SERVICES

TOURISM. The Maldives' principal assets are its beauty, geographical isolation, and rich marine resources. When an Italian entrepreneur set up some uninhabited islands as resorts for foreign visitors in the early 1970s, the tourism sector began to develop very rapidly. Tourists come to spend time relaxing in one of the Maldives' 85 idyllic resort islands. A key pastime for tourists is diving in the cleanest ocean in the world amongst more than 1,000 species of fish, constituting one of world's most species-rich marine areas.

The influx of tourists to the Maldives has been increasing steadily since the 1970s. In 1993, 241,020 tourists travelled to experience the beauty of the Maldives, and by 1997, this number had risen nearly 50 percent to 365,563. Of these, the vast majority came from Western Europe, Japan, and from nearby countries in South Asia. The increase in tourist arrivals has significantly improved the country's receipts from tourism, which increased from $146 million in 1993 to $286 million in 1997. The recent purchase of resorts by the multinational hotel groups, Hilton and Four Seasons, is a clear indication of the projected growth of the Maldives' tourism sector. Yet the cultural effect of foreign influences has been controlled by the government policy of restricting tourist access to resort islands, unless they specifically apply for permission. Also, no Maldivians have their permanent residence on resort islands. The purpose of this is to maintain the population's apparent cultural unity as based upon the Islamic faith.

INTERNATIONAL TRADE

The Maldives is increasingly relying upon imports. This is due to a lack of agricultural production and fossil fuel resources, a growing population and household incomes, and the high influx of tourists since the 1970s who demand certain foodstuffs and luxuries. In 1977, imports totalled $11.1 million, whereas by 1998 they had boomed to $354 million. The Maldives receives its imports from a wide range of countries. The European Union countries supplied $65 million in 1998, of which the 2 largest partners, the UK and the Netherlands, provided $18.5 million and $12.5 million, respectively. In the same year, Singapore supplied $40.9 million in imports, India $39.3 million, Malaysia $34.9 million, Sri Lanka $30.9 million, the United Arab Emirates $23.8 million, Japan $22.3 million, and the United States $19.1 million.

Maldivian exports totalled $76.2 million in 1998—a considerable growth from a 1977 level of $4.8 million. The main destination was the EU countries, which consumed $20.1 million. The UK was the primary partner here and purchased $14.7 million in Maldivian exports, Germany imported $5.1 million. Exports to the United States totalled $15.7 million, nearby Sri Lanka $13.1 million, Japan $10.9 million, and Thailand $9.8 million.

The Republic of Maldives is an active member of the South Asian Association for Regional Co-operation (SAARC), whose other members are Bangladesh, Bhutan, India, Nepal, Pakistan, and Sri Lanka. Of these countries, the Maldives can boast the second highest GDP growth in the 1990s and the highest level of average individual incomes.

MONEY

There is no stock market in the Maldives, although at times some of the larger parastatals issue shares. According to the CIA *World Factbook 2001*, the national currency has had a fixed exchange rate since 1995 when it was pegged to the U.S. dollar at a rate of Rf11.77:US$1. This contributed to a low **inflation rate** of 3 percent in 1998. As a result, the price of **consumer goods** has remained fairly consistent, and the cost of living is steady. The Maldives Monetary Authority regulates the banking system and the money supply. It also functions as the central bank.

POVERTY AND WEALTH

Throughout the 1990s, nearly all of the available measures used to classify sustainable human development indicated that there had been considerable positive progression in the material and social conditions in the

Trade (expressed in billions of US$): Maldives

	Exports	Imports
1975	.003	.007
1980	.008	.029
1985	.023	.053
1990	.052	.138
1995	.050	.268
1998	.076	.354

SOURCE: International Monetary Fund. *International Financial Statistics Yearbook 1999.*

Exchange rates: Maldives

rufiyaa (Rf) per US$1	
2001	11.770
2000	11.770
1999	11.770
1998	11.770
1997	11.770
1996	11.770

Note: Currency has had a fixed rate since 1995.

SOURCE: CIA *World Factbook 2001* [ONLINE].

GDP per Capita (US$)

Country	1975	1980	1985	1990	1998
Maldives	N/A	N/A	650	917	1,247
United States	19,364	21,529	23,200	25,363	29,683
India	222	231	270	331	444
Sri Lanka	382	452	536	590	802

SOURCE: United Nations. *Human Development Report 2000; Trends in human development and per capita income.*

lives of Maldivians. The **United Nations Development Program** has marked the Maldives out as being one of just two countries in the South Asian region to be a medium human development country. Between 1977 and 1995, the life expectancy of the average Maldivian increased by 20 years to 71 years, which is a remarkable level for a developing country.

Despite that, it is estimated by the Maldives Ministry of Planning and National Development that almost 50 percent of children suffer, to different degrees, from stunting and wasting in their physical development. This is due to malnutrition in the more remote and less easily accessible islands. This is mainly caused by limited agricultural potential and the high cost of imports. Consequently, the majority of Maldivians consume a relatively restricted range of foodstuffs, with rice, fish, and coconut being the staples. A 1993 survey found that less than 30 percent of children ate fruits and vegetables. On the other hand, the annual average intake of protein rose from 69 grams (1980–82) to 94.6 grams (1995–97), and over the same period caloric intake improved from 2,194.3 to 2,505.1.

WORKING CONDITIONS

The Maldives is not a member of the International Labor Organisation. Although the national constitution does not explicitly bar the formation of trade unions, they do not exist in the Maldives. This is partly due to the lack of the legal right to stage strikes or engage in collective bargaining processes. Also, most workers are employed outside of the formal sector. In fact, due to the low recognition of workers' rights by the Maldives government, in 1995 the United States temporarily suspended the Maldives' tariff preferences within the U.S. Generalized System of Preferences.

While enrollment at primary schools is very high (98 percent in 1999), secondary school enrollment is only about 50 percent of the relevant age group. This results from having only 2 secondary schools outside of Malé (even though the government spent 17.6 percent of its 1999 budget on education). This not only has the effect of limiting secondary education to the more wealthy tiers of Maldivian society but acts against equal educational opportunities for girls. Girls are considerably more socially restricted in their movement than boys and have fewer employment opportunities. In addition, a recent UNDP survey found that there were only around 250 Maldivians with university degrees. The end result is that professional, skilled, and even semi-skilled workers are lacking in the Maldives. For example, 70 percent of primary and secondary school teachers are foreign workers. The total amount of imported labor grew from 2,000 in 1986 to 18,500 in 1995, which places an additional drain on already sparse **foreign exchange reserves**.

COUNTRY HISTORY AND ECONOMIC DEVELOPMENT

12TH CENTURY. The population adopts the Islamic faith.

1558. The Portuguese colonize the islands (only to be driven out in 1573).

17TH CENTURY. Maldives becomes a protectorate under the Dutch rulers of Sri Lanka (then Ceylon).

1887. The British officially declared the Maldives a protectorate.

1965. The Maldives become fully independent on 26 July.

1968. A national referendum votes in favor of the abolition of the sultanate in favor of a republic. Amir Ibrahim Nasir is elected president.

1978. Maumoon Abdul Gayoom is elected president.

1981. Maldives Monetary Authority is established and Malé International Airport is opened.

1988. Coup attempt by Tamil mercenaries is successfully halted with the aid of Indian forces.

1998. Gayoom is re-elected as president for the fifth consecutive term.

FUTURE TRENDS

In mid-2001, the two most important issues in the continued development of the Maldives are the partly linked factors of population growth and anticipated global environment problems. If projected population growth proves correct (a doubling of late 1990s levels by 2010), there will simply not be enough jobs in the country to employ the country's young people. Slightly less than 50 percent of the population are under 15 years old and the Maldives future will be dominated by the effects of a large proportion of young people entering the labor market, with estimated annual levels of 5,000 new job seekers looking for work. Similarly, population growth exerts considerable strain on already highly depleted reserves of potable water and building materials (particularly coral). Moreover, if pollution in the world's ecosystem continues to have the effect of raising the temperate of global climates thereby increasing sea-levels (a phenomenon know as the "greenhouse effect"), then the majority of the low-level land mass of the Maldives will simply disappear.

On a more positive note, the economy has consistently grown throughout the 1990s, and foreign investment is on the increase. With the decline of stocks of fish in most of the world's other oceans, the Maldives' access to the rich fish reserves of the Indian Ocean means that this industry will remain of significant importance, especially if the modernizing trend in the domestic canning and refrigeration of fish continues. In addition, except for some slight drops in tourism receipts during the financial crises of the late 1990s, the tourism sector is likely to continue to grow as is indicated by the recent investment of multinational hotel groups there.

DEPENDENCIES

Maldives has no territories or colonies.

BIBLIOGRAPHY

Amnesty International. *Amnesty International: Report 2000.* London: Amnesty International, 2000.

British Broadcasting Corporation (BBC). *Country Profile: The Maldives.* <http://news.bbc.co.uk//hi/english/world/south_asia/country_profiles/newsid_11660000/1166511.stm> Accessed May 2001.

Camerapix. *Spectrum Guide to the Maldives,* Nairobi: Camerapix, 1993.

Ciment, J., and I. Ness, *The Encyclopaedia of Global Population and Demographics,* Chicago: Fitzroy Dearborn, 1999.

De Laroque, T., with R. Ellis. *Toni The Maldive Lady: My Story.* Singapore: Times Editions, 1999.

Ellis, K. *Introduction to the Maldives.* Hong Kong: Odyssey, 1991.

The Far East and Australasia 2001. 32nd edition. London: Europa Publications, 2001.

Freedom House. *Freedom in the World: The Annual Survey of Political Rights and Civil Liberties 1999–2000.* New York: Freedom House, 2000.

Foreign Investment Services Bureau, Ministry of Trade, Industries and Labor . <http://www.investmaldives.com>. Accessed May 2001.

Food and Agriculture Organisation. *FAO Yearbook: Trade: Vol.52, 1998.* Rome: FAO, 1999.

———. *Fishery Statistics: Capture Production: Vol. 86/1, 1998.* Rome: FAO, 2000.

———. *Fishery Statistics: Commodities: Vol. 87, 1998.* Rome: FAO, 2000.

International Monetary Fund. *International Financial Statistics Yearbook 2000.* Washington D.C.: IMF, 2000

Ministry of Planning and National Development, Republic of Maldives. *Country Strategy Note: A Strategy for the United Nations Development System in Maldives.* (Malé: Republic of Maldives, November 1998). <http://www.mv.undp.org>. Accessed May 2001.

Ministry of Tourism, Republic of Maldives. <http://www.visitmaldives.com>. Accessed May 2001.

United Nations. *International Trade Statistics Yearbook, 1998.* New York: United Nations, 1999.

United Nations. *Statistical Yearbook Forty-Fourth Issue.* New York: United Nations, 2000.

United Nations Conference on Trade and Development (UNCTAD). *World Investment Report 2000: Cross-border Mergers and Acquisitions and Development.* Geneva: United Nations, 2000.

United Nations Development Programme. <http://www.undp.org>. Accessed May 2001.

United Nations Development Programme in the Republic of Maldives. <http://www.mv.undp.org>. Accessed May 2001.

United Nations Economic and Social Commission for Asia and the Pacific. *Asia-Pacific in Figures,* 14th edition. New York: United Nations, February 2001.

Upham, M. *Trade Unions of the World.* 4th edition. London: Cartermill, 1996.

U.S. Central Intelligence Agency. *CIA World Factbook.* <http://www.odci.gov/cia/publications/ factbook/index.html>. Accessed May 2001.

U.S. Energy Information Administration. <http://www.eia.doe.gov/emeu/cabs/maldives.html>. Accessed May 2001.

U.S. Department of State. *Financial Year 2000 Country Commercial Guide: Maldives.* <http://www.state.gov/www/about_state/business/com_guides/2000/sa/maldives_ccg2000.pdf>. Accessed May 2001.

World Bank. *Maldives Data Profile* and *Maldives at a Glance.* <http://www.worldbank.org>. Accessed May 2001.

—Liam Campling

MARSHALL ISLANDS

Republic of the Marshall Islands

CAPITAL: Majuro.

MONETARY UNIT: United States dollar ($). One U.S. dollar equals 100 cents. There are notes of 1, 2, 5, 10, 20, 50, and 100 dollars. Coins come in denominations of 1, 5, 10, 25, and 50 cents and 1 dollar.

CHIEF EXPORTS: Fish, coconut products, and shells.

CHIEF IMPORTS: Foodstuffs, machinery and equipment, fuels, beverages, and tobacco.

GROSS DOMESTIC PRODUCT: US$105 million (1998 est.).

BALANCE OF TRADE: **Exports:** US$28 million (1997 est.). **Imports:** US$58 million (1997 est.).

COUNTRY OVERVIEW

LOCATION AND SIZE. The Marshall Islands are located in the North Pacific Ocean some 4,000 kilometers (2,486 miles) northeast of Australia. They consist of 2 groups of small islands, atolls (coral islands), and reefs running from the northwest to the southeast. The more easterly of these is the Ratak Chain, the more westerly, the Ralik Chain. It is estimated that there are 1,152 islands and 30 atolls, but only 4 islands and 19 atolls are inhabited. With terrains of coral, limestone, and sand, none of the islands have any high ground, and the most elevated location of the islands is 10 meters (33 feet). The total land area is 181 square kilometers (70 square miles), and about 60 percent is taken up by crops. There are phosphate deposits and the possibility of minerals in the seabed within the 200 nautical mile economic zone claimed by the Marshall Islands. The capital is Majuro, which is located on an atoll of the same name.

The Marshall Islands are located within the tropics, and the weather is generally hot and very humid. Temperatures average around 27°C (81°F), and vary little during the year. There is a rainy season from May to November, with annual rainfall of about 4,000 millimeters (157 inches), but the sandy terrain means that little water is collected, and the shortage of drinking water is a continual problem. The islands are occasionally hit by typhoons.

POPULATION. The population was estimated at 68,126 in 2000, giving a population density of 375 persons per square kilometer (971 per square mile), quite a bit higher than in neighboring island states in the Pacific. The population was estimated to be growing at 3.9 percent a year in 2000, which is considered a very rapid rate. The birth rate was 45 births per 1,000 population, and the death rate was 6 persons per 1,000. The figures indicate negligible migration, but the International Monetary Fund (IMF) has indicated that there is in fact significant out-migration to the United States. The average fertility rate is 6.6 children per woman. With such a rapid rate of growth, the population can be expected to have a young age structure. The 0–14 age group contains 50 percent of the population, the 15–64 group contains 48 percent, while only 2 percent are 65 and over. Slightly more than half of the population lives on Majuro Atoll, and a further 20 percent live on Kwajalein. The urban population is about 70 percent of the total.

Almost all of the people on the Marshall Islands belong to the Micronesian ethnic group and follow the Christian religion. Most are Protestant, although there are some Catholics and small communities of Seventh-Day Adventists, Mormons, Jehovah's Witnesses, and Bahai. English is the official language and is spoken by everyone. Two local Malayo-Polynesian dialects are in use as local languages, and they are used in parliament and for some radio broadcasts. Overall life expectancy is 66 years, with a 64-year expectancy for males and a 67-year expectancy for females. The adult literacy rate was 93 percent in 1980, with practically all adult males and 88 percent of females being literate.

OVERVIEW OF ECONOMY

Given its small size in terms of population, its inaccessible location, and the absence of any minerals apart

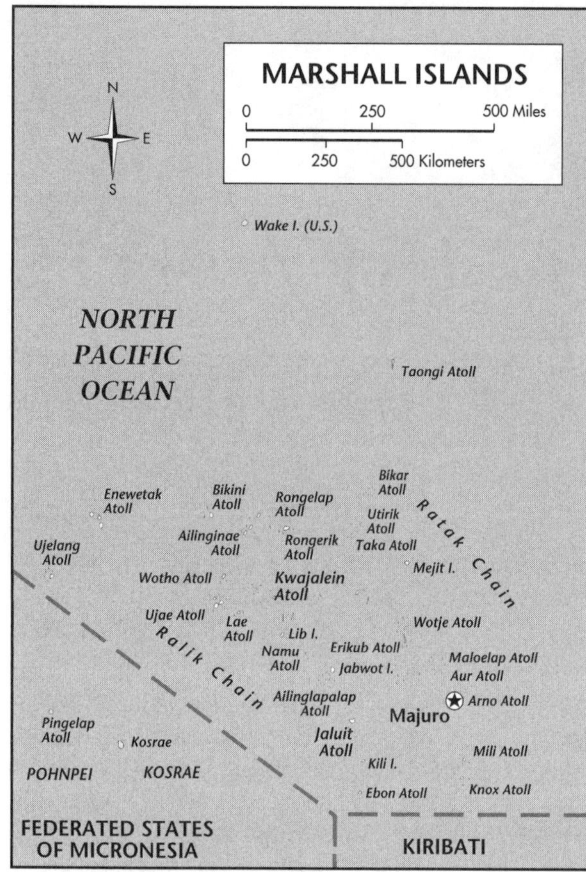

from phosphates (which are not currently exploited), it is surprising that the economy of the Marshall Islands generates as much income for its citizens as it does. The per capita **gross domestic product** (GDP) was estimated at $1,670 (**purchasing power parity**, 1998 est.), and this rate would just squeeze the Marshall Islands into the lower-middle income group. In addition, the Marshall Islands receive very substantial receipts from the United States—partly aid and partly rents for the use of military bases—which add more than 50 percent to the income that is generated domestically.

Most employment is in the services sector, which, because of the receipts from the United States, is able to support health workers, teachers, and government administrators. The agriculture sector is quite small in terms of both its contribution to total output and employment. The small industry sector, primarily engaged in crop and fish processing, is about what would be expected given the general level of development of the islands.

Coconut products and fish are the main exports, and these earnings are supplemented by tourism. Almost everything, aside from some food products, is imported and, without U.S. aid there would be a drastic fall in imports.

The growth of the economy varies from year to year and is affected by the impact of climatic conditions on agriculture. In recent years, output has declined by 2 percent to 5 percent per year, although El Niño weather conditions caused severe disruption in 1996, when output fell by 13 percent.

POLITICS, GOVERNMENT, AND TAXATION

The Marshall Islands were originally settled by people from neighboring Pacific islands. In the 16th century, Spain claimed the islands, although Germany was allowed trading rights. With decline of Spanish influence, the islands came under the control of Germany, who established a protectorate. At the outbreak of World War I (1914–18), the Japanese took over the islands and administered them under a United Nations (UN) mandate. World War II (1939–45) saw clashes between the United States and the occupying Japanese, with the United States finally establishing control of the islands in 1944. The United States administered the islands as a trustee for the United Nations and used them to begin a series of nuclear tests. The tests subjected the islanders to serious radiation and made Bikini Atoll uninhabitable. This was to have long-term implications for the Marshall Islands, leading to the United States providing considerable financial support while continuing to operate its military bases. In 1965, movements for self-determination of the islands began, culminating in full independence in 1990. The Marshall Islands has a Compact of Free Association with the United States, agreed to in 1986, by which the United States is responsible for defense of the Marshall Islands, rents military bases, and provides financial assistance. The initial agreement was valid for 15 years from 1986 and is being renegotiated.

The 1979 constitution established a parliamentary government, with a president as chief executive and head of state. The parliament is known as the Nitijela. Directly elected for 4-year terms, the parliament has 33 members, known as Senators. The president is elected by the parliament, and the president chooses his cabinet from among the members of parliament. The voting age is 18. Although elections were typically non-partisan on the Marshall Islands, opposition began to emerge in 1991, and subsequent elections have seen incumbents losing their seats. In 2000, the opposition gained 40 percent of the seats in the parliament and established a significant presence. Parliamentary candidates tend to contest elections on the basis of their personalities, rather than their party affiliations, and it is sometimes not clear which party an elected member supports. In 2001, during a no confidence vote (which decides if the ruling government has enough support to survive), 2 ostensible government members voted with the opposition and 1 opposition member voted with the government.

The legal system is based on the former Trust Territory laws, but has been modified by the legislature, mu-

Communications

Country	Telephones[a]	Telephones, Mobile/Cellular[a]	Radio Stations[b]	Radios[a]	TV Stations[a]	Televisions[a]	Internet Service Providers[c]	Internet Users[c]
Marshall Islands	3,000 (1996)	365 (1996)	AM 3; FM 4; shortwave 0	N/A	3	N/A	1	500
United States	194 M	69.209 M (1998)	AM 4,762; FM 5,542; shortwave 18	575 M	1,500	219 M	7,800	148 M
Philippines	1.9 M	1.959 M (1998)	AM 366; FM 290; shortwave 3 (1999)	11.5 M	31	3.7 M	33	500,000
Solomon Islands	8,000	658	AM 3; FM 0; shortwave 0	57,000	0	3,000	1	3,000

[a]Data is for 1997 unless otherwise noted.
[b]Data is for 1998 unless otherwise noted.
[c]Data is for 2000 unless otherwise noted.

SOURCE: CIA *World Factbook 2001* [Online].

nicipal bodies, customary law, and common law. There are 4 levels of judicial courts: the Supreme Court, High Court, district and community courts, and traditional courts. The traditional courts are limited mainly to jurisdiction over traditional titles and land issues.

In the **fiscal year** 1997–98, the budget anticipated that government revenues would be 25 percent of GDP. **Income tax** raised 32 percent of government revenue (excluding grants), import **duties** 28 percent, sales taxes 13 percent, and other income (interest, fees, licenses) 27 percent. There is a continuing program to try to improve tax performance by tightening administration, reducing tax **arrears**, simplifying import duties to a basic duty of 12 percent (with some exceptions), doubling the fuel tax, reducing tax exemptions, introducing a **value-added tax** (VAT) and taxes on commercial rentals, and the introduction of user charges.

Total spending in 1997–98 was projected at 53 percent of GDP. On the recurrent expenditure side, general administration takes up 12 percent of total government spending, education 23 percent, health 12 percent, and foreign affairs 10 percent. The gap between revenues and expenditures was more than met by receipts from the United States of 40 percent of GDP, and on this basis, a **budgetary surplus** of 11 percent of GDP was forecast. Budget surpluses have not always been the norm. Between 1992 and 1995, **budget deficits** averaged 14 percent of GDP.

INFRASTRUCTURE, POWER, AND COMMUNICATIONS

Perhaps because the country's limited roadways are scattered widely across the many islands, there are no measurements of roadway length on the Marshall Islands. The main settlements on Majuro Atoll and Kwajalein have paved roads, and the roads in Majuro have recently been upgraded. Elsewhere there are coral surfaced roads and sandy tracks. There are no railways. The main port is at Majuro, and this is the only port that is able to receive large ocean-going vessels. A dry-dock facility was recently completed on Majuro Atoll for the islands' fleet of 143 ships, mostly bulk and cargo carriers, petroleum tankers, and a vehicle carrier. Sixteen of the inhabited atolls and islands have airports and 4 have paved runways.

All of the Marshall Islands' electricity is supplied by diesel generators. In 1994, the Marshall Islands generated and consumed 57 million kilowatt hours (kWh). There is some domestic use of bottled gas, and many families use kerosene stoves or wood as cooking fuel. The water supply is erratic, and there are projects to increase water storage facilities and to construct desalinization plants.

In 1994, there were an estimated 3,000 land line telephones in use and 280 mobile telephones. The 3 major settlements of Majuro Atoll and the islands of Ebeye and Kwajalein are connected by a direct dial system; the other locations are linked by short-wave radiotelephone, mainly used by the government. International links are provided by 2 Intelsat satellite earth stations. There is a U.S. government satellite link on Kwajalein Island.

The islands had 3 AM radio stations and 4 FM stations in 1998, and in 1997, there were 3 television stations, although 2 of these were provided by the U.S. military on Kwajalein Island. The local newspaper is the weekly *Marshall Islands Journal.*

ECONOMIC SECTORS

The services sector dominates the economy, and is primarily composed of the large number of government employees, those providing services for the U.S. military installation on Kwajalein Island, and the tourism industry. In 1995, services generated 72 percent of GDP. The most recent employment figures, from 1988, indicate that the services sector employed 58 percent of the **labor force**. Incomes in this sector are above average. The smallest sector in terms of output is industry, which produced 13 percent of output in 1995 and engaged 23 percent of the labor force in 1988. The agriculture sector (which includes fishing) only employed 19 percent of the labor force in 1998, generating 15 percent of output in 1995.

AGRICULTURE

Copra (dried coconut) is the main **cash crop**, though its output has been falling. There was a 16 percent fall in 1996 as a result of El Niño rains, but this was followed by an 11 percent fall in 1997. The poor transport links between the islands, atolls, and Majuro is a problem, as the crop has to come to the capital for processing and packaging before exportation. The price earned by growers has fallen (the price halved between 1994 and 1997), reducing their incentive to produce, but it was still above the world price due to a government **subsidy**. The long-term problem is that the coconut trees are declining in productivity as they become older and, with lower prices, the growers have little incentive to replace the tree stock. The lack of private land titles and a land market is a further problem. Without land as collateral, farmers find it difficult to raise loans to finance replanting.

Fish exports appear substantial and fast-growing, but much of the catch is in fact caught by Chinese and Japanese vessels, taken to land, and then shipped from the islands in refrigerated cargo boats. The main benefits to the islands are fishing license fees, supplying the fishing fleet, and some processing and packaging of the catch. The Marshall Islands do have some government-owned boats, but their catches were very low. They ceased operation in 1996. Trochus shells are collected from the reefs. They are exported to be made into buttons and ornaments, and they can be ground to produce an ingredient for lacquers.

Marshall Islands
GDP–COMPOSITION BY SECTOR–1995

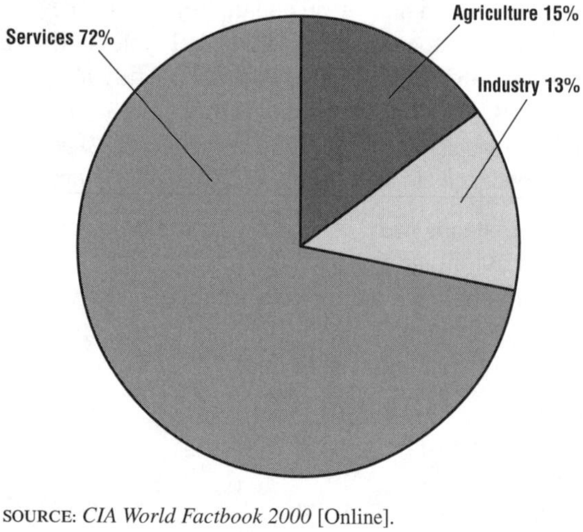

Services 72%
Agriculture 15%
Industry 13%

SOURCE: *CIA World Factbook 2000* [Online].

Food and livestock production has grown modestly in the period from 1993 to 1997 (by about 3.5 percent annually), basically reflecting the increase in the population. However, production is not encouraged due to the low prices of imported food as compared with domestic output. A total of 60 percent of caloric intake comes from imports. Local food producers are hampered by poor transportation, which raises the cost of their products. The main food crops are bananas, breadfruit (a large fruit with edible pulp and seeds), pandanus (a fruit with edible nuts), taro (a starchy root crop similar to the potato), vegetables, and tropical fruits. Livestock is mostly poultry and pigs, with some cattle.

INDUSTRY

There is no mining on the Marshall Islands, although there are some phosphate deposits. The main manufacturing enterprise is the Tobolar Copra Processing Authority, which is government-owned but run by a private management team. It is the only purchaser of copra, which it crushes to produce coconut oil. Currently, it is unable to purchase enough copra and operates at about one-third of its capacity. A garment factory was established in 1998 in a **joint venture** with China. Other manufacturers are involved in the production of drinking water and beer, and the processing of breadfruit and taro.

The Marshalls Electricity Company is government-owned, and manages to cover its costs, as does the publicly-owned Majuro Water and Sewage Services. The construction sector is made up of small private enterprises that mainly construct private dwellings. An international construction company undertakes any large project, such as the new port at Majuro, and the local workforce provides only some unskilled labor.

SERVICES

The services sector is the largest employer, and generates almost three-quarters of GDP. Transport and communications generate 7 percent of GDP; distribution, restaurants and hotels, 18 percent; financial services 14 percent; and public administration and community services, 30 percent.

Much of the high value of this sector comes from servicing the U.S. installation on Kwajalein Island, which is used for missile tracking and weapons testing. Another source of service sector income has been the sale of Marshall Islands passports since 1996. These were initially offered at $350,000 each, and later at $100,000. The islands indicated that they were prepared to sell up to 3,000 passports, and to date the sales have realized about $10 million. The sales were suspended in 1997 but there are plans for resumption. The services sector also supplies the international fishing fleets operating in the waters that surround the islands, serves as an onshore leave destination, and generates further income from the sale of fishing licenses (about $1.5 million to $3 million, a year).

The National Telecommunications Authority is still majority-owned by the government. By virtue of being a **monopoly** and making relatively high charges for international calls, it manages to cover its costs. Air Marshall Islands is government-owned. It sustained large losses in 1996 and 1997, and its routes have been restructured with plans of eventual **privatization**.

BANKING AND FINANCES. The banking sector includes 2 U.S. commercial banks, the domestic Bank of the Marshall Islands, and the Marshall Islands Development Bank. Most lending consists of consumer loans for construction, travel, and education. The lack of private titles to land or a land market makes lending to the agriculture sector difficult.

TOURISM. Tourism offers some prospects for expansion. In 1997, there were 6,000 arrivals in the islands, but less than 1,000 were tourists; the rest were on business or in transit. There are presently less than 200 hotel beds, although a new government-owned hotel of 150 beds is under construction. In 1997, tourism is estimated to have earned $3 million for the Marshall Islands. Visitors are presently deterred by the lack of facilities (particularly outside Majuro), the relatively high cost of transportation to the islands, the radiation contamination of some of the atolls by nuclear testing, and the current program of weapons testing on Kwajalein. It is thought, however, that the islands have some possibilities in establishing a specialty market in tourism, based on sport fishing, diving and snorkeling, gambling (approved in 1996), and the general tropical attractions of the islands.

INTERNATIONAL TRADE

Merchandise exports of $28 million were made up entirely of coconut products (11 percent) and fish products (89 percent) in 1997. Frozen fish exports have increased from $1.3 million in 1993 to $21.9 million in 1997 as a result of a Chinese fishing fleet that based itself at Majuro. Exports of trochus shells for buttons, ornaments, and making lacquers are not recorded, but there is probably some small informal trade. Diesel used to be **re-exported** to Micronesia, but this ended in 1996. Exports go mostly to China as a result of the frozen fish expansion, with the United States, Japan, and Australia being other export destinations.

Merchandise imports were $58 million in 1997, with food and beverages making up 31 percent and fuels 23 percent. The rest consisted of consumer manufactures, machinery and transport equipment, and chemicals. The United States supplied 52 percent of imports in 1997, much of which was goods for the U.S. workers at the Kwajalein installation. The next biggest supplier was Singapore with 4 percent.

MONEY

The Marshall Islands use the U.S. dollar as their currency. This has the advantages of not having the expense of running a central bank, the currency is completely convertible, and price stability is reasonably well ensured as the Marshallese do not have the ability to print currency. The rate of **inflation** has been in single digits in the period from 1993 to 1997, ranging from 4.8 percent to 9.6 percent. The only drawback for "dollarized" economies is that they do not earn the seigniorage (profit from the minting of coins) they would gain if they issued their own currency. The increasing number of countries that have been attracted to using the U.S. dollar in place of a domestic currency has caused the United States to consider sharing some of the seigniorage it earns as currency issuer.

POVERTY AND WEALTH

The are no figures on the numbers below the dollar-a-day poverty line, but given the income level and the structure of the economy, perhaps 20 percent of Marshallese might live poverty. Most of those affected will be among the 30 percent of the population living on the atolls other than Majuro and Kwajalein, relying on small-scale agriculture and fishing for their livelihoods.

Life expectancy (at 65 years in 2000) is considered high, and the level of adult literacy, last surveyed in 1980, was 93 percent. Together with its lower-middle

Exchange rates: Marshall Islands

US$	
Jan 2001	1.0000
2000	1.0000
1999	1.0000
1998	1.0000
1997	1.0000
1996	1.0000

Note: US currency is used in the Marshall Islands.

SOURCE: CIA *World Factbook 2001* [ONLINE].

GDP per Capita (US$)

Country	1996	1997	1998	1999	2000
Marshall Islands	1,680	N/A	1,450	1,670	N/A
United States	28,600	30,200	31,500	33,900	36,200
Philippines	2,600	3,200	3,500	3,600	3,800
Solomon Islands	3,000	3,000	2,600	2,650	2,000

Note: Data are estimates.

SOURCE: *Handbook of the Nations*, 17th, 18th, 19th and 20th editions for 1996, 1997, 1998 and 1999 data; CIA *World Factbook 2001* [Online] for 2000 data.

income status, the Marshall Islands has a medium level of human development when evaluated by the criteria used by the UN. Infant mortality is high, however, at 41 per 1,000 births in 2000 (in the United States the rate is 6 per 1,000).

WORKING CONDITIONS

The economically active labor force was estimated at 11,500 in 1988, of which 73 percent were males. Approximately 12 percent of the labor force was recorded as being unemployed. However, the unemployment rate has little meaning in an economy like that of the Marshall Islands, as it relates to those registering as looking for jobs in the urban areas as a percentage of the formal labor force. A substantial part of the labor force of the Marshall Islands is in the agriculture and fishing sectors, much of it in small-scale family enterprises outside the formal sector. With negligible social security provisions, those without work or support from families or charities cannot survive. It is likely that there is considerable disguised unemployment in the rural areas, meaning that the work could be carried by a smaller workforce than is used.

There is a Marshall Islands Social Security Administration, but it is under investigation for mismanagement, and it is not able to make much of a contribution to helping those who are out-of-work or in need.

COUNTRY HISTORY AND ECONOMIC DEVELOPMENT

1000 B.C. Migration to the Marshall Islands from other Pacific Ocean islands begins.

1525. Spanish navigator Alonso de Salasar is the first European to sight the islands.

1529. Alvaaro de Saavedra lands on the islands and claims them for Spain.

1788. The British sea captain, John Marshall, visits the islands.

1874. Pope Leo XIII, acting as a European mediator, confirms Spanish dominion over the islands, while also allocating trading rights to Germany.

1885. Germany establishes a protectorate over the islands.

1914. With the outbreak of World War I, Japan assumes administration of the islands.

1920. Japan receives a United Nations mandate to administer the islands.

1944. After fierce fighting between Japanese and American forces during World War II, the United States occupies the islands.

1945. Japanese settlers are **repatriated**.

1947. The UN assigns the islands (which are known as the Trust Territory of the Pacific Ocean) to the United States. The U.S. Navy undertakes their day-to-day administration.

1948. The United States begins a series of nuclear test explosions on the islands, which subject the islanders to high levels of radiation.

1965. The Congress of Micronesia is formed by delegates from Pacific islands to press for independence.

1970. A commission on self-government confirms that the peoples of Micronesia have a right to sovereignty, self-rule, and to terminate association with the United States.

1979. Marshall Islands District, named after the British explorer who visited the islands in 1788, drafts and approves a constitution, which is recognized by the United States. Amata Kabua, who holds the traditional position of High Chief, is elected as the first president.

1982. The United States signs a Compact of Free Association, which outlines proposals for the end of its trustee relationship with the Marshall Islands.

1983. Marshall Islanders vote to accept the Compact of Free Association. Kabua is reelected as president.

1986. The Compact of Free Association, after several mutually agreed amendments, comes into operation, and the islands become self-governing.

1987. Kabua reelected as president.

1990. The UN removes the trustee status of the islands, establishing the Republic of the Marshall Islands.

1991. The Marshall Islands joins the UN as an independent, sovereign nation. The Ralik-Ratak Democratic Party is formed to oppose the supporters of Kabua, and wins 2 seats in the parliament.

1995. Kabua is reelected as president. The Government Party (or Kabua Party, as it is often known) wins

23 seats, and the newly formed United Democratic Party (UDP) wins 10 seats.

1996. President Kabua dies and is succeeded by Imata Kabua, the paramount chief. The Kabua Party becomes Our Islands Party (OIP).

2000. Elections give the OIP 20 seats and the UDP 13 seats. Kessai Note, who had held no traditional post, is elected president.

2001. The United States Nuclear Claims Tribunal awards Marshall Islands $563 million, but the tribunal has no powers to enforce payment.

FUTURE TRENDS

It is clearly very important that the islands extend the agreement with the United States relating to the use of Kwajalein for missile testing. About 1,500 Islanders work at the complex, making up about 13 percent of the labor force, and the jobs are particularly well-paid. The major success in recent years has been the expansion of the frozen fish export sector, and the government would be wise to make sure that the agreements with the Chinese fishing fleets are continued. Tourism has some possibilities as a specialty market, but foreign investment will be vital if significant expansion is to be achieved.

The main sector of concern is the production of coconut products. In the long-term, many of these problems can be solved by registering land-titles and extending loans to farmers to replace exhausted trees. This is particularly important from a social standpoint, as the coconut farmers are among the poorest members of the community. In the short-term, some efforts to improve transport between the islands and atolls would help both the coconut farmers and the small fishermen.

DEPENDENCIES

Marshall Islands has no territories or colonies.

BIBLIOGRAPHY

Bank of Hawaii. *Republic of Marshall Islands.* <http://www.boh.com/econ/pacific/rmiaer.asp>. Accessed April 2001.

International Monetary Fund. *Marshall Islands: Recent Economic Developments.* Washington, DC: International Monetary Fund, 1998.

U.S. Central Intelligence Agency. *CIA World Factbook 2000.* <http://www.cia.gov/cia/publications/factbook/geos/rm.html>. Accessed April 2001.

U.S. Department of State. *Background Notes: Marshall Islands.* <http://www.state.gov/www/background_notes/marshall_0007_bgn.html>. Accessed September 2001.

—Michael Hodd

MICRONESIA

Federated States of Micronesia

CAPITAL: Palikir, Pohnpei Island.

MONETARY UNIT: The official currency of Micronesia is the United States dollar ($). One dollar equals 100 cents. There are coins of 1, 5, 10, 25, and 50 cents and 1 dollar. There are notes of 1, 2, 5, 10, 20, 50, and 100 dollars.

CHIEF EXPORTS: Fish, garments, bananas, and black pepper.

CHIEF IMPORTS: Food, manufactured goods, machinery and equipment, and beverages.

GROSS DOMESTIC PRODUCT: US$263 million (1999 est.).

BALANCE OF TRADE: **Exports:** US$73 million (1996 est.). **Imports:** US$168 million (1996 est.).

COUNTRY OVERVIEW

LOCATION AND SIZE. The Federated States of Micronesia forms (with Palau) the archipelago of the Caroline Islands, and lies about 800 kilometers (497 miles) east of the Philippines. The Federated States of Micronesia (FSM) consists of 607 islands and includes (from west to east) the states of Yap, Chuuk (formerly Truk), Pohnpei (formerly Ponape), and Kosrae. Micronesia covers about 702 square kilometers of land (271 square miles), has a coastline of 6,112 kilometers (3,798 miles) and is scattered over more than 2.7 million square kilometers (1 million square miles) of the ocean. Micronesia's largest island cluster is Pohnpei (163 islands), with an area of 344 square kilometers (133 square miles), while the smallest cluster is Kosrae (5 islands), spanning 110 square kilometers (42.5 square miles). The islands include a variety of terrains, ranging from mountainous islands to low, coral atolls and volcanic outcrops.

POPULATION. The population of Micronesia was estimated at 134,597 in July 2001, up 18 percent from 114,000 in 1998. The current annual population growth rate is 3.28 percent, which will result in a population of 176,815 by 2010. The birth rate is 27.09 per 1,000 population, with a fertility rate of 3.83 children per woman. The death rate is 5.95 per 1,000 population. The **immigration** rate is 11.65 migrants per 1,000 population. The infant mortality rate in July 2000 was 33.48 per 1,000 births (the U.S. rate was 7 per 1,000).

There are 9 ethnic Micronesian and Polynesian groups, spread across the islands. In 1994, around 53,319 people lived in Chuuk; 33,692 in Pohnpei; 11,178 in Yap; and 7,317 in Kosrae. The highest population density was estimated in Chuuk island with 419.8 people per square kilometer (1,087 per square mile) in 1994.

OVERVIEW OF ECONOMY

Previously administered by the United States as a Trust Territory of the United Nations, the Federated States of Micronesia became self-governing in domestic matters in 1986, and fully independent in 1991.

The small size of Micronesia, both in terms of geographical area and population size, its remote location, and its lack of commercially viable mineral resources all combine to set limits on the economy. The nation's main assets are its tropical location (which provides good potential for tourism), productive fishing grounds, and reasonably well-educated **workforce**.

Micronesia's estimated **GDP per capita** is $2,000, which places it near the top of 45 world economies the World Bank classifies as Lower Middle-Income (countries with GDP per capita in a range from $700-$2,800). Financial support from the United States has been a vital feature of the period since self-government was introduced in 1986, with $1.3 billion allocated over the period from 1986 to 2001, an enormous sum for a community of 134,000—almost $100,000 per person. The money has been allocated to improving educational and health provisions, providing **infrastructure**, training for political and community leaders, bolstering **public**

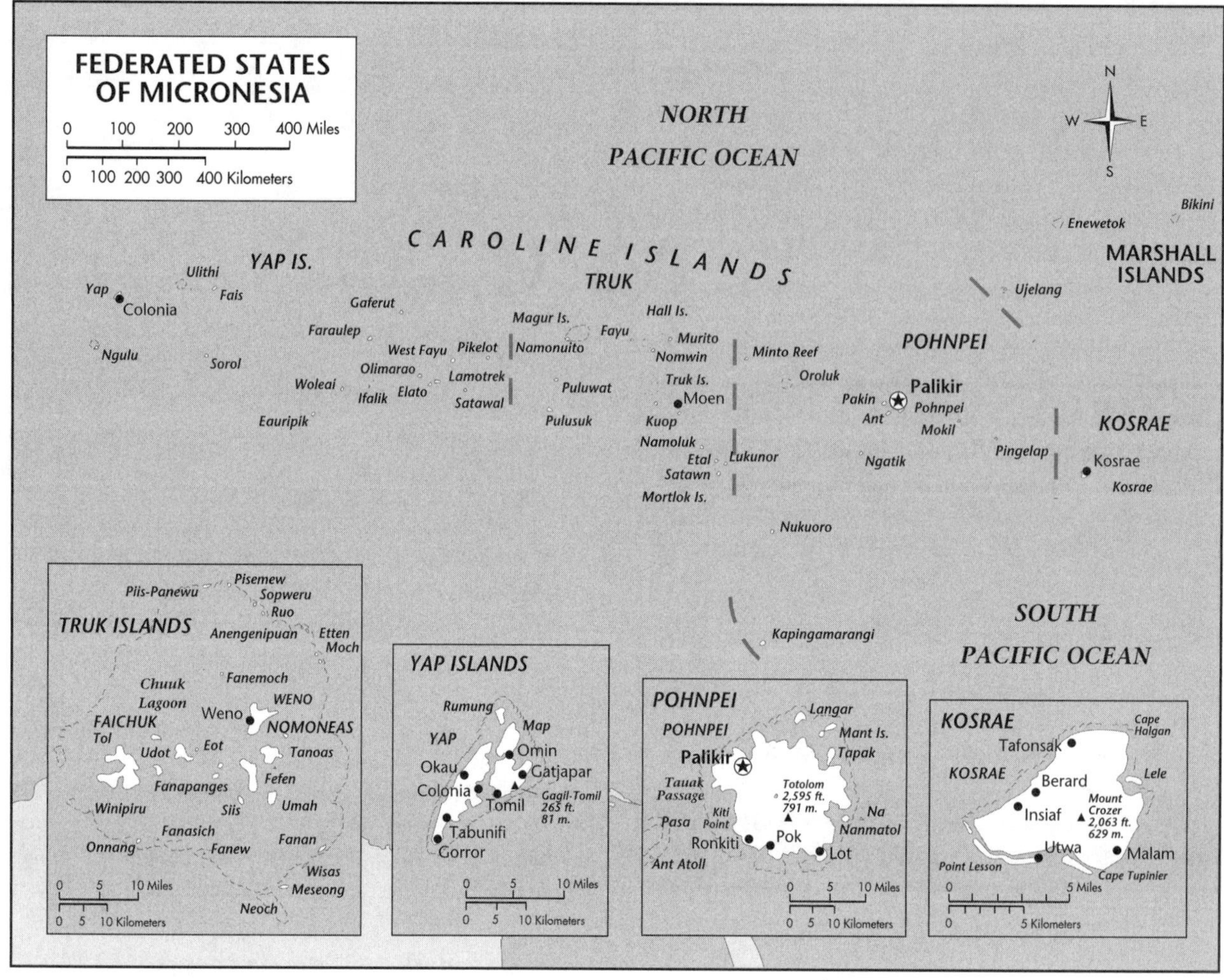

sector efficiency, and encouraging the **private sector**. Grants from external sources amounted to some $91.5 million in 1996–97 (equivalent to 43 percent of GDP).

The most significant cash export is fish, which accounted for 82 percent of total exports in 1996. Micronesia has established an **exclusive economic zone**, which covers an ocean area of more than 2.5 million square kilometers (965,250 square miles) of particularly productive fishing grounds yielding tuna, red snapper, and grouper. Local producers fish these waters, and licenses are granted to foreign fishing fleets to work these waters as well. Other marine resources include phosphate deposits, and there are currently trials under way to see if these deposits on the ocean floor can be exploited commercially.

In the past, copra (the sun-dried white flesh of the coconut, from which coconut oil is extracted) was Micronesia's main **cash crop**. However, low world prices have led to production plummeting from 8,500 tons in 1979 to 200 in 1992, and it has remained around that level since, although in some years no exports of copra are recorded at all, and this despite a government **subsidy** to try to maintain production. Copra now makes a small contribution to income in Micronesia, and the economy is no longer buffeted by fluctuations in world copra prices. Also, Micronesia no longer faces a dilemma of whether to continue production in the face of current low prices. Needless to say, the decline in copra production is a particular blow for farmers on the outer islands for whom coconuts have been an important source of income.

The islands all have some tree cover, and timber, including wood from the coconut tree, is used for house construction, furniture, and household utensils. The climate in the Micronesia is tropical, and there is a healthy amount of rainfall. The soil is rich, and fruits indigenous to the islands include bananas, mangos, pineapples, and papayas.

Economic growth in the Micronesia is heavily influenced by changes in global and regional commodity prices and the climate. The nation is mainly made up of small, flat islands, which makes it difficult to support large-scale cultivation. The main form of agriculture is therefore subsistence production. It is difficult for subsistence producers to create a large surplus due to the lack of storage facilities and transportation. The strongest areas for economic growth are tourism, fishing, manufacturing and mining.

The government employed as much as two-thirds of the population before 1997. However, in 1997, the Asian Development Bank approved a loan of $17.68 million for the funding of a program of major economic structural adjustment. This was done in preparation for the ending of U.S. assistance under the Compact of Free Association at the beginning of the 21st century. The reform package included measures for attracting new sources of foreign aid and private investment, for fiscal reform, and for the strengthening of the private sector, as well as severe reductions in the number of public-sector employees. The year 1997 saw the balance of the workforce begin to tilt toward the private sector, and in 1998, government expenditures declined by 27 percent, spurred by continuing **privatization**. In terms of GDP components, the government's recent efforts to encourage privatization of certain industries seem to be working. Non-market production dropped 4.3 percent as more citizens chose to work in the money economy.

In exchange for allowing the United States exclusive access to its waters, Micronesia receives an annual fixed payment from the U.S. government.

POLITICS, GOVERNMENT, AND TAXATION

The Federated States of Micronesia emerged as a nation from the former United Nations Trust Territory of the Pacific Islands (TTPI) administered by the United States from the end of World War II. The Federated States of Micronesia became self-governing in 1986.

Political legitimacy rests on a majority vote through elections in accordance with the constitution. On May 10, 1979, the locally drafted Constitution of the Federated States of Micronesia incorporated the 4 states of Kosrae, Yap, Ponape (later Pohnpei), and Truk (later Chuuk). The Congress includes 14 members, called Senators. The 4 states each elect 1 "Senator-at-Large" for a 4-year term. The remaining 10 Senators are elected for 2-year terms: their seats are distributed in proportion to the population of each state. Each of the 4 states has its own constitution, governor, and legislature. The federal president and vice-president are elected by the Congress from among the 4 "Senators-at-Large." The president of the Federated States of Micronesia since May 1999 has been Leo A. Falcam.

The state governments are fairly autonomous and work like state governments in the United States, with individual executive, legislative, and judicial systems. In each state, traditional leaders work closely with the local governments to maintain cultural traditions.

There are 3 branches of government: an executive branch led by a president who also serves as head of state; a **unicameral** (single house) legislature elected from the 4 constituent states; and a judicial system that applies criminal and civil laws and procedures closely paralleling those of the United States. Under the Compact of Free Association, the United States is responsible for defence.

The Council of the Micronesian Government Executives aims to facilitate discussion of economic developments in the region and to examine possibilities for reducing the considerable cost of shipping essential goods between the islands.

The main tax that all businesses in Micronesia pay is the Gross Receipts Tax. The tax is assessed on the gross revenues of businesses, which includes all receipts without deductions. The rate is $80 on the first $10,000 of gross revenues and 3 percent of any excess for the calendar year. Businesses with less than $2,000 gross revenue in a year are eligible for a refund of the taxes paid for that year. A Wages and Salaries Tax is assessed on an employee's income. The **Social Security Tax** requires the employer to pay half of the tax and the employee to pay the other half. The current rate is 4 percent of wages paid by both the employee and the employer.

INFRASTRUCTURE, POWER, AND COMMUNICATIONS

Micronesia has a total of 240 kilometers (149 miles) of roadways, 42 kilometers (26 miles) of which are paved. Macadam (a mix of small broken stone and concrete or asphalt) and concrete roads are found in the more important islands. Other islands have stone and coral-surfaced roads and tracks. There are no rail lines in the islands.

The country has a total of 6 airports, of which 5 have paved runways. International airports which can accommodate medium-sized jets can be found in Pohnpei, Chuuk, Yap, and Kosrae, and there are airstrips in the outer islands of Onoun and Ta in Chuuk. The Federated States of Micronesia is considering expanding air terminals in order to meet the increasing demand for air traffic. The islands are served by Continental Micronesia, Air Nauru, and Continental Airlines (USA). Pacific Missionary Aviation, based in Pohnpei and Yap, provides domestic air services.

There are several ports and harbors, such as Colonia (Yap), Kolonia (Pohnpei), Lele, and Moen. All of the states in the Federated States of Micronesia have deep draft harbors capable of handling almost all commercial shipping needs. Each port is capable of providing containerized cargo handling, as well as some warehousing and transshipment capabilities. All ports offer cold storage

Communications

Country	Telephones[a]	Telephones, Mobile/Cellular[a]	Radio Stations[b]	Radios[a]	TV Stations[a]	Televisions[a]	Internet Service Providers[c]	Internet Users[c]
Micronesia	11,000 (2001)	N/A	AM 5; FM 1; shortwave 0	N/A	2	N/A	1	2,000
United States	194 M	69.209 M (1998)	AM 4,762; FM 5,542; shortwave 18	575 M	1,500	219 M	7,800	148 M
Philippines	1.9 M	1.959 M (1998)	AM 366; FM 290; shortwave 3 (1999)	11.5 M	31	3.7 M	33	500,000
Solomon Islands	8,000	658	AM 3; FM 0; shortwave 0	57,000	0	3,000	1	3,000

[a]Data is for 1997 unless otherwise noted.
[b]Data is for 1998 unless otherwise noted.
[c]Data is for 2000 unless otherwise noted.

SOURCE: CIA *World Factbook 2001* [Online].

facilities. Shipping services are available to anywhere in the world on a monthly schedule by PM & O Line, Pacific Micronesia Line, Kyowa Lines, Palau Shipping Lines, Tiger Lines, and Saipan Shipping Company. Freight rates are relatively high, as volume shipping is rarely possible.

The 4 urban centers all have public water and sewer systems. Outside of the urban centers, the populations rely on water catchments (devices for trapping water), wells, and septic tank systems. Charges for water usage range from $1.50 to $5.40 per 6,000 gallons of water. Kosrae does not charge for water and sewerage.

With the exception of some small hydroelectric facilities in Kosrae and Pohnpei, electricity in the Federated States of Micronesia is produced by diesel generators. The principal energy source in Micronesia is imported petroleum. From 1993 to 1997, Micronesia spent $10 to $20 million per year for petroleum products. Power is generally available only in the 4 urban centers. The power system in Pohnpei is operated as a state enterprise fund and is the most reliable system. The other 3 states are moving in a similar direction. The existing power system can accommodate additional users, and the government is willing to provide such means when necessary. Electricity generating costs are $0.19 a kilowatt-hour, while charges range from $.05 a kilowatt-hour to $0.25 a kilowatt-hour.

The telecommunications system in the Federated States of Micronesia is highly developed and offers satellite access for telephone, telex, and facsimile to any location worldwide. There were 8,000 main telephone lines in use in 1995. For domestic purposes, the islands are interconnected by short-wave radiotelephones (used mostly for government business). For international links there are 4 Intelsat (Pacific Ocean) satellite earth stations.

The Federated States of Micronesia Postal Service delivers and sends mail by air. The Federated States of Micronesia is part of the U.S. zip code system. Postage rates between the Federated States of Micronesia and the United States are the same as U.S. domestic rates.

There are 5 AM radio stations and 1 FM radio station. The majority of stations broadcast in English. There are 2 broadcasting television stations.

ECONOMIC SECTORS

Economic activity in Micronesia consists primarily of **subsistence farming** and fishing as well as revenues from external licensing (the U.S. government, for example, makes a fixed payment to the Federated States of

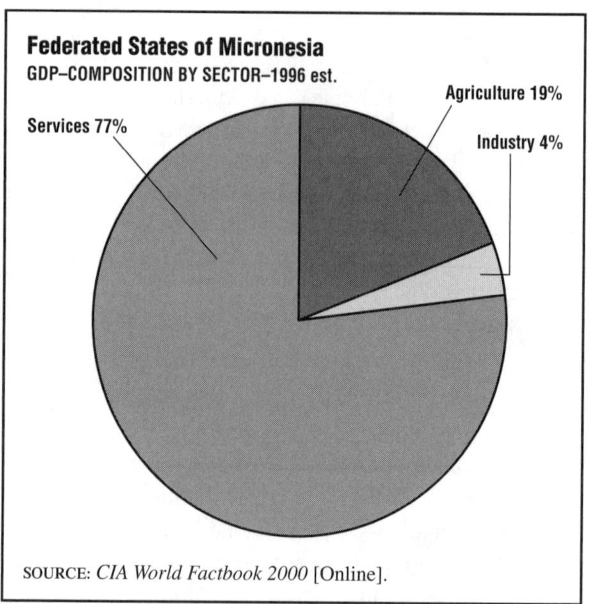

SOURCE: *CIA World Factbook 2000* [Online].

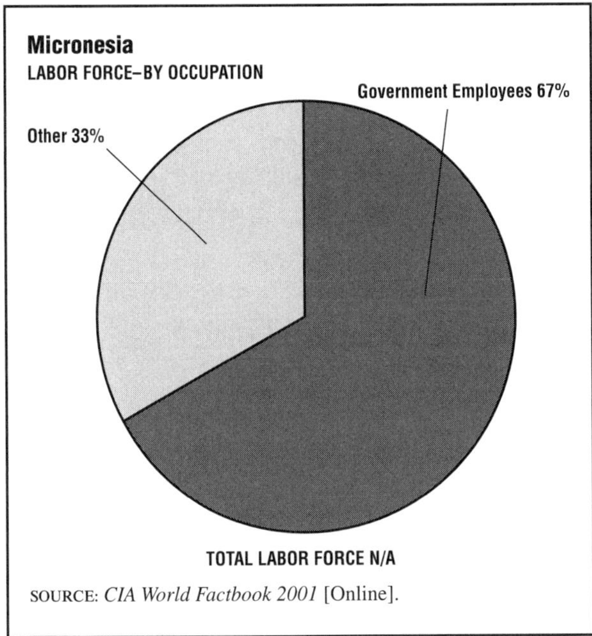

SOURCE: *CIA World Factbook 2001* [Online].

Micronesia for exclusive access to its waters). In the financial year ending September 30, 1997, fees from fisheries licensing agreements, mainly with Japan, contributed some 30 percent of domestic budgetary revenues.

The islands have no mineral deposits worth exploiting, with the possible exception of off-shore phosphate, but it is uncertain whether these deposits can be extracted commercially. The potential for a tourist industry exists, but the remoteness of the location and a lack of adequate facilities hinder development. Currently, monetary aid from the United States provides the majority of revenue for both the government and the national economy.

The government's main economic priority is to develop a sustainable, independent economy by bolstering the private sector and reforming the public sector with the objective of reducing dependence on foreign aid and encouraging economic self-sufficiency. In addition, the government supports international efforts to stop global warming and pollution in general, in order to protect the islands and their agricultural sectors. In recent years, the climate has been very unstable with typhoons, flooding, and mudslides followed by a drought.

AGRICULTURE

Farming is mainly on a subsistence level, although its importance is diminishing. The principal agricultural crops are coconuts, bananas, betel nuts, cassava, and sweet potatoes. The agricultural sector contributed 19 percent of GDP in 1996 and engaged 27 percent of the total labor force in 1994. Exports of agricultural products (excluding fish) accounted for 6 percent of export earnings in 1996, while exports of marine products accounted for 84 percent of total export revenues in that year. The annual rainfall received each year varies from 2,500 millimeters (98 inches) in Yap to 4,500–7,500 millimeters (177–295 inches) in Pohnpei. The limited water reserves in both Chuuk and Yap are a source of concern for the long term.

INDUSTRY

Industry (including mining, manufacturing, utilities, and construction) provided 4 percent of GDP in 1996, and engaged 10 percent of the total labor force in 1994. The major industrial productions are construction, fish processing, and craft items from shells, wood, and pearls. There is little manufacturing, other than garment production (in Yap) and the manufacture of buttons using troche shells.

SERVICES

The service sector provided an estimated 77 percent of GDP in 1996, and government services alone contributed 42.1 percent. The national and state governments in 1996–97 employed a total of 6,015 people, and services as a whole employed 63 percent of the labor force. Tourism is an increasingly important industry, and it is hoped that several projects to improve communications will further stimulate the sector, which has been hindered by the territory's remote location. The tourism industry was identified in the Asian Development Bank in mid-1995 as having the greatest potential for development and thus contributing to Micronesia's economic growth. Presently, most of the Federated States of Micronesia's tourism industry is inadequate and not competitive with destinations such as Guam and, soon, Palau. As of 1991, the most recent year for which such data are available, the Federated States of Micronesia's entire tourism industry (hotel, motel, and other accommodations) amounted to only 290 rooms, 144 of which were in Pohnpei, 80 in Chuuk, 26 in Yap, and 30 in Kosrae. Among the visitors from overseas, 60 percent are from the United States and 25 percent from Japan.

INTERNATIONAL TRADE

Thanks to its lack of exportable goods, Micronesia has traditionally run a large trade imbalance. In 1996, the **trade deficit** was $95 million, on exports of $73 million and imports of $168 million. The main exports of the Federated States of Micronesia are marine products, while the main imports are food, manufactured goods, machinery and equipment, beverages, and fuels. Micronesia's main trading partners are the United States, Japan, Australia, and Guam. In 1996, the United States supplied 73.2 percent of Micronesia's imports and Japan 11.9 percent.

Exchange rates: Micronesia

US$	
Jan 2001	1.0000
2000	1.0000
1999	1.0000
1998	1.0000
1997	1.0000
1996	1.0000

Note: US currency is used in the Federated States of Micronesia.

SOURCE: CIA *World Factbook 2001* [ONLINE].

MONEY

The United States dollar is the official currency of Federated States of Micronesia. Its value fluctuates in terms of the other main currencies of the world, but remains relatively stable. Financial regulation is provided by the Federated States of Micronesia Banking Board. Commercial banks include the Bank of the Federated States of Micronesia, the Bank of Guam, and the Bank of Hawaii. There is also the Federated States of Micronesia Development Bank, which has branches in all of the states, and which makes low-interest, long-term loans primarily to local investors.

POVERTY AND WEALTH

The average per capita income was estimated at $2,000 in 1998 (in the United States, by way of comparison, per capita income in 1998 was $29,340). Although manufactured goods are expensive, as they are mostly imported, basic foodstuffs are cheap, and this does much to alleviate poverty. The government has a considerable amount of income at its disposal as a result of the financial support from the United States, and as a result, it is able to support sections of the community (such as farmers in the outlying islands, with the subsidy of copra production) that might otherwise be in poverty.

GDP per Capita (US$)

Country	1996	1997	1998	1999	2000
Federated States of Micronesia	1,760	2,000	N/A	2,000	N/A
United States	28,600	30,200	31,500	33,900	36,200
Philippines	2,600	3,200	3,500	3,600	3,800
Solomon Islands	3,000	3,000	2,600	2,650	2,000

Note: Data are estimates.

SOURCE: *Handbook of the Nations*, 17th, 18th, 19th and 20th editions for 1996, 1997, 1998 and 1999 data; CIA *World Factbook 2001* [Online] for 2000 data.

There is a compulsory education law that requires all children to begin school at the age of 6. Children may leave school when they reach the age of 14 or after completing the eighth grade. There are virtually 100 percent enrollment rates in primary and, until the age of 14, in secondary education. The adult literacy rate was estimated at 89 percent in 1980. The government maintains a free medical service.

WORKING CONDITIONS

The unemployment rate in Federated States of Micronesia was estimated at 27 percent in 1989, but had fallen to 16 percent by 1999. These figures are high, the degree of under-utilization of the labor force is somewhat greater than even these figures suggest. For much of the year in small-scale family farming there is relatively little work to do, and this is shared among the family members. During planting and harvesting, there is more work to be done, and everyone is more fully occupied. Everyone sharing the work appears to have an occupation in agriculture, but many workers are not engaged full time for all the year, and hence there is some "disguised unemployment."

The government respects the human rights of its citizens. There is no law dealing specifically with trade unions or with the right to collective bargaining. Individual employers, the largest of which are the national and state governments, set wages.

Neither the constitution nor the law specifically prohibits forced and bonded labor by children, but such practices are not known to occur. There is no law establishing a minimum age for employment of children. While in practice there is no employment of children for wages, they often assist their families in subsistence farming activities.

The 4 state governments have established minimum wage rates for government workers. Pohnpei has a minimum hourly wage rate of $2.00 an hour for government and $1.35 an hour for private workers. The other 3 states have established minimum hourly rates only for government workers of $1.25 for Chuuk, $1.49 for Kosrae, and $0.80 for Yap. The minimum hourly wage for employment with the national government is $1.68. These minimum wage structures and the wages customarily paid to skilled workers are sufficient to provide an adequate standard of living under local conditions.

There are no laws regulating hours of work (although a 40-hour workweek is standard practice) or prescribing standards of occupational safety and health. A federal regulation requires that employers provide a safe workplace. The Department of Health has no enforcement capability and working conditions vary in practice. Foreign laborers are paid at a lower rate than citizens, work longer hours per day, and work a 6-day week in contrast to the 5-day week for citizens.

COUNTRY HISTORY AND ECONOMIC DEVELOPMENT

1525. Portuguese navigators in search of the Spice Islands (Indonesia) come upon Yap and Ulithi. Spanish expeditions later explored the rest of the Caroline Islands and make the first European contact with native peoples.

1526–1899. The Spanish Empire claims sovereignty over the Caroline Islands.

1899. Facing insurmountable management challenges in its Pacific empire as war with the United States looms, Spain sells the islands to Germany. The German administration encourages the development of trade and the production of copra (dried coconuts).

1914. German administration ends when Japanese naval squadrons take possession of the Caroline Islands, the Marshall Islands, and the islands of the Marianas at the start of World War I (1914–18).

1918. Japanese economic interest and settlement in the islands expands. The Japanese population in Micronesia exceeds 100,000, compared with an indigenous population of about 40,000. Sugar cane, other tropical crops, mining, and fishing are developed as major industries.

1939–1945. World War II abruptly ends the relative prosperity experienced during the period of Japanese civil administration.

1947. The United Nations establishes the Trust Territory of the Pacific Islands (TTPI), and the United States takes on the role of trustee as administering authority. The TTPI consists of the 4 island groups that will later become the states of the Federated States of Micronesia.

1965. The Congress of Micronesia formed.

1967. A commission is established to examine the future political status of the islands.

1970. Micronesians declare their rights to sovereignty over their own lands, to self-determination, to devise their own constitution, and to revoke their association with the United States.

1977. U.S. President Jimmy Carter announces that his administration intends to terminate the trusteeship agreement.

1978. Following a constitutional convention, the Federated States of Micronesia drafts a constitution that provides for federation of the 4 states: Chuuk (formerly Truk), Pohnpei (formerly Ponape), Kosrae (formerly Kusaie), and Yap.

1979. The 4 states ratify the constitution, and the Federated States of Micronesia comes into being.

1982. The United States signs a Compact of Free Association with the Federated States of Micronesia.

1986. The Federated States of Micronesia becomes self-governing.

1991. Micronesia achieves full independence and becomes a member of the United Nations.

1993. Micronesia joins the International Monetary Fund.

2001. Micronesia begins a renegotiation of Compact of Free Association with the United States to secure the continuation of financial support. The government announces a privatization plan.

FUTURE TRENDS

Although Micronesia will continue to be hampered economically by its isolated location, small geographical area, and population size, it has the enormous benefit of the generous financial support of the United States. The level of this support is undergoing renegotiation, with the United States offering $74 million a year and Micronesia requesting $84 million. Even at the lower level of support, this would secure Micronesia's living standards for the next 15 years of the agreement (the level of U.S. assistance in 2000 was $79 million).

Micronesia had a positive GDP growth rate in 2000 of 2.5 percent, and although this is encouraging in view of the negative growth rates recorded from 1996 to 1999, it is still below the population growth rate of 3.3 percent a year. There is pressure on the government from the IMF to reduce expenditures and increase revenue collection to maintain the **budget surplus** achieved since 1996, and to maintain the current low **inflation rate** (2.8 percent in 2000). The government has announced a privatization program to try to improve efficiency in the economy, and this is to be supported by loans from the Asian Development Bank

Fisheries is targeted as one the industries presenting the greatest potential for growth in the private sector. The fishing industry should see improvements in the near future as Japan is funding a $2.8 million project to train fishermen in Micronesia. However, both Taiwan and Japan are seeking to reduce the license payments they make for fishing in Micronesia's waters. They argue that the current low price for tuna on the world market makes this necessary, and they also claim that tuna have begun to migrate away from Micronesia's waters to other parts of the Pacific.

Tourism is the second sector with expansion potential. In 2000, the islands received 17,152 visitors. The number of visitors has fallen slightly for each of the past 4 years. Initially, the fall was credited to the Asian financial crisis, particularly affecting the number of Japanese tourists. However, the fact that the fall has continued indicates that there is much to be done in regenerating the sector, and this will require foreign investment in hotels and an international marketing program. A British firm, Travel Research International, has been engaged to promote Micronesia's tourism, concentrating on diving, cultural tourism, deep-sea fishing, and **eco-tourism** as the main attractions.

In common with many other South Pacific countries, Micronesia is alarmed by the effect continuing global warming will have on its islands. The consequent rise in the level of the oceans threatens low-lying islands with flooding and, eventually, with submergence.

DEPENDENCIES

Micronesia has no territories or colonies.

BIBLIOGRAPHY

Economist Intelligence Unit. *Country Profile: Federated States of Micronesia.* London: Economist Intelligence Unit, 2001.

Embassy of the Federated States of Micronesia, Washington, D.C. <http://www.fsmembassy.org>. Accessed September 2001.

Goetzfridt, N. J., and W. L. Wuerch. *Micronesia 1975–1987.* Westport, CT: Greenwood Publishing, 1989.

Pacific Islands Business Network. *Federated States of Micronesia: Country Profile.* <http://pidp.ewc.hawaii.edu/pibn/countries/fsm.htm>. Accessed September 2001.

U.S. Central Intelligence Agency. *World Factbook 2000.* <http://www.odci.gov/cia/publications/factbook/index.html>. Accessed August 2001.

U.S. Department of State. *Background Notes: Federated States of Micronesia, June 1996.* <http://www.state.gov/www/background_notes/micronesia_0696_bgn.html>. Accessed September 2001.

—Oygul Musakhanova

MONGOLIA

Mongol Uls

CAPITAL: Ulaanbaatar (formerly spelled Ulan Bator).

MONETARY UNIT: Mongolian tughrik (togrog) (MT), equal to 100 mongos. There are coins of 1, 5, 10, and 50 mongos. Paper money comes in notes of 1, 5, 10, 20, 50, 100, 500, 1,000, 5,000, and 10,000 tughriks.

CHIEF EXPORTS: Copper, gold, non-ferrous metals and animal products, including cashmere, wool, livestock.

CHIEF IMPORTS: Machinery and equipment, chemicals, industrial consumer goods, fuel and food products, including sugar and tea.

GROSS DOMESTIC PRODUCT: US$6.1 billion (1999 est.).

BALANCE OF TRADE: **Exports:** US$454.3 million (1999 est.). **Imports:** US$510.7 million (1999 est.).

COUNTRY OVERVIEW

LOCATION AND SIZE. Formerly known as Outer Mongolia, the Republic of Mongolia is a landlocked country located between the Russian Federation and the People's Republic of China. The country has an area of 1,565,000 square kilometers (604,246 square miles), slightly smaller than the state of Alaska. Mongolia's capital city, Ulaanbaatar, is located in the northeast of the country, 200 kilometers (124 miles) from the Russian border.

POPULATION. The population of Mongolia was estimated at 2,650,952 in July 2000. It has almost doubled since the 1960s, due to improved health and medical facilities, and longer life expectancy. In 2000 the birth rate stood at 21.53 per 1,000 while the death rate stood at 6.14 per 1,000. The estimated annual population growth ratc is 1.54 percent; if the current trend remains unchanged, the population is expected to double once more within the next 25–30 years.

With ethnic Mongols making up almost 90 percent of the population, Mongolia is ethnically homogenous (uniform). Kazakhs make up 4 percent, and other ethnic groups, including Chinese and Russians, round out the total. The Mongolian population is young, with 34 percent below the age of 15 and just 4 percent older than 65. Urbanization started only in the 1960s, but by the late 1990s almost 58 percent of Mongolians lived in urban areas. Ulaanbaatar and its suburbs are home to 773,700 people, or nearly one-third of the country's total.

At the beginning of the 20th century, the Mongolians were under threat of extinction due to the absence of medical services, high infant mortality, diseases and epidemics, and natural disasters. After independence in 1921, the government in this sparsely populated country began promoting population growth. This policy reversed the decline and stimulated a rapid increase in the population during the second half of the 20th century. However, population density remains one of the lowest in the world, with about 1.6 people per square kilometer (3.9 people per square mile). The country's low population can be explained in part by its geographic and climatic extremes: Mongolia is home to soaring mountains and burning deserts, including the Gobi Desert in the southern third of the country; because of the country's high average altitude, winters are long and temperatures extreme.

OVERVIEW OF ECONOMY

Mining, agriculture, and the processing of agricultural products are the 3 main sectors of the Mongolian economy. For centuries, the Mongolians have been engaged in animal husbandry, raising horses, sheep, goats, cattle, and camels. Since the vast prairie land could support millions of cattle and sheep, but not sustain crop cultivation, the Mongolians often bought wheat, barley, and oats from their neighbors, and crop production was of secondary importance for them. Animal husbandry and hunting provided other important sources of livelihood and products for trade, such as marmot and squirrels found in the rich forests of northern Mongolia.

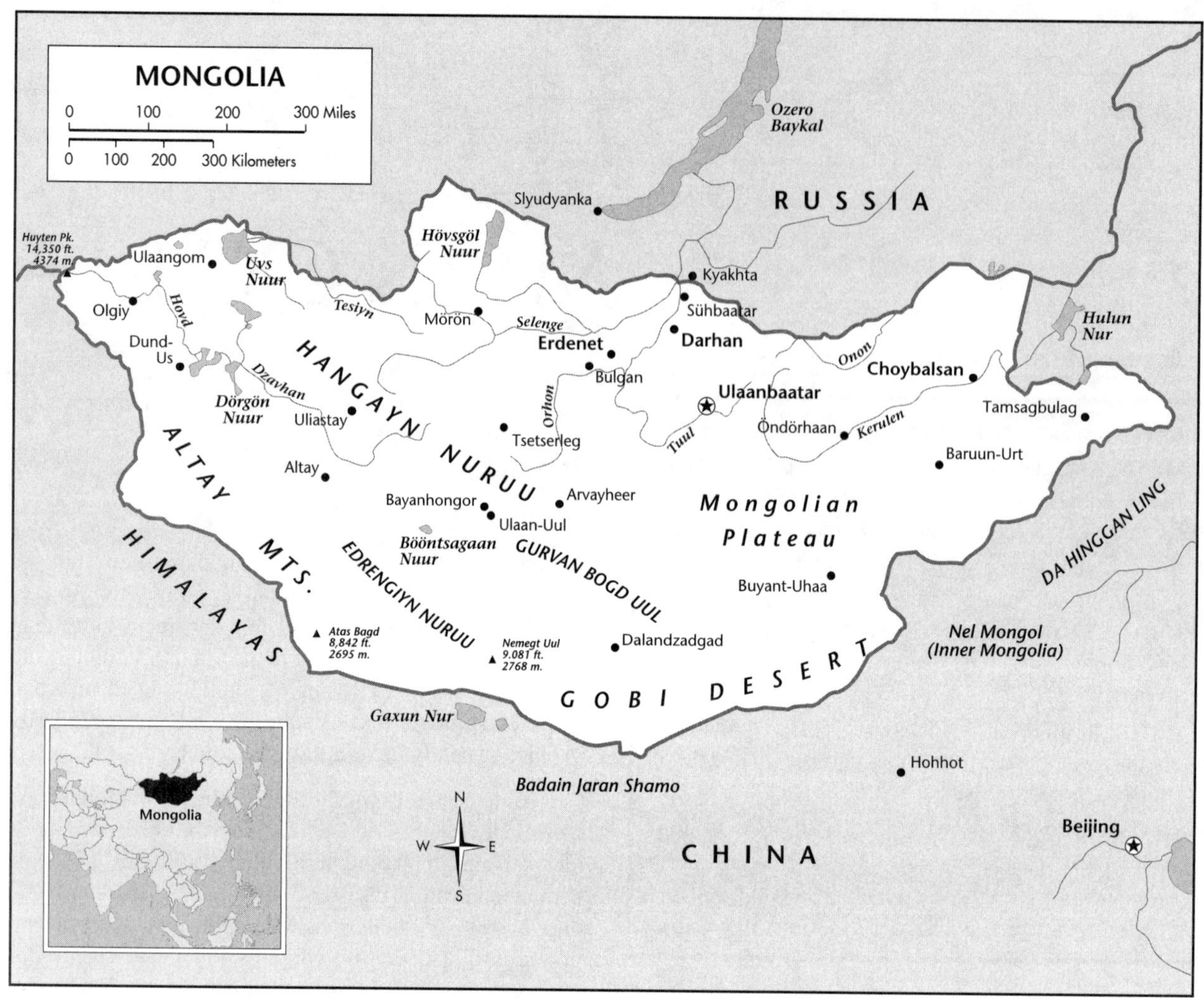

The Mongolians long had close relations with neighboring China, which historically was one of its biggest trading partners. However, relations between Mongolians and Chinese were often interrupted by devastating wars and military conflicts and, gradually, the Chinese Empire established political control over Mongolia. These wars damaged Mongolian economic and social development. Consequently, Mongolia entered the 20th century as an underdeveloped, feudal country.

Most of the major economic and social changes in the 20th century came as a result of **communist** revolutions in neighboring countries. The Chinese Revolution of 1911 and the Russian Revolution of 1917, which were directed against imperial regimes and promised social justice, had profound effects on the Mongolian elite. In 1921, with Soviet assistance, Mongolia established an independent provisional government and declared independence from China. In 1924 the Mongolian People's Revolutionary Party came to power, remaining in control for the next 70 years. It introduced radical political and economic changes, state control, and central state planning, modeled on the Soviet political and economic systems. With Soviet assistance, the Mongolian government introduced large-scale farming centered around state-controlled collective farms. It also established light industry and mining operations. As in most **socialist** countries, almost all economic activities in Mongolia were state-controlled, and private entrepreneurial initiatives were limited. Until the 1990s, the Soviet Union and its eastern European territories remained Mongolia's main trading partners, the main market for its products, and the main source of foreign aid. According to the International Monetary Fund (IMF), the Mongolian economy grew at an average annual rate of 6.0 percent between 1979 and 1989, which was one of the highest growth rates in communist countries.

Major changes came in the late 1980s with the introduction of democratization and market-oriented reforms. These changes were largely peaceful since they were started by the ruling class under the influence of the neighboring Soviet Union and China. In early 1990s, the Mongolian government formulated its program of radical economic change (the so-called "shock therapy" approach) with the assistance of international organizations such as the World Bank and the IMF. This program was based on 3 main strategies: rapid **privatization**, rapid price **liberalization**, and currency reform. According to the IMF, Mongolia's economy declined at an average annual rate of 0.1 percent between 1989 and 1999.

The modern Mongolian economy largely relies on the export of raw materials to international markets. The country's main exports are copper concentrate (which accounted for almost 47 percent of its total export earnings in 1998), cashmere (the country produces almost 30 percent of the world's cashmere), and textile and meat products. Mongolia depends heavily on imports of machinery, fuels, industrial and **consumer goods**, and food products. Because of the transitional **recession** and disappearance of aid from the former USSR, Mongolia's economy increasingly relies on foreign aid and credits. Total **external debt** has reached almost US$738.8 million (1998), quite a large figure for a nation of only 2.6 million people.

POLITICS, GOVERNMENT, AND TAXATION

Since achieving independence from China in 1921, Mongolia has made consistent attempts to expand political participation beyond tribal and religious identities and affiliations. An attempt was made to build a Soviet-type political regime based on political parties, a parliamentary system, and Communist ideology. The Mongolian People's Party was founded in 1921, and renamed the Mongolian People's Revolutionary Party (MPRP) in 1924. Until 1990, Mongolia preserved a one-party political system in which the MPRP remained the main political force.

Influenced by the late 1980s reforms of USSR leader Mikhail Gorbachev, the Mongolian Constitution was amended in 1990, and the first multiparty election for the Great Hural (Parliament) took place that same year. The MPRP was challenged by the newly formed Mongolian National Democratic Party (MNDP), the Mongolian Socialist Democratic Party (MSDP), and several others. The MPRP gained almost 80 percent of the seats in the new Parliament and formed a government led by President Punsalmaagiin Ochirbat. Despite their overwhelming victory, the former Communists showed a great sense of tolerance toward the opposition and promoted genuine reforms in liberalizing the political and economic system, introducing a new constitution (1992) and a new **unicameral** (one house) Parliament. However, the MPRP had a serious setback when President Ochirbat broke with his party; in 1993 he won the first direct presidential elections as an opposition candidate. In 1996, the Democratic Coalition, led by the MNDP and the MSDP, defeated the MPRP, taking 49 of the 76 seats in Parliament. The Democratic Coalition advocated a greater opening up of the economy and full privatization. In the 1997 presidential election, President Orchibat, the Democratic Coalition candidate, lost to MPRP candidate Natsagiin Bagabandi, who came to power calling for greater social assistance and more balanced reforms. The MPRP further strengthened its position in the July 2000 Parliamentary election, taking 72 seats. This latest Mongolian transition was largely peaceful, and its military does not play any active role in its politics.

Throughout the 1990s, the government promoted market-oriented reforms, abandoning the **centrally planned economy** and focusing on privatization, price liberalization, and a new monetary system. However, the state's sudden withdrawal of **subsidies** led to a steep transitional recession affecting almost all sectors of the economy, especially construction and industries. The weakness of the legal system and the inability of state institutions to implement property rights and contract law undermined confidence among local and foreign investors.

INFRASTRUCTURE, POWER, AND COMMUNICATIONS

During the Cold War (1945–89), Mongolia's transportation **infrastructure** enjoyed a relatively high level of investment to insure its military usefulness. After-

Communications

Country	Newspapers	Radios	TV Sets[a]	Cable subscribers[a]	Mobile Phones[a]	Fax Machines[a]	Personal Computers[a]	Internet Hosts[b]	Internet Users[b]
	1996	1997	1998	1998	1998	1998	1998	1999	1999
Mongolia	27	151	63	10.8	1	2.7	5.4	0.04	6
United States	215	2,146	847	244.3	256	78.4	458.6	1,508.77	74,100
China	N/A	333	272	40.0	19	1.6	8.9	0.50	8,900
Kazakhstan	N/A	384	231	N/A	2	0.1	N/A	1.42	70

[a]Data are from International Telecommunication Union, *World Telecommunication Development Report 1999* and are per 1,000 people.
[b]Data are from the Internet Software Consortium (http://www.isc.org) and are per 10,000 people.

SOURCE: World Bank. *World Development Indicators 2000.*

wards, investments in transportation infrastructure diminished considerably, and the quality of the roads is declining. The country is served by the 1,928 kilometer (1,198 mile) Trans-Mongolian railway, which connects it with both Beijing and Moscow. Mongolia also has 49,250 kilometers (30,603 miles) of unevenly distributed highways, of which only 1,674 kilometers (1,040 miles) are paved, mainly in the northern part of the country. In the south and southwest, horses and camels are still important modes of transportation. An international airport connects Ulaanbaatar with Beijing, Moscow, and other destinations, and there are 34 smaller airports, only 7 of which have paved runways.

Electrical power is supplied by the Central Electricity System (CES), which produces around 2.66 billion kilowatt hours (1998) of power. Five coal-fired power stations provide almost 85 percent of the total, with the balance imported from Russia. During the 1990s, attempts were made to renovate the CES with international aid and to build small hydroelectric and wind-powered stations. Power interruptions are common, and some remote areas remain without electricity, where diesel oil, wood, and dried horse and camel dung is used as fuel.

Telecommunication services in Mongolia have been under reconstruction since the early 1990s. In 1997, there were 93,800 telephone lines, 2,000 mobile-phone subscribers, and 13,000 personal computers. Internet access was established in 1996.

ECONOMIC SECTORS

In 1999, Mongolia derived its GDP from 3 principal sectors: agriculture, fishing, and hunting (33 percent), industry (24 percent), and services (43 percent). Historically, livestock breeding and agriculture have been the cornerstones of the national economy. With Soviet assistance, Mongolia established an industrial sector based mainly on mining and the processing of agricultural products. Mongolian economic development is limited by its landlocked isolation, harsh continental climate, and small population. Significant economic potential lies in its unexploited natural resources including copper, molybdenum, tin, tungsten, and gold. Domestic reserves of coal can satisfy growing energy consumption, and the discovery of oil reserves in 1994 raises the possibility that Mongolia might eventually become a petroleum-exporting country.

Mongolia
GDP–COMPOSITION BY SECTOR–1999 est.

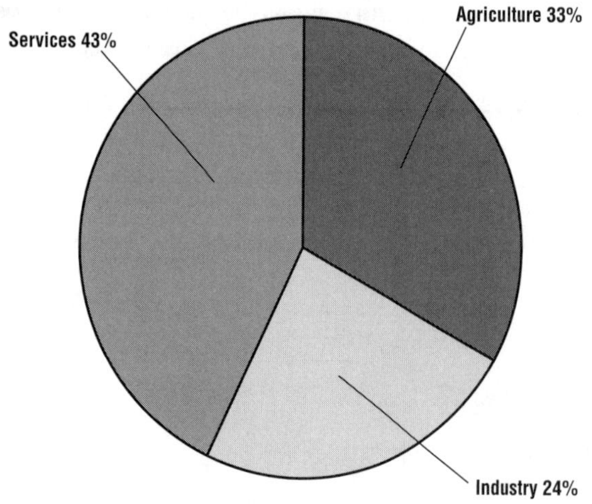

Agriculture 33%
Services 43%
Industry 24%

SOURCE: *CIA World Factbook 2000* [Online].

During the 1990s, Mongolia experienced a deep recession with the disappearance of Soviet economic assistance and the disintegration of the Soviet-backed Council for Mutual Economic Assistance (CMEA), which had been a major market for Mongolian exports. The country increasingly relies on the export of raw materials to the international market, and it is extremely vulnerable to fluctuations in world prices for its major export products, copper and cashmere. Mongolia needs large **foreign direct investments** and international assistance to modernize existing technologies and to begin major economic changes. In the 1990s, the Mongolian government undertook a series of free-market oriented economic reforms focusing on privatization, internal and external trade liberalization, and promotion of private entrepreneurs. In 1997, because of its rapid and extended economic liberalization, Mongolia became one of the first of the former socialist countries to be accepted into the World Trade Organization (WTO), opening up Western markets for Mongolian goods.

AGRICULTURE

The agricultural sector, which employs about half of Mongolia's population, underwent major **deregulation** during the 1990s. In September 1991, the *negdels* (state-controlled collective farms) were privatized and reformed into smaller units. A combination of mismanagement and harsh weather led to higher meat prices and a depression in the agricultural processing industries. Since 1991 many herders, having no experience outside their negdels, have struggled to adapt themselves to the new economic realities. Both animal herding and crop cultivation are extremely vulnerable to the region's harsh weather and climate changes, which include occasional drought. In 1996, forest and prairie fires caused damage estimated at $1.4 billion and seriously damaged the region's environment. In the winter of 1999–2000, approximately 2.4 million animals died as a result of extremely cold and icy weather, bringing poverty and hunger to many Mongolian farmers.

ANIMAL HERDING. Animal herding is the most important sector of Mongolian agriculture, providing almost two-thirds of agricultural production. It provides a source of income, food, and a mode of transportation for a significant part of the population as well as being an important part of Mongolia's exports. Mongols still migrate around vast prairies, raising horses, sheep, goats, cattle, and camels. By the second half of the 1990s, the livestock population had reached a record high of 31.2 million, almost 90 percent of which was privately owned. With the liberalization of international trade, many herders turned to raising goats to produce valuable cashmere, and the number of goats almost doubled to 11 million between 1992 and 1998. In 1998 Mongolia produced 502.1 tons of cashmere, but fluctuations in the world price of this commodity have hurt profits. Overgrazing of pasture land, especially by goats, could potentially cause environmental degradation in the fragile prairie ecosystem, and there are limited resources available to reverse the trend.

CROP CULTIVATION. In 1998 Mongolia produced 194,900 tons of cereals (down from 330,700 tons in 1994), 65.2 tons of potatoes, and 45.7 tons of vegetables. Crop cultivation is limited, due to the harsh continental climate (the growing season is just more than 100 days long) and a shortage of arable (cultivatable) land, though this sector plays an important role in sustaining self-sufficiency in foodstuffs. After the privatization of the large state-controlled farms in the 1990s, crop production fell sharply, a decline blamed on a lack of management skills, funds, and technologies, and on an ill-considered and ill-implemented privatization program. Other sectors of Mongolian agriculture include forestry, fishery, and fur production, all relatively minor.

INDUSTRY

Industrialization was introduced into Mongolia in the 1970s, with large investments from the Soviet Union, especially for mining and the processing of agricultural products. Through the 1970s and 1980s, the Mongolian government implemented an industrialization program that emphasized increasing investments and diversifying the country's exports. In the 1990s, because of prevailing conditions in the international market and the collapse of the traditional Soviet market, Mongolian industry underwent considerable restructuring. By 2001, Mongolia increasingly relied on export of its mineral resources, although there have been considerable efforts made to revive its manufacturing sector.

MINING. Copper, gold, molybdenum and fluorspar concentrates are the major natural resources of export significance in Mongolia. In 1998 Mongolia exported 485,000 tons of copper concentrate, valued at $124 million; around 12.5 tons of gold, valued at $117.2 million; and 4,131 tons of molybdenum concentrate, valued at $12.1 million. Export of these mineral resources provided around 60 percent of total export earnings in 1998. Mongolian coal reserves are estimated at approximately 100 billion tons, but the country extracts coal mainly for domestic consumption, at a level of around 5.1 million tons per year.

Mining is a relatively new sector in the Mongolian economy. Although the country is rich in various natural resources, until the 1970s they were under-exploited. Major mining plants were built in the 1970s with Soviet assistance. The biggest, Erdenet and Darhan, are situated in the north of the country, close to the Russian border. In the 1990s, the Mongolian government struggled to attract international investors into the mining sector. Mongolia still largely relies on Russian technology in this sector of the economy, although Russian involvement began to diminish during the 1990s as **multinational corporations** started to move into the mining sector.

In the mid-1990s, oil reserves were discovered, estimated at around 5 billion barrels, that could be used both for domestic consumption and for export to China. Extraction of oil from Tamsag basin began in 1997 and completion of an oil refinery is expected in Nalaikh, near Ulaanbaatar, in 2002. International investment is needed to develop its oil reserves at full scale.

MANUFACTURING. Mongolia's manufacturing sector accounted for 24 percent of GDP in 1998, employing 12.4 percent of the **labor force** in the production of agricultural products, garments, leather goods, and carpets. During the era of state-controlled industry (1924–91), these goods were produced mainly in small and medium-sized, state-owned enterprises for export to the Soviet Union and Eastern Europe. Russia was also the main market for Mongolia's food processing industry, which produced sausages and canned meat.

The manufacturing industry was one of the fastest growing sectors of the economy in the 1970s and 1980s, but because of excessive state control, it was relatively inefficient and made low quality products. In the 1990s, the government introduced a privatization program aimed at stimulating private initiative and increasing productivity, but the sector could not compete internationally because of a lack of management skills, lack of investments, and inefficient technologies. A steep recession, which threatened thousands of jobs and provoked social protests, followed. Between 1994 and 1998, production of leather footwear declined from 407,000 pairs to 33,000, leather coats from 35,000 to zero, sheepskin coats from 57,000 to 1,000, and woolen fabrics from 77,000 square meters to 5,000 square meters.

SERVICES

Between 1924 and 1991, Mongolia's services sector was heavily state-controlled and was significantly underdeveloped. Since the early 1990s, the Mongolian government has made considerable efforts to deregulate this sector, with special attention focused on reforming the financial services industry. The **monopoly** of the state bank was broken and commercial banks were allowed to compete. This sector was restructured with assistance from the World Bank and the International Monetary Fund (IMF). In 2000 there were 12 banks, 6 state-owned and 6 privately owned.

Tourism is an underdeveloped sector of the economy, limited by lack of accommodation facilities and transportation infrastructure. Thanks to the combination of Mongolia's landscape and its position on the old Silk Road (the trade route connecting China with Western Europe in medieval times), adventure tourism offers a high growth potential. Mongolia welcomed about 160,000 tourists in 1999, and the government passed a law establishing the National Tourism Development Program: 2000–2015 in order to boost this sector.

The **retail** sector is quite underdeveloped by Western standards, consisting mainly of small shops and restaurants. With the growth in tourism since the 1990s, the quality of the retail sector and diversity of services have been improving.

INTERNATIONAL TRADE

Mongolian international trade has fluctuated considerably during last 3 decades. After the collapse of both the Council for Mutual Economic Assistance (CMEA) and trade with the former Soviet Union, Mongolian international trade experienced a dramatic decline that continued until the mid-1990s. Since then, Mongolian trade has started a slow recovery, boosted by growing exports of gold and other mineral resources. Mongolia joined the World Trade Organization (WTO) in 1997.

During the 1990s Mongolia managed to diversify its markets, and China became one of its fastest-growing trade partners. In 1998 exports to China amounted to 30.1 percent of total Mongolian exports, followed by Switzerland (21.5 percent), Russia (12.1 percent), South Korea (9.7 percent) and the United States (8.1 percent). In that year, Russia remained the primary source of imports (30.6 percent), followed by China (13.3 percent), Japan (11.7 percent), South Korea (7.5 percent), and the United States (6.9 percent.) In 1998 Mongolia exported a total of $316.8 million in goods and imported $472.4 million in goods.

Exchange rates: Mongolia

tughriks per US$1	
Dec 2000	1,097.00
2000	1,076.67
1999	1,072.37
1998	840.83
1997	789.99
1996	548.40

SOURCE: CIA *World Factbook 2001* [ONLINE].

Trade (expressed in billions of US$): Mongolia

	Exports	Imports
1975	N/A	N/A
1980	.403	.548
1985	.689	1.096
1990	.661	.924
1995	.473	.415
1998	N/A	N/A

SOURCE: International Monetary Fund. *International Financial Statistics Yearbook 1999.*

MONEY

During the era of state control (1924–91), the Mongolian tughrik had a fixed rate (4 to the U.S. dollar in 1989), and was not freely convertible. With the introduction of convertibility in the early 1990s, there was a sudden surge in **hard currency** demand and the tughrik depreciated (dropped in value) sharply (MT448.61 to the U.S. dollar in 1995 and MT1,072.37 to the U.S. dollar in 1999). The Mongolian government has tried to stabilize its currency and its economy by relying heavily on international assistance from the World Bank and the IMF. The annual rate of **inflation**, which soared to around 300 percent in 1993, was reduced to 15 percent in 2000. The Bank of Mongolia, the nation's central bank, seeks to maintain a tight **monetary policy** in order to stabilize the value of the currency and reduce inflation.

POVERTY AND WEALTH

Reforms during the 1990s brought mixed results to the Mongolian people. While they removed state control over the economy, allowed private businesses, and di-

GDP per Capita (US$)

Country	1975	1980	1985	1990	1998
Mongolia	N/A	N/A	479	498	408
United States	19,364	21,529	23,200	25,363	29,683
China	138	168	261	349	727
Kazakhstan	N/A	N/A	N/A	2,073	1,281

SOURCE: United Nations. *Human Development Report 2000; Trends in human development and per capita income.*

Distribution of Income or Consumption by Percentage Share: Mongolia

Lowest 10%	2.9
Lowest 20%	7.3
Second 20%	12.2
Third 20%	16.6
Fourth 20%	23.0
Highest 20%	40.9
Highest 10%	24.5

Survey year: 1995

Note: This information refers to expenditure shares by percentiles of the population and is ranked by per capita expenditure.

SOURCE: *2000 World Development Indicators* [CD-ROM].

versified international trade, they also brought widespread poverty, a diminishing **social-welfare system**, especially in health care and education, a rise in organized crime, and huge gaps in personal income.

In 1999, per capita GDP was estimated at US$2,320. According to the United Nations Development Program's Human Development Report, a statistical survey of the standard of living of the world's nations, Mongolia was ranked 110th, just behind China and Egypt, but just ahead of El Salvador and Bolivia. This is largely because of the strong education and health systems built during the single party (1924–1991) era, which remain strong despite declines in the 1990s. In 2000, the enrollment rate at primary and secondary schools stood at 84 percent, and most people had access to health care services. The government plans to increase spending in these areas, however, to return them to the levels the country enjoyed before 1991.

WORKING CONDITIONS

Since the abandonment of state guarantees of employment in 1993, the unemployment rate among Mongolia's workforce of 1.256 million has been rising, reaching an official rate of 4.5 percent in 1998. In 1998, there were 49,800 workers registered as unemployed, but some estimates put the figure as high as 200,000, especially in remote small towns and villages. Working conditions remain far from ideal because of low wages and harsh economic conditions. Until the 1990s, the trade-union movement was state-controlled; with the introduction of market-oriented reforms Mongolia's trade unions have struggled to gain membership, though they still maintain close affiliations with political parties.

COUNTRY HISTORY AND ECONOMIC DEVELOPMENT

1921. Mongolia declares independence from China.

1924. Mongolian People's Revolutionary Party (MPRP) comes to power, remaining the ruling party for the next 70 years.

1946. China formally recognizes Mongolia's independence.

1961. Mongolia joins the United Nations.

1987. Mongolia normalizes its relations with China and signs a treaty concerning the resolution of border disputes.

1990. Mongolian Constitution is amended, and the first multiparty election for Parliament takes place.

1992. New constitution is adopted by the Great Hural (Parliament).

1993. Punsalmaagiin Ochirbat is elected president in the first direct presidential election.

1993. Mongolian tughrik is made freely convertible.

1996. For the first time in modern Mongolian electoral history, the MPRP is defeated by a Democratic Coalition led by the MNDP and the MSDP.

1997. Mongolia joins the World Trade Organization.

2000. MPRP returns to power, taking 72 seats in parliamentary elections.

Household Consumption in PPP Terms

Country	All food	Clothing and footwear	Fuel and power[a]	Health care[b]	Education[b]	Transport & Communications	Other
Mongolia	56	14	9	8	14	1	−2
United States	13	9	9	4	6	8	51
China	N/A	N/A	N/A	N/A	N/A	N/A	N/A
Kazakhstan	37	10	20	9	6	6	12

Data represent percentage of consumption in PPP terms.

[a]Excludes energy used for transport.

[b]Includes government and private expenditures.

SOURCE: World Bank. *World Development Indicators 2000.*

FUTURE TRENDS

By 2001, Mongolia was able to achieve **macroeconomic** (large-scale, overall) stability, although at the very high cost of growing poverty and inequality. It will likely take another decade before the country achieves full recovery from its transition from state control to private control of the economy. Mongolia's future is uncertain because of its geographical isolation, difficulties in attracting foreign investors, growing debt, and increasing dependence on international humanitarian assistance. Global climate changes may threaten the very existence of agriculture and animal husbandry in Mongolia. However, Mongolia should be able to depend on its strengths in exporting raw materials, and it has potential oil fields that could also contribute to export earnings—if oil field development receives the necessary investments. Moreover, private enterprise has proved surprisingly strong, outperforming state-controlled industries in head-to-head competition. As more private businesses gain experience and financial strength, the Mongolian economy should become more diversified and stable.

DEPENDENCIES

Mongolia has no territories or colonies.

BIBLIOGRAPHY

Akiner, Shirin, editor. *Mongolia Today.* London: Routledge,1991.

Economist Intelligence Unit. *Country Report: Mongolia, November 2000.* London: Economist Intelligence Unit, 2000.

Fletcher, Sanjay, Catriona Purfield, and Sergei Dodzin. *Mongolia. Statistical Annex.* Washington, D.C.: World Bank, January 2000.

Human Development Report Mongolia 2000: Reorienting the State. Ulaanbaatar: UNDP and Government of Mongolia, 2000.

Mongolia: Toward a Market Economy. Washington, D.C.: World Bank, December 1992.

The Mongol Messenger. <http://www.mongolnet.mn/mglmsg>. Accessed February 2001.

Nixon, F.I., B. Walters, B. Suvd, and P. Luvsandori, editors. *The Mongolian Economy: A Manual of Applied Economics of an Economy in Transition.* Aldershot, UK: Edward Elgar, 2000.

UB-Post. <http://www.ulaanbaatar.net/ubpost>. Accessed February 2001.

United Nations in Mongolia. <http://www.un-mongolia.mn>. Accessed February 2001.

U.S. Central Intelligence Agency. *The World Factbook, 2000.* <http://www.cia.gov/cia/publications/factbook>. Accessed June 2001.

—Rafis Abazov

NAURU

Republic of Nauru

CAPITAL: No official capital, but the Yaren District houses the government offices.

MONETARY UNIT: Nauru uses the Australian dollar (A$). One Australian dollar equals 100 cents. There are coins of 2 dollars, 1 dollar, 50 cents, 20 cents, 10 cents, and 5 cents. There is no 1 cent coin. Banknotes come in denominations of 100, 50, 20, 10, and 5 dollars.

CHIEF EXPORTS: Phosphate.

CHIEF IMPORTS: Food, fuel, manufactured goods, building materials, machinery.

GROSS DOMESTIC PRODUCT: US$201.3 million (1999 est.).

BALANCE OF TRADE: **Exports:** US$19 million (1997). **Imports:** US$17.2 million (1996).

COUNTRY OVERVIEW

LOCATION AND SIZE. Nauru is a tiny island in the Pacific Ocean, located just south of the equator, to the northeast of New Guinea and the Solomon Islands. Nauru is only 21 square kilometers (8.1 square miles) in size, making it one of the smallest nations in the world. As an island country, Nauru has no land borders with other countries. It is roughly circular in shape and has about 30 kilometers (18 miles) of coastline. Comparatively, Nauru is about one-tenth the size of Washington, D.C. Nauru has no cities and its population lives in small settlements along the coast.

POPULATION. Nauru's population was estimated at 11,845 in July 2000. About 58 percent of the total consists of indigenous Nauruans, a Pacific people of mixed Melanesian, Micronesian, and Polynesian ancestry. About 26 percent of the population consists of other Pacific peoples (mainly from the neighboring island countries of Kiribati and Tuvalu). Nauru's smaller minority populations are 8 percent Chinese and 8 percent European. The population growth rate was 2.4 percent in 1998. Nauru has no official population policy.

About 80 percent of Nauru's territory consists of land that has been mined for phosphate. This land is not inhabited and is not suitable for agriculture. Nauru's people live entirely in the fertile coastal areas, especially along the southwest coast.

Nauru's population is very young. About 41 percent of the total population is under the age of 15, while about 57 percent are between the ages of 15 and 64. Only about 2 percent of the population is above the age of 65.

OVERVIEW OF ECONOMY

Nauru's economy is dominated by the export of phosphate, a mineral used as a fertilizer. Supplies of phosphate are running out and are expected to last no more than 5 years. The government is encouraging new industries, such as **offshore banking** and tourism, to replace the declining phosphate industry.

Phosphate has been the basis of Nauru's economy since 1906, when the island was a German colony. The decay of marine microorganisms on an atoll (a coral island made up of a reef surrounding a lagoon), supplemented by thousands of years of bird droppings, have made Nauru into an island made almost entirely of phosphate. Phosphate has been exported mainly to Australia and New Zealand, where it improved the poor soils in those countries. After Germany's defeat in World War I, Nauru was made a trust territory by the League of Nations (and later the United Nations) and governed jointly by Australia, New Zealand, and Great Britain, although Australia effectively handled all of the administration. Nauru became independent in 1968.

During the colonial administration, a trust fund was established in which part of the income from phosphate sales was deposited. This fund was set up to provide the country with income when phosphate supplies run out. This trust fund—the Nauru Phosphate Royalties

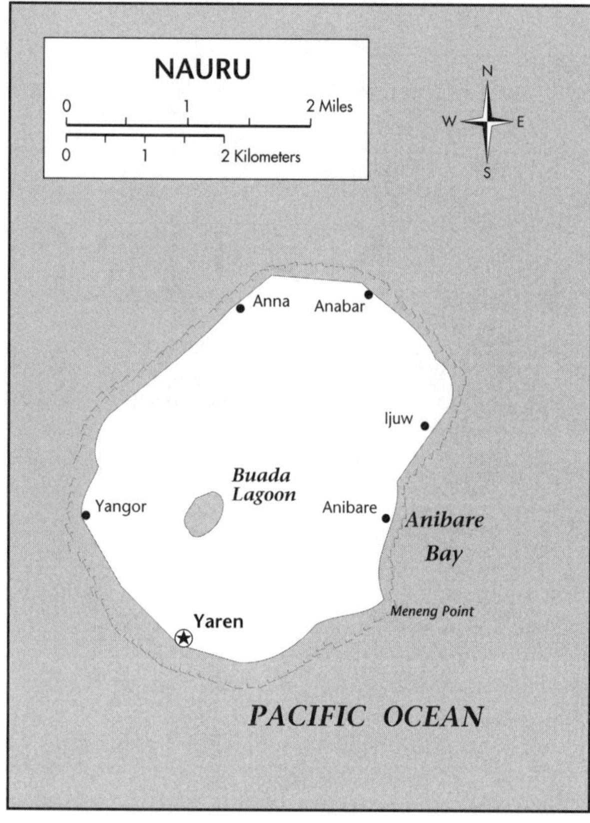

Trust—as well as the phosphate mining company, are controlled by the Nauruan government.

Phosphate mining has made Nauru very rich and provides citizens with some of the highest per capita incomes in the Pacific region. But phosphate mining has also seriously damaged Nauru's environment. About 80 percent of the land consists of mined-over territory that is now uninhabitable. Nauru's extreme dependence on phosphate means that it has to import nearly everything else, including food, fresh water, fuel, and all manufactured products.

As the country's reserves of phosphate have dwindled, the Nauruan government has encouraged other industries, especially tourism and off-shore banking, to locate in the country. Tourism is limited by Nauru's remote location and lack of major attractions. Off-shore banking has proved more successful, but has been marred by corruption and scandals involving **money laundering**. For example, the Russian mafia has been accused of using Nauruan banks to process its illegal revenues. Apart from Internet-based banking, there is almost no foreign investment in Nauru and no foreign investment policy.

POLITICS, GOVERNMENT, AND TAXATION

Nauru became an independent republic in 1968; it is the smallest republic in the world. Nauru is a member of the British Commonwealth and was admitted as a full member of the United Nations in 1999. Nauru generally follows the political system of Great Britain and has a **unicameral** (one chamber) Parliament with 18 members who hold office for 3 years. The Parliament elects the president, speaker, and deputy speaker. The cabinet, which consists of the president and 5 other members of Parliament, holds executive power. Members are elected as independents rather than from political parties. Nauru has had 8 changes of government since independence. Lately Nauru's government has become increasingly fractious, with a constant reshuffling of leaders and ministers.

The Nauruan government controls most aspects of the country's economy. The government owns most of the large businesses, including the Nauru Phosphate Corporation, the national airline, and the national bank. The government also controls the Nauru Phosphate Royalties Trust, which collects and invests phosphate royalties. The fund is currently estimated to have a value somewhere between $100 million and $800 million, but no details are publicly released. There are no taxes in Nauru, and government activity is financed entirely from phosphate revenues. The government is the largest employer and provides free health care and education to all citizens. As the Nauruan government is extremely secretive, it is difficult to obtain exact figures for many aspects of the country's economy.

Nauru has no military, but the Nauruan police are responsible for law and order and for national defense. Nauru generally has good relations with neighboring island countries. Nauru has had disputes with France because of French nuclear testing in the South Pacific in 1995, and the passage of French ships carrying plutonium and nuclear waste through Nauruan waters in 1992 and 1997.

The Asian Development Bank is the only provider of external financial assistance, in the form of loans, to Nauru. This aid is used to help reform the Nauruan government, to make it more open, to help diversify the economy away from phosphate mining, and to provide for health care, sanitation, and education.

In 1994, Nauru agreed to an out-of-court settlement in a lawsuit it had brought against Australia, New Zealand, and Great Britain. The basis of the lawsuit was to seek compensation for environmental damage to the country during the pre-independence period when phosphate mining was controlled by these countries. Australia agreed to pay Nauru US$73 million as part of the settlement. Great Britain and New Zealand reimbursed Australia for a small portion of this payment.

Communications

Country	Telephones[a]	Telephones, Mobile/Cellular[a]	Radio Stations[b]	Radios[a]	TV Stations[a]	Televisions[a]	Internet Service Providers[c]	Internet Users[c]
Nauru	2,000 (1996)	450 (1994)	AM 1; FM 0; shortwave 0	7,000	1	500	1	N/A
United States	194 M	69.209 M (1998)	AM 4,762; FM 5,542; shortwave 18	575 M	1,500	219 M	7,800	148 M
Philippines	1.9 M	1.959 M (1998)	AM 366; FM 290; shortwave 3 (1999)	11.5 M	31	3.7 M	33	500,000
Solomon Islands	8,000	658	AM 3; FM 0; shortwave 0	57,000	0	3,000	1	3,000

[a]Data is for 1997 unless otherwise noted.
[b]Data is for 1998 unless otherwise noted.
[c]Data is for 2000 unless otherwise noted.

SOURCE: CIA *World Factbook 2001* [Online].

INFRASTRUCTURE, POWER, AND COMMUNICATIONS

Nauru has 30 kilometers (19 miles) of roads, of which about 80 percent are paved. The major road circles the island, while the others connect the phosphate mines with coastal settlements. The only rail facilities on Nauru are narrow-gauge and run 5.2 kilometers (3.2 miles) from the phosphate mines to a processing plant. Nauru has no port or harbor, but it does have a deep water anchorage and facilities for loading phosphate onto ships. Nauru operates its own airline, called Air Nauru, with 2 aircraft (Boeing 737s), based at Nauru's international airport. The airline connects Nauru with Australia and other Pacific and Asian countries. The government heavily subsidizes Air Nauru, and its future is questionable. Nauru has international telephone connections by satellite. The country is completely electrified and power is supplied by diesel generators, the fuel for which is imported.

ECONOMIC SECTORS

Nauru has only 2 important economic sectors: mining and financial services. Nauru's economy is dominated by phosphate mining, while Internet-based banking is an emerging sector. Nauru's agriculture is extremely small-scale and cannot provide enough food for the population. Despite being an island, Nauru has no real fishing industry. Apart from a few handicrafts, there is no manufacturing industry on Nauru.

AGRICULTURE

Agriculture accounts for only a tiny portion of Nauru's economic activity, making up only 5 percent of GDP in 1995. Apart from some market gardens, the only agricultural products of any significance are coconuts, in addition to chickens and pigs for domestic consumption. Because of environmental damage from phosphate mining, less than 20 percent of Nauru's land is suitable for agricultural production.

INDUSTRY

MINING. Phosphate mining dominates Nauru's economy and has done so throughout the 20th century. The large phosphate mines are located in the center of the island, an area called Topside. Between 1920 and the country's independence in 1968, Nauru was administered by Australia, and the phosphate mines were owned and operated by the British Phosphate Commission (BPC). After independence, the Nauruan government took control of the phosphate mines and created the Nauru Phosphate Corporation. The Nauru phosphate deposits are among the world's richest. Phosphate was and continues to be exported, primarily to Australia, New Zealand, Japan, South Korea, and Indonesia. Phosphate supplies are expected to run out within 5 years.

Mining has had a severe environmental impact on the country. About 80 percent of the land area has been devastated after phosphate has been removed, leaving a landscape unsuitable for any other kind of industry or as residential land.

SERVICES

TOURISM. The tourism sector in Nauru is very small, as the country does not offer many attractions and cannot compete with neighboring Pacific island countries. Nauru is remote and expensive to get to, and tourist facilities are extremely limited. There are only 2 hotels and no resorts.

Nevertheless, the Nauruan government is attempting to develop the tourist industry to replace dependence on phosphate mining, but little has been done so far.

FINANCIAL SERVICES. Nauru has developed a large Internet-based "offshore" banking industry, with more than 400 banks registered in the country (all of which are listed at the same address, that of the government-owned Nauru Agency Corporation). The advantages of banking in Nauru are the absence of taxes and banking secrecy. It costs only about US$5,680 to establish a bank in the country, and US$4,980 per year in registration fees after that. In 1998, Nauru was accused by the Russian government of accepting an estimated US$70 billion in deposits from the Russian mafia, and providing cover for organized crime (this money does not actually come to Nauru, but is electronically transferred through the Nauru banks). Other countries, including the United States, have also protested against Nauru's "laundering" of illegally-obtained funds. The United States even threatened to abolish Nauru's right to trade in U.S. dollars. In 1999, Nauru bowed to these international pressures and vowed to clean up its banking industry.

The government controls the Nauru Phosphate Royalties Trust, which receives a share of the profits from phosphate sales. The assets of the fund have been estimated as being anywhere between $100 million and $800 million. Most of the assets consist of overseas real estate as well as stocks and bonds. Major real estate developments owned by the Nauru Phosphate Royalties Trust include Nauru House, which is one of the largest office buildings in Melbourne, Australia, and hotel developments in Hawaii and Fiji. The secrecy of the Nauruan government prevents exact figures from being known, but most experts suggest that the lower end of the estimated asset range is more accurate. The trust fund has been the subject of numerous allegations of corruption and mismanagement.

INTERNATIONAL TRADE

Nauru's major trading partner is Australia. Other important partners are New Zealand, Japan, South Korea, and Indonesia. These countries purchase Nauruan phosphate for use as a fertilizer. Phosphate is Nauru's only export. Apart from some locally-produced foods (fruit, coconuts, chickens, and pigs), virtually everything is imported into Nauru, including most foods, fresh water, fuels, motor vehicles, building materials, and machinery. Most of these goods are imported from Australia.

MONEY

Nauru does not have its own currency, but uses the Australian dollar. By doing so, it gains the advantages of allying its economy with a stronger, larger neighbor. As Australia is Nauru's largest trading partner, using the Australian dollar simplifies trade because currencies do not need to be converted. On the other hand, Nauru's **monetary policy** is linked to changes in the Australian dollar, which has dramatically depreciated (decreased in value) against the U.S. dollar over the past several years. **Inflation** in Nauru has generally been quite low.

Exchange rates: Nauru

Australian dollars per US$	
Jan 2001	1.7995
2000	1.7173
1999	1.5497
1998	1.5888
1997	1.3439
1996	1.2773

SOURCE: CIA *World Factbook 2001* [ONLINE].

POVERTY AND WEALTH

Nauru's phosphate wealth has made it one of the richest countries in the Pacific and, on a per capita basis, one of the richest countries in the world. Revenues from phosphate mining provide an extensive system of social support for Nauruan citizens. Nauru is a true **welfare state**, and everything is provided by the Nauru government, including free health care and education. Many Nauruans also receive various kinds of payments from the government, including a share of mining royalties, compensation for damage to land, and unemployment insurance. This has led to complete dependence on government. Nauruans have been described as living a life of "luxury and leisure."

Residents' luxurious lifestyles have come with a high price, however. The change in the local diet, which is now rich in high-fat imported foods, has given Nauru one of the highest rates of diabetes in the world. Nauru also has

GDP per Capita (US$)

Country	1996	1997	1998	1999	2000
Nauru	N/A	N/A	N/A	N/A	5,000
United States	28,600	30,200	31,500	33,900	36,200
Philippines	2,600	3,200	3,500	3,600	3,800
Solomon Islands	3,000	3,000	2,600	2,650	2,000

Note: Data are estimates.

SOURCE: *Handbook of the Nations*, 17th, 18th, 19th and 20th editions for 1996, 1997, 1998 and 1999 data; CIA *World Factbook 2001* [Online] for 2000 data.

high rates of unemployment and alcoholism, among other health and social problems. Unemployment has not become a major concern, however, as the government, as well as family members, provide support for non-workers. According to the Asian Development Bank, there is no evidence of absolute poverty in Nauru. The entire population has access to safe drinking water, and 97 percent have access to good sanitation.

WORKING CONDITIONS

The government is the main employer in Nauru, and the **private sector** employs only 1 percent of the workforce. Major branches of government employment include the government-owned Nauru Phosphate Corporation and the administrative and bureaucratic branches of government. Many Nauruans do not work but receive assistance from the government. Much of the mining work is done by foreigners, especially temporary workers from China, the Philippines, and the neighboring island countries of Kiribati and Tuvalu. About 3,000 foreign workers live in Nauru. Non-Nauruans face many restrictions, including limitations on travel in and out of the country and limitations on their political rights.

Nauruan workers have the right to form unions, but none have yet been established. Women's access to employment is restricted by social conventions, and there are few women employed by government companies and no women in Parliament. Because the government takes care of all its citizens' needs, there has been little incentive for education in Nauru, and few Nauruans travel overseas to study at universities.

COUNTRY HISTORY AND ECONOMIC DEVELOPMENT

1798. British whaler Captain John Fearn is the first European to visit Nauru and names it "Pleasant Island."

1888. Nauru annexed by Germany.

1899. Phosphate deposits discovered.

1906. Phosphate mining started by a British-Australian company.

1914. Nauru occupied by Australia after World War I begins.

1920. Australia begins administration of Nauru on behalf of the 3 trustees: Australia, New Zealand, and Great Britain.

1941. Nauru's industrial plant and housing facilities are completely destroyed by Japanese bombings.

1942. Nauru occupied by Japanese forces until 1945.

1951. A local government council set up to handle local affairs.

1968. Nauru achieves independence.

1994. Australia agrees to out-of-court settlement of US$73 million for environmental damage caused by phosphate mining during the Australian administration of the island.

1998. Russian mafia transfers an estimated US$70 billion to Nauru banks to evade taxes.

1999. Nauru bows to international pressures to control its banking industry; Nauru admitted as a member of the United Nations.

1999. Nauru government borrows US$100 million from General Electric Corporation; trust fund assets used as collateral.

2000. Fiji government seizes the Nauru-owned Grand Hotel in Fiji on the grounds that the Nauru government failed to develop the property as agreed.

2001. Nauru agrees to process more than 300 refugee "boat people" (mainly from Afghanistan, Iraq, and Pakistan) originally bound for Australia. Australian government agrees to give Nauru US$10 million and pay all costs of housing and feeding refugees. A refugee camp is built in the center of the island.

2001. Australia grounds Air Nauru's 2 Boeing 737 aircraft, claiming that the airline did not have sound management and that the Nauru airport was unsafe.

2001. Bank of Nauru closes because of lack of cash. Economists warn that the value of the Nauru Phosphate Royalties Trust Fund may be approaching zero.

FUTURE TRENDS

Nauru's phosphate industry has reached the end of its life, with the last supplies expected to run out within a few years. It is unclear how the country will support itself once the mines close. Diversification into other economic sectors, such as tourism and offshore banking, have not proven especially successful. Tourism has remained small due to the country's remoteness and lack of attractions. Offshore banking has been marred by scandals involving money laundering and corruption, and the country has been heavily criticized for this. With its tarnished reputation, many foreign companies will be hesitant about investing in Nauru.

The imminent closure of Nauru's phosphate mines mean that the country will be left with no major source of income and with severe environmental problems. About 80 percent of the country has been ecologically devastated by mining, and this land is not suitable for agriculture or for residential property. The cost of rehabilitating the mined-out land is expected to cost at least

US$200 million and it is unclear where this money will come from. Nauru's water supply is becoming more limited because of the depletion of natural underground reserves. The country already has to import drinking water.

Income from the country's Nauru Phosphate Royalties Trust will help tide over the country when the mines first close, but it will not be sufficient to replace the income from mining royalties themselves. The trust fund itself has been marred by allegations of corruption and mismanagement, and the ability of the trust fund to keep producing income is questionable.

With its mines closing and its environment in ruins, Nauru faces a grim future. The careful and wise investment of the country's remaining assets—in its trust fund—is the most likely source of salvation for Nauru.

DEPENDENCIES

Nauru has no territories or colonies.

BIBLIOGRAPHY

Asian Development Bank. "Country Performance Assessment: Nauru." <http://www.adb.org/Documents/CAPs/NAU/0100.asp>. Accessed December 2000.

CountryWatch. "Country Review: Nauru." <http://www.countrywatch.com>. Accessed February 2001.

Hanson Cooke Ltd. "The Republic of Nauru." <http://www.earth.nwu.edu/people/emile/nauru.html>. Accessed December 2000.

Lal, Brij V., and Kate Fortune, eds. *The Pacific Islands: An Encyclopedia.* Honolulu: University of Hawaii Press, 2000.

U.S. Central Intelligence Agency. "World Factbook 2000: Nauru." <http://www.odci.gov/cia/publications/factbook/gcos/nr.html>. Accessed December 2000.

Viviani, Nancy. *Nauru: Phosphate and Political Progress.* Canberra: Australian National University Press, 1970.

Weeramantry, Christopher. *Nauru: Environmental Damage Under International Trusteeship.* Melbourne: Oxford University Press, 1992.

—Michael Pretes

NEPAL

Kingdom of Nepal

CAPITAL: Kathmandu.

MONETARY UNIT: Nepalese rupee (NR). One Nepali rupee is made up of 100 paisa. Rupee notes come in denominations of NR1, 2, 5, 10, 20, 25, 50, 100, 250, 500, and 1,000. Coins are denominated as 5, 10, 25, and 50 paisa and NR1, 2, and 5.

CHIEF EXPORTS: Carpets, clothing, leather goods, jute goods, grain.

CHIEF IMPORTS: Gold, machinery and equipment, petroleum products, fertilizer.

GROSS DOMESTIC PRODUCT: US$27.4 billion (purchasing power parity, 1999 est.).

BALANCE OF TRADE: **Exports:** US$485 million (f.o.b., 1998). **Imports:** US$1.2 billion (f.o.b., 1998).

COUNTRY OVERVIEW

LOCATION AND SIZE. Nepal is a landlocked country in South Asia, bordered by India on 3 sides and by China to the north. It has an area of 140,800 square kilometers (54,363 square miles), a border of 2,926 kilometers (1,818 miles), and is slightly larger than Arkansas. Roughly rectangular in shape, Nepal can be divided lengthwise into 3 ecological zones from south to north: the fertile alluvial plains of the Tarai region, the mountains and valleys of the central Hilly region, and the inhospitable Mountain region, home to the Himalayas and the world's highest mountain, Everest. Nepal is drained by over 6,000 rivers which form the Karnali, Narayani, and Koshi river systems. Its capital, Kathmandu, is in the central part of the country.

POPULATION. Nepal had a population of 24,702,119 in 2000, up from 19,145,800 in 1990. Government sources estimate a population of 28,618,668 by 2010. While the death rate has declined significantly over the last few decades to 10.41 per 1,000 people, the birth rate has remained high at 33.83 per 1,000. The infant mortality rate declined from 147 deaths per 1,000 in 1985 to 64 deaths per 1,000 in 2000, but while health services have improved, high fertility rates have led to a population growth rate that increased from less than 2 percent in the 1950s to about 2.6 percent in the 1980s. According to the World Bank, the growth rate in 1999 was 2.3 percent.

Nepal is one of the few countries in the world where men live longer than women. Female life expectancy is 57.3 years, compared to 58.3 years for males. Forty-one percent of the population is aged 0–14 years, 56 percent are between 15 and 64, and only 3 percent are above 65 years of age in 2000. The population can be grouped by 3 major ethnicities: Indo-Nepalese, Tibeto-Nepalese, and indigenous Nepalese. In 1991 46.7 percent of the people resided in the southernmost plains of the Tarai region, 45.5 percent in the central Hilly region, and 7.8 percent in the northernmost Mountain region, but large-scale internal migration in recent years has led to overcrowding in the fertile Tarai region. The population of Nepal is overwhelmingly rural, with just over 9 percent living in urban areas such as the Kathmandu Valley. Population density stands at 175 people per square kilometer (453 per square mile).

Family planning in Nepal began in the late 1950s. An increase in government expenditure on family planning offices and door-to-door campaigns have contributed towards the adoption of family planning. In 1969, only 7,774 people used some form of contraception; this number rose to 419,950 by 1999. Difficulties in rural access to family planning services and cultural and socioeconomic considerations which favor large families continue to impede the implementation of a coherent population control policy.

In addition to the established Nepalese population, there are approximately 96,500 Bhutanese refugees in Nepal, 90 percent of whom are accommodated in 7 camps run by the United Nations Office of the High Commissioner for Refugees (UNHCR).

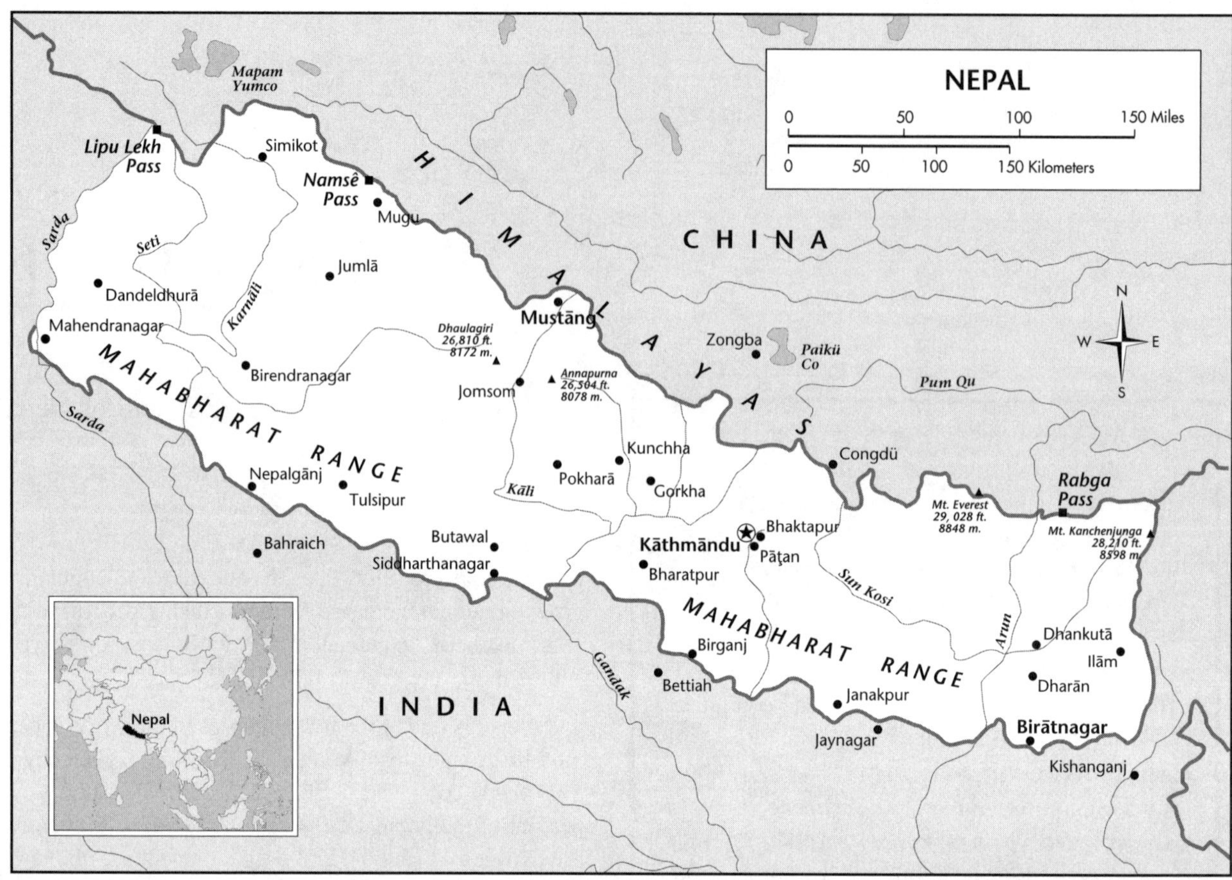

OVERVIEW OF ECONOMY

Nepal's place in the western imagination as a latter-day Shangri-La stems from its historical isolation, maintained until the overthrow of the Rana oligarchy (a small group of people who rule a nation) in 1951. Development planning commenced soon after, but half a century on, the country still struggles to free itself from its feudal legacy and temper the effects of an unpredictable global economy. Today, Nepal is one of the least developed countries in the world, with nearly half of its inhabitants living below the poverty line. Decentralization and **privatization** of government-run businesses have not worked for this agricultural nation; the 1989 trade-transit crisis with India, which caused severe commodity shortages, demonstrated how frail the economy was. Popular protests brought about multiparty democracy in 1990, and the reigning Hindu monarch was relegated to constitutional status. Ever since, recurring political instability culminating in a massacre within the royal family in June 2001 has hampered the implementation of economic reforms designed to relax trade regulations, attract foreign investment, and cut government expenditure.

Nepal's spectacular landscape, while attracting the tourism that both pays and pollutes the country, has been the major hindrance to its economic development. Rugged mountains cover over 80 percent of the land, isolating communities from each other and from the Kathmandu Valley. Trade, industrial growth, and foreign investment have been defeated by the terrain, despite significant efforts to improve the transport and communications **infrastructure**. As a landlocked nation, Nepal is heavily dependent on India economically. The industrial sector employs only 3 percent of the population, while the successful cottage industries that produce carpets and garments bring in up to 80 percent of foreign exchange earnings from countries other than India. Exports consist largely of primary produce sent to India, and trade with nations other than India is expanding. Imports include industrial and agricultural inputs such as machinery, fertilizers, petroleum products, and additional primary produce.

For now, agriculture constitutes most of Nepal's economy, with 81 percent of the population engaged in farming activities that account for over 40 percent of **gross domestic product** (GDP). The major food crops are rice, wheat, and maize, while sugar cane, oilseed, tobacco, and potatoes are other major **cash crops**. Despite government programs to introduce fertilizers and modern techniques, most farms still generate only enough produce to feed the farmer's family, with little or nothing left over to sell. **Underemployment** is high in the farming sector. The lack of irrigation facilities has left the average farmer dependent on the seasonal monsoon rains, and increased production has resulted mostly from the extension of arable land. The growth of a population heavily reliant on firewood has led to deforestation, which contributes to erosion and floods with serious consequences for communities in southern Nepal, India, and Bangladesh.

While efforts to develop the Nepalese economy systematically through the implementation of the government's 5-year plans have established a basic infrastructure, the benefits have been reaped by the urbanized, educated minority of Nepalese rather than by the rural poor. However, impoverished peasants and highly qualified urbanites alike **emigrate** and migrate within the country in search of better prospects, with serious implications for the economy. Foreign aid, which has supplied over 60 percent of development expenditure over the decades, has been underutilized and mismanaged. The increasing loan component of such aid has added to the country's **foreign debt**, which totaled US$1.5 billion in 1998.

POLITICS, GOVERNMENT, AND TAXATION

The unification of Nepal in 1769 under the Shah dynasty of Gorkha failed to prevent 2 centuries of intrigue among the aristocratic families of Kathmandu. From 1846 onwards, hereditary prime ministers from the Rana family governed in the name of the Shah kings. Their downfall in 1951 led to a succession of governments appointed by royalty. Nepal had its first democratic elections in 1959, and the Nepali Congress Party governed until a royal coup d'etat, or takeover, a year later. The partyless system known as *Panchayat* followed. This comprised public assemblies at village, district, and national levels, who were ultimately accountable to the king. Undercurrents of political dissent periodically rumbled beneath the Himalayan kingdom's facade of tranquility, but it took an economic crisis, a coalition of political parties, and widespread urban demonstrations before the ruling Hindu monarch, King Birendra Bir Bikram Shah Dev, was forced to dismantle the Panchayat system in favor of a multiparty democracy within a constitutional monarchy in 1990. More than a decade on from the introduction of democracy, Nepal has failed to achieve political stability. The turmoil of years past echoes among antagonistic factions and has led to much discontent, particularly in the neglected countryside, where a Maoist insurgency has claimed over 1,600 lives in the 5 years from 1996. In June 2001, a massacre within the royal family, instigated by the Crown Prince, led to rioting and curfews in the Kathmandu Valley. The political situation remains fragile.

With the transition to democracy in 1990, the Nepali Congress Party was voted into power. Established in 1947, this party is the largest political organization in the country and has governed for most of the last decade. The old guard of political leaders, represented by Prime Minister Girija Prasad Koirala and Krishna Prasad Bhattarai, has held sway over this reform-oriented centrist party. The Nepali Congress had its roots in democratic **socialism**, but in the 1980s it modified its program to espouse a mixed economy. During a relatively stable tenure from 1991 to 1994, the party implemented various economic reforms that facilitated privatization and foreign investment, and attempted to improve public enterprise management.

Left of the political spectrum, **communist** parties briefly worked with the Nepali Congress during the revolution of 1990. Parties within this United Left Front Coalition, however, differed widely in their socialist ideologies. The centrist United **Marxist**-Leninist Party (UML), which supports the creation of a **welfare state** (a political system in which the government assumes primary responsibility for the social welfare of its citizens), is the second largest party in Nepal, and remains a potent force despite a damaging split in 1998. The appointment of a minority UML government in 1994 slowed the process of **liberalization**, and **subsidies** to public enterprises increased. Other parties include 2 factions of the monarchist National Democratic Party and the Nepal Sadbhavana Party, which is based in the Tarai region and favors closer economic integration with India. Political bickering has consumed the national agenda, resulting in 9 changes of government between 1991 and 2001. The struggle for political power has filtered down to **public sectors**, which have witnessed widespread corruption and politicization. Though **inflation** has remained moderate and the urban population has benefited from exposure to the global economy, there has been little progress in reducing rural poverty. If the current state of affairs continues, problems with law and order may seriously jeopardize the internal security of Nepal.

The political system is based on the British parliamentary system. The king is head of state, and, along with the Council of Ministers retains executive powers. There are 2 legislative bodies: the National Council and the House of Representatives. Members of the National Council are appointed by the House, the king, and an electoral college. Members of the House of Representatives are elected by popular vote for 5-year terms. The political party with a majority in the House of Representatives appoints the prime minister. The judiciary is headed by the Supreme Court, and is composed of a network of appellate courts and district courts.

Management of the Nepalese economy has changed significantly over time. Prior to the 1950s, while feudal overlords vied for economic gain at the expense of the rural population, little planned development took place. Under the Panchayat regime, a succession of 5-year plans attempted to impose government control over all aspects of the economy. However, against a background of poor infrastructure, the country's geographical difficulties, and the spread of corruption, the lot of the rural majority was little changed. Attempts to accelerate growth through increased government spending resulted in economic instability in the early 1980s. Under pressure from financial institutions such as the International Monetary Fund (IMF) and the World Bank (WB), certain structural reforms were implemented, which helped the growth of the **private sector**.

Before 1951, Nepalese administrations extracted revenue in the form of land tax and a **tariff** on foreign trade. Their reliance on middlemen reduced the revenue available and subjected traders and producers to exploitation that discouraged economic activity. Moreover, the income derived was rarely used for purposes of benefiting the economy. From the late 1950s, a combination of income, sales, and property taxes were introduced. Today, corporate tax stands at 25 percent, though certain industries are taxed at a maximum of 20 percent of their income. **Income tax** is progressive, with different exemption limits for individuals and families. Relative to average Nepalese incomes, income tax exemption is fairly high. Agreements are underway with other governments to avoid double taxation and encourage foreign investors. Government revenues have increased substantially in recent years, from just over 6 billion rupees in 1989 to a high of over 24 billion rupees in 1997, but falling to 17 billion the following year. Customs and consumption taxes (such as taxes of food and drink) have been the primary sources of revenue. A **value-added tax** was introduced from 1995. However, a weak tax administration, resulting in low tax compliance, limits this important source of development funds.

INFRASTRUCTURE, POWER, AND COMMUNICATIONS

In post-1950s Nepal, planners and foreign aid donors viewed the creation of infrastructure as vital to the success of the country's economic development. Five-year plans prioritized transportation and communications, but although the results were significant, they remain inadequate. Nepal has 13,849 kilometers (8,522 miles) of paved, graveled, and fair-weather roads, with the major highways linking east to west and north to south. However, monsoon rains work on the unstable mountain geology, causing widespread landslides and driving up road maintenance costs. There were 253,407 vehicles registered in 1999, of which 142,000 were in the Kathmandu Valley. Airports operate in 44 out of 75 districts, and include domestic airports in remote areas which link up with the international airport in Kathmandu. This network is crucial to the tourist industry. Recently, Nepal adopted an open-sky policy, allowing private airlines to operate domestic and international services.

Other forms of transportation are underdeveloped. There is a single narrow gauge railway line covering a distance of 52 kilometers (32 miles) from Janakpur to Jayanagar in the south, and an under-utilized 42-kilometer (26-mile) ropeway (suspended cable-car line) from Hetauda to Kathmandu, which transported 10,684 metric tons of goods in 1995. A limited trolley bus service operates in the Kathmandu Valley. Access to the sea is only possible through the Indian ports of Calcutta (1,150 kilometers, or 713 miles, from the Nepalese border) and Haldia.

Much has been said about the potential of Nepal's hydropower to fulfill local power needs, drive industrialization, and boost revenues through the sale of surplus power to India. Of a feasible potential of 27,000 megawatts (MW), Nepal currently uses a mere 332.7 MW. "Megaprojects," sponsored by institutions such as the World Bank, have been embraced and publicized by successive governments as a panacea to some of the country's eco-

Communications

Country	Newspapers	Radios	TV Sets[a]	Cable subscribers[a]	Mobile Phones[a]	Fax Machines[a]	Personal Computers[a]	Internet Hosts[b]	Internet Users[b]
	1996	1997	1998	1998	1998	1998	1998	1999	1999
Nepal	11	38	6	0.2	0	N/A	N/A	0.07	35
United States	215	2,146	847	244.3	256	78.4	458.6	1,508.77	74,100
China	N/A	333	272	40.0	19	1.6	8.9	0.50	8,900
Thailand	63	232	236	10.1	32	2.5	21.6	4.49	800

[a]Data are from International Telecommunication Union, *World Telecommunication Development Report 1999* and are per 1,000 people.

[b]Data are from the Internet Software Consortium (http://www.isc.org) and are per 10,000 people.

SOURCE: World Bank. *World Development Indicators 2000.*

nomic ills without sufficient consideration to the displacement of people and the environmental damage they may cause. Examples of power-generating mega-projects under consideration are those in Chisapani (10,800 MW), Pancheshwor (6,480 MW), and the Arun Valley (643 MW). Local opponents have cited the inherently unsustainable and wasteful nature of such projects, which stand to plunge the country into serious debt. Locally based small to medium hydropower schemes have met with success, but this approach needs government support.

Nepal has considerably improved its postal and telephone services, though they remain deficient in rural areas. The Nepalese telecommunications network is digitized, and the Nepal Telecommunications Corporation (NTC) provides basic services for the country. Television programming began in 1985 and many families receive (not always legally) transmissions from foreign networks such as Star TV. Radio Nepal has existed since the 1950s and has a significant rural audience.

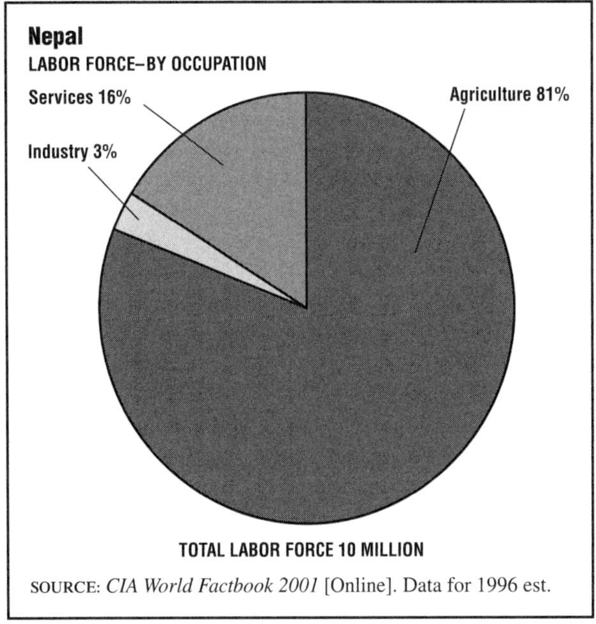

SOURCE: *CIA World Factbook 2001* [Online]. Data for 1996 est.

ECONOMIC SECTORS

The agricultural economy has failed to make the transition from **subsistence farming**, and is still largely dependent on weather conditions. Despite its undeveloped nature, agriculture supplied 41 percent of the country's GDP in 1998. The industrial sector only involves a minority of the population. In recent years, successive governments have passed legislation intended to encourage investment and privatization. Industry contributed some 22 percent to GDP in 1998. In contrast to the stagnation in both these sectors, the service industry derives major impetus from tourism, where the Himalayan kingdom enjoys a comparative advantage rivaled by few other nations. All told, the services sector contributed 37 percent to GDP in 1998. While the particular configuration of Nepal's topography and landlocked status have acted as limiting factors on the full development of its economy, this alone cannot explain the problems that continue to trouble a country with one of the highest per capita shares of foreign aid in the world today.

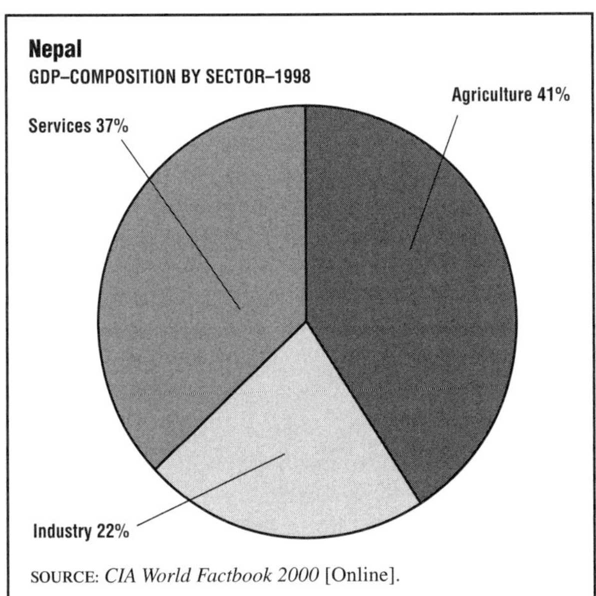

SOURCE: *CIA World Factbook 2000* [Online].

AGRICULTURE

Agriculture in Nepal has long been based on subsistence farming, particularly in the hilly regions where peasants derive their living from fragmented plots of land cultivated in difficult conditions. Government programs to introduce irrigation facilities and fertilizers have proved inadequate, their delivery hampered by the mountainous terrain. Population increases and environmental degradation have ensured that the minimal gains in agricultural production, owing more to the extension of arable land than to improvements in farming practices, have been cancelled out. Once an exporter of rice, Nepal now has a food deficit.

Over 80 percent of the population is involved in agriculture, which constitutes 41 percent of GDP. The seasonal nature of farming leads to widespread underemployment, but programs to grow cash crops and encourage cottage industries have had some success over the years. Two-sevenths of the total land is cultivated, of which 1.5 million hectares produced 3.7 million metric tons of the staple crop of rice in 1999. Wheat and maize together take up a similar portion of the available land, with harvests of 1 million metric tons and 1.5 million metric tons, respectively, in 1999. Production of cash crops increased substantially in the 1970s, and sugarcane, oilseed, tobacco, and potatoes (a staple food in some areas) were the major crops. Agricultural production accounted for about three-fourths of total exports in the late 1980s. As noted earlier, most exports consist of primary agricultural produce which goes to India. In general the majority of Nepalese farmers are subsistence farmers and do not export surplus; this does not prevent a minority in the fertile southern Tarai region from being able to do so. Most of the country is mountainous, and there are pockets of food-deficit areas. The difficulties of transportation make it far easier to export across the border to India than to transport surplus to remote mountain regions within Nepal. A considerable livestock population of cattle, goats, and poultry exists, but the quality is poor and produces insufficient food for local needs.

Government efforts to boost the agricultural economy have focused on easing dependence on weather conditions, increasing productivity, and diversifying the range of crops for local consumption, export, and industrial inputs. Solutions have included the deployment of irrigation, chemical fertilizers, and improved seed varieties, together with credit provision, technical advice, and limited mechanization. This has had some effect. Land under irrigation increased from 6,200 hectares in 1956 to 583,000 hectares in 1990. The use of chemical fertilizers, introduced in the 1950s, climbed to about 47,000 metric tons by 1998. Still, the weather continues to determine good and bad years for the average farmer. On a national scale, while production of both food and cash crops grew annually by 2.4 percent from 1974 to 1989, population increased at a rate of 2.6 percent over the same period.

Increased agricultural activity has placed tremendous stress on the fragile ecosystems of the mountains, with severe deforestation leading to erosion and flooding that threatens the livelihoods of farmers throughout the country. In the rush to open up arable land in the early years of development, Nepal lost half its forest cover in the space of 3 decades. Government plans to maintain cover at 37 percent depend on the success of community forestry programs, which merge traditional and modern agro-forestry and conservation practices. Responsibility is placed in the hands of Forest User Groups, which included almost 800,000 households in 1999.

A potent issue is that of land reform. Before 1950, a feudal system held sway. Land ownership was concentrated in the hands of landlords who contracted out to tenant farmers. Increased productivity may have been suppressed by such a system. Even though the legal mechanisms for land reform (such as placing limits on the amount of land owned) do exist, in practice most farmers still have pitifully small holdings. Predictably, land reform has been the mandate of every political party in Nepal, particularly the communists.

INDUSTRY

The industrial sector in Nepal is very undeveloped. Early industrial ventures, spurred by domestic shortages in the 1930s and 1940s, fared badly due to inexperience. By 1960 there were 63 registered industries, unsupported by adequate institutional organization or infrastructure. With the influx of foreign aid targeted at both the industrial sector and the transport and communications infrastructure, a mix of modern industries and cottage industries slowly developed, numbering 3,557 institutions by 1997. They are small by international standards. Industrial activity, accounting for about 21 percent of GDP, employs only 3 percent of the population. Most of these industries are located around urban centers such as the Kathmandu Valley and in the Tarai region.

Nepal suffers from a lack of both internal and external investment. This stems from low domestic savings, a small domestic market, a severe shortage of skilled labor, chronically corrupt and inefficient public administrations, high transport and operating costs, the inadequacy of power resources and, increasingly, political instability. There have been recent attempts to encourage investment and privatization through the Industrial Policy 1992 and Foreign Investment and One Window Policy 1992, and the creation of industrial centers with governmental land and buildings on lease for private ventures.

MODERN INDUSTRIES. The largest manufacturing industries in Nepal produce jute, sugar, cigarettes, beer, chemicals, tea, vegetable ghee (clarified butter used in Indian and Nepali cooking) and oil, matches, soap, shoes, and processed leather. While industries such as jute, tea, and sugar use local raw materials, other industries have to import inputs from India. Mining is based on deposits of limestone (for cement), clay, garnet, magnetite, and talc. Surveys of other deposits have been sporadic and inadequate, and the difficulty of the terrain has limited development.

COTTAGE INDUSTRIES. As early as 1952, the Nepalese government recognized that industrialization would have to take into account the severe limitations imposed by the country's geography. Cottage industries—the local production of traditional handicrafts—were seen as a way to engage the underemployed rural population and contribute towards export earnings. In Nepal, these industries have included pottery, handmade paper and products, woodwork, metal work, weaving, embroidery, and basket making, and draw on artistic traditions dating back centuries. However, even with the creation of Cottage Industries Training Centers across the country, many of these crafts have been in decline. Still, they contribute about 60 percent of industrial production, with the garment and carpet industries showing rapid growth since the 1980s and earning 84.3 percent of export earnings from countries other than India.

SERVICES

TOURISM. While the topography of Nepal has hampered economic development, it has also blessed the country with the matchless beauty of the mighty Himalayan mountain range in the north, rugged hills and valleys with cultural centers such as Kathmandu, and sub-tropical climes in the south that house rare species of wildlife such as tigers, rhinos, and gharial crocodiles. Ever since the successful ascent of Mount Everest in 1953, the tourist industry has been booming. For a country that was closed to the world until the mid-20th century, tourist arrivals of almost half a million in 1999 are impressive. A network of trekking agencies, hotels, and restaurants exists. There were a total of 708 hotels in 1999, with 31,355 beds. Tourism is an important contributor to the economy, constituting 3.6 percent of GDP and 26.3 percent of export earnings. Recognizing this, the state has supported the industry by building airports in otherwise inaccessible areas and opening up tourist routes.

Through the 1960s and 1970s, Nepal's allure as a tourist destination stemmed as much from the Himalayas as it did from its exotic appeal and the relatively easy availability of marijuana. Today, the industry is more broad-based, and mountaineering, trekking, white-water rafting, wildlife tours, cultural tours, and pilgrimages attract young and old, rich and poor alike. Almost a third of visitors are from neighboring India. The influx of tourists has been a strong influence on the Nepalese people. Ethnic groups such as the Sherpas, who escort mountaineering expeditions, have benefited considerably from their involvement with tourist activities. Culturally, Nepal has been exposed to western influence. Environmentally, the country has suffered adverse effects from tourism, though awareness of environmental issues is growing.

Tourism will continue to represent an important renewable resource, with government targets of a million visitors a year promoted through campaigns such as "Visit Nepal Year 1998" and "Destination Nepal 2002." Lately, pollution in the Kathmandu Valley, political violence, strikes in the hotel industry, and the royal massacre of 2001 have threatened to dent the number of tourist arrivals. Nevertheless, the potential for the expansion of tourism-related activities such as the provision of rural infrastructure and the local production of specialized food and equipment remains high.

FINANCIAL SERVICES. The use of institutional financial services has been slow to spread in rural areas. Until the mid-1990s, most Nepalese banks were state controlled or owned. The country's first commercial bank, Nepal Bank Ltd., opened in 1937. The central bank, Nepal Rastra Bank, opened in 1956, and Rastriya Banijya Bank opened in 1966. Specialized financial institutions such as the Nepal Industrial Development Corporation (NIDC) and the Agricultural Development Bank (ADB) were also established to provide assistance to private industry and small farmers, respectively. These have had mixed success since traditional moneylenders still play a central role in village financial affairs. By 1990 the ADB had only granted loans to 9 percent of all farming families. Since 1984, foreign banks have been allowed to operate in Nepal as part of a strategy to encourage foreign investment. By the beginning of the 21st century, there were 14 commercial banks and 45 finance companies in Nepal.

RETAIL. **Retail** services in Nepal are mostly small, independent, family businesses. Large franchises do not exist and, with the exception of Indian-owned businesses, foreign investment is limited. Ethnic groups such as the Marwaris and the Newars are noted for their entrepreneurial skills and have a large share of the retail sector.

INTERNATIONAL TRADE

Nepal is a landlocked nation, surrounded by India on 3 sides and by Tibet (now a province of China) in the north. Historically, international trade before the 1950s was with these countries. Exports have consisted of primary agricultural produce, while everything not produced locally has been imported. Throughout the years of development, these imports have included industrial inputs, fertilizers, and petroleum. Since the 1970s, the **balance of trade** has been increasingly negative. During the same period, however, exports of garments and carpets have grown, reaching sales close to US$300 million, and trade with other countries has increased to the detriment of the trade with India.

Until the 1950s, 90 percent of Nepal's trade was with its giant neighbor, India. The essentially open border facilitates trade, but also makes unquantifiable smuggling hard to control. Exports to India are generally supplied

Trade (expressed in billions of US$): Nepal

	Exports	Imports
1975	.100	.171
1980	.080	.342
1985	.160	.453
1990	.204	.672
1995	.345	1.330
1998	.474	1.239

SOURCE: International Monetary Fund. *International Financial Statistics Yearbook 1999.*

by agricultural surplus from the fertile Tarai region—mostly rice, but also tobacco, jute, and vegetable oils. Raw materials such as hides, skins, herbs, textile fibers, metal ores, and some manufactured goods, such as bamboo products, wooden furniture, and textiles, are also exported. Imports consist of daily necessities such as salt, sugar, tea, medicines, petroleum products, and items such as chemicals, machines, cement, coal, and spare parts that are needed for development work. The trading relationship with India was first codified in 1950 with the Treaty of Trade and Transit, which lowered tariffs and tax **duties** on goods passing between Nepal and India. In successive modifications and renewals of the treaty (notably in 1960), transit facilities for trade between Nepal and other countries were established in India at the port of Calcutta. The decline in India's percentage of trade with Nepal to just above 30 percent in 1998 demonstrates the success of these arrangements. In March 1989, delayed negotiations led to the expiration of the treaty, and all but 2 trading points were closed for a year. This crippled the Nepalese economy, as internal trade (much of which had to pass through Indian territory) and external trade with India was subjected to virtual closure. Shortages of basic goods such as salt and petroleum caused considerable strife, leading to both anti-India and anti-government demonstrations in Nepal, and were partly responsible for the downfall of the Panchayat system. An interim government successfully reinstated the treaty in June 1990.

Trade with Tibet, mostly the **bartering** of agricultural produce, went into decline at the turn of the 20th century when the British in India opened alternative routes. The limited Tibetan market and its inaccessibility further hindered the development of this barter trade. Negotiations on maritime access via Bangladesh, traversing 26 kilometers (16 miles) of Indian territory, have been difficult. Nepal has been more successful in expanding its exports with countries such as the United States, Britain, Germany, and Japan, the value of which rose from 14.4 million rupees in 1965 to over 16 billion rupees in 1996.

Nepal's trade balance is skewed towards imports, partly because the demand for industrial inputs and **consumer goods** has grown while local production has not. In 1998, Nepal imported US$1.2 billion in goods while exporting just US$474 million. India, Hong Kong, and Singapore are the country's major import partners. Governments have attempted to increase export earnings by diversifying products, and also to reduce import costs by substituting imports with local production. Policies such as the Exporter's Exchange Entitlement Scheme and both a Dual Exchange Rate and a Single Exchange Rate were formulated to facilitate these objectives. To its credit, Nepal has obtained favorable agreements with its trade partners to offset its landlocked status. But the treaty crisis with India and the failure to agree on Bangladeshi access highlight the country's limited bargaining power. Still very much a developing nation, Nepal is unable to influence the global market to which it exports primary goods at prices that are generally both low and unpredictable; the geographical diversification of its trade needs to include a shift towards a wider array of manufactured products.

MONEY

With the establishment of the central Nepal Rastra Bank, Nepal began to gain control of its **foreign exchange reserves**, which until 1960 were channeled through the Central Bank of India. Indian currency, prevalent throughout the country and freely convertible, was separated from other foreign currencies. In 1983, in order to counter economic instability and increased inflation, the **exchange rate** of the Nepalese rupee was weighted against a basket of important currencies such as the U.S. dollar. In reality, the Nepalese currency is quite strongly influenced by fluctuations of the Indian rupee. The value of the Nepalese rupee has been in decline for years; as of June 2001, US$1 was equivalent to 74.66 Nepalese rupees. Inflation was moderate at 11.8 percent in 1999, but imported goods are still beyond the reach of many Nepalese. While economic growth was strong in the late 1980s, the temporary breakdown of the trade treaty with India significantly damaged the economy.

In 1993, the Nepal Stock Exchange was born out of the Securities Exchange Centre. Interest has exceeded expectations, though only a minority of the urban population is involved in the stock market. The minimal development of the industrial sector limits opportunities for investment.

POVERTY AND WEALTH

Nepal's largely rural population depends on subsistence agriculture for a living. As this is outside the realm of the quantifiable modern economy, the low **GDP per capita** of US$217 in 1998 may be misleading. Nonetheless, 42 percent of the population lives below the poverty

Exchange rates: Nepal

Nepalese rupees per US$1	
Jan 2001	74.129
2000	71.104
1999	68.239
1998	65.976
1997	58.010
1996	56.692

SOURCE: CIA *World Factbook 2001* [ONLINE].

GDP per Capita (US$)

Country	1975	1980	1985	1990	1998
Nepal	149	148	165	182	217
United States	19,364	21,529	23,200	25,363	29,683
China	138	168	261	349	727
Bhutan	N/A	232	292	387	493

SOURCE: United Nations. *Human Development Report 2000; Trends in human development and per capita income.*

Distribution of Income or Consumption by Percentage Share: Nepal

Lowest 10%	3.2
Lowest 20%	7.6
Second 20%	11.5
Third 20%	15.1
Fourth 20%	21.0
Highest 20%	44.8
Highest 10%	29.8

Survey year: 1995–96

Note: This information refers to expenditure shares by percentiles of the population and is ranked by per capita expenditure.

SOURCE: *2000 World Development Indicators* [CD-ROM].

line (1996), and patterns of income and resource distribution reveal chronic inequalities within a population separated along the lines of the caste system (a hierarchical class system), gender, and place of residence.

Hindus fleeing Muslim invaders in India hundreds of years ago brought the caste system to Nepal. The educational and technological superiority of the Indo-Nepalese migrants allowed them to dominate both the indigenous and Tibeto-Nepalese ethnic groups. The caste system—with its notions of hereditary superiority and traditional rights to power, access, and livelihood—was imposed upon Hindus and non-Hindus. In order of status, the Brahmins (priests) were followed by Chhetris (administrators), Vaishyas (merchants), Sudras (farmers, artisans, and laborers), and untouchables (outcasts and the socially polluted). These divisions are not as sharply defined in the changing Nepal of today where caste has no legal justification, but a 1991 study revealed that 80 percent of civil service, army, and police posts were held by Brahmins and Chhetris of the hills (less than 50 percent of the population). The Newars of the Kathmandu Valley have also occupied an important niche in the political and economic culture of Nepal relative to their numbers.

Not surprisingly, land and income distribution is skewed. A 1983 study indicated that more than 50 percent of landholdings in the Hill region were smaller than half a hectare. In 1990, 75 percent of the families in Nepal earned less than 35 percent of the total national income. The harsh reality behind these figures has forced many in the Hill and Mountain regions to migrate to urban centers, the Tarai, and abroad to seek employment as soldiers, laborers, and domestic help. The burden of poverty is particularly hard on women, and a growing population of Nepalese sex workers in the brothels of India is sad testimonial to this problem.

Although government planning has channeled resources into the health and education sectors, doctors and health care centers are concentrated in urban areas, and rural services are still inadequate. Health services barely cope with widespread malnutrition, gastrointestinal diseases, tuberculosis, and polio. There is a rising incidence of cardiovascular disease in urban centers and a shortage of trained medical personnel and supplies. Those who can afford it prefer to be treated for serious illnesses abroad. Though many Nepalese are aware of the link between education and socio-economic betterment, regular attendance at school (conventional school is usually the only option; there are no distance/part-time/private tuition type educational courses in the villages) means time away from vital household and farming chores. Primary education is free, but standards in public schools are low, and literacy was still only 45 percent in 1999 among those over the age of 15. A college education abroad is much coveted, and is the prerogative of the rich or the fortunate few who secure scholarships.

So far, government policies have not significantly improved the lot of the poor Nepalese peasant. Programs targeting rural areas often end up enriching local officials and prosperous farmers. Ironically, the "development industry," fueled by foreign aid, has provided income for many in Kathmandu, while conditions remain bleak in the countryside. Governmental neglect of rural areas and ongoing political instability only add to the resentments that are manifest in the violence surrounding the Maoist "People's War" in the country.

THE LIVES OF THE POOR AND RICH. A rural family often lives under precarious conditions. In a typical village in the hills, a poor household relies on the produce from a small plot of land that has no irrigation facilities and is subject to erosion every year. A woman usually lives in her husband's house with his parents and siblings. The family house is made of stone and provides only 1 or 2 shared rooms. Cooking is done over an open stove in the main room. If they are fortunate, the family might own livestock such as cattle or chickens. Very little can be set aside from year to year, so they are unable to afford basic necessities. Such pleasures as a varied diet, clean water, fuel, medicines, decent clothing, and electricity may not be available. Education is considered a luxury that detracts from the time the children, especially the girls, can spend working. Water is drawn from the

Household Consumption in PPP Terms

Country	All food	Clothing and footwear	Fuel and power[a]	Health care[b]	Education[b]	Transport & Communications	Other
Nepal	44	9	7	5	14	5	15
United States	13	9	9	4	6	8	51
China	N/A	N/A	N/A	N/A	N/A	N/A	N/A
Bhutan	N/A	N/A	N/A	N/A	N/A	N/A	N/A

Data represent percentage of consumption in PPP terms.
[a]Excludes energy used for transport.
[b]Includes government and private expenditures.

SOURCE: World Bank. *World Development Indicators 2000.*

local stream. Dependence on firewood has led to severe deforestation in the hills, and the women have to walk hours to forage. Health facilities are limited. If a member of the family falls sick, they may be carried along treacherous mountain paths for hours to reach a health post. Often, the men in the household leave the village in search of jobs to help support the family.

A prosperous family in Kathmandu may derive its wealth from an aristocratic legacy, or modern occupations such as business, law, or medicine. They may have houses in the urban center that can be rented out, and also own land worked by tenant farmers outside the Kathmandu Valley. Together, a wealthy married couple can earn upwards of US$6,000 a year. The easy availability of domestic workers from rural villages allows the wife to delegate household chores. The education of the children is perceived as fundamentally important in securing a future in modern Nepal. They study in private English-medium boarding schools and go on to complete college degrees abroad. Health services in Kathmandu are good in comparison to the rest of the country, but serious problems such as cardiovascular disease are entrusted to doctors in India or Thailand. Despite the irregular supply of electricity in the Valley, the family will have a range of electrical appliances and might have invested in a computer with Internet access. Their lives in Kathmandu are very comfortable, but they share with the poor the common problems of water and electricity shortages, frequent strikes, and the threat of political violence.

WORKING CONDITIONS

Working conditions in Nepal are largely unregulated. For the minority of the population working in the formal economy, labor laws allow for a 6-day, 48-hour week with 30 days of annual leave, 15 days of sick leave, basic health and safety standards, and some benefits. The amended Factories and Factory Workers' Act 1977, which set out these standards, was revised following the democratic transition in 1990. In the Kathmandu Valley, a 5-day, 40-hour week with 25 days of annual leave has been implemented. In 2000, unemployment was 14 percent, and underemployment 47.5 percent. The latter is a common feature of the agricultural sector, where work patterns are determined by the planting and harvest seasons, and alternate opportunities may be either unavailable or culturally unattractive. Skilled labor is severely limited in Nepal, and a quarter of the **labor force** is composed of Indians. This shortage has hampered the development of the industrial economy.

In practice, laws passed to protect workers have hardly been implemented. Working conditions in the family-run farms and businesses that drive the economy retain both positive and negative features of power structures within the family. So while arrangements may be more cooperative, women and girls bear the brunt of the drudgery, leaving the men to reap the benefits and have time for leisure. This is particularly true of rural Nepal. Larger farms which employ tenant farmers often maintain feudalistic structures of patronage. Safety and health standards in industry are also widely neglected.

The democratic change in 1990, especially in the light of communist success, has altered the dynamics of labor in Nepal. Labor unions, restricted prior to 1991 along with political parties, now operate nationally, overseen by the General Federation of Nepalese Trade Unions (GEFONT). In 1991, labor union membership included 30 percent of non-agricultural workers. Workers regularly carry out strikes, and deadlocks in negotiations with government and industry have caused great inconvenience in urban centers such as Kathmandu. Strikes in recent years by public transport drivers and trash collectors are examples of this disruption. In early 2001, a dispute between workers in the tourist industry and the hotel association concerning the inclusion of service charges led to a temporary breakdown in services. Nepal's export-oriented industries have also had to adjust to the demands of Western consumers. In 1994, the Nepalese government responded to negative publicity in Europe over the prevalence of child labor in the carpet industry, and continues to work with non-governmental organizations to eliminate this problem.

COUNTRY HISTORY AND ECONOMIC DEVELOPMENT

c. 563 B.C. The Buddha (Prince Siddhartha) is born in Lumbini, in the Tarai region of Nepal.

c. 400–750 A.D. Licchhavi kingdom in power in Kathmandu.

1100–1484. Khasa Malla kings rule in western Nepal.

1484. Malla kingdom divided; the 3 kingdoms of Kathmandu, Bhadgaon, and Patan are established.

1769. Nepal emerges as a unified state under the leadership of Prithivi Narayan Shah, who has waged his campaign from Gorkha in midwest Nepal. For the next half century, the economy is geared towards military expansion pursued by successive Shah rulers and their administrators.

1791–92. War between Nepal and China.

1814–16. Nepal is at war with Britain; hostilities are ended with the Treaty of Sugauli, which reduces the territory of Nepal.

1846. Jang Bahadur establishes hereditary Rana rule.

1854. The country's first legal code is proclaimed.

1855. Nepal goes to war with Tibet, which results in duty-free privileges for Nepalese traders and payment of tribute from Tibet.

1923. Treaty of Friendship is signed with Britain, confirming the independence of Nepal and a special relationship with the British Empire.

1950–51. The first democratic revolution takes place in Nepal, leading to the end of the Rana regime and the rehabilitation of the Shah dynasty. The government signs the Treaty of Trade and Commerce with India.

1955. Nepal is admitted to the United Nations.

1956. The first 5-year plan of economic development is drawn up.

1959. The first general elections are held in Nepal. The Nepali Congress Party is elected to government with Bishweswor Prasad Koirala as prime minister.

1960. Important revisions are made to the Trade and Transit Treaty with India. King Mahendra dismisses the elected Nepalese government and imprisons political leaders.

1962. The Panchayat system is established. The Land Reorganization Act and a new legal code are established.

1972. King Mahendra dies and is succeeded by King Birendra.

1980. A national referendum votes to support the Panchayat system.

1985. Nepal becomes a founding member of the South Asian Association for Regional Cooperation (SAARC).

1989. Failure to renegotiate the trade and transit treaties with India results in economic disruption.

1990. Popular protests led by the Nepali Congress and the United Left Front Coalition lead to the establishment of multiparty democracy.

1991. General elections are won by the Nepali Congress. Girija Prasad Koirala becomes prime minister.

1994. The Communist Party of Nepal (UML) wins mid-term elections and forms a minority government under Man Mohan Adhikari.

1995. A coalition government is formed under Sher Bahadur Deuba of the Nepali Congress.

1997–98. Successive coalition governments take power following the collapse of the Deuba government.

1999. General elections bring a new government under Krishna Prasad Bhattarai of the Nepali Congress. He is replaced by Girija Prasad Koirala the following year.

2001. The Crown Prince Dipendra opens fire on a family gathering at the royal palace, killing 9 members of the royal family, including the king and the queen. Dipendra dies of a self-inflicted wound. Widespread mourning and rioting accompanies the ascension to the throne of Gyanendra, the surviving brother of the late king.

FUTURE TRENDS

Many observers have characterized Nepal as a country spanning the medieval and modern ages. The urban-rural divide illustrates this split. Nepal is in limbo, a condition that has managed to perpetuate itself through half a century of development planning and massive infusions of foreign aid. Undeniably, the country has made great progress since it opened up to the world, particularly in establishing a basic infrastructure in transport, communications, health, and education. However, its difficult topography, coupled with inefficiencies that are the legacy of an enduring system of feudalistic patronage in society and government, mean that the results of development plans rarely match expectations.

Economic gains in various sectors have been offset by population growth and environmental degradation, both poised to become even more problematic in the future. The disparity between rich and poor is growing, and discontent in the countryside bodes ill for the stability of a country that depends heavily on tourism. While Nepal has continued to prioritize liberalization and privatization of its economy in order to encourage growth and attract investment, the political problems of the last decade have hardly fostered a conducive environment. Until these policies are allowed to bear fruit, Nepal will not be able to break out of the shackles of its subsistence agriculture economy and develop industrially.

Cottage industries exporting goods such as carpets and garments will continue to grow. Tourism, as long as visitors remain safe from internal instability, will remain crucial to the economy. Foreign aid—so far mismanaged, underutilized, and responsible for a debt burden that demands servicing—is set to provide the bulk of development funds in the years to come. The development of large hydroelectricity projects could bring considerable benefits, but these carry inevitable social and environmental consequences. Ultimately, until Nepal achieves democratic stability and the institutional culture demonstrates that it is prepared to deal with corruption at every level, it will fail to achieve economic prosperity. The emigration of peasants and highly educated urbanites will also continue, draining Nepal of valuable population resources. The benefits of development have accrued to the rich, privileged, and educated; as in olden times, the country lives in the shadow of the Kathmandu Valley.

DEPENDENCIES

Nepal has no territories or colonies.

BIBLIOGRAPHY

Economist Intelligence Unit. *Country Profile: Nepal.* London: Economist Intelligence Unit, 2000.

Pant, Y. P., and G. P. Pant. *Some Aspects of Economic Planning: A Case Study of Nepal.* New Delhi, India: Vikas Publishing House, 1999.

Pant, Y.P. *Economic Development of Nepal.* Allahabad, India: Kitab Mahal, 1982.

Savada, A.M., editor. *Nepal and Bhutan Country Studies.* Third Edition. Washington D.C.: Library of Congress, 1993.

Statistical Yearbook of Nepal 1999. Kathmandu, Nepal: Central Bureau of Statistics, 1999.

U.S. Central Intelligence Agency. *World Factbook 2000.* <http://www.odci.gov/cia/publications/factbook/index.html>. Accessed July 2001.

Zivetz, L. *Private Enterprise and the State in Modern Nepal.* Madras, India: Oxford University Press, 1992.

—Rabi Thapa

NEW ZEALAND

CAPITAL: Wellington.

MONETARY UNIT: New Zealand dollar (NZ$). One dollar equals 100 cents. There are coins of 5, 10, 20, and 50 cents, and of 1 and 2 dollars. Notes are of 5, 10, 20, 50, and 100 dollars.

CHIEF EXPORTS: Dairy products, meat, forestry products, fish, fruit and nuts, wool, manufactures.

CHIEF IMPORTS: Mechanical machinery, vehicles, electrical machinery, fuels, plastics, technical equipment, aircraft, paper products, pharmaceuticals.

GROSS DOMESTIC PRODUCT: US$63.8 billion (purchasing power parity, 1999 est.).

BALANCE OF TRADE: **Exports:** US$12.2 billion (f.o.b., 1998). **Imports:** US$11.2 billion (f.o.b., 1998).

COUNTRY OVERVIEW

LOCATION AND SIZE. New Zealand is an archipelago (group of islands) located in Oceania, southeast of Australia. The 2 main islands are North Island (Te Ika a Maui) and South Island (Pounamu), with some near onshore islands and smaller outlying islands including Chatham Islands, Kermadec Islands, and Auckland Islands. Its total land area is 268,670 square kilometers (103,733 square miles), making it about the size of the state of Colorado, with a coastline of 15,134 kilometers (9,404 miles). The capital, Wellington, is located at the south end of North Island.

POPULATION. The population of New Zealand was estimated at 3,862,000 in mid-2000, an increase of 12.4 percent from the 1996 census population of 3,434,950. Between the censuses of 1991 and 1996, New Zealand had the highest rate of growth in the Organization for Economic Cooperation and Development (OECD), partly resulting from high levels of **immigration**, but also as a result of a relatively young population. In 2000 the birth rate stood at 15.3 per 1,000 population while the death rate was 7.8 per 1,000 population. With a projected annual population growth rate of about 1 percent between 1996 and 2010, the population is expected to reach 4,207,000 by 2010.

In most years, New Zealand has a net migration loss of New Zealand citizens who move to Australia, the United Kingdom, and elsewhere, so one of the objectives of its recent immigration policy (1987) is to offset this loss with new migrants, preferrably those with skills and investment capital. While migrants from the United Kingdom continued to arrive as they had throughout the 20th century, a significant new migration stream came from Asia especially from China, Taiwan, Hong Kong, and Korea. These new populations, together with Pacific peoples who arrived in earlier decades, have resulted in an increasingly multicultural society. In 1996 about 72 percent of the population considered themselves of European ethnicity, down from about 81 percent 10 years earlier. The indigenous Maori made up nearly 15 percent of the population, Pacific people 6 percent, and Asians about 5 percent. The Asian population had increased the most rapidly, from only 1.5 percent 10 years earlier.

By most standards, New Zealand is sparsely populated, with an average of only 13 persons per square kilometer. This population is unevenly distributed, with three-quarters on North Island, and one-third in the largest city, Auckland. Over the years, Auckland has grown faster than the rest of the country, being the center of much manufacturing and, more recently, service industries. More than half of all migrants have settled in Auckland, and of new migrants from the Pacific and Asia, about two-thirds have settled there.

OVERVIEW OF ECONOMY

Throughout the 20th century, New Zealand has been considered to be a nation of primary production, with exports being predominated by meat, wool, dairy products, timber, and fish. However, by 1999 agricultural exports had declined to about half of all exports, and less than 10 percent of the workforce were employed in agriculture. Nevertheless, agriculture remains an important

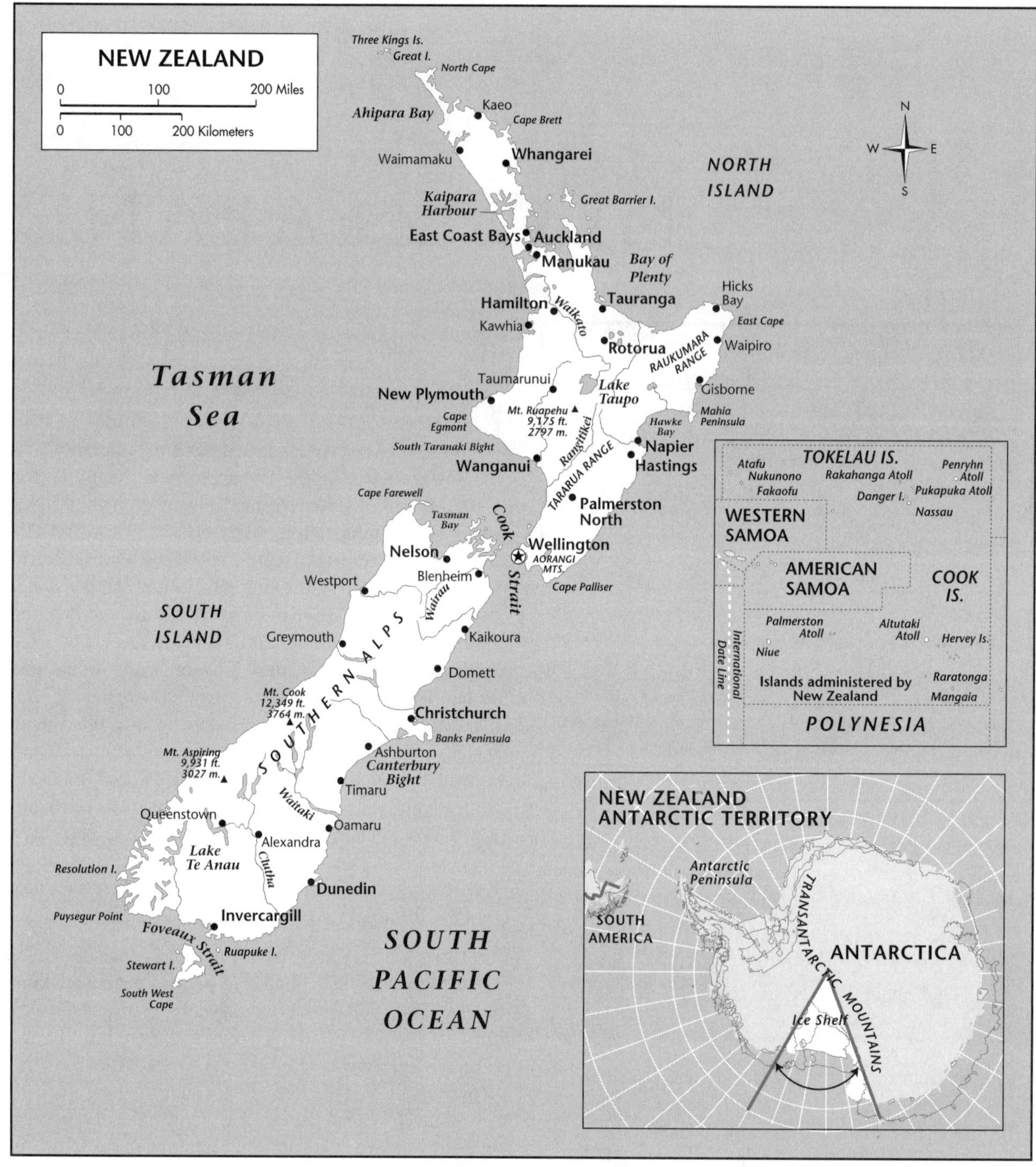

element in the economy and there have been ongoing moves to diversify the agricultural base. In recent years, horticulture has become more important; significant exports include apples, citrus fruit, kiwifruit, stone fruit, squash, and many other products. Wine production has increased rapidly in the last 2 decades, and New Zealand's reputation for its wines is growing.

Traditional sectors of agriculture still have great potential. With the **devaluation** of New Zealand's currency in recent years, producers of dairy products, meats, and wool have found their products very competitive on the world market and have increased their incomes substantially. Further, it is expected that as international trade **tariffs** decline, New Zealand will gain access to markets in which its products will be even more competitive.

Manufacturing has increased dramatically since World War II. With a comparative advantage in food processing, this sector led the post-war manufacturing boom.

With the protectionism of the 1950s and 1960s (i.e. high tariffs/taxes on imports), manufacturing diversified into many areas of **import substitution**, including textiles and footwear, home appliances, furniture, machine construction, automobile assembly, and many others. Following an economic restructuring program that began in 1984 with the election of a new government, some of these industries were exposed to increased international competition with the progressive reduction of tariffs. Some have done well, others have declined, and one has disappeared (the automobile assembly industry).

Most industrialized countries have had the greatest growth in services in the late 20th century. By 1998 in New Zealand, services accounted for 69 percent of **gross domestic product** (GDP) and fully 65 percent of wage and salary employment. Important sectors include government services such as general administration, education, and health. In the **private sector**, major growth areas have been tourism and specialized services in business advice, real estate, computing, and telecommunications. Tourism is often seen as the industry of the future, and New Zealand has experienced a steady increase in visitor numbers and an expansion of tourist **infrastructure**. Financial services have been especially affected by **deregulation** after 1984, and much of that sector has been acquired by foreign corporations.

POLITICS, GOVERNMENT, AND TAXATION

New Zealand is a parliamentary democracy with the British queen as the nominal head of state. It has a **unicameral** (1 house) parliament with 120 seats; half of these represent constituencies and the other half are "list" seats. In the mixed member proportional (MMP) system established in 1996, each voter has 2 votes: 1 for the constituency member of parliament and 1 for a party. After the constituencies are declared, the list seats are calculated so that a party's representation in parliament is similar to the party vote that they received in an election. In contrast to the "first past the post" system in which 2 parties predominate (as in the United States), MMP has allowed smaller parties to be represented, although they must either have a constituency member of parliament elected or get a minimum of 5 percent of the national party vote to qualify for list seats.

Throughout the 20th century, until 1996, the political system was dominated by 2 political parties: a conservative party called "National" since the 1930s and a liberal/left wing party called "Labour." The first Labour Party government was elected in 1935 and began constructing a **welfare state**, building state housing, and investing in health and education. New state enterprises were established. From the 1940s to the 1970s the Labour and National parties exchanged control several times, but the welfare state remained intact. Ironically, the election of a new Labour government in 1984 began a movement to weaken the welfare state and to reduce the role of government in the economy (a "monetarist" approach). The reforms instituted by the new government included progressive tariff reductions, **privatization** of many state enterprises, and cutbacks in some social services. These policies were pursued and, in some cases, strengthened by the National Party government elected in 1990; for example, there were cutbacks in social welfare payments and more privatizations. It was not until the election of 1999 that some of these policies were slowed or reversed with the election of a coalition government led by the "reformed" Labour Party in coalition with the "left-wing" Alliance Party.

The impact of MMP on the political system has been considerable. The 2 governments elected since 1996 have been coalitions, first of "the right" and then of "the left." In each parliament, several smaller parties have held 5 or more seats and, in some cases, have had an influence on coalition government policy. The smaller parties range from the ACT Party, which advocates more radical "monetarist" reforms than those already undertaken, to the Green Party, which has among its parliamentary members advocates for legalization of marijuana and environmentalists of various types.

Income tax is the largest source of revenue for the government, accounting for 46 percent of all taxes in 1998–99 (with an additional 5 percent withholding tax on interest and dividends). A Goods and Services Tax (GST) was instituted in 1996 and currently stands at 12.5 percent on virtually all goods and services; this tax contributed 26 percent of tax revenue. Company tax contributed only 12 percent to revenue in 1998–99 while the other 11 percent of tax came from various **duties**. There is a 3-layered income tax system, with income up to NZ$38,000 a year taxed at 19.5 percent, then income above this and up to NZ$60,000 taxed at 33 percent, and income above that is taxed at 39 percent. Companies are taxed at a flat rate of 33 percent.

INFRASTRUCTURE, POWER, AND COMMUNICATIONS

New Zealand's transport network is relatively modern. Of its 92,075 kilometers (57,086 miles) of roads, about 60 percent are paved, and over US$225 million was spent on road construction and maintenance in 1999. Most major cities and towns are linked by bus services and some by rail, but the private car is the predominant mode of transport. There are 3,973 kilometers (2,463 miles) of railways running the length of the country, although these now mostly carry freight rather than

Communications

Country	Newspapers	Radios	TV Sets[a]	Cable subscribers[a]	Mobile Phones[a]	Fax Machines[a]	Personal Computers[a]	Internet Hosts[b]	Internet Users[b]
	1996	1997	1998	1998	1998	1998	1998	1999	1999
New Zealand	216	990	508	1.3	203	N/A	282.1	476.18	700
United States	215	2,146	847	244.3	256	78.4	458.6	1,508.77	74,100
Australia	293	1,376	639	43.6	286	48.6	411.6	477.85	6,000
Papua New Guinea	15	97	24	N/A	1	N/A	N/A	0.49	2

[a]Data are from International Telecommunication Union, *World Telecommunication Development Report 1999* and are per 1,000 people.
[b]Data are from the Internet Software Consortium (http://www.isc.org) and are per 10,000 people.

SOURCE: World Bank. *World Development Indicators 2000.*

passengers. In North Island about 500 kilometers of the railway network is electrified. Large train/truck/car ferries link the North and South Islands with frequent services.

Throughout the country there are 111 airports, with 44 of these having paved runways. Domestic air services are predominantly provided by 2 airlines: Air New Zealand and Qantas New Zealand (which bought out Ansett New Zealand in 2001). Air New Zealand flies to at least 21 destinations in Australia, Asia, North America, Europe, and the Pacific Islands. In 2000, 24 international passenger airlines and at least 4 freight-only airlines flew into New Zealand. In addition to commercial flying, New Zealand is a global leader in the number of aviators per capita who pilot small, privately-owned aircraft: there is roughly 1 pilot for every 430 people, and 1 aircraft for every 1,170 people. At least 5 ports in the country can service large international shipping.

New Zealand's system of utilities is extensive and modern. Large hydroelectric dams, mainly in South Island, generate about 65 percent of electricity. Most of the rest is generated by fossil fuels, although 6 percent comes from geothermal plants, and small amounts from wind, wood, and biogas. Gas is piped from oilfields in the west of North Island, mostly to larger population centers.

The telephone system is modern and extensive with 96 percent of New Zealand households having a telephone in 1996. In 2000, about 30 percent of New Zealanders also had a cellular phone. As part of the privatization program of the 1980s, the telephone system was sold to a consortium of American companies. Currently, Telecom is the largest operator, but other companies have entered this very lucrative market.

In 1999 there were at least 80 Internet service providers in New Zealand and in the following year over 1 million Internet users; around 52 percent of the population had some sort of Internet access. In 2000 there were 46,000 .nz domain names, although some New Zealand websites also used generic names such as .com and .org.

ECONOMIC SECTORS

Despite its reputation as a country of primary production, the contribution of agriculture, fishing, and hunting to New Zealand's gross domestic product was only 8.4 percent in 1999. This proportion has been slowly declining since the early 1980s. The relative decline in industry has been even more dramatic, falling from 32.1 percent in 1975 to 23.2 percent of GDP in 1999. This has been partly a result of economic restructuring under which tariffs have been dramatically reduced on manufactured imports, but it also follows the trend in most industrialized countries away from manufacturing and other sectors in "industry" to services. However, the growth of the latter has not been great in relative terms in New Zealand. Services have increased only slightly from 45.3 percent in 1975 to 47.2 percent of GDP in 1999. Aspects of the economy which do not fit into the 3 service sector categories have increased the most over the last quarter century. These include gen-

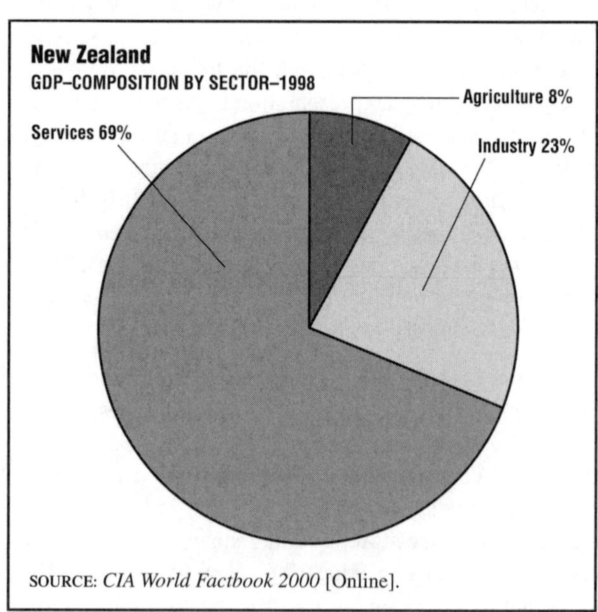

SOURCE: *CIA World Factbook 2000* [Online].

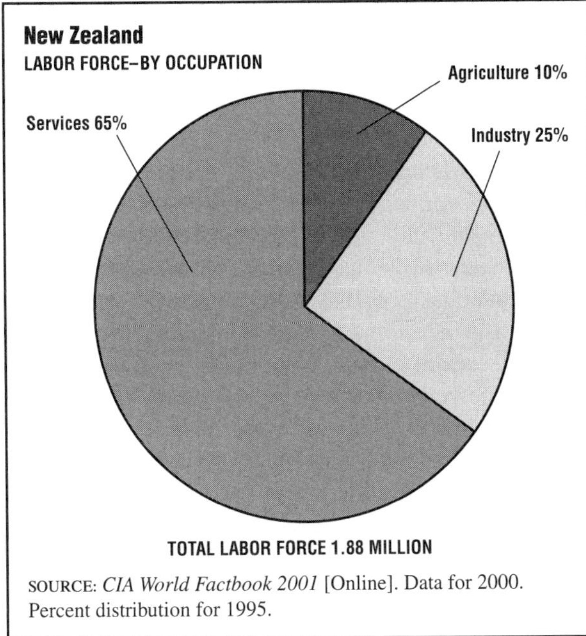

SOURCE: *CIA World Factbook 2001* [Online]. Data for 2000. Percent distribution for 1995.

eral government transactions and the increasing value of owner-occupied dwellings.

AGRICULTURE

New Zealand has been considered an agricultural country since the 19th century, when the introduction of refrigerated transport allowed its sheep and dairy industries to expand to provide the United Kingdom with meat, wool, butter, and other agricultural products. Throughout the 20th century agricultural imports have remained important to the New Zealand economy, contributing 50 percent of all export income in 1999. At the same time, with increasing mechanization and the rapid growth of other sectors, the proportion of the population working in agriculture (including fishing and forestry) declined steadily from about 37 percent in 1901 to 9.4 percent in 1999.

Pastoral farming involves the raising of sheep, cattle, and more recently other animals such as deer and goats. An often-heard statistic is that there are 20 sheep for every person in New Zealand, and this was true in 1981 when there were 80 million sheep on the land. As other types of farming have become popular, the number of sheep has declined to 45 million, so there are only about 12 sheep per person now. There are also about 5 million beef cattle, 4 million dairy cattle, and 1.2 million domestic deer. Sheep and beef meats comprised 12.5 percent of exports in 1999 and are processed at plants in various parts of the country for shipment to many parts of the world, notably Europe and North America, but also increasingly Asia. Wool is also an important export, and while Europe is the traditional destination for this export, increasing amounts are going to China for processing.

In terms of export income, dairy products have the highest value of agricultural products, making up 17 percent of exports in 1999. Dairy farms are found throughout the country, but certain areas are particularly well known as dairying areas, such as Waikato and Taranaki in North Island. The supply of fresh milk to New Zealanders explains the location of dairy farms near larger towns, but most dairy production is destined for international markets, and farms which produce for this market must locate wherever production conditions allow. There are a range of dairy products exported, but the most important are butter, cheese, and milk powders. The market for these products is wide; for example, in 1999 there were exports to all continents, with substantial quantities going to Latin America and Africa.

After pastoral farming, the next most important type of farming is horticulture, the growing of fruits and vegetables. New Zealand's climate is suitable for a large variety of fruit ranging from temperate fruit such as apples, pears, peaches, plums, and cherries, to subtropicals such as avocados, passionfruit, grapes, and kiwifruit, as well as many other citrus fruits. In terms of area planted and exports sales, the 2 most important of these in recent years have been apples and kiwifruit. The latter were rebranded from Chinese gooseberry when New Zealand producers started commercial production, and then controlled most of the world supply of this fruit in the early 1980s. Since that time, many other countries have started growing kiwifruit, and the New Zealand industry had a difficult time in the 1990s with problems of oversupply and low world prices (at least compared to the 1980s).

Another important and rapidly growing part of the horticultural industry is grape growing, especially for production of wine. Although wine has been produced in New Zealand for 150 years, the growth of the wine industry has been most dramatic in the last 20 years. The land area in grape production has steadily increased and the areas of production have diversified so that drinkable wine is now produced near the northern tip of the country as well as in the south-central area of South Island. Favored grape varieties include cabernet sauvignon, merlot, pinot noir, and chardonnay, but New Zealand has become best known for its sauvignon blanc. The most important destinations for New Zealand wine are the United Kingdom and Australia.

FORESTRY. Products based on the forestry industry, including logs, processed wood, wood pulp, and paper, make up just over 10 percent of exports by value. In the past, logging has taken place in the indigenous forests of New Zealand, but the depletion of these forests and the strong political support for their conservation have resulted in an end to this practice. The timber industry is now centered on the exotic forests, mainly of pine, first planted during the depression of the 1930s, but much expanded from the 1970s onwards. The original planting was done by the state, but in recent years private companies have undertaken nearly all new planting. The largest forests are in the center of North Island, but smaller plantations are found in various parts of the country. The main destinations for forestry products are Australia, Japan, Korea, and the United States, and while a great deal of processing takes place in New Zealand, there is also a large trade in unprocessed logs.

FISHING. New Zealand has an **Exclusive Economic Zone** (EEZ) of 1.3 million square nautical miles, an area about 15 times its land mass (the EEZ extends 200 miles from the coast and is the area in which a country has rights to economic resources such as fish). However, in much of this area the waters are extremely deep and not suitable for many of the commercially significant fish species. Nevertheless, fishing is still an important industry accounting for about 5 percent of exports, as well as supplying the domestic market. Each year the government assesses the maximum sustainable yields of each major species and sets a quota which is divided up between those who hold quota rights. The fishing fleet is made up of foreign-based boats as well as those based in New Zealand, which process their catch within the country. The indigenous Maori have some traditional fishing rights which are separate from the quota system, but in recent years Maori corporations have also become important in the commercial industry, having bought a company which owns about one-third of the fishing quota. A growing part of the fishing industry more generally is aquaculture, especially the cultivation of salmon, greenshell mussels, and Pacific oysters.

INDUSTRY

MINING. There is a diverse range of minerals found in New Zealand, although minerals make up only about 3 percent of exports (not counting the export of aluminum; see below). Gold has been mined since the 19th century and there is a small but steady production, as well as of silver, which is usually associated with gold. The highest value mineral production is of iron and steel, processed from black ironsands on the west coast of North Island. A nearby smelter provides iron and steel for the domestic market as well as for export. At the southern tip of South Island is a large aluminum smelter which processes bauxite from Queensland using power from nearby hydroelectric stations. The output from this smelter accounted for 4.2 percent of exports in 1999.

MANUFACTURING. Manufacturing employed the full time equivalent of 234,220 people in 1999, but this number has fluctuated considerably through time. The processing of food products has been a significant part of manufacturing throughout the 20th century, but it was after World War II that many other types developed when the government placed high tariffs on most imports. As part of the economic restructuring from 1984 onwards, that process has been reversed with a rapid reduction in tariffs on most imported manufactured goods. Often these imported manufactures come from countries with low labor costs, and New Zealand manufacturing enterprises are not able to compete on the basis of price. In some cases New Zealand industries benefitted from lower input costs, although a considerable amount of the raw materials originated in the country, and there was little saving in the costs of production. This has resulted in the decline of some sectors such as clothing and footwear and the closure of the automotive assembly industry. The impacts on other sectors have varied. The processing of food has a comparative advantage related to the strength and diversity of agricultural production in New Zealand and the fact that most food processing takes place near a source of supply. Still there has been some restructuring of this sector related to technological changes and to changing company structures (e.g. the purchase of Watties Industries by the transnational company Heinz). New Zealand has established a reputation for the production of carpets, especially those made with high quality wool. Sectors supplying the construction industry have done well during the 1990s under conditions of rapid population growth, especially in the Auckland region. With its ongoing successes in international yachting, New Zealand is also establishing a reputation for the construction of both hi-tech sailing yachts and luxury leisure boats.

SERVICES

TOURISM. Consistent with a worldwide trend, tourism has been rapidly growing in New Zealand. In 1970, there were less than 200,000 visitors each year to New Zealand, but in 1999 this number surpassed 1.5 million. About half of these can be considered as tourists, the other half being involved with business, visiting friends and relatives and other activities (although even these are likely to be "partly tourists"). The economic impacts of tourism are great, although they are difficult to measure because tourism has an impact in many different economic sectors. In 1995 it was estimated that tourism provided about 58,000 full-time equivalent jobs directly and 60,000 indirectly. In the same year it brought in about NZ$4.3 billion (US$2.7 billion), more than all dairy exports (the largest agricultural export sector).

Tourism in New Zealand is based on a variety of attractions. Most generally the country is seen as having many natural assets, including mountains, subtropical forests, beautiful beaches, active volcanoes, geothermal pools, and geysers. Many also come to see the culture of the indigenous Maori, which is expressed in many ways, including dance and art. As international tourism has become more competitive and diverse, tourists tend to demand a broad range of attractions, so dynamic urban spaces may also be seen to be part of the total tourist experience. Thus, for example, the waterfront village in Auckland built to host New Zealand's defense of the America's Cup has become an important part of the tourist infrastructure, as has the spectacular new national museum in Wellington, Te Papa. Other forms of tourism are also expanding. **Eco-tourists** come to watch whales and dolphins or simply to walk in the forests. New Zealand has also become well known for adventure tourism with such sports as bungee jumping, white water rafting, and hang-gliding.

FINANCIAL SERVICES. Since the economic restructuring which started in 1984, there has been considerable change in the financial sector. Most controls on the financial sector were removed and there has been a rapid growth in the money market since then, especially in relation to foreign exchange. New financial institutions entered the country, and foreign investment in the financial sector accelerated, as it did in other sectors. By 1999 there were 18 banks registered in New Zealand, only 1 of which was wholly New Zealand owned. About 70 percent of this foreign ownership was Australian. In 2001 the coalition government was set to introduce a state-owned enterprise "People's Bank" which would use the existing network of New Zealand Post outlets.

The Reserve Bank of New Zealand has several roles: 1) operating **monetary policy** to maintain price stability, 2) maintaining an efficient financial system, and 3) meeting currency needs. Thus, despite the distancing of the government from intervention in the financial system, the Reserve Bank may intervene to stabilize the currency or influence interest rates or the rate of **inflation**.

RETAIL. Wholesale and **retail** trade accounted for about 16 percent of GDP in 1999. During the 1990s the parts of the retail sector that grew most rapidly were food retailing, accommodation, hotels, liquor, cafes, restaurants, and takeaways. The 2 major factors in stimulating these sub-sectors were increases in tourist numbers and changing lifestyles among New Zealanders to favor more convenience foods, eating out, and diversity of food choice. These are trends common to other industrial countries. Other parts of the retail sector are also following international trends. The move to suburban shopping malls has taken place for several decades, but a relatively recent variation is the "mega-mall" with huge barn-like stores, each catering to a particular range of products (electronics, home furnishings, sports, etc.). At the same time, huge cut-price department stores have undercut traditional department stores. In New Zealand the most successful of these has been The Warehouse whose success is similar to that of Wal-Mart in the United States.

Another international trend experienced in New Zealand in the last 2 decades is international franchising. International brand names introduced during that period include McDonald's, Burger King, Pizza Hut, Starbucks, Planet Hollywood, Borders, and Body Shop. Of course, the same trend has occurred for specific product lines.

INTERNATIONAL TRADE

Over the years, New Zealand has tended to import more than it exports, but the trade imbalance is relatively small.

The major destinations of New Zealand's exports, in order of importance, are Australia, United States, Japan, United Kingdom, South Korea, Germany, and China. The products exported to each of these countries varies considerably. For example, there is a great contrast between Australia and United States. Since Australia produces many of the same agricultural products as New Zealand, the most important exports are manufactures such as machinery, textiles, and paper products, as well as wood and mineral fuels. Exports to the United States, however, are more agricultural: meat, dairy products, fish, fruit, and nuts, followed by specialized manufactures. There is a mixture of agricultural and manufactured products flowing to Japan, while to the United Kingdom the pattern is similar to the United States.

The sources of New Zealand's imports are similar to the export destinations: Australia, United States, Japan, China, Germany, and United Kingdom. From Australia, New Zealand imports products in many of the same categories as it exports, mainly fuels and manufactures. From the United States the most important imports are machinery, aircraft, plastics, and vehicles. More than half of the imports from Japan are of vehicles, with various types of machinery making most of the rest. Through the 1990s, as trade tariffs have been reduced, New Zealand's trade within Asian countries, especially China, has increased and is likely to increase further.

Trade (expressed in billions of US$): New Zealand

	Exports	Imports
1975	2.162	3.155
1980	5.421	5.472
1985	5.720	5.992
1990	9.488	9.501
1995	13.738	13.958
1998	12.070	12.496

SOURCE: International Monetary Fund. *International Financial Statistics Yearbook 1999.*

Exchange rates: New Zealand

New Zealand dollars (NZ$) per US$1	
Jan 2001	2.2502
2000	2.1863
1999	1.8886
1998	1.8632
1997	1.5083
1996	1.4543

SOURCE: CIA *World Factbook 2001* [ONLINE].

GDP per Capita (US$)

Country	1975	1980	1985	1990	1998
New Zealand	14,005	13,961	15,416	15,026	16,427
United States	19,364	21,529	23,200	25,363	29,683
Australia	14,317	15,721	17,078	18,023	21,881
Papua New Guinea	1,048	975	936	888	1,085

SOURCE: United Nations. *Human Development Report 2000; Trends in human development and per capita income.*

MONEY

A **floating exchange rate** was adopted in 1985 as part of the economic restructuring started the previous year. Before that time, the **exchange rate** was controlled in relation to a basket of currencies, and in 1984 it appeared that the New Zealand dollar was overvalued, since it was held at a value higher than was justified in terms of the country's trade and investment transactions. Through the 1990s the exchange rate has fluctuated, but from 1996 it has been steadily devalued against the American dollar, a process accelerated during 2000. The impact on the rate of inflation in the late 1990s was not as great as might be expected. One reason was that there was still a downward trend in the price of many manufactures, and many of these originated in countries whose currencies were also declining against the American dollar. Even for products originating in the United States, such as computer software, companies often kept prices down to remain competitive.

The New Zealand Stock Exchange is the only one in the country. At the beginning of 1999 there were 146 New Zealand companies and 83 overseas companies listed with the exchange. There are 3 types of stocks bought and sold on this exchange: company shares, bonds, and debentures and other loans, although the bulk of the trading is in the first of these.

POVERTY AND WEALTH

According to **United Nations Development Program**'s (UNDP) Human Development Indicator (HDI), New Zealand ranked 19th on the list of countries in terms of education, health, and the quality of life in 2001. This ranking is lower than it once was, but still definitely qualifies New Zealand as one of the world's "wealthy" countries. In terms of per capita GDP it is substantially below the American level, although between 1975 and 1998 **real GDP** per capita showed steady growth.

In the past, New Zealand has had a reputation as an equitable society because it was the first country in the world to give women the vote (1893), and it was one of the first to develop a welfare state, among other things. Yet a look at the income distribution in 1996 reveals that income is very unequally distributed, with the lowest 20 percent of income earners accounting for only 2.4 percent of all income, while the top 20 percent earned 51.8 percent, and the top 10 percent more than one-third of the total. A comparison of the data for 5 years earlier shows that in each of these last 2 categories the percentages have increased by nearly 5 percent (from 46.9 and 29.8 percent, respectively).

When gender differences are considered, it is shown that in the top 10 percent of income earners, only 22 percent are females. Although the equivalent comparison is not available by ethnicity, a comparison of median income is clear: men of European ethnic background earned 20 percent more than Maori men and 38 percent more than those of Pacific island origin.

Inequalities in income have existed for a very long time and result partly from large wage differences between professionals and managers on the one hand and unskilled laborers on the other. Minority ethnic groups and women tend to hold a disproportionate number of jobs in certain sectors, often those that are most vulnerable to economic change, such as seasonal work (e.g. fruit harvesting, food processing) and casual work (e.g. out-

Distribution of Income or Consumption by Percentage Share: New Zealand

Lowest 10%	0.3
Lowest 20%	2.7
Second 20%	10.0
Third 20%	16.3
Fourth 20%	24.1
Highest 20%	46.9
Highest 10%	29.8

Survey year: 1991

Note: This information refers to income shares by percentiles of the population and is ranked by per capita income.

SOURCE: *2000 World Development Indicators* [CD-ROM].

Household Consumption in PPP Terms

Country	All food	Clothing and footwear	Fuel and power[a]	Health care[b]	Education[b]	Transport & Communications	Other
New Zealand	21	5	12	3	2	8	49
United States	13	9	9	4	6	8	51
Australia	24	5	9	2	16	9	36
Papua New Guinea	N/A	N/A	N/A	N/A	N/A	N/A	N/A

Data represent percentage of consumption in PPP terms.
[a]Excludes energy used for transport.
[b]Includes government and private expenditures.

SOURCE: World Bank. *World Development Indicators 2000.*

work on clothing). In New Zealand the restructuring which took place after 1984 had a considerable impact on work patterns, with many becoming unemployed in the private sector as tariffs were lowered or **subsidies** withdrawn, and in the **public sector** as government services were reduced. In the late 1980s ethnic minorities in particular were affected, with unemployment rates 2 or 3 times the national average. Workers were also affected by changes in labor legislation which reduced the power of unions (see Working Conditions section). On the other hand, many investors made large profits in the recently deregulated finance sector.

WORKING CONDITIONS

Many of the reforms that resulted in a welfare state in New Zealand were brought into effect in the 1930s and again in the 1970s by the Labour Party, which was strongly supported by labor unions. This suggests that labor unions were quite powerful in some periods. However, as the economy became increasingly service-oriented the power of the traditional unions—associated with unskilled and semi-skilled workers—declined. In 1991, a new National Party (conservative) government brought in the Employment Contracts Act (ECA), which weakened the power of labor unions. In particular it abolished compulsory unionism in which, if a high proportion of workers in a workplace voted to have a union represent them, then all workers were obliged to join. It also made it more difficult to take strike action, restricted the rights of union representatives to enter a workplace, and instituted several other restrictions which ultimately weakened union power. Soon after the Labour Party was elected in 1999, new legislation, the Employment Relations Act, overturned some aspects of the ECA once again increasing the role of unions in the workplace.

Working conditions are regulated by several acts of parliament. The minimum wage in 2000 was NZ$7 an hour for adult workers and NZ$4.20 an hour for those aged 16 to 19. Minimum annual leave after 1 year of employment is 3 weeks, and there are 11 public holidays a year for which a worker must be paid if they fall on days which would otherwise be working days for them (Christmas and New Year's Day must be compensated regardless). The number of hours in the workweek are not legislated, but must be outlined as part of an employment contract; if nothing is explicitly stated in the contract, it defaults to a 40-hour workweek. Parental leave is available to either a mother or a father, and time periods vary according to particular conditions. Parental leave is currently unpaid, but under debate during 2001 is a more comprehensive system of paid parental leave.

COUNTRY HISTORY AND ECONOMIC DEVELOPMENT

1300 A.D. Evidence of human habitation on Aotearoa (New Zealand).

1642. Dutchman Tasman first European to sight "Staten Landt"; later renamed "Nieuw Zeeland."

1769. James Cook claims country for Great Britain.

1790s-1800s. Ongoing Maori-European (Pakeha) contacts: whaling, timber, spread of disease.

1840. Treaty of Waitangi between British Crown and many Maori chiefs cedes some political powers to British but maintains indigenous rights in perpetuity.

1860s. Land wars fought between Maori and British administration/settlers; Maori armed resistance ends in 1872 after loss of much land.

1882. First shipment of frozen meat to England.

1907. New Zealand becomes a dominion.

1914–18. World War I; New Zealand takes over Samoa from Germany.

1935. First Labour government elected; state housing program started.

1939–45. World War II; New Zealand troops in Africa, Europe, Pacific; bulk purchases of farm produce for war effort.

1950s. Manufacturing industry expands; Maori urbanization for employment; beginning of substantial Pacific immigration.

1960s. National government in power; open access to British market for farm products.

1972–75. Labour government in power.

1975–84. National government in power; New Zealand butter quotas set by European Commission; wage and price freeze.

1984–91. Labour government undertakes economic restructuring including reduction of tariffs, abolition of subsidies to agriculture, regions etc., privatization, reduction of government services.

1987. International and New Zealand stock market crash following period of much property speculation in New Zealand.

1991–99. National coalition government in power; Employment Contracts Act introduced; welfare benefits cut; further privatization.

1999. Labour-Alliance coalition government elected on reformed policies focusing on preservation of government services, more pro-labor stance.

FUTURE TRENDS

At the turn of the century there were mixed feelings about the economic future of New Zealand. The country has been quite successful in diversifying its agricultural base, and there is optimism that international trade **liberalization** will benefit producers who are efficient by world standards. There is an ongoing focus on identifying new niche markets whether they are in new varieties of wine, more exotic varieties of subtropical fruit, or in ostrich feathers. In the manufacturing sector there is ongoing concern about the degree to which New Zealand industries can compete with countries with low labor costs in Asia and elsewhere. Once again, there is some optimism that niche markets will boost manufacturing, with recent examples including carpet weaving and yacht construction. At the same time, there are regular reminders of the problems of global trade liberalization, with factories being closed or relocated to other countries which have lower rates of pay and government subsidies.

Further hope is found in the service sector. In particular, tourism is likely to continue to expand, although to some extent this may depend on the cost of international air travel. If airfares continue to decline in real terms as they have for some years, that will benefit New Zealand, distant as it is from major markets. However, if prices are increased substantially by fuel increases or the impact of global alliances, then New Zealand's tourism future may be more problematic. There have also been some successes in areas of high technology such as the software industry, and if New Zealand manages to fulfill its objective of achieving a "high knowledge" economy there are likely to be many other possibilities.

There are also areas of concern or even pessimism. For some, the socioeconomic inequalities which have increased during the period of economic restructuring are likely to increase under ongoing trade and investment liberalization. The restructuring has driven down wages for unskilled workers while at the same time provided large profits for investors in some sectors. The way in which these issues are resolved will depend on the economic and social policies of the new government.

DEPENDENCIES

New Zealand has no territories or colonies.

BIBLIOGRAPHY

Asia Pacific Viewpoint (special edition on New Zealand economy). Vol. 26, No. 2, 2000.

Economist Intelligence Unit. *Country Profile: New Zealand.* London: Economist Intelligence Unit, 2001.

Statistics New Zealand. *New Zealand Official Yearbook 2000.* Wellington: Statistics N.Z., 2000.

Statistics New Zealand. *People and Places.* Wellington: Statistics N.Z., 1997.

U.S. Central Intelligence Agency. *World Factbook 2000.* <http://www.odci.gov/cia/publications/factbook/index.html>. Accessed August 2001.

—***Wardlow Friesen***

OMAN

Sultanate of Oman
Saltanat 'Uman

CAPITAL: Muscat.

MONETARY UNIT: Omani riyal (OR). One OR equals 1,000 baiza. Coins are in denominations of 500, 250, 200, 100, 50, 25, 10, and 5 baiza. Paper currency comes in denominations of OR50, 20, 10, 5, and 1, as well as 500, 250, 200, and 100 baiza.

CHIEF EXPORTS: Petroleum, re-exports, fish, metals, and textiles.

CHIEF IMPORTS: Machinery and transport equipment, manufactured goods, food, livestock, and lubricants.

GROSS DOMESTIC PRODUCT: US$19.6 billion (purchasing power parity, 1999 est.).

BALANCE OF TRADE: **Exports:** US$7.63 billion (f.o.b., 1997 est.). **Imports:** US$5.682 billion (f.o.b., 1997 est.).

COUNTRY OVERVIEW

LOCATION AND SIZE. The Sultanate of Oman borders the Arabian Sea, the Gulf of Oman, and the Persian Gulf and shares borders with Yemen, the United Arab Emirates, and Saudi Arabia. Oman has an area of 212,460 square kilometers (82,030 square miles) and a coastline that totals 2,092 kilometers (1,299 miles). Comparatively, Oman occupies an area slightly smaller than Kansas. Muscat, Oman's capital, is located on the country's northeastern coastline.

POPULATION. In July 2000 the population of Oman was estimated at 2,533,389, of whom 2,006,311 were Omani and 527,078 were non-Omani. Large expatriate communities (communities of foreigners who have left their own country to live and work abroad) are very common in the Gulf countries on account of the oil and services industries. In Oman many unskilled expatriates from Asia are employed to carry out menial jobs, although this community has been declining slowly since 1996. The Omani population increases on average by 2.7 percent a year and, as a result, the country has a very young population. Some 47 percent of Omanis are under the age of 20 compared to only 4 percent who are over the age of 60. In 2000 the birth rate stood at 38.08 births per 1,000 population, while the death rate stood at 4.16 per 1,000. With a projected annual population growth rate of 3.46 percent, the population is expected to reach 3,848,217 by the year 2015.

The majority of the Omani population is Sunni Muslim, but a substantial number of people—including the ruling family—follow Ibahism, an offshoot of Shia Islam. Given Oman's long trading history, its population is a mixture of different races and even one of its most prominent mercantile families is of Hindu descent. Oman was a hub for the slave trade in the 18th and 19th century and although this practice was abolished in the 20th century, many continue to work for the families that previously owned their ancestors.

Employment in Oman is largely dependent on nationality. In the **public sector**, Omanis held 70 percent of the jobs in 1999, while in the **private sector**—which contains most of the lower-paying jobs—90 percent of the employees were from foreign countries. Rising unemployment in Oman has forced the government to realize that it can no longer pursue its policy of guaranteeing jobs to young Omanis entering the labor market and it is now focusing on increasing employment opportunities for Omanis in the private sector. Oman has seen a dramatic migration of people to the cities in search of better jobs; the largest proportion of thc population is found in the capital city Muscat and in the larger northern towns of Suhar, Nizwa, and Sur.

OVERVIEW OF ECONOMY

Historically, Oman has been a gateway for trade between Asia and the Middle East. Its capital, Muscat, is

the country's most developed city as well as the center of economic activity, thanks to its coastal location. The strategic Musandam peninsula gives Oman control over the land adjacent to the vital Strait of Hormuz, through which a majority of the world's oil passes. Oil is the most important factor in the Omani economy and it is the oil industry that is the catalyst for growth in **gross domestic product** (GDP). GDP growth averaged 4.4 percent between 1993 and 1996, reached 6.2 percent in 1997, and fell to 2.9 percent in 1998 due to the crash in global oil prices. Crude oil has accounted for over 30 percent of Oman's GDP since 1980. Oman differs from other Gulf countries such as Saudi Arabia and the United Arab Emirates in that its reserves of oil are difficult to extract from the ground, limited in quantity, and predicted to run out in 17 years. Given that the oil industry is not labor intensive, the population in the Sultanate is growing rapidly, and the public sector is over-staffed, there is a serious unemployment problem in the country. However, the government has never released any unemployment statistics and no credible estimates have been made since 1995 due to international skepticism about the official population figures.

Oman is a free market economy, but the government is at present the most important factor in the economy, both as an employer and as a purchaser of goods and services. The Omani economy has been growing steadily over the last 25 years and considerable development has taken place. However, with the fluctuations in the global price of oil, an oil industry that will soon be negligible, massive investments made in **infrastructure**, and hence shrinking **foreign exchange reserves**, there is a pressing need to diversify the economy. It is especially important to expand the sources of export earnings as well as to provide jobs for a growing population. These 2 goals form the basis of Oman's policy initiatives. The government has encouraged private domestic and foreign investors to take the lead in promoting these initiatives, and a period of structural transformation from primary to manufactured exports has begun. In the late 1980s the government's commitment to economic diversification coincided with the discovery of abundant natural gas and since this time, drilling sites for both gas and oil are to be found all over the country. The Omani government has announced that it intends to implement a 5-year plan (2001–2006) in order to address these important challenges. In addition, policymakers will also have to focus on Oman's membership in the World Trade Organization (WTO). This will expose the country to even more foreign competition.

Political parties in Oman are not legal, but the major trading families who control the bulk of the country's trade and industry are very powerful groups and are represented in the government. In 1998 Oman received US$509,100,000 in official development assistance, the largest portion of which came from the United Kingdom, a country with which Oman enjoys strong ties. Oman also has a good relationship with the European Union and much improved relations with the United States; its main trading partners are Japan and China. The economy's main exports are oil, live animals, animal products, textiles, base metals, and mineral products. Before the discovery of oil in the 1960s, the Omani economy was dependent on agriculture, however, in 1999 this sector accounted for 2 percent of GDP due to the lack of water supply. Nevertheless, it still employs a large number of people along the northern coast and in the south.

POLITICS, GOVERNMENT, AND TAXATION

Oman has been ruled by the Royal Al Bu Sa'id family since the 18th century. Political parties are not allowed in the country and there are no directly elected representatives. The current sultan, Qaboos Bin Sa'id Al Sa'id, overthrew his father in a palace coup in 1970 and seized the throne. Although the family has traditionally ruled over all state affairs, the new sultan has been careful to balance tribal, ethnic, and regional interests and as a result he has placed several tribal leaders in the government. In 1991 the sultan established the 59-seat Consultative Council, or Majlis Ash-Shura, to act as a consultative body, thus allowing a limited form of political expression. The government selects council members from lists of nominees proposed by each of the 59 wilayats (regions). Nevertheless, the country is an absolute hereditary monarchy and the sultan still rules by royal decree. He can appoint and fire all council ministers as well as ministers in the defense department, the department of foreign affairs, and the department of finance.

Oman did not have a constitution until 1996, when the sultan promulgated (proclaimed) the "Basic Law" by decree. This basic law clarifies the royal succession, provides for a prime minister, bars ministers from holding interests in companies doing business with the government, establishes a **bicameral** legislature, and guarantees basic civil liberties for Omani citizens. The legislature has no power to overturn the sultan's wishes. Its role has been purposefully ill-defined so as to render it a fairly ineffective body. The state promises to provide health care and education for all citizens as well as maintain security through the use of the army. Basic freedoms such as freedom of the press are touched upon, however, they are not clearly defined and are still very restricted. The Omani legal system is based both on English common law and Islamic law. The ultimate authority in law remains the sultan and he has not yet accepted compulsory jurisdiction of the International Court of Justice (this institution has its seat in The Hague and is the principal judicial organ of the United Nations).

The major source of government revenue does not come from taxation but from oil revenues. The only **direct taxes** in Oman are **income tax** (which ranges from 15 to 45 percent) and some regional taxes; the only **indirect tax** is customs **duty**. There are 5 percent taxes on hotel and restaurant bills, a 2 percent tax on electricity bills exceeding OR50. Oman makes no distinction between resident and non-resident companies. If a company has income from Oman that requires occasional visits to the Sultanate, the income will be considered taxable. Tax rates on non-petroleum, foreign-owned firms were lowered in October 1996 for all except those firms with greater than 90 percent foreign ownership. The nature of the relationship between the petroleum companies and the government will often govern taxation and royalties on petroleum producers. Labor law and the Oman tax law also affects a foreigner's ability to do business in Oman. There is no complete body of regulations codifying these laws and many government decisions are made on an ad hoc basis.

INFRASTRUCTURE, POWER, AND COMMUNICATIONS

Due to the large-scale program of road construction carried out by the Ministry of Communications over the past 3 decades, there are now approximately 6,000 kilometers (3,720 miles) of paved roads and 24,000 kilometers (14,880 miles) of unpaved roads in Oman. In 1970 there were only 10 kilometers (6 miles) of paved roads and about 1,700 kilometers (1,054 miles) of unpaved road in the entire country. The number of licensed automobiles on the road increased from 261,627 in 1992 to 404,375 in 1998 and this increase in traffic also led to an increase in the number of road deaths from 218 in 1992 to 478 in 1998. Oman does not have a rail system.

The country's main airport, Muscat Seeb International, has a capacity of 1.3 million passengers. The

Communications

Country	Newspapers	Radios	TV Sets[a]	Cable subscribers[a]	Mobile Phones[a]	Fax Machines[a]	Personal Computers[a]	Internet Hosts[b]	Internet Users[b]
	1996	1997	1998	1998	1998	1998	1998	1999	1999
Oman	29	598	595	0	43	2.7	21	2.87	50
United States	215	2,146	847	244.3	256	78.4	458.6	1,508.77	74,100
Saudi Arabia	57	321	262	N/A	31	N/A	49.6	1.17	300
Yemen	15	64	29	N/A	1	N/A	1.2	0.02	10

[a]Data are from International Telecommunication Union, *World Telecommunication Development Report 1999* and are per 1,000 people.
[b]Data are from the Internet Software Consortium (http://www.isc.org) and are per 10,000 people.

SOURCE: World Bank. *World Development Indicators 2000.*

airport has been fully modernized and boasts duty-free shopping areas, impressive lounges, and large transit areas. The main runway has been extended to 3,585 meters (11,760 feet) and the passenger terminals have been expanded to handle 3,000 passengers an hour. In 1995 the total number of passengers passing through Seeb International airport amounted to 2,176,033. Salalah, the country's second airport, which was built initially as a military installation, began operating a passenger terminal in 1986 and the main runway was extended in 1992. Oman now has 6 civil airports in total at Seeb, Salalah, Sur, Masirah, Khasab, and Diba in Musandam. The country's main port is Mina Sultan Qaboos, which was completed in 1974 with a capacity to handle 2.2 million tons annually. Many improvements have since been made, including dredging the harbor entrance to a depth of 13 meters (42 feet). The second-largest port is called Mina Raysut and it is this port that serves Salalah and the Governorate of Dhofar. The construction of a third port in Suhar started in 1999 and the project is expected to cost US$250 million.

Electrical power in Oman is supplied both by the public sector and by the private sector. In 1999 the total national production amounted to 5.2 billion kilowatt hours (kWh) with consumption reaching 4.9 billion kWh. In 1999 there were 31 power stations with a total installed capacity of 1,662 megawatts. The government-owned General Telecommunications Organization (GTO) was established in 1980 and was responsible for setting up the modern telephone system throughout the country. Thirty years ago there were only 500 lines in and around the capital and international telephone calls could be made only through radio channels. As of 1998, all the telephone exchanges became digital and one can now telephone all over the world. Oman has an overall telephone capacity of 420,000 lines, both fixed and mobile, and given the widespread use of the telephone, it is estimated that Oman will need about 500,000 telephone lines by the year 2020, which will require massive investment.

ECONOMIC SECTORS

The Omani economy is a diverse one with services contributing 57 percent of GDP and industry contributing approximately 40 percent. However, over the past 40 years there has been a major shift in the structure of the economy. In the 1950s and 1960s, when the oil fields had not yet been discovered, the agricultural sector drove the economy. This sector has diminished in importance since the early 1970s, representing only 3 percent of GDP in 1999, whereas the export of oil and petroleum-related products and the manufacturing of goods such as textiles has increased. The sector's output is heavily dependent upon the weather, and accurate figures on employment in agriculture remain unknown.

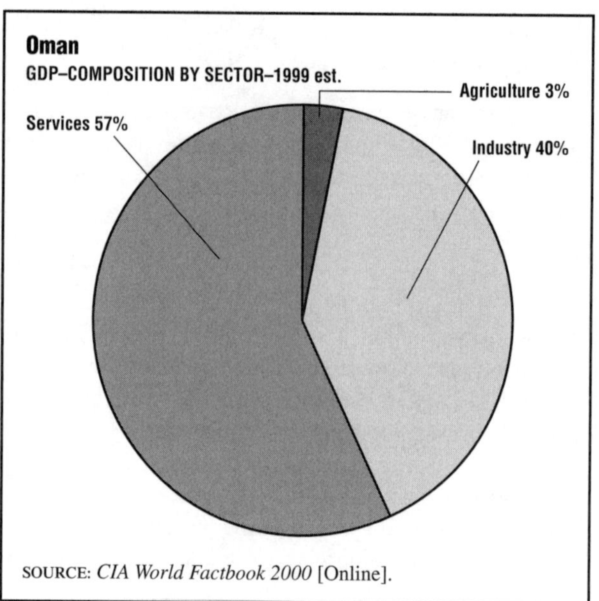

SOURCE: *CIA World Factbook 2000* [Online].

AGRICULTURE

Prior to the discovery of oil in the 1960s, the agricultural sector was central in the Omani economy. However, in 1999 the sector contributed only 3 percent to GDP and was heavily subsidized by the government. Oman is not self-sufficient in food and in 1995 the country spent US$572 million on food and live animals. This figure rose to US$650 million in 1999. There are efforts underway to develop self-sufficiency in staple foods. The main crops grown in Oman are tomatoes, eggplant, dates, bananas, limes, and carrots. The principal agricultural area is found along the Batinah coast, in the northeast between Muscat and Diba al-Hisn, which accounts for about half the total crop area of approximately 101,000 acres. In the south, agriculture is centered on a small coastal plain that is fed by monsoon rain coming from the Indian Ocean. In spite of its small contribution to GDP, the agricultural sector is still a major employer. In 1994, the World Bank estimated that over half the Omani **labor force** was working in the agricultural sector. The Omani government reports that a total of 140,000 people are employed permanently in this sector and that 47,000 of these people are unpaid family workers. Agricultural employees are primarily of Omani descent.

Oman is famed for producing very high quality agricultural goods and the highest quality products are usually exported to the neighboring Gulf Cooperation Council (GCC) countries. (On 26 May 1981 an agreement was signed between the 6 conservative monarchies of the Gulf: Saudi Arabia, Bahrain, United Arab Emirates, Kuwait, Oman, and Qatar to coordinate their economic, political, cultural, and security policy.) However, the agricultural farm is threatened by many problems, including outdated technology and an increase in the salinity of the water. The government has responded to these issues by investing more into the sector. Its goal is to obtain self-sufficiency in food production by improving agricultural conditions. In working to make the agricultural sector internationally competitive, the government has introduced incentives for foreign investors. These exemptions include tax reductions, utilities discounts, loans, and **tariff** protection. The government has also helped Omani firms in exporting their products.

FISHING. With 2,092 kilometers (1,297 miles) of coastline running from the mouth of the Gulf in the north to the border with Yemen in the south, Oman has very rich fishing potential which has yet to be fully developed. There is a 200-mile **exclusive economic zone** which extends from Oman out to sea and over 150 species of fish and crustaceans have been identified in Omani waters ranging from tuna and crayfish to lobster and shrimp. Large amounts of lobsters are caught off the Masirah islands and off the coast of Dhofar, and they are exported to Saudi Arabia and the United Arab Emirates where they are in great demand. In 1998, approximately 26,940 Omanis were employed in the fishing industry and a total of 116,780 tons of fish were caught. The number of fish caught per annum has been slowly declining over the past 20 years due to pollution and the depletion of fish stocks. In response to this, the Omani government has put restrictions on the amount of fish catches. Lobster may now be harvested only twice a year. The annual fish catch remains at over 100,000 tons per year, and efforts to produce **value-added**, manufactured fish products are underway. Processing and packaging for export are key concerns, as is the use of better technology at sea.

IRRIGATION. Oman's position in a semi-arid climatic zone results in the serious problem of water scarcity. The government has been pursuing programs of improved water efficiency and water resource development and some far-reaching legislation has been passed through the government. In 1999 there were 48 dams all over the country that collect rainwater as well as a major project underway to decrease water consumption through the use of water-saving devices on taps. The government has also initiated a plan for the supply of water to Muscat up until 2010 that involves extending the existing pipelines. Two additional reservoirs have been built around Muscat at a cost of US$3 million.

INDUSTRY

OIL. Similar to many of the Gulf countries, the Omani industrial sector makes up a large proportion of GDP, accounting for 40 percent of it in 1999. However, Oman is not a typical Persian Gulf oil producer due to its small, scattered oil fields and, as a result, production costs are much higher per barrel than those in other GCC countries. The average Omani oil field produces one-tenth the volume per well that Saudi Arabia or Iran produce. Oil was not discovered in commercial amounts until 1962, much later than most oil-producing Gulf states. Oman is not a member of the Organization of Petroleum Exporting Countries (OPEC). (OPEC is an international organization of 11 developing countries which are heavily reliant on oil revenues as their main source of income. The current members are Algeria, Indonesia, Iran, Iraq, Kuwait, Libya, Nigeria, Qatar, Saudi Arabia, the United Arab Emirates, and Venezuela.) However, in the past Oman has cut production in co-operation with OPEC in an attempt to raise prices. Oman's oil production has wavered between 910,000 barrels a day (b/d) and 890,000 b/d since April 1999. The Omani government has announced a new 5-year plan which is to run from 2001 to 2005 and which aims to increase production to 1 million b/d. The bulk of Oman's 5.28 billion barrels in proven reserves is situated in the north and in the center of the country. In the north the largest fields are Yibal, Natih, Fahud, al-Huwaisah, and Lekhwair. The largest field is Yibal, producing 180,000 b/d and, together, these fields produce half of the total Omani oil production. The crude oil produced in the north is mainly light or medium crude and is found alongside natural gas. The oil fields further south tend to produce heavier crude and are usually not associated with natural gas.

With oil reserves amounting to 5.28 billion barrels, Oman has a further 17-year supply of oil if it continues to produce at 910,000 b/d. Since the discovery of oil, the oil and gas industry has been the catalyst of growth for the Omani economy, contributing approximately 37 percent to GDP each year and as much as 55 percent of GDP up until the early 1980s. In addition, oil provides 75.3 percent of state revenues. The oil industry is largely run by Petroleum Development Oman (PDO) which has a government majority ownership. PDO controls 90 percent of the country's output. Shell owns 34 percent of the company and operates the majority of Oman's large fields. In 1999, Oman exported 95.8 million barrels of oil to Japan, 65.6 million barrels to Thailand, 55.9 million barrels to South Korea, and 39.4 million barrels to China.

GAS. The gas sector in Oman is considered to be the cornerstone of the government's economic growth strategy and great efforts have been made to turn natural gas into a thriving export industry. There are abundant gas reserves in Oman and 1999 estimates put the proven reserves at 29.28 trillion cubic feet (tcf). The government has projected that by the year 2002 natural gas will contribute 15 percent of GDP. Most of the gas reserves are located in areas that are controlled by PDO. Oman has entered into a number of projects with overseas companies such as Gulfstream resources of Canada and Neste Oy of

Finland to develop, explore, and produce natural gas in the northern part of the country.

MANUFACTURING. Following the discovery of large gas deposits, attention moved away from the manufacturing industry and in 1999, manufacturing contributed 5 percent to GDP. Most of the country's industrial enterprises are involved in light industry. Existing companies manufacture soft drinks, textiles, perfume, and cement. The sector grew by 3 percent between 1994 and 1998, but it relies heavily on skilled expatriate labor and therefore does not contribute much to the creation of local jobs.

SERVICES

TOURISM. Evidence of Oman's rich cultural and architectural heritage can be seen in its hundreds of historic sites and its many beautiful beaches. The country's varied geography and range of climatic conditions give it enormous potential in the tourism industry, a sector which is still very undeveloped. Given Oman's current unemployment problem, combined with the thousands of young Omanis entering the workforce every year, the expansion of the tourism sector could create much-needed jobs. The government initiated a 15-year tourism plan in 1990, easing visa restrictions in order to open up the country to more tourists, and very quickly the number of visitors rose from 290,000 in 1994 to 503,000 in 1999.

In 2000, tourism represented less than 1 percent of GDP even though there was an 11 percent increase in the number of visitors between 1988 and 1992. In 1994 there were only 37 hotels in Oman and in 2000 there were 89. The government has made an attempt to attract visitors from the Gulf region, signing an agreement with Dubai whereby nationals of both countries can easily obtain visas. However, the government's plan is to attract affluent European visitors to the country who are happy to take supervised coach tours instead of exploring the country on their own. Government concerns about local sensitivities as well as the continuing high tax on alcohol serve as major constraints to the growth of this potentially lucrative industry.

FINANCIAL SERVICES. The Omani government has made serious attempts to ensure the stability of the banking sector and in 2000 there were 16 commercial banks in the country, of which 9 were branches of foreign banks. In addition to the commercial banks, the government has set up 2 credit institutions that provide small loans for Omani citizens. The Omani Housing Bank provides loans to finance the construction of homes and the Oman Development Bank provides general **microcredit**. The Central Bank of Oman places restrictions on the amount of foreign exchange that banks are allowed to lend and invest and in addition sets the total amount of capital to be held by local banks at US$26 million and by foreign banks at US$9 million.

Oman's stock exchange was established in 1989 and is called the Muscat Securities Market (MSM). There are over 100 banks and companies listed on the exchange with a current capitalization of over US$2 billion. In 1999 Oman was included in the International Finance Corporation's **emerging market** index and the government has made concerted efforts to make the stock market more transparent and more regulated. Electronic trading was introduced in 1999 as well as a regulatory agency called the Capital Markets Authority (CMA).

INTERNATIONAL TRADE

In 1999, Oman's exports amounted to US$7.2 billion and its imports were valued at US$5.4 billion. The country's principal export is oil and in 1999 the commodity accounted for 76 percent of all exports. In the 1980s, however, oil accounted for over 90 percent but its share has declined due to the falling price of crude oil. The second major export in Oman is **re-exports** which totaled US$1.3 billion in 1999. Given that the Omani economy is not very diversified, the smallest proportion of exports is non-oil exports such as foodstuffs and animal products. These accounted for 35 percent of total non-oil Omani exports in 1999. In 1999 the principle importer of Omani crude oil was Japan. Japan imported a total of 95.8 million barrels followed by Thailand, which imported 65.6 million barrels.

Oman has slowly increased its production of crude oil and as a result the country has enjoyed **trade surpluses** throughout the last decade even though it has increased its imports. Nevertheless, the size of these surpluses varies considerably from year to year due to the world prices of crude oil. When Iraq invaded Kuwait in 1990 the price of oil increased substantially and that year Oman's trade surplus amounted to US$2.9 billion. However, when world oil prices fell drastically in 1998, Oman's surplus fell to just US$291 million. In 1993 the

Trade (expressed in billions of US$): Oman

	Exports	Imports
1975	1.044	.765
1980	2.386	1.732
1985	4.705	3.153
1990	5.508	2.681
1995	5.962	4.248
1998	N/A	5.682

SOURCE: International Monetary Fund. *International Financial Statistics Yearbook 1999.*

surplus stood at US$1.3 billion and in 1996 the rise in the price of crude oil pushed it up to US$3 billion.

Over the past 30 years, Oman has come to rely more and more on imports because it has a very small industrial sector and an agricultural sector that is unable to meet the demand for the variety and quantity of food that the middle- and upper-class Omanis desire. Imports of food amounted to 14 percent of the total value of imports in 1999. The bulk of imports come from the United Arab Emirates and Japan, representing 26.3 percent and 15.8 percent of all imports, respectively. Major Omani imports include food and live animals, beverages and tobacco, crude materials, and minerals. In 1999, Oman's imports totaled US$4.67 billion. Oman's main trading partners are Japan, China, Thailand, South Korea, the United Arab Emirates, and the United States.

In October 2000 the General Council of the World Trade Organization approved Omani membership and in November Oman became the 139th member. Prior to its accession, Oman had to make several changes in order to conform to WTO's membership rules. Not only did the authorities have to agree upon a custom duty ceiling, allow foreign firms with under 70 percent foreign ownership to be taxed the same rates as Omani firms, but also it had to establish intellectual property rights. The consequence of this new membership will open up the Omani markets further and expose local companies to increased competition. By 2003, Oman is required to allow fully foreign-owned computer companies, banks, and insurance companies to operate within the country.

MONEY

Due to the small size of the Omani economy, the country's **monetary policy** is quite straightforward. The goal of the Omani Central Bank is to maintain a stable riyal so that the economy can function competitively abroad. The riyal has been pegged to the dollar since 1973. In 1986 the riyal was devalued by 10.2 percent and since then it has been stable at about US$2.60 to 1 riyal. All the money flowing into the economy is regulated by the Central Bank of Oman. The central bank also regulates the commercial banks through a variety of measures.

POVERTY AND WEALTH

In 1970 Oman initiated a comprehensive sustainable development program and it was among one of the first developing countries to place a real emphasis on the social sector. The program was called Oman 2020 and, since its inception, it has achieved some of the fastest-ever recorded growth in the history of human development. In 1970 there was no formal education system in place apart from 3 primary schools in Muscat that had a maximum capacity of 900 boys. By the end of 1994, 920 schools had opened all over the country and approximately 450,000 students were enrolled in formal education of whom about 50 percent were girls. In 1999, 70 percent of all Omani children attended primary school. In addition to the improvements in education, there have been far-reaching improvements in life expectancy and infant mortality. Life expectancy has increased by 24 years from 47 in 1970 to 71 in 1997, and infant mortality has been reduced 10 times over from more than 215 per 1,000 live births to less than 18 in 1997.

Before the development program began, there were many health problems that were prevalent in Oman due to the poverty and the lack of education. One of the most serious diseases that afflicted more than half of all Omani school children was trachoma, a disease that leads to blindness. This disease is spread through the bite of a blackfly, which breeds in fast-flowing rivers and streams. When the fly bites, it deposits the larvae of a parasitic worm which moves rapidly through the body, causing severe eyesight damage and possible blindness when it enters the eyes. This disease has now been totally wiped out. Additional gains in social and health conditions have led to improvements in the sanitation system; almost three-quarters of all houses have clean running water and toilets that flush. The vast majority of homes have electric light, electricity, and gas with which to cook. The government provides pensions for the elderly and the disabled as well as widows, orphans,

Exchange rates: Oman

Omani riyals per US$1	
2001	0.3845
2000	0.3845
1999	0.3845
1998	0.3845
1997	0.3845
1996	0.3845

Note: Currency rates have been fixed since 1986.

SOURCE: CIA *World Factbook 2001* [ONLINE].

GDP per Capita (US$)

Country	1975	1980	1985	1990	1998
Oman	3,516	3,509	5,607	5,581	N/A
United States	19,364	21,529	23,200	25,363	29,683
Saudi Arabia	9,658	11,553	7,437	7,100	6,516
Yemen	N/A	N/A	N/A	266	254

SOURCE: United Nations. *Human Development Report 2000; Trends in human development and per capita income.*

Household Consumption in PPP Terms

Country	All food	Clothing and footwear	Fuel and power[a]	Health care[b]	Education[b]	Transport & Communications	Other
Oman	22	8	25	13	21	5	7
United States	13	9	9	4	6	8	51
Saudi Arabia	N/A	N/A	N/A	N/A	N/A	N/A	N/A
Yemen	25	5	26	3	5	5	31

Data represent percentage of consumption in PPP terms.
[a]Excludes energy used for transport.
[b]Includes government and private expenditures.

SOURCE: World Bank. *World Development Indicators 2000.*

and divorced women. This massive investment in human capital was made possible by the revenues that the state collected from the oil industry. Without this income it is unlikely that Oman would have made such groundbreaking progress in achieving better standards of living for a large part of its population.

Although Oman serves as a good example for other less-developed countries, there is still much room for improvement due to the high income inequality. The female literacy rate is still less than half that of the male literacy rate, and the total fertility rate (the number of children the average woman will have in her lifetime) is 6.9, one of the highest in the world.

WORKING CONDITIONS

Oman is heavily dependent on expatriate labor with an expatriate community of 527,078 and a total labor force of 650,000. Expatriate workers send large amounts of their wages back home, and in 1997 these earnings amounted to US$1.5 billion or 9.5 percent of GDP. Foreign labor mostly comes from India, Bangladesh, Pakistan, and Sri Lanka, and in most cases these expatriates perform menial and physical jobs. In some cases they have managerial jobs. There are an estimated 30,000 young Omanis entering the workforce every year, and the government has realized that it can no longer provide jobs for the entire workforce. To this end, it has been pursuing a policy of "Omanization" whereby expatriate labor is slowly replaced by Omani labor. Foreigners are not allowed to work in agriculture or public relations, nor are they allowed to be Arabic typists, guards, or technical assistants unless the employer can show that no Omanis are capable of filling the position. Taxi drivers and fishermen must be Omani. In 1994 Oman joined the International Labor Organization (ILO). (This is a UN agency that seeks the promotion of social justice and human and labor rights.) As a consequence, Oman must follow international standards covering a wide range of issues in the world of work, including certain basic human rights, the abolition of forced labor, the elimination of discrimination in employment, the employment of women, and the employment of children.

Oman's labor code lays out basic workers' rights and in 1998 the minimum wage was raised by the government and set at US$260 (100 riyals) per month plus US$52 (20 riyals) for transport costs and housing costs. However, the minimum wage does not apply to all occupations such as small businesses that employ fewer than 5 people, domestic servants, dependent family members working in a family business, and some manual labor jobs. The government has been reluctant to enforce the minimum wage for foreign workers employed in menial jobs. In contrast, the foreign workers who are highly skilled and in managerial positions are often paid much more than their Omani counterparts. The working week is 5 days in the public sector and 5 and a half days in the private sector. Non-Omanis working in construction, **retail**, in the personal service outlets, or in the petroleum fields usually work a 7-day week.

Foreign men and women employed in manual labor or as domestic servants have made official complaints in the past about employers withholding salaries and inhumane treatment. In many cases the government has been unhelpful or undertaken investigative procedures that have been detrimental to the employee concerned, which clearly goes directly against the principles of the International Labor Organization. Employers who mistreat their foreign domestic servants are not always held accountable for their actions and several foreign women working in Oman have been forced to contact their governments' embassies to seek shelter and escape from abuse.

COUNTRY HISTORY AND ECONOMIC DEVELOPMENT

1921. Treaty of Sib is signed, which marks the British takeover of the government of Oman. A council of Ministers governs with British advisers and the British take control of customs revenue. Also during this time, new Western strategic interests develop in Oman in the form of air routes and oil prospecting.

1951. British recognize Oman as an independent state.

1962. Oil is discovered.

1967. Oil production starts.

1970. Sultan Sa'id is overthrown by his own son, Qaboos Bin Sa'id, in a palace coup. Sultan Qaboos **liberalizes** the political system, and starts many development projects. Oman is plagued by civil war.

1980. Military agreement signed with the United States which reflects the Western strategic interest in Oman for the planning of rapid deployment force capabilities to secure Western access to gulf oil.

1981. Oman forms the Gulf Cooperation. This agreement is signed between the 6 conservative monarchies of the Gulf: Saudi Arabia, Bahrain, United Arab Emirates, Kuwait, Oman, and Qatar to coordinate their economic, political, cultural, and security policy.

1991. Sultan Qaboos expands and **restructures** Oman's consultative council.

1994. Oman joins the International Labor Organization (ILO).

1999. Oman is included in the International Finance Corporation's emerging market index. Electronic trading is introduced.

2000. Oman becomes a member of the World Trade Organization.

FUTURE TRENDS

Oman looks to the future with both pessimism and optimism. The pessimism comes from the certainty that the country's major source of revenue—oil—will run out before the year 2020. Oil accounted for the great majority of Oman's exports and GDP ever since it was discovered in the early 1960s. The oil boom had a widespread impact on the economy: it allowed Oman to provide jobs for many of its people in the public sector, it allowed the country to import labor to perform the least wanted jobs in the economy, and it allowed Oman to avoid developing other industries. With the coming decline of the oil economy, Oman must seek alternative means for economic development.

Fortunately, Oman's government has taken a number of steps to ease the country into new economic patterns. The government plans to develop the production of its natural gas and other non-oil energy-based industries. Its 4 previous 5-year plans have been successful and the current 5-year plan focuses on the private sector as the catalyst for non-petroleum economic growth. The government is moving ahead with **privatization** of its utilities, the development of a body of commercial law to facilitate foreign investment, and increased budgetary outlays. However, Oman will have to continue to liberalize its markets in conjunction with its accession to the World Trade Organization (WTO).

Managing the transition from an oil-based to a more diversified economy will not be easy. Even though Oman has a reputation for stability and cooperation, the country's future success is likely to depend on the wisdom and political will of the country's leaders.

DEPENDENCIES

Oman has no territories or colonies.

BIBLIOGRAPHY

Chatty, Dawn. *Mobile Pastoralists: Development Planning and Social Change in Oman.* New York: Columbia University Press, 1996.

Economist Intelligence Unit. *Country Profile: Oman, 2000.* London: Economist Intelligence Unit, 2000.

International Monetary Fund. *International Financial Statistics Yearbook 1999.* Washington, D.C.: International Monetary Fund, 1999.

Skeet, Ian. *Oman: Politics and Development.* London: Macmillan, 1992.

U.S. Central Intelligence Agency. *World Factbook 2000: Oman.* <http://www.cia.gov/cia/publications/factbook/geos/mu.html>. Accessed February 2001.

U.S Department of State. *FY 2000 Country Commercial Guide: Oman.* <http://www.state.gov/www/about_state/business/com_guides/2000/nea/index.html>. Accessed February 2001.

World Bank. *World Development Report 2000/2001: Attacking Poverty.* <http://www.worldbank.org/poverty/wdrpoverty/report/index.htm>. Accessed February 2001.

—Salamander Davoudi

PAKISTAN

Islamic Republic of Pakistan
Islami Jamhooria Pakistan

CAPITAL: Islamabad.

MONETARY UNIT: Pakistani rupee (R). 1 Pakistani rupee equals 100 paisa. Currency notes of 1, 2, 5, 10, 50, 100, 500, and 1,000 rupees are in use.

CHIEF EXPORTS: Cotton, fabrics and yarn, rice, other agricultural products.

CHIEF IMPORTS: Machinery, petroleum, petroleum products, chemicals, transportation equipment, edible oils, grains, pulses, flour.

GROSS DOMESTIC PRODUCT: US$282 billion (purchasing power parity, 1999 est.).

BALANCE OF TRADE: **Exports:** US$8.4 billion (f.o.b., 1999). **Imports:** US$9.8 billion (f.o.b., 1999).

COUNTRY OVERVIEW

LOCATION AND SIZE. Pakistan is a country located in South Asia that covers an area of 796,095 square kilometers (310,410 square miles), almost twice the size of California. In the south, it borders the Arabian Sea, with a coastline of 1,046 kilometers (650 miles) and stretches north to the great Hindukush and Karakoram mountain ranges, with peaks as high as the Nanga Parbat (8,126 meters, 26,660 feet) and the K2 (8,611 meters, 28,251 feet). Pakistan is edged between India, with whom it shares a 2,192-kilometer (1,362-mile) borderline to the east, and Afghanistan and Iran, with whom it has 2,430 kilometers (1,510 miles) and 909 kilometers (565 miles), respectively, of common border. It also shares a 523-kilometer (325-mile) border with China in the north.

The country's temperatures are amongst the most extreme on earth, ranging from 50 degrees Celsius (122 degrees Fahrenheit) or more at the height of summer in the deserts of Sindh to -50 degrees Celsius (-58 degrees Fahrenheit) and below in the depths of winter on the northern mountain ranges. Until 1947, Pakistan was part of British India, which was then divided into the largely Hindu India and the Muslim state of Pakistan. Until 1971, this state consisted of a large territory to the west of the newly established Republic of India and a smaller territory in the northeastern part of historic British India, separated from each other by 1,600 kilometers (995 miles). East Pakistan succeeded in that year to become independent Bangladesh.

POPULATION. The government of Pakistan estimated that Pakistan's population was 137.5 million in June 2000, excluding about 1.5 million refugees from Afghanistan. Pakistan's Afghani refugee population increased significantly in the fall of 2001 after a U.S. bombing campaign against Afghanistan's ruling Taliban regime caused thousands to flee to Pakistan. A large majority of Pakistanis are very young, owing to the high rate of population growth in recent decades. About 41 percent of the population is under the age of 14 years, and 55 percent is between the ages of 15 and 64 years. Population growth is still quite high at around 2.2 percent in 2000. Pakistan has a very high infant mortality rate, with 88 deaths per 1,000 live births, but, on average, every woman in the country gives birth to more than 4 children. According to government figures, only about a third of the population lives in towns (33 percent in 2000), while two-thirds (67 percent) are rural. The population density was 175 people per square kilometer in 1999, according to World Bank figures, which makes Pakistan a heavily populated country despite its size. The largest towns are Karachi with 9.3 million inhabitants, Lahore (5.1 million), and Faisalabad (2 million).

Pakistan has 4 major provinces: the Punjab, Sindh, Baluchistan, and the North-West Frontier Province (NWFP), as well as some federally administered tribal areas. In 1998, 55.6 percent of the population lived in Punjab, 23.0 percent in Sindh, 13.4 percent in the NWFP, 5 percent in Baluchistan, 2.4 percent in the Federally Administered Tribal Areas (FATA), and 0.6 percent in the northern areas and the federal capital of Islamabad.

The provinces are, by and large, based on the 5 major ethnic groups prevalent in Pakistan. Punjabis live mainly in the fertile and most populous region, Punjab, in the center and east of the country. Sindhis live in the south; the Pashtuns share a common ethnic heritage with most Afghanis and live in the west. Baluchis live in the mountainous areas in the southwestern part of the country. Finally, the immigrants from India at the time of the partition and their descendants are called Muhajir (Muhajireen), after the Arabic term for immigrant.

Urdu is the national language of the state, and English is the official language, most widely used among the elite and in government ministries, since only 10 percent of the population speak Urdu as their native tongue. Punjabi is spoken by 48 percent of the population, while Sindhi is used by 12 percent; Siraiki, a Punjabi variant, is spoken by 10 percent, and Pashtu by 8 percent of the population. Only 40 percent of Pakistanis are able to read and write, compared to an average of 49 percent in South Asia and 53 percent in low-income countries worldwide. The literacy rate for women is even lower than for men, showing gender disparities in education.

Islam is the state religion of Pakistan, which was designed to be the homeland for Muslims living in British India. At the time of the census in 1998, 96.7 percent of Pakistanis were Muslims. The remaining 3.3 percent consist of non-Muslim minorities, such as Christians (1.6 percent of total population), Hindus (1.5 percent), and others. The majority of Muslims are adherents to the Sunni branch of Islam, but a minority, variously estimated at 15 to 25 percent, are Shia Muslims. An offshoot Shia sect, the Ismailis, led by Prince Karim Aga Khan, are prominent in some northern areas. Shia-Sunni tensions have increased in recent years and there have been occasional clashes.

OVERVIEW OF ECONOMY

Pakistan is a poor, heavily populated country on which internal political instability, phases of military dictatorship, and inefficient, corrupt governmental rule have taken a toll as much as the costly confrontation with neighboring India ever since partition in 1947. The economy is dominated by services, but agriculture still plays an important role. Pakistan's most important industry is textiles, which alone represents about 60 percent of the country's exports. After growing at an average rate of over 6 percent per year from 1980 to 1991, **real gross domestic product** (GDP) growth slowed during the 1990s and dropped to 1.3 percent in 1996–97 due to a poor cotton crop and related setbacks in the textile industry. In 1997–98, growth hit 4.3 percent against a governmental target of 6 percent. Real GDP grew only by 3.1 percent in 1998–99 but went up to 4.5 percent during 1999–2000. Pakistan's **GDP per capita** was US$450 in 1999, which puts it slightly above the South-Asian average of US$440 per capita.

Since the late 1980s, Pakistan has pursued a program of market-oriented economic adjustment, reform, and development. With the support of international financial institutions—mainly the International Monetary Fund (IMF) and bilateral donors—this program has aimed at enhancing **macroeconomic** stability, promoting the **private sector** and export-led industrial development, and reversing past neglect of key social sectors such as health, education, and population planning. Specifically, the government has sought to reduce monetary and external imbalances, reduce trade barriers, modernize the financial sector, **privatize** state-owned industries, and offer specific incentives to attract foreign investment. Unfortunately, the implementation of this program has mostly lagged behind expectations.

Despite the availability of cheap labor, a large domestic market, and access to regional markets, foreign investors have shied away from investing their money in Pakistan because of its widespread corruption, lack of skilled labor, law and order problems (especially in Karachi, the industrial hub), and an outdated **infrastructure**. Domestic investment has also slowed in recent years. According to official figures, total investment has declined from an average of 17.1 percent of GDP a year between 1984 and 1994 to 7.9 percent between 1994 and 2000. One reason is that manufacturers, who are traditionally served by the domestic banking system (particularly yarn spinners and sugar refiners), have often failed to honor their debts, contributing to a banking crisis.

Underlying most of the economic problems faced by Pakistan is the "crisis of governance," as the World Bank calls it. This phrase refers to the poor performance of the public institutions in terms of accountability, efficient management, corruption, and tax collection. Among these, corruption is one of the most pressing problems. Transparency International, an international non-governmental organization monitoring governments, ranked Pakistan 2nd, 5th, and 11th, in its annual reports on the most corrupt countries in the world between 1996 and 1998. Corruption hurts the economy by raising transaction costs. Even if these payoffs are considered part of the cost of doing business, there is an economic loss as these payments are neither available for expansion and improvement in the quality of public services, nor for private sector investment. A 1994 survey conducted by the World Bank among 200 business firms in Pakistan revealed that a significant amount of time and money was wasted in numerous unpredictable interactions with petty and higher-level bureaucrats seeking bribes. Entrepreneurs reported spending about 12 percent of their time dealing with tax and regulatory requirements. Also, corruption depresses economic growth by lowering public investment. Only a part of the amount appearing in budget documents as expenditure on public projects may actually get spent on these projects; the rest is siphoned off by government functionaries and contractors. One study estimated that the value for money obtained in government construction of school buildings may be only 50 to 60 percent.

Another major problem is Pakistan's huge **external debt** and its continued dependence on financial aid. Foreign loans and grants provide approximately 25 percent of government revenue, and **debt service** obligations total nearly 50 percent of government expenditure, which means that as much as half of all government expenditures are used to repay loans. Defense and debt service together absorb more than two-thirds of total federal expenditure, or almost all revenues from federal taxes. Improving tax collection in the medium- to long-term is crucial if Pakistan is to maintain repayments on its combined foreign and domestic debt of about US$62 billion, almost equivalent to Pakistan's annual GDP. It is estimated that the country needs at least US$21 billion of aid up to 2004 just for debt repayment, a large figure for a nation with annual exports of less than US$9 billion and very little **foreign exchange reserves**. In the case of the provinces, the bulk of expenditure is taken up by establishment costs (civil servants' salaries, benefits, and pensions), interest payments, and **subsidies**. The government under General Pervez Musharraf, which overthrew the government under Nawaz Sharif in 1999, faced US$32 billion in external debt. General Musharraf's ambitious economic agenda includes measures to widen the tax net, privatize **public sector** assets, and improve its **balance of trade** position. Commitment to these reforms, however, has to withstand strong opposition from interest groups such as employees of state-owned corporations, private traders, landlords, and government bureaucrats. It is unclear how the U.S. war against the Taliban regime in neighboring Afghanistan, begun in 2001, will impact Pakistan's economy.

POLITICS, GOVERNMENT, AND TAXATION

Democracy has not yet taken root in Pakistan. The military has intervened several times in Pakistan's history and has always remained an important political player even when not in power. A military intervention occurred as recently as 12 October 1999, when elected institutions were suspended. Under the suspended constitution, the parliament consists of 2 houses: a National Assembly elected directly through universal suffrage (voter eligibility begins at 21 years of age), and a Senate elected by the provincial legislatures. The prime minister is the head of government and is elected by and from the National Assembly. The president is the head of state and is chosen by an electoral college consisting of the National Assembly, the Senate, and the provincial assemblies. The constitution requires that the president be a Muslim and provides for a 5-year term. For all practical purposes, the prime minister has to be a Muslim as well.

Each of Pakistan's 4 provinces had its own directly elected provincial assembly, a government headed by a chief minister, and a governor appointed by the president upon recommendation by the prime minister. After 12 October 1999, however, provinces had only governors, with no assemblies or chief ministers. The 217-member National Assembly is elected for a 5-year term and the 87-member Senate for a 6-year term. The National Assembly seats are currently divided, with 8 going to the Federally-Administered Tribal Areas (FATA), 1 to the federal capital of Islamabad, and 10 additional seats reserved for religious minorities. Each of the 4 provinces has 19 senators; there are 8 senators from the FATA and 3 from the federal capital area. Indirect elections for half the members of the Senate are held at 3-year intervals.

The constitution guarantees an independent judiciary. The supreme court is the highest court in the country; high courts in the provincial capitals of Lahore, Karachi, Peshawar, and Quetta stand at the head of the provincial judicial systems. In principle, Pakistan's press publishes freely. However, self-censorship is widely practiced by journalists, and advertising and other tactics are used by the government to influence media content. About 90 percent of Pakistan's paper-reading public reads papers and magazines in the Urdu language which are not noted for their objectivity, fairness, or accuracy. The electronic media are strictly controlled by the state and are notorious for their propaganda against domestic political opposition and India.

Pakistan came into existence in August 1947 with the partition of British India and has had a turbulent political history ever since. The country was designed to be the homeland for Muslims living in British India. The creation of a separate Muslim nation was accomplished largely through the efforts of Mohammed Ali Jinnah, Pakistan's first governor general, who is also remembered as "Quaid-e-Azam" (The Great Leader). Between 1947 and 1948, Pakistan and India fought the first of 3 wars over the Muslim-majority territory of Kashmir, claimed by both states. The conflict ended in a stalemate. Kashmir continues to be a disputed territory and the principal subject of discussion within the Pakistani establishment and media.

Initially, Pakistan consisted of 2 parts: East Pakistan and West Pakistan, separated by 1,610 kilometers (nearly 1,000 miles) of Indian territory. In 1970 general elections resulted in the Awami League sweeping the East Pakistan seats to gain a majority in Pakistan as a whole. The Pakistan People's Party (PPP), founded by Zulfikar Ali Bhutto, won a majority of the seats in West Pakistan. The outcome was a country completely divided, with neither major party having support in the other area. Negotiations to form a coalition government broke down, and a civil war ensued. In 1971, the eastern section declared itself the independent nation of Bangladesh. Leadership of the western part of Pakistan was handed over to Bhutto, who became prime minister and the first civilian chief martial law administrator.

In July 1977, Bhutto was deposed by the chief of army staff, General Zia-ul-Haq, who became president in 1978. (Bhutto was executed in 1979.) Under Zia, the government of Pakistan became increasingly Islamized and benefited from supporting mujahideen (holy warriors) efforts to counter the Soviet invasion of Afghanistan. General elections were held in November 1988 after General Zia died in a plane crash, and the PPP, headed by Benazir Bhutto, daughter of the late prime minister, won a majority of seats in parliament and formed a coalition government. In August 1990, President Ghulam Ishaq Khan exercised his right under the constitution to dissolve the National Assembly, dismiss the prime minister, and call for new elections. In the general election held in October 1990, the Islamic Democratic Alliance won the largest number of seats, and Mian Nawaz Sharif, leader of its largest component party, the Pakistan Muslim League (PML), became prime minister. Nawaz Sharif, the first industrialist to lead Pakistan, continued a trend toward **liberalization** of the economy and promotion of private sector growth, though largely unsuccessfully.

In 1997, Nawaz Sharif was re-elected prime minister with a substantial majority, but on 12 October 1999 his government was removed in a bloodless military coup. The chief of army staff, General Pervez Musharraf, took over as "chief executive," suspended the constitution, established a military-dominated National Security Council as the country's supreme decision-making body, and named a mostly civilian cabinet. Many western countries, led by the United States—Pakistan's Cold War ally and partner in the jihad (holy war) of the 1980s that expelled the Soviets from neighboring Afghanistan—tolerated the coup, even though it seemed a throwback to a pre-Cold War era. After the nuclear standoff with India over the Kashmir dispute, it seemed favorable to have the army in command rather than have Islamists take over the country from a run-down civilian government.

Upon assuming power, General Musharraf set an ambitious reform agenda, which included fighting corruption, devolving power to the local level, and fighting sectarianism. In May 2000, the supreme court validated the coup, but gave General Musharraf 3 years from 12 October to return to a civilian government. Musharraf agreed to this time frame. Tensions with India, religious sectarianism, corruption, and political uncertainty are among the many challenges his government faces.

Plans have been put forward to implement well-designed and comprehensive civil service reforms. These reforms, as favored by the World Bank, could foster economic growth and sustained poverty reduction by reducing the obstacles to private sector development that the poorly performing public sector now creates. They are also designed to expand access of the poor to good-quality basic social services, and address serious problems of governance, such as corruption. The country's civil service is largely unchanged since the days of British colonial rule and is characterized by rigid, often irrelevant, and unevenly enforced rules and mismanagement. The erosion of **real wages** even of high-level officials (which is the consequence of high rates of **inflation** without attendant pay raises in the civil service) add to the factors that have eroded accountability and transparency, and led to widespread corruption. At the same time, the government is burdened by wage costs and rising pension costs, which are making important non-wage expenditures impossible.

An economic team, headed by the finance minister, has identified tax reform as the single most urgent measure needed to hold Pakistan together. Without a rise in tax revenues the state will simply not have the money to tackle any of the major problems facing the country. Economists warn that Pakistan must eventually raise its annual tax collection to 20 percent of GDP, up from a range of 10.7 to 15.5 percent in the past decade, to begin balancing its budget. At the moment, annual tax revenues just about pay for debt servicing and national defense, leaving other crucial areas to be financed through more loans. Only about 1 percent of the country's population of nearly 140 million pay **income tax**.

INFRASTRUCTURE, POWER, AND COMMUNICATIONS

Pakistan's infrastructure is poor and suffers from decades of neglect. Roads and railways are insufficient and in poor condition. Both the telephone system and the provision of electricity are hampered by corrupt and inefficient governmental service providers, which increasingly face competition from private entrepreneurs.

TRANSPORTATION. Pakistan has a total of 247,811 kilometers (153,990 miles) of roads, of which 141,252

Communications

Country	Telephones[a]	Telephones, Mobile/Cellular[a]	Radio Stations[b]	Radios[a]	TV Stations[a]	Televisions[a]	Internet Service Providers[c]	Internet Users[c]
Pakistan	2.861 M (1999)	158,000 (1998)	AM 27; FM 1; shortwave 21	13.5 M	22	3.1 M	30	1.2 M
United States	194 M	69.209 M (1998)	AM 4,762; FM 5,542; shortwave 18	575 M	1,500	219 M	7,800	148 M
India	27.7 M (October 2000)	2.93 M (2000)	AM 153; FM 91; shortwave 68	116 M	562	63 M	43	4.5 M
Afghanistan	29,000 (1996)	N/A	AM 7; FM 1; shortwave 1 (1999)	167,000 (1999)	10	100,000 (1999)	1	N/A

[a]Data is for 1997 unless otherwise noted.
[b]Data is for 1998 unless otherwise noted.
[c]Data is for 2000 unless otherwise noted.

SOURCE: CIA *World Factbook 2001* [Online].

kilometers (87,774 miles) are paved. There are only 339 kilometers (211 miles) of expressway. Almost 90 percent of Pakistan's freight and passenger traffic travels by road. The major north-south and east-west link is Lahore and Rawalpindi to Peshawar and carries over half of Pakistan's goods and passenger traffic. The World Bank reports that Pakistan's road network is notable for its poor condition. Over two-thirds of paved arterial roads are not wide enough for 2 lanes. At both federal and provincial levels, Pakistan provides insufficient funding for road maintenance. According to the World Bank, these poorly maintained roads can result in 30 to 40 percent higher transportation costs.

Trains, the classic means of public transportation in British India, diminished in importance during the last decade of the 20th century. There are 8,163 kilometers (5,072 miles) of railway tracks. Pakistan Railways, an autonomous agency under the Ministry of Railways, operates the railroad system. Over the past 15 years, there has been a marked shift in freight traffic from rail to highways, a trend that the government hopes to stabilize and reverse. Railways carry about 15 percent of freight traffic and road vehicles 85 percent. The rail system comprises 781 stations. Rolling stock includes about 550 locomotives, 4,250 passenger coaches, and 32,000 freight cars. Pakistan Railways plans to improve railroad's share of long-haul freight traffic, upgrade track to permit trains to operate at higher speeds, and rehabilitate infrastructure to make better use of capacity.

Pakistan's major ports are Karachi and Port Muhammad bin Qasim, where Pakistan's merchant fleet of 20 ships is based; the country also has 2 proposed sites for future facilities at Gwadar and Pasni, both on Baluchistan's Makran Coast. Karachi is the main port, handling the majority of all dry and liquid cargo. During 1999 and 2000, Karachi Port handled 18 million tons of cargo, an increase of 2.4 percent from the preceding year. Port Qasim during the same period handled 9.5 million tons of cargo, showing an impressive increase of 19 percent over the corresponding period. To facilitate this expansion, the Pakistani government has allowed 2 shipping companies to construct and operate specialized integrated container terminals at Port Qasim and on Karachi's West and East Wharves.

The government-owned national air carrier, Pakistan International Airlines (PIA), has a fleet of 48 planes and serves 35 domestic and 37 international destinations. Karachi's Quaid-i-Azam International Airport, whose Jinnah Terminal opened in August 1992, is the principal international gateway to Pakistan, although Islamabad, Lahore, Peshawar, Faisalabad, and Quetta also have a number of international flights. In line with plans to continue modernizing and upgrading its civil aviation facilities, a new international airport is being constructed at Lahore. New airports and improvements in runways are also planned for Islamabad and other cities. The government recently opened the domestic aviation market to private sector competition. As of July 2000, 3 private airlines—Aero Asia, Shaheen Air, and Bhoja Air—are operating on local and international routes, while a fourth private sector airline, Safe Air, is operating on domestic routes only.

POWER. The combined generating capacity of the 2 public energy producers and distributors—the Water and Power Development Authority (WAPDA) and the Karachi Electricity Supply Corporation (KESC)—reached 11,701 megawatts (MW) in 1999–2000. Private producers contributed an extra 4,674 MW, bringing the total installed capacity to 16,375 MW. Pakistan's energy supply comes from a combination of oil (42.8 percent), natural gas (38.6 percent), water (12.8 percent), coal (5.2 percent), liquid petroleum gas (0.4 percent), and nuclear production (0.2 percent). Pakistan has faced chronic energy shortages, and domestic energy demand has outstripped supply. The development of the energy sector remains a high priority. From July 1998 to June 1999, the largest electricity consumption was by the industrial and transport sectors (34.4 percent each), followed by domestic (22.1 percent), commercial (3.2 percent), agriculture (3.0 percent), and other government sectors (2.9 percent). Pakistan's commercial energy demand is estimated to double over the next 10 years and, despite recent gas discoveries, the energy shortfall is expected to increase.

Even after recent rationalization of power **tariffs**, industrial and commercial tariffs are quite high in Pakistan. Nevertheless, the state-run WAPDA remains close to bankruptcy due to numerous unpaid bills. Unpaid bills (many in dispute) mounted from R15 billion at the end of June 1998 to R28 billion by the end of February 1999. KESC, which is supposed to be privatized, owes WAPDA R8 billion. The government reacted by using armed forces personnel to collect overdue electricity bills from private consumers and to check for theft of electricity. The successful drive against illegal connections led to a fall in sales demand as illegal connections were removed by WAPDA as well as by the consumers themselves. Although bill collection from private consumers is greatly improved, collection from government agencies is still a serious problem.

TELECOMMUNICATIONS. Pakistan has a mediocre but improving domestic telephone system. Service is adequate for government and business use, in part because major businesses have established their own private systems. Since 1988, the government has promoted investment in the national telecommunications system on a priority basis, significantly increasing network capacity. However, despite improvements in urban systems, telecommunication services are still not readily available to the majority of the rural population. There were 2.861 million fixed lines in 1999 and another 400,000 applications are being processed, yet Pakistan's Telecommunication Corporation (PTC) is meeting less than half of this demand each year. One reason is that much of the demand is from customers in rural areas where two-thirds of the population lives and where the payback takes much longer and is less lucrative.

In December 1990, the Pakistan Telephone and Telegraph (PTT) Department, which was directly controlled by the Ministry of Communications, was converted into the Pakistan Telecommunications Corporation (PTC), which still is the only provider of basic telephone services. PTC today employs 60,000 civil servants and is the country's most lucrative state-owned franchise. PTC earned net profits of about R18 billion on sales of R60 billion in the first half of 2001. Nevertheless, the government is eager to privatize PTC by first selling 26 percent ownership to a "strategic investor," and then selling further parts after the firm is on a solid footing. This new urgency to sell parts of PTC stems from a desire to lay a telecom infrastructure that supports a wider ambition. Pakistan, with an eye on India's IT success, wants to develop a software sector, but IT companies will invest only if they have access to affordable bandwidth capacity. Since private-sector inflows are necessary to achieve this goal, the sector is being **deregulated** in rapid fashion.

At present there are 3 cellular mobile phone operators. Cellular phones are a small market, with a penetration of only 0.24 percent, but it is growing quickly as deregulation lowers tariffs and as the cost of handsets falls. In 1998, there was only 1 operator, which had 158,000 subscribers. The current 350,000 cellular phone subscribers is forecast to swell to 1 million by 2003. There were 49 radio stations in 1998, broadcasting to about 13.5 million radios. In 1997, the country had 22 television broadcast stations, and Pakistanis owned 3.1 million televisions. In 1999, there were 26 different Internet service providers (ISPs); by 2000, this number had increased above 30 ISPs. Internet bandwidth usage grew heavily as access expanded from 29 cities in August 2000 to 350 population centers in a 4-month crash program. The number of Internet accounts is about 150,000, sharpening a market struggle between several Internet service providers.

Pakistan's IT policy focuses on education, and the budget reflects the emphasis: the allocation to science and technology went from R120 million in 2000 to R5 billion in 2001. The aim is to equip and upgrade universities; train teachers and public servants; improve economic rewards for PhDs; draw women into the IT net by training them for, say, medical transcription services; and teach the computer language Java on a mass scale, especially to the large number of jobless young people. At the same time, 15-year tax breaks are being offered to create the right business environment for foreign investment.

ECONOMIC SECTORS

Services dominate the Pakistani economy. In 1998, they contributed 48.2 percent to GDP, while agriculture and industry each accounted for about a quarter of **gross domestic production** (25.2 percent and 26.6 percent, respectively). After the crisis following the nuclear standoff with India and the subsequent international **sanctions** against Pakistan in May 1998, **value-added** large-scale manufacturing was projected to grow by only 2.4 percent in 1998–99, sharply down from 6.2 percent in 1997–98. Growth of the agricultural sector, too, was expected to be only about half the level of the previous year. The manufacturing sector has seen dramatic fluctuations, averaging 9 percent per year during the first 2 decades of independence, but dropping to less than 3 percent in the 1970s, when large-scale **nationalization** significantly reduced investment levels. The rate recovered in the 1980s, averaging 7.6 percent, but fell back to 3.9 percent in the 5 years prior to 1999–2000.

A common feature in developing countries is the **informal sector**, often making up a good deal of the services sector. The popular view of informal sector activities is that they are primarily those of petty traders, smugglers, drug traffickers, street **hawkers**, shoeshine boys, and other groups **underemployed** on the streets of the big towns. Evidence suggests that the bulk of employment in the informal sector, far from being only marginally productive, is economically efficient and profit-making, though mostly small in scale and limited by

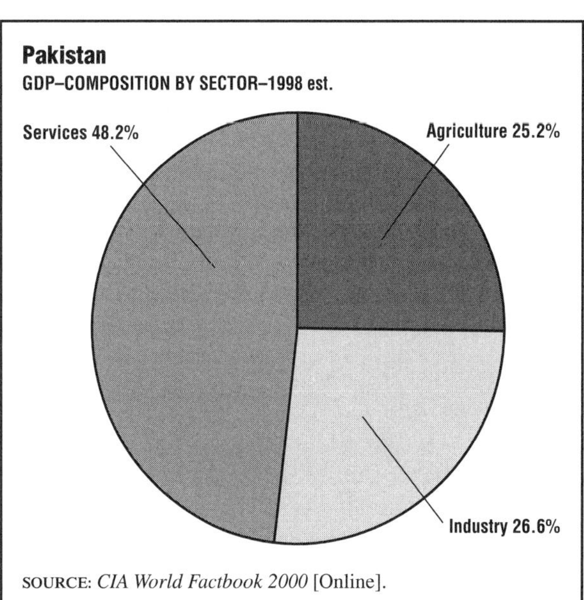

SOURCE: *CIA World Factbook 2000* [Online].

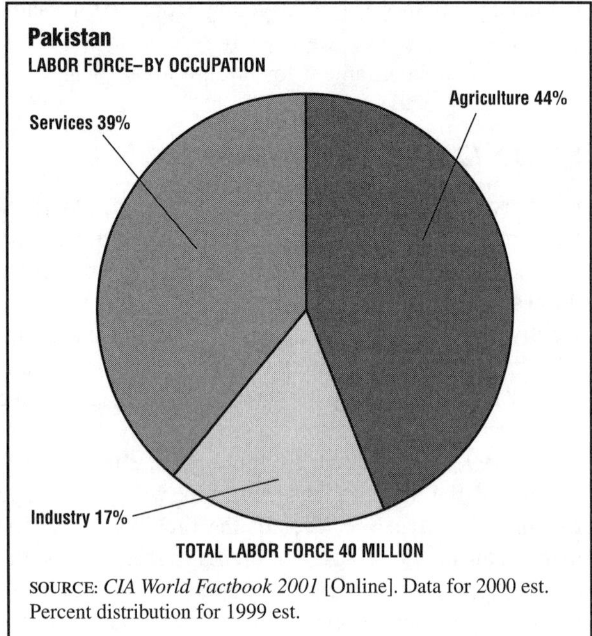

SOURCE: *CIA World Factbook 2001* [Online]. Data for 2000 est. Percent distribution for 1999 est.

simple technologies and little capital. The informal sector employs a variety of tradesmen offering virtually the full range of basic skills needed to provide goods and services for a large though often poor section of the population. Persons employed in this sector are not documented, meaning they do not have access to public services and do not pay income tax. The informal sector also includes the heroin manufacturers flourishing in the North-West Frontier Province and Baluchistan, who compensate for the bareness of their soil and the neglect of successive central governments by resorting to the "**black market**" economy, notably the processing of opium, grown in neighboring Afghanistan, into heroin. Smuggling across the porous border with Afghanistan is also a large constituent of the economy. However, the opium smuggling trade with Afghanistan will no doubt be undercut by the U.S. bombing campaign in Afghanistan, which targeted Afghani poppy fields as well as Taliban military operations. Acting in cooperation with the United States, Pakistan officially closed its border with Afghanistan, which could also stem the flow of drugs into Pakistan.

AGRICULTURE

Agriculture is a vital sector of Pakistan's economy and accounted for 25.9 percent of GDP in 1999–2000, according to government estimates. The sector directly supports three-quarters of the country's population, employs half the **labor force**, and contributes a large share of foreign exchange earnings. The main agricultural products are cotton, wheat, rice, sugarcane, fruits, and vegetables, in addition to milk, beef, mutton, and eggs. Pakistan depends on one of the world's largest irrigation systems to support production. There are 2 principal seasons. Cotton, rice, and sugarcane are produced during the *kharif* season, which lasts from May to November. Wheat is the major *rabi* crop, which extends from November to April. The key to a much-needed improvement of productivity lies in a more efficient use of resources, principally land and water. However, change is dependent on the large landowners who own 40 percent of the arable land and control most of the irrigation system, which makes widespread reform difficult. Assessments by independent agencies, including the World Bank, show these large landholdings to be very unproductive. Pakistan is a net importer of agricultural commodities. Annual imports total about US$2 billion and include wheat, edible oils, pulses, and consumer foods.

Pakistan is one of the world's largest producers of raw cotton. The size of the annual cotton crop—the bulk of it grown in Punjab province—is a crucial barometer of the health of the overall economy, as it determines the availability and cost of the main raw material for the yarn-spinning industry, much of which is concentrated around the southern port city of Karachi. Official estimates put the 1999–2000 harvest at some 11.2 million 170-kilogram bales, compared with the 1998–99 outturn of 8.8 million bales and the record 12.8 million bales achieved in 1991–92. The government recently actively intervened in the market to boost prices and to encourage production. A major problem is that the cotton crop is highly susceptible to adverse weather and pest damage, which is reflected in crop figures. After peaking at 2.18 million tons in 1991–92, the lint harvest has since fluctuated considerably, ranging from a low of 1.37 million tons in 1993–94 to a high of 1.9 million tons in 1999–2000.

The 2000–01 wheat crop was forecast at a record 19.3 million tons, compared to 17.8 million tons produced during the previous year. This increase is due largely to favorable weather and a 25-percent increase in the **procurement** price to about US$135 per ton. About 85 percent of the crop is irrigated. Despite the record production, Pakistan will continue to be a major wheat importer. The government has imported an average of US$2.4 million annually over the past 5 years. The United States and Australia are the major suppliers. Demand for wheat is increasing from Pakistan's rapidly growing population as well as from cross-border trade with Afghanistan.

Pakistan is a major rice exporter and annually exports about 2 million tons, or about 10 percent of world trade. About 25 percent of exports is Pakistan's famous fragrant Basmati rice. Rice is Pakistan's second leading source of export earnings. Private traders handle all exports. Pakistan's main competitors in rice trade are Thailand, Vietnam, and India.

Tobacco is grown mainly in the North-West Frontier Province and Punjab and is an important **cash crop**. Yields in Pakistan are about twice those for neighboring countries largely due to the extension services provided by the industry. Quality, however, is improving only slowly due to problems related to climate and soil. Farmers have started inter-cropping tobacco with vegetables and sugarcane to increase returns. About half of the total production is used for cigarette manufacturing and the remainder used in traditional ways of smoking (in hand-rolled cigarettes called birris, in water pipes, and as snuff). The share of imported tobacco is increasing gradually in response to an increased demand for high-quality cigarettes.

Minor crops account for only 5 percent of total cultivated area; these include oilseeds (sunflower, soybean), chilies, potatoes, and onions. Domestic oilseed production accounts only for about 25 percent of Pakistan total edible oil needs. As a result, Pakistan spends more than US$1 billion annually in scarce foreign exchange to import edible oils, while its oilseed processing industry operates at less than 25 percent of capacity due to an inadequate supply of oilseeds. For 2000–01 total oilseed production was forecast to decrease 10 percent to 3.6 million tons. The government has highlighted development of the oilseed sector as a priority.

Pakistan's fishing industry is relatively modest, but has shown strong growth in recent years. The domestic market is quite small, with per capita annual consumption of approximately 2 kilograms. About 80 percent of production comes from marine fisheries from 2 main areas, the Sindh coast east from Karachi to the Indian border, and the Makran coast of Baluchistan. Ninety percent of the total marine catch is fish; the shrimp which constitute the remainder are prized because of their greater relative value and demand in foreign markets. During 1999–00, total fish production was 620,000 tons, of which 440,000 tons consisted of sea fish and the remainder were fresh-water species. About one-third of the catch is consumed fresh, 9 percent is frozen, 8 percent canned, and about 43 percent used as fish meal for animal food.

Livestock accounts for 40 percent of the agricultural sector and 9 percent of the total GDP. Principal products are milk, beef, mutton, poultry, and wool. During 1999, the livestock population increased to 120 million head. That same year Pakistan generated 970,000 tons of beef, 640,000 tons of mutton, and 190,000 tons of poultry. In an effort to enhance milk and meat production, the government recently launched a comprehensive livestock development project with Asian Development Bank assistance. Poultry production provides an increasingly popular low-cost source of protein. Modern poultry production is constrained by high mortality, high incidence of disease, poor quality chicks, and poor quality feed, combined with an inadequate marketing system. Frozen poultry have only recently been introduced.

Forests cover an area of 4.2 million hectares or about 5 percent of the total area of Pakistan. The principal forest products are timber, principally for house construction, furniture, and firewood. Many of the country's wooded areas are severely depleted as a result of over-exploitation. The government has restricted cutting to protect remaining resources—though corruption often jeopardizes environmental efforts—and has lowered **duties** to encourage imports. Forestry production has since declined from 1.07 million cubic meters in 1990–91 to 475,000 cubic meters in 1998–99. Pakistan imports an estimated US$150 million of wood products annually to meet the requirements of a growing population and rising demand by a wealthy elite.

INDUSTRY

Pakistan, which had almost no large industrial units at the time of partition in 1947, now has a fairly broad industrial base, and manufacturing accounts for about 17 percent of GDP. Cotton textile production is the single most important industry, accounting for about 19 percent of large-scale industrial employment. Cotton yarn, cotton cloth, made-up textiles, ready-made garments, and knitwear collectively accounted for nearly 60 percent of Pakistan's exports in 1999–2000. Other important industries are cement, vegetable oil, fertilizer, sugar, steel, machinery, tobacco, paper and paperboard, chemicals, and food processing. The government is attempting to diversify the country's industrial base and to increase the emphasis on export industries. Small-scale and cottage industries are numerically significant but account for a relatively small proportion of the GDP at about 6 percent. Small-scale industry includes facilities, which employ fewer than 50 workers, and cottage industries (industrial units in which the owner works and is aided by family members but employs no hired labor). In 1999, industrial production grew by 3.8 percent.

Privatization of many state-owned enterprises is a key element of Pakistan's reform program. In 1991, the government identified a group of 118 state-owned industrial units for privatization. Of these, 97 units have been sold off. Industrial units—including factories producing cement, chemicals, automobiles, food products, etc.—have mainly attracted domestic private investors. The government plans to spend 90 percent of privatization proceeds for debt repayment and 10 percent for poverty alleviation. The government has laid out a time frame for privatization of various organizations in the financial, oil and gas, power, industrial, and telecommunication sectors, and the privatization process is to be completed by 30 June 2002. In most cases, the government aims to find "strategic investors" to buy up a certain stake of these firms and gain management control. The privatization process is a very complex undertaking, since new regulations of private sector entities in these sectors are still being established.

MINING/HYDROCARBONS. Unless there are major new discoveries, crude oil production—which satisfies under 18 percent of the country's requirements, compared with 35 percent in 1991–92—will ultimately run out. Recoverable reserves were estimated at 225 million barrels. Crude oil and related product imports cost R100.4 billion (US$1.7 billion) during the first 9 months of 1999–2000, accounting for 25.9 percent of all imports.

There have been promising gas discoveries in recent years. Natural gas production averaged 2.22 billion cubic feet per day in 1999–2000, about 10 percent above the previous year, while known recoverable reserves were estimated at over 19.5 trillion cubic feet at the end of March 2000. The government faced the prospect of buying this gas at international oil prices, since it had earlier promised to do so. However, it can hardly afford the price, which caused problems with the gas exploration companies.

There is an extensive range of non-fuel minerals. Deposits of limestone, marble, china clay, dolomite, gypsum, silica, ochre, sulfur, barytes, bauxite, iron ore, and emeralds are being exploited, but all on a very low scale. International exploration and development companies would, if they could, flock to Baluchistan, which is believed to possess massive reserves, particularly of natural gas. The problem is that the province's tribal chiefs, over whom the central government exerts little control, have been demanding too high a price for permission to drill. Most of the foreign companies initially awarded concessions were not able to make use of them when faced with obstruction from Baluchi tribesmen. An exception is the country's biggest development project in the remote Chagai district of Baluchistan, where the Metallurgical Construction Corporation of China is mining blister copper. It is also hoping to exploit some of the area's gold and silver reserves.

MANUFACTURING. Before 1947 there was little manufacturing in the area that makes up present-day Pakistan. Its primary role was as a supplier of raw materials, including cotton, to industrial hubs across British India, such as Bombay. In general, manufacturing still works with relatively basic technologies, generates few value-added products, and has a narrow production base, i.e., it does not diversify into many different product groups. Textiles are Pakistan's primary industry, and in 1999 accounted for 8.5 percent of the gross domestic product, 31 percent of total investment, 38 percent of industrial employment, and almost 60 percent of total exports. Pakistan is Asia's eighth-biggest textiles exporter, with export revenues of US$5.7 billion in the first half of 2000. Export growth has been declining since a recent peak of 6.1 percent in 1996. The trend is reversing, encouraged by large cotton crops in the past 2 years which have lifted output to about 11 million bales (each bale weighing 170 kilograms), the bulk of which is consumed at home, and large-scale capital investment to modernize plants. However, progress is still expected to fall short of targets, notably to be among Asia's top 5 exporters with sales of US$14 billion by 2005.

As a rule, large textile firms concentrate on spinning and weaving, leaving garment manufacturing to highly fragmented small to medium-scale producers. The industry, particularly its spinning and weaving sectors, has been under pressure since the mid-1990s, owing to increased competition in the international market, financial mismanagement within the industry, and rising global demand for value-added textiles, as well as the increase in production capacity in other developing countries. Pakistan's textile sector must move to higher value-added production to meet challenges and opportunities beyond 2005, when quotas are removed and tariff barriers lowered, as mandated by the World Trade Organization (WTO). This will expose Pakistan's mills to intense competition from China, Asia's largest textile exporter.

Food processing is a large industry, generating an estimated 27 percent of value-added production and making up 16 percent of the total employment in the manufacturing sector. Major sub-sectors of Pakistan's food industry are cooking oils and hydrogenated vegetable oils, sugar, flour, tea, dairy products, beverages, and canned foods. The fish, meat, and fruit and vegetable sectors remain underdeveloped, partly for lack of adequate infrastructure, including storage and transportation facilities. A small quantity of processed foods is imported to feed a few supermarkets catering to the country's elite. The vast agricultural resources and the country's geographic location make Pakistan an ideal country for investment in the food sector. Several foreign firms have entered the market and established their own presence as manufacturers, or established **joint ventures** with local partners. The fastest growing sectors are beverages—including carbonated soft drinks and juice and juice-flavored drinks—poultry, and edible oils.

Pakistan Steel, with an annual capacity of 1.1 million tons, is Pakistan's only integrated steel plant. It is located near Port Bin Qasim, 25 kilometers (15.5 miles) east of Karachi. The steel mill was constructed with technical assistance from the former Soviet Union, and currently employs about 20,000 workers. Iron ore, manganese, and cocking coal for the plant are all imported.

Leather is one of the major foreign exchange earners for Pakistan. The leather and leather products industry is labor-intensive (directly employing more than 200,000 workers), and there are over 500 tanneries in Pakistan. The recent growth of the industry is due in large part to its successful progression from the export of raw hides and skins and semi-processed leather towards high value-added finished leathers and leather products (including leather jackets, gloves, footwear, and sporting goods). The tanning sector is concentrated in Punjab, where manufacturing units process primarily buffalo and cow hides; tanneries in Sindh process primarily goat and sheep skins. The local market for leather is limited, and about 80 percent of production is exported. More sophisticated machinery and productivity increases can be expected to further boost exports. Pollution, especially through tannic acid and dyes, is a serious problem for this industry.

SERVICES

In 2000, services contributed about 49 percent to GDP. Wholesale and **retail** trade alone accounted for 14.9 percent of GDP, while transport, storage, and communications contributed 10.1 percent, public administration and defense 6.3 percent, ownership of dwellings another 6 percent, and finance and insurance 2.5 percent. Other services contributed 9.3 percent to GDP.

FINANCIAL SERVICES. A ruling by the Pakistani supreme court in December 1999 obliged the government under General Pervez Musharraf to finalize arrangements for an Islamic banking system by the end of the 2001 financial year. The issue of converting to an Islamic banking system, under which fixed interest is abolished in favor of a regime where profits and losses are shared between depositors and borrowers, has never been as central in the country's history as it is now. Some of the existing instruments, such as leasing, are considered compatible with Islam and could be offered on a wider variety of products to respond to demand. Bankers assert that once the issue of Islamic banking is resolved Pakistan will launch the privatization of 1 or 2 of its 3 large public sector banks: Habib Bank, United Bank, and National Bank.

Financial reforms introduced in 1990 have liberalized Pakistan's banking sector, which had long been dominated by state-owned banks, and private banks are gradually playing a more significant role. In December 1990, the government announced plans to privatize state-owned banks and to allow the establishment of private domestic banks. As of 2001 the government had privatized 2 formerly nationalized banks: Allied Bank Limited (ABL) and Muslim Commercial Bank. There are 44 banks operating in the country, of which 25 are domestic, while 19 are foreign banks. The 25 Pakistani commercial banks have over 8,000 branches nationwide. Commercial banks are engaged predominantly in corporate lending. Consumer banking in Pakistan is largely undeveloped. There is no tradition of lending to small individual consumers, and purchases of automobiles, housing, and **consumer goods** are generally made on a cash basis. High interest rates combine with high start-up costs to discourage initiatives in the consumer sector.

In 1996, the banking system was on the verge of collapse due to the breakdown of governance and loss of financial discipline. Over the years there had been widespread political interference in both lending and loan recovery by banks, and borrowers had come to expect not to repay loans they took, especially from the state-owned banks. As a result, the stock of **non-performing loans** (NPLs) grew by almost 600 percent between the end of June 1989 and the end of June 1998, when the total amount of NPLs stood at R146 billion. Since December 1997 a reform program has been implemented, with support from the World Bank. Corporate governance has been improved through changes in management of the state-owned banks and protection given to the new management from political interference. The legal and judicial processes for recovery of loans have been strengthened. Operating losses have been reduced through staff separations and closures of non-viable bank branches. Much remains to be done to further strengthen banking regulation and supervision, and develop a well-functioning legal and judicial system. At the same time, privatization needs to be accelerated while ensuring that banks are sold to sponsors that bring in internationally recognized good corporate governance.

COMMERCE. Commercial activities such as wholesale and retail trade have the largest share of business in the service sector at around 30 percent.

In 2000, General Pervez Musharraf, the military ruler, ordered his troops to accompany teams of tax inspectors to visit neighborhoods to collect information on the expenditures of individual Pakistanis. The move sparked resistance from traders in parts of the country, eventually forcing the government to make some concessions. Many of the tax board's employees are poorly paid and have wide-ranging powers, a combination that breeds corruption. Businessmen complain of being harassed by tax officials and subjected to complicated bureaucratic procedures as penalties for not paying bribes. Concessions made to traders included the abolition of a newly introduced general sales tax at retail level. This measure did not meet International Monetary Fund (IMF) conditionality, and the organization subsequently stalled the payment of a sizeable adjustment loan.

TOURISM. The number of foreign tourist arrivals in the South Asia region was 5 million in 1998; Pakistan's share of tourist arrivals in this region was 7.6 percent. More than half of foreign tourists in 1999 traveled to Pakistan to visit friends and relatives, followed by business travelers (18.3

percent), holidays and recreational travelers (13.4 percent), and religious tourists (2.5 percent). Most of the total tourists from overseas visited main cities like Karachi, Rawalpindi/Islamabad, and Lahore. Of the 420,000 tourists visiting in 1999, the largest share of around 125,000 came from the United Kingdom, mostly native Pakistanis working and living in Great Britain.

INTERNATIONAL TRADE

The external sector was seriously affected by the economic sanctions imposed on Pakistan after it conducted nuclear tests in May 1998. The lack of foreign investor confidence following the freeze on foreign currency deposits led to a decline in foreign private capital inflows and a sharp decline in money sent home from citizens working abroad, or so called "workers' **remittances**." The level of **foreign direct investment** declined by 32.1 percent per year to a low of US$296 million in 1998–99, according to official data. Remittances from Pakistanis abroad, most of them in the Gulf, the United Kingdom, and North America, peaked at US$2.89 billion in 1982–83, but fell to under US$1.5 billion in 1998–99. These adverse developments, along with suspension of new economic assistance by major donors, pushed Pakistan's foreign exchange reserves down from US$1,533 million at the end of April 1998 to US$415 million (the lowest level reached during the crisis) by 12 November 1998, hardly sufficient to finance 2–3 weeks worth of imports.

Disappointing foreign sales performances have given Pakistan a trade deficit every year since 1972–73. This is partly due to the narrow range of export products. Five categories of goods—cotton yarn, garments, cotton cloth, raw cotton, and rice—still account for over 60 percent of export earnings. A second major reason is the vulnerability of key products, notably cotton, to droughts, floods, and pestilence. However, there are other reasons for the poor performance, including the small proportion of high value-added goods in the sales mix, low product quality, and poor marketing.

Trade (expressed in billions of US$): Pakistan

	Exports	Imports
1975	1.054	2.161
1980	2.623	5.359
1985	2.744	5.900
1990	5.598	7.388
1995	8.005	11.480
1998	8.501	9.315

SOURCE: International Monetary Fund. *International Financial Statistics Yearbook 1999.*

The United States has long been Pakistan's largest export market, absorbing over 21 percent of total sales in 1999–2000. The United Kingdom, Hong Kong, and Germany have also been major outlets. In recent years, Japan and the United States have alternated as Pakistan's top supplier, although Gulf countries took a bigger share in 1999–2000, reflecting the sharp increase in the cost of oil imports. In 1999, Pakistan exported goods worth US$8.4 billion; it imported goods in the value of US$9.8 billion, creating a trade deficit of US$1.4 billion. Pakistan's main exports are cotton, fabrics, yarn, rice, and other agricultural products, most of which go to the United States (21 percent), Hong Kong (7 percent), the United Kingdom (7 percent), Germany (7 percent), and the United Arab Emirates (5 percent). Imports are mainly machinery, oil and oil-related products, chemicals, transportation equipment, grains, pulses, and flour. They come mainly from the United States (8 percent), Japan (8 percent), Malaysia (7 percent), Saudi Arabia (7 percent), and the United Arab Emirates (7 percent). Exports of goods and services represent roughly 15 to 16 percent of GDP, and imports equal around 18 percent of GDP.

Pakistan is a member of the World Trade Organization (WTO). Though not a member of any regional free trade arrangement, the country is party to 2 arrangements which are progressing toward regional trade liberalization. The Economic Cooperation Organization (ECO), whose founding members are Pakistan, Turkey, and Iran, grants a 10 percent tariff preference on several goods. ECO membership was expanded to 10 in 1993, when Afghanistan, Azerbaijan, and the 5 former Soviet Muslim republics of central Asia were admitted. The second arrangement, the South Asian Association for Regional Cooperation (SAARC), is comprised of India, Pakistan, Bangladesh, Sri Lanka, Nepal, Bhutan, and the Maldives. Because of competition in key export sectors such as textiles among the larger member states, this association is not expected to stimulate regional trade flows. Pakistan's leading regional trading partners are Bangladesh (its former eastern part), India, and Sri Lanka. Pakistan is also a member (along with India and Nepal) of the Asian Clearing Union, which was founded in 1976 and aims to facilitate multilateral payments through the use of currencies of participating countries in regional transactions in order to expand intra-regional trade and save convertible foreign exchange.

MONEY

In June 2001, 1 U.S. dollar equaled 63 Pakistani rupees. The rupee's average value against the dollar had been R12.7 for US$1 in 1982–83. This shows that inflation has been running high since that time. For the decade from 1980 to 1990, the **inflation rate** averaged 7 percent per year, and from 1990 to 1995, it reached an average

Exchange rates: Pakistan

Pakistani rupees per US$1	
Jan 2001	59.152
2000	52.814
1999	49.118
1998	44.943
1997	40.918
1996	35.909

SOURCE: CIA *World Factbook 2001* [ONLINE].

GDP per Capita (US$)

Country	1975	1980	1985	1990	1998
Pakistan	274	318	385	448	511
United States	19,364	21,529	23,200	25,363	29,683
China	138	168	261	349	727
India	222	231	270	331	444

SOURCE: United Nations. *Human Development Report 2000; Trends in human development and per capita income.*

of more than 11 percent annually. After the economic crisis that came as a consequence of the nuclear standoff with India and international sanctions against Pakistan in 1998, it went down to about 7 percent again. There are 3 stock exchanges in Pakistan: Karachi, Lahore, and Islamabad. In 2001 the Karachi stock exchange had about 780 listed companies with trading volume increasing from 1.1 million shares a day in 1990 to about 95 million in 2001. Lahore and Islamabad stock exchanges are substantially smaller than Karachi.

The State Bank of Pakistan (SBP), the central bank, controls the money supply and credit, supervises the operations of banks, administers the country's international reserves, and acts as banker to the federal and provincial governments. The government of Pakistan has followed a liberal **monetary policy** from 1999 to 2000 in order to provide cheap credit to the industrial sector. The demand for credit, however, has not come forth from the private sector. Although domestic credit expansion was higher this year due to large borrowing by the government sector, conversion of non-resident foreign currency accounts into rupees, and an increase in liquid reserves, actual growth in money supply has remained stagnant due to low credit demand from the private sector. The government and the SBP are attempting structural reforms in an effort to move toward more indirect, market-based methods of monetary control along with greater autonomy for the SBP. The central bank's autonomy was considerably strengthened with the passage of new banking laws in the State Bank Act in May 1997.

Pakistan's external debt increased significantly during the 1990s, mainly due to growth of private debt. Total external debt, including private sector debt, increased from US$27.5 billion in 1993–94 to US$32.6 billion in 1997–98, equivalent to 50.6 percent of GNP.

POVERTY AND WEALTH

A third of the population of Pakistan lives below the poverty line (34 percent in 1991). While the lowest 10 percent of the population has a share of only 4.1 percent in the overall household income and consumption, the richest 10 percent of the population has a share of 27.6 percent. The slowdown of economic growth in recent years has resulted in an increase in the incidence of poverty in the 1990s. Thus, there is a compelling need for a clear strategy focusing on reviving and sustaining high economic growth in a stable macroeconomic environment (i.e. low fiscal and external deficits with single digit inflation). It includes the provision of quality basic social services—particularly education, health, and drinking water—and an efficient and responsive social safety net program for the very poor. Low inflation in the prices of food and other mass consumption goods are also very important for the welfare of the poor.

Pakistan's human development indicators, especially those for women, fall significantly below those of countries with comparable levels of per-capita income. Only 40 percent of the population is literate (28 percent of women), compared with 49 percent in South Asia and 53 percent in low-income countries. About two-fifths of the population has no access to safe drinking water, and more than half has no access to sanitation. The infant mortality rate of 88 per 1,000 live births is higher than the average of 73 in South Asian countries and 83 for low-income countries. Pakistan's population growth rate of 2.6 percent remains among the highest in the world and frustrates efforts to increase the coverage of social services.

Distribution of Income or Consumption by Percentage Share: Pakistan

Lowest 10%	4.1
Lowest 20%	9.5
Second 20%	12.9
Third 20%	16.0
Fourth 20%	20.5
Highest 20%	41.1
Highest 10%	27.6

Survey year: 1996–97

Note: This information refers to expenditure shares by percentiles of the population and is ranked by per capita expenditure.

SOURCE: *2000 World Development Indicators* [CD-ROM].

Household Consumption in PPP Terms

Country	All food	Clothing and footwear	Fuel and power[a]	Health care[b]	Education[b]	Transport & Communications	Other
Pakistan	45	7	19	6	5	7	11
United States	13	9	9	4	6	8	51
India	N/A	N/A	N/A	N/A	N/A	N/A	N/A
Afghanistan	N/A	N/A	N/A	N/A	N/A	N/A	N/A

Data represent percentage of consumption in PPP terms.
[a]Excludes energy used for transport.
[b]Includes government and private expenditures.

SOURCE: World Bank. *World Development Indicators 2000.*

To address these problems, the government initiated a Social Action Plan (SAP) in 1993. Increasingly, the design and implementation of social service programs involve active participation from communities and non-governmental organizations (NGOs). To make further progress in the social sectors, the second phase of the SAP was initiated in 1997–98. A key part of the poverty reduction strategy is the provision of adequate basic social services—particularly elementary education and basic health services—to a much higher proportion of the poor. Only through better education and improved health can the life-long earning capacity of the poor be enhanced.

Pakistan is a major transit and consumer country for opiates (opium, heroin, morphine) from neighboring Afghanistan, the world's largest producer of opium. In 2000, Afghanistan cultivated 82,000 hectares of opium poppies, yielding 3,275 metric tons of fresh opium. As a result of the high levels of opium production in the region over the past 2 decades, Pakistan now has one the highest addiction rates in the world. Drug addiction is a common reason for the incidence of poverty for individuals and families. A recent shift to injecting heroin instead of smoking or sniffing it has heightened fears of an HIV/AIDS epidemic.

WORKING CONDITIONS

The workforce comprises of 38.6 million people, growing at an annual average rate of 2.7 percent in 1992–99. There is an extensive export of labor, mostly to the rich Middle Eastern states in the Gulf region, where Pakistanis, alongside Sri Lankis, Indians, and Filipinos find work as cleaners and domestic servants, but also in industry, commerce, and governmental services. The convenience of affordable travel to the oil-rich Arabian Gulf states and the expectation of work opportunities makes those countries attractive destinations for Pakistanis seeking jobs.

Officially, about 7 percent of the workforce is currently unemployed, a crude measure in most countries, but even more so in a country with a massive undocumented labor force. Pakistan's employment statistics are incomplete, omitting a range of wage earners and self-employed persons, male as well as female, in what is termed "the informal sector." According to unofficial estimates, unemployment may reach about 15 percent, and represents a growing problem for the government. With a majority of the population poised to enter a job market with few employment prospects, the provision of jobs, especially in rural areas, is of increasing importance. Due to the low quality or absence of educational services, again particularly in rural areas, there is a lack of skilled labor.

Several attempts have been made to eradicate bonded labor over the past decade in Pakistan, but the system remains partially in place. The bonded labor system is a lending structure in which the debtor/worker is bound to the creditor/employer as long as all or part of the debt remains outstanding. In case of sickness or death, the family of the individual is responsible for the debt, which often passes down from generation to generation. The problem of child bonded labor is especially serious: bonded money is paid to a parent or guardian, who then provides the child to work off the debt. The most severe conditions have been detected among the *haris* (landless tenant farmers) in the Sindh region, as documented by the Human Rights Commission of Pakistan. Some 1,000 laborers surveyed revealed that three-quarters had been subject to physical restraint, such as private jails, and that some 90 percent of the children had been compelled to work. To alleviate this problem the Human Rights Commission of Pakistan has purchased land and set up temporary camps in order for families to take refuge, and the government has allowed haris to settle on government land.

A related but distinct problem is that of child labor. Although most Pakistani children work in the agricultural sector, a large number of children work in urban centers weaving carpets, manufacturing surgical instruments, and producing sporting goods for export. A 1992

UNICEF/Government of Pakistan study reported that 90 percent of the 1 million workers in the carpet industry are children, many of whom began working in the industry before 10 years of age. Just as the data on Pakistan's labor force is unreliable, figures on child labor remain somewhat unclear. Nevertheless, there is little doubt that child labor has assumed massive proportions in Pakistan. The actual total number of working children in Pakistan is probably somewhere between 8 and 10 million.

COUNTRY HISTORY AND ECONOMIC DEVELOPMENT

1930. The idea of establishing a separate state for all Muslims of South Asia is conceived by the poet-philosopher Allama Muhammad Iqbal.

1947. On 14 August, the British divide the crown colony of India into 2 territories: the Republic of India and the future Islamic Republic of Pakistan, essentially establishing separate Hindu and Muslim states. Several millions of Muslims and Hindus are killed in sporadic fighting between the 2 groups as people migrate across the border into the country aligned with their religious affiliation.

1948. On 30 July, Pakistan signs the General Agreement on Tariffs and Trade (GATT), an agreement aimed at regulating international trade.

1950s-60s. Pakistan uses military and economic aid from its Cold-War alliances to create an artificial prosperity.

1970–71. Zulfikar Bhutto's Pakistan People's Party (PPP) wins elections in West Pakistan, while the Awami League wins the overall majority due to its clear victory in East Pakistan. After the ensuing civil war, East Pakistan declares its independence as the People's Republic of Bangladesh. Bhutto becomes prime minister of the remaining Pakistan.

1970s. The 1970s oil boom in the nearby manpower-starved Persian Gulf enables Pakistan to export manpower in large numbers. Money from Gulf workers transferred home to Pakistan in large amounts helps to sustain the economy in the 1970s.

1977–79. The chief of army staff, General Zia-ul-Haq, overthrows Bhutto in a military coup on 5 July 1977 and becomes president in 1978. Bhutto is executed in April 1979.

1980s. Pakistan's opposition to the Soviet invasion of neighboring Afghanistan in late 1979 helps it procure heavy doses of financial aid from Western nations also opposed to the Soviet action. However, when the aid dries up with the end of the Cold War towards the close of the decade, Pakistan's economy becomes saddled with huge amounts of **foreign debt**.

1988. Pakistan returns to democratic rule after Zia-ul Haq dies in an airplane crash. The country once again comes under the rule of the Pakistan People's Party, now led by Bhutto's daughter, Benazir. The constitution is restored with some amendments on 30 December.

1996–97. The Bhutto government is dismissed by the president due to charges of corruption, mismanagement, and involvement in extra-judicial killings. Elections in February 1997 result in an overwhelming victory for the Pakistan Muslim League and Nawaz Sharif, who becomes prime minister.

1998. In May, India and Pakistan both conduct nuclear tests, demonstrating their strength and bringing the region to the verge of nuclear war over the disputed Kashmir province. The ensuing international economic sanctions and the related drying up of most capital inflows lead to severe financial difficulties.

1999. The government of Sharif is overthrown by the chief of army staff, General Pervez Musharraf, who jails Sharif and declares himself chief executive of the state. The supreme court validates the military coup against Sharif but restricts the rule of the chief executive to a period of 3 years.

FUTURE TRENDS

Pakistan's prospects for the immediate future are bleak. There is uncertainty as to the political future of the country; the supreme court legitimized General Musharraf's military coup of 12 October 1999 in the course of 2000, but also restricted the rule of the chief executive to 3 years. Nobody knows whether the country will return to democratic rule or whether this new phase of democracy will be equally dominated by the large landowners and characterized by widespread corruption as it was in the past. Observers warn that Pakistan's economic outlook and the extent to which its communities outside Punjab feel that they live in an unjust system could be the key determinant of the country's political future rather than the system of government it follows. The pending return of Benazir Bhutto, the former prime minister convicted of bribery and corruption, to Pakistan and possibly into politics further complicates the picture. The ongoing dispute with India over the province of Kashmir, where frequent ambushes have led to casualties and brought the 2 countries to the verge of nuclear confrontation, is unlikely to be resolved in the near future.

While Pakistan's military regime earns credit from Western economists for having a deeper commitment to reforms than previous rulers, many add that the pace of change is not fast enough. With a short-term mechanism in place to service the debt, the long-term challenge is to seek a significant increase in annual export income and large inputs of foreign inward investment. Another challenge to face is the public sector's poor performance. Public sector companies alone run a combined annual deficit equivalent to about 2 percent of GDP. The government promised to begin privatizing some large companies in 2001 and eventually sell some loss-making ones in an attempt to improve the risky state of public finances. It is vital for the country that it keeps the support of the IMF and other donors as it struggles to maintain payments. Improving tax collection in the medium- to long-term is crucial if Pakistan is to maintain repayments on its combined foreign and domestic debt of about US$62 billion, almost equivalent to Pakistan's annual GDP. It is estimated that the country needs at least US$21 billion of aid up to 2004 just for debt repayment, a large figure for a nation with annual exports of less than US$9 billion and reserves of below US$1 billion—sufficient to pay for about 5 weeks of imports.

Pakistan, it seems, has plans for reforms, but the success of its program will ultimately depend on how quickly and comprehensively it can deal with low social indicators, attract investors, and convince lenders that the future management of the economy will be different from the past.

DEPENDENCIES

Pakistan has no territories or colonies.

BIBLIOGRAPHY

Government of Pakistan, Ministry of Finance. <http://www.finance.gov.pk>. Accessed August 2001.

Harrison, Selig S. *India and Pakistan: The First Fifty Years.* Cambridge: Woodrow Wilson Center Press, 1999.

Naipaul, V. S. *Among the Believers.* Harmondsworth: Penguin, 1982.

Noman, Omar. *Pakistan: Political and Economic History Since 1947.* London: Kegan Paul, 1990.

U.S. Department of State. *FY 2001 Country Commercial Guide: Pakistan.* <http://www.state.gov/www/about_state/business/com_guides/2001/sa/pakistan_ccg2001.pdf>. Accessed August 2001.

Zaidi, S. Akbar. *Issues in Pakistan's Economy.* Oxford: Oxford University Press, 1999.

—Markus R. Bouillon and Ralph Stobwasser

PALAU

Republic of Palau
Belau

CAPITAL: Koror (a new capital is being constructed on the nearby island of Babeldoab).

MONETARY UNIT: United States dollar ($).

CHIEF EXPORTS: Fish, coconut products, shells, handicrafts.

CHIEF IMPORTS: Foodstuffs, beverages, tobacco, petroleum, cement, machinery, transport equipment, consumer manufactures.

GROSS DOMESTIC PRODUCT: US$160 million (1997 est.) [includes U.S. spending].

BALANCE OF TRADE: **Exports:** US$11 million (1998 est.). **Imports:** US$63 million (1998 est.).

COUNTRY OVERVIEW

LOCATION AND SIZE. Palau is located in the north Pacific Ocean some 2,000 kilometers (1,242.8 miles) north of Australia. It estimated that there are more than 200 islands in a chain running from northeast to southwest, although only 8 are inhabited. The islands are rocky and mountainous, with the highest point being Mount Ngerchelchauus at 242 meters. The largest island is Babeldoab (also spelled Babelthuap). The total land area is 458 square kilometers (176.8 square miles). There are gold deposits (although unmined) and the possibility of further minerals in the seabed within the 200 nautical mile economic zone claimed by the islands. The capital is Koror on Koror Island. However, the constitution calls for the capital to be sited at Melekeok on the nearby island of Babeldoab, and construction is under way to fulfill that requirement. The country is ranked as the fourteenth smallest nation in the world.

Palau is located in the tropics, and the weather is generally hot and very humid. Temperatures average around 27 degrees Celsius (80 degrees Farenheit), and vary little during the year. A rainy season lasts from May to November, with annual rainfall of around 3,600 milimeters (142 inches). The islands are hit by typhoons from time-to-time, and the main typhoon season is in the second half of the calendar year.

POPULATION. The population was estimated at 18,766 in mid-2000, giving a population density of 41 persons per square kilometer (106 per square mile), quite a bit lower than the neighboring Marshall Islands, which have a density of 375 persons per square kilometer (971 per square mile). The population was estimated to be growing at 1.8 percent a year in 2000. The birth rate is 20 per 1,000 people, and the death rate is 7 persons per 1,000. Migration is low, with about 90 citizens leaving each year. The average fertility rate is 2.5 children per woman. With this modest rate of population growth, the population can be expected to have most of its population in the working age groups. The 0 to 14 age group contains 27 percent of the population, and the 15 to 64 group contains 68 percent. Five percent are 65 and over. More than half the population live in the current capital, Koror, and urban residents account for 80 percent of the total population.

Almost all the people on the islands originate from Polynesian, Malayan, and Melanesian ethnic groups, and mostly follow the Christian religion, although a local traditional belief, Modekngei, is practiced by more than 30 percent of the population. English is the main official language. In 13 states Palauan is also an official language; in Sonsoral, Sonsoralese is also official; in Tobi, the Tobi language is also official; and in Angaur, Anguar and Japanese are also official. Overall life expectancy is 69 years, with male life expectancy being 65 years and female life expectancy 72 years. The adult literacy rate in 1980 was 92 percent, with 93 percent of adult males and 90 percent of females achieving literacy.

OVERVIEW OF ECONOMY

Given its small population, its inaccessible location, poor **infrastructure**, lack of skilled labor, and the absence

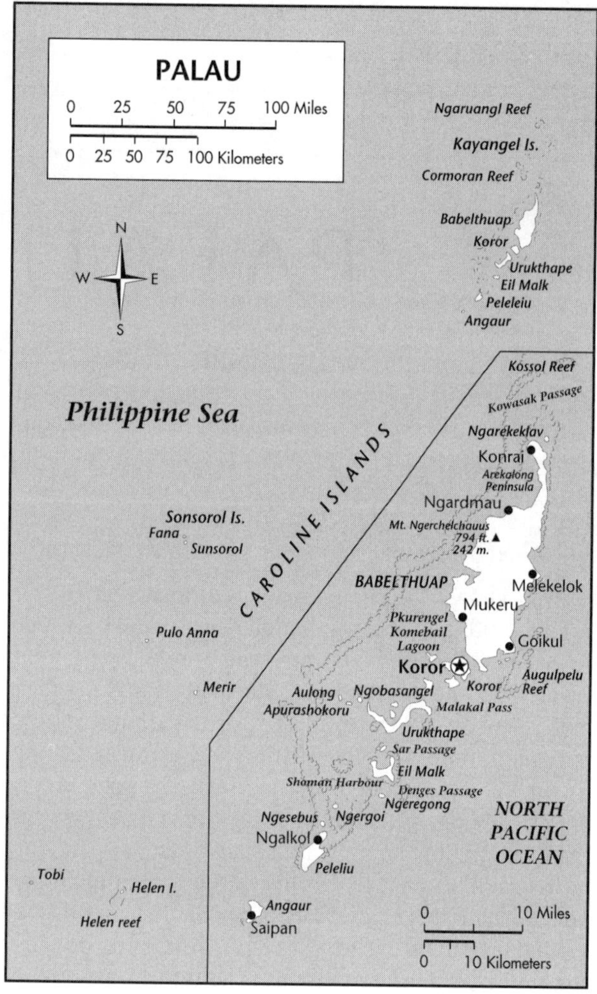

of any significant minerals, it is remarkable that the economy generates as much income for its citizens as it does. **Gross domestic product (GDP) per capita**, at $6,696 in 1998, places Palau in the upper-middle income group of countries in the world economy. This is increased by significant receipts from the United States, which add around 16 percent to the income generated domestically.

Most employment, 89 percent in 1995, was in the services sector. The agriculture sector is very small in terms of both its contribution to total output and employment, while the industry sector is also small and is mainly made up of construction. Fish is the main export, and tourism is the main foreign exchange earner. Almost all commodities, apart from some food, are imported.

Economic growth can vary yearly, affected by fashions in tourism and by the economic conditions in the countries of origin of tourists. Since 1992, the level of GDP has remained almost unchanged, with a zero growth rate over the period. However, the volatility is observed in a fall in GDP of 12.3 percent in 1993 and an expansion of 14.3 percent in 1995.

POLITICS, GOVERNMENT, AND TAXATION

The islands of Palau were originally settled by people from neighboring Pacific islands. In the 16th century, Spain claimed the islands, although Germany was allowed trading rights. With the decline of Spanish influence, the islands came under German control. The Germans established Palau as a protectorate. At the outbreak of World War I, the Japanese took over the islands and administered them under a United Nations (UN) mandate. This was a period of considerable development, with the creation of schools, hospitals, and a change in land tenure that allowed private land rights. By the end of their administration period, the Japanese in Palau numbered 26,000, outnumbering the local inhabitants. During World War II, the United States clashed with the occupying Japanese, and the United States established control of the islands in 1944. From 1947, the United States administered Palau as Trustees for the United Nations. Talk of self-determination for Palau began in 1965. In 1979, Palau approved a constitution, and in 1981 became the Republic of Palau, although not fully independent of the United States. Efforts to have approval for a Compact of Free Association with the United States (which would allow the United States to provide defense and contribute financial support) were continually thwarted by an inability to have the proposals approved by 75 percent of the vote in a referendum. After changing the constitution to allow approval by simple majority, the compact was approved in 1993, and Palau became fully independent in 1994.

The Palau government is a democracy modeled on the United States. Although the country has a long history of traditional tribal rule, democracy has been accepted and any citizen is eligible for high office. The 1979 constitution established a parliamentary government, with 2 houses. The Senate (Oibiil Era Kelulau) has 14 seats, and members are elected for 4-year terms by popular vote. The House of Delegates has 16 members, one for each state, and members are elected by popular vote, also for 4-year terms. Parliamentary candidates contest elections on the basis of their personalities and platforms; there are no party affiliations. There is a president and vice-president. There are 3 levels of court, headed by a Supreme Court, supported by a National Court, and Courts of Common Pleas.

Palau has been successful at blending its traditional heritage with its new democratic government, and that resulting government has helped to mix Palau's traditional economy with its new, more market-oriented one. Land ownership is one example of Palau's success at blending traditional practices with its new economy. As with many Pacific island nations, Palau has a long history of sharing income and land within a clan and community. Market economies are based on private ownership of land. The Palau government has taken legislative steps to accommodate the traditional sharing of lands with the free market economy by designing laws that provide guidelines for issuing land titles on land traditionally held by a family or clan.

In the year 1997–98, that government revenue (including grants) was anticipated in the budget as 57 percent of GDP. Of this, 59 percent was raised by government tax and other non-tax income, and 41 percent was grants from the United States. **Income tax** raised 11 percent of government revenues (excluding grants), import **duties** 10 percent, gross revenue tax on business 14 percent, other taxes 8 percent, and non-tax revenue (licenses, fees, trust fund income, investment income) 56 percent.

Total spending in 1997–98 was projected at 50 percent of GDP. General administration makes up 57 percent of total government spending, education 14 percent, health 14 percent, and capital expenditures 15 percent. A **budgetary surplus** of 6 percent of GDP was realized. The budget has been in overall surplus from 1992 to 1998, although the annual outcome has varied between a 119 percent surplus in 1994–95 (as a result of a substantial grant from the United States on the final acceptance of the Compact agreement), and a projected deficit of 18 percent in 1997–98.

The main tax rates are: 6 percent on incomes from employment, rising to 12 percent; 4 percent on the gross revenues of businesses; 4 percent on the net incomes of financial institutions; import duties varying between 3 percent (most goods) to 150 percent (tobacco); hotel room tax (10 percent); departure tax ($20); and road tax ($50 to $150).

INFRASTRUCTURE, POWER, AND COMMUNICATIONS

There are 61 kilometers (38 miles) of roads, of which 36 kilometers (22.4 miles) are paved. The road round Beldaob, 100 kilometers (62 miles) in length, is a major improvement in the road system. The unpaved roads are coral-surfaced roads and provide practical, if bumpy, highways. There are no railways. The main port is on Koror, and this is the only port that is able to receive large ocean-going vessels. The mountainous terrain makes thc construction of airports a problem, but there are 3 airports. The only one with a paved runway is the international airport located across from the capital Koror on Babeldoab island.

Palau's electricity is supplied mostly by diesel generators (85 percent in 1996), but the terrain does allow for the construction of dams, and 15 percent of electricity comes from hydroelectricity. In 1996 the Palau generated 200 million kWh. There is some domestic use of bottled gas for cooking. Water supply is adequate.

In 1988, there were an estimated 1,500 land line telephones in use and no mobile telephones. It is to be expected that provision of telephones, both land lines and mobiles, have increased substantially since then. International links are provided by an Intelsat satellite earth station.

The islands had 1 AM radio station and 1 shortwave station in 1998, and in 1997 there was 1 television station, and 11,000 television receivers. The *Palau Gazette* is published monthly by the government, and *Tia Belau* is published bi-weekly in both English and Palauan.

ECONOMIC SECTORS

The services sector dominates the economy, with a large number of **public sector** employees. In 1998, services generated 87 percent of GDP and employed 76 per-

Communications

Country	Telephones[a]	Telephones, Mobile/Cellular[a]	Radio Stations[b]	Radios[a]	TV Stations[a]	Televisions[a]	Internet Service Providers[c]	Internet Users[c]
Palau	1,500 (1988)	0 (1988)	AM 1; FM 0; shortwave 1	12,000	1	11,000	N/A	N/A
United States	194 M	69.209 M (1998)	AM 4,762; FM 5,542; shortwave 18	575 M	1,500	219 M	7,800	148 M
Philippines	1.9 M	1.959 M (1998)	AM 366; FM 290; shortwave 3 (1999)	11.5 M	31	3.7M	33	500,000
Solomon Islands	8,000	658	AM 3; FM 0; shortwave 0	57,000	0	3,000	1	3,000

[a]Data is for 1997 unless otherwise noted.
[b]Data is for 1998 unless otherwise noted.
[c]Data is for 2000 unless otherwise noted.

SOURCE: CIA *World Factbook 2001* [Online].

cent of the **labor force** in 1995. The incomes in this sector are above average. The smallest sector in terms of output is agriculture (which includes fishing), which produced 5 percent of output in 1998 and engaged 9 percent of the labor force in 1995. The industry sector only employed 15 percent of the labor force in 1995, generating 8 percent of GDP in 1998.

AGRICULTURE

Palau does not produce enough food to support itself, mainly because the cost of doing so is higher than the cost of importing needed items. The main crops are coconuts, bananas, root crops such as taro (similar to the potato), vegetables, and tropical fruits. Poultry, pigs, and dairy cows are the main livestock. Crops and livestock generated only about 2 percent of GDP in 1998. Since Palau cannot incorporate any economies of scale in agricultural production, the likelihood of significant increases in the sector are slim. Fisheries generated about 3 percent of GDP in 1998, but output from the fisheries sector appears to be in a steady decline—in 1992, the value of fish landed was almost 4 times greater, and the fishing fleet has halved to 150 vessels in 1998.

Much of the catch from Palau's waters is taken by Chinese and Japanese vessels, and Palau receives income from licence fees of around $200,000 a year. It is felt that there is considerable illegal fishing. In addition, local boats meet with Chinese and Japanese vessels at sea and sell their catches to them, leading to under-recording of the Palau catch.

INDUSTRY

There is little mining and quarrying, being almost entirely the quarrying of coral for construction. The main manufacturing enterprise is a garment factory, employing some 300 workers. Other manufacturing includes bakeries, building material, furniture, and handicrafts, all of which serve the domestic market.

There are 2 power plants at Aimeliik and Malakai. The construction sector is the largest part of the industry sector, and it generates 8 percent of GDP and employs 14 percent of the workforce.

SERVICES

The services sector employs three-quarters of the workforce and generates more than four-fifths of GDP. Transport and communications generate 16 percent of GDP; distribution, restaurants and hotels, 27 percent; financial services 6 percent; and public administration, community and other services, 51 percent.

The banking sector is made up of 3 U.S. commercial banks, 5 domestically-owned commercial banks, and the National Development Bank of Palau (NDBP). Most lending by the commercial banks is made up of consumer loans for construction, travel, and education. The NDBP is responsible for most business loans. There was concern over the operation of the domestically-owned commercial banks in 1999, which were not subject to any banking regulation. A ban was imposed on certain international transactions, as it was thought that the banks were being used for **money laundering**. There have subsequently been U.S.-assisted initiatives to tighten control of the banks.

The publicly-owned Palau National Communication Corporation, by virtue of operating a **monopoly**, generally manages to cover its costs. However, the 1997–98 reduction in tourism, as a result of the Asian economic crisis, led to a fall in the number of lucrative international calls, and the corporation posted a loss.

Tourism is a major source of foreign exchange earnings. In 1997, there were 73,000 arrivals in the Islands, and the sector generated $70 million, equivalent to 53 percent of GDP. The sector is expanding rapidly—in 1993, tourism receipts were $18 million. At present there are 1,200 hotel beds, and a further 560 are planned to be in operation by the end of 2001.

INTERNATIONAL TRADE

Merchandise exports of $11 million in 1997–98 were made up almost entirely of fish products. There are some exports of copra (dried coconut), garments and handicrafts. Exports of seashells for buttons, ornaments, and making lacquers are not recorded, but there is probably a small amount of informal trade. The fishing sector appears to be in a steady decline. In 1992–93, fish exports were around $17.7 million. The decline is partly because of changes in the available fish stocks, as a result of oceanographic factors. In addition, fish prices fell after 1996 as a result of the Asian economic crisis, reducing demand for fish. Exports of fish have also been hindered by a shortage of refrigerated air freight services from Palau. Exports go mostly to the United States and Japan.

Merchandise imports were $52 million in 1997–99. Food products made up 14 percent of imports by value, beverages and tobacco 8 percent, petroleum 25 percent, chemicals 3 percent, machinery and transport equipment 23 percent, and manufactured **consumer goods** 26 percent. The main sources of imports were the United States (40 percent), Guam (18 percent), Japan (13 percent), Singapore (13 percent), and Taiwan (5 percent).

MONEY

Palau uses the U.S. dollar as its currency. This has the advantage of bypassing the expense of running a central bank. Also, the currency is completely convertible,

Exchange rates: Palau

US$	
Jan 2001	1.0000
2000	1.0000
1999	1.0000
1998	1.0000
1997	1.0000
1996	1.0000

Note: US currency is used in Palau.

SOURCE: CIA *World Factbook 2001* [ONLINE].

and price stability is reasonably well ensured, as Palau does not have the ability to print currency. The rate of **inflation** was less than 3 percent a year from 1996–98. The only drawback for "dollarised" economies is that they do not earn the seigniorage (the profit earned from the minting of coins) they would gain if they issued their own currency. The increasing number of countries that have been attracted to using the U.S. dollar in place of a domestic currency has caused the United States to consider sharing some of the seigniorage it earns as a currency issuer.

POVERTY AND WEALTH

There are no figures on the numbers below the poverty line, but given the income level and the structure of the economy, probably less than 10 percent of the population live in poverty. Most of those affected are among the 30 percent of the population living outside Koror, who rely on small-scale agriculture and fishing for their livelihoods. Infant mortality is 18 per 1,000 births in 2000 (in the United States, the rate is 6 per 1,000). The per capita GDP of Palau ($6,987 in 1998) was one-third that of Guam and about one-quarter that of Hawaii. Household and agricultural workers had the lowest wages, while bankers, insurance agents, and lawyers had the highest.

GDP per Capita (US$)

Country	1996	1997	1998	1999	2000
Palau	N/A	8,800	7,100	N/A	N/A
United States	28,600	30,200	31,500	33,900	36,200
Philippines	2,600	3,200	3,500	3,600	3,800
Solomon Islands	3,000	3,000	2,600	2,650	2,000

Note: Data are estimates.

SOURCE: *Handbook of the Nations*, 17th, 18th, 19th and 20th editions for 1996, 1997, 1998 and 1999 data; CIA *World Factbook 2001* [Online] for 2000 data.

Retail workers made up the largest category of wage earners and reported an average yearly wage ($6,044) that was slightly lower than the **GDP per capita**.

A life expectancy in 2000 of 69 years is high, and the level of adult literacy, last surveyed in 1980, was 92 percent. Taken together with its upper-middle income status, these factors, when evaluated by the criteria used by the UN, give Palau a position near the top of the countries with a medium level of human development.

WORKING CONDITIONS

The economically active labor force was estimated at 8,300 in 1988, and 7 percent of the labor force was recorded as being unemployed. However, the unemployment rate has little meaning in an economy like that of Palau—it relates to those registering as looking for jobs in the urban areas as a percentage of the formal labor force. A substantial part of the labor force is in the agriculture and fishing sectors, much of it in small-scale family enterprises outside the formal sector. There are no unemployment benefits, and those without work or support from families or charities cannot survive. It is likely that there is considerable disguised unemployment in the rural areas, with tasks being shared and the work capable of being carried out by a smaller workforce.

COUNTRY HISTORY AND ECONOMIC DEVELOPMENT

1000 B.C. Migration to Palau Islands from other Pacific Ocean islands begins.

1525. Spanish navigator Alonso de Salasar is first European to sight the archipelago of the Caroline Islands, of which present-day Palau is a part.

1529. Alvaaro de Saavedra lands on the Caroline Islands, and claims them for Spain.

1783. British vessel, under Captain Henry Wilson is shipwrecked near Koror, and the crew stays 3 months rebuilding the ship.

1885. Pope Leo XIII, acting as a European mediator, confirms Spanish dominion over the Caroline Islands, while also allocating Germany trading rights.

1899. Spain sells islands to Germany, who begin phosphate mining in Anguar, plant coconuts and begin to reduce the impact of influenza and dysentery which were causing widespread loss of life.

1914. With the outbreak of World War I, Japan assumes control of the islands.

1920. Japan receives a UN mandate to administer the islands, establish schools and land property rights, and develop Koror.

1922. Japan establishes administration of all of its Micronesian territories from Koror.

1944. After fierce fighting between Japanese and American forces, the United States occupies the islands.

1945. Japanese settlers are **repatriated**.

1947. UN assigns the Caroline Islands, as the Trust Territory of the Pacific Ocean, to the United States. The U.S. Navy undertakes day-to-day administration.

1965. Congress of Micronesia formed by delegates from Pacific islands to press for independence.

1967. Commission established to make recommendations on the future government of the islands of Micronesia.

1970. Commission confirms that the peoples of Micronesia have a right to sovereignty, self-rule, and to terminate association with the United States.

1979. Referendum in Palau District approves constitution, which forbids presence of nuclear weapons, including those on visiting vessels.

1981. Constitution comes into effect, and the islands become the Republic of Palau, although not independent of the United States. Haruo Remeliik becomes first president.

1982. The United States signs Compact of Free Association which will allow an independent Palau to rely on the United States for defense and to receive U.S. aid.

1983. Referendum in Palau fails to endorse Compact of Free Association (which allows transit and storage of nuclear materials) by requisite 75 percent of votes cast.

1984. Referendum again fails to endorse Compact.

1985. President Remeliik assassinated. Lazarus Salii elected to succeed Remeliik.

1986. Despite the United States agreeing to observe ban on nuclear material, Compact again fails to be endorsed in 2 successive referenda.

1987. Fifth referendum on Compact fails. President suspends 70 percent of public sector employees on the grounds of financial crisis. Further referendum approves change in constitution to require only simple majority for the endorsement of the Compact. In December, Compact is approved by referendum on a simple majority.

1988. Supreme Court rules against approval of Compact by a simple majority. President Salii, under investigation for corruption by U.S. General Accounting Office, commits suicide. Ngiratkel Etpison elected president.

1990. Seventh referendum again fails to approve Compact by required 75 percent.

1992. Kuniwo Nakamura wins presidential election. Second referendum to allow simple majority for endorsement of Compact is approved by 62 percent of voters. Challenge to decision in courts is unsuccessful.

1993. Eighth referendum on the Compact is endorsed by 68 percent of voters, but the decision is challenged in the courts.

1994. Court challenges fail. Palau finally becomes independent on October 1, under the terms of the Compact of Free Association.

1996. During presidential election, bridge between the islands of Koror and Babeldoab collapses, killing 2. Nakamura re-elected president.

1997. Legal settlement for collapse of bridge between Koror and Babeldoab with payment of $13.8 million to Palau. New bridge approved at cost of $3.8 million.

1999. Palau is subject to an international banking transactions ban as a result of practices thought to facilitate money laundering.

2000. Tommy Remengesau elected president. New $100 million road around the island of Babeldoab is announced which will allow capital to be moved to Melekeok.

FUTURE TRENDS

The economy is heavily dependent on the grants received from the United States as part of the Compact agreement. In the 1998–99 budget the Compact grants were $13 million (10 percent of GDP), and other grants from the United States were $11 million (8.5 percent of GDP). The Compact grants are scheduled to be phased out, and to end in 2008–09. Palau has invested some of the large early payments under the Compact agreement, and income from these investments will serve to cushion the position when the Compact agreement is due to end. It is expected that the Compact agreement will be renewed, as the defense provisions are an important consideration for Palau, and it is possible that Compact grants will be continued. Even if they are not, it is likely that the United States will increase grants under other headings to compensate, so that the situation after 2008–09 is not likely to be as severe as at one time anticipated.

Tourism is clearly the best long-term prospect for generating income in Palau, given the scenic attractions of the mountainous islands and the strong association with Japan (Japanese is an official language in one of the states). However, international investment will be necessary for the development of tourism, but a barrier at present is the regulation that prevents foreigners from owning land.

DEPENDENCIES

Palau has no territories or colonies.

BIBLIOGRAPHY

Bank of Hawaii. *Republic of Palau Economic Report: 2000.* <http://www.boh.com/econ/pacific/pal/2000/palau2000.pdf>. Accessed August 2001.

International Monetary Fund. *Republic of Palau: Recent Economic Developments.* Washington D.C.: IMF, 1999.

U.S. Central Intelligence Agency. *CIA World Factbook 2000: Palau.*<http://www.cia.gov/cia/publications/factbook/geos/ps.html>. Accessed August 2001.

World Yearbook. London: Europa Publications, 2000.

—Michael Hodd

PAPUA NEW GUINEA

Independent State of Papua New Guinea

CAPITAL: Port Moresby.

MONETARY UNIT: Kina (K). One kina equals 100 toea. There are coins of 1, 2, 5, 10, and 20 toea, and 1 kina. There are notes of 2, 5, 10, 20, and 50 kina.

CHIEF EXPORTS: Oil, gold, copper ore, timber, palm oil, coffee, cocoa, coconut products.

CHIEF IMPORTS: Machinery and transport equipment, manufactured goods, food, fuels, chemicals.

GROSS DOMESTIC PRODUCT: US$11.6 billion (purchasing power parity, 1999 est.).

BALANCE OF TRADE: **Exports:** US$1.9 billion (f.o.b., 1999 est.). **Imports:** US$1 billion (f.o.b., 1999 est.).

COUNTRY OVERVIEW

LOCATION AND SIZE. Papua New Guinea occupies the eastern half of the island of New Guinea (the western half, called Irian Jaya or West Papua, is part of Indonesia), as well as some nearby islands. New Guinea is part of the Pacific island region known as Melanesia. Papua New Guinea lies at the southeastern edge of Southeast Asia, to the east of Indonesia, and north of Australia. The total area of Papua New Guinea is 459,854 square kilometers (285,753 square miles). Papua New Guinea's only land border is with Indonesia, and it is 820 kilometers (509 miles) long. The country's coastline is 5,152 kilometers (3,201 miles) long. Papua New Guinea is about the same size as California. The capital, Port Moresby, is located on the southern side of the mainland, on the Coral Sea.

POPULATION. Papua New Guinea has perhaps the world's most diverse population, with at least 846 indigenous languages spoken. The population is almost entirely indigenous Melanesian, with small numbers of European and Asian immigrants. The population was estimated at 4.7 million in 2000. The growth rate of the population was estimated at 2.3 percent in the same year. Although the overall population density of Papua New Guinea remains low, there are great differences between regions. In general, the low-lying, coastal parts of the country have fairly low population densities, while the mountain valleys, or "highlands," have much greater population densities. For example, the Western Province averages only 1 person per square kilometer (2.6 per square mile), while parts of the highlands average up to 100 people per square kilometer (260 per square mile).

Papua New Guinea has few large cities. The largest is the capital, Port Moresby, with a population over 400,000. The most serious population issue facing the country is the migration of rural residents to the cities, especially to Port Moresby and to the second largest city, Lae. Many of these migrants are unable to find jobs, leading to crime and other social problems. The Papua New Guinea government has sought ways to control population growth but faces an uphill battle.

The population of Papua New Guinea is generally quite young, with 39 percent between the ages of 0–14, 58 percent between the ages of 15–64, and only 3 percent over the age of 64.

OVERVIEW OF ECONOMY

The extraction of Papua New Guinea's rich mineral and petroleum resource base dominates the national economy, accounting for 72 percent of export earnings. Gold, copper, and petroleum are the most important of these resources. Mining, however, is concentrated in only a few areas, employs only a small percentage of the country's population, and is dominated by international corporations. Most Papua New Guineans (85 percent) depend on **subsistence agriculture**, in which crops are grown for family and local use and not exported. Papua New Guinea's tropical climate and rich soil allow both subsistence and commercial agriculture to flourish. The commercial agricultural sector, which once dominated

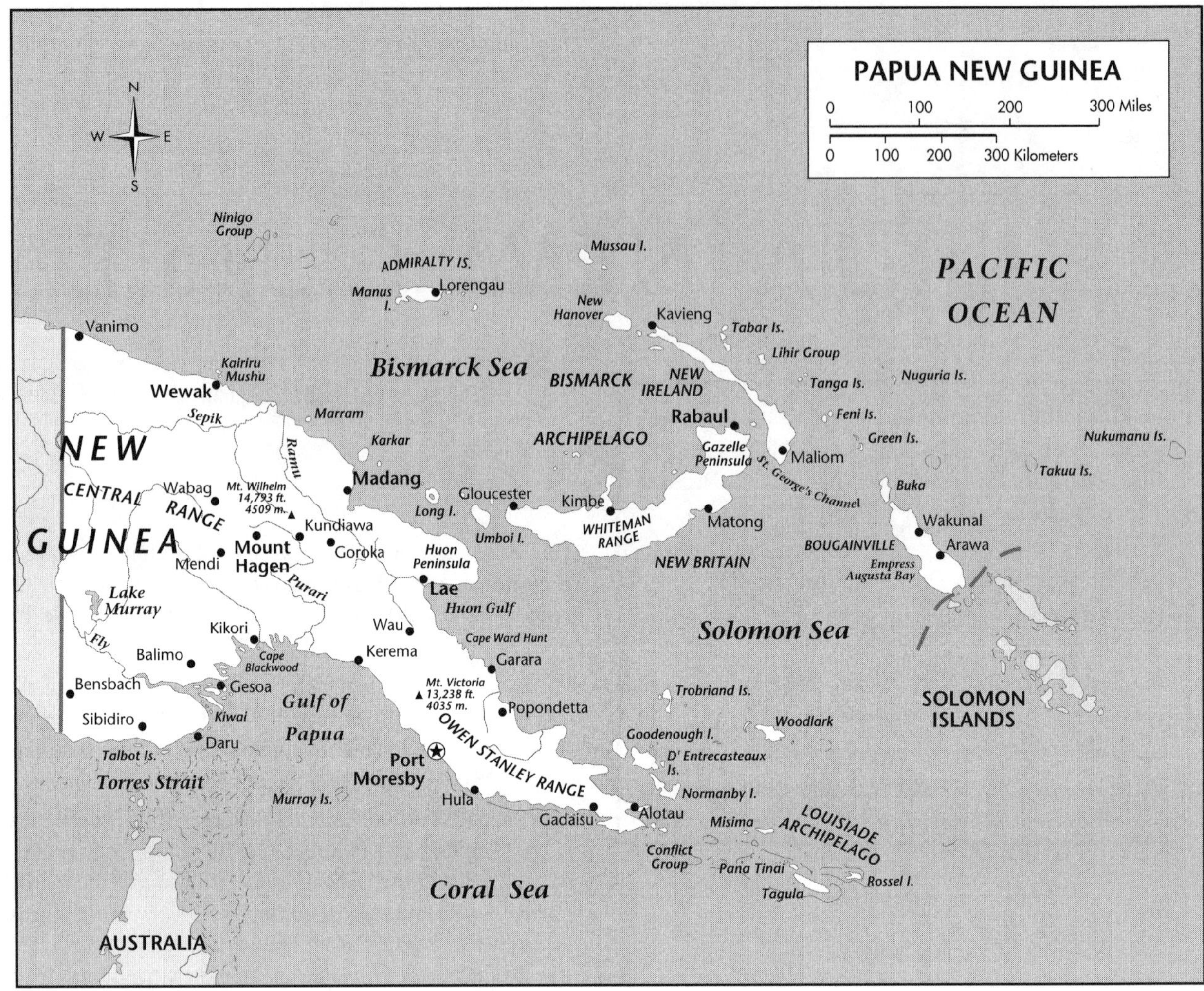

the economy, has greatly decreased in size relative to the growing mining sector. Coffee, palm oil, cocoa, and coconut products (a dried form called copra and coconut oil) are the most important agricultural exports. Forestry is also a growing economic sector. Despite its rich mineral and agricultural resource base, Papua New Guinea has limited manufacturing and service sectors, and must import most manufactured products such as machinery, motor vehicles, and many foods.

The diversity of the population, political disputes, and the ruggedness of Papua New Guinea's landscape have been the key factors limiting economic development in the country. Changing political leadership and policies since independence in 1975 have hampered long-term planning. Additionally, the rugged terrain of much of the country, with extensive swamps, mountains, and scattered islands, requires expensive communications and extraction **infrastructure** with high maintenance costs. Conflicts between the national and provincial governments reflect the country's diversity and add to the difficulties of formulating economic policy. A revolutionary movement on the island of Bougainville, the location of one of Papua New Guinea's largest mines, led to sabotage and closure of the mine in 1989. The mine has not reopened but recent peace talks are putting an end to the conflict.

Papua New Guinea's total **external debt** is estimated at US$2.4 billion (1999). In 1998, the country's **debt service** stood at US$178 million. Australia is by far the largest donor of foreign aid, giving about US$150 million each year. Much of this aid is used for the development of health services, infrastructure, education, and the maintenance of law and order. Papua New Guinea also receives aid from other donors such as the Asian Development Bank. Donors have also provided additional aid in times of crisis, such as during the devastating 1997 drought.

POLITICS, GOVERNMENT, AND TAXATION

The territory comprising today's Papua New Guinea was colonized in the 19th century by both Germany and Great Britain. The British territory was transferred to Australia in 1906. During World War I, Great Britain acquired the German territory and in 1920 transferred control of this territory to Australia as well. Australian policy and culture shaped much of modern Papua New Guinea, and the country remains a constitutional monarchy within the British Commonwealth, with Queen Elizabeth II as the ceremonial head of state. The parliament is **unicameral** (it has only 1 chamber) and the prime minister is a member of parliament. Mekere Morauta became prime minister in 1999 at the head of a coalition government. Papua New Guinea's parliamentary, political, and judicial institutions are similar to those in Australia and Great Britain.

The cultural and regional diversity of Papua New Guinea's population means that there are many political parties. The main ones are the Black Action Party, Bougainville Unity Alliance, Christian Democratic Party, Hausman Party, League for National Advancement, Liberal Party, Melanesian Alliance, Melanesian Labour Party, Milne Bay Party, Movement for Greater Autonomy, National Alliance, National Party, Papua New Guinea First Party, Christian Country Party, Papua New Guinea United Party, Peoples Action Party, and Peoples Democratic Movement. In the 1997 elections the People's Progress Party won the most votes, with just 15 percent, and led the coalition government. Because of the high number of parties, governments are composed of coalitions between several parties.

Papua New Guinea is divided into 19 provinces plus the national capital district. Legally, the national government retains most political power, and the provinces are therefore politically quite weak. In practice, however, the national government is often unable to exert its authority in provincial matters. The weakness of the national government in practice is demonstrated in the continuing difficulties on the island of Bougainville. In 1989, a rebel movement called the Bougainville Revolutionary Army (BRA) seized control of the Panguna mine on the island and demanded full independence for the province. The mine was closed and is not likely to reopen. Peace negotiations have been taking place over the past 3 years and are close to being resolved.

Papua New Guinea's government has in general encouraged foreign investment, especially in the mining industry. This is done by offering favorable tax rates for mining companies. The national government often takes a part interest in large mining projects by owning a portion of the stock in these projects, which provides revenue for the government. The national government also gathers revenue from personal taxes (on property and vehicles), a **value-added tax** (VAT), corporate **income taxes**, and mining taxes.

INFRASTRUCTURE, POWER, AND COMMUNICATIONS

Papua New Guinea currently has a limited infrastructure, largely due to the country's rugged terrain. Extreme weather, such as storms and floods, means that roads and other infrastructure deteriorate quickly. Political disputes and corruption, leading to unnecessary infrastructure and the diversion of money away from useful projects, also contributes to the problem. Papua New Guinea has 19,600 kilometers (12,179 miles) of roads, of which only 686 kilometers (426 miles) are paved (approximately 3.5 percent of the total). The main ports are at Port Moresby, Lae, Madang, and Rabaul. There are 492 airports, but only 19 have paved runways. The national air carrier is Air Niugini, which flies domestically as well as to Australia, several Asian countries, and the Solomon Islands. There is no rail system in the country.

About 70 percent of Papua New Guinea's electricity comes from fossil fuels, with hydroelectric power providing the remaining 30 percent. The total electricity consumption in 1998 was 1.618 billion kilowatt hours (kWh).

Telecommunication systems in the country are generally adequate. Papua New Guinea had 44,000 telephone mainlines in use in 1995, and has recently established a cellular telephone network in several areas. By 1997,

Communications

Country	Newspapers	Radios	TV Sets[a]	Cable subscribers[a]	Mobile Phones[a]	Fax Machines[a]	Personal Computers[a]	Internet Hosts[b]	Internet Users[b]
	1996	1997	1998	1998	1998	1998	1998	1999	1999
Papua New Guinea	15	97	24	N/A	1	N/A	N/A	0.49	2
United States	215	2,146	847	244.3	256	78.4	458.6	1,508.77	74,100
Australia	293	1,376	639	43.6	286	48.6	411.6	477.85	6,000
Indonesia	24	156	136	N/A	5	0.9	8.2	0.76	900

[a]Data are from International Telecommunication Union, *World Telecommunication Development Report 1999* and are per 1,000 people.
[b]Data are from the Internet Software Consortium (http://www.isc.org) and are per 10,000 people.

SOURCE: World Bank. *World Development Indicators 2000.*

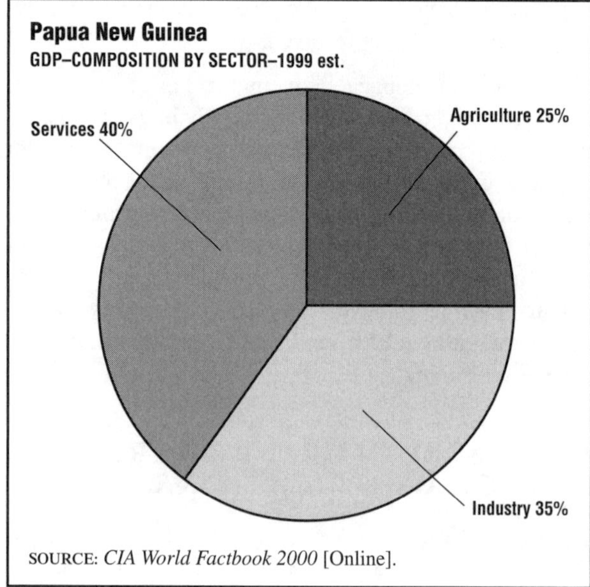

SOURCE: *CIA World Factbook 2000* [Online].

there were 3,053 mobile cellular subscribers. In 1999, the country had 2 Internet service providers.

ECONOMIC SECTORS

Papua New Guinea is heavily dependent on the development of its natural resources. Its rich mineral deposits make the country a leading world supplier of gold and copper. Mining began on a large scale in the 1970s and rapidly surpassed agriculture as the largest source of export earnings. However, the mining industry is concentrated in a few areas and does not employ many people. Most of the population still depends on subsistence agriculture for its livelihood. The manufacturing and service sectors remain extremely small in comparison. In 1999, agriculture represented 25 percent of GDP, industry represented 35 percent, and services 40 percent. Papua New Guinea's mineral-based economy is subject to world market fluctuations in commodity demand and prices.

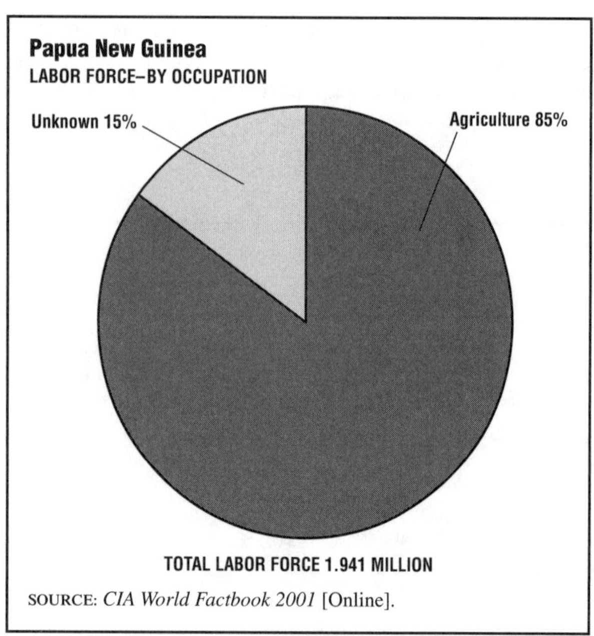

SOURCE: *CIA World Factbook 2001* [Online].

AGRICULTURE

Agriculture is important to Papua New Guinea for both income and as a source of food. In total, the agricultural sector contributes 25 percent of **gross domestic product** (GDP), not including subsistence agriculture. This contribution comes primarily from the production of crops such as coffee, oil palms, cocoa, and coconuts, all of which grow well in the country's tropical climate. Coffee, palm oil, cocoa, and coconut products (copra and oil) are the main agricultural export revenue earners, with US$240.3 million total value in 1998, and their production employs an estimated 77 percent of labor in the country. The bulk of Papua New Guinea's export agricultural products are produced by villagers. Australia, Japan, and South Korea have consistently been the major buyers of the country's agricultural exports since 1970.

Most Papua New Guineans own the land on which they grow their own food crops, of which sweet potatoes, sago, bananas, coconuts, taro, and yams are the most important.

Forestry is an emerging part of the agricultural sector, and about one-third of forest lands have been opened to commercial exploitation. Much of the timber industry is dominated by Malaysian companies. Papua New Guinea is now the world's second-largest exporter of round tropical logs, most of these going to Japan and Korea.

INDUSTRY

MINING. Since the 1970s the mining of rich mineral deposits has dominated the Papua New Guinea economy. In contrast to the agricultural sector, mining in Papua New Guinea is characterized by large and highly mechanized operations. Copper, gold, and crude oil are the key income earners for the country.

In 1970 mineral exports were a mere 1 percent of total exports. Within 2 years, this figure had risen to 55 percent. By the start of the 1990s the contribution of the mining sector to total exports had continued to rise, reaching 70 percent. The large Panguna mine on the island of Bougainville opened in 1972, and until its closure in 1989 was one of the largest copper mines in the world. The shutdown of the mine was due to what many people have charged was environmental havoc created by the mine. It also became a flashpoint for resentment against the

Papua New Guinean government by the indigenous people on Bougainville.

Since the closure of the Panguna mine, gold has been the main mineral export earner for the country, with a peak contribution to export value of 50.9 percent in 1991. In 1994, gold was contributing 26.4 percent of the value of total exports, equal to crude oil as the dominant export earner. Gold is mined at Porgera in the highlands and at several other locations, and in 1997 a new gold mine on Lihir Island opened. The Lihir mine reserves are estimated to be 103.4 million tons of ore, with a mine life of approximately 37 years, making it one of the world's largest gold reserves.

The Ok Tedi copper mine near the border with Indonesia has in some respects replaced production from the closed Panguna mine. Ok Tedi is expected to operate for about 10 more years, though because of a lawsuit resulting from environmental damage caused by mining, the main operating company, Broken Hill Proprietary (BHP), would like to close the mine earlier, against the wishes of the Papua New Guinea government.

MANUFACTURING. The manufacturing sector in Papua New Guinea is small. In the 15 years between 1977 and 1992, the manufacturing sector's contribution to GDP varied between 15–18 percent. Food processing, beverage production, and tobacco processing are the main products manufactured in the country.

The Papua New Guinea government uses **tariffs** and **subsidies**, as well as direct industry support, to keep this sector afloat. While the industry has become dependent upon such measures, the government sees the manufacturing sector as providing employment for the increasing number of urban migrants. Most manufacturing is for domestic consumption only, and does not generate any export earnings.

SERVICES

The services sector in Papua New Guinea is small and almost entirely in the **public sector**. This sector employs an estimated 17.2 percent of the **labor force**, consisting mainly of government employees such as administrators, teachers, and health care workers. Approximately 66,000 tourist visas were issued in 1997, though under 10,000 of these are "real" tourists, with the others being people visiting relatives and other temporary visitors. Tourism generated US$72 million in 1997, but the high cost of travel to and within the country limits tourism development at present. Financial services are likewise a limited sector.

INTERNATIONAL TRADE

Papua New Guinea's traditional trading partners have been consistent for both exports and imports since the early 1970s. Prior to independence in 1975, Australia was the main buyer of Papua New Guinean exports, and while this relationship has continued, Japan, South Korea, Germany, and New Zealand have since played major roles as importers of Papua New Guinean goods. In 1998 20 percent of Papua New Guinea's goods went to Australia, 13 percent to Japan, 7 percent to Germany, 5 percent to South Korea, 4 percent to the Philippines, and 3 percent to the United Kingdom. Traditionally, the major exports to these countries have been **cash crops** such as copra, cocoa, and coffee. Australia has been a major buyer of Papua New Guinea's gold. Minerals are also exported to such countries as Japan and Germany. Papua New Guinea purchases most of its imports (machinery, foods, and technology) from these same countries, and especially from Australia. In 1998 Australia accounted for 51 percent of the country's imports, Singapore 10 percent, Japan 8 percent, the United States and New Zealand 5 percent, and Malaysia 3 percent. In 1999 the country enjoyed a positive trade balance of nearly a billion dollars on exports of US$1.9 billion and imports of US$1.0 billion.

Trade (expressed in billions of US$): Papua New Guinea

	Exports	Imports
1975	.441	.592
1980	1.031	1.176
1985	.912	1.008
1990	1.144	1.193
1995	2.644	1.452
1998	1.677	1.189

SOURCE: International Monetary Fund. *International Financial Statistics Yearbook 1999.*

MONEY

Since 1994 the kina has fallen dramatically relative to the U.S. dollar. The depreciation of the kina means that imports into the country become more expensive, limiting Papua New Guinea's ability to purchase technology and manufactured goods. In general, the coun-

Exchange rates: Papua New Guinea

kina (K) per US$1	
Oct 2000	2.810
2000	2.696
1999	2.539
1998	2.058
1997	1.434
1996	1.318

SOURCE: CIA *World Factbook 2001* [ONLINE].

try's finances have been characterized by relatively low **inflation** since independence, except for a period of higher inflation in the 1990s. The **inflation rate** was 16.5 percent in 1999.

Papua New Guinea's first stock exchange, in Port Moresby, opened in 1999. The first 4 companies listed were Oil Search, Orogen Minerals, Lihir Gold, and Steamships Trading.

POVERTY AND WEALTH

Papua New Guinea has a complex distribution of wealth. The extremely varied and rugged terrain kept some indigenous people of the country isolated from any connection with the "modern world" until as late as 1970. This factor, combined with the belated and rapid economic development from the 1970s, has produced a highly variable distribution of income and wealth. While much of the wealth from economic development has been concentrated in urban centers, cultural factors also feature in the distribution of poverty and wealth. Much of Papua New Guinean society is still very traditional, and differs from European-based societies in several important ways. Papua New Guinean society is centered around agriculture and attachment to the land. Land is rarely sold, but instead is inherited by children. Papua New Guinean society has a complex structure, with many bonds among family members, distant relatives, and neighbors. These bonds include obligations to share wealth, and to give and receive gifts. Papua New Guinean society did not and does not have a tradition of chiefs or leaders who gain their status through inheritance. Instead, in traditional Papua New Guinea society men become leaders through their own efforts, especially through the gaining and sharing of wealth. All of these factors are important in the way that wealth is distributed in the country.

Despite these cultural factors, the Papua New Guinea government has made some efforts to decentralize services—especially health and education—and to provide equal access to them throughout the country. These efforts, begun in the 1970s, have made little difference, if any, in greatly varying levels of income and wealth between urban and remote areas. About 85 percent of the population still depends on subsistence agriculture, and 37 percent of these people are below the poverty line.

GDP per Capita (US$)

Country	1975	1980	1985	1990	1998
Papua New Guinea	1,048	975	936	888	1,085
United States	19,364	21,529	23,200	25,363	29,683
Australia	14,317	15,721	17,078	18,023	21,881
Indonesia	385	504	603	778	972

SOURCE: United Nations. *Human Development Report 2000; Trends in human development and per capita income.*

Distribution of Income or Consumption by Percentage Share: Papua New Guinea

Lowest 10%	1.7
Lowest 20%	4.5
Second 20%	7.9
Third 20%	11.9
Fourth 20%	19.2
Highest 20%	56.5
Highest 10%	40.5

Survey year: 1996

Note: This information refers to expenditure shares by percentiles of the population and is ranked by per capita expenditure.

SOURCE: *2000 World Development Indicators* [CD-ROM].

WORKING CONDITIONS

Papua New Guinea has a total workforce of 1.941 million, and the unemployment rate has fluctuated between 3 and 10 percent since the 1980s. The development of new sectors in the Papua New Guinea economy has shaped the characteristics of employment. Before 1950, plantations provided almost the sole source of employment for both women and men, with only a fraction of the workforce employed formally. Little changed until after World War II, when both a legal minimum wage was set and the transition to a formal cash wage system was under way. By the 1950s Papua New Guineans were extensively employed in all areas of the country's economy. Women's participation in the formal employment sector has remained very small, with an estimated 14 percent of wage employment in 1980. Women and unskilled men are still subject to difficulties in job advancement. Regional differences in employment are extreme. Most formal employment is in the urban centers, especially Port Moresby.

Working conditions vary accordingly. The plantations have traditionally required a young workforce, owing to the early retirement of plantation employees, whose work is hard and largely unregulated. In contrast, those sectors such as mining, which have been driven by the infrastructure created by international corporations, provide considerable salaries (and benefits to land owners). However, the value of mineral exports in relation to agricultural subsistence or commodity exports means that the proportion of those involved in the mining sector remains very small in comparison. Papua New Guinea also has a substantial **informal sector**, consisting of small businesses that do not typically pay taxes or keep accounting records. Such businesses receive little support from the government, even though they may be in great need of loans to help start and expand their activities. Life for these small businesses is made even more difficult by laws that require them to, for example, obtain licenses or record their profits.

COUNTRY HISTORY AND ECONOMIC DEVELOPMENT

1526. First European exploration by Spaniard Don Jorge de Meneses, naming the principal island "Papua."

1545. Spaniard Ynigo Ortis de Retez names the island "New Guinea."

1828. The Dutch East India company, which controls the western part of the island, declares the island to be a colonial possession attached to the Dutch East Indies.

1884. Germany takes possession of the northeast part of the main island and the nearby smaller islands, while Great Britain establishes a protectorate on the southern coast of Papua.

1920. Britain, which took control of German possessions on the island during World War I (1914–1918), grants control of the entire territory to Australia.

1942. Japan takes possession of the Australian territories of New Guinea and Papua early in World War II. Following the Japanese surrender in 1945, the Territory of Papua is joined in administrative union with the Territory of New Guinea.

1964. The first House of Assembly opens, replacing the Legislative Council.

1972. The name of the territory is changed to Papua New Guinea; the Panguna copper mine on Bougainville island opens.

1973. Papua New Guinea receives self-government.

1975. Papua New Guinea achieves independence.

1984. The Ok Tedi copper and gold mine opens near the Indonesian border.

1990. The environmental consequences of mining come under scrutiny following natural disasters at Wau and Bulolo from disposal of tailings into Bulolo River.

1997. Lihir gold mine opens on Lihir Island.

1999. Port Moresby Stock Exchange opens; Sir Mekere Morauta becomes prime minister following the resignation of Bill Skate.

FUTURE TRENDS

Papua New Guinea will continue to depend heavily on mineral exports for the bulk of its foreign currency earnings, while simultaneously remaining a largely agricultural country in terms of employment and food production. Exploration for new mineral deposits continues on a large scale, and several projects, such as a nickel mine in Ramu, are likely to open within the next few years. The Lihir gold mine, one of the world's largest, has recently started operating and production is expected to increase. As always, the mining sector is subject to international market conditions, especially demand for minerals and changing prices.

The country's mining sector is coming under increased international scrutiny for its environmental practices. For example, villagers downstream from the Ok Tedi mine have accused the mining company of negligence in releasing toxic materials into local rivers and other water sources.

Papua New Guinea is also likely to see a continuation of political tension, especially with respect to tensions between the national and provincial governments. The independence movement on Bougainville island still simmers, although there is hope that peace talks will finally resolve the dispute. Other provincial governments are demanding greater powers and the national government will have to come to terms with these demands.

DEPENDENCIES

Papua New Guinea has no territories or colonies.

BIBLIOGRAPHY

Australian Agency for International Development (AusAID). *Papua New Guinea: Improving the Investment Climate.* Canberra, Australia: ANUTECH, 1995.

Connell, John. *Papua New Guinea: The Struggle for Development.* London: Routledge, 1997.

Economic Insights Pty Ltd. *The Economy of Papua New Guinea.* Canberra: Australian Agency for International Development (AusAID), 2000.

Economist Intelligence Unit. *Country Report: Papua New Guinea.* London: Economist Intelligence Unit, 2001.

Lal, Brij V., and Kate Fortune, eds. *The Pacific Islands: An Encyclopedia.* Honolulu: University of Hawaii Press, 2000.

U.S. Central Intelligence Agency. *World Factbook 2000.* <http://www.odci.gov/cia/publications/factbook/index.html>. Accessed August 2001.

U.S. Department of State. *Background Notes: Papua New Guinea.* <http://www.state.gov/www/background_notes/png_0011_bgn.html>. Accessed August 2001.

—Michael Pretes and Rory Eames

PHILIPPINES

Republic of the Philippines
Republika ng Pilipinas

CAPITAL: Manila.

MONETARY UNIT: Philippine peso (P). Paper money is printed in bills of 1,000, 500, 100, 50, 20, and 10 pesos. There are coins of 5 and 1 pesos and 25, 10, and 5 centavos. There are 100 centavos in 1 peso.

CHIEF EXPORTS: Electronic equipment, machinery and transport equipment, garments, and coconut products.

CHIEF IMPORTS: Raw materials and intermediate goods, capital goods, consumer goods, and fuels.

GROSS DOMESTIC PRODUCT: US$282 billion (1999 est.).

BALANCE OF TRADE: **Exports:** US$34.8 billion (1999 est.). **Imports:** US$30.7 billion (1998 est.).

COUNTRY OVERVIEW

LOCATION AND SIZE. Made up of about 7,100 islands, the Philippines is on the southeastern rim of Asia and is bordered by the Philippine Sea on the east, the South China Sea on the west, the Luzon Strait on the north, and the Celebes Sea on the south. Its land area, which is slightly larger than that of Arizona, measures 300,000 square kilometers (115,830 square miles), and its coastline is 36,289 kilometers (22,550 miles). The capital, Manila, is on the island of Luzon in the highly urbanized National Capital Region, which is made up of 12 other urban areas including the cities of Mandaluyong, Marikina, Pasig, Quezon, Kalookan, Valenzuela, Las Piñas, Makati, Muntinlupa, Parañaque, and Pasay. The main financial district is in Makati City.

POPULATION. The Philippine population has more than tripled since 1948, from 19 million to an official estimate of 81.16 million in 2000. From 1995 to 2000, and the annual population growth rate stood at 2.02 percent, slightly lower than in 1990 and one-third less than the growth rate of 3 percent during the 1960s.

The population of the Philippines is young, with people aged between 15–64 years making up 59 percent of the population, while those under 15 make up 37 percent of the population. Those aged 65 years and above make up only 4 percent of the population.

In January 2000, the U.S. Agency for International Development (USAID) warned of the serious consequences of the booming Philippine population. It predicted the population will double by 2030 based on its 1999 growth rate of 2.3 percent, giving the Philippines "the equivalent of 58 percent of the current population of the United States [living] on 3 percent of its land area," a situation with "grave consequences" for the Philippine economy, society, and the environment.

The country is divided into 3 island groups: Luzon, Visayas, and Mindanao, known together as Luzviminda. These 3 groups are further subdivided into 16 regions. The 2000 National Census lists 61 chartered cities and 73 provinces in the Philippines, with the most populated regions in Luzon. Four out of ten persons in the Philippines lives in the National Capital Region and the adjoining regions of Central Luzon and Southern Tagalog.

OVERVIEW OF ECONOMY

The Philippine economy has experienced repeated boom-and-bust cycles in the 5 decades since the nation achieved independence from the United States in 1946. In the 1950s and early 1960s its economy ranked as the second most progressive in Asia, next to that of Japan. After 1965, when Ferdinand E. Marcos became president, the nation experienced economic problems and social unrest, especially from the 1970s, when corruption and cronyism (the practice of appointing friends to well-paid posts regardless of their qualifications) took hold. In 1972, Marcos declared a state of emergency and placed the country under martial law to stifle unrest and control economic development. By his third term in

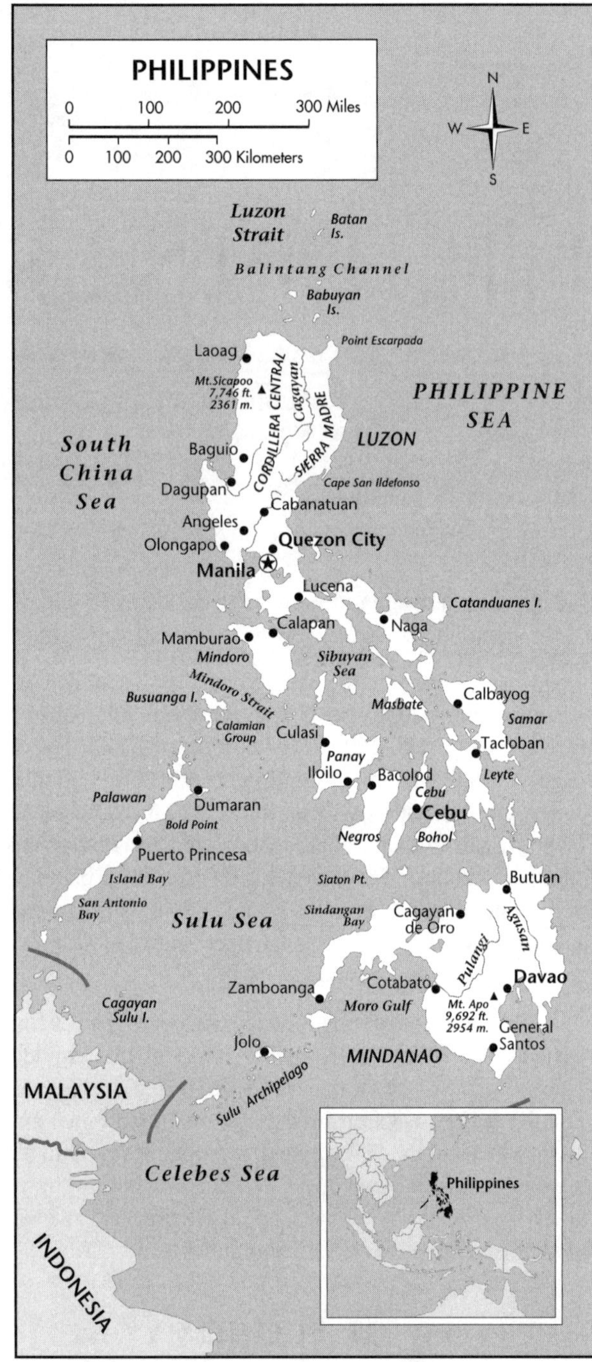

1981, democratic institutions in the country had severely eroded, **foreign debt** ballooned, and the country's economy plummeted. In less than 20 years, the Philippines had gone from relative prosperity to becoming the "sick man of Asia." In 1983, the leader of the political opposition, former senator Benigno Aquino, was assassinated upon his returned from exile in the United States.

Marcos was removed from office in 1986 through a peaceful "People Power" revolution in which millions of people demonstrated in the streets. Aquino's widow, Corazon, became president, and a new constitution was approved in 1987. Meanwhile, the GDP growth rate increased steadily from 3.5 percent in 1986 to 4.3 percent in 1987, peaking in 1988 at 6.7 percent. The Aquino administration endured many troubles, including 6 coup d'etat attempts, many natural disasters (e.g. earthquakes, the Mt. Pinatubo eruption), and a power shortage problem that caused economic activities to stop. During this period, the Aquino administration passed various critical laws such as a liberal Foreign Investment Act, the Comprehensive Agrarian Reform Law, and the **privatization** of government corporations that brought the economy back to its feet.

Aquino's successor, Fidel Ramos, embarked on an ambitious development plan dubbed "Philippines 2000." Under the plan, several industries critical to economic development were privatized, such as electricity, telecommunications, banking, domestic shipping, and oil. The taxation system was reformed, and **external debt** was brought to more manageable levels by debt restructuring and sensible fiscal management. By 1996, GNP was growing at a rate of 7.2 percent and GDP at 5.2 percent. The annual **inflation rate** had dropped to 5.9 percent from its high of 9.1 percent in 1995. By the late 1990s, the Philippines' economic growth gained favorable comparisons with other Asian countries such as Taiwan, Thailand, South Korea, and Malaysia.

The Philippine economy took a sharp downturn during the Asian financial crisis of 1997. Its fiscal deficit in 1998 reached P49.981 billion from a surplus of P1.564 billion in 1997. The peso depreciated (fell in value) to P40.89 per U.S. dollar from its previous rate of P29.47 to a dollar. The annual growth rate of the GNP fell to 0.1 percent in 1998 from 5.3 percent in 1997. Despite these setbacks, the Philippine economy fared better than that of some of its Asian neighbors, and other nations praised the Ramos administration for its "good housekeeping."

In 1998, Joseph Estrada was elected president. Even with its strong economic team, the Estrada administration failed to capitalize on the gains of the previous administration. His administration was severely criticized for cronyism, incompetence, and corruption, causing it to lose the confidence of foreign investors. Foreign investors' confidence was further damaged when, in his second year, Estrada was accused of exerting influence in an investigation of a friend's involvement in stock market manipulation. Social unrest brought about by numerous bombing threats, actual bombings, kidnappings, and other criminal activities contributed to the economy's troubles. Economic performance was also hurt by climatic disturbance that caused extremes of dry and wet weather. Toward the end of Estrada's administration, the fiscal deficit had doubled to more than P100 billion from a low of P49 billion in 1998. Despite such setbacks, the rate of GNP in 1999 increased to 3.6 percent from 0.1 percent in 1998, and the GDP posted a 3.2 percent growth rate, up from a low of -0.5 percent in 1998. Debt reached P2.1 trillion in 1999. Domestic debt amounted to P986.7 billion while foreign debt stood at US$52.2 billion. In January 2001 Estrada was removed from office by a second peaceful "People Power" revolution engineered primarily by youth, non-governmental organizations, and the business sector. President Estrada was the first Philippine president to be impeached by Congress, and his vice-president, Gloria Macapagal-Arroyo, became the fourteenth President of the Republic.

The economy of the Philippines is hampered by huge foreign debt, a low savings rate, inefficient tax collection, inadequate **infrastructure**, especially outside major cities, and poor agricultural performance. The Philippine economy is vulnerable to oil-price increases, interest-rate shifts by the U.S. Federal Reserve, and the performance of international stock exchanges. Social factors that have a negative impact on the economy include a high crime rate, especially kidnappings and rape, pockets of **Communist** rebels in rural areas, threats from Muslim separatist movements, high rates of poverty and unemployment, and the government's inability to begin its land-distribution program. Environmental factors also damage economic development, including frequent typhoons and drought. Worker productivity is adversely affected by illnesses brought on by air and water pollution. In metropolitan Manila alone, the effect of pollution on health and labor productivity has been estimated to be equal to a loss of about 1 percent of **gross national product** annually.

Foreign aid, or official development assistance (ODA) funds, have contributed immensely to the development of the nation's economy. Through grants and loans extended by development agencies and international creditors, the government is able to finance infrastructure development (bridges, roads, highways, railways, transportation systems) and social programs (livelihood projects, training seminars, immunization programs, and environmental projects). Since the late 1990s, ODA funds have helped improve living conditions in the most depressed rural areas, especially in Mindanao, Southern Philippines, mostly via agricultural programs. In 1999 most funds were allocated to agricultural programs. About 95 percent of ODA assistance is distributed in loans, with the remainder in grants.

POLITICS, GOVERNMENT, AND TAXATION

The government of the Republic of the Philippines is composed of 3 equal branches: the executive, legislative, and judicial, with checks and balances on each other. The popularly elected president is the nation's highest executive official. The legislature is divided into 2 chambers, a Senate (upper chamber) of 24 members and a House of Representatives (lower chamber) of a maximum of 260 members. The Supreme Court, led by the Chief Justice and 14 associate justices, is the highest judicial body, and acts as the final arbiter of the legal validity of any executive or legislative policy. In 1991 a Local Government Code was enacted that transferred some of national government powers to local government officials. Administratively, the country is divided into political subdivisions such as provinces, cities, municipalities, and barangays (villages). Each political subdivision has its own local government, which enjoys a certain level of autonomy (self-governance) and is legally entitled to an equitable share of the national wealth called the Internal Revenue Allotment.

The country practices a multi-party system. Political parties are required to register with the Commission on Elections (COMELEC) to which they must present a constitution, by-laws, and platform. In practice, parties in the Philippines are very weak and merely exist to host individual political ambitions. Hence, it is not unusual for new political parties to crop up just weeks before election time and dissolve after the elections, with winning candidates merely transferring to the dominant party.

Elections in the Philippines are often swayed by patronage (support given by a moneyed or influential individual) and the personality of the candidate. In fact, it is unusual for candidates to discuss their platforms during campaign rallies since many of those who attend such rallies are usually more interested in watching the entertainers that accompany these candidates than the candidates themselves. In 2001, after the ouster of former president Joseph Estrada, formerly a well-known movie star, reformers called for an end to personality-oriented elections and for campaigns built around a relevant discussion of national issues.

The military plays a significant role in the economy by ensuring peace and order in the country, particularly in Mindanao, southern Philippines, where a long-term war against rebels continues to be waged. In special instances, military personnel are partnered with police personnel to patrol the cities and minimize urban crime. The navy also guards the country's coastal borders against poachers and illegal fishing vessels, which deplete the country's coastal resources.

The policies and programs of government are funded by various taxes imposed at the national and local levels, and by borrowing. Taxes are collected by the Bureau of Internal Revenue and the Bureau of Customs. Domestic corporations, resident citizens, and resident aliens are taxed on their net income from all sources, worldwide, while resident foreign corporations are taxed on their Philippine net income. Government also generates funds from other offices, such as the Land Transportation Office, which collect taxes for specific government services. Other sources of revenue are derived from the sale of government corporations to the **private sector**, fees and service incomes of various government agencies, foreign grants, and proceeds from the sale of transferred, surrendered, and privatized assets.

Revenue earned by government is usually inadequate to finance its programs and activities. Bernardo Villegas, an economist at the University of Asia and the Pacific, explains that for a developing country like the Philippines to remedy this situation, the government must resort to borrowing money either from external or domestic sources, such as via **treasury bills**, notes, and bonds issued as collateral (property pledged by a borrower to guarantee the investment of a lender) for domestic loans. Foreign sources are used because there is no adequate, long-term source of capital in the country, a situation that is made worse by the country's low savings rate. Funds borrowed abroad are readily available and come with lower interest rates. International lending institutions such as the Asian Development Bank, the International Monetary Fund, and the Japan Bank for International Cooperation are some of the country's foreign creditors. Borrowing has increased the **national debt** to P2.1 trillion. Domestic debt at the end of 1999 reached P986.7 billion, while foreign debt stood at US$52.2 billion.

In the past, the government has played an active role in influencing the country's economy, often to the displeasure of the business sector, which wants the economy left to market forces with minimal government intervention. Like many developing countries, the Philippines' economic policies include **import substitution** policies and the promotion of labor-intensive industries to support a burgeoning workforce. The government also exerts control over the economy through the regulation or prohibition of **monopolies**, the sourcing and formation of capital, the provision of private incentives, and through the regulation of strategic sectors that are vital to national interests.

Government in developing countries, such as the Philippines, must take charge of building strategic infrastructure, such as farm-to-market roads and bridges linking landlocked areas, to stimulate the exchange of goods and services between localities. It is also the government's function to protect natural resources from illegal exploitation.

INFRASTRUCTURE, POWER, AND COMMUNICATIONS

The transport infrastructure includes 492 kilometers (306 miles) of working railroads and 199,950 kilometers (124,249 miles) of roads, of which 39,590 kilometers (24,601 miles) are paved. In the first quarter of 2000, infrastructure projects got the biggest share of official development assistance (ODA) loans, taking 66 percent of the $11.4 billion ODA package extended to the Philippines. Among the projects are plans to decongest traffic by expanding roads and building bridges and highway interchanges.

The Philippine archipelago has more than 1,490 ports that serve to connect its major islands. As of 1996, there were 566 registered cargo and container ships, and total cargo handled was estimated at 140.1 million tons. The busiest national port is in Manila. Ninety percent of the country's imports and more than 20 percent of its exports pass through its South Harbor and the Manila International Container Terminal. In February 2001 the Philippine Ports Authority earmarked US$122 million to upgrade port services here and in even other locations.

As of 1999, there were 266 registered airports and 5 domestic airlines operating in the Philippines. Beginning in 2000, the government and its private-sector partners speeded up the schedule for the construction and upgrading of at least 20 airports to enable them to meet world standards by 2004.

Communications

Country	Newspapers	Radios	TV Sets[a]	Cable subscribers[a]	Mobile Phones[a]	Fax Machines[a]	Personal Computers[a]	Internet Hosts[b]	Internet Users[b]
	1996	1997	1998	1998	1998	1998	1998	1999	1999
Philippines	79	159	108	8.2	22	N/A	15.1	1.29	500
United States	215	2,146	847	244.3	256	78.4	458.6	1,508.77	74,100
China	N/A	333	272	40.0	19	1.6	8.9	0.50	8,900
Indonesia	24	156	136	N/A	5	0.9	8.2	0.76	900

[a]Data are from International Telecommunication Union, *World Telecommunication Development Report 1999* and are per 1,000 people.
[b]Data are from the Internet Software Consortium (http://www.isc.org) and are per 10,000 people.

SOURCE: World Bank. *World Development Indicators 2000.*

In 1986 the country's economy was severely crippled by continuous power shortages that lasted more than 10 hours daily, paralyzing the manufacturing sector. In 1992 the Ramos administration took steps to resolve this problem by allowing private operators to build more power plants that substantially improved the country's power-generating capacity. By March 2000, 74 percent of the country's households had access to electric service, and dependence on oil-run power plants was reduced to 19 percent from a previous high of 80 percent. Power is now generated from several sources, including coal (38 percent), geothermal (27 percent), and hydroelectric (16 percent). The opening of the offshore Malampaya gas field in Palawan will further reduce dependence on foreign oil with its initial production rate of 145 billion cubic feet annually, which can be used to create 2,700 megawatts of power.

Under the Ramos administration, the monopolistic (one company in control) telecommunications industry was opened up to competition and by 2001 there were more than 50 firms offering service. Telephone density per 100 inhabitants nearly tripled during the 1990s, from 3 lines per 100 inhabitants in 1992 to 8 lines in 1998. In 1999 there were 1.9 million main lines in use and another 1.95 million cellular telephones, plus 93 Internet service providers. In September 2000, Globe Telecom and 7 other telecommunication carriers in the Asia-Pacific region agreed to create the C2C Cable Network, an undersea fiber-optic-cable system, worth US$2 billion. Upon completion, the C2C network will be able to accommodate 90 million conversations simultaneously.

The Philippines has been recognized as the global capital for text messaging, a feature of digital mobile phones virtually ignored in other countries. This allows the user to type brief messages and send it to another mobile phone. Each day, more than 18 million text messages are transmitted in the country, twice as many as in all of Europe. However, high fees make this service still out of reach for most people.

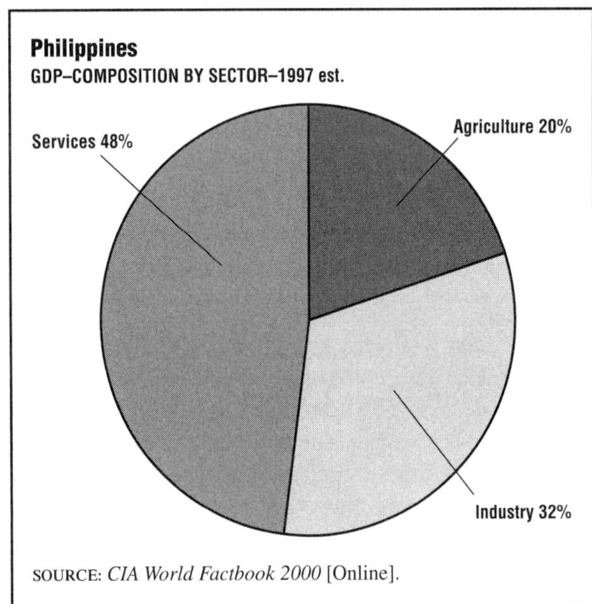

SOURCE: *CIA World Factbook 2000* [Online].

ECONOMIC SECTORS

In the Philippines, the 3 largest economic sectors are industry, service, and agriculture, in terms of contribution to GDP. In past years, the service sector has exhibited continuous growth. Agriculture, although still substantial, continues to decline. Estimates from 1997 reveal that agriculture contributed 20 percent to GDP, industry contributed 32 percent, and services dominated the economy with 48 percent of GDP.

In 1999 the rate of growth of the GDP stood at 3.2 percent. Economists blamed the sluggish growth on the lackluster performance of the industry sector, which grew by 0.5 percent. With the end of the dry spell brought about by El Niño weather conditions, the agriculture sector's performance rebounded and grew 6.6 percent, the highest rate in decades. Services grew by 3.9 percent that year because of the strong performance in **retail**.

Maximum economic growth for 1999 and 2000 was slowed by successive political crises in the Estrada administration that caused foreign and international lending agencies to lose confidence. In 2000 GDP posted a 3.9 percent positive growth rate, with industry growing 4 times faster than it did in 1999. Services continued its strong performance, with a 4.4 percent increase over its 1999 figures.

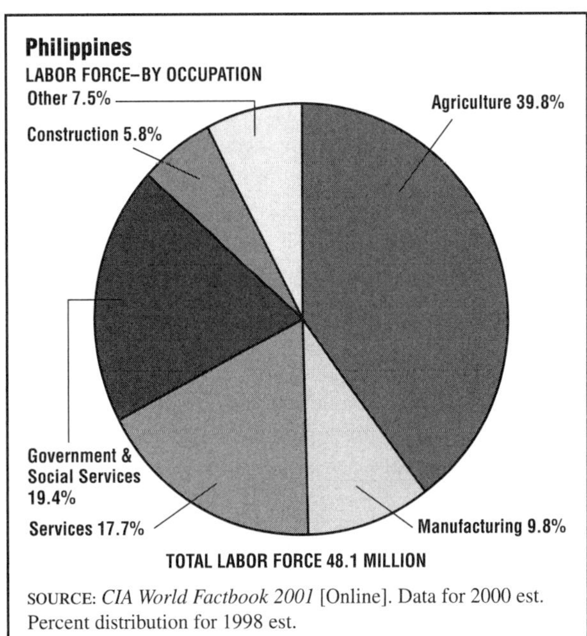

SOURCE: *CIA World Factbook 2001* [Online]. Data for 2000 est. Percent distribution for 1998 est.

AGRICULTURE

The Philippines is still primarily an agricultural country despite the plan to make it an industrialized economy by 2000. Most citizens still live in rural areas and support themselves through agriculture. The country's agriculture sector is made up of 4 sub-sectors: farming, fisheries, livestock, and forestry (the latter 2 sectors are very small), which together employ 39.8 percent of the **labor force** and contribute 20 percent of GDP.

The country's main agricultural crops are rice, corn, coconut, sugarcane, bananas, pineapple, coffee, mangoes, tobacco, and abaca (a banana-like plant). Secondary crops include peanut, cassava, camote (a type of rootcrop), garlic, onion, cabbage, eggplant, calamansi (a variety of lemon), rubber, and cotton. The year 1998 was a bad year for agriculture because of adverse weather conditions. Sector output shrank by 8.3 percent, but it posted growth the following year. Yet, hog farming and commercial fishing posted declines in their gross revenues in 1999. The sector is burdened with low productivity for most of its crops.

The Philippines exports its agricultural products around the world, including the United States, Japan, Europe, and ASEAN countries (members of the Association of Southeast Asian Nations). Major export products are coconut oil and other coconut products, fruits and vegetables, bananas, and prawns (a type of shrimp). Other exports include the Cavendish banana, Cayenne pineapple, tuna, seaweed, and carrageenan. The value of coconut-product exports amounted to US$989 million in 1995 but declined to US$569 million by 2000. Imported agricultural products include unmilled wheat and meslin, oilcake and other soybean residues, malt and malt flour, urea, flour, meals and pellets of fish, soybeans and whey.

One of the most pressing concerns of the agricultural sector is the rampant conversion of agricultural land into golf courses, residential subdivisions, and industrial parks or resorts. In 1993 the nation was losing irrigated rice lands at a rate of 2,300 hectares per year. Small landholders find it more profitable to sell their land to developers in exchange for cash, especially since they lack capital for seeds, fertilizers, pesticides, and wages for hiring workers to plant and harvest the crops. Another concern is farmers' continued reliance on chemical-based fertilizers or pesticides that have destroyed soil productivity over time. In recent years however, farmers have been slowly turning to organic fertilizer, or at least to a combination of chemical and organic inputs.

Environmental damage is another major concern. Coral-reef destruction, pollution of coastal and marine resources, mangrove forest destruction, and siltation (the clogging of bodies of water with silt deposits) are significant problems.

The agriculture sector has not received adequate resources for the funding of critical programs or projects, such as the construction of efficient irrigation systems. According to the World Bank, the share of irrigated crop land in the Philippines averaged only about 19.5 percent in the mid-1990s, compared with 37.5 percent for China, 24.8 percent for Thailand, and 30.8 percent for Vietnam. In the late 1990s, the government attempted to modernize the agriculture sector with the Medium Term Agricultural Development Plan and the Agricultural Fisheries Modernization Act.

The fisheries sector is divided into 3 sub-sectors: commercial, municipal, and aquaculture (cultivation of the natural produce of bodies of water). In 1995, the Philippines contributed 2.2 million tons, or 2 percent of total world catch, ranking it twelfth among the top 80 fish-producing countries. In the same year, the country also earned the distinction of being the fourth biggest producer of seaweed and ninth biggest producer of world aquaculture products.

In 1999 the fisheries sector contributed P80.4 billion at current prices, or 16 percent of gross **value added** in agriculture. Total production in 1999 reached 2.7 million tons. Aquaculture contributed the most, with 949,000 tons, followed closely by commercial fishing with 948,000 tons, and municipal fisheries with 910,000 tons. Domestic demand for fish is substantial, with average yearly fish consumption at 36kg per person compared to a 12kg figure for consumption of meat and other food products.

INDUSTRY

In 2000 following the Asian economic slump of the late 1990s, industrial sectors (manufacturing, transportation, communication and storage, mining and quarrying) all posted positive growth rates, lifting the entire economy from the previous year's lackluster performance. Yet, the construction industry suffered because of the lack of long-term investments by the private sector. Although public construction grew by 15 percent from 1998 to 1999, private construction sank to 11 percent because of real estate oversupply. Mining and quarrying continued to suffer from low metal prices in the world market.

In the Philippines, small and medium enterprises make up 99 percent of all manufacturing companies. Revenue of the top 420 manufacturing firms increased by 9.9 percent in 1998. In 2000 manufacturing accounted for almost a quarter of the country's production. According to the Labor Department's January 2001 Labor Force Survey, 9.8 percent of all workers were employed in this sector.

The manufacturing sector produces the country's top export products such as semiconductors, electronics, machinery and transport equipment, and garments. Exports of electronics and semiconductors generated US$17.4 billion in 1998 and US$21.6 billion in 1999. Other chief imports of this sector include paper and paper products, textile yarn and fabrics, nonmetallic minerals, iron and steel, and metal products. Most of the large and medium manufacturing companies are in special export-processing zones or industrial parks. Some provinces have been specially designated to host these companies, such as the CALABARZON area which is made up of 4 provinces: Cavite, Laguna, Batangas, and Quezon.

SERVICES

According to the 2001 Labor Force Survey, employment in the service sector rose to 13.2 million in 2000, up from 12.7 million in 1999. The proportion of workers in the Philippines service sector increased accordingly, from 45.8 percent to 46.8 percent.

RETAIL. The Philippines has a variety of retail establishments scattered throughout the country, from small village-based general stores that supply all the needs of a small community to a web of specialized stores in the larger cities. The wholesale and retail sector was affected by the economic slowdown in 1998, so retailers and wholesalers tried to increase consumer spending with aggressive marketing campaigns, quarterly sales, and discount promotions. In 1999 revenue rose to P145.41 billion from a low of P138.64 in 1998. Around this time, the retail sector was opened to foreign competition by the Retail Trade **Liberalization** Act, which allows foreign retailers to conduct business and fully own enterprises as long as they meet certain capitalization (available funds) requirements.

TOURISM. According to the Department of Tourism (DOT), which works with other government agencies to improve infrastructure and guarantee peace and order in the country, the Philippines was the twelfth ranked tourist destination in Asia in 1997. In Southeast Asia, the Philippines ranked fifth, behind Thailand, Singapore, Malaysia and Indonesia. In 1999, 2.17 million tourists visited the country, mostly from East Asia, followed by North America and Europe. These tourists spent $2.55 billion in the country. The country offers nearly 12,000 rooms in numerous hotels. To attract more tourists, as well as to encourage locals to travel to other areas of the country, the government implemented 5 major programs in 1999. Among these programs were the promotion of community-based tourism, the rehabilitation of the world-renowned Ifugao rice terraces, and the promotion of Manila as a multi-faceted destination. Also introduced were programs geared toward overseas workers and attracting expatriate (living abroad), third- and fourth-generation Filipinos to visit their homeland, and programs highlighting cultural artifacts and national heritage. The Philippines boasts some of the best scuba diving in the world, and its World War II sites are also major tourist attractions.

COMMUNICATIONS. In the early 1990s, the monopoly of the Philippine Long Distance Telephone Company (PLDT) was abolished and the sector was opened to competition. Two telecommunications companies, Globe Communications and Smart Communications, are locked in battle over mobile-phone market share. By 1999, Globe was leading with 720,000 subscribers, but Smart followed closely behind. The call-center service business is thriving with the entry of foreign companies like America Online, Etelecare International, People Support, and Getronics. Although still in its infancy, the industry is expected to expand, aided by the availability of workers proficient in English, suitable facilities, and government incentives.

INTERNATIONAL TRADE

EXPORTS. The growth and stability of the Philippine economy is dependent on foreign trade, particularly on the dollar revenue generated from export. For this reason, the Department of Trade and Industry (DTI) has established an Export Development Council to oversee the growth of this sector as guided by the Philippine Export Development Plan. The plan uses a comprehensive approach in promoting Philippine exports to world markets. Another organization that assists the DTI in export promotion is the Center for International Trade Exposition Missions (CITEM), which assists Filipino exporters in marketing and promoting their products through regular trade fairs, trade missions, and other export-promotion programs and activities at home and abroad.

The primary trading partners of the Philippines have always been the United States and Japan, both former colonizers. Trade with these 2 countries has accounted for 50 to 60 percent of Philippine exports for the last 10 years. The Philippines also trades with Singapore, the

Trade (expressed in billions of US$): Philippines

	Exports	Imports
1975	2.294	3.756
1980	5.741	8.295
1985	4.607	5.459
1990	8.068	13.041
1995	17.502	28.337
1998	27.783	30.705

SOURCE: International Monetary Fund. *International Financial Statistics Yearbook 1999.*

Netherlands, Taiwan, Hong Kong, the United Kingdom, Malaysia, Germany, and Thailand.

Labor-intensive industrial manufacturers dominate the Philippine export scene. Electronics and semiconductors continue to lead the country's top-10 export products, generating US$1.74 billion in 1998 and US$2.16 billion in 1999. Officials of the Department of Science and Technology predict that earnings from electronic exports will reach US$4.7 billion by 2004. A 1997 government survey revealed that 75 percent of the 784 firms in the country's export-processing zones were electronics manufacturers, and that these firms account for 59 percent of the country's exports. Other important export products are machinery and transport equipment, garments and coconut products, furniture and fixtures, bananas, processed food and beverages, and textile yarns.

Trade officials have forecast that Philippine merchandise exports are likely to hit the US$50 billion mark by the end of 2001, up from $35 billion in 1999. Philippine foreign trade continues to increase every year. In 1998 and 1998, the Philippines posted positive export growth rates—16.9 percent and 18.8 percent—when those of other Asian countries were in decline.

IMPORTS. Imports for 1999 were $30.7 billion. The country's top 10 imports are electronic components, telecommunications equipment and electrical machinery, mineral fuels and lubricants, industrial machinery and equipment, textile yarn and fabric, transport equipment, iron and steel, and organic and inorganic chemicals. The Philippines has attempted several strategies to correct the trade imbalance where imports exceed exports. These strategies range from exchange and import controls to raising **tariffs** for imported products. Despite these efforts, imports have continued to surpass exports for the last 30 years, except in 1973. This forces the government to borrow from international lending agencies to pay for the products that it imports, which are paid for in foreign currencies, commonly in U.S. dollars. These loans are compounded by interest, which further increases the national debt. Over the last 2 decades, this imbalance has been eased somewhat by the money sent by Filipinos working abroad to their families, estimated at US$6.8 million in 1999, a substantial rise over the US$4.5 million figure for 1998.

The major countries importing goods to the Philippines are the United States (22 percent), Japan (20 percent), South Korea (8 percent), Singapore (6 percent), Taiwan (5 percent), and Hong Kong (4 percent), according to 1998 estimates.

MONEY

In the late 1950s, the **exchange rate** for the Philippine peso against the U.S. dollar was 2 to 1. Because the country's economy was undermined by flawed economic policies, innumerable political crises, and a ballooning foreign debt, the peso continued to weaken so that by 1972, the average exchange rate was P6.67 to $1 and, by 1982, at P8.54 to $1. By 1986, the peso had depreciated (lost its value) further and the average exchange rate was P20.39 to US$1, sinking to P40.8 during the 1997 Asian financial crisis. In 2000, at the height of the political crisis that hit the Estrada administration, the peso hit rock bottom at P55 to US$1. Immediately upon Estrada's ouster, the peso gained strength against the U.S. dollar and stabilized at the average exchange rate of P48.50 to a dollar.

Exchange rates: Philippines

Philippine pesos (P) per US$1	
Jan 2001	50.969
2000	44.192
1999	39.089
1998	40.893
1997	29.471
1996	26.216

SOURCE: CIA *World Factbook 2001* [ONLINE].

In the late 1980s, the government began a series of financial reforms aimed at strengthening the banking sector. One of the most important was the restructuring and infusion of fresh capital to the nation's central bank, Bangko Sentral ng Pilipinas, which had become bankrupt following successive political and economic crises in the 1980s. Under the New Central Bank Act of 1993, the central bank was granted "increased fiscal and administrative autonomy (self-government) from other sectors of the government." The act also prohibits the Central Bank from engaging in development banking or financing.

The most important of the agencies overseeing the **monetary policy** of the Philippines are the Department of Finance, the Department of Budget and Management, and the Bangko Sentral ng Pilipinas (Central Bank of the Philippines).

The Department of Finance is the government's central finance office, which manages and mobilizes resources to insure that government policies inspire confidence in foreign investors. This Department manages the bureaus of Internal Revenue, Customs, Treasury and Local Government Finance, and supervises the Securities and Exchange Commission and the Philippine Deposit Insurance Corporation, charged with overseeing the stock market and guaranteeing bank deposits. The Department of Budget and Management is responsible for the formulation and implementation of the national budget and for the sound utilization of government funds to achieve the country's development goals. The re-organized Bangko Sentral ng Pilipinas conducts monetary policy, issues currency, supervises lending to other banks and the government, manages foreign currency reserves, determines exchange rate policy, and provides other banking functions to the government.

BANKING SECTOR. There are 5 types of banks in the Philippines: universal banks (also called "expanded commercial banks"), commercial banks, thrift banks, rural banks, and government-owned banks. Thrift banks, which include savings and mortgage banks, private development banks, and stock and savings associations, service mainly the consumer retail market and small- and medium-size enterprises. The rural banking system services the needs of the agricultural sector, farmers, and rural cooperatives. There are 3 fully government-owned banks: the Land Bank of the Philippines, the Development Bank of the Philippines, and the Al Amanah Islamic Investment Bank of the Philippines. The banking sector encountered great difficulty during the Asian financial crisis in 1997, but owing to past reforms, the financial condition of the Philippine banking system has been more stable compared to several of its neighboring countries, and major bank failures have been avoided.

STOCK EXCHANGES. The Manila Stock Exchange was established by American businessmen in 1927 after a gold boom. In order to protect its investors, the Securities and Exchange Commission (SEC) was set up in 1936, making it the oldest securities regulatory body in Asia. The Makati Stock Exchange was founded in 1956 by some Filipino brokers who felt dominated by the Americans. For many years, the 2 stock exchanges competed against each other for clients, but they merged in 1992 after a Supreme Court ruling. The newly merged stock exchanges commenced commercial operations in March 1994. Standard and Poor's estimated the **market capitalization** of the merged exchanges at US$48.105 million and trading value was at US$19.673 million.

GDP per Capita (US$)

Country	1975	1980	1985	1990	1998
Philippines	974	1,166	967	1,064	1,092
United States	19,364	21,529	23,200	25,363	29,683
China	138	168	261	349	727
Indonesia	385	504	603	778	972

SOURCE: United Nations. *Human Development Report 2000; Trends in human development and per capita income.*

POVERTY AND WEALTH

Poverty remains a serious problem in the Philippines, which is the only populous country in East Asia in which the absolute number of people living on less than $1 a day remained constant over the 1981–1995 period, according to figures compiled by the World Bank. That body estimates that even if the Philippine economy posts a 6 to 8 percent growth through 2005, it will still not be possible to bring the poverty level below 15 percent. Economists believe that it may take some 20 years of continuous economic reforms and implementation of social programs before the country can match the single-digit poverty figures of its more wealthy neighbors. In general, widespread poverty in the country is a direct result of inappropriate and unresponsive economic policies, mismanagement of resources, corruption, and failure of the government to implement anti-poverty programs.

Economic policies from the 1960s to the 1980s focused on a capital-intensive, import-substituting strategy, which bred inefficient industries and contributed to the neglect of the agricultural sector. Policies promoting industrialization favored the development of urban areas to the detriment of rural areas, most of which remained underdeveloped. At the outset, urban areas, especially Metro Manila, cornered major infrastructure and social projects, thereby attracting most of the investments and jobs in the manufacturing and industrial sectors. In contrast, living standards in the rural areas continued to decline, leaving most of the peasant communities to subsist on a hand-to-mouth existence.

Starting in the mid-1980s, policies adopted by the government moved toward a more open, market-friendly economy. However, as government continued to pursue industrialization, the country's foreign debt ballooned and most of the government's resources went for debt and interest payments. This greatly hindered the government's ability to finance infrastructure and social programs for the neglected sectors of the population.

The mid-1990s witnessed a significant increase in income inequality. Only the top 10 percent of the population increased its share of total income, while the remaining 90

Distribution of Income or Consumption by Percentage Share: Philippines

Lowest 10%	2.3
Lowest 20%	5.4
Second 20%	8.8
Third 20%	13.2
Fourth 20%	20.3
Highest 20%	52.3
Highest 10%	36.6

Survey year: 1997

Note: This information refers to expenditure shares by percentiles of the population and is ranked by per capita expenditure.

SOURCE: *2000 World Development Indicators* [CD-ROM].

Household Consumption in PPP Terms

Country	All food	Clothing and footwear	Fuel and power[a]	Health care[b]	Education[b]	Transport & Communications	Other
Philippines	37	3	11	1	14	1	32
United States	13	9	9	4	6	8	51
China	N/A	N/A	N/A	N/A	N/A	N/A	N/A
Indonesia	47	3	6	5	14	3	22

Data represent percentage of consumption in PPP terms.
[a]Excludes energy used for transport.
[b]Includes government and private expenditures.

SOURCE: World Bank. *World Development Indicators 2000.*

percent lost income share. A 1997 government survey revealed that more than a third of the population (36.7 percent) lived below acceptable standards. Still, the incidence of extreme poverty had declined since 1985, when the comparable figure was 49.2 percent. In 1999, the National Statistics Office estimated that, of the 14.7 million families in the Philippines, the top 20 percent earned 14 times more (P502.1 billion) than the lowest 20 percent (P35.8 billion).

A survey by the National Statistics Office of income distribution in the period from 1991 to 1997 shows the combined earnings of 80 percent of Filipino families amounted to only 44 percent of total income in the country, while the top 10 percent of families owned 39.3 percent. In 1999, almost half (46.6 percent) of the total income, or P417.9 billion, came from wages and salaries, and about a quarter (23.5 percent), or P210.3 billion, from entrepreneurial activities.

Among the poorest Filipinos, most family income is derived from entrepreneurial activities such as selling food on street corners or collecting recyclable materials to sell at the junkyards. Those belonging to the higher income strata obtain a bigger share of their incomes from wages and salaries. Most of the poor are lowland landless agricultural workers, lowland small farm owners and cultivators, industrial wage laborers, **hawkers**, microentrepreneurs, and scavengers. Most poor Filipinos live in rural areas, where they are subject to the low productivity of agricultural employment. Urban poverty is caused by low household incomes and the internal migration of poor rural families to urban areas.

Due to inadequate access to community health centers, members of poor households are not able to maximize health services benefits, such as family planning, the lack of which results in larger families with more malnourished and uneducated children. The condition of the poor is made worse by lack of housing, clean water and electricity, especially in the urban areas.

In 1987 Congress enacted the Cooperative Code of the Philippines in order to improve income opportunities, promote self-reliance, and encourage the entrepreneurial spirit in the countryside. As of December 2000, there were 57,470 cooperatives (a collective organization owned and operated by the people drawing benefits from it) registered with the Cooperative Development Authority. In 1991, Congress enacted the Local Government Code, which expanded basic social services on the grassroots level. The Social Reform Agenda (1993), formulated during the Ramos administration, is one of the government's most comprehensive development frameworks for combating poverty; its strategies aim at improving access to basic social services, increasing opportunities for employment, income generation, and self-reliance. The Estrada administration established the National Anti-Poverty Commission and allocated P2.5 billion for suitable programs.

WORKING CONDITIONS

Working conditions in the Philippines are closely related to one's social class. Those belonging to the upper class enjoy the best opportunities in terms of job satisfaction, facilities, advancement, and choice of career. Those from the middle class are usually able to land white-collar jobs with some room for advancement by capitalizing on education, company loyalty, and hard work. Those belonging to the lower class, due to their lack of education or capital, largely engage in poorly paid manual labor or blue-collar jobs, viewed as menial in Philippine society.

The unemployment rate in the Philippines rose to 10.1 percent in October 2000 during a political crisis provoked by President Estrada's impeachment trial on charges of graft (illegal or unfair gain) and corruption. The performance of the manufacturing industry sank to an historic low and investor confidence hit rock-bottom. Nearly 3 million Filipinos were unemployed and the unemployment rate in Metro Manila reached 17.8 percent.

The Department of Labor and Employment is the main agency making and implementing labor policies and government programs. Guidelines set by the Labor Code of the Philippines guarantee equal work opportunities to all, equal compensation for work of equal value, secure work tenure, overtime and vacation benefits, safe working conditions, the right to collective bargaining, and social-security benefits.

OVERSEAS FILIPINO WORKERS (OFWS). Beginning in the 1980s, lack of employment opportunities and **inflation** at home caused many Filipinos to seek employment in Europe, the Middle East, and neighboring countries in Southeast Asia through legal and illegal means. According to labor statistics released in January 2001, a total of 789,000 documented OFWs left to work abroad from January to November 2000 as information technology workers, engineers, seafarers, housekeepers, and nurses, among others. As of December 2000 labor statistics released by the Inter-Agency Committee on Tourism and Overseas Employment Statistics reveal that there are 7,383,122 Filipino professionals working abroad. Money sent home by the OFWs in 1999 amounted to US$6.8 million, a big jump from US$4.5 million in 1998. The social costs of this phenomenon were also substantial, for it caused the breakdown of the family unit, carrying with it attendant problems such as extramarital affairs and increased delinquency among unsupervised children. An equally disturbing problem was the rampant sexual and physical abuse of OFWs, especially women, and those victimized by illegal recruiters.

WOMEN AND CHILDREN IN THE WORKFORCE. On one hand, economic growth has opened up more opportunities for women, particularly in export industries; on the other hand, women are first to be terminated when industries are forced to downsize. Since the Asian financial crisis in 1997, women have been forced to seek additional sources of income to supplement their meager take-home pay and are thus working longer hours than men. A 1998 study revealed that the number of women employed in the manufacturing sector had decreased by 12 percent, while those engaged in mining and quarrying increased by more than 16 percent.

A government agency, the National Commission on the Role of Filipino Women (NCRFW), is mandated to conduct gender consciousness-raising programs among government policymakers, planners, implementers, women in government, and non-government institutions. Through its initiative, the Philippine Development Plan for Women was formulated and adopted by the government. Another agency, the Bureau of Women and Young Workers, a subordinate agency of the Department of Labor and Employment, looks after the interests of working women and children. There are laws in place protecting women from gender discrimination and sexual harassment and establishing community day-care centers for children, but the implementation of these laws is not always strictly monitored.

Though the minimum age of employment is 18 years for hazardous jobs and 15 years for non-hazardous jobs, it is not unusual to see children engaged in some form of labor to contribute to their family's daily survival. A government survey in 1995 estimates that 3.6 million children, mostly boys aged 5 to 17 years, were engaged in some form of child labor. At least 1 in 10 of them is engaged in heavy physical work.

COUNTRY HISTORY AND ECONOMIC DEVELOPMENT

1521. In his search for the Moluccas, Ferdinand Magellan docks in the Philippines and is slain by native chieftain Lapu-Lapu in battle.

1543. Spanish conquistador Ruy Lopez de Villalobos names the islands Filipinas after Spain's Philip II.

1565. Miguel Lopes de Legazpe establishes his base in the province of Cebu and later moves it to Manila.

1575. Spain takes control of non-Islamic areas and monopolizes trade.

1896. Nationalist Jose Rizal is executed by the Spaniards. He is later honored as a national hero.

1898. Spain sells the Philippines to the United States for $20 million after a mock battle in Manila Bay.

1900. The United States establishes a commonwealth government and enacts a law that will grant the Philippines independence by 1944.

1935. Manuel L. Quezon is elected president and a new constitution is adopted.

1941. Japanese forces invade Luzon.

1942. Japanese forces conquer Manila as U.S. troops on the Bataan peninsula surrender to Gen. Yamashita.

1945. Japanese occupation ends. The Philippines joins the United Nations as a charter member.

1946. The Philippines gains independence from the United States on July 4, becoming an independent republic with Manuel Roxas as president.

1947. The Philippines and the United States sign a Military Bases Agreement.

1948. President Roxas dies and is succeeded in office by Elpidio Quirino.

1950S. The Communist Hukbalahap Movement collapses. The country rebuilds itself and earns the distinction of becoming the second most prosperous nation in Asia, next to Japan.

1953. Ramon Magsaysay is elected to the presidency as standard bearer of the Nacionalista Party.

1957. President Magsaysay dies in an air crash and is succeeded in office by Vice President Carlos P. Garcia.

1961. Vice President Diosdado Macapagal is elected president over incumbent Garcia.

1965. Ferdinand E. Marcos is elected president, defeating incumbent Macapagal.

1967. The Philippines joins the Association of Southeast Asian Nations (ASEAN).

1969. President Marcos is re-elected and becomes the first president ever to be sworn in for a second time. The New People's Army is founded.

1972. President Marcos declares martial law in the guise of controlling a Communist rebellion. He orders the arrest of all opposition leaders, suspends the constitution, and dissolves the National Assembly. A new constitution is approved in a national referendum that proposes a return to a parliamentary form of government. President Marcos serves as president while Cesar Virata serves as prime minister. Muslim insurgency in the South intensifies.

1981. President Marcos ends 8 years of martial law and wins elections for a second 6-year term.

1983. Senator Benigno S. Aquino Jr. returns from exile in the United States and is assassinated on his arrival at the Manila airport. Marcos calls for a quick election to quell domestic unrest and international pressure.

1986. Millions of Filipinos hold a peaceful "People Power" revolution protesting President Marcos's victory amidst charges of ballot tampering. Marcos and his family are exiled to Hawaii, and Corazon C. Aquino, wife of the slain Senator Aquino, assumes the presidency. A new constitution is soon ratified.

1989. Limited autonomy is granted to Muslim provinces. Dispute escalates with China over the Spratly Islands. Military stages a coup d'état.

1990. A destructive earthquake, measuring 7.7 on the Richter scale, kills more than 1,600 and destroys property amounting to hundreds of millions of pesos. Typhoons batter the Visayas region.

1991. Eruption of the volcano Mount Pinatubo, burying many towns under lava including the ones where 2 American bases, Clark Air Base and the Subic Naval Bay Station, were located.

1992. Fidel V. Ramos is elected president. He unveils his blueprint for development called Philippines 2000. The Philippine Senate votes against the continued presence of U.S. military bases in the country.

1990s. The Philippine economy registers positive growth. International agencies express optimism about the country's development and dubs the country as one of Asia's "tiger cub" economies.

1998. Joseph E. Estrada, running under a social-justice platform, wins the presidency by a wide margin. The Philippines' fiscal deficit balloons to P111.66 billion from a deficit of P11.14 billion in 1986.

2000. President Estrada becomes the first Philippine president to be impeached by Congress. After mass "People Power" demonstrations, vice president Gloria Macapagal-Arroyo becomes the fourteenth President of the Republic.

FUTURE TRENDS

The greatest task at hand for the government of President Gloria Macapagal-Arroyo is to stimulate the economy to sustained growth and reduce poverty by ensuring that the benefits of development are evenly distributed. In order to achieve this, government must manage its huge **budget deficit** and the national debt, and both the private and **public sectors** must reduce unemployment by attracting more foreign investors or generating employment locally through entrepreneurship. The new president is an economist by training, and it is believed she can inspire confidence in investment. By 2001, forecasters were revising upward their predictions of GDP growth from 2.7 percent to 4 percent.

In May 2001, voters will elect 13 senators, 209 representatives, 53 party-list representatives, and 79 governors and vice-governors. The outcome of the elections is crucial to the political and economic stability of the country. Any perception of election irregularities such as vote-buying or cheating will diminish investor confidence. In fact, most foreign investors are postponing business decisions until the outcome of the elections is known. In addition, it is crucial that the candidates of the current administration win a majority of the positions in order to affirm its mandate and ensure the smooth passage of its priority bills in both the Senate and the House of Representatives.

Some of the existing problems that can cause destabilization are the remaining pockets of Communist insurgency, the continuing struggle by Muslim separatists, and the feeble, but divisive, attempts of the former president to regain the presidency. The precarious state of the country's environment and natural resources can also hurt political stability and economic growth. In 2000, the government was severely criticized for not being able to effectively address the crisis in waste management. Dozens of slum dwellers living near the Payatas dumpsite were buried alive under mountains of trash that collapsed on their houses after continuing rains. A temporary shutdown of the dumpsite resulted in the accumulation of uncollected garbage in Metro Manila and added to public perceptions of the government as incompetent and ineffective. The continuing degradation of the environment is negatively affecting health and livelihood. The heavily polluted air in Metro Manila is the primary cause of respiratory illnesses, which harms labor productivity. Water pollution disrupts marine-dependent livelihoods, as well as the country's source of food. Although initiatives for resource conservation and environmental protection have gone a long way, there is still much to be done in terms of strict implementation of the laws and instilling respect for the environment.

DEPENDENCIES

Philippines has no territories or colonies.

BIBLIOGRAPHY

Aganon, Marie E. *National Report, Philippines: Changing Labor Market and Women Employment.* Tokyo: Asian Productivity Organization, 2000.

Asian Development Outlook 2000. New York: Oxford University Press, 2000.

Austria, Edna Villencio et. al. *Philippines: Asian Approach to Resource Conservation and Environmental Protection.* Tokyo: Asian Productivity Organization, 2000.

Cabanilla, L.S. et. al. *Measuring Sustainability, Efficiency and Equitability of Philippine Agriculture.* Working Paper No. 98–05. Institute for Strategic Planning and Policy Studies, 1998.

Chew, Victor T. *Southeast Asian Tax Handbook.* International Bureau for Fiscal Documentation, 1996.

De Leon, Hector S. *The Fundamentals of Taxation.* 11th ed. Manila: Rex, 1993.

Department of Labor and Employment. <http://www.info.com.ph/~dolemis>. Accessed July 2001.

Department of Tourism. <http://www.tourism.gov.ph>. Accessed July 2001.

Department of Trade and Industry. <http://www.dti.gov.ph>. Accessed July 2001.

Gonzales, Felix R. *Updates on Philippine Fisheries.* Philippine Chamber of Food and Agriculture, 2000.

Harrison, Matthew. *Asia-Pacific Securities Markets.* Hong Kong: Financial Times, 1997.

Hoorway, James. "Philippines, Asian Economic Survey." *The Asian Wall Street Journal.* 23 October 2000.

Hutchcroft, Paul D. "Sustaining Economic and Political Reform: The Challenges Ahead." *The Philippines: New Directions in Domestic Policy and Foreign Relations.* David G. Timberman, ed. Asia Society, 1998.

Lamberte, Mario B. *The Philippines: Challenges for Sustaining the Economic Recovery.* Discussion Paper Series No. 2000–02. Philippine Institute for Development Studies, January 2000.

Mana-Ay, Ambrocio. "Philippines." *Rural Poverty Alleviation in Asia and the Pacific.* Tokyo: Asian Productivity Organization, 1999.

Panganiban, Artemio V. "An Introduction to the Supreme Court." *Law.* Vol. XXIV, No. 8, Integrated Bar of the Philippines, 1998.

Rodlauer, M. et. al. *Philippines: Toward Sustainable and Rapid Growth.* Occasional Paper 187. Washington: International Monetary Fund, 2000.

U.S. Central Intelligence Agency. *The World Factbook, 2000.* <http://www.cia.gov/cia/publications/factbook>. Accessed December 2000.

Villegas, Bernardo M. *Philippine Economic Prospects under the Estrada Administration.* <http://www.asiasociety.org/publications/update_cris_villegas.html>. Accessed December 2000.

—Maria Cecilia T. Ubarra

QATAR

State of Qatar
Dawlat Qatar

CAPITAL: Doha (Ad-Dawhah).

MONETARY UNIT: Qatari riyal (QR). One riyal equals 100 dirhams. Coins are in denominations of 50, 25, 10, 5, and 1 dirhams. Paper currency is in denominations of QR500, 100, 50, 10, 5, and 1.

CHIEF EXPORTS: Petroleum products, fertilizers, and steel.

CHIEF IMPORTS: Machinery and transport equipment, food, and chemicals.

GROSS DOMESTIC PRODUCT: US$15.1 billion (purchasing power parity, 2000 est.).

BALANCE OF TRADE: **Exports:** US$9.8 billion (f.o.b., 2000 est.). **Imports:** US$3.8 billion (f.o.b., 2000 est.).

COUNTRY OVERVIEW

LOCATION AND SIZE. Qatar is a tiny peninsula jutting into the Persian Gulf and bordering only Saudi Arabia. With an area of 11,437 square kilometers (4,416 square miles) and a short coastline of 563 kilometers (345 miles), Qatar is slightly smaller than the state of Connecticut. Qatar's capital city, Doha, is located in the east on the Persian Gulf and is home to 320,000 people. Other major cities include Umm Sa'id and al-Khawr.

POPULATION. The population of Qatar was estimated at 769,152 in July of 2001, a marked increase from the 1990 population of about 486,000. Arabs make up 40 percent of the population, but there are also Pakistanis (18 percent), Indians (18 percent), Iranians (10 percent). Non-Qataris make up the largest proportion of the country's **labor force**. Since 1998, the population growth has slowed down, as evidenced in the 5.3 percent drop in the population in 1998. The slowdown is believed to come as a result of the government's "Qatarizing" movement—to encourage the employment of local workers—following the sharp decline in oil prices in 1997 and 1998.

Qatar's population growth has accelerated since the 1960s, mainly as the result of the influx of large numbers of expatriate workers into the country. Between the late 1960s and 1997, the population grew from 70,000 to 522,000, of whom only 160,000 are Qatari nationals. According to the Economist Intelligence Unit (EIU) *Country Profile* for 2000, the population growth rate reached 1.5 percent in 1999, and is projected to reach 1.8 percent in the coming decade. The expatriate worker community, which accounts for 70 percent of the population, is largely made up of Indians and Pakistanis.

Like most Arab countries, Qatar's population is mostly young; 27 percent of the population is younger than 15. Also like many developing countries, a majority of Qataris (90 percent) are concentrated in urban areas. Major cities have been growing at the rate of 2 percent annually. Almost 80 percent of the population is concentrated in the capital, Doha. Other major cities include Messaieed, an industrial township 124 kilometers (77 miles) south of Doha.

OVERVIEW OF ECONOMY

Qatar's domestic economy is heavily dependent on the hydrocarbons sector. Oil accounts for about 40 percent of **gross domestic product** (GDP) and about 63 percent of government revenues. Qatar's oil reserves are small relative to its Persian Gulf neighbors, although its output has tripled in recent years with the exploration of new fields. Other non-oil industries exist, but they are heavily dependent on the oil sector, which means that Qatar's dependence on oil is likely to continue for a long time to come.

More importantly, Qatar has the third-largest reserves of natural gas in the world. Its reserves are expected to last for 250 years at the current rate of production. The government has increased emphasis on the natural gas sector since 1990 with the goal of replacing oil as the main

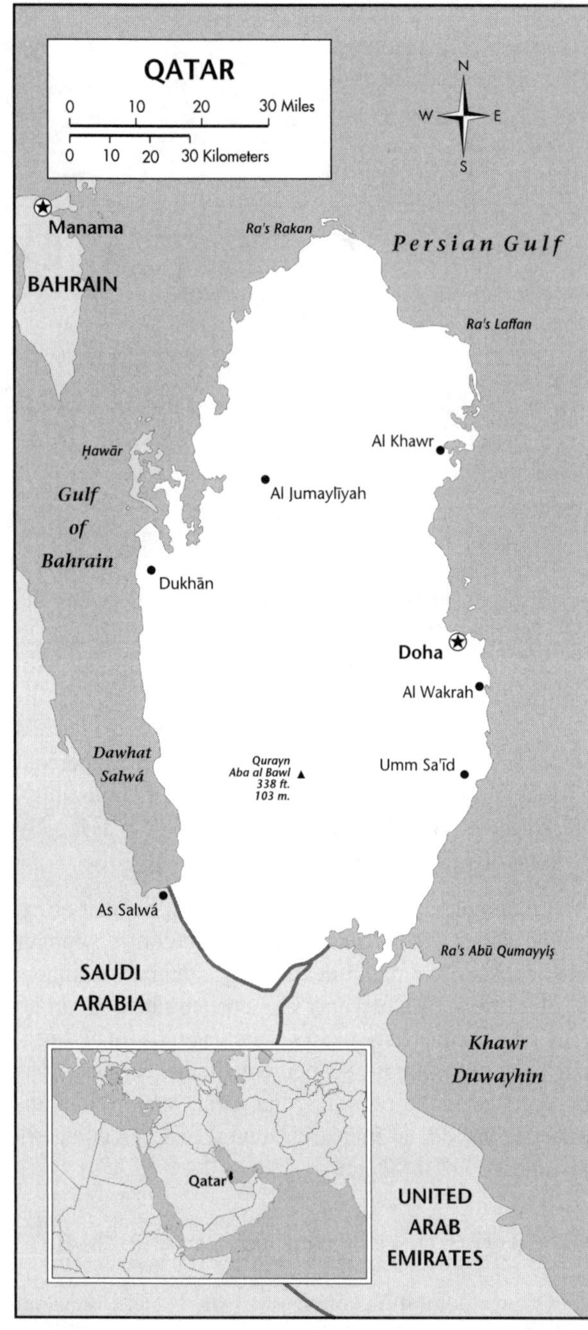

source of revenue. Several hydrocarbon-related industries, mainly petrochemicals, have also been set up since 1990. It is likely to take years before this diversification strategy begins to yield profit, however, largely because of the huge investments and heavy foreign borrowing that the government needed for the development of the natural gas sector. These loans would have to be paid before the government could show a profit.

Agriculture is not a major contributor to the economy. The state, which owns all agricultural land, has attempted to promote production by increasing the number of small farms. These efforts have been largely unsuccessful, mainly because of the lack of water for irrigation.

Qatar entered the 20th century as a tribal settlement on the peninsula nominally controlled by the al-Thani tribe, whose exact origins remain unknown. Real power, however, rested with the British, who effectively controlled the country's foreign relations. The al-Thani ruling family had signed a series of treaties with the British in the 19th century. In return the British promised protection against other powerful regional tribes, especially the Wahhabis from neighboring Saudi Arabia and against Bahrain, which claimed Qatar as its own. By the end of World War I, however, Qatar's importance had waned, largely due to the diversion of British trade routes to India after the opening of the Suez Canal. Unlike bigger oil producers in the Gulf region, oil was not discovered in Qatar until the 1950s. Until the 1970s, foreign companies, who owned and managed the oil industry in return for fees paid to the al-Thani family, dominated oil production. By the early 1990s, many of the foreign subsidiaries had become completely state-owned. After several Gulf sheikhdoms declared their independence from the British, Qatar followed suit on September 3, 1971, after securing continued support from the al-Saud tribe that ruled neighboring Saudi Arabia.

Since the early 1970s, increased oil revenue has allowed the government to embark on massive development projects that brought rapid material and social change. The state's role in the economy remains central, as the government controls the oil revenue. Income from oil fluctuates according to changes in world oil prices. The government's dependence on oil revenue and decades of government overspending have resulted in recurring **budget deficits**, especially during low oil prices, and a high **external debt**, which was estimated by the EIU to have reached US$12.2 billion in 1999.

Since 1997, at the recommendation of the International Monetary Fund (IMF), Qatar has embarked on a program to reduce **subsidies** on utilities, gasoline, wheat, and sugar and to introduce charges for health care and education for the purpose of stabilizing the **exchange rate**. As a result, the expatriate community in Qatar no longer enjoys free medical benefits. Services to Qataris, however, continue to be heavily subsidized by the state. In 1999, an official stock market was set up and the government issued 2 domestic bonds and 1 international bond as a means to develop alternative financing methods. In 2001, the government plans to **privatize** the generation, transmission, and distribution of utilities, and to continue its policy of encouraging locals to seek employment to reduce the country's dependence on foreign workers. The government is also expected to continue to encourage the **private sector** to play a bigger role in the economy.

POLITICS, GOVERNMENT, AND TAXATION

Qatar is an absolute monarchy that has been ruled by the al-Thani family since the mid-1800s. It is currently headed by Sheikh Hamad, who ousted his father, Sheikh Khalifa, in a bloodless *coup d'etat* (a takeover of a government) in June 1995. Although autocratic (ruling through absolute power), the ruling family has been committed to building the state and developing its resources. Since taking over, the widely popular Sheikh Hamad has embarked on an ambitious political and economic reform program to modernize the state and address the decline in economic performance that began in the early 1990s. In 1999, the first municipal elections in the country's history were held, followed by the establishment of a constituent assembly in mid-1999 entrusted with the task of drawing up a permanent constitution and providing for an elected parliament. Sheikh Hamad has also allowed greater political freedoms. Despite these efforts, however, ultimate authority continues to rest with him and his circle of advisors. The sheikh remains the source of absolute authority and enjoys the power to dissolve the Consultative Council (a 35-member advisory council appointed by the sheikh) and rule by decree, powers given to him by the 1970 provisional constitution.

Qatar is a **welfare state**, where health care and education are almost free. Since 1998, the government has moved to introduce small charges for these services, especially for health care, in an effort to boost the government's budget by reducing spending. However, most utilities in 2001 continue to be heavily subsidized by the government, and education remains entirely free. Qataris do not pay taxes and the government's budget continues to rely heavily on oil revenue.

INFRASTRUCTURE, POWER, AND COMMUNICATIONS

Qatar enjoys an extensive and highly-developed **infrastructure** that has been built and developed with oil wealth since the 1950s. The country is served by a network of over 1,230 kilometers (764 miles) of primary and secondary roads, linking Doha with major industrial and oil producing areas. Most of these roads, some 1,107 kilometers (688 miles), are paved. The country has no railway system. Qatar has 4 airports, 2 of which have unpaved runways. Doha International Airport is the country's major airport. Twenty-eight airlines service Doha and bring in most of the country's tourists. Qatar has 3 ports and harbors: Doha, Halul Island, and Umm Sa'id.

Electrical power is provided to Qataris from the Ras Aby Aboud and Ras Abu Fontas power stations. In addition, there are 6 gas turbines and an estimated 5,000 diesel units spread across the country. Altogether, Qatar's total power capacity is estimated at 2,019 megawatts (MW). In 2000, the government drew up plans to build an independent power station with a capacity of 1,902 MW to meet the increasing demands of industrial projects and satisfy rising power demand, which peaks in the summer due to soaring temperatures. Several foreign companies, which are expected to own 60 percent of the project, have submitted bids, but the project's completion date remained unknown in 2001.

Telecommunications services in Qatar are thoroughly modern. Telephone service is provided by the Qatar Public Telecommunications Corporation (Q-Tel), which is 55 percent government owned. There are 430,000 landlines in the country, and in 2001, Q-Tel will be installing additional exchanges for Doha and Ras Laffan. Q-Tel also provides Internet and cable television access.

Communications

Country	Telephones[a]	Telephones, Mobile/Cellular[a]	Radio Stations[b]	Radios[a]	TV Stations[a]	Televisions[a]	Internet Service Providers[c]	Internet Users[c]
Qatar	142,000	43,476	AM 6; FM 5; shortwave 1	256,000	2	230,000	1	45,000
United States	194 M	69.209 M (1998)	AM 4,762; FM 5,542; shortwave 18	575 M	1,500	219 M	7,800	148 M
Saudi Arabia	3.1 M (1998)	1 M (1998)	AM 43; FM 31; shortwave 2	6.25 M	117	5.1 M	42 (2001)	400,000 (2001)
Bahrain	152,000	58,543	AM 2, FM 3, shortwave 0	338,000	4	275,000	1	37,500

[a]Data is for 1997 unless otherwise noted.
[b]Data is for 1998 unless otherwise noted.
[c]Data is for 2000 unless otherwise noted.

SOURCE: CIA *World Factbook 2001* [Online].

ECONOMIC SECTORS

Qatar's economic sectors reflect the small size of the country. Qatar relies heavily on the oil sector, exporting some 650,000 barrels a day, mostly to Europe and eastern Asia. The services sector is the country's second-largest economic sector and most important non-oil sector. According to the CIA *World Factbook* for 2001, the sector's contribution to GDP reached 50 percent in 1996. The industrial sector is also an important contributor to the economy, accounting for 49 percent of GDP in 1996. This sector is dominated by the oil industry, which accounts for a little over 40 percent of GDP. The non-oil manufacturing sector, on the other hand, accounts for only 8.8 percent, according to the EIU. Agriculture is an insignificant contributor to the economy, accounting for roughly 1 percent of GDP.

One of the greatest problems facing all of Qatar's economic sectors is the dependence on oil revenue and the adverse impact of the fluctuation of oil prices on the country's investment climate and fiscal deficit. Lower oil prices generally mean lower revenue for the government. Reduced government revenues in turn translate into lower government spending on economic projects, a situation that brings about an overall slowdown in the economy.

Recognizing these obstacles, Qatar has moved to diversify its sources of income by developing its liquefied natural gas (LNG) industry and expanding its industrial base. Qatar's efforts to diversify its economic base have not been very successful. Most economic activity continues to be centered on oil. Qatar has 2 natural gas plants that have been in existence since 1980. With the help of international oil companies, Qatar launched 2 LNG projects in 1992, the North Field development at Ras Laffan city. The first phase of the project was completed in 1992, and the second project is scheduled to start in 2001. According to the EIU *Country Profile* for 2000, once completed, the North Field will be "the largest single concentration of natural gas" in the world. The government invested some US$20 billion in the development of the North Field between 1995 and 2000. However, it is not expected to make a profit from these projects until its debts to the companies that financed the exploration projects are paid. Therefore, Qatar's dependence on oil is likely to continue.

Qatar
GDP–COMPOSITION BY SECTOR–1996 est.

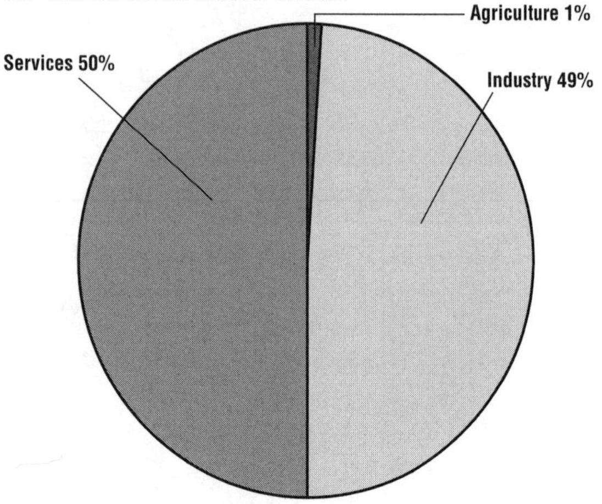

SOURCE: *CIA World Factbook 2000* [Online].

AGRICULTURE

The government, which owns all agricultural land, has attempted to encourage agricultural production, accounting for only 1 percent of GDP. Given the scarcity of fresh surface water, however, most agricultural activity is dependent on wells. The government has also attempted to increase the number of small farms. As a result, the number of farms has increased from 338 in 1975 to 891 in 1995. Most farmers are absentee landlords, who are relatively uninterested in investing in agriculture, and the land is mostly cultivated by foreign workers.

Qatar's agricultural products are consumed locally, providing 70 percent and 40 percent of the consumption of summer and winter vegetables, respectively. In addition to vegetables, Qatar produces cereals, fruits and dates, eggs, poultry, and dairy products. Despite a noticeable increase in agricultural production in the course of the past 20 years, however, Qatar continues to rely on food imports, especially foodstuffs and live animals, which account for roughly 10 percent of total imports.

INDUSTRY

MINING. Qatar's economy is heavily dependent on oil. Oil accounts for 40 percent of GDP and 63 percent of the state's income. The Qatar General Petroleum Corporation estimates that Qatar's total oil reserves have reached 12.2 billion barrels, up from 3.7 billion in 1995, due to the exploration of new oil fields by western companies since 1990. Oil production has risen consistently since 1994. Average production reached 854,000 barrels a day in May 2000, up from 410,000 barrels a day in 1994. Despite the increased production levels, Qatar's output is relatively low by regional standards.

In addition to oil, Qatar has been a producer and exporter of natural gas since 1980, when the first liquefied natural gas (LNG) plant was opened. Altogether, there are 3 LNG plants in the country, and a fourth is being constructed. The first plant was opened in 1980, producing up to 1,284 tons a day of propane, 851 tons a day of butane, 588 tons a day of condensate, and 1,350 tons a day of ethane-rich gas. A second LNG factory was opened in 1982, and it also produces large quantities of propane, butane, condensate, and other gases. The third LNG project was completed at Ras Laffan in 1992 as the first phase of the North Field Project. According to the EIU, the plant produces some 22.6 million cubic meters a day of gas and around 50,000 barrels a day of condensates. A fourth project, phase two of the Ras Laffan North Field project, is being constructed in 2001 to produce ethylene and polyethylene for use as feedstock (raw materials used for chemical and biological processes) by Qatar Chemical Complex. The project also aims to export 22 million cubic meters of gas a day to neighboring Persian Gulf states. LNG products are mostly exported to generate foreign exchange but are also used as feedstock for the emerging petrochemical industry.

MANUFACTURING. Qatar's non-oil industrial base is relatively small. However, the contribution of the non-oil manufacturing sector to the economy has increased steadily since the 1970s, in large part thanks to the huge investments and efforts by the country to build a non-oil industrial base. Since 1992, the government has moved to establish the Ministry of Energy and Industry to encourage industrialization and to set up the Qatar Industrial Development Bank to provide loans with easy terms to would-be investors. In 2001, Qatar enacted a law allowing foreign companies a 100-percent ownership of projects in some sectors, including education, tourism, and health care. Despite these efforts, however, industrial output remains low. The sector's contribution to GDP reached 8.8 percent in 1999.

Qatar's industrial base is dominated by the petrochemicals sector, which is controlled by the government. It is the biggest producer of low-density polyethylene and chemical fertilizers in the world. The sector has traditionally accounted for 40 percent of GDP. However, since 1998, the sector's contribution to GDP has been affected by the economic slowdown in Asia, the primary market for Qatar's oil products. Efforts are underway in 2001 to set up new petrochemical ventures that are expected to resume exports once the economic slump affecting Asia is over. In addition to petrochemicals, there is a small steel production operated by the 100-percent state-owned Qatar Steel Company. The sector produces 500,000 metric tons a year. Since 1998, the government has attempted to privatize the company by selling 49 percent of its shares on the Doha Securities Market to improve its profitability and as part of an overall scheme to reform the economy. The government, however, was forced to delay the partial privatization of the company as a result of the poor performance of the Doha Securities Market since 1998, which meant that the company's shares will be sold for much less than the government had hoped for.

SERVICES

TOURISM. Tourism is a very negligible contributor to Qatar's economy. Since 1996, the government has attempted to establish a tourism industry and to turn Qatar into a major destination for international sporting events. The government has, as a result, invested heavily in the construction sector. These efforts came to a halt in the wake of the 1998 spending cuts, which were prompted by the sharp fall in world oil prices, but were revived in the 2001 budget, as oil prices rose again in 2000.

FINANCIAL SERVICES. Qatar has a fledgling financial sector regulated by the Central Bank of Qatar. There are 14 banks operating in the country, including 5 locally-owned banks that hold 80 percent of the financial sector's assets. There are also 16 currency exchange companies. There are no investment banks. The Qatar National Bank, the country's largest bank, is the only bank involved in the government's hydrocarbon development program, and handles all the government's business. Other banks include the Qatar International Islamic Bank, Doha Bank, and the Commercial Bank of Qatar.

The government introduced new regulations in August 1995 to ease earlier restrictions placed on financial transactions. Despite these efforts, some restrictions continue to affect interest rates paid by banks on deposit accounts. Although the Central Bank requires banks to disclose accounts according to international standards, there is growing concern that some banks do not disclose their **non-performing loans**.

The Doha Securities Market (DSM) was established in 1997 with QR21 billion (US$5.8 billion) in assets. Nineteen companies are listed on the DSM, but trading has been generally weak, resulting in a 0.5 percent drop in the stock market index at the end of 1999.

RETAIL. Lacking many large commercial centers other than Doha and its suburbs, Qatar has a relatively undeveloped **retail** sector. While Doha is home to a variety of retail stores, including fast food franchises such as McDonald's, the majority of towns in the interior of the country have small family-owned shops, farmer's markets, and temporary roadside stands.

INTERNATIONAL TRADE

Over the past decade, Qatar has relied more and more on imports. The value of imports more than doubled since 1990, peaking to US$3.9 billion in 1999, up from US$1.2 billion in 1989. Imports have traditionally varied from basic foodstuffs to **consumer goods**. Since the early 1990s, however, capital purchases for gas development projects have accounted for approximately 40 percent of imports. The volume of imports is expected to rise by

Trade (expressed in billions of US$): Qatar

	Exports	Imports
1975	1.805	.413
1980	5.672	1.423
1985	N/A	1.139
1990	N/A	1.695
1995	N/A	N/A
1998	N/A	N/A

SOURCE: International Monetary Fund. *International Financial Statistics Yearbook 1999.*

Exchange rates: Qatar

Qatari riyals (QR) per US$1	
2001	3.6400
2000	N/A
1999	N/A
1998	N/A
1997	N/A
1996	N/A

Note: Rate is fixed.

SOURCE: CIA *World Factbook 2001* [ONLINE].

2002, largely because of revived government spending in the construction business.

Imports of foreign goods are dominated by Organization for Economic Development and Cooperation (OECD) suppliers, namely Japan, the United Kingdom, the United States, Italy, and Germany. (The OECD is a 30-member organization that provides governments with a forum to discuss and develop economic and social policy.) In 1998, Japan overtook the United Kingdom as Qatar's major supplier of machinery and manufactures, providing 15.4 percent of total imports. Imports from the United Kingdom accounted for 13.9 percent of total imports, followed by France, the United States, and Germany.

Qatar's exports are dominated by crude oil, although its importance has begun to decline in recent years due to the increase in the export of LNGs. As a result of its dependence on crude oil, which roughly accounts for 56 percent of exports, Qatar's export bill has fluctuated with world oil prices. Export revenue surged from US$4.36 billion in 1998 to US$6.6 billion in 1999. In 1998, Japan was also Qatar's largest export partner, accounting for 58.1 percent of the total export bill. South Korea came next at 11.0 percent, followed by Singapore, the United States, and Thailand.

The substantial oil revenue has allowed Qatar to maintain a **trade surplus**. However, the transfer of large amounts of money in **remittances** by the large expatriate workers community has consistently resulted in a deficit in the current account for most of the past decade. The deficit peaked to US$1.6 billion in 1993, and the government's efforts to reduce the number of expatriate workers is expected to reverse the trend in the coming years. Similarly, the service balance has registered a deficit for much of the past decade, due to the government's heavy spending on defense and capital imports related to the LNG development. In 1999, the deficit in the service balance reached US$1.5 billion. The income balance also has registered a deficit as a result of the interest on the country's mounting **foreign debt**.

MONEY

The value of the Qatari riyal has remained stable since it was first issued in 1969. The majority of Qatar's exports are denominated by the U.S. dollar. The Central Bank of Qatar has kept a **fixed exchange rate** of QR3.64: US$1, despite a fall in the value of the dollar in 1995, mainly to prevent **inflation**.

POVERTY AND WEALTH

Qataris enjoy one of the highest living standards in the world. Per capita income is high by both regional and international standards. In 1999, per capita income was estimated at US$21,841, US$1,803 higher than 1998. By contrast, per capita income in the United States is US$29,683.

The country's vast wealth from oil revenue and its relatively small population have allowed the government to invest heavily in education and in providing first-class health and educational services to its citizens since the 1970s. As a result, the literacy rate in the country is estimated by the United Nations to have reached 80 percent in 1995. Vast oil wealth has also allowed the government to offer heavily-subsidized or free services, such as public education.

GDP per Capita (US$)

Country	1996	1997	1998	1999	2000
Qatar	21,300	16,700	17,100	17,000	20,300
United States	28,600	30,200	31,500	33,900	36,200
Saudi Arabia	10,600	10,300	9,000	9,000	10,500
Bahrain	13,000	13,700	13,100	13,700	15,900

Note: Data are estimates.

SOURCE: *Handbook of the Nations*, 17th, 18th, 19th and 20th editions for 1996, 1997, 1998 and 1999 data; CIA *World Factbook 2001* [Online] for 2000 data.

Household Consumption in PPP Terms

Country	All food	Clothing and footwear	Fuel and power[a]	Health care[b]	Education[b]	Transport & Communications	Other
Qatar	22	12	11	5	13	8	29
United States	13	9	9	4	6	8	51
Saudi Arabia	N/A	N/A	N/A	N/A	N/A	N/A	N/A
Bahrain	32	7	8	1	6	9	37

Data represent percentage of consumption in PPP terms.
[a]Excludes energy used for transport.
[b]Includes government and private expenditures.

SOURCE: World Bank. *World Development Indicators 2000.*

No information is available about the distribution of wealth in Qatar, but poverty among Qataris is believed to be virtually non-existent.

WORKING CONDITIONS

Qataris have traditionally been uninterested in working at menial jobs and have instead relied on foreign workers in the administration of their country. Locals generally tend to occupy high positions in government ministries and private businesses, but the bulk of the manual labor is performed by Indians and Pakistanis. Unemployment among nationals is believed to be quite low (figures are unavailable). Since 1998, the government has launched a program to encourage Qataris to replace foreign-born laborers. This program also expanded labor training programs for Qatari nationals. No official statistics are available to assess its success.

The Ministry of Interior controls all transactions relating to foreign workers in the country. There is no minimum wage requirement. Salaries are negotiable. Expatriate workers pay for health care and are required to pay annual residency fees in the amount of US$275. According to the U.S. State Department *Country Commercial Guide, 2001*, the wives and children of expatriate workers are required to pay US$137 and US$82 respectively in residency fees. Qatar has no tradition of labor unions, although trade associations and labor unions are not forbidden by law.

COUNTRY HISTORY AND ECONOMIC DEVELOPMENT

MID-1800s. Al Khalifa, Bahrain's ruling family, establish Qatar.

1915. Al Khalifa family expels the Turks from Qatar.

1916. Qatar signs treaty to receive protection from United Kingdom.

1949. Sheikh Abdullah abdicates in favor of his son Ali.

1950s. Oil is discovered in commercial quantities.

1971. Qatar declares independence from the British.

1973. World oil crisis. Qatar's oil revenue increases dramatically.

1981. Qatar, Kuwait, Bahrain, Saudi Arabia, Oman, and the United Arab Emirates form the Gulf Cooperation Council.

1995. Sheikh Hamad deposes his father, Sheikh Khalifa, in a bloodless coup.

1997. Economic reform program launched.

1999. The first municipal elections are held.

FUTURE TRENDS

Qatar entered the 21st century under a cloud of uncertainty. Despite the large sums of money that have entered the government's coffers from the sale of oil in the last 50 years, decades of government overspending and misuse have created serious financial constraints, mainly large foreign debt and recurring budget deficits. Despite the government's attempts to address these 2 problems by diversifying the country's economic base and introducing reform, Qatar's dependence on oil and the government's large role in the economy have meant that economic performance will continue to fluctuate according to oil prices. As a result, economic performance will be best when oil prices are high.

Given the structure of the economy, the government is expected to proceed with the "Qatarization" of its labor force. The government is also expected to forge ahead with the economic reform program started in 1997, which will seek to increase the role of the private sector, and to push for the privatization of more state-owned enterprises. Given that Qatar's budgetary problems are unlikely to be resolved until revenue from the sale of liquid natural gas exports begins to flow, the government will have no choice but to proceed with the promised democratization process and to engage the population politically to deflect the potentially disruptive impact of declining conditions. Political participation will engage citizens in the decision-making process by allowing them to elect their representatives through a popular vote, hence reducing the perception among the largest proportion of Qataris that they are outside the political process.

DEPENDENCIES

Qatar has no territories or colonies.

BIBLIOGRAPHY

Economist Intelligence Unit. *Country Profile, Qatar*. London: Economist Intelligence Unit, 2000.

U.S. Central Intelligence Agency. *World Factbook 2000.* <http://www.odci.gov/cia/publications/factbook/index.html>. Accessed August 2001.

U.S. Department of State. *FY 2001 Country Commercial Guide: Qatar.* <http://www.state.gov/www/about_state/business/com_guides/ 2001/nea/index.html>. Accessed January 2001.

—Reem Nuseibeh

SAMOA

Independent State of Samoa
Malo Sa'oloto Tuto'atasi o Samoa i Sisifo

CAPITAL: Apia.

MONETARY UNIT: Tala (WST). One tala equals 100 sene. Coins are 1, 2, 5, 10, 20, and 50 sene and 1 tala. Notes are 2, 5, 10, 20, 50 and 100 talas.

CHIEF EXPORTS: Copra, coconut oil, coconut cream, taro, fish, and kava.

CHIEF IMPORTS: Food, machines and transport equipment, manufactures, and fuels.

GROSS DOMESTIC PRODUCT: US$571 million (purchasing power parity, 2000 est.).

BALANCE OF TRADE: **Exports:** US$17 million (f.o.b., 2000). **Imports:** US$90 million (f.o.b., 2000).

COUNTRY OVERVIEW

LOCATION AND SIZE. Located in the South Pacific Ocean, about halfway between Hawaii and New Zealand and just east of the International Date Line. The country consists of 2 large islands—Savai'i to the west and Upolu to the east—and several smaller islands. It has a land area of 2,850 square kilometers (1,100 square miles) and a coastline of 403 kilometers (250 miles), making it slightly smaller than Rhode Island. The capital city, Apia is located on the north coast of Upolu.

POPULATION. The population of Samoa was estimated at 169,200 in mid-2000, an increase of 17 percent since the census of 1991. In 2000 the birth rate stood at 30.3 per 1,000 people, while the death rate was 6.4 per 1,000. With a projected annual population growth rate of only 0.6 percent between 2000 and 2010, Samoa would have 179,000 by 2010; the U.S. Central Intelligence Agency (CIA) *World Factbook 2001* estimated the population at 179,058 for 2001, though. The low growth rate resulted mainly from a high rate of outward-migration, which in 2000 was estimated at 17.6 per 1,000. This migration is mostly to the United States and New Zealand.

The population is predominantly of Samoan (Polynesian) ethnic origin, although about 7 percent also have European origins. Only 21 percent of the population live in an urban area, with Apia accounting for most of this. The urban growth rate is twice as high as the general growth rate, but at 1.2 percent per year still relatively low by Pacific standards.

OVERVIEW OF ECONOMY

As a small island country in the South Pacific, Samoa (formerly Western Samoa) has an economy largely based on agriculture, government and tourist services, and **remittances** from Samoans living abroad. The majority of households in Samoa are dependent on subsistence production for at least part of their food supply and other basic items. At the same time, most households rely on cash income to provide basics that are not available from subsistence. In other words, food products grown or caught for personal consumption—such as taro, coconut, banana, fish, and crayfish—are also sold to generate cash for village households.

The export economy mainly relies on agricultural products. The most important of these are coconut products such as copra (the dried flesh of the coconut), copra meal, coconut oil, and coconut cream. In the early 1990s taro (a tropical Asian plant) was an important export but was destroyed by disease in 1993 and is only starting to re-emerge as an export. In the late 1990s the development of a commercial fishing operation illustrated the competitive advantage Samoa has in this industry, with its proximity to fish canning facilities in American Samoa. Timber has been a modest source of export income in the past, but is not likely to be significant for 25 years when recently planted trees mature.

Manufacturing in Samoa is mainly to supply the domestic market, although there have been some initiatives to foster export manufacturing using tax breaks. Tourism grew steadily through the 1990s and has

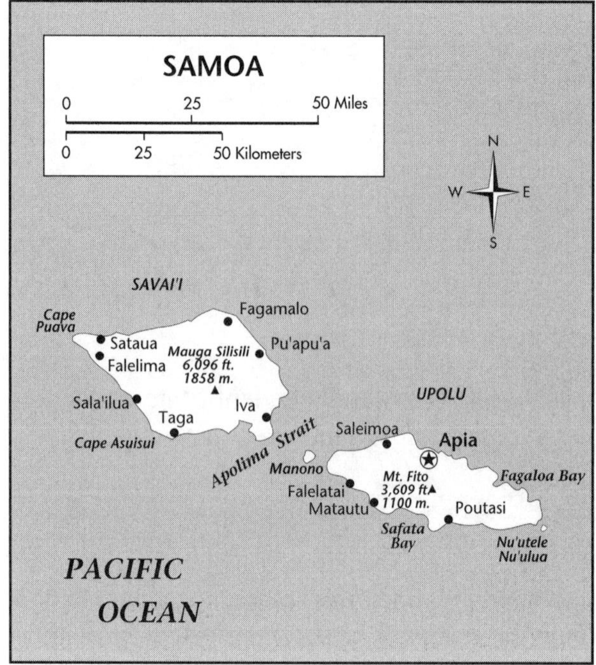

considerable potential, especially if tourism **infrastructure** is developed.

Besides tourism, remittances and international aid offset Samoa's annual trade imbalance. Remittances from relatives overseas are an important source of income for many families in Samoa and a significant source of foreign exchange for the country. The largest source of remittance income, comes from the Samoan population living in New Zealand. Another substantial amount comes Samoan communities in Hawaii and California. International aid contributes about one-quarter of **gross domestic product** (GDP) and supports many of the government's development projects. The largest aid donors are Japan, Australia, and New Zealand followed by multilateral aid agencies such as the Asian Development Bank.

POLITICS, GOVERNMENT, AND TAXATION

Traditionally, political power in Samoa was held by matai (chiefs), whose positions were generally inherited, although individuals with charisma and power can earn positions. The matai system survives to the present day, but was changed during the colonial and post-colonial periods. Political turbulence characterized the 19th century in Samoa, during which matai-lead governments formed and reformed, often with support from traders, missionaries, and other foreigners. In 1899 the colonial powers of Germany, Great Britain, and the United States resolved this impasse for their own purposes by signing a treaty granting Germany control of Western Samoa and the United States control of Eastern (American) Samoa. Western Samoa, however, was occupied by New Zealand during World War I and was a colony of that country until it gained independence in 1962. In the 1920s the Mau movement, advocating non-payment of tax and whose ultimate goal was independence, was formed. The movement was suppressed by New Zealander troops in the late 1920s but it remains a symbol of nationalism to the present day.

Samoa has a parliamentary system with the Paramount Chief of Samoa as the ceremonial head of state. Until 1991, members of Parliament were elected by the matai, but in that year universal suffrage for all citizens 21 years and over was introduced. Tradition is still maintained, however, since only matai can be elected to 1 of the 49 parliamentary seats. There are 2 main parties, the Human Rights Protection Party and the Samoa National Development Party, but these parties tend to revolve around personalities more than political positions that allow them to be labeled left, center, or right.

Until recently the main domestic sources of government revenue were trade **tariffs** and, to a lesser extent, **income taxes**. In 1994, a **value added** goods and services tax (VAGST) was introduced despite popular opposition. The VAGST of 10 percent is imposed on most items of consumption including imports, with exceptions including unprocessed local primary production, financial services, and hospital and educational services. Since this tax's creation, most individuals do not have to pay income tax and trade tariffs have been reduced.

INFRASTRUCTURE, POWER, AND COMMUNICATIONS

The 2 main islands of Upolu and Savai'i are quite well serviced by 790 kilometers (491 miles) of roads, of which about 40 percent are paved. Nearly all villages can be accessed by road, and bus services reach most parts of the country. The 2 islands are linked by passenger and car ferries with frequent sailings. The size of the country and the existence of road and ferry services mean that internal air travel is relatively rare. The sole international airport, Faleolo Airport, on the northwest coast of Upolu, provides international air passage to New Zealand, Fiji, Tonga, American Samoa, Australia, and Honolulu, Hawaii. Polynesian Airlines, owned by the Samoan government, and Samoa Air are 2 of the main regional carriers. Samoa also has 2 unpaved airports on Savai'i for domestic travel.

While about 62 percent of Samoa's electricity is generated with the use of imported fuel, the remainder is generated by a local hydroelectric station. Telephone services extend to most parts of the country, although only about 1 in 4 households has a telephone and public telephones are rare. International telephone service is usually good. In 2000 there was at least 1 Internet service provider.

Communications

Country	Telephones[a]	Telephones, Mobile/Cellular[a]	Radio Stations[b]	Radios[a]	TV Stations[a]	Televisions[a]	Internet Service Providers[c]	Internet Users[c]
Samoa	8,000	1,545 (1998)	AM 1; FM 3; shortwave 0	178,000	6	11,000	2	500
United States	194 M	69.209 M (1998)	AM 4,762; FM 5,542; shortwave 18	575 M	1,500	219 M	7,800	148 M
Philippines	1.9 M	1.959 M (1998)	AM 366; FM 290; shortwave 3 (1999)	11.5 M	31	3.7 M	33	500,000
Solomon Islands	8,000	658	AM 3; FM 0; shortwave 0	57,000	0	3,000	1	3,000

[a]Data is for 1997 unless otherwise noted.
[b]Data is for 1998 unless otherwise noted.
[c]Data is for 2000 unless otherwise noted.

SOURCE: CIA *World Factbook 2001* [Online].

ECONOMIC SECTORS

Calculating the size of different economic sectors is very difficult for Samoa's economy because a large proportion of the population works in the informal subsistence sector. In Samoa, there has been a relative decline in subsistence activities during the 1990s dropping as a percentage of GDP from 29.7 percent in 1992 to 17.7 percent in 1998, according to the Asian Development Bank. Over the same period, agriculture declined slightly from 21.2 percent to 19.3 percent of GDP. On the other hand, industry increased considerably from 15.8 to 23.7 percent as did services from 32 to 38.6 percent of GDP. In the **labor force** data, much of the agricultural employment is in unpaid village work—either informal or subsistence—so that it is difficult to compare these data with those from other countries. Official counts, however, show about 23,000 workers in the formal sector out of a total labor force of 42,494.

AGRICULTURE

About two-thirds of all households in Samoa depend on a mixture of **subsistence agriculture** and **cash cropping**. The non-monetary agricultural production of the country was estimated to comprise 17.7 percent of GDP in 1998, falling from 29.7 percent in 1992. This was partly a result of the growth of other parts of the economy, rather than a contraction of the subsistence economy. In 1998 non-subsistence agriculture and fishing

Samoa
GDP–COMPOSITION BY SECTOR–1996 est.

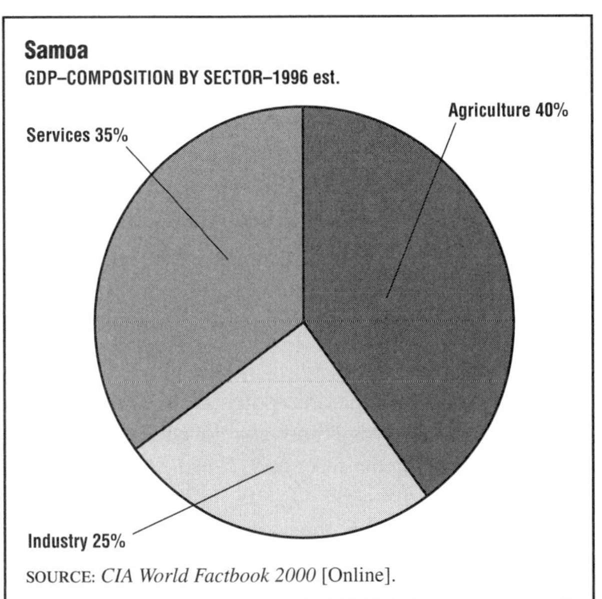

SOURCE: *CIA World Factbook 2000* [Online].

Samoa
LABOR FORCE–BY OCCUPATION

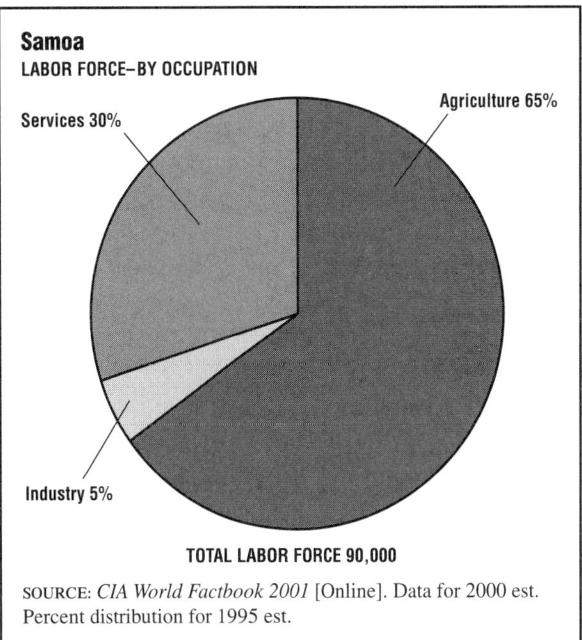

SOURCE: *CIA World Factbook 2001* [Online]. Data for 2000 est. Percent distribution for 1995 est.

made up 19.3 percent of GDP. Agriculture contributed about 30 percent of all export revenue in 1999. The main export products, in order of importance in the late 1990s were copra (dried coconut flesh), coconut oil, copra meal, coconut cream, and kava (a mildly narcotic drink traditional to the South Pacific). The importance of coconut products is obvious, but unlike many Pacific countries that only export copra, Samoa has added value to these products. For example, coconut cream canned in Samoa is worth several times its equivalent in copra. The vulnerability of dependence on a crop such as coconuts was illustrated when cyclones in 1990 and 1991 caused considerable damage to tree crops.

During the 1980s, Samoa identified an international niche market for taro, a traditional prestige root crop. The taro exported from Samoa was sold mostly to Samoan and other Pacific communities and, in 1992, made up more than one-half of all agricultural exports by value, surpassing the cyclone-depleted coconut products. In 1993, taro blight destroyed the whole crop, however, and by the late 1990s taro production was only beginning to recover.

In recent years, the government and international aid donors have been promoting agricultural diversification. Although there have been small amounts of other food crops exported (such as bananas), the only crop that has generated significant export income is kava, which has recently gained an international reputation as a soothing and therapeutic substance. In 1998, kava exports were valued at WST5.5 million (US$1.8 million), a sum similar to the copra exports in that year. Other agricultural products currently being promoted include cattle and tropical fruits.

FISHING. The Asian Development Bank estimated that 30 to 40 percent of all households in Samoa fish for their own consumption and that 12 percent of households rely on fishing as their primary source of income. Many subsistence fishers may also sell some of their catch. Larger commercial fishing endeavors have developed, though, mainly resulting from the introduction of long-line tuna boats. Thus, fishing's contribution to GDP rose from 4 percent in 1995 to 8 percent in 1999, with further expansion expected. Most of the catch is processed in the canneries of American Samoa, giving Samoa a competitive advantage because of the proximity of these facilities and because they allow access to the American market.

FORESTRY. In the past, there was relatively large-scale logging on the island of Savai'i, but logging has become small-scale and limited mostly to customary (village owned) land. Exports of timber are small as most production is for the local market. Large-scale establishment of forest plantations began in the 1970s, but most of these forests were destroyed by the cyclones of 1990 and 1991. Recent planting of high-value hardwood species such as mahogany will take about 25 years to mature, so there are few prospects of timber re-establishing itself as an important export before then.

INDUSTRY

Of the formal labor force, about 17 percent worked in industry, with about half of these working in construction and just over one-quarter in manufacturing in 1991. More recent data show that all industrial sectors together accounted for 23.7 percent of GDP in 1998. This percentage has grown through the 1990s.

MANUFACTURING. Much of the manufacturing sector, mostly located in Apia, serves the purpose of **import substitution**. Thus, the most important industries include food processing, beer production, furniture, and construction materials. There are, however, some export-oriented industries. Notable is the production of canned coconut cream, mainly for export. Beer and cigarette factories export some of their product. A small industries center has been established at Vaitele, near Apia. The most uncommon of the new endeavors, in a Pacific sense, is the Yazaki automobile electrical wiring assembly plant, which was transferred from Melbourne in 1991. This plant exports about US$50 million in automotive parts to Australia each year, however, the benefit to Samoa may be low since wages are low and the company pays no taxes or **duties**.

SERVICES

Services accounted for 51 percent of all formal sector employment in 1991, and this proportion has probably risen since then. In 1998 all services accounted for 38.6 percent of GDP, up from 32 percent in 1992. The largest subsector of employment was social and personal services, which accounted for just over half of all employment in the services sector, with many of these being government employees.

TOURISM. Through the 1990s there has been a steady increase in the number of visitors to Samoa, from just over 48,000 in 1990 to about 78,000 in 1998. Only about one-third of these can be considered as tourists, however, since another third are Samoan expatriates visiting friends and relatives while another third are traveling on business. Still, tourism contributed an estimated 15.4 percent of GDP in 1997.

Samoa has considerable potential as a tourist destination. It has a strong and visible culture and many Samoans consider their country *Hawai'iki* (the original home of all Polynesians). On this basis the Samoa Visitors Bureau presents Samoa as "The Cradle of Polynesia" in its international promotions. The visibility of Samoan culture—epitomized by traditional open-sided houses—the many beautiful beaches, waterfalls, and other features of a "tropical paradise"; and the scale and architectural variety of Samoan churches exceed normal tourist expectations of a country its size. There are several international standard hotels, mostly in Apia and elsewhere on Upolu. Smaller hotels and guesthouses have seen growing competition from village-based tourist operations. Most local accommodations include fales (leaf houses), usually on a beach, with locally cooked food on offer. These are relatively low impact ventures, though, in which most of the profits stay in the village.

FINANCIAL SERVICES. Following the example of Vanuatu and Cook Islands, Samoa established an **offshore banking** center in 1988. About 500 banks and other companies have established themselves in Samoa, although information is not available to identify the costs and benefits of this operation to the Samoan economy. Domestic financial services are provided by Bank of Samoa (owned by ANZ Bank), Pacific Commercial Bank (a **joint venture** between Bank of Hawaii and Westpac) and National Bank.

RETAIL. The **retail** sector is similar to that in other Pacific countries of similar size. Apia has a number of medium-sized shops and small supermarkets that sell food imported from New Zealand and manufactures from Asia as well as local produce. Elsewhere in the country, shops stock mainly basic items necessary for everyday life. The largest market is in Apia, selling fruit, vegetables, fish, basic manufactured goods, and handicrafts. Smaller markets are found in other towns where the range of products is related to the size of the local population.

INTERNATIONAL TRADE

The difference between the level of Samoa's exports and imports is considerable. In the years shown in the table, the trade imbalance ranges from just over 3 to 1 in 1985 to more than 10 to 1 in 1995, and the general trend is an increasing imbalance. The value of exports has not kept pace with the expansion of the economy, which requires increased imports. Also, 2 cyclones in 1990 and 1991 and the taro blight in 1993 had a severe impact on the level of exports in the mid 1990s.

Australia has been the most important destination for exports in recent years, ranging between 50 and 85 percent of all exports between 1995 and 1999. New Zealand is the most important source of imports, but Australia, Japan, Fiji, and the United States are also significant.

The large negative balance of trade is possible because of other international transfers. Tourism contributes some international income. At the household level the most important source of income is remittances from relatives living overseas, particularly in New Zealand, the United States, and Australia. At the government level, international aid helps to counterbalance the **trade deficit**.

MONEY

The Samoan tala has depreciated against the U.S. dollar since 1982. This may be partly attributed to the vulnerable export base of the country, but a range of other factors in the international economy are less easy to identify. In the late 1990s a strong U.S. dollar devalued most currencies of the Pacific region that most influence the Samoan tala, including the New Zealand and Australian dollars.

POVERTY AND WEALTH

A total of 174 countries are ranked in the **United Nations Development Program**'s (UNDP) *Human Development Report 2000* according to the Human Development Indicator (HDI), which measures a country's state of well-being using income, education, and health measures. The HDI rank for Samoa was 95 which puts it in the middle range of countries, similar to other countries in Polynesia but higher than Melanesian countries. **GDP per capita** in 1998 was US$998, about one-thirtieth that of the United States.

There is no adequate information on income distribution in Samoa, but this may be inferred from other

Trade (expressed in billions of US$): Samoa

	Exports	Imports
1975	.007	.037
1980	.017	.062
1985	.016	.051
1990	.009	.080
1995	.009	.095
1998	.015	.097

SOURCE: International Monetary Fund. *International Financial Statistics Yearbook 1999.*

Exchange rates: Samoa

talas per US$1	
Jan 2001	3.3400
2000	3.2712
1999	3.0120
1998	2.9429
1997	2.5562
1996	2.4618

SOURCE: CIA *World Factbook 2001* [ONLINE].

GDP per Capita (US$)

Country	1975	1980	1985	1990	1998
Samoa	N/A	974	915	931	998
United States	19,364	21,529	23,200	25,363	29,683
Philippines	974	1,166	967	1,064	1,092
Solomon Islands	419	583	666	784	753

SOURCE: United Nations. *Human Development Report 2000; Trends in human development and per capita income.*

information. Another indicator developed by the UNDP is the Human Poverty Index (HPI). It measures conditions for those worst off in a country, such as their educational level, health status, access to health services, access to safe water, and incidence of malnutrition in children. Of 15 Pacific countries measured by the HPI, Samoa falls in the middle, meaning that the people worst off in Samoa are comparatively better off than the worst off in most Melanesian countries. On indicators of education, Samoa boasts 96 percent literacy and a high participation rate in education. School attendance is mandatory up to age 14 and there are no central government fees, although local communities may levy them to cover maintenance of buildings.

In health, the indicators are generally high, with universal access to health services and with most households having access to safe water. Health service is free and available through clinics as well as at 5 public hospitals. There is not a system of universal pensions, but those who have worked in formal employment are likely to have provided for a pension through the National Provident Fund. Most other older people depend on their nuclear or extended families, in Samoa and overseas. Since 1999, migrants returning from working in New Zealand are able to bring their New Zealand pensions with them, and this is expected to be an increasing source of income in Samoa as the number of these migrants increases.

WORKING CONDITIONS

There is a minimum wage in the **private sector** of WST1.40 per hour, which has been readjusted to the cost of living over the last 20 years. This rate makes living in town problematic, although many households will have some people working for wages as well as others undertaking subsistence production. The minimum wage is about 10 percent of the salary that a new senior manager might get in the private sector.

Men make up an estimated 78 percent of the formal workforce. In almost all sectors they predominate. In public service men comprise only 47 percent of the full-time salaried workers but two-thirds of the temporary government workers. The unemployment rate of 13 percent is quite high, but it would be even higher if all those in the rural sector who wanted paid employment were counted. There is no unemployment benefit. Unionization is relatively strong with the Teacher's Association being formed in the 1950s and the Western Samoa Public Service Association starting in 1969. In the private sector, unions have been a recent development with the formation of the Western Samoa National Union of Workers in 1994.

COUNTRY HISTORY AND ECONOMIC DEVELOPMENT

1721. The first European "explorer" visits Samoa. Metal tools and weapons are introduced.

1830s-1890s. A series of governments under Samoan chieftainship and foreign support come and go. German coconut plantations are founded.

1899. Treaties are signed between Britain, Germany, and the United States giving Western Samoa to Germany and American (Eastern) Samoa to the United States.

1914. New Zealand takes control of Western Samoa during World War I.

1920s. The nonviolent Mau movement, formed to oppose taxes and support independence, is suppressed by force; 11 Samoans, including a matai, are killed.

1962. Western Samoa becomes the first independent nation in the Pacific Islands.

1982. Samoa experiences a constitutional crisis with 3 governments in 1 year. Tension continues between parliamentary and traditional matai systems.

1991. Universal voting franchise is introduced for all citizens over age 21; previously only matai could vote.

1997. The country's name changes from Western Samoa to Samoa.

FUTURE TRENDS

During the 1990s Samoa's economy experienced several blows related to natural disaster, but at the turn of the century, there is optimism about future development. The fishing industry has grown rapidly in recent years with further potential apparent. Tourism has grown slowly but steadily, and to some extent the degree to which this expands may depend not only on the government's promotion of it but also on the public's attitude to the desirable scale of the industry. The agricultural sector is likely to continue to be affected by weather, disease, and fluctuating world prices, but probably will continue as an important source of export income, even if the product mix changes. For many years there have been predictions that migrant remittances will eventually slow down as expatriates become more settled in their countries of residence, but so far this does not seem be the case. Though international aid payments are being reduced in some cases, most small Pacific countries—such as Samoa—have managed to attract high per capita levels of aid, and this ought to continue into the foreseeable future.

DEPENDENCIES

Samoa has no territories or colonies.

BIBLIOGRAPHY

Economist Intelligence Unit. *Country Profile: Samoa.* London: Economist Intelligence Unit, 2001.

"Key Indicators for Developing Asian and Pacific Countries." *Asian Development Bank.* <http://www.adb.org/Samoa>. Accessed February 2001

"Samoa 2000: Building on Recent Reforms." *Asian Development Bank.* Manila: ADB, 2000.

Lal, Brij V., and Kate Fortune. *The Pacific Islands: An Encyclopedia.* Honolulu: University of Hawai'i Press, 2000.

U.S. Central Intelligence Agency. *World Factbook 2001.* <http://www.odci.gov/cia/publications/factbook/index.html>. Accessed August 2001.

United Nations Development Programme. *Pacific Human Development Report 1999: Creating Opportunities.* Suva: UNDP, 1999.

Vaai, Kolone. "Recent Economic Development in Western Samoa." *Pacific Economic Bulletin.* Vol. 11, No. 2, 1996.

—Wardlow Friesen

SAUDI ARABIA

Kingdom of Sa'udi Arabia
Al-Mamlakah al-'Arabiyah as-Sa'udiyah

CAPITAL: Riyadh (Ar-Riyad).

MONETARY UNIT: Saudi Riyal (SR). One riyal equals 100 halalahs. There are coins of 5, 10, 25, 50, and 100 halalahs, and notes of 1, 5, 10, 50, 100, and 500 riyals. Since July 1986 the Saudi riyal has been pegged to the U.S. dollar at a rate of SR3.745:US$1.

CHIEF EXPORTS: Petroleum and petroleum products (90 percent).

CHIEF IMPORTS: Machinery and equipment, foodstuffs, chemicals, motor vehicles, textiles.

GROSS DOMESTIC PRODUCT: US$191 billion (purchasing power parity, 1999 est.).

BALANCE OF TRADE: **Exports:** US$48 billion (f.o.b., 1999). **Imports:** US$28 billion (f.o.b., 1999).

COUNTRY OVERVIEW

LOCATION AND SIZE. Saudi Arabia is located in the Middle East between the Persian Gulf and the Red Sea. It borders Jordan, Iraq, and Kuwait to the north, Yemen to the south, and Oman, the United Arab Emirates (UAE), and Qatar to the east. The country, which is divided into 13 provinces, is composed primarily of desert. Each region has a governor appointed by the king. With a land area of about 1.96 million square kilometers (756,981 square miles), Saudi Arabia is about one-fourth the size of the continental United States. Riyadh, the capital, is located in the central eastern part of the country.

POPULATION. The population of Saudi Arabia was estimated at 22,023,506 in July of 2000, a figure growing at about 3.3 percent a year. Saudi nationals account for close to 75 percent of the population. The remaining residents, nearly 6 million people, are expatriates comprised primarily of foreign workers. About 90 percent of Saudi nationals are Arabs. The rest of the indigenous population, according to CIA statistics, are Afro-Asian.

In 2000, the birth rate stood at 37.47 per 1,000 population, compared with a death rate of 6.02 per 1,000. According to a Saudi census taken in the early 1990s, a little over 50 percent of the population is male. While men make up a majority of the population, due primarily to the high concentration of males among expatriate workers, women are expected to live longer. Women on average live 69 years in Saudi Arabia, while the men live 66.

An overwhelming majority of the Saudi population is young. In 1999, according to the Saudi Ministry of Planning, 46 percent of the population was under 15. Another 38 percent was under 40. Those over 40 accounted for only 16 percent of the population. Efforts to accommodate the rising numbers of young adults entering the **workforce** each year have been only partly successful, and the consequent rise in unemployment has begun to aggravate the underlying tensions between the country's richest and poorest citizens.

Up until the 1960s a majority of the Saudi population were either nomadic or semi-nomadic desert dwellers with no fixed homes. However, after petroleum was discovered in Saudi Arabia in the 1930s, state revenues quickly began to rise. As the oil industry matured, the economy quickly modernized and nomadic herding faded as an economic base. By 2000, 95 percent of the Saudi population was settled.

The Saudi royal family and a majority of the population are Sunni Muslim. About 5 percent of the population, around 1 million people, are Shia Muslim. Tensions between the Sunni majority and the Shia minority have been especially high since the 1979 Iranian Revolution, when Saudi Shiites rioted in parts of the Eastern Province. Shia Muslims routinely suffer from religious discrimination.

OVERVIEW OF ECONOMY

The Saudi Arabian economy is fueled almost entirely by the production and distribution of petroleum and its derivative products. Over the past decade oil sales have generated, on average, 90 percent of the country's yearly export earnings, 35 percent of annual **gross domestic product** (GDP), and 75 percent of all budget revenues. High oil prices in the 1970s led to rapid economic expansion, with GDP growing over the course of the decade by 10 percent per year. As oil prices dropped in the 1980s, GDP growth slowed, averaging just 1.3 percent per year between 1980 and 1998. Rising oil prices beginning in 1999 again boded well for the economy.

Oil was discovered in Saudi Arabia by American geologists in the 1930s, but high level production did not begin until after World War II (1939–45). In the 1960s, the Saudi oil industry began to mature, resulting in a massive accumulation of wealth, fast paced economic growth, and rapid urban development. However, it was not until the 1970s that Saudi Arabia emerged as one of the Middle East's preeminent political and economic powers.

Two events in the 1970s were crucial to Saudi Arabia's economic development. One was the Arab oil **embargo** of 1973, during which time Arab countries withheld oil from the world market, raising world oil prices dramatically. The other was the 1979 Iranian Revolution, when Shiites overthrew the western-backed monarchy in Iran and assumed control of the country. Both events disrupted oil supplies, causing the commodity's cost to rise. Throughout the 1970s, Saudi Arabia was able to export oil at substantially elevated prices, leading it to become one of the fastest growing economies in the world. The massive inflow of revenue allowed the kingdom to increase import levels and still maintain a favorable **balance of trade**. Spending on defense and **infrastructure** rose, and Saudi Arabia became a benefactor nation to the rest of the Arab world, supplying large amounts of financial aid. (Aid has averaged 4 percent of GDP per year over the past 25 years, making Saudi Arabia's average aid-to-GDP ratio the highest in the world.) In a matter of decades, Saudi Arabia transformed itself from a desert kingdom populated by nomadic tribes to a modern economic entity which controls over a quarter of the world's oil.

While petroleum exports are indeed lucrative, Saudi Arabia's dependence on oil as its primary source of revenue is potentially problematic. In the near term, the Saudi economy is left vulnerable to shifts in the price of oil, lowered demand, or disrupted production due to any number of factors, including regional conflicts and the Organization of Petroleum Exporting Countries (OPEC) shifting oil production quotas. In the long term there is the problem of dwindling supplies. While the Saudis maintain over a quarter of the world's known oil reserves (about 263 billion barrels at the end of 1999), these reserves, at the current rate of production, will last only 87.5 years. If, in that time, Saudi Arabia fails to sufficiently diversify its economy or discover new sources of oil, the country will be faced with a serious shortfall in revenues. And even if the kingdom does discover new reserves (as will likely be the case—some estimates put undiscovered reserves in Saudi Arabia at nearly a trillion barrels) the price of oil will probably steadily drop in the coming years as supplies and production efficiency increase.

The need to begin generating alternative sources of income was recognized as early as 1970, when the government issued the first in an ongoing series of 5 year plans aimed at expanding the non-oil sectors of the economy. While infrastructure expansion and urban development—both natural outgrowths of the oil industry—have proceeded at an impressive pace, attempts to diversify the economy have produced limited results. Similarly, efforts to decentralize the state run economy through broad **privatization** schemes have been largely unsuccessful.

THE FIVE YEAR PLANS. The first 5-year plans, covering the 1970s, focused on developing the national infrastructure (see Infrastructure, Power, and Communications). The third plan (1980–85) focused less on infrastructure and more on education, health, and social services. It also included efforts to expand the productive sectors of the economy, namely industry—a goal which was only partly achieved. While the building of 2 new industrial cities, Jubail and Yanbu, was completed, no broad industrial expansion occurred, leaving primary components of the plan unfulfilled.

The fourth plan, which covered the latter half of the 1980s, remained focused on education and training. It also sought to reduce government spending while generating growth in the **private sector**. **Joint ventures** were encouraged between foreign companies and Saudi state enterprises in the hope of increasing foreign investment. The role of the private sector grew during this time, rising to 70 percent of non-oil GDP by 1987.

Starting in 1990, the fifth 5-year plan concentrated on expanding the infrastructure and strengthening the Saudi national defense. The perceived need for a stronger military was reinforced by the Iraqi invasion of Kuwait, a move which destabilized the region and precipitated the 1991 Persian Gulf War. Between 1990–94 34 percent of Saudi expenditures went toward national defense. The fifth plan also sought to increase private sector employment opportunities for Saudi citizens by limiting the number of foreign workers on Saudi soil. Efforts to "Saudi-ize" the workforce—raise the percentage of Saudi workers—continued through the sixth plan (1995–2000), which also focused on the diversification of economic activity through private sector growth, especially in the areas of industry and agriculture.

The Saudi government will continue in its efforts to create jobs for Saudi citizens over the next 5 years and beyond. Indeed, with 100,000 nationals entering the workforce each year, job creation will remain a priority for the foreseeable future.

GOVERNMENT SPENDING. High petroleum prices in the 1970s boosted Saudi revenues and allowed increased spending. A series of ambitious, high cost initiatives were launched to develop the nation's infrastructure, expand industry and agriculture, overhaul health and education, and modernize the military (as outlined above). These efforts eventually put a strain on the government budget, as spending began to outpace the flow of revenues. In the 1970s, the problem was mitigated by the high price of oil, but in the 1980s, when oil prices declined, revenues fell and the government deficit grew, reaching 19.6 percent of GDP by 1986. Financial resources were further strained in 1990 when Iraq's invasion of Kuwait prompted the Saudis to appropriate US$30 billion in emergency defense spending. Though the value of Saudi exports exceeds that of its imports, the trade surplus has historically been unable to offset the deficit, which is generally financed through domestic borrowing. Eighty percent of the debt is held by autonomous government institutions, such as pension funds and social security. The other 20 percent is held by commercial banks.

Over the past decade, measures have been taken to lower government spending and reduce the fiscal imbalances created in the 1980s. In 1996 and 1997, spending cuts coupled with rising oil prices helped lower domestic debt and ease the pressure on government finances. However, this trend was interrupted in 1998 when oil prices fell, prompting calls for additional austerity measures and general economic reform. In 1999, government spending was reduced by an additional 13 percent. That year, with financial pressure building, the government also implemented new revenue-generating measures, a move it had resisted in the past. It raised domestic gasoline prices by 50 percent, introduced airport taxes, and doubled work permit fees. In 2000, surging oil prices produced the first government surplus in 17 years. However, the surplus may be shortlived, as the Saudi government plans to increase spending in 2001, a decision based primarily on expectations of rising oil prices.

While spending in 2001 is expected to be higher than in 2000, total spending between 2000–04 is actually slated to go down. The seventh 5-year plan (2000–04) calls for spending no more than US$200 billion, down from US$258 billion over the previous 5 years.

The Saudi government has expressed an interest in decentralizing the economy and increasing private sector participation. Although a number of privatization schemes have been considered, the government has yet to relinquish control over most major industries. Plans to privatize telecommunications and electric companies have stalled, as have plans to privatize the state-owned Saudi Arabian airlines.

Privatization efforts will likely be revitalized as Saudi Arabia attempts to gain entry into the World Trade Organization (WTO), an international regulatory body that sets standards for international trading practices and arbitrates disputes between member nations. (The WTO holds that free market, rules-based economies are more transparent than state-run economies and sees them as more fit for membership.) Joining the WTO will force Saudi Arabia to further **liberalize** its economy and would place its economic policies under international scrutiny, depriving Saudi policy makers of a certain degree of freedom. But once Saudi Arabia was admitted to the WTO it would have protection against the arbitrary exclusion of its imports by other members, a trade-off most Saudi officials find favorable. Among the measures the kingdom will have to take to gain entry into the organization are the removal of protectionist trade barriers, the lowering of import **tariffs**, and the opening of key service sectors to foreign participation—all policies which remove protection for local producers from competition. Saudi Arabia will also have to improve its protections for intellectual property rights. These measures will likely improve the investment climate in Saudi Arabia, paving the way for greater inflows of foreign exchange and smaller outflows of **remittances**.

Many workers in Saudi Arabia are from other countries, and send home much of their earnings. These worker remittances amount to approximately US$16 billion a year. Opening the private sector up to greater foreign participation—allowing, for instance, non-Saudis to buy homes and invest in local companies—could provide a means for keeping more capital in local markets.

POLITICS, GOVERNMENT, AND TAXATION

HISTORY OF THE RULING FAMILY. The foundations for a modern Saudi state were laid in 1744 when Muhammad bin Saud, the ruler of a local tribe, joined forces with a religious reformer, Muhammad Abd Al-Wahhab, in an attempt to unify the Arabian peninsula under strict Islamic law. Within 60 years, the Al Saud family, through a mixture of religious proselytizing and military conquest, had taken control of a majority of what is now Saudi Arabia, including the holy cities of Mecca and Medina. (Mecca is where the prophet Mohammed, the founder of Islam, was born in 570 A.D. and Medina is where, in 633, he died.)

The success of the Al Saud attracted the attention of the Ottoman Turks, who held the Arabian peninsula as part of their empire. In 1816, employing an Egyptian force, the Ottomans launched a campaign to recapture areas under Saudi control. The Al Saud, outnumbered and overpowered, were driven back by Egyptian forces and by 1818 had lost a majority of their empire.

Over the course of the 19th century, the Al Saud made numerous attempts to regain their lost territory, but superior Ottoman forces, as well as resistance from rival clans, proved difficult to overcome. By 1890 the Al Saud had been driven into exile in Kuwait.

In 1902, the Saudi prince Abdul Aziz Al Saud (who was to become known internationally as Ibn Saud) was able to recapture Riyadh, his family's ancestral home, from the rival Al Rashid clan. From there, Ibn Saud launched his campaign to reunify the peninsula. By the end of the First World War, in 1918, the Ottoman empire had collapsed, paving the way for Arabian independence. In 1924, having established a foothold in central Arabia, Ibn Saud moved west into the hejaz region where his army of fanatically religious desert dwellers known as the "Ikhwan" (brethren), defeated Sherif Hussein and took possession of the holy cities of Mecca and Medina. By 1932, Ibn Saud, with the support of the Ikhwan, had consolidated control over nearly the entire peninsula. That year he declared the Kingdom of Saudi Arabia with himself as its king.

Over the next 30 years the Al Saud and Al Rashid, vying for control over the peninsula of Arabia, remained at war. In the end, the Saudis emerged victorious, primarily due to Ibn Saud's ability to gain the loyalty of the Ikhwan. Ibn Saud, upon his death in 1953, had 34 surviving sons, who continue to sit at the center of the nation's political apparatus. Ibn Saud was succeeded after his death by his eldest son Saud, who, in his first year of rule, established the Council of Ministers, a body formed to advise the king on state policy and direct the development of the rapidly growing Saudi bureaucracy. Despite ruling for a full 11 years, King Saud was perceived as an ineffective leader. In 1964, under heavy pressure from religious elites and members of the royal family, Saud stepped down in favor of his half brother, Faisal, who had previously served as foreign minister.

As king, Faisal attempted to address issues to which Saud, and even Abdul Aziz, had given little thought, such as how to effectively modernize the country in the face of its emerging wealth. He also struggled with how to maximize the benefits of the kingdom's bountiful petroleum resources. Decisions on oil policy were not always easy to make, especially when matters of Arab solidarity conflicted with the country's drive toward economic prosperity.

When Arab oil producers decided to cut petroleum sales to the United States in 1973, this conflict came into full view. That year, the ever-present tensions between Israel and its neighbors erupted as Israeli and Egyptian forces clashed in the Sinai desert. U.S. aid to Israel during the war led to fierce protests in the Arab world, culminating in an Arab boycott of oil sales to the United States and other western countries. Saudi Arabia, which participated in the boycott, learned a hard lesson as a result: it could not maintain its economy without doing business in the West, for even though the price of oil went up during the boycott due to the cut in supply, the price spikes were insufficient to cover the loss in sales. In 1974, despite opposition from other Arab oil producers, the Saudis froze oil prices and resumed sales to the United States. That year, in a series of negotiations, the United States and Saudi Arabia came to an agreement by which America would provide the kingdom with military support in exchange for an uninterrupted flow of oil. Over the remainder of the decade, Saudi Arabia sold vast quantities of oil at inflated prices, leading it to become one of the fastest growing economies in the world.

King Faisal, who presided over the oil boycott and the subsequent agreement with the United States, was assassinated in 1975 by a member the royal family. The alleged assassin was executed for the crime. Faisal was replaced by his half brother, Crown Prince Khalid. Fahd, another half brother who would later become king, was appointed as the new Crown Prince and first deputy prime minister, where he was given the responsibility of overseeing a wide range of the country's international and domestic affairs.

Economic development was rapid under King Khalid. Saudi Arabia's acquisition of national wealth enhanced its political influence in the Middle East and heightened its role in world economic affairs. At the same time, however, the kingdom's growing relationship with the West began to concern religious hard-liners who feared that Western influence would corrupt the nation's Islamic ideals. In November 1979, about 250 armed followers of Sunni Muslim cleric Juhaiman Ibn Seif al-Oteif took over the Grand Mosque in Mecca. After a standoff, government troops ousted the militants by force. The incident was not without effect, as it alerted the royal family to the extent of the religious opposition it was fostering by failing to display a more overt commitment to the preservation of Islamic ideals. In response, a committee was established, chaired by interior minister Prince Nayef, to establish a set of societal rules based on Islamic principles. Still, opposition from Islamist religious forces continues to pose the greatest single threat to the royal family.

In June 1982, Khalid died and, in a smooth transition, Prince Fahd became king. Prince Abdullah, Fahd's half brother and commander of the Saudi National Guard, was appointed crown prince and deputy prime minister. The role of second deputy prime minister was filled by Fahd's brother, Prince Sultan, who also served as the minister of Defense and Aviation.

King Fahd, despite inheriting a weakening economy, quickly became a central figure in Middle East politics. In 1988, he played a key role in bringing about a cease fire in the Iran-Iraq war. He also helped reorganize and strengthen the Gulf Cooperation Council (GCC), a group of 6 gulf states (Saudi Arabia, Oman, Kuwait, Qatar, the United Arab Emirates, and Bahrain) formed to facilitate regional economic cooperation and peaceful development. Additionally, in the 1990–91 Gulf War, King Fahd used his influence as arbiter over Islam's holiest sites (Mecca and Medina) to help organize and hold together the U.S.-led war coalition that liberated Kuwait from Iraq. King Fahd suffered a stroke in November of 1995. By 1997, Crown Prince Abdullah had taken effective control of the state.

Over the decades, tensions between the royal family and radical religious forces have persisted as various Saudi kings have sought to balance the nation's dependence on the West with efforts to preserve the kingdom's cultural and religious heritage. Currently, opposition from Islamist religious forces poses the greatest single threat to the Saudi government. The royal family tries to maintain close ties with the religious leaders, who, it is hoped, can keep the extremist members of the clergy in line. However, religious radicals have, especially over the past decade, attracted a growing number of followers. The reasons for this vary. The kingdom's uneven distribution of wealth is partly to blame, as it has led to rising discontent among the nation's poorest citizens. But more importantly, there is deep seeded resentment stemming from the presence of non-Muslim military forces on Saudi soil. U.S. troops and British soldiers have been stationed in Saudi Arabia since the Gulf War, a situation religious fundamentalists fiercely oppose. This opposition on more than one occasion has been expressed through violence. In November 1995, a car bomb exploded near a U.S. military installation, killing 7 people. In June 1996, there was another, more lethal attack in which a bomb blew up outside the Khobar Towers military barracks, killing 19 American servicemen. A Saudi dissident, Osama bin Laden, has been blamed for planning the attack. However, as of 2001, no arrests had been made.

GOVERNMENT STRUCTURE. Saudi Arabia is an absolute monarchy where the king essentially rules by decree. That does not mean, however, that judicial structures are entirely absent, or that the king's powers are limitless. The Basic Law, the closest thing the Saudis have to a written constitution, was introduced in 1992 to be used in conjunction with Islamic Sharia law, whose dictates up to that point had been the sole source of legal guidelines. Neither the Basic Law nor the king's decrees are meant to violate Sharia law.

The Mutawaa'in, or religious police, constitute the Committee to Prevent Vice and Promote Virtue. The semi-autonomous group enforces compliance with Islamic customs. Abuses by the Mutawaa'in are known to occur, especially in its treatment of Saudi Arabia's Shia minority.

The Council of Ministers, established in 1953, holds executive and legislative powers, but any of its decisions can be overruled by the king. The council is appointed by the king and is primarily made up of members of the royal family. There is also a Consultative Council, which was formed in 1993. Its members are also appointed by the king. Originally comprised of 60 members, the council was expanded to 90 members in 1997. Made up of tribal leaders, government officials, and educated elites, the council plays an advisory role to the king and has no governing power. Each of Saudi Arabia's 13 regions has its own council as well as a regional governor who is appointed by the king.

TAXATION. Saudi Arabia has a very limited tax regime, as it relies mostly on oil receipts, customs **duties**, and licensing fees to produce government revenue. Saudi nationals, rather than paying income or property taxes, pay what is called the zakat, an annual 2.5 percent assessment of a person's net personal wealth. Revenue from zakat collection helps pay for social services, such as health care and education. Foreign companies and self-employed foreigners in Saudi Arabia are not obliged to pay the zakat, but are, on the other hand, charged with **income taxes**, which range from 25 percent on income under US$26,667 to 45 percent on income over US$266,667.

Saudi Arabia also charges tariffs on imported goods which range from 12 percent to 20 percent. In order to gain entry into the WTO, the government will have to lower these tariffs to a maximum of 7.5 percent.

INFRASTRUCTURE, POWER, AND COMMUNICATIONS

In the 1970s, in order to accommodate its burgeoning oil industry, the Saudi government took extensive measures to expand the kingdom's infrastructure. Roads and railways were built, airports were expanded, and seaports were enhanced to handle heavy volumes of traffic.

By the end of 1999, the kingdom had around 150,000 kilometers (93,210 miles) of roads, about a third of them paved. Major arteries provide passage between urban and industrial centers. Jeddah, Mecca, and Medina in the west are linked to Riyadh and to the Eastern Province oil fields

Communications

Country	Newspapers	Radios	TV Sets[a]	Cable subscribers[a]	Mobile Phones[a]	Fax Machines[a]	Personal Computers[a]	Internet Hosts[b]	Internet Users[b]
	1996	1997	1998	1998	1998	1998	1998	1999	1999
Saudi Arabia	57	321	262	N/A	31	N/A	49.8	1.17	300
United States	215	2,146	847	244.3	256	78.4	458.6	1,508.77	74,100
Egypt	40	324	122	N/A	1	0.5	9.1	0.28	200
Iran	28	265	157	0.0	6	N/A	31.9	0.05	100

[a]Data are from International Telecommunication Union, *World Telecommunication Development Report 1999* and are per 1,000 people.
[b]Data are from the Internet Software Consortium (http://www.isc.org) and are per 10,000 people.

SOURCE: World Bank. *World Development Indicators 2000.*

by the trans-peninsular highway. The Tapline road provides a link between Damman, on the gulf coast, and the Jordanian border. The Red Sea road runs north-south, the length of the western shore.

Saudi Arabia's rail network is currently limited to a 571-kilometer (355-mile) single track line running between Damman and Riyadh, and a 322-kilometer (200-mile) line between Riyadh and Hufuf. As of 2000, new lines had been proposed to connect cities on the gulf coast in the east, such as Damman and Jubail, to mineral deposits in the northwest. A cross-peninsula line connecting the Red Sea port of Jeddah with the gulf port of Damman had also been proposed.

There are 6 major seaports in Saudi Arabia, along with 14 minor ones, sufficient to handle the country's importing and exporting needs. Four of the major ports—Duba, Yanbu, Jeddah, and Jizan—are on the Red Sea. The other 2, Damman and Jubail, are on the Persian Gulf. Yanbu and Jubail are industrial ports and together account for more than half of the country's import and export handling. As part of a larger effort to decentralize the economy, operation and maintenance of the seaports were turned over to the private sector in 1997.

Saudi Arabia has 3 international airports located at Jeddah, Damman, and Riyadh. These airports also act as the primary hubs for domestic flights. Other domestic airports include Medina, Jizan, Taif, Qassim, Tabuk, and Abha. Saudi Arabian Airlines, the national carrier, is owned and operated by the government. While privatizing the airline has been considered, as of 2000 no concrete moves had been made to that effect.

The expansion of the Saudi infrastructure was rapid in the 1970s, when oil revenues were at their peak. The completion of a number of major projects in the 1980s coincided with a downturn in the price of oil and a subsequent loss of revenues. As a result, spending on infrastructure declined. The growth in the transport sector, which between 1975 and 1979 reached 19.3 percent, had, by the early 1990s, dropped below 2 percent.

In 1998, despite a growth in investment, the telecommunications sector in Saudi Arabia was fairly limited. By 1999, the expansion of the industry had become a priority. The U.S. firm Lucent Technologies won a US$4 billion contract in 1994 to install fixed phone lines throughout the kingdom, but 4 years later the 2.9 million existing lines still represented under 15 lines per 100 inhabitants, according to the International Telecommunication Union. In an effort to bring the system in line with emerging East European economies, the government is seeking to increase the number of lines to at least 30 per 100 residents by 2002. Lucent, on top of its initial contract, was hired in 1998 to expand mobile phone service in a deal worth US$700 million. The government hopes the expansion will enable the kingdom to accommodate 5 million cell phone subscribers by the end of 2001.

In a bid to privatize the telecommunications industry, the government in April 1998 approved the creation of the Saudi Telecommunications Company, an entity which originally comprised the telecommunications arm of the Post, Telegraphs, and Telephone ministry (PTT). According to the initial plan, shares in the company were to be sold starting at the beginning of 2000, with the government stake in the company being eventually reduced to zero. However, when talks broke down over the transfer of a large bulk of shares to the American firm SBC (Southern Bell Communications), government withdrawal of operations was delayed. By 2001, a deadline for complete privatization had still not been set.

By the end of the 1990s, the demand for energy in Saudi Arabia had reached an all-time high, outstripping supply and, in some cities, causing frequent power outages during periods of high use. Short-term solutions, such as raising prices to curb demand, proved ineffective. For instance, in 2000, price increases totaling almost 78 percent were introduced for electricity. However, after 6 months, vehement public protests were launched in response to high electricity bills. As a result, the price hikes were rescinded before they could have any substantial effect. To meet growing energy needs over the long term, the government has set out to **restructure** the industry and increase investment from both the public and private sectors.

In November of 1998, it was announced that the 10 separate electricity companies in Saudi Arabia would be consolidated into a single company, the Saudi Electric Company. The government has expressed its intention to eventually relinquish its 85 percent stake in the sector. By consolidating the sector, the government hopes to streamline operations and improve efficiency, making the industry more dependable and more profitable, and in turn more attractive to outside investors. By 2020, the government's aim is to increase power generation capacity by over 3 times from where it stood in 1990, from 22,000 megawatts (MW) to 69,000 MW. Saudi Arabia, which imports no energy, is entirely dependent upon oil for the generation of its power.

ECONOMIC SECTORS

Saudi Arabia, despite moves to diversify its economy, is still almost entirely dependent upon oil. Petroleum sales provide the kingdom with 90 percent of its export earnings and 75 percent of its annual budget revenues. Saudi Arabia is a founding member of the Organization of Petroleum Exporting Countries (OPEC) which was founded in Baghdad, Iraq, in September of 1960 to unify and coordinate members' petroleum prices.

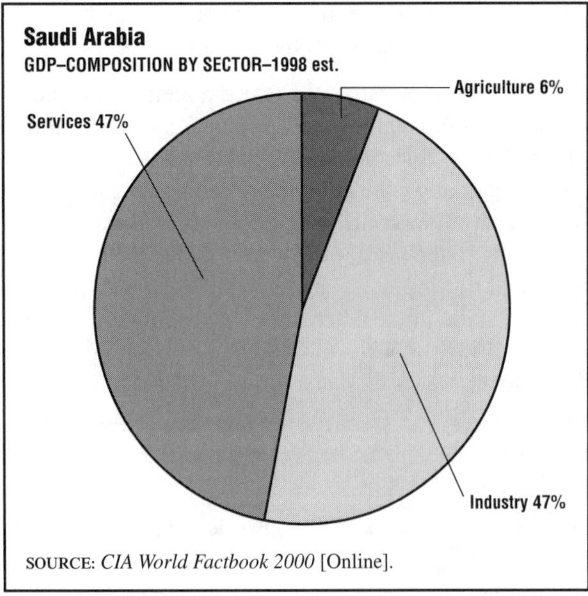

SOURCE: *CIA World Factbook 2000* [Online].

Iraq, Iran, Venezuela, and Kuwait were OPEC's other founding members. Qatar, Indonesia, Libya, the United Arab Emirates, Algeria, and Nigeria are also current members. OPEC countries are responsible for 40 percent of the world's oil production and 77 percent of its known reserves. Saudi Arabian oil exports make up nearly 30 percent of OPEC's yearly total exports. The government hopes to increase non-oil GDP by 4 percent between 2000 and 2004, with agriculture projected to expand by 3.1 percent per year, industry by 5.1 percent, and utilities (electricity, gas, and water) by 4.6 percent. Construction activity is expected to increase annually by over 6 percent. And non-oil mining had been targeted for an expansion of 8.3 percent per year, which would make it the fastest growing sector of the economy. Despite all such efforts to increase non-petroleum related economic functions, it will be difficult to move the country away from dominance by the petroleum sector.

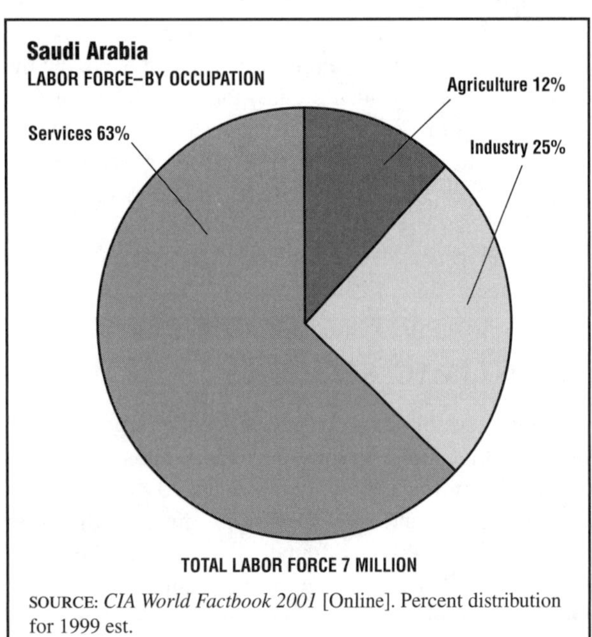

SOURCE: *CIA World Factbook 2001* [Online]. Percent distribution for 1999 est.

In 1998, industry, which included oil production, contributed 47 percent of GDP and employed 25 percent of the total workforce of 7 million. Agriculture contributed just 6 percent of GDP and employed 12 percent of the workforce, while the services sector contributed another 47 percent and employed 63 percent of the workforce.

AGRICULTURE

In the 1980s, in moves to diversify the economy, the Saudi government sought to expand the agricultural sector. It was hoped that eventually the nation would become self sufficient for food. This was an ambitious goal considering a majority of Saudi Arabia is desert where the potential for crop cultivation is limited. Still, the Saudis had some success with their plan. Food cultivation expanded in the 1980s, and as oil revenues fell, agriculture's share of GDP rose, stabilizing in the 1990s between 6 and 7 percent. By 1998, agricultural jobs provided work for 12 percent of the labor force.

Less than 2 percent of Saudi Arabian land is used for cultivation. Crops are grown mainly in the southwest of the kingdom, where there is rainfall sufficient for farming, or in areas where oases provide enough ground water for irrigation. Desalinated sea water, which is used for some purposes in Saudi Arabia, is too saline, even after treatment, to be used for farming.

The Saudi government, in its push to increase food production, had by the mid-1990s turned over 2.8 million hectares of public land to the private sector for agricultural use. About a fifth of the land was turned over to individual farmers, while the rest was designated for **agribusiness** projects or turned over to agricultural companies.

Government involvement in agriculture peaked in the 1980s. With production heavily subsidized, the **value added** in agriculture grew by 70 percent between 1985 and 1991. (Value added is the increase in the market value of a product at a particular stage of production. It is calculated by subtracting the value of all inputs bought from other firms from the value of the firm's output. For example, the value added by the cotton textile industry is the value of the textiles when they leave the factory minus the value of raw cotton and other materials used in their manufacture.) In the 1991–92 crop year, wheat production rose to an all-time high of 4 million tons, with Saudi Arabia becoming the world's sixth largest wheat exporter. However, earnings from sales were nullified by the high costs of production. The government was spending 5 times the market price to produce a ton of grain.

With the outbreak of the Gulf War (1990–91), agricultural **subsidies** were reduced and, with funds needed for military expenditures, quotas were imposed on government purchases of grain from local farmers. By 1995–96, the land area devoted to grain production had fallen by over 65 percent. The harvest that year fell to 1.2 million tons. Meanwhile, domestic consumption stood at 1.8 million tons. Although the production of barley and grain had markedly declined by the late 1990s, fruit and vegetable production rose.

INDUSTRY

OIL. Due to vast petroleum reserves, low production costs, and high levels of distribution, the oil industry is the most vibrant sector in the Saudi economy, providing the country with the bulk of its capital. Oil revenues account for 35 percent to 40 percent of the Saudi GDP annually.

As of 2001, Saudi Arabia's proven oil reserves amounted to over 263 billion barrels, representing about a quarter of the world's known oil supply. Assuming production rates were to remain what they were in 2000, Saudi Arabia's reserves would last about 87.5 years. It is probable, however, that more reserves will be discovered in the future, extending the industry's viability. As of 2001, Saudi Arabia was the largest producer and exporter of oil in the world.

Sales of Saudi oil are highly profitable due to low production costs. The sheer abundance of oil in Saudi Arabia and its close proximity to the earth's surface makes it easy to find and cheap to extract. According to the kingdom's oil minister, Ali bin Ibrahim al-Nuaimi, the production of a barrel of oil in the kingdom costs about US$1.5 compared with an average cost of US$5/barrel elsewhere in the world. Discovery costs are also low—about 10 U.S. cents per barrel as opposed to the worldwide average of US$4/barrel. Of the 400 billion barrels of recoverable oil discovered in the last 20 years, about a quarter was discovered in Saudi Arabia. The low discovery costs and high yields in Saudi Arabia are very attractive to foreign oil companies, who work in conjunction with the Saudi government to extract and deliver oil to world markets.

A majority of Saudi oil is produced from fields near Riyadh, in the Eastern Province, the largest of which are Ghawar, Safaniyah, Abqaiq, and Berri. Ghawar, with 70 billion barrels, is thought to be the largest oil field in the world. These 4 fields alone account for nearly half of the kingdom's reserves and 85 percent of its production capacity. Oil fields in the "Neutral Zone"—lands shared between Saudi Arabia and Kuwait—contain about 5 billion barrels.

Saudi Arabia exports a majority of its oil by tanker. Tankers loaded daily on the Persian Gulf coast have a full capacity of 14 million barrels a day (b/d). The other primary distribution route is through the 1,200-kilometer (746-mile) Trans-Arabian pipeline linking the Abqaiq oil field, near Riyadh, with Yanbu on the Red Sea. The pipeline has a capacity of 5 million b/d. Most of the oil arriving in Yanbu is loaded onto tankers for transport out of the Red Sea. Some of the oil continues on through the Sumed pipeline to Sidi Krier on Egypt's Mediterranean coast.

As of 2000 the most recently developed field in Saudi Arabia was the Shaybah oil field in the Empty Quarter, which holds reserves of up to 7 billion barrels. The Empty Quarter is the harsh desert region covering the southeastern part of the peninsula. Sand dunes in the Empty Quarter average 600 feet in height. In the summer, daytime temperatures reach 122 degrees Fahrenheit, then plummet to 32 degrees at night. Because of the harsh climate and terrain, much of the Empty Quarter remains unexplored. The field came on line in 1999 after the completion of a 635-kilometer (395-mile) pipeline linking it to distribution points in Abqaiq.

Practically all oil production in Saudi Arabia is controlled by the state-run Saudi Arabian oil company, Saudi Aramco. While foreign companies are contracted to build infrastructure and install equipment, the Saudi government maintains ownership of the facilities.

Saudi Arabia played a lead role in orchestrating the 1973–74 oil embargo against the United States. The resultant rise in oil prices was not enough to offset losses in sales, prompting the Saudis to soften their position and resume business in the West. Over the course of the next 25 years a stable partnership formed between Saudi Arabia and the United States, with the United States guaranteeing Saudi security in return for an uninterrupted flow of oil. Saudi Arabia now generally favors only moderate price increases, realizing it is in the country's long-term interests to keep demand steady by ensuring that oil remains competitive with other forms of energy. Out of a total workforce of 7.12 million people, 127,000 are employed in the oil and mining industry.

The kingdom is also planning to expand the production of natural gas, a venture that will involve the participation of a number of foreign companies. In 1991, natural gas reserves in Saudi Arabia were estimated at 6.1 trillion cubic meters, about 3.9 percent of the world's total. While most of this gas is acquired as a derivative of crude oil production, non-oil associated reservoirs are thought to exist in abundance. It is the mining of gas from these reservoirs that the government will focus on in the coming years, being that the use of oil-associated gas is constrained due to OPEC production quotas. It has been estimated that new foreign investment under the initiative could total tens of billions of dollars, more than the total level of foreign investment currently in the country.

NON-OIL MINING. Saudi Arabia is a country rich in minerals. Large deposits of gold, silver, iron ore, copper, bauxite, coal, tungsten, phosphates, lead, zinc, and uranium are known to exist, but have yet to be fully exploited. The reasons for this vary. For one, the kingdom's concentration on oil has led it to neglect other forms of mining. Furthermore, the mineral deposits are in remote areas where the lack of roads and water make extraction difficult. Still, the government views non-oil mining as a potentially lucrative industry, one that might help reorient the economy away from its dependence on oil. Thus, despite the difficulties, the government has decided to move forward in its efforts to exploit the country's mineral resources. Working in conjunction with the private sector, the government hopes to see the non-oil mining sector grow, on average, by 8.3 percent per year between 2000–04.

The newly formed Saudi Arabian Mining Company (Maadin) is at the center of the government's plans. The state-owned company, in partnership with privately run firms, has taken over key government mining operations with a goal to improve efficiency and increase production. Maadin is already active at the Mahd al-Dahab mine, from which over 100,000 ounces of gold are produced a year. In 2001, plans were approved to begin operations at Al Hajjar, in Asir province, with an anticipated annual yield of 55,000 ounces of gold. Renewed interest in phosphate mining is also expected to have an impact on the country's economy. If the deposits in the northern and center part of the kingdom can be feasibly removed, a major new processing plant may be constructed in Jubail to refine the high level yields.

Maadin is also involved in zinc mining near Riyadh, where results have been promising. In order to stimulate growth in the industry, the government may move to further **deregulate** mining in the second half of 2001.

MANUFACTURING. The Saudi government, in its bid to diversify the economy and increase employment opportunities, has encouraged growth in the non-oil industrial sector. However, results have been limited. The number of licenses issued and industries established did not grow by a significant margin in the last half of the 1990s. During this time, the sector's contribution to GDP remained steady at around 15 percent.

Although an informal manufacturing base (involving the production of such various items as textiles, soap, and furniture) has existed in Saudi Arabia for centuries, these small-scale private industries contribute relatively little to the GDP, and the government is doing little to promote their development. Primarily the government has focused on the growth of heavy industry—petrochemicals, fertilizer, and steel—in its efforts to stimulate the economy.

CONSTRUCTION. The rapid growth of the Saudi oil industry has led to fast-paced urban development and an ever-expanding infrastructure. As a result, construction is one of the more active sectors of the non-oil economy. It provided jobs for 16 percent of the workforce in 1998 and, in 1999, accounted for almost 9 percent of GDP.

Despite the construction sector's importance to the economy, growth in the industry during the 1990s was slow, averaging just 1.5 percent. This was partly due to the decline in infrastructure work following the completion of a number of major projects in the 1980s. However, industry prospects look good for 2001, with the pace of urban development once again on the rise. In 2000, the government issued over 27,000 work permits, with the number of contracts awarded rising 49 percent in the first 9 months of the year. The heightened activity pushed up the sales of cement by 6 percent.

SERVICES

TOURISM. Hoping to capitalize on its Red Sea coastline, unspoiled desert landscapes, and a slew of archeological sites, the Saudi Arabian government has expressed an interest in expanding the country's tourism sector. However, this task will likely be complicated by the country's rigid social structures and its fear of outside influence. Visitors have little freedom of movement in Saudi Arabia. All tourist activities are controlled by a sponsor, or guide, who is responsible for ferrying tourists to and from points of interest. Outsiders are expected to adhere to Saudi conventions. Western women, for instance, are required to abide by the country's conservative dress codes, covering their heads, arms, and legs whenever they are in public. Pants for women are not permitted, nor are women allowed to drive. Furthermore, unmarried couples may not stay in the same hotel rooms. There have been reports of Saudi citizens harassing or assaulting foreigners who fail to comply with Saudi norms of behavior. These restrictive social rules could be off-putting to some western tourists. Nonetheless, steps are being taken to increase the kingdom's annual number of visitors.

New guidelines were recently approved for issuing tourist visas to foreigners, making it easier for travel companies in Saudi Arabia to arrange group tours. The kingdom's efforts to accommodate non-Muslim, recreational travelers only began in 1998, when a tour group visited the kingdom for the first time. It was an archeological tour limited to married couples and women over the age of 45. Expanding the tourism industry amid the country's restrictive social environment will not be easy. Still, the government hopes that between 2000 and 2004, it will grant some 3 million tourist visas to foreigners, generating revenues worth approximately US$2.67 billion.

A majority of the kingdom's tourism currently comes from Muslims performing the "haj," the pilgrimage to the country's holy sites. All Muslims are instructed to make the pilgrimage at least once in their lives. In 1999, the government moved to expand the travel rights of foreign Muslims, allowing them to venture beyond Mecca and Medina. In March 2000, it is estimated that over 1 million foreigners and 700,000 Saudis made their way to the western region of Hejaz to visit the holy cities.

FINANCIAL SERVICES. Ten commercial banks operate within Saudi Arabia. Seven of them are joint ventures with foreign banks which operate according to international norms. The other 3 banks—the National Commercial Bank (NCB), the Al Rajhi Banking and Investment Company, and the Riyadh Bank—are state-owned and are run in accordance with Islamic law. This forbids them from charging interest on their loans. Any expansion of the banking system appears unlikely, at least in the near future, as the government considers the current number of banks to be sufficient to serve the economy.

Saudi Arabia has a viable over-the-counter stock market where investors, primarily the domestic commercial banks, trade **equity** in 75 Saudi companies, up from 70 companies in 1996. The number of shares traded and the value of those shares rose dramatically in the last half of the 1990s, gaining 43.6 percent in 1999 alone. In 2000, the market rose another 11 percent, making Saudi Arabia the only Arab country outside of Tunisia whose stock market posted overall gains for the year.

The Saudi Arabian stock market has traditionally been closed to non-Saudi investors. However, laws barring foreign participation were amended in 1997, and foreign nationals are now allowed to trade in the market, although on a limited scale (generally through investment in mutual funds).

INTERNATIONAL TRADE

Saudi Arabia has maintained a trade surplus since 1967 (when its trade statistics were first compiled in their current form). As the kingdom generates a majority of its revenue from petroleum exports, this surplus tends to rise and fall with the price and production of oil. After the oil embargo of 1973, when oil prices were high, the kingdom's trade surplus rose, increasing steadily until 1978. This trend continued after the Iranian revolution of 1979 when oil prices rose to new levels. Between 1978 and 1981 Saudi Arabia's trade surplus doubled, reaching a peak of US$82.5 billion.

Trade (expressed in billions of US$): Saudi Arabia

	Exports	Imports
1975	29.682	4.213
1980	109.083	30.166
1985	27.481	23.622
1990	44.417	24.069
1995	50.040	28.091
1998	N/A	N/A

SOURCE: International Monetary Fund. *International Financial Statistics Yearbook 1999.*

The surplus declined steadily throughout the 1980s as export volume diminished and oil prices fell. By 1985, the balance of trade had fallen to just US$7 billion. In 1990, Iraq invaded Kuwait, prompting the United Nations to place an embargo on Iraqi oil. The cut in supply sent prices back up, and as Saudi Arabia heightened production to meet world demand (from 5.1 million b/d in 1989 to 8.2 million b/d in 1991), export revenues increased and the trade surplus rose once again. In 1996, export revenues exceeded import expenditures by US$35.3 billion.

In 1998, the world economy slowed. At the same time, oil production by both OPEC and non-OPEC members increased. The higher production levels coupled with lowered demand caused the price of oil to fall by almost US$7/barrel, from US$19.12/barrel in 1997 to US$12.76/barrel in 1998. In Saudi Arabia, oil receipts fell and the trade surplus dropped to US$11.2 billion. In 1999, oil producers worldwide lowered production, and the corresponding rise in prices helped boost Saudi Arabia's export revenues, pushing the trade surplus to US$25 billion. This upward trend continued throughout 2000 when the surplus rose to US$52.4 billion.

Saudi Arabia imported US$28 billion worth of goods in 1999. A majority of that expenditure went toward the purchase of machinery, electrical equipment, chemicals, foodstuffs, and transportation equipment (cars, trucks, buses). Agricultural imports accounted for 17 percent of the total in 1999, up 11 percent since 1992, reflecting cuts in farm subsidies and the consequent decline in domestic food production. Electrical equipment and machinery accounted for 24 percent of the kingdom's total imports in 1999.

Saudi Arabia's exports totaled US$48 billion in 1999. Over 90 percent of those earnings were derived from the export of oil.

A majority of Saudi Arabia's trade is conducted with the United States. U.S. goods in 1998 accounted for 21 percent of Saudi imports, over twice as much as the kingdom's next leading suppliers, the United Kingdom and

Japan, whose imports to Saudi Arabia amounted to 9 percent each. Germany, France, and Italy were other major suppliers of goods.

Japan emerged as the leading buyer of Saudi goods in 1998, purchasing 17 percent of the kingdom's exports. The United States was close behind with 15 percent of Saudi exports. Saudi Arabia provides the United States with approximately 20 percent of its imported crude oil. The kingdom also is a major exporter to South Korea, Singapore, India, and France.

Saudi Arabia and its fellow members of the Gulf Cooperation Council (GCC)—Kuwait, Qatar, the United Arab Emirates, Bahrain, and Oman—have, over the past decade, been trying to promote higher levels of trade between themselves by removing barriers to the free exchange of goods, services, and capital between member states. One of these barriers, the lack of a common external tariff, has continued to complicate moves toward greater economic integration.

Saudi Arabia generally applies a 12 percent tax on imported goods, unless those goods compete with locally produced items, wherein the tax is issued at 20 percent. (Taxing certain imported items at higher rates raises the price at which the items are then sold. This helps keep local manufacturers competitive.) This is the highest import tax in the Middle East and is a point of contention between Saudi Arabia and other GCC members. In order to gain entry into the WTO, Saudi Arabia will be forced to lower tariffs to a maximum of 7.5 percent, bringing import taxes in line with other WTO member states. Imported medical goods, basic foodstuffs, and other items considered essential are exempt from the tax.

Some items, either for religious reasons or purposes of state security, are banned in Saudi Arabia. The import of non-medical drugs and alcohol is forbidden, as is any religious material which might be deemed offensive to the principles of Islam. Furthermore, the import of weapons and electronic equipment is tightly controlled.

MONEY

The Saudi Arabian Monetary Agency (SAMA) regulates the kingdom's money supply. Since June 1986, the Saudi riyal had been informally pegged to the U.S. dollar at SR3.745:US$1. The fixed rate cuts down on revenue volatility, being that a majority of Saudi oil exports are sold to America and denominated in U.S. dollars. Keeping the riyal consistent in its relation to the dollar also helps keep the currency stable, and this, in turn, makes Saudi Arabia a more attractive market for international investment capital. At the same time, the pegged rate provides a stable **exchange rate** with other GCC countries whose currencies are also generally pegged to the dollar.

Exchange rates: Saudi Arabia

Saudi riyals (SR) per US$1	
2001	3.7450
2000	3.7450
1999	3.7450
1998	3.7450
1997	3.7450
1996	3.7450

Note: The rate of Saudi currency has been fixed since June 1986.

SOURCE: CIA *World Factbook 2001* [ONLINE].

POVERTY AND WEALTH

Saudi Arabians generally enjoy a decent standard of living, due in large part to government programs designed to minimize poverty. Saudi citizens are given free education (although enrollment is not required and has historically been low, accounting for relatively high illiteracy rates) and health care, and all adult Saudis are entitled to a plot of land and a loan of US$80,000 with which to build a house.

The **GDP per capita** in Saudi Arabia reached its peak in the late 1970s and early 1980s, when elevated oil prices were generating high levels of revenue. In 1981, GDP per head reached US$16,650. Slumping oil prices and declining production in the ensuing years caused the per capita GDP to fall. By the end of the decade the figure dropped to US$5,500. Rising oil prices following the Gulf War coupled with increased Saudi production helped raise the per capita GDP once again. In 1999 the figure stood at US$9,000.

Despite the extensive social safety net in Saudi Arabia, the unequal distribution of wealth in the country is fostering resentment among the country's poorest citizens. In 1999, the National Commercial Bank estimated that out of a population of 20 million, there were 120,000 millionaires controlling a combined fortune of over US$400 billion. Meanwhile, according to the Saudi American Bank, 20 percent of Saudi men between the

GDP per Capita (US$)

Country	1975	1980	1985	1990	1998
Saudi Arabia	9,658	11,553	7,437	7,100	6,516
United States	19,364	21,529	23,200	25,363	29,683
Egypt	516	731	890	971	1,146
Iran	1,611	1,129	1,208	1,056	1,275

SOURCE: United Nations. *Human Development Report 2000; Trends in human development and per capita income.*

ages of 20 and 29 had no paid work. As a result, larger families were increasingly finding themselves under financial strain. The government, in recognition of the problem, began taking steps in 1995 to open more jobs to Saudi citizens. Two successive 5-year plans, from 1995 through 2004, have listed the Saudiization of the workforce as a primary objective. To this end, the government has passed laws requiring that at least 5 percent of the private sector be made up of Saudi citizens. Also, all firms have been ordered to increase the number of Saudi workers by 5 percent a year. At the same time, the government has attempted to limit the employment of foreign nationals by prohibiting the renewal of their work contracts and by raising the visa fees employers must pay to hire them.

Illiteracy rates are high in Saudi Arabia, hovering at around 20 percent in 1999. Consequently, the government in its development plans has placed heavy emphasis on improving education. Outside of defense expenditures, education spending accounts for the largest portion of the government budget (27 percent in 2000). Between 2000 and 2004 the government hopes to build over 1,000 primary schools, 819 middle schools, and over 900 high schools. During this time student enrollment is projected to rise from 3.9 million to 5.1 million. In efforts to create more highly skilled high school graduates, the government is also attempting to increase student enrollment in the kingdom's vocational schools and technical colleges. Efforts thus far have been successful, with vocational enrollment rising by over 20 percent between 1998 and 1999.

Health care also receives a great deal of government attention. Facilities are generally good. According to a 2001 report issued by the Ministry of Health, the 314 private hospitals provide 1 bed for every 461 people. The 2001 budget provided spending for the construction of 30 new hospitals.

WORKING CONDITIONS

The Saudi Arabian labor force is comprised of approximately 7.12 million workers. These workers enjoy few rights. The formation of unions is strictly prohibited, strikes are forbidden, and there is no collective bargaining. In the absence of a minimum wage, employers are free to pay their workers as they see fit.

While forced labor is against the law, abuses do occur, especially in remote areas and in the domestic service industry, where there have been reports of maids being forced to work up to 16 hours a day, 7 days a week. Employees have little freedom of movement, and cannot leave the country or even travel out of the region without their employer's permission.

According to labor regulations, the work week is 48 hours. Employers can require 12 additional hours of overtime at time-and-a-half pay. The law requires workers to be given a rest period of 24 hours, which is generally granted on Fridays, the Muslim sabbath. Labor laws, however, do not apply to domestic servants, who have little redress for any poor treatment they might receive. Those who run away are generally returned to their employers.

The International Labor Organization has cited Saudi Arabia for failing to adhere to conventions on equal pay, for continuing gender segregation in the work place, and for limiting vocational programs for women. Additionally, in 1995 Saudi Arabia was suspended from the U.S. Overseas Private Investment Corporation (OPIC) insurance programs for its failure to guarantee the rights of its workers as recognized by international norms.

According to human rights reports, foreign workers run the risk of being exploited. Workers recruited in foreign countries may be pressured after arriving in Saudi Arabia to sign new contracts with less favorable terms, or they may be pressured to accept lower pay than originally promised. Once in Saudi Arabia, workers may also find their freedom of movement restricted. Employers may refuse to grant them exit visas, making it impossible for them to return home.

Saudi nationals in general receive higher pay than non-nationals, especially in the agricultural sector, where Saudi citizens can make up to 3 times that of their foreign counterparts. The Saudi government has taken steps to introduce minimum wage requirements for foreign workers, making it more costly for employers to hire them. In this way the government hopes to spur more employment opportunities for Saudi citizens.

COUNTRY HISTORY AND ECONOMIC DEVELOPMENT

1745. Muhammad Abd Al-Wahhab, a religious reformer, allies with Muhammad bin Saud, a local ruler, and the 2 begin a religious/military campaign to unite the Arabian Peninsula under a new brand of strict Islamic law. They and their followers are known as Saudis.

1801. Saudi forces capture Mecca, an important religious site.

1805. Saudi forces capture Medina, another important religious site. The Ottoman Turkish government, which rules the region, launches a campaign to drive Saudi forces out of Arabia. By 1818 the Saudis have lost most of the territory previously captured and eventually take up exile in Kuwait.

1902. The Saudis renew their efforts to unify Arabia. King Abdul Aziz Al Saud (later known as Ibn Saud) recaptures Riyadh, the Al Saud ancestral home, from the Al Rashid, who are ruling in Arabia with Turkish support.

1932. Present-day Saudi Arabia is consolidated under Ibn Saud's rule. Ibn Saud declares himself king.

1953. Ibn Saud dies, leaving his kingdom to his surviving sons. His eldest son, Saud, becomes king and establishes the Council of Ministers, an advisory body made up of members of the royal family.

1962. Civil war breaks out in Yemen between Royalists and Republicans. Egypt backs the Republicans while Saudi Arabia backs the Royalists. Tensions between Egypt and Saudi Arabia are high over the next 5 years until 1967, when Egyptian forces withdraw from Yemen.

1964. King Saud steps down in favor of his half brother Faisal bin Abdul Aziz.

1967. War breaks out between Israel and 4 Arab nations, Egypt, Jordan, Syria, and Iraq. Saudi Arabia sits out the war, but later provides economic assistance to Egypt, Jordan, and Syria.

1973. War erupts once again between Israel and its Arab neighbors. Saudi Arabia and other Arab oil producers boycott the sale of oil to the United States to protest American financial aid to Israel. The price of oil rises steeply, but Saudi Arabian earnings still suffer due to loss of sales to the West.

1974. Despite Arab opposition, Saudi Arabia abandons the 1973 boycott, negotiating an economic and military cooperation agreement with the United States whereby the United States provides the kingdom with military protection in return for the guaranteed flow of oil. Saudi wealth begins to grow rapidly, heightening its political and economic influence throughout the world.

1975. King Faisal is assassinated. He is succeeded by his half brother, Crown Prince Khalid. Another half brother, Fahd, is appointed crown prince and first deputy prime minister.

1979. Armed religious militants take over the Grand Mosque in Mecca. The 250 men, followers of the Sunni Muslim cleric Juhaiman Ibn Seif al-Oteibi, are removed by force. The incident alerts the royal family to growing dissatisfaction in the kingdom among religious conservatives. In response, the government establishes a committee to lay out a system of societal laws based on Islamic principles.

1982. King Khalid dies and is succeeded by Crown Prince Fahd. Fahd becomes a key player in Middle East politics.

1988. A Saudi-brokered cease fire is declared in the 8-year-old Iran-Iraq war, bringing stability to the Middle East.

1990. Iraq invades Kuwait, drawing international condemnation and starting the Gulf War. The UN places an embargo on Iraqi oil. The cut in world supply causes oil prices to rise. Saudi Arabia begins to increase production to help meet world demand. King Fahd helps organize and hold together the coalition of Arab military forces which, in conjunction with a large contingent of U.S. forces, drives Iraq from Kuwait.

1995. King Fahd suffers a stroke. Over the next 2 years, Crown Prince Abdullah emerges as the de facto head of state.

1996. A car bomb explodes outside U.S. military housing at the Al Khobar military base in Eastern Province, killing 19 American servicemen. Responsibility is linked to Osama bin Laden, a Saudi dissident claiming to resent the Western presence on Saudi soil.

1999. Saudi Arabia cuts oil production by over 2 million barrels a day to boost prices.

2000. New laws are passed to facilitate foreign investment.

2001. Saudi Arabia and Iran sign a security pact pledging cooperation in combatting terrorism, drug trafficking, and **money laundering**.

FUTURE TRENDS

Barring the discovery of a new energy supply that renders oil obsolete, Saudi Arabia will be able to maintain its economy through the production and distribution of oil for nearly another century. The discovery of new reserves, which appears likely, will extend the viability of the oil-based economy even further. However, as oil supplies rise and efficiency increases, prices will likely go down. To compensate for lower oil revenues, the Saudi government will continue to take steps toward economic diversification, expanding its agricultural, non-oil mining, and tourism sectors. The government will also continue to push for private sector growth as it loosens its grip on the economy.

In the meantime, Saudi Arabia will continue to implement oil policies that are favorable to the West for 2 main reasons. One, Saudi Arabia is dependent on the West, primarily the United States, for trade and military protection. And two, it is in Saudi Arabia's own interests to maintain stable oil prices to keep the commodity competitive with other forms of energy.

Saudi Arabia will also further its efforts to attract foreign investment, especially in heavy industrial sectors where the government is encouraging the creation of public-private partnerships. Although the government has expressed interest in decentralizing the economy, full privatization in most industries has yet to occur.

Cooperation between the United States and Saudi Arabia should continue, at least into the near future. However, relations could become strained if the situation in Israel continues to deteriorate. Historically, U.S. support for Israel has generated hostility in the Arab world. If the violence in Israel escalates and the Palestinians are perceived as being grossly victimized, the Saudi population, for reasons of Muslim solidarity, may begin pushing for intervention. Any move in that direction would complicate U.S.-Saudi relations.

Young Saudis will continue to enter the labor market in growing numbers. As such, the so-called Saudiization of the workforce will remain a government priority for the foreseeable future. Hiring fees will be raised for foreign workers, and those workers with expired visas may be forbidden to renew them. The Saudi infrastructure will also expand in the coming decades as new oil fields are discovered and the non-oil mining sector grows. Saudi Arabia's push to gain entry into the World Trade Organization will accelerate the pace of economic reforms currently underway.

DEPENDENCIES

Saudi Arabia has no territories or colonies.

BIBLIOGRAPHY

Asad, Muhammad. *The Road to Mecca.* 1954; Louisville, KY: Fons Vitae, 2001.

Commercial Office, Royal Embassy of Saudi Arabia in Washington, D.C. <http://www.saudicommercialoffice.com>. Accessed September 2001.

Economist Intelligence Unit. *Country Profile: Saudi Arabia.* London: Economist Intelligence Unit, 2001.

Metz, Helen Chapin, editor. *Saudi Arabia: A Country Study.* Washington, DC: Library of Congress, Federal Research Division, 1993.

The Saudi Arabian Cultural Mission to the U.S.A. <http://www.sacm.org>. Accessed September 2001.

U.S. Central Intelligence Agency. *World Factbook 2000.* <http://www.odci.gov/cia/publications/factbook/index.html>. Accessed August 2001.

U.S. Department of State. *Background Notes: Saudi Arabia, September 1998.* <http://www.state.gov/www/background_notes/saudi_0998_bgn.html>. Accessed September 2001.

U.S. Department of State, Bureau of Democracy, Human Rights, and Labor. *Country Reports on Human Rights Practices, 1999: Saudi Arabia.* Released February 2000. <http://www.usis.usemb.se/human/human1999/saudiara.html>. Accessed September 2001.

U.S. Department of State. *FY 2001 Country Commercial Guide: Saudi Arabia.* <http://www.state.gov/www/about_state/business/com_guides/2001/near/index.html>. Accessed September 2001.

—John Mazor

SINGAPORE

Republic of Singapore

> **CAPITAL:** Singapore.
>
> **MONETARY UNIT:** Singapore dollar (S$). One dollar equals 100 cents. There are coins of 1, 5, 10, 20, 50 cents, and 1 dollar. There are notes of 2, 5, 10, 20, 50, 100, 500, 1,000, and 10,000 dollars.
>
> **CHIEF EXPORTS:** Machinery and equipment (including electronics), chemicals, and mineral fuels.
>
> **CHIEF IMPORTS:** Machinery and equipment, mineral fuel, chemicals, and foodstuffs.
>
> **GROSS DOMESTIC PRODUCT:** US$109.8 billion (2000 est.).
>
> **BALANCE OF TRADE:** **Exports:** US$137 billion (2000 est.). **Imports:** US$127 billion (2000 est.).

COUNTRY OVERVIEW

LOCATION AND SIZE. Singapore is a city-state in Southeast Asia, located about 137 kilometers (85 miles) north of the Equator. It consists of 1 major island and 59 small islands. Singapore lies at the center of a major sea route connecting the Far East to Asia, Europe, and the Middle East, which gives the country its strategic importance. It is separated from Malaysia to the north by the narrow Johore Strait and from Indonesia to the south by the wider Singapore Strait. The country has a land area of 637.5 square kilometers (247 square miles), but no land boundaries, and its total coastline is 193 kilometers (120 miles). The territory of Singapore covers a slightly smaller area than that of New York City.

POPULATION. The population of Singapore, which is entirely urban, was estimated at 4,151,264 in July 2000. In 2000, the birth rate stood at 12.79 per 1000 people, a low level attributed to urbanization and birth control policies, and the death rate stood at 4.21 per 1000. The estimated population growth rate is 3.54 percent. Such a high rate is due to the high net **immigration** rate, which stood at 26.8 immigrants per 1000 people. These immigrants form a large community of foreign temporary workers estimated at about 10 percent of the total population. Singapore has one of the highest population densities in the world, with about 6,500 people per square kilometer (or 16,800 per square mile).

The Singaporean population is diverse and represents 3 major ethnic groups. Ethnic Chinese make up almost 77 percent of the population, Malays make up 14 percent, Indians 7.6 percent, and other ethnic groups 1.4 percent. Around 18 percent of the population is below

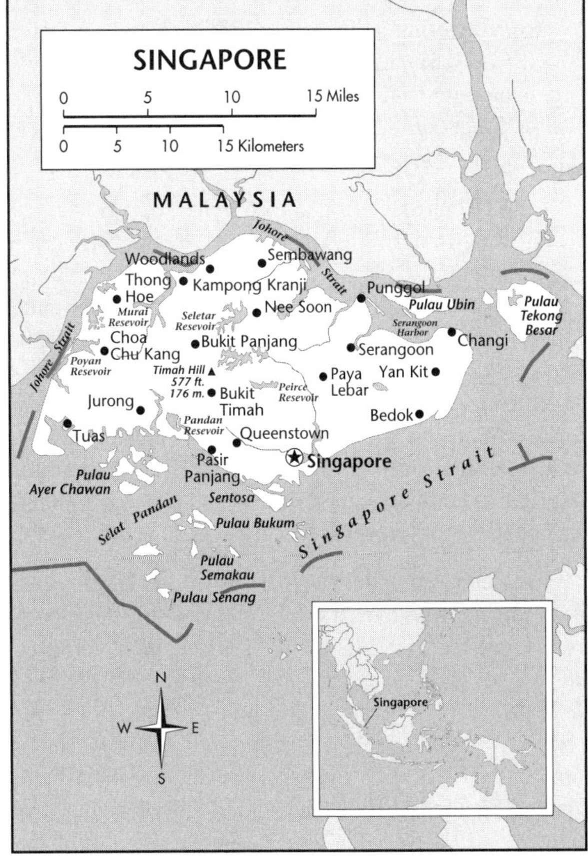

the age of 14, and just 7 percent is older than 65. The current ethnic distribution was formed in the 19th century when the British administration encouraged people to migrate to Singapore from neighboring Malacca, the Indonesian islands, India and especially China.

In 1957, Singapore's population was approximately 1.45 million, and there was a relatively high birth rate. Aware of the country's extremely limited natural resources and small territory, the government introduced birth control policies in the late 1960s. In the late 1990s, the population was aging, with fewer people entering the labor market and a shortage of skilled workers. In a dramatic reversal of policy, the Singapore government now plans to introduce a "baby bonus" scheme in 2001 that will encourage couples to have more children.

Singapore wants to limit the inflow of illegal immigrants. The effect of drugs and drug trafficking is another important issue, since Singapore lies near the "Golden Triangle," an area between Burma, Laos, and Thailand that is the world's largest producer of illicit drugs such as opium. Singapore is among the few countries in the world to have adopted the death penalty for possession and sale of drugs. New chronic diseases like AIDS are also of great concern to the Singaporean government, since the country is a busy tourist destination.

OVERVIEW OF ECONOMY

Manufacturing and services are the 2 main features of the modern Singaporean economy, but the economy's main economic engine is its seaport, one of the world's busiest. Singapore also has one of the largest commercial shipping registers in the world.

In 1819, when the British East India Company leased this territory from the Sultan of Johore to establish a trade and communication post, it was a small settlement in a swampy area. However, the British administration quickly cleared jungles, reclaimed marshes, and established a merchant seaport. This port expanded into a major regional trading post due to its strategic and convenient location along the main sea route connecting the Far East to British India and to Europe. The rise of Singapore as a communication hub would prove a foundation for its future prosperity.

As a free port and a major British naval base in East Asia, Singapore enjoyed a special status within the British protectorate for a long time. In 1959, Singapore achieved full self-governance, and in 1963, it joined the Federation of Malaysia. However, sharp political disagreements arose with the federal government, and in 1965, Singapore left the Federation and became an independent state. Having a small territory and no natural resources, the government staked everything on the transformation of the country's economic base from a trade mediator and regional transport hub to a manufacturing center, specializing in capital-intensive industries, high technologies, and financial services. Singapore's government promoted a free-market economy and export oriented industrialization (EOI), combined with a measure of state intervention, subsidized credits to selected industries, and high public investment in applied research and certain export targets. Export to the international market promoted efficient use of resources and generated **hard currency**, which was necessary for catching up with further development of technologies and industrial innovation. This policy brought unprecedented economic expansion, with an annual average growth rate of 6.4 percent from the 1960s through the 1980s. This development transformed Singapore into one of the "economic tigers" of Asia.

There are different interpretations about the causes of this high performance. A World Bank report argued that this success was because of a mix of private investors and available human resources. Others argue that state initiatives and government economic policies were important. In Singapore's transformation, the Economic Development Board, which is the government agency responsible for the formulation and implementation of economic and industrial development strategies established in 1961, played a crucial role.

The country's major export products are electronic goods, machinery, and equipment produced by major **multinational corporations**. Tourism is important. In 1996, Singapore hosted 4,795 international and regional conventions and received more than 7 million tourists, providing revenues of about 9 percent of **gross domestic product** (GDP). Finance and business services are other important sectors of the economy, accounting for almost 30 percent of GDP in 1996. Transport and communications contributed an estimated 10 percent of GDP in 1996.

The Singapore government is persistent in the promotion of initiatives to keep the country competitive in the international arena. One of these initiatives is IT2000, which depends on a vision of Singapore as an "Intellectual Island" where information technologies penetrate all aspects of life. Another initiative is Jurong Town Corporation, which offers ready-built factories and manages 33 industrial parks housing 7,000 companies. The government supported the selected sectors in manufacturing and other industries through different means. It owns the Government-Linked Companies (GLCs) that operate as commercial entities. Singapore has the second highest number of state-controlled firms (45 percent) in the world, higher than Korea or Japan.

One of the important features of the Singaporean economy is that the financial sector has been guided by conservative **fiscal policies**. In 1998, in response to the 1997 Asian financial crisis, the Singapore government announced financial reforms to improve the country's international competitiveness, which included further **liberalization** of the financial sector and tax initiatives.

High economic performance and development kept unemployment at a low level during the last decades of the 20th century in all sectors of the economy including manufacturing, tourism, and finance. In 1999 unemployment was just 3.2 percent (by comparison, unemployment in the United States was 4.2 percent in the same year). Because of the speed of its economic expansion, Singapore began to experience shortages of skilled labor in the late 1990s and early 2000s.

POLITICS, GOVERNMENT, AND TAXATION

Singapore is a parliamentary democracy with a president as the constitutional head of state. The president plays a ceremonial role in the political life of the country and until 1991 was elected by the parliament. In 1991, the constitution was amended, allowing citizens to vote for their president in direct popular elections. Current president S. R. Nathan took office for a 6-year term in 1999. Singapore's **unicameral** (one house) parliament has 83 members elected by popular vote. Executive power rests with the cabinet, led by the prime minister who is responsible to the parliament.

Several political parties have been active since Singapore's independence in 1965. Five of these parties have a high profile and influence in the country. These are: People's Action Party (PAP); National Solidarity Party (NSP); Singapore Democratic Party (SDP); Singapore People's Party (SPP); and Worker's Party (WP). Unlike many neighboring countries, the Communist Party does not have mass support in Singapore, and there has been no violent confrontation with communists. The military has never been an influential force in the political arena of the country. Politically, Singapore has remained remarkably stable and nearly untouched by political violence since independence.

Since the end of World War II, the major issues shaping political competition in Singapore have been the promotion of political stability, economic growth, and maintaining a balance among the 3 main ethnic groups. The PAP came to power spreading an ideal of national consolidation, economic growth, and state paternalism. It has remained the country's dominant political force for the past 40 years, controlling parliament in every election since independence. The PAP's strong man, Lee Kuan Yew, became prime minister in 1959 when Singapore acquired self-governance, and retained this position until 1990. After his resignation, Goh Chok Tong, Lee's chosen successor, became the new prime minister. One of the unique features of Singaporean political development is the governing by a single party since gaining independence in 1965. This has led prominent human rights groups to criticize the Singaporean government over its failure to promote and protect the political and civil rights of its citizens.

Since the early 1960s, under the leadership of both Lee Kuan Yew and then Goh Chok Tong, the Singapore government has promoted a free-market and export-oriented economy. This policy has been successful and the country has experienced unprecedented economic growth and prosperity. Leading **technocrats** were able to capture major trends in technological change in the modern world and utilize the benefits of globalization. In 1992, as a member of the Association of South East Asian Nations (ASEAN), Singapore created a regional **free trade zone**, to be known as the ASEAN Free Trade Zone (AFTA). Singapore managed to minimize the negative effects of the oil crisis of 1979 and the Asian financial meltdown in 1997.

The country has continually attracted **foreign direct investment** and technological transfers from developed countries such as Japan and the United States. One of the important tools in the hands of the government has been its taxation policy and its initiatives. With few exceptions, capital gains are not taxed in Singapore. Both resident and non-resident companies are taxed at the same rate as the corporate tax rate, which stays at 25.5 percent. The typical withholding tax rate on interest payable to non-residents stays at 15 percent, but this could be reduced or even exempted by tax treaties in the future. A Goods and Services Tax (GST) was introduced in April 1994 at 3 percent, but was accompanied by compensatory reductions in **direct taxation**. Qualified employees may enjoy tax exemptions of 50 percent for up to S$10 million of stock option gains arising over a period of 10 years for stock options granted after June 2000.

INFRASTRUCTURE, POWER, AND COMMUNICATIONS

Singapore inherited from the colonial era a superior **infrastructure** and well-developed transport network. After independence, the Singaporean government made many efforts and sizable investments to improve these even further. This small city-state is served by a network of 3,122 kilometers (1,940 miles) of highways, 99 percent of which are paved. In the 1970s and 1980s, there was a steep increase in private car ownership, which led to traffic congestion and rising air pollution. The government reacted swiftly, investing significant sums in public transport, especially the mass transit system. It also restricted private car usage on Singaporean roads, using different measures, including taxes and Certificates of Entitlement. By the 1990s, 83 kilometers (51

Communications

Country	Newspapers	Radios	TV Sets[a]	Cable subscribers[a]	Mobile Phones[a]	Fax Machines[a]	Personal Computers[a]	Internet Hosts[b]	Internet Users[b]
	1996	1997	1998	1998	1998	1998	1998	1999	1999
Singapore	360	822	348	49.5	346	31.6	458.4	322.30	950
United States	215	2,146	847	244.3	256	78.4	458.6	1,508.77	74,100
China	N/A	333	272	40.0	19	1.6	8.9	0.50	8,900
Japan	578	955	707	114.8	374	126.8	237.2	163.75	27,060

[a]Data are from International Telecommunication Union, *World Telecommunication Development Report 1999* and are per 1,000 people.
[b]Data are from the Internet Software Consortium (http://www.isc.org) and are per 10,000 people.

SOURCE: World Bank. *World Development Indicators 2000.*

miles) of mass rapid transit system, and 11 kilometers (6 miles) of light rapid transit system had been built, and the country could boast of an excellent public transport system, praised for its safety, quality of service, and punctuality. In 1998, the government launched a S$1.7 billion project to build a new transit line. There were at that time 681,924 registered motor vehicles, including 378,090 cars, 11,410 buses, 133,382 motorcycles and scooters, and other vehicles.

Throughout the colonial era, the port of Singapore was an important military base and commercial seaport. After gaining independence, Singapore maintained its status as an important regional transport hub. Its seaport is believed to be one of the world's busiest ports in tonnage terms, with 140,922 vessels making up a shipping weight of 858 gross tons calling at the port and total container traffic of 15.14 million 20-foot equivalent units. It also has one of the largest commercial shipping registers in the world. Its merchant marine included 891 ships (1,000 gross registered tonnage and over) in 1998. Singapore also houses the third-largest oil refinery in the world with a capacity of 1 million barrels a day (1998). Major petroleum companies, including Shell, ESSO, Caltex, British Petroleum, and Mobil, operate there.

The government has invested heavily in the development of aviation, signing air service agreements with 90 countries, including "open skies" agreements with the United States, New Zealand, and Brunei Darussalam. The Civil Aviation Authority of Singapore (CAAS) oversees and regulates development in this sector. There were 9 airports in Singapore in 1999. The largest is Changi airport (a subsidiary of CAAS), which hosted 61 airlines and handled 23.8 million passengers in 1998 alone, making Singapore one of the major airports in the region. The 47-hectare (116-acre) Changi Airfreight Center handled 1.43 million tons of air freight movement in 1998. The government planned to invest a further S$1.5 billion in upgrading the airport facilities in the first decade of the 21st century. Singapore Airline (SIA) was created in 1972 after the split of Malaysia-Singapore Airline. SIA and its subsidiary, SilkAir, operated 87 aircraft, employed 18,800 people, and carried 12 million passengers a year in 1998. In 1998, SIA was ranked fourth in terms of international freight measured in ton-kilometers, and eighth in international passenger-kilometers.

Singapore is fully reliant on imports of mineral fuel for domestic consumption, and these imports accounted for 9.3 percent of merchandise imports in 1996. This makes the country vulnerable to unfavorable fluctuations in world oil prices. Electric power is produced from fossil fuel at 3 power stations. Electricity production was recorded at 28.586 billion kilowatt-hours (kWh) in 1998.

Telecommunication services in Singapore remain under state control. Telephone service is provided by the state-controlled Singapore Telecom (ST). The country had 54.6 million telephone lines and 1.02 million mobile cellular telephones in 1998. The government has attempted to end ST's **monopoly**. In 1993, it sold about 7 percent of its share to private companies and, in 1997, ST's monopoly on mobile and pager services came to an end. In 1998, there were 8 Internet service providers in the country and 458.4 computers per 1,000 people, which is more than in the United States. In 2000, the Singapore government announced a S$1.5 billion investment over 3 years into the e-Government Action Plan, which should enable Singaporeans to access a wide range of online services.

ECONOMIC SECTORS

Singapore's separation from the Federation of Malaysia in 1965 had advantages and disadvantages. On the one hand, its economic development has been constrained by its small territory, small population, and extremely limited natural resources, and the country has always been fully reliant on the importation of foodstuffs. Yet Singapore has a huge advantage in its location in a major sea route connecting the Far East to South Asia, Europe and the Middle East. The country has a well-

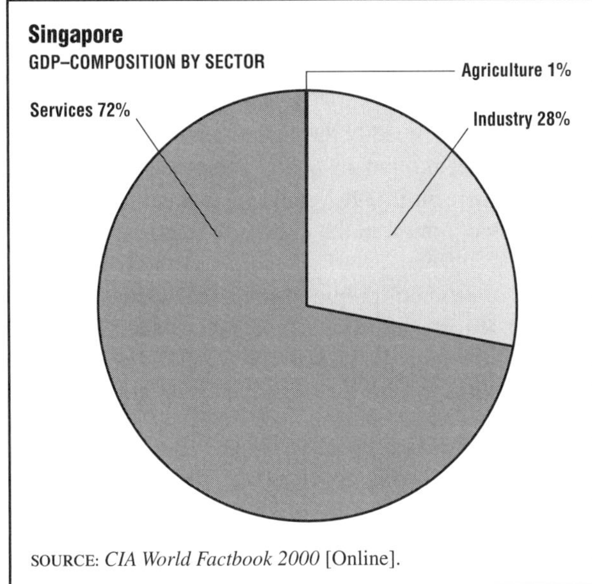

SOURCE: *CIA World Factbook 2000* [Online].

trained, well-educated, disciplined **labor force** and has attracted major multinational corporations from Europe, Japan, and the United States. Many of them, such as Sony, NEC, Matsushita, Texas Instruments, and others, have established their manufacturing and assembly plants or distribution centers there.

Singapore has fully used the advantage of its superior location, reinventing itself as a major communication hub in Southeast Asia. The policy of encouraging private entrepreneurship, giving priority to the development of an export-oriented economy, and encouraging capital intensive industries combined with selective state intervention, brought Singapore unprecedented economic growth from the 1960s through the 1990s. By 2000, industry and services had become the 2 largest sectors of the modern Singaporean economy, contributing 30 percent and 70 percent of GDP, respectively, in 2000. (Agriculture's contribution was negligible.) Although there was a substantial slowing down in economic growth in all sectors of the economy after the 1997 Asian financial crisis, Singapore managed to avoid economic decline like neighboring Indonesia or Thailand.

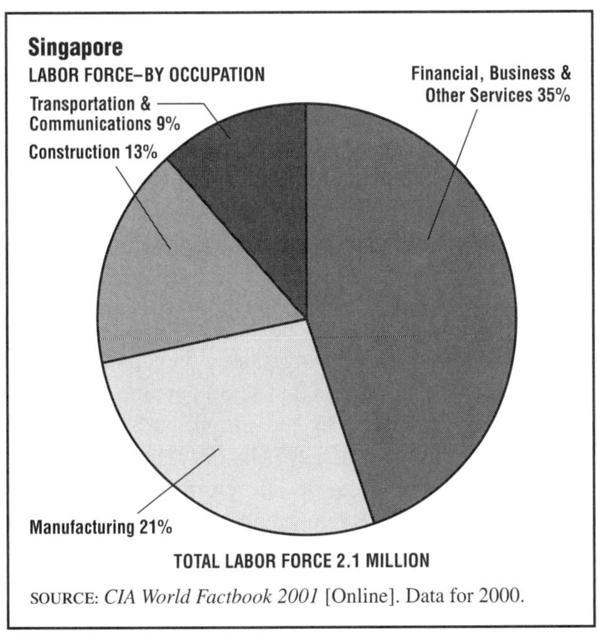

SOURCE: *CIA World Factbook 2001* [Online]. Data for 2000.

AGRICULTURE

Agriculture, including fishery, is an insignificant part of Singapore's economy, accounting for just 0.2 percent of GDP and employing 0.2 percent of the workforce. Since the 19th century Singapore has been fully reliant on the import of foodstuffs, obtained from its neighbors. The country has a small fishing industry consisting of a small fleet and marine fish farms. There has been some interest in the greenhouse production of certain fruits and vegetables for domestic consumption, but it has not developed and remains small. Singapore does cultivate orchids for domestic and export markets.

In the late 1990s, Singapore businessmen expressed interest in biotechnology and genetically modified food production. The public outcry in Europe and the United States over genetically modified food has cooled this interest for the time being. Some private entrepreneurs invested in the agricultural sector in neighboring Malaysia and Thailand, aiming to export the products back to Singapore.

INDUSTRY

Singapore belongs to the "New Industrialized States" (NIS), the countries that underwent rapid industrialization from the 1960s to the 1980s. During these 2 decades, Singapore managed to attract technology transfers from the developed world as well as sizable foreign direct investment (FDI). The island has a small mining industry that is of no importance in the national economy.

MANUFACTURING. Singapore has a diverse, well-established, and economically important manufacturing sector, which contributed 28 percent to GDP and provided employment for 417,300 people, or 21.6 percent of the workforce, in 1999. Since the early 1990s, the manufacturing sector's share in GDP has been slowly declining due to the steady rise in competition from neighboring countries and the expansion of its own service sector. The United States remains the single largest investor in Singapore's economy. In 1999, about 57 percent of FDI commitments came from the United States.

Singapore began its industrial sector in the 1960s, using its superior location and well-trained and educated labor force. The industrial sector initially consisted of electrical assembly, oil refining, and shipping facilities. The electronic sector became the country's most important manufacturing element. This sector underwent a rapid expansion in the late 1960s when Texas Instruments and other multinational corporations established assembly plants in Singapore.

In the 1990s, there was further growth in the manufacturing of different electronic products and computer components. In the late 1990s, Singapore became the world's largest producer of computer disk drives. In 1999, electronics accounted for 43.4 percent of **value-added** manufacturing in the country, making Singapore vulnerable to downturns in the international market. Most of these goods are produced in foreign-owned plants for export to the United States, Europe, and East Asia. Electronics manufacture was affected by the 1997 Asian financial crisis, although the Singaporean government supported the sector by tax breaks and other initiatives. After 1997, several multinational corporations such as Seagate, Western Digital of the United States, and others laid off staff and began **restructuring** their production capacity. Some considered moving their manufacturing operations to neighboring countries such as Malaysia, Indonesia, and the Philippines, where wages are lower than in Singapore.

Chemical production, petroleum production, and printing are also important contributors to the country's economy. Singapore has a well-developed chemical and chemical production sector. This sector experienced steady growth in the 1980s and 1990s by attracting substantial FDI. Chemical production contributed 18.1 percent of valued-added manufacturing in 1999.

Petroleum production underwent rapid expansion in the 1960s and 1970s, benefiting from the country's large and efficient seaport and modern oil refining facilities. This sector produces 18.8 million metric tons (20.68 million tons) of distillate fuel oils and 15.7 million metric tons (17.27 million tons) of residual fuel oil, and other petroleum-based products. Singapore has the world's third largest oil-refining industry. Petroleum production contributes 4.4 percent of valued-added manufacturing.

Singapore has developed high-quality color printing processes, producing several publications for major clients from the United States and Europe. Printing and publishing contributes 4.0 percent of value-added manufacturing (1999). The other manufacturing sectors produce transport equipment, machinery, and fabricated metal products.

SERVICES

TOURISM. Tourism is an important sector of Singapore's economy, providing employment for 118,900 people. Although Singapore was long known as a tourist destination for sailors, business people, and adventurers, mass tourism began in earnest in the 1970s and 1980s with the increase in international air travel. The number of tourists visiting the country rose steadily throughout the 1980s and 1990s, reaching 7.29 million in 1996. There was a decline of about 1.3 percent in 1997 and 13.3 percent in 1998, due to economic turmoil in the region. In response to this decline, the Singapore Tourism Board started "Tourism Unlimited," a program promoting regional tourism and developing tourist projects near Singapore. In 1999, about 6.96 million tourists visited the country, contributing S$11.2 billion dollars to the national economy.

Singapore promotes itself as a "dream destination," offering excellent service, a multicultural environment, local hospitality, exotic festivals, and tax-free shopping. To boost its competitiveness it has also signed visa-free agreements with most countries in Asia, Europe, and the Americas. According to the national authorities, in 1998 Singapore had 108 hotels with total room capacity of 32,000. Most visitors come from the ASEAN countries, Japan, Taiwan, Australia, the United Kingdom, and the United States. In the 1990s, Singapore reinvented itself as Asia's convention city. In 1996, the capital hosted 4,795 international and regional conventions with 426,000 foreign participants. According to the Union des Associations Internationales, Singapore ranks seventh among the world's major convention cities.

FINANCIAL SERVICES. The financial and business services sector is one of the most important sectors to the Singapore economy and provides employment for 266,000 people. Finance rests on the traditional foundations of the banking system, investments, insurance, and foreign exchange. There were 154 commercial banks in 1997, although banking was dominated by the "Big Four": the DBS Bank, the United Overseas Bank (UOB), the Overseas Union Bank (OUB), and the Overseas-Chinese Banking Corporation (OCBS). According to the IMF, Singapore is the world's fourth-largest global exchange center. The financial sector, particularly its banking component, has been tightly regulated by the Monetary Authority of Singapore (MAS), prompting sharp criticism from the United States and the World Trade Organization (WTO).

Although the 1997 Asian financial crisis affected the financial sector, there were no major bank collapses or bankruptcies. In 1997, Singapore's benchmark Strait Times Industrial Index (STII) fell 30 percent, leading to the STII being replaced by the simplified Straits Times Index (STI) in August of 1997. In 1999, the STI experienced some recovery due to an upturn in the manufacturing sector. The MAS reinforced its strict policy against internationalizing the Singapore dollar by limiting overseas lending and borrowing by non-residents. This policy restricts use of the currency outside the country for activities unrelated to the domestic economic development. However, economic recovery has improved the Singapore government's fiscal position, and it intends to **deregulate** and gradually liberalize the financial sector.

The business services sector (including property services, accountancy, and information technology), the fourth-most important economic sector in 1999, experienced difficult times in the late 1990s. During this period, economic **recession** and declining investments in neighboring countries led to less demand for financial and business services and brought a sharp decline in spending in the property market.

RETAIL. Singapore's well-developed **retail** sector provides excellent service to the local population and to foreign tourists. Large, state-of-the-art supermarkets are complemented by thousands of small retail shops where tourists and local consumers can buy different products. Singapore has long been recognized as a major tourist shopping destination offering, among other things, the latest electronic products free of tax. In 1998, there were 281,200 people employed in the wholesale and retail trades. After the decline of 1997 and 1998 this sector recovered, with the value of retail sales up by 12.1 percent and their volume up by 14.1 percent.

INTERNATIONAL TRADE

Since the 1960s, Singapore has adopted a policy of export-oriented industrialization, promoting the export of goods and services in the international markets. It has few barriers against the import of goods and services, although the government's well-known interventionist policy in the regulation and ownership of many Singapore companies has been widely criticized. Singapore more than doubled its exports, from US$52.752 billion in 1990 to US$118.268 billion, in 1995. Exports dipped after 1997, but recovered to reach US$137 billion in 2000. The United States is Singapore's single largest trading partner, accounting for 19 percent of all exports in 1999, primarily from the sale of manufactured electronics and computer peripherals. A large part of these exports originates from U.S.-owned companies, which are traditionally the largest investors in the Singapore economy. Neighboring Malaysia is the second largest export market, accounting for 17 percent of total exports. Hong Kong and Japan are also important export destinations, accounting for 8 percent and 7 percent of exports respectively. Other important partners include Taiwan, Thailand, the United Kingdom, the Netherlands, China, South Korea, and Germany.

The United States and Japan are the largest suppliers of imports to Singapore, with both countries supplying 17 percent of imports. Malaysia remained one of the traditional sources of imports, accounting for 16 percent of the total. Major imports from Malaysia include **consumer goods** like foodstuffs and raw materials. China (5 percent), Thailand (5 percent), Taiwan (4.0 percent), Saudi Arabia (3 percent), and Germany (3 percent) are other major sources of imports. In 2000, the value of imports totaled US$127 billion.

Trade (expressed in billions of US$): Singapore

	Exports	Imports
1975	5.375	8.133
1980	19.376	24.007
1985	22.812	26.285
1990	52.752	60.899
1995	118.268	124.507
1998	109.895	104.719

SOURCE: International Monetary Fund. *International Financial Statistics Yearbook 1999.*

Singapore's government considers the development of free trade as an important factor for the country's future economic growth. Singapore strongly supported free trade negotiations between the members of the Asia Pacific Economic Cooperation organization (APEC), which tried to remove trade barriers between member countries, including the United States, Canada, Japan, Australia, and others. Singapore also strongly supported the creation of a regional free trade zone for the Association of South East Asian Nations (ASEAN), to be known as the ASEAN Free Trade Zone (AFTA). In 2001, Singapore announced its intention to discuss bilateral free-trade arrangements with Australia, Canada, Japan, and the United States.

Singapore's international trade rose during the last 3 decades of the 20th century, when the country managed its trade balance to achieve a **trade surplus** of US$10 billion by 2000. Singapore demonstrated its immunity to the sharp oil price rises in 2000 and 2001; however, it faces increasing competition from neighboring countries and has become vulnerable to changes in global market demands for electronic products. Nevertheless, political and economic uncertainty in neighboring Indonesia, the Philippines, and Thailand have strengthened Singapore's position, confirming its image as one of the most stable and business-friendly countries in the region.

MONEY

Over the last 2 decades, the value of the Singapore dollar showed remarkable stability because of the country's steady economic growth. During this period of unprecedented growth, Singapore managed to avoid high **inflation** or economic recession. The Asian financial crisis

Exchange rates: Singapore

Singapore dollars (S$) per US$1	
Jan 2001	1.7365
2000	1.7240
1999	1.6950
1998	1.6736
1997	1.4848
1996	1.4100

SOURCE: CIA *World Factbook 2001* [ONLINE].

GDP per Capita (US$)

Country	1975	1980	1985	1990	1998
Singapore	8,722	11,709	14,532	19,967	31,139
United States	19,364	21,529	23,200	25,363	29,683
China	138	168	261	349	727
Japan	23,296	27,672	31,588	38,713	42,081

SOURCE: United Nations. *Human Development Report 2000; Trends in human development and per capita income.*

of 1997 did affect Singapore's economy, but the country was able to avoid the political and economic calamities that brought high inflation and sizable recession to neighboring Indonesia and Thailand. There was slowdown of the Singapore economy in 1997 and 1998, affecting all sectors and bringing a small rise in inflation. In 1999 and 2000, the country overcame the difficulties and produced significant growth. Inflation stabilized at about 0.4 percent and GDP growth at about 5.5 percent in 1999.

According to the IMF classification, the Singapore dollar is a freely floating currency determined by the foreign exchange market. The Monetary Authority of Singapore (MAS), which acts as the central bank, closely monitors the **exchange rate** and ensures the stability of the currency against international currency speculators. Due to the regional economic downturn, the value of the Singapore dollar declined slightly against the U.S. dollar, from 1.4174 in 1995 to 1.6733 in January 2000. This stability was supported by Singapore's huge stocks of foreign reserves, the world's largest in per capita terms (US$23,864 per head against US$14,070 per head in Hong Kong). These foreign reserves are even larger than those of the United States. Singapore is also the world's fourth-largest global exchange center after London, New York, and Tokyo, with Chase Manhattan Bank, Citibank, Deutsche Bank, Morgan Guaranty, and others, operating in this market.

Singapore has a single stock market, which until 1997 was known as the Strait Times Industrial Index (STII). In August 1997, it was replaced by the Straits Times Index (STI). In 1997 and 1998 the STI was affected by the regional recession, recovering in 1999 and 2000. According to the Singapore Exchange (SGX) statistics, 388 companies, representing total capitalization of S$389.5 billion (US$236 billion), were listed in the SGX main board in December 2000.

POVERTY AND WEALTH

Extraordinary economic growth during the past 3 decades brought wealth and prosperity to Singapore. This growth was impressive during the 1980s and 1990s. In 1959, when Singapore gained self-governance, its per capita GDP was just US$400. In 2000, Singapore was ranked fifth in the world in terms of per capita GDP, ahead of the United States, Canada, and the United Kingdom. In 2000, the per capita GDP, figured at **purchasing power parity**, was US$26,500. A Central Provident Fund, to which employers and employees pay compulsory contributions, provides benefits in case of work injury, old age, and disability. Most people live in small apartments in high-rise buildings.

Social polarization is visible in education. The social prestige of a good education is traditionally very high in Singapore society. Private schools are very expensive and those who can spend a considerable part of their income on providing the best education for their children. Although the government is trying to encourage the development of a "knowledge society," education is not compulsory, and the poorer members of Singaporean society are disadvantaged, while the wealthy send their children to leading British, Australian, and North American universities.

In Singapore's society, as elsewhere, some people acquire wealth while others need to work hard merely to maintain a decent life. There are no statistics on the distribution of income, and therefore it is difficult to assess socio-economic and social division in the country. Traditionally, recent immigrants, both legal and illegal, have been the most disadvantaged members of the society. There is evidence, too, that social polarization exists along ethnic lines, with the ethnic Chinese community considered better off than the Malay community. In formulating social policy, the government has to take the importance of ethnic issues into consideration. The Singapore government supports such traditional values as a strong work ethic and the importance of family, promoting them as "Asian values" in opposition to the perceived "individualism" of Western societies. The National Council of Social Services, with the help of 150 voluntary bodies, provides most of the welfare services to individuals and families in need. The government also provides services for families in distress, with mandatory

Household Consumption in PPP Terms

Country	All food	Clothing and footwear	Fuel and power[a]	Health care[b]	Education[b]	Transport & Communications	Other
Singapore	15	7	5	3	14	7	48
United States	13	9	9	4	6	8	51
China	N/A	N/A	N/A	N/A	N/A	N/A	N/A
Japan	12	7	7	2	22	13	37

Data represent percentage of consumption in PPP terms.
[a]Excludes energy used for transport.
[b]Includes government and private expenditures.

SOURCE: World Bank. *World Development Indicators 2000.*

counseling in cases of family violence, monthly **subsidies** for working mothers with children in child-care centers, and financial assistance to low-income families. All residents, regardless of social status, are eligible for low-cost medical care.

WORKING CONDITIONS

In 1998, Singapore's labor force was 1.932 million people, with the unemployment rate about 3.2 percent, or 61,700 people. Over the last 3 decades of the 20th century, unemployment has never been high, thanks to the country's robust economic performance across almost all sectors of the economy. Singapore's economy experienced 2 difficult years in 1997 and 1998, when unemployment rose, but since the beginning of economic recovery in 1999 and 2000 there has been strong demand in the labor market. The Employment Act established a 44-hour working week, although there is no official minimum wage or unemployment compensation.

Singapore's economy demands a highly trained and flexible workforce. The government strongly promotes the acquisition of different skills, supporting several higher education centers, and vocational and technical institutes. Facing shortages in the workforce, the government encourages women to work by providing different initiatives and support for working mothers. Women made up about 40 percent of the workforce in 1999. Due to the nature of the labor market and the nation's growing prosperity, there is no child labor problem. The law prohibits employment of children under age 12. Due to labor shortages, there is a growing number of foreign workers in Singapore, unskilled and concentrated in the service and construction sectors.

The activities of trade unions are allowed in the country within the framework of the Societies Act, labor laws, and other regulations. According to the U.S. State Department, in the late 1990s there were 255,020 union members, organized into 83 unions. Most of them are affiliated with the National Trades Union Congress (NTUC), which is closely associated with the ruling People's Action Party. Strikes, slow-downs, and other workers' protests are rare in Singapore. Collective bargaining is common in management-labor relations, but most disagreements are solved through informal consultations and, in disputed cases, through the Industrial Arbitration Court.

The rise of the "new economy" caused a surge in demand for information technology (IT) workers. It is expected that, with annual growth of 10 percent in the IT sector, manpower in this area will need to more than double from 95,000 in 2000 to 220,000 in 2008. The government intends to develop the existing workforce rather than rely on immigration for the acquisition of skilled personnel in the sector. To facilitate retraining, in April 2000 the Ministry of Manpower and the Infocomm Development Authority jointly launched the Strategic Manpower Conversion Program, emphasizing information technologies and "technopreneurship."

COUNTRY HISTORY AND ECONOMIC DEVELOPMENT

1819. Sir Thomas Stamford Raffles of the British East India Company leases a small territory from the Sultan of Johore and founds Singapore.

1821. First large group of Chinese migrants arrive from Xiamen.

1826. Singapore is incorporated into the Straits Settlements, a British colony.

1860. First census indicates a population of 80,792 in Singapore.

1858. Straits Settlements become a British Crown colony under the jurisdiction of the Colonial Office in London.

1914. Indentured labor system abolished.

1921. Singapore becomes a principal naval base for the British Navy in East Asia.

1942. The country is occupied by Japan during World War II.

1945. Allied forces liberate Singapore from Japanese occupation.

1946. Singapore becomes a Crown colony separate from Malaysia.

1955. A new constitution is adopted, introducing a measure of self-government.

1959. Singapore gains full self-governance under Prime Minister Lee Kuan Yew.

1961. Establishment of the Economic Development Board, a government agency responsible for the formulation and implementation of economic and industrial development strategies.

1963. Singapore joins the Federation of Malaysia.

1965. Singapore withdraws from the Federation of Malaysia and becomes independent.

1965. Singapore joins the United Nations.

1967. Singapore becomes a founding member of the Association of South East Asian Nations (ASEAN).

1970. Independent Monetary Authority of Singapore is established.

1971. Final withdrawal of British troops from Singapore.

1973. Last major ties with Malaysia renounced.

1979. Government begins a program of economic restructuring in response to the shock of the oil crisis.

1987. English is made the language of instruction in schools.

1990. Lee Kuan Yew resigns.

1991. The constitution is amended to allow Singapore citizens to directly elect their president.

1995. Huge losses made by a Singapore-based derivatives trader causes the collapse of Barings, the oldest British banking group.

1997. The ruling People's Action Party wins parliamentary elections, capturing 81 of 83 parliamentary seats.

1998. In response to the 1997 Asian financial crisis, the government announces financial reforms to improve the country's international competitiveness.

1999. The "Industry 21" Program, a new economic blueprint for the development of Singapore in the 21st century, is launched.

FUTURE TRENDS

Singapore has benefited from the globalization of the world economy and experienced 3 decades of extraordinary economic growth, which has brought prosperity and confidence to the people of this small city-state. Able to withstand economic turmoil such as the 1997 Asian financial crisis and the surge in world oil prices at the beginning of the 21st century, Singapore has proved that its economy has grown on a sustainable and strong basis. Inflation remains under control and the Singaporean exchange rate is stable. The quality of life has improved steadily and society has benefited from rising prosperity. The government's policies aim to maintain political and social stability by promoting economic growth from capital- and skill-intensive technologies, although it has been criticized for restricting freedom of press and associations, and for its interventionist economic policies.

In the long term, Singapore needs to maintain its international edge against growing competition from neighboring countries. It is also exposed to economic, political, and environmental developments in the neighboring countries of Indonesia and Malaysia. Continuous political turmoil and social unrest in Indonesia might threaten Singapore by causing an influx of refugees and regional instability. Recent forest fires in the Indonesian part of Borneo brought air pollution to dangerous levels, affecting tourism and the health of the Singapore population.

DEPENDENCIES

Singapore has no territories or colonies.

BIBLIOGRAPHY

The East Asian Miracle: Economic Growth and Public Policy. Washington, DC: The World Bank, 1993.

Economist Intelligence Unit. *Country Profile: Singapore.* London: Economist Intelligence Unit, 2001.

Economist Intelligence Unit. *Country Report: Singapore.* London: Economist Intelligent Unit, January 2001.

Eliot, Joshua, and Jane Bickersteth. *Singapore Handbook.* NTC Publishing Group, 1999.

Kuan Yew, Lee. *From Third World to First: The Singapore Story: 1965–2000.* New York: HarperCollins Publishers, 2000.

Monetary Authority of Singapore. <http://www.mas.gov.sg>. Accessed October 2001.

Peebles, Gavin, and Peter Wilson. *The Singapore Economy.* New York: Edward Elgar, 1996.

Singapore Exchange. <http://www.ses.com.sg>. Accessed October 2001.

Singapore Government Web Site. <http://www.gov.sg>. Accessed October 2001.

Singapore: Selected Issues. IMF Staff Country Report No. 00/83. Washington, DC: International Monetary Fund, July 2000.

Singapore: Your Compelling Global Hub for Business and Investment. <http://www.sedb.com/edbcorp/index.jsp>. Accessed October 2001.

U.S. Central Intelligence Agency. *World Factbook 2001.* <http://www.odci.gov/cia/publications/factbook/index.html>. Accessed September 2001.

—Rafis Abazov

SOLOMON ISLANDS

CAPITAL: Honiara.

MONETARY UNIT: Solomon Islands dollar (SI$). 100 cents equals 1 dollar. Coin denominations include 1, 2, 5, 10, 20, and 50 cents, and 1 dollar. Paper notes include 2, 5, 10, 20, and 50 dollars.

CHIEF EXPORTS: Timber, fish, coconut products, cocoa.

CHIEF IMPORTS: Machinery and transport equipment, manufactured goods, food, mineral fuels, chemicals.

GROSS DOMESTIC PRODUCT: US$1.21 billion (purchasing power parity, 1999 est.).

BALANCE OF TRADE: **Exports:** US$142 million (f.o.b., 1998 est.). **Imports:** US$160 million (c.i.f., 1998 est.).

COUNTRY OVERVIEW

LOCATION AND SIZE. The Solomon Islands is an archipelago (a group of islands) in the South Pacific Ocean, about 485 kilometers (300 miles) east of Papua New Guinea, and about 1,900 kilometers (1,200 miles) northeast of Australia. Solomon Islands has a land area of 27,540 square kilometers (10,633 square miles) and a total coastline of 5,313 kilometers (3,301 miles). The land area of Solomon Islands is slightly less than that of the state of Maryland. Guadalcanal is the largest island, about 5,300 square kilometers (2,047 square miles). Other islands include Makira, San Cristobal, Vella Lavella Rennell, and Santa Cruz. Honiara, the capital, is located on the north coast of the island of Guadalcanal.

POPULATION. The population of Solomon Islands was estimated to be 466,194 in July 2000, based on a census taken in November 1999, the first since 1986. Over that period, the population increased by 43 percent, corresponding to an average annual increase of 2.8 percent. This was a substantial decline from the average rate of 3.5 percent per year between 1976 and 1986, but the current rate is still high by world standards. The birth rate was estimated at 40.9 per 1,000 population in 2000, one of the highest in the Pacific, and the death rate was 6.8 per 1,000 population. The projected population by the year 2010 is 620,500.

The great majority (93 percent) of the population is of Melanesian ethnicity, with about 70 different language groups, mostly located on the larger islands of the archipelago. A minority (4 percent) is of Polynesian descent comprising about 8 different languages; these people mainly originate on the small outlying islands, although many are now settled elsewhere. An even smaller minority (about 1.5 percent) is of Micronesian ethnicity, mainly descendants of those resettled from the Gilbert Islands (now Kiribati) during the colonial period. The rest of the population is mainly of European or Chinese ethnicity. Of the major countries of the Pacific, Solomon Islands is the least urbanized, with only 13 percent living in urban areas. The only significant urban center is the capital Honiara, with about 50,000 people; in recent years Honiara has been growing about 35 percent faster than the rest of the country.

Despite high birth rates, Solomon Islands governments have not aggressively promoted family planning. For several years, there has been a low-key population planning policy, which promotes smaller family sizes and infant and maternal well-being. According to the 2000 census, birth rates have declined considerably, perhaps due to improvements in infant health and greater availability of contraceptives.

OVERVIEW OF ECONOMY

The Solomon Islands' economy is largely dependent on agriculture, forestry, and fishing. For a high proportion of the population (mainly village-based), the Solomon economy involves the production of subsistence foods and other items for personal consumption. The main item of production for cash at the village level is copra (the dried flesh of coconut), but also significant in some areas is cocoa, market vegetables, and marine products including fish and shells.

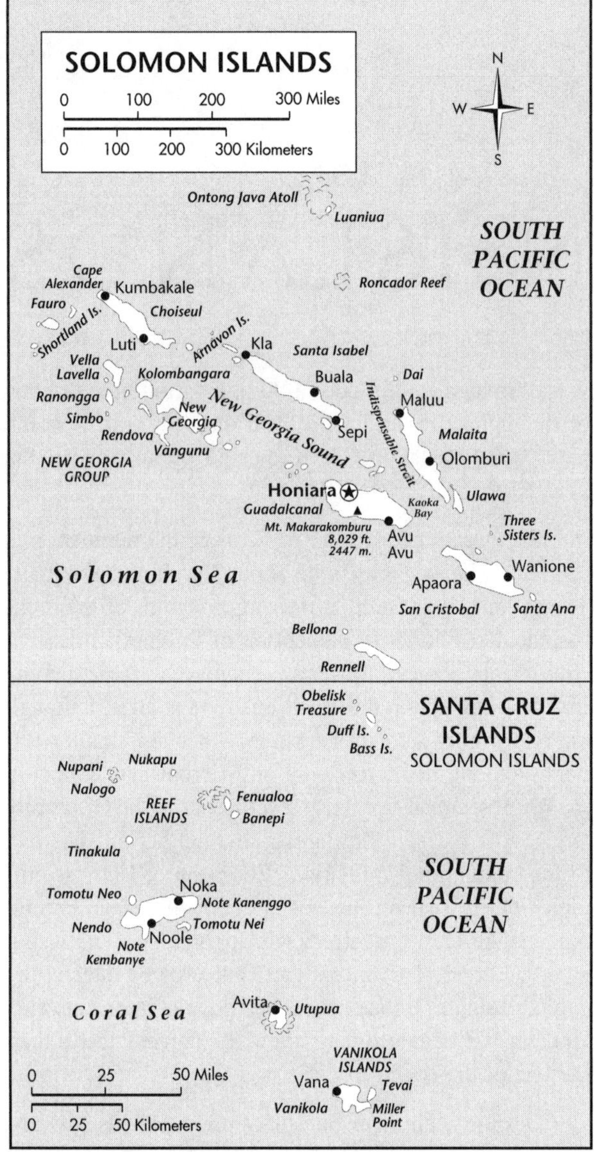

The agricultural cash economy is a legacy from the British colonial period. After the establishment of the British Solomon Islands Protectorate in 1893, the colonial administration facilitated the establishment of plantations, usually run by British settlers, and the recruitment of local labor. While there were some attempts to introduce new crops into the subsistence economy, the colonial administration took few initiatives to diversify the economy before independence in 1978.

During the 1970s the logging, fishing, and rice industries increased production as a result of new private investments and international aid programs. Through the 1980s and 1990s the 2 most significant items of production for export were timber and fish. Ethnic tensions on Guadalcanal in 1999 and 2000 caused some disruptions, but a peace settlement was reached in October 2000, and these economic activities are projected to reach previous levels. Large-scale mining started in 1998, and this sector is expected to expand if political stability is maintained.

Various small-scale manufacturing enterprises in recent decades have resulted in some **import substitution** (replacing imports of some food, furniture, and similar items with locally made products) and limited exports of food, beverages, construction materials, and furniture. Local processing within the fishing industry is also important.

Services have been mainly confined to the **public sector**, particularly in civil administration and education. Tourism has remained a small-scale activity, partly because the government did not actively promote tourism as an economic alternative until the mid-1990s. An 18-month civil war disrupted economic activity in the country, but by 2001 the economy was rebounding even though tourists were warned to steer clear of Guadalcanal, where most of the fighting had occurred.

POLITICS, GOVERNMENT, AND TAXATION

Since independence in 1978, Solomon Islands has modeled the Westminster (British-style) system of government. The British monarch serves as head of state, and there is a **unicameral** parliament made up of 50 members (MPs) elected by voters over 21 years of age at least every 4 years. Each electoral constituency is represented by the MP who gains the most votes. The prime minister is elected by majority vote in parliament.

There is considerable fluidity in the party system, and parties have formed and reformed both during and between elections. Since independence in 1978, most governments have been coalitions, with the prime minister representing the party that gained the most votes in an election.

There are 9 provinces (Choiseul, Western, Isabel, Central, Rennell-Bellona, Guadalcanal, Malaita, Makira, and Temotu) and 1 Town Council (Honiara). Each has its own elected members and has authority over various aspects of development, including parts of the education, health, and transport systems. In response to ethnic tensions in 1999 and 2000, the central government has worked to increase the powers of the provincial governments.

Since the Solomon Islands has about 80 distinctive language groups, political parties have usually attempted to attract members and appoint cabinet ministers from various parts of the country in the interests of ethnic diversity. However, some degree of ethnic tension has persisted, and there have been calls for regional independence. In 1999 these tensions came to a head when the Guadalcanal Revolutionary Army attacked settlers from the neighboring island of Malaita who had settled on Guadalcanal, amid fears that Malaitans were beginning to dominate the government and parts of the economy. In early 2000, the Malaitan Eagle Force took over the capital, forced out most Guadalcanalese and essentially overthrew the government. In October 2000 a peace settlement was signed, and international monitors arrived, mainly from Australia and New Zealand. By early 2001, there had been only minor breaches of the agreement.

Before the ethnic tension, the government had embarked on a modest **restructuring** program that involved some cutbacks in government expenditure, especially by reducing the number of civil servants. This was partly a response to high levels of government debt, and major fluctuations in revenue as a result of varying levels of exports and commodity prices. During the tension, the government approached insolvency (an inability to pay its debts), but was rescued by international aid, especially from the Republic of China (Taiwan). During this period, aid from Australia and New Zealand was channeled into peacekeeping activities.

The major sources of government tax revenue are customs revenue and inland (internal) revenue, which in 1997 accounted for about equal amounts of the total. Customs revenue is also equally divided between import taxes and export taxes, particularly on logs. Inland revenue originates from personal taxes, business taxes, and from other sources. A relatively small proportion of inland revenue is derived from individual **income tax** since only a small proportion of the population works in the paid **labor force**.

INFRASTRUCTURE, POWER, AND COMMUNICATIONS

The nation's numerous islands make its transportation **infrastructure** heavily dependent on maritime transport. Until the 1970s inter-island transport consisted mainly of canoes, mission ships, copra trading boats, and the occasional government boat. Regular passenger transport is now handled by government boats and increasingly by private companies.

The country is served by 1,360 kilometers (845 miles) of roads, but well over half of these are private plantation roads. Only about 34 kilometers (21 miles) of these roads are paved, mainly in Honiara. Most outlying islands have few or no roads, with a transportation infrastructure consisting of walking trails or outboard motor canoes.

Solomon Islands is served by 1 international airport, Henderson Field near Honiara, built by the U.S. military during World War II and since upgraded by aid from Japan and other sources. Another airport, at Munda in the Western Province, can also accommodate international (usually charter) flights. It was also built during World War II and has runways paved with coral. There are 31 other airports with unpaved runways throughout the islands, mostly for smaller aircraft operated by Solomon Airlines, but domestic airfares are high. During the ethnic conflicts in 2000, international and domestic flights were interrupted. By early 2001, Solomon Airlines was again flying to Brisbane and Nadi and operating most domestic flights, but other international airlines were still weighing the risks of resuming service.

Most households in Solomon Islands do not have access to electricity. In Honiara and in other provincial centers, power is generated by diesel generators operating on imported fuel. During the 1990s attempts were made to develop hydroelectric power for Honiara, but these plans were delayed due to problems related to land and compensation.

Telephone service is available only in Honiara and some towns. Domestic and international connections,

Communications

Country	Telephones[a]	Telephones, Mobile/Cellular[a]	Radio Stations[b]	Radios[a]	TV Stations[a]	Televisions[a]	Internet Service Providers[c]	Internet Users[c]
Solomon Islands	8,000	658	AM 3; FM 0; shortwave 0	57,000	0	3,000	1	3,000
United States	194 M	69.209 M (1998)	AM 4,762; FM 5,542; shortwave 18	575 M	1,500	219 M	7,800	148 M
Philippines	1.9 M	1.959 M (1998)	AM 366; FM 290; shortwave 3 (1999)	11.5 M	31	3.7 M	33	500,000
Micronesia	11,000 (2001)	N/A	AM 5; FM 1; shortwave 0	N/A	2	N/A	1	2,000

[a]Data is for 1997 unless otherwise noted.
[b]Data is for 1998 unless otherwise noted.
[c]Data is for 2000 unless otherwise noted.

SOURCE: CIA *World Factbook 2001* [Online].

including Internet access, are usually good. These connections are provided via satellite by Solomons Telekom, a **joint venture** between the government and Cable and Wireless, Limited, and which holds a **monopoly** on telephone services. In 1997, Solomon Islands had 3 radio but no television stations, although there are about 3,000 television sets in the country. The civil war in 2000 destroyed many telecommunications buildings and equipment. All expansion was temporarily postponed during the conflict.

ECONOMIC SECTORS

While a very high proportion of the population lives in rural areas, agriculture, fishing, and hunting have contributed only about one-third of GDP in recent years, and this proportion has declined slightly since the early 1980s. In terms of formal employment, agriculture made up only 21.8 percent of the 34,000-strong labor force in 1998, although the subsistence and village **cash cropping** sector employs large numbers who are not enumerated in these surveys. Industry has shown slight growth in recent years, and made up 17.4 percent of the formal labor force in 1998. The service economy, which includes everything from domestic labor to work by skilled professionals, is the dominant sector, contributing about 40 percent of GDP, and supplying 60.8 percent of the formal labor force in 1998. The economy was devastated by the civil conflict that lasted between June and October of 2000. In the wake of the war, many major companies closed and farmers had difficulties moving their products to market. Foreign aid has helped the country weather the economic difficulties.

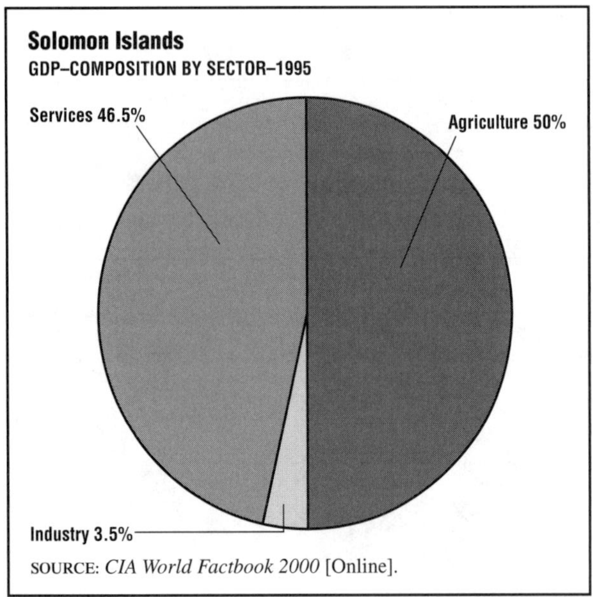

SOURCE: *CIA World Factbook 2000* [Online].

AGRICULTURE

AGRICULTURE. Through much of the 20th century, under British colonial rule, Solomon Islands represented a classic example of a plantation economy, with coconut production being the primary activity of both village **smallholders** (individual farmers) and large-scale expatriate (foreign) plantation owners. For village producers, the production of copra (dried flesh of coconuts) is still an important source of cash, and several large coconut plantations are still operating. As a source of export income, coconut products have steadily declined since the 1960s. During the 1990s, a number of coconut oil presses were installed in various parts of the country, and this has increased the value of this product.

For many years, government and international aid donors have sponsored initiatives to diversify the agricultural base of both smallholder and large-scale farmers by promoting the production of cocoa as a new crop. In 1998, cocoa comprised about 5 percent of export income. Also moderately successful has been the production of chilies, mostly at the village level.

In the late 1970s, large-scale rice production was established by an American company on the Guadalcanal Plains, leading to a small export trade. The industry collapsed in the next decade due to flagging domestic demand and the destruction of much of the crop in 1986 by Cyclone Namu. Production resumed in the mid-1990s on large plantations on Guadalcanal and on a smaller scale in many villages. The UN Food and Agricultural Organization estimated that 4,500 metric tons of rice were produced in 2000, up from 1,300 metric tons in 1998.

FORESTRY. Most timber exports have been of whole logs, with only about 10 percent of total production in the 1990s being milled within the country. Logging began during the British colonial period and escalated considerably after independence in 1978. It is estimated that accessible timber resources may be exhausted by about 2010 if present levels of logging continue. The rate of exploitation was a major political issue during the 1990s and into the 21st century.

FISHING. Fishing is an important activity at 3 different levels: subsistence production (production that only meets the immediate needs of the producer), small-scale cash fishing, and the large-scale offshore fishing industry. Small-scale cash fishing is most successful near urban markets, especially Honiara. Since the early 1980s, 31 fishery centers providing refrigeration and marketing services have been established throughout the country, although many of these have since failed. In the late 1990s, some centers were being renovated amidst attempts to facilitate the marketing of fish to Honiara and to Australia.

There were 2 major local fishing companies in 1999: Solomon Taiyo Ltd. (STL) and National Fisheries Development (NFD). STL has a large cannery at Noro in Western Province which produced nearly a million cases of canned tuna in 1999, about one-quarter of which was sold domestically. While domestic prices for fish remained high during the year, the world price of tuna plummeted, causing NFD to cease operations late in the year. STL closed during the period of ethnic tension, but is expected to open again.

INDUSTRY

MINING. Small-scale mining during the 20th century consisted mainly of gold-panning operations on Guadalcanal; the Gold Ridge mine in the central part of the island did not begin production until 1998. Developed by Ross Mining, this operation was expected to produce gold for about 10 years. The mine was closed down in June 2000 as ethnic tensions reached a peak. As of early 2001, the mine had not reopened, although negotiations were underway with landowners and the government about issues of compensation and security.

MANUFACTURING. Except for the production of traditional handicrafts, manufacturing has never been a major industry in Solomon Islands. In the late 1990s it contributed about 5 percent of the country's GDP. The most important manufacturing enterprises cater to the local market in such sectors as food processing, beer, furniture, construction materials, and construction of outboard canoes. Traditional handicrafts such as woodcarvings, weavings, and shell ornaments are sold to tourists or exported on a small scale.

SERVICES

TOURISM. Despite its beautiful beaches and calm lagoons, Solomon Islands has always had a relatively small tourist industry. About 12,000 people visited the islands each year, with relatively little increase until 1997–98. Although official figures are not available, the numbers of visitors dramatically fell in 1999 and 2000 as a result of ethnic tensions and the interruption of air services into the country.

Guadalcanal and the nearby islands were major battlegrounds during World War II, and in the decades after the war most tourists were returning veterans or their families, both American and Japanese. Following the end of the war, the landscape was strewn with downed airplanes, tanks, and other war material, and the beaches of Guadalcanal and some of the other islands were littered with landing craft. Much of this material has since been exported as scrap, but even in 2001 there are remnants. Both the Japanese and the Americans have constructed hilltop monuments for the many thousands of troops killed during the war. More recently the country has become a center for scuba diving and snorkeling; along with spectacular coral reefs, there are many sunken warships still intact for divers to explore. Many tourists are attracted by the great cultural diversity of the country and its traditional villages.

Tourist infrastructure is limited, with only a few international standard hotels, mostly in Honiara, although there are guesthouses in most areas. Since the mid-1990s, efforts have been made to develop **ecotourism** (nature holidays), mostly village-based but in many cases supported through international aid programs. Unlike neighboring countries such as Papua New Guinea, Vanuatu, and Fiji, the Solomon Islands has no flight and accommodation packages available to international travelers.

FINANCIAL SERVICES. The financial services sector is small and mainly serves the local market. International banks such as Westpac and ANZ are located in Honiara and 2 provincial centers. The National Bank of Solomon Islands (a joint venture between Bank of Hawaii and the local National Provident Fund) is the only commercial bank with branches in smaller towns. The Central Bank of Solomon Islands (CBSI) regulates money supply and is responsible for general economic monitoring, and the Development Bank of Solomon Islands (DBSI) offers small-scale lending for development projects.

RETAIL. The **retail** sector is not well developed. Most retail operations are in Honiara and other towns, but the range of goods is limited. Villages are served by small locally-run shops selling basics such as soap, kerosene, rice, tea, sugar, biscuits, and fishhooks, or by copra trading boats that also serve as retail outlets.

INTERNATIONAL TRADE

According to the International Monetary Fund and other sources, Solomon Islands' exports in 1999 were valued at US$116 million (a drop from US$168 million in 1995) and imports at US$110 million (a drop from US$154 million in 1995). The drop can be attributed in part to the economic crisis in Asia, which lowered demand for the logging exports of the Solomon Islands. Despite the drop in overall trade activity, Solomon Islands has had a positive **balance of trade** in recent years, a situation rare among Pacific countries. This may be attributed to high volumes of log exports during the 1990s and, to a lesser extent, the steady export of fish products.

Japan is by far the largest destination for exports, taking about one-third of all exports by value in 1999. It is also an important destination for timber products, even though companies operating in this industry are mainly Korean. The largest fishing enterprise in Solomon Islands

Trade (expressed in billions of US$): Solomon Islands

	Exports	Imports
1975	.015	.033
1980	.074	.089
1985	.070	.083
1990	.070	.091
1995	.168	.154
1998	N/A	N/A

SOURCE: International Monetary Fund. *International Financial Statistics Yearbook 1999.*

GDP per Capita (US$)

Country	1975	1980	1985	1990	1998
Solomon Islands	419	583	666	784	753
United States	19,364	21,529	23,200	25,363	29,683
Philippines	974	1,166	967	1,064	1,092
Fiji	2,086	2,319	2,102	2,356	2,416

SOURCE: United Nations. *Human Development Report 2000; Trends in human development and per capita income.*

is a subsidiary of the Japanese Taiyo Company, and many of the fish products are destined for the Japanese market. Other important export destinations for its timber and fish are Thailand and the Philippines.

Imports from Australia account for 37 percent of the total imports to Solomon Islands, making it the single largest source. The next largest import sources are Singapore, Japan, and New Zealand, which provide a variety of foodstuffs, fuels, and machinery.

MONEY

Since independence in 1978 the Solomon Islands dollar has floated freely. In 1982, its dollar was worth slightly more than the U.S. dollar (SI$.9711 to US$1), but fell to about one-fifth of the U.S. dollar by 2001 (SI$5.0745 to US$1). In the 1980s, this was partly a result of a negative trade balance, but this does not seem to have been a factor in recent years, when exports have tended to be of greater value than imports. During the 1990s, the rate of **inflation** has averaged 10.7 percent per year.

POVERTY AND WEALTH

The **United Nations Development Program**'s Human Development Indicator (HDI), which measures a country's welfare using income, education, and health statistics, ranks Solomon Islands 121st out of 174 countries. Although it ranks as the second poorest nation in the Pacific, it is better off than many African countries. Per capita GDP in 1998 was only US$753, about one-fortieth that of the United States. This is a decline from the peak figure of US$784 in 1990. Still, in most parts of Solomon Islands there is little evidence of the desperate poverty found in some parts of the Third World. Most households have sufficient food, although nutrition surveys have found some cases of malnutrition, particularly in urban areas where food is expensive.

Other indicators show that Solomon Islands is a poor country. Seventy percent of adults are illiterate, and only 41 percent of boys and 36 percent of girls aged 5 to 14 were enrolled in primary school in 1999. Health services have improved in recent years, but infant mortality is relatively high at 38 per 1,000, and there is only 1 doctor for every 7,292 persons.

Exchange rates: Solomon Islands

Solomon Islands dollars (SI$) per US$1	
Nov 2000	5.0968
2000	5.0864
1999	4.8381
1998	4.8156
1997	3.7169
1996	3.5664

SOURCE: CIA *World Factbook 2001* [ONLINE].

WORKING CONDITIONS

Only about 16 percent of the working-age population participate in wage and salary employment, much of this centered in Honiara. There is far more demand for employment than there are jobs, especially for the unskilled. Wages for unskilled work are low, at SI$1.20 in agriculture and fishing and SI$1.50 in other sectors. Since many products consumed in urban areas are imported, these wages are inadequate for living well in town.

There are 2 major unions: The Solomon Islands National Union of Workers (SINUW), representing workers in the **private sector**, and Solomon Islands Public Employees Union (SIPEU), for government workers. Unions in the private sector have become weaker in recent years, possibly as a result of the surplus of potential labor; the public-sector union has been more successful in promoting the interests of its members.

COUNTRY HISTORY AND ECONOMIC DEVELOPMENT

1000 B.C. Evidence of human settlement on some islands.

140–670 A.D. Evidence of Lapita pottery culture on some islands.

1568. Spanish explorer Alvaro de Mendaña visits several islands in search of the fabled mines of King Solomon. Islands given Spanish names include Guadalcanal, Santa Isabel, San Cristobal.

1600–1700s. Explorers visit from Spain, the Netherlands, England, and France.

1800s. Regular contact between Solomon Islanders and whalers, missionaries, and traders. Labor recruitment ("blackbirding") for plantations in Fiji and Queensland. Lever's Pacific Plantations begins establishing large-scale plantations.

1893. British Solomon Islands Protectorate (BSIP) declared.

1942. Japanese invade Solomons; Allied forces counterattack.

1943. Allied forces occupy Guadalcanal in February; Japanese evacuate in December.

1940s. Rise of "Marching Rule," an indigenous movement on Malaita that advocates independence, non-payment of taxes, and return to tradition; leaders are jailed in 1948.

1978. On 7 July, Solomon Islands becomes independent; first prime minister is Peter Kenilorea.

1986. Cyclone Namu strikes; many people on Guadalcanal buried by landslides, plantations destroyed.

1990s. Escalation of ethnic tensions as vigilante groups (Guadalcanal Revolutionary Army, then Isatabu Freedom Movement) begin to drive Malaitan settlers off the land.

2000. Malaitan group (Malaita Eagle Force) takes control of Honiara in June; Townsville Peace agreement, with international monitoring, is signed in October, allowing full access to Honiara by all groups. It guarantees compensation to offended parties and mandates confiscation of weapons.

FUTURE TRENDS

There was much optimism about the economic future of Solomon Islands in the 1990s because of its wealth of timber, fish, minerals, and other resources. At the same time, there was a recognition that the timber resource was being exploited at an unsustainable rate, and that it would be only about a decade before the accessible forests were logged out. There was also some apprehension late in the 1990s about the oversupply of the global fishing infrastructure and the increasingly competitive nature of the industry in the Pacific. By 2000, ethnic tension between groups on Guadalcanal and Malaita raised fears about the survival of the nation-state. By early 2001 there was some optimism that the peace agreement of October 2000 would hold, and that the economy would eventually return to normal. However, many critical industries were still closed awaiting assurances of ongoing security. The future of the Islands' forests remains uncertain, but some efforts to improve the effects of over-fishing included sustainable harvesting of black pearls.

DEPENDENCIES

Solomon Islands has no territories or colonies.

BIBLIOGRAPHY

Asian Development Bank. *Solomon Islands 1997 Economic Report.* Manila: ADB, 1998.

Central Bank of Solomon Islands (CBSI). *Annual Report. Honiara: CBSI,* various years 1980–1999.

Solomon Islands Employment 1998. Honiara: Solomon Islands Statistics Office, 2000.

"Solomon Islands Ministry of Commerce." <http://www.commerce.gov.sb>. Accessed May 2001.

United Nations Development Programme. *Pacific Human Development Report 1999: Creating Opportunities.* Suva: UNDP, 1999.

U.S. Central Intelligence Agency. *The World Factbook, 2000.* <http://www.cia.gov/cia/publications/factbook>. Accessed May 2001.

—***Wardlow Friesen***

SRI LANKA

Democratic Socialist Republic of Sri Lanka
Sri Lanka Prajathanthrika Samajavadi Janarajaya

CAPITAL: Colombo.

MONETARY UNIT: Sri Lanka rupee (R). One rupee equals 100 cents. There are coins of 1, 2, 5, 10, 25, and 50 cents, and 1, 2, 5, and 10 rupees. There are bills of 10, 20, 50, 100, 200, 500, and 1,000 rupees.

CHIEF EXPORTS: Textile and apparel, tea, gems and jewelry, coconut products, rubber and rubber-based products, and spices.

CHIEF IMPORTS: Machinery and equipment, textiles, petroleum, foodstuffs.

GROSS DOMESTIC PRODUCT: US$62.7 billion (purchasing power parity, 2000 est.).

BALANCE OF TRADE: **Exports:** US$5.2 billion (f.o.b., 2000). **Imports:** US$6.1 billion (f.o.b., 2000).

COUNTRY OVERVIEW

LOCATION AND SIZE. Sri Lanka is an island nation-state in the Indian Ocean. It is located 880 kilometers (547 miles) north of the equator, off the southern tip of India, and has a maximum length of 432 kilometers (268 miles) and a maximum width of 224 kilometers (139 miles). The island has an area of 65,610 square kilometers (25,332 square miles) and a total coastline of 1,700 kilometers (1,056 miles). Sri Lanka is slightly larger than West Virginia. Its capital, Colombo, lies on the country's western coast.

POPULATION. Sri Lanka's population was estimated at 19.24 million in 2000, indicating growth of 11.5 percent compared with the 1991 population of 17.25 million. Sri Lanka has the slowest-growing population in southern Asia—estimated at 0.9 percent yearly—and its population is projected to increase to 23.55 million by the year 2025. The density of Sri Lanka's population is fairly high, at 280 persons per square kilometer (725 per square mile). In 2000 the birth rate was estimated at 16.8 per 1,000 people and the death rate at 6.4 per 1,000 people. The majority of Sri Lanka's people live in the rural sector (67 percent), in urban areas (22 percent), and on plantation estates (11 percent). The infant mortality rate (16.5 per 1,000) and overall death rate are low for a developing country, and the average life expectancy (69 years for men and 73 years for women) is the highest in southern Asia. The low fertility rate and high life expectancy has led to a larger increase in the older population than the younger population. It took most western countries 45 to 135 years for their elderly population to double, while in Sri Lanka this process is expected to take only 2 decades. Sri Lanka is expected to have the third oldest population in Asia in 2025. The rising burden of maintaining an aged population could exert considerable restraints on the government's fiscal resources, and the need to provide retirement support income and health care will have serious consequences on the economy as a whole during the next 2 decades.

An important characteristic of the Sri Lankan population is its ethnic and cultural diversity. Approximately 74 percent of the population are Sinhalese, 12.6 percent are Sri Lankan Tamils, 5.5 percent Indian Tamils, 5 percent Muslims, and the remainder consists of Burghers, Malays, and others (2.9 percent). Among the ethnic groups, the Sinhalese were the earliest inhabitants of Sri Lanka and are descendants of the first colonists who occupied the island during the 5th century B.C. Most of them are Buddhist, and speak a language called Sinhala, derived from several Indo-Aryan languages. The Sri Lankan Tamils are the descendants of the early Dravidian invaders from southern India. They are predominantly Hindu and speak Tamil, one of the major Dravidian languages of southern India. Indian Tamils are the descendants of laborers brought by the British planters in the 19th century to work on plantations. The Muslims are the descendants of early Arab traders who settled in Sri

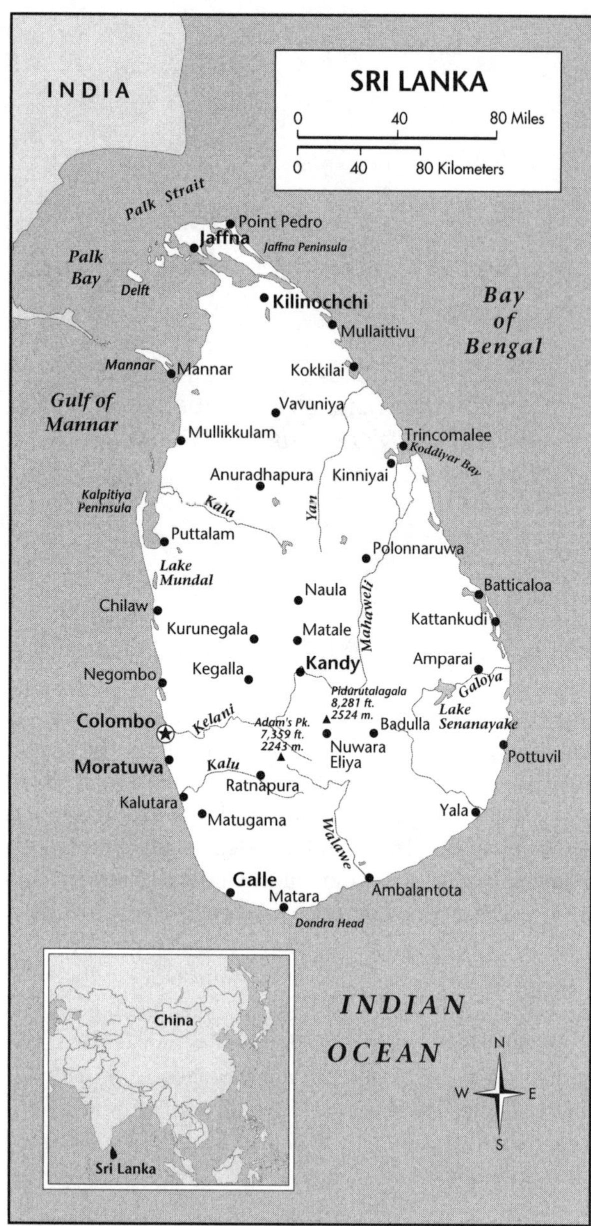

Lanka during the 10th century. The Burghers are the descendants of the Portuguese, Dutch, and British who occupied the island from the 16th to the mid-20th century. The Burghers are predominantly Christian and speak English as their first language.

OVERVIEW OF ECONOMY

Sri Lanka is a developing economy based largely on agriculture, services, and light industry. Agriculture accounts for approximately 21 percent of the **gross domestic product** (GDP) and employs 38 percent of the workforce. Agricultural output is divided between **cash crops** from plantation agriculture and food crops from subsistence agriculture. Cash crops—namely tea, rubber, and coconuts—are largely grown on plantations. Rice is the principal food crop and the main livelihood for over 70 percent of Sri Lanka's rural population. Manufacturing industries account for approximately 19 percent of the gross domestic product and employ about 17 percent of the workforce. Chief manufactures include textiles, ceramics, petroleum products, vegetable oils, fertilizers, and cement. The service sector is the largest of the Sri Lanka economy, employing 45 percent of the workforce and contributing roughly 60 percent of GDP. Tourism, banking, finance, and **retail** trade are the major components of the service sector.

The country is endowed with many natural resources. It has an equatorial climate with a high average rainfall. The land is fertile and suitable for growing a variety of crops, and one-third of the land is arable. Rivers cascading from the central hill country provide energy to generate hydropower, the major source of electricity in Sri Lanka. The country also has rich fishing resources. Sri Lanka's mineral resources include titanium ore, graphite, kaolin, and gemstones. It also has large deposits of unexploited iron ore.

Foreign trade is an important segment of the Sri Lankan economy. Major imports include petroleum, consumables, machinery and capital equipment, motor vehicles, and various manufactured goods. Major exports include garments, tea, rubber, coconut products, foodstuffs, gems, and jewelry. Sri Lanka is the largest exporter of black tea in the world and the third largest producer of natural rubber. A variety of gemstones, for which Sri Lanka is world famous, are also exported. Significant quantities of high-grade graphite, for which Sri Lanka is a world leader, are also exported. The industrialized countries taken together as a group accounted for 75 percent of Sri Lanka's total exports in 1999 and the United States is the largest single buyer of Sri Lanka's exports, with 39 percent in 1999. Other major export markets are the United Kingdom, Germany, Japan, Russia (tea), China (rubber), India, and the Middle East. In terms of imports, Japan is the single largest exporter to Sri Lanka. Motor vehicles, spare parts, and woven fabrics are the major items imported from Japan. India is the second largest exporter, followed by Singapore, South Korea, Taiwan, the United Kingdom, and the United States.

Sri Lanka is a mixed economy, in which both the **private sector** and the state sector engage in the production process. Foreign investments are encouraged and several **free zones** have been established. The country's banking system is well developed, so that both foreign and local banks function in the economy. Sri Lanka is committed to a free market ideology and has one of the most liberal foreign trade regimes in the world. This contrasts greatly to what the Sri Lankan economy looked like during the first 3 decades after the country gained independence from

Great Britain in 1948. The economy that evolved in Sri Lanka under British rule was predominantly oriented towards agriculture, with plantation agriculture being the major contributor to the nation's growth. The 3 plantation crops—tea, rubber, and coconuts—accounted for 30 percent of the gross domestic product in 1948 and the bulk of the output was exported. Manufacturing was an insignificant activity in the economy. Banking and commerce were, for the most part, only used to support plantation agriculture. Nearly all foreign exchange earnings were derived from the plantations. The country depended on imports for nearly three-fourths of its food requirements and almost all of its manufactured goods.

The Sri Lankan economy has since become highly diversified; it has rapidly growing manufacturing and service sectors, agricultural activities have been modernized, and the country is nearly self-sufficient in rice production. The significance of the 3 major export crops (tea, rubber, and coconuts) as the main source of export earnings has fallen (from 90 percent in the 1950s to 16 percent in 1999) and the significance of manufacturing has risen (from 1 percent of exports in 1950 to 60 percent in 1999). These changes in the structure of the Sri Lankan economy are a result of varying economic policy measures adopted by the government since independence. Development strategies that shaped the Sri Lankan economy over the last 5 decades may be distinguished under 2 eras: the first era covering the period between 1948–76, and the second era during the post-1977 period.

During the first era, development policy focused on achieving the objectives of **equity** and economic growth. The instruments adopted to achieve economic growth were aimed at **import substitution** industrialization, both in manufacturing and foodstuffs. The key measures used to achieve this growth strategy were the imposition of various restrictions on imports, and the encouragement of domestic production. Extensive social welfare programs such as price **subsidies** on food, statutory **price controls** on **consumer goods**, and the provision of free education and health services were the instruments used to achieve greater equity. The welfare programs achieved significant improvements in the area of human development, including lower mortality rates, increased life expectancy, and high literacy rates. However, high welfare expenditures restrained the nation's capital growth and ability to invest, slowing economic growth and causing high unemployment and low wages. During the 1951–1976 period, per capita gross domestic product grew only at an average of 0.2 percent per year. The achievements of the import substitution policies were even less noticeable, except in the production of rice and subsidiary food crops. With a worsening trade balance crisis, most newly established industries operated well below capacity due to a shortage of imported goods. This, coupled with increased government participation in industrial development, hindered industrial growth and the ability to remain commercially viable. The continued government intervention in all spheres of economic life reached its climax at the end of the first policy era.

The second era of Sri Lankan economic development (post-1977) marked a shift towards a free market economy. The strategy aimed at **liberalizing** the economy from excessive government controls and it chose the private sector as the engine of growth. Policies were designed to accelerate economic growth by stimulating private investment through various incentives and also to increase the country's foreign earnings by promoting export-oriented economic activities. The liberalization policies, pursued under the watchful eye and participation of the International Monetary Fund and the World Bank, met with success at the beginning. Stimulated by enhanced levels of foreign aid and investment, the economy was successful, recording real growth rates of about 6 percent per year until 1986. During the following 5 years, however, there was a marked deceleration of growth caused mainly by the disruptive effects of the ethnic conflict on economic activities. Gross domestic product grew at an annual average of 2.7 percent between 1986–1989, and at an annual average of 5 percent between 1990–2000. During the second era, the level of income in the economy grew significantly with per capita gross domestic product more than doubling (from US$382 in 1975 to US$802 by 2000).

The transition to a free market economy based on a liberalized trade and **exchange rate** regime has brought benefits to the Sri Lankan economy. Unemployment, a problem for decades, has reduced significantly, and remains at historically low levels (8 percent in 2000). Nonetheless, the high levels of **inflation**, fueled by the sharp deterioration of the Sri Lankan currency, combined with the mounting cost of civil war has raised the cost of living to very high levels. The soaring cost of living has made many Sri Lankans struggle to satisfy their basic needs. Over 45 percent of the population depends on benefits under the income supplement programs initiated by the government. The **balance of payments** problem remains unresolved. The persistent **trade deficit** has led to increased reliance on foreign aid to meet the country's import requirements, leading to an inevitably mounting **foreign debt**. Foreign debt as a percentage of the gross domestic product, which accounted for 21 percent in 1975, grew to 75 percent in 1994, and amounted to 59 percent in 1999.

POLITICS, GOVERNMENT, AND TAXATION

When Sri Lanka obtained its independence from Britain in 1948 it had an educated electorate conscious of its voting rights and the concept of majority rule. The judiciary was respected and the rule of law was well established. The political party system was also established with the United National Party (UNP) as the foremost party of the time. Sri Lanka also had a written constitution incorporating some of the principles of the British Westminster system of government. There is a **unicameral** Parliament with 225 members elected to 6-year terms. The president is popularly elected to a 6-year term and is the chief executive.

The UNP was in power for 8 years until it lost the 1956 election to Sirimavo Bandaranaike. His Sri Lanka Freedom Party (SLFP)-led coalition swept into power on the promise to make Sinhala the national language. This created disquiet among minorities, especially among Tamils. Tamil leaders opposed the introduction of Sinhala as the official language because they wanted to speak Tamil; their opposition soon led to violence. The seeds of the separatist war in Sri Lanka can be traced to incidents that occurred in 1958. But the conflict grew into a large-scale military confrontation only after 1983, when a group of Liberation Tigers of Tamil Elam (LTTE) followers ambushed Sinhalese troops. The LTTE, who are the Tamil protagonists of the war, have used terrorist methods to finance and promote their cause. They have assassinated moderate Tamil leaders, including President Premadasa, and several Sri Lankan ministers and party leaders. They also killed Indian prime minister Rajiv Gandhi because he withdrew his support of the LTTE.

Another serious problem was the emergence of a Sinhalese youth revolutionary party called the JVP, which staged an armed insurrection in 1971, lasting for 2 years and followed by 3 years of sporadic outbursts. The JVP resurrected itself in the late 1980s with a subtle form of urban terrorism, but it was brought under control by a ruthless program of suppression by the government. Both the LTTE and the JVP have been serious impediments to steady economic growth in Sri Lanka. However, Sri Lanka has been endowed with a very strong democratic tradition which has managed to survive these major conflicts, even during periods of poor economic management.

The 2 dominant parties during 50 years of independence have been the UNP (conservative) and the SLFP (**socialist**-left, and more recently center-left). The 2 political parties have alternated in positions of power for half a century, with the UNP heading the government from 1948 to 1956, 1965 to 1970, and 1977 to 1994. An SLFP-led coalition government was in power from 1956 to 1965, 1970 to 1977, and since 1994 as a coalition called the Peoples Alliance (PA).

The Sri Lankan government epitomizes a classic democratic 2-party political system in operation. The UNP regimes during the period 1948 to 1970 placed emphasis on private sector participation with several ongoing subsidized programs such as free education, free health care, village land settlement, and colonization. The SLFP regimes continued the welfare programs and moved increasingly to public ownership and **nationalization** with limited private sector participation. In the early and the mid-1970s, they placed strict restrictions on imports and currency movement.

In 1977 the UNP government came into power and decided to run an open economy with few restrictions. The private sector became the main engine of growth. The rupee was devalued by 46 percent from its former artificial value. This immediately stimulated growth and received the backing and financial support of the World Bank. This UNP government lasted for 17 years. When the SLFP-led coalition known as the Peoples Alliance was elected to government in 1994, it accepted the importance of this open market economy as a positive growth strategy for the country.

A short time before the end of the first term of the Peoples Alliance in 2000, the LTTE attempted to assassinate the president of Sri Lanka, Chandrika Bandaranaike Kumarathunga. The bomb caused damage to one eye but she survived, and her party was elected for a second term. The PA has had a very difficult period in government because of the financial and political pressures generated by the escalation of the armed conflict with the LTTE. The election itself generated a degree of conflict never experienced before in Sri Lankan politics, but democracy survived as it had in every one of the elections held after 1948.

TAXATION AND REVENUE. The major source of government revenue in Sri Lanka is taxes (86 percent). However, unlike the United States, the contribution of **income taxes** to government revenue is negligible, at 13 percent, while **indirect taxes** dominate government revenue. There are 3 major sources of indirect taxes: the goods and services tax (GST), **excise tax**, and the national security **levy** (NSL). The GST is a recent addition to the tax system (introduced in April 1998), replacing the business **turnover** tax. The GST is levied on a **value-added** basis at a uniform rate of 12.5 percent with full credit given to all inputs. GST revenue accounted for 26 percent of the total tax revenues in 2000. An excise tax, which contributed 23 percent of the total tax revenue during the same period, is levied mainly on liquor, tobacco, petroleum, and motor vehicles. The third important source of government revenue, the NSL, was initially introduced as an interim measure to finance the rising cost of war in the north and the east. It has become an important contributor to national tax revenue, contributing 17.5 percent. The NSL is levied at a rate of 6.5 percent. Taxes on international trade account for 16 percent of the total tax revenue. With the liberalization of trade and **restructur-**

ing of the **tariff** regime, which began in the late 1980s, revenue from taxes on foreign trade has been declining.

The personal income tax (PIT) rate in Sri Lanka has 4 brackets, ranging from 10 percent to 35 percent. The PIT's contribution to the government tax revenue is small (about 1 percent of gross domestic product) and is lower than most other countries. The economy's high dependence on subsistence agriculture, low levels of income and tax compliance, and inefficient tax administration are the key contributors to low levels of PIT revenue. The corporate income tax (CIT) in Sri Lanka of 35 percent (flat rate) is relatively modest and is similar to the rates in other Asian economies. However, the CIT tax yield in Sri Lanka is quite low, as many firms are offered tax incentives to encourage investment.

INFRASTRUCTURE, POWER, AND COMMUNICATIONS

Sri Lanka has a well-developed transport system, including a road network of approximately 100,000 kilometers (62,140 miles). A rail network consisting of about 1,944 kilometers (1,208 miles) of tracks links Colombo with the rest of the country. Road networks are under severe strain due to the rapid increase in the number of vehicles since the 1980s. The number of registered vehicles nearly tripled from 478,000 in the mid-1980s to 1.38 million in 2000, generating severe traffic congestion. With a rising number of vehicles, and the need for a more efficient road network to facilitate the movements of goods and services, the government is actively engaged in improving, rehabilitating, and extending the existing network.

Sri Lanka has 14 airfields, the largest of which is the Katunayake International Airport, the principal gateway to Sri Lanka. The country is serviced by 32 airlines, both domestic and foreign, and the national carrier, SriLankan Airlines, handles about 56 percent of international passengers to and from Sri Lanka. It has scheduled operations to 35 destinations in 26 countries covering Australia, the Indian subcontinent, the Far East, Europe, and the Middle East. The Sri Lanka Ports Authority (SLPA) is responsible for operating the ports. The SLPA operates 4 major ports in Colombo, Galle (in the south), Trincomalee (in the east), and Kankasanturai (in the north). In addition, limited shipping facilities are provided by the Ceylon Shipping Corporation and by several private sector shipping companies. A major restructuring of the cargo handling facilities in Colombo port is now taking place in conjunction with the British PNO company.

Hydropower is the major source of electricity, accounting for 66 percent of the nation's electricity supply. One of the main sources of hydropower is the gigantic Mahaweli Scheme, which has harnessed the flow of Sri Lanka's longest river in several stages. The remainder is generated through thermal power (34 percent) and most recently, wind power. Electricity generation and distribution has traditionally been a government **monopoly**. However, the private sector has become much more involved in power generation during the past decades.

Telecommunications is the fastest growing sector in the country. During the first half of 2000, the telecommunications sector grew by 11 percent. Sri Lanka Telecom Ltd. (SLT) is the major supplier; its network provided 44,228 new telephone connections during the first half of 2000, with total network subscriptions of 621,394. The demand for telephones is growing much faster than supply: at the end of June 2000, there were 246,560 applicants on the waiting list. To meet rising demand the SLT is expanding its capacity with assistance from international donors. In addition to the SLT subscriber network, there are 4 cellular phone operators with a subscription of 307,027. Other service providers include wireless local loop telephones (2 operators with 101,093 subscribers), data communication services such as Internet and e-mail (15 operators with 32,633 subscribers), and public phones (6 operators with 7,491 public phone booths).

Communications

Country	Newspapers	Radios	TV Sets[a]	Cable subscribers[a]	Mobile Phones[a]	Fax Machines[a]	Personal Computers[a]	Internet Hosts[b]	Internet Users[b]
	1996	1997	1998	1998	1998	1998	1998	1999	1999
Sri Lanka	29	209	92	0.0	9	N/A	4.1	0.52	65
United States	215	2,146	847	244.3	256	78.4	458.6	1,508.77	74,100
India	N/A	121	69	18.8	1	0.2	2.7	0.18	2,800
Bangladesh	9	50	6	N/A	1	N/A	N/A	0.00	50

[a]Data are from International Telecommunication Union, *World Telecommunication Development Report 1999* and are per 1,000 people.
[b]Data are from the Internet Software Consortium (http://www.isc.org) and are per 10,000 people.

SOURCE: World Bank. *World Development Indicators 2000.*

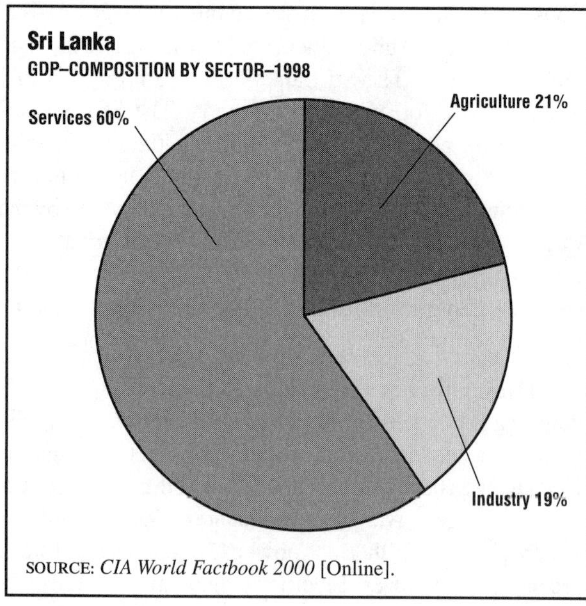

SOURCE: *CIA World Factbook 2000* [Online].

ECONOMIC SECTORS

The changing structure of the economy mirrored in the relative contribution of the key industrial sectors reflect the country's potential to realize substantial growth. It also reflects the transition of the agriculture-dominated economy to a more diversified one with growing industrial and modern service sectors. In 1950, agriculture accounted for half the gross domestic product and by the year 2000, its significance was reduced to one-fifth of the gross domestic product. The contribution of industry more than doubled from about 11 percent to 19 percent while the service sector expanded significantly from 39 percent to 60 percent during the same period. Sri Lanka is rich in resources, both natural and human. It has several unexploited mineral resources (such as iron ore) and underexploited mineral and fisheries resources with substantial potential for future growth. Another area with substantial growth potential is tourism, which is interrupted by the prolonged civil unrest in the economy.

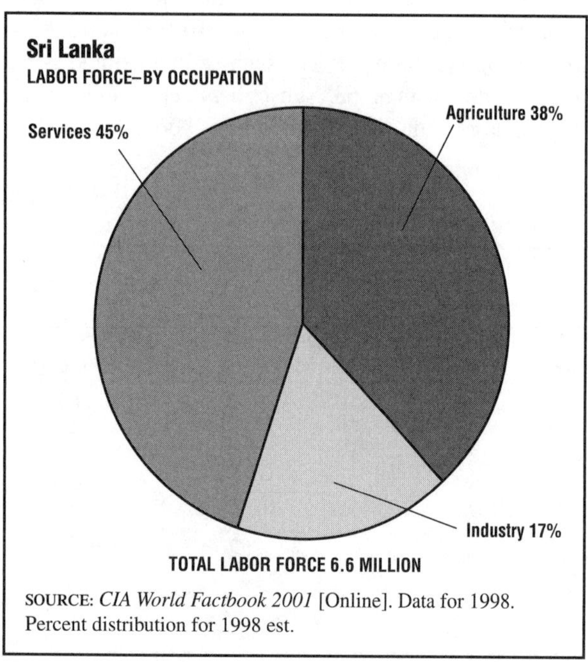

SOURCE: *CIA World Factbook 2001* [Online]. Data for 1998. Percent distribution for 1998 est.

AGRICULTURE

Agriculture is the most important sector of the Sri Lankan economy. Even though its contribution to the gross domestic product declined substantially during the past 3 decades (from 30 percent in 1970 to 21 percent in 2000), it is the most important source of employment for the majority of the Sri Lankan workforce. Approximately 38 percent of the total **labor force** was engaged in agriculture in 1999. In the subsistence sector, rice is the main crop and farming rice is the most important economic activity for the majority of the people living in rural areas. During the last 5 decades the rice sector grew rapidly and output more than tripled, reaching the highest ever output of 2.9 million metric tons in 1999. Increases in the area under cultivation, and improved productivity due to the modernization of agriculture are the main reasons for an increase in production. The rehabilitation of Sri Lanka's extensive ancient irrigation network and massive new investment in construction and maintenance of irrigation **infrastructure** led to a large increase in the area under rice cultivation. Between 1960–2000, the area used to grow rice increased 6 times to 546,249 hectares. The modernization of farming methods, such as the use of high-yielding seeds, tractors, and chemical fertilizers also led to increased productivity in the rice sector. Between 1960–1999, rice yield per hectare doubled from 1,877 kilograms to 3,672 kilograms. In addition to rice, various other food crops are produced for local consumption. They include yams, pulses, grains, vegetables, and fruits. Most of these crops are cultivated in family gardens, except for potatoes and sugar. Sugar cane is cultivated in the dry zone, and Sri Lanka produces only 15 percent of what it consumes domestically.

The major plantation crops of tea, rubber, and coconuts continue to figure prominently in the economy of Sri Lanka; however, the contribution of these commercial crops to gross domestic product declined from 11.5 percent in 1970 to 5 percent in 2000. Tea, the prominent crop of the plantation sector, grows in many parts of the wet zone, and in particular in the central hill country. Sri Lanka is famous for its high quality black tea, and is the largest supplier in the world. In 1999, 269.3 million kilograms of tea (95 percent of total tea production) was exported, earning US$621 million in foreign exchange. The

United Kingdom, Russia, and the Middle East are the major export markets.

The second major commercial crop is rubber, growing in the ridge and valley country of the wet zone interior. Of 159,000 hectares under cultivation, about 80 percent was being tapped (harvested) and in 1999, 96.6 million kilograms of rubber were produced. A sizable proportion of rubber production is used in the domestic manufacturing sector (56 percent in 1999) and the remainder is exported. In 1999 export earnings amounted to US$33 million. China is traditionally the major buyer of Sri Lankan rubber. The performance of this sector has been subject to instability due to unfavorable movements in world prices. Competition from synthetic rubber producers has caused rubber prices to drop. However, with rising petroleum prices (the major ingredient for synthetic rubber) there is a chance for world rubber prices to improve.

The third commercial crop, coconuts, is grown mainly in the hinterland of the western seaboard. Production in 1999 accounted for 2,828 million nuts, the highest output since 1986. Coconut (mainly coconut milk) is a major ingredient used in food preparation in Sri Lanka, and nearly 65 percent of the output is consumed locally. The remainder is exported in the form of kernel products (desiccated coconut, coconut oil, copra), coconut cream, and coconut milk powder. In 1999, kernel products generated US$129 million in foreign exchange.

Forestry and fishing are less important components of the economy. Forests in the dry zone were cleared for settlement and agriculture early on. Unsustainable agricultural practices such as chena cultivation and logging resulted in land degradation and a reduction in the size of forest reserves. The country has abundant fishing resources, with an **exclusive economic zone** covering over 500,000 square kilometers (193,050 miles), a coastline of about 1,700 kilometers (1,056 miles), and a massive network of inland water reservoirs suitable for fish farming. However, this potential has not yet been exploited. Most marine fishing is concentrated in coastal areas, which account for about 12 percent of the exclusive economic zone. Total fish production in 1999 was estimated at 280 thousand metric tons, and the contribution of this activity to gross domestic product was about 3 percent in 1999. Fishing is a traditional livelihood for people living in coastal areas: in 1999 about 145,000 people were employed in fishing activities. A slow-growing sector, fish production increased at an annual average of only about 3 percent between 1992 and 1999. Poor production is mainly due to a lack of technical knowledge and equipment.

The livestock sector in Sri Lanka is small, consisting mainly of the dairy and the poultry subsections. Unlike in the United States, where dairy production takes place on large farms, in Sri Lanka dairy farming is a small-scale domestic activity. Total milk production in 1999 accounted for 342 million liters, sufficient only to meet about one-fourth of local needs. The remainder is imported in the form of powdered milk (in 1999, 54,000 metric tons of milk powder was imported). An important development in the livestock sector was the rapid increase in the poultry production. In 1999 approximately 57 million metric tons of poultry meat was produced, increasingly becoming a common source of animal protein in Sri Lanka.

INDUSTRY

INDUSTRY. Manufacturing accounts for 16 percent of the gross domestic product and employs nearly 400,000 people. The textile industry is the largest of Sri Lanka's industries, contributing 63 percent to industrial sector growth (1999). Other major manufacturing industries include processed diamonds, food and beverages, light engineering, chemicals, petroleum, rubber and plastics, and machinery and equipment. The manufacturing sector that evolved under the import substitution development strategy in the 1960s to cater mainly to the domestic market has transformed into a sector catering to the foreign market. Much of the industrial output is exported and it is the single major export earner in the economy (in 1999, industrial exports accounted for 54 percent of total export earnings). This remarkable achievement is attributable to the policy reforms introduced during the post-1977 period. Under the reforms, the private sector was encouraged to participate in export-oriented industries through various incentives, and several free zones were established. This resulted in a significant inflow of foreign investment; the private sector emerged as the major contributor to industrial output. Overall, market-oriented policy reforms introduced during the post-1977 period have led to far-reaching changes in the structure and performance of the manufacturing sector.

MINING. Mining is a minor economic activity contributing about 2 percent of the gross domestic product (1999). The country's mineral extraction industries include the mining of gemstones and graphite; excavation of beach sands containing ilmenite and monazite; and quarrying quartz sand, clay, and salt. Gem mining is traditionally the most important activity, producing high value gemstones such as sapphire, ruby, and topaz, and a variety of semiprecious stones, most of which are exported. Sri Lanka leads the world in high-grade graphite mining.

SERVICES

TRADE. Wholesale and retail trade, the largest subcategory in the service sector, accounts for about 21 percent of the gross domestic product (1999) and employs about 22 percent of the workforce (2000). With the lifting of import controls and the government monopoly in the importation and distribution of essential consumer goods during the post-1977 period, the trade sector expanded rapidly. Domestic trade accounts for half the value of the trade sector. Increased participation by foreign firms in domestic trade in Sri Lanka is a relatively recent phenomenon, with international food franchises such as McDonald's and Pizza Hut in operation. Numerous small outlets including street stalls serve the retail trade, and in the major cities there are large shopping centers and supermarkets.

FINANCIAL SERVICES. Banking, insurance, and real estate accounted for 8 percent of gross domestic product in 2000. This sector expanded rapidly following the 1977 policy reforms that dismantled the virtual government monopoly in the insurance industry and lifted the restrictions in the banking industry. The increased incentives for the private sector led to the emergence of several new insurance companies and banks. A total of 6 new local banks were established and 11 foreign banks opened branches. The banking system consists of 11 local and 16 foreign banks. Two development finance institutions and several merchant and investment banks are also active participants in the financial markets in Sri Lanka. In addition, 22 financial institutions providing credit facilities are in operation. The Sri Lankan financial system comes under the regulation of the Central Bank of Sri Lanka, which is the monetary authority of the country.

TOURISM. Tourism is an important activity with potential for growth. The country known as the paradise in the Indian Ocean offers a diversity of environments and tourist attractions, from tropical beaches and arid lands to lush forests, tea plantations, and a rich archaeological heritage. Promotion of tourism in Sri Lanka began in the late 1960s with the establishment of the Ceylon Tourist Board. Between 1976 and 1982, the number of tourist arrivals grew rapidly at an annual average rate of almost 24 percent, reaching a peak of 407,230 before declining to 337,342 in 1983 as a result of the civil unrest in the country. As the political violence in the country intensified, international tourist arrivals continued to fluctuate with a general trend of decline. Tourist arrivals increased to 436,440 in 1999. Tourism generates US$275 million in foreign exchange annually and employs approximately 87,600 workers. The majority of tourists to Sri Lanka come from Western Europe (65 percent), Asia (26 percent), and North America (5 percent).

INTERNATIONAL TRADE

One feature of the Sri Lankan economy, both in the past and present, is the high dependency on foreign trade. The country's dependency on trade, measured by the Trade Dependency Ratio (TDR), defined as the ratio of the sum of exports and imports to gross domestic product, stood at 66 in 1999 compared with a TDR of 33 for the period 1970–1977. In 2000 exports stood at US$5.2 billion while imports stood at US$6.1 billion. The changing degree of trade dependency evident in the post-liberalization era has been accompanied by significant changes in the structure of Sri Lankan foreign trade. The dominance of tea, rubber, and coconuts, which accounted for 74 percent of the total exports in 1977, had fallen to 21 percent in 1999. Industrial exports have become the major contributor to export earnings with their share rising from 14 percent to 76 percent during the same period. Of industrial exports, textiles and garments are the leading sub-category, contributing 68 percent to total industrial exports in 1999. The balance consisted of machinery and equipment (6 percent), rubber-based products (5 percent), travel goods and processed diamonds (4 percent each), petroleum products and footwear (2 percent each), crustaceans and mollusks and ceramic products (1 percent each), and other industrial products (7 percent). Despite the changes in the structure of exports, tea continues to be the leading export with a share of 65 percent of total agricultural exports while textiles dominate the industrial exports with a share of 67 percent of the total industrial exports.

Trade (expressed in billions of US$): Sri Lanka

	Exports	Imports
1975	.603	.816
1980	1.067	2.037
1985	1.293	1.843
1990	1.983	2.685
1995	3.798	5.185
1998	4.732	5.917

SOURCE: International Monetary Fund. *International Financial Statistics Yearbook 1999.*

Intermediate goods dominate Sri Lanka's imports (51 percent of total imports), followed by investment goods (27 percent), and consumer goods (21 percent). This is in contrast to the composition of imports in the pre-liberalization era, which was dominated by consumer goods (50 percent of total imports in 1977), followed by intermediate goods (36 percent), and investment goods (12 percent). Rice, flour, and sugar dominated consumer goods in the past, accounting for 80 percent of total consumer goods imported. Their significance, however, fell to 21 percent in 1999. This changing structure of imports reflects the new economic environment resulting from the economic reforms introduced in 1977. The improvement in the domestic supply of rice and other food items helped to limit food imports. The expansion in the industrial sector resulted in higher imports of intermediate goods. Developments in infrastructure facilities, construction and the transport sector, combined with increased use of advanced technology, increased the import of investment goods.

The destination of Sri Lankan foreign trade also has changed. The United States has become the single most important trading partner, and has continued to be the largest single buyer of Sri Lanka's exports (accounting for 39 percent of exports in 1999). Garment exports accounted for 74 percent of total exports in 1999. The United Kingdom accounted for 13 percent, while Germany accounted for 5 percent of Sri Lanka's exports. On average, one-third of the Sri Lankan imports come from the industrial countries. Japan is the largest source of imports to Sri Lanka, with 10 percent in 1999. Motor vehicles, spare parts, and woven fabrics are the major items imported from Japan. India is the second largest exporter (with 9 percent), followed by Hong Kong and Singapore (8 percent each), South Korea (6 percent), Taiwan, the United Kingdom, and the United States. Wheat, gold, agricultural equipment, and textiles are among the major items imported from the United Kingdom, while wheat accounted for 31 percent of imports from the United States. Textiles, tools and accessories for the garment industry, and fruits are the other major items imported from the United States.

Sri Lanka's trade with the rest of the world has changed in terms of composition, direction, and volume. However, the country has not been able to solve its fundamental problem, the unfavorable trade balance. As exports continued to grow, so did imports. Despite the persistent unfavorable trade balance, the country has managed to maintain its import levels with foreign assistance, capital flows, and an important and growing source of foreign exchange: **remittances** by Sri Lankan migrant workers in the Middle East. Prior to 1977 policy reforms, the fortunes of Sri Lankan exports depended primarily on the movements of world prices for the 3 major export commodities. While the export sector has diversified, the dependence on trade has also increased markedly. As the country's trade relations with industrialized countries rises, the Sri Lankan economy is vulnerable not only to changes in price levels of the major exports, but also to fluctuations in the levels of economic activity in industrialized countries.

MONEY

With the liberalization of the foreign **exchange rate regime** in 1977, which changed from a **fixed exchange rate** regime to a flexible one, the value of the Sri Lankan currency has continued to fall against major currencies. The Sri Lanka rupee (R) which was 16.5 per U.S. dollar in 1980 fell to R40 per dollar by 1990, and collapsed to R85 in 2001. With the high dependence on imports, the falling value of the currency means that the prices of imports continue to rise, pushing up domestic inflation.

Exchange rates: Sri Lanka

Sri Lankan rupees per US$1	
Jan 2001	83.506
2000	77.005
1999	70.635
1998	64.450
1997	58.995
1996	55.271

SOURCE: CIA *World Factbook 2001* [ONLINE].

Sri Lanka has an active stock market, the Colombo Stock Exchange (CSE), the origin of which dates back to the 19th century. Share trading in Sri Lanka began in 1886 when the Colombo Brokers Association commenced the trading of shares in limited liability companies. Share trading grew since then and Colombo had a very active share market throughout the 20th century except during the 1960s and 1970s where a spate of nationalization, including the insurance companies and plantations, effectively reduced the trading to insignificant proportions. This decline was short lived, and the stock market recovered quickly following the policy reforms introduced in the latter part of 1970s, which created free and open market ideals where the private sector was given the key role in economic activities. Today the exchange has 238 companies listed with a **market capitalization** of approximately 10 percent of gross domestic product.

POVERTY AND WEALTH

The wealthy, representing those engaged in commerce and industry, are largely concentrated in urban areas, while the poorest live on plantations and in rural areas. While the rich live in luxury, many urban poor live

GDP per Capita (US$)

Country	1975	1980	1985	1990	1998
Sri Lanka	382	452	536	590	802
United States	19,364	21,529	23,200	25,363	29,683
India	222	231	270	331	444
Bangladesh	203	220	253	274	348

SOURCE: United Nations. *Human Development Report 2000; Trends in human development and per capita income.*

Distribution of Income or Consumption by Percentage Share: Sri Lanka

Lowest 10%	3.5
Lowest 20%	8.0
Second 20%	11.8
Third 20%	15.8
Fourth 20%	21.5
Highest 20%	42.8
Highest 10%	28.0

Survey year: 1995

Note: This information refers to expenditure shares by percentiles of the population and is ranked by per capita expenditure.

SOURCE: *2000 World Development Indicators* [CD-ROM].

in shanty houses with no sanitary facilities. The urban poor in Sri Lanka are found mainly in the capital, Colombo. The majority of the Sri Lankan population live in rural areas, and the major source of wealth among them is land. Landlessness and unequal distribution of land are key determinants of rural poverty. Those living on plantations are laborers with no access to land ownership or alternative employment opportunities. They live in substandard houses supplied by the owners of plantations. A fourth group of poor, those displaced by the continuing war in the north and east, live in various refugee camps with no access to any amenity or opportunities.

The overall degree of disparity in wealth is reflected in the distribution of incomes. The wealthiest 20 percent of the population account for over 52 percent of the nation's income while the poorest 10 percent account for only 2 percent. Disparities in wealth have risen steadily during the post-1977 period, a result of policy reforms that paved the way for more wealth generation through the increased participation of the private sector. An important byproduct of the policy reforms was the soaring inflation induced by the falling value of Sri Lankan currency, raising the cost of living of the poor disproportionately. Meeting basic needs is a struggle to the poor, because average Sri Lankans spend over 40 percent of their income on food alone. Rising poverty has led to considerable social unrest; strikes in work places and protest rallies are common occurrences. The government maintains several subsidy programs to improve the position of the poor. Over 45 percent of the population benefits from one such income supplementary program called Samurdhi. Another, the dry ration program, is aimed at helping displaced families of the north and east due to the continuing civil war. International agencies such as the World Bank and Asian Development Bank have sought to help Sri Lanka reduce poverty. Several funded projects have directly targeted the poorest segments of the population. Despite low per capita income levels, and high levels of the incidence of poverty, the quality of life in Sri Lanka is relatively high when compared with its neighbor, India.

WORKING CONDITIONS

According to the Department of Census and Statistics, the labor force in Sri Lanka is about 7 million and the total number of employed persons is 6.5 million. The unemployment rate is at around 8 percent (2000). While the overall unemployment rate is lower than in the past (which was about 15 percent in 1992), unemployment among youth is relatively high. Around 22.5 percent of the youth of age between 15 and 19 were unemployed and 15 percent in the age group 20 to 29. Of the total workforce, 66.5 percent are males and 33.5 percent are females. Women play an important role in the economic life of Sri Lanka. The largest concentration of women in professions is in the areas of teaching, nursing, and clerical work. In the plantation industry, women make up 68 percent of the workforce and, in the garment industry, about 90 percent of the workforce.

The basic minimum age for employment in Sri Lanka is 15 years, and the government has enforced laws to prevent child labor. The forced or bonded labor of children is prohibited. Despite the laws governing child labor, underage children work as street vendors and hold menial jobs in tile factories, coir-making operations,

Household Consumption in PPP Terms

Country	All food	Clothing and footwear	Fuel and power[a]	Health care[b]	Education[b]	Transport & Communications	Other
Sri Lanka	43	0	7	4	8	4	33
United States	13	9	9	4	6	8	51
India	N/A	N/A	N/A	N/A	N/A	N/A	N/A
Bangladesh	49	4	18	8	9	4	8

Data represent percentage of consumption in PPP terms.
[a]Excludes energy used for transport.
[b]Includes government and private expenditures.

SOURCE: World Bank. *World Development Indicators 2000.*

fishing, and in domestic service. Poverty leads most of these children to work. According to a government study, about 60 percent of the employed children are secondary income earners, contributing as much as 30–40 percent of household income.

The constitution of Sri Lanka guarantees the right of workers to organize and establish labor or trade unions, except those employed by the security forces and members of the judiciary. All public and private sector employees possess the right to bargain collectively. The Department of Labor provides conciliation and arbitration services to resolve labor disputes. Although trade union freedom is substantial, it has been subject to periodic modification or curtailment during times of political strife. In Sri Lanka, there is no universal basic minimum wage, and the minimum wages differ from industry to industry. Sector-specific minimum wages are set by wage boards. There are about 39 wage boards, which set minimum wages for more than 100 occupations in industry, commerce, services, and agriculture. Remuneration tribunals also set minimum wages in some cases.

In Sri Lanka, working conditions and workers' rights are well protected by legislation. However, disruptions in the workplace are common. In recent years there were a number of labor actions such as strikes and protests. The rising cost of living has driven many workers to demand higher wages. There are instances where even those in the medical profession have gone on strike for higher wages. Because of the inability of most workers to make ends meet, many Sri Lankans seek employment abroad. The total number of Sri Lankan workers abroad was estimated to be around 788,000 in 1999, of whom nearly 90 percent are employed in the Middle East.

COUNTRY HISTORY AND ECONOMIC DEVELOPMENT

427 B.C. The legendary Sinhalese Prince Vijaya colonizes the north-central part of Sri Lanka.

250 B.C. The king of Anuradhapura, Devanpiya Tissa, embraces Buddhism.

210 B.C. Sinhala kingdom is invaded by Cholas from southern India and Elara becomes king.

161 B.C. King Dutthagamini defeats Elara and reestablishes Sinhala rule.

1055. Sinhala kingdom moves its capital to Polonnaruwa under King Vijayabahu I.

1232–1815. Sinhala kingdom moves south.

1371–1408. Dambadeniyan, Gampolan, and Kotten kingdoms.

1469–1815. Kandyan kingdom.

1521–1581. Sitawakan kingdom.

1505. The Portuguese capture the coastal belt and rule it until the Dutch oust them.

1658. The Dutch capture coastal areas.

1659. The British regain the coastal areas, displacing the Dutch.

1660. The British are invited by the Kandyan chiefs to usurp the king, gaining control. They maintain a colony in Sri Lanka until the 20th century.

1948. Sri Lanka gains political independence from the British on 4th February.

1948. The UNP is elected in Ceylon under the leadership of D. S. Senanayake.

1956. A coalition of parties (MEP) led by S. W. R. D. Bandaranaike is elected.

1959. The SLFP leader is assassinated and his widow becomes prime minister in 1960.

1965. The UNP regains power under the leadership of Dudley Senanayake.

1971. Sri Lanka becomes a republic, but retains membership in the British Commonwealth.

1977. The UNP, under the leadership of J. R. Jayawardane, comes to power.

1978. Jayawardane becomes the first president of Sri Lanka. Liberalization reforms begin.

1979. Riots in response to the ambush and killing of 13 Singhalese soldiers by Tamil Tigers.

1980. Military action launched against the Tamil Tigers, with help from India.

1981. R. Premadasa becomes the second president of Sri Lanka.

1993. Premadasa's authoritarian rule ends as he becomes a victim of the LTTE.

1994. Chandrika Bandaranaike Kumaratunga and the Peoples Alliance gain political power.

2000. Kumaratunga wins a second term as president.

FUTURE TRENDS

Since independence, despite low levels of per capita income, Sri Lanka has achieved an impressive human development record, with many of Sri Lanka's social indicators comparing favorably to those of more advanced economies. The country has broken away from a **public-sector**-dominated, highly regulated economic system and has laid the foundation for dynamic growth based on a free market, liberalized trade and exchange rates, and **deregulated** foreign investment. This transition has led to rapid economic growth, a significant reduction in the level of unemployment, and a rise in the level of per capita income. However, the impressive growth of the economy evident during the 1977–1982 period has generated increasing economic inequality. The soaring inflation fueled by the deterioration of the value of the Sri Lankan currency has worsened the relative position of the poor. Despite the reduced levels of unemployment and the increased opportunities, nearly half of the population depends on government subsidies to meet their basic needs. The balance of payments, a fundamental problem of the economy that has persisted since the 1950s, has continued to worsen. Mounting foreign debt and the **debt servicing** obligations has added further burden to the already critical balance of payments.

The slowdown in the pace of economic growth over the last 2 decades, coupled with the rising costs of the civil war, seriously threatens the economy's ability to meet the challenges and changing socioeconomic needs of its population. With a rapidly aging population, the need for more resources to provide health care and income support will exert considerable pressure on the government's fiscal resources and the tax system during the coming decades. The solutions to most of the burning problems, and those bound to emerge in the near future, lie in the country's ability to achieve sustained levels of long-term economic growth. The continuing civil conflict poses the biggest obstacle to the country's growth prospects. The need for an immediate solution to the 18-year-old civil war is imperative. Given that the Sri Lankan economy managed to realize an average growth rate of about 5 percent during the last decade in spite of severe interruptions caused by the civil war, lasting peace would undoubtedly bring prosperity to the nation.

DEPENDENCIES

Sri Lanka has no territories or colonies.

BIBLIOGRAPHY

Central Bank of Sri Lanka. <http://www.centralbanklanka.org>. Accessed March 2000.

"Country Profile of Sri Lanka." *Indian Ocean Rim Network.* <http://www.iornet.org/newiornet/Srilanka.htm>. Accessed September 2001.

Department of Census and National Statistics (DCS), Sri Lanka. <http://www.statistics.gov.lk>. Accessed September 2001.

Economist Intelligence Unit. *Country Profile: Sri Lanka.* London: Economist Intelligence Unit, 2001.

Embassy of Sri Lanka Online. <http://users.erols.com/slembassy/index2.html>. Accessed September 2001.

Fernando, T., and R. N. Kearney. *Modern Sri Lanka: A Society in Transition.* New York: Syracuse University Press, 1979.

Lakshaman, W. D. *Dilemmas of Development.* Colombo: Sri Lanka Association of Economists, 1997.

Lakshaman, W. D., and C.A. Tisdell. *Facets of Development of Sri Lanka since Independence.* Australia: University of Queensland, 1999.

U.S. Central Intelligence Agency. *World Factbook 2001.* <http://www.odci.gov/cia/publications/factbook/index.html>. Accessed September 2001.

U.S. Department of State. *FY 2001 Country Commercial Guide: Sri Lanka.* <http://www.state.gov/www/about_state/business/com_guides/2001/sa/index.html>. Accessed September 2001.

—Sarath Divisekera

SYRIA

Syrian Arab Republic
Al-Jumhuriyah al-'Arabiyah as-Suriyah

CAPITAL: Damascus.

MONETARY UNIT: Syrian Pound (S£). One Syrian pound equals 100 piasters. There are coins of 25 and 50 piasters and 1 Syrian pound. There are notes of 1, 5, 10, 25, 50, 100, and 500 Syrian pounds.

CHIEF EXPORTS: Petroleum, textiles, manufactured goods, fruits and vegetables, raw cotton, live sheep, phosphates.

CHIEF IMPORTS: Machinery and equipment, foodstuffs/animals, metal and metal products, textiles, chemicals.

GROSS DOMESTIC PRODUCT: US$50.9 billion (2000 est.).

BALANCE OF TRADE: **Exports:** US$4.8 billion (f.o.b., 2000). **Imports:** US$3.5 billion (f.o.b., 2000).

COUNTRY OVERVIEW

LOCATION AND SIZE. Syria, a Middle Eastern country, is located on the east coast of the Mediterranean Sea. It is bounded by Turkey to the north, by Iraq to the east and southeast, by Jordan to the south, and by Lebanon and Israel to the southwest. Syria has an area of 185,180 square kilometers (71,500 square miles), including 1,295 square kilometers (500 square miles) of territory in the Golan Heights captured by Israel in the Six Day War of 1967. There are 2,253 kilometers (1,400 miles) of boundary length, with a coastline of 193 kilometers (120 miles). The area occupied by Syria is slightly larger than the state of North Dakota. The capital city, Damascus, is located on the Barada River in southwest Syria. Other major cities, Latakia and Aleppo, are situated on the Mediterranean coast in the west and in northern Syria, respectively.

POPULATION. The population of Syria was estimated at 16,305,659 in July 2000, an increase of 3.4 percent from the 1990 population of 12,116,000. In addition, there are about 38,200 people living in the Israeli-controlled Golan Heights (excluding nearly 20,000 Israeli settlers). Syria has one of the highest population growth rates in the world. Over the last decade, however, Syria's population growth rate has gradually decreased from 3.30 percent in 1990 to approximately 2.58 percent in 2000. Despite the steady decline in its growth rate, the population is expected to reach 20.9 million by the year 2010.

Syrians are divided along profound ethnic and sectarian (groups divided by politics, language, and religion) cleavages. Arabs constitute the major ethnic group with 90.3 percent, while other minority groups such as Kurds, Armenians, Turcomans, and Assyrians make up the remaining 9.7 percent of the population. Sectarian divisions include Sunni Muslims (about 74 percent), Alawites (an extreme Shi'ite subsect), Druze (a secret Middle-Eastern sect and doctrine combining different Islamic, Jewish, and Christian elements), and other Muslim sects (about 16 percent). The Christian population in Syria is small (about 10 percent), and Jews number only a few thousand.

Syria's population is overwhelmingly young, with 41 percent below the age of 15 and only 3 percent older than 65. The urban-rural population ratio has been reversed over the last decade in favor of the urban population, which increased at a rate of 4.1 percent from 49.4 percent in 1988 to 53.5 in 1998. Because of this trend, major cities like Damascus, Latakia, and Aleppo have become the main venue of rural **emigration** within the country.

OVERVIEW OF ECONOMY

According to the World Bank, in 2000 the Syrian economy was classified as a low middle-income economy with a **gross national product** (GNP) per capita of about US$1,000. Although it does not possess the extensive natural resources of its richer neighbors, Syria was able to sustain one of the most integrated and productive economies in the region for several decades after gaining

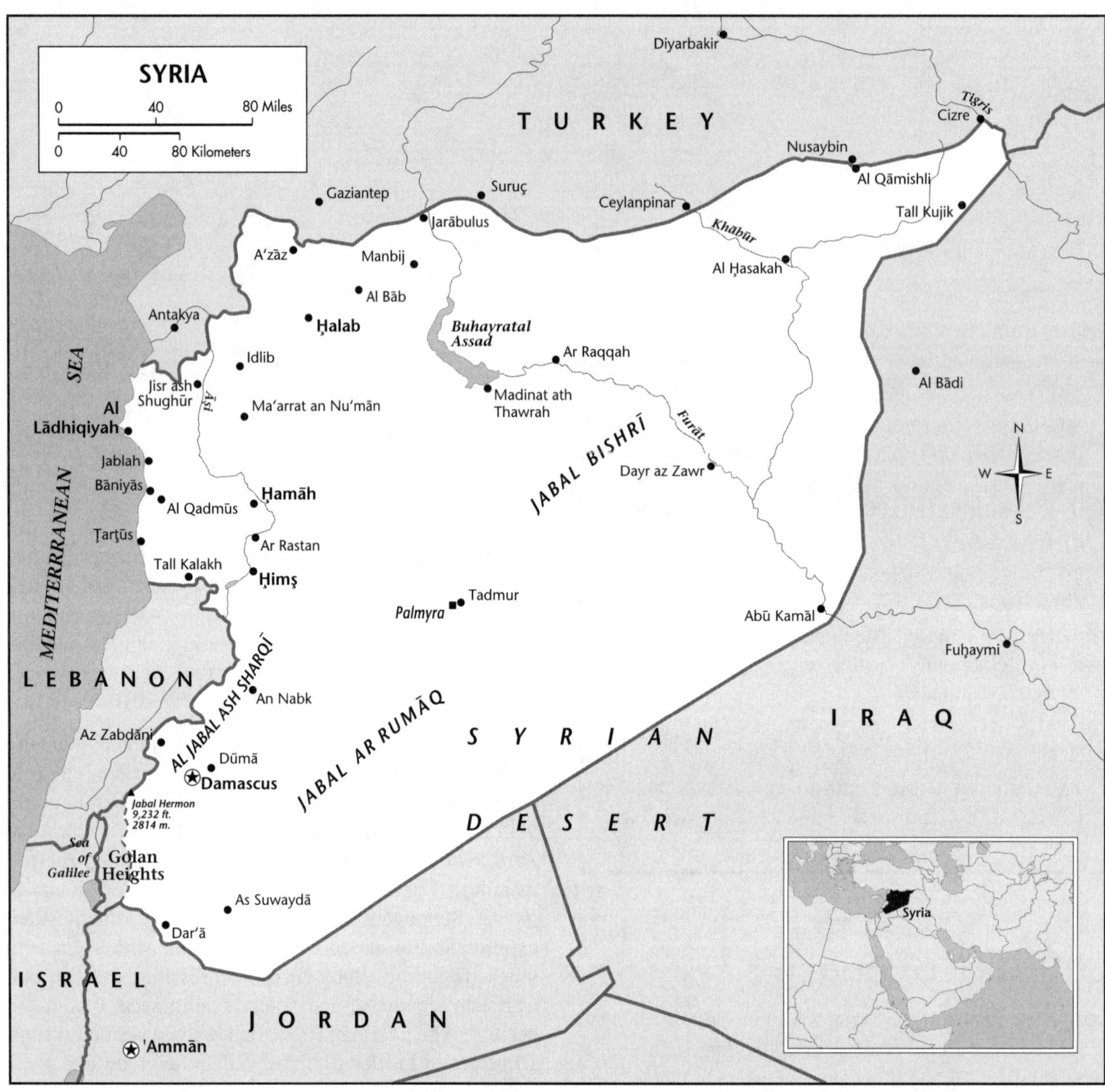

its independence in 1946. Following unification with Gamal Abdel Nasser's Egypt under the United Arab Republic and the rise of the Ba'ath Party, however, **socialism** became the official economic policy in 1958. Although Syria left the United Arab Republic in 1961, government-sponsored land reforms and the **nationalization** of major industries and foreign investments had confirmed the new socialist direction of Syria's economic policy by the mid-1960s.

During the 1970s, Syria achieved high rates of economic growth. The dramatic rise of world oil prices from 1973 to 1974 led to increased production in domestic refineries. Moreover, higher prices for agricultural and oil exports, as well as the state's limited economic **liberalization** policy, encouraged growth. The October War in 1973 and later ostracism of Egypt from the Arab League due to its peace agreement with Israel put Syria, as a front-line state, in a position of leadership in the Arab-Israeli conflict. Because of this, Syria began to receive substantial quantities of foreign aid from the oil-rich Gulf states. Besides these higher levels of aid, Syria's economic boom was furthered by increased **remittances** from Syrians working in the oil-rich Arab states. By the end of the decade, the Syrian economy had shifted from its traditional agrarian base to an economy dominated by the service, industrial, and commercial sectors. Massive expenditures for development of irrigation, electricity, water, road building projects, and the expansion of health services and education to rural areas contributed to prosperity.

By the mid-1980s, the country's economic climate had shifted from prosperity to austerity. Syria's economic boom collapsed for a variety of reasons: a reduction in worker remittances, declining world oil prices, lower export revenues, agricultural devastation due to drought, and costly military involvement with Lebanon. A drastic decline in Arab aid, due to Syria's support for Iran against Iraq in the Iran-Iraq War (1980–88), also contributed to the country's economic woes.

The final collapse of Soviet Russia after 1989 left Syria without the generous Soviet economic and military aid on which it had depended. Syria did receive aid through substantial financial rewards—in the form of large injections of credits from Saudi Arabia, the Gulf states, the United States, the European Community, and Japan—for its decision to support the coalition forces in the Gulf War of 1991 against Iraq.

Agriculture remains the dominant sector in Syria, yet only 20 percent of arable land is irrigated. Although Syria has sufficient water supplies, the great distance between major water supplies and population centers poses serious distribution problems. The water problem is exacerbated by rapid population growth, industrial expansion, and increased water pollution. Oil production is leveling off, and the efforts of the non-oil sector to penetrate international markets have fallen short. A vibrant **black market**, smugglers, corruption, cumbersome bureaucracy, and inefficient state-owned enterprises are huge barriers to growth and development.

Besides these economic burdens, Syria suffers from a substantial **external debt**, which was estimated about US$22 billion in 1999, including US$10 to 12 billion owed to the former Soviet Union and US$900 million to the former East Germany which many observers doubt will ever be repaid. Much of the US$22 billion owed dates back to the Cold War (a period in history, lasting from approximately 1945–89, characterized by the arms race between the United States and former Soviet Union), stemming from arms transfers. Russia and Germany argue that the debt should be paid, but Syria claims that the debt is no longer valid because the predecessor states no longer exist.

POLITICS, GOVERNMENT, AND TAXATION

Syria is a socialist republic ruled by the Ba'ath Socialist Party dictatorship. According to the Syrian Constitution of 1973, the president governs with the assistance of an appointed Council of Ministers, headed by a prime minister. The president also functions as commander-in-chief of the armed forces and secretary-general of the Syrian Ba'ath Party. Since 1970, Syria has been under the patrimonial rule of the Assad family. During the reign of Hafez Assad, the Ba'ath Party became the major instrument in implementing economic and **fiscal policies**. Assad's takeover in 1970 gave new momentum to the Syrian economy. He relaxed many socialist restrictions and measures by previous Ba'ath leaders and adopted a moderate foreign policy toward the conservative oil-rich Arab states to accumulate their oil money in Syria.

A second phase of economic reform in 1986 and 1987 added to Assad's economic reform and relaxation policies of the early 1970s. In this second phase, the government largely surrendered its control over foreign exchange to the market. The state-owned banking sector, instead of being an instrument of control over private exports and imports, was gradually reduced to the role of an intermediary. It passed a new investment law in May 1991 (Investment Law #10), lengthening the list of goods that the **private sector** can either produce or import. Apart from foreign trade and currency regulations, this second phase involved a substantial liberalization of Syria's agricultural economy (pricing, production, and marketing of fruits and vegetables have been placed in private hands by the government). Although these limited liberalization schemes served their purposes well, they were not enough for a complete transformation from a socialist to a market economy. Throughout the 1990s, Syria's economy suffered from instability, **recession**, unemployment, rising external debts, and capital shortages.

Thanks to the liberalization schemes of the 1970s and the 1980s, by 2001 Syria developed a mixed economy based on agriculture, trade, mining, and manufacturing. The government controls the most vital sectors of the country's economy and regulates private businesses. The economy, where the public and private sectors have an almost equal share, is managed through a central planning system. The **public sector** (composed of enterprises wholly or partly owned by the state and controlled through a public authority which does focus entirely on commercial profit) is dominant in oil, banking, construction, electricity, chemicals, and much of the textile and food processing industries. The private sector (composed of enterprises owned by individuals in pursuit of profit) is dominant in agriculture, tourism, domestic trade, and certain light industries. State control in commerce is restricted to foreign exchange operations.

The Syrian government depends heavily on oil revenue, foreign aid, remittances from Syrian workers abroad, tourism, and tax revenues. In 1997, tax revenue constituted 16.4 percent of the GDP. For the same year, taxes levied on goods and services made up 20.72 percent of the current government revenue whereas **income taxes** and taxes levied on international trade accounted for 30.15 percent and 10.58 percent, respectively. Income taxes are levied on 3 main categories of income: 1) profits from an industrial, commercial, or noncommercial activity; 2) wages; and 3) income derived from moveable capital assets. All businesses are charged a "profits tax" based on net profits derived from professional, industrial, commercial, and non-commercial activities. The business profit tax is applied in progressive rates (between 10 percent and 45 percent) depending on the amount of taxable income. Shareholding companies and industrial limited liability companies are taxed at a flat rate of 32 percent and 42 percent, respectively. An individual is liable for the same taxes as a company on his business income, income from movable capital, and real property. Individuals are also subject to a wage and salary tax; the rate varies from 5 percent to 12.5 percent. Tax on movable capital incomes, which is levied at a flat rate of 7.5 percent, applies to interest, royalties, and foreign source dividends.

INFRASTRUCTURE, POWER, AND COMMUNICATIONS

Syria has an inadequate and outdated **infrastructure** and transport system that is mainly controlled by state-run agencies. The highways, which provide the chief means of transporting goods and passengers, run about 36,377 kilometers (22,604 miles), nearly 10,000 kilometers (6,214 miles) of which are unpaved. The major Syrian cities are linked by the 2,750-kilometer (1,709-mile) long railway network all around the country, but the service is slow because of the obsolete trains.

Syria has 104 airports, including military airports, 24 of which have paved runways. The international airlines are in the capital of Damascus and Aleppo, where facilities can handle jet aircrafts. Syrian Airlines connects Syria with other Arab, Asian, and major European countries. Although Syria has a short coastline, which stretches for about 193 kilometers (120 miles) along the Mediterranean Sea between Turkey and Lebanon, it has a commercial fleet composed of 137 ships and 4 major ports and harbors in Baniyas, Jablah, Latakia, and Tartus.

Syria's electrical power is handled by the Public Establishment of Electricity for Generation and Transmission and the Public Establishment for Distribution and Exploitation of Electrical Energy. Syria's annual electricity production was 17.5 billion kilowatt hours (kWh) in 1998, 42.8 percent of which was generated from fossil fuel, whereas the remaining 57.2 percent was produced from hydroelectric resources. The main problems in the Syrian electricity sector are inefficiency and technical power losses that lead to periodic power outages.

The Syrian telecommunication system is undergoing a number of significant improvements and digital upgrades, including fiber-optic technology. The government-owned Syrian Telecommunication Establishment provides all services in this sector. The country had 1.4 million telephone lines in 1998. In addition, a pilot global system for mobile communications (GSM) cellular telephone network was launched in Syria in February 2000, with capacity for 60,000 subscribers in the Damascus and Aleppo areas. A permanent GSM telephone system to replace the pilot scheme was expected to launch in February 2001, according to an *EIU Country Report* of October 2000. Recently, the Syrian government approved the Syrian Computer Society (SCS) as the country's first Internet service provider. Only SCS members (Syrian scholars, university professors, engineers, computer specialists, public sector professionals, and some private entrepreneurs) are allowed access to the Internet. Their activities are subject to strict government control and monitoring. Most Internet services remain blocked, including most web mail and voice/telephony services.

ECONOMIC SECTORS

Since the 1970s, the Syrian economy underwent several sectoral changes not common in developing countries. Industry, especially service, has developed a great deal. Agriculture remains vital to the economy despite its diminishing contribution to GDP. In 1996 agriculture employed about 40 percent of the **labor force** and supplied

Communications

Country	Newspapers	Radios	TV Sets[a]	Cable subscribers[a]	Mobile Phones[a]	Fax Machines[a]	Personal Computers[a]	Internet Hosts[b]	Internet Users[b]
	1996	1997	1998	1998	1998	1998	1998	1999	1999
Syria	20	278	70	N/A	0	1.4	1.7	0.00	20
United States	215	2,146	847	244.3	256	78.4	458.6	1,508.77	74,100
Turkey	111	180	286	9.2	53	1.7	23.2	8.06	1,500
Israel	290	520	318	184.0	359	24.9	217.2	187.41	800

[a]Data are from International Telecommunication Union, *World Telecommunication Development Report 1999* and are per 1,000 people.
[b]Data are from the Internet Software Consortium (http://www.isc.org) and are per 10,000 people.

SOURCE: World Bank. *World Development Indicators 2000.*

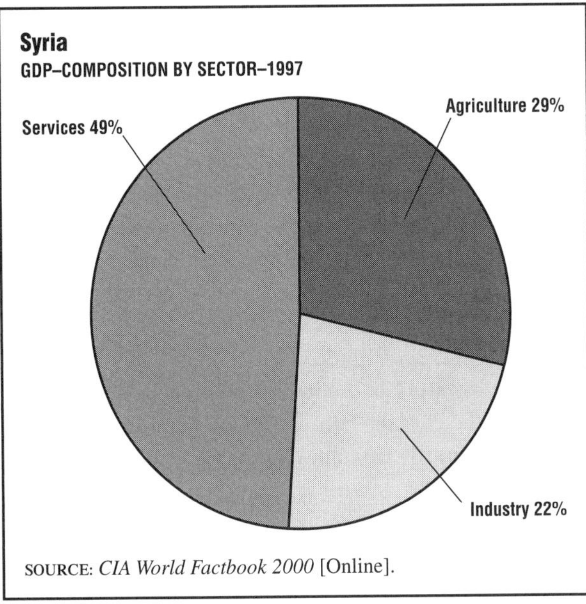

SOURCE: *CIA World Factbook 2000* [Online].

necessary products to the industrial sector. The oil sector is a driving force behind Syrian industry. Crude oil exports of US$1.342 billion accounted for nearly 43 percent of Syria's total exports in 1998. The Syrian services sector also made up 49 percent of its GDP in 1997 and employed about another 40 percent of the labor force.

Since the second half of the 1990s, the Syrian economy has been undergoing a recession. According to the 2000 *EIU Country Profile,* the Syrian agricultural sector has suffered in the last 3 years because of rapid climate changes and severe droughts in the region. The continuing rise of crude oil prices in international markets may promise an increase in Syria's export earnings, while service sectors such as construction, transport, and telecommunications have been steadily growing since the Gulf War in 1991.

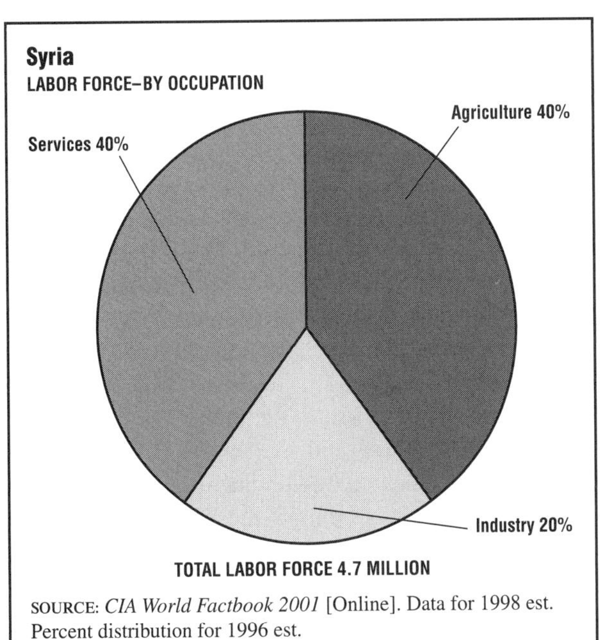

TOTAL LABOR FORCE 4.7 MILLION

SOURCE: *CIA World Factbook 2001* [Online]. Data for 1998 est. Percent distribution for 1996 est.

AGRICULTURE

The agricultural sector in Syria accounted for 29 percent of the GDP in 1997 and employed an estimated 40 percent of labor in 1996, including a significant proportion of townspeople. The primary agricultural products are cotton, olives, wheat, barley, lentils, chickpeas, sugar beets, beef, mutton, eggs, poultry, and milk. Cotton, grown on irrigated land, is Syria's premier **cash crop**. Besides providing employment and income for a significant amount of the population, it also has provided Syria with much needed **hard currency**. Until 1974, when it was superseded by oil as the largest Syrian export, cotton accounted for about one-third of Syria's total exports. By the late 1990s, cotton accounted for almost 50 percent of the agricultural sector's contribution to GDP. Nearly half of the cotton produced is used for local consumption by the largely export-oriented clothing and textile industry. Syria is also the second largest olive exporter in the Arab world after Tunisia and is sixth in the world after Spain, Greece, Tunisia, Italy, and Turkey. According to the *EIU Country Report,* the total value of agricultural exports in 1998 was about 24 percent of total exports, while the share of agricultural imports in 1998 was nearly 16 percent of total imports.

The average farmer's reliance on outdated and inefficient irrigation methods is a major obstacle to improving agricultural outputs. The introduction of drip, sprinkler, and subsurface irrigation methods is handicapped because of the limited amount of money available to the common farmer. Because of these shortcomings, Syria is susceptible to food shortages during long droughts.

Because of the government's revitalization efforts during the 1980s and 1990s, the agricultural sector recorded a 10 percent increase in its share of GDP in 1998. This kind of liberalization effort has been essential to increased agricultural production. The enactment of Decree #10 in 1986 allowed **joint sector** companies to be established with a minimum 25 percent stake to be held by the public sector. Pricing, production, and marketing of fruits and vegetables have also been placed in private hands. Liberalization measures since 1991 include the lifting of **subsidies** for seeds and pesticides, and the reduction of the fertilizer subsidy.

Because of geographic and topographic conditions, Syria has no forestry sector. Fishing is also quite limited, with a few small and medium-sized boats fishing off the Mediterranean coast.

INDUSTRY

The Syrian industrial sector contributed 22 percent of the GDP in 1997 and 20 percent of the labor force in 1996. State-owned organizations dominate heavy industry. Mining and quarrying (mostly oil) generates about 28 percent of gross industrial output, followed by the agro-food and chemical industries. The textiles and clothing industry comes next, and accounts for about 12 percent of industrial output.

MINING. Petroleum is Syria's chief mineral product. Most of the petroleum comes from fields in the northeastern part of the country. Phosphate rock is another important source of income. Phosphate, which is used to make fertilizer, is mined in the Palmyra area of central Syria. The principal limestone quarries are located north and west of Damascus, near the city of Aleppo. Marl is used in the cement industry with quarries near Damascus, Aleppo, and Rastan. Sandstone suitable for glass manufacture is mined in the Palmyra Mountains. The country's other mineral products include asphalt, gypsum, natural gas, and table salt.

OIL. Most of Syria's oil fields are located on the Euphrates Graben, which runs across the northeastern region of the country. The discovery of large crude fields in the mid-1980s boosted the role that oil plays in the Syrian economy. Since this time, output has expanded rapidly and reached a peak of 604,000 barrels per day in 1996. Production has been falling in recent years, because many fields discovered in the 1960s reached maturity. According to the International Energy Agency (IEA), as of 2000, Syria's production was about 520,000 barrels per day, of which some 325,000 barrels per day have been exported, accounting for some 65 percent of export revenue. Because of Syria's old, small, and dispersed oil fields, the *EIU Country Report* claims that the decline in Syrian oil production will continue in 2001, and most observers agree that the decline will continue for years to come.

Intense exploitation in the late 1980s and early 1990s saw oil production rise rapidly, fuelling economic growth, but at a cost. Fields were damaged as groundwater seeped into reservoirs and reservoir pressure fell, requiring injection projects to maintain pressure. Additionally, harsh government terms caused many foreign oil firms to leave the country. Investors have complained about the restrictive terms for exploration and development in the Syrian oil sector. In fact, international observers have forecasted that Syria will revert to being a net importer of oil within a few years as production declines and domestic consumption rises, unless new, substantial, and financially viable reserves are soon found. Syria exports Syrian Light, a blend of light and sweet crude oils produced from the Deir ez-Zour and Ash Sham fields. The country also exports fuel oil and other products. Syria is a member of OAPEC (Organization of Arab Petroleum Exporting Countries), but not OPEC (Organization of Petroleum Exporting Countries).

The oil exploitation of the 1980s attracted international interest to the Syrian oil sector, and several consortiums (companies formed to undertake an enterprise beyond the resources of any one member) were formed. Companies such as Agip, Bay Oil, Chevron, Conoco, Marc Rich, Shell, Elf, Total, and Veba are the most prominent involved in the sector. The largest of these is the Shell consortium made up of Pecten, Shell, and Deminex. In 1985 the Shell consortium entered a **joint venture** with the Syrian Petroleum Company (SPC) to create the Al-Furat Petroleum Company. This joint venture produces about two-thirds of Syria's oil output. All Syrian oil, including that produced by foreign companies, is sold on a monthly basis by the state-owned marketing company Sytrol. Since January 1994, Sytrol has had a clause in its term contracts prohibiting customers from re-selling Syrian crudes without written permission from Sytrol. This is intended to curb spot trading in Syrian crudes, especially sales to Israel. The unfavorable contract terms for exploration, development, and poor exploration results have only left 3 (Elf, Shell, and Deminex) out of the 14 companies that were operating in the country in 1991.

Syria's 2 oil refineries are located at Banias and Homs. Total production from these refineries was 242,140 barrels per day in 2001. Syria is planning to construct a third refinery, with an initial capacity of 60,000 barrels per day, at Deir ez-Zour to supply products to the eastern part of the country. The country's major oil export terminals are at Banias and Tartous on the Mediterranean, with a small tanker terminal at Latakia. Tartous is connected through a pipeline to the Banias terminal. The Syrian Company for Oil Transport (SCOT) operates all 3 terminals and is in charge of Syria's pipelines.

GAS. Syria's proven natural gas reserves are estimated at 8.5 trillion cubic feet (Tcf). Most (73 percent) of these reserves are owned by SPC, including about 3.6 Tcf in the Palmyra area, 1.6 Tcf at the al-Furat fields, 1.2 Tcf at Suwaidiyah, 0.8 Tcf at Jibsah, 0.7 Tcf at Deir ez-Zour, and the remainder at al-Hol, al-Ghona, and Marqada. In 1998, Syria produced about 208 billion cubic feet of natural gas, a 5-fold increase over the previous decade. As part of a strategy to substitute natural gas for oil in power generation to free up as much oil as possible for export, Syria plans to increase this production even further in the coming years. According to the *EIU Country Report* of 2000, Syria produced about 460 million cubic feet per day of gas, but this will nearly double by 2005 to 850 million cubic feet per day, as new gas sources are extracted.

SPC has been working to increase Syria's gas production through several projects. The Palmyra area in central Syria is the site of much of this activity, including the development of the Al Arak gas field, which came on stream at the end of 1995. In October 1997 the Syrian government announced the discovery of a large new gas field in the Abi Rabah area of the Palmyra region. One of the main problems for the gas sector is the location of gas in the northeast regions of the country, while the population centers are in the southwest. According to EIU reports, in July 2000 a step to ease the disparity was taken with the announcement that a Dutch company, A Halk Pijpleidingen, had been awarded a contract to construct a US$46 million pipeline from newly developed gas fields in the Palmyra area to the city of Aleppo. The 124-mile pipeline will be used to supply gas to a 1,000 megawatt power station in the city, constructed by Mitsubishi Heavy Industries of Japan. Bids are being measured to build a gas pipeline from Homs to the Mediterranean port of Banias.

Given the small size of Syria's gas fields, most of the large oil companies have shown little interest in the market, given the complex government bureaucracy that they must navigate. One of the exceptions is Conoco, the only U.S. oil company operating in Syria. Another is Elf of France, with whom Syria Petroleum Company signed a US$430 million service agreement in November 1998 to utilize associated gas in the Deir ez-Zour oil fields. Elf and Conoco each hold a 50 percent interest in the project, with Conoco as the lead operator. In March 2000 the 2 companies awarded Houston-based Kvaerner ENC a US$160-million contract to engineer, procure, and construct the infrastructure for the project. The Deir ez-Zour gas development work will include the construction of a gas gathering system and processing plant, and a 155-mile pipeline that will connect the system to the national grid near Palmyra that serves western Syria. When completed in late 2001, gas output from 22 fields should be about 280 million cubic feet per day. According to the *EIU Country Report,* Syria is planning to supply 3 million cubic meters per day of gas to Lebanon via a 107-mile pipeline that will run from the Syrian city of Homs to northern Lebanon. Elf announced that it is also considering joining the US$175-million pipeline project that would supply power stations in Lebanon with natural gas from Syria.

MANUFACTURING. Manufacturing accounts for about 6 percent of the value of Syria's production. The main industries are cement, glass, food processing, iron and steel, leather goods, brassware, fertilizers, and textiles. Cotton fabrics, wool, and nylon are Syria's most important manufactures. The textile industry is in Aleppo, Damascus, Homs, and Hamah. Natural silk is produced at Latakia. Technical engineering industries, most of which are in Damascus, are active in producing cement, glass panes, bottles, utensils, pharmaceuticals, plywood, and batteries. The food processing industry produces salt, vegetable oils, cotton cake, canned fruit and vegetables, tobacco, and a variety of dairy products. While manufactured goods made up 10 percent of total Syrian exports in 1998, the well-established textile industry contributed another 10 percent of export earnings and employed one-third of the industrial workforce.

Syrian manufacturing industries grew substantially in the 1960s. The government encouraged industrialization by raising **tariffs** on imported **consumer goods** and providing tax exemptions and credit for domestic industries. Therefore, most of the traditional handmade manufactures (damask steel, swords and blades, brass and copper work, wood engravings, gold and silver ornaments, mother-of-pearl inlays, silk brocades) have dramatically decreased since the introduction of industrial processing. Private sector participation in manufacturing has taken off in the 1990s, with the total capital investment in the industrial private sector growing from US$273 million in 1991 to US$735 million in 1995. Of the 1.1 million workers in manufacturing, more than 75 percent are now employed in the private or mixed sectors. While private sector involvement has been limited to the textile, food processing, leather, paper, and chemical industries, the government started to open heavy industry to private investment in areas where the public sector is unable to meet increasing demand.

SERVICES

TOURISM. Syria's rich history attracts large numbers of tourists. Artifacts from the ancient Mesopotamian civilization, castles from the crusaders, and many other diverse historical sites appeal to world travelers. The United Nations Educational, Scientific, and Cultural Organization has declared Damascus and Aleppo world heritage sites because these date to the early development of civilization, well before the Greek and Roman empires.

With such a rich cultural heritage and a Mediterranean coastline, Syria's tourism sector shows great potential, and the number of tourists who visit the country each year is on the rise. Since the Gulf War in 1990–91, an average of about 900,000 visitors have visited Syria each year. But regional instability after 1996 has hindered the tourist sector, evidenced by the drop in tourists to 400,000 in 1999 from 2.5 million in 1998. In the same time span, tourism revenue declined from US$1.3 billion in 1998 to US$712 million in 1999. Arab tourists continue to visit Syria in increasing numbers, enjoying the improved luxuries offered by the sector. According to the *EIU Country Report,* capacity at the luxury end of the market is about 8,000 beds in the five-star hotels, with occupancy estimated at 80 percent during the summer season of 2000.

There are a number of problems in the tourism sector, including a lack of marketing activities on an international level, the low number of airline carriers to Syria, and the lack of a nationally coordinated policy for the development of tourism. The hazy divisions between public and private sectors and the non-existence of large centers for tourist entertainment and cultural activities are other major weaknesses inhibiting growth. The most important challenge that the tourism industry faces is the lack of big investments in this vital economic sector. To encourage private sector and foreign investment in Syrian tourism projects, the government has made several aggressive decisions since 1986. Incentives include tax exemptions on all tourism-based projects. All imports needed to build tourism installations, if these imports do not exceed 50 percent of total investment, are tax exempt. There is also a 7-year corporate tax exemption, after which taxes are paid at 50 percent of the normal rate.

FINANCIAL SERVICES. The Syrian financial system has been run by the state since nationalization in the 1960s. The banking functions have been designed to cater to the financial requirements of the public sector. Because loans to the private sector are unknown, private businesses must finance projects with cash or through external loans. The Central Bank of Syria and the Commercial Bank of Syria are 2 of the 5 government-owned banks that deal in hard currency. Although previously only foreigners were allowed to open accounts with foreign currency in the Commercial Bank of Syria, beginning in September 1996 the government allowed Syrians to deposit foreign currency at government banks without disclosing the source of such currency, and plans to allow citizens to possess foreign currency. The new decision eliminates provisions in an old currency law that prevented Syrians from dealing in hard currency. The new decree allows hard currency to be transferred abroad provided it is used for education expenses, payments of books, medical treatment, newspaper subscriptions, and other non-commercial transactions. Changing money at rates other than official rates remains illegal and all transfers in and out of the country must be declared.

The EIU reports that the current banking system is in urgent need of reform. The system is criticized by business leaders for being inefficient and offering only basic services. There are, for example, no ATMs, checks, or credit cards in Syria. Commercial loans are hard to obtain without using political party or government connections or traditional patronage relations (a system of relations in which government or any other sectarian, tribal domineering authority distributes the sources at its expense to its supporters as rewards). The new Syrian government has acknowledged the need for reform of the financial system and these new moves show that progress is being made. Some modernization efforts have been initiated with the computerization of the Central Bank and other commercial banks.

The government has also announced that foreign banks will be allowed to open branches in Syria for the first time. Banks with at least US$11 million in capital will be permitted to operate in the country's **free zones** (an area where goods may be landed, handled, manufactured, reconfigured, and **re-exported** without the intervention of the customs authorities) to finance commercial and industrial activity. In August 2000 3 Lebanese banks were issued licenses while some non-Arab international banks expressed their wishes to enter the full international market rather than be restricted to the small free zones. The United Nations Industrial Development Organization (UNIDO) has estimated that Syria would gain US$8 billion in foreign investment if it allowed the establishment of private banks, opened a stock market, and unified **exchange rates**.

INTERNATIONAL TRADE

According to International Monetary Fund sources, because of the discovery of large oil fields, Syria's foreign trade volume has immensely increased over the last 3 decades. During this period, exports have grown from US$203 million in 1970 to US$4.8 billion in 2000, while imports have risen from US$360 million in 1970 to US$3.5 billion in 2000. Syria's foreign trade is highly dependent on its oil revenues and oil prices on the international markets. For the year 2000, the EIU reported that increasing oil prices have continued to boost export revenue and Syria recorded a surplus of more than US$1 billion for the first time since the Gulf War.

Syria's chief exports are petroleum, textiles, food, live animals, and manufactured goods which are exported to Germany (which received 21 percent of exports in 1999), Italy (12 percent), France (10 percent), Saudi Arabia (9 percent), and Turkey (8 percent). Syria's main import products are machinery, food and live animals, transport equipment, and chemicals. The country's main import partners include France (which purchased 11 percent of imports in 1999), Italy (8 percent), Germany (7 percent), Turkey (5 percent), and China (4 percent). Additionally, a large amount of trade (nearly US$200 million) with Lebanon, Turkey, and Iraq goes unrecorded. It is estimated that these invisible flows favor Syria, as evidenced by the use of its military and political influence on Lebanon to create a common market between the 2 countries, from which Syria will benefit.

As of 2001, there were about 200 state-owned trading companies that enjoyed prohibitive tariff protection, overvalued exchange rates, and restrictions on private-sector competition. These state-run companies regulated most of Syria's exports. According to the Syrian Min-

Trade (expressed in billions of US$): Syria

	Exports	Imports
1975	.930	1.685
1980	2.108	4.124
1985	1.637	3.967
1990	4.212	2.400
1995	3.563	4.709
1998	2.890	3.895

SOURCE: International Monetary Fund. *International Financial Statistics Yearbook 1999.*

GDP per Capita (US$)

Country	1975	1980	1985	1990	1998
Syria	907	1,071	1,036	956	1,209
United States	19,364	21,529	23,200	25,363	29,683
Turkey	1,898	1,959	2,197	2,589	3,167
Israel	10,620	11,412	12,093	13,566	15,978

SOURCE: United Nations. *Human Development Report 2000; Trends in human development and per capita income.*

istry of Economic and Foreign Trade statistics, in 1998 72 percent of exports were made by the public sector.

MONEY

Syria maintains a multiple **fixed exchange rate** system that pegs the value of currency to the U.S. dollar. All the official rates overvalue the Syrian pound to varying degrees. Two principal exchange rates are used: the Official Rate that devalued the national currency in 1988 from S£3.925 to S£11.225 per U.S. dollar, and the Neighboring Countries Rate (NCR) that was introduced in 1990 and is periodically adjusted. The NCR was S£46.50 per U.S. dollar, according to EIU estimates in 2000. Tourist hotels use the Official Rate. Most local transactions are carried out at the NCR rate. A blended rate applies provisionally to certain public sector transactions, including sales of oil and gas. The black market rate has hovered between S£46 and S£54 per U.S. dollar since the early 1990s.

Over the last decade, the Syrian government has contracted the **inflation rate** from 34 percent in 1988 to minus 0.5 in 1999. The EIU forecasts that weak Syrian growth and the current low level of economic productivity in the local economy will further help the government keep **inflation** in check. The potential increase in government spending due to public sector wages and a steady growth in global non-oil commodity and raw material prices might threaten to reverse this trend over the forecast period.

Exchange rates: Syria

Syrian pounds per US$1	
2001	N/A
2000	46
1999	N/A
1998	46
Jan 1997	41.9
1996	N/A

SOURCE: CIA *World Factbook 2001* [ONLINE].

POVERTY AND WEALTH

Besides existing ethnic and sectarian cleavages, Syrian society is also stratified along tense social and economic class divisions. The class structure is characterized by a high degree of maldistribution of wealth, meaning that much of the wealth is concentrated in the hands of the few, while large numbers of people live in poverty. Moreover, there is a high correlation between wealth and sectarian-ethnic background. The upper income group is composed of Alawite high-ranking officials, military officers, Sunni landowners, small industrial business owners, and important merchants. The middle-income group comprises most Alawite and Sunni government officials, shopkeepers, professionals, and farmers. The lower income group is made up of Alawite workers, peasants (farmers who do not own all the land they cultivate), and employees.

Although the Ba'athist Syrian government has directed its welfare policies—such as land reform—at easing social problems, an estimated 20 percent of the Syrian population lives under the poverty line. In the last 30 years, the pace of change from an agricultural to an industrial economy and the accompanying migration of people to the cities has worsened income distribution and caused the mushrooming of high-poverty shantytowns (poorly constructed temporary housing) on the edge of populous cities. To compensate for disparities in the distribution of wealth, the Ministry of Municipal and Rural Affairs has constructed blocks of low-income flats in these areas. Meanwhile, the Ministry of Social Welfare and Labor has been empowered to find work for and distribute cash allowances to the unemployed. The Ministry also encourages such youth activities as athletics, scouting, literacy campaigns, and the organization of cooperatives. The government gives substantial grants to private welfare societies in solving poverty problems. According to World Bank sources, however, the share of GDP allocated to the social security and welfare policies was barely 0.7 percent a year between 1992 and 1997.

WORKING CONDITIONS

The Syrian labor force was estimated at about 4.8 million by the International Labor Organization in 1998. The service and agriculture sectors employ the majority of the labor force, each accounting for about a 40 percent stake. Although government figures put unemployment at below 10 percent, unofficial estimates more than double this figure, with under-employment accounting for another 25 percent. Syria has one of the highest population growth rates in the world, with an annual increase of 2.58 percent. Because of the high growth rate, an extra 200,000 new workers enter the labor market every year. According to the *EIU Country Report,* the unemployment rate among 15 to 29-year-olds is unofficially reported to be as high as 85 percent. As a part of an emergency plan in its 2000 budget, the government has allocated S£80 billion for the creation of 92,322 new jobs, but this falls far short of the number entering the labor market each year.

Due to these harsh conditions in the labor market, many Syrians go to Lebanon and the Gulf States to work. For that reason, in recent years, Syria has become economically dependent on Lebanon. Sources in Lebanon estimate that about 500,000 to 1 million Syrians work in the country. In Beirut, Syrian workers can earn twice what they make in their own country. Jobs in Lebanon reduce unemployment in Syria and the remittances of these workers to their families back home are estimated at US$1–3 billion dollars per year. The condition exacerbates economic deprivation in Lebanon, however. Lebanese Shiites and Palestinian refugees are hard hit by the influx of Syrian workers.

The 1973 Syrian constitution provides for the right of the "popular sectors" (workers, peasants, and state employees) of society to form trade unions. The government insists that there is in practice trade union pluralism (a condition in which a multiple number of unions with different particular interests can freely exist). Despite this, workers are not free to form labor unions independent of the government-prescribed structure. The General Federation of Trade Unions (GFTU) is the major independent popular organization. The government uses it as a framework for controlling nearly all aspects of union activity. The GFTU is charged with providing opinions on legislation, devising rules for workers, and organizing labor. In the private sector, unions are active in monitoring compliance with the laws and ensuring workers' health and safety. Strikes are not prohibited (except in the agricultural sector), but in practice they are discouraged.

COUNTRY HISTORY AND ECONOMIC DEVELOPMENT

1250. Mamluks take control of most of Syria.

1516. Syria is incorporated into the Ottoman Empire.

1869. The opening of the Suez Canal leads to a decline in Syria's economic importance.

1916. The Sykes-Picot agreement between Great Britain and France, made during World War I, places Syria and Lebanon under French "influence."

1922. The League of Nations approves the French Mandate for Syria and Lebanon.

1945. Syria becomes a member of the United Nations.

1946. Syria and Lebanon declare their independence from France.

1948. In the Arab-Israeli war, Syria joins the joint Arab forces fighting against Israel.

1958. Establishment of the United Arab Republic (UAR), a union of Syria and Egypt. Egyptian Gamal Abdel Nasser becomes president of the union and dissolves all political parties in Syria. He also introduces regulations on the size of land property.

1961. Opposition to the UAR grows in Syria, particularly against the socialist economic policies implemented by Nasser. The army takes control of Damascus, and declares a new independence for Syria.

1963. The Ba'athist party takes control of the country.

1967. In the Six Day War, Israel seizes the Golan Heights from Syria.

1970. Hafez Assad seizes power in a "corrective coup."

1971. Assad is elected president for a 7-year term in a plebiscite (a vote of the people).

1973. Syria and Egypt go to war with Israel to retake the Golan Heights.

1976. The Syrian army intervenes in the Lebanese civil war.

1981. Israel formally annexes the Golan Heights.

1982. An Islamic extremist uprising in Hama is crushed and thousands are killed. Israel invades Lebanon.

1987. Assad sends troops into Lebanon for a second time to enforce a cease-fire in Beirut.

1990. Following the Iraqi invasion of Kuwait, Syria joins the U.S.-led coalition against Iraq. This leads to improved relations with Egypt and the United States.

1991. Syria participates in the Middle East peace conference in Madrid, and holds bilateral talks with Israel. The Damascus Declaration aid and defense pact is signed with Egypt, Saudi Arabia, Kuwait, the United Arab Emirates, Qatar, Bahrain, and Oman.

2000. Assad dies and is succeeded by his son, Bashar, soon afterwards.

FUTURE TRENDS

In order to overcome its existing economic problems, Syria will need to attract major international investors. This does not seem likely in the near future due to domestic and international problems. In the domestic arena, the 34-year-old Bashar Assad, son of the late Hafez Assad, tried to cement his position while launching his liberal political and economic agenda. Bashar and his reformist elite tried to bring a new openness to the country, but efforts were thwarted by the "old guard" of military and political veterans who remained loyal to the legacy of Hafez Assad.

With regard to regional politics, it is clear that Bashar Assad must strengthen his domestic political standing before entering into peace talks with Israel. Syria's other main foreign policy concern, Lebanon, has become akin to a domestic policy issue. Syria has politically dominated Lebanon for a decade, making foreign and defense policy decisions for the country, and approving all senior politicians. Under the elder Assad, no opposition was allowed to Syria's dominant position in Lebanon. After Israel withdrew from Lebanon in May 2000, many Lebanese continue to resent the presence of Syria and call for the removal of its troops. Bashar Assad might be forced to make a vital decision regarding his policy towards Lebanon. Most likely, the Syrian government will ask Lebanon for some concessions because of the economic advantages they gain from about 500,000 to 1 million Syrian workers in Lebanon.

Syria has long sheltered revolutionaries and terrorists to get leverage in regional politics. If the government wants to attract foreign investors, it must reconsider its support for international terrorism. Depending on policy options embraced by the new president, the outcomes of these domestic and international policy decisions will shape Syria's economic performance in the next decade. Because of population and unemployment problems, Syria's reliance on oil revenue puts it in an unstable situation. Decreasing production in the sector might have a negative impact on the economy in the end, while increasing oil prices on the international markets seems to continue boosting export revenues in the short-run.

DEPENDENCIES

Syria has no territories or colonies.

BIBLIOGRAPHY

Arab World Online. "Country Profile: Syrian Arab Republic." <http://www.awo.net/country/overview/crsyr.asp>. Accessed September 2001.

Economist Intelligence Unit. *Country Profile: Syria.* London: Economist Intelligence Unit, 2001.

Energy Information Administration. "Syria." <http://www.eia.doe.gov/emeu/cabs/syria.html>. Accessed September 2001.

Syrian Embassy. <http://www.syrianembassy.org>. Accessed September 2001.

U.S. Central Intelligence Agency. *World Factbook 2001.* <http://www.odci.gov/cia/publications/factbook/index.html>. Accessed September 2001.

U.S. Department of State. *FY 2001 Country Commercial Guide: Syria.* <http://www.state.gov/www/about_state/business/com_guides/2001.nea/index.html>. Accessed September 2001.

—Yüksel Sezgin

TAIWAN

Republic of China
Chung Hwa Min Kuo

CAPITAL: Taipei.

MONETARY UNIT: New Taiwan dollar (NT$). One dollar equals 100 cents. There are notes of 50, 100, 500, and 1,000 dollars. There are coins of 50 cents, and 1, 5, and 10 dollars.

CHIEF EXPORTS: Machinery and electrical equipment (51 percent), metals, textiles, plastics, chemicals.

CHIEF IMPORTS: Machinery and electrical equipment (51 percent), minerals, precision equipment.

GROSS DOMESTIC PRODUCT: US$386 billion (purchasing power parity, 2000 est.).

BALANCE OF TRADE: **Exports:** US$148.38 billion (f.o.b., 2000). **Imports:** US$140.01 billion (c.i.f., 2000).

COUNTRY OVERVIEW

LOCATION AND SIZE. The island of Taiwan, in Eastern Asia, is about 161 kilometers (100 miles) away from the southeast part of mainland China, and about 483 kilometers (300 miles) north of the Philippine island of Luzon. The East China Sea forms the northern border of Taiwan, the Taiwan Straits are to the west, the Philippine Sea to the south, and the Pacific Ocean on the east coast. The territory is slightly smaller than the combined area of Maryland and Delaware in the United States. Taiwan occupies a total area of 35,980 square kilometers (13,892 square miles). Its capital city, Taipei, is in the northeast, and is the most densely populated area in the territory.

POPULATION. As of November 2000, the population of Taiwan was estimated at 22,257,000. People aged 14 years and under comprise 22 percent of the total population, while 70 percent belong in the 15 to 64 age bracket. The earliest government census records, dated 1905, set the island's population at 3.12 million, which doubled to 6.02 million by 1945. Subsequently, the Taiwanese population increased at an average of 3.84 percent, prompting the government to implement strict population control measures such as family planning. By 1997, the population growth rate had dropped to 1 percent.

Besides government family planning programs, the decline in population growth can be linked to the change of attitude in the younger generation who, due to better education and career opportunities, now tend to marry later. There has been a decrease in potential mothers between the ages of 20 and 34. Of the 326,002 births registered in Taiwan in 1997, the ratio was 109.04 boys for every 100 girls. The greater male-to-female ratio on the island is in keeping with Chinese culture, which traditionally values sons above daughters.

The population distribution curve measured by age groups indicates an aging population. In 1990 people aged 65 and over comprised about 6.1 percent of Taiwan's population. This figure increased to 8 percent in 2000 and, with average life expectancy at 76.35 years, the government estimates that the percentage of its elderly population will increase to 19.1 percent by 2030. In an attempt to encourage a moderate *increase* in population, the government modified its former population reduction slogan from, "One [child] is not too few; two are just right," to "Two are just right."

Because of the increasing industrialization of Taiwan, people are flocking to the urban-metropolitan areas of the island, which absorb 67.8 percent of the total population. In 1997 the population density of Taiwan was the second highest in the world next to Bangladesh, with 601 people per square kilometer (1,557 per square mile). The capital city, Taipei, which covers 272 square kilometers (105 square miles), is the most densely populated area with 9,560 persons per square kilometer (24,760 per square mile). Second to Taipei is Kaohsiung City with an area of 154 square kilometers (59 square miles), which is home to 9,350 persons per square kilometer (24,216

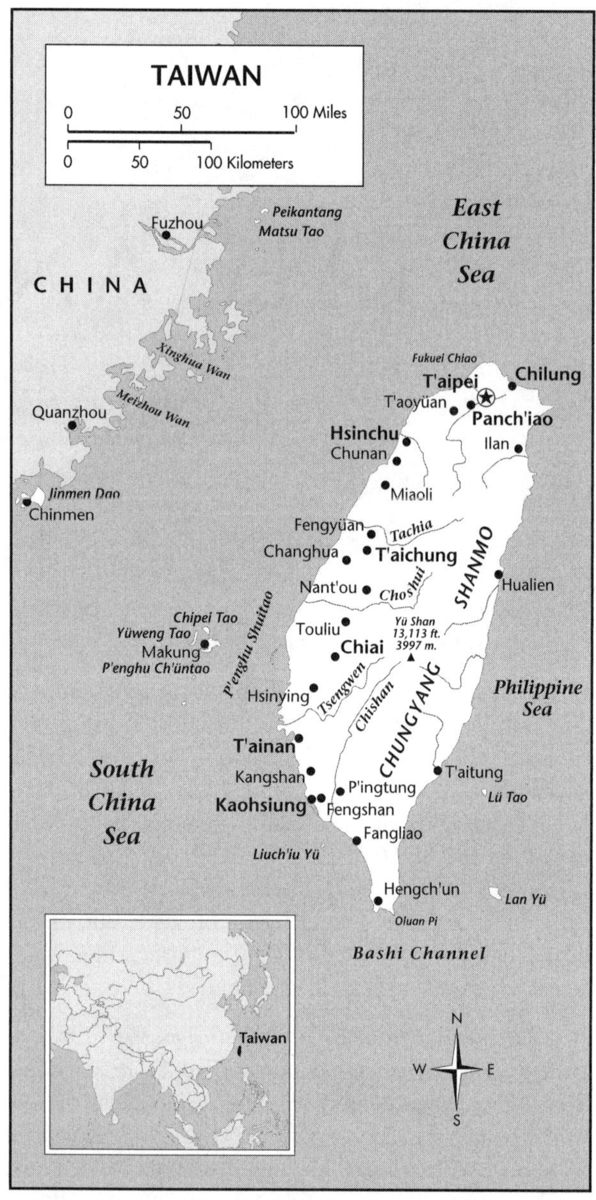

per square mile), while Taichung City, with an area of 163 square kilometers (63 square miles), has 5,519 inhabitants per square kilometer (14,294 per square mile).

OVERVIEW OF ECONOMY

The economic development of Taiwan can be broken down into 5 stages. In the 1950s, the main goal of the government was to stabilize the economy and ensure an adequate and regular food supply for the population. Hand in hand with agricultural production, the government encouraged the development of labor-intensive industries to provide much-needed employment to a growing **labor force**, and to ease the need for imported products by manufacturing substitute products locally.

In the 1960s, the government continued to promote the same labor-intensive industries, but this time the focus was on manufacturing products for export. By the end of the decade, the export industry was thriving and had stimulated local demand for the machinery needed to produce export goods. This export-led strategy had several positive results. Employment opportunities increased and a greater variety of manufactured products were developed. Expansion advanced local knowledge of management skills and the development of industrial technology. Moreover, receipts of foreign currency greatly enhanced the financial standing and stability of the government.

Supported by these developments, in the 1970s the government shifted its strategy to the encouragement of basic and heavy industries. These industries were designed to produce and promote domestic substitutes for imported products, and to develop those industries that would require heavy capital expenditures. By thus reducing Taiwan's reliance on foreign suppliers for components, government expenditure decreased.

By the 1980s, Taiwan's foreign trade was posting huge surpluses. The government directed these funds to building **infrastructure** such as roads, bridges, airports, and seaports, and to improve the quality of life on the island. The surplus was also able to finance the further development of capital-intensive and high-technology industries such as electronics, information, and machinery. At the turn of the decade, the government focused on building a world-class infrastructure and 1994 saw the approval of a plan known as the Twelve Major Construction Projects. The scope of the plan included transportation, culture, and education, improvement of living standards, development of water resources, and environmental protection.

In just 50 years, Taiwan had achieved rapid economic growth, characterized by stable prices and equitable distribution of income. Its rapid industrial advancement between 1980 and 2000 has earned the island recognition as one of the "tiger" economies of Asia.

One of the most important events that set the stage for Taiwan's economic development was its implementation of genuine land reform. Under this program, rents were reduced, public lands were distributed to the landless, and farmers were given the opportunity to own the land they had been tilling for many years. In 1953, 60 percent of the rural population became owner-farmers, and owner-cultivated land increased to more than 75 percent of the total land tilled. In the meantime, those land owners who were compelled to sell their property under the land reform program were compensated in government bonds. Dissatisfied with the government's action and highly suspicious of the value of the bonds, many of the landowners immediately sold them. At the same time, land prices went down in anticipation of the effects of land reform. Taken together, these events contributed to eradicating the land-owning class and the landlord-tenant relationship, a transformation that saved Taiwan from the fate of other societies where huge income disparity between landowners and their workers set the stage for social and economic injustice.

Land reform also led to the reorganization of rural Chinese society. It brought the end of patriarchy, whereby authority was vested only in men, and saw the loosening of family ties. As agricultural processes were modernized, production became more efficient, allowing younger people to leave the farms and pursue other careers in the urban areas. This migration triggered urbanization which, in turn, fostered job specialization, lowered class barriers, promoted social equality, and increased cultural and social interaction.

As social interaction increased, people no longer confined close relationships to the family circle but made outside friends, thus further contributing to social stability and harmony. Under government guidance, the Taiwanese found themselves sharing a common vision and working toward a common goal. Besides economic policies, the government implemented policies that extended compulsory education to 9 years and established schools for vocational and technical training. By encouraging young people to acquire new ideas and skills, Taiwan created a well-trained and industrious labor force, which has served as the backbone of the nation's economic development.

The major economic sectors in Taiwan are composed of services, manufacturing, and agriculture. Since 1985, the service sector has contributed greatly to economic development by generating more than half the **gross domestic product** (GDP), increasing to 64 percent in 1999, while industry and agriculture accounted for 33 percent and 3 percent of GDP, respectively.

Small and medium enterprises (SMEs) in Taiwan are engaged in the manufacturing of products from toys and textiles to personal computers. SMEs can also be found in the construction industry, and in the service sector, particularly in financial, social, and personal services. According to the Ministry of Finance, 97.76 percent of the businesses in Taiwan can be classified as SMEs. In 1998, SMEs provided employment for 4 out of 5 workers in Taiwan, or 7.27 million out of 9.55 million workers.

The government of Taiwan is optimistic about the island's continued economic growth. Its optimism is based on past economic performance. Even at the height of the 1997 Asian financial crisis, which had a negative impact on the leading economies of Asia, Taiwan's gross domestic product still amounted to US$283.4 billion.

Taiwan's government is continually drawing up plans to create more businesses on the island to provide more employment and to strengthen its position against the re-occurrence of a regional or global economic crisis. For the 21st century, the government is working hard to secure the next step of that process. In his inaugural speech of May 2000, President Chen declared that Taiwan must respond to international developments by moving toward a knowledge-based economy in which high-tech industries constantly innovate, while traditional industries progressively transform and upgrade.

POLITICS, GOVERNMENT, AND TAXATION

In the early stages of its development, in the 1950s, Taiwan's economy was closely managed and controlled by the government. After the economy showed signs of rapid growth and continued development, government gradually exerted less control to give the economy free rein.

Government control during the early stages of Taiwan's economy was crucial to the provision of much-needed direction, guidance, and motivation of the population. The government's role included the maintenance of a stable and law-abiding society, strict implementation of their policies, and the formulation of programs to spur national development.

From the 1950s to the 1960s, the government assumed the role of an economic caretaker, exercising control and influence. The government gave support to emerging industries and acted to protect them against external competition. In the 1950s, foreign aid from the United States assisted the development of the textile and milling industries, while export industries tapped the country's limited foreign reserves. During this period, the government also encouraged the growth of Taiwan's domestic automobile industry by shielding it from foreign competition. Citizens wanting to buy foreign-made cars were penalized by a tax equivalent to the price of the imported car itself.

At this stage of Taiwan's economic development, the government demonstrated creativity in its plans to advance economic development. First, it maximized the contribution of state-run enterprises to the national coffers by taking a part of the profits in **indirect tax**. Second, the government provided incentives for private enterprise to thrive, lowering the price of electricity for industrial use, while increasing the price for commercial use. As intended, this ploy encouraged business into the manufacturing rather than the **retail** sector.

In the 1970s, the government took the initiative in building necessary infrastructure such as roads, bridges, airports, new cities, highways, and railways. It launched large-scale public investment projects, since dubbed the Ten, Twelve, and Fourteen Major Construction Projects;

the Six-Year National Development Plan; and the Twelve Economic Construction Projects.

Because of the government's protection and economic intervention, Taiwan's economy grew by leaps and bounds in just 4 decades. By the 1990s, private enterprise had grown strong and steady and needed little state assistance, although the expectation remains that government will continue to foster a healthy investment environment and move with the times in implementing new regulations. The role of the government, in short, has shifted from that of caretaker to that of teacher. As teacher, it has provided private enterprise with information on economic growth and technology, as well as assistance in training personnel.

Over the years, the government and people of Taiwan have attempted to uphold democratic principles and strengthen the island's political institutions. Political activities, especially elections which appear tainted by corrupt practices (buying votes, peddling influence, or provoking violence) are greeted with outrage. Beginning in the mid-1990s, certain reform-minded politicians campaigned for electoral reform. They tried to strengthen the role of political parties, improve their image, and highlight the importance of issues in elections. They aimed, too, to attract political candidates of a higher caliber, reduce the influence of personal connections and, finally, to combat factionalism (the breaking into smaller, differing factions or groups within a political party).

Taiwan's government is a multi-party democracy based on a constitution created in 1947 and amended in 1992, 1994, 1997, and 1999. The president and vice president are elected on the same ticket by popular vote and serve a 4-year term. The legislative branch consists of a **unicameral** (single-house) Legislative Yuan with a total of 225 members serving 3-year terms, 168 of whom are elected by popular vote, 41 of whom are elected by proportional vote by party, 8 elected from overseas constituencies based on proportional vote, and 8 elected by popular vote from among the country's aboriginal population, which constitutes 2 percent of the population. There is also a unicameral National Assembly of 300 members, all of whom are elected by **proportional representation** based on election of the Legislative Yuan and serve 4-year terms.

The year 2000 marked a significant political event in Taiwan when the candidates of the Kuomintang (KMT), Taiwan's ruling party for over 50 years, were defeated by the candidates of the leading opposition party, the 14-year-old Democratic Progressive Party (DPP). Taiwan's highest political office, the presidency, went to the DPP's Chen Shui-bian, the country's tenth president. His running mate, Hsiu-lien Annette Lu, became vice president, marking a victory not only for the DPP but also for the women's movement. Vice President Lu is known to have championed gender equality and women's rights since the beginning of her political career.

In the 2000 national elections, there were 3 major issues aside from the economy on which candidates had to make their attitudes clear to win votes. These were mainland policy, national defense, and foreign relations. Mainland policy dictates whether Taiwan should pursue its independence from mainland China or maintain the status quo. Currently, Taiwan upholds the principle of "one China, two political entities." Under the constitution, Taiwan is referred to as the Republic of China and regards itself as the national government of China, while the People's Republic of China is a political entity that controls mainland China. The issue is a cause of political tension not only for the 2 territories but also for other countries. Mainland China continues to use the threat of political and economic **sanctions** against those countries willing to recognize Taiwan as a separate country. Due to the scale of China's economic resources, its huge population, and its military capability, the threats are not taken lightly.

The KMT, or Nationalist Party, has the longest running political record in Taiwan. Founded by Dr. Sun Yat-sen in 1894, the KMT celebrated its one hundredth anniversary on 24 November 1994. The party is of major significance in Taiwan's history, and was involved in the war against Japanese invaders, struggles against **communist** rebellion, implementation of the constitution, and the economic development of the island. The KMT enjoys wide support, with a membership of approximately 2.1 million. At the lowest level, members are organized into cells. Moving upwards, there are district, county, and provincial congresses and committees. The highest level includes the National Congress and the Central Committee. With its historic defeat in 2000, KMT's leadership began an evaluation of the party platform, direction, and standing, compared with the other political parties.

The Democratic Progressive Party (DPP) was long the leading opposition party to the KMT. It was established on 28 September 1986 and has approximately 200,000 members. Its main policy is in direct opposition to the KMT because it calls for Taiwan's complete independence from mainland China. In recent elections, the more senior officers of DPP have tended to attach less importance to the party's stance on independence in an attempt to attract more voter support. The lack of consensus on this issue has caused some dissent within the party and has resulted in the breaking away of members who are passionate advocates of Taiwanese independence. Several of these dissatisfied DPP members have left the party and, with new recruits, have formed the Taiwan Independence Party and the New Nation Association.

In the 2000 elections, the economic platform espoused by the DPP included the introduction of a **pro-**

gressive tax system, elimination of unemployment, the promotion of balanced development in every sector of the economy, the opening of state-run enterprise to private investment, and protection of the environment against further destruction.

Another opposition party that has emerged is the New Party (NP), formed in August 1993 by a KMT breakaway group composed of 6 Legislative Yuan (a branch of government) members and 1 former lawmaker. Their official statement of resignation from the KMT, as documented in Taiwan's 1999 Yearbook, gave as their reason the "undemocratic practices of the KMT" as well as ideological differences. The New Party has been led by such prominent political personalities as the former finance minister, Wang Chien-shien, and former head of the Environmental Protection Administration, Jaw Shau-kong. The party champions 2 major issues: anti-corruption and social justice. The goal of the NP is to attract those voters who were dissatisfied with the performance of the ruling KMT, but who are opposed to the DPP's support for independence. The NP now claims a registered membership of nearly 68,500.

One of the newest parties to emerge because of Taiwan's ongoing democratization is the People First Party (PFP), established on 31 March 2000 by former Taiwan governor James Soong. The PFP is distinct from the other parties in allowing eligibility for membership at age 16, 2 years younger than the minimum age required by the other parties. James Soong, who was elected as the party's first chairman, ran as an independent in the 2000 presidential elections, but was defeated. The PFP is still in the process of establishing its structure and political base.

GOVERNMENT EXPENDITURES AND TAXATION. Data generated by the Directorate General of Budget, Accounting and Statistics (DGBAS) shows that the government spent NT$1.164 trillion in 1999. A big percentage of the budget went to national defense (22.6 percent); followed by education, science, and culture (17.4 percent); economic programs (14.8 percent); social welfare (13.5 percent); general administration (11.6 percent); and pension and survivor's benefits (11.1 percent). In the same year, the government posted a **budget surplus** amounting to NT$64.6 billion, while **external debt** amounted to US$35 billion.

Taiwan's government collects 18 different categories of taxation, which provide the revenue for national expenditures. Nine of these categories are classified as **direct taxes**: corporate **income tax**, individual income tax, rural land tax, land value tax, land value increment tax, estate and gift tax, mining-lot tax, house tax, and deed tax. The other 9 taxes are indirect and include customs **duty**, business tax, commodity tax, stamp duty, vehicle license tax, securities transaction tax, amusement tax, slaughter tax, and harbor dues.

Taxes are collected by the National Tax Administration, which administers different tax collection offices in the different provinces and municipalities. In 1999 tax revenue alone accounted for 62.7 percent of the government's total revenues. In the same period, the government was able to collect a little over NT$770 billion in taxes according to DGBAS statistics.

INFRASTRUCTURE, POWER, AND COMMUNICATIONS

One of the key factors in Taiwan's rapid economic development is its well-planned and efficient transport network. As an export-oriented economy, its many businesses are heavily dependent on shipping, by air and sea, for the transport of their goods to overseas markets.

On 5 January 1995, Taiwan approved the Asia-Pacific Regional Operations Center (APROC) Plan, an

Communications

Country	Telephones[a]	Telephones, Mobile/Cellular[a]	Radio Stations[b]	Radios[a]	TV Stations[a]	Televisions[a]	Internet Service Providers[c]	Internet Users[c]
Taiwan	12.49 M (2000)	16 M (2000)	AM 218; FM 333; shortwave 50 (1999)	16 M (1994)	29	8.8 M (1998)	8	6.4 M
United States	194 M	69.209 M (1998)	AM 4,762; FM 5,542; shortwave 18	575 M	1,500	219 M	7,800	148 M
China	135 M (2000)	65 M (2001)	AM 369; FM 259; shortwave 45	417 M	3,240	400 M	3	22 M (2001)
Singapore	1.928 M (2000)	2.333 M (2000)	AM 0; FM 16; shortwave 2	2.6 M (2000)	6 (2000)	1.33 M	9	1.74 M

[a]Data is for 1997 unless otherwise noted.
[b]Data is for 1998 unless otherwise noted.
[c]Data is for 2000 unless otherwise noted.

SOURCE: CIA *World Factbook 2001* [Online].

ambitious project that will transform the island into a center of business and investment in the Asia-Pacific region. With APROC, Taiwan plans to attract the establishment of new local, as well as foreign, companies on the island. Taiwan's world-class and well-organized facilities would see such companies conveniently placed to take advantage of opportunities in the flourishing Southeast Asian markets, and the much coveted market of mainland China.

There are a total of 34,901 kilometers (21,687 miles) of roads in Taiwan, 90 percent of which are paved. Taiwan has a modern railway system that provides frequent and convenient passenger service between major cities on the island. As of 1999, Taiwan's railway network totaled 2,481 kilometers (1,542 miles). Railways in Taiwan are operated by the Taiwan Railway Administration (TRA), the Taiwan Sugar Corporation, and the Taiwan Forestry Bureau. The TRA provides passenger and freight services to the general public, while the Taiwan Sugar Corporation and the Taiwan Forestry Bureau haul their own products and offer only limited passenger service.

The government has already begun the development of a high-speed railway (HSR) that is expected to begin operating in June 2003. The planned HSR route, 340 kilometers (212 miles) long, will pass through the west corridor of the island. Ten stations will be located from Taipei to Kaohsiung to serve about 22 million residents in the region. The estimated construction cost of the project is US$13.05 billion, and the HSR will cut the present travel time from north to south by train or highway vehicles from 4 hours to 90 minutes.

As of December 1997, Taiwan's shipping industry had a fleet of 255 vessels weighing over 100 gross tons. Taiwan claims to have one of the largest fleets of cargo container ships in the world. Taiwan has 6 international harbors: Chilung, Suao, Taichung, Hualien, Anping, and Kaohsiung. Waterborne imports and exports handled by these ports amounted to 166.1 million tons in 1997.

As of 1997 51 airlines have been providing flight services to destinations in Taiwan. There are 34 foreign carriers, and 5 domestic-based airlines: EVA Airways, Mandarin Airlines, China Airlines, Transasia Airways, and Far Eastern Air Transport Corporation. Three Taiwan-based carriers offer international charter services: UNI Airways Corporation, Great China Airlines, and U-Land Airlines.

Taiwan has 2 international airports: Chiang Kai-shek International Airport at Taoyuan in northern Taiwan and Kaohsiung International Airport in the south. In addition, there are several domestic airports.

COMMUNICATIONS. The government is laying the foundation for a national information infrastructure through 30 different projects designed to make the country into a competitive and knowledge-based society. The different projects are focused on enhancing broadband access, improving the quality of Internet service, improving and diversifying the content of local web sites, and promoting electronic commerce and other Internet-based applications. As of 1 July 1999, Taiwan had 15 Internet service providers and 4.13 million Internet users. Based on official estimates, there are at least 52,000 locally authored web sites in Taiwan, 89.6 percent of which are dot-coms (Internet-based companies offering different types of conventional and innovative goods and services). Most of these web sites are written in Chinese, although many provide English versions.

As of April 2000, the Directorate General of Telecommunications estimated the mobile phone subscribers at 13.78 million, a number that was higher than the estimated 12.49 million telephone main lines. In July 2000, Taiwan reduced its international direct dialing (IDD) fees by an average of 15 percent. Earlier, charges on local and mobile phones, leased lines and Internet service had seen reductions of between 2 percent and 5 percent. Further reductions are expected once a separate accounting system has been established and an evaluation of the state-run telecom company carried out.

ECONOMIC SECTORS

According to a study by the Nomura Research Center of Japan, the competitive advantage of Taiwan's manufacturing industry lies in information, telecommunications, and other high technology industries. Correspondingly, the government has identified and appropriated funding for the development of 10 high technology industries that will be the foundation of Taiwan's economic success in the first few decades of the 21st cen-

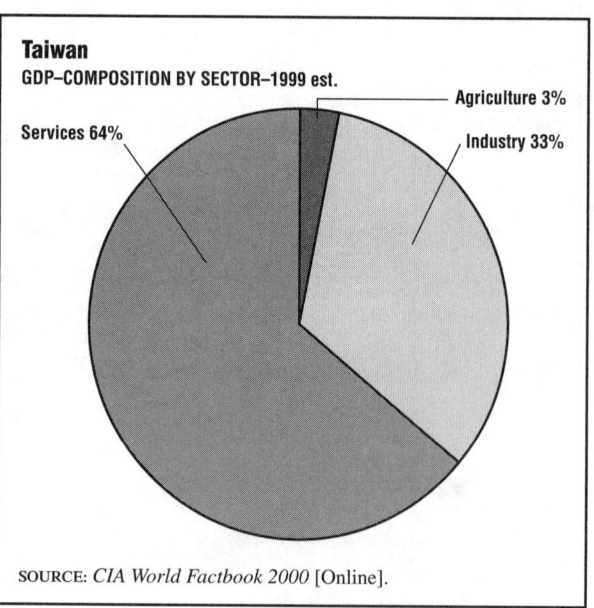

SOURCE: *CIA World Factbook 2000* [Online].

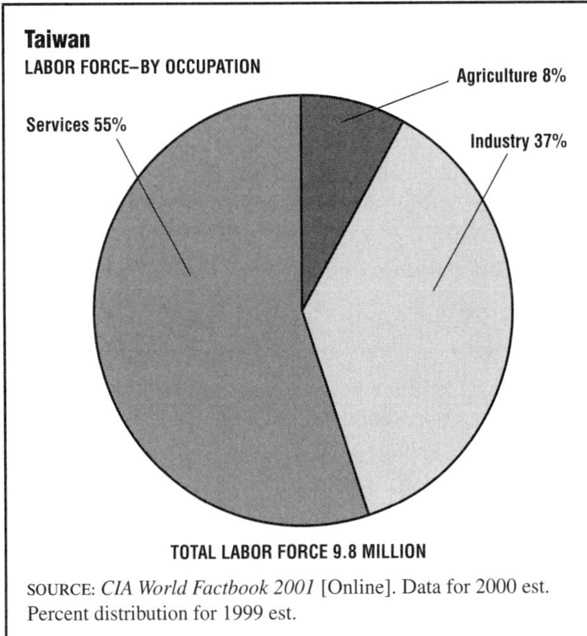

SOURCE: *CIA World Factbook 2001* [Online]. Data for 2000 est. Percent distribution for 1999 est.

tury. The 10 industries are: (1) communications, (2) information, (3) consumer electronics, (4) semiconductors, (5) precision machinery and automation, (6) aerospace, (7) advanced materials, (8) specialty chemicals and pharmaceuticals, (9) medical and health care equipment, and (10) pollution control and treatment.

Labor-intensive industries such as processed foods, leather products, and wood and bamboo products have gradually been replaced by capital- and technology-intensive industries. Examples of these industries are chemicals, petrochemicals, information technology, electrical equipment, and electronics. Electronics and information technology are the biggest players in the manufacturing sector, which employs 26 percent of the national workforce.

The service sector is thriving and shows promise of further growth as the spending power of the population increases. By the end of 1995, the growth of the service sector exceeded that of the agricultural and manufacturing sectors by more than 60 percent and has continued to do so. The different businesses that fall under the service sector in Taiwan are: finance, insurance, and real estate; commerce, including wholesale and retail business, food and beverages, and international trade; social and individual services; transport, storage, and telecommunications; commercial services, including legal, accounting, civil engineering, information, advertising, designing, and leasing; governmental services, and miscellaneous others. Among these businesses, finance, insurance, and real estate are the most dominant. The service sector creates the largest competitive employment opportunities and employs the bulk of Taiwan's labor force.

Meanwhile, the contribution of the agricultural sector to GDP has been steadily declining since the 1980s when Taiwan's government shifted the focus of its economic strategy to industrialization. Few of the younger generation are willing to work in the agricultural sector, preferring to pursue better opportunities in the other sectors. Farmers make up only 8 percent of the labor force and produce less than 3 percent of the island's total GDP according to 1999 statistics. Consequently, the sector diminished in importance while the manufacturing sector has risen to the forefront. The agricultural sector will face even more problems when the country is finally accepted as a member of the World Trade Organization (WTO). To comply with the WTO's requirements, the government has been systematically reducing the trade barriers on its traditionally well-protected agricultural goods, leaving local produce to face increased competition from the foreign agricultural products that will flood the domestic market when Taiwan becomes a full-fledged member in the WTO.

Manufacturing has long been overtaken by the service sector in terms of contribution to GDP. In 1999, the service sector contributed the biggest slice of GDP at 64 percent, with industry accounting for 33 percent, and agriculture 3 percent.

AGRICULTURE

In the 1950s, 90 percent of Taiwan's residents lived in farming communities growing rice, sugar, tea, camphor, and other crops. Two decades later, the government aggressively pursued industrialization, causing agricultural exports to fall behind agricultural imports. By 1999, agriculture constituted only 3 percent of Taiwan's GDP compared with 32.2 percent in 1952. Although the total area under cultivation decreased by one-third between the 1960s and the 1990s, the value of agricultural output to the national economy has increased by half because of improvements in overall productivity. Taiwan's biggest export markets are Japan, Hong Kong, and the United States.

In 1998, rice was Taiwan's most valuable crop, followed by betel nuts, corn, sugar cane, mangos, watermelons, tea, pineapples, pears, and grapes. In the 2 crop seasons of 1998, Taiwan harvested 1.49 million tons of brown rice. According to the Taiwan Provincial Department of Food (TPDF), this was more than was needed to meet local demand. The oversupply of rice is expected to peak as Taiwan braces itself for intensive competition from foreign rice imports as the country moves toward membership in the WTO.

Next to hogs, rice, and chickens, betel nuts rank as Taiwan's fourth most valuable farm product according to TPDF. Demand steadily increased in the 1990s, resulting in the expansion of areas cultivated for betel nuts. In 1997,

56,300 hectares of land were planted with betel nuts and produced almost 156,000 metric tons. Farmers were keen to plant betel nuts because, in a good year, the income can be 10 times higher than that from growing rice.

In 1998, 178,000 hectares of land were devoted to vegetable cultivation, which yielded 2,872,571 metric tons of produce. More than 100 kinds of vegetables are grown in Taiwan. The primary vegetables grown in planted areas are bamboo shoots, watermelon, leafy vegetables, vegetable soybeans, cabbage, cantaloupe, garlic, scallions, celery cabbage, Chinese cabbage, and radishes.

Taiwan produces 30 varieties of fruit, including apples, pears, peaches, citrus fruits, bananas, pineapples, lychees, longans, mangos, papayas, persimmons, loquats, and guavas. The main crops are citrus, mangos, lychees, bananas, pineapples, wax apples, and Asian pears. Pineapples and lychees are canned to satisfy domestic and international demand, while other fruits are processed into juice for local consumption.

FLORICULTURE. From 1986 to 1998, Taiwan's floriculture (flower-growing industry) underwent huge and profitable expansion, and its export value increased from US$3.7 million to US$41.5 million. As demand and sales increased, Taiwan's floral nurseries were expanded from 3,500 hectares to 10,000 hectares. The major export markets for flowers are Japan, Hong Kong, and the United States. Most flower farms allocate half of their planting area to producing cut flowers, that is, flowers sold as single stems for vases and floral arrangements, while the other half is used for nursery production. Annual production of cut flowers is 1.4 billion stems and 25 million potted plants.

FISHING. In 1998, the Taiwanese fishing industry harvested fish worth US$2.9 billion, of which 62 percent came from deep-sea fishing, 20 percent from aquaculture, 15 percent from offshore fishing, and 3 percent from coastal fishing. Skipjack and eel are Taiwan's biggest water-based export items. The export value of eel, most of which goes to Japan, exceeded US$400 million in 1998.

To protect natural resources and further develop the island's fishing industry, Taiwan's government invested in the construction of fishing harbors, wholesale markets, modern equipment, and other infrastructure during the 1980s. During the 1990s, the government complemented this initiative with renewed efforts to raise public awareness of environmental and conservation issues. Several environmental laws were passed, such as the Water Pollution Control Act in 1991 and the Environmental Impact Assessment Act in 1994.

Taiwan's mountainous terrain serves as a natural hazard to its thriving fishing industry, especially in the rainy season when mud and silt are deposited in the island's wide and shallow river beds. The government, therefore, set aside and developed areas especially suited to aquaculture (the production of scientifically farmed fish), and Taiwan has become a world leader in aquacultural development. The industry flourished in the 1980s, but received a setback when the grass shrimp industry was hit by an epidemic in 1987. During the 1990s, government further boosted production by promoting automation, encouraging the use of biotechnology, and improving its marketing strategy.

LIVESTOCK. In the 1950s, the farming of livestock in Taiwan was a backyard enterprise. In just 4 decades since, livestock grew into a multi-billion dollar industry and has become a major export product. In 1998, livestock production was valued at more than US$3.6 billion, accounting for 41.56 percent of the total value of agricultural production. Hog farming still ranks first in the livestock industry, followed by broiler chickens, eggs, and milk. However, an outbreak of foot and mouth disease in March 1997 caused a temporary decline in export sales. The official estimate of hog farms stricken by the disease is 6,147 across 20 cities. To control the spread of the disease, the government ordered the extermination of all affected animals and the immediate vaccination of those unaffected. Roughly 21 million doses of vaccines were used to bring the disease under control. Since then, the hog industry has recovered and export sales have returned to the normal level.

Taiwan attributes the growth of its agricultural industry to the dedication of its farmers, the development of a farmers' organization, continual improvements in techniques and infrastructure, and the implementation of a beneficial land reform program. The government continues to support its farmers with price guarantees, low-interest loans, economic incentives, and other helpful measures.

Through technological improvements such as new cultivars, growth regulators, and mechanization, crop yields per hectare of land jumped from 8,600 kilos in 1945 to 16,384 kilos in 1998. Taiwanese fruit growers have applied advanced horticultural technology to modernize their operations. Through the effective control of plant diseases, adjustments to fruit maturation periods, the cultivation of improved fruit strains, and the implementation of multiple annual harvests, the fruit sector has witnessed profitable growth.

Taiwan has used information technology to create the National Agricultural Information Service, an integrated agricultural information database that includes planning, production, and marketing information related to domestic farming, forestry, fishing, and animal husbandry. This database provides rapid access to information and communication, and allows players in the agricultural sector to exchange ideas at an international level.

Taiwan's agricultural sector faces several challenges. Efficient farming is hindered by the rapidly aging agrarian workforce and a severe shortage of new young workers, who have abandoned the rural life for more profitable careers in the cities. Farmers are having to confront falling incomes, rising costs, and increased foreign competition, and as Taiwan's entry into the WTO approaches, the farmers' predicament will worsen before it gets better.

Another factor that serves to hinder agricultural growth is the island's mountainous topography, which restricts farming to the arable western slopes and alluvial plains. To make matters worse, plots are small with most farmers having less than 1 hectare of cultivable land. This restricts the application of advanced agricultural methods such as mechanization, since these depend on economies of scale (large output) to be cost-effective. Promotion of efficiency in the farming industry has not kept pace with other sectors. About 10 percent of Taiwan's total farmland has been neglected because farming has ceased to be profitable.

The development of aquaculture is seriously threatened by environmental degradation. Freshwater aquaculture uses huge amounts of ground water, sometimes causing land to shift or cave in. Two of Taiwan's government agencies, the Ministry of Economic Affairs and the Council of Agriculture, have jointly promoted recycling systems that use fresh water more efficiently, and have encouraged aquaculturists to switch to marine ranching.

Taiwan's fishing and aquaculture industries are endangered by the pollution of its rivers and coastal waters caused primarily by the expansion of urban communities. There are 21 primary, 29 secondary, and 79 ordinary rivers in Taiwan. According to the Environmental Protection Administration (EPA), 33.8 percent of primary and secondary rivers are polluted to different degrees. Most industrial, agricultural, and residential wastewater drains directly into rivers, seriously polluting the water downstream. By April 1998 only 240,000 households (33.25 percent) were connected to the sewage system.

INDUSTRY

INFORMATION TECHNOLOGY. According to the Institute for Information Industry, Taiwan's software market will have reached up to NT$150 billion in production value by 2001 due to rising global demand for software. Continued investment and a steady supply of competent human resources are 2 major factors behind the sharp growth of Taiwan's software industry in recent years. The industry will have the opportunity to upgrade its production value further in the future, especially as **e-commerce** becomes increasingly popular among domestic enterprises in Taiwan.

In 1998 Taiwan's hardware information technology industry registered a total production value of US$33.8 billion, up by 11.9 percent from US$30 billion of the previous year, making it Taiwan's most important foreign exchange earner. Since 1995, Taiwan has been the world's third-largest computer hardware supplier after the United States and Japan. Taiwan has about 900 computer hardware manufacturers employing close to 100,000 workers. These companies manufacture laptop computers, monitors, desktop PCs, and motherboards which, in 1998, accounted for about 80 percent of the production value of the information technology industry. To secure a lion's share of the world market, Taiwan's manufacturers strive to maintain high quality and competitive prices. According to statistics released by the Institute for Information Industry, Taiwan has already replaced Singapore as Japan's second largest supplier of information products after the United States. In March 2000, Taiwan earned the distinction of becoming the world's leading manufacturer of CD-ROM drives, a feat made possible by Japan's withdrawal from the CD-ROM market in 1998. In 1999 Taiwan also claimed to be the world's largest supplier of notebook PCs, with an estimated world market share of 49 percent.

AUTOMOBILES. Thirteen automobile manufacturers have plants in Taiwan. Most of these are working in partnership with foreign carmakers, mostly Japanese. These companies produce and import automobiles. In 1998, roughly 402,000 automobiles were produced in Taiwan, and the value of the automotive industry reached US$9.93 billion.

However, limited parking space and the efficient mass transit systems in urban districts have resulted in the decline of the domestic car market. From a high of 542,000 units sold in 1995, only 476,000 were purchased in 1998, with 80 percent of the demand being for sedans. In recent years, competition between locally made and imported vehicles has gradually decreased. In 1998 the domestic automobile industry, although threatened by imports from Japan and the United States, still managed to capture about 84 percent of the market, with over 70 percent of the 292,000 domestically made sedans supplied by 3 companies: Ford Lio Ho Motor Co., Ltd. (20.3 percent), Yulon Motor Co., Ltd. (28.6 percent), and Kuozui Motors, Ltd. (22.4 percent). In the commercial vehicle market, China Motor Corporation maintained its traditional top position, producing over half of the 115,700 commercial vehicles sold.

To strengthen the industry, automobile manufacturers need to invest in research and design (R&D), and to improve their own technology in engines, computerized gearing systems, and several other components, to enhance their design capability. One of the industry's weaknesses is its dependence on foreign engines and its inability to produce other key parts such as airbags, which has curtailed its plans to export vehicles. Since 1999, the Ministry of Economic Affairs has allocated funding to encourage R&D and thus alleviate the automobile industry's dependence on imports from Japan and elsewhere.

TEXTILES. The Taiwanese textile industry produces synthetic fibers, yarns, fabrics, clothing, and clothes accessories. In the last few years, local manufacturers have attempted to develop man-made fibers and fabrics to compensate for Taiwan's inability to produce cotton or wool, and its limited production of silk and linen. In 1998, Taiwan produced 3.25 million metric tons of man-made fiber, the third highest volume in the world. The country's output of polyester fiber, at 2.68 million tons, occupied second place globally. Nylon production was the world's highest at 301,000 tons. Taiwan has also started mass-producing carbon, spandex, and viscose fibers. The chief export markets for Taiwan's textile exports are the United States, Hong Kong, and other Southeast Asian countries.

SERVICES

FINANCIAL SERVICES. As in the past, Taiwan's banking system is dominated by state-run institutions. Despite pressure from foreign investors, the financial sector has not been **liberalized** and remains under government control. Consequently, the financial services sector is underdeveloped. In 1995, the combined factors of the Mexican peso crisis, the flight of foreign capital from Taiwan, and the collapse of several savings institutions brought even more restrictive government controls, the severity of which caused an increase in **black market** activities. In 1991, the Bureau of Investigation launched a campaign against unlicensed investment houses and underground futures brokers that resulted in prosecutions of certain companies charged with stock manipulation. Despite such moves, the sector continued to draw criticism for its perceived dubious and risky practices.

RETAIL. One of the biggest retailers in Taiwan is the 7–11 chain of convenience stores. In terms of store-to-population density, Taiwan has the highest ratio in the world with one 7–11 outlet for every 10,000 people. Owned by the President Chain Store Group, the company's revenues amounted to US$1.29 billion in 1998. The President Group is a household name in Taiwan, where almost everybody has used its products or services at one time or another. Moreover, it is the largest Taiwanese investor in mainland China. In October 1999, the Ministry of Economic Affairs approved a US$328 million mainland-bound investment project proposed by the President Group. The company is diversifying its operations by reinvesting in the Starbucks coffee shop chain and the Conforama home furniture and appliance chain.

Aside from food and beverages, an emerging retail market in Taiwan is the home improvement and furniture market. With the population's increased spending power, ever-increasing numbers of people are renovating their homes and surroundings. In 1992, internationally renowned companies like Ethan Allen, ID-design, Ikea, and B&Q entered the Taiwanese market. In an interview with the *Free China Journal* in 1999, an Ikea official estimated the annual value of the furniture sector in Taiwan at US$203 million. This estimate did not include the home improvement sector.

In 1998, Ikea's international chain of stores posted earnings worth US$7.02 billion. According to the Taiwan Furniture Manufacturers' Association, the huge potential of the sector evidenced by the earnings of the foreign companies has attracted Taiwan-based furniture exporters to offer their products to the domestic market as well.

INTERNATIONAL TRADE

The phenomenal growth of Taiwan's economy can be credited to its brisk foreign trade. From 1970 until 1990, the country amassed huge surpluses from its earnings in international trade, which peaked in 1987 when the **trade surplus** reached US$18.7 billion. However, several other countries became alarmed at Taiwan's huge surpluses and the corresponding economic power it might exert on other economies. The United States demanded that Taiwan remove trade restrictions and allow more foreign products into the country. Since then, Taiwan has reduced or removed a significant number of trade barriers, thus allowing foreign products to compete with local products in the domestic market. From 1992 to 1996, Taiwan's trade surplus declined by nearly 30 percent. However, from 1998, trade figures have once more shown a steady rise and, according to the Central Bank of China, Taiwan's **foreign exchange reserves** in 1999 amounted to US$106.2 billion, one of the highest in the world. In 2000, Taiwanese exports reached US$148.38 billion against imports of US$140.01 billion, producing a trade surplus of US$8.37 billion.

Taiwan is a major exporter of industrial products ranging from mechanical appliances and accessories, electronics, electrical appliances, personal computers and peripherals, metal products and transport equipment, to furniture and clothing. The United States has been Taiwan's most important trading partner over decades. However, as Taiwan pursued the expansion of its economy, it began seeking out other trading partners, which resulted in a decrease in trade with the United States. In the 1980s, 40 percent of Taiwan's total exports were U.S.-bound; by 2000 only 23.5 percent of the island's total exports were destined for the American market.

Trade (expressed in billions of US$): Taiwan

	Exports	Imports
1975	5.302	5.959
1980	19.785	19.764
1985	30.704	20.124
1990	67.142	54.830
1995	111.585	103.698
1998	110.454	104.946

SOURCE: International Monetary Fund. *International Financial Statistics Yearbook 1999.*

Until 1999, Japan was Taiwan's biggest export destination after the United States. However, since 1999, Hong Kong has replaced Japan as the second leading export partner, since Taiwan uses it as an indirect link to send goods to mainland China. Major items exported to Hong Kong include electrical and electronic equipment and peripherals, machinery, accessories, raw plastic materials, and textiles. In 2000, exports to Hong Kong amounted to 21.1 percent of Taiwan's total exports, while those to Japan, due also to the slowdown of the Japanese economy, only accounted for 11.2 percent.

Southeast Asia has become an attractive trading partner for Taiwan. Many Taiwanese businesses have set up in Southeast Asian countries such as Thailand and the Philippines to take advantage of abundant skilled labor, availability of raw materials, and lower land prices. In 1986, only 5 percent of Taiwan's exports were bound for countries in the Association of South-East Asian Nations (ASEAN), but by 2000 the figure had climbed to 12.2 percent.

Taiwan has also set its sights on the large and economically strong European market. In 2000, Taiwan recorded exports to Europe at 16 percent of its total. The country's top 4 European trading partners are Germany, France, the United Kingdom, and the Netherlands, which, together, account for more than 60 percent of exports to the continent.

With huge exports fueling the economy, the spending capacity of the government and the population has multiplied. In the past, the government aggressively discouraged the entrance of imported products to the island by trade barriers and restrictive laws. However, with the new economy, the government has liberalized the situation and, in 2000, Taiwan's total imports amounted to roughly US$110 billion. More than a quarter, or 27.5 percent, of these imports came from Japan. Taiwan's industries, especially the information and automobile industries, rely heavily on the supply of parts and the transfer of technology from Japan. Most of the items imported from Japan are machinery, auto parts, electrical appliances, electronics, chemicals, and metal products. Other imports come from the United States (17.9 percent) and Europe (13.6 percent).

Despite the absence of direct transport links to mainland China, Taiwan's economic ties with the country are strengthening through the substantial Taiwanese investment being poured into China. Taiwanese businesses are eager to invest in mainland China, one of the most sought-after markets in the world. With a population approximately a billion strong, China is not only a huge market for any country's products, but also has one of the biggest manpower resources in the whole world. Trade relations between the 2 economies are so intertwined that breaking them off would bring major repercussions. Mainland China is a big contributor to Taiwan's overall trade surplus. In 1987, Taiwan had a trade surplus of just over US$1 billion with mainland China, and by 1998, this had grown to US$15.7 billion.

Based on data from Taiwan's Mainland Affairs Council, the value of 2-way trade between Taiwan and mainland China amounted to US$23.95 billion in 1998. More than 82 percent of the indirect trade consisted of exports from Taiwan, which totaled US$19.84 billion. Some major items exported to mainland China are industrial machinery and equipment, electronic parts, plastics, man-made fibers, and industrial textiles. Meanwhile, imports from China climbed to 4.1 percent in 1999 from 3.9 percent in 1998. Agricultural and industrial raw materials accounted for a huge percentage of these imported goods. However, in view of the uneasy political relations that prevail between the 2 territories, Taiwan does not concentrate too great a part of its investments in China. Taiwan is mindful that political upheaval in its dealings with China would jeopardize its own economic development.

Taiwan is gearing itself for membership in the WTO and is setting the proper economic policies in motion to ensure its acceptance. One of the long-standing trade issues for which Taiwan is criticized is its violation of agreements on the protection of intellectual property. Piracy in different forms—such as copying and reselling the contents of entertainment and software CDs—remains a serious matter. To its credit, Taiwan's government is addressing the problem through a combination of rules and regulations to control piracy, and efforts to raise awareness of the issues involved with it.

MONEY

The financial industry in Taiwan operates within 3 important legal frameworks: the Banking Law, the Securities and Exchange Law, and the Insurance Law. Three government agencies oversee financial operations: the Ministry of Finance (MOF), the Central Bank of China

Exchange rates: Taiwan

New Taiwan dollars per US$1	
2001	N/A
2000	33.082
1999	31.395
1998	32.216
1997	32.052
1996	27.5

SOURCE: CIA *World Factbook 2001* [ONLINE].

(CBC), and the Departments of Finance of each municipal or provincial government.

The MOF is in charge of supervising the financial markets and allied financial institutions in Taiwan through its subordinate agencies: the Bureau of Monetary Affairs, the Securities and Exchange Commission, and the Department of Insurance. In addition, it formulates policies that contribute to the development and efficiency of Taiwan's financial service sector. The CBC controls the strict implementation of the **monetary policies** of Taiwan as outlined in the provisions of the Banking Law and the Law Governing the CBC.

Each of the provincial or municipal governments has its own Department of Finance. Collectively, these departments direct and control community financial institutions such as credit cooperatives and the credit of farming and fishing associations.

The several agencies and institutions that comprise the structure of Taiwan's financial sector offer a wide variety of financial services, designed to cater to clients from big business to individual account holders.

Banks fall into several categories such as commercial banks, specialized banks, local branches of foreign banks, and others, established under Taiwan's banking laws, which undertake savings and trust business and deal in securities. In the past, the sector was dominated by government-owned banks, but, as a result of increasing competition and government **privatization** policies, 15 new private commercial banks were established in 1991. These new arrivals now dominate the market.

Credit cooperatives provide banking services in regional communities where the customer base is small and it is not economically viable to establish commercial banks. Grassroots organizations such as farming and fishing associations usually have credit departments to take charge of promoting economic development in their particular areas. Investment and trust companies act as fund managers of trust funds and trust properties.

The Postal Savings System of Taiwan has more than 1,600 post offices throughout the island where people can remit or deposit money. Money may be withdrawn and re-deposited into banks, or reinvested in different financial instruments.

The insurance industry offers life and other insurance. Life insurance includes simple life insurance, health insurance, and accident insurance. Other policies offer fire insurance, marine insurance, land and air transportation insurance, liability insurance, and other non-life insurance.

In 1960 the Securities and Exchange Commission was founded in Taiwan, based on American and Japanese models. In 1961, the Taiwan Stock Exchange (TSE) was established and began operating in 1967, and the Securities and Exchange Law was passed in 1968.

The first securities traded in Taiwan were issued by the Taiwanese government in 1949, and were called "Patriot bonds." Trading in stocks began on an informal basis in 1953 when the government launched its "Land to the Tillers" program. The objective of the program was for government to buy land from large landowners and distribute it equitably among farmers with no land of their own. Rather than money, landlords were issued government shares in previously **nationalized** enterprises. Since the landowners were not interested in holding these stocks, an informal market developed to trade these shares.

POVERTY AND WEALTH

Poverty in Taiwan has almost been eradicated, with less than 1 percent of the population (129,968 people or 56,720 households) considered as poor or belonging to the low-income bracket. This means that more than 99 percent of the population enjoys the benefits of Taiwan's economic prosperity and greatly improved quality of life.

Families are classified as belonging to the low-income bracket if their average monthly income does not reach the estimated monthly minimum set by each city or province. To meet the family's basic needs (food, shelter, clothing, and education) in Taipei City, one would need to earn at least US$337 monthly. This amount changes depending on the city's standard of living; for example, one would only need to earn US$171 monthly to live in Kinmen County.

In 1999, the government spent US$5.08 billion on social welfare programs, and offers many kinds of assistance to individuals and families from low-income groups. In addition to cash, job-placement assistance is provided to the wage earners in families, along with educational aid for school-age children and health programs for mothers and children. There are also civic organizations, academic institutions, and private foundations that

GDP per Capita (US$)

Country	1996	1997	1998	1999	2000
Taiwan	920	14,200	16,500	16,100	17,400
United States	28,600	30,200	31,500	33,900	36,200
China	2,800	3,460	3,600	3,800	3,600
Singapore	21,200	24,600	26,300	27,800	26,500

Note: Data are estimates.

SOURCE: *Handbook of the Nations*, 17th, 18th, 19th and 20th editions for 1996, 1997, 1998 and 1999 data; CIA *World Factbook 2001* [Online] for 2000 data.

coordinate with government agencies in assisting displaced or disadvantaged citizens.

Aside from low-income families, the government gives support to people, such as the elderly and the handicapped, who are unable to work. In July 1993, the government began providing a monthly **subsidy** to the low-income elderly. Citizens over the age of 65 whose average family income is less than, or equal to, 1.5 times the minimum monthly expenses are qualified to receive a monthly subsidy of US$174. Elderly people whose average family income is between 1.5 and 2.5 times the minimum expense are eligible for a monthly relief subsidy of US$87. In addition, the government pays the health insurance premium in full for low-income households and emergency aid where needed.

WORKING CONDITIONS

A well-trained labor force is the backbone of a developing economy, and Taiwan's economic growth over the past 50 years has been bolstered by a diversified and skilled workforce of about 9.7 million people. Approximately 6.6 million of these are employees, while the rest are either self-employed or have some other working status. The unemployment rate in 2000 was at a very low 3 percent.

Taiwan protects the rights of workers by law, while other important labor issues such as workers' welfare, gender equality, labor-management relations, safety and health, and appropriate quotas for foreign workers, are also clarified by legislation.

The Labor Insurance Act, which was passed into law in 1958, mandates the provision of insurance coverage to employees in the **private sector**, including industrial workers, journalists, fishermen, persons receiving vocational training in institutes registered with the government, union members, and those working in non-profit organizations. Teachers and employees working in government agencies who are not eligible for teachers' or civil servants' insurance are also covered under this law.

One of the most important labor laws in Taiwan is the 1984 Labor Standards Law. It supplies the basic legal definitions of worker, employer, wages, and contract, and outlines the rights and obligations of workers and employers. The law prescribes the minimum requirements for labor contracts, and makes provisions for working hours, work leave, and the employment of women and children. Furthermore, the law offers protections against unreasonable work hours and forced labor, and grants workers the right to receive compensation for occupational injuries and layoffs, as well as a retirement pension.

On the initiative of the Employment and Vocational Training Administration of the Council of Labor Affairs (EVTA), the Employment Promotion Measures law was formulated in 1985. This law aims to assist target groups such as women, people aged 45 and above, the disabled, aborigines (people from local indigenous groups), low-income households, and dispossessed workers to find decent employment. Under this program, the government assists women by promoting job equality between the sexes, providing women with vocational training, and surveying the demand for part-time and freelance opportunities to enlarge the employment market for women. The government also provides daycare centers for preschool children, after-school classes for elementary students, and day care for the elderly to relieve the pressure on women to stay at home.

In 1991 the Labor Safety and Health Law was amended to include many new requirements for the installation of safety and health equipment in work places such as dockyards and fireworks factories. The law covers almost all major industries in the industrial, agricultural, commercial, and service sectors, and specifically prohibits women and employees under the age of 16 from working in dangerous or harmful environments.

Passed into law on 8 May 1992, the Employment Services Act is a comprehensive law that seeks to ensure equal job opportunities and access to employment services for all. Specifically, the act calls for a balance of manpower supply and demand, efficient use of human resources, and the establishment of an employment information network. Further, the act requires the central government to encourage management, labor unions, and workers to negotiate reductions in working hours, wage adjustments, and in-service training to avoid layoffs, and for government to protect workers' rights during times of economic slowdown. The Employment Services Act also regulates public and private employment service agencies.

The Labor Inspection Law replaces the old Factory Law. It empowers the Council of Labor Affairs and local governments to inspect conditions in the workplace to ensure the safety and health of workers. The scope of inspections carried out under the law covers health and safety, labor insurance, employee welfare funds, and the hiring of foreign workers. Employment at potentially dangerous sites requires approval from labor inspectors before employees can begin work on the project. Labor laws ensure the rights of workers to organize unions for the protection of their collective interests.

Under the revised Collective Agreement Law, labor unions are designated as the sole labor representative in the signing of collective agreements. Such agreements promote labor-management cooperation and cover working conditions such as wages, work hours, layoffs, pensions, compensation for occupational injuries, and the handling of labor complaints and disputes.

In Taiwan, women have been traditionally considered inferior to men and are expected to stay at home and submit to the decisions of fathers or husbands. However, new attitudes have slowly developed with the lobbying of women's groups for equal opportunities, and as Taiwan's society has become exposed to modern ideas. Over the last decade, society's expectations of women have changed as more women complete higher education, compete with men in the workplace, become financially independent, and postpone marriage to pursue a career. On average, first-time brides were 28.1 years old in 1998 compared to 25.8 in 1990. Almost half of Taiwan's women are regular wage earners and help support their families financially.

In 1998, the Ministry of Education reported that 56 percent of junior college graduates, 51 percent of university and college graduates, and 26 percent of graduate school graduates were women. This was a significantly large change from the figures of 20 years earlier, and marked the first time that female graduates outnumbered male graduates.

As in any country with a bustling economy, Taiwan cannot depend on its domestic labor force because the demand for workers exceeds available supply. In the high-tech industries, Taiwan produces 20,000 new workers annually, but 30,000 workers are needed. A sample survey of 302 Taiwan-based high-tech industries conducted by the Taipei Computer Association revealed that 80 percent of companies experience difficulty in finding suitable employees, particularly software specialists. Situations such as these call for the hiring of foreign workers to meet the labor shortage and, in August 2000, there were 316,078 foreigners working in Taiwan. Most of these workers come from Thailand, followed by the Philippines and Indonesia.

Aside from the large demand for labor, foreign workers are attracted to Taiwan by the range of job opportunities. The Taiwanese are now reluctant to take low-paying jobs or work in fields that demand heavy physical labor, and the agricultural sector is suffering shortages. An aging population and a low birth rate add to the problem. More workers are retiring than are entering the workforce, and the influx of foreigners is growing. The presence of a foreign workforce has created a degree of tension in Taiwan. Locals have expressed apprehension that their indigenous culture might be destroyed by foreign influences and, in practical terms, there is a possibility that wages will decrease because foreign workers are willing to accept less pay than the Taiwanese.

In July 2000, the unemployment rate of Taiwanese workers increased to 3.06 percent (300,000 workers) from 2.9 percent for the years 1999 and 1998. The main cause of unemployment is the layoffs in traditional manufacturing businesses, which are **re-structuring** or downsizing (cutting down the number of employees). The availability of sophisticated technology that can do the work of 2 or more people is one reason for downsizing, especially since the government is encouraging industries to shift from labor-intensive operations to high-tech manufacturing and services.

COUNTRY HISTORY AND ECONOMIC DEVELOPMENT

1206. The Island of Taiwan is declared a protectorate of the Chinese Empire.

1622. The Dutch establish a trading post and control much of the Republic of China (ROC) until 1662 when the Chinese expel them.

1887. Taiwan is granted provincial status by the Chinese mainland government.

1895–1945. Taiwan is declared a Japanese colony after the Sino-Japanese war in 1895, and remains a Japanese colony until the end of World War II in 1945.

1947. The Constitution of Taiwan is adopted.

1949. Chinese nationalist forces under Chiang Kai-Shek retreat from the Communist armies on the mainland to Taiwan and take power in Taiwan.

1949–91. Taiwan is officially in a state of war with the Peoples' Republic of China (PRC).

1951–64. The United States injects US$100 million annually into Taiwan's economy, supplying needed capital to Taiwan's industries, which grow rapidly during this period.

1953. The Taiwanese government begins a series of 4-year plans, setting goals and guidelines for economic development.

1961. The Securities and Exchange Commission (SEC) is established.

1969. For the first time, a popular national election is held and a handful of national politicians are elected with tenure for life.

1973–74. Taiwan's economic growth suffers a temporary setback due to the world oil crisis.

1975. President Chiang Kai-shek dies. For the next 3 years, the vast powers of the presidency rest in the hands of Premier Chiang Ching-kuo, chairman of the Kuomintang (KMT), the country's sole political party.

1978. Chiang Ching-kuo is elected president. The United States announces its decision to end recognition of the government of Taiwan and to transfer recognition and the United States embassy to the Peoples' Republic of China.

1983. The government opens the stock market to foreign investment.

1987. A vocal opposition, the Democratic Progressive Party (DPP), is established, thereby challenging the long-running dominance of the Kuomintang (KMT).

1988. The government lifts restrictions on the publication of new daily newspapers.

1989–93. Elections are described by foreign observers as progressively freer, leaving the KMT in power but facing a strong parliamentary opposition.

1993. The Ministry of Finance and the Central Bank of China allow the establishment of foreign exchange brokerage businesses and foreign insurance companies.

1994. The government assigns top priority to the implementation of the Twelve Major Construction Projects. A Comprehensive Physical Development Plan is initiated with a view to rationalizing land use, improving the investment climate, and upgrading the quality of life.

1994. President Lee and Premier Lien initiate the White Paper on China, which redefines Taiwan's one-China principle. The leaders of China bitterly oppose Taiwan's new one-China principle and accuse it of trying to establish an independent Taiwan.

1996. Conduct of the first presidential election results in victory for the KMT, with President Lee Teng Hui garnering 54 percent of the vote.

1996. Foreign mutual fund companies are allowed to invest in the stock market.

1997. The Plan for National Development into the Next Century is introduced. Aimed at accelerating Taiwan's transformation into a modern industrialized society, this plan is centered on the achievement of 3 goals: strengthening national competitiveness, improving the quality of life, and promoting sustainable development.

1999. President Lee provokes Beijing's fury in July when he declares that, in the future, Taiwan and China should conduct relations on a "special state-to-state basis," a move away from the official formula that they constituted one temporarily divided country.

2000. The opposition party, DPP, captures the top national positions as Chen Shui-bian and running mate Annette Lu are elected as president and vice-president respectively, breaking 55 years of uninterrupted rule by the KMT.

FUTURE TRENDS

Despite the current instability caused by the political realignment in the new administration of President Chen Shui-bian, Taiwan's future remains optimistic. Economic forecasts made by the Taipei-based World Economics Society point to continued growth, estimating that GDP growth over the next 10 years will not fall below 5.5 percent annually. The figure approximates the fluctuations of Taiwan's GDP annual growth performance in recent years: 8.2 percent in 1989, 6.68 percent in 1997, 4.57 percent in 1998, and 5.7 percent in 1999. This means that Taiwan's economy will continue to display stability and expansion, propelled by exemplary performance in the service and manufacturing sectors. Both sectors are expected to perform even better because of technological innovations and improved productivity. Moreover, employment levels and living costs are expected to remain manageable. Taiwan is also likely to benefit from its strategic position in the information technology industry. It aims to be known as the "Silicon Island of East Asia." This goal is not far-fetched since, in 2000, Taiwan ranked third in the world in the production of computer hardware and software, next to the United States and Japan. With its aggressive implementation of its growth plans, Taiwan is likely to attract more foreign businesses to the island and thus become a major international **procurement** and logistics base. The International Monetary Fund has recognized Taiwan's consistent economic performance by affiliating it with the rest of the world's advanced economies.

Politically, Taiwan's relationship with mainland China is still of major concern. To protect its economic achievement, Taiwan must tread slowly and wisely in setting the direction of its relations with mainland China. It must make sure that the relationship between the 2 territories is based on mutual respect and benefit. With regard to domestic politics, the government must continue to strengthen its democratic institutions.

The government is also taking steps to check the social and environmental impact of its economic programs and policies. Environmental programs focusing on protection and conservation are being implemented across the island in line with President Chen Shui-bian's electoral promises, and research into green technologies is also promised.

Meanwhile, the newfound affluence of Taiwanese society has, inevitably, produced certain social problems that need to be nipped in the bud. The government has realized that the younger generation must be encouraged to retain the work ethic of their elders. This is crucial to the health of the country's economic future. The "nouveau riche" mentality that characterizes the poor who suddenly acquire wealth can result in people opening themselves to financial profligacy, profiteering, corrupt practices, and other social ills that accompany irresponsible wealth. Other emerging social concerns involve the rise in crime and criminal gangs, the breakdown of the family, and the neglect of children as parents become too involved with their careers.

DEPENDENCIES

Taiwan has no territories or colonies.

BIBLIOGRAPHY

"A Brief Introduction to the Republic of China." *Republic of China on Taiwan Government Information Office.* <http://www.gio.gov.tw/taiwan-website/5-gp/brief>. Accessed October 2001.

Copper, John F. *Taiwan: Nation-State or Province.* London: Westview Press, 1990.

Council for Economic Planning and Development. *Economic Development, Taiwan, Republic of China 2000.* Taipei: Council for Economic Planning and Development, 2000.

Directorate General of Budget, Accounting and Statistics, Executive Yuan. <http://www.dgbasey.gov.tw>. Accessed December 2000.

Economist Intelligence Unit. *Country Profile: Taiwan.* London: Economist Intelligence Unit, 2001.

Feldman, Harvey, and Ilpyong J. Kim, eds. *Taiwan in a Time of Transition.* New York: Paradigm House, 1988.

Ministry of Economic Affairs R.O.C. <http://www.moea.gov.tw>. Accessed October 2001.

"The Republic of China Yearbook 2000." *Republic of China on Taiwan Government Information Office.* <http://www.gio.gov.tw/info/book2000>. Accessed October 2001.

Taipei Economic and Cultural Office in the United States. *Taiwan Online.* <http://www.roc-taiwan.org/usoffice/dc.htm>. Accessed October 2001.

"Taiwan Factbook." *China Economic News Service.* <http://www.cens.com.tw./info/factbook.html>. Accessed December 2000.

Taiwan Headlines. <http://www.taiwanheadlines.gov.tw>. Accessed October 2001.

U.S. Central Intelligence Agency. *World Factbook 2001.* <http://www.odci.gov/cia/publications/factbook/index.html>. Accessed September 2001.

U.S. Department of State. *FY 2001 Country Commercial Guide: Taiwan.* <http://www.state.gov/www/about_state/business/com_guides/2001/eap/index.html>. Accessed October 2001.

—Maria Cecilia T. Ubarra

TAJIKISTAN

Republic of Tajikistan
Jumhurii Tojikiston

CAPITAL: Dushanbe.

MONETARY UNIT: Somoni (SM). Introduced in 2000 to replace the Tajik ruble. SM1 equals 1,000 Tajik rubles. Somoni are issued as notes of SM1, 5, 10, 20, 50, and 100. Also 1, 4, 20, and 50 diram notes (100 dirams in SM1).

CHIEF EXPORTS: Aluminum, electricity, cotton, gold, fruits, and textiles.

CHIEF IMPORTS: Electricity, petroleum products, natural gas, aluminum oxide, machinery and equipment, and foodstuffs.

GROSS DOMESTIC PRODUCT: US$7.3 billion (purchasing power parity, 2000 est.).

BALANCE OF TRADE: **Exports:** US$761 million (2000 est.). **Imports:** US$782 million (2000 est.).

COUNTRY OVERVIEW

LOCATION AND SIZE. Tajikistan is a landlocked country situated in Central Asia. Slightly smaller than the state of Wisconsin, Tajikistan's territory is measured at 143,100 square kilometers (55,251 square miles). It shares borders with Uzbekistan (1,161 kilometers) to the west, China (414 kilometers) to the east, Afghanistan (1,206 kilometers) to the south, and Kyrgyzstan (870 kilometers) to the north. The capital, Dushanbe, is in the west, near the Uzbekistan border.

POPULATION. The U.S. Central Intelligence Agency's estimated July 2001 population for Tajikistan was almost 6.6 million. The country's population density of 143 people per square kilometer is low except that 93 percent of the country is mountainous, resulting in a more real population density of 488 people per square kilometer; this figure is one of the highest in the world. Tajikistan's growth rate is about 2.12 percent. It also has a high infant mortality rate, estimated at 117.4 deaths per every 1,000 live births. Compared to many other countries, life expectancy at birth in Tajikistan is low, estimated at 64 years. Unlike many other countries, Tajikistan's rural population is rising due to a higher fertility rate in the countryside and reduced opportunities for employment in urban centers.

Tajiks comprise approximately 65 percent, Uzbeks about 25 percent, and Russians—due to economic and political reasons—less than 3.5 percent of the population. The autonomous (self-governing) Badakhshan province is primarily inhabited by Pamiri Tajiks whose various dialects can be considered separate languages from other Tajik dialects spoken in Tajikistan. Furthermore, whereas Tajiks and Uzbeks are mostly Sunni Muslims, the far majority of the people of Badakhshan are Shia Muslims. Other ethnic groups, such as Turkmen, Kyrgyz, and Tatars live in Tajikistan. While Tajik is the official language of the country, Russian and Uzbek are widely used, especially in business circles.

OVERVIEW OF ECONOMY

Civil conflict from 1992 to 1997 weakened Tajikistan's economy. It is estimated to have shrunk by 60 percent since 1991, when the Soviet Union broke up and its 14 former republics, including Tajikistan, declared their independence. Despite some economic gains in the past several years, Tajikistan still has one of the lowest **gross domestic products (GDP) per capita** among the former Soviet republics and Soviet bloc countries of eastern Europe. The country's primary source of foreign currency is the export of aluminum.

As in many other former **socialist** countries, Tajikistan has been implementing a **privatization** program. Since privatization began in 1991, the state has sold nearly 5,500 of its smaller properties. In 1999, nearly 300 auctions were held, resulting in more than 1,400 sales and generating the equivalent of US$14.4 million for the state treasury. One of the relatively larger privatized industries was most of the 26 factories for converting raw

cotton to cotton fiber. The government hopes that continued privatization in the agricultural and industrial sectors will lead to higher economic output.

POLITICS, GOVERNMENT, AND TAXATION

Soon after declaring its independence from the Soviet Union in 1991, the country was engulfed in a bloody civil war (1992–1997) fought along ideological and regional lines. That violent conflict took approximately 35,000 lives and led to massive amounts of **internally displaced persons** and refugees fleeing to other countries. The former communists, who had controlled the government, fought against a coalition of opposition parties dominated by the Islamic Renaissance Party and mostly composed of people with Gharm/Qarateguine regional origin. In June 1997, the opponents signed a peace accord, pledged to cease all hostilities, and promised to form a government of national unity.

The constitution, adopted in 1994 and amended in 2000, replaced the Soviet-era version. It established executive, legislative and judicial branches of government. The president of Tajikistan is considered the head of state, elected every 7 years for a maximum of 2 terms. The president appoints cabinet members, the prime minister, and the justices within the court systems, all subject to approval by the legislature. The ruling party in 2001 was the People's Democratic Party of Tajikistan, associated with President Imomali Rahmonov. He has been in power since 1994 but his final term will expire in 2006. The prime minister acts as the head of government and directs the cabinet. In February 2000, elections were held to create a **bicameral** parliament.

The government generates most of its revenue from taxes. During 1996 and 1997, it maintained large **budget deficits**. There was a significant reduction of the deficit in 1999 to 3.2 percent of GDP and 3.8 percent in 1998. The government broadened the tax base and boosted revenue through the introduction of a new tax code in January 1999. The new code cut the number of tax categories from 45 to 17 and reduced the top rate of **income tax**. The government's budget deficit fell to a low of 2.2 percent of GDP in 2000. This was based mainly on the increased efficiency in tax collection and the revenue generated from privatization. The change was thought to increase tax revenue by as much as 1 percent of GDP.

INFRASTRUCTURE, POWER, AND COMMUNICATIONS

Tajikistan's **infrastructure** is relatively well developed. For example, a network of 13,000 kilometers (8,100 miles) of roads, mostly paved—though not in the best of conditions—covers large parts of the country. Despite the extensive road system, however, there is only 1 road linking Dushanbe with Khudzhand, the second biggest city in the country, which is located in the northern Leninabad region. Because climatic conditions often make this land route unusable, plans are underway to build the 13-kilometer (8.1-mile) Anzob Tunnel. The total cost for the project will likely surpass US$300 million.

The railway system is only 480 kilometers (298 miles) long and connects a few main towns to the Uzbekistan railway network. A major project nearing completion by end of 2001 is the construction of a railway from Qurghonteppa to Kulob, the 2 largest towns in the south. The country has 59 airports, 14 having paved concourses, though not all are operational due to lack of maintenance. The largest airports are in Dushanbe, Khudzhand, and Kulob. International destinations are limited and travelling on Tajikistan Airlines's dilapidated fleet is considered dangerous. Travel to Tajikistan from other parts of the world is time consuming, expensive, and cumbersome.

Access to information and communication tools are limited, with only an estimated 38 people out of every 1,000 having private access to a telephone. Moreover, the existing telecommunications system is prone to breakdowns and is in dire need of upgrading. Tajikistan was the last country among the former East European countries and the **Commonwealth of Independent States** (CIS) that was connected to the Internet. At least 2 Internet service providers and several cellular telephone companies of limited range operate in the country.

The 4 most important types of household fuel in Tajikistan are firewood, electricity, cow dung, and natural gas. Households and industry rely heavily on imported petroleum, natural gas, and—to a lesser extent—electricity, primarily from Uzbekistan. Tajikistan has an estimated 5.6 billion cubic meters of recoverable natural gas reserves, but due to financial barriers, it has been unable to increase its production. The government is attempting to encourage foreign companies to invest in **joint ventures** in the extraction of natural gas. The country's own oil production is about 3,000 barrels per day, while the consumption need of the country is more than 29,000 barrels per day. Tajikistan could be one of the world's leading per capita producers of energy if it were to expand its system of dams and hydroelectric plants. As it stands, due to the east-west configuration of its electricity grids, the country imports and exports electric energy without satisfying or affording its electricity needs. Large parts of the country, especially small towns and villages, face frequent and long periods of blackouts.

ECONOMIC SECTORS

In 2000, according to the Economist Intelligence Unit, Tajikistan registered a **real GDP** of US$1.1 billion. To find an estimate of its per capita income, GDP is divided by the estimated population of 6.6 million, arriving at a per capita GDP of a mere US$167 per year—

Communications

Country	Newspapers	Radios	TV Sets[a]	Cable subscribers[a]	Mobile Phones[a]	Fax Machines[a]	Personal Computers[a]	Internet Hosts[b]	Internet Users[b]
	1996	1997	1998	1998	1998	1998	1998	1999	1999
Tajikistan	20	142	285	N/A	0	0.3	N/A	0.24	2
United States	215	2,146	847	244.3	256	78.4	458.6	1,508.77	74,100
Russia	105	418	420	78.5	5	0.4	40.6	13.06	2,700
Kyrgyzstan	15	112	45	N/A	0	N/A	N/A	4.13	10

[a]Data are from International Telecommunication Union, *World Telecommunication Development Report 1999* and are per 1,000 people.
[b]Data are from the Internet Software Consortium (http://www.isc.org) and are per 10,000 people.

SOURCE: World Bank. *World Development Indicators 2000.*

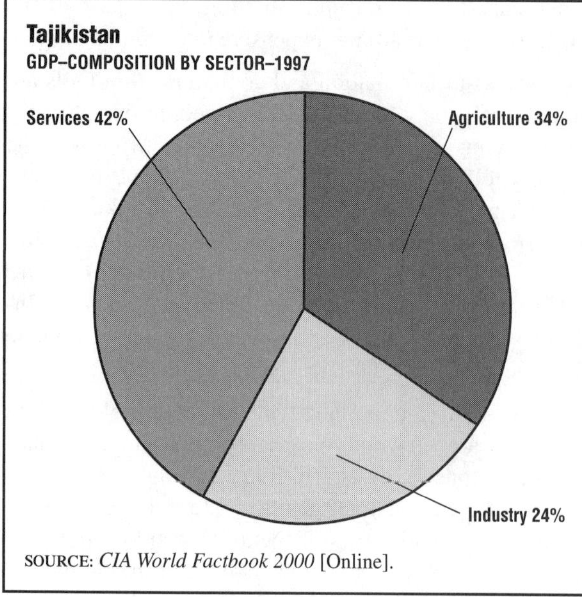

SOURCE: *CIA World Factbook 2000* [Online].

one of the lowest among East European and former Soviet republics. The economy of Tajikistan is heavily reliant on the export of 2 commodities—aluminum and cotton—and is highly susceptible to trade fluctuations. Trials of independence, a destructive civil war, and deteriorating terms of trade have combined to significantly reduce the capacity of the country to produce cotton and aluminum at levels comparable to pre-independence times. Furthermore, in 1998, due to stagnating world prices of both resources, a wide **trade deficit** of US$145 million and an equally large negative **current account balance** of US$107 million were incurred. Donor inflows, primarily from the United States and the European Union, and loans from the World Bank and International Monetary Fund (IMF), have helped moderate the current account deficit. However, **foreign direct investment** (FDI) in Tajikistan has been low, averaging only US$22 million per year between 1994 and 1998.

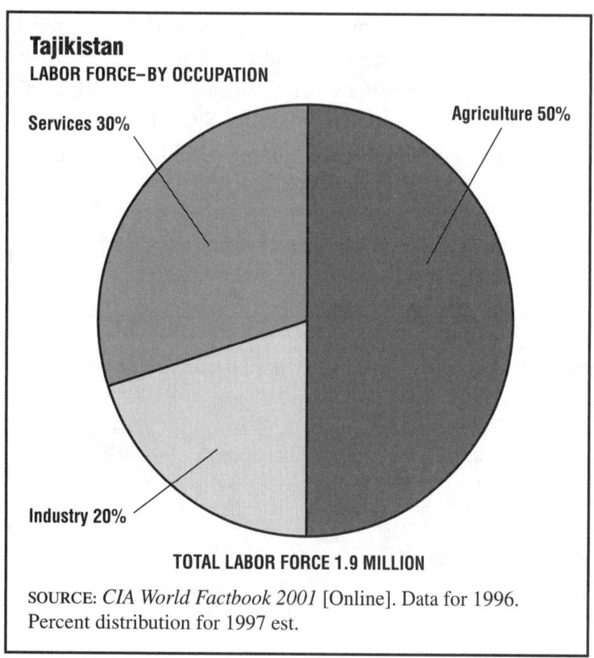

SOURCE: *CIA World Factbook 2001* [Online]. Data for 1996. Percent distribution for 1997 est.

AGRICULTURE

Tajikistan is primarily an agricultural country, with as much as 70 percent of its population living in rural areas and 65 percent of the workforce being employed in the agricultural sector, especially the cultivation and production of cotton. The Soviet Union had designated much of Central Asia's agriculture, including Tajkistan's, as a cotton monoculture (production of one type of crop). Before independence, production of raw cotton averaged more than 800,000 metric tons per year. In 1999, by contrast, raw cotton production was only 316,000 metric tons. Cotton still accounts for two-thirds of total agricultural output, however. Export of cotton fiber in 1999 accounted for a relatively low figure of US$92 million or 13 percent of GDP. The main reasons for a decline of cotton production are the substantial reduction in state **subsidies** to farms, the consequent inability of farms to purchase sufficient inputs such as fertilizers and other agronomic goods, and the deterioration of the irrigation system and agricultural machinery.

The primary food crops are wheat, barley, maize, potatoes, and rice. There are more than 800,000 hectares (2 million acres) of arable land in Tajikistan, which is equivalent to merely 6 percent of the country's land mass. The far majority of the arable land is located in the flood plains of the Kofarnihon, Vakhsh, Yakhsu, and Ghizilsu Rivers, all of which flow toward the Amudarya and Syrdarya rivers. In addition to the cropland, there are an estimated 3.5 million hectares (13,500 square miles) of permanent pastures. With its fast-growing population, Tajikistan has a comparatively and increasingly low per capita cropland. Wise use of agricultural lands, therefore, is an extremely important issue for Tajikistan. Since 1995, with the encouragement of semi-private farming and the distribution of more than 50,000 hectares (125,000 acres) of land to mostly rural households, there has been a significant increase in the production of grain, however, inclement weather since 1999 has severely affected overall agricultural production, including grain and cotton. The effects of floods have been exacerbated by the lack of proper land and water management by local governments, as in not maintaining riverbeds and allowing for the overgrazing of hills and valleys. The combined natural and human effects, have, among other things, led to a lowering of grain harvests, which had been an abundant 550,000 metric tons in 1997. This total fell by 57 percent to a low of 236,000 metric tons in 2000.

INDUSTRY

ALUMINUM. Following years of sharp decline, the end of the civil war in 1997 permitted relatively strong industrial sector growth, including real increases of 8 percent in 1998 and 5 percent in 1999. The mainstay of the industrial sector of Tajikistan is the production of aluminum, which requires alumina and large amounts of electrical energy. Even though Tajikistan does not have its own source of alumina, due to its potential for excess electrical energy, the Soviet Union built the Tursonzoda smelter, one of the world's largest aluminum smelters, near Dushanbe. The factory can produce as much as 500,000 metric tons of aluminum annually. Due to similar economic problems as the agricultural sector, however, since independence, aluminum production has declined. More than 90 percent of the aluminum produced is exported. Whereas the production of aluminum in 1990 was at a peak of 450,000 metric tons, by 1997, it had reached a low of 189,000 metric tons. Recently, however, the government has attempted to provide for the necessary inputs to increase aluminum production. Consequently, aluminum production in 2000 was estimated at about 300,000 metric tons.

MINING. Tajikistan has significant, largely unexplored, mineral deposits, such as gold, silver, antimony, and coal. Physical access to the sites—in remote areas with limited infrastructure—has been difficult and costly. A joint venture between British-owned Nelson Gold Company and the Tajik government, Zeravshan Gold Company, has been a success. In 1999, gold production in Tajikistan totalled 2.7 metric tons. In addition to gold, Tajikistan contains one of the world's largest silver deposits, Adrasmanskoye, which the country hopes to develop with the aid of foreign investors. Nine of the former Soviet Union's 34 antimony deposits are in Tajikistan. In 1997, 800 metric tons of lead was produced.

ENERGY. Tajikistan is a net importer of energy. In 1999, it consumed about 29,000 barrels of oil per day. The country has some petroleum deposits, and as much as 3,500 barrels of crude oil are extracted daily. There is no oil refinery, however, so all oil is imported—nearly 70 percent from Uzbekistan. Tajikistan has small natural gas reserves of about 200 billion cubic feet, and only minor domestic production. About 3 billion cubic feet of natural gas per year is produced domestically. In 1998, 37 billion cubic feet of gas was consumed, the majority imported from Uzbekistan and Turkmenistan. Gas pipelines run from Uzbekistan to Dushanbe, and from Uzbekistan to northern Tajikistan. Tajik authorities supply gas to Uzbekistan in exchange for Uzbekistan's free use of a rail transport corridor, a gas pipeline across northern Tajikistan (for **re-export** to Kyrgyzstan), and other incentives.

Due to the country's terrain and plentiful water, the major domestic energy resource is hydroelectric power: in 1998, Tajikistan produced 13.1 billion kilowatt hours (kWh). The southern and the northern power grids are linked to Uzbekistan. Over the past decade, depending on rainfall and domestic needs, Tajikistan has been both a net exporter and net importer of electricity. Due to a regional drought, begun in 2000, the country has experienced serious electricity shortages. It has imported more electricity and imposed increased power cuts on residential customers. Electricity prices were raised in April 2000 to limit demand. The Tursonzoda aluminum plant consumes 40 percent of the country's generated electric power. A new hydroelectric power dam, Sangtuda, is under construction with Russian and Iranian financing. It is expected to eliminate Tajikistan's need for power imports in the north and leave sufficient surpluses for export. A link between the northern and southern power grids is also planned. A study on improvements to the Tajik power grid, funded by the Kuwaiti government has been underway since 2001.

SERVICES

Services is the largest sector of the economy in Tajikistan. It constituted more than 60 percent of the country's GDP in 1998 and employs a significant part of the **labor force**. Much of the service economy is in the form of **retail** trade through micro- and small-enterprises scattered throughout mostly urban markets or bazaars. According to estimates from the state statistical agency of Tajikistan, the northern province of Leninabad sees more than one-third of retail trade, Dushanbe another third, and the southern province of Khatlon one-fifth. Despite the size of Badakhshan province—nearly half the territory of Tajikistan—its heavily mountainous geography limits its population to around 3 percent and its share of retail trade to even less. The primary products sold by small- and micro-businesses are domestically-produced agricultural goods and imported consumer items. Most of the consumer items sold by businesses are imported from Uzbekistan, Kyrgyzstan, and Kazakhstan. Increasingly, however, Tajik entrepreneurs—especially larger businesses—travel to Iran and Dubai to secure consumer items for import and sale. According to a 1998 survey of small- and micro-businesses throughout the country, the top 3 constraints facing them are racketeers demanding illegal fees, political instability, and taxation (the tax police).

FINANCIAL SERVICES. There were 17 registered banks in 1999. Four major commercial banks—Agroinvestbank, Orion Bank, Vnesheconombank, and Savings Bank—account for nearly three-quarters of all deposits and loans in the country. The banking sector, however, is marred by mismanagement and a history of extending **bad loans**. There are also few programs specializing in small loans to the agricultural and small business sectors, which are a crucial part of the economy. One study estimated that owners of micro- and small businesses pay as much as 130 percent interest rates on loans.

INTERNATIONAL TRADE

International trade plays a significant role in the country's economy. Total trade in 2000 reached an estimated US$1.5 billion, equally split between imports and exports. In 2000, the country registered a small trade surplus of US$17 million. Main export items were aluminum (constituting roughly 40 percent of export earnings), electricity (19 percent), and cotton fiber (18 percent). From 1929 to 1991, Tajikistan was able to trade freely with the other Soviet republics. During that time, Tajikistan exported its minerals, cotton, and aluminum (starting in 1974) to the rest of the Soviet Union in return for **consumer goods**, grain, fuel, and technology. During the Soviet period, however, Tajikistan consistently registered a trade deficit and regularly received union budgetary transfers from the central government. Such budgetary assistance during the Soviet era constituted as much as 23 percent of Tajikistan's GDP.

Independence in 1991 broke much of the trade and government ties with the former USSR. Since then, most exports have gone to countries outside of the CIS. Exports to the CIS countries have been primarily electricity to Uzbekistan and vegetables and raw tobacco to Russia. The major destinations of exports with their corresponding percentage of the total value of exports are: Uzbekistan 37 percent, Liechtenstein 26 percent, Russia 16 percent, and Kazakhstan 6 percent (1997 data). The origin of most imports, however, is still the CIS. For example, the vast majority of imported electricity, natural gas, and oil are from Uzbekistan and Russia. Most grain imports are still from Kazakhstan, though as much as 100,000 tons/year of wheat and other foodstuffs are imported from western Europe and the United States as food aid. Tajikistan also has imported large amounts of alumina, the raw component needed for the production of aluminum, from Ukraine. The major sources of imports with their corresponding percentage of total value of imports are: Netherlands 32 percent, Uzbekistan 29 percent, Switzerland 20 percent, and Russia 9 percent (1997 data). Government **tariffs** stand at around 8 percent. Based on international standards, this is considered a liberal trade regime.

MONEY

Tajikistan's choice of currency has normally been according to the will of Moscow. Even after independence in 1991, for example, it began to use the new Russian ruble. In May 1995, however, it finally created its own legal tender, the Tajik ruble (TR). At that time, the National Bank of Tajikistan set the **exchange rate** as TR100 to US$1. Between 1995 to 1999, consumer price **inflation** increased by a rate of 1,680 percent, or an average annual compound rate of 420 percent. In 1999, however, the **inflation rate** was 28 percent. The depreciation of the Tajik ruble throughout the years is attributable to internal and external factors that diminished confidence in the local currency. Civil unrest and political instability, continued lack of economic opportunities for the average citizen, and the government's loose monetary and **fiscal policies** were among internal factors. External factors include Russia's 1998 economic woes, rise of petroleum prices, fluctuations of world cotton and aluminum prices, and a region-wide drought. By January 2001, the exchange rate reached TR2,200 to US$1.

Meanwhile, the government embarked on a new currency called the somoni in October 2000 to take into account several years of high inflation. Hence, cash transactions no longer require large wads of currency. The name change "ruble" to "somoni" was also a tactical move by the government to use the currency as a symbol for Tajik nationalism. As of April 2001, the somoni was to have been the sole legal tender of the republic. At its introduction SM1 was equivalent to TR1,000. The exchange rate of the somoni is expected to reach SM2.5 to US$1 by the end of 2001.

Trade (expressed in millions of US$): Tajikistan

	Exports	Imports
1994	482	577
1995	748	809
1996	651	763
1997	745	750
1998	601	771
1999	N/A	N/A

SOURCE: United Nations. *Monthly Bulletin of Statistics* (September 2000).

Exchange rates: Tajikistan

Tajikistani somoni per US$	
Jan 2001	2.2
Jan 2000	1550
Jan 1999	998
Jan 1998	N/A
Jan 1997	350
Jan 1996	284

Note: The new unit of exchange was introduced on October 30, 2000, with one somoni equal to 1,000 of the old Tajikistani rubles.

SOURCE: CIA *World Factbook 2001* [ONLINE].

GDP per Capita (US$)

Country	1975	1980	1985	1990	1998
Tajikistan	N/A	N/A	N/A	718	345
United States	19,364	21,529	23,200	25,363	29,683
Russia	2,555	3,654	3,463	3,668	2,138
Kyrgyzstan	N/A	N/A	N/A	1,562	863

SOURCE: United Nations. *Human Development Report 2000; Trends in human development and per capita income.*

POVERTY AND WEALTH

Tajikistan is the poorest country among the East European and CIS nations. It had the lowest per capita income among the same groups during the Soviet era. In earlier years, though, the Tajikistan economy was much more robust, with industry and agriculture being doubly productive than today. Furthermore, the central government of the Soviet Union used to provide Tajikistan with a significant amount of its national budgetary requirements. Despite its relatively low ranking during the **communist** era, Tajikistan was not poor. The population was healthy, wages were paid, and public services were fully functional. In 2001, on the other hand, due to independence and civil war related issues, Tajikistan *is* poor. There are limited employment opportunities, wages are low—particularly in the agricultural sector—and a variety of financial and material input necessary for proper agricultural and industrial activities is sorely lacking. Poverty in Tajikistan is also evident in the decreasing access to basic public services such as education, health care, and clean water.

Income generated from employment remains the most important source of revenue for households. Other sources of income, however, such as revenue from micro- and small businesses and the sale of food and household goods, cover equally large shares of overall household incomes. The well-to-do and poor segments of the population—and between some urban folk and the mostly rural population—exhibit clear economic divergence. Expenditures at the richest households are 4 times those of the poorest. The poorest households spend 79 percent of their budget on food. They cover most of this need through **subsistence farming**, some **remittances** from abroad, and humanitarian aid. More female-headed households are considered poor than male-headed, partially due to the facts that Tajik women tend to be less educated, have fewer opportunities for business, and work in the public health and education spheres, where pay levels are significantly lower. Due to the continuing economic crisis, at best, the government can only provide minimal real provisions for social welfare to the needy. This is difficult for a population that still remembers the Soviet-era's generally good provision of health, education, and welfare services. A 1998 survey of households and small businesses throughout the country found that when asked what type of economy they hope Tajikistan to resemble in the future, 53 percent chose the USSR.

WORKING CONDITIONS

The fall of the Soviet Union, the civil war of 1992–1997 that resulted in several billions of dollars of damages, and the continued economic slump have led to a drop in the standard of living for the majority. **Public-sector** wages are among the lowest in the world. According to the World Bank, about two-thirds of the population of Tajikistan subsists on less than US$2 a day. Though the official unemployment rate was 3 percent at the end of 2000, it did not include more than 220,000 government employees not receiving their salaries. These figures would yield an unemployment rate higher than 16 percent. The average wages per month among the CIS countries is highest in Kazakhstan at US$101 and lowest in Tajikistan at US$8.8. The highest average monthly salaries in Tajikistan belong to people working in the sectors of finance and banking, where they earn about US$40; the lowest belong to those in education (US$6), health care (US$4), and agriculture (US$3).

Household Consumption in PPP Terms

Country	All food	Clothing and footwear	Fuel and power[a]	Health care[b]	Education[b]	Transport & Communications	Other
Tajikistan	48	7	10	0	14	5	16
United States	13	9	9	4	6	8	51
Russia	28	11	16	7	15	8	16
Kyrgyzstan	33	11	11	3	22	6	14

Data represent percentage of consumption in PPP terms.
[a]Excludes energy used for transport.
[b]Includes government and private expenditures.

SOURCE: World Bank. *World Development Indicators 2000.*

Some sector-specific labor organizations exist, but they cannot be considered unions. They are remnants of the communist past, when labor rights were ingrained in the system. Due to the widespread economic slump and high unemployment rate, few workers dare to organize against their employers, who can replace protesting workers with any of the thousands of unemployed. Many people are not engaged in their learned professions, due to paltry government salaries. Some use a self-owned micro-business to supplement their government salaries. The **informal economy** consists of thousands of micro-businesses in the various bazaars around the country, where one can find doctors, accountants and engineers selling anything from potatoes to baby clothing.

COUNTRY HISTORY AND ECONOMIC DEVELOPMENT

875. Samanid dynasty, with its Persian speaking court, begins a 175-year reign over territory that includes much of today's Uzbekistan and Tajikistan.

1895. A treaty signed by Russia and Britain determines the southern borders and what becomes Eastern Turkestan, a Russian protectorate, which covers the territory of today's Central Asian republics and some parts of eastern China. The 1895 treaty considers Amudarya as the border between Russian and British influence.

1920. The Bolshevik army occupies Bukhara, forcing the emir to flee to Afghanistan.

1924. Tajikistan becomes an autonomous republic within the Soviet Socialist Republic of Uzbekistan.

1926. The first Tajik language newspaper in Soviet Tajikistan begins publication.

1929. Territory is annexed from Uzbekistan by orders of Stalin, and included as part of Tajikistan. Tajikistan is then declared an independent Soviet Socialist republic.

1930. Aggressive collectivization of agriculture is imposed on Tajikistan by Soviet planners, with an eye on expansion of cotton monoculture (the cultivation of a single crop).

1937. The Great Terror of Stalin purges much of the local communist elite, replacing them in favor of ethnic Russians and Europeans.

1991. Tajikistan declares independence from the Soviet Union. A coalition government is formed involving elements of the Islamic opposition as well as former communists. By June, civil war breaks out between supporters of the former communist incumbent president, Rahmon Nabiyev, and the Islamic and secular opposition groups. Shortly after, parliament appoints Imomali Rahmonov as head of state after Nabiyev's resignation in September. Civil war between government supporters and the Islamic and democratic forces begins.

1993. UTO, the Islamic opposition, which is based in Afghansitan and partly in Iran, forms an effective guerrilla force that carries out cross-border raids and eventually captures much of east-central Tajikistan.

1994. Rahmonov defeats a candidate from northern Tajikistan in a controversial election with 58 percent of the vote.

1995. Parliamentary elections are held; no opposition parties are allowed to take part.

1997. A peace accord brokered by the UN, Iran, and Russia is signed in Moscow between the government and the UTO. Refugees begin to return from Afghanistan.

1999. Voters re-elect Rahmonov as president. The UN's Organization for Security and Co-operation in Europe (OSCE) and Human Rights Watch accuse the government of vote rigging, manipulation of the media, intimidation of opponents and illegal disqualification of several political parties.

2000. The pro-government People's Democratic Party takes the majority of seats in elections to the new bicameral parliament.

2001. Despite relative calm in the country, assassinations occur sporadically and the drug trade is on the rise.

FUTURE TRENDS

Tajikistan is still in a nation-building stage. Because its territory is cut off from the centers of Tajik civilization—the cities of Bukhara and Samarqand, which are part of Uzbekistan—any central government in Tajikistan faces political and social maneuvering and challenges to unite an ethnically mixed and geographically dispersed population. In addition, recent government propaganda on the "Tajik" nature of the country, despite ethnic Tajiks comprising only 65 percent of the population, may not easily be accepted by an ethnically diverse population. Therefore, in addition to economic woes, which continue to cause barriers to the well-being of the country, the lack of democracy and security also wreak havoc. The presidential and parliamentary elections of 1999 and 2000, for example, were thought to be mired with improper intervention and influence by the ruling elite. Furthermore, although some level of banditry may have diminished due to the government's incorporation of many former opposition forces, other problems of insecurity are on the rise. Two of the most critical are the increase in the drug trafficking from Afghanistan and armed guerillas of the Islamic Movement of Uzbekistan (IMU) using Tajikistan as a base to invade neighboring Uzbekistan and Kyrgyzstan.

The future well-being of Tajikistan depends on a variety of factors, among which are whether the armed conflicts of Afghanistan and the sporadic guerrilla warfare of the IMU will eventually come to peaceful resolutions. Other factors are the will of the government to extend more democracy, human rights, and freedom of expression. The allowance of an independent media and encouragement of a strong civil society will be steps in the right direction. Provision of loans and logistics for small farmers and small businesses could truly alleviate the economic pains of the people. A plan to protect the natural environment in the form of establishing large parts of the country as national parks and creating accommodations for tourists via the creation of small locally-owned hotels throughout the country could encourage the establishment of a potentially lucrative **ecotourism** industry. This could simultaneously generate income for the local population, provide foreign capital for the central government, and preserve the natural environment. Finally, moves toward economic and cultural integration with other Central Asian republics and easing of travel throughout the region will be highly beneficial for the future of Tajikistan and the region as a whole.

DEPENDENCIES

Tajikistan has no territories or colonies.

BIBLIOGRAPHY

Economist Intelligence Unit. *Country Profile: Kyrgyz Republic and Tajikistan: 2000–2001.* London: EIU, 2000.

European Bank for Reconstruction and Development. *Tajikistan, 2000 Country Investment Profile.* Geneva: EBRD, 2000.

Foroughi, Payam. *1998 Socio-Economic Survey of Households, Farms and Bazaars in Tajikistan.* USAID and SCF, 1999.

International Monetary Fund. *Republic of Tajikistan: Recent Economic Developments,* Washington, DC: IMF, 2000.

U.S. Central Intelligence Agency. *World Factbook 2000.* <http://www.odci.gov/cia/publications/factbook/index.html>. Accessed August 2001.

United Nations Development Programme. *Human Development Report 2000.* New York: UNDP, 2000.

"United Nations Statistical Yearbook 2000." *United Nations.* <http://jlnt2s.imf.org/ICA/stayear.ica>. Accessed February 2001.

World Bank. *Tajikistan: A World Bank Country Study.* Washington, DC: World Bank, 1994.

"World Outlook 2000." *International Monetary Fund.* <http://dsbb.imf.org/category.htm>. Accessed February 2001.

—Payam Foroughi and Raissa Muhutdinova-Foroughi

THAILAND

Kingdom of Thailand

CAPITAL: Bangkok.

MONETARY UNIT: Thai baht (B). One baht equals 100 satangs. There are notes of 50 satang and 1, 5, 10, 20, 50, 60, 100, 500, and 1,000 baht, and coins of 1, 5, 10, 25, and 50 satangs and 1, 5, and 10 baht.

CHIEF EXPORTS: Computers and parts, textiles, rice.

CHIEF IMPORTS: Capital goods, intermediate goods and raw materials, consumer goods, fuels.

GROSS DOMESTIC PRODUCT: US$388.7 billion (purchasing power parity, 1999 est.).

BALANCE OF TRADE: **Exports:** US$58.5 billion (f.o.b., 1999). **Imports:** US$45 billion (f.o.b., 1999). [*International Financial Statistics 1999* reports 1998 exports of US$54.46 billion and imports of US$42.97 billion.]

COUNTRY OVERVIEW

LOCATION AND SIZE. Situated in Southeast Asia, Thailand is adjoined to Laos and Burma (Myanmar) to the north, Cambodia and the Gulf of Thailand to the east, Burma and the Andaman Sea to the west, and Malaysia to the south. Its total area, which is about twice the size of Wyoming, measures 514,000 square kilometers (198,455 square miles). The length of its coastline measures 3,219 kilometers (2,000 miles). Its capital city, Bangkok, is the most populated city in Thailand. Located in the central region, Bangkok is the center of Thailand's economic and political activities. Major cities in the north are Chiang Mai and Chiang Rai, Nakhon Ratchasima, Khon Kaen, Udon Thani, Phitsanulok, Nakhon Sawan, and Ubon Ratchathani. Meanwhile, major cities in the south are Nakhon Si Thammarat, Songkhla, Surat Thani, and Hat Yai.

POPULATION. The country's population in 2000 stood at 61.2 million, compared to 55.2 million in 1989, according to the *CIA World Factbook.* The country's population growth rate from 1988 to 1998 has been estimated at an average of 1.05 percent, according to the *Asian Economic Survey*. The population is expected to increase by 0.93 percent by 2010. The population is predominantly composed of young people, with 70 percent between the ages of 15 and 64, 24 percent below 15 years old, and only 6 percent older than 64 years.

The majority of the population still resides in rural areas. In 2000, the World Bank reported that approximately 40 percent of the country's population, or 25 million Thais, lived in urban areas and estimates that this will increase to 53 percent by 2010. Bangkok hosts about 12 million Thais.

The majority of the Thai population—75 percent—is of the Thai ethnic group, while 14 percent are Chinese and 11 percent are other ethnic groups. Fully 95 percent of the population is Buddhist, while 3.8 percent are Muslims and the remainder represent a variety of religions.

OVERVIEW OF ECONOMY

The Thai economy is one of the most robust in Asia. In the 1960s it was a predominantly agricultural economy largely dependent on its rich produce of crops such as rice, cassava, maize, rubber, and sugar cane, along with its seafood production, primarily of shrimp. Its strategic location and bountiful natural resources has enabled the country to maximize trade opportunities. The 1980s to mid-1990s marked its boom years and its emergence as a diverse, modern, and industrialized economy.

The economy's growth can be attributed to several factors. First, Thailand has pursued a rational approach to industrialization. Prior to its attempt at industrialization, Thailand already had a stable agricultural sector which became the springboard for industrialization. In the 1960s, its first attempt at industrialization was characterized by the strategy of **import substitution** which centered mainly on food processing. Hence, Thailand used the produce of its agricultural sector to initiate a

shift into industrialization. The availability of local laborers, combined with abundant natural produce, enabled the country to increase production and shift to manufacturing or processing products for export purposes. This led to the rapid expansion of the manufacturing sector and a marked increase in exports. This approach enabled Thailand to avoid the usual path taken by newly industrialized economies (NIEs) of pursuing industrialization at the expense of the agricultural sector. The strategy was to gradually build upon existing resources in order to facilitate the development of the economy.

A second important factor was Thailand's diversification of its economy. This is a pervasive trend in the development of the economy, which is rooted in the innate flexibility of the Thai people. This is exemplified by the stages of growth of the industrial sector which began with simple agri-based manufacturing, and steadily progressed to more sophisticated industries through the use of available resources such as rich natural resources and cheap labor. Diversification was also aided by huge inflows of **foreign direct investment** geared towards a wide range of products, namely electronics, chemicals, property, and processed food. In the 1980s, foreign direct investment totaled US$8 billion, with US$2.5 billion coming from Japan and the rest from Chinese, Korean, and American investors. In fact, 50 percent of the country's industrial output and 20 percent of its industrial workforce are attributable to foreign investors who are attracted by lower manufacturing costs, according to *Thailand's Turn.*

A third factor in Thailand's growth is government stability. The administration of Prime Minister Prem Tinsulanonda, which lasted from 1980 to 1988, developed a continuity in policies and programs that inspired the confidence of the **private sector** in both the government and the economy. This translated to a greater willingness to invest in the growing manufacturing industry and support further expansion of export activities.

Fourth, the dynamism of the private sector propelled export production. In 1981, a landmark policy was implemented which facilitated the formation of the Joint Public-Private Consultative Committee on Economic Problems that enabled businesspersons to influence public policy through their associations. This, in turn, led to an increased participation of the private sector in the development of state enterprises. Economic development in the country was largely propelled by the private sector, which invested heavily in industrial growth; the government had a limited role in determining the direction of the economy.

These factors have contributed greatly to the growth of the country's major economic sectors, namely agriculture and fishing, manufacturing and industry, and services, particularly tourism. In 1991, 98.6 percent of all Thai business enterprises were mainly small and medium enterprises, accounting for 90.7 percent and 7.6 percent, respectively. The Ministry of Industry defines small-scale enterprises as those with a maximum of 50 employees with an **equity** of 10 million baht, while medium-scale enterprises employ 50–200 personnel and have an equity of 10–100 million baht.

The country's inability to produce oil has negatively impacted its growth, particularly during periods of oil crisis such as the world oil crisis between 1970 and 1979. The country's dependence on oil has been reduced with the discovery of its first natural gas field in the Gulf of Thailand in 1981. The country also taps alternative domestic sources of energy such as hydropower, liquefied natural gas, and coal. It is also in the process of studying the use of nuclear power.

At the end of 1990, the country's long-term **external debt** stood at about US$16 billion. However, annual **debt service** payments were only equivalent to 10 percent of the total earnings from exports, which means that the debt payments were manageable. The 1997 Asian financial crisis reversed this situation as the combination of US$90.5 billion in debt in 1996–97 and high levels of **non-performing loans** caused the near collapse of Thailand's financial sector. The troubles of the financial sector spilled over to the other sectors of the economy which were dependent on the financial sector for credit. Banks had to set aside finances to cover loans which creditors were not able to pay, so they no longer had any money to lend borrowers who were capable of paying. This forced the government to increase its allocation for **foreign debt** payments to take the pressure away from the financial sector. This resulted in a significant increase in **public sector** debt, which was only equivalent to 4 percent of GDP in 1996 but rose to 18 percent of GDP by mid-1999.

To alleviate the effects of the crisis, the International Monetary Fund (IMF) gave Thailand a US$17.2 billion assistance package in August 1997. With the help of these funds, reforms in the financial sector were implemented along with the **restructuring** of the industrial and agricultural sector to increase productivity. Policy reforms to increase accountability and transparency, as well as social reforms to improve education, social services, and human resource development are also being implemented by the government with assistance from the IMF, the Asian Development Bank (ADB), the Overseas Economic Co-Operation and Development (OECD) Fund, and the World Bank.

POLITICS, GOVERNMENT, AND TAXATION

On 24 June 1932, Thailand's political system changed from an absolute monarchy to a constitutional monarchy. The king is the head of state and is very much revered by the Thais. Presently, the monarch is King Bhumibol Adulyadej, who ascended the throne in 1946. King Bhumibol Adulyadej has been specially recognized for bringing the Thai monarchy closer to the people. In 1955, he visited the poorest regions of Thailand in order to see for himself the living conditions of the people. Since then, the king and his family have spent 7 months of every year visiting each of the 76 provinces of Thailand. As a result, the king is very well informed of the distinct needs of each region.

To date, the king has implemented over a thousand projects to improve the living conditions in the remotest rural areas, including the introduction of new crops, water conservation, irrigation, swamp drainage, preservation of national forests, and crop substitution. One of the king's most publicized projects is the Royal Rainmaking Project, wherein after years of careful experimentation, 14 different formulae were invented to address the problem of dry spells in Thailand.

The Thai Constitution mandates that the government should be placed under the administrative power of a prime minister, a cabinet, and a **bicameral** legislature composed of a 253-member appointed Senate and a 500-member, popularly-elected House of Representatives. The prime minister is selected from the majority party in the ruling coalition in the House of Representatives. Since 1932, Thailand has promulgated 16 constitutions, the latest of which was adopted in 1997.

The cabinet is composed of 13 ministries together with the Office of the Prime Minister and the Office of State Universities. Each ministry is led by a minister who is assisted by one or more deputy ministers. In addition, there are ministers holding the portfolio of "Minister Attached to the Prime Minister's Office." These ministers take charge of the sectors assigned to them and assist the government in the formulation and implementation of national programs. The National Economic and Social Development Board (NESDB) is the agency in charge of longer term development planning, which is implemented in 5-year periods. Aside from the NESDB, other important government agencies for economic planning are the Board of Investment (BOI), which provides incentives for investment, the Office of the Technical and Economic Cooperation Department, and the Office of the National Education Commission.

The Ministry of Industry is crucial in assisting the government in all industry and manufacturing-related activities such as formulating policies, licensing of factories, issuing mineral leases, formulating and supervising industrial standards, providing technical assistance to industries, and supervising the Small Industries Finance Office. Meanwhile, the Ministry of Commerce oversees external and internal trade. Specifically, it controls or supervises prices of certain strategic commodities such as rice and provides export promotion services to export companies.

The Thai government believes that the private sector should lead the country in its quest for progress and development. In this endeavor, the government's major contribution to economic growth was to provide economic and social services; provide financial resources for the construction of physical **infrastructure** like highways, irrigation, and power facilities; and to formulate and offer various incentives and financial assistance to promote private investments, export businesses, and agricultural enterprises.

Since the 1950s, the government followed a clear direction towards private enterprise. International organizations like the World Bank and the United States Agency for International Development as well as the United States have strongly encouraged Thailand towards adopting that strategy.

Presently, the Thai government is at the forefront, alongside the business sector, in implementing a wide range of economic reforms to promote Thailand's economic recovery from the 1997 **recession**. Improvements have also been made in the implementation of economic and social welfare programs. This effort is guided by the new constitution, which promotes a stronger, more accountable, decentralized, and transparent government.

POLITICAL PARTIES. As of 1998, Thailand had at least 11 registered political parties, the biggest of which are the Democratic Party (Prachathipat Party) and Thai Nation Party (Chat Thai Party). The other political parties are the Liberal Democratic Party, Mass Party, National Development Party, New Aspiration Party, Phalang Dharma Party, Social Action Party, Solidarity Party, Thai Citizen's Party, and the Thai Rak Thai Party.

Political parties in Thailand serve as the breeding ground for future leaders and bureaucrats. They provide the venue by which those with political ambitions are able to familiarize themselves with the country's democratic structure and processes and obtain a certain measure of political leadership training. However, the political party system in Thailand is still in a state of evolution and can be best described as fragmented, structurally weak, and vulnerable to corruption. The cost of staging a national campaign is very high and the funds needed to finance such an endeavor are generally only available to those in the business world. Hence, businesspeople dominate most of the political parties in Thailand. Moreover, political parties in Thailand are not mass-based, have no distinct ideological differences, and lack full-time, dedicated, and qualified personnel to formulate and implement the party's programs. Since one Thai political party cannot really be differentiated from the other, switching party loyalties is not unusual in Thailand.

REVENUES. A huge percentage of government revenue comes from taxes which are collected at the national and local level. At the national level, the central government collects an **income tax** and a profit remittance tax, while the most important **indirect tax** is the **value-added tax** (VAT). In September 1997, the government announced an increase in the VAT from 7 percent to 10 percent in order to raise revenue and to meet the conditions of the US$17.2 billion loan extended by the IMF to Thailand. However, businesses making less than US$24,000 per annum were still exempted. The government levies taxes on all personal incomes including income from business, commerce, agriculture, industry, transport, construction, or contracting work. The corporate tax rate is currently 30 percent of net profits for all firms. Other taxes imposed by the central government are customs and **excise taxes**, and stamp **duty**. Local governments are authorized to collect different types of taxes such as property and land tax. Tourism and its allied services are the biggest source of revenue of the government, especially in terms of foreign currency earnings.

THE ROLE OF THE MILITARY. The military has played a large role in Thailand's political history and national development. In less than 3 decades, from 1932 to 1958, Thailand underwent 12 coups d'etat. Since 1958 there have been 6 more coups, half of which were successful in overthrowing the government. Since the transition from an absolute monarchy to a constitutional monarchy in 1932, the country has been led mostly by military leaders.

Against this scenario, it is important to analyze the contribution of military leaders to Thailand's current economic development since they had a hand in crafting most of Thailand's economic strategies. For instance, the rule of Field Marshal Sarit Thanarat after a coup in 1957 laid the foundation for Thailand's economic development. One of the most important contributions of his regime was the formulation of a national economic development policy, the first of its kind, which was implemented beginning in 1961. Numerous **technocrats** were tapped in the crafting of Thailand's economic strategy for development. His other achievements include the establishment of universities in the north, northeast, and southern regions, the enticement of foreign investors to invest in Thailand by offering incentives such as **tax holidays**, and hastening the completion of infrastructure projects such as dams, roads, and bridges. Succeeding regimes followed Sarit's example and crafted their respective development strategies after his, a key factor in Thailand's present economic progress.

INFRASTRUCTURE, POWER, AND COMMUNICATIONS

In the late 1980s, Thailand's infrastructure failed to cope with the rapid expansion of the economy. In fact, many experts believe that the country's economy could have grown more were it not for hindrances caused by inadequate infrastructure, a problem that is more pro-

Communications

Country	Newspapers	Radios	TV Sets[a]	Cable subscribers[a]	Mobile Phones[a]	Fax Machines[a]	Personal Computers[a]	Internet Hosts[b]	Internet Users[b]
	1996	1997	1998	1998	1998	1998	1998	1999	1999
Thailand	63	232	236	10.1	32	2.5	21.6	4.49	800
United States	215	2,146	847	244.3	256	78.4	458.6	1,508.77	74,100
China	N/A	333	272	40.0	19	1.6	8.9	0.50	8,900
Vietnam	4	107	47	N/A	2	0.3	6.4	0.00	100

[a]Data are from International Telecommunication Union, *World Telecommunication Development Report 1999* and are per 1,000 people.
[b]Data are from the Internet Software Consortium (http://www.isc.org) and are per 10,000 people.

SOURCE: World Bank. *World Development Indicators 2000.*

nounced in the rural areas. Thailand's problem with inadequate transportation infrastructure is so severe that the Bangkok Metropolitan Region has become internationally notorious for its legendary traffic jams. Infrastructure for water, sewerage, and energy are also lagging behind the rate of urbanization and development. Secondary cities and rural areas are suffering because of their inability to attract investors due to poor infrastructure.

To address these problems, the Thai government has formulated a long-term infrastructure plan to meet the demands and requirements of a newly industrialized country. The government has prioritized the improvement of existing infrastructure and construction of new projects to alleviate the problem. Building on the goals of the previous economic plans, the Eighth National Economic Plan (1997–2001) allocated US$7.5 billion for infrastructure development, which is 47 percent more funds than the previous plan. The government also identified priority projects such as expressways, rapid mass transportation, port development, water supply, and telecommunications. At the same time, legal reforms are being instituted to enable the private sector to participate in infrastructure development.

However, the immediate implementation of the projects was stalled due to various reasons, the foremost of which was the onset of the Asian Financial Crisis in July 1997, which caused a serious economic recession. The immediate effect was a lack of adequate funds to continue on-going projects or to start construction of planned projects. Other obstacles were disputes with foreign builders and negotiations with potential operators of toll roads as well as last-minute changes in contract specifications and bureaucratic requirements like land-use permits.

Beginning in 1999 Thailand has slowly recovered from the debilitating effects of the recession. Combining funds from different sources like annual budgets, independent development loans, borrowings, and the private sector, a total of US$78 billion was allotted for infrastructure projects. The government is utilizing different strategies such as the Build-Operate-Transfer (BOT) scheme to fund construction of expressways and Mass Rapid Transfer (MRT) systems in Bangkok, to the installation of more telephone lines and the construction of privately-owned and operated power generating plants.

LAND TRANSPORTATION. Thailand's road networks cover over 170,000 kilometers (105,638 miles). To help alleviate the traffic in Bangkok, an elevated train system was opened in December 1999. An underground subway system is also under construction and is expected to be operational by 2003. A total of US$700 million was allotted for these mass transportation projects. Originating from Bangkok, Thailand's rail network spans 3,981 kilometers (2,474 miles) and transports people to the major regions, namely Chiang Mai, Nong Khai, Ubon Ratchathani, Padang Besar, and Sungai Kolok. The State Railway of Thailand expressed its plans to spend US$4.2 billion between 1997 and 2001 to improve and expand its rail network.

AIR TRANSPORTATION. Thailand is working on its goal to become the aviation hub of Southeast Asia. It is expanding its existing international airport to accommodate 36 million people by 2003. At the same time, a second international airport, 30 kilometers east of Bangkok, is currently under construction. Presently, Thailand has a total of 106 airports. Of these, 6 are international airports while 29 are domestic airports, with several more provincial airports in the offing.

WATER TRANSPORTATION. There are 8 international deep seaports in different parts of Thailand, with the major ports in Bangkok, Laem Chabang, Phuket, and Songkhla. In order to reduce the traffic in the over-utilized main port in Bangkok's Klong Toey district, the government is upgrading and constructing additional ports, particularly in the Eastern Seaboard and southern region, along the Gulf of Thailand and the Andaman Sea.

The importance of the Eastern Seaboard is increasing due to the establishment of industrial parks and export processing zones around the sea port in Laem Chabang. The government foresees that the port areas in the south will grow in importance to equal existing main ports.

COMMUNICATIONS. As of 1998, there were 5.4 million land lines and 2.3 million mobile phone subscribers in the country. As incorporated in the Telecommunications Master Plan for 1997–2006, Thai authorities have set a goal of increasing the number of telephones per 100 people from 4 in 1993 to 18.2 by 2001. In 1999, the government completed the Rural Long Distance Telephone project and is currently operating a total of 20,732 lines or 47 percent of its target. A number of projects are currently underway, including the Fibre Optic Submarine Cable Network Development and the Telecommunication Satellite Network Development.

As of 1999, Thailand had 204 AM stations, 334 FM stations, and 6 short wave facilities servicing about 13.96 million radios. In addition, 5 television broadcast stations provide service to 15.19 million television sets in all of Thailand as of 1997.

POWER. In the past, Thailand was heavily dependent on imported crude oil. After the world oil crisis in the 1970s, however, Thailand began to explore indigenous sources of energy and was rewarded with the discovery of a natural gas field in the Gulf of Thailand in 1981. As of 1996, 20 fields are in operation with daily oil production reaching 2,500 barrels per day, and of gas reaching 1,200 million cubic feet per day.

Due to the continued expansion of industries, the future demand for energy has been forecasted to increase by 7 percent in the period between 2002 and 2006. Demand for petroleum will still lead this increase at 49 percent, followed by imported coal at 12.4 percent. Demand for electricity has been forecasted to double from 10,203 megawatts in 1996 to 20,400 megawatts in 2006, according to the *Asia Pacific Economic Compendium* (1996).

Thailand continues to explore other sources of energy within its territory and from neighboring countries. In addition, it continues to construct different projects to meet its energy requirements. Among these are the Greater Bangkok Area Transmission System, the Yadana-Ratchaburi Gas Pipeline, the Ratchaburi Power Plant, and the Eighth Power Distribution System Improvement and Expansion Plan.

ECONOMIC SECTORS

Thailand's economy has grown steadily by an average of 8 percent for the past decade. There is a wide base for growth, with each sector contributing to the development of the economy. Starting out as an agrarian economy, Thailand's bid for industrialization strengthened its industry sector, while the boom in the tourism industry strengthened the service sector. In the 1990s, manufacturing and tourism are the 2 largest contributors to GDP.

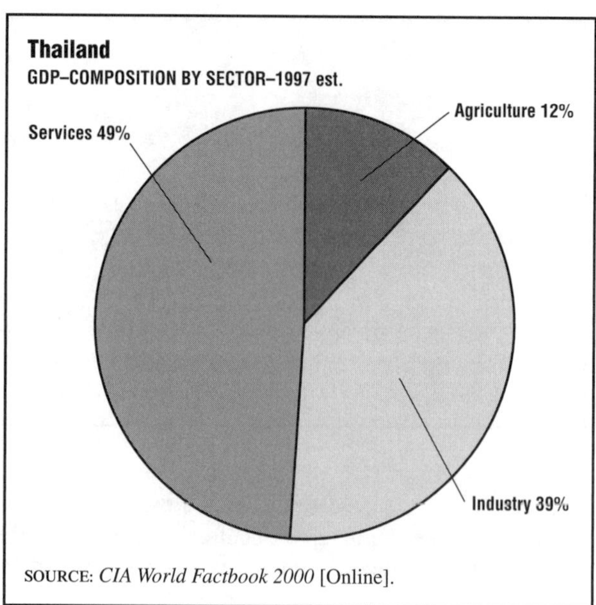

SOURCE: *CIA World Factbook 2000* [Online].

Agriculture has been the traditional backbone of the economy, with Thailand being ranked among the top 5 producers of food in the world. In the 1970s, the country supplied 30 percent to 40 percent of rice in the world market. In the 1990s, it continued to be the leading exporter of rice, tapioca, and frozen shrimp. It is also the world's largest producer of rubber, the demand for which has increased due to the AIDS epidemic, which has increased the demand for condoms. Thailand is also one of

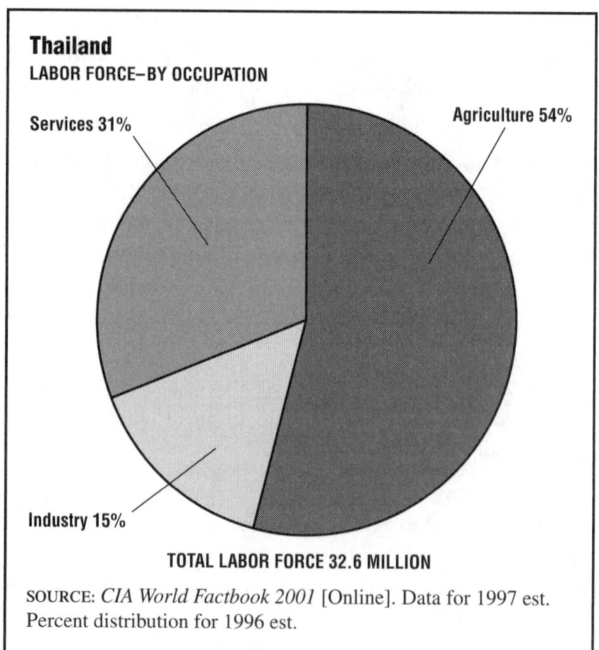

SOURCE: *CIA World Factbook 2001* [Online]. Data for 1997 est. Percent distribution for 1996 est.

the world's biggest suppliers of flowers, particularly orchids, which it exports mainly to Japan and Europe. Despite its output, the agricultural sector is on the decline, and is slowly being overtaken by the industry and service sectors in terms of contribution to GDP.

With the re-orientation of production from import substitution to producing for export, and the drive towards industrialization, the manufacturing industry grew steadily until it exceeded agriculture in terms of contribution to GDP. According to Bank of Thailand statistics reflected in the 2000 Business Monitor International Annual Report, the manufacturing industry accounted for 86.8 percent of the country's total exports in 1999. The country's first step into manufacturing was food processing, effectively building on its strong agricultural sector. Today, it is the world's largest exporter of canned pineapple, with one-third of all the canned pineapple sold in the United States coming from Thailand. It is also Asia's biggest exporter of tuna after Unicord, a local company, purchased Bumble Bee Seafoods, the third largest tuna canner in the United States. It now supplies 20 percent of the world market for canned tuna.

The country's service sector is experiencing steady growth, with the boom in the tourism industry. In 1992, tourism accounted for 10 percent of the GDP, with 600 tourists arriving every hour, or 5,256,000 tourists for the year, spending an average of US$1,000 each, equivalent to about US$5 billion a year. This amount is equal to 50 percent of the country's total exports. In 2000, revenues from tourism were expected to hit 343 billion baht or US$6.86 billion, with a total of 9,438,000 tourists expected to visit the country throughout the year.

Strong local corporations—such as Charoen Pokphand, which earns revenue of US$2.5 billion annually; Thai Union Frozen Products, the largest canned seafood exporter; and Boonrawd Brewery—work together with various **multinational corporations** to energize the manufacturing industry. Forecasts for the year 2000 predicted that multinational corporations which have set up shop in the country—such as Mitsubishi, Isuzu, and Honda for automobiles; Fujitsu, Seagate, IBM, Sony, and Matsushita Electronic for electronics; Heineken and Carlsberg breweries, and Nestle and Kellogg for food processing; and Exxon, Montell, and Bayer for petrochemicals—will expand their operations in the country and pump in more investment.

AGRICULTURE

Traditionally an agrarian economy with rice as its main product, the country's agricultural sector has since expanded to cope with the demands of its newly industrialized state. Thai agriculture has a clear advantage over other newly industrializing economies, namely the large portion of land allocated for cultivation, a climate suited to the growth of a wide variety of crops, and high quality strains of agricultural products.

In 1960, agriculture contributed over 40 percent of the national income. This contribution steadily declined due to the intense and rapid growth of the manufacturing sector. By the end of the 1980s, agriculture merely accounted for 17 percent of GDP, which declined even further to 12 percent until the late 1990s, to below 10 percent in 1999. The same pattern exists in terms of its contribution to exports, which stood at 46.9 percent in 1980 and plummeted to 9 percent by 1998.

However, these figures do not indicate a weakening of the sector's significance to the Thai economy, but more a strengthening of the industry and service sectors. Agriculture still accounts for 4 of the country's top exports—rice, canned fish, frozen or chilled shrimp, and rubber—and continues to serve as the foundation of booming manufacturing ventures such as food processing. Processed food such as canned fruits, vegetables, seafoods, and ready-to-eat meals, also enjoy a healthy domestic market, along with sugar and flour.

The agricultural sector has consistently employed about 50 percent of Thailand's 30 million-strong workforce. In 1993, farm population accounted for about 57 percent of the total workforce. If those indirectly engaged in **agribusiness** industries were included, the estimate would be even higher. Economists predicted that the 1 to 4 million people left unemployed by the 1997 financial crisis in the late 1990s would be absorbed by the agricultural sector.

FIELD CROPS. Agricultural production is focused on 7 major crops—namely rice, tapioca, rubber, maize, sugarcane, mung beans, and tobacco leaves—which are grown mostly for export purposes. Fifty percent of the country's cultivated land is devoted to planting rice; Thailand continues to be the world's top exporter of rice, exporting 6.8 million tons of its total production of 23.3 million tons in 1999, worth 7.1 billion baht. Based on Bank of Thailand statistics, exports of rubber amounted to 2 million tons worth 43.9 billion baht, while maize amounted to 80.7 thousand tons worth 528 million baht, according to *Business Monitor International.* Crop production is expected to increase as genetic research on plants improves yields and as cultivated areas are expanded. However, falling global prices and adverse weather conditions are likely to reduce farm incomes.

LIVESTOCK. The second largest component of agriculture is livestock production, which accounted for 1.3 percent of GDP in 1993. The decline in the prices of field crops and the reduced productivity of land have caused farmers to turn to contract farming of broiler chickens, cows, and pigs. A single broiler contract growing project employs about 145 families who earn an equivalent of US$350 monthly, after paying for the bank loans needed to buy broiler houses and equipment. Research to improve egg production and feed conversion has also been successfully undertaken, making Thailand a leading producer and exporter of frozen chicken. The government also helps this sector by facilitating the improvement of beef and dairy production through cross-breeding and artificial insemination using high-grade breeds imported from the United States, Switzerland, Germany, Denmark, and Australia. Thai beef is exported to Singapore and Hong Kong, and the sector is angling to gain entrance to the Japanese market.

FORESTRY. The wood industry relies on the wide variety of hard and softwood available in the country's forests. Among these are tropical evergreens, hill evergreens, mangroves, and other trees which are processed to produce firewood, stick lac, gum benzoin, rattan, and bamboo. Rattan is then manufactured into furniture, while bamboo is used for furniture and paper. Dyes, tanning bark, and medicinal herbs are also harvested. The growth of the output from forestry fell from 2.6 percent in the period between 1967–71 to 0.25 percent in the 1982–86 period due to the massive depletion of the country's forest resources. The devastation is caused mainly by the destructive practice of slash-and-burn agriculture by villagers as well as illegal logging. Uncontrolled logging resulted in the felling of 1.5 percent of the country's total forest acreage every year. After heavy floods in 1988 washed away entire villages, the government banned logging and conducted reforestation efforts. Currently, 23 percent of the country is covered with forests following legislation in the early 1990s which called for the maintenance of a proper percentage of forestland.

FISHING. The country's 3,000-kilometer (1,864-mile) coastline produces an average of over 3 million metric tons of marine products annually, which amounts to about US$2 million. Its fishing industry, which is one of the largest in Asia, exports frozen shrimp, tuna, squid, and cuttlefish. There is also an abundance of freshwater fish in rivers, lakes, and streams as well as flooded paddy fields where farmers purposely raise them. The Fisheries Department also promotes freshwater aquaculture by farmers in large ponds. Forty-five freshwater fishery stations have been set up by the government to promote freshwater aquaculture. In 1999, fishery products accounted for 3.6 percent of total exports. However, its total contribution to GDP has diminished due to the exhaustion of resources in Thailand's coastal waters.

INDUSTRY

The country's industry and agriculture sectors were traditionally intertwined. Today, however, industry has eclipsed agriculture in terms of contribution to GDP, contributing 39 percent in 1997. The rapid growth of this sector can be attributed to free market forces, limited government assistance, and the private sector's quick response to shifting market demands. However, the Asian financial crisis from 1997 to 1998 heavily impacted industries and caused the closure of 8,000 businesses. The increasing cost of labor has also led to a departure from labor-intensive ventures. To date, only the manufacturing industry contributes substantially to national income, particularly the 4 sub-sectors of food processing, automobiles, electronics, and petrochemicals.

The initial move into industrialization in the 1960s was characterized by import substitution, which mainly involved the processing of its bountiful agricultural produce. In 1972, a new Industrial Promotion Act signaled the shift in government policy to an export-oriented economy. This new emphasis began the rapid diversification of the industry sector which saw the rise of several industries, including petrochemicals, textiles, transportation equipment, electronics, iron and steel, and minerals.

The manufacturing sector constitutes Thailand's main industry, producing a wide variety of goods such as textiles and garments, plastics, footwear, electronics, integrated circuits, computers and components, automobiles and parts, and cement. Manufacturing facilities are mostly located in Bangkok and on the Eastern Seaboard, which was launched in 1977 as the long-term site for large-scale small, medium, and heavy industries. In 1993, the manufacturing sector employed 10 percent of the entire **labor force**. By 1998, however, the sector already employed approximately 20 percent of the Thai workforce, who are among the highest paid workers in the country along with those working in the service industry, according to the *Ministry of Foreign Affairs Handbook.*

The manufacturing sector expanded its contribution to GDP from 16 percent in 1960 to 37 percent in 1993 to 39 percent in 1997. Given that manufactured goods are produced largely for export purposes, its share of export earnings grew steadily from 32 percent in 1980 to 74.7 percent in 1990 to 84.5 percent in 1999. Presently, its top export markets are the United States, Japan, the European Union, Singapore, Malaysia, Hong Kong, Taiwan, and China, with the United States and Japan jointly absorbing 36 percent of the country's exports.

FOOD PROCESSING. Canned foods constitute the main export earner of this sector, and Thailand is the world's leading exporter of canned pineapple and tuna. Its export growth rate increased by 6.8 percent between 1998 and 1999. This sector has shifted from basic refining to **value-adding** (increasing the value of a good in the process of production), hence, the biggest growth segments include ready-to-eat meals like canned traditional Thai dishes, processed seafood, and snacks. Though still largely patronized by the domestic market, 2 rice dishes—namely *khaolam*, a rice dessert baked in bamboo trunks, and *krayasart*, a sticky rice dessert—are already being sold in China and Japan. Production of ready-to-eat halal food is another avenue to be explored, to tap the regional Islamic market.

The government has thrown its support behind agro-processing by promoting the establishment of industrial estates that are located near prime sources of raw material. Several multinational companies have also established their presence in the country, namely the Heineken and Carlsberg breweries; Nestle, whose 8 plants are producing a wide range of products from ice cream to mineral water; and Kellogg, which uses local rice as raw material for its ready-to-eat cereals.

MOTOR INDUSTRIES AND AUTOMOBILE ASSEMBLY. The country is currently the regional center for vehicle assembly and the manufacturing of motor parts, and is the second leading manufacturer of pick-up trucks in addition to the long-established motorcycle industry. Between 1991 and 1996, vehicle assembly peaked at 560,000 per year, in addition to 1.5 million units of motorcycles. The financial crisis debilitated this sector in 1997 and 1998, but it managed to rebound and produced 327,233 units of vehicles following a sharp increase in export orders in 1999, along with 725,425 units of motorcycles. Shipments in motor vehicles and parts in 1999 amounted to US$1.6 billion. Among the auto companies who have established factories in the Eastern Seaboard are Ford, GM, Mazda, Honda, and Toyota.

ELECTRONICS. This sub-sector produces a wide range of products from low-tech **consumer goods**, such as TV tubes and computer monitors, to advanced microchips. In 1999, total electronic exports amounted to US$21.4 billion. The government has encouraged its growth by offering official investment incentives to foreign investors. Among the multinational corporations that have been attracted by these incentives are Fujitsu, Seagate, IBM, Sony, and Matsushita Electronics, which produces the National Panasonic brand. However, the sector is undermined by lack of skilled scientific and professional workers and heavy reliance on foreign technology.

PETROCHEMICALS. Natural gas discovered in the Gulf of Thailand is being tapped for the raw materials upon which to develop a globally competitive petrochemical industry. This sub-sector was greatly affected by the financial crisis due to the massive debts that it accumulated during its development in the early 1990s. However, its performance is picking up with an increase of 2.1 percent in output in 1999, due to higher export demands. Foreign investment is expected to fuel its resurgence with Germany's Phenolchemie, Chevron, Bayer, and Montell pumping in fresh investments.

SERVICES

The services sector is Thailand's fastest growing sector, largely fueled by the boom in tourism. In 1997, services accounted for over 49 percent of GDP and employed over 4.1 million, or 31 percent of, Thai workers.

TOURISM. The beauty of the country attracts millions of tourists annually. Thailand boasts beautiful beaches, cultural attractions such as Buddhist temples, bountiful food, affordable high-quality goods such as textiles, and hospitable people. Beckoned by these attractions, tourists have steadily generated income for the country since 1982, with tourism posting a growth rate of 16 percent per year. In 1994, 6.16 million tourists visited Thailand. In 1998, 7.76 million tourists spent nearly US$8 billion. This was exceeded by the 1999 figure, which posted the arrival of 8.5 million tourists. In 1992, tourism employed 1,693,005 workers (5.1 percent of the total labor force), with 923,822 employed directly and 769,183 employed indirectly. The boom in tourism spurred the growth of related service industries which generated employment. Of the total number of workers in the tourism industry, 37 percent were hired by hotels, 26 percent by restaurants and food shops, 11 percent by leisure and entertainment, and 26 percent by the souvenir industry, travel agencies, and other related enterprises. In recognition of the importance of this industry, the Tourism Authority of Thailand works closely with other agencies to develop tourism resources efficiently by promoting investment in tourist-related facilities.

BUSINESS SERVICES. The continuous expansion of the Thai economy led to the increase in the need for business services including legal, advertising, employment, and general management. In 1997, legal and accounting firms reported the highest revenue while advertising bore the brunt of the financial crisis. The demand for financial restructuring services including merger, acquisitions, and debt collection remained high in 1998, which led to an increase in the sector's employment. To illustrate, one accounting company expanded its debt restructuring division from 2 to 20 people in 1997. Top international consulting firms have offices in Thailand, including Baker & McKenzie and Tilleke & Gibbins for law; Andersen Consulting and Boston Consulting Group for management consulting; Arthur Andersen and Price Waterhouse for accounting; and J. Walter Thompson and AC Neilsen for advertising and media.

RETAIL. The **retail** sector is composed of department stores, hypermarkets, supermarkets, and convenience stores, most of which are local companies. Among the international retailer stores are Carrefour, 7-Eleven, Marks & Spencer, and Makro.

FOOD. As of 1999, Thailand had 639 international restaurants and 328 local restaurants, and about 15,000 fast food, mid-level family style restaurants, coffee shops, noodle shops, specialty food shops, and delivery shops to fuel the food services sector. It also had 2,350 hotels, 364 resorts, and 784 bungalows which account for higher food sales than restaurants. In 1998, total food sales amounted to US$5.385 million. In 1992, restaurants and food shops employed approximately 440,000 workers. Even though the dollar value of food service sales decreased due to the **devaluation** of the baht during the 1997 Asian financial crisis, the sector grew by 7 percent based on actual sales.

FINANCIAL SERVICES. Thailand has 34 commercial banks, of which 13 are domestic and 21 are foreign. Among the foreign banks are Bank of America, Chase Manhattan, and Citibank. Leading local banks include Krung Thai Bank, with 646 local branches and 10 overseas branches; Bangkok Bank PCL, with 526 local branches and 21 overseas branches; and Thai Farmers Bank, with 497 local branches and 12 overseas branches. As a result of the financial crisis, some local banks have been taken over by the government and are in the process of reorganization and eventual **privatization**. The public financial sector includes banks geared for specific purposes including 1) the Government Savings Bank for small savings deposits; 2) the Bank for Agriculture and Agricultural Cooperatives for farm credit; 3) the Government Housing Bank for middle- and low-income housing mortgages; 4) the Industrial Finance Corporation of Thailand for industrial development projects; and 5) the Export Import bank for importers and exporters. Other financial services include finance companies, mortgage lenders, life and non-life insurance companies, and financial cooperatives.

INTERNATIONAL TRADE

Thailand has a long history of international trade. Beginning in the 15th to 18th centuries, during the reign of the Ayutthaya monarchy, foreign merchants who lived near the kingdom's capital conducted trade with foreigners. The country's first significant trade treaty was the Bowring Treaty in 1855 with Britain. Shortly after that, it also signed treaties with 14 other countries including the United States, France, Russia, Sweden, Spain, and Japan.

Trade (expressed in billions of US$): Thailand

	Exports	Imports
1975	2.208	3.280
1980	6.505	9.214
1985	7.121	9.242
1990	23.070	33.379
1995	56.439	70.776
1998	54.456	42.971

SOURCE: International Monetary Fund. *International Financial Statistics Yearbook 1999.*

Today, the United States, Japan, and the European Union continue to be its top trading partners, absorbing 52.6 percent of all exports in 1999 and supplying 48.8 percent of total imports in the same period. Its other partners are Hong Kong, China, and the Association of South-East Asian Nations (ASEAN) countries, the most significant of which are Singapore and Malaysia. Other countries apart from those mentioned accounted for 18.4 percent of exports and 21.6 percent of imports in the same period.

Thailand's major exports are rice, tapioca products, cane sugar and molasses, and rubber for agriculture; chemicals, polymers, and plastics for the manufacturing industry; and gypsum, natural gas, and feldspar for the mining industry. Bank of Thailand statistics as reflected in the Asian Economic Survey of 2000 identified the country's major export products as machine parts, circuits, frozen shrimp, prawns, sundry items, computer parts, garments, vehicle parts, and plastic products. On the other hand, its major imports are petroleum, integrated circuit parts, and chemicals.

The **balance of trade** was consistently negative until 1998, which means that the value of the country's imports was bigger than the value of its exports. The discrepancy was minimal in 1970, with import value exceeding export value by only US$541 million. In 1975, imports exceeded exports by US$1.072 billion, which doubled in 1980 to US$2.709 billion. In 1985, imports still exceeded exports by US$2.21 billion, which had quadrupled by 1990 to US$10.309 billion. In 1995, the balance still stood in favor of imports by US$14.337 billion. In a considerable reversal, imports in 1997 exceeded exports by US$5.319 billion but the following year, exports exceeded imports by US$11.485 billion.

Despite the uneven balance of trade, the Thai economy continued to grow by an average of 6.8 percent in the 1970s, 7.5 percent in the 1980s, and 8 percent in the early 1990s before the Asian financial crisis. This growth can be attributed to 2 factors, namely the boom of the tourism industry and the inflow of foreign direct investment. According to *International Historical Statistics,* in 1970, the services sector contributed 44.1 percent of GDP, which increased in 1980 to 49.7 percent. Though this contribution fell to 46.9 percent in 1999, it is safe to say that the dollar earnings from the tourism industry generated a substantial amount, enough to offset the trade imbalance.

Foreign direct investment (FDI) is another major factor in the growth of the economy since the mid-1980s. In 1988, FDI infused US$1.25 billion into the economy, partly explaining the 7.5 percent growth despite a US$4.332 billion discrepancy in balance of trade in favor of imports. Foreign direct investment doubled to US$2.5 billion in 1990.

Thailand is a member of several international trade organizations including the ASEAN Free Trade Area (AFTA), the Asia Pacific Economic Cooperation (APEC), and the World Trade Organization (WTO).

MONEY

The Thai economy grew with the formulation of the first 5-year National Economic Development Plan in 1958. During the 1960s, the country grew by an average of 8 percent annually. In the 1970s the fluctuation of commodity prices, a rise in interest rates, and the 150 percent increase in world oil prices slowed the economy, although it continued to grow at the rate of 6.8 percent annually. Political instabilit—including student uprisings in 1973, 2 military coups, and increased **communist** insurgency—hindered the government in its adjustment of economic plans and structures to meet the challenges of the next decade. Surprisingly however, the economy continued to perform well in the 1980s with a 7.5 percent GNP growth rate. The year 1986 is significant because of the fall of the excess value of imports over exports to a mere US$301 million compared to the previous year's deficit of US$2.121 billion, indicating a substantial growth of the value of Thailand's exports. This can be attributed to economic adjustments launched by the government.

The first half of the 1990s was marked by similar growth until the Asian financial crisis hit the region. In 1996, **real GDP** growth rate fell sharply from 8.8 percent in 1995 to 5.2 percent and during the period of the crisis between 1997 and 1998, real GDP growth dropped to –0.43 percent and –10.18 percent, respectively, according to the *International Financial Statistics Yearbook.* The government spent much of the country's foreign reserves to stabilize the value of the baht, causing the further devaluation of the currency. The crisis led to a temporary increase in poverty levels in the city and unemployment due to massive lay-offs specifically in the construction and service industries. These unemployed city-dwellers went back to rural areas hoping to find employment, which led to a rise in poverty levels in the south, central, and northeast regions. Thailand's recession also started a domino effect that led to the fall of the economies of its South East Asian neighbors.

There has been a remarkable resurgence in the economy since then, fueled by the US$17.2 billion assistance package given by the World Bank, reforms in the financial sector, and increased foreign investment. For the first time since 1969, the economy posted a positive balance of trade with the value of exports exceeding imports by US$11.485 billion in 1999, according to the *International Financial Statistics Yearbook.*

The average **exchange rate** of the Thai baht from 1984 to 1997 was B25 to US$1. However, the baht was devalued by the administration of Prime Minister Prem Tinsulanonda by 8.7 percent in 1981, and again in November 1984 by 14.9 percent, as part of its austerity measures. This devaluation led to the decline in the cost of production, which resulted in increased revenue from exports.

With the onset of the financial crisis, the baht fell from its B25 to US$1 average to B31.36 to US$1 in 1997, and to an all-time low of B41.36 in 1998. The infusion of direct foreign investment in 1998 led to the recovery of the economy and the increase in the value of the baht to B37.81 against the dollar in 1999, which went even higher to B37.349 in January 2000. By 12 October 2000, however, the baht had devalued once more to a 27-month low of B43.27, which threatened to increase **inflation**. The depreciation was caused by external factors, including weak regional currencies such as the Philippine peso and the Indonesian rupiah, the strong showing of the dollar compared to currencies such as the Euro, and increase in world oil prices which used up the country's surpluses. Internal factors that were identified include weak economic policies and practices and the country's unstable political situation.

The Stock Exchange of Thailand (SET) was established through the passage of the SET Act in May 1974, and began operation on 30 April 1975. The second revision of the SET Act in 1992 produced the Securities and Exchange Act (SEA) which established a Securities and Exchange Commission to serve as the only supervisor of the securities business.

Exchange rates: Thailand

baht (B) per US$1	
Jan 2001	43.078
2000	40.112
1999	37.814
1998	41.359
1997	31.364
1996	25.343

SOURCE: CIA *World Factbook 2001* [ONLINE].

POVERTY AND WEALTH

In Thailand, the incidence of poverty or wealth is dependent on a person's occupation, location of residence or work, and level of educational attainment. From the 1970s until the early 1990s the poor were mostly agricultural workers in the rural areas, particularly in the

GDP per Capita (US$)

Country	1975	1980	1985	1990	1998
Thailand	863	1,121	1,335	2,006	2,593
United States	19,364	21,529	23,200	25,363	29,683
China	138	168	261	349	727
Vietnam	N/A	N/A	183	206	331

SOURCE: United Nations. *Human Development Report 2000; Trends in human development and per capita income.*

Distribution of Income or Consumption by Percentage Share: Thailand

Lowest 10%	2.8
Lowest 20%	6.4
Second 20%	9.8
Third 20%	14.2
Fourth 20%	21.2
Highest 20%	48.4
Highest 10%	32.4

Survey year: 1998

Note: This information refers to expenditure shares by percentiles of the population and is ranked by per capita expenditure.

SOURCE: *2000 World Development Indicators* [CD-ROM].

north, northeast, or southern regions, whose highest level of education was 6 years of primary schooling. Meanwhile, those working in the manufacturing or service sectors in the major cities or in the central region—specifically in the Bangkok metropolitan region—who completed at least 12 years of formal education, were more likely to be economically well-off. Due to the concentration of economic activities in the capital, such as construction of physical infrastructure and job creation, the regional disparities in income and wealth slowly began to widen. As Thailand slowly shifted from an agrarian economy to an industrialized economy, economic resources were shifted to the industrial sector and huge demand for factory workers created huge differences in wage rates between farmers and factory workers. As the contribution of the agricultural sector to the economy decreased so did the demand for farm workers. In the latter years of the 1980s, 80 percent of the people living below the poverty line worked in the agricultural sector.

Poverty in Thailand is not so much a problem of an increasing number of families being unable to provide for their most basic needs, as it is a problem of the huge difference in income between the upper 30 percent and the rest of the population. Thailand's impressive economic growth in the 1980s and 1990s has improved overall living conditions, but the benefits of this national affluence have not been distributed equitably. Those belonging to the lower 30 percent of the population are merely surviving while the upper 30 percent are enjoying the fruits of the country's affluence with brand new houses and cars, overseas education for their children, and increased savings for emergencies. Despite the fact that more and more Thai families are climbing out of the poverty pit, their earning capacity remains low compared to that of the upper 30 percent.

The government has addressed the increasing incidence of poverty in the different national development plans that are formulated every 5 years. From the second to the seventh National Economic Development Plan, the government formulated different strategies in order to achieve a fairer distribution of income and social services, to create more employment opportunities in the rural areas, to assist parents in their children's education, and to provide credit facilities for small-time business ventures.

Before the Asian financial crisis hit Thailand in 1997, government efforts to alleviate poverty were slowly gaining ground with poverty levels falling from 33 percent in 1988 to 11.4 percent in 1996, according to the World Bank. However, the income distribution remained inequitable with the top 20 percent earning 12.2 times more than the bottom 20 percent in 1988. The disparity

Household Consumption in PPP Terms

Country	All food	Clothing and footwear	Fuel and power[a]	Health care[b]	Education[b]	Transport & Communications	Other
Thailand	23	8	5	3	13	11	37
United States	13	9	9	4	6	8	51
China	N/A	N/A	N/A	N/A	N/A	N/A	N/A
Vietnam	49	7	15	4	18	6	2

Data represent percentage of consumption in PPP terms.

[a]Excludes energy used for transport.

[b]Includes government and private expenditures.

SOURCE: World Bank. *World Development Indicators 2000.*

worsened further in 1993 with the top 20 percent earning 15.8 times more than the lowest 20 percent of the population. Average income in the most impoverished region in the northeast was 11.9 times lower compared to Bangkok in 1994. Consequently, rural workers tried to find work in the urban areas, especially in the Bangkok metropolitan area, causing the proliferation of slum areas in the urban cities.

In July 1997, as the Asian financial crisis ravaged the Thai economy, hundreds of workers in the construction and service industries in Bangkok were laid off. These newly unemployed workers moved back to the rural areas to find work in the agricultural sector which was performing strongly in those times. This migration caused the incidence of poverty to increase in the agricultural regions because not all of the unemployed could be absorbed in the agricultural sector. The northeast region experienced the largest increase in poverty during this period, rising from 19.4 percent in 1996 to 30.8 percent in 1999. Overall poverty incidence in Thailand rose from 11.4 percent in 1996 to 13 percent in 1998 as an additional 1.1 million people fell below the poverty line.

Poverty in Thailand can be attributed to several factors. First is the concentration of economic activities in Bangkok and a number of other urban areas. Investment, goods and services, government programs, and well-paying jobs are still largely concentrated in the capital and nearby urban areas despite government efforts to decentralize economic development. The concentration of resources and investment in Bangkok is evidenced by the fact that it contributes over 50 percent of the country's GDP despite hosting only about 10 percent of the population. In contrast, other regions, especially rural areas, suffer from inadequate investment and employment opportunities.

Another reason stems from the failure of the Thai government to provide social safety nets amid the country's rapid growth and industrialization. The government over-prioritized the implementation of financial and industrial reforms and neglected to formulate and implement a comprehensive social service program to protect the most unprepared sectors from the ill effects of rapid industrialization. Moreover, experts have expressed that, had Thai authorities given the same attention to the social sector, it might have even surpassed its current development and would have ensured its future development with a steady source of well-educated and multi-skilled labor as it shifts to technologically sophisticated industries.

A third problem is the weak educational system in the country. Inferior and inadequate education is the root of the growing income gap between city dwellers and villagers. As poverty in the rural areas worsened, many rural folk could not afford to send their children beyond the 6 years of compulsory schooling, making them unqualified for the higher paying jobs in the manufacturing and service sectors. As a consequence, these families were trapped in the vicious cycle of poverty where living conditions of the succeeding generations do not improve due to lack of education.

Another problem is the failure of the government to implement agricultural land reform policies. This failure has resulted in insecure land ownership and increasing tenancy, or production on rented land. As the population increased, people in the rural areas encroached into the forest areas to settle and plant. After several years of residence in these areas, they claim illegal ownership of the land which results in periodic conflicts with government authorities. Due to the government's refusal to issue land titles to legalize the ownership of the land to the farmers who are tilling it, rural workers lack the proper legal documents to secure agricultural support such as credit facilities and technical support and have no security of ownership over the land. This leads to low productivity from the land. Another problem is the increase in the number of farm tenants who till other peoples' land because they either have no land of their own or because they had to sell their own land to pay off accumulated debts.

In 2000, the World Bank reported that Thailand has not fully recovered from its economic recession in 1997. The most recent data revealed that the number of poor increased from 11.4 percent in 1996 to 15.9 percent in 1999. Just like in the past, Bangkok remains affluent while other regions suffer. According to the World Bank's country report for 2000, poverty incidence in 1999 increased from 5.8 percent to 8.8 percent at the outskirts of the urban areas and 14.9 percent to 21.5 percent in the rural areas. At the same time, Thailand continues to suffer from unequal income distribution with the richest 30 percent accounting for some 80 percent of the aggregate national income while the other 70 percent account for roughly 20 percent of the aggregate national income.

According to the World Bank, during the 1990s the Thai government became more aggressive in addressing the root problems of poverty and the ever-widening income disparity. In 1993, the Ministry of Interior launched the Poverty Alleviation project which provides interest-free loans to poor rural households who want to engage in micro-enterprise. Meanwhile, the Ministry of Education is implementing the Educational Loans Program, which provides loans to students from low-income households to encourage them to continue their studies beyond the 6 years of compulsory schooling. The Thai government has likewise launched programs to create jobs in the rural areas by hiring villagers for the construction of rural infrastructure, such as in the case of the Tambon Development Program.

WORKING CONDITIONS

In 1999, more than 50 percent of the 362,683 establishments in Thailand were located in Bangkok and nearby provinces. Based on 1999 labor statistics, Thailand's total labor force was 8,134,644, with males (4,253,327) edging out females (3,881,317). About 4.4 million are working in the **informal sector**—which involves domestic work, traditional handicraft production, and manufacturing of export goods—and small-scale enterprises with less than 10 workers.

During the 1997 recession, it was estimated that about 8,000 businesses closed down while those that continued to operate had to lay off staff, reduce wages, and cut bonuses in order to stay afloat. Women were the first to be laid off in most of the industries except in printing and advertising, retail and wholesale, and furniture and wood products.

The unemployment rate fluctuated from 2.2 percent in February 1997 to 4.6 percent in February 1998 and 5.2 percent in February 1999 before dropping to 4.3 percent in February 2000. In the first 2 quarters of 1999, the total number of unemployed persons peaked at about 1.7 million. The recession has caused **real wages** to fall, with agriculture being the hardest hit sector. Between August 1997 and August 1999, overall real wages fell by 6.1 percent, with real wages falling by 15 percent in agriculture, 8 percent in manufacturing, and 7 percent in construction.

LABOR UNIONS AND ISSUES. In 1999, Thailand had a total of 1,087 private enterprise labor unions, 44 state enterprise labor unions, 19 labor union federations, 8 labor union councils, 226 employer associations, 3 employer association federations, and 10 employer councils, according to the Department of Labor Protection and Welfare. Membership in these voluntary organizations may vary from 250 to 8,000 workers. In specific industries such as textile, doll, and artificial flower making, it can be expected that the majority of the union members will be female. Female union leaders, however, are a rarity in Thailand.

One of the effects of the recession in 1997 was a marked increase in labor disputes compared to figures in the past 17 years. Approximately 80 percent of these cases involved the collection of severance pay.

Different government agencies, led by the Ministry of Labor and Social Welfare, ensure that working conditions, especially in the factories, conform to legally-established standards. However, despite periodic inspections, working conditions in the factories still need improvement. One study reports that over 20,000 Thai workers suffer occupational afflictions every year. In 1993, the Committee for Workers' Health and Safety was established after a tragic blaze that killed 188 Kader workers.

In general, Thai workers complain about low pay, excessive working hours, and inadequate medical benefits. The textile industry has been specifically cited in many studies as having some of the most dismal working conditions characterized by deafening noise, poor lighting, inadequate medical facilities, and improper ventilation. Each year about 30 percent of the industry's female workers suffer from byssinosis or "cotton sickness" from cotton dust particles. Meanwhile, women in other industries likewise suffer from other occupational hazards.

Based on 1998 labor statistics, of the total 186,498 cases covered by the workers' compensation fund, 67.8 percent involved temporary disability requiring less than 3 days of leave, 29.7 percent involved temporary disability requiring more than 3 days of leave, 2 percent involved permanent partial disability, while 0.4 percent involved death.

Thailand's 1997 constitution mandates equal rights and protection for men and women. However, the results of various surveys reveal that there is still some discrimination against Thai women in terms of professional advancement and wages. Most employers in the private sector hire women only when there is a difference in wage rates. Commonly, firms would rather not hire women or promote them to more important jobs because of traditional attitudes against women working outside the home. Likewise, women are not prioritized for skills training and upgrading since it is unlikely that they will be promoted to higher positions anyway. Women are commonly employed in labor-intensive industries, service and entertainment jobs, and the informal sector.

One of the negative consequences of Thailand's tourism industry is the prostitution of its women and children, especially those who have no formal schooling or only finished the first 6 years of schooling. The law prohibits women under 18 from working in nightclubs, dance halls, schools for dancing, bath and massage houses, and hotels, however, there are not enough government personnel to conduct inspections.

Thailand has been severely criticized by the international community for the proliferation of child domestic workers in its factories and brothels, or houses of prostitution. Child labor involves not only Thai children but also children of migrant workers of neighboring countries. Determining the exact number of child laborers in Thailand is difficult since parents or companies do not want to cooperate with authorities for fear of prosecution or loss of income. Different agencies have conflicting estimates of number of prostituted children in Thailand. The estimates range from 40,000 (1997) by the Thai government, to 200,000 (1997) by the international organization End Child Prostitution, and 400,000 (1998) by the BBC News. Based on the provisions of the Labor Protection Act (1998), persons between the ages of 15 to 18 can only work in non-hazardous jobs and must secure permission from the Department of Labor. Moreover, they cannot work at night or during holidays.

In the mid-1990s, only 40 percent of the Thai labor force had completed secondary or post-secondary education. Enrollment in secondary education is slowly increasing, although it is still low compared to other countries in the region. The gross enrollment ratio of formal secondary education increased from 64.8 percent in 1997 to 70.6 percent in 1999. The New Education Act of 1999, as provided for in the 1997 constitution, has mandated the extension of compulsory schooling to 9 years from the current term of 6 years and the implementation of a 12-year free education program by 2004. Moreover, the act has reduced the power of the central ministry in favor of new school districts within the next 3 years.

In its early years of development, Thailand placed too much priority on developing the primary level of education to the detriment of the quality of secondary and tertiary education. As a consequence, Thailand lagged behind other countries in terms of research and development in science and technology, which meant that its workforce was ill-equipped to handle the emerging opportunities in high technology industries. As a result, the companies that were engaged in these industries chose to set up the center of their operations in other Asian countries. It was only after the 1997 financial crisis that Thailand started paying attention to the improvement of its educational system.

Over the years, the Thai government has formulated different strategies to improve the skill level of its workforce (World Bank, 2000). Among these programs are the Vocational Training Promotion Act (1994), the Training Tax Exemption Decree (1995), and the Skills Development Fund (1997), which grants low-interest short-term loans for approved training courses that would provide skills certification.

COUNTRY HISTORY AND ECONOMIC DEVELOPMENT

1300s TO 1500s. Thailand's very first kingdom, Sukhothai, is established. It is remembered for its contribution to Thailand's art, architecture, and politics.

1378. King Borommaracha I of Ayutthaya conquers Sukhothai's frontier city of Chakangrao. The Kingdom of Ayutthaya becomes the dominant power in the Chao Phraya Basin, site of the present capital, Bangkok. This period, which ends in 1767, marks Thailand's earliest achievements in the area of international trade.

1767–82. General Phraya Taksin, former governor of Tak, defeats the Burmese invaders that destroyed the Ayutthaya kingdom and establishes his kingdom at Thon Buri, across the river from what is presently Bangkok.

1782–1809. Rama I, ancestor of the present monarch, establishes Bangkok as the capital of Thailand and rebuilds the Thai state. Some of Thailand's greatest structures are built during King Rama I's reign, including the Grand Palace and the Temple of the Emerald Buddha.

1821–68. The Thai Kingdom faces the challenge of avoiding Western imperialism during the consecutive reigns of the monarchs Rama II and his 2 sons, Rama III and Rama IV. Under the reign of King Rama IV, Thailand signs a significant trade treaty with Britain in 1855 called the Bowring Treaty which paves the way for greater Thai presence in the world market.

1868–1910. Under King Chulalongkorn's reign, Thailand's communication system is modernized with the introduction of post and telegraph services. Mass transportation is also introduced with the construction of a railway network. Under his reign, a more centralized and bureaucratic political structure is established, the slave system is abolished, and Thailand becomes more outward looking.

1910–32. The reigns of Rama VI and VIII are marked by their contributions to Thailand's educational system. In 1917, Thailand's first university, Chulalongkorn University, is founded. In 1921, Rama VI issues a law on compulsory primary education. Upon his brother's death, Rama VIII accedes the throne. He works on establishing Thailand in the international community.

1932. Thailand becomes a constitutional monarchy after a bloodless coup d'etat on 24 June. A formal constitution is promulgated and a National Assembly is established with the monarch as Head of State. In the same year, the first formal comprehensive education plan is implemented.

1942. The Bank of Thailand Act establishes the country's central bank. The Bank of Thailand holds the main accounts of the Thai government including those of government enterprises.

1946. On 9 June, King Bhumibol Adulyadej ascends to the throne. In the same year, Thailand becomes a member of the United Nations.

1949. Thailand becomes a member of the World Bank.

1955. King Bhumibol Adulyadej becomes the first Thai ruler to travel to the poorest provinces of Thailand, in the northeast region, to check for himself the living conditions of the people. This begins the implementation of more than a thousand social projects.

1957. The premiership transfers from Field Marshal Pibul to Field Marshal Sarit Thanarat. The policies of his administration are focused on economic development and national security. Under his administration, the first national economic development plan is formulated.

1959. Thailand's Board of Investment is established. Its main tasks are to promote investment of both foreign and local capital in the private sector.

1962. The automobile industry is established as part of the government's import substitution policy.

1967. Through the primary initiative of Thailand, the Association of South-East Asian Nations (ASEAN) is established in accordance with the Bangkok Declaration.

1972. In December, Field Marshall Thanom Kittikachorn announces a new interim constitution that provides for a totally appointed legislative assembly, two-thirds of the members of which would be drawn from the military and police.

1973. In May and June, students and workers rally in the streets to demand a more democratic constitution and genuine parliamentary elections. On 14 October the military government of Field Marshal Thanom Kittikachorn and Field Marshal Prapass Charusathien is overthrown by student-led mass demonstrations which culminate in shoot-outs with almost 100 people killed.

1974. The Stock Exchange of Thailand is established and placed under the supervision of the Ministry of Finance and the Bank of Thailand.

1975. The pullout of 27,000 United States military personnel based in Thailand as part of the Vietnam War effort begins in March and is completed in mid-1976.

1976. A bloody coup d'etat is staged at the Thammasat University on 6 October.

1977. Another violent coup d'etat brings to an end the 1-year civilian regime of Thanin Kraivichien. General Kriengsak Chamanand becomes the prime minister. Under his administration, Thailand achieves some kind of political stability, thereby attracting foreign investors who establish businesses in the country.

1978. A new constitution is promulgated in December.

1980. In February, the government's decision to increase the prices of oil, gas, and electricity provokes opposition from elected politicians and demonstrations by students and workers, reminiscent of the 1973 demonstrations. As opposition grows, Prime Minister Kriangsak resigns and is replaced in March by General Prem Tinsulanonda.

1984. The Thai baht is devalued after much pressure from the International Monetary Fund and as part of the government's austerity measures.

1987. The manufacturing sector surpasses the performance of the agricultural sector in exports by a wide margin, marking the beginning of Thailand's industry-led economic development.

1989. Thailand becomes a founding member of the Asia Pacific Economic Cooperation (APEC).

1991. In February, a coup d'etat establishes yet another military government led by General Suchinda Kraprayoon.

1992. The Office of the Securities and Exchange Commission is established to closely monitor and supervise the operations of Thailand's stock exchange.

1995. Thailand joins the World Trade Organization as one of its founding members.

1997. A financial crisis hits the East Asian region, causing the Thai economy to nosedive with GDP growth falling to –0.14 percent from the previous year's 5.52 percent.

1998. Thailand's economy makes an impressive recovery. For the first time, the country registers a positive trade balance caused by an influx of foreign direct investment.

2000. National elections are conducted and culminate in the election of Thaksin Shinawatra, a successful Thai businessman and leader of the Thai Rak Thai Party.

FUTURE TRENDS

The success of the country's economic programs rely on the effective implementation of reforms that the government is presently putting in place after the financial crisis revealed the weaknesses and gaps in Thailand's economy. The Thai economy is poised for greater involvement in heavy industries, including automobile assembly, petrochemicals, electronics, and a more diversified food processing sector focused on value-added products such as ready-to-eat meals and canned foods. The economy has rebounded from the Asian financial crisis of 1997–98, although the World Bank believes that it has yet to fully recover. Challenges facing the economy include weak infrastructure, labor skills that do not match the needs of an increasingly industrialized economy, and the need to re-organize the financial sector to ensure that loans are paid in order to avoid a crisis similar to that of 1997.

Thailand has greatly benefitted from the US$17.2 billion World Bank assistance package in terms of recovering from the crisis. However, due credit must also be given to the strong inflow of foreign direct investment and the robust performance of the tourism industry that enabled the economy to rebound and pose the first positive balance of trade since the 1960s.

Efforts at decentralizing political power to local governments and communities must be stepped up in order to ensure that the rest of the country progresses along with Bangkok. Another important factor is the development of physical infrastructure in the rest of the country to promote the growth of rural communities and increase their contribution to Thailand's economic development. To achieve this, the government's proposed strategy to actively partner with non-government organizations in assisting rural communities must be implemented effectively since using this approach would also ease the disparity in income among the regions and within the different economic classes. Furthermore, the government must actively pursue the stamping out of corruption in order to bring about an even higher rate of economic growth.

Among the other concerns that government must address in the years ahead is the pending maturation of HIV-infected citizens into full-blown AIDS carriers. As of 1999, 700,000 Thai people are infected with HIV. The World Bank predicted that in the year 2000, 55,000 Thais will have developed AIDS and 29,000 more will have become infected with HIV. This will negatively affect the productivity of the country's labor force since those who are afflicted with the disease are mostly women in their prime productive years.

Thailand's industrialization has taken a toll on its environment, as its resources were depleted of raw materials that were needed to support the growing industries. Having realized the impact of environmental degradation, the government is stepping up efforts to rehabilitate its denuded forests and heavily polluted and over-fished coastal resources. In agriculture, research and technology has produced strains of crops that are high yielding and suitable to rotation which enables the land to recover from the effects of monoculture (the cultivation of a single type of crop). However, the continuous use of pesticides and herbicides still inflict considerable environmental damage.

DEPENDENCIES

Thailand has no territories or colonies.

BIBLIOGRAPHY

Asian Development Bank. *Asian Development Outlook 2000.* New York: Oxford University Press, 2000.

Bank of Thailand. *Inflation Report.* Bangkok, October 2000.

Barlow, Colin. *Institutions and Economic Change in Southeast Asia.* Edward Elgar Publications Inc., 1999.

Bunbongkarn, Suchit. *State of the Nation: Thailand.* Singapore: Institute of Southeast Asian Nations, 1996.

Business Monitor International Ltd. *Thailand 2000.* BMI, 2000.

Chavalpait, Orothai. *Asian Approach to Resource Conservation and Environmental Protection.* Tokyo: Asian Productivity Organization, 2000.

Chew, Victor T. *Southeast Asian Tax Handbook.* International Bureau for Fiscal Documentation, 1996.

Cumming-Bruce, Nick. "Thailand, Asian Economic Survey." *Asian Wall Street Journal.* 23 October 2000.

Dhiravegin, Likhit. *Democracy in Thailand.* Bangkok, 1994.

Harrison, Matthew. *Asia-Pacific Securities Markets.* Hong Kong: Financial Times, 1997.

House, Maurice W. *Thailand Market Development Reports: HRI Food Services Sector Report.* Global Agriculture Information Network, 1999.

International Monetary Fund. *International Financial Statistics Yearbook.* New York: IMF, 1999.

Kingdom of Thailand. *Thailand in the 1990s.* Bangkok: National Identity Board Office of the Prime Minister, 1995.

Komin, Suntaree. "A Social Analysis of the Environmental Problems in Thailand." In *Asia's Environmental Crisis,* edited by Michael C. Howard. Oxford: Westview Press, 1993.

Kulich, Elliot, and Dick Wilson. *Thailand's Turn: Profile of a New Dragon.* London: Westmillan Press, 1992.

National Economic and Social Development Board of Thailand. *Asia-Pacific Economic Compendium.* Global Projects Group, 1996.

Satyasivaraman. "Farmers Back in Business." *Manila Chronicle.* 3 January 1998.

Sri-ngam, Sri. "Thailand." In *Rural Poverty Alleviation in Asia and the Pacific.* Tokyo: Asian Productivity Organization, 1999.

U.S. Central Intelligence Agency. *World Factbook 2000.* <http://www.odci.gov/cia/publications/factbook/index.html>. Accessed August 2001.

World Bank. *Thailand Country Dialogue Monitor.* <http://www.worldbank.org/eap>. Accessed April 2001.

—Maria Cecilia T. Ubarra

TONGA

Kingdom of Tonga
Pule'anga Tonga

CAPITAL: Nuku'alofa.

MONETARY UNIT: Pa'anga (T$ or TOP). There are coins of 1, 2, 5, 20, 50 seniti and 1 and 2 pa'anga, and notes of 1, 2, 5, 20, and 50 pa'anga. One pa'anga equals 100 seniti.

CHIEF EXPORTS: Squash, fish, vanilla beans.

CHIEF IMPORTS: Food, machinery and transport equipment, fuels, chemicals.

GROSS DOMESTIC PRODUCT: US$238 million.

BALANCE OF TRADE: **Exports:** US$8 million (1998 est.). **Imports:** US$69 million (1998 est.).

COUNTRY OVERVIEW

LOCATION AND SIZE. The Tonga archipelago (group of islands) is in the Pacific Ocean about 4,000 kilometers (2,500 miles) southwest of Hawaii and about 1,600 kilometers (1,000 miles) northeast of New Zealand. The country consists of a series of islands, clustered into 3 main groups: Tongatapu, Ha'apai, and Vava'u; these were formerly known as the Friendly Islands. The total land area is 748 square kilometers (289 square miles), about 4 times the size of Washington, D.C. The coastline is 419 kilometers (260 miles). The capital is located on Tongatapu island.

POPULATION. The population of Tonga was estimated at 102,321 in mid-2000, a slight increase over the 1996 census population of 97,784. In 2000 the birth rate stood at 27.2 per 1,000 while the death rate stood at 6.1 per 1,000. With a projected annual population growth rate of 0.6 percent in the decade beginning with 2001, the population is expected to reach 104,100 by 2010. This relatively slow rate of growth is a result of an annual net migration rate of 15.1 per 1,000 population. Much of this migration is to New Zealand, but Tongans have also settled in Australia, the United States, and Europe.

The population is predominantly of Tongan (Polynesian) ethnic origin, although there are small numbers of Europeans and Chinese. Only 32 percent of the population live in urban areas, mainly the capital, Nuku'alofa. The urban growth rate is only slightly higher than the total growth rate, which was estimated at 1.91 percent in 2000. The Tongan population is very young, with nearly 42 percent under 15 years of age. Those between the ages of 15 and 64 make up 54 percent of the population, with the remaining 4 percent 65 years old and over. Various branches of Christianity, including Roman Catholicism, the Tokaikolo Church of Christ, and Free Wesleyan, are among those practiced on Tonga.

OVERVIEW OF ECONOMY

On a chain of small islands in the South Pacific, Tonga's economy relies on several basic elements, including subsistence production (making enough to survive), agricultural exports, the **remittances** (money sent home by former citizens working abroad) of Tongan migrants, and international aid. In the villages of Tonga, there is a great reliance on subsistence production of food and other items. There is no reliable survey of the number of people working in subsistence activities, but if it is assumed that most of the adult population not formally employed are primarily subsistence producers, then about 28,000 are in this category. In 1996, about 29,400 persons were engaged in wage and salary employment, with a further 4,500 listed as unemployed.

Agricultural products and fish have always been the mainstays of the export economy. Tourism is relatively small-scale, employing only about 1,400 people in the mid-1990s, but it showed some growth in the decade up to 1997, with the number of visitors increasing by about 5 percent per year.

The Tongan economy also remains heavily dependent on 2 types of transfers from overseas, which together account for 27 percent of GDP. The private remittances

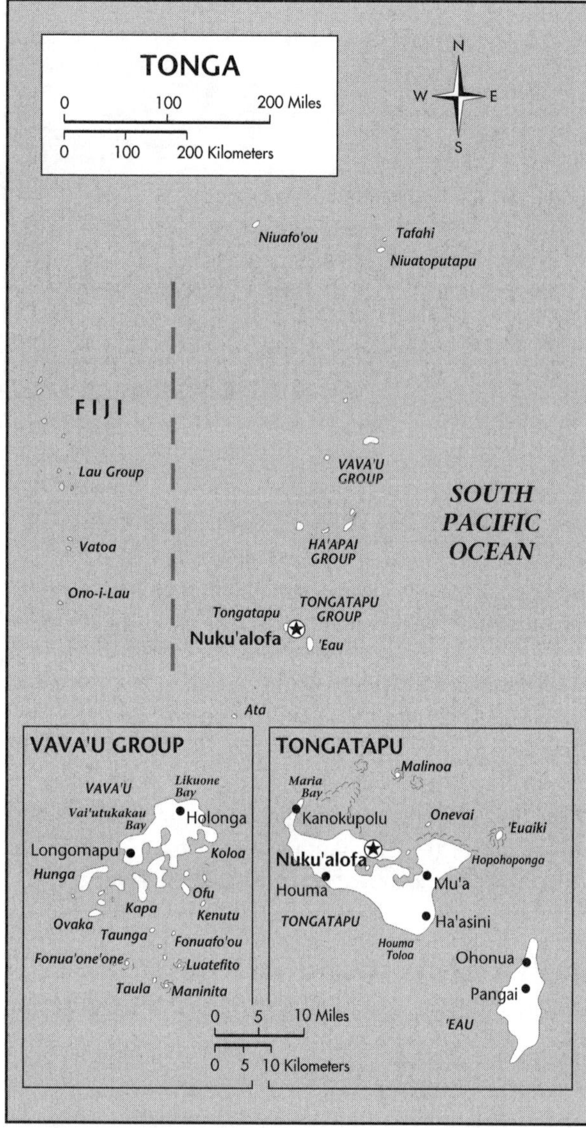

of Tongan migrants in other countries are an important source of income for many families in Tonga. Government expenditure is supported by international aid, mainly originating from Australia, Japan, New Zealand, the Asian Development Bank, and the European Union.

POLITICS, GOVERNMENT, AND TAXATION

Tonga is the only surviving kingdom in the Pacific. Its 1875 constitution is the oldest one in the Pacific islands, and although Tonga was a "protected state" of Great Britain from 1900 to 1970, most Tongans maintain that their country was never a colony. The current system of government is a hereditary constitutional monarchy, with King Taufa'ahau Tupou IV ruling since 1965. Beneath the monarch, there are 33 nobles, who control most of the land in the country. The nobility was established in the constitution of 1875 and is based on inheritance. The prime minister, deputy prime minister, and cabinet are appointed by the king from this group. The **unicameral** (single house) Legislative Assembly (Fale Alea) is made up of 30 seats, 12 of which are reserved for the cabinet appointed by the monarch, 9 are selected by the nobles, and another 9 are elected by popular vote of all citizens over the age of 21 years.

The most important political development in recent years has been the formation of a party called the Human Rights and Democracy Movement (HRDM). In 1994 the HRDM was formed under the leadership of 'Akilisi Pohiva; in the 1999 elections this party won 5 of the 9 "commoner" seats in the Assembly. The HRDM has advocated a broader democratic base and land reforms that would reduce the power of the nobles; for these activities, Pohiva and others have been jailed for short periods for "contempt of Parliament."

About 20 percent of GDP in 1994–95 was raised by taxation, and this accounts for nearly 70 percent of government revenue. Trade taxes are the most important, making up 68 percent of tax revenues, and this is almost equally split between customs **duties** and port and services taxes. Direct and **indirect taxes** each make up a further 14 percent of tax revenue. Personal **income tax** is set at 10 percent and corporate tax is typically around 30 percent. In each case there are many possible exemptions, so these taxes raise less revenue than they might.

INFRASTRUCTURE, POWER, AND COMMUNICATIONS

Transport needs within Tonga are served by roads, shipping services, and air. There are about 680 kilometers (423 miles) of roads, with 184 kilometers (114 miles) paved. These serve most areas within the main islands, with transport provided by private vehicles and bus services. Shipping among the 3 main island groups is provided by the government-owned Shipping Corporation of Polynesia and the private Uata Shipping Lines. These offer regular passenger, cargo, and car ferry services throughout the country.

Royal Tongan Airlines provides international air services from Fua'amotu Airport, the only of the country's 5 airports that has a paved runway. It also links the 3 island groups with regular domestic flights.

Parts of Tonga's telecommunications network are old. Domestic phone services link most of the country via the government-owned Tonga Telecommunications Commission, but there has been little upgrading since the 1950s. International communications via satellite are provided by Cable and Wireless Limited. Electricity is widespread and is generated completely by imported fuels. Tonga had 1 Internet service provider as of 1999.

Communications

Country	Telephones[a]	Telephones, Mobile/Cellular[a]	Radio Stations[b]	Radios[a]	TV Stations[a]	Televisions[a]	Internet Service Providers[c]	Internet Users[c]
Tonga	8,000 (1996)	302 (1996)	AM 1; FM 2; shortwave 1 (2001)	61,000	1 (2001)	2,000	2	1,000
United States	194 M	69.209 M (1998)	AM 4,762; FM 5,542; shortwave 18	575 M	1,500	219 M	7,800	148 M
Philippines	1.9 M	1.959 M (1998)	AM 366; FM 290; shortwave 3 (1999)	11.5 M	31	3.7 M	33	500,000
Solomon Islands	8,000	658	AM 3; FM 0; shortwave 0	57,000	0	3,000	1	3,000

[a]Data is for 1997 unless otherwise noted.
[b]Data is for 1998 unless otherwise noted.
[c]Data is for 2000 unless otherwise noted.

SOURCE: CIA *World Factbook 2001* [Online].

ECONOMIC SECTORS

According to the Asian Development Bank, Tonga's economic sectors contributed to total GDP in 1999 in the following proportion: agriculture, fishing, and hunting, 29.9 percent; industry, 10.7 percent; services, 43.8 percent; other, 15.7 percent. In 1996, the same source reported that the total **labor force** of 33,900 was distributed in these sectors as follows: agriculture, 34 percent; industry, 22.8 percent; services, 43.2 percent.

The agriculture sector's contribution to GDP has been fairly consistent, dropping slightly from 31.6 percent in 1984 to 29.9 percent in 1999. Between 1994 and 1996, Tonga experienced a downturn in agricultural performance, along with declining price competitiveness internationally, and a weakening level of remittances from overseas migrants. This caused high unemployment in 1996. Industry, which contributed 10.7 percent of GDP in 1999, is made up of relatively small-scale processing of food and timber products for the local market, as well as small factories making products for export, including woolen goods. The service sector is the largest, made up mostly of the government subsector, and a smaller tourism one.

AGRICULTURE

Agriculture contributed 29.9 percent of GDP in 1999, and in 1996 employed 34 percent of the labor force. In terms of GDP this proportion has been fairly consistent through the 1980s and 1990s, despite fluctuations

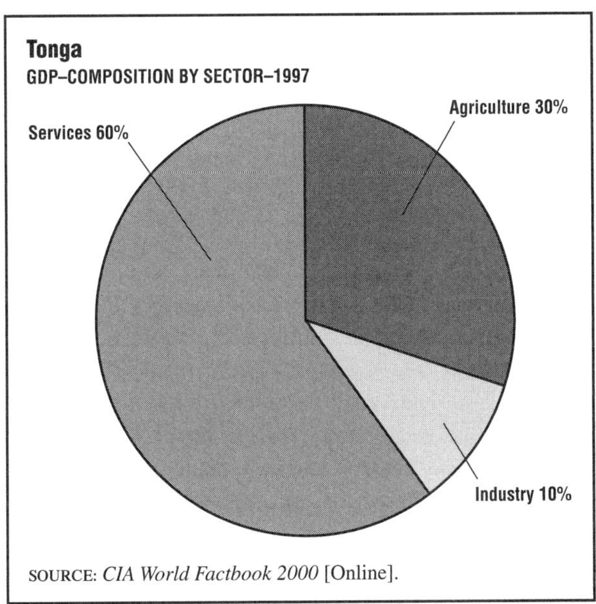

SOURCE: *CIA World Factbook 2000* [Online].

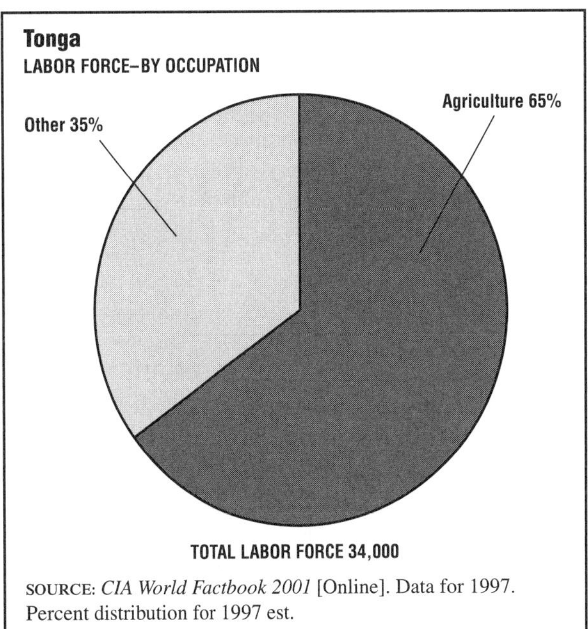

SOURCE: *CIA World Factbook 2001* [Online]. Data for 1997. Percent distribution for 1997 est.

due to weather and unstable world market prices for agricultural products.

As in most Pacific countries, subsistence production for domestic use is an important part of the economy, although not well recorded. The export of agricultural products has been highly unpredictable over time. Through most of the 20th century, Tonga's main export was coconut products, mainly copra (dried coconut meat yielding coconut oil), but at various times other products have been exported in sizeable quantities, particularly bananas.

A specialized market for squash was established in the 1980s when Tonga secured a quota to supply the vegetable to Japan during several months of the year when other sources, especially New Zealand, were not pro ducing. In the early 1990s, this source of export income grew, but in the second half of that decade, production fluctuated considerably as a result of disease, weather, and oversupply. Other squash producers from Vanuatu and Mexico have also offered competition by entering the same market.

Other agricultural products, such as bananas and market vegetables, are significant in the domestic market but have contributed very little to export income in recent years. Even vanilla beans, which were significant exports in the early 1990s, have declined in importance because of international competition. There has been a small but steady export of root crops, mostly to supply Tongan and other Pacific communities, especially in New Zealand. Kava (a mild legal narcotic) production has increased recently, and this has considerable export potential as illustrated by the success of this industry in Vanuatu.

Fish was the second most important export during the 1990s, mainly high-grade tuna and snapper. The potential sustainable harvest of tuna is about 30,000 tons a year, which is several times higher than the existing harvest. Most fish is exported unprocessed to the United States, Fiji, and American Samoa. A cannery in Tonga is under consideration, but a restraining factor is government legislation requiring that 90 percent of sales from such a venture would have to be to overseas buyers.

INDUSTRY

Industry contributed 10.7 percent of GDP in 1999, a slight decline from 1984, when it contributed 13.8 percent of GDP. The importance of industry to employment is somewhat greater than this, however, since 22.8 percent of the labor force is industrial. Construction was the biggest single sector, followed by manufacturing. The contribution of construction is variable, depending on the expansion of tourism **infrastructure** (especially hotels) and new businesses in any one year.

The most important manufacturing activities are related to food and timber processing, mainly for the local market. Under a trade agreement with Australia and New Zealand (SPARTECA), Tonga is allowed to export manufactured goods duty-free, and at times has been successful in establishing a market for woolen goods and other products produced in small factories or from home. The advantages of this trade agreement have declined with trade **liberalization**, which has opened up the Australian and New Zealand markets to cheaper Asian products.

SERVICES

The largest sector in terms of GDP and employment is services, making up 43.8 percent of GDP in 1999 and providing 43.2 percent of jobs in 1996. Within this sector, the largest employer is the government, in the areas of public administration and education. In terms of GDP the next largest subsector is trade (including hotels and restaurants), followed by transport, communications, and finance. It is not possible to separate tourism out from these data since it makes contributions to several of these subsectors.

TOURISM. Tourism's contribution to GDP is rather minimal (about 2 to 3 percent), and it employs about 1,400 people. The industry began expanding in the late 1980s, when it welcomed 20,000 visitors per year, to 1995, when it welcomed 29,000, though there have been some fluctuations since then. Improvements in domestic and international air services have contributed to this growth, especially after the **restructuring** of Royal Air Tonga, the national airline. This carrier has flights to and from Australia, New Zealand, Fiji, Samoa, and Niue. Other airlines serving Tonga include Air New Zealand, Air Pacific, Polynesian Airlines, and Samoa Air. Tourists visit Tonga for beaches, sun, and diving, but also to explore sites unique to the region, such as the 19th century royal palace and the Ha'amonga-a-Maui, a large trilithon (stone archway) built by a Tongan king sometime before the 13th century. Also on the island of Tongatapu are trees full of sacred bats, which only the monarch is allowed to kill, although presumably does not because of their tourist value.

FINANCIAL SERVICES. International financial services are limited in Tonga. The domestic market is mostly served by the Bank of Tonga, ANZ (Australia New Zealand) Bank, and MBF (Malaysian Borneo Finance).

RETAIL. Retail services are typical of those available in a small Pacific nation. In the capital, Nuku'alofa, shops provide a reasonable range of products, mainly food goods from New Zealand and manufactured goods from Asia. In other parts of the country, small village shops supply only the most basic goods. Many Tongans also rely on goods packages from relatives living overseas, which are consumed within the family or sold to others.

INTERNATIONAL TRADE

According to statistics from the International Monetary Fund (IMF), Tonga has had a negative trade balance since 1975. In 1975, Tonga's imports totaled $17 million and its exports $6 million. By 1998, according to the *CIA World Factbook 2000*, imports had risen to $69 million and exports to $8 million. This illustrates Tonga's very narrow export base, as it relies mainly on squash and fish, with small contributions from other agricultural and manufacturing products. Since squash is the most valuable export and the total production goes to Japan to be used in soups and various food products, that country accounts for more than 40 percent of Tonga's exports. The United States and New Zealand are the other significant export destinations, importing fish and small agricultural and manufacturing products respectively.

The most important imports into Tonga are foodstuffs, machines, and transport equipment. New Zealand is the most important source of foodstuffs and of some manufactures and is the source of about 35 percent of all imports. The next most important import sources are Australia, the United States, and Fiji.

The large negative trade balance is offset by other international transfers. Tourism contributes some international income, and there is potential for expansion in this sector. At the household level, the most important source of income is remittances from relatives living overseas, particularly in New Zealand, the United States and Australia. At the government level, international aid helps to counterbalance the large imbalance in trade.

Exchange rates: Tonga

pa'anga (T$) per US$1	
Jan 2001	1.9885
2000	1.7585
1999	1.5991
1998	1.4920
1997	1.2635
1996	1.2323

SOURCE: CIA *World Factbook 2001* [ONLINE].

MONEY

The value of the pa'anga against the U.S. dollar has halved over the past 2 decades, from 0.9859 to the U.S. dollar in 1982 to 1.997 in February 2001. Much of this **devaluation** took place during the early 1980s, and then again in the late 1990s. During the 1980s, the export value of coconut products and vanilla declined, and remittance income fluctuated, causing an impact on the currency. In the late 1990s and early 2000s a further serious devaluation occurred, and this may be partly attributed to the strong American dollar against the currencies of the Pacific region, including the New Zealand and Australian dollars, which are part of a number of currencies to which the pa'anga is linked.

The National Reserve Bank of Tonga (NRBT) has several functions. One of these is to stabilize the Tongan currency. This is only possible, though, within the network of the other currencies to which the pa'anga is linked. The NRBT also monitors the economy by maintaining databases and providing advice on government spending and revenue, the supply of money, interest rates, and the trade balance.

POVERTY AND WEALTH

GDP per capita rose from $1,300 in 1975 to $1,868 in 1998, according to the Asian Development Bank. The *CIA World Factbook 2000* reports a slightly higher figure, which it estimated at US$2,200 for 1998. Although the Human Development Indicator (HDI) for Tonga does not appear among the 174 countries which are ranked in the UNDP's *Human Development Report 2000*, it does appear in the UNDP's *Pacific Human*

Trade (expressed in billions of US$): Tonga

	Exports	Imports
1975	.006	.017
1980	.007	.038
1985	.005	.041
1990	.011	.062
1995	.014	.077
1998	N/A	N/A

SOURCE: International Monetary Fund. *International Financial Statistics Yearbook 1999.*

GDP per Capita (US$)

Country	1996	1997	1998	1999	2000
Tonga	2,250	2,100	2,200	N/A	2,200
United States	28,600	30,200	31,500	33,900	36,200
Philippines	2,600	3,200	3,500	3,600	3,800
Solomon Islands	3,000	3,000	2,600	2,650	2,000

Note: Data are estimates.

SOURCE: *Handbook of the Nations*, 17th, 18th, 19th and 20th editions for 1996, 1997, 1998 and 1999 data; CIA *World Factbook 2001* [Online] for 2000 data.

Development Report 1999. In that report, Tonga has the sixth highest HDI of the 15 Pacific countries considered. Its GDP per capita is only the eighth highest of these countries, but it makes up for this with high indicators of education and health. Adult literacy for both men and women is reported to be near 99 percent, the highest of any Pacific country. Infant mortality, at 19 per 1,000, is one of the lowest in the Pacific, and this is illustrative of a good system of health delivery and a safe water system. Primary education is free and compulsory, and participation at secondary school is also high, resulting in a combined enrollment rate of 83 percent.

Still, there is some evidence of inequalities within the country. No calculated measures of the distribution of income or consumption are available, but there is some inequality of income between urban and rural areas. Squatter (one who lives somewhere without paying rent) settlements around the capital, Nuku'alofa, have a poor standard of housing and inadequate water and sanitation systems. In some rural areas, land access is inequitably distributed, despite the fact that all adult males on reaching their sixteenth birthday are supposed to be granted a plot of land by the local noble.

WORKING CONDITIONS

According to official statistics, about one-third of the workforce is not "economically active." These people are mainly village-based subsistence workers, a disproportionate number of whom are women, who are producing goods and services that are not exchanged for cash. Many of these aspire to become part of the country's formal sector. The situation for those who want wage employment does not appear good. It is estimated that of the 2,000 school graduates each year, only about 500 will find work in the formal sector. The rest must either return to the subsistence economy, continue job searching and become officially unemployed, or migrate. It is the latter option that many choose, and this partly explains why there are an estimated 50,000 Tongans living in other countries.

In the formal sector, about 37 percent of the workforce is female. While it is difficult to calculate, about 12 percent of the labor force is said to be unemployed. There is no comprehensive system of unemployment compensation, nor is there a general pension scheme. The country does not have a minimum wage law; workers did have some amount of protection in that they could live without a monetary income with the support of extended families and **subsistence farming**, if needed. There is no legal provision for labor unions in Tonga, although 2 associations that represent working groups are the Tonga Nurses' Association and the Friendly Islands Teachers' Association.

COUNTRY HISTORY AND ECONOMIC DEVELOPMENT

1140 B.C. Evidence of human habitation and Lapita pottery.

950 A.D. Tuíi Tonga is the dominant leader.

1643. First European (Dutch) sighting of Tonga by Schouten and Le Maire.

1643–1800s. Many European contacts include visits by "explorers" from the Netherlands, Great Britain, France, and Spain, who introduce many new trade goods and diseases.

1777. British Captain James Cook explores what he calls the "Friendly Isles."

1822. First Christian conversions, by Wesleyan missionaries; Tonga becomes nominally Christian over the next 20 years.

1845. After civil wars, King Taufa'ahau Tupou I (George Tupou I) of the Ha'apai group becomes first ruler of a united Tonga.

1875. New constitution proclaims Tonga an independent constitutional monarchy.

1900. Great Britain declares Tonga a "protected state" but does not impose full colonial rule.

1918. Queen Salote Tupou III is crowned, and rules until 1965.

1960s. Large-scale migrations to New Zealand and elsewhere begin.

1965. King Taufa'ahau Tupou IV, the current monarch, is crowned.

1990s. Rise of republican movement proposing full democracy and end of monarchy; squash becomes primary export, to Japanese market.

FUTURE TRENDS

The late 1990s was a period of economic stagnation by some indicators. Primary exports in agriculture, forestry, and fishing had declined as a result of drought, hurricane damage and unstable world prices. However, the **balance of payments** was still positive as a result of some growth in services and a steady flow of remittances. Both the private and **public sectors** have been making an ongoing attempt to identify niche markets for Tongan enterprise, ranging from the export of new agricultural products such as the vaguely narcotic but reputedly therapeutic kava, to the acquisition of a number of satellite television bands, which Tonga has successfully leased. Despite a relative lack of resources, there is some optimism for the future based on the high educational levels of Tonga's population and the international networks established by Tongan migrants. At the same time, there will be ongoing pressure to further democratize Tonga's political system. In the long term, the monarchy may survive, accompanied by a more democratic Parliament, although such a change is not likely to have a significant economic impact, other than perhaps allowing a more equitable distribution of wealth.

DEPENDENCIES

Tonga has no territories or colonies.

BIBLIOGRAPHY

Asian Development Bank. "Key Indicators for Developing Asian and Pacific Countries." <http://www.adb.org/Tonga>. Accessed February.2001.

———. *Country Assistance Plan 2001–2003.* Tonga: ADB, 2000.

———. *Tonga: Economic Performance and Selected Development Issues.* Manila: ADB, 1996.

Fairbairn, Te'o I.J. "The Tongan Economy: Recent Performance and Future Challenges." *Pacific Economic Bulletin.* Vol. 13, No. 1, 1998.

Lal, Brij V. & Kate Fortune. *The Pacific Islands: An Encyclopedia.* Honolulu: University of Hawai'i Press, 2000.

United Nations Development Programme, *Pacific Human Development Report 1999: Creating Opportunities.* Suva: UNDP, 1999.

U.S. Central Intelligence Agency. "The World Factbook, 2000." <http://www.cia.gov/cia/publications/factbook>. Accessed January 2001.

—Wardlow Friesen

TURKEY

Republic of Turkey
Türkiye Cumhuriyeti

CAPITAL: Ankara.

MONETARY UNIT: Turkish lira (TL). One Turkish lira equals 100 kurus (pronounced kouroush). However, because of the high inflation rates Turkey has faced in the past 20 years, kurus are no longer used due to the low purchasing power. As of the end of 2000, there are coins of 10,000, 25,000, 50,000, and 100,000 liras. The 10,000 and 25,000-lira coins were expected to be phased out by 2001, and probably replaced with new coins of 500,000 and 1 million liras.

CHIEF EXPORTS: Clothing, foodstuffs, textiles, metal manufactures.

CHIEF IMPORTS: Machinery, semi-finished goods, chemicals, transport equipment, fuels.

GROSS DOMESTIC PRODUCT: US$444 billion (purchasing power parity, 2000 est.).

BALANCE OF TRADE: **Exports:** US$26.9 billion (f.o.b., 2000 est.). **Imports:** US$55.7 billion (c.i.f., 2000 est.).

COUNTRY OVERVIEW

LOCATION AND SIZE. Turkey is a peninsula that, uniquely, straddles 2 continents. Located in southeastern Europe and southwestern Asia, 97 percent of its area occupies Anatolia, the peninsula of land that lies between the Black Sea on the northern coast of the country, and the Mediterranean to the south, where the continents of Asia and Europe meet. The remaining 3 percent of the country is in Thrace, a region in the southeastern Balkan peninsula, north of the Aegean Sea. Turkey has an area of 780,580 square kilometers (301,382 square miles) with a total coastline of 8,430 kilometers (5,238 miles), and shares its land borders with Armenia, Azerbaijan, Bulgaria, Georgia, Greece, Iran, Iraq, and Syria. The country is strategically situated since it controls the Turkish Straits, comprised of the Bosphorus, the Sea of Marmara, and the Dardanelles, which connect the Black Sea to the Aegean on the west coast. Comparatively, Turkey is slightly larger than the state of Texas. The capital city, Ankara, is located in the northwest center of Anatolia.

POPULATION. In July of 2000, Turkey's current population was estimated at 65,666,677. Between 1990 and 2000, the average annual growth rate of the population was 1.27 percent, with a total fertility rate of 2.16 children born per woman. The World Bank expects Turkey's population to reach 91 million by 2025. Since 1986, the state has actively promoted population control but, ironically, for about 40 years following the establishment of the republic in 1923 the government actually encouraged population growth.

The Turkish population is very young with only 6 percent aged 65 and over, and 65 percent between the ages of 15 and 65. In 1995, approximately 67 percent of the population lived in urban areas. As of 1999, urban dwellers increased to 75.3 percent of the total population. Approximately 20 percent of them live in Istanbul, making it the most heavily populated city in the country.

Turks constitute almost 80 percent of population and Kurds 20 percent. The rest of the population is made up of small minorities of Arabs, people from the Caucasus, Greeks, Armenians, and Jews. The ethnic Turks are a diverse people who differ from one another in dialect, customs, and outlook. The 3 major groups are the Anatolian Turks, who have lived in the Central Anatolian Plateau for centuries; the Rumelian Turks, who were originally mainly immigrants from the Ottoman territories in the Balkans; and the Central Asian Turks, descended from Turkic-speaking immigrants from the Caucasus region, southern Russia, and Central Asia. Turkey is the only country with a Muslim majority population (99.8 percent) that operates under a secular constitution and a democratic government.

OVERVIEW OF ECONOMY

Modern Turkey is a free market economy oriented to Western markets. While the **private sector** continues to be the country's powerful engine of rapid economic growth, the state has a significant involvement in essential sectors such as communication, transport, and banking. Modern industry and commerce play the majority role in the economy, although traditional village agriculture and crafts are still nurtured.

By the end of World War I, the long, drawn-out collapse of the Ottoman Empire was complete. Having lost the war, Turkey was not left with much in the way of an economy. The few factories that remained were in foreign hands, agricultural output had dropped significantly, and, with the loss of the Ottoman territories, many traditional markets disappeared. The country's technology was out-dated and there was a shortage of skilled labor. The several years of struggle for independence following World War I offered little opportunity for recovery.

With the establishment of the republic in 1923, the government was faced with the formidable task of rebuilding the country's economy. Initially, the focus was on returning agricultural production to pre-war levels while building a transport **infrastructure**, particularly railroads. Meanwhile, steady encouragement of private enterprise was evident in various government policies and measures. The economy exhibited impressive growth levels until 1930, when the Great Depression caused the collapse of external markets for Turkey's agricultural products. This prompted the state to take a more active role in the economy, adopting a policy of etatism (an economic doctrine where individual enterprise retains its fundamental role in the economy, but active government intervention is considered necessary. It applies particularly to basic industries and public services).

The economic role of the state continued until the early 1980s, when Turkey's policy makers embarked on a new course of **liberalization**, abandoning **protectionist policies** and initiating several reforms aimed at opening up the Turkish economy to foreign trade and investment. These new policies brought an annual growth rate averaging 5 percent over the last 2 decades of the twentieth century, giving Turkey the highest growth rate of any OECD (Organisation for Economic Co-operation and Development) country. By 2001, Turkey was one of the 20 largest economies in the world.

The path to economic growth in Turkey, however, has not been smooth. Since the 1950s, the country has suffered serious disruption to its economy every 10 years. At times, this has been due to poor political leadership, at other times, the cause has been structural inadequacies and **balance of payment** problems. In 1994, the country faced one of its worst **recessions**, bringing an end to 13 straight years of growth, but the economy bounced back strongly over the next 3 years, growing by over 8 percent. In 1998, slowdown returned as a result of the Asian and Russian financial crises; in 1999, disaster struck in the form of 2 deadly earthquakes, measuring 7.4 and 7.2 on the Richter scale, which hit northwestern Turkey right in the middle of its industrial heartland. The World Bank estimated the economic loss at approximately US$10 billion, and Turkey suffered its worst contraction since World War II. That the country has survived this miserable period is seen as a positive sign for its economic future. A larger problem is that of persistent **inflation**, which has been over 60 percent annually for 5 years, and remained in the double digits in 2001. The expectation of inflation has become a way of life in Turkey, bringing an inertia that has made it extremely difficult to tackle the situation.

Despite these problems, several factors have allowed Turkey to remain attractive to foreign investors. A population of 64 million with significant purchasing power represents a big and fast-growing market, with strong potential for further development. Also, Turkey lies in the middle of the rich oil-producing area of the Caspian Sea and the consumer markets in Europe, while its strategic geopolitical position at the crossroads of Europe, Asia, and the Middle East makes it a prime gateway. In addition, Turkey has close relations with the Central Asian Republics, forged by ethnic and linguistic ties, and is the leading investor in many of these countries. Last, but certainly not least, Turkey entered a customs union agreement with the European Union (EU) in 1996, thus enabling the free flow of goods to and from other European markets. All these factors make Turkey an attractive destination for trade as well as for cost-effective export industries.

Turkey's economic profile is multi-dimensional in nature. Tourism is a significant economic sector, while textiles and clothing are the most important manufacturing industries, supplying the largest percentage of goods for export. Other important industries include iron, steel, cement, chemicals, and the automotive industry. The Turkish private sector is dominated by a number of large **holding companies**, whose senior management is controlled by prominent families. The best known and strongest of these are the Sabanci Holding and Koc Holding companies, both of which have a significant presence in most sectors of the economy. In order to limit outside interference in company management, most large businesses only float a small portion of company shares in the public market.

POLITICS, GOVERNMENT, AND TAXATION

The Turkish political system is a secular parliamentary democracy that recognizes the separation of executive, legislative, and judicial powers. The executive branch of government includes the president, the prime minister, and the cabinet (council of ministers responsible for a variety of governmental tasks). The president is elected by parliament for a period of 7 years. He serves as the head of state, has broad powers of appointment and supervision, and is non-partisan. The prime minister is the head of the government and is responsible for appointing the cabinet. The Turkish Grand National Assembly (TBMM), or parliament, is the legislative branch of government and consists of 550 elected representatives voted for by the citizens of Turkey. The judicial system consists of a constitutional court, a series of state courts, a council of state, and a high council of judges and prosecutors.

Modern Turkey has suffered several periods of instability and authoritarian rule. When the Turkish Republic was established in 1923, Turkey was governed under 1-party rule by the Republican People's Party (CHP) established by Kemal Ataturk, who founded the modern republic. This situation lasted until 1945, when the multi-party era commenced. The first change of power took place in 1950 when the Democrat Party won the national elections. They ruled until 1960, when power was seized in a military coup intended to end internal political tensions and growing economic problems. Democracy returned in 1961 as soon as a new constitution was written, but only lasted until 1971 when, after a 3-year period of political strife and resultant domestic violence, another coup was staged, replacing the civilian government with a succession of semi-military, non-partisan governments. In 1973, general elections were held once again in an effort to re-start the democratic process but, by 1980, a military coup was again necessary to restore order and stop political violence that was claiming more than 20 victims daily.

Another new constitution was drafted in 1982. It was approved in a national referendum, and elections were held 1983. The Motherland Party, formed by Turgut Ozal, won an absolute majority, formed a government, and won a second election in 1987, making for 6 years of stable rule until, in 1989, Turgut Ozal left the Motherland Party to become Turkey's new president. Many of the structural and economic reforms that have led to liberal trade policies and reduced the government's role in the economy were initiated during this period in the 1980s. Since then, however, no single party has been able to capture a majority in elections, and the Turkish political scene has witnessed one coalition after another failing in attempts to bring stability back to government.

In the 55 years since the beginning of the multiparty era, Turkey has had 43 governments (in addition to the 14 different governments in the single-party era). In 1999, the country witnessed the fall of yet another government, the establishment of an interim government, and the election of a third. With each government averaging just over 15 months in power, it is not surprising that the country has found it difficult to develop and execute a stable, long-term economic plan. The fundamental problem lies with the fact that there are too many political parties in operation (21 parties participated in the 1999 elections), many of them following similar pro-reform, centrist policies, offering little difference of choice other than between the distinctive personalities of their various leaders.

The last elections were held in April 1999. The Democratic Left Party (DSP), led by Bulent Ecevit, received 22 percent of the votes and won the most seats in parliament. This was not enough to secure a majority and, in June 1999, DSP formed a coalition with the National Action Party (MHP) and the Motherland Party (ANAP). If this coalition proves stable, the next elections will be held in 2004. There are grounds for optimism, since the 3-party coalition has a strong parliamentary majority, and has been aggressive in pushing an ambitious reform program, well supported both domestically and externally.

Of the 21 parties that participated in the 1999 elections, 6 are prominent. Two of these are center-left parties: the Democratic Left Party (DSP), who is the majority partner in the current coalition government, and the Republican People's Party (CHP). Bulent Ecevit, the current prime minister, leads the DSP, a social democratic party with a strong free-market economic agenda. Ecevit has had decades of experience in Turkish politics (he was prime minister 3 times during the 1970s). The CHP tries to carry on the tradition of the party's early days as the first political party in Turkey, but in the last elections it failed to get the 10 percent of the vote necessary to enter parliament. Thus excluded from parliament for the first time in its history, the CHP has embarked on a process of rebuilding itself.

On the opposite side of the political spectrum are 2 center-right parties: the Motherland Party (ANAP), a junior coalition partner in the current government, and the True Path Party (DYP), which holds 85 parliamentary seats. Both are parties of the conservative mass, have similar ideologies (social and political beliefs), and, in common with the center-left, support free trade and growth led by the private sector. However, such slight policy differences as there are have favored ANAP popularity in urban areas, while the DYP has more visibility in smaller towns and villages.

The Nationalist Movement Party (MHP) was the big surprise of the 1999 elections, capturing second place with 18 percent of the national vote and a partnership in the coalition government. It has a strong nationalist agenda, and has been historically connected to right-wing organizations partly responsible for the violence preceding the military coup in 1980. Despite retaining hard-line attitudes on certain issues, the MHP seems, overall, to have softened somewhat. It has strongly supported the economic reforms and has co-operated in maintaining the stability and continuity of the coalition government.

The Virtue Party (FP) is the successor to the Welfare Party, which was in government in 1996–97 but was shut down in 1998 for undermining the principles of Ataturk and secular Turkey. FP has a religious agenda, and rejects the secular principles on which the republic is based in favor of Islam. It won 15 percent of the vote in the 1999 elections, making it the main opposition party to the 3-party coalition government.

In Turkey, the military has traditionally exerted significant pressure on ruling parties, and military intervention in government has been frequent. Since the first coup in 1960, representatives of the army, air force, and navy join the president, the prime minister, several key ministers, and the Chief of the Turkish General Staff on the National Security Council (NSC), an advisory body that oversees the president and the cabinet. At times, the NSC has had a marked effect on the political agenda. The military played a major role in the resignation of the Welfare Party government by publicly supporting a popular opposition movement comprised of businesses, labor, and community groups. The influence of the military (which has closer ties with the center-right parties) seems to have diminished in the new government, although its stance on several sensitive issues is well known to the public.

The Ecevit government restarted structural reform, trying to make up for the time lost during the political uncertainties of the 1990s. In addition to social security reforms, one of the primary tasks of the new government was the reduction of the national deficit through accelerated **privatization**. A series of legislative measures have been designed to allow for the process to be as smooth as possible. These privatization projects will make Turkish industry more efficient and globally competitive, and will bring increased revenue to the government. The government is also trying to tighten its fiscal discipline by cutting expenditures and tightening up on tax collection. This latter measure is important, since Turkey has a large unregistered economy that could account for an increase in the official GNP by up to 50 percent. Indeed, although Turkey's population has grown by 30 percent over the last 15 years, its taxpayer base has remained static, indicating the seriousness of the problem. If the government can succeed in reducing this unregistered economy, the tax base will broaden and bring some much-needed relief to the country's finances.

INFRASTRUCTURE, POWER, AND COMMUNICATIONS

As an **emerging market** Turkey has a competitive commercial infrastructure. However, the government faces a continual challenge to meet the demands of a rapidly growing economy, and gives special priority to major infrastructure projects, particularly in the transport and energy sectors.

By the end of 1999, Turkey had 118 airports, 22 of which were open to international traffic. However, a large majority of international traffic targets 3 main airports: Ataturk International Airport in Istanbul, Adnan Menderes Airport in Izmir, and Esenboga Airport in the capital, Ankara. The new international passenger terminal in Istanbul, which opened in January 2000, is one of the largest in Europe. Several more new airports are under construction, including one on the Asian side of Istanbul. Over 300 foreign airlines serve Turkey, in addition to Turkish Airlines (THY). THY, with its fleet of 73 passenger planes, operates to both domestic and international destinations. There are 15 additional public and private domestic airlines operating on a smaller scale.

Shipping plays an important role in the Turkish economy. This is no surprise, since over 70 percent of Turkey's boundaries consist of 4 seas: the Black Sea in the north, the Marmara in the northwest, the Aegean in the west, and the Mediterranean in the south-southwest. The country's 8,430-kilometer coastline is covered with large and small ports, 21 of them international. Five ports, all state-owned, handle most of the country's sea freight: Istanbul and Kocaeli on the Sea of Marmara, Izmir on the Aegean, and Mersin and Iskenderun on the Mediterranean. Seaports on the Black Sea coast mainly handle export cargo of steel products, tea, and hazelnuts, and import cargo of coal, iron ore, raw minerals, fertilizers, and bulk construction materials. The area around the Marmara Sea is the country's industrial heartland and these ports serve a vital function in Turkey's economy, handling cargo carrying raw industrial materials, semi-finished materials, chemicals, steel, and petroleum. The Marmara Sea is also the only connection between the Black Sea and the Mediterranean through 2 straits, and is therefore one of the busiest maritime routes in the world. The Mediterranean ports also handle domestic and international cargo traffic. Iskenderun handles 75 percent of Turkey's steel exports, while a nearby port serves both the domestic and the Iraqi oil pipeline. Mersin, one of the main ports of the eastern Mediterranean, acts as an export hub for southeast Anatolia's products.

The railway system is one of the weakest modes of transportation in Turkey. Although the country has 10,933 kilometers (6,778 miles) of railways running between its western and eastern borders, only 2,133 kilometers (1,322 miles) are electrified. The railroads are state-owned and operated, but rail expansion has not been politically popular for the last several decades and has lacked funding. Most commercial and public transportation, therefore, must rely on other means while the aging rail system, badly in need of renovation, is primarily used to carry minerals and bulk commodities over long distances. The government has, however, begun engaging in plans for both the modernization of existing lines and the addition of up to 2,000 kilometers (1,240 miles) of railway.

The highway transport system carries over 95 percent of passenger transport and over 90 percent of the surface transport of goods in Turkey. The country's road network is extensive, with over 382,000 kilometers (nearly 237,000 miles) of roads. By the end of 1999, 1,726 kilometers (1,070 miles) of this network consisted of motorways, and a total of 96,000 kilometers (59,520 miles) was tarred. The government has made strenuous efforts to extend and improve its road network, especially in the building of additional motorways. The economic crisis of 1998 and the earthquakes of 1999 caused some of these projects to be postponed, but they, and others, are expected to go ahead.

Turkish telecommunications services are undergoing rapid modernization and expansion. As of 1999, Turkey

Communications

Country	Newspapers	Radios	TV Sets[a]	Cable subscribers[a]	Mobile Phones[a]	Fax Machines[a]	Personal Computers[a]	Internet Hosts[b]	Internet Users[b]
	1996	1997	1998	1998	1998	1998	1998	1999	1999
Turkey	111	180	286	9.2	53	1.7	23.2	8.06	1,500
United States	215	2,146	847	244.3	256	78.4	458.6	1,508.77	74,100
United Kingdom	329	1,436	645	45.9	252	33.9	263.0	270.60	12,500
Greece	153	477	466	1.2	194	3.8	51.9	59.57	750

[a]Data are from International Telecommunication Union, *World Telecommunication Development Report 1999* and are per 1,000 people.
[b]Data are from the Internet Software Consortium (http://www.isc.org) and are per 10,000 people.

SOURCE: World Bank. *World Development Indicators 2000.*

had more than 19 million telephone lines, exceeding a density of 25 percent. The target density for 2005 is 40 percent. Turk Telekom, a state-owned enterprise, provides basic telephone services in the country, utilizing a variety of communication systems including satellite, submarine cable, and fiber-optic cable. The government has announced plans to privatize up to 49 percent of the company in the near future. The country is also seeing a rapid expansion in cellular telephone services, with many licenses sold to private companies. The current cellular density is estimated at 15 percent and is expected to reach 30 percent by 2010. Cellular phones have received widespread acceptance in the large cities, where they have become a part of daily life among both business executives and teenagers. The Internet is also a well-accepted communication/information medium in Turkey, again primarily in the urban areas. At the end of 1999, Turkey had 1.7 million Internet users, 70 Internet service providers, and 8.06 Internet hosts per 10,000 people. Internet usage is seeing rapid growth, primarily due to cutting-edge Internet banking operations.

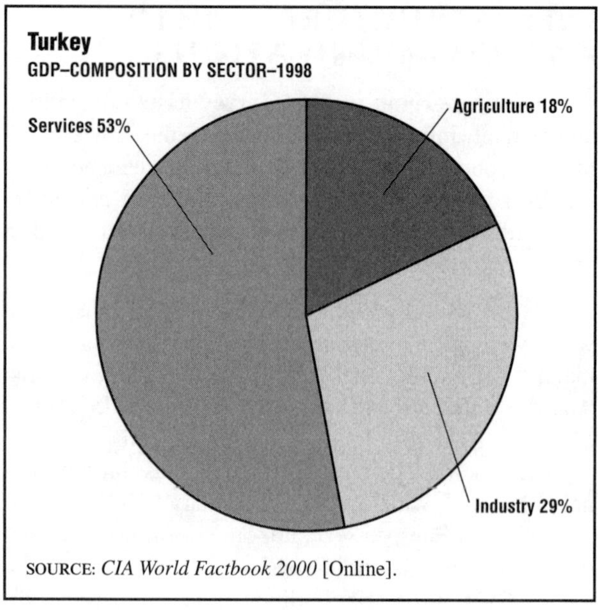

SOURCE: *CIA World Factbook 2000* [Online].

Turkey faces one of its biggest challenges in the energy sector. Rapid urbanization and strong economic growth have led to one of the fastest growing power markets in the world. It is no secret that Turkey is facing a major hurdle in trying to meet the demands of such growth. In 1999, imported energy supplied 60 percent of the country's primary energy consumption, and energy imports are expected to reach 75 percent by 2020. Turkey has an installed electric capacity of 26,500 megawatts, of which about 11,000 megawatts is hydroelectric and the balance is thermal power. This capacity not only cannot meet the 8–10 percent projected annual increase in demand, but is also insufficient for present needs. The Turkish government has been actively seeking investments and developing projects to triple energy production by 2010. The Southeastern Anatolia Project (GAP) is expected to be completed in 2005, and is the most crucial public project in Turkey. When complete, the 22 dams and 19 hydroelectric power plants that are a part of this project will produce 22 percent of Turkey's projected electricity requirements. Due to the current shortage of electric capacity, the 220-volt power system has suffered from occasional blackouts.

ECONOMIC SECTORS

Turkey's economy has been able to supply a broad range of goods and services since the early 1950s. Since then, the mix of domestic production has seen a shift from agriculture to manufacturing, and then to services. In the early 1950s, agriculture made up a little under 50 percent of **gross domestic product** (GDP), while the manufacturing sector's share was about 20 percent. In the 1970s, with the government's continued emphasis on industrialization, manufacturing caught up with agriculture for the first time and surpassed it. This trend continued until the 1980s. With the economic reforms of the 1980s, the economic shift accelerated as all sectors exhibited strong growth, though both manufacturing and services grew much more rapidly. By the late 1990s, the services sector began to dominate the domestic economy: in 1999, the services sector made up 56 percent of GDP, while manufacturing was at 29 percent and agriculture at 15 percent. However, all 3 remain vital to the Turkish economy.

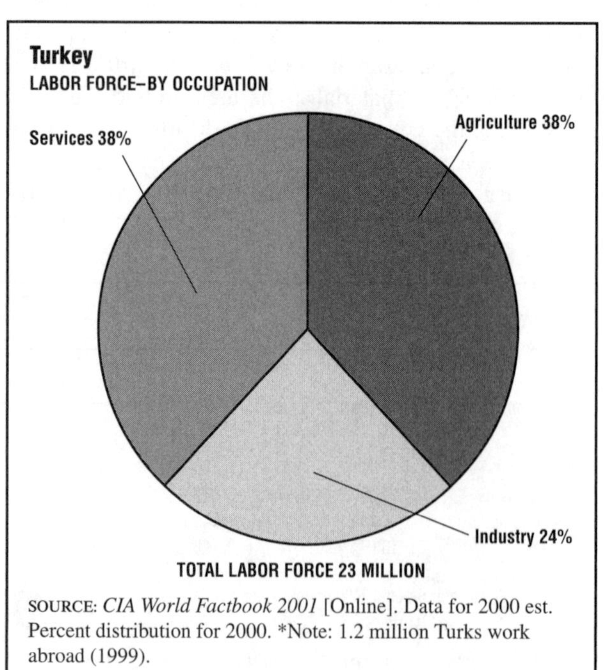

SOURCE: *CIA World Factbook 2001* [Online]. Data for 2000 est. Percent distribution for 2000. *Note: 1.2 million Turks work abroad (1999).

AGRICULTURE

Historically, the agriculture sector has been Turkey's largest employer and a major contributor to the country's GDP, although its share of the economy has fallen consistently over several decades. In 1999, it accounted for 15 percent of GDP, while employing about half of the **labor force**. Although the sector has grown over time, the growth has been only about 1 percent faster than the country's population, and much slower than that of the industrial and services sectors. Farmers have been slow to adopt modern techniques, and much of the potential land and water resources are inefficiently managed.

Nevertheless, Turkey is one of the few countries in the world that is self-sufficient in terms of food. The country's fertile soil, access to sufficient water, a suitable climate, and hard-working farmers, all make for a successful agricultural sector. In addition, a broad range of crops can be raised because of the variety of different climates throughout the land. This has allowed Turkey to become the largest producer and exporter of agricultural products in the Near East and North African regions. In fact, according to *The Economist*'s world rankings, Turkey is one of the top 10 producers of fruit, wheat, and cotton in the world. More impressively, it ranks among the top 5 producers of vegetables, tea, and raw wool. As a result of this massive production base, Turkey enjoys a comparative advantage in many agricultural products, and a positive trade balance in agriculture that contributes significant relief to an overall **trade deficit**. The country's main export markets are the EU and the United States, to which Turkey exports dried fruit and nuts, cotton, and tobacco. Another major export market is the Middle East, which buys fresh fruit, vegetables, and meats from Turkey. By 1999, the value of agricultural exports had risen to US$2.4 billion and accounted for 9 percent of Turkey's export earnings (down from 60 percent in 1980). However, these figures could be misleading insofar as almost 50 percent of the manufactured exports also originate in the agricultural sector (primarily textiles and clothing). Therefore, the agricultural sector's direct and indirect total contribution would still account for 50 percent of total exports. Of Turkey's agricultural sector, crops account for 55 percent of the gross value, livestock represents 34 percent, and forestry and fishing make up the rest.

The vegetal (of, or relating to, plants and vegetables) production is primarily made up of cereals, pulses (edible seeds of various pod-bearing plants such as peas, beans, or lentils), industrial crops, and perishables. Of these, cereal crops occupy more than half of the cultivated land. The main species of cereal crops produced in Turkey are wheat, barley, oats, rye, maize, millet, and rice. These crops are produced in most parts of the country, with a heavier concentration in the central regions. Of all these, wheat has a special place in the Turkish economy. Turkey is both a top 10 producer and a top 10 consumer of wheat in the world. It is the essential food element in the Turkish diet, generally eaten in the form of bread. Production increases in the late 1970s enabled the country to become a wheat exporter and, although the output slowed down in the early 1980s, renewed efforts have seen wheat production continue to expand. In 1998, the total wheat production was 21 million tons.

Turkey is also the main pulse producer in the Middle East and one of the leading producers in the world. The pulse output increased from 617,000 tons in the early 1970s to 1.1 million tons in the 1980s and 1.6 million tons in 1998. Since the mid-1990s, over 60 countries import Turkish pulses, primarily chickpeas and lentils.

The major industrial crops produced in Turkey are cotton, tobacco, and sugar beets. Cotton is crucial to the wider economy since it provides the fiber for textiles, the leading category of Turkish exports. Cotton is primarily grown on the coastal plains of the Mediterranean and Aegean seas, in the south and southwest. Cotton production in 1999 was 855,000 tons. Only 10 percent of cotton is exported in raw form, while the rest feeds the domestic textile industry. The Southeastern Anatolian Project is Turkey's largest development project. It seeks improvements in energy production, tourism, mining, gasoline, education, health, communications, industry and transport, and in active farming by means of extensive irrigation systems. When the project is completed, it is estimated that Turkey's cotton production will expand to twice the level of production in the year 2000. Another industrial crop, sugar beets, saw a dramatic increase in production in the 1980s and 1990s. In the 1970s, annual production was around 650,000 tons, meeting only domestic needs. In the 1980s, this increased to 1.5 million tons, and in 1998 the total production of sugar beets was 22 million tons.

Tobacco has been grown in Turkey for many centuries, and the tobacco industry is a major player in the Turkish economy, contributing 18 percent of total agricultural exports. Turkey ranks as the fifth largest tobacco-producing country in the world, and its number-one producer of Oriental tobacco, of which it grows over half of the world's supply. The country is also the world's fourth largest tobacco exporter. The crops are primarily concentrated on the Aegean coast and Black Sea regions, but eastern Anatolia also contributes to the output. The crop yield varies considerably from year to year due to climatic changes, but averages around 200,000 to 300,000 tons annually. On average, 30 percent of this output is exported to the United States and another 20 percent to the EU.

Perishable fruit and vegetables are also important to the Turkish economy. Out of the 140 perishables grown in the world, the country produces 80 varieties of fresh fruits and vegetables and exports 30 kinds of vegetable and 20 kinds of fruit. These include grapes, citrus fruit, melons, potatoes, onions, tomatoes, olives, and cucumbers. These exports are worth over US$1 billion annually to Turkey.

Turkey is prominent, too, in the world trade of edible nuts and dried fruits. In this category of agricultural products, hazelnuts, pistachios, sultanas, dried apricots, and dried figs are important exports. Records indicate that hazelnuts have been grown along the Black Sea coast since 300 B.C. and Turkey is a major producer, competing with Spain, Italy, and the United States in the international markets. In 1998, Turkish hazelnut production reached 580,000 tons. Turkey also leads the world in figs, producing 36 percent of the world's total production and accounting for 70–75 percent of total world exports.

Animal husbandry is also significant in the agricultural sector. Turkey has traditionally been an important supplier of live sheep, lamb, and mutton to the Middle East, especially Iran and Iraq, but the United Nations (UN) **embargo** on Iraq, following the Gulf War, adversely affected domestic meat exporters and led to a significant decline in exports in the 1990s. Sheep constitute 59 percent of the existing animal total in Turkey, followed by cattle (22 percent) and goats, both the common goat and the Angora breed (16 percent). Most livestock is grazed in the central and eastern Anatolian plains, as well as in the western Anatolian region. Turkey is self-sufficient in milk products, supplying around 10 million tons per year.

Turkey's basic agricultural resources are vast and offer considerable potential for expansion. However, to maximize this potential and increase efficiency, the agricultural sector needs government involvement in structural reforms and development projects. One of the several aims of the Southeastern Anatolian Project (GAP) is to strengthen and expand the agricultural resource base for one of the most underdeveloped parts of the country. Indeed, GAP is possibly one of the most crucial projects for Turkey, since the large economic disparity between urban and rural areas has created social tension, and contributed to damaging levels of migration from the countryside to the cities, primarily in the southeast. This situation poses a serious threat to future agricultural development and to the general economic health of Turkey.

INDUSTRY

The industrial sector in Turkey has been the primary focus of government policies since the early 1950s. Industrial policy until 1980 was based on an **import-substitution** strategy. This protectionist approach was very successful for several decades, and the sector grew at an average rate of 8.6 percent annually until the late 1970s. The first factories built in the country processed food and non-durable **consumer goods**, and remain among Turkey's most competitive manufactures. The next phase of development was in industries such as iron and steel, chemicals, and cement. By the end of the 1970s, **capital goods** and high-technology products had become the primary focus, but the rapid industrialization was taking its toll on the sector. Efficiency problems and energy shortages began to slow down growth, and prevented industry from becoming competitive in the international markets. The **liberal economic** policies introduced in 1980 were designed to address these issues by establishing a less protectionist, more outward-looking industrial policy. The idea was to use market signals to identify uncompetitive industries, transfer their resources to those industries where Turkey enjoys a comparative advantage, and thus compete in world markets. This strategy necessitated a greater emphasis on private sector-led growth. Accordingly, policies and reforms were designed to facilitate rapid expansion of the private sector.

While much progress has been made in the industrial sector since 1980, the process is still not complete. **Public sector** companies continue to dominate a number of critical industries, particularly those such as energy and steel whose products are crucial to private sector companies. Still, the industrial sector has achieved an average growth rate of 6 percent since 1990, and Turkey competes successfully in several areas of the international market. The country's abundance of natural resources, its geographical proximity to export markets, and the existence of a large domestic market give Turkey competitive strength in a diversity of industrial sectors. In 1999, the industrial sector in Turkey contributed to 29 percent of GDP and employed 27 percent of the labor force. More remarkably, industry accounts for 89.4 percent of Turkey's total export earnings. The key industries in Turkey are textiles, iron and steel, chemicals, cement, food processing, motor vehicles, construction, glass and ceramics, and mining.

TEXTILES AND CLOTHING. Industrial expansion in the 1960s and 1970s gave birth to the modern textile industry in Turkey. Currently, it is one of the most important sectors in the Turkish economy, accounting for 10 percent of GDP, 20 percent of the labor force, and 40 percent of total manufacturing output. This sector is the largest in the country and it is the largest supplier of exports as well. Today, Turkey is extremely competitive in international markets and was ranked sixth in world exports of clothing in 1998.

The fact that Turkey is a major grower of cotton is a great advantage for the textile and clothing sector. Thanks to the easy availability of the raw materials, Turkish spinning and weaving industries have developed significantly, creating integrated and diversified production in all sub-sectors of the textile industry. In terms of cotton spinning, the installed capacity in Turkey is equivalent to around 33 percent of that of the EU as a whole. The export value of cotton and cotton textile products was US$777 million in 1999 and the main destinations were the EU countries and the United States.

In addition to the cotton-based textile industry, Turkey makes a strong showing in both woolen textiles and man-made fibers. It is the third largest mohair producer and has the sixth largest synthetics capacity in the world. In 1999, the export value of wool or woolen textile products was US$107 million, while the man-made fibers industry accounted for US$1.1 billion.

The Turkish home textile industry has also been a strong competitor in world markets. Turkish towels and bathrobes, produced primarily around the western cities of Denizli and Bursa, enjoy a worldwide reputation for quality, and the home textiles sector accounted for 3.2 percent of Turkey's total exports in 1999, bringing in US$859 million.

The clothing industry has shown stable growth over the years and is today one of the most important manufacturing sectors. In 1999, the production volume of clothing equaled 223,000 tons, and its export revenues reached US$6.2 billion, giving it a 23 percent share of Turkey's total exports. The major markets for clothing exports are again the EU and the United States. The EU accounts for 71 percent of all clothing exports, and Germany leads all European countries with 38 percent of total exports. The clothing manufacturers are spread through the west and south of the country, with the majority based in Istanbul.

IRON AND STEEL. The foundations of the iron and steel industry were laid in the late 1930s with the establishment of the first integrated steel mill (a steel mill that takes raw materials in the form of iron ore and coke to produce molten iron, which is further processed to produce finished steel products) in 1939. At present, there are 3 integrated steel mills: the recently privatized KDCI (Karabuk, Black Sea region) plant and the 2 public-sector plants, Erdemir (Eregli, Black Sea region) and Isdemir (Iskenderun, East Mediterranean region). With the 1980 reforms, private sector investments accelerated, and several private electric arc furnaces (lower capacity mini-mills that produce steel from iron-bearing scrap) were established. Today, there are 17 electric arc furnaces (EAFs), only one of which is state-owned. The total steel production capacity of these 20 plants is 19.9 million tons, of which over 70 percent comes from EAFs.

Since 1980, the Turkish iron and steel industry has been one of the fastest growing in the world. In 1999, Turkey's raw steel production rose to 14.3 million tons, with a 1.9 percent share of the total world production. Turkey currently ranks seventeenth among the 66 steel-making countries in the world and fifth in Europe. In 1999 steel products were exported to 149 countries, with the top 6 buyers being Italy, Israel, the United Kingdom (UK), the United States, the United Arab Emirates, and Greece. With a total export value of US$2.1 billion in 1999, the steel industry is the second most important export sector in the country, after textiles and clothing.

CHEMICALS. Turkey has been manufacturing chemicals since the very early years of the republic. Although it has not been a high-flying sector, it has shown slow but steady improvement over time. Currently, it is one of the country's largest industries in terms of value, and is the fourth major export sector, accounting for 6.6 percent of Turkey's total exports and worth US$1.7 billion. The major chemical exports are plastic raw materials and plastic products, followed by rubber and rubber products. There are 6,000 companies manufacturing chemicals in Turkey, the most prominent being Petkim, a state-owned petrochemical company established in 1965, which supplies around 40 percent of the domestic market. Petkim's 2 major complexes are located at Kocaeli (Marmara Region) and Izmir (Aegean Region). Aside from Izmir and Kocaeli, most of the private sector companies are located in Istanbul, Ankara, and Adana. Primary chemicals produced in Turkey include boron products, caustic soda, chlorine, industrial chemicals, and sodium phosphates.

CEMENT. In comparison with the rest of Europe, Turkey was a latecomer to the cement industry. However, with accelerated investments and a number of structural reforms such as the elimination of government price-setting practices in 1984 and privatization of the industry from 1989, Turkey has become self-sufficient in this sector. Today, there are 51 cement plants in Turkey, all of which are private companies. By 2001, the country was the eighth largest cement producer in the world with a 2.5 percent share of the world market, and the largest producer in Europe. In 1999, Turkey produced 38.1 million tons of cement. While 34.7 million tons of it went to the domestic market, the balance was exported. The chief markets for Turkish cement are the United States, Spain, Israel, Egypt, and France.

CONSTRUCTION. A domestic construction sector did not exist in the founding days of the Turkish Republic, with almost all building done by foreign companies. The sector developed steadily over 50 years following the establishment of the Republic. The 1970s and early 1980s saw a period of international expansion for Turkey's construction sector, and Turkish firms became quite successful in the oil-producing states of the Middle East. The industry contracted with the Iran-Iraq war, but large domestic infrastructure projects enabled it to survive the difficult period. The break-up of the Soviet Union marked the beginning of a new era in the Turkish construction sector, and led to the diffusion of Turkish construction firms throughout Russia and Central Asia. Today, the construction sector makes up about 6 percent of the **gross national product** (GNP), and Turkey's share in international global contracting services is about 2–3 percent. (Since most construction is offered outside the country, the industry contributes only to GNP, and not to GDP.) During the 1990s, 34 percent of construction services performed were located in the Russian Federation, while Libya accounted for another 15 percent, followed by Kazakhstan, Pakistan, Turkmenistan, Uzbekistan, and Saudi Arabia.

MINING. Geologically complex, Turkey possesses some of the richest and most diverse mineral deposits in the world numbering 4,400, excluding petroleum and coal. Today, 53 minerals are produced in the Turkish mining sector, with 85 percent of production belonging to the state-owned enterprises that predominate in the production of mineral fuels and metallic ore. The 15 percent that belongs to the private sector is concentrated in industrial minerals. Turkey is a major producer of boron, chromite, marble, barites, magnesite, pumice, feldspar, celestite, and emery. Two-thirds of boron reserves and 40 percent of marble reserves in the world are located in Turkey, and the country provides 80 percent of the world demand of emery. In 1999, mining products accounted for 1.4 percent of total exports, worth US$353 million—down from 1998, when mining exports accounted for a 1.9 percent share of total exports, worth US$531.6 million.

SERVICES

The services sector accounted for 64 percent of GDP in 1999, while employing over one-third of the total labor force. Tourism and banking are the 2 primary service industries in Turkey.

TOURISM. With a share of nearly 26 percent of GDP, the tourism industry in Turkey is strategically important to the Turkish economy. The industry entered the 1980s with 1.5 million tourists annually and a global market share of 0.3 percent. However, the sector took off between 1983 and 1993, growing at an average annual rate of 18 percent, the highest tourism growth rate in the world for the period. In 1998, the number of foreign visitors reached 9.7 million, bringing revenues estimated at US$7.1 billion. As such, Turkey is currently in the world's top 20 tourist destinations, both in terms of visitor numbers and earnings.

Despite these statistics, Turkey remains a relatively undiscovered land for tourists. The country's long and gorgeous coastline, high mountains and lakes, and wealth of historical, religious, and archaeological sites offer opportunities for massive development of tourism. However, the growth of the sector has been plagued with problems, chief among them the fallout from the nuclear disaster at Chernobyl in the Soviet Union, Kurdish terrorist campaigns, and economic problems in neighboring regions. In addition, access to natural and historical wonders is difficult in most parts of the country, and much investment in transportation, waste management, and infrastructure is required to remedy this problem. Since the 1980s, the government has identified tourism as a high-priority industry and has been steadily developing the sector, encouraging both private and foreign investment through new laws and incentive programs.

Today tourism is considered to be one of the leading industries in the Turkish economy. It creates jobs for at least 10 million Turkish citizens and offers a capacity of 563,000 beds. Further capacity of nearly 8,500 beds is available on some 990 yachts that cruise the Aegean and Mediterranean coasts. These are operated by over 100 yacht agencies. The largest number of tourists are from Germany, the **Commonwealth of Independent States** (CIS, formerly the USSR), the United Kingdom, the United States, and France.

FINANCIAL SERVICES. The Turkish financial system is based upon a universal banking system that legally enables commercial banks to operate in all financial markets. As such, banks carry out nearly all of the activities in the money and capital markets in Turkey, and the banking sector has become almost synonymous with the Turkish financial system. The only 2 areas prohibited to commercial banks are leasing and the trading of goods for commercial purposes. On the other hand, development and investment banks may not accept deposits, but can engage in the 2 activities prohibited to the commercial banks. Excluding the Central Bank of Turkey, there were 80 banks operating in Turkey by the end of 1999. Of these, 61 are commercial banks and 19 are development and investment banks. Seven of the banks are state-owned. Much like their counterparts in Germany and Japan, the major private banks have ownership linkages with large non-financial conglomerates. Most state banks are located in Ankara, while many of the private banks are centered in Istanbul.

The banking system has undergone a rapid technological transformation in the last decade. According to the U.S. Department of Commerce, in terms of trade finance, treasury operations, electronic banking, and information management, the dozen leading Turkish banks are as sophisticated as their counterparts in developed countries. Certainly, Turkish banks are among the most profitable in Europe, but this statistic could prove misleading in the long term. Given the high **budget deficit** and high inflation, operations have a short-term focus and profits come primarily from banking investment in short-term government securities and short-term loans with high real interest rates. Therefore, profitability has not been loan-based (contrary to their counterparts in developed countries) and banks lack a lending culture and risk-asset management systems. Therefore, as inflation responds to recent measures and begins to fall, banks will begin losing their highly profitable short-term operations, and will have to focus more on core banking operations with low margins.

The Central Bank of Turkey is responsible for the supervision of the banking sector in order to guarantee that banks meet **liquidity** requirements and operate responsibly. However, banking has suffered in the past from weak supervision and inconsistent accounting practices. The banking sector passed through a crisis in 1999 when 3 small banks failed. The same year, a new law was passed calling for the creation of an independent regulatory agency, toughening operating conditions, and giving weight to regulatory and sanctioning powers. It is expected that, under stricter supervision, the financial sector will grow considerably stronger.

INTERNATIONAL TRADE

Trade played a minor role in the Turkish economy before 1980, but grew rapidly after economic reforms promoted liberalization of foreign trade. These reforms were designed to remove **price controls**, decrease **subsidies**, reduce **tariffs**, and promote exports. In addition to rapid growth in both exports and imports, the reforms brought a change in the structure of foreign trade, and the predominant role of agricultural products came to an end with the emergence of a greater emphasis on industrial products.

In addition to being a World Trade Organization (WTO) member, Turkey has also entered a number of multilateral trade relationships to increase its presence in the world trade arena. It signed a free trade agreement with the European Free Trade Association (EFTA) in 1991. In 1992, Turkey and 10 other nations in the Black Sea region formed the Black Sea Economic Cooperation Organization. Turkey is also a member of the Organization for Economic Cooperation (covering Central Asian countries) and the Organization of the Islamic Conference. Separately, Turkey has entered into free trade agreements with Israel, and with several Central and Eastern European countries.

On 1 January 1996 the EU and Turkey entered into a customs union, covering industrial products and processed agricultural goods, but excluding traditional agricultural products from the agreement. Turkey's adoption of the EU's Common External Tariff has resulted in lower **duty** rates for third-party countries, including the United States.

In 1980, Turkey's total merchandise exports yielded US$2.9 billion. The share of agricultural products was 56.7 percent, while industrial products made up only 36.3 percent. Another 6.5 percent consisted of mineral products. In 1999, Turkish exports reached US$26.6 billion, a figure actually 1.4 percent lower than in 1998. The drop was primarily due to the difficult economic conditions that prevailed in Turkey as a result of the Asian financial crisis and the 2 earthquakes. The share of agricultural products in 1999 was only 9 percent, and mineral products 1.4 percent. By contrast, the share of manufactured products, on the other hand, made up 89.4 percent of total exports in 1999.

The 1991 Gulf war between the U.S.-led coalition and Iraq, and its resultant economic embargo against Iraq, have had adverse effects on Turkish exporters. While exports to Iraq were US$986 million in 1988, this figure had fallen to US$124.1 million by 1995. As a result, Iraq's share in Turkey's exports dropped from 8.4 percent (which would have been enough to rank Iraq as the third largest export market) to 0.56 percent in 1995. The 1992–95 war in Bosnia also took a toll on Turkish exports. Since most of Turkey's exports are to the European markets, the main method of transportation is surface freight. The Bosnian war brought a significant increase in freight costs, as well as causing numerous administrative difficulties. The 1997 Asian financial crisis also had a large impact on Turkey's exports, since the Asian countries are important competitors for Turkish products in overseas markets. The **devaluation** in Asian countries lowered their export prices and gave them a clear advantage over Turkey.

Edible fruits constitute a majority of Turkey's agricultural exports, and this trend continued in 1999. Among industrial products, textiles and ready-to-wear industries remained the major contributor. Other important industrial export sectors were iron and steel, electrical machinery, and motor vehicles and equipment. While Turkey's export markets are highly diversified, OECD countries make up a majority of the trade and took 67.8 percent of exports for 1999. Germany is the largest single export market for Turkey. In 2000, Germany took up 18.7 percent of Turkey's exports. The United States is the second largest

Trade (expressed in billions of US$): Turkey

	Exports	Imports
1975	1.401	4.739
1980	2.910	7.910
1985	7.958	11.343
1990	12.959	22.302
1995	21.637	35.709
1998	25.938	45.369

SOURCE: International Monetary Fund. *International Financial Statistics Yearbook 1999.*

export market, with a share of 11.4 percent, and the United Kingdom the third largest, with 7.4 percent. Italy and France take up the remaining 12.3 percent.

Turkish imports exhibit similar patterns of growth to their exports. In 1980, total imports amounted to US$7.9 billion. The figure grew to US$45.9 billion by 1998 and, by 1999, with economic difficulties affecting domestic demand, imports decreased by 11.4 percent to US$40.7 billion. In 2000, imports totaled US$55.7 billion. In 1999, 28.3 percent of Turkey's imports were made up of machinery, while chemicals made up 15.2 percent, semi-finished goods made up 14.5 percent, fuels made up 11 percent, and transport equipment made up another 9.5 percent.

Looking at the suppliers of the Turkish market, the patterns are very similar to the Turkish exports. OECD countries have taken the largest share of imports, a fact unchanged by 1999 when OECD countries constituted 69.6 percent of total supplies. Imports from the EU countries have the largest share within the OECD group, and 52.6 percent of total imports in 1999. Germany is the first import source for Turkey with a share of 14.5 percent. Italy ranks second with 7.8 percent, and France is third with 7.7 percent. The United States was the fourth most important source of Turkish imports, with a share of 7.6 percent.

MONEY

Inflation remains Turkey's principal economic problem. During the 1970s, inflation averaged about 20 percent, rising to 40 percent during 1981–87, 65 percent during 1989–93 and 85 percent during 1994–95. In late 1997, inflation reached 100 percent before the government launched another attempt at deflating the economy in mid-1998.

The extensive role of the government in the Turkish economy, coupled with weak political leadership, is the primary reason behind the country's chronic inflation. While the program of structural change and liberalization in the 1980s proved successful in promoting economic growth, the government remained hesitant in relinquishing the economic power it held through the strong public sector. However, inefficiencies in the public sector—primarily the expenditure on state economic enterprises—resulted in large, ever-increasing budget deficits. The situation was made worse by political uncertainty as the lack of a stable majority government led to frequent elections. Prior to each election, governments have tended to boost spending in an effort to gain short-term popularity, a ploy that results in even larger **national debt**. Such serious deficits naturally lead to very high rates of inflation.

In 1994, high inflation, coupled with government attempts to manipulate interest rates and an overvalued currency, brought financial crisis and economic recession. Things picked up in 1995, and financial expansion continued until 1998, when the economic difficulties of Russia impacted Turkey. This led to an 18-month program of **deflationary** measures, which was followed up by an IMF-backed 3-year program initiated in December 1999. This aggressive program rested on 3 pillars: an up-front fiscal adjustment to decrease the public deficit in the short-term, structural reforms to ensure long-term stability and a balanced fiscal budget, and a firm **exchange rate** commitment to control external factors. Based on the first 6 months' performance, it seems that the budget deficits have largely been brought under control. Several steps have been taken, and the rate of inflation has been visibly declining. However, more structural reforms need to be completed if this long-term problem is to find a permanent solution.

The Turkish lira (TL) has been a **fully convertible currency** since 1990. With the major economic reforms of the early 1980s, the financial policies were also revamped. For the first 5 years following these reforms, the Central Bank determined the foreign exchange rates on a daily basis, targeting a 5–10 percent per year real depreciation of the Turkish lira as an incentive to exports. After the first 5 years, the foreign exchange rates were completely freed. In 1994, the financial crisis led to a major depreciation of the lira against the U.S. dollar. From 1994 until the end of 1999, the Central Bank allowed the lira to depreciate against a trade-weighted dollar/Euro basket. In 1995, 1 U.S. dollar was worth 45,845 Turkish liras. In January 2000, the same U.S. dollar was worth 545,584 liras. Since the end of 1999, with the initiation of the 3-year deflationary program, the TL is allowed to depreciate based on a targeted **inflation rate**. By 2003, it is expected that the currency will be allowed to float freely, assuming that the deflationary goals are met. However, the uncertainty caused by the high inflation rate has led to the "dollarization" of the economy, where most business transactions and major consumer transactions are usually denominated in U.S. dollars or German marks.

Exchange rates: Turkey

Turkish liras (TL) per US$1	
Dec 2000	677,621
2000	625,219
1999	418,783
1998	260,724
1997	151,865
1996	81,405

SOURCE: CIA *World Factbook 2001* [ONLINE].

This limits the Central Bank's ability to maintain price stability and control inflation.

The Istanbul Stock Exchange (ISE) is the only securities exchange in Turkey. It allow the trading of a wide variety of instruments including stocks, depository receipts, government bonds, **treasury bills**, and real estate certificates. The exchange only began its operations in 1986, but it grew quickly to become one of the top emerging market exchanges of the world. In 1993, the ISE was the best performing stock market in the world, and foreign investment accounted for 25 percent of daily trading volume. By mid-1999 there were 268 companies listed on the exchange. In comparison, the New York Stock Exchange has 3,025 companies listed. The main indicator of the market is the ISE National-100 Index, comprising 100 companies with high **market capitalization** that are also representative of the major economic sectors.

POVERTY AND WEALTH

Using per capita income statistics, Turkey is ranked internationally in the low to medium income group. When compared to countries that were once at the same level but have gone on to make dramatic improvements in their income distribution, it is easy to see that Turkish efforts have been largely unsuccessful. In fact, the renewed and accelerated effort toward economic development and industrialization that began in the early 1980s has had the effect of sharpening the extreme income divide in Turkey. Between 1987 and 1994 the share of the national income earned by the bottom 20 percent of the population dropped by 7.25 percent, and in 1994 the richest 20 percent of the population controlled 47.7 percent of the wealth, while the poorest 20 percent controlled only 5.8 percent.

In addition to their primary residence, a wealthy family in Turkey typically owns several homes around the country. These usually include a second establishment for renting out, and one or more summer homes, mostly in the coastal regions of the Mediterranean or Aegean. Family ties are quite strong in Turkey; therefore most families invest in real estate and rent those homes out until their children grow up and move into them. The children of such families thus have the advantage of starting out in life as well-educated homeowners.

GDP per Capita (US$)

Country	1975	1980	1985	1990	1998
Turkey	1,898	1,959	2,197	2,589	3,167
United States	19,364	21,529	23,200	25,363	29,683
United Kingdom	13,015	14,205	15,546	18,032	20,237
Greece	8,302	9,645	10,005	10,735	12,069

SOURCE: United Nations. *Human Development Report 2000; Trends in human development and per capita income.*

Distribution of Income or Consumption by Percentage Share: Turkey

Lowest 10%	2.3
Lowest 20%	5.8
Second 20%	10.2
Third 20%	14.8
Fourth 20%	21.6
Highest 20%	47.7
Highest 10%	32.3

Survey year: 1994

Note: This information refers to expenditure shares by percentiles of the population and is ranked by per capita expenditure.

SOURCE: *2000 World Development Indicators* [CD-ROM].

A poor family in Turkey might own a home. This could be a farming shelter in a rural area or a makeshift home on the outskirts of urban areas. Some poor families rent low-level apartments, or move into their parents' homes. Where numerous people share one dwelling, unsafe conditions can result from the overcrowding. The children of these families get some education through the public school system, and might occasionally even make it to college, but in rural areas where the nearest school is miles away, the family might choose not to send their children to school. As in the rest of the world, for those in poverty, life in general is hard.

The fostering of industrialization by Turkish governments has had a negative effect on the farming communities. Even though the agricultural sector has, historically, been Turkey's largest employer, it has declined in importance relative to the rapidly developing industrial sector. As a result, the disparity in income between the rural and urban parts of the country has also widened, and has been the cause of significant migration from rural to urban areas. Primarily due to economic instability, **emigration** to other countries has also been a factor since the 1970s.

High inflation and the constantly decreasing purchasing power of the Turkish lira create additional problems. Typically, wages and salaries have failed to keep pace with the increasing prices of consumer goods and services. The average consumer **price index** inflation in 1999 was 65 percent, reflecting a monthly increase in the prices of goods and services of approximately 5 percent. Even when earnings are adjusted for inflation, the adjustments are generally made at the end of the year, forcing consumers to absorb the mid-year price increases until the year-end.

Household Consumption in PPP Terms

Country	All food	Clothing and footwear	Fuel and power[a]	Health care[b]	Education[b]	Transport & Communications	Other
Turkey	45	7	18	6	5	2	16
United States	13	9	9	4	6	8	51
United Kingdom	14	7	9	3	3	6	58
Greece	32	11	14	5	14	8	16

Data represent percentage of consumption in PPP terms.
[a]Excludes energy used for transport.
[b]Includes government and private expenditures.

SOURCE: World Bank. *World Development Indicators 2000.*

The structure of social classes in Turkey is similar in all large cities where the population exceeds 100,000 and evolved with urbanization and industrialization. The urban upper class is mainly made up of government officials, wealthy business people, and professionals, and is primarily determined by political power and/or education. The urban upper class is smaller than the urban middle class and less diverse. Education, particularly a college degree, is the passport to joining the urban middle class. Even though the middle class was expanding steadily during the early 1980s, persistently high inflation rates impeded its stability and growth. The biggest social class to influence the growth of cities since the 1950s is the rural working class. Large numbers of rural poor migrated to the cities, and the movement continues. Prior to the 1950s, more than 80 percent of Turkish residents lived in rural areas, and most of the migrants who came to the cities were unable to find affordable housing. They built shelters on the outskirts of the cities without official permission or approval and, by 1980, up to 60 percent of the inhabitants of big cities were living in these primitive settlements, with no electricity, plumbing, or paved roads. Eventually, some of these neighborhoods were incorporated into the cities and provided with those amenities. About 65 percent of the poor classes depend on unskilled work for their livelihood.

The Turkish government subsidizes education at all levels, from pre-school to university, for all citizens. The law enforces attendance at primary and secondary schools, which accounts for 8 years of education and takes pupils to age 14 or 15. However, due to the insufficient number of higher education institutions, only a select few candidates for college actually get to attend. The selection process is conducted through a nationwide examination held every year, from which students with the highest scores are placed in accordance with their choices. There are also a limited number of private universities for those who can afford to pay.

The Ministry of Health is legally empowered to provide medical and preventive health care services. It establishes and operates hospitals and other health care centers, trains health personnel, and supervises private health facilities. The ministry also supervises the medical and health care personnel who work for the public sector. The pay for state-employed physicians is considerably lower than the earnings of private-practice doctors, and medical facilities are still concentrated in urban areas. Consequently, although steadily improving, access to medical and health care in most rural areas is inadequate.

WORKING CONDITIONS

Statistics for 1995 declared that the Turkish workforce is comprised of approximately 36 percent of the population, or 23.8 million people, 1.5 million of whom work abroad. The agricultural sector employs 46 percent of this workforce. Even though the number of female workers has increased considerably, the Turkish workforce is still male-dominated, with men making up 71 percent of the workforce.

The unemployment rate for 1999 was 7.3 percent, though the U.S. Department of State's *Country Commercial Guide* notes that it could be considerably higher, especially in urban areas, due to discouraged workers leaving the labor force. Even though Turkey has large numbers of unskilled and semi-skilled workers, there is a relative shortage of skilled labor, but the *Country Commercial Guide* also reports that the Turkish labor force is hardworking, productive, and dependable. In addition, labor-management relations have been generally good in recent years.

Labor laws in Turkey support a nominal 45-hour workweek, and the amount of overtime that employers may request is limited. Non-wage benefits that most workers receive include transportation and meals, and some jobs include housing and subsidized vacations. In recent years, fringe benefits have accounted for as much as two-thirds of total remuneration in the industrial sector. Even though the law mandates occupational safety and health regulations and procedures, limited resources and lack of safety awareness often result in inadequate enforcement.

With the exception of the police and the armed forces, Turkish workers have the right to unionize or join existing labor unions. The right to strike exists for most workers except those employed in the public utilities, education, and the petroleum, sanitation, and national defense industries, as well as those who are responsible for life and property protection. The law requires collective bargaining to have taken place before a strike. In order for a union to become a bargaining agent, the law requires that it must represent "50 percent plus one" of the employees at a particular work place and 10 percent of all workers in the particular branch of industry nationwide. However, since 1980 Turkey has been criticized by the International Labor Organization (ILO) for some of the above restrictions. The government has passed constitutional amendments to allow civil servants, who include central government employees such as teachers, to form unions, but it is still illegal for them to strike or bargain collectively.

Under the labor laws and constitution of Turkey, workers must be at least 15 years of age to qualify for full-time employment. Children of ages 13 and 14 can work in jobs that are not physically demanding or part-time if they are enrolled in school or in vocational training. Children are also prohibited from working at night or in physically demanding jobs such as mining. However, in practice, many under-age children continue to work in order to provide badly needed supplementary income for their families. In farming communities for example, the whole family can be seen at work during harvest times. The Turkish government has identified the child labor problem and is working with the ILO to find a solution.

COUNTRY HISTORY AND ECONOMIC DEVELOPMENT

2000 B.C. Hittites begin migrating to the Anatolian (Asia Minor) area of Turkey. Phrygians, Persians, Greeks, and Romans follow this migratory pattern.

1000–1100 A.D. Immigrants from Russia and Mongolia arrive in the area.

1100–1200. Islam becomes entrenched in Turkey and the residents are involved in the Crusade battles.

1300–1400. The Ottoman Empire is established and prevails as a vast trans-continental empire for several centuries. At the peak of its powers, the empire rules vast areas of northern Africa, southeastern Europe, and western Asia. However, it is unable to keep up socio-logically and technologically with developments in Europe. The influence of nationalism causes the diverse ethnic groups within the empire to seek independence, which leads to the fragmentation of the 600-year-old empire.

1923. After World War I and the collapse of the Ottoman Empire, Mustafa Kemal Ataturk founds the Republic of Turkey. Under Ataturk's leadership, the new republic focuses on reform—political, linguistic, economic, and social. Ataturk forms the Republican People's Party, which stays in control until 1950. A republic based on secular governance replaces the once religious and monarchist rule of the Ottoman Empire.

1938. Ataturk dies, having established the ideological base of Turkey as secular, nationalistic, and modern. Since then, the Turkish military has assumed the guardianship of Ataturk's vision.

1945. Turkey joins the United Nations (UN). The Democratic Party is founded and the multi-party era begins in Turkish politics.

1949. Turkey becomes a member of the North Atlantic Treaty Organization (NATO).

1950. The Republican People's Party loses the elections to the Democratic Party.

1960. Growing economic and internal political problems under the Democratic Party government result in a military takeover.

1961. The civilian government is reinstated and a new constitution written, which enshrines the formation of a National Security Council, composed of the president, the prime minister and other key ministers, and representatives of the army, air force, and navy.

1968. Political disturbance erupts between political extremists of the left and right, bringing domestic instability.

1971. The military interferes in order to deal with domestic disturbance, and calls for a replacement government.

1973. General elections result in a coalition government, which falters a year later.

1974. Turkey occupies Northern Cyprus in order to prevent a Greek takeover of the island.

1975. Until 1980, political and social instability increases under the coalition governments of Suleyman Demirel and Bulent Ecevit.

1980. Under the direction of General Kenan Evren, the National Security Council moves to restore public order and remains in control of the government for 2 years. During this time, a national referendum appoints General Evren as president for a 7-year term. A temporary law bans former political party leaders from political involvement for 10 years.

1983. New elections bring in the Motherland Party under Prime Minister Turgut Ozal. Under Ozal's leadership, the country sees the introduction of liberalizing economic reform.

1987. The 10-year ban on former politicians is lifted by a referendum and the government calls a national election. Turgut Ozal wins a second 5-year appointment as prime minister.

1989. Parliament elects Ozal as president of Turkey.

1991. Early elections are held and result in former prime minister Suleyman Demirel's new True Path Party forming a coalition government with the Social Democratic Populist Party.

1993. Demirel is elected president after Ozal's death and Tansu Ciller becomes the country's first female prime minister.

1994. Turkey suffers its worst recession since World War II after government attempts to influence interest rates. In local elections, the Welfare Party wins local elections.

1995. After much political turbulence during a very short period of time, the True Path Party, Welfare Party, and Motherland Party each emerge with a similar number of electoral seats. The coalition collapses in a year and the True Path Party forms a coalition with the Welfare Party, making Necmettin Erbakan the first Islamic prime minister of Turkey.

1996. Turkey enters into a customs union with the European Union.

1997. The coalition government is as unsuccessful as the previous one. The military's political role is challenged by Erbakan's anti-secular efforts, and the military supports business and community groups calling for the government's resignation. In order to ensure compliance with the secular state, the military takes measures that include banning Erbakan from government participation.

1999. The country experiences 2 devastating earthquakes and 3 changes of government. The economy holds up despite expectations of an economic downturn. The 57th government of Turkey, like its predecessors a coalition, is elected. The new government restarts structural reforms to bring stability back to the Turkish economy. In December, the European Union declares Turkey a candidate for full membership.

FUTURE TRENDS

Turkey entered the new millennium with renewed hopes of economic, political, and social development and reform. The 3-party coalition that came into power in April 1999 has shown signs of stability, and many international sources are hopeful that the government will achieve its aims in the next 3–5 years. Its aggressive reform program addresses most of the country's outstanding critical issues, including the often appalling human rights record, undisciplined **fiscal policy**, and state interference in the economy. These financial measures should help to reduce inflation, and speed up privatization of public sector enterprises. There is also a program for structural reform in the social security and taxation systems. With the completion of the Southeastern Anatolian Project (GAP) within the next few years, the Turkish economy should receive a boost. In addition, the project could accomplish much in terms of reducing the disparities in income in different regions of the country, and between rural and urban areas. The possibility of joining the EU in due course should act as a major incentive for the nation to continue on a path of democratization, industrialization, and modernization.

DEPENDENCIES

Turkey has no territories or colonies.

BIBLIOGRAPHY

Colakoglu, N.M. *Executive's Handbook: Turkey Almanac 1998.* Istanbul: InterMedia, 1998.

Economist Intelligence Unit. *Country Profile: Turkey.* London: Economist Intelligence Unit, 2001.

Export Promotion Center of Turkey (IGEME), Trade Point Ankara. *Economic Outlook 2000.* <http://www.igeme.org.tr/english/economy/economy.htm>. Accessed January 2001.

Export Promotion Center of Turkey (IGEME), Trade Point Ankara. *Foreign Trade of Turkey.* <http://www.igeme.org.tr/english/trade/foreign.htm>. Accessed January 2001.

International Monetary Fund, Staff Country Reports. *Turkey: Selected Issues and Statistical Appendix.* <http://www.imf.org/external/pubs/CAT/longres.cfm?sk=3408.0>. Accessed December 2000.

Republic of Turkey. <http://www.turkey.org/start.html>. Accessed September 2001.

U.S. Central Intelligence Agency. *World Factbook 2001: Turkey.* <http://www.odci.gov/cia/publications/factbook/geos/tu.html>. Accessed September 2001.

U.S. Department of State, Bureau of European Affairs. *Background Notes: Turkey.* <http://www.state.gov/www/background_notes/turkey_9910_bgn.html>. Accessed December 2000.

U.S. Department of State. *1999 Country Reports on Economic Policy and Trade Practices.* <http://www.state.gov/www/

issues/economic/trade_reports/1999/turkey.pdf>. Accessed December 2000.

U.S. Department of State. *FY 2001 Country Commercial Guide: Turkey.* <http://www.state.gov/www/about_state/business/com_guides/2001/europe/index.html>. Accessed September 2001.

U.S. Library of Congress. *Turkey: A Country Study.* <http://lcweb2.loc.gov/frd/cs/trtoc.html>. Accessed December 2000.

World Trade Organization, Ministry of Foreign Affairs and Trade. *Trade Policy Review: Turkey: October 1998.* <http://www.wto.org/english/tratop_e/tpr_e/tp83_e.htm>. Accessed December 2000.

—Tunga Kiyak

TURKMENISTAN

CAPITAL: Ashgabat.

MONETARY UNIT: Turkmen manat (TMM). One manat equals 100 tenge. There are notes of TMM1, 5, 10, 50, 100, 500, and 1,000. Coins come in denominations of 1, 5, 10, 20, and 50 tenge.

CHIEF EXPORTS: Natural gas, petroleum, cotton, chemicals, processed food, minerals.

CHIEF IMPORTS: Machinery and transportation equipment, chemicals, fuel, food and dairy products, sugar, textiles.

GROSS DOMESTIC PRODUCT: US$19.6 billion (purchasing power parity, 2000 est.).

BALANCE OF TRADE: **Exports:** US$2.4 billion (f.o.b., 2000 est.). **Imports:** US$1.65 billion (c.i.f., 2000 est.).

COUNTRY OVERVIEW

LOCATION AND SIZE. Turkmenistan is located in central Asia, bordered by Iran (992 kilometers/616 miles) to the south, Uzbekistan (1,621 kilometers/1,007 miles) to the northeast, Kazakhstan (379 kilometers/235 miles) to the north, Afghanistan (744 kilometers/462 miles) to the southeast, and the Caspian Sea (1,786 kilometers/1,110 miles) to the west. Turkmenistan has an area of 488,100 square kilometers (188,455 square miles), slightly larger than the state of California. The capital, Ashgabat, is located in the south-central part of the country, near the border with Iran.

POPULATION. The Turkmenistan population is smaller than in other central Asian states. According to the last Soviet census in 1989, 2.54 million Turkmens lived in the republic. In 1989 Turkmens comprised 68.4 percent of the population, Russians 9.5 percent, Uzbeks 9 percent, and Kazakhs 2 percent. Due to the **emigration** of Russians, in 1998 Turkmens made up 77 percent of the population, and Russians only 6.7 percent. Of all the former Soviet Republics, Turkmenistan had the highest infant mortality rate—73.25 per 1,000 in 1997—and the shortest life expectancy, 61 years in 2001 (both figures estimated). During the next decade, population growth is expected to slow considerably as infant mortality rates increase and health care deteriorates.

Only 3 percent of Turkmenistan's land is arable. The Kara Kum, or Black Sand Desert, occupies almost 75 percent of Turkmenistan's territory. The 16 urban areas along its borders and coastline account for 45 percent of the population. Almost 50 percent of the population lives around the capital, Ashgabat, and only 2 other cities have populations with more than 100,000 inhabitants.

OVERVIEW OF ECONOMY

Turkmenistan is one of the most politically conservative and impoverished of the former Soviet republics. It has made little progress toward **restructuring** its economic foundation. Between 1991 and 1998, Turkmenistan's economic activity plummeted 45 percent. Its economy is agricultural, accounting for almost half of the **gross domestic product** (GDP), primarily marked by livestock raising and cotton production. Prior to independence in 1991, Turkmenistan was the second-largest cotton producer in the Soviet Union (behind Uzbekistan) and tenth largest in the world. It produces more cotton per capita than any other country in the world. Turkmenistan has the world's fifth largest reserves of natural gas and considerable oil resources. Turkmenistan is also known for subtropical fruits, melons, and nuts, especially pomegranates, figs, olives, and almonds.

Since gaining independence in 1991, Turkmenistan's government has emphasized grain production to increase its self-sufficiency and to limit Russian influence. The government has taken a cautious approach to economic reform, though. In 1992 the government of President Saparmurat Niyazov introduced his Ten Years of Prosperity program, which provided for Soviet-style **subsidies** for natural gas, electricity, and drinking water to all households in the republic. The program was afterwards modified to Ten Years of Stability, yet continues to subsidize for social needs, accounting for almost 60 percent of the state budgetary expenditures.

In the 1970s the Soviets made major investments in oil and gas production in Turkmenistan. By 1992 gas

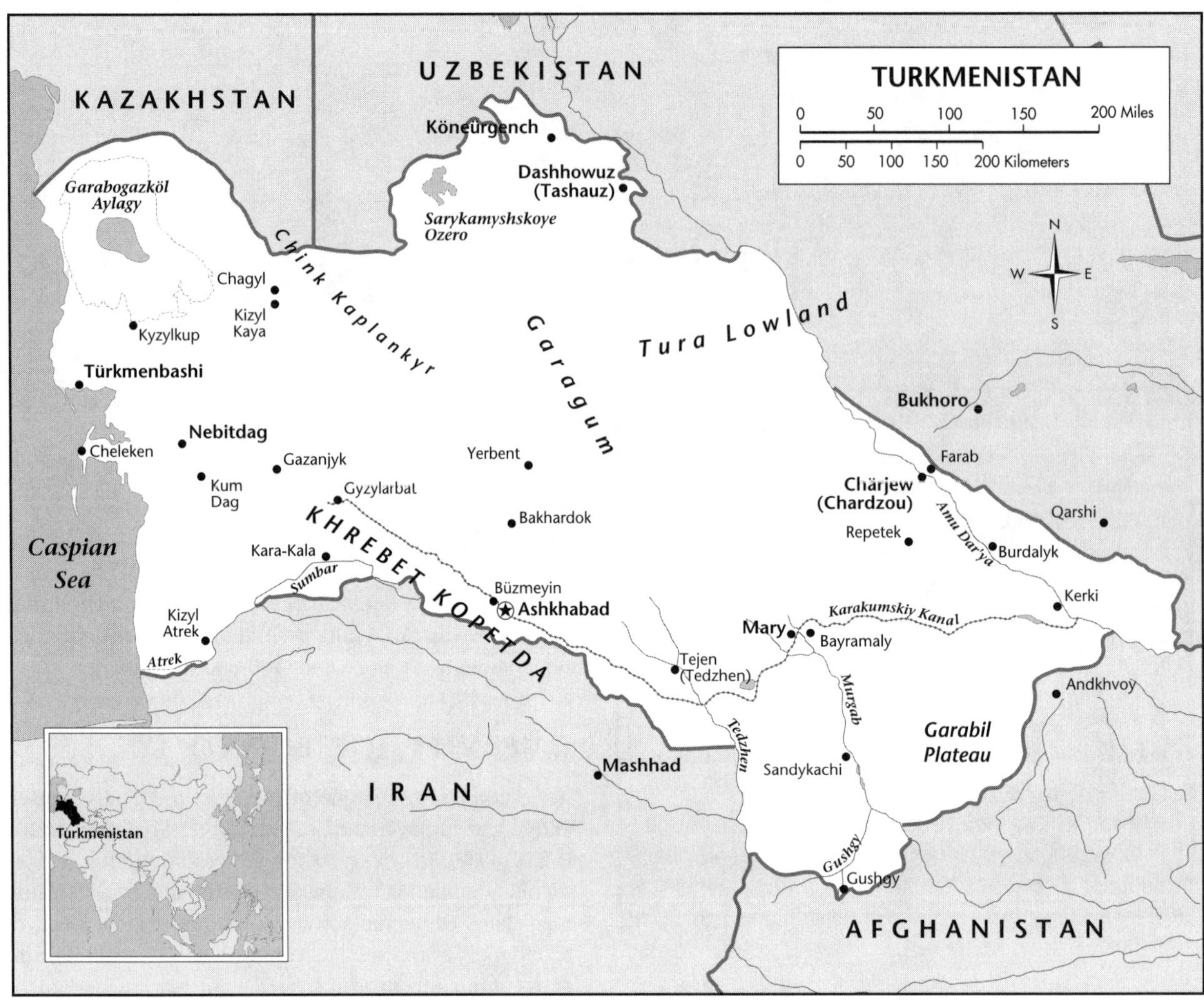

production accounted for almost 60 percent of GDP. Combined with the failure of trading partners to make payments, Russia's refusal to allow Turkmenistan gas transportation through its territory resulted in reduced output by more than 40 percent, mounting debts, and a sharp decline in overall industrial production. Turkmenistan continues to rely upon its abundant natural resources and cotton production to sustain its inefficient and declining economy.

Sources differ greatly on Turkmenistan's **macroeconomic** indicators since 1991. Government figures are often inflated to provide a more positive picture. Unemployment statistics for Turkmenistan are unreliable, but according to government sources in 1997 it was 5 percent. **Real wages** have declined by 25 percent since 1997 and **inflation**, which peaked in 1993 at more than 3,000 percent, dropped to 30 percent in 1999. The chief reason for the economic collapse was the failure of Russia, Ukraine, and other central Asian republics to pay for goods. In addition, the decline in energy prices hurt the economy.

POLITICS, GOVERNMENT, AND TAXATION

Turkmenistan was the first central Asian republic to create a new constitution, which proclaimed the country a presidential republic. It is dominated by Saparmurat Niyazov, who won election in June 1992. In January 1994 a referendum extended his rule from a 5-year term to a ten-year term; in December 1999 he was made president for life. He is the leader of the state and supreme commander of the armed forces. In accordance with the Turkmenistan constitution, he also appoints all cabinet ministers. Presidential powers extend to all facets of the country's economic and political life, even including the right to issue edicts that have the force of law.

The 1992 Turkmenistan constitution established a national assembly with 50 members elected to 5-year terms. Its primary duties are to enact and approve criminal legislation and ratify presidential decrees. In practice, however, international observers have criticized this body for its failure to limit the expansion of presidential powers over domestic and foreign affairs. In addition, there are the national council and a council of elders, both of which wield little power or influence in political affairs.

In December 1991 the Communist Party of Turkmenistan was renamed the Democratic Party of Turkmenistan (DPT). It controls all political activity in Turkmenistan, though ostensibly allowing political opposition. In 1992, under an initiative proposed by Niyazov, a party called the Peasant Justice Party was formed, consisting of regional secretaries of the DPT. A small opposition party, independent of government sanction, was formed in 1989 but was banned in 1990. The Agzybirlik (Unity) Party operates mostly in exile from Moscow.

Since 1991 Turkmenistan has attempted to establish relations with neighboring countries and potential trading partners in order to exploit its natural resources. Internal reform, however, has hampered economic development. In 1992 and 1993 the government passed laws on foreign investment, banking, property ownership, and intellectual property rights designed to attract foreign investment. The laws allow 100 percent ownership by foreign investors, but in practice the government restricts this right and prefers **joint ventures** rather than the full purchase of plants, factories, and other facilities by foreigners.

In 1993 the government began an ambitious 10-year plan that was designed to double per capita income, which was less than US$3,000 per year in **purchasing power parity** terms. The government freed the population from certain fees, such as for heating and electricity, and initiated in December 1992 the Ten Years of Prosperity program, which envisioned a transition to a free market economy, the dismantling of Soviet-style planned management, and extensive social welfare services. Soon thereafter, however, the government changed the slogan to Ten Years of Stability when anticipated investments and profits failed to materialize. Nevertheless, the government took great strides to attract investment for the plan, as Turkmenistan struggled to upgrade its basic **infrastructure**. The government started a national airline and built a new airport, along with new roads, buildings, and hotels in Ashgabat. Emphasis later shifted to constructing new pipelines, or expanding capacity in old ones, to diversify its markets and avoid further dependency upon Russia to export its natural gas.

In 1994 Turkmenistan was in the midst of a severe economic crisis. The government was forced to ration food, GDP fell more than 20 percent, and inflation was growing at 1,100 percent. In 1995, the government fixed the minimum wage at TMM1,000, which, according to some sources, corresponded to roughly 4 kilograms (8.8 pounds) of meat or potatoes.

Roughly two-thirds of Turkmenistan's revenues come directly from gas exports. The decline in international energy prices forced the government to broaden the tax base to lessen the impact of revenue shortfalls. No information is available on tax compliance, but it has been estimated that it is quite limited. Corporate and **income tax** rates range from 25 percent to 35 percent, although collection procedures, liability, and individual rates are often complicated, contradictory, subject to abuse, and arbitrarily applied.

INFRASTRUCTURE, POWER, AND COMMUNICATIONS

Turkmenistan inherited an aging infrastructure from the Soviet Union, with 13,000 seriously depreciated railway cars, insufficient signaling and communication equipment, and inadequate staffing. The Turkmenistan government has ambitious plans for a highly extended transport infrastructure, with priorities devoted to railroad and pipelines development. Turkmenistan's transport system carries freight chiefly via rail, roads, internal waterways, and pipelines. Air transport accounted for less than 1 percent of transportation in the early 1990s. Turkmenistan still uses the Turkmenbashi-Ashgabat-Chardzhou Line as its primary railroad, which links Turkmenistan with Russia and Europe through Uzbekistan. Construction of this

Communications

Country	Newspapers	Radios	TV Sets[a]	Cable subscribers[a]	Mobile Phones[a]	Fax Machines[a]	Personal Computers[a]	Internet Hosts[b]	Internet Users[b]
	1996	1997	1998	1998	1998	1998	1998	1999	1999
Turkmenistan	N/A	276	201	N/A	1	N/A	N/A	0.56	2
United States	215	2,146	847	244.3	256	78.4	458.6	1,508.77	74,100
Russia	105	418	420	78.5	5	0.4	40.6	13.06	2,700
Iran	28	265	157	0.0	6	N/A	31.9	0.05	100

[a]Data are from International Telecommunication Union, *World Telecommunication Development Report 1999* and are per 1,000 people.

[b]Data are from the Internet Software Consortium (http://www.isc.org) and are per 10,000 people.

SOURCE: World Bank. *World Development Indicators 2000.*

railroad began in the 1880s to connect Turkestan with the Russian Empire. In recent years, construction has begun on a line expected to link Turkmenistan with Iran, although most observers do not expect it to develop as a primary trade route. Plans are being made to build 1,000 kilometers (621 miles) of new railroads, but this requires substantial foreign investment which is lacking. Another plan has called for a railroad that would connect Istanbul with Beijing, running through Turkmenistan, but this too has failed to materialize.

Turkmenistan has focused considerable attention on expanding its present pipeline capacity and building new pipelines. In April 1993, Niyazov announced that an agreement had been reached with Iran to construct a new pipeline to transport natural gas from Turkmenistan through Iran to the Persian Gulf. These plans were met with serious international opposition, particularly from the United States and Russia. The Russians profit from the Turkmenistan dependence upon old Soviet transport routes; however, aging pipelines and insufficient capacity subject Turkmenistan to the whims of Moscow and the inability of former Soviet consumers to make payment. The United States encouraged Ashgabat to construct a line under the Caspian Sea to Turkey, or increase merchant fleet trade, in order to export its most valuable commodity.

Roads in Turkmenistan vary considerably in quality, with 2 major highways that crisscross the country. In 1990, there were nearly 23,000 kilometers (14,292 miles) of roads, of which a little more than 15,000 kilometers (9,321 miles) were paved. Poor maintenance and increased freight and passenger traffic have severely strained the system.

Turkmenistan has 64 airports of varying sizes and capacities, with only 22 having permanently surfaced runways. The main airport, in Ashgabat, includes a new international complex connecting the country to China, Russia, Iran, Pakistan, Turkey, and European locations. There are plans to upgrade Turkmenistan Airlines with Boeing airplanes, replacing some of the aging Aeroflot aircraft.

Telecommunications is provided exclusively by the Turkmenistan Ministry of Communications, which also manages the country's postal services. There are 2 state-controlled broadcasting centers, the Orbita station in the capital and another in Nebitdag. The telephone network is inadequately maintained and insufficiently developed. Less than 30 percent of households have a telephone, and those are principally in the capital. The government has been upgrading the system, including signing agreements with Turkey to install electronic exchanges and international circuit capacity designed to improve local, long distance, and international communications.

Electrical power is one resource that Turkmenistan exports. Approximately 99.94 percent is supplied by fossil fuel, particularly natural gas, and 0.06 percent is hydraulically produced. In 1998, 8.745 billion kilowatt-hours (kwh) of electricity was produced, of which 2.7 billion kwh were exported. In May 1998, a new line was developed to export electricity to Iran. Plans to export electricity to Afghanistan and Turkey are also being negotiated.

ECONOMIC SECTORS

Turkmenistan's economy is dominated by state control of agriculture and industry, legacies of Soviet economic developments and regional links. The CIA *World Factbook* indicated that agriculture accounted for 25 percent of GDP and industry for 43 percent in 1999. Given that about 44 percent of the population is involved in agriculture, Turkmenistan has attempted **privatization** schemes, but with little success. Moreover, Turkmenistan, which has never opted for a market economy, continues Soviet-like systems with multiple **exchange rates**, state orders, and regulated prices, making expanded trade with neighboring states extremely difficult.

The best option for Turkmenistan to restructure its economy, and to develop some sort of sustainable growth, appears to be its ability to market and sell its natural resources, in particular natural gas. The absence of infrastructure, however, raises doubts about Turkmenistan's ability to do so at the pace necessary for economic expansion. Since transportation and export problems have caused problems throughout Turkmenistan's entire economy, especially for the international trade of its energy resources, establishing new markets and routes for trade

Turkmenistan
GDP–COMPOSITION BY SECTOR–1997 est.

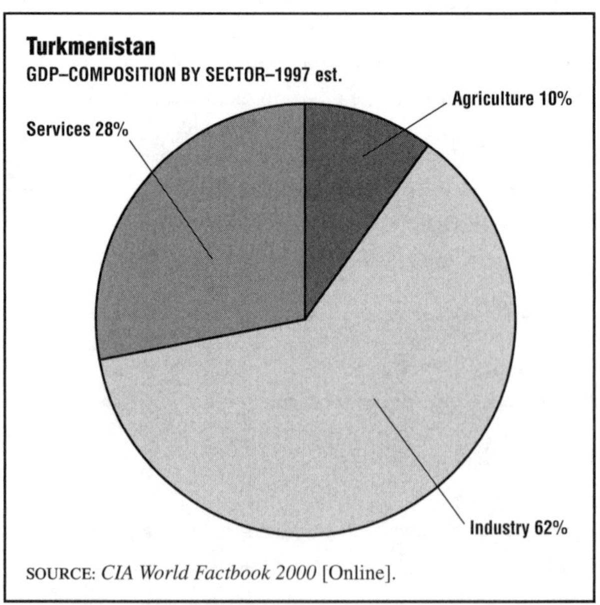

SOURCE: *CIA World Factbook 2000* [Online].

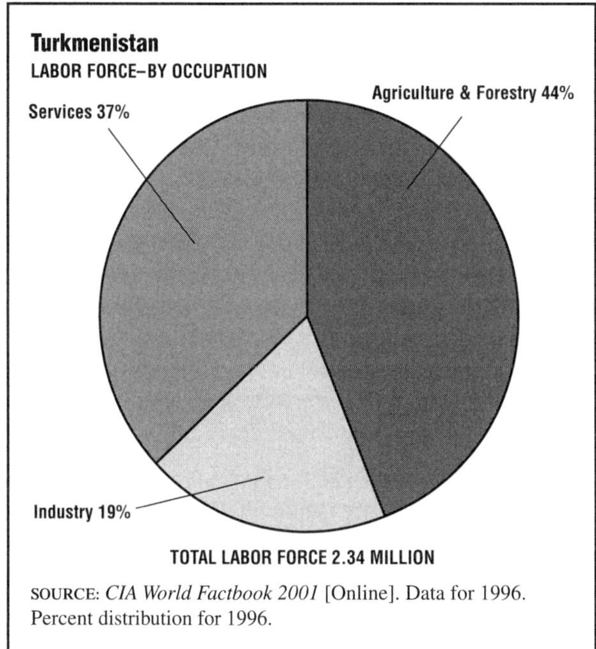

SOURCE: *CIA World Factbook 2001* [Online]. Data for 1996. Percent distribution for 1996.

is of crucial importance. Foreign investment in Turkmenistan has been substantial, although due to the political environment it has decreased almost 70 percent since 1995. In 1992 investment was US$11 million, peaking in 1995 at US$233 million, but falling to only US$62 million in 1998.

AGRICULTURE

Since 1991, Turkmenistan has attempted to restructure the agricultural sector to reduce its dependency upon other former Soviet republics. Agricultural policy has focused upon grain production, which has resulted in significant increases in non-cotton production, but the new crops are unlikely to thrive unless changes are also made to the **procurement** and transportation sectors. Due to the distance between farms and processing plants, less than 10 percent of fruits, vegetables, and cereals are processed in the country. Livestock raising remains an important part of Turkmenistan's agricultural sector, primarily in meat products such as beef, mutton, and chicken. In 1997 agricultural exports, chiefly cotton, amounted to US$364.5 million, whereas the value of agricultural imports was US$271.7 million.

To understand Turkmenistan's agriculture, it is necessary to understand Soviet practices and collectivization schemes. Roughly 50 percent of arable land is planted in cotton. Due to Soviet planning and economic specialization, Turkmenistan has few textile factories and manufactures less than 1 percent of the cotton grown. It must continue to import cotton fabrics and clothing from Russia and other states in the region. Turkmenistan has made little progress in restructuring the agricultural economy, with only limited privatization and expanded diversification of crop production. Moreover, Turkmenistan is heavily dependent upon irrigation for agriculture. Dilapidated canals and inefficient water management, however, result in only half of the water being delivered to the fields.

The Soviets practiced surface level irrigation, in which water is provided along furrows rather than direct application. Consequently, watering sometimes took days instead of hours, even with around-the-clock irrigation. In addition, the Soviets abandoned nighttime irrigation in favor of daytime irrigation, increasing water usage substantially. Almost no mechanism was in place to determine optimal application, or if there was adequate monitoring equipment, it was in disrepair. The result was endemic over-watering and a casual disregard for resource management.

Management and maintenance of the country's irrigation network is expensive. The budget allocated for maintaining the existing irrigation canals has fallen from US$3.2 million to only US$20,000. In addition, the government has failed to reduce sediment in the canal, due to failing equipment and insufficient financial resources, cutting annual clearance requirements by more than 50 percent. Staffing for the irrigation network has also become a critical problem for Turkmenistan, falling from 1,700 personnel in 1987 to only 640 in 1999. Relatively few young people are employed in irrigation and water management, so Turkmenistan could be facing a severe crisis unless newly-skilled replacement personnel are found.

INDUSTRY

Soviet industrialization left a legacy of ecological devastation, uneven development, and an obsolete, rapidly deteriorating infrastructure. Furthermore, Soviet industrialization often ignored local conditions, conflicting with a traditional society hesitant to embrace new technology. Thus, the Soviets proceeded to emphasize heavy industry that was more and more based upon imported labor from the European regions of the Soviet Union. Local labor has not materialized to replace this technically skilled workforce. Turkmenistan has a strong resource base but inadequate training and financial resources to expand its domestic industry in the near future. Nevertheless, the government is taking steps to lessen its dependency upon industrial trade.

Turkmenistan has a critical shortage of industrial capacity to process its agricultural products and natural resources, a situation that has deteriorated considerably since 1991. Most industrial development in Turkmenistan under Soviet rule was oriented toward heavy industry, especially in chemicals and petrochemicals such as sulfuric acid, ammonia, detergents, and fertilizers. Small-scale steel production was used to manufacture water pumps and construction. Since independence, Turkmenistan has invested in the development of cement production and farm machinery; however, these form a very limited part of Turkmenistan industry. Turkmenistan has also begun to develop local leather works and foodstuffs industries, which remain underdeveloped due to low mechanization and an insufficiently trained workforce. Turkmenistan has no textile factories, only spinning and clothing; however, the Turkmenistan carpet industry remains vibrant and has an international reputation for excellent quality. The Turkmenistan Carpet Production Association manages 10 factories, although household production accounts for a considerable share of overall production.

Turkmenistan has developed numerous joint ventures with international companies in order to update its industrial capacities, increase productivity, and lower pollution levels, which remain high. In addition, it has increased investment in light industry, particularly in consumer and durable goods, but Turkmenistan relies on trade for most products.

SERVICES

The service sector in Turkmenistan accounted for roughly 32 percent of GDP in 1999 and employed an estimated 37 percent of the workforce in 1996. Transportation, energy, and health care are particularly important. Tourism is relatively small, although in 1997 more than 250,000 tourists traveled to Turkmenistan, an increase of more than 400 percent from 1993.

Financial services are strictly controlled by the government, particularly currency exchanges and lending. Loans are provided to finance projects in the republic, with particular emphasize given to agriculture. The **retail** sector is rather primitive, with few major retail centers, as most citizens buy products at local bazaars and through state-run stores.

Health care in Turkmenistan continues to be free to all citizens, although the system lacks modern technology. Basic medicines are in critically short supply and treatment is crude at best. Medical training has also deteriorated since 1991. According to one study, in Dashhowez Province half of the patients treated died because physicians lacked proper training and surgical supplies. Moreover, most facilities do not have running water and central heating. In addition, pharmaceuticals must be purchased with **hard currency**, which is scarce and costly. In rural areas, many Turkmens must rely solely upon traditional healers, who use prayer and herbs.

INTERNATIONAL TRADE

Since independence, Turkmenistan has sought to advance its sovereignty by entering only bilateral trade agreements. The country's potential prosperity is dependent upon its ability to maintain peace and stability in a possibly volatile region. Thus, its international relations and trade are focused within former Soviet territories of central Asia, Russia, and the Caucasus, while seeking to cultivate new relations with Asia, Europe, and America. Since transportation and export problems have caused problems for Turkmenistan's economy, especially for the international trade of its energy resources, establishing new markets and routes is of crucial importance. Foreign investors are, however, hesitant to work in Turkmenistan, usually because the socioeconomic infrastructure has deteriorated or laws necessary to protect their investments can be violated by presidential decree.

Russia continues to be the most important partner for Turkmenistan's international trade. Russia dominates 50 percent of all trade within the **Commonwealth of Independent States** (CIS), particularly among natural resources, and appears unlikely to relinquish control in the near future because it commands the transportation grid built during the Soviet era. Thus, for example, with oil and gas, the pipelines run through Russia, which has often punitively regulated the amount of central Asian goods allowed to traverse its territory.

Russia was the only CIS country to export natural gas to the outside world until Turkmenistan signed an agreement with Iran in 1997. A pricing feud over supplies to Ukraine with Russia's state-run petroleum and natural gas company Gazprom severely disrupted Turkmenistan's ability to export any gas. Shipments were halted with the concomitant effect of handicapping all Turkmenistan trade, causing its exports to fall 61 percent in 1997 and GDP tumble 26 percent. Opening an export route through Iran eased some of Turkmenistan's economic woes. A resolution with Gazprom was reached, but the prices were so high that Turkmenistan will realize minimal profits.

Turkmenistan's trade with CIS states hovered around 50 percent in 1997. This was a slight decrease from previous years and represented Turkmenistan's somewhat successful efforts to reduce its dependency on Russia. Nevertheless, its export-import income has fallen significantly since independence. Export trade in 1992 was roughly US$1.5 billion and US$751 million in 1997. Exports have increased slightly since then, but the low volume reflects the country's continuing struggle to sell its natural gas. Imports, however, rose dramatically from the 1992 figure of US$446 million, jumping the next year to US$2.1 billion, but decreasing to US$1.2 billion by 1997. Because trade with the CIS consists mostly of energy resources, rather than manufactured goods, Turkmenistan has generally maintained a positive trade balance, but it has fluctuated widely since 1992. It is the only former Soviet republic to have a consistently positive trade balance since the collapse of the Soviet Union.

Efforts have been made by central Asian leaders to increase trade, but these have generally been rebuffed by Turkmenistan, which prefers bilateral trade agreements. Turkmenistan rejected Kazakhstan's attempt to create a Euroasiatic Union, but Niyazov agreed to join the Economic Cooperation Organization (ECO), which was founded by Turkey, Iran, and Pakistan in 1960. The ECO was designed to coordinate economic policies between these states and was given new life by the inclusion of the 5 central Asian republics. The move strengthened relations between Turkmenistan and Iran, a feature that disturbed Russia. Russia's demand that they choose between membership in the CIS or the ECO was hardly acknowledged.

Outside of the CIS, Turkey is Turkmenistan's most important trading partner and continues to be Turkmenistan's most vital supplier of technical and financial support. In 1993, for example, it provided the Turkmenistan government with credits worth US$92 million. Turkey further regards Turkmenistan as a country of transit to central Asian markets. Moreover, Turkmenistan is valued by Turkey essentially as a seller of natural gas. In a basic accord signed in October 1994, Turkey agreed to purchase natural gas from Turkmenistan for the next 30 years.

Turkmenistan has signed natural gas export agreements with Iran, believing its southern neighbor to be the most logical conveyor of Turkmenistan resources, even though the United States opposes the arrangement and central Asian leaders have strongly criticized Niyazov's attempts to enhance this relationship. In 1993 Turkmenistan and Iran signed a 25-year accord with the objective of delivering 28 billion cubic meters of natural gas. Delivery will be through a pipeline, jointly built but principally financed by Iran. In order to accelerate the process, in 1995 the countries agreed to transfer 8 billion cubic meters of natural gas annually.

MONEY

Turkmenistan maintains an official exchange rate (US$1=TMM5,200), but currency exchanges on the **black market** are often 3 times the official rate. The government has not significantly intervened to artificially support the national currency, although in January and again in April 1995 the Central Bank attempted unsuccessfully to unify the 2 exchange rates. Subsequently, the government decided to limit foreign exchange sites, which resulted in greater disparities between the official and black-market rates. Most banks in Turkmenistan are government owned and the principle lending task is to channel foreign loans into designated state-run enterprises. In 1998, prudent steps taken by the government required businesses to have minimum capital equal to US$1 million; however, audits to determine **solvency** and adherence to banking laws have been sporadic. In December 1998, the government suspended free convertibility of hard currency to limit **capital flight**.

Turkmenistan has a single stock market, with 300 joint-stock companies. In 1993, the Law on Securities and Stock exchanges was adopted, although companies have not been allowed to issue stock freely. The success of Turkmenistan's stock market will depend upon further privatization projects and a more transparent legal and accounting system, which remain the same from Soviet times and are not likely to be changed in the near future.

POVERTY AND WEALTH

By most accounts, living standards in Turkmenistan have not dropped as dramatically since 1991 as they have in other former Soviet republics, although conditions are worsening. During the Soviet era, Turkmenistan was considered one of the poorest republics, with roughly 45 percent of the population living below the official poverty line in 1989. The CIA *World Factbook* reported that, by 1999, 58 percent of the population lived below the poverty line. Since the collapse of the Soviet Union, uneven economic developments have served to create a tiny stratum of the population in Turkmenistan that holds most of the wealth. For the average Turkmenistan citizen, the availability of food and **consumer goods** has declined while prices have risen. Most people continue to receive their income from state employment. Wages are based upon the old Soviet method, with people working in in-

Exchange rates: Turkmenistan

Turkmen manats per US$1	
Jan 2001	5,200
Jan 2000	5,200
Jan 1999	5,350
Jan 1998	N/A
Jan 1997	4,070
Jan 1996	2,400

SOURCE: CIA *World Factbook 2001* [ONLINE].

GDP per Capita (US$)

Country	1975	1980	1985	1990	1998
Turkmenistan	N/A	N/A	N/A	1,154	486
United States	19,364	21,529	23,200	25,363	29,683
Russia	2,555	3,654	3,463	3,668	2,138
Iran	1,611	1,129	1,208	1,056	1,275

SOURCE: United Nations. *Human Development Report 2000; Trends in human development and per capita income.*

Distribution of Income or Consumption by Percentage Share: Turkmenistan

Lowest 10%	2.6
Lowest 20%	6.1
Second 20%	10.2
Third 20%	14.7
Fourth 20%	21.5
Highest 20%	47.5
Highest 10%	31.7

Survey year: 1998

Note: This information refers to expenditure shares by percentiles of the population and is ranked by per capita expenditure.

SOURCE: *2000 World Development Indicators* [CD-ROM].

dustry, transportation, and science faring better than individuals employed in health, education, and services. By 1995, real wages had dropped nearly 48 percent since independence. Conditions in rural areas are often much worse than in urban, where unemployment is as high as 60 percent, although this is difficult to determine with any precision. It was estimated in 1997 that households in Turkmenistan spent 63 percent of income on food, which will likely increase as prices continue to rise and real wages decline.

Since independence, Turkmenistan has experienced significant increases in the rural population. This growth is expected to aggravate economic conditions in rural areas. Worsening economic conditions might force many to leave the rural areas to find work in the country's urban centers. Turkmenistan's cities are not able to accommodate rural migrants seeking employment in urban industries, however, thereby keeping wages below subsistence levels.

WORKING CONDITIONS

Working conditions in Turkmenistan have declined since independence, chiefly because the government has made almost no progress toward economic reform. Most Turkmens are employed in state enterprises and guaranteed a minimum wage. The CIA *World Factbook* reported that the **labor force** consisted of 2.34 million people (roughly 50 percent of the population) in 1996. Some sources indicate that the labor force is declining due to emigration and relative population stagnation. The majority of the population works in agriculture and decreased productivity and failing infrastructure means growing impoverishment for most Turkmens. Extremely limited privatization in rural areas also will lead to distressing economic and social conditions in the near future.

A Soviet-style trade union, the Federation of Trade Unions, is the only labor union in Turkmenistan. The government does not permit collective bargaining. The political environment acts as a sufficient obstacle to independent union formation and activity, however. Child labor laws are comprehensive, although children in rural areas often must work. Moreover, high school students are often deployed in the fields during intensive harvest periods, particularly in cotton fields. Women make up a significant percentage of the workforce, although they face discrimination. Labor disputes often go unresolved because the judiciary serves at the pleasure of the president, who appoints and can dismiss them at will.

COUNTRY HISTORY AND ECONOMIC DEVELOPMENT

1881. Russians defeat Turkmenistan tribes and annex Turkmenistan into the Governorship of Turkestan.

1888. Russians start construction of railway from Krasnovodsk (now Turkmenbashi) to Ashgabat.

1916. Widespread revolt in central Asia against the tsarist government's use of local troops during World War I.

1917. Russian Revolution and Civil War begin.

1920. Soviet General Frunze captures Ashgabat, ending the anti-Soviet government in Turkmenistan.

Household Consumption in PPP Terms

Country	All food	Clothing and footwear	Fuel and power[a]	Health care[b]	Education[b]	Transport & Communications	Other
Turkmenistan	32	6	14	6	18	11	14
United States	13	9	9	4	6	8	51
Russia	28	11	16	7	15	8	16
Iran	20	10	32	12	8	9	10

Data represent percentage of consumption in PPP terms.

[a]Excludes energy used for transport.

[b]Includes government and private expenditures.

SOURCE: World Bank. *World Development Indicators 2000.*

1921. New Economic Policy begins in Soviet Union.

1924. The Turkmenistan Soviet Socialist Republic is established.

1929. Collectivization begins in central Asia, widespread famine as Turkmens resist.

1930s. Pastoral nomadism ends in Turkmenistan; cotton production increases.

1959. Construction begins on the Karakum Main Canal.

1990. Turkmenistan declares its autonomy from the Soviet Union in August.

1990. Saparmurat Niyazov is elected president in October.

1991. Turkmenistan declares its independence from the Soviet Union.

1991. The Communist Party is renamed the Democratic Party of Turkmenistan in December.

1992. Niyazov introduces the Ten Years of Prosperity economic reforms.

1992. Turkmenistan joins the Economic Cooperation Organization (ECO), designed to coordinate economic policies among Iran, Turkey, and Pakistan and given new life by the inclusion of the 5 Central Asian Soviet republics.

1993. New Turkmenistan currency, the manat, is introduced.

1998. The financial collapse in Russia affects Turkmenistan's energy trade.

1999. Niyazov is named president for life.

FUTURE TRENDS

Turkmenistan is regarded by most observers as the most restrictive state in the region. Human rights organizations have consistently criticized the political and economic environment in Turkmenistan. President Niyazov has promoted a political system that rigorously opposes any **liberalization** or reform programs. Many specialists believe that Turkmenistan has the natural resources necessary to make an effective economic recovery; however, the political environment is considered by most to be a major impediment to future prosperity. For instance, the investments made by major transnational petroleum companies have thus far ended up in the bank accounts of political elite.

The best option for Turkmenistan to restructure its economy and develop some sort of sustainable growth appears to be its ability to market and sell its natural resources, in particular its natural gas. The absence of infrastructural preconditions, economic reforms, and political liberalization raises doubts about Turkmenistan's ability to do so quickly enough for expansion. The most serious non-political obstacle to Turkmenistan's economic future is its lack of access to markets with clients capable of paying for Turkmenistan's trade resources.

DEPENDENCIES

Turkmenistan has no territories or colonies.

BIBLIOGRAPHY

Capisani, Giampaolo. *The Handbook of Central Asia: A Comprehensive Survey of the New Republics.* New York and London: I. B. Tauris, 2000.

Country Watch. *Turkmenistan 1999/2000.* <http://countrywatch.com/files/175/cw_country.asp?vCOUNTRY=175>. Accessed March 2001.

Curtis, Glenn, editor. *Kazakhstan, Kyrgyzstan, Tajikistan, Turkmenistan, and Uzbekistan: Country Studies.* Washington, DC: Library of Congress, 1996.

Freedom House. "Turkmenistan." <http://freedomhouse.org/nit98/turkmen.html>. Accessed February 2001.

Freitag-Wirminghaus, Rainer. "Turkmenistan's Place in Central Asia and the World." In *Post-Soviet Central Asia,* edited by Touraj Atabaki and John O'Kane. London and New York: Tauris Academic Studies, 1998.

Gurgen, Emine, and others. *Economic Reforms in Kazakhstan, Kyrgyz Republic, Tajikistan, Turkmenistan, and Uzbekistan.* Washington DC: International Monetary Fund, 1999.

O'Hara, Sarah, and Tim Hannan. "Irrigation and Water Management in Turkmenistan: Past Systems, Present Problems and Future Scenarios." *Europe-Asia Studies.* Vol. 51, 1999.

—Steven Sabol

TUVALU

CAPITAL: Funafuti.

MONETARY UNIT: Tuvaluan dollar (T$). There are coins of 1, 5, 10, 25, 50 cents, and 1 dollar. One Tuvaluan dollar equals 100 cents. The currency is tied to the Australian dollar at an exchange rate of 1 Tuvaluan dollar per 1 Australian dollar.

CHIEF EXPORTS: Copra, clothing, footwear.

CHIEF IMPORTS: Food, animals, mineral fuels, machinery, manufactured goods.

GROSS DOMESTIC PRODUCT: US$7.8 million (1995 est.).

BALANCE OF TRADE: **Exports:** US$165,000 (f.o.b., 1989). **Imports:** US$4.4 million (c.i.f., 1989).

COUNTRY OVERVIEW

LOCATION AND SIZE. Tuvalu is an island group of 5 atolls (coral islands consisting of a reef surrounding a lagoon) and 4 islands in the South Pacific Ocean. It is located midway between Australia and Hawaii. The island chain stretches some 676 kilometers (420 miles) from the southern island of Niulakita to the northern-most island of Nanumea and covers 757,000 square kilometers (292,278 square miles) of ocean, but it has a total land area of only 26 square kilometers (10 square miles), including 24 kilometers (15 miles) of coastline. Tuvalu's land area is one-tenth the size of the city of Washington, D.C., making it one of the smallest nations in the world. Funafuti, the capital and largest city, is located on the islet of Fongafale in the Funafuti Atoll. The nation's largest island is Vaitupu at 4.9 square kilometers (1.89 square miles) and the smallest is Niulakita at 0.41 square kilometers (0.16 square miles). All of Tuvalu is less than 4.5 meters (15 feet) above sea-level. Due to environmental factors such as rising ocean levels and soil erosion, Tuvalu is slowly shrinking in land mass at a rate of 2 millimeters per year. It is expected that some time in the future Tuvalu will be entirely underwater.

POPULATION. The population of Tuvalu was estimated at 10,838 in July of 2000, up from 8,229 in 1985 and 9,043 in 1991. The current annual population growth rate is 1.41 percent, which would result in a population of 12,600 by 2010. However, the loss of island territory has spurred many Tuvaluans to abandon their homes to start over in New Zealand, a population shift that is certain to become more pronounced as the islands gradually disappear underwater. New Zealand has agreed to take in the entire Tuvaluan population as "environmental refugees" at a rate of 60 people per year. The birth rate is 21.78 births per 1,000 population or 3.11 children born per woman. The death rate is 7.66 deaths per 1,000 population.

Most Tuvaluans are young. Some 34 percent of the population is younger than age 15, while just 5 percent is over age 65. Most Tuvaluans are ethnically Polynesian

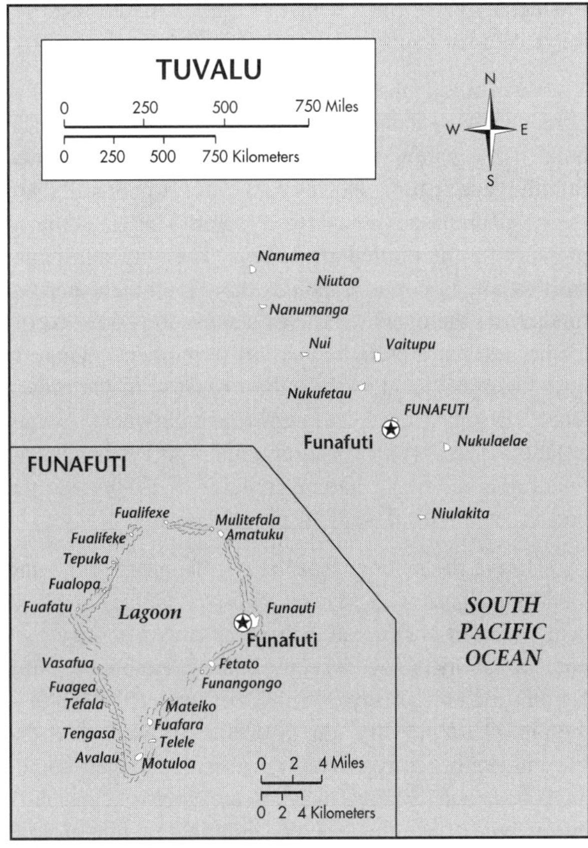

(96 percent), but the inhabitants of the island of Nui are Micronesian. The population is mainly urban and more than half live on the islet of Fongafale. This has led to a high population density in the area. Partially because of sanitation problems caused by the lack of fresh water, Tuvalu has a high infant mortality rate (23.3 deaths per 1,000 live births).

OVERVIEW OF ECONOMY

A tiny nation with a tiny economy, Tuvalu spent much of its history under the control of foreign powers. The islands were originally populated by immigrants from other South Pacific islands nearly 2,000 years ago. Later, Europeans seized many of the islands' inhabitants to serve as slaves; during the 19th century, slave traders from South America reduced Tuvalu's population by nearly 80 percent. Efforts to harvest copra (dried coconut meat which produces coconut oil) and mine guano (seafowl excrement used as fertilizer) led the United States to claim the 4 southern islands in 1856 and the British to claim the northern territory in 1892 as part of its Gilbert Islands Protectorate. Many Tuvaluans **emigrated** to the larger Gilbert Islands to find employment, especially after World War II. In 1974, Tuvaluans voted for independence from the other Gilbert Islands (now Kiribati). Tuvalu became independent from the British Commonwealth in 1978, but the new nation possessed few economic resources. In 1979, the United States relinquished its claim to the 4 southern islands.

Even among the developing nations of the South Pacific, Tuvalu's economy is relatively undeveloped. The bulk of the nation's economy is based on **subsistence farming** and fishing. However, the soil is poor and there are no natural sources of fresh water. This has created pressure for the limited arable land. The only significant cash export is copra, although the government derives funds from the overseas sale of stamps and coins to collectors and there is limited export of garments. There is little unemployment in the nation because of the prevalence of subsistence farming (unemployment hovers around 4 percent). The nation's main port is located in Funafuti and a major harbor dredging in 1980 made the port accessible to deep-draft ocean vessels.

During the latter part of the twentieth century, some 1,000 Tuvaluans worked in the phosphate mines in the island nation of Nauru and their **remittances** (money sent home to family or friends) contributed substantially to the nation's economy. However, by the turn of the century, the phosphate industry was in decline in Nauru and the government began **repatriating** (returning to their homeland) Tuvaluans. Many Tuvaluans are employed as sailors on foreign-based ships and also contribute remittances.

Until the year 2000, the principal source of foreign revenue for Tuvalu was international aid. In 1987, Australia, New Zealand, and the United Kingdom established a US$17 million trust fund for the territory. Later, Japan and South Korea also made contributions. Tuvaluan governments have only cautiously made withdrawals from the fund and generally adopted a conservative investment strategy which has substantially grown the fund. By 1999, the fund was valued at US$35 million. In addition, the United States makes payments to Tuvalu for fishing rights under the terms of a 1988 treaty between the 2 nations. In 1999, these payments totaled US$9 million.

The government has traditionally played a major role in the economy and controls many of the main economic sectors. In an effort to improve the economy, the government has undertaken a variety of reforms, including the **privatization** of many functions and personnel cuts of 7 percent. These reforms are especially significant in light of the fact that almost 20 percent of the Tuvaluan workforce is employed by the government. To raise revenue, the government began licensing Tuvalu's area code of 688 to international companies to use for "900" number calls in 1998. The arrangement has generated US$1.2 million per year. After it was discovered that a Hong Kong company was using the number for adult businesses, the overwhelmingly Protestant population of Tuvalu forced the government to revoke the licenses. In 1998, the government negotiated a contract to lease its Internet domain name ".tv" to companies in exchange for an estimated US$50 million over the next decade. Under the terms of the agreement, Tuvalu will receive a minimum of US$4 million annually for 10 years. These new sources of income could triple Tuvalu's GDP.

POLITICS, GOVERNMENT, AND TAXATION

The first parliamentary elections in the independent nation of Tuvalu were held in 1981, and the nation is now governed by a revised constitution which was adopted in 1986. Under the terms of the new constitution, the British monarch is the nation's head of state and is represented by a governor-general chosen from among the Tuvaluans by the prime minister. Tuvalu does not have formal political parties, but the 12 members of the **unicameral** (single-chamber) parliament often align themselves in factions. In 1999, Ionatana Ionatana was elected prime minister on a platform devoted to governmental reform to **liberalize** the economy and to bolster Tuvalu's international standing.

From independence onward, the government has been a major actor in the national economy. For instance, the only hotel in the nation is government-owned as is the islands' only radio station. In addition, the government owns about one-fourth of the land on the islands (most of these lands are leased to clans to be farmed on a communal basis), and almost one-quarter of the nation's population works for the government. Until his death in December 2000, Ionatana sought to divest the government from these publicly-held ventures and encourage private enterprise. The main policy used to encourage new business and to attract foreign companies is the designation of "pioneer status" for certain new businesses (including tourism) which gives them tax-exempt status.

The government has also endeavored to lessen its reliance on foreign aid. The arrangement to lease its Internet domain name, ".tv," to the Canadian company dotTV is a major part of this effort. In order to assure input into the marketing of the domain name, the government is a significant minority shareholder in dotTV and has a seat on the company's board. The government merged the operations of the nation's 2 main banks in order to improve efficiency and reduce redundancy. In addition, the government has sought to improve the economies of the outer islands through a US$4 million program underwritten by the Asian Development Bank and through the construction of airfields on all of the nation's islands. A central goal of this effort is to direct power away from the central government and into the hands of localities. As the national government lessens its reliance on foreign aid to conduct day-to-day operations, it plans to shift the bulk of the funds it receives into programs to improve the health and living conditions on the outer islands where some two-thirds of the population live below the national poverty line with incomes of less than US$1,000 per year.

There is a fixed **income tax** of 30 percent on all income above US$1,900, and all corporate profits are also taxed at the flat rate of 30 percent. There are also sales taxes on certain goods and services. The government also taxes stamp sales, copra, and fishing licenses. The government maintains price limits on fuel and basic food items.

Under Ionatana, Tuvalu became the 189th member of the United Nations and a full member of the Commonwealth of Nations. The government also supports the establishment of a **free-trade zone** in the region. One of the major political issues is the status of the islands, as an increasing number of Tuvaluans support the removal of Queen Elizabeth II as their head of state and the establishment of a full republic. Tuvalu has likewise been a vocal supporter of international efforts to stop global warming, believed to be a factor in the rising ocean levels that are reducing the nation's land.

INFRASTRUCTURE, POWER, AND COMMUNICATIONS

The **infrastructure** of Tuvalu is rudimentary. Only the island of Funafuti has a network of paved roads (the government owns only 1 paving tractor to maintain the roadways). The other islands have either no or only limited paved roads. In fact, there are only 8 kilometers (5 miles) of paved roads in the entire nation. There are a few privately-owned vehicles and some government-owned ones. The most prevalent methods of transportation are bicycle and small motorcycle. The only airport is located on Funafuti. Government plans to build an airfield on each island have long been opposed for environmental and economic reasons. Estimates are that 3,000–4,000 palm trees would have to be cut down to make a serviceable landing strip. Since there is little arable land on any of the islands, such palm depletion would seriously undermine the local economies.

Inter-island shipping on small craft remains the main form of transport between the islands. The capital island and the island of Nui have navigable harbors in their la-

Communications

Country	Telephones[a]	Telephones, Mobile/Cellular[a]	Radio Stations[b]	Radios[a]	TV Stations[a]	Televisions[a]	Internet Service Providers[c]	Internet Users[c]
Tuvalu	1,000	0 (1994)	AM 1; FM 0; shortwave 0	4,000	0	800	1	N/A
United States	194 M	69.209 M (1998)	AM 4,762; FM 5,542; shortwave 18	575 M	1,500	219 M	7,800	148 M
Philippines	1.9 M	1.959 M (1998)	AM 366; FM 290; shortwave 3 (1999)	11.5 M	31	3.7 M	33	500,000
Solomon Islands	8,000	658	AM 3; FM 0; shortwave 0	57,000	0	3,000	1	3,000

[a]Data is for 1997 unless otherwise noted.
[b]Data is for 1998 unless otherwise noted.
[c]Data is for 2000 unless otherwise noted.

SOURCE: CIA *World Factbook 2001* [Online].

goons, but only Funafuti is capable of servicing deep-draft ships after a harbor dredging was completed in 1980.

There is a satellite dish in the capital and the government has put receivers on each of the islands so that transmissions are available to those with electricity and televisions. There is telephone service on Funafuti with about 700 subscribers in 1999 and radiophone communications exist between all of the inhabited islands. Electricity is available in the capital and in a limited fashion on some of the islands. While there are no broadcast stations, there is 1 Internet service provider and 1 local radio station. The government publishes the only newspaper, *Tuvalu Echoes*. Funafuti has a hospital, and each island has a dispensary (an office to dispense medical supplies). With the proceeds from the licensing of ".tv," the government expects to engage in several major infrastructure programs, although the main concern is the development of measures to protect the islands from flooding caused by storms.

ECONOMIC SECTORS

Tuvalu's economy is limited due to its small size and narrow range of natural resources. The nation's economic base is divided into 2 main sectors: agriculture and revenues from external licensing. Agriculture remains based on subsistence farming, with minor exports of copra. Concurrently, licensing of fishing, the nation's phone prefix, and the ".tv" domain name provide the majority of revenue for both the government and the national economy.

The government's main economic priority is to develop the economy to such an extent that foreign aid is no longer required. In addition, the government is endeavoring to support international efforts to stop global warming and pollution in general in order to protect both the islands themselves and the agricultural sector on the lands. For instance, in the spring of 2000, floods of 3.2 meters (11 feet) left most of the islands underwater. The government subsequently entered into agreements which would allow those Tuvaluans permanently displaced by global warming to **immigrate** to Australia or New Zealand. Finally, although substantial revenues are expected from the ".tv" licenses, the government is attempting to protect the local way of life from overt commercialism.

AGRICULTURE

As much as 75 percent of the population of Tuvalu is involved in agricultural production of some sort. Subsistence farming is the main source of both food and income for many Tuvaluans. Agriculture, in the form of the production of copra, also provides the nation's only true export. Total agricultural exports in 1998 amounted to US$400,000, and agriculture accounted for 25 percent of the nation's total GDP.

The main crops include copra, taro (a large tuber), bananas, and sugarcane. There is little or no livestock production, although many families keep small numbers of pigs and chickens for personal consumption. While copra is harvested from coconut trees, the other crops are planted according to traditional practices. The islands receive about 2,500 millimeters (100 inches) of rainfall per year, but the porous, volcanic nature of the soil means that islanders have to use cisterns to collect rainwater as the water rapidly soaks through the ground and there are no natural springs or wells on any of the islands. Because there is little fresh water, islanders often use coconut milk in place of drinking water. Water constraints have also led to the evolution of a distinctive form of planting. Crops are planted in trenches that are 3 to 6 meters (10 to 20 feet) wide and dug down to the water table (usually a depth of between 2 to 4 meters or 6 to 12 feet). In order to compensate for the nation's poor soil, these trenches are filled with leaves and natural fertilizers to produce a mulch capable of sustaining the crops. Indigenous foodstuffs such as breadfruit (a round seedless fruit from the mulberry family the texture of which resembles bread when cooked) are often cultivated on the banks and edges of the trenches for local consumption.

Most farms are small (less than an acre in size) and communally owned. The Agriculture Division has been implementing programs designed to join together communal lands into larger farms in order to increase efficiency with the ultimate goal of ensuring that no land capable of agriculture remains unproductive. As the communal farms are joined together, profits from production would be divided into 3 parts: one-third for the original land owners; one-third for the agricultural workers; and the final third would be deposited in a communal fund in a bank. This group fund would serve as a resource for future land improvements or to offset periods of underproduction or price declines.

Fishing is done extensively throughout the islands, but the majority of the catch is used for local consumption. Tuvalu allows other nations, including South Korea, Taiwan, and the United States, to fish for tuna in its territorial waters in exchange for license fees that totaled US$5.5 million in 1998. In addition, small quantities of sea cucumbers are harvested by Tuvaluans for export to China.

INDUSTRY

Industry in Tuvalu is quite limited. Copra production is the main industry and provides the nation with its main export. In addition, about 600 Tuvaluans are employed by foreign firms on merchant ships and 750 are employed in the phosphate mines of Nauru. Many families are supported by the remittances from these 2 groups. There is some local manufacture of handcrafts, clothing, and footwear for tourists and for export.

SERVICES

There is a small, but steady, tourist sector which generates some US$300,000 per year. The nation receives about 1,000 tourists per year. In addition to the 16-room hotel in Funafuti, there are about 12 guest houses on the islands. Because of the relative isolation of the islands, many indigenous Polynesian customs and traditions have survived. Tourists are exposed to dancing, singing, and variety of local crafts. There is also extensive diving, snorkeling, and fishing. Efforts to encourage tourism have resulted in government policies that give new tourist businesses tax-exempt status.

The subsistence nature of most of the population and strong cultural influences have combined to prevent the development of any significant **retail** trade. Instead local markets and home production of products is the norm. Each island has a cooperative store (Fusi) to sell local crops and products. All stores are closed on Sunday.

INTERNATIONAL TRADE

Tuvalu has an import-driven economy and relies upon products produced elsewhere. Though import and export statistics are outdated, they give a sense of the reliance upon imports: in 1989, the country imported US$4.4 million in goods and services while exporting just US$165,000 worth of goods and services. The main export of Tuvalu is copra, while the nation's main imports include food, animals, mineral fuels, machinery, and manufactured goods. Tuvalu's main trading partners are Australia, Fiji, New Zealand, and the United States.

MONEY

The Australian dollar is legal currency in Tuvalu, but the nation mints its own coins. Since Tuvalu's currency is tied to that of Australia, it is relatively stable and its value is determined by supply and demand in international exchange markets. The government-owned National Bank of Tuvalu is responsible for most financial services; however, the limited capital of the institution means that funds for development must come from abroad. In 1995, 1 U.S. dollar equaled 1.35 Australian dollars and in 2000, 1 U.S. dollar equaled 1.52 Australian dollars.

Exchange rates: Tuvalu

Tuvaluan dollars (T$) per US$1	
Jan 2001	1.7995
2000	1.7173
1999	1.5497
1998	1.5888
1997	1.3439
1996	1.2773

SOURCE: CIA *World Factbook 2001* [ONLINE].

GDP per Capita (US$)

Country	1996	1997	1998	1999	2000
Tuvalu	N/A	N/A	N/A	1,100	N/A
United States	28,600	30,200	31,500	33,900	36,200
Philippines	2,600	3,200	3,500	3,600	3,800
Solomon Islands	3,000	3,000	2,600	2,650	2,000

Note: Data are estimates.

SOURCE: *Handbook of the Nations*, 17th, 18th, 19th and 20th editions for 1996, 1997, 1998 and 1999 data; CIA *World Factbook 2001* [Online] for 2000 data.

POVERTY AND WEALTH

Of the nation's inhabitants (not including persons employed outside of Tuvalu), only about 1,500 are formally employed. The average per capita income is only about US$1,000 per year, making Tuvalu one of the poorest nations on earth. However, education is free and compulsory for children between the ages of 6 and 13. Health care is also free, though limited by access (each of the main islands has a dispensary, but the only hospital is on Funafuti).

The society is egalitarian and democratic. Low income levels are mitigated by the strong social and village support networks. In 1998, Tuvalu was judged to be the only nation in the world above reproach for human rights violations.

WORKING CONDITIONS

Forced or compulsory labor is prohibited. Labor laws set a minimum wage and 8-hour work day, but the market determines most wage scales in Tuvalu. Average hourly wages in Tuvalu for unskilled workers are between 40 and 92 U.S. cents an hour with 47 cents per hour being the average. The current minimum wage is US$81.25 biweekly, regardless of age or gender. Managerial or technical wages range from US$3,000 to US$9,000 per year. Although workers may organize and have the right of collective bargaining, there has never been a strike in the nation's history. The only registered trade union is the Tuvalu Seamen's Union which is affiliated with the International Transportation Workers' Federation. However, government workers belong to associations that have some features of unions.

Children under the age of 14 are prohibited from working, and children under the age of 15 are prohibited from working on ships or in industry. Employers are required to provide adequate potable water, sanitary facilities, and medical care. The Ministry of Labor, Works, and Communications is responsible for overseeing labor practices and law.

COUNTRY HISTORY AND ECONOMIC DEVELOPMENT

0–100 A.D. Polynesians colonize Tuvalu; Samoans settle in the southern atolls, while Tongans settle in the north; Micronesians from Kiribati conquer Nui.

1861. Elekana, a Cook Islander castaway, brings Christianity to Tuvalu.

1863. Slave traders take 450 Tuvaluans as slaves to work in the guano mines of Peru.

1865. Elekana returns to islands with a Congregationalist missionary, A. W. Murray.

1877. Tuvalu comes under British control.

1880s. European traders establish a post on Tuvalu in order to acquire copra.

1892. In an effort to forestall American expansion in the area, Great Britain declares a protectorate over the northern islands.

1916. Tuvalu becomes a formal British colony.

1942–45. The United States lands military troops in the region during World War II and builds the nation's current airfield at Funafuti.

1974. The United Kingdom grants Tuvalu self-governing status; Tuvaluans vote for independence.

1976. Tuvalu is formally separated from the Gilbert Islands.

1978. Tuvalu becomes an independent nation and a special member of the Commonwealth of Nations (a voluntary association of nations giving symbolic or actual allegiance to the British crown).

1997. Three cyclones devastate the islands.

1998. Tuvalu signs a 10-year deal worth at least US$50 million to license the nation's Internet domain name, ".tv."

2000. Tuvalu becomes a member of the United Nations and a full member of the Commonwealth of Nations.

FUTURE TRENDS

With its Internet deal, Tuvalu entered the 21st century with prospects for dramatic economic growth. Royalties from the first year provided over US$20 million or US$2,272 for every Tuvaluan. These funds formed the core of a new government trust fund. If the royalties are as much as expected, the standard of living on Tuvalu will rise considerably. The government indicated that some of the revenues would be spent on communication links with the outer islands and the rest of the world. Some observers are concerned that the newfound wealth of the nation may destroy the traditional society and lifestyles of the islands. In addition, continued global warming, with the subsequent rise in ocean levels, and population increases have exerted considerable land pressure on the tiny nation.

DEPENDENCIES

Tuvalu has no territories or colonies.

BIBLIOGRAPHY

Icon Group. *Strategic Assessment of Tuvalu, 2000.* San Diego: Icon Group, 2000.

Kelly, Robert C., Stanton Doyle, and N. Denise Youngblood. *Country Review: Tuvalu, 1999/2000.* Houston: CountryWatch.com, 2000.

Laracy, Hugh, ed. *Tuvalu: A History.* Suva, Fiji: University of South Pacific, 1983.

Pacific Island Business Network. "Tuvalu: Country Profile." <http://pidp.ewc.hawaii.edu/pibn/countries/tuvalu.htm>. Accessed December 2000.

U.S. Central Intelligence Agency. *CIA World Factbook 2000: Tuvalu.* <http://www.odci.gov/cia/publications/factbook/index.html>. Accessed February 2000.

U.S. Department of State. *1999 Country Reports on Human Rights Practices: Tuvalu.* <http://www.state.gov/www/global/human_rights/1999_hrp_report/99hrp_toc.html>. Accessed February 2000.

—Tom Lansford

UNITED ARAB EMIRATES

CAPITAL: Abu Dhabi.

MONETARY UNIT: Emirian dirham (Dh). One Emirian dirham equals 100 fils. There are coins of 1, 5, 10, 25, and 50 fils and 1 and 5 dirhams. Paper notes include 5, 10, 50, 100, 200, 500, and 1,000 dirhams.

CHIEF EXPORTS: Crude oil, natural gas, re-exports, dried fish, and dates.

CHIEF IMPORTS: Machinery, transport equipment, chemicals, and food.

GROSS DOMESTIC PRODUCT: US$54 billion (2000 est.).

BALANCE OF TRADE: **Exports:** US$46 billion (f.o.b., 2000 est.). **Imports:** US$34 billion (f.o.b., 2000 est.).

COUNTRY OVERVIEW

LOCATION AND SIZE. The United Arab Emirates (UAE) controls the southeastern portion of the Arabian peninsula south of the states of Bahrain and Qatar. The federation covers 82,820 square kilometers (31,976 square miles) and is bordered on the north by the Persian Gulf and Iran, on the east by Oman, and on the south and west by Saudi Arabia. The UAE separates Oman from the Musandam peninsula and extends 90 kilometers (145 miles) along the Gulf of Oman, an area known as the al-Batinah coast. The UAE is slightly smaller than the U.S. state of Maine.

POPULATION. The population of the UAE is between 2.8 million and 3 million. About 85 percent of them live in cities that straddle the country's Arabian/Persian Gulf coastline. UAE cities tend to be ethnically heterogeneous and male, while there are more women and UAE nationals in rural areas. The 3 largest emirates—Abu Dhabi, Dubai, and Sharjah—collectively govern 84.3 percent of the population. Close to 80 percent of the population is comprised of expatriate nationals and nearly 63 percent of the population is male. Nearly 96 percent of Emiratis are Muslim. South Asians, mainly Indians and Pakistanis, make up 50 percent of the population. The next 3 largest expatriate ethnic groups are Iranians (2.5 percent), Arabs from other parts of the Middle East (13 percent), and Westerners (1 percent).

By all accounts the population is growing very rapidly. According to the UAE's Central Bank, the UAE's population grew by 5.5 percent between 1993 and 1997. The UAE government expects population to double by 2010, whereas Dubai projects the emirate's population to double by 2005. The World Bank projected a 37 percent increase in population, but with 30 percent of the current population under the age of 15, this still represents an important demographic shift. By contrast, the United Nations anticipates the UAE's population to double by 2029.

The principal causes of this rapid population growth are the federation's booming economy and the government's encouragement of UAE nationals to have large families. The UAE government provides substantial financial incentives for UAE nationals to marry each other and to raise large families. The UAE government hopes that this would help to balance the federation's population, which is overwhelmingly composed of expatriates.

OVERVIEW OF ECONOMY

The UAE is a tribal federation of 7 emirates occupying a portion of the southeastern Arabian peninsula. It is one of the most economically secure states in the world. The UAE controls 98 billion barrels of oil—10 percent of the world's proven oil reserves—as well as 212 trillion cubic feet of gas, the fourth largest amount in the world after Russia, Iran, and Qatar. The UAE has employed its natural resources and its strategic location to become one of the most modern and wealthiest states in the world. It boasts both large petroleum and non-petroleum sectors. Economic growth in large part has hinged on the price of oil and the ability of UAE governments, whose proceeds come almost entirely from oil sales, to invest in large **infrastructure** projects.

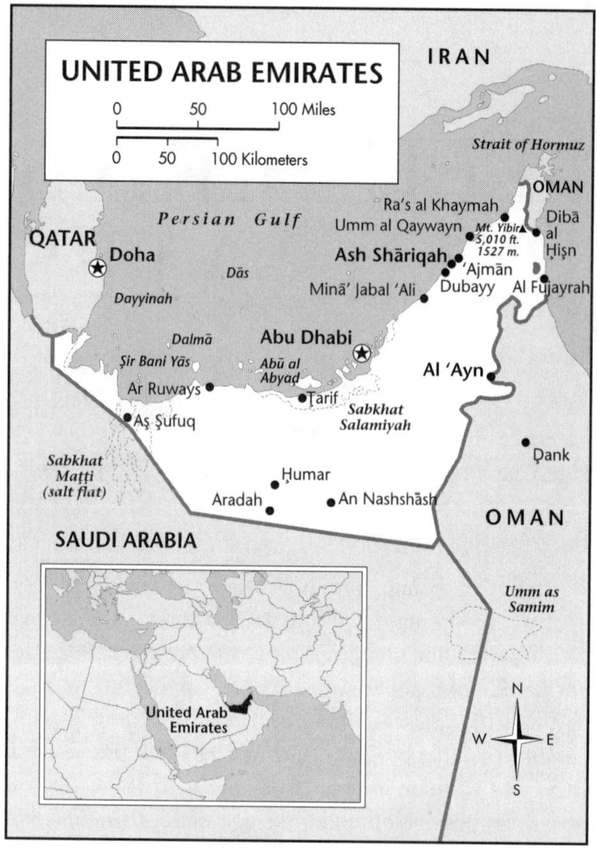

For much of the last 2 centuries, the inhabitants of the UAE depended on pearling, fishing, commerce, and, allegedly, piracy of commerce in the Indian Ocean. To protect its trade routes to India, Great Britain attacked many communities along the UAE's Arabian/Persian Gulf coast in 1819 and 1820 and for the next 50 years extended an informal protectorate (protection and partial control of one region or dependent country by another country) over the region, which became known as the "Trucial Coast" because of the non-aggression pacts (or truces) that Great Britain forced regional emirates to sign with each other and Britain.

The region "entered" the 20th century in the 1950s with the discovery of oil in Abu Dhabi and subsequent discoveries of oil in Dubai and Sharjah in the 1960s. Following Britain's withdrawal from the Trucial Coast in 1971, the UAE became an independent state composed of 7 of the original 9 emirates. The other 2 emirates, Bahrain and Qatar, became separate independent states. Abu Dhabi, Dubai, and to a lesser extent, Sharjah, used the proceeds from oil sales to build modern, urban societies. Dubai, with substantially smaller oil supplies than Abu Dhabi, sought to build commercial institutions, leisure industries, manufacturing, port and transportation facilities, and other service industries that were not dependent on oil proceeds. The crown jewel of this project is the Jebel Ali **Free Zone**, which opened in 1985 and now boasts 1,600 international companies from over 70 different nations. Sharjah too has sought to broaden its economy by investing in manufacturing. Since the early 1980s, Abu Dhabi has invested billions of dollars in non-oil industries, including manufacturing, services, and agriculture. After the Gulf War, the UAE used the **glut** in the world arms industry to mandate an "offsets" program requiring all firms selling weapons to the federation to invest in its non-oil related industries.

Because the UAE had a relatively poor and unskilled population when oil was discovered there, the federation has depended on expatriate laborers and managers to meet close to 90 percent of its labor demands. The vast majority of these expatriate workers are South Asian, though there are large numbers of Arab and Western expatriate workers. Expatriates earn half as much as UAE nationals but present 3 significant problems. First, expatriate workers may undermine the UAE by promoting their own governments' interests or that of organized crime within the federation. Second, expatriate workers often require high payments for social services and send virtually all of their salary home rather than spending it in the UAE. Third, expatriate workers intensify preexisting social divisions within the UAE since they tend to be the principal workers in non-oil UAE industries, while UAE nationals generally prefer to work for the government.

The federation cannot regularly feed itself or meet its water and electrical needs without significant imports or technological assistance. The UAE's hot and arid climate has few regions hospitable to large-scale farming. While the UAE has invested heavily in new technologies and irrigation systems, the federation's agricultural production cannot produce adequate amounts of the most basic commodities. Nor can the UAE meet the water needs of the federation for much longer due to the gradual poisoning through salinization (to become concentrated with salt) of the federation's extensive underground network of wells. Similarly, the demand for electricity is quickly outpacing supply and forcing the UAE to turn to desalinization plants as a way to provide adequate water and power resources for the federation since they generate energy as a byproduct of turning salt water into fresh water. These problems are particularly acute in the northern emirates, which lack the resources to meet the demand of their population for either water or electricity.

Still, the UAE has the financial and institutional resources to solve these problems. The UAE can depend on the proceeds from the sale of its petroleum and natural gas. Abu Dhabi has US$150 billion in overseas assets that can either cover budget shortfalls due to excessive spending or a sharp decline in oil prices. Equally importantly, the UAE's **free market system** and open economy has fostered the creation of numerous medium and large corporations that produce highly competitive goods for the regional and world markets.

POLITICS, GOVERNMENT, AND TAXATION

The UAE is a federation of 7 tribally-based emirates (Arab royal houses): Abu Dhabi, Dubai, Sharjah, Ras al-Khaimah, Ajman, Fujairah, and Umm al-Qawain. Even though it has a central government based in Abu Dhabi, each emirate controls its own economy and retains broad autonomy. The federation's highest constitutional authority, the UAE Supreme Council of Ministers, is composed of the 7 emirate rulers; it establishes federal policies and sanctions legislation. Most council decisions are reached through a consensus of the emirates' rulers and leading families. Since the council meets 4 times a year, the UAE cabinet runs the day-to-day affairs of the federation. Through an informal agreement, the ruler of Abu Dhabi serves as president, and the ruler of Dubai serves as vice president and prime minister. The president chooses the cabinet and members of the federal judiciary. The Federal National Council, composed of representatives appointed by the ruler of each emirate, can comment on legislation proposed by the UAE cabinet. There is also a UAE Supreme Court composed of 5 judges that carries out 3 functions: it settles disputes between different emirates, settles disputes between individual emirates and the federal government, and decides on the constitutionality of federal laws.

Throughout the UAE's 3 decades of existence, the Ruler of Abu Dhabi, Shaykh Zayid al-Nahyan, has served as the federation's president and worked to unite the emirates, which had previously been virtual protectorates of Britain (the so-called Trucial States) from the 1820s until the 1970s. Zayid has used his political skills and Abu Dhabi's oil wealth to keep the federation together through times of crisis which strained the sometimes tenuous ties of the 7 emirates. Zayid has been most successful in mediating Abu Dhabi's rivalry with Dubai and convincing Dubai's ruling family to take on key positions in the UAE federal government. In recent years, however, Zayid's advanced age and poor health have forced him to delegate greater responsibility to his eldest son, Shaykh Khalifa. While it is certain that Khalifa will succeed Zayid as UAE president and ruler of Abu Dhabi, it is not clear how strong of a ruler he will be because of his fierce rivalry with his half brother, Shaykh Muhammad, the chief of staff of the UAE army.

Though the UAE's permanent constitution stipulates that each emirate provide half of its revenues to the federal government, Abu Dhabi annually uses the proceeds from its oil sales to provide between 60 percent to 90 percent of the UAE's federal budget. Dubai and revenues from the UAE ministries generally have covered the remainder. These revenues come from the 20 percent surcharge foreign banks pay on their profits, taxes and royalties from the proceeds on foreign oil companies, and a 4 percent customs **duty** on all imported products except tobacco and alcoholic beverages. Another key problem is the fact that there is little transparency in UAE budgets, and it is estimated that as much as a third of UAE's oil revenues do not appear on national accounts. Over the last 4 years, the UAE budget has been US$7 to US$8 billion in deficit, but this is not considered a great problem because the income from Abu Dhabi's US$150 billion in overseas investments more than covers **budget deficits** of that size. In addition, the UAE government maintains an extensive cradle-to-grave **social welfare system**. There are no income or consumption taxes within the UAE.

INFRASTRUCTURE, POWER, AND COMMUNICATIONS

The UAE has a modern infrastructure that has made it a regional transportation center. According to government statistics, the UAE has 1,088 kilometers of roads (676 miles) as of 1998, all of which are paved. The Abu Dhabi-Dubai highway has been upgraded several times, and the links from Dubai to the northern emirates are in

Communications

Country	Newspapers	Radios	TV Sets[a]	Cable subscribers[a]	Mobile Phones[a]	Fax Machines[a]	Personal Computers[a]	Internet Hosts[b]	Internet Users[b]
	1996	1997	1998	1998	1998	1998	1998	1999	1999
United Arab Emirates	156	345	294	N/A	210	21.0	106.2	39.44	400
United States	215	2,146	847	244.3	256	78.4	458.6	1,508.77	74,100
Saudi Arabia	57	321	262	N/A	31	N/A	49.6	1.17	300
Iran	28	265	157	0.0	6	N/A	31.9	0.05	100

[a]Data are from International Telecommunication Union, *World Telecommunication Development Report 1999* and are per 1,000 people.
[b]Data are from the Internet Software Consortium (http://www.isc.org) and are per 10,000 people.

SOURCE: World Bank. *World Development Indicators 2000.*

good repair as well. Rashid and Jebel Ali in Dubai are the largest of the UAE's 15 ports; together they handled 2.84 billion 20-foot container equivalent units of cargo in 1999, among the largest volumes in the world. Dubai has also won port and free zone management contracts in Djibouti, Sudan, Saudi Arabia, and Beirut since 1998. Dubai's airport is the largest of the UAE's 40 airports and, following the completion of the Shaykh Rashid terminal in March 2000, is now widely considered a first-class international airport. A significant expansion of the Abu Dhabi airport is expected to be completed in 2005. There are no railroads in the UAE, nor is there any domestic air transportation network.

Average annual rainfall in the UAE is very low (generally 42 millimeters) and there are few fertile areas except in the north (where annual rainfall is 150 mm per year) and among the oases. The U.S. State Department expects the UAE demand for water to increase by 50 percent by 2015 and warns that the demand will soon outstrip supply. The UAE has addressed this problem through the development of underground wells—which have rapidly depleted the water table—and desalinization. Many underground wells have gone dry or were rendered unusable because of increased salinity from salt leaching into ground reservoirs. Today, 82 desalinization plants, many of which are also power plants, meet 75 percent of the UAE's total non-agricultural water needs. Due to the depletion of renewable resources through farming and excessive urbanization, there is no alternative to desalinization. Other options, such as importing water from Turkey via pipeline, are not considered viable because of security considerations.

The UAE's desalinization plants are key components of an electrical network that witnessed phenomenal growth in recent decades from 5.5 billion kilowatt-hours (kWh) in 1980 to 19 billion kWh in 1998. Installed generating capability is 7,466 megawatts, with Abu Dhabi accounting for 45 percent of the total and Dubai 26 percent. Especially acute is the demand for gas; in Abu Dhabi and Dubai, demand doubled from 1996 to 2000. The UAE expects to spend $3.5 billion on new projects over the next 4 years to meet increased demand for electricity, which is expected to be 10 percent annually between 2000–2001. Among the most important of these projects is the $10 billion Dolphin Gas Project which aims to ship gas from Qatar's North Field to Abu Dhabi, Dubai, Oman, and Pakistan. A federation-wide electrical network is also being planned and will most likely be connected to the Omani electric grid. This would be the first step towards creating an electrical network throughout all Gulf Cooperation Council (GCC) countries: Bahrain, Kuwait, Oman, Qatar, Saudi Arabia, and the UAE. In addition, the UAE federal government and the largest emirates have **privatized** most of the power system along with the water system.

Telecommunications services in the UAE are among the most advanced in the world. They are managed by Etisalat, which is 60 percent owned by the UAE government. According to the *CIA World Factbook,* there are 915,223 main phone lines in use in the UAE and nearly 1 million mobile cellular phones. In 2000, the country had 1 Internet provider but there should be many more by 2005 as the UAE **deregulates** its telecommunications industry to comply with World Trade Organization guidelines. The management of Dubai Internet City has also confirmed that independent Internet service providers will be allowed to operate in Dubai.

ECONOMIC SECTORS

The UAE is a mixed free-market economy based on oil and natural gas production, and these industries combined take up more than a quarter of UAE **gross domestic product** (GDP). Over the past 2 decades, the UAE's economic diversification program has led to the rise of several non-oil sectors that now make up a significant percentage of the UAE's GDP: manufacturing (12.6 percent), commerce and hotels (11.4 percent), real estate (9.1 percent), construction (8.6 percent), transportation (7.3 percent), and finance and insurance (6.4 percent). The UAE also has a strong **re-export** sector. Government services account for nearly 11 percent of GDP. Industrial growth has been assisted by free trade zones, including Jebel Ali in Dubai, which have been magnets for international firms. In recent years Dubai has succeeded in attracting high-profile technology firms to the emirate's "Internet City," including Microsoft, Oracle, Hewlett Packard, and Cisco Systems.

Nonetheless, the health of the UAE's economy as a whole continues to fluctuate with the world price of hy-

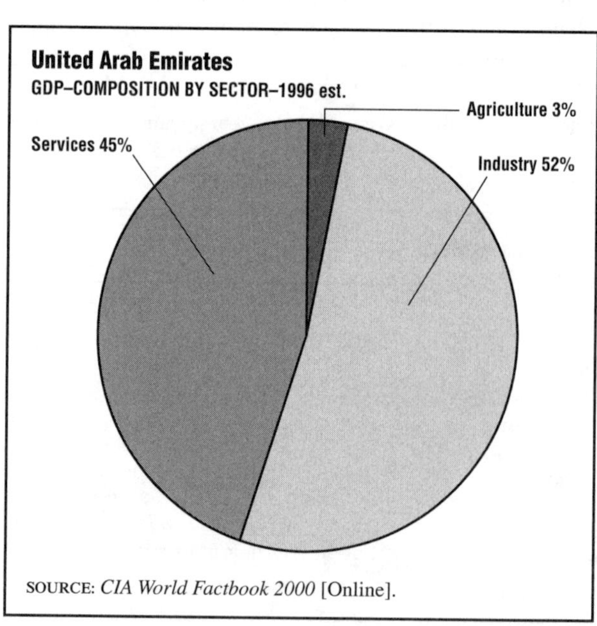

SOURCE: *CIA World Factbook 2000* [Online].

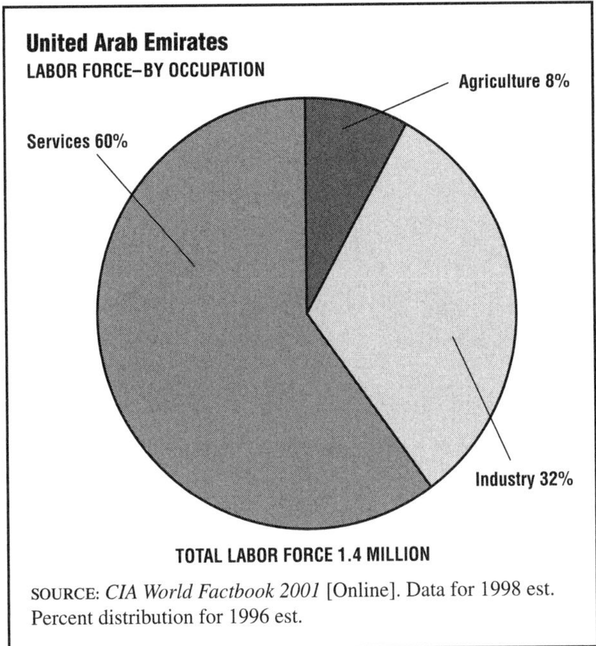

SOURCE: *CIA World Factbook 2001* [Online]. Data for 1998 est. Percent distribution for 1996 est.

drocarbons and the economic vitality of its largest trading partners, particularly Japan, which accounts for close to a third of UAE petroleum exports. In part this is due to the large percentage of GDP taken up by petroleum and in part to the fact that government revenues—70 to 80 percent of which come from oil—and spending are closely linked to oil prices. These links have meant that different sectors of the economy have risen rapidly in recent years as oil prices increased sharply after oil prices hit historic lows in 1998. One exception to this trend is the demand for electricity and power: demand for power grew by nearly 400 percent between 1980 and 1998.

Among the most important corporations based in the UAE is the Abu Dhabi National Oil Company (ADNOC). It manages the petroleum and gas extraction operations in Abu Dhabi along with the 2 major petroleum refineries in the UAE. Other key corporations are: Dubai state-owned Dubai Aluminum, a leading supplier of aluminum to the states of the Gulf Cooperation Council; Etisalat, the Abu Dhabi state-owned telecommunications firm; and Emirates Airlines, Dubai's state-owned airline. The airline has won a plethora of international "Best Airline" awards and maintains one of the most modern airline fleets in the world. It has outclassed "Gulf Air" (a consortium owned by Abu Dhabi, Qatar, Bahrain, and Oman), which remains one of the leading airlines in the Arabian/Persian Gulf region despite experiencing steep losses in the 1990s.

AGRICULTURE

Agriculture accounts for only 3 percent of the UAE's GDP due to the federation's severe climatic conditions, although it accounts for 20 percent of all water consumed, much from rapidly-depleting natural water supplies or desalinization projects. The UAE's agricultural sector annually produces about 600,000 tons of produce. The federation's chief crops are cereals. The UAE produces enough poultry and salad to meet its needs for most of the year. Some crops, such as tomatoes, are grown in quantities greater than what the UAE consumes in a whole year. The agriculture sector also produces watermelons, eggs, cucumbers, gherkins, aubergines (eggplants), green chilies, peppers, and dates.

For much of the 19th and 20th centuries, fishing and pearl diving were mainstays of UAE commerce. Today the government works to conserve fish stocks and protect the economic livelihood of the remaining fishing communities. The annual fish catch—96,000 tons—slightly exceeds domestic consumption.

Because a high proportion of UAE nationals are employed in fishing and agriculture, these 2 sectors receive a disproportionate amount of federal and local funding. For political reasons, the UAE government will continue to encourage agricultural self-sufficiency but it is aware that this goal is unattainable in either the short- or long-term.

INDUSTRY

MINING. Oil is the foundation of the UAE's economy and will be so for many years to come. Current estimates suggest that the federation has more than a century of oil supplies. Oil production represented more than a third of GDP in 1999 and virtually all of the government's revenues. These revenues are also important to government spending, on which most non-oil UAE industries are dependent. Abu Dhabi, Dubai, Sharjah, and Ras al-Khaimah all have some level of oil production, but Abu Dhabi dominates both the UAE's production and reserves. According to the U.S. Energy Information Agency (EIA), Abu Dhabi has crude reserves of 92.2 billion barrels, or slightly less than 10 percent of the world's total, and 92 percent of UAE reserves. The EIA also reported that total UAE oil production for 2000 reached 2.29 million barrels of oil a day but that Abu Dhabi's recent investments could push production closer to 2.7 to 2.9 million barrels. Generally Abu Dhabi has reduced its production to ensure that the UAE stays within OPEC (Organization of the Petroleum Exporting Countries) production guidelines.

The UAE is also blessed with the fourth largest gas reserves in the world: 212 trillion cubic feet, which is about 4 percent of the world's total. These reserves are expected to last for about 150 to 170 years. Abu Dhabi controls 92 percent of the UAE total, while Dubai, Sharjah, and Ras al-Khaimah control the rest. The UAE has soaring domestic demands for gas production. Abu Dhabi has initiated a multi-billion-dollar program to address this need. The most ambitious part is the Dolphin gas project, which proposes to ship gas from Qatar's North Field to the UAE (principally Abu Dhabi and Dubai), Oman, and eventually to Pakistan. Significant funding is still needed for the project, but the *Economist* expected managers will be able to find the necessary funding because the project involves 4 national governments.

Finally, there is copper in Fujairah and Ras al-Khaimah, talc in Fujairah, and manganese in all of the northern emirates. It not clear whether there is enough of any of these minerals to justify commercial mining.

MANUFACTURING. The *Economist* estimated that the UAE has invested $6.8 billion in industrial development over the last 30 years, spurring the creation of 1,000 factories with more than US$20 billion in direct investment. The dominant industries have been chemicals and plastics (closely connected to UAE crude oil supplies) along with aluminum. Dubai Aluminum is a leading supplier of aluminum to the GCC states and accounts for 60 percent of Dubai's non-oil exports. The UAE government also has made significant investments in petrochemicals and other "downstream" hydrocarbon industries—"downstream" meaning those that involve refining petroleum. In addition, the government is encouraging local-foreign ventures to invest in manufacturing and offering low-interest loans through the Emirates Industrial Bank to private financiers willing to invest in manufacturing in the UAE. Fifty percent of all manufacturing centers are in Abu Dhabi, while Abu Dhabi, Dubai, and Sharjah collectively controlled 93 percent of the UAE's industrial production in 1998.

OFFSETS PROGRAM. A key source of local-foreign investment in manufacturing is the "offsets" program, launched in 1991. It requires arms manufacturing and military aerospace firms to invest 60 percent of the value of their sales to the UAE in non-oil UAE industries. It is designed to take advantage of the current glut on the world arms market and to escape the traditional dilemma of choosing between spending on guns or food. By law, a UAE citizen must retain 51 percent of the capital in the partnership. Virtually all offset projects must be completed within 7 years. If the obligations are not met by the target dates, the company is penalized 8.5 percent of the unfulfilled portion of the obligation.

FREE TRADE ZONES. Another key contributor to UAE industry has been free trade zones. The most important free trade zone is Jebel Ali Free Trade Zone in Dubai. Jebel Ali in 1999 boasted 1,600 corporations and nearly $2.5 billion in investments. The zone's principal advantage was that it allowed companies investing more than Dh1 million (US$272,479) to be 100 percent foreign owned. It also boasts some of the best transportation facilities in the world and has become a regional transportation center, servicing the U.S. Navy, among others. Since the founding of Jebel Ali in 1985, the other UAE emirates established their own free trade zones, which have sought to replicate Jebel Ali's success.

SERVICES

BANKING. According to the *CIA World Factbook,* nearly 60 percent of the UAE workforce is involved in the service sector of the economy. The most important of these industries is banking, which has grown far too large. The National U.S.-Arab Chamber of Commerce estimated that there were 20 UAE-owned banks with more than 200 branches and 28 foreign banks with 119 branches in the UAE. Much of the industry is controlled by the "big five" commercial banks—Abu Dhabi Commercial Bank, Emirates Bank International, National Bank of Dubai, MashreqBank, and National Bank of Abu Dhabi. The UAE Central Bank is responsible for regulating the UAE banking industry and preventing fraud, a continuing problem in the UAE banking system in the 1990s. The UAE was closely involved in the 1991 Bank of Commerce and Credit International scandal and eventually paid nearly US$2 billion in compensation. In 1998 it was revealed that the Dubai Islamic Bank lost US$200 million due to the actions of a corrupt employee. A year later, Madhav Bhagubhai Pater, an Indian businessman, fled from Sharjah, leaving behind debts of US$130.5 million to UAE and foreign creditors.

TOURISM AND RETAIL. The UAE has a thriving tourist industry centered in Dubai, which has 70 percent of the country's hotels. Dubai features horse races, desert safaris, golf courses, and a number of five- and four-star hotels. The emirate also has shopping festivals, such as the Dubai Shopping Festival, where goods are heavily discounted. The purpose of these festivals is to attract visitors. According to the festivals' organizers, nearly 2.5 million people vacationed in the emirates in 2000: they came mostly from Britain, from surrounding states, and from the states of the former Soviet Union. Fujairah, which faces the Indian Ocean, has witnessed a considerable upsurge in vacationers in recent years. **Retail** has generally benefited from this upsurge except when a strong yen increases the price of imported Japanese **consumer goods**.

CONSTRUCTION AND REAL ESTATE. For much of the 1980s and 1990s, the UAE underwent a building boom with new office buildings rising daily in the UAE's major cities, particularly Dubai and Abu Dhabi. In recent years, there have been reports that the boom is slowing, that UAE developers are taking a more reasoned/scientific approach to building, and that there is even a sign of a glut of office space in Dubai. Still, Dubai continues to build new hotels. The Saadiyat project in Abu Dhabi promises 28,000 new homes, a bridge valued at US$220 million, and a new trade center valued at US$95 million.

RE-EXPORT. Finally, a rapidly emerging sector in the UAE economy is re-export, whose value, according to UAE government statistics, almost doubled between 1990 and 1998. At that time, foreign trade hit US$10.6 billion. The center of UAE re-export trade is Dubai, which accounted for 40 percent of the federation's re-export trade in the late 1990s. Among the most important markets for Dubai's re-export trade are Iran and the southern countries of the former Soviet Union. Reportedly Dubai also served as an entryway for smugglers attempting to circumvent U.S. **sanctions** against Iran imposed in the mid-1990s.

INTERNATIONAL TRADE

Since independence, the UAE has maintained an open, free market system with close links to the international economy. Historically the UAE's prime industries were pearling and fishing. Since the discovery of oil in the 1960s, the federation's closest trading partners have been industrialized nations in Europe and Asia, primarily France, Germany, Great Britain, Italy, Japan, India, and South Korea. The UAE exchanged crude oil for machinery, cars, transportation equipment, and food. Japan is critical since it usually accounts for a third of UAE petroleum exports: the EIA estimated that 80 percent of the UAE's crude oil exports in 1999 went to Japan and other east Asian countries. The UAE's modern infrastructure and port facilities also have allowed it to serve as an important re-export and transportation hub, particularly for Iran through Dubai.

Generally the health of the UAE's economy has depended on the price of oil and the economic vitality of its leading trading partners. At the same time, the federation's economy also has been impacted adversely by the politics of the Arabian/Persian Gulf region. Because of the UAE's perceived support for Iraq in the Iran-Iraq war, Iran attacked UAE oil tankers in the Arabian/Persian Gulf and compelled the UAE government to seek the protection of the U.S. Navy through a reflagging operation (UAE ships hoisted the U.S. flag and carried U.S. servicemen). The UAE and Iran also continue to dispute ownership over 3 islands in the Arabian/Persian Gulf: Abu Musa and the Greater and Lesser Tunbs. During the Gulf War, the UAE sought a close relationship with the United States as a way to protect the federation's economic assets from Iraqi threats. The UAE also benefited from the relocation of a number of businesses from Kuwait to the federation, especially to Dubai. Still, it is important to remember that the UAE's dependence on desalination plants for power and water ensures that the state's economy is especially vulnerable because economies of scale dictate that desalination plants should be large and located on the coast.

Since the Gulf War and the collapse of the Soviet Union, the UAE has faced new competitors and steadily increased its trade with China, the United States, and the former Soviet republics. Throughout the first two-thirds of the 1990s, large numbers of Russians traveled to the UAE and purchased products for sale at home, often using small transport planes or traveling through the emirate of Sharjah. U.S. firms also have made steady inroads into the UAE, helping the United States overtake Japan in 1996 as the leading exporter to the federation. U.S. exports to the UAE increased by 14.5 percent alone in 1999. Finally, erstwhile GCC-ally Saudi Arabia fought hard—but ultimately failed—to steal the UAE's share of the Japanese petroleum market throughout the late 1990s.

MONEY

Since 1981, the UAE's currency, the Emirian dirham, has been linked directly to the U.S. dollar at a rate of Dh3.67 to $1. The connection reflects the fact that crude oil—the UAE's chief export and the driving force in its economy—is denominated and sold in U.S. dollars. It also reflects the desire of the UAE government to ensure that domestic interest rates will move in sequence with those prevailing in the United States.

Trade (expressed in billions of US$): United Arab Emirates

	Exports	Imports
1975	7.262	2.685
1980	20.676	8.746
1985	14.043	6.549
1990	23.544	11.199
1995	N/A	20.984
1998	N/A	N/A

SOURCE: International Monetary Fund. *International Financial Statistics Yearbook 1999.*

Exchange rates: United Arab Emirates

Emirian dirhams (Dh) per US$1	
2001	3.6725
2000	N/A
1999	N/A
1998	N/A
1997	3.6711
1996	3.6710

Note: Central bank mid-point rate of 3.6725 has been in effect since 1998.

SOURCE: CIA *World Factbook 2001* [ONLINE].

The UAE has achieved this stability through a tight **monetary policy** that regulates domestic **liquidity** under an open exchange and payments system: there are no prohibitions on the import or export of currencies into the UAE except for Israeli currency and countries subject to United Nations sanctions. The UAE Central Bank also adjusts the stock of domestic liquidity through the issuance of certificates of deposit (CDs) to the federation's commercial banks. The UAE is currently considering introducing an auction system for these CDs. The UAE government has no **external debt**, and its private debt-to-service ratio has been improving steadily since the 1980s.

Generally the dirham linkage has helped the UAE maintain **macroeconomic** stability and relatively low rates of **inflation**, generally between 4 percent and 5 percent annually. The principal problem for the system occurred in the late 1980s and again in the mid-1990s as the U.S. dollar dropped in value against the Japanese yen. This process created **balance of payments** concerns for the UAE since its principal trading partner at the time was Japan. There have been periodic discussions over the last decade of linking the dirham to a "basket" of currencies, including the U.S. dollar, the Japanese yen, and leading European currencies.

Dubai Financial Market (DFM), the UAE's first fully-regulated stock exchange, and its sister exchange, the Abu Dhabi Financial Market, both opened in 2000. Although initial interest in the stock exchanges was light, the UAE Central Bank expects that investors will flock to the 2 markets over the next decade. There have been discussions between representatives of DFM and the U.S. NASDAQ about a possible link up of the bourses (stock exchanges). The UAE Central Bank also has encouraged the development of a local bond market but has been hindered by several high-profile fraud cases involving large UAE investors.

POVERTY AND WEALTH

The United Arab Emirates is one of the wealthiest nations in the world and its citizens enjoy the highest standard of living in the Middle East: per capita income was estimated at US$17,700 in 1999. Although illiteracy was relatively high for wealthy nations at 25.4 percent in 1998, more than 90 percent of the UAE population has access to safe water, health services, and sanitation. In comparison, nearly 57 percent of the population was illiterate in 1975. The UAE government spends close to 16 percent of its annual budget on schools and has produced one of the lowest student-to-teacher ratios in the world, 12 pupils per teacher. Generous spending on health care has produced similar results in a number of key health indicators that are far better than the world average: life expectancy, infant mortality rates, births attended by trained physicians, and numbers of doctors per 100,000 people in the population. Overall, UAE citizens can depend on a cradle-to-grave **welfare state** that has few peers in the world.

GDP per Capita (US$)

Country	1975	1980	1985	1990	1998
United Arab Emirates	37,520	37,841	24,971	20,989	16,666
United States	19,364	21,529	23,200	25,363	29,683
Saudi Arabia	9,658	11,553	7,437	7,100	6,516
Iran	1,611	1,129	1,208	1,056	1,275

SOURCE: United Nations. *Human Development Report 2000; Trends in human development and per capita income.*

There are enormous socio-economic cleavages in the UAE, however, as wealth is not distributed evenly. Collectively, Abu Dhabi and Dubai control 83.2 percent of the UAE's GDP in large part because of Abu Dhabi's large oil production and Dubai's oil supply and commercial base. Sharjah has built its economy on trade and oil but has also depended on manufacturing. It is held back by large loans taken out in the 1970s and 1980s, reportedly receiving annual **subsidies** from Saudi Arabia. All 3 emirates feature modern cities that are as advanced as any in the major industrialized nations.

The other 4 emirates have little oil. In 1999 together they accounted for only 6.9 percent of GDP. They depend heavily on subsidies from the UAE central government. The economic future of these poorer emirates may revolve mostly around who emerges as the dominant figure in UAE affairs after Zayid's death. The *Economist* reported that Abu Dhabi Crown Prince Shaykh Khalifa wants to limit Abu Dhabi's assistance to the poorer emirates and accelerate privatization programs of large state industries. Army Chief of Staff Shaykh Muhammad favors a more federal system in which Abu Dhabi would help develop the economy of the entire federation.

Within individual emirates, there are also clear economic distinctions based on nationality and gender. While many basic social services are provided to expatriates at reduced rates, UAE citizens command salaries roughly double those of expatriates in similar jobs and have access to numerous subsidies, grants, loans, free services, and pensions unavailable to expatriate workers. UAE citizens also receive preferential treatment for many government jobs. Women are routinely discriminated against in hiring decisions. Very infrequently, they are sent abroad for post-secondary education in the United States or Europe. Increasingly, members of the UAE elite are educated in foreign universities rather than in the UAE.

WORKING CONDITIONS

One of the most striking features of the UAE is the demographic composition of its workforce and the striking differences between the working conditions. Nearly 70 percent of the UAE government's workforce is comprised of Emirati nationals, while expatriates overwhelmingly dominate the **private sector**. There is no minimum wage. All workers are prohibited from organizing unions, bargaining collectively, and going on strike. In 1995 the United States suspended the UAE from the U.S. Overseas Private Investment Corporation Insurance Program because of the government's failure to comply with internationally recognized worker rights and standards.

The UAE, however, does regulate workplace health and safety standards rigorously, and injured workers are entitled to fair compensation by law. Forced and compulsory labor is illegal and rare. Children under the age of 15 are not permitted to work, and there are special regulations for workers between the ages of 15 and 18. Most UAE workers work 8 hours a day, 6 days a week, and are not required to work outside when the temperature exceeds 44 degrees Celsius (112 degrees Fahrenheit)—a key consideration in a climate as hot as that of the UAE. The UAE Ministry of Labor and Social Affairs (MLSA) generally rejects contracts that provide excessively low wages and attempts to investigate all complaints made by workers. Workers also may seek redress in courts, including special labor courts established by the MLSA. Unemployment rates are believed to be very low.

Still, these labor regulations do not cover government employees, domestic servants, agricultural workers, and women. Such groups are at times obliged to work longer than mandatory hours, and domestic servants are often victims of abuse or work conditions approaching indentured servitude. Even expatriate workers, who are covered by labor laws, frequently are not protected because the costs of seeking redress in the courts can be prohibitively high and because the MLSA is understaffed. Expatriate workers also face the threat of immediate deportation because many are in the UAE on temporary work visas. Though not officially sanctioned, discrimination is often practiced against women. As a result, unemployment for female university graduates is far higher than that of their male counterparts.

Child laborers perhaps are in the greatest danger. There have been consistent reports for at least a decade of underage boys—sometimes as young as 5- or 8-years old—working as camel jockeys. Although the government in 1993 prohibited children younger than 15 serving as camel jockeys, the State Department's *1999 Human Rights Report for the UAE* speculated that the employers of underage camel jockeys are from powerful Emirati families considered to be above the law. Equally vulnerable are the large number of women from the former Soviet Union, Africa, and Asia who engage in prostitution and other acts associated with organized crime.

COUNTRY HISTORY AND ECONOMIC DEVELOPMENT

1820. Britain imposes a non-aggression pact on the rulers of the UAE for disrupting Indian-bound trade.

1892. Britain and the local rulers agree to transform the region into a British protectorate.

1958. Large quantities of oil are discovered in Abu Dhabi.

1971. Iran seizes 3 UAE administered islands: Abu Musa and the Tunb islands.

1971. Britain withdraws. The UAE is formed with all of the current emirates except Ras al-Khaimah.

1971. The UAE joins the United Nations and the Arab League.

1972. Ras al-Khaimah joins the UAE.

1973. OPEC raises the price, and cuts the supply, of oil. UAE GDP growth is 10 percent annually in the 1970s.

1981. Iran-Iraq war begins. The UAE financially supports Iraq. The UAE joins the Gulf Cooperation Council and pegs the dirham to the U.S. dollar.

1985. Dubai launches the Jebel Ali Free Zone.

1991. Gulf War begins. The UAE pays US$10 billion to support the anti-Iraq coalition.

1996. The UAE constitution becomes permanent. Abu Dhabi city is recognized as the UAE capital.

1996. The UAE agrees to a defense pact with the United States.

1999. Dubai Internet City and the Dolphin Gas Project are both unveiled.

2000. The first regulated UAE stock market, Dubai Financial Markets, opens for trading.

FUTURE TRENDS

There appears to be little doubt that the UAE has a bright economic future. The UAE controls nearly a century of oil reserves, maintains a modern infrastructure and a stable political system, lacks significant overseas debt, and has the financial resources necessary to address the economic, environmental, and social challenges of demographics, the dominance of oil in the state, and the paucity of water supplies before they become overwhelming. At the same time, the UAE's economic and social problems are very real and will intensify if they are not addressed.

Most of the UAE's proposed solutions to these problems have exacerbated certain aspects of them. The gap in wealth between the poorer and richer emirates could exacerbate tensions in the future. Abu Dhabi has combined its privatization programs with deep cuts in subsidies to the northern emirates, a move that has only enlarged this gap. This issue will be paramount if Shaykh Khalifa emerges as the dominant figure in the UAE government after the death of Shaykh Zayid. Privatization also favors the UAE's service sector, which is dominated by expatriates. This, too, could cause very serious social tensions. In addition, the offset program is contingent upon the UAE's spending billions on arms for decades, an expenditure that is likely to become a great burden. Thus, the UAE's principal challenge in the next century will be to build a viable society whose economic success does not undermine its economic and political stability.

DEPENDENCIES

United Arab Emirates has no territories or colonies.

BIBLIOGRAPHY

Cordesman, Anthony. *Bahrain, Oman, Qatar and the UAE: Challenges of Security.* Boulder, Colorado: Westview Press, 1997.

El-Din, Amin Badr. "The UAE Offsets Program." *Middle East Policy.* Vol. 5, January 1997.

Economist Intelligence Unit. *United Arab Emirates Country Profile.* London: Economist Intelligence Unit, 1998.

Economist Intelligence Unit. *United Arab Emirates Country Report.* London: Economist Intelligence Unit, 1997.

Emirate of Dubai Official Trade Statistics and Commerce Statistics. 2000.

Energy Information Agency. *Country Analysis Brief: UAE.* <http://www.eia.doe.gov/cabs/uae.html>. Accessed January 30, 2001.

Foley, Sean. "The UAE: Political Issues and Security Dilemmas." *Middle Eastern Review of International Affairs.* Vol. 3, No. 1, March 1999.

Gause, F. Gregory. *Oil Monarchies: Domestic Security Challenges in the Arab Gulf States.* New York: Council on Foreign Relations Press, 1994.

International Monetary Fund. *Direction of Trade Statistics Yearbook.* Washington, DC: International Monetary Fund Press, 1999.

Kelly, J.B. *Arabia: The Gulf and The West.* New York: Basic Books, 1980.

Kemp, Geoffrey, and Robert E. Harkavy. *Strategic Geography and the Changing Middle East.* Washington, DC: Carnegie Endowment for International Peace and Brookings Institution, 1997.

National U.S.-Arab Chamber of Commerce. *2000 Commercial and Economic Guide: UAE.* <http://www.nusacc.org/entry/profiles/uae.asp>. Accessed January 14, 2001.

Rugh, William. "The Foreign Policy of the United Arab Emirates." *Middle East Journal.* Vol. 50, Winter 1996.

———. "What Are the Sources of UAE Stability?" *Middle East Policy.* Vol. 5, September 1997.

Schofield, Richard. "Border Disputes in the Gulf: Past, Present and Future." *The Persian Gulf at the Millennium: Essays on Politics, Economics, Security , and Religion,* edited by Gary G. Sick and Lawrence G. Potter. New York: St. Martin's Press, 1987.

Sick, Gary. "The Coming Crisis in the Persian Gulf." *The Persian Gulf at the Millennium: Essays on Politics, Economics, Security, and Religion,* edited by Gary G. Sick and Lawrence G. Potter. New York: St. Martin's Press, 1997.

al-Shayeji, Abdullah. "Gulf Views of U.S. Foreign Policy in the Region." *Middle East Policy.* Vol. 5, September 1997.

United Nations. *Human Development Report.* London: Oxford University Press, 2000.

———. Department of Economic and Social Affairs, Population Division. *World Population Projections to 2150.* New York: United Nations, 1998.

———. Department of Economic and Social Affairs, Population Division, *World Population Prospects: The 1998 Revision.* New York: United Nations, 1999.

U.S. Central Intelligence Agency. *World Factbook 2000.* <http://www.odci.gov/cia/publications/factbook/index.html>. Accessed August 2001.

U.S. Department of Commerce. *1997 Country Commercial Guide: United Arab Emirates.* Washington, DC: United States Printing Office, 1997.

U.S. Department of State. "1998 Report on Economic Policies and Trade Practices: United Arab Emirates." *Tradeport.* <http://www.tradeport.org/ts/countries/uae/ecopol.html>. Accessed January 30, 2001.

———. "1999 Report on the United Arab Emirates Human Rights Practices." <http://www.state.gov/www/global/human_rights/1999_hrp_report/uae.html>. Accessed January 31, 2001.

———. *FY 2001 Country Commercial Guide: United Arab Emirates.* Washington, DC: United States Printing Office, 2000.

U.S. Library of Congress. *United Arab Emirates: A Country Study.* <http://lcweb2.loc.gov/frd/cs/aetoc.html>. Accessed January 1, 2001.

World Bank. *World Development Indicators 2000.* Baltimore: Johns Hopkins University Press, 2000.

World Bank. *World Population Projections 1994–1995.* Baltimore: Johns Hopkins University Press, 1996.

—Sean Foley

UZBEKISTAN

Republic of Uzbekistan
Uzbekiston Respublikasi

CAPITAL: Tashkent (Toshkent).

MONETARY UNIT: Uzbekistani sum (UZS). One sum equals 100 tyyn. Notes come in denominations of 100, 50, 25, 5, and 1 sum. Coins include 1, 5, 10, 20, and 50 tyyn.

CHIEF EXPORTS: Cotton, gold, natural gas, mineral fertilizers, ferrous metals, textiles, food products, and automobiles.

CHIEF IMPORTS: Machinery and equipment, chemicals, metals, and foodstuffs.

GROSS DOMESTIC PRODUCT: US$60 billion (purchasing power parity, 2000 est.).

BALANCE OF TRADE: **Exports:** US$2.9 billion (f.o.b., 2000 est.). **Imports:** US$2.6 billion (f.o.b., 2000 est.).

COUNTRY OVERVIEW

LOCATION AND SIZE. Uzbekistan is located in central Asia, bounded on the north and west by Kazakhstan (2,203 kilometers/1,369 miles), on the east by Kyrgyzstan (1,099 kilometers/683 miles) and Tajikistan (1,161 kilometers/721 miles), on the south by Afghanistan (137 kilometers/85 miles), and on the southwest by Turkmenistan (1,621 kilometers/1,007 miles). Uzbekistan has an area of 447,400 square kilometers (172,741 square miles), which is slightly smaller than California. Uzbekistan's area includes 22,000 square kilometers (8,494 square miles) of inland water, mainly the Aral Sea. It is one of only two countries in the world bounded only by other landlocked countries. The capital, Tashkent, is located in the eastern arm of the country, near the Kazakhstan border.

POPULATION. The population of Uzbekistan was estimated at 25.1 million in July 2001 and it was youthful, with 36.3 percent aged 14 years or younger, and only 4.6 percent 65 or older. The birth rate was 26.1 births per 1,000 and the death rate was 8 per 1,000 people. The population growth rate was 1.6 percent in 2001, and the fertility rate was approximately 3 children per woman. Life expectancy was lower than in industrialized countries, 63.81 years total; 60.24 for men, and 67.56 for women. The average population density was 51.2 people per square kilometer (132.6 per square mile), but 1995 figures show that most of the population was concentrated in the fertile Fergana Valley at 474.5 persons per square kilometer (1,229 per square mile). The central and western desert areas were sparsely populated, at only 6.6 persons per square kilometer in the region of Navoi, and 8.5 in the region of Karakalpakstan in 1995. In Tashkent, the largest city in central Asia with a population of 2.1 million in 2000, the population density reached higher than 7,000 persons per square kilometer (18,130 per square mile). About 35 percent of the population in 2000 was urban, down from 41 percent in 1995.

Uzbeks, a Turkic people, comprised 80 percent of the population in 1996, while Russians (5.5 percent), Tajiks (5 percent), Kazakhs (3 percent), Karakalpaks (2.5 percent), Tatars (1.5 percent), and Koreans (1 percent) made up the rest. Religious groups include mostly Muslims (88 percent, mostly Sunni), and Orthodox Christians (9 percent). The official language is Uzbek, spoken by 74.3 percent of the population. Russian is spoken by 14.2 percent and is still predominant in business and science, while Tajik is spoken by 4.4 percent of the population.

OVERVIEW OF ECONOMY

Although rich in natural resources, particularly natural gas and gold, Uzbekistan was among the poorest republics of the Soviet Union before its independence in 1991. The Soviet regime stressed the development of heavy industry, particularly mining, machines, and chemicals, while neglecting **consumer goods** production and the country's **infrastructure**. Although it developed as a major producer and exporter of natural gas

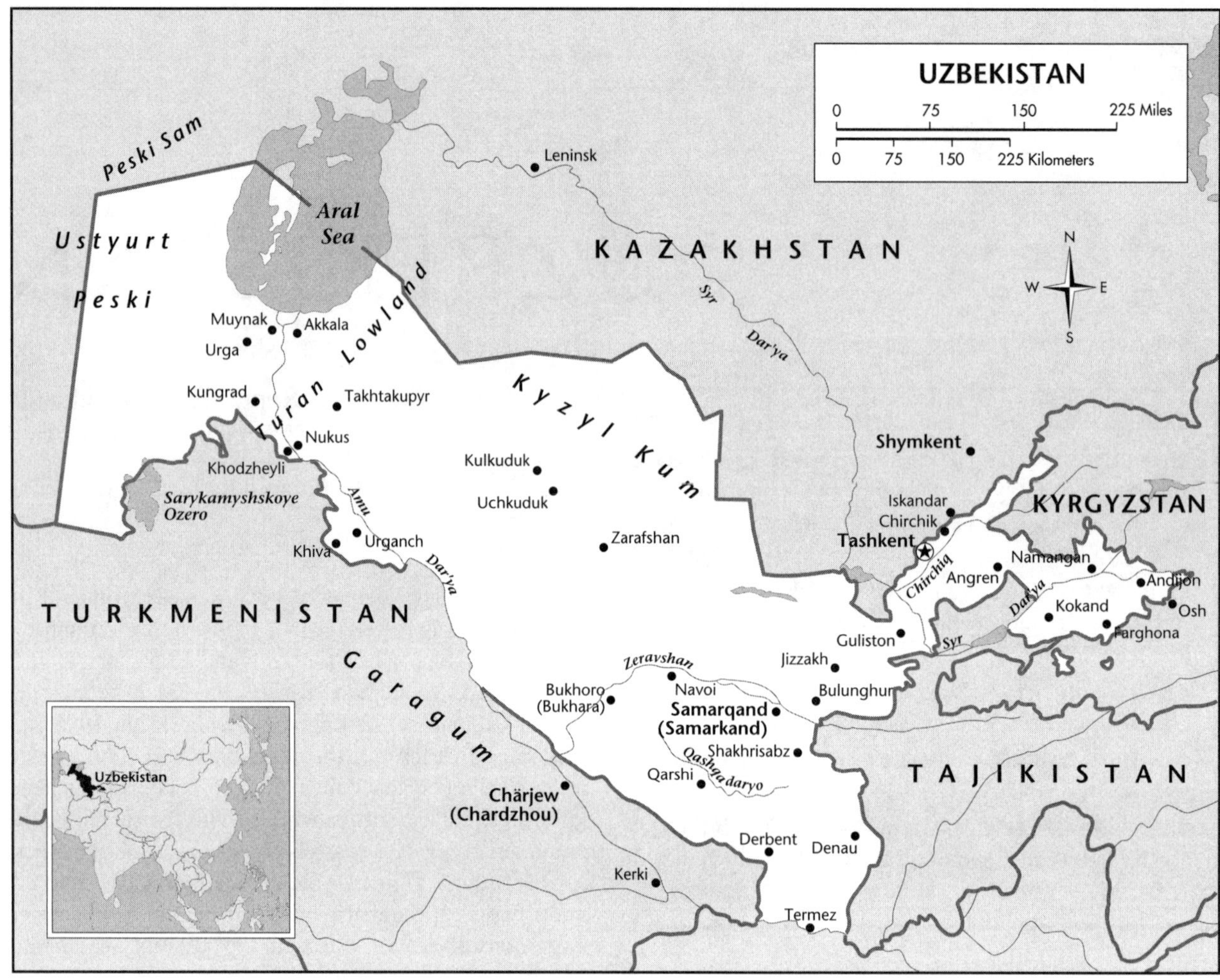

and gold and a sizable regional manufacturer of automobiles, aircraft, machinery, textiles, and chemicals, Uzbekistan remained predominantly rural. Nearly two-thirds of its population was concentrated in the heavily farmed river valleys where cotton production was the top priority of the central government. Uzbekistan was the principal cotton supplier to the Soviet Union and became the third largest cotton exporter worldwide in 2000. Monocultural (production of a single crop) agriculture and extensive irrigation in the arid Uzbek plains, however, caused severe environmental problems during the 1970s and 1980s. Poor land management resulted in the depletion of water supplies, the partial drying of the Amu Darya and Sir Darya rivers and the Aral Sea, heavy water and soil contamination, and newly formed patches of desert.

Following the collapse of the Soviet Union, Uzbek manufacturing experienced some decline in demand from its former Soviet markets, but the industrial sector protected the economy from the massive contraction seen in other former Soviet republics. The government of **communist** leader Islam Karimov, who stayed in office as president throughout the 1990s, subsidized state-owned, loss-making companies to keep them open. Karimov adopted **protectionist policies** in order to boost domestic industry, leading to expensive and inefficient industrial **import substitutions**. Industrialization was achieved but with the accumulation of a large **external debt** (US$3.3 billion in 1999) that was to be repaid with cotton and gold exports. In the late 1990s, however, the world prices of these key exports dropped, and the lack of competitiveness of the new Uzbeki industrial sector produced a **hard currency** shortage. The situation was aggravated by the government's reluctance to introduce current-account convertibility of the sum. The sum is not freely convertible to foreign currencies, and **exchange rates** for different purposes are set by the administration. The financial crises in Asia and Russia in the late 1990s and the lack of sufficient foreign investment caused economic stagnation and additionally-tightened import controls, fueling **inflation** and a deficit of goods in the domestic consumer market. Poor cotton harvests in the 1990s added to the growing **budget deficit**, and by 1995, Uzbekistan had received US$276.6 million in foreign aid to help meet its financial obligations.

To counter the negative trend towards debt, by the mid-1990s, the government introduced tighter monetary controls, launched a **privatization** program, and tried to lure foreign investors. However, its legal regimes still lacked transparency and many foreign partners complained about slow decision-making and persistent bureaucratic control complicated by red tape. Before 2000 there were several designated **strategic industries** that were not subject to privatization, such as mining of precious metals and gems, oil and gas drilling and processing, defense, aerospace, and communications. But by 2000, about 20 enterprises with foreign capital were expected to manufacture a wide variety of consumer and other goods, from tomato paste to electrodes to marble and granite. Unfortunately, a large South Korean investor, Daewoo Motors, went bankrupt in late 2000, threatening the future of its automotive plant in Uzbekistan.

By 1995 the country had returned to the level of industrial production that it had reached before the collapse of the Soviet Union. By the late 1990s, however, reforms had not been able to **restructure** the economy. The International Monetary Fund (IMF) suspended a US$185 million loan due to the failure of Uzbekistan to meet its **structural adjustment program** requirements. Without IMF aid and without hard currency, external debt default (suspension of all debt repayments) became likely. However, the IMF insisted that Uzbekistan adopt a stabilization program requiring a radical change in economic policy, including further privatization, an end to import substitutions, and a shift to the convertibility of the sum.

In early 2001 a 2-year government program was launched, envisaging the privatization of 1,244 enterprises. Thirty-eight of these, including several strategic enterprises and banks, were to be turned into joint-stock companies with the participation of foreign investors who would be offered between 39 percent and 70 percent of the shares. Approximately 49 enterprises were to be sold directly to foreign investors on the understanding that they would renovate their production processes, introducing modern technology and management. The number of firms with shares placed on the securities market and the off-exchange market to foreign investors in early 2001 reached 535, covering practically all sectors of the economy. Convertibility of the sum, however, was not yet on the government's agenda in 2001.

POLITICS, GOVERNMENT, AND TAXATION

Uzbekistan declared its independence from the Soviet Union in 1991 and a new constitution was adopted in 1992, declaring a multiparty democracy and a presidential republic. Since reelection in 2000, President Karimov has consolidated the government's power to run more like a dictatorship than a democracy. The 250-seat **unicameral** Ali Majlis (supreme council/parliament) has very little political clout. Although there has been universal suffrage since early Soviet times, members of parliament are nominated by local governors or selected from the People's Democratic Party (the former communist party) and other pro-government groups. The cabinet is headed by a prime minister who is nominated by the president, exerting total control on all other high-ranking national- and local-level officials. Other pro-government parties include the Homeland Progress, the National Revival, and the People's Unity Movement. Opposition groups, such as Birlik (Unity) and Erk (Will), were either silenced or banned in the early 1990s, and their leaders were banished. Only 2 human rights groups have survived under the strict government control. None of them has any large political role or represents any particular social group, and no opposition party at all existed legally in 2000. Adolat (Justice), an Islamic movement, was disbanded in 1992 and most of its members were incarcerated.

President Karimov considers Islamic fundamentalism and terrorism a major threat to the country, repeatedly citing it to justify his authoritarian rule to the public and the international community. Tajikistan is seen as a potential source of Islamic fundamentalist terrorism against Uzbekistan, as was Afghanistan prior to the toppling of that country's ruling fundamentalist Taliban regime in 2001. In many cases, the government's overreaction to real or imagined terrorist threats had the unintended effect of arousing sympathy from Uzbekistani citizens and pushing devout Muslims towards fundamentalism. Economic hardship also became a fertile ground for religious dissent during the 1990s. During the pre-1990 Soviet atheist regime, knowledge of Islam was minimal in central Asia. Even in early 2001, an attempt to overthrow the secular government and to establish Islamic rule was hardly thinkable. But in the late 1990s, tens of thousands of people were arrested by the government for their fundamentalism and put on trial to discourage the possibility of an Islamic fundamentalist revolution.

The key to understanding Uzbekistan politics lies in the domestic society's traditional clan structure, based on both kinship and territorial proximity. This society has survived the cultural impositions of both the czarist and the communist Russian regimes. Uzbekistan is ruled by representatives of the renowned Samarkand-Bukhoro clan. The clan's leader, President Karimov, took office in 1989 as a result of a compromise between the country's major clans, but he was resented by the powerful Fergana and Tashkent clans. In 1992 Vice President Shukrullo Mirsaidov, the chieftain of the Tashkent clan, along with the Birlik and Erk opposition groups tried to uproot Karimov but failed. The weakness of the opposition groups was mostly due to their inability to agree on one leader. In the early 1990s several independent organizations were created by young **technocrats** and businessmen, forming an important talent pool that the president was able to draw on for technical and political support for his policies. The importance of traditional clans is expected to shrink with the modernization of the country.

After the breakup of the Soviet Union, Turkey was regarded as the bridge between Europe and the central Asian states, including the ethnically Turkic Uzbekistan. By 2000 Turkey's importance as a mediator declined considerably because Uzbekistan turned eastward to its former trading partners for political and economic support. Post-Soviet integration was more active than western European integration, and Uzbekistan was still dependent on Russia for its security and for more than half of its trade. Since the mid-1990s, the United States has also boosted its presence in Uzbekistan and considers it as an important ally against the spreading of Islamic fundamentalism and terrorism in central Asia.

Taxation in Uzbekistan is considered rather restrictive, although the actual collection rate is quite low. In 2001, the government proposed a reduction of the **income tax** rate from 31 percent to 26 percent to boost investment. **Foreign debt** service problems are very serious given the country's lack of foreign exchange revenues and shrinking exports. The government plans to pay off its official debt, which is owed to other governments, before paying back its debt to private creditors. In this manner, Uzbekistan hopes to stay in the good graces of multilateral lenders such as the IMF, from which it receives debt assistance.

INFRASTRUCTURE, POWER, AND COMMUNICATIONS

Uzbekistan's infrastructure is extensive, but badly needs modernization. In 1993 there were 3,380 kilometers (2,113 miles) of railroads, 300 kilometers (187.5 miles) of which were electrified, and 81,600 kilometers (51,000 miles) of highways, 71,237 kilometers (44,523 miles) of which were paved, including gravel. The construction of a 2,300 kilometer (1,437.5 miles) long high-speed highway is expected to start in 2002. An international tender will be announced for implementing the project, and credits from international organizations and local budget resources are to be mobilized. The system of inland waterways included 1,100 kilometers (687.5 miles) in 1990: crude oil pipelines 250 kilometers (156 miles), petroleum products pipelines 40 kilometers (25 miles), and natural gas pipelines 810 kilometers (506 miles) in 1992. There was 1 port at Termiz on the Amu Darya River and 3 airports with paved runways in 1997.

The policy of import substitution has made Uzbekistan self-sufficient in energy. Since independence, oil production increased by 189 percent to 8.1 million tons in 1998, thereby eliminating oil imports. This self-sufficiency was not achieved with foreign investment, but through the compulsory allocation of national credit and large amounts of government-guaranteed foreign debt. Natural gas production rose from 41.9 billion cubic meters in 1991 to 54.8 billion cubic meters in 1998, but most natural gas is exported to former Soviet markets that pay late, if at all. Relations with neighboring Kyrgyzstan deteriorated in 2000 when the Uzbekistan government demanded that Kyrgyzstan hand over part of its land as payment for natural gas.

The Uzbeki energy sector has lost efficiency since 1991 because of government-controlled energy prices favoring individuals over industries. According to the IMF, industrial gas users payed 812.5 percent more than private families in 1997, though this disparity fell to 203 percent in 1998. Smuggling oil out of Uzbekistan is a widespread occurrence since the domestic price is very low when converted at the free market exchange rate. Despite self-sufficiency in fuel production, fuel is in short supply, encouraging drivers to buy smuggled imported gasoline from private traders at a premium of more than 45 percent above the official price. Electricity production generally meets the needs of the country, standing at 43.47

Communications

Country	Newspapers	Radios	TV Sets[a]	Cable subscribers[a]	Mobile Phones[a]	Fax Machines[a]	Personal Computers[a]	Internet Hosts[b]	Internet Users[b]
	1996	1997	1998	1998	1998	1998	1998	1999	1999
Uzbekistan	3	465	275	N/A	1	N/A	N/A	0.05	8
United States	215	2,146	847	244.3	256	78.4	458.6	1,508.77	74,100
Russia	105	418	420	78.5	5	0.4	40.6	13.06	2,700
Turkmenistan	N/A	276	201	N/A	1	N/A	N/A	0.56	2

[a]Data are from International Telecommunication Union, *World Telecommunication Development Report 1999* and are per 1,000 people.
[b]Data are from the Internet Software Consortium (http://www.isc.org) and are per 10,000 people.

SOURCE: World Bank. *World Development Indicators 2000.*

billion kilowatt hours in 1998. Approximately 85.2 percent of Uzbekistan's electricity is generated in thermal plants, and 14.2 percent is generated at hydropower stations in the mountains. In 2000, the government launched a US$113 million import substitution program for power-sector machinery. It also planned to increase local coal production at the Angren mine from 3 million tons in 1999 to 5 million tons by 2007. Elimination of energy imports has come at the heavy price of high foreign debt, which Uzbekistan is finding difficult to service.

The Uzbekistan telephone system is outdated, with only 1.976 million main lines in 1999, and 26,000 cellular phones in 1998. In the late 1990s, the telephone system was expanded and improved under contracts with foreign companies, particularly in and around Tashkent and Samarkand. By 1998, 6 cellular networks were in operation, 4 of them of the European GSM type (Groupe Spéciale Mobile; or Global System for Mobile Communications). Uzbekistan communications are linked with other post-Soviet republics and other countries by a leased connection via the Moscow international switch. With the opening of a link to the Trans-Asia-Europe (TAE) fiber-optic cable, the country will become independent of Russia for its international communications. There was only 1 Internet service provider in 1999 and computer usage was low. In 2000 a shortage of hard currency made the state-owned telecommunications company Uzbektelekom repay its US$1.2 million debt to Kazakhstan's Kazakhtelekom in supplies of Uzbek telephone boxes and natural gas. Kazakhtelekom cut off calls coming from Uzbekistan in August 2000, claiming that the debt was in fact US$4.4 million.

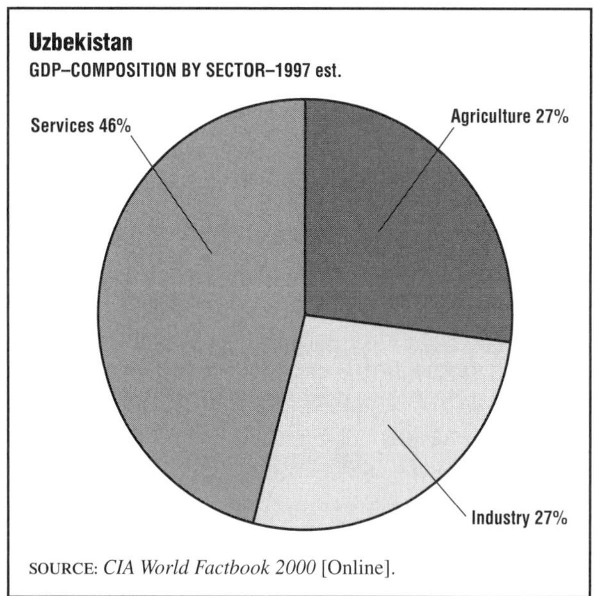

SOURCE: *CIA World Factbook 2000* [Online].

ECONOMIC SECTORS

Agriculture contributed 28 percent of **gross domestic product** (GDP) in 1999 and employed 44 percent of the workforce in 1995. Most agricultural and light industry output is related to cotton, accounting for 30.8 percent of total exports in 1999. Lack of environmental and management reform has plagued the agricultural sector. The cotton crop failed twice, in 1996 and 1998, and remained below the government's target of 4 million tons in 1999. The government's pursuit of self-sufficiency in food production led to some land reserved for cotton being reassigned for food growing.

Industry produced 21 percent of GDP in 1999, employing 20 percent of the workforce in 1995. Manufacturing made up the greatest part of the industrial sector and accounted for 13.9 percent of GDP and 12.8 percent of the workforce in 1999. A car factory in Andijan assembled Daewoo cars from imported components, while an aircraft factory assembled Russian aircraft. The rest of the industrial sector was comprised of truck and bus assembly, electrical engineering, textiles, agricultural machinery, and agricultural processing. Gold mining and refining is the country's next largest industrial endeavor, accounting for 10.4 percent of GDP in 1999. Most gold is mined at Muruntau in Navoi, where annual output is about 80 tons per year. Gold brings in less money than it did during Soviet times due to a drop in its price in the late 1990s.

Approximately 51 percent of GDP came from services in 1999; the sector employed 36 percent of the workforce in 1995. Economic volatility and isolation, the lack of consumer credit, and government controls have

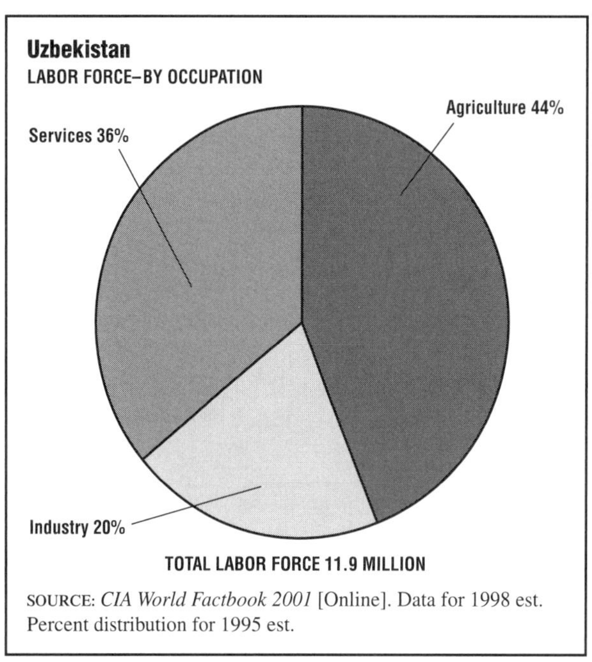

SOURCE: *CIA World Factbook 2001* [Online]. Data for 1998 est. Percent distribution for 1995 est.

inhibited the development of a modern services sector. Outside of education and health, there were 398,000 employees in the services sector in 2000, or just 4.5 percent of the total workforce.

AGRICULTURE

Agriculture in arid central Asia is heavily dependent on irrigation. Arable land comprises only 9 percent of the territory because much of the land is desert. Only 1 percent is covered by permanent crops, about 3 percent is occupied by forests, and 46 percent is permanent pastures used by sheep and other livestock. Under the Soviet regime vast formerly-deserted terrain has been reclaimed for cotton growing, and agriculture was collectivized into large state-controlled farms. These lands remain under the control of the Uzbekistani government. The cotton sector is still the most important employer and export producer, characterized by the extensive use of machines and chemicals. The drying up of the Aral Sea due to excessive irrigation in the cotton fields has resulted in growing concentrations of pesticides and salts blown from the exposed bed of the lake. Mismanaged irrigation has contributed to soil contamination, **desertification**, water pollution, and many health disorders.

Apart from cotton, leading products include vegetables, fruits, grain, livestock, and animal products, including the world-famous karakul sheep. In 1998, President Karimov threatened to impose criminal penalties on local leaders who anticipated food shortages and restricted the sale of food at market in order to stockpile food locally. In 2000 the grain and cotton harvests were low due to persistent drought and mismanagement of water resources. The government would not raise water prices to encourage farmers to use it more efficiently, because allowing the sale of water at market prices defies the communist ideal of a state-run economy. To ensure that water shortages would not happen again in 2001, the government reached an agreement with Tajikistan (where its rivers originate) to cooperate on water use. Another pricing problem exists in the cotton industry: the domestic cotton fiber price was just 43 percent of the world price in 2000. In order to achieve self-sufficiency in grain production, the government is still shifting land from cotton to grain production, which deprives the economy of export revenue. A ton of cotton on the world market in 2000 was worth around US$1,100 in export revenue, while a ton of grain was worth approximately US$200.

INDUSTRY

Manufacturing in Uzbekistan is based on its wealth of natural resources including natural gas, petroleum, coal, gold, uranium, silver, copper, lead, zinc, tungsten, and molybdenum. Mining and metallurgy are the most important areas, but textiles, food processing, machine building, and electrical engineering are also well developed. Due to self-sufficiency policies, the industrial production growth rate was 6 percent in 1999, but the sector was performing poorly financially.

OIL AND GAS. Uzbekistan has failed so far to promote oil and gas exports due to its isolationist economic policy. The prices that Uzbekistan gets for its oil and gas exports in post-Soviet markets are low, and payments are insecure. Approximately 41.5 billion cubic meters of gas was produced in the first 9 months of 2000, up by 1 percent from 1999. Most gas is consumed locally by enterprises at prices above the cost of production, and by households at subsidized prices. Officially recorded crude oil production fell in the first 9 months of 2000 to 5.7 million tons, down by 6.2 percent from 1999. Refined oil production was rising though. It is likely that oil is illicitly exported to Kazakhstan. Fuel oil production, at 1.3 million tons, increased slightly during 2000, and the kerosene output of 300,000 tons rose by 17.1 percent in 2000. The government intended to increase investment in the state-owned oil and gas giant Uzbekneftegaz by taking on further external debts, expanding exploration and production in 2001. Free-market domestic prices were seen as a more efficient method to generate the capital for industrial investment domestically, without increasing the large external debt burden. The government also planned to sell 49 percent of Uzbekneftegaz to foreign investors in 2001. The subsidiaries of Uzbekneftegaz also were scheduled for partial sale to foreign investors, including 44 percent in Uzneftegazdobycha (exploration and development), and 39 percent in each of Uzneftepererabotka (oil refineries), Uzburneftegaz (drilling), and Uzneftegazstroi (oil and gas construction).

GOLD. Uzbekistan is the world's eighth largest producer of gold. The gold mine is owned by the Navoi Mining and Metallurgical Combine (NGMK), a Soviet-era, state-owned firm that the government refuses to privatize or reform. The estimated output in 1999 was 80 tons but there was no independent confirmation. Gold accounts for 10 to 20 percent of export earnings and the drop in its price since 1997 has discouraged foreign companies from investing. Yet, Newmont Mining of the United States has entered a **joint venture** with NGMK to extract gold from a 242 million-ton pile of tailings left beside the mine from the Soviet era. The project, with European Bank for Reconstruction and Development (EBRD) funding, should produce almost 143 million grams (5 million ounces) over 17 years.

MOTOR VEHICLES. As a result of the policy of import substitution, most industrial production supplies the domestic market and is not export-oriented. Even Uzdaemotors, a joint venture between Daewoo Motors and state-owned Uzavtosanaot that assembles motor vehicles, produces cars primarily for the Russian and domestic market. Production started in 1996 when investment was expected to reach US$658 million. Supplies were ordered from Russia and South Korea. Uzbekistan was to provide the labor; however, Russia's economic problems in 1998 damaged export prospects, and few locals could afford to buy Daewoo cars. As a result, production in 2000 was even less than the 1997 target of 125,000 units and the 1998 target of 80,000 units. Although Daewoo's stake reached 70 percent in 1998, the Uzbekistan government kept the venture operational after the bankruptcy of Daewoo in 2000, switching it from a foreign investment into another government asset backed with foreign debt.

FOOD PROCESSING. In 1997 Jahn International of Denmark joined Intertrade from the United States and local Tashkent Sud to form Sun Juice, a fruit juice company. Nestle of Switzerland plans to invest US$30 million for the construction of a chocolate factory in Namangan, while British companies have invested in the Uzbek tobacco industry.

SERVICES

FINANCIAL SERVICES. Due to excessive government restrictions and controls, financial services are poorly developed. The central bank is not independent and acts as a money printing press for the finance ministry. Banks do not act as financial intermediaries for their clients, rather they pay negative interest rates on deposits, confiscate savings, and funnel government credit and foreign loans to enterprises and sectors selected by the government. The government refuses to push insolvent state-owned enterprises into bankruptcy, allowing them to stay in business. Banks fund their operations by refusing to pay back creditors, suppliers, and workers, eroding the banking sector. Of the 31 banks in Uzbekistan in 2000, just 4 small ones were private. Most banks were considered insolvent by international lenders, relying on further foreign debt inflows for survival. The largest bank was the state-owned National Bank of Uzbekistan (NBU), with 70 percent of the total loan portfolio and around 66 percent of the foreign exchange **turnover** in the country. The NBU is 1 of 4 banks allowed to deal in foreign exchange and makes a good profit by borrowing from the EBRD, nearly doubling the interest rate when lending to Uzbekistan firms. The government planned—but failed—to sell a 40 percent stake in the NBU in 1999. The main foreign-owned bank is ABN-AMRO (Netherlands), which operates in a joint venture with NBU.

RETAIL. Trading in domestically produced food and imported consumer goods in the vibrant traditional oriental bazaars is a major economic activity and important income source. Many government and other employees add to their income as small traders, and the vast majority of Uzbekistan people shop at the local bazaar. The largely unregulated bazaars have so far survived the government's restrictions, with illegal currency traders providing the dollars that fund the smuggling of consumer items into the country. Outside of the bazaars, Tashkent is the fourth most expensive city in the world, and its modern **retail** complexes are reserved for the rich and for foreigners. Levi Strauss (United States) and Benetton (Italy) have outlets in both, and Sony (Japan) and Daewoo have large consumer electronics stores. Several other international retailers entered the market in the late 1990s, including Jahn International, and Nestle. Uzbekistan may have a future in imported consumer goods trade since it shares a border with all central Asian states and has the largest domestic population, making it a natural distribution center. Yet in 2000, most consumer goods were flowing into Uzbekistan illegally from its neighbors.

TOURISM. Uzbekistan has many important historic and cultural monuments in the medieval capitals of Samarkand, Bukhoro, and elsewhere. The lack of adequate facilities and high prices for western goods have prevented the development of any significant international tourism. No particular government plans in the area have been revealed.

INTERNATIONAL TRADE

The Uzbeki policy of self-sufficiency prevents active international trade. The country exports cotton, gold, natural gas, mineral fertilizers, ferrous metals, textiles, foods, and automobiles; it imports machinery and equipment, chemicals, metals, and foods. Russia is Uzbekistan's principal trade partner, responsible for 53 percent of volume (1999). Russian imports include machinery and tools, metals, chemicals, pharmaceuticals, paper and lumber, and grains; exports to Russia include raw cotton (70 percent of all Russian imports in 1999), metals, chemicals, and farm products. There were about 250 Russo-Uzbekistani joint ventures in 2000. Other major export destinations included Switzerland (10 percent), the United Kingdom (10 percent), Belgium (4 percent),

Trade (expressed in millions of US$): Uzbekistan

	Exports	Imports
1994	3044	2478
1995	3100	2900
1996	4590	4721
1997	4387	4522
1998	3528	3288
1999	N/A	N/A

SOURCE: United Nations. *Monthly Bulletin of Statistics* (September 2000).

Kazakhstan (4 percent), and Tajikistan (4 percent) in 1998. Imports to Uzbekistan originated from South Korea (11 percent), Germany (8 percent), the United States (7 percent), Turkey (6 percent), and Kazakhstan (5 percent) in 1998. Uzbekistan has a large current-account deficit and the ratio of external debt to exports in 1999 was 96 percent. With a more precise account of exchange rates, however, it might be as high as 137 percent.

GDP per Capita (US$)

Country	1975	1980	1985	1990	1998
Uzbekistan	N/A	N/A	N/A	1,338	1,007
United States	19,364	21,529	23,200	25,363	29,683
Russia	2,555	3,654	3,463	3,668	2,138
Turkmenistan	N/A	N/A	N/A	1,154	486

SOURCE: United Nations. *Human Development Report 2000; Trends in human development and per capita income.*

MONEY

Despite government pledges that in 2000 the sum would be convertible (freely exchangeable for foreign currencies at market rates), Uzbekistan continued to operate a system of administratively-set multiple exchange rates in 2001. These were used to protect import substitution industrialization, including a set commercial bank rate and an administratively set commercial exchange rate, which kept the sum at around 50 percent of the commercial bank rate. The **black market** is widely used. In December 2000 President Karimov said that convertibility would take 3 to 5 years, but he was pushed to take action when a default on the country's external debt was imminent because of a threatened halt to IMF funding. Uzbekistan is plagued by a hard currency shortage and has serious problems with servicing its debt. It was scheduled to make US$900 million of repayments in 2000.

The Tashkent Stock Exchange is 26 percent government-owned, and most of the stocks in companies that are listed are owned by the employees of those companies. Trade at the Tashkent Stock Exchange is predominantly conducted through **treasury bills** because they are considered a liquid and safe asset, despite the fact that yields are negative and the market is extremely small.

POVERTY AND WEALTH

Under the Soviet regime, Uzbekistan was arguably a land of economic equality, although among the poorest republics of the Soviet Union. The vast majority of the population was state-employed, no private initiative was allowed, and central funds were allocated comparatively equitably as free health care, higher education, pensions, and other benefits. The only exceptions of the modest standard of living were the *nomenklatura* (the communist party elite) and the organized crime and black market economy players. The market reforms in the 1990s generated new wealth for a limited number of entrepreneurs who were well connected to the government yet understood the economic hardships of everyday Uzbeki life. In 1995 the country's **Gini index** was 33.3, lower than that of the United States and the United Kingdom but higher than in most former communist countries. Due to the government's policies of protectionism and import substitution, unemployment is still a minor problem, but the loss-making state industries and struggling agricultural sector are no longer able to sustain the living standards of the 1980s. Monthly salaries in the state manufacturing sector reached as low as US$34 in 1994, and had increased only slightly by 2001. Inflation, at 29 percent in 1999, is also a concern. Many Uzbekistanis suffer from problems other than financial insolvency such as a poor health system, the lack of safe water, epidemics, and excessive soil pollution and desertification. These problems are most apparent in the intensely farmed river valleys, where almost two-thirds of the population are concentrated. On many occasions throughout the 1990s, the government has appealed to international organizations for aid in dealing with severe droughts. In particu-

Exchange rates: Uzbekistan

Uzbekistani soms per US$1	
Jan 2001	325.0
2000	141.4
1999	111.9
1998	110.95
1997	75.8
1996	41.1

SOURCE: CIA *World Factbook 2001* [ONLINE].

Distribution of Income or Consumption by Percentage Share: Uzbekistan

Lowest 10%	3.1
Lowest 20%	7.4
Second 20%	12.0
Third 20%	16.7
Fourth 20%	23.0
Highest 20%	40.9
Highest 10%	25.2

Survey year: 1993

Note: This information refers to income shares by percentiles of the population and is ranked by per capita income.

SOURCE: *2000 World Development Indicators* [CD-ROM].

Household Consumption in PPP Terms

Country	All food	Clothing and footwear	Fuel and power[a]	Health care[b]	Education[b]	Transport & Communications	Other
Uzbekistan	34	3	13	4	7	9	30
United States	13	9	9	4	6	8	51
Russia	28	11	16	7	15	8	16
Turkmenistan	32	6	14	6	18	11	14

Data represent percentage of consumption in PPP terms.
[a]Excludes energy used for transport.
[b]Includes government and private expenditures.

SOURCE: World Bank. *World Development Indicators 2000.*

lar, Karakalpakstan has been an environmental disaster area plagued by the drying up of the Aral Sea and unprecedented scarcity of water.

WORKING CONDITIONS

Uzbekistan is party to all major universal legal instruments on economic and social rights, the rights of the child, the right to equal compensation and collective bargaining, and the elimination of employment discrimination. Its **labor force** numbered 12 million in 1999, and official unemployment was low at 2.2 percent in 1995, but no data have been released since. The hidden unemployment figure, made up of workers who receive no pay from cash-stripped companies or who are put on mandatory leave, affected about 1 million people in the agricultural sector in 2000. State employees' wages increased by 36 percent in 1996 (from a US$34 monthly average in 1994) but remained among the lowest of the former Soviet republics. The government has tried to hold wages in check to prevent inflation, setting the minimum wage to 75 percent of a typical consumer's spending. Pay raises in both the state and **private sector** are limited to a maximum of 70 percent of the sector's increase in output and are subject to government approval. Labor unions are government controlled. Many labor practices are inefficient due to obsolete technology, lack of management skills, and import substitutions.

COUNTRY HISTORY AND ECONOMIC DEVELOPMENT

100s B.C. The territory that is now Uzbekistan becomes a part of the Silk Road, linking China with the Middle East and Europe.

600s A.D. Arab invaders conquer Uzbekistan and introduce Islam.

1300s. The land is ruled by the empire of Tamerlane. Samarqand becomes the capital in 1369. Nomadic Turkic tribes form the Uzbek confederation and start moving south into Uzbekistan.

1700s. The Kokand principality emerges in the Fergana Valley. The Turkic-speaking Karakalpaks in the Amu Darya delta are subjugated by the new khanate of Khiva. Feudal agricultural economy develops.

1850. Russian forces march on Kokand, Tashkent, Bukhoro, and Khiva and take them over by 1876. A modern commodity economy starts developing but many locals resent the non-Muslim administration and colonists.

1916. Burdened with Russian demands to aid in its World War I effort, the locals revolt against a military draft but are suppressed.

1917. The Bolsheviks seize power in Russia and establish new political divisions in central Asia ruled by local soviets (councils), which are opposed by guerrillas of the Action for National Liberation party (called *Basmachi* by the Russians).

1918. Southern central Asia, including part of Uzbekistan, is organized into the Turkistan Autonomous Soviet Socialist Republic (ASSR) within the Russian Soviet Federated Socialist Republic.

1919. The Uzbek Soviet Socialist Republic is carved out from Turkestan (with the Bukharan and the Khorezmian republics), officially becoming a republic of the Soviet Union in 1922.

1928. Land is collectivized into state farms.

1931. The Uzbek S.S.R. is enlarged with the addition of the Karakalpak ASSR.

1941. In World War II, many industries are relocated to Uzbekistan from the western regions of the Soviet Union. Many non-Uzbek nationals **immigrate** to the republic.

1960s. Excessive irrigation brings an ecological disaster in the Aral Sea basin.

1991. Uzbekistan declares independence from the Soviet Union and joins the new **Commonwealth of Independent States** (CIS). Presidential elections, in which most opposition groups are not allowed to participate, leave Islam Karimov—the incumbent president and former communist leader—in office. Karimov establishes an authoritarian regime, banning opposition parties and claiming that more democracy would render the country vulnerable to Islamic fundamentalism.

FUTURE TRENDS

With President Karimov firmly in office, Uzbekistan will likely be characterized by political stability, but the policy of import substitution and the lack of sufficient structural reform may further aggravate economic problems. Poor cotton crops and recurrent droughts may add to the crisis. If accompanied by economic crisis, the president's exaggerated security threats—particularly about Islamic groups—could contribute to the authoritarian character of the regime and lead towards further political violence.

Particularly troublesome will be the persistent inconvertibility of the sum, the lack of hard currency, and the growing external debt. The country will not be able to serve its financial obligations in the 21st century without IMF help, but the IMF requires the closure of many loss-making industrial enterprises that would be particularly difficult for the government to effect. Significant reforms were promised in 2000, and there were hints that some harmful old policies would be abandoned.

Growth in the former Soviet area, Uzbekistan's main export market, is expected to be robust, but a weakening global economy in 2001 will restrain growth because of its impact on key commodity prices, especially of cotton and gold. Due to its natural wealth and strategic location, Uzbekistan has significant growth prospects once it implements market reforms and controls environmental hazards.

DEPENDENCIES

Uzbekistan has no territories or colonies.

BIBLIOGRAPHY

Curtis, Glenn E., editor. *Kazakhstan, Kyrgyzstan, Tajikistan, Turkmenistan, and Uzbekistan: Country Studies.* Library of Congress: Washington, D.C., 1997.

Economist Intelligence Unit. *Country Profile: Uzbekistan.* London: Economist Intelligence Unit, 2001.

Eurasia Information Analytic Center. *Uzbekistan.* <http://www.eurasia.org.ru/main/inform.html>. Accessed April 2001.

U.S. Central Intelligence Agency. *World Factbook 2001.* <http://www.odci.gov/cia/publications/factbook/index.html>. Accessed September 2001.

—Valentin Hadjiyski

VANUATU

Republic of Vanuatu
République de Vanuatu
Ripablik blong Vanuatu

CAPITAL: Port Vila.

MONETARY UNIT: Vatu (VT). There are coins of 1, 2, 5, 10, 20, 50 and 100 vatu and notes of 500, 1,000 and 5,000 vatu. One vatu equals 100 centimes, although there are no centime coins still in circulation.

CHIEF EXPORTS: Copra, beef, cocoa, coffee, timber, kava, squash.

CHIEF IMPORTS: Food, machinery and equipment, fuels.

GROSS DOMESTIC PRODUCT: US$245 million (1999 est.).

BALANCE OF TRADE: **Exports:** US$33.8 million (1998 est.). **Imports:** US$76.2 million (1998 est.).

COUNTRY OVERVIEW

LOCATION AND SIZE. Vanuatu is located in Oceania, about 2,000 kilometers (1,243 miles) to the northeast of Australia, to the south of Solomon Islands, and north of New Caledonia. It consists of a group of more than 80 islands with a land area of 14,760 square kilometers (5,699 square miles) (slightly larger than the state of Connecticut) and a coastline of 2,528 kilometers (1,570 miles).

POPULATION. The population of Vanuatu was estimated at 199,800 in mid-2000, an increase of 3.4 percent from the 1999 census population of 193,219. In 2000, the birth rate was 36.0 per 1,000 while the death rate stood at 6.2 per 1,000. With a projected annual population growth rate of 3.0 percent between 2000 and 2010, the population is expected to reach 267,600 by 2010 and to double in 23 years.

About 94 percent of the population are Melanesian by origin, made up of about 100 different cultural groups. A further 4 percent is French, and there are small but significant populations of Vietnamese and Chinese.

With a high total fertility rate of 5.3, the population is very young, with about 37 percent under the age of 15 and only about 3 percent over 65 years. This is a result of both the high birth rate and a relatively low life expectancy. The majority of the population is rural, with only 21 percent of the people living in urban areas. However, the urban growth rate is about 50 percent higher than the total growth rate, and this growth is mainly centered on the 2 largest urban centers, Port Vila and Luganville.

OVERVIEW OF ECONOMY

Lying in the Western Pacific Ocean, Vanuatu is made up of a chain of islands with diverse physical characteristics and economic potential. The islands range from small coral atolls to relatively large islands of volcanic origin. Nearly 80 percent of the population of Vanuatu live in villages, so subsistence production of food, housing, and other items is the mainstay of the household economy. Most households also participate in some cash production, mainly of agricultural products such as copra (dried coconut flesh), cocoa, and coffee. Recently, new items that have entered the village cash economy, and which are of relatively high value, are kava and squash.

The formal economy of Vanuatu is based mainly on agricultural products and services. Copra and coconut oil are produced on large-scale plantations as well as in the villages. Coconut plantations often have cattle as well. Other products common to the village economy are also produced in plantations, in particular cocoa and coffee. Fishing supplies the internal market and is also a source of export income.

Vanuatu regularly has a negative **balance of trade**, and this is balanced by the services sector. Tourism has been growing steadily in recent years, partly because of heavy promotion in nearby countries such as Australia

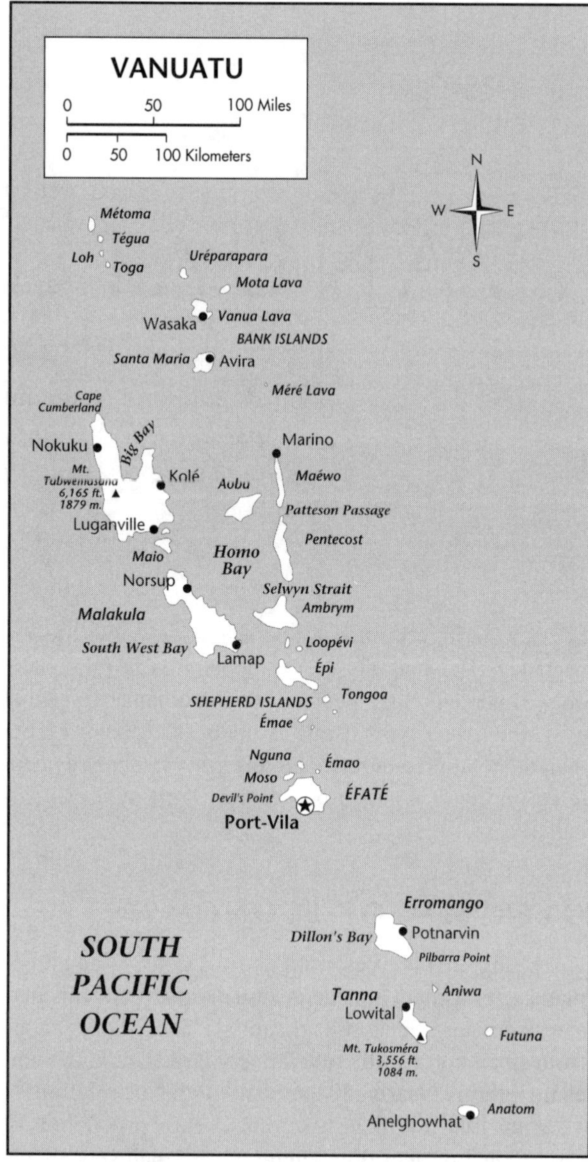

and New Zealand. Another significant source of employment and government revenues is the Offshore Financial Centre (OFC), which provides a **tax haven** for **offshore banks**, trust companies, insurance companies, and shipping companies.

International aid accounts for about 35 percent of GDP and development expenditure since independence in 1980 has been mainly financed by aid. Australia is the largest aid donor, followed by Asian Development Bank, France, Japan, and New Zealand.

POLITICS, GOVERNMENT, AND TAXATION

During the colonial period from 1906 to 1980, Vanuatu, then known as the New Hebrides, had the distinction of being ruled by 2 colonial powers, Great Britain and France. This "condominium" arrangement has sometimes been termed "pandemonium" since there were 2 systems of administration, education, and courts. Furthermore, in addition to the 2 colonial languages of English and French, inhabitants spoke one or more of about 100 indigenous languages. For most ni-Vanuatu (people of Vanuatu) the only effective language of communication was, and is, Bislama (a kind of Pidgin which has strong elements of English vocabulary and Melanesian grammar).

After obtaining independence from Great Britain and France in 1980, dual systems continued to operate in some contexts, especially education. Systems of administration, courts, etc. were combined, but still operated in at least 2 languages. The country adopted a republican system, with a president as head of state (elected by an electoral college of parliament and regional council presidents), and a prime minister selected by a parliament of 52 members elected by universal suffrage of all citizens aged 18 and over. A considerable number of political parties have formed and reformed since independence, but in most cases they are based on the colonial language split, either being Anglophone (English-speaking) or Francophone (French-speaking) parties.

The primarily Anglophone Vanua'aku Party, with Father Walter Lini as prime minister, held power from 1980 to 1991, when parliament voted him out in a no-confidence motion. Subsequently, Francophone parties, usually in coalition, have tended to form the governments. In the late 1990s, there was a great deal of political turmoil as governments changed and various political leaders were accused of corruption. In early 2001, Barak Sope, an English speaker, was selected as prime minister of a coalition government. Following much political turmoil in the late 1990s, the English-French divide appeared to be less important, as coalitions were sometimes forged across languages.

Local government is administered by 6 regional councils, and there are municipal councils in the 2 urban areas of Port Vila and Luganville. Authority over matters of tradition is held by *malvatumauri* (national council of chiefs) who are elected by district councils. These chiefs usually represent land-holding groups. As in many parts of Melanesia, they do not necessarily gain their position by inheritance but rather through skill in achieving economic and political power at the local level.

There is no corporate or personal **income tax** in Vanuatu. Import taxes accounted for 66 percent of all tax revenues in the country in 1997. There are also export **tariffs** that account for most of the other tax revenues. Application for membership in the World Trade Organization (WTO) means that in the future, these trade taxes will have to be progressively reduced. This means other types of tax may have to be imposed, according to David Ambrose and Savenaca Siwatibau in the *Pacific Economic Bulletin.*

Communications

Country	Telephones[a]	Telephones, Mobile/Cellular[a]	Radio Stations[b]	Radios[a]	TV Stations[a]	Televisions[a]	Internet Service Providers[c]	Internet Users[c]
Vanuatu	4,000 (1996)	154 (1996)	AM 2; FM 2; shortwave 1	62,000	1	2,000	1	3,000
United States	194 M	69.209 M (1998)	AM 4,762; FM 5,542; shortwave 18	575 M	1,500	219 M	7,800	148 M
Philippines	1.9 M	1.959 M (1998)	AM 366; FM 290; shortwave 3 (1999)	11.5 M	31	3.7 M	33	500,000
Solomon Islands	8,000	658	AM 3; FM 0; shortwave 0	57,000	0	3,000	1	3,000

[a]Data is for 1997 unless otherwise noted.
[b]Data is for 1998 unless otherwise noted.
[c]Data is for 2000 unless otherwise noted.

SOURCE: CIA *World Factbook 2001* [Online].

INFRASTRUCTURE, POWER, AND COMMUNICATIONS

Because of the numerous islands in the country, the main internal transport linkages are by sea and air. The islands are served by a number of government and private passenger and cargo ships, although they do not usually run on a schedule and are not much cheaper than flying. International sea linkages are well served by shipping lines from Australia, New Zealand, and Asia. However, because Vanuatu is a flag of convenience registry, there were 78 vessels (some very large) from 15 different countries registered in Vanuatu in 1998. Most of these are not seen in Vanuatu waters.

Internal air services are provided by the government-owned Vanair, which flies to 29 destinations within the country. International air services link neighboring Pacific states including Fiji, New Caledonia, and Solomon Islands and most longer distance air linkages are routed through Brisbane, Australia, and Nadi, Fiji. The national airline Air Vanuatu flies to Sydney, Brisbane, Melbourne, Auckland, and Nadi. Within the country there are 32 airports, 2 of which have paved runways, but nearly all international traffic is channeled through Port Vila.

Electricity is mainly concentrated in the towns and is generated exclusively using imported fuels. Similarly, telephone services are mainly available in towns, and communication with rural areas is generally by 2-way radio or radio bulletins on the government-owned radio station.

ECONOMIC SECTORS

In 1999, agriculture contributed 25.7 percent of Vanuatu's **gross domestic product** (GDP), while industry made up 14.0 percent and services contributed 60.4 percent of GDP. Some value is attributed to subsistence agriculture in the statistics for agriculture, and other significant contributors are copra production and beef production. Industry is mostly made up of small-scale manufacturing and construction. The large proportion of GDP that derives from services can be attributed to government employment, especially in education, as well as the tourism industry and offshore banking facilities. The only data available about the **labor force** in Vanuatu are from the 1989 census, and these are quite different from the GDP data (and 10 years older). Since the subsistence sector is such an important element in the economy, it was decided by Vanuatu's statistics department that "labor force" should include all workers, whether they were working for cash or not. Thus, the statistics show that about 75 percent of the labor force in 1989 was in agriculture, and this percent-

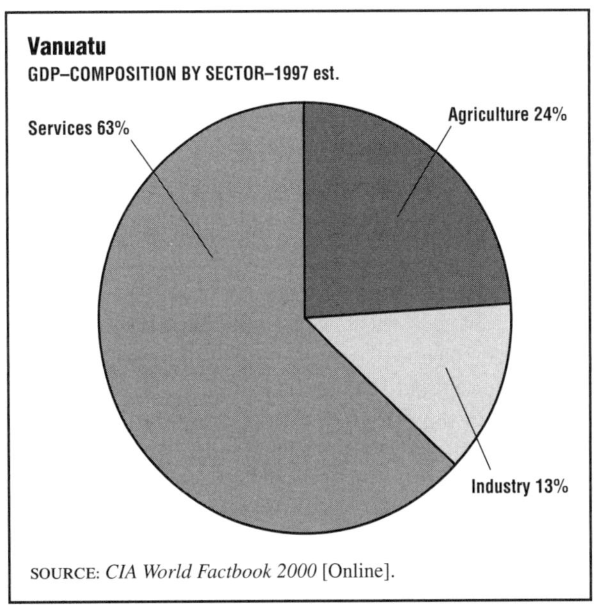

SOURCE: *CIA World Factbook 2000* [Online].

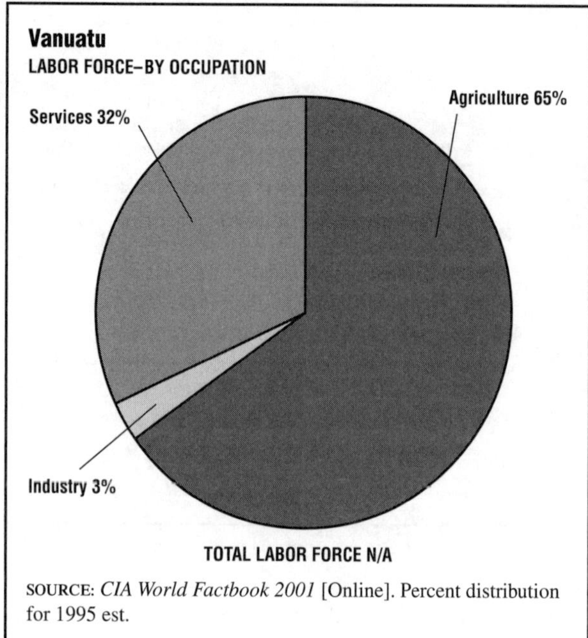

SOURCE: *CIA World Factbook 2001* [Online]. Percent distribution for 1995 est.

age includes all of those growing their own food for consumption as well as those selling crops and those working for wages on a plantation. Industry accounted for only 1.3 percent of the labor force, and services 23.9 percent; however, nearly all of those in industry and services were in the formal sector. Also, it is likely that these proportions will have increased during the 1990s, even when the subsistence component is included.

AGRICULTURE

The most recent economic data available show that agriculture, forestry and fishing contributed 25.7 percent of Vanuatu's GDP in 1999. Although a further breakdown is not available from that year, data from 1995 shows that subsistence agriculture made up about a third of this sector, forestry and logging another third, and the rest made up of commercial agriculture, particularly copra production and beef production.

According to the Asian Development Bank, agriculture is more important to the Vanuatu economy than it is to any other Pacific economy, since it does not have the mineral and forestry resources of Papua New Guinea or Solomon Islands, the manufacturing base of Fiji, the marine resources of Micronesia, or the **remittances** of Polynesia. Throughout Vanuatu, subsistence agriculture is the mainstay of the village economy, since 80 percent of the population lives in villages. Food crops produced include taro, yams, kumara (sweet potato), bananas, coconut, and a great range of fruit and vegetables.

The most important agricultural product, in terms of cash production in the villages and in terms of export, is copra. This is the dried flesh of coconuts, produced by individual households and on large-scale plantations. Production of copra is highly variable year to year depending on weather conditions and world prices, although a general downward trend in production is noticeable since the early 1980s. One explanation is that the price in real terms paid to producers has declined over this period.

In recent decades there has been an attempt to diversify the rural economy away from coconuts to a variety of crops. Much effort went into the promotion of cocoa during the 1980s, but this was not very successful. By the late 1990s, cocoa exports were still only a small fraction of the value of exported coconut products. There has also been considerable promotion of coffee, but this too has not been very successful.

After copra, the second most important agricultural product by value is beef. Vanuatu is the only significant beef exporter in the Pacific, and this accounted for about 10 percent of all exports by value in the late 1990s. Cattle are often raised under coconut trees and serve both as a source of income and as a means of keeping plantations clear of weeds. The main export markets for beef have been Japan and the neighboring countries of Melanesia.

Two other crops that have increased in value recently are kava and squash. Kava, which is made into a drink that induces relaxation and mild euphoria, is a traditional crop that has recently been commercialized. The establishment of kava bars in the towns has accelerated since the 1980s, and in the 1990s kava was being exported around the world, where it can often be found in drugstores. The success of Tonga in securing a niche in the Japanese squash market caused other Pacific nations to look at this as a potential new crop. Vanuatu was one of the first to start squash production, but it is too early to determine whether this will be a successful case of agricultural diversification.

Logging in Vanuatu has never been on the scale seen in the neighboring countries of Solomon Islands or Papua New Guinea. Nevertheless, in 1997 and 1998, timber was the second most important export by value, after copra. The logging industry has maintained a relatively small but steady rate of production for many years, and involves both foreign companies and village-based sawmills. A ban on the exports of whole logs was implemented in 1989. Although temporarily lifted in 1993, the ban has been quite successful in adding value to the industry within the country by generating jobs in sawmilling and related activities.

Fish are an important food source in most parts of Vanuatu. However, commercial exploitation of fish is much less than in neighboring countries, considering the large area of ocean within Vanuatu's **Exclusive Eco-**

nomic Zone (EEZ). Fishing fleets based in the country in the 1960s and 1970s ceased operations in the 1980s after considerable losses. Thus, fish are not a significant source of export income. Vanuatu does, however, receive some income from royalties paid by offshore fleets fishing within its EEZ, especially Taiwanese and American. The catches of these offshore fleets are landed mainly in Fiji and American Samoa, so relatively little employment is generated within Vanuatu from these activities.

INDUSTRY

In 1999, industry made up 14 percent of GDP. Data from 4 years earlier showed that construction contributed about 48 percent of this sector. This contribution, however, varies considerably from year to year depending on new developments in the tourist sector and in private industry. Manufacturing made up 39 percent of the industry sector, and its contribution has been steady and slowly growing.

There was a manganese mine operating on the island of Efate in the 1960s and 1970s, but currently there is no significant mineral production. Nevertheless, there is much interest in the mineral possibilities of the country, since Vanuatu is similar geologically to Papua New Guinea and Solomon Islands, where gold and other minerals are currently being mined. In the mid-1990s, Australian aid allowed a countrywide survey of mineral potential, and following this, a number of exploration licenses were taken out by private companies.

Manufacturing is a relatively minor industry in Vanuatu, although in the late 1990s it contributed just over 5 percent of GDP. The most important manufacturing enterprises cater for the local market in areas such as food processing (especially meat), wood processing and construction materials. Most of the manufacturing is located in the capital, Port Vila, although small operations such as production of soap from coconut oil take place elsewhere. The growth of tourism has encouraged the production of traditional handicrafts.

SERVICES

The services sector is the largest broad economic sector in the Vanuatu economy, contributing 60.4 percent of GDP in 1999. The makeup of this sector is suggested by data from 1995, which showed that the most important service subsectors, in order, were wholesale and **retail** trade, government services, transport, storage and communication, finance and insurance, real estate, and hotels and restaurants. Although the last of these subsectors is mostly generated by tourism, a considerable amount of the income generated in other subsectors also relates to tourism. Specific amounts were not available.

The sector that is often thought to have the greater future potential in the Pacific is tourism, and it has been heavily promoted in Vanuatu in recent years. Visitor arrivals have doubled in the 2 decades since independence in 1980, rising from about 25,000 per year at that time to about 50,000 in the late 1990s. Tourism in Vanuatu is still a small industry compared to Fiji, but larger than neighboring Solomon Islands. The majority of tourists (about 60 percent) come from Australia, with smaller numbers from New Zealand and New Caledonia. So far, relatively few have come from the largest potential markets of Japan, North America, and Europe.

Tourism is largely focussed on the capital, Port Vila, on the island of Efate. There are several international standard hotels in Port Vila, but in the rest of the country tourist facilities are rare, despite the great potential of some islands. With over 100 indigenous cultural groups, one of the main attractions of Vanuatu is its cultural diversity, represented in different housing styles, dances, and artforms, especially carvings. There are also the typical Pacific attractions of beaches, diving and a tropical climate.

The national airline Air Vanuatu links Port Vila to Noumea, Brisbane, Sydney, Auckland, Nadi and Honiara, and other airlines serve the capital as well, including Air Pacific, Aircalin (New Caledonia) and Solomon Airlines.

Vanuatu is one of several tax havens in the South Pacific. The Offshore Financial Centre (OFC) was established in 1971 and has been maintained since independence. This provides a tax haven for offshore banks, trust companies, insurance companies, and shipping companies. It has been estimated that the OFC employs about 400 people. OFC pays registration fees to the government, which contribute about 2.5 percent of the overall gross domestic product, according to Ambrose and Siwatibau. Local banking services are provided by the National Bank of Vanuatu, ANZ (Australia New Zealand) Bank, Bank of Hawaii, and Westpac.

Like many Pacific countries, retail services are somewhat limited. In Port Vila there are medium-sized shops and supermarkets, but in most of the country there are only small shops with a very limited range of goods.

INTERNATIONAL TRADE

Vanuatu has a large imbalance in trade, with imports exceeding exports by 3 or 4 times. This imbalance is made up for by income from tourism, tax haven revenue, and international aid.

Copra has dominated Vanuatu's exports for many years; it made up 45 percent of all exports in the years 1995 to 1998. In those years, beef and timber were almost as equally important as each other, making up about

Trade (expressed in billions of US$): Vanuatu

	Exports	Imports
1975	.012	.040
1980	.036	.073
1985	.031	.070
1990	.019	.096
1995	.028	.095
1998	N/A	N/A

SOURCE: International Monetary Fund. *International Financial Statistics Yearbook 1999.*

12 percent each, while cocoa made up about 5 percent of all exports. For copra, timber, and cocoa, the processing countries of these products are significant; the 3 most important export destinations were Japan, Belgium, and Germany. Beef was mostly exported to the nearby countries of New Caledonia, Solomon Islands, and Fiji, and to more distant Japan.

The most important imports into Vanuatu are machines and transport equipment, foodstuffs, basic manufactures, and fuels. Japan is the most important source of imports, accounting for about half of these in value. Australia is the next major source of imports, especially for food and certain types of manufactures, followed by United States, Singapore, and New Zealand.

MONEY

In the period since 1982, the vatu has declined in value against the American dollar by about 40 percent. However, this is not as great a relative decline as experienced in many other Pacific countries. This may be because, despite a negative balance of trade, Vanuatu has a reasonably consistent source of foreign revenue coming from tourism and its tax haven activities. Also, the vatu is pegged against a group of currencies, and although these currencies are secret, it is believed that the most important are the Australian and U.S. dollars, with smaller weight given to the Japanese yen and French franc, according to the Asian Development Bank.

The Reserve Bank of Vanuatu has the usual functions of a central bank, including regulating the money supply, providing economic advice to the government, and general economic monitoring.

POVERTY AND WEALTH

A total of 174 countries are ranked in the United Nations Development Programme's (UNDP) *Human Development Report 2000* according to the Human Development Indicator (HDI), which measures a country's state of well-being using income, education, and health measures. The HDI rank for Vanuatu was 118, meaning that it was better off than many African countries, but was the third poorest country in the Pacific. **GDP per capita** in 1998 was US$1403, nearly twice as much as neighboring Solomon Islands but only about one-twentieth that of the United States.

While there is no adequate information on income distribution, partly because subsistence income is hard to measure, there is evidence that there are varying levels of well-being within the country. Another indicator developed by UNDP is the Human Poverty Index (HPI). It measures conditions for those worst off in a country, such as their health status, education level, access to health services, access to safe water, and malnutrition in children. While to a traveler in Vanuatu there appears to be a kind of "subsistence affluence" in most areas, the HPI suggests that Vanuatu is still a poor country, with the third lowest HPI in the Pacific, at a level similar to that of many of the poorest African countries. For example, illiteracy is estimated at 66 percent, about 23 percent of children under 5 are underweight, and about 20 percent of the population does not have access to adequate health services, according to the UNDP. However, since there is no poverty index in Vanuatu, it is not possible to determine how many people or households can be considered to be poor. The government has many different programs underway to try to overcome some of these problems, and often these are funded by international aid, especially in the areas of education and health.

Exchange rates: Vanuatu

vatu (VT) per US$1	
Dec 2000	143.95
2000	137.82
1999	129.08
1998	127.52
1997	115.87
1996	111.72

SOURCE: CIA *World Factbook 2001* [ONLINE].

GDP per Capita (US$)

Country	1975	1980	1985	1990	1998
Vanuatu	N/A	1,426	1,672	1,596	1,403
United States	19,364	21,529	23,200	25,363	29,683
Philippines	974	1,166	967	1,064	1,092
Solomon Islands	419	583	666	784	753

SOURCE: United Nations. *Human Development Report 2000; Trends in human development and per capita income.*

WORKING CONDITIONS

The situation of the labor force is difficult to determine, due to a lack of recent data. Using Vanuatu's definition of labor force, the bulk of the adult population is said to be in the labor force, with most of these being involved in village agriculture. Most of those working in the wage and salary economy are located in Port Vila or Luganville, the 2 largest urban centers. At the time of the last census, the unemployment rate was calculated to be only 1 percent, although there appeared to be a great deal of **underemployment** involving people who were working only part time. As in most Pacific island nations, there is no unemployment benefit. The minimum wage was set at 16,000 vatu (US$140) per month in 1995, and this applied to both rural and urban employment. Earlier minimum wage levels had been lower in the rural sector, and it was felt by some that the rural minimum was above market rates and would inhibit job creation, according to the Asian Development Bank.

Workers in the formal sector are represented by at least 16 trade unions, generally organized according to industrial sector, but coordinated by the Vanuatu Council of Trade Unions.

COUNTRY HISTORY AND ECONOMIC DEVELOPMENT

1000 B.C. Evidence of human settlement on many islands.

1606 A.D. First European sighting of Vanuatu by Pedro Fernandez de Quiros, who founded an unsuccessful settlement on Espiritu Santo, the largest island in the Vanuatu group, and claimed the islands for Spain.

1768–89. Various European explorers—most commonly British and French—visit islands and introduce metal tools and weapons and new trade goods.

1825. Sandalwood trade starts, which accelerated trade even though the sandalwood resource was exhausted quickly.

1839. First Christian missionaries land; progress in conversion is slow, and some areas resist Christianity to the present day.

1864–1911. Labor recruitment for plantations in Fiji and Queensland, sometimes called "blackbirding."

1887. Condominium of New Hebrides established by French and British.

1940–41. New Hebrides joins Free French in WWII; Vila and Santo become American bases; Jon Frum movement starts proposing that Americans can deliver followers from missionaries and other Europeans.

1960s. Nagriamel, first political party, forms and demands independence and the return of some land.

1971. Tax haven established.

1980. Vanuatu granted independence; islands of Espiritu Santo and Tanna declare themselves independent under Nagriamel and Jon Frum movements; Britain and France refuse to take military action, so troops from Papua New Guinea defeat rebels and secure country for first prime minister, Walter Lini, leader of the Vanua'aku Party.

1982. Vanuatu declares itself nuclear free.

1991–2001. Series of coalition governments, often involving French-English party coalitions.

FUTURE TRENDS

In the late 1990s, much attention was being paid to the political struggles pitting one party against another. However, the party disputes tended to be based on regional and language interests rather than fundamental differences of opinion on economic policy. There was not much dynamism in the economy, with agricultural production and tourist numbers being relatively stable. In the future, the greatest hope appears to be held for tourism, since the country has many undeveloped possibilities. There is some potential for expansion in other sectors; for example, some localization in the fishing industry is possible, although these possibilities will depend to a great extent on a higher degree of political stability than has been seen recently. In terms of the development of human resources, especially in education and health, there will be an ongoing dependence on international aid.

DEPENDENCIES

Vanuatu has no territories or colonies.

BIBLIOGRAPHY

Ambrose, David, and Savenaca Siwatibau. "Recent Development in Vanuatu." *Pacific Economic Bulletin.* Vol. 12, No. 1, 1997.

Asian Development Bank. *Vanuatu: Economic Performance, Policy and Reform Issues.* Manila: Asian Development Bank, 1997.

Economist Intelligence Unit. *Country Profile: Vanuatu.* London: Economist Intelligence Unit, 2001.

"Key Indicators for Developing Asian and Pacific Countries." *Asian Development Bank.* <http://www.adb.org/Vanuatu>. Accessed February 2001.

United Nations Development Programme, *Pacific Human Development Report 1999: Creating Opportunities.* Suva: United Nations Development Programme, 1999.

U.S. Central Intelligence Agency. *World Factbook 2000.* <http://www.odci.gov/cia/publications/factbook/index.html>. Accessed August 2001.

—Wardlow Friesen

VIETNAM

Socialist Republic of Vietnam
Cong Hoa Xa Hoi Chu Nghia Viet Nam

CAPITAL: Hanoi.

MONETARY UNIT: Vietnamese dong. One dong equals 10 hao and 100 xu. There are no coins in Vietnam. Only banknotes are used, and there are notes of 5,000, 10,000, 50,000, and 100,000 dong. While U.S. dollars are commonly accepted in Vietnam, the government policy is to foster the use of the local dong currency.

CHIEF EXPORTS: Crude oil, marine products, rice, coffee, rubber, tea, garments, and shoes.

CHIEF IMPORTS: Machinery and equipment, petroleum products, fertilizer, steel products, raw cotton, grain, cement, and motorcycles.

GROSS DOMESTIC PRODUCT: US$154.4 billion (2000 est.).

BALANCE OF TRADE: **Exports:** US$14.3 billion (2000 est.). **Imports:** US$15.2 billion (2000 est.).

COUNTRY OVERVIEW

LOCATION AND SIZE. Vietnam is bordered on the north by China and to the west by Laos and Cambodia. To the east is the South China Sea (called "Eastern Sea" by the Vietnamese). The country's shape and size is often compared to a bamboo pole with loads at the end (north and south). In the central part of the country Vietnam is only 40 kilometers (25 miles) across. The total land area of Vietnam is 329,569 square kilometers (127,247 square miles), making it slightly larger than New Mexico. It has a long coast of 3,444 kilometers (2,140 miles). Its 2 major cities are the capital Hanoi in the north and Ho Chi Minh City (formerly Saigon) in the south. Other major cities are the ancient capital of Hue in central Vietnam, the coastal cities of Danang and Haiphong, and Dalat in the central highlands.

POPULATION. Vietnam, in terms of population, is the second largest country in Southeast Asia after Indonesia. Its current population was estimated to be 79,939,014 in July 2001, making it the 13th largest country in the world. This compares with a population of 52,741,766 in 1979, 64,411,713 in 1989, and 75,355,200 in 1996. It has one of the higher population densities in the world, at 242.6 persons per square kilometer (628 per square mile). Vietnam has a little less than one-third of the population of the United States in an area that is only 3.5 percent as large.

The current population growth rate is estimated to be 1.45 percent (2001). If this growth rate were to persist into the future, the Vietnamese population would double to approximately 160 million by the year 2051. The Vietnamese woman on average currently has 2.49 children. In recent years, Vietnam has had considerable success in lowering both its population growth rate and fertility rate. Vietnam has a relatively young population with 32 percent of the population under 15.

The population of Vietnam has considerable diversity, with 54 ethnic nationalities. However, 85 to 90 percent of the population are Vietnamese. The second largest ethnic group is Sino-Vietnamese, concentrated in the Ho Chi Minh City area. Among the most numerous of other ethnic nationalities are the Tay-Thai Group (1,200,000), Khmer (1,000,000), Hmong (558,000), and the Cham (99,000).

OVERVIEW OF ECONOMY

Vietnam is one of the world's poorest countries, having suffered from years of war (1940–89) that damaged its economy and basic **infrastructure**. Thus, economic development is the nation's highest priority. It is still largely an agricultural economy, with 72 percent of its workforce engaged in that sector. Much of the country is made up of mountains and forests, with only 17 percent of its land arable.

Vietnam has a long history dating back to around 2879 B.C. when the first Viet state called Vān Lang was

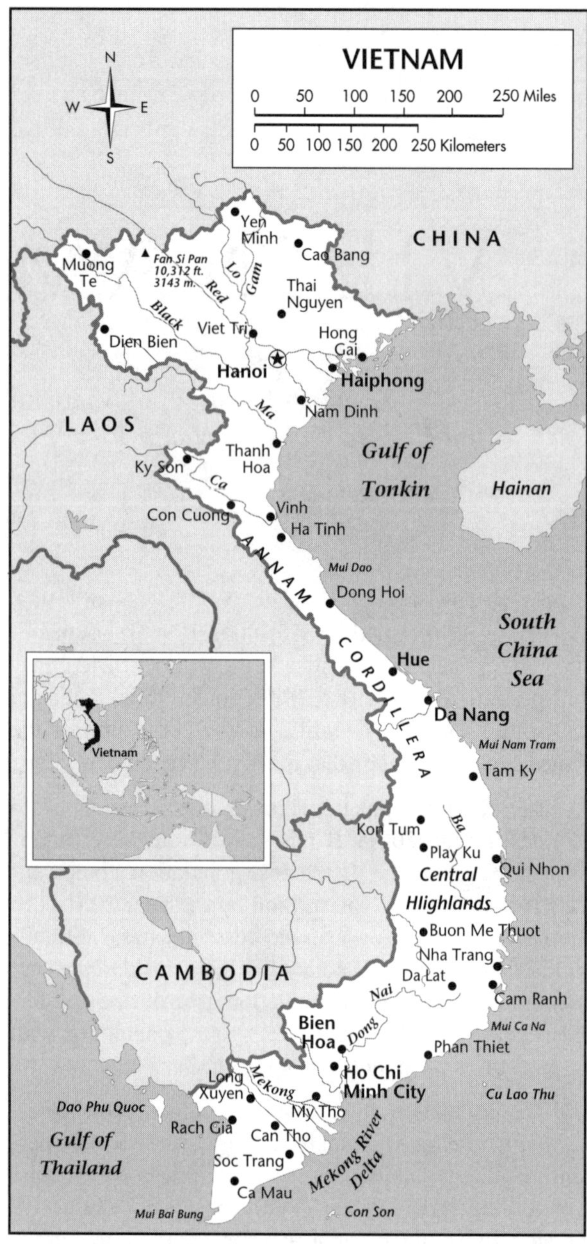

founded. Later there was a state called Âu Lạc (257 B.C.-208 B.C.) and then a subsequent state called Nam Viêt (207 B.C.-39 A.D.). Almost 1,000 years of Chinese domination followed, until 939 A.D. when an independent Ngô Dynasty was established.

In terms of Vietnamese economic history, 5 themes are important. The first is the continual Vietnamese struggle to free itself from foreign domination, starting with roughly 1,000 years of Chinese rule, threats from the Mongols, and then external domination by the French, Japanese, and the United States. The second theme is the struggle against natural disasters such as floods and typhoons. Reflective of this struggle are the huge dikes protecting the capital, Hanoi, from possible flooding by the Red River. A third theme is *nam tiên* (expansion to the south), the need for additional land and territory, given the high population density of Vietnam. Through this process the Vietnamese moved south over time and took over lands which were once part of the Kingdom of Champa (1471) and the area of what is now southern Vietnam was once part of the Khmer Empire. Thus, the Vietnamese came to control both the rich Red River delta in the north and the Mekong River Delta in the south.

A fourth theme relates to Chinese cultural and intellectual influences, particularly in the cities. Close to 1,000 years of Chinese domination left an indelible influence on Vietnam, its culture, customs, and language. This influence has direct relevance to Vietnamese education and potential for human resource development. Unlike its Southeast Asian neighbors such as Thailand, Cambodia, and Laos, Vietnam is part of the Confucian world, as are Japan, Korea, and Singapore. Part of this cultural heritage is the great importance attached to learning and special respect for teachers, scholars, and mentors. A fifth theme is the importance of village life as the heart of Vietnamese culture and related wet rice cooperative culture. It is impossible to understand Vietnam without understanding its villages and their rich cultural traditions.

Vietnam historically had a royal system with imperial dynasties. The imperial capital of Vietnam was in central Vietnam in Hue. In 1858, France invaded Vietnam, capturing Saigon in 1861. By 1884 France controlled all of Vietnam, occupying 3 areas of the country known as Cochin-China (in the south), Annam (in the central region), and Tonkin (in the north). In 1887, France established the colony of Indochina, which included Vietnam, Cambodia, and Laos. Vietnam was the power center of the colony and the French trained the Vietnamese to help them administer the colony "backwaters" in Laos and Cambodia. The local populations in Laos and Cambodia both resented this practice. As in Cambodia, the French co-opted the imperial leaders and used them in their colonization process.

France's interest in Vietnam was economically motivated and the French thought that the Mekong River could be a gateway to the huge China market. Unfortunately, the Mekong turned out not to be a navigable river. To generate profits to run its Indochinese colony, the French introduced a plantation economy to facilitate rubber extraction and exports. Land alienation (transferring ownership to another) was the cornerstone of economic exploitation under the colonial government. The French also introduced **consumer goods** such as opium, alcohol, and cigarettes to generate revenues to support the running of their Vietnamese colony. The French film *Indochine* provides dramatic visual images of life (economic and social) during the French colonial period. Various rebellious movements against the French emerged and the

French were extremely harsh in punishing those Vietnamese for their disloyalty.

During the Second World War, Vietnamese nationalists and revolutionaries cooperated with the West in fighting against Japanese occupation. On December 2, 1945, nationalist leader Ho Chi Minh declared an independent Democratic Republic of Vietnam and was hoping for U.S. support of the new regime. Instead, the French decided to reassert their colonial authority in Vietnam, resulting in the first Indochina War from 1946 to 1954, which eventually led to the French defeat at Dien Bien Phu in May, 1954. The Geneva Accords of 1954 then resulted in Vietnam being temporarily divided into North and South Vietnam at the 17th parallel. The United States opposed 1956 national elections called for by the Geneva Accords, which could have led to the peaceful unification of Vietnam under the leadership of Ho Chi Minh. Instead the south-north division persisted and eventually the U.S. war in Vietnam ensued (1959–75) with tremendous destruction and loss of life in many areas of Vietnam. Vietnam was eventually unified with the "fall of Saigon" on April 30, 1975.

For its first eleven years after unification, Vietnam became a fully **socialist**, state-planned economy with agricultural collectivization. Its international economic relations were almost entirely with the Eastern bloc countries such as the USSR, which provided most of its economic assistance. In December 1979, the Vietnamese army invaded Cambodia to remove the hated Khmer Rouge regime, led by Pol Pot. For the next 10 years, the Vietnamese army became bogged down in Cambodia fighting the Khmer Rouge insurgents who retreated to the remote jungles of west and northwestern Cambodia. Vietnam's Cambodian adventure proved an adverse economic drag on the economy as well. Finally, Vietnam agreed to remove its troops from Cambodia in 1989 as part of a Cambodian peace process. Thus, the modern Vietnamese economy has really known only 12 years of peace, coming since the end of the Cambodian conflict in 1989.

In December 1986, at the Sixth National Party Congress, a new policy of *doi moi* (economic renovation) was introduced. This was a Vietnamese version of what the Soviets called *perestroika*. It basically used free-market mechanisms as a strategy to improve the economy and its productivity, and, in particular, to provide greater incentives for economic effort and performance. Prior to the introduction of this new economic policy, the economy was plagued by economic stagnation and excessive, triple-digit **inflation**. Vietnam's war-torn economy had multiple and extensive economic problems that required a fundamental rethinking of the economic system. Central to the economic renovation was also a commitment to reduce the large size of the state sector and state-owned-enterprises (SEOs). In 1988, the socialist cooperative method of agriculture was abandoned. While under the current economic system all land is still owned by the state, individuals can have long-term leases on land for their and their descendants' use.

With the new *doi moi* policy, the Vietnamese economy began to demonstrate impressive **macroeconomic** (economic system as a whole) performance in the 1990s. With the collapse of the USSR in 1991, Vietnam also opened its economy internationally, with dramatic increases in both international investments in Vietnam and international economic assistance. Still, a major stumbling block was the U.S. trade **embargo**, which was finally lifted in 1994. That was followed by Vietnam's joining the Association of Southeast Asian Nations (ASEAN) in 1995, and later the Asia-Pacific Economic Cooperation forum (APEC).

While the 1997 Asian economic crisis hurt the Vietnamese economy, the Vietnamese economy had much more immunity to this crisis than many neighboring economies, primarily because Vietnam did not have a stock market, nor an internationally traded currency. Also, rather than being part of the "Baht Zone" (areas with close economic interconnections with Thailand), Vietnam was partially a dollarized economy with strong economic links to greater China, an area showing greater currency stability during the Asian economic crisis.

Also, the 2001 global slump in the high technology sector has had minimal impact on Vietnam since it is producing more basic manufacturing/industrial products at the lower end of the technology scale, such as garments and footwear. Thus, Vietnam in 2001 had one of the highest economic growth rates (7.1 percent) in the world. In October 2001, the U.S. Congress finally approved the bilateral trade bill with Vietnam. This provides an important new opening for Vietnam to export to the large U.S. market and eventually to join the World Trade Organization (WTO). Vietnam has suggested the goal of becoming an industrialized country by the year 2020.

POLITICS, GOVERNMENT, AND TAXATION

Vietnam remains a one-party state with complete domination by the **Communist** Party of Vietnam (CPV). Vietnam has a **unicameral** National Assembly whose 450 members are elected every 5 years. As in neighboring Laos, non-party members may compete for seats in the National Assembly. In the last election for the National Assembly in 1997, 92 percent of those elected were CPV members. Economic policies are primarily determined by the Party Politburo, Central Committee of the Party, Party Congresses (every 5 years), and the National Assembly. Some argue that debates within these bodies represent a diverse spectrum of views and perspectives that may even be broader than within the United States' own two-party Congress, where both parties are often fairly close in terms of basic ideology. With Vietnam trying to maintain a socialist political system and an increasingly capitalistic economic system, there is considerable space for divergence of policy perspectives, particularly with respect to how fast economic reforms should proceed.

As an example of an area in which government policy has changed in accord with the *doi moi* policy in the 1990s, the government opened the door for **privatization** in the higher education sector. The government realized that it did not have the economic resources to meet the growing social demand for higher education. The result was the emergence of a number of private universities. As of 2001, 82,902 students (approximately 8.9 percent of all Vietnamese college students) were studying in private universities or colleges.

Most of the government's tax revenues come from the following: sales tax (60 percent), taxes on profits (20 percent), license fees (10 percent), and property taxes (6.5 percent). Tax collection among non-state enterprises tends to be rather small. In Vietnam, local governments lack the capability to raise revenue through taxes. The customs department collects import-export taxes and the General Taxation Department (GTD) collects other taxes through its branches in the various provinces and districts of the country. Local governments are allowed to keep taxes collected in excess of specified targets. This provides an excellent incentive for local authorities to enforce tax collections.

INFRASTRUCTURE, POWER, AND COMMUNICATIONS

As the result of years of war, Vietnam's infrastructure is weak, but steadily improving. In the French colonial period, a 1,730-kilometer (1,075-mile) rail system was developed which connected Saigon to Hanoi, and the port city of Haiphong to Yunnan, China. Later in the 1950s, the Chinese assisted with the development of a rail link between Hanoi and Guangxi Province in China. All of these lines were badly damaged during the wars. Total railway length is 2,652 kilometers (1,650 miles), and many tracks need renovation. In 1999, it took 32 hours to travel by rail from Hanoi to Ho Chi Minh City. Vietnam has 93,300 kilometers (57,977 miles) of highways, 25 percent of which are paved. However, many of the paved roads are in poor condition. Notable improvements have occurred in recent years. For example, there is now an excellent highway from Hanoi to the International Airport and the road from Hanoi to Haiphong and Ha Long Bay is being steadily improved, as is Highway Number One, which links Hanoi and Ho Chi Minh City. A considerable amount of international economic assistance is being used to upgrade Vietnam's weak road infrastructure.

Vietnam's major ports are Haiphong (in the north), Da Nang (central region) and Ho Chi Minh City (in the south). To supplement these, additional ports have been developed at Cua Lo, Quy Nhon, and Nha Trang. Vietnam has 2 international airports (Hanoi and Ho Chi Minh City) and 32 local airports. Travel to distant remote provinces is often done by air.

With Vietnam's rapid economic development in the 1990s, energy demand has been increasing at about 20 percent per year, frequently outstripping supplies of electricity. In 1999, Vietnam generated 22.985 billion kilowatt-hours (kWh) of electricity, of which 47.1 percent was from fossil fuels and 52.3 percent from hydroelectric power. In the future, Vietnam could import electricity from Laos, which has great hydroelectric potential.

While Vietnam's telecommunications system has steadily improved, it remains inadequate. There were only 2.6 million conventional phone lines in 2000 and 730,155 cellular phones for a population of approximately 80 million. Vietnam has 101 radio stations, 7 television stations, and 5 Internet service providers. It is estimated that there

Communications

Country	Newspapers	Radios	TV Sets[a]	Cable subscribers[a]	Mobile Phones[a]	Fax Machines[a]	Personal Computers[a]	Internet Hosts[b]	Internet Users[b]
	1996	1997	1998	1998	1998	1998	1998	1999	1999
Vietnam	4	107	47	N/A	2	0.3	6.4	0.00	100
United States	215	2,146	847	244.3	256	78.4	458.6	1,508.77	74,100
China	N/A	333	272	40.0	19	1.6	8.9	0.50	8,900
Thailand	63	232	236	10.1	32	2.5	21.6	4.49	800

[a]Data are from International Telecommunication Union, *World Telecommunication Development Report 1999* and are per 1,000 people.
[b]Data are from the Internet Software Consortium (http://www.isc.org) and are per 10,000 people.

SOURCE: World Bank. *World Development Indicators 2000.*

are 8.2 million radios, 3.57 million televisions, and 121,000 Internet users in Vietnam in 2000. Internet service in Vietnam tends to be slow and expensive.

ECONOMIC SECTORS

The economic structure of Vietnam has changed a great deal since the end of warfare in the country in 1989, with agriculture declining in importance from 40.8 percent of GDP in 1989 to 27.1 percent in 1999. Industry has gained proportionally in importance, growing from a percentage contribution of GDP in 1989 of 22.9 percent to 36.7 percent in 1999. During this period, the contribution of the services sector remained virtually unchanged at 36 percent. The annual growth rates of these sectors show similar trends, with agricultural growth rates averaging 3.9 percent since 1995, while industrial sector growth rates averaged 11.4 percent over the same period. These changes reflect the impact of the *doi moi* economic renovation policy.

Despite these structural changes, Vietnam remains an agricultural economy in terms of employment. Around 72 percent of Vietnam's **labor force**, or approximately 28 million individuals, is engaged in agriculture.

With its *doi moi* reform policy and the goal of reducing the size of the **public sector**, as of the late 1990s the state sector employed only 9 percent of Vietnam's labor force of 39 million. In the industrial sector, about 25 percent of all employees were working in the state sector. In the commercial service sector, state employment consisted of only 13 percent of employment in 1997.

The Vietnamese service sector is comprised primarily of those in government work (including teachers), a growing modern **retail** trade sector, small-scale retail shops, a growing tourist industry, and an expanding finance/banking sector.

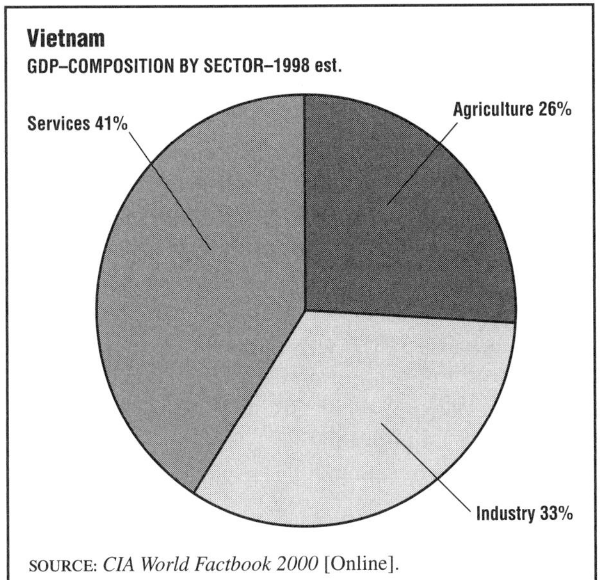

SOURCE: *CIA World Factbook 2000* [Online].

AGRICULTURE

Despite its limited amount of arable land, Vietnam's agricultural economy has demonstrated impressive success, particularly in the 15 years since the introduction of *doi moi.* The shift to the use of market mechanisms and price incentives contributed significantly to this success. Vietnam has not only achieved self-sufficiency in rice production, but is now a major global food exporter and is the world's third leading exporter of rice, competing actively with Thailand and the United States in this global market. Between 1988 and 1997, total food production in Vietnam increased 50 percent. This extraordinary agricultural success not only contributed positively to Vietnam's foreign exchange earnings, but also contributed to a reduction in the incidence of poverty.

In addition to rice, Vietnam has had success with other agricultural **cash crops**. In recent years Vietnam has become a major exporter of both groundnuts and cashew nuts. The export of cashew nuts in 1997 brought in US$125 million. Also, Vietnam has become Asia's second largest producer of robusta coffee, and coffee is now Vietnam's second leading agricultural export. Other important export crops are rubber and tea.

FISHING. With its long coastline, Vietnam has an active fishing sector. Most of its catch is marine fish (94 percent). Many of Vietnam's marine products are being exported to countries such as Japan, and marine products now represent 9.2 percent of Vietnam's total exports (in terms of value).

FORESTRY. Deforestation remains a major problem in Vietnam. In 1943, 44 percent of Vietnam was forests. By 1995, the forest area of Vietnam had declined to 23 percent. During the U.S. war in Vietnam, 5 percent of the forest was destroyed, and 50 percent was damaged. Deforestation has also been caused by uncontrolled logging, agricultural expansion caused by population growth, slash-and-burn agriculture, and the use of forest wood for firewood. To reverse this pattern of deforestation, the government has introduced 18 forest farming projects and a system of designated national parks.

INDUSTRY

During the colonial period, the French did not promote the development of Vietnamese industry in order to keep it from competing with their own industries. In the period following 1954, socialist northern Vietnam used a Soviet-type economic system emphasizing the development of Vietnamese heavy industry by the state sector. In the capitalist south, the emphasis was on the development of light industry such as the assembly of small-scale consumer goods. By the 1980s, a unified Vietnam was shifting to an emphasis on greater light industry to meet the basic needs of the population.

MANUFACTURING. The 1990s saw the emergence of Vietnam as a major player in 5 key manufacturing sectors: textiles, footwear and garments, agro-processing, electric and electronic industries, and automobile and motorcycle assembly. For example, Nike is now sourcing significant production of both footwear and apparel in Vietnam, and this has caused controversy related to alleged sweatshop conditions. On the improved road from Hanoi to Haiphong, there is a new Ford Motor Assembly plant; 45 different models of cars arc now bcing assembled in Vietnam. Among the companies investing in car assembly production, in addition to Ford, are Mercedes-Benz, Toyota, Isuzu, Daihatsu, Suzuki, and several Korean auto companies. There are a total of 14 **joint ventures** in the emerging Vietnamese automobile industry. In Vietnam, there is a huge domestic market for motorcycles, the major mode of transportation for Vietnamese living in urban areas. Twenty percent of this huge demand is now being met by the local assembly. Vietnam's electronics assembly manufacturing sector also grew rapidly in the 1990s. Among the major international investors were Daewoo, Hitachi, and Phillips. The assembly of television sets almost tripled to a level of 364,000 in 1998.

Steel and cement production were also given high priority, primarily as a strategy for reducing or eliminating steel and cement imports. Another important new manufacturing area is plastics. Given its impressive oil and gas resources, this is a natural industry for Vietnam to develop.

ELECTRICITY. With Vietnam's rapid industrialization and urbanization, there has been a dramatic increase in energy needs. To respond to this need and to avoid frequent power shortages, Vietnam has completed a number of hydroelectric power projects to generate increased electricity. Among the new power stations and plants are Ba Ria-Vung Tau, Da Nhim, Tri An, Hoa Binh, YALY, and Thamco. Many of these are in the south, to serve the growing manufacturing sector in the Ho Chi Minh/Saigon area. The goal of the government is to achieve a generating capacity of 33 billion kWh by 2002. The government also has a goal of providing electricity to 80 percent of rural households by the year 2005.

MINING. Mineral resources were a major factor attracting the French to Vietnam. Vietnam has commercially viable reserves of coal, iron ore, bauxite, chromite, copper, titanium, zinc, gold, apatite, and gemstones. However, other than coal many are underexploited. In 1996, Vietnamese coal exports were worth US$115 million. Vietnam also mines unrefined salt and phosphate rock.

OIL AND NATURAL GAS. Vietnam has now become a player in the international petroleum industry. In 1998, its petroleum exports were worth US$2.1 billion. It has potentially huge offshore oil and natural gas deposits in the South China Sea (known in Vietnam as the Eastern Sea), many of which remain unexplored. Though the international Law of the Sea has articulated elaborate rules for determining claims to the natural resources of the oceans, numerous disputed island groups in the South China Sea (such as the Spratlys) have led to considerable controversy. Nations such as Vietnam, China, Brunei, the Philippines, and Taiwan claim rights to these vast reserves of oil and natural gas. Several international oil companies are active in Vietnam, trying to profit from the nation's oil wealth. The Russians are active in this arena as well, in a joint venture with Vietnam, Vietsovpetro. Vietnam also plans to build oil refineries.

CONSTRUCTION. The 1990s has seen a construction boom in Vietnam in areas such as infrastructure (highway and bridge construction and renovation), hotel construction for the emerging tourist industry, office and apartment buildings for Vietnam's growing modern service sector, factory construction for the emerging manufacturing sector, and improved residential dwellings for occupancy or rent. Ho Chi Minh City now has many impressive, modern new high-rises. Also visible are many renovated and/or new Buddhist pagodas and Catholic churches, especially in the south. Funding for such religious projects has often come from **remittances** from overseas Vietnamese.

SERVICES

BANKING. Subsequent to the introduction of the doi moi economic reform in 1986, in 1988 financial reforms began. Spun off from the State Bank of Vietnam (the country's central bank) were 2 new commercial banks: the Agricultural Bank of Vietnam (VBA) and the Industrial and Commercial Bank of Vietnam. Prior to the economic reforms, most bank lending in Vietnam was to state-owned enterprises (SOEs). However, by 1995 38 percent of credit went to the non-state sector. The newly created Agricultural Bank took an active role in expanding credit to farm households, reaching approximately 7 million households in 1995. The government subsidized lending rates. The central bank also continues to subsidize state commercial banks. Technically, the central bank is responsible for monitoring all financial sector organizations, though its implementation of this mandate has been weak.

GOVERNMENT AND STATE ENTERPRISE EMPLOYMENT. Integral to the *doi moi* economic reforms was a downsizing of the government sector of the economy.

There has been, for example, considerable demobilization of the Vietnamese army, especially after the end of the Cambodian conflict. By 1991, state enterprise employment represented only 6.2 percent of all employment. After initially reducing the size of the state sector in terms of employment, this sector has leveled off, and this part of the economy no longer is an engine to generate new employment.

TOURISM. Vietnam has considerable tourism potential and in 1998 it had 1,520,100 visitors. The country features multiple attractions, including the historical sites related to the war, majestic Ha Long Bay in the north, the ancient imperial capital of Hue, the former seaport of Hoi-an, attractive beach resorts, adventure tourism in the remote northwest, and the delightful central highlands. A Vietnam-U.S. joint venture in Dalat has produced a world-class golf course and club in the center of Dalat. Vietnam's tourism infrastructure has improved significantly in recent years, with the building of many new hotels and the remodeling of others, such as the famous Continental Hotel in Saigon. The new roads to the International Airport in Hanoi and to Ha Long Bay also reflect the commitment to improve the tourism infrastructure.

Vietnam's tourism, however, is constrained by cumbersome visa requirements and an emphasis on the building of expensive up-scale hotels in both Hanoi and Ho Chi Minh City. Tourist development in the Vung Tau beach area near Saigon will work well for domestic tourism, but will not attract international tourists, since it is competing with destinations such as Bali and Phuket. An area of considerable potential is Vietnam's possible collaboration with Cambodia, Thailand, Laos, and Burma in promoting joint tourism. Visitors to majestic Angkor Wat in Cambodia, for example, could also include Vietnam in their itinerary, or visitors to the world heritage site at Ha Long Bay, could include Luang Prabang, Laos, in their itinerary.

RETAIL AND INFORMAL ECONOMY. In Vietnamese urban areas there has been a rapidly growing small-scale retail sector and large **informal economy**. Much of this sector involves the retail sale of a wide variety of consumer products and services. They range, for example, from the large and formal Saigon Bowl to vendors selling fruits and vegetables on the streets. It is common to even find barbers setting up shop on a sidewalk using a wall to hang their mirrors. Unfortunately, exact data are not available on the exact size and scope of the informal sector, but it is substantial and largely unmeasured.

INTERNATIONAL TRADE

Prior to the collapse of the Soviet Union, most of Vietnam's trade was with the former Soviet Union and Eastern European countries. Since 1991, the country's trade has diversified significantly. It has also expanded dramatically, reflecting an internationalization of the Vietnamese economy. In 1999, exports plus imports divided by GDP reached the level of 84.5 percent, a useful indicator for the level of internationalization of an economy.

Trade (expressed in millions of US$): Vietnam

	Exports	Imports
1994	4054	5825
1995	5448	8155
1996	7255	11144
1997	9184	11592
1998	9360	11494
1999	N/A	N/A

SOURCE: United Nations. *Monthly Bulletin of Statistics* (September 2000).

Though Vietnam has consistently had **trade deficits**, the amount has narrowed with the boom in Vietnamese exports. For example, in 1989 exports were only 73.7 percent of imports. In 1999, exports had risen to be 98.9 percent of imports. With the passage of the bilateral trade law with the United States in October 2001, and the granting of most-favored nation status to Vietnam, there is potential for Vietnam soon to become a net exporter with a positive trade balance.

In terms of value (stated in US$), Vietnam's leading exports from January to September 2000 were: crude oil (2,471.8 million); textiles and garments (1,355.4 million); marine products (1,017.7 million); rice (531.5 million); computers and computer parts (460 million); coffee (384.1 million); handicrafts (185.4 million); fruits and vegetables (149.4 million); pepper (137 million); and diverse other products (2,603.5 million). Leading imports for the same period were: machinery, equipment, and other small parts (1,793.6 million); petroleum products (1,472.4 million); textiles and leather materials (941.3 million); iron and steel (577.1 million); electronic parts (520.3 million); motorcycles and parts (478.3 million); fertilizers of all kinds (373 million); plastic products (359.8 million); fabrics (234.4 million); chemical products (225.1 million); and miscellaneous other imports (4,004.8 million).

In terms of trading partners, based on data for the same period Vietnam's leading export markets were: Japan (18 percent), China (9.7 percent), Australia (8 percent), Singapore (6.5 percent), the United States (5.3 percent), Taiwan (5.2 percent), Germany (5.0 percent), the Philippines (4.0 percent), the United Kingdom (3.4 percent), and the Netherlands (2.8 percent). These data clearly indicate how successful Vietnam has been in diversifying its export markets, which tends to minimize risk. In terms of imports, Vietnam purchased the most from the following countries: Singapore (18.8 percent), Japan (14.5 percent), Taiwan (12.4 percent), South Korea (11.6 percent), China (8.2 percent), Thailand (4.9 percent), Hong Kong (4.8 percent), the United States (2.6 percent), Malaysia (2.5 percent), and Indonesia (2.3 percent). Thus, in terms of trade deficit, Vietnam has the most important trade imbalances with Singapore, South Korea, Taiwan, Thailand, and Hong Kong. In terms of favorable trade balances, Vietnam is doing well with the United States, Germany, and the Philippines. Trade with Japan and China appears fairly balanced.

Despite Vietnam's trade expansion and its membership in ASEAN, the ASEAN Free Trade Area (AFTFA), and APEC, its trade regime remains restrictive by international standards. This policy is obviously a legacy of the system of central planning. With the final conclusion of the bilateral trade law with the United States in October, 2001, Vietnam is obliged to relax various economic restrictions and obstacles which should pave the way for Vietnam's entry to the World Trade Organization.

Related to Vietnam's **balance of payments**, the country was extremely fortunate to have Russia agree to forgive 85 percent of its US$11 billion debt, accumulated during the Soviet period. It is only necessary for Vietnam to pay Russia US$1.7 billion over the next 23 years with only 10 percent in **hard currency**, and the rest being commodities or other products. In 1999, Vietnam's total **external debt** was US$11.142 billion, according to the World Bank. Its **debt service** payments as a percent of its export earnings was a manageable 13.7 percent.

MONEY

The central bank is responsible for **monetary policy**. During recent years, its performance in terms of keeping inflation low and the currency relatively stable has been impressively successful. For example, the inflation rate for the year 2001 is estimated to be 0.6 percent. Inflation in Vietnam since 1996 has normally been around 5 percent or less and has not exceeded 10 percent. While the Vietnamese dong has dropped in value in recent years, the decreases have been much less than in other Southeast Asian countries such as Thailand, Laos, the Philippines, and Indonesia. In the last 7 years, the dong has declined by only a total of 32 percent, from 11,000 dong to the dollar in 1994 to 14,530 dong to the dollar in January 2001.

POVERTY AND WEALTH

In 1999, average GNP per capita in Vietnam was only US$370, giving Vietnam the rank of 170th in the world on this indicator. This statistic, however, is quite misleading, since it does not reflect differential costs of living in different countries and societies. It is much more meaningful to think in terms of GNP per capita being 5,365,000 dong and then to assess what can be purchased locally with that amount of income. The World Bank has made such adjustments and the estimated **GDP per capita** (in terms of **purchasing power parity**) is a much higher $1,950. In 1998, it was estimated that 37 percent of the population was living below the poverty line, though this estimate seems too high and may not adequately reflect local purchasing power.

Rapid economic development in Vietnam has not been accompanied by worsening income distribution, as is common in many other countries at this stage of development. One reason for this outcome is the commitment of the government of Vietnam to target basic and key services to alleviate poverty, spread literacy, and improve health for individuals in all provinces in all areas of the country. A significant portion of revenues generated in the richer provinces are redistributed to poorer, more disadvantaged provinces. Such a policy reflects the government's commitment to prevent large regional disparities and social injustices. However, some researchers have found increasing gender inequality.

A major economic problem facing the Vietnamese economy is the large number of individuals who are unemployed or **underemployed**. This problem is exacerbated (made worse) by several factors: the improvement of agricultural productivity and limited land for expansion has driven farmers off the land; the reduction in the

Exchange rates: Vietnam

new dong (D) per US$1	
Jan 2001	14,530
Jan 2000	14,020
Dec 1998	13,900
Dec 1996	11,100
1995	11,193
Oct 1994	11,000

SOURCE: CIA *World Factbook 2001* [ONLINE].

GDP per Capita (US$)

Country	1975	1980	1985	1990	1998
Vietnam	N/A	N/A	183	206	331
United States	19,364	21,529	23,200	25,363	29,683
China	138	168	261	349	727
Thailand	863	1,121	1,335	2,006	2,593

SOURCE: United Nations. *Human Development Report 2000; Trends in human development and per capita income.*

Distribution of Income or Consumption by Percentage Share: Vietnam

Lowest 10%	3.6
Lowest 20%	8.0
Second 20%	11.4
Third 20%	15.2
Fourth 20%	20.9
Highest 20%	44.5
Highest 10%	29.9

Survey year: 1998

Note: This information refers to expenditure shares by percentiles of the population and is ranked by per capita expenditure.

SOURCE: *2000 World Development Indicators* [CD-ROM].

size of the state sector; and Vietnam's historically rapid population growth rate and young population. Despite the excellent macroeconomic success of the economy in the 1990s, it is insufficient to generate adequate numbers of jobs for new entrants to the labor force. Also, over the next several years state-owned enterprises are expected to reduce employees as part of Vietnam's continuing economic reform process. In July 2001, a freeze on the establishment of new state companies was announced. The unemployment rate in 1995 was estimated to be an extremely high 25 percent. In 1996, an estimated 2 million rural residents migrated to the cities in search of employment (approximately 7 percent of the nation's workforce). The National Assembly has set a strategic target to create 1.4 million new jobs. The major source of new jobs will be from **private sector** development.

WORKING CONDITIONS

Vietnam has in place an extremely progressive national labor law which is designed to regulate working conditions. The major challenge is to ensure that the labor law is being properly and appropriately implemented. The high visibility of Nike, Inc., which decided to add Vietnam as an important site to source its production of footwear and apparel, generated considerable controversy in the United States, especially among activist labor rights groups such as the Workers' Rights Consortium. Accusations of sweatshop conditions and negligible pay were made by a number of journalists.

Actually, Nike's dynamic and creative marketing strategy has enabled the company to expand its production to a country that desperately needs expanded job opportunities. Unfortunately, the subcontractors (Korean and Taiwanese) producing for Nike in Vietnam were without question guilty in some instances of certain abuses and violated Vietnam's labor law. Managers found guilty of such abuses were deported. Though salaries in the Vietnamese garment, textile, and footwear factories are extremely low by U.S. standards, this additional income is often pooled in an extended family context and contributes importantly to families' economic welfare. With companies such as Nike active in Vietnam, in 1998 Vietnam was able to export US$1.4 billion worth of footwear overseas.

Those unable to find formal employment in the Vietnamese economy must seek income-generating activities in the informal economy. Conditions in the informal economy vary rather dramatically, depending on the activity involved. Some informal sector jobs provide individuals with far more freedom and independence than if they were working in a formal factory setting. In other instances, work in the informal economy can be rather humiliating, such as those involved in "begging" tourists to buy their souvenirs, for example. Unfortunately, an illegal commercial sex industry has emerged in Vietnam, especially in the Ho Chi Minh City area. Undereducated, unemployed women can be vulnerable to such an industry. Primarily as the result of the growth of this industry, it is estimated that approximately 100,000 Vietnamese have HIV/AIDS.

COUNTRY HISTORY AND ECONOMIC DEVELOPMENT

2879 B.C. Vān Lang becomes the first emperor of Vietnam, known as the Vān Lang Kingdom.

Household Consumption in PPP Terms

Country	All food	Clothing and footwear	Fuel and power[a]	Health care[b]	Education[b]	Transport & Communications	Other
Vietnam	49	7	15	4	18	6	2
United States	13	9	9	4	6	8	51
China	N/A	N/A	N/A	N/A	N/A	N/A	N/A
Thailand	23	8	5	3	13	11	37

Data represent percentage of consumption in PPP terms.

[a]Excludes energy used for transport.

[b]Includes government and private expenditures.

SOURCE: World Bank. *World Development Indicators 2000.*

111 B.C. TO 939 A.D. Vietnam is under Chinese rule.

939. Vietnam becomes independent of China.

13TH CENTURY. Vietnam repels Mongol forces of Kublai Khan 3 times.

15TH CENTURY. Vietnam repels Ming China's attempt to control the country.

1801. The beginning of the unified reign of Emperor Gia Long, and the beginning of the Nguyen Dynasty.

1858. France begins its invasion of Vietnam, capturing Saigon in 1861. Eventually French control extends beyond Vietnam to all of Indochina.

1924. Vietnamese revolutionary Ho Chi Minh leaves for southern China where he establishes the first **Marxist** organization to promote revolution in Indochina.

1930. Formation of Indochinese Communist Party in Hong Kong.

1941. Ho, after extensive overseas travel, returns to Vietnam to establish the Viet Minh, a revolutionary organization.

1945. On 2 September, Ho announces the birth of Vietnam as an independent, unified nation.

1946–1954. Vietnam fights a war against the French, while the United States provides military and financial aid to the French. In 1954, the French are defeated at Dien Bien Phu by the Viet Minh. Vietnam is later divided at the 17th parallel into North and South Vietnam, with the United States providing aid to the pro-capitalist South Vietnam and opposing the communist North Vietnam.

1959–73. The American war in Vietnam begins, with the United States siding with South Vietnam against North Vietnam. The United States finally leaves the country in 1973.

1975. Following the fall/liberation of the South Vietnamese city of Saigon, the 2 Vietnams are united as the Socialist Republic of Viet Nam on 30 April.

1977. The Socialist Republic of Vietnam is admitted to the United Nations.

1978. Vietnam invades Cambodia and overthrows the Pol Pot regime, which leads to prolonged civil war in Cambodia between Pol Pot's Khmer Rouge forces and the Vietnamese-installed government in Phnom Penh, the capital of Cambodia.

1986. New *doi moi* economic policy calls for economic **liberalization** and the use of market forces and mechanisms.

1989. Vietnam withdraws its troops from Cambodia.

1994. The United States lifts its economic embargo against Vietnam.

1995. Vietnam is accepted as the 7th member of ASEAN.

1995. U.S. president Bill Clinton announces the normalization of relations with Vietnam. Clinton visits Vietnam in 2000.

2001. In October, a Bilateral Trade Agreement between the United States and Vietnam is approved by the U.S. Congress.

FUTURE TRENDS

There is considerable debate about the economic future of Vietnam. Pessimists focus on the country's inadequate physical infrastructure and its powerful state bureaucracy which makes doing business in Vietnam complex and difficult. They also point to persisting ambiguities in Vietnam's evolving legal structure and issues of corruption. These obstacles are normally more of an obstacle for those from the West than those from other Asian countries such as China, Taiwan, and Thailand.

In contrast, there are many reasons to be optimistic about Vietnam and its economic future. First, Vietnam has the good fortune of having access to Pacific ports and being strategically and centrally located near China, India, and Indonesia, all among the world's largest countries. These are potentially huge markets for possible Vietnamese exports.

Second, with its Confucian traditions, Vietnam has demonstrated a strong commitment to education and human resource development. The country's overall literacy rate is an impressively high 93.7 percent. Already, Vietnamese students are performing well in the Scientific Olympics in areas such as math and science. On several key educational indicators, Vietnam has equaled or surpassed Thailand, despite having a much weaker educational infrastructure. Vietnam may have the highest quality labor relative to cost of any country in the world.

Third, Vietnam shares a number of common characteristics with Japan and now seems in a number of ways similar to Japan during its post-war phase of development, though, of course, Vietnam does not have the industrial pre-war base that Japan had. Both countries had their infrastructures destroyed in war, and both were highly motivated to rebuild their societies and economies after suffering from war. The demographics of Japan and Vietnam are similar, with high population density and a relatively small portion of arable land, necessitating the ability to use limited space productively and creatively. Eventually Vietnam's population will be larger than that of Japan. Thus, like Japan it has important economies of scale and related people resources.

Fourth, Vietnam has excellent tourism potential which can be a valuable source of foreign exchange. It also benefits from substantial and increasing international remittances of overseas Vietnamese. Fifth, in fighting the Chinese, the French, and then the United States, the Vietnamese demonstrated impressive courage, determination, flexibility, and creativity. These traits bode well for the entrepreneurial potential of Vietnam.

Finally, the October 2001 approval by the U.S. Congress of a trade agreement between the 2 countries will provide Vietnam with greatly improved export access to the large U.S. market for a wide variety of products. Here there is also a parallel with the earlier economic history of Japan.

DEPENDENCIES

Vietnam has no territories or colonies.

BIBLIOGRAPHY

Boothroyd, Peter, and Pham xuan Nam, editors. *Socioeconomic Renovation in Viet Nam: The Origin, Evolution, and Impact of Doi Moi.* Ottawa: International Development Research Centre, and Singapore: Institute of Southeast Asian Studies, 2000.

Doling, Tim. *Mountains and Ethnic Minorities: North West Vietnam.* Hanoi: The Gioi Publishers, 1999.

Do Phuong. *Vietnam: Image of the Community of 54 Ethnic Groups.* Hanoi: The Ethnic Cultures Publishing House, 1998.

Economist Intelligence Unit. *Country Profile: Vietnam.* London: Economist Intelligence Unit, 2001.

Export-Import Bank of Thailand. <http://www.exim.go.th>. Accessed October 2001.

Luong, Hy V. *Revolution in the Village: Tradition and Transformation in North Vietnam, 1925–1988.* Honolulu: University of Hawaii Press, 1992.

McCarty, Adam. "Vietnam." *Far East and Australasia 2001.* London: Europa, 2001.

Osborne, Milton E. *The Mekong, Turbulent Past, Uncertain Future.* Washington, D.C.: Atlantic Monthly Press, 2000.

Phan Huy Le, et al. *The Traditional Village in Vietnam.* Hanoi: The Gioi Publishers, 1993.

Rao, M. Govinda. "Fiscal Decentralization in Vietnam: Emerging Issues." *Hitosubashi Journal of Economics.* No. 41, 2000.

Romnås, Per, and Bhargavi Ramamurthy, editors. *Entrepreneurship in Vietnam: Transformation and Dynamics.* Copenhagen: Nordic Institute of Asian Studies Publishing, and Singapore: Institute of Southeast Asian Studies, 2001.

Simon, Julian L. *Population Matters: People, Resources, Environment, and Immigration.* New Brunswick: Transaction Books, 1990.

Sloper, David, and Le Thac Can, editors. *Higher Education in Vietnam: Change and Response.* Singapore: Institute of Southeast Asian Studies, 1995.

Templer, Robert. *Shadows and Wind: A View of Modern Vietnam.* New York: Penguin Books, 1999.

Tran Hong Duc and Ha Anh Thu. *A Brief Chronology of Vietnam's History.* Hanoi: The Gioi Publishers, 2000.

Tran Thi Van Anh and Le Ngoc Hung. *Women and Doi Moi in Vietnam.*

Truong Do Xuan. "Vietnam's Economy After the Asian Economic Crisis." *Asia-Pacific Economic Literature.* Vol. 14, No. 1, 2000.

Tu Wei-ming. *Confucian Traditions in East Asian Modernization: Moral Education and Economic Culture in the Four Mini-Dragons.* Cambridge, Ma.: Harvard University Press, 1996.

U.S. Central Intelligence Agency. *World Factbook 2001.* <http://www.odci.gov/cia/publications/factbook/index.html>. Accessed September 2001.

U.S. Department of State. *FY 2001 Country Commercial Guide: Vietnam.* <http://www.state.gov/www/about_state/business/com_guides/2001/eap/index.html>. Accessed October 2001.

Vietnam: Embassy of the Socialist Republic of Vietnam in the United States of America. <http://www.vietnamembassy-usa.org>. Accessed October 2001.

"Vietnam Media Reports." *Intellasia.* <http://www.intellasia.com>. Accessed October 2001.

Westlake, Michael, editor. "Vietnam." *Asia 2001 Yearbook.* Hong Kong: Far Eastern Economic Review, 2000.

The World Bank. *Vietnam: Education Financing.* Washington, D.C.: The World Bank, 1997.

—Gerald Fry

YEMEN

Republic of Yemen
Al-Jumhuriyah al-Yamaniyah

CAPITAL: Sanaa.

MONETARY UNIT: Yemeni riyal (YR). One riyal equals 100 fils. There are coins of 1, 5, 10, 25, and 50 fils riyals, and notes of 1, 5, 10, 20, 50, and 100 riyals.

CHIEF EXPORTS: Crude oil, cotton, coffee, and dried and salted fish.

CHIEF IMPORTS: Food, live animals, machinery and equipment, and manufactured goods.

GROSS DOMESTIC PRODUCT: US$14.4 billion (purchasing power parity, 2000 est.).

BALANCE OF TRADE: **Exports:** US$4.2 billion (f.o.b., 2000). **Imports:** US$2.7 billion (f.o.b., 2000).

COUNTRY OVERVIEW

LOCATION AND SIZE. Yemen is located in the Middle East at the southern end of the Arabian Peninsula. The Arabian Sea, the Gulf of Aden, and the Red Sea bound its south and west. It is also bordered by Saudi Arabia to the north and Oman to the east. Yemen also includes the island of Socotra in the Indian Ocean, and the Kamaran group in the Red Sea. With an area of 527,970 square kilometers (203,849 square miles) and a coastline of 1,906 kilometers (1,184 miles), Yemen is slightly larger than twice the size of Wyoming. The capital city, Sanaa, is located in the west. Other major cities include Aden in the south and al-Hudaydah on the Red Sea coast.

POPULATION. With a population of 18,078,035 (est. July 2001), Yemen is one of the most populous countries on the Arabian Peninsula. The 1990 population estimate was only 11.88 million. The population growth rate in 2000 was estimated at 3.36 percent, but is expected to drop significantly in the coming decade. With a projected growth rate of 2.8 percent between 2000 and 2015, the population is expected to reach 36 million by the year 2029. The majority of the population are Muslims of the Sunni Shaf'i and the Shi'ite Zaydi traditions. There is also a small minority of Jews and Christians.

Yemen's population growth is very high by world standards, and the highest in the Middle East. The population is generally young, with some 50 percent below the age of 15. About 25 percent of the population live below the poverty line, up from 19 percent in 1992, and the average annual income is less than US$400. Widespread malnutrition and diseases make the infant mortality rate in Yemen one of the highest in the region. An estimated 38 percent of Yemenis age 15 or older could read and write in 1990. Among women, the rate was only 26 percent.

OVERVIEW OF ECONOMY

Yemen's domestic economy is largely dependent on oil, which accounts for about 85 percent of export earnings and 75 percent of government revenue. Yemen's oil reserves, however, are small in comparison to its larger oil-producing neighbors, such as Saudi Arabia. Oil reserves are concentrated in the north and south, with the southern field of Masila being the largest, followed by the Ma'rib field, also in the south. Agriculture, the second largest sector, accounts for 20 percent of **real gross domestic product** (GDP) and employs over half of the **labor force**. Higher oil prices fueled GDP growth of 2.8 percent in 1999 and 6.0 percent in 2000, and that upward trend is expected to continue in the coming years, barring a drop in oil prices.

Yemen entered the 20th century as part of the Ottoman Empire, administered by officials appointed by the Ottoman sultan based in Istanbul. For most of the 20th century Yemen was divided into 2 separate states: South Yemen and North Yemen. South Yemen was carved out by the British, who had established a protectorate area

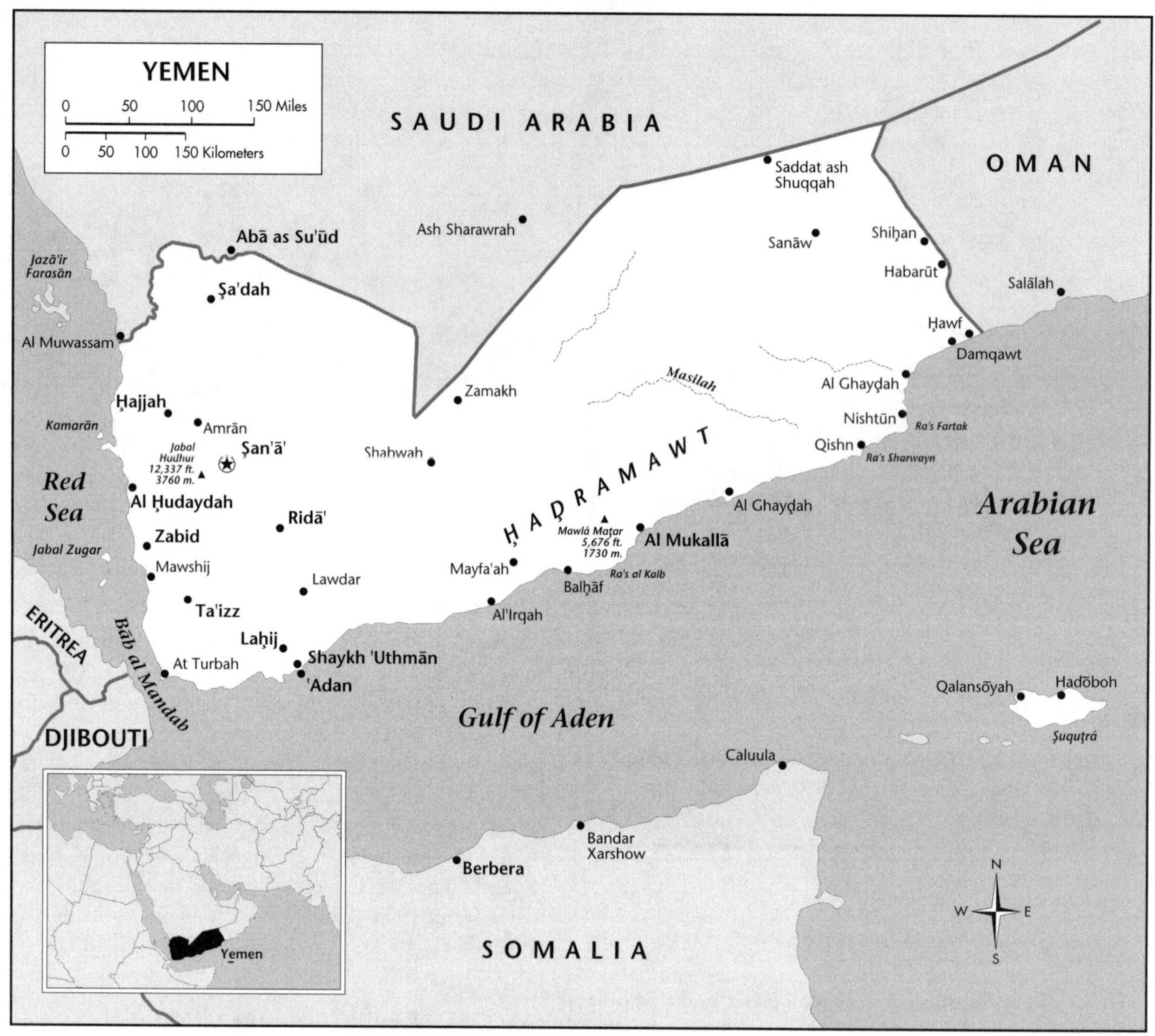

around the southern port of Aden in the 19th century. The British withdrew their forces from Aden in 1967. In 1970, when the government declared a **Marxist** state in the south, hundreds of thousands of Yemenis relocated to northern Yemen. North Yemen became an independent state in 1918, after the collapse of the Ottoman Empire.

In 1990, after years of hostilities and occasional conflict, north and south Yemen formally united to form the Republic of Yemen. Since unification, the country has struggled to overcome the legacy of the civil war that broke out between the north and the south in 1994, and to reform the economy. In 1995, Yemen launched an economic reform program in coordination with the International Monetary Fund (IMF). By the end of the 20th century, however, Yemen still had not created a vibrant economy or diversified its sources of income. As a result, Yemen remains dependent on oil revenue and on international lending agencies for financial assistance.

Yemen's economy is an underdeveloped free market economy with limited state control. Despite political violence, it has a fairly stable multiparty system and enjoys the support of the United States and the European Union. The economy's main exports are cotton, coffee, and dried and salted fish, but oil remains by far the largest single contributor to the national economy. Agricultural products account for one-fifth of GDP. Industry and mining, which are concentrated in Masila in the north and Ma'rib in the south, account for approximately one-fifth of GDP. Limited manufacturing, **retail** trade, and services are centered in the urban centers of Sanaa and Aden. Because of its limited productive capacity and industrial base, the country is heavily dependent on imported goods and on **foreign debt** relief and assistance to sustain its struggling economy.

Neither the agricultural sector nor the oil sector is capable of providing enough jobs to counteract long-standing problems with unemployment, which is exacerbated by rapid population growth. Unemployment reached 35 percent in Yemen during 1998, while the unemployment rate in the United States was just 4.2 percent in 1999. Despite the government's efforts to address the problem, unemployment will continue to present a serious challenge to the government for a long time to come.

Yemen's economic difficulties—sluggish GDP growth and high unemployment—have traditionally been offset by **remittances** from Yemeni workers abroad, and foreign aid from neighboring countries, especially Saudi Arabia. The Saudi government, however, both expelled Yemeni workers and cut off aid in 1990, due to Yemen's support for the Iraqi invasion of Kuwait that started the Gulf War. The country has also sustained a heavy foreign debt as a result of the 1990 unification, which, at its peak in 1990, was valued at almost twice the **gross national product**. Unable to make its debt payments, Yemen was forced to reschedule its debt to the Paris Club (a grouping of country creditors that extends loans to poor developing countries) in 1996. However, foreign assistance in the form of grants and loans, mainly from the United States and Europe, has alleviated the country's debt burden.

Corruption is a major problem in Yemen, and is especially so in the overstaffed and underpaid government bureaucracy. Chief illicit practices include soliciting bribes, evading taxes, and nepotism (favoring relatives, especially in hiring). The government has taken a tough stand against corruption, but with little success.

POLITICS, GOVERNMENT, AND TAXATION

Since independence, Yemen has been ruled by one party, the General People's Congress (GPC), which holds an absolute majority in parliament. The party is liberal and committed to reform. The emerging multiparty political system coexists with a feudal tribal system, and suffers from a legacy of deeply embedded rivalry between the north and the south. Until its unification with North Yemen, a Marxist-oriented government dominated South Yemen, and its economy was in ruins at the time of unification. For the first 3 years after unification in 1990, the country was governed by a transitional legal code under which the government was a hybrid of the pre-unification cabinets and parliaments of North and South Yemen. Before the 1994 civil war, the Marxist Yemeni Socialist Party ruled South Yemen. Its role diminished greatly after its leaders were sent into exile by the northern government as a pre-condition for peace.

Following the marginalization of the Socialist Party, the government was able to launch an economic reform program in 1995, which was formally endorsed by the IMF in 1997. The program stipulated deep spending cuts and the **privatization** of numerous state-owned facilities, including the National Bank of Yemen, the Yemen Cement Company, and Yemenia airlines, among other state-owned enterprises. It also aimed at keeping **inflation** levels low and encouraging foreign investment in the country. Although some progress has been achieved in the areas of cost-cutting and expanding the government's revenue base, the overall performance of the economy has been rather weak.

Taxes are an insignificant source of government revenue. As a result of the reform program, however, the government has attempted to improve its tax revenue collection system by computerizing its customs clearance at ports and airports. The government, however, has been largely reluctant to reform the **income tax** system in line with the IMF's recommendations. These efforts have been complicated by economic and political uncertainties, such as high unemployment rates, widespread poverty, and a high incidence of political violence. As a result, dependence on the oil sector for revenue is likely to persist.

INFRASTRUCTURE, POWER, AND COMMUNICATIONS

Yemen's **infrastructure** is relatively poor and underdeveloped. The country is serviced by a network of over 67,000 kilometers (41,634 miles) of primary and secondary roads, only 7,700 kilometers (4,785 miles) of which are paved. Southern Yemen's road system is in especially bad condition, as parts of many roads are washed away by flash floods and heavy rains. As a result, the country's road system constitutes a serious obstacle to economic development. There is no railway system.

Yemen has 5 major airports: the Sanaa, Aden, Rayyan, Taiz, and Hodeida airports. Renovation of the Sanaa and Aden airports began in 2000. Yemenia airline is the country's official airline and is largely protected against foreign competition. The carrier is slated for privatization, but the government has been reluctant to sell its 51 percent share in the airline. Yemen has 6 ports. With the exception of the Port of Aden, all ports experience delays in loading and unloading. Most domestic activity is concentrated at the Port of Hodeidah. Aden Container Terminal, which opened in March 1999 and is still being expanded, is gradually taking over as the country's main port.

Electrical power is supplied to Yemenis by the Public Electricity Corporation, which has a capacity of 400 Megawatts of power. The company can barely meet local demand; electricity reaches only 30 percent of the population. As a result of repeated blackouts and severe shortages—especially in Mukalla and Hadramawt, both

Communications

Country	Newspapers	Radios	TV Sets[a]	Cable subscribers[a]	Mobile Phones[a]	Fax Machines[a]	Personal Computers[a]	Internet Hosts[b]	Internet Users[b]
	1996	1997	1998	1998	1998	1998	1998	1999	1999
Yemen	15	64	29	N/A	1	N/A	1.2	0.02	10
United States	215	2,146	847	244.3	256	78.4	458.6	1,508.77	74,100
Saudi Arabia	57	321	262	N/A	31	N/A	49.6	1.17	300
Oman	29	598	595	0.0	43	2.7	21.0	2.87	50

[a]Data are from International Telecommunication Union, *World Telecommunication Development Report 1999* and are per 1,000 people.
[b]Data are from the Internet Software Consortium (http://www.isc.org) and are per 10,000 people.

SOURCE: World Bank. *World Development Indicators 2000.*

of which are not connected to the national grid—several factories and residences either have their own generators, or are forced to operate only one shift a day. The situation is worse in rural areas, where an estimated 60 percent of households have no electricity. The government has launched a program to upgrade and extend power supplies, largely with the help of the World Bank.

Telecommunications services in Yemen are unreliable. The country had 249,515 working lines in 1998, with a capacity of 296,129 lines. Telephone service, mobile included, is often interrupted for security reasons. Internet service is available, but is both costly and unreliable. In 2000, the country had just 1 Internet service provider for its 12,000 Internet users.

ECONOMIC SECTORS

Yemen's economic sectors reflect the small size of the economy. The 2 largest economic sectors are agriculture and oil. Agriculture accounted for 20 percent of GDP in 1998, industry (including oil) for 42 percent, and services for 38 percent. Oil accounts for 85 percent of export earnings and is the largest source of government revenue. Two of the greatest obstacles to growth in all of Yemen's economic sectors are overstaffing in all of the state institutions and the sensitivity of the oil sector to changes in world oil prices. Since 1995, the government has targeted certain areas of economic growth—especially the manufacturing and construction sectors—to fuel growth and to diversify the sources of revenue by investing in both the oil and non-oil sectors. Growth in these sectors, however, has been rather sluggish.

Yemen
GDP–COMPOSITION BY SECTOR–1998

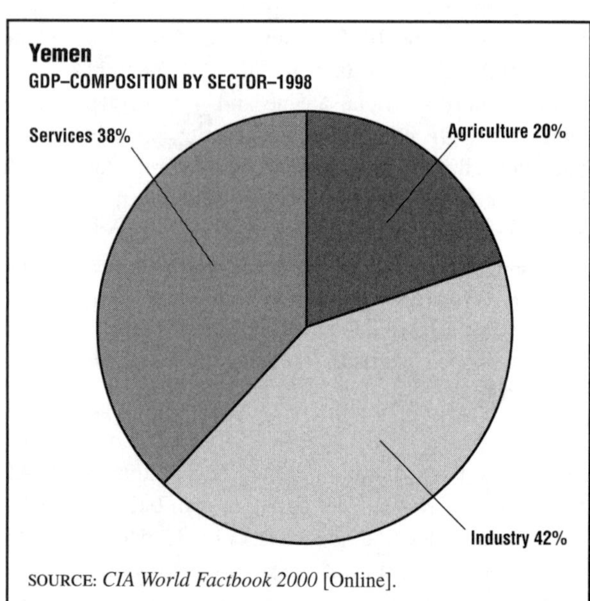

SOURCE: *CIA World Factbook 2000* [Online].

AGRICULTURE

Agricultural production is the single most important contributor to Yemen's economy, accounting for 20 percent of GDP. The agricultural sector provides approximately 58 percent of the country's employment. The labor-intensive sector is largely underdeveloped and inefficient, as a result of soil erosion, the high cost of credit and land, a lack of investment, and the scarcity of water. Most of the cultivated land is irrigated and dependent on groundwater, but high demand could exhaust water supplies by 2008. Although agricultural output has increased steadily in the past few years, crop yields remain low relative to those produced by comparable countries.

Major agricultural products include fruits, vegetables, and cereals, but production is rarely sufficient to meet domestic demand. As a result, Yemen continues to import most of its food. Yemen also cultivates qat, a mildly narcotic plant indigenous to Africa. Although legal, the government has recently moved to ban its consumption in public offices and on army duty due to economic and social costs associated with those under the influence. It continues to be widely consumed, and future efforts to ban it are unlikely.

FISHING. Though Yemen's location would suggest a booming fishing industry, actual fishing production remains low, largely due to under-exploitation. Most fishing activity continues to center around small boats and family-owned businesses. The sector employs some 41,000 people and produced over 127,000 tons of fish catch in 1998. Yemeni fishing would likely benefit from regulation and effective enforcement to avoid the over-fishing of some species.

INDUSTRY

MINING. Oil is a significant source of revenue for the government and of export earnings. Yemen's oil reserves, however, are small by regional standards. Oil reserves, proven and unproven, are estimated to be about 4 billion barrels, in comparison to Saudi Arabia, which has over 260 billion barrels of proven and unproven reserves. Most of the oil production is concentrated in the country's 2 largest fields at Ma'rib and Masila. There are also significant oil fields in Jannah, East Shabwa, and Iyad. Unlike neighboring Arab oil producing states, oil production is dominated by foreign companies. Several foreign companies, such as Hunt Oil Company (U.S.) and Canadian Occidental, enjoy production-sharing agreements, but Yemen's uncertain political atmosphere and dim oil prospects have limited the number of foreign companies interested in the oil sector. The sector's future lies in the successful exploration of new fields.

In addition to oil, Yemen's Ma'rib region is home to natural gas reserves estimated at 16.9 trillion cubic feet. Although small by regional standards, the gas is produced in commercial quantities, but competition and the lack of potential clients have thus far hindered the development of this endeavor. Other minerals include gypsum, salt, and gold.

MANUFACTURING. The manufacturing sector is an important and growing contributor to the Yemeni economy, accounting for about 12 percent of GDP in 1998. The sector has grown steadily in the last decade, but its growth is hindered by competition from imported goods and the lack of funding. Oil refining accounts for half of manufacturing activity. Refining activities are mostly concentrated in Aden and Ma'rib.

Yemen's small industrial base is built around small-sized, family-owned enterprises. Yemen has some 33,284 industrial establishments employing 1 to 4 workers. All large- and medium-sized establishments account for 5 percent of the total number of industrial enterprises. The bulk of Yemen's industrial base is centered on food processing and beverages, but production of cooking oil and flour has increased in recent years. The production of mixed metal products, such as water storage tanks, doors, and windows is the second largest industry, followed by the production of non-metallic products.

SERVICES

TOURISM. Tourism is not a significant contributor to Yemen's economy, despite the government's continuous effort to promote the country as a tourist destination. The sector suffers from a number of problems, foremost among which are political instability and the absence of modern facilities and infrastructure. Furthermore, at least 100 foreigners were reported kidnapped in 1999. Western countries have been advising their nationals against travel to Yemen since the 1998 abduction and killing of 18 foreigners. The number of tourists visiting the country dropped significantly after the 1998 incident, from 87,000 in 1987 to 45,000 in 1999.

FINANCIAL SERVICES. Yemen's banking system is poor and suffers from a number of problems, including a poor loan collection record, low bank monetary assets, and questionable policies regarding the extension of loans to clients. Despite government efforts to reform the financial sector by setting new standards for local banks in 1997, the sector continues to suffer from poor enforcement and compliance, a weak judicial system to ensure collection, and a general lack of public trust in the banking system as a whole. Furthermore, the government's efforts to sell its 2 major commercial banks have been rather slow, mainly due to the long preparation time required to bring these banks up to standard for sale.

Both public and private banks operate in Yemen. Both state-owned commercial banks and 3 of the 12 private banks follow Islamic banking practices, which includes not charging interest on loans. There are also 4 foreign-operated banks. Banking facilities are virtually absent in rural areas, and most loans are extended to well-known businessmen or on the basis of personal connections, making it hard for independent entrepreneurs to access funding.

RETAIL. Yemen lacks well-developed commercial centers —even in the larger coastal cities—and, therefore, has a poorly developed retail sector. The majority of shops in major cities are small and family-owned and run. Small family shops and temporary road stands characterize this sector in the majority of inland towns.

INTERNATIONAL TRADE

Over the past several decades, Yemen has relied more and more on imports, but, despite periodic peaks in the amount of imports, Yemen's oil exports have kept its trade balance positive. In 2000, exports stood at US$4.2 billion, while imports were worth US$2.7 billion. In addition to legitimate trade, the smuggling of firearms, alcohol, and **consumer goods** to and from Saudi Arabia is rampant on the Red Sea. Yemen imports a wide variety of goods, except oil and oil products. Neighboring Gulf countries, mainly Saudi Arabia and the United Arab Emirates, supply the majority of Yemen's imports, followed by France, the United States, and Italy.

Oil accounts for over 85 percent of total sales abroad. Non-oil exports include semi-processed agricultural products, mostly foods. Given its weak industrial base, oil is expected to remain the country's major export. Sales of liquefied natural gas are expected to surge, but the prospects for that eventuality are far from certain. Yemen exports the majority of its oil to Asia, especially Thailand, China, South Korea, and Singapore.

MONEY

Since 1996, the government has allowed the value of the Yemeni riyal to float—meaning its value is determined by supply and demand, not by the government. Before 1996, the government officially set the price, which led to it being widely sold on the **black market**. The riyal was devalued in 1996 from YR12 per US$1 to YR50 per US$1. Since 1996, the value has fluctuated sharply. Between 1996 and 1997, the value of the riyal remained stable, selling for an average of YR125 per US$1 for most of that period. Since 1998, however, the value of the riyal has declined steadily, mainly due to rising fears about Yemen's increasing foreign debt and **budget deficit**. As a result, the riyal traded at YR170 per US$1 in mid-1999. The Central Bank's efforts to keep the value at a stable rate since then have been largely successful. Since late 1999, it has been trading at an average of YR160 per US$1.

POVERTY AND WEALTH

With a per capita income of US$254 annually, Yemen is by far the poorest country in the region. Living standards in the country have fallen sharply since 1990 as a result of high inflation, which in 1995 peaked at 56.3 percent. Although inflation dropped to 10 percent in 2000, the value of wages also decreased, forcing Yemenis to spend more than half their income on food and beverages and limiting their ability to purchase imported goods. An estimated 25 percent of the population lived below the poverty line in 1997, up from 19 percent in 1992.

Exchange rates: Yemen

Yemeni rials per US$1	
Oct 2000	164.590
2000	160.683
1999	155.718
1998	135.882
1997	129.281
1996	94.157

SOURCE: CIA *World Factbook 2001* [ONLINE].

GDP per Capita (US$)

Country	1975	1980	1985	1990	1998
Yemen	N/A	N/A	N/A	266	254
United States	19,364	21,529	23,200	25,363	29,683
Saudi Arabia	9,658	11,553	7,437	7,100	6,516
Oman	3,516	3,509	5,607	5,581	N/A

SOURCE: United Nations. *Human Development Report 2000; Trends in human development and per capita income.*

Distribution of Income or Consumption by Percentage Share: Yemen

Lowest 10%	2.3
Lowest 20%	6.1
Second 20%	10.9
Third 20%	15.3
Fourth 20%	21.6
Highest 20%	46.1
Highest 10%	30.8

Survey year: 1992

Note: This information refers to expenditure shares by percentiles of the population and is ranked by per capita expenditure.

SOURCE: *2000 World Development Indicators* [CD-ROM].

WORKING CONDITIONS

Yemen's poor education system has meant that the majority of Yemen's labor force is unskilled. About 62 percent of Yemeni adults are unable to read and write. This problem is aggravated by the fact that the majority of Yemen's labor force is concentrated in the agricultural sector, in jobs that do not require advanced skills. The unemployment rate in the country is quite high by regional and international standards, reaching 35 percent in 1998. Local training programs are also poor by regional standards, and job opportunities for graduates of local universities are limited. As a result, thousands of skilled and semi-skilled laborers are forced to seek employment opportunities in neighboring Arab countries. Child labor has been prohibited since 1999, but it remains widespread, especially in the agricultural sector. Government work hours are from 8:00 AM to 2:00 PM. Private businesses maintain a different work schedule, which runs in 2 shifts: from 8:00 AM to 1:00 PM, and from 4:00 PM to 8:00 PM.

Household Consumption in PPP Terms

Country	All food	Clothing and footwear	Fuel and power[a]	Health care[b]	Education[b]	Transport & Communications	Other
Yemen	25	5	26	3	5	5	31
United States	13	9	9	4	6	8	51
Saudi Arabia	N/A	N/A	N/A	N/A	N/A	N/A	N/A
Oman	22	8	25	13	21	5	7

Data represent percentage of consumption in PPP terms.
[a]Excludes energy used for transport.
[b]Includes government and private expenditures.

SOURCE: World Bank. *World Development Indicators 2000.*

COUNTRY HISTORY AND ECONOMIC DEVELOPMENT

1538. Yemen falls under Ottoman rule.

1839. The British occupy Aden in southern Yemen.

1918. North Yemen gains independence from the Ottoman Empire at the end of World War I (1914–1918), calling itself the Yemen Arab Republic.

1935. The British create the Aden Protectorates.

1962. A group of nationalist officers revolt against the British and proclaim the Yemen Arab Republic (YAR) under the leadership of Abdullah al-Sallal.

1967. South Yemen gains independence from the United Kingdom.

1970. South Yemen, renamed the People's Democratic Republic of Yemen, **nationalizes** foreign-owned properties and establishes close ties with the Soviet Union.

1974–1978. A series of military coups in North Yemen leads to the ascendancy of President Ali Abdullah Saleh, who rules until the 1990 unification.

1986. A 12-day civil war erupts within the government of South Yemen. Former premier Haydar Bakr al-Attas is elected president in October.

1990. The Republic of Yemen is established peacefully on 22 May.

1993. Fair, multi-party, universal-suffrage elections are won by the General People's Congress.

1994. The south rebels against northern domination. The north wins, and the constitution is amended to establish a multiparty democracy.

1995. The government launches an economic reform program.

1999. In the first direct presidential election, Saleh returns to office.

2001. First municipal elections in country's history. The ruling General People's Congress wins the majority of seats. The constitution is amended to extend the term of the president from 5 to 7 years and parliamentary terms from 4 to 6.

FUTURE TRENDS

Yemen entered the 20th century under a cloud of economic decline. For much of the century, the rivalry between northern Yemen and the Marxist-led government of the south sapped the country's resources. The legacy of **socialism** left the southern economy in ruins. The reunification of the countries in 1990 and the subsequent civil war in 1994 further contributed to Yemen's economic decline. Government policies to stabilize the economy enacted in the mid-1990s have significantly improved the country's **macroeconomic** and structural conditions.

Yemen will likely address the unemployment problem, attempt to curb population growth, and implement the privatization policy in hopes of achieving long-term economic growth. The government has yet to lift **subsidies** on diesel fuel completely, cut military spending, downsize the public bureaucracy, or quash corruption in its public institutions and ministries. Much work will need to be done on the political front to achieve social and political stability, particularly to soothe the tensions between the current government and rural tribal groups and southern Marxists.

DEPENDENCIES

Yemen has no territories or colonies.

BIBLIOGRAPHY

Economist Intelligence Unit. *Country Profile: Yemen*. London: Economist Intelligence Unit, 2001.

Embassy of the Republic of Yemen. <http://www.yemenembassy.org>. Accessed September 2001.

U.S. Central Intelligence Agency. *World Factbook 2001.* <http://www.odci.gov/cia/publications/factbook/index.html>. Accessed September 2001.

U.S. Department of State. *FY 2001 Country Commercial Guide: Yemen.* <http://www.state.gov/www/about_state/business/com_guides/2001/nea/index.html>. Accessed September 2001.

—Reem Nuseibeh

GLOSSARY

Advance Tax: A percentage of the previous year's tax bill which is paid at the beginning of the new fiscal year and later credited back at its end.

Agribusiness: Agricultural and livestock production on a large scale, often engaged in by large, multinational companies; also used to refer to the companies themselves.

Arrear: Usually plural, **arrears**. Unpaid, overdue debt.

Bad Loan: An unrecoverable loan; the amount cannot be reclaimed by the lender.

Balance of Payments: The measure of all the money coming into a country and all the money leaving the country in a given period, usually a year. The balance of payments includes merchandise exports and imports, the measure of which is called the **balance of trade**, as well as several other factors.

Balance of Trade: A measure of the value of exports and imports, not including services. When imports exceed exports, there is a trade deficit. When exports exceed imports, there is a trade surplus.

Bank of Issue: The bank that is given the right to issue and circulate currency in a country.

Barter System: An exchange of goods and/or services for other goods and/or services, rather than for money.

Bear Market: A sustained period of negative growth in the stock market.

Bicameral: A legislative body consisting of two houses or chambers.

Black Market: An informal market in which buyers and sellers can negotiate and exchange prohibited or illegal goods (such as exchanging local money for foreign currency). Black markets often exist to avoid government controls. *See also* **Informal Sector.**

Budget Deficit: A government budget deficit occurs when a government spends more money on government programs than it generates in revenues. Governments must borrow money or print currency to pay for this excess spending, thus creating potential financial difficulties. *See also* **Budget Surplus.**

Budget Surplus: A government budget surplus occurs when a government generates more revenues than it spends on government programs. Governments can adjust to surpluses by lowering tax rates, paying down the national debt, or stockpiling the money. *See also* **Budget Deficit.**

Cadre: A group of important and influential members of political parties who direct the actions of that party.

Capital Adequacy: The state of a bank having enough capital to maintain its loans and operating costs.

Capital Flight; also called **Capital Outflow:** Money sent abroad because investors fear that economic conditions within a country are too risky.

Capital Good: A manufactured good used in the production of other goods. For example, factories or machinery used to produce goods are considered capital goods.

Capitalism: An economic system based on the private ownership of the means of production and on an open system of competitive markets. It is assumed that producers in a capitalist system can use their skills and capital in the pursuit of profit.

Capital Outflow: *See* **Capital Flight.**

Cash Crop: An agricultural good produced for direct sale on the market.

Centrally-planned Economy: An economy in which the government exerts a great deal of control over economic planning, including the control of production, the allocation of goods, distribution, and prices. Common in **socialist** countries.

c.i.f.: Abbreviation of **cost, insurance, and freight**; a method of determining the value of imports or exports that includes cost, insurance, and freight in determining the total amount.

Commonwealth of Independent States (CIS): A loose union of 12 of the former republics of the Soviet Union, excluding Estonia, Latvia, and Lithuania.

Communism: An economic system in which the means of production and distribution are held in common by all members of the society, and in which the rewards are distributed based on need. In actual communist countries, the state usually controls all the capital and land, and the economy is centrally planned. *See also* **Centrally-planned Economy.**

Consumer Good: A product sold directly to the end user, or consumer, such as food and clothing.

Crawling Peg: A fixed **exchange rate** between two currencies which is adjusted incrementally based on the movement of an economic indicator such as inflation.

Currency Board: An arrangement whereby a currency's value is fixed in some proportion to a strong foreign currency and such an exchange rate is guaranteed by the country's foreign exchange reserves.

Current Account Balance: The portion of the **balance of payments** that includes merchandise imports and exports (known as the **balance of trade**) plus imports and exports of services.

Debt Relief: Partial or full forgiveness of debts, offered to impoverished countries by lenders, usually after it becomes clear that continued payment on such debt is likely to ruin the country's economy.

Debt Service: Payment of interest on a loan or other debt. Debt servicing can be very expensive and debilitating for developing countries.

Deflation: Falling prices across an economy, expressed as a percentage per year. *See also* **Inflation.**

Dependency Ratio: The ratio of **pensioners** to the number of people employed.

Deregulation: A lessening of government restrictions on the economy.

Desertification: The progressive drying of the land.

Devaluation: An act by the government or central bank which decreases the official price of a nation's currency. When a currency is devalued, it can result in the country's exports becoming cheaper and more attractive.

Direct Tax: A tax levied directly on individuals or companies, such as income and property taxes. *See also* **Indirect Tax.**

Disposable Income: Those parts of a household income not needed for essentials such as food, healthcare, or housing costs. Disposable income may be saved, invested, or spent on non-essential goods.

Duty: A tax imposed on imported goods. *See also* **Indirect Tax.**

E-commerce: Economic activity conducted on the Internet.

Ecotourism: Tourism to natural and cultural areas which tries to minimize environmental impacts.

Embargo: A prohibition by a government against some or all trade with a foreign nation. *See also* **Sanctions.**

Emerging Market: A country with still evolving economic, social, and political structures that shows evidence of moving toward an open market system.

Emigration: To leave one's country to live elsewhere.

Enterprise Entry: The creation of new, predominantly small and medium size enterprises.

Enterprise Exit: The removal of businesses from an economy, either through bankruptcy or downsizing.

Equity: The value of all the shares in a company.

Estate Tax: A tax on inherited property and wealth.

Exchange Rate: The rate at which one country's currency is exchanged for that of another country.

Exchange Rate Mechanism (ERM): A mechanism set up in 1978 to handle fluctuations in the **exchange rates** of various European currencies. Each currency in the ERM may fluctuate only within agreed limits against any other currency.

Exchange Rate Regime: The mode of determining the **exchange rate** between the national currency and other major foreign currencies. In a fixed exchange rate regime, a currency is fixed or "pegged" to the currency of another, usually very stable currency, such as that of the United States. In a **floating** or flexible exchange rate regime, governments allow the value of their currency to be determined by supply and demand in the foreign exchange market.

Excise Tax: A tax on the sale or use of certain products or transactions, sometimes luxury or non-essential items.

Exclusive Economic Zone (EEZ): The area extending from a country's coastline over which that country has exclusive control of its resources.

External Debt: The total amount of money in a country's economy owed to enterprises and financial institutions outside the country.

Fiduciary: Related to a trust or trusteeship.

Fiscal Policy: The programs of a national government relating to spending on goods, services, **transfer payments**, and the tax system.

Fiscal Year: Any period of 12 consecutive months for which a company or a government calculates earnings, profits, and losses.

Fixed Exchange Rate: *See* **Exchange Rate Regime.**

Floating Exchange Rate: *See* **Exchange Rate Regime.**

Floor Price: The minimum price for a good or service which normally cannot be further reduced due to political, economic, or trade considerations.

f.o.b.: Abbreviation of **Free on board**; a method of determining the value of exports or imports that considers the value of goods excluding the cost of insurance and freight charges.

Foreign Debt: *See* **External Debt.**

Foreign Direct Investment (FDI): The total value of investment by foreign entities in a country, usually expressed on an annual or cumulative basis.

Foreign Exchange Reserves: The amount of money a country has in its treasury consisting of currency from foreign countries.

Free Market System: An economic system based on little government intervention and the freedom of private association and control of goods. *See also* **Capitalism.**

Free Trade Zone: Also called **Free Zone.** An industrial area where foreign companies may import, store, and sometimes export goods without paying taxes.

Full Employment: The level of employment at which a minimal amount of involuntary unemployment exists. It is considered the maximum level of employment in an economy.

Fully Convertible Currency: A currency that can be freely traded in international foreign exchanges for units of another currency.

GDP per Capita: Gross domestic product divided by the number of people in a country. GDP per capita is a convenient way to measure comparative international wealth.

Gini Index: An index used to measure the extent to which the distribution of income within an economy deviates from perfectly equal distribution. A score of 0 would mean perfect equality (with everyone having the same level of wealth) and 100 would signify perfect inequality (with a few extraordinarily wealthy people and the large majority living in dire poverty).

Glut: An excess of goods in a particular market, which typically causes the price of that good to fall.

Grey Economy: Economic activity that takes place in both the formal and **informal economy,** meaning that some but not all economic activity is reported to authorities such as tax collectors.

Gross Domestic Product (GDP): The total market value of all goods and services produced inside a country in a given year, which excludes money made by citizens or companies working abroad.

Gross National Product (GNP): The total market value of all goods and services produced in a year by a nation, including those goods produced by citizens or companies working abroad.

Guarantor: An institution or individual that guarantees to pay the debts of another institution or individual in the case of bankruptcy.

Guest Worker: Persons from a foreign country who are allowed to live in a host country so long as they are employed. Many guest workers send **remittances** to their native country.

Hard Currency: Money that can be exchanged on the foreign market and is stable enough to purchase goods from other countries.

Hawking: Selling wares, often pirated goods, in the **informal sector.**

Holding Company: A company that owns or controls several other companies.

Immigration: To move into a country that is not one's native country.

Import Substitution: A policy which calls for the local production of goods that have traditionally been imported. The goal of import substitution is to lessen a country's dependence on foreign suppliers.

Income Tax: A **direct tax** on an individual's earned income.

Indirect Tax: A tax which is not paid directly, but is passed on as part of the cost of an item or service. For instance, **tariffs** and **value-added taxes** are passed on to the consumer and included in the final price of the product. *See also* **Direct Tax.**

Inflation: A persistent increase in the average price of goods in an economy, usually accompanied by declining purchasing power of the national currency.

Inflation Rate: The rate at which prices rise from one period to the next.

Informal Sector: Also called **Informal Economy**. The part of an economy that lies outside government regulations and tax systems. It usually consists of small-scale and usually labor-intensive activities; it often includes illegal activities. *See also* **Black Market.**

Infrastructure: The system of public facilities, services, and resources in a country, including roads, railways, airports, power generation, and communication systems.

Intermediate Good: A good used as an ingredient or component in the production of other goods. For instance, wood pulp is used to produce paper.

Internally Displaced Person: A person fleeing danger (such as war or persecution) who has not crossed international boundaries. Those who relocate to another country are called "refugees."

Joint Sector: An economic sector in which private enterprise and the government invest jointly.

Joint Venture: A special economic initiative or company formed by a foreign firm and a domestic company, usually in a developing state. The domestic partner often holds a majority interest, thus allowing the host country to control the amount and kind of foreign economic activity. Can also be a simple joint operation by two or more companies.

Labor Force: Also called **Workforce**. The total number of people employed in a country plus the number of people unemployed and looking for a job.

Labor Mobility: The ability and readiness of workers to move to regions or sectors of higher growth within a country or economy.

Levy: A tax based on the assessed value of personal property and/or income.

Liberal Economy: An economy in which markets operate with minimal government interference and in which individual choice and private ownership are the guiding forces.

Liberalization: The opening of an economy to free competition and a self-regulating market, with minimal government-imposed regulations or limitations.

Liquidity: Generally, the amount of money on hand. When related to government, it refers to the amount of money in circulation.

Macroeconomics: Economic issues large enough to impact the nation as a whole.

Market Capitalization: The total market value of a company, expressed by multiplying the value of a company's outstanding shares by the current price of the stock.

Marxism: A set of economic and political theories based on the work of 19th century theorists Karl Marx and Friedrich Engels that holds that human history is a struggle between classes, especially those who own property and those who do not (the workers). Marxism provided the theoretical basis for the economic systems of modern **communism** and **socialism.**

Microcredit: The lending of small amounts of startup capital to the very poor as a way of helping them out of poverty. The World Bank and other aid agencies often make mircrocredit loans to small-scale entrepreneurs in the developing world.

Monetary Policy: A government policy designed to regulate the money supply and interest rates in an economy. These policies are usually determined by the central bank or treasury in order to react to or to anticipate inflationary trends and other factors that affect an economy. They are said to be "tight" when interest rates are raised and other measures are implemented in an effort to control inflation and stabilize currency values.

Monetized Economy: An economy based on money as opposed to barter.

Money Laundering: A method used by criminal organizations to hide income gained from illicit activities, such as drug smuggling, by manipulating banks to provide a legitimate explanation for the source of money.

Monopoly: A company or corporation that has exclusive control over the distribution and availability of a product or service.

Multinational Corporation (MNC): A corporation which has economic ties to or operations in two or more countries.

National Debt: The amount of money owed to lenders by a government. The debt occurs when a government spends more each year than it has raised through taxes. Thus, to spend more than it has, the government must borrow money from banks or through the issuance of bonds.

Nationalization: The movement of privately-owned (and usually foreign-owned) companies into government ownership. Companies have often been nationalized by the developing countries whose government argued that the foreign firms involved did not pay their fair share of the profits to the host country and unfairly exploited it in other ways.

Nomenklatura: The elite members of the Communist Party in communist nations, who were often given privileges not extended to ordinary citizens.

Nomenklatura Privatization: A system of **privatization** in communist nations that openly or covertly transferred ownership of state assets to the **nomenklatura.**

Non-performing Loan: A delinquent loan or one in danger of going into default.

Offshore Banking: Banking operations that offer financial services to people and companies from other countries, usually with associated tax benefits. Offshore banking operations are often suspected as a cover for **money laundering** or other illegal financial activities.

Overheated Economy: An economy that is growing at a very high annual rate, which leads to low interest rates, a high borrowing rate, and an abundance of money in the economy—all of which can lead to **inflation.**

Parastatal: A partly or wholly government-owned enterprise.

Participation Rate: The ratio between the labor force and the total population, which indicates how many people are either working or actively seeking work.

Pensioner: A retired person who lives off a government pension.

Price Control: Artificial limitation on the prices of goods set by the government, usually in a **centrally-planned economy.**

Price Index: An index that shows how the average price of a commodity or bundle of goods has changed over a period of time, usually by comparing their value in constant dollars.

Primary Commodity: A commodity, such as a particular crop or mineral, which is a natural rather than manufactured resource.

Private Sector: The part of an economy that is not directly controlled by the government, including businesses and households.

Privatization: The transition of a company or companies from state ownership or control to private ownership. Privatization often takes place in societies that are making a transition from a **socialist** or mixed-socialist economy to a **capitalist** economy.

Procurement: The purchase of goods or services by the government.

Progressive Taxation: An income taxation system in which tax rates rise in accordance with income levels. Thus, a person making a large salary will be taxed at a higher rate than someone who makes less money.

Proportional Representation: An electoral system whereby the number of legislative seats allocated to a particular political party is decided in proportion to the number of votes that party won in an election.

Protectionist Policy: A government policy used to protect local producers from competition from imported foreign goods. Countries may erect various trade barriers such as **tariffs** or quotas in an effort to protect domestic firms or products.

Public Sector: The part of the economy that is owned and operated by the government.

Purchasing Power Parity (PPP): The purchasing power parity method attempts to determine that relative purchasing power of different currencies over equivalent goods and services. For example, if it costs someone in the United States US$300 to buy a month's worth of groceries, but it costs someone in Ghana only US$100 to buy the same amount of groceries, then the person in Ghana can purchase three times as much for the same amount of money. This means that though the average citizen of Ghana may earn less money than the average citizen of the United States, that money buys more because goods and services cost less in Ghana. The PPP calculation attempts to account for these differences in prices and is used to calculate **GDP** and **GDP per capita** figures that are comparable across nations. Note: GDP figured at purchasing power parity may be three or more times as large as GDP figured at **exchange rate** parity.

Pyramid Scheme: Fraudulent investment strategy involving a series of buying and selling transactions that generate a paper profit, which, in turn, is used to buy more stocks. They were prevalent in Eastern Europe following the fall of the Soviet Union, and preyed on the average citizen's lack of understanding of **free-market** investment transactions.

Real GDP: The **gross domestic product** of a country expressed in constant prices which are determined by a baseline year. Real GDP thus ignores the effects of inflation and deflation and allows for comparisons over time.

Real Wage: Income measured in constant dollars, and thus corrected to account for the effects of inflation.

Recession: A period of negative growth in an economy, usually defined as two consecutive quarters of negative **GDP** growth. A recession is characterized by factors such as low consumer spending, low output, and high unemployment.

Re-export: An imported good that does not undergo any changes (e.g., not turned into a new product) before being exported.

Relative Income Poverty: This is a measure of the overall equality in income among employed workers. Relative income poverty is high when a high percentage of the sum of total income is concentrated in the hands of a small percentage of the working population, and it is low when income is more equally spread among all workers.

Remittance: Money that is sent back to people, usually relatives, living in the home country of a national working abroad.

Repatriation: Taking money out of a foreign country in which it had been invested and reinvesting it in the country where it originated.

Reserve Ratio: The percentage of a bank's assets in reserve against the possibility of customers withdrawing their deposited funds. Some governments impose a minimum percentage, usually enforced by a central bank in proportion to the total amount of currency in circulation.

Restructuring: A catch-all phrase for turning around a company, involving cutting costs, restoring finances, and improving products.

Retail: The sale of goods and services to individuals in small amounts.

Sanction: A penalty, often in the form of a trade restriction, placed on one country by one or several other countries as a penalty for an action by the country under sanctions. Sanctions are designed to force the country experiencing them to change a policy, such as its human rights practices.

Shadow Economy: Economic interactions that are invisible to standard accounting and taxing procedures. See **Informal Economy.**

Sharecropper: A farmer who works someone else's land in exchange for a share of the crops they produce.

Smallholder: A farmer who has only a very small farm or plot of land.

Social Security Tax: A **direct tax** levied partly on the worker and partly on the employer in order to provide funds for a nation's **social welfare system.**

Social Welfare System: A set of government programs that provides for the needs of the unemployed, aged, disabled, or other groups deemed in need of government assistance.

Socialism: An economic system in which means of production and distribution are owned by the community, and profits are shared among the community. Countries with socialist economies put a premium on centralized control over an economy rather than allowing market forces to operate, and tend to have a relatively equal distribution of income.

Solvency: Financial stability.

Statist Economic Policy: A policy in **capitalist** or quasi-capitalist countries that favor state control or guidance of companies or sectors of the economy that are thought to be vital.

Strategic Industry: An industry considered extremely important to the well being of a country.

Structural Adjustment Program (SAP): A set of economic programs and policies aimed at stabilizing the overall structure of a troubled economy. Structural adjustment programs are often required by international lending agencies such as the World Bank and the International Monetary Fund. These programs often involve devaluing the currency, reducing government spending, and increasing exports.

Structural Unemployment: Unemployment caused by a mismatch between the needs of employers and the skills and training of the labor force.

Subsidy: A payment made by a government to an individual or company that produces a specific good or commodity. Some countries subsidize the production of certain agricultural crops, while others may subsidize mass transit or public art.

Subsistence Farming: Farming which generates only enough produce to feed the farmer's family, with little or nothing left over to sell.

Tariff: An **indirect tax** that is applied to an imported product or class of products.

Tax Haven: A place where investors shield their money from the national taxes of their own country. *See also* **Offshore Banking.**

Tax Holiday: A period of time in which businesses or investors enjoy exemptions from paying taxes. Tax holidays are offered as a lure to investment or business development.

Technocrat: Government official who is expert in specialized—usually technological—areas.

Trade Deficit: *See* **Balance of Trade.**

Trade Surplus: *See* **Balance of Trade.**

Transfer Payment: Cash paid directly to individuals by a government, usually as part of a **social welfare system.**

Transfer Pricing: A method used by foreign firms to overprice their overseas costs and thereby reduce their local tax liabilities.

Treasury Bill: Also called a **T-bill**. A guaranteed government investment bond sold to the public. They usually reach maturity after short periods, for example, three months or six months.

Trickle Down: An economic theory that contends that tax relief and other governmental incentives should be given primarily to the highest income earners in a society, on the assumption that their increased economic investment and other activity will provide benefits that "trickle down" to the lower- and middle-income wage-earners.

Turnover: The measure of trade activity in terms of the aggregated prices of all goods and services sold in the country during a year.

Two-tier Economy: An economy where skilled or educated workers enjoy a high standard of living, but unskilled workers are trapped in poverty.

Underemployment: A situation in which people are not reaching their economic potential because they are employed in low-paying or part-time jobs. For example, an engineer who is working in a fast food restaurant would be said to be experiencing underemployment.

Underground Economy: Economic transactions that are not reported to government, and therefore not taxable. **Informal sectors** and **black markets** are examples of underground economic activity.

Unicameral: A legislative body consisting of a single house or chamber.

United Nations Development Program (UNDP): The United Nations' principal provider of development advice, advocacy, and grant support.

Value Added: The increase in the value of a good at each stage in the production process. When a company adds value to its products it is able to gain a higher price for them, but it may be liable for a **value-added tax.**

Value-added Tax (VAT): A tax levied on the amount of **value added** to a total product at each stage of its manufacture.

Vertical Integration: Control over all stages of the production and distribution of a certain product. For example, if one company owns the mines, the steel plant, the transportation network, the factories, and the dealerships involved in making and selling automobiles, it is vertically integrated.

Voucher Privatization: A system for selling off state-owned companies in which citizens are given "vouchers" which they may invest in such companies. This system was devised to allow all citizens the opportunity to invest in formerly state-owned businesses; however, in practice many citizens invest their vouchers in voucher funds, which are professionally managed investment groups who amass vouchers in order to exert control over the direction of companies.

Welfare State: A government that assumes the responsibility for the well-being of its citizens by providing institutions and organizations that contribute to their care. *See also* **Social Welfare System.**

Workforce: *See* **Labor Force.**

INDEX

Page numbers appearing in boldface indicate major treatment of entries. A page number accompanied by an italicized "t" indicates that there is a table on that page, while a page number accompanied by an italicized "f" indicates there is a figure on that page.

G

H

I

M

P

Q

R

X

Y

Z